KAVOUSI

The Results of the Excavations at Kavousi in Eastern Crete

Directed by

Geraldine C. Gesell, Leslie Preston Day,
and William D.E. Coulson

Sponsored by

The University of Tennessee

Under the auspices of

The American School of Classical Studies at Athens

Frontispiece. Large pedestaled krater (**GR27 P4**), Early Orientalizing. Watercolor D. Faulmann.

PREHISTORY MONOGRAPHS 71

KAVOUSI IV

The Early Iron Age Cemeteries at Vronda

Part 1

TEXT

By

Leslie Preston Day and Maria A. Liston

Contributions by

Kimberly Flint-Hamilton, Kevin T. Glowacki, Eleni Nodarou,
Effie Photos-Jones, David S. Reese, Lynn M. Snyder, and Julie Unruh

Edited by

Geraldine C. Gesell and Leslie Preston Day

Published by
INSTAP Academic Press
Philadelphia, Pennsylvania
2023

Design and Production
INSTAP Academic Press, Philadelphia, PA

Printing and Binding
HF Group – Acmebinding, Charlestown, MA

INSTAP Academic Press, a part of the Institute for Aegean Prehistory (INSTAP), was established to publish projects relevant to the history of the Aegean world, in particular from the Paleolithic to the 8th century B.C. It is a scholarly nonprofit publisher specializing in high-quality publications of primary source material from archaeological excavations as well as individual studies dealing with material from the prehistoric periods—exemplified by its *Prehistory Monographs* series of volumes. INSTAP is committed to engaging a variety of audiences by disseminating knowledge through its scholarly publishing program, which produces award-winning monographs at reasonable prices that are both academically and popularly acclaimed.

Library of Congress Cataloging-in-Publication Data

Names: Day, Leslie Preston, author, editor. | Liston, Maria A., author. | Flint-Hamilton, Kimberly, contributor. | Glowacki, Kevin T. (Kevin Thomas), 1961- contributor | Nodarou, Eleni, contributor | Photos-Jones, Effie, contributor | Reese, David S., 1954- contributor | Snyder, Lynn M., contributor | Unruh, Julie contributor. | Gesell, Geraldine Cornelia, editor. Title: Kavousi IV : the early Iron Age cemetaries at Vronda / by Leslie Preston Day and Maria A. Liston ; contributions by Kimberly Flint-Hamilton, Kevin T. Glowacki, Eleni Nodarou, Effie Photos-Jones, David S. Reese, Lynn M. Snyder, and Julie Unruh ; edited by Geraldine C. Gesell and Leslie Preston Day.
Description: Philadelphia, Pennsylvania : INSTAP Academic Press, 2023. | Series: Prehistory monographs ; 71 | Includes bibliographical references and index. | Contents: Introduction / Leslie Preston Day -- Tholos tombs at Vronda / Leslie Preston Day and Maria A. Liston -- Enclosure burials at Vronda / Leslie Preston Day, Maria A. Liston, Kimberly Flint-Hamilton, David S. Reese, and Lynn M. Snyder -- Cremation process / Maria A. Liston -- Human remains / Maria A. Liston -- Faunal and botanical remains / Lynn M. Snyder, David S. Reese, and Kimberly Flint-Hamilton -- Funerary architecture / Leslie Preston Day -- Early Iron Age pottery / Leslie Preston Day -- Petrographic analysis of the grave ceramic assemblage / Eleni Nodarou -- Finds other than pottery / Leslie Preston Day, with a contribution by Julie Unruh -- Burial customs / Leslie Preston Day -- History and society in the Vronda graves / Leslie Preston Day. | Summary: "This volume presents the results of the excavation of two cemeteries at the site of Vronda Kavousi in East Crete: the cemetery of tholos tombs belong to the Subminoan to Protogeometric periods (with some use in the eighth century B.C.) and the cemetery of enclosure graves with cremation burials belonging to the Late Geometric to Late Orientalizing periods. A discussion of individual graves (including the stratigraphy, architecture, human remains, faunal and botanical remains, pottery, and other finds) is followed by the analysis of the cremation process and human remains, the faunal and botanical remains, the pottery, the petrographic analysis of the pottery, the metalsand other finds, the burial customs, and the history and society of the burying population. A study of the capacities of some of the pottery vessels and a metallurgical analysis of the iron objects appear in appendices"-- Provided by publisher.
Identifiers: LCCN 2022055543 (print) | LCCN 2022055544 (ebook) | ISBN 9781931534369 (v. 1 ; hardback) | ISBN 9781931534369 (v. 2 ; hardback) | ISBN 9781623034412 (pdf)
Subjects: LCSH: Excavations (Archaeology)--Greece--Kavousi Region. | Cemeteries--Greece--Kavousi Region. | Grave goods--Greece--Kavousi Region. | Human remains--Greece--Kavousi Region. | Tombs--Greece--Kavousi Region. | Iron Age--Greece--Kavousi Region. | Kavousi Region (Greece)--Antiquities.
Classification: LCC DF261.K4 D397 2023 (print) | LCC DF261.K4 (ebook) | DDC 938--dc23/eng/20230505
LC record available at https://lccn.loc.gov/2022055543
LC ebook record available at https://lccn.loc.gov/2022055544

Copyright © 2023
INSTAP Academic Press
Philadelphia, Pennsylvania
All rights reserved
Printed in the United States of America

Table of Contents

Preface ix

List of Abbreviations xiii

Glossary xv

1. Introduction, *Leslie Preston Day* 1
    Methodology 3
    Stratigraphy 5
    Excavation and Recording of Graves 6
    Presentation of the Material 7
    Catalogs 8
    Pottery 8
    Other Objects 13
    History and Chronology of the Vronda Remains 14

2. Tholos Tombs at Vronda, *Leslie Preston Day and Maria A. Liston*...15
    Vronda Tomb I (Boyd's Tomb A)..16
    Vronda Tomb II (Boyd's Tomb 1)...18
    Vronda Tomb III (Boyd's Tomb B)..20
    Vronda Tomb IV (Boyd's Tomb 3)...20
    Vronda Tomb V (Boyds Tomb C)...27
    Vronda Tomb VI (Boyd's Tomb D)..28
    Vronda Tomb VII (Boyd's Tomb 4)...29
    Vronda Tomb VIII (Boyd's Tomb 2, Grave 18)..31
    Vronda Tombs II, VII, or VIII (Boyd's Tombs 1, 4, or 2)...34
    Vronda Tomb IX...35
    Vronda Tomb X..44
    Vronda Tomb XI...48
    Addendum: Other Vessels Possibly from Vronda Tholos Tombs 51

3. Enclosure Burials at Vronda, *Leslie Preston Day, Maria A. Liston, Kimberly Flint-Hamilton, David S. Reese, and Lynn M. Snyder* 53
    Grave 1 53
    Grave 2 59
    Grave 3 61
    Grave 4 67
    Graves 5 and 11 73
    Grave 6 81
    Grave 8 90
    Graves 9 and 14 92
    Grave 10..109
    Grave 12..111
    Grave 13..124
    Grave 15..127
    Grave 16..129
    Grave 17..134
    Grave 19..139
    Grave 20..143
    Graves 21 and 22...151
    Grave 23..156
    Grave 24..161
    Grave 26..162
    Grave 27..168
    Grave 28..172
    Grave 29..181
    Graves 30, 33, and 7 183

Grave 31	192
Graves 32 and 25	193
Grave 34	198
Grave 35	200
Grave 36	201
Grave 37	208
Other Possible Enclosure Burials	209

4. Cremation Process, *Maria A. Liston* 211
- Excavation 211
- Inventory and Measurement 211
- Reconstructing the Cremation Process 212
- Classification of Cremation Burials 215
- Cremation Process at Vronda 216

5. Human Remains, *Maria A. Liston* 219
- Tholos Tombs: Demography, Health, and Pathology 219
- Enclosure Graves: Demography, Health, and Pathology 220

6. Faunal and Botanical Remains, *Lynn M. Snyder, David S. Reese, and Kimberly Flint-Hamilton* 235
- Animal Bones, *Lynn M. Snyder* 235
- Marine Shells, *David S. Reese* 242
- Palaeobotanical Remains, *Kimberly Flint-Hamilton* 242

7. Funerary Architecture, *Leslie Preston Day* 245
- Tholos Tombs 245
- Enclosure Graves 248
- Other Types of Burials without Architectural Features 250

8. Early Iron Age Pottery, *Leslie Preston Day* 253
- Discussion by Shape 254
- General Observations about the Pottery 291
- Potters' Marks and Graffiti 294

9. Petrographic Analysis of the Grave Ceramic Assemblage, *Eleni Nodarou* 297
- Kavousi Fabrics and the Aim of the Study 297
- Analytical Results 298
- Provenance and Consumption Patterns 303
- An East Cretan Assemblage—An East Cretan Community? 304

10. Finds Other than Pottery, *Leslie Preston Day, with a contribution by Julie Unruh* 305
- Metal 305
- Ivory or Bone 321
- Glass 321
- Stone 322

  Terracotta 323

  Textile Remains 324

  Analysis of Textiles, *Julie Unruh* 325

11. Burial Customs, *Leslie Preston Day* 327

  Tholos Tombs 328

  Enclosure Burials 331

  Comparison of Burial Customs in Tholos Tombs and Enclosures 350

  Reconstructing the Burial Rituals 352

12. History and Society in the Vronda Graves, *Leslie Preston Day* 355

  History of Mortuary Use of the Vronda Ridge 355

  Burying Population and Location of Cemeteries 358

  Introduction of Cremation 362

  Social Structure and Burial 365

  Conclusions 373

Appendix A. Estimates of Vessel Capacities, *Kevin T. Glowacki* 375

  Cups 376

  Skyphoi and Kraters 377

Appendix B. Metallographic and Analytical (SEM-EDAX) Investigation of Metalwork from
 Early Iron Age Kavousi, *Effie Photos-Jones* 379

  Iron Production Using the Bloomery Process 380

  Iron Artifacts from Vronda and Kastro and Their Examination with Optical and Scanning
   Electron Microscopy and Microhardness Testing 381

  Results and Discussion 382

Appendix C. Concordance of Excavation Inventory Numbers with Catalog Numbers and
 Museum Numbers 385

References 395

Index 413

Preface

This volume is the fifth in the final report of the cleaning and excavations at Kavousi Vronda, which were conducted between 1981 and 1992 by Geraldine C. Gesell, Leslie Preston Day, and the late William D.E. Coulson. The volume includes two distinct cemeteries: the tholos tombs at Vronda, which were uncovered by Harriet Boyd or local landowners and cleaned as part of the Kavousi Project between 1900 and 1990; and the cremation enclosures excavated by members of the Kavousi Project from 1984 through 1992. Preliminary analysis of the material from the tholos tombs was carried out by Geraldine Gesell (architecture), William Coulson† (pottery), and Leslie Day (objects), and it formed the basis for preliminary reports (Gesell, Day, and Coulson 1983; Day 1984; Gesell 1985). Preliminary reports on the cremation enclosures also have appeared (Day, Coulson, and Gesell 1986; Gesell, Coulson, and Day 1991; Day 1995, 2011a; Gesell, Day, and Coulson 1988, 1995). The skeletal remains from all of the tombs in the Kavousi area were studied and written up by Maria Liston (1993, 2007; Liston and Day 2009). This volume supersedes all of these earlier works.

The reports on the houses of the earlier LM IIIC settlement can be found in three previous volumes. *Kavousi* IIA (Day, Klein, and Turner 2009) describes the buildings on top of the Vronda ridge: Building A-B; Building Complexes C-D and J-K; and Buildings P, Q, and R. *Kavousi* IIB (Day and Glowacki 2012) presents the buildings on the slopes of the Vronda ridge: Building Complexes E, I-O-N, and L-M; Building F; the pottery kiln; and areas excavated on the periphery that did not belong to any of these buildings. *Kavousi* IIC (Day et al. 2016) contains detailed analyses of the architecture, pottery, other finds (including figurines and stone tools), and botanical and faunal remains, along with a complete history of the site and a reconstruction of the social, political, and religious organization of the LM IIIC settlement. *Kavousi* III: *The Late Minoan IIIC Shrine* presents the architecture and ritual equipment of the shrine in the settlement (Gesell, Glowacki, and Klein, in prep.). For building and room designations, the reader should consult earlier volumes.

The Kavousi series also will include volumes on the excavations at the Kastro, a site high on the mountain above and to the east of Vronda. The Kastro report will include volumes on the pottery, stratigraphy, architecture, and finds from the settlement on the peak, as well as the material from the tombs on the slopes surrounding the Kastro that were recovered by earlier archaeologists.

A detailed history of excavations at Kavousi can be found in *Kavousi* I (Haggis 2005, xvii–xix) and *Kavousi* IIA (Day, Klein, and Turner 2009, xxv–xxviii, 3–5). It thus will not be repeated here.

The complete list of acknowledgments for the work at Kavousi was provided in *Kavousi* IIA (Day, Klein, and Turner 2009, xxix–xxxv), but since that time others have contributed to the study and publication of the Vronda material. The work has been done with the support of the 24th Ephorate of Prehistoric and Classical Antiquities (now the Ephorate of Antiquities of Lasithi) and especially its directors, Vili Apostolakou and Chrysa Sofianou. We are most grateful for the continuing support of the Institute for Aegean Prehistory (INSTAP). The INSTAP Study Center for East Crete (INSTAP SCEC) has facilitated the studies and has provided the use of publication teams to complete drawings and photography; we are especially grateful to the director, Thomas Brogan, who personally has done so much to support our work. We wish to thank the American School of Classical Studies at Athens (ASCSA) for its support, and in particular the Blegen Library, the facilities of which were a major source of information for our research. We also greatly appreciate the financial support that came from our associated institutions: Wabash College, the University of Tennessee, and Texas A&M University.

The University of Tennessee supported the preliminary studies of the human remains from the graves, and the Wiener Laboratory (ASCSA) and its former and current directors, Sherry Fox and Panagiotis Karkanas, have provided resources and advice for the human bone studies. The data on crania were shared with an undergraduate student, Sarah Swingler, who initially analyzed them for her undergraduate honors thesis and identified some of the patterns in the data.

Others have been generous with their time and expertise. The pottery studies were informed by discussions with a number of individuals, including Antonios Kotsonas, Margaret Mook, Penelope Mountjoy, Metaxia Tsipopoulou, and the late Nicolas Coldstream. The petrographic analysis was conducted at the INSTAP SCEC. Ryan Collier, Matthew Hurley, Shireen Kanakri, Matthew Miller, Megan Oehrlein, and Mark Willingham helped with the estimation of vessel capacities. Analysis of the few stone tools found in the graves was carried out by Heidi Dierckx, who also wrote the catalog entries. Harriet Blitzer and Tristan Carter provided the identification of stones used in objects that were not tools. Initial faunal analysis of the material from the tholos tombs was provided by Sheilagh Wall-Crowther. Walter Klippel collaborated with Lynn Snyder in the species identification of the animal bones from all of the graves, and Dimitra Mylona was enormously helpful in pulling material for analysis and photography. The marine shells were studied by David Reese; an overall discussion of these shells can be found in *Kavousi* IIC (Day et al. 2016). The botanical remains from the graves have been analyzed by Kimberly Flint-Hamilton, and the overall results have been presented in *Kavousi* IIC (Day et al. 2016).

The metallurgical analysis of the iron artifacts from Vronda and the Kastro was carried out by Effie Photos-Jones, of the University of Glasgow and Scottish Analytical Services for Art and Archaeology (Ltd.), Glasgow. The study took place in the 1990s, and it reflects the state of research at that time. There has been no serious opportunity to discuss these results in the context of more recent research on the topic of Early Iron Age metallurgy in Greece. Bloomery iron (early or late) is not a glamorous material, and yet it has been pivotal in the development of the Greek world. Its full story, on its own and vis-a-vis bronze, remains largely unwritten. Unfortunately, it has not been possible to update it with respect to recent comparable work elsewhere in Crete or in other parts of Greece, other than to acknowledge the analytical study by Eleni Filippaki, Yannis Bassiakos, and Barbara Hayden (2014) on mainly Late Roman to Byzantine iron slag from Priniatikos Pyrgos near Hagios Nikolaos in East Crete.

The following individuals worked specifically on the graves, and their contributions are much appreciated. The cleaning of Tholos Tombs I, II, IV–VI, IX, and X was carried out by William Coulson, Leslie Day, and Geraldine Gesell. Tholos VIII was uncovered again by Pedar Foss, and Tholos XI was cleaned by Jane Carter. Trench supervisors of the enclosure graves included Kevin Baldwin (Grave 11), Thomas Brogan (Grave 19), Jane Carter (Grave 34), William Coulson (Grave 1), Leslie Day (Graves 1 and 2), Deanne Dicer (Grave 36), Pedar Foss (Grave 13), Kevin Glowacki (Graves 6–8, 15, 23, 24, 28, 30, 33, 35), James Higginbotham (Grave 16), Nancy Klein (Grave 31), Mark Lawall (Grave 19), Heidi Mittelstadt (Grave 20), Jonathan Reynolds (Grave 20), Julia Shear (Graves 9, 14), Jeffrey Soles (Grave 3), Susan Springer (Graves 4, 5), Lee Ann Turner (Graves 10, 12, 17, 21, 22, 25–27, 32), Benjamin Venable (Grave 29), and Catherine Woolfit (Grave 29). Maria Liston and anthropological assistants (Melinda Carter, Jonathan Reynolds, and Susan Kirkpatrick Smith) worked together with the trench supervisors in excavating the enclosures, overseeing the plotting and removal of the bones and the grave goods.

Plans and sections of the tholos tombs were drawn by William Coulson, Leslie Day, Jeffrey Soles, Pedar Foss, and Konstantinos Chalikias. Charles L. Hall, Douglas H. Pierce, Faye C. Polillo, James Rehard, and Vanessa A. Rousseau drew the state plans of the enclosures. Plans of the tholoi and enclosures were inked by Roxana Docsan.

The difficult task of conservation of the pottery and objects from the enclosure burials was undertaken over the years by a number of conservators, including Jane Allison, Richard Barden, Ann Brysbaert, Nancy Buschimi, Stefania Chlouveraki, Matthew Crawford, Kathy Hall, Barbara Hamman, Katherine Holbrow, Helen Kingsley, Linda Landry, Catherine Magee, Katherine Nightingale, Albert Nyboer, Noël Siver, Kirsten Svenson-Taylor, Christine Thede, Katerina Triandafyllou, Katherine Untch, and Gayle Wever. The pottery and objects from the tholos tombs were drawn by William Coulson, Leslie Day, Geraldine Gesell, and Roxana Docsan; drawings were inked by Roxana Docsan. Pottery from the enclosure burials was drawn primarily by Roxana Docsan and Leslie Day, but also by David Cummins, Stephen T. Moody, and Christopher White; while most of the pottery was inked by Roxana Docsan, a few vessels were done by Doug Faulmann and Elizabeth Safran. The metal artifacts were drawn and inked by Lyla Pinch Brock. Terry Faulkner drew and inked the figures of the semi-articulated skeletons based on the field drawings. Kathy Hall provided testing, X-ray analysis, and perceptive observations about the metal artifacts, including the textile impressions.

Photography was carried out by Kavousi Project staff photographers from 1981–1996: Duane Bingham, Steven Hamilton, Karen Moukheiber, Christina Paterakis, Joanne Polley, Julie Smith, and John Zimmerman. From 1997 to the present, photography has been carried out at the INSTAP SCEC by Kathy May and Chronis Papanikolopoulos. William Coulson, Leslie Day, Geraldine Gesell, Kevin Glowacki, Nancy Klein, and Melissa Eaby were responsible for additional site photography. The photographs of the material excavated by Boyd were taken by Geraldine Gesell. Theodora Kopestonsky kindly helped with the digitization of many of the photographs.

Quentin Dodd worked on a digital reconstruction of the contents of Grave 9 for his senior undergraduate thesis at Wabash College. Because this occurred early in the use of computers in archaeology, it was not entirely successful. Nevertheless, he was instrumental in determining the stratigraphy of this complicated enclosure.

Kevin Glowacki estimated the capacities of vessel types from the enclosure burials found in Appendix A. The iron artifacts formed the basis for a metallurgical study by Effie Photos-Jones, a report on which is included as Appendix B. Additional information about the metal objects came from X-ray analysis by Kathy Hall at the INSTAP SCEC.

The material from the Vronda cemeteries is to be found in several museums and storerooms in Crete at the time of publication. Pottery and objects from Boyd's excavation of the tholos tombs are in the Herakleion Archaeological Museum (inventory numbers prefaced by HM). The majority of the material from the cleaning and excavation by the Kavousi Project can be found in the storerooms of the INSTAP SCEC. Some vessels are on display or in the storerooms of the Archaeological Collection of Ierapetra (IM), while others (including some that had been inventoried in the Ierapetra museum) have been taken to the Archaeological Museum of Hagios Nikolaos (HNM).

List of Abbreviations

The following chronological abbreviations are used (Bronze Age dates are based on Warren and Hankey 1989; Early Iron Age dates are based on Coldstream 2001 and Kotsonas 2008).

FN	Final Neolithic (ca. 4500–3200 B.C.)	LG	Late Geometric (ca. 745–710/700 B.C.)
EM	Early Minoan (ca. 3200–2100 B.C.)	CA I	Cypro-Archaic I (ca. 750–600 B.C.)
MM	Middle Minoan (ca. 2100–1600 B.C.)	SubG	Subgeometric (ca. 680–650 B.C.)
LM	Late Minoan (ca. 1600–1050 B.C.)	SubLG	Sub-Late Geometric (ca. 680–650 B.C.)
SM	Subminoan (ca. 1050–1000/970 B.C.)	O	Orientalizing (ca. 700–600 B.C.)
EIA	Early Iron Age (ca. 1100–700 B.C.)	EO	Early Orientalizing (ca. 710/700–670 B.C.)
CG	Cypro-Geometric (ca. 1050–750 B.C.)	MO	Middle Orientalizing (ca. 670–640 B.C.)
PG	Protogeometric (ca. 970–810 B.C.)	LO	Late Orientalizing (ca. 640–600 B.C.)
EPG	Early Protogeometric (ca. 970–920 B.C.)	EPAR	Early Protoarchaic (ca. 710/700–640 B.C.)
MPG	Middle Protogeometric (ca. 920–875 B.C.)	LPAR	Late Protoarchaic (ca. 640–600/570 B.C.)
LPG	Late Protogeometric (ca. 875–845 B.C.)	A	Archaic (ca. 600–480 B.C.)
SubPG	Sub-Protogeometric (ca. 850–800 B.C.)	C	Classical (ca. 480–331 B.C.)
PGB	Protogeometric B (ca. 845–810 B.C.)	V	Venetian (13th–17th century A.D.)
G	Geometric (810–700 B.C.)	Ott.	Ottoman (17th century–1900 A.D.)
EG	Early Geometric (ca. 810–790 B.C.)	Mod.	Modern (1900 A.D.–present)
MG	Middle Geometric (ca. 790–745 B.C.)		

The following additional abbreviations are also used in this volume.

AutoCAD	computer-aided design software	**M**	metal
avg.	average	m	meter(s)
B	bone or ivory	m asl	meters above sea level
brec	breccia	m^2	square meter(s)
ca.	approximately	m^3	cubic meter(s)
cf.	comparable to (in faunal analyses)	max.	maximum
		mm	millimeter(s)
cm	centimeter(s)	MNI	minimum number of individuals
d.	diameter	μm	micron(s)/micrometer(s)
EDM	electronic distance measurement	nm	not measured
esp.	especially	no(s).	number(s)
est.	estimated	**P**	pottery
ext.	exterior	para	parallel
G	glass	PB	polished block
G.	Grave	perp	perpendicular
g	gram(s)	pers. comm.	personal communication
GPS	Global Positioning System	pl.	plural
h.	height	PMD	petrography sample by Peter M. Day
H/DR	ratio of height of an open vessel to the diameter of the rim	pres.	preserved
		S	stone
HM	Herakleion Archaeological Museum catalog number	SEM-BS	back-scattered mode scanning electron microscopy
HNM	Archaeological Museum of Hagios Nikolaos catalog number	SEM-EDX	scanning electron microscopy with energy-dispersive X-ray analysis
H_v	Vickers hardness (test for measuring microhardness)	SEM-SE	secondary emission mode scanning electron microscopy
IM	Archaeological Collection of Ierapetra catalog number	SHB	smithing hearth bottom
INSTAP	Institute for Aegean Prehistory	**ST**	stone tool
INSTAP SCEC	Institute for Aegean Prehistory Study Center for East Crete	**TC**	terracotta
		th.	thickness
int.	interior	TMJ	temporo-mandibular joint
KAV	prefix (Kavousi) for petrographic and metallurgical samples	VE	Vronda East
		VN	Vronda North
kcal	kilocalorie(s)	VS	Vronda South
kg	kilogram(s)	VW	Vronda West
km	kilometer(s)	w.	width
L	liter(s)	wh	whole
L.	length	wt.	weight
LCH	Langerhans cell histiocytosis	XPL	cross-polarized light
lime	limestone		
LEH	linear enamel hypoplasia		

Glossary

The text uses the following terms, which are specialized terminology or do not have exact English equivalents.

dromos	passage leading to the entrance of a tholos tomb, often just a pit in front of the stomion
enclosure grave	a stone-lined enclosure containing multiple cremation burials that were burned on the pyre and left in place; formerly called a cist grave
jift	solid and semisolid residue from olive pressing
pseudo-dromos	area in front of a tholos tomb that is not lined with stones and is often merely a pit
stomion	doorway for entering a tholos tomb
tholos	type of tomb that is generally round in plan and covered with a corbeled vault (pl. tholoi)
tsakali	soft marl bedrock that can be cut easily; also called *kouskouras*
zembili	large rubber basket with two handles used for carrying dirt and stones; approximate capacity of 25.00 L (pl. *zembilia*).

1

Introduction

Leslie Preston Day

The site of Kavousi Vronda is located on a ridge in northeastern Crete, ca. 4.00–5.00 km east of the isthmus of Ierapetra and 1.25 km south of the modern village of Kavousi, on the eastern edge of the Gulf of Mirabello (Figs. 1, 2; Pls. 1A, 1B). The top of the ridge, which rises to 427.00 m asl, was inhabited in the EM II, MM IB–II, MM III–LM I, and especially LM IIIC period (Day et al. 2016, 119–209). From the 11th century into the 7th century, however, a period here referred to as EIA (for the problems in labeling this period, see Kotsonas 2016), the ridge and its surrounding slopes were used exclusively for burials, first in small tholos tombs on the periphery of the former village, and then in stone-lined enclosures set within the collapsed walls of the LM IIIC settlement (Figs. 3, 4, 6; Pls. 2, 3).

The archaeological importance of the Kavousi area in the Late Bronze and Early Iron Ages was, in fact, first recognized on the basis of graves found there by local farmers. When Arthur Evans traveled through Kavousi on his trip to eastern Crete in 1896 or 1899, he reported a group of objects said to have come from tombs on the slopes of the Kastro peak at Plai tou Kastrou (Gesell, Day, and Coulson 1983, 389, 412–413). In 1900, Harriet Boyd Hawes uncovered eight tholos tombs at Vronda, most of which were already known to local landowners and completely or partially robbed of their contents (Boyd 1901, 132–137). Although a report of her activities at Kavousi appeared in the next year (Boyd 1901), the pottery was given to Lida Shaw King for study, but no detailed publication of the tombs and their material ever appeared. Two photographs of pottery from the tholos tombs appeared in the 1901 report (Boyd 1901, pls. 1, 2), along with a few illustrations of other objects, but no other information was forthcoming.

In 1979 a new study of the Kavousi material was begun by William Coulson†, Leslie Day, and Geraldine Gesell (Gesell, Day, and Coulson 1983). This study included the pottery and objects from Boyd's excavations now in the Herakleion Archaeological Museum and those from the tholos tomb uncovered by a local landowner in 1951 in the Archaeological Collection of Ierapetra. In 1981, Boyd's tombs and the others that had subsequently been discovered were cleaned, drawn, and photographed. Cleaning of the Kastro in 1982 and the Vronda settlement in

1983 and 1984 demonstrated that the Kavousi sites could provide important new evidence for the transitional period between the palatial cultures of the Bronze Age and the rise of the Greek city-state. As a result, excavations were carried out from 1987–1990 and in 1992 at both Vronda and the Kastro.

Boyd gave number or letter designations to the tholos tombs she discovered at Vronda, depending on whether they had been totally robbed of their contents or not. Letters were used for robbed tombs, and numbers for those still containing material. These numbers were confusing, and in the 1983 report the tombs were sequentially numbered with Roman numerals. The sequence begins with Boyd's Tombs I–VIII; other tholos tombs found by the local landowner and those discovered during the course of cleaning and excavation have been numbered as Tombs IX–XI.

The cleaning on the Vronda ridge in 1984 brought to light two cremation burials, and excavations from 1987 to 1990 revealed more burials within the ruined buildings of the earlier settlement. The cremations within enclosures were originally labeled cist graves because the enclosures formed boxes in which the cremation occurred and the body was left (Gesell, Day, and Coulson 1988, 1995; Gesell, Coulson, and Day 1991). The term "cist grave" has been used for this type of burial in Greece (Dickinson 1983, 57) and elsewhere (e.g., in Early Bronze Age Denmark; see Sørensen and Bille 2008, 257–260), but its use to identify the Kavousi graves has led to confusion on the part of archaeologists who use the term cist for graves constructed of upright slabs (e.g., Kanta and Davaras 2004, 151). Because of this lack of clarity, Kanta identified the Vronda graves erroneously as shaft graves, despite the fact that they are not constructed at the bottom of a deep shaft. Following Melissa Eaby (2007, 326–329), who distinguishes enclosures from cist graves, for the sake of clarity we are now identifying this type of grave as an enclosure burial, although problems of definition still exist (Gaignerot-Driessen 2016, 131).

From the beginning of the excavations in 1987, it was decided to give each deposit of human bones consecutive Arabic numerals, and these numbers were consistently applied. Thus, while the tholos tombs are Tombs I–XI, the graves discovered within the settlement remains are Graves 1–37. Of these 37 graves, 21 were cremations within rectangular enclosures, one was a pithos inhumation in an enclosure, seven were dumps of material from some of these enclosures, and seven were other types of burials. Among the seven are a possible pit burial (Grave 8), two possible pyre sites (Graves 13 and 31), a child burial cast into an abandoned room (Grave 24), and three others of uncertain form. The designation of Grave 18 was initially given to what turned out to be Boyd's Tomb VIII, which had been covered over since her time (Grave 18 thus appears as Tomb VIII in this vol., Ch. 2, pp. 31–34; it does not appear in Ch. 3). It is also possible that Boyd's workmen uncovered one of these enclosure burials in 1900. She reports the finding of a hoard of iron objects in one of the rooms of the large building on the summit of the ridge (Boyd 1901, 132). Cremations at Vronda are difficult to distinguish, and Boyd's workmen may have overlooked the fragmentary burned bones and pottery and not recognized the remains as a grave. The iron tools and weapons resemble the objects found in the other enclosure burials more than any finds from the LM IIIC houses, and they are here considered possible grave goods. These iron objects are cataloged after Grave 37, traces of which were also found in the same general area.

Graves 1 and 2 were encountered just below the modern surface during the 1984 cleaning. Graves 3–8 were cleared in 1987, 9–20 in 1988, 21–29 in 1989, and 26, 29, and 30–36 in 1990. Fragments of a human cranium from south of Building B, Room B7 found in 1992 were ascribed to Grave 37. These graves differed from the tholos tombs found by Boyd in a variety of ways. First, they had a different form: they were stone-lined rectangular enclosures instead of built beehive-shaped tombs. Second, they were constructed within the confines of the LM IIIC settlement, often utilizing the still visible walls of those buildings rather than being placed around the periphery of the earlier settlement. Third, these graves contained for the most part primary cremations rather than the inhumations made in the tholos tombs. Finally, the cremation enclosures seem to have been used in the LG to LO periods (mid-eighth to late seventh centuries B.C.), at a later time than the tholos tombs, which were in use from the Subminoan period, shortly after the abandonment of the settlement, into the Geometric period. It is not entirely clear if there was any overlap between the last uses of the tholoi on Vronda and the first appearance of the cremation enclosures, but the last-used of the tholos tombs, Vronda Tomb IX, contained material similar to what may be the earliest burial in the enclosures (Grave 9), and other tholoi contained some possible LG pottery as well.

Thus, the last uses of the tholos tombs may have occurred around the same time as the first use of the cremation enclosures.

Methodology

Not much is known about the way in which Boyd excavated the tholos tombs. She had four workmen looking for tombs, and they cleared out the tholoi they found, probably from above. She reports that two boys removed a stone from the wall of Tomb IV, creating a window, and in order to remove the pithos within they had to remove the capstone and go in from the top (Boyd 1901, 134). It seems likely that her workmen generally entered the tombs from above and handed out the pottery and objects. There is little information on the disposition of the skeletons or the grave goods within, except in the case of the unlooted Tomb IV. Although some of the material still exists in the Herakleion museum, many of the vessels mentioned or illustrated were no longer to be found in 1979. The skeletal material has also disappeared. When the tombs were cleaned in 1981, it was apparent that the entranceways had not been excavated by Boyd, and we were able to clean out the stomion (doorway) and a pit or pseudodromos that existed in front of each tomb. Cleaning of the floors of the tombs also produced pottery fragments and some bones. The tomb cleared by the local landowner (Vronda IX) had been filled in after he removed the whole vessels; the soil was redeposited in the tomb for the planting of an olive tree. When this tomb was cleaned in 1981 and 1987, we were able to recover more broken fragments of pottery, a few iron objects, and some bones.

The enclosure graves, in contrast, were carefully excavated for maximum recovery of information. The methodology employed for excavation at Vronda changed over the years as we refined and adapted the system to meet changing needs. During the cleaning seasons in 1981 and 1983, when the tholos tombs and the rooms of Building A-B were still visible on the surface, excavation was carried out by rooms, graves, or areas. Within each grave, room, or area, every soil layer was given a designation as a level. In this volume, the word "Level" (with capital letter) will be used as a technical term for the stratigraphic layers observed in the first three seasons of cleaning. Thus, for example, within Tholos Tomb X, the surface soil was removed as Level 1, slope wash was designated Level 2, a harder-packed layer with stones was labeled Level 3, a layer of loose-packed stones was Level 4, two layers of rubble fill were called Levels 5 and 6, the deep fill in the pit was labeled Level 7, and the fine soil at the bottom was Level 8. Pottery was collected in bags in each level, but the bags were not assigned numbers.

During the 1984 expansion of the cleaning to areas along the slopes of the ridge, where walls and rooms were less clearly visible, a grid was imposed on the site to make it easier to plot the architecture and the finds (Fig. 5). The original grid was oriented due north, and consisted of 5.00 x 5.00 m squares, arranged five across and numbered consecutively (V 000–V 7900) from west to east. This grid proved to be inadequate for the size of the ridge, and during the course of the 1984 cleaning the grid was expanded to include five more squares to the west, again numbered consecutively from the southwestern corner (V 8000–V 15900). Thus, contiguous trenches do not always have consecutive numbers (e.g., V 4000 is adjacent to V 12400). Balks 1.00 m wide were initially left on the northern and eastern sides of each trench, although many of these were subsequently removed. Within each trench, every wall, room, or space was defined as a "Locus" and given a locus number that would replace the final digit(s) of the trench designation (e.g., Trench V 12400, Locus 1 = V 12401). Stratigraphic layers continued to be recognized as different levels, designated, for example, as Locus 12401 Level 2. Pottery pails were labeled consecutively within each locus, for example, Locus 12401 Level 2, pottery pail 1, which is expressed as V 12401.1, Level 2 in the catalogs. Also, objects were given consecutive numbers within each locus. This system caused some confusion, since it was never clear to the excavators whether the pottery pails were to be numbered consecutively in the level or in the locus; it was abandoned after 1984.

In 1987, four new grids were established to cover the remainder of the settlement. These include two large grids, Vronda West (VW) and Vronda North (VN), and two smaller grids, Vronda South (VS) and Vronda East (VE). The abrupt drop on the east and the lack of surface remains there prevented much exploration in this area, while excavations carried out to the south suggested little ancient activity. Both areas were used for the excavation dump.

Beginning in 1987, excavation was carried out according to the locus system. Within each trench, every feature was given a locus designation, whether a horizontal division (wall, room, enclosure, hearth, pit) or a vertical one (different soil layers). Within each locus, pottery pails were numbered consecutively, and object numbers were also consecutive; the pail numbers may reflect that fragments came from a specific area of the grave or those removed on different days. Although this system proved clear (if a trifle unwieldy), it was not always understood by new trench supervisors, and a variety of systems came into being for short periods of time; these will be mentioned in individual contexts.

The use of the trench system with balks helped to pinpoint the precise location of architectural, stratigraphic, and artifactual features in the excavation in an era before modern surveying technology (e.g., total station electronic distance measurement [EDM]) and the Global Positioning System (GPS). Nevertheless, the system had certain drawbacks, particularly with regard to the enclosure burials. Occasionally, a grave was located in more than one trench or even at the junction of four trenches. Grave 3 was the first burial uncovered in more than one trench. The initial attempt to excavate the parts of the grave in each trench separately proved impracticable because of the stones within the enclosure and the disposition of the pottery and bones across trench lines. Therefore, we decided to dig the entire grave as a single locus with dual designations: VW 18104/VW 18203 and later VW 18108/18104. The dual designations were cumbersome, however, and after this experiment, other graves that straddled trenches were dug as a unit with the designation of the trench in which the greatest part of the grave lay or in which the human remains were first recognized.

The first two enclosure graves appeared during the 1984 cleaning. At first they were not recognized as burials because of the fragmentary nature of the skeletal material. Both graves lay so close to the surface that the tumble and soft soil were not immediately distinguished from the topsoil, and the tiny pieces of bone were not recognized as human remains. Once these two burials were recognized, however, every attempt was made to recover all of the associated material. Beginning in the 1987 season, all of the graves were excavated by a biological anthropologist, who collaborated with the trench supervisors. Any changes in soil or differentiated areas within the enclosure were assigned different locus numbers. Although the cremated bodies were not articulated, the last burial within each enclosure was often in anatomical order, and the recognizable body parts were plotted on the grave plan. Major bones of earlier burials that had been swept to the sides were also recorded on the plans, along with recognizable grave goods. Attempts were made to remove pottery clusters in groups, and these groups were often given special designations that differed from excavator to excavator (for example, they might be given different pottery pail numbers or a cluster number that correlated with the excavator's drawing).

In the graves dug in 1987, there were some anomalies in the ways in which the human remains were initially numbered and labeled that may cause confusion to those using the records or reading preliminary reports. During the first excavation season, numbers were given to every identifiable individual, and these numbers were consecutive in the order they were recognized over the whole site. Thus, for example, burials 1 and 2 were in Grave 3, burials 3 and 6 were in Grave 4, and burials 4 and 7 were in Grave 5. Because this system was inherently confusing it was soon abandoned, and all the burials were renumbered according to their sequence within each grave. Within a grave, each burial was identified with a letter, beginning with the first encountered (e.g., Grave 9, Burial A). After the study of the skeletal material, these designations were changed to numerical labels that reflect the order in which the burials were made; for example, Grave 9, Burial A (the first encountered) became Grave 9, Burials 5, 6, and 7 (two adults and an infant), the last burials made in the enclosure. These are the numbers presented in this final report.

Once a grave was identified by the presence of human remains, soil was retained for flotation in a water sieve. In 1987 large samples were collected for water sieving, but from 1988 onward 100% of the soil was kept. Much skeletal material was recovered from the residue from water sieving, including the small bones of children, infants, and even fetuses. Tiny objects of metal, such as pins, were also found, as well as fragments of pottery that were too small to have been observed during excavation. While most of the sherds were so small and worn that they were of little use, some were large enough to join onto vessels as they were reconstructed, often providing a link between parts of vessels that otherwise could not have been joined.

Because of the hardness of the soil, a variety of tools were utilized in the excavation. Large picks were used on occasion, particularly in removing the stones that covered the cremation burials. Trowels, shave hooks, dental picks, and brushes were also employed for the graves. The biological anthropologist supervised the excavation of the graves and usually did the actual digging, plotting the bone fragments on a plan made together with the trench supervisor, who kept track of the elevations, recorded the finds, and managed the disposition of finds and pottery fragments into labeled bags. When, as was common in the 1988 season, several enclosures were under excavation at the same time, anthropological assistants carried out the actual digging with the help of trench supervisors and consultation with the biological anthropologist.

Stratigraphy

No stratigraphy was reported for the tholos tombs, and the only one excavated by the project (Tomb X) had been disturbed. The basic stratigraphy in the enclosure graves was generally quite simple and reflects the way in which the burials were made and covered over. Those enclosures found on the top of the ridge had little soil accumulation over them, whether due to erosion, human modification, or earlier excavation. Boyd commented on the poor preservation of remains on the top of the hill (1901, 132), so it seems likely that there was little accumulation of soil at the time of her excavation, or indeed ever. This lack of deposition can be seen most clearly in the area of Graves 12 and 17. The wall that formed the southern boundary of Grave 12 and the northern boundary of Grave 17 was a house wall belonging to the LM IIIC Building J, Room J4, and it must have been standing at least as high as it is preserved today. The same wall was also used in the Venetian period for Building R (Day, Klein, and Turner 2009, 159). Clearly there had not been much deposition during the thousand years that separated the Late Geometric grave from the Venetian building. Along the sides of the ridge, where terrace walls, both ancient and modern, prevented erosion, the deposits were deeper.

Topsoil represents the surface over the site at the time modern excavations began; in some areas, it had accumulated only since Boyd's time. Topsoil was typically a loose, dry, crumbly loam, brown to pale brown in color (Munsell 10YR 4/3–6/3) and mixed with pebbles and small stones. Below the topsoil there was occasionally a layer of wash: soft or compacted, yellowish-brown (10YR 5/4–6/4) to very pale brown (10YR 7/3) soil. Below the topsoil and wash, excavators generally encountered a layer of stones mixed with large quantities of shells from land snails; loose stones are the natural habitat for snails in this area, as we discovered when modern examples were collected by workmen taking down modern terrace walls and brought to us later for lunch. Below these stones, interpreted as having been heaped over the enclosure after the last burial, was the actual grave soil. This soil was generally soft, loose, ashy, and very dark brown (10YR 3/3) to grayish brown (10YR 5/2) in color. There were slight variations in the texture and color of the soil in different levels and different areas of the enclosures, and these deposits were given different locus numbers.

In most cases the different burials were not arranged stratigraphically, one on top of another. Rather, the bones and material from the earlier burials had been pushed to the sides of the enclosure and were in some cases dumped outside the enclosure walls. Grave 28 was unusual in having two largely undisturbed primary cremations. Most of the graves had been used for cremations on multiple occasions, and the sequence for each burial event became clear. A pyre was erected within the enclosure, and the body (or bodies—there was evidence for more than one person, often an adult and a child or infant) was burned, perhaps wearing jewelry or accompanied by some grave goods. After the cremation was completed (an event that took many hours), pottery and other objects were placed in the enclosure. The bodies were left in situ, as can be seen from the semi-articulation of the last cremations in an enclosure. The enclosure was then covered with a pile of stones until its next use. Markers in the form of amphorae or other large ceramic vessels may have stood over or near the enclosures, particularly on the summit of the ridge.

When the enclosure was used again for another cremation, the pile of stones was removed, and the ashy soil containing the bones and grave goods was swept to the walls of the enclosure or tossed outside if the interior space was too full. Thus, we have called the burials within the enclosures primary cremations in order to indicate that the bodies were burned there on a pyre and the human remains were left in situ, not removed for burial in a tomb elsewhere as was most common with cremations elsewhere in the Greek world (for different types of cremations, see McKinley 2013, 149). The remains that were pushed aside within the enclosure during subsequent cremations are called disturbed primary cremations. The term secondary cremation is used here to designate the bones that were removed from the pyre and placed in ceramic vessels; often these vessels were deposited in the enclosures, as was the case with the container burials in Graves 21, 26, and 28. Cremated bones that were removed from the enclosures for subsequent burials are termed discard deposits. These were often close to the enclosures and were originally given grave numbers (Graves 7, 11, 14, 22, 25, and 33 thus appear in this vol., Ch. 3, with their associated main enclosure burial number). The enclosures produced some inhumations as well, most often the last burial in a grave, as in Graves 5, 6, and 23. Also, at least two children were buried in pithoi in Graves 10 and 21, in the latter accompanying the cremation burials of two adults.

Excavation and Recording of Graves

Architecture

The orientation and location of the tholos tombs varied a good deal. In describing their architecture, the location of the entrance has determined the orientation, and it is generally given in terms of the closest cardinal direction (north, south, east, west).

The enclosure graves were also oriented in different ways, but they had no entrances. Some, but not all, were arranged on a north–south axis and presented no difficulties for description. Those that were not oriented north–south or east–west, however, have been described as if they had been rotated so that one side faced north and the others south, east, and west. For example, if the walls were oriented to the northeast, southeast, southwest, and northwest (as with Grave 5), they are described as north (for northeast), south (for southwest), east (for southeast), and west (for northwest). Generally, a glance at the state drawings of the grave should clarify which walls are being described.

Cataloging of Finds

Pottery was collected in "pails" (although plastic bags were actually used) numbered consecutively by locus or by locus/level in 1984. Recognizable objects were assigned object numbers that were sequential by locus (e.g., V 5312.1, object 1). Those objects deemed worthy were inventoried. The inventory number includes the letter V followed by the last two digits of the year of excavation and a sequential set of numbers (e.g., V88.4). These inventoried objects were ultimately put into a database, using Dbase II software. Many of the objects were also entered into the catalog of the Archaeological Collection of Ierapetra, and these were physically moved to the Ierapetra storerooms in 1998; the remainder of the material is stored in the Institute for Aegean Prehistory Study Center for East Crete (INSTAP SCEC). The metal objects were subsequently returned to the INSTAP SCEC, where they are currently stored in a climate-controlled area. In the grave catalogs, the Ierapetra museum catalog number is entered when appropriate after the Kavousi inventory number (e.g., IM 1187). Some of the material from the enclosures is now in the Archaeological Museum of Hagios Nikolaos, and its inventory number from that museum is listed after the Vronda inventory and Ierapetra museum number (e.g., HNM 15743). The material from Boyd's excavations is in the Herakleion museum, and it was studied in 1979. The Herakleion museum inventory number is included in the catalogs (e.g., HM 1960). The material uncovered in Vronda IX by the local landowner was inventoried in the Ierapetra museum, and it has Ierapetra inventory numbers; it remains in Ierapetra. The fragments collected during the cleaning of Vronda IX are stored at the INSTAP SCEC.

Presentation of the Material

The tholos tombs discovered by Boyd are presented first in this volume, since they were generally earlier in date and were excavated earlier (this vol., Ch. 2). The enclosure graves appear next (Ch. 3), followed by specialist studies. For both types of graves, the discussion includes grave-by-grave descriptions of the architecture, stratigraphy (Leslie Day), human remains (Maria Liston), faunal (Lynn Snyder and David Reese) and botanical (Kimberly Flint-Hamilton) remains, pottery, objects, and chronology (Leslie Day), followed by a catalog and description of the pottery and objects within each grave (Leslie Day). Chapters with the detailed final analysis of the cremations (Ch. 4), human remains (Ch. 5), faunal and botanical remains (Ch. 6), architecture (Ch. 7), pottery (Chs. 8, 9), and objects (Ch. 10) follow. Finally, there are general discussions of the burial customs, the society of the burying population, and the history of use of Vronda as a cemetery site (Chs. 11, 12). Three appendices provide additional information on the following: the capacities of drinking vesesls (App. A), the metallurgical analysis of iron objects (App. B), and lists of inventory and museum catalog numbers (App. C).

With regard to the enclosure graves, a grave number has been assigned to any feature containing human bone, whether or not it has any identifiable funerary structures or grave goods. A burial number has been assigned to each individual skeleton or collection of bone representing no more than one individual. A grave is an archaeological feature; a burial is a body and its associated deposit. Detailed descriptions of the human bones—their weight, preservation and signs of burning, evidence for the ages and sexes of the individuals, and any macroscopically visible signs of pathologies or anomalies—are presented with each grave.

The enclosure graves were numbered sequentially as they were found at the site, but some numbers were subsequently eliminated. Grave 18, numbered when human bone was found, turned out to be a tholos tomb, identified as Boyd's tomb 2, now Vronda VIII. Other deposits assigned grave numbers were later associated with adjacent enclosure graves on the basis of pottery joins (Graves 7, 11, 14, 22, 25, 33); the bones and other objects associated with those graves have been incorporated into their original deposits. The burials have been designated by the number of the grave in which they were found, and the skeletons were assigned numbers in the order in which they were placed in the grave (to the extent that this could be reconstructed, based on the position of the remains and stratigraphic sequences within the graves).

Assemblages of faunal remains are mentioned in the discussion of each grave and are presented in tabular form; we have deliberately refrained from reporting the minimal number of individuals (MNI) because the small numbers, fragmentation, and poor preservation make such figures meaningless. For shells, however, these figures are appropriate and are given in the tables whenever possible.

The discussion of each grave also includes descriptions of the architecture and stratigraphy, as well as a catalog and description of the pottery and objects. Because the tholos tombs were excavated unsystematically, there is no information that permits us to assign the finds to individual burials. Although there was recognizable stratigraphy in some of the enclosure graves, for the most part the material found within was disturbed by later burial events, natural processes, and human activity, making association of individual finds with particular burials difficult. For these reasons all of the material from a single tholos or enclosure has been cataloged together, although mention is made when the finds can be associated with a particular burial event.

With a few exceptions (a possible Neolithic bowl from Grave 17 [**GR17 P10**], fragments from the fill placed in Tomb VIII), only the pottery that seems to belong with the burials has been cataloged, including diagnostic pieces (whole or nearly complete vessels, rims, bases, handles, and decorated body fragments). Recognizable shapes that are too small or of uncertain shape are mentioned in the discussion of the pottery with each grave, and the pottery from each of the two cemeteries (tholos tombs and enclosure graves) is discussed in detail in a later chapter. The remainder of the pottery from the enclosure graves, probably fragments from the LM IIIC settlement embedded in the soil matrix of the graves and walls, is not discussed, but the amount by ware type is given for each grave. Objects are cataloged with the discussion of each grave and are also analyzed separately.

Catalogs

The catalogs of the material are included with the grave descriptions rather than being presented with the discussion of the individual types of objects. Within each room, the objects are cataloged by grave in the following order: pottery (**P**), metal (**M**), bone or ivory (**B**), glass (**G**), terracotta (**TC**), and stone, including stone objects (**S**) and stone tools (**ST**). The catalog number is given in bold and includes the tomb or grave in which the object was found (e.g., **TIV** or **GR3**) followed by letters that designate the material and sequential numbers for objects of that material in that tomb or grave. The catalog entries are arranged as follows:

Catalog Number (Inventory number, museum accession number; find spot [locus/pottery pail, object number]; Fig. no.; Pl. no.). Identification of object. Preservation. Measurements. Description of material and details of manufacture (including fabric, color, wear, and surface appearance). Details of shape or decoration. Type if applicable. *Bibliography. Comparanda. Date.*

Pottery

The pottery is cataloged according to ware in the following order: fine wares, medium-coarse wares, cooking wares, coarse wares, and pithos wares. Within each of these categories, pottery fragments are listed according to their surface treatment: painted (that is, light on dark, dark on light, or monochrome) and plain.

Wares

Fine Decorated

Fine decorated wares are characterized by the use of dark paint on a light background or white paint on a black background. The dark-on-light wares are most common, but because the surfaces are generally worn, it is often difficult to determine if a piece was decorated; often the paint adhered to the sediment, which was removed when the pieces were washed. Sometimes the decoration can only be seen as the area that is dull against a shiny slip. When badly burned, the paint and slip can become like a photographic negative, with the slip a darker color and the paint a lighter color. Because of the preservation, the drawings give more information than photographs, and photographs are used in this publication more as an indication of preservation than as a record of the original appearance of the vessels. The light-on-dark wares are less common; because of the poor preservation of the surface, added white paint is rarely preserved, and some of the material cataloged as monochrome may originally have been decorated with white paint. Pottery with decoration in white on a dark background is usually EO to LO in date.

Fine Monochrome

Fine monochrome pottery is particularly difficult to read, especially when it is found in small fragments. Monochrome fragments might come from a vase that was entirely painted or from one that had been partially dipped in paint. The latter form of decoration is regularly called blob decoration and can be distinguished only when the line marking the edge of the blob is preserved. The majority of the drinking vessels from the enclosures are monochrome, but some of those from the tholos tombs are dipped or blob.

Fine Plain

There is very little plain ware, and what exists may actually represent the unpainted portion of a vessel with blob or dipped decoration, or a vessel on which the decoration is no longer preserved.

Medium Coarse

Pottery that has frequent small or infrequent large inclusions has been classified as medium coarse. Generally, such vessels are similar to coarse wares but with less numerous or finer inclusions.

Cooking

Cooking wares are rare in the grave assemblages, although many fragments appear in the soil of the graves.

Coarse

Generally, all of the utilitarian pottery shapes, including small jars, jugs, kraters, basins, and assorted specialty shapes, fall into this category.

Pithos

This category includes the large, thick-walled storage jars used as containers or markers.

Shape Descriptions

Within the wares, open vessels are discussed first, then closed, proceeding from smaller to larger vessels. Within each shape, complete examples are described first, then fragments of the rims, handles, and bases, beginning with the better-preserved examples in each of these diagnostic categories. Such descriptions are minimal, providing only information that is not clear from the drawings and photographs; the vessels are described from the top down.

Terminology for Pottery Shapes

For the most part, we have adhered to the names established by Nicolas Coldstream (2001) for the pottery shapes. However, his terminology for storage jars does not fit the ceramics at Vronda. Coldstream, following James Brock (1957), recognizes three categories of jars at Knossos: amphorae, pithoi, and pyxides. The category of amphora is clear and can be recognized in the Vronda assemblages. Amphorae have closed necks and either two vertical handles on their necks (neck amphorae) or two horizontal handles on their bellies (belly-handled amphorae). At Knossos, the term pithos is used for all large jars, whether necked or neckless, that were used as cremation urns (Coldstream 2001, 24–31). All smaller containers, often of shapes similar to the urns, are termed pyxides (Coldstream 2001, 35–37). Other scholars have accepted this terminology (e.g., Tsipopoulou 2005, 349–355, 379–386; Rethemiotakis and Englezou 2010, 111–114, 146–149; Kaiser 2013, 19–40, 106–111). While this categorization makes sense for the Knossos cemeteries, with their rich sequence of secondary cremation burials in urns, it is not so useful for other sites, as Antonis Kotsonas (2008, 100–101) makes clear. It is particularly inappropriate at Vronda, because the bodies were left in situ, and the bones and ashes were not generally collected and placed in containers. The few secondary cremations were placed either in amphorae or in jars. In this publication, we will use the term necked jar for any jar with a rather restricted neck, whether large or small. The term pyxis is applied to neckless jars, regardless of their size. The term pithos is used only for two large, coarse storage jars that contained inhumations, vessels that resemble the coarse domestic storage jars.

Measurements

All measurements for the pottery and objects are given in centimeters (cm). Rim measurements are taken at the point where the rim meets a horizontal line, unless otherwise indicated. All weights are given in grams (g).

Fabrics

In the catalogs, fabrics have been generally divided into three categories according to the frequency and size of the inclusions: fine, medium coarse, and coarse. These categories were established on the basis of macroscopic observation, and they do not correspond precisely to the categories identified petrographically (fine, semi-fine, and semi-coarse).

Fine wares generally have no inclusions, but they occasionally may include a few larger stones (often phyllites) or many almost microscopic inclusions. Many of these fabrics are local, but there are a substantial number of imported vessels. Medium-coarse wares tend to have more inclusions than fine wares and thinner walls than coarse wares, but the category is a fluid one.

Coarse wares have been identified on the basis of the types established for the Kavousi area by Donald Haggis and Margaret Mook (1993) and published in the first volume of the Kavousi series (Haggis 2005). A brief description based on the work by Mook (2005) appears in *Kavousi* IIA (Mook and Day 2009). Many of the LM IIIC coarse wares are the same as those used for the cult objects from the Vronda shrine, and these were presented in a discussion of that material (Day et al. 2006). Others are to be discussed with the coarse wares from the Kastro in a future volume.

Only a few vessels from the graves were originally tested petrographically, and these are recorded in the catalog as sampled by PMD (for Peter M. Day), with the last two digits of the year followed by the sample number (e.g., sampled PMD 94/10). A further petrographic analysis of the grave pottery, which also included some vessels from one of the tholos tombs (Vronda Tomb IX), was conducted by Eleni Nodarou in 2015, and these sampled items are identified in the catalogs as follows: sampled KAV15/1–15/104. The results of the petrographic analysis are given in Chapter 9 of this volume.

Slips and Paint

Most of the fine ware had a slipped surface, whether as a result of painting the surface with a fine suspension of the clay used to make the vessel or from rubbing the surface. The surface was often slipped even when monochrome paint was added. Some of the medium-coarse and coarse wares were also slipped.

Decoration was in a darker color, and we have chosen to call this "paint," although it is not a real paint but is instead similar to the slip. Most of the decoration was probably intended to be black, although it fired red and brown as well.

Hardness

Fine wares are generally soft, either due to conditions during firing or as the result of the local soil conditions. Standard descriptions of hardness (e.g., the Mohs scale) are not helpful, as almost all Vronda fine ware falls within the soft range. There are, however, some differences within the category of soft. Fabrics that we term "very soft" are like chalk, coming off on the fingers at a touch. "Soft" fabrics are easily scratched with a fingernail, and the clay comes off on the fingers if rubbed. "Medium-soft" fabrics can also be scratched with a fingernail, but the clay does not rub off on the fingers. Occasionally, there are fragments of harder fabric ("medium-hard") or even ones that are impervious to the fingernail ("hard"). Such fabrics are probably not local. Medium-coarse and coarse wares are also soft or hard.

Color

Color presents a difficult problem in the description of pottery. Munsell soil chart designations (Munsell Color 1998, 2000) were given to each piece of pottery in an attempt to achieve standardization. Whenever possible Munsell numbers were taken in sunlight, with the sun behind the viewer. At times, however, the readings were made indoors or in shade, and they were made at different times of day and by different people. As people see colors differently even using the Munsell charts, there was a good deal of variation in the readings. With pottery that was partly burned, we have tried to take a reading on the unburned portions. For vessels that were heavily burned, we gave the closest possible reading of the gray. Fabrics that were completely blackened have simply been termed black.

Preservation

For nearly complete vessels, an attempt has been made to provide the approximate percentage of the original that is preserved. These percentages are estimates. Whenever possible, a record of the number of fragments is provided; we have always attempted to estimate the number of fragments that the vessel was broken into before excavation, so we have not counted the fresh breaks. Some vessels exist in a number of fragments, some of which themselves had been mended from broken pieces that will be referred to as sherds, and whenever possible the number of sherds making up the fragments is noted.

The pottery has poorly preserved surfaces, particularly in the enclosure graves. The fabrics are soft, and they were found coated with soil that was not easy to remove. The soil adhering to the surfaces was often harder than the clay of the pot, and the paint flaked off with the soil or was scrubbed off during the washing process. Faint traces of the painted decoration could often, but not always, be discerned, often by observation in raking light where there was still slip and where it was missing. In addition, the surface condition was affected by the heat and fire of the funeral pyre, which changed the color and consistency of many of the fabrics. A particularly soft and chalky fabric was common in the cremation burials, and the edges of vessels of such fabric were often too worn to make reconstruction possible. Edges of fragments had to be thoroughly cleaned and consolidated before vessels could be mended. Most were only mended sufficiently to make drawing possible, but some vessels were restored with plaster. Sometimes the vessels that had been in the fire were too warped to be put back together.

Quantification

All of the pottery from the enclosure graves was weighed and counted, and information was kept on the numbers of rims, bases, and handles that were found. Whenever possible, coarse wares that were not cataloged were identified according to the Kavousi coarse fabric types (Haggis and Mook 1993; Mook and Day 2009), so there is some information on the recognizable types in any given grave deposit. Frequently, in the areas of the graves fragments were removed from their pottery contexts by the conservation staff before the study began, often because they were seen to join with other fragments of vessels that were pulled out and inventoried. Whenever possible the count and weight of these pieces is given. Most of the pottery from the water sieve, however, was preserved in tiny crumbs that were not identifiable, and although these were retained, counted, and weighed, they have not been included in the statistical analysis.

Dating

Whenever possible, a date has been assigned to all cataloged pottery. The chronological sequence of the pottery (Table 1) has presented difficulties for three major reasons (for a good discussion of the problems, see Kotsonas 2008, 31–41). The first problem is the paucity of stratified deposits from the relevant periods on Crete. The majority of the pottery comes from graves that were often used over a period of time and disturbed, where vessels of different styles were not placed one over the other or found in their original positions. The dating of this pottery must be based on a typology of shapes and style of decoration. To date, only at Knossos have habitation deposits from the SM, PG (subdivided into Early, Middle, Late, and B phases: EPG, MPG, LPG, PGB), G (subdivided into EG, MG, and LG), and O (divided into the early and late phases EO and LO) periods been excavated, published, and correlated with the pottery from the graves (Coldstream 2001, 21). The second difficulty lies in the fact that earlier styles of pottery may have continued in circulation or been deemed appropriate for deposition in graves; there is evidence of this custom in the Vronda grave assemblages, where earlier PG styles are found together with LG and even EO–LO pottery. The third problem in the dating of the EIA pottery on Crete is regionalism. Ceramic phases established for Knossos do not correlate precisely with the sequences in other areas of the island, and East Crete in particular developed its own idiosyncratic styles that often lagged behind those in Central Crete. Evidence from the settlement at Kavousi Kastro shows that the earlier PG styles were being produced or at least still in circulation in LG (Mook 2004, 169–173), and that LG styles lingered into the 7th century there (pers. comm., M.S. Mook). In addition, while the many imports from Attica and Euboea at Knossos help to correlate the Central Cretan sequence with that of the rest of Greece, the lack of such imports and even of pottery from Knossos makes such correlations in East Crete difficult. The problem is particularly acute in the SM, PG, and earlier G periods, but somewhat less so in LG, EO, and LO.

The period known as Subminoan was identified by Vincent Desborough (1964, 169) and James Brock (1957, 8), but it has not been found stratified between LM IIIC and EPG contexts anywhere, a fact that has led some scholars to think that it is a style (Mook 2004, 169; Hallager 2010, 153) rather than a chronological unit, as it is viewed by others (e.g, Catling 1996d, 295–297; D'Agata 2011, 53; Day et al. 2016, 103–104). At Knossos four phases of SM were recognized above the LM IIIC deposits, but no succeeding EPG stratum was identified (Warren 1982–1983, 76–87). Two phases of SM have been identified at Sybrita/Thronos, but the material comes from unstratified deposits or discrete ritual pits (D'Agata 1999; 2003; 2007, 101; 2011). Elsewhere on Crete, SM appears primarily in graves, many of which were used over a period of time and contained material of several ceramic phases, as in the North Cemetery at Knossos (Coldstream 2001) and at Eltyna (Rethemiotakis and Englezou 2010), Chamaizi Phatsi (Tsipopoulou 1997), and Vasiliki (Tsipopoulou, Vagnetti, and Liston 2003).

Because SM material appears so commonly in tombs, it has been argued that the SM pottery style was created especially for funerary contexts, as was proposed some time ago for Submycenaean on the mainland (Rutter 1978) and recently reiterated (Papadopoulos, Damiata, and Marston 2011). Thus, it would have been contemporary with late Late M IIIC, but the specialized shapes found in the tombs were not used in the settlements (Gaignerot-Driessen 2016, 17). Florence Gaignerot-Driessen has refined this, suggesting that the style was used exclusively for burial in Eastern Crete, if not elsewhere (2016, 17). Reexamination of the pottery from Karphi, however, where tholos tombs lay scattered around the LM IIIC settlement, revealed that many of the tombs contained material similar to what was used in the LM IIIC houses, as well as some later material including SM and EPG (Day 2011b, 221–242). Thus, the idea that SM was a functional category of pottery made only for funerary use seems not to hold true for that site. In the Kavousi area, one phase (IV) on the Kastro is stratified between LM IIIC and EPG and contains material from both periods (Mook 2004, 169). The excavators have rejected the term SM for this material, preferring to call it "transitional," but it is in many ways similar to that identified at Sybrita/Thronos as SM II (D'Agata 2011, 55). Material at Azoria has also been identified as transitional between LM IIIC and PG (Haggis et al. 2007a, 696–697).

As has been argued elsewhere (Day et al. 2016, 197–198), there is evidence for SM as a distinct chronological phase at Vronda. While a few vessels approaching SM in style appeared just before the abandonment of the settlement, the majority of the final pottery was of LM IIIC date. Pottery of clear SM date, similar to that found in the earliest tombs of the North Cemetery at Knossos, only began to appear in the tholos tombs, and the tombs were used (if not constructed) after the houses of the settlement had gone out of use. The fact that one of the tholoi was built over a house in the LM IIIC settlement shows that the tombs represent a later phase in the use of the Vronda ridge (Day et al. 2016, 197), although unfortunately this tholos (Tomb VIII) provided little material for dating, and the only preserved vessel (**VIII P1**) that can be securely identified is of LM IIIC date.

It seems clear that a distinct chronological phase existed between LM IIIC and EPG, although there is some disagreement about the terminology that should be applied to it and whether it came late to the eastern part of the island. Should SM be seen as the latest phase of LM IIIC or the earliest appearance of PG? This question is not merely a matter of terminology, because the change to PG has been seen as evidence for the arrival of Greek speakers in Crete (Warren 1982–1983, 83). It seems best, as there is a phase in the Cretan ceramic sequence already identified as transitional between LM IIIC and EPG, with the long-standing label of SM, to retain this designation and hope for future findings to refine its definition.

The identification of PG through MG material is also problematic at Kavousi. There are few imports of pottery from Central Crete or elsewhere in this period, making correlation of the East Cretan ceramic sequence with the rest of the island difficult, and there may be a regional style of PG. At first the EPG period in East Crete seems to conform to that of Central Crete, although it is possible that the SM style lingered longer in the east. The ceramic styles identified as MPG, LPG, PGB, EG, and MG at Knossos and elsewhere on the island, however, cannot be recognized in the east, where PG styles continued well into the 8th century. Thus, many of the graves, both tholos tombs and enclosure burials, contain pottery that is PG in style (sometimes with parallels in shape or decoration to specific subperiods in Central Crete) but is associated with later LG vessels (Mook 2004, 169–173; Tsipopoulou 2005, 346–347; Kotsonas 2008, 36–37). Mook suggested that the East Cretan pottery of PG style but contemporary with EG and MG in Central Crete (810–745 B.C.; Coldstream 2001, 22) be termed "SubPG" on analogy with certain areas on the mainland (e.g., Euboea; Popham, Sackett, and Themelis 1979–1980, 362) where PG styles continued even after the introduction of Geometric motifs and shapes. Because it is difficult to know if a vessel of PG style was an antique placed with the dead or was produced in an earlier style, the term is not applied to the Vronda grave pottery, although it is used for comparanda from other sites.

During the first half of the 8th century, East Crete began to pick up some of the Geometric styles of Central Crete, and we term this period Geometric. Although some PG styles lingered into the second half of the 8th century in East Crete, the LG pottery seems to correlate with the Central Cretan sequence for LG. However, there may have been a time lag in adopting the LG styles at Kavousi, and LG pottery may have continued to be produced even after the EO styles were popular in Central Crete. On analogy with the term SubPG, the labels "SubG" and "SubLG" have been used by some scholars to indicate pottery made in LG style in the 7th century, but those labels are not applied to the Vronda material.

There is much pottery of 7th century date that we call Early or even Late Orientalizing at Vronda. The term "Orientalizing" carries a great deal of baggage, and many scholars have abandoned it (for a good discussion of the problems of terminology, see Kotsonas 2008, 40). Kotsonas prefers the term "Protoarchaic." Orientalizing pottery in East Crete is rarely figured and does not seem to follow styles elsewhere in Crete or in the Aegean. This style may not have been adopted locally in East Crete until it was already established elsewhere on the island. While the latest burials at Vronda contain much EO pottery, most of them produced a few pieces that find parallels elsewhere from the end of the 7th century, a fact that suggests a lag in the adoption of Orientalizing styles.

In the catalogs, the date given for any individual piece of pottery is its stylistic date, based upon the shape and decoration of the vessel rather than the context, which is usually SM–PG in the tholoi, and LG—but occasionally G, EO, or LO—in the enclosures.

Other Objects

Besides the pottery, other objects from the graves have been cataloged according to their material as follows: metals, bone or ivory, glass, stone, and terracotta. We have made some attempt at dating these objects, especially the metal pins and fibulae, but for the most part the metal, stone, and terracotta objects did not change as much as the pottery, and they cannot be closely dated.

Metals

Metal objects are made of bronze, iron, or lead, and they are cataloged by material in that order. Within each metal group, jewelry is presented first, then decorative metalwork followed by weapons and tools. Jewelry includes pins, fibulae, earrings, rings, and bracelets. Decorative metalwork generally occurs in the form of bronze sheeting that was attached to another material. Weapons are presented according to size from small to large, beginning with arrowheads, followed by spearheads, and finally by short swords (dirks) or daggers. Knives are here considered primarily to have been tools, although admittedly some were also useful as weapons. Tools are discussed in the following order: knives, axes, scrapers, chisels, hammers, files, tongs, awls, tweezers, fleshhooks, and miscellaneous. Every attempt has been made to identify these objects despite their corroded state, but some metal objects defy identification. Weapons present particular difficulties in determining precise functions. For example, it is uncertain whether a socketed head belonged to an iron spear (used for thrusting) or a javelin (used for throwing), so these objects have generally been cataloged as spearheads. Similarly, the differences between a sword, a small sword (dirk), and a dagger are uncertain. The images of the cataloged metal objects include both photographs and line drawings. The photographs show the objects as they are, while the line drawings indicate how they might have looked before their shapes were corroded and warped.

Bone or Ivory

Objects of bone or ivory are rare and are often completely burned, making identification difficult. This material was generally used for beads, but it could also have been used for inlays or decorative handles.

Glass

Glass was rare in the graves and was used only for beads.

Stone

Stone objects include beads and lids. Most of the beads were made of serpentinite, but a single bead of carnelian (**GR1 S1**) and one of rock crystal (**GR36 S1**) were also found. Most of the lids were simply flat slabs of stones that had been chipped around the edges to make a circle and used to seal container burials, such as those in Graves 10 (**GR10 P1**) and 28 (**GR28 P3, GR28 P22**). A single knobbed lid (**IV S1**) was found in Tomb IV that may have been an antique or a found object. A few fragments of obsidian blades were also found, but these may well have dated to earlier periods of the site's use. Other stone tools found infrequently within the enclosures probably also belonged to the period of the settlement's use.

History and Chronology of the Vronda Remains

The tholos tombs found by Boyd around the periphery of the Vronda settlement produced pottery considerably later than that discovered in the abandonment levels of the LM IIIC settlement, and it is clear that they were used after the site was no longer inhabited. These tombs began to be used soon after the abandonment of the settlement, with major interruptions until they were reused in the 8th century, probably by the inhabitants of the Kastro.

In the late 8th century the new type of cremation burials in stone-lined enclosures appeared within the abandoned buildings of the earlier settlement. Although most of the cremation enclosures belong to the LG period (second half of the 8th century), several graves (4, 15, 17, 23, 30, 32) continued in use into EO (early 7th century) or even LO (late 7th century). After this time, Vronda was truly abandoned until the Venetian era, when it again became a site for houses (Buildings F and R).

2

Tholos Tombs at Vronda

Leslie Preston Day and Maria A. Liston

In 1900, Boyd excavated eight tholos tombs on Vronda (Thunder Hill), the spur of the mountain above Kavousi village (Figs. 1–4, 6; Pls. 2, 3; Boyd 1901, 132–137). At that time her workmen cleaned off the tops of the tombs and entered them from above. Only four of these tombs contained objects, while the remainder were robbed. The tombs that produced objects were given number designations (1–4), while those that were empty were assigned letters (A–D). Boyd published the tholoi briefly, giving dimensions of the tombs and listing their contents, if any still remained. The number of ceramic vessels was recorded for each tomb, and some of the pottery was illustrated. One photograph (Boyd 1901, pl. I) shows the pottery from Tomb 3, while another (1901, pl. II) illustrates vessels from Tombs 1, 2, and 4 without further identification. When the material from Boyd's excavations was studied in 1979 by the directors of the Kavousi Project (Gesell, Day, and Coulson 1983, 389–409), it was impossible to identify many of these vessels unless they still bore the original pencil label, and some of them (even those illustrated in the publication) were no longer to be found in the Herakleion Archaeological Museum. Another tholos tomb excavated in 1951 by a local landowner lay down the slopes to the north of Boyd's tombs at a place now called Xerambela (Fig. 6; Pl. 2), and it was only mentioned briefly in publication (Platon 1951, 445). The pottery from this tholos, which was taken to the Ierapetra museum, was also studied in 1979 with the permission of Nicholas Platon.

Five of Boyd's original eight tombs were cleaned in 1981 by members of the Kavousi Project, and material was recovered, some from within the tholoi, but more from the entryways (the stomion and the pit or pseudo-dromos in front). These entrances had remained unexcavated by Boyd's workmen, who went into the tombs from the top. Three of the tombs (Boyd's tombs 2, 4, and B) were not located at that time. In the preliminary report the numbers that Boyd gave the tombs were changed so that all the tombs on Vronda would have consecutive Roman numeral designations (Gesell, Day, and Coulson 1983, 394). The concordance of these numbers is as follows: Boyd tomb A = Vronda Tomb I; Boyd tomb B = Vronda Tomb III; Boyd tomb C = Vronda Tomb V; Boyd tomb D = Vronda Tomb VI; Boyd tomb 1 = Vronda Tomb II; Boyd tomb 2 = Vronda

Tomb VIII; Boyd tomb 3 = Vronda Tomb IV; Boyd tomb 4 = Vronda Tomb VII; 1951 tomb = Vronda Tomb IX; 1981 tomb = Vronda Tomb X; 1990 tomb = Vronda Tomb XI.

Another tomb, labeled Vronda X, was excavated in 1981, and although it had been robbed, a small amount of material was found inside (Gesell, Day, and Coulson 1983, 405–409). During the excavations at Vronda from 1987–1992, some further excavation was done in and around Boyd's tombs. It was apparent that just to the south of Tomb IV lay Boyd's dump, which was excavated and produced some bones and objects belonging to Tomb IV. When Building L-M was uncovered in 1988, another tholos appeared in the area of Building L, Rooms L2 and L3, and it became evident that this tomb was one of Boyd's tombs that had been covered over; its location conforms to that shown on her plan as tomb 2 (now Tholos VIII), which had not been located in 1981 (Gesell, Coulson, and Day 1991, 160–161; Day and Glowacki 2012, 144, 146–148). Another tomb came to light in the area just north of LM IIIC Building Complex I-O-N in 1990 (Gesell, Day, and Coulson 1995; Day and Glowacki 2012, 170–171). At first this was believed to be one of Boyd's that had not been located in 1979 (Tholos VII; Gesell, Day, and Coulson 1995, 91–92), as it conformed to the location Boyd indicated on her schematic plan of the cemetery (Boyd 1901, 132 n. 1). Subsequently, however, it became clear that the well-preserved tomb did not match the description given by Boyd, and the tomb was given a new designation of Tholos XI. In 1988 some cleaning also was done in Tholos IX, where it appeared that the landowner had only removed whole vessels and had left fragments of pottery and iron objects behind in the fill put in after the planting of an olive tree.

The significance of these tombs and their relationship to the LM IIIC settlement is difficult to determine, and dating has been problematic. None of the material from the tombs looks as early as that found in the LM IIIC settlement (see Day et al. 2016, 197), although fragments around the floors and in the stomion and pseudo-dromos of the tombs look LM IIIC in date. Tomb VIII cut into one of the LM IIIC buildings, and it is possible that Tomb XI did as well. The other tombs are to the north and the west of the earlier settlement, possibly outside its boundaries. While it is possible that these tombs were constructed and first used by the inhabitants of the Vronda settlement in LM IIIC, one would have to suppose that subsequent users removed all of the material belonging to those earlier burials. It is more likely that these tholos tombs were constructed after the abandonment of the LM IIIC settlement. Our interpretation is also hampered by the fragmentary state of the evidence, as so many of the vessels excavated by Boyd are now missing or their find spots could not be determined. Most of the published material dates to SM–PG, but there is some later Geometric material, perhaps not as late as that which was found in the cremation cemetery on the ridge above. From Boyd's publication, it is impossible to assign groups of pots to particular burials within the tombs, and dating must be done purely on stylistic grounds. As the pottery sequence for East Crete in this period is still a matter for debate, dating often becomes difficult or impossible, especially with small jugs and cups. Desborough (1952, 268) was uncomfortable with some of the material illustrated for Tombs II, VIII, and VII (Boyd tombs 1, 2, 4), but he thought that if Tomb IV (Boyd tomb 3) was a homogeneous group, then probably II, VIII, and VII were also. After examining some of the unpublished material from Tombs IV and IX, it is clear that there is some later material in the tombs, showing, at least, that they were used over a considerable period of time by several generations. It is thus probable that none of the tombs is homogeneous in date.

Vronda Tomb I (Boyd's Tomb A)

In 1900, Boyd found Vronda Tomb I in a ruined state and thoroughly plundered (Boyd 1901, 132). The tomb was located and cleaned in 1981. At that time the interior circle was visible, but the stomion and the area in front of it had not been cleared (Pl. 4A). Cleaning revealed a stone-lined dromos leading into the tomb. Some fragments of pottery were recovered, primarily from the dromos and stomion (Gesell, Day, and Coulson 1983, 396–397).

Architecture and Features

Vronda Tomb I is not well preserved; it rises only four courses high in the south and three courses on the north for a maximum preserved height of 0.86 m (Fig. 7). In the shape of an irregular circle, it has an interior diameter of 1.64–1.68 m (Fig. 8). During construction some of the *tsakali* bedrock had been cut away around the exterior, and the blocks of the walls were shoved up against it, particularly on the east and north; on the south, the stones seem to have been pushed up against the slope of the hill. The entrance is on the west through a long (1.60 m) dromos and a stomion or doorway (Fig. 8; Pl. 4B). The dromos runs parallel to the slope of the ridge, and the stomion opens out to the west onto what is today a flat terrace. The bottom of the grave had been carved out of the local *tsakali*, and a dirt floor had been laid over it. The walls were constructed almost entirely of the local breccia, with some limestone blocks used for the stomion. The stomion was 0.50 m high, 0.72 m wide, and 0.64 m deep. While some limestone was employed in the sides of this doorway, the lintel is a single block of breccia. The area in front of the stomion had been excavated out of the *tsakali* by the builders as a long pit, which was then lined with stones, forming a dromos. This dromos consists of two nearly parallel rows of single limestone or breccia blocks, four on the north and three on the south. The north wall of the dromos is longer than the south, and it bends out slightly toward the north. The floor of the dromos slopes downward from the exterior to the stomion.

Stratigraphy

The burial chamber was found filled with tightly packed soil and medium- to large-sized stones, all of which appeared to have accumulated since Boyd's time. The stomion and dromos, however, had not been previously excavated. The stomion had been blocked in antiquity with two large, flat stones set one on top of the other, with some soil above, below, and between the stones (Pl. 4B). The dromos was found filled with hard light brown soil mixed with stones, and over the top of this soil a large quantity of stones was encountered, perhaps a sort of cairn marking the position of the entrance (Pl. 4C).

Burials

During cleaning, remains of a single burial were discovered.

Burial 1

Type: disturbed inhumation
Age: adult
Sex: unknown

Tomb I contained 18.00 g of bone, consisting of four fragments of long bone shaft that appear to be from an adult human.

Faunal Remains

A single bone was identified from the dromos (Table 2). It is a sheep or goat unsided femur diaphysis fragment. The element is eroded.

Pottery

Several fragments that may represent material from the use of the tomb were recovered from the cleaning within the chamber. These include a bell skyphos (**I P1**), a very small rim fragment that may come from a krater or a jar (**I P2**), and a kalathos or lekane (**I P3**). The bell skyphos is unusual in shape because of the ridge at the base of the neck. A similar shape, with a more flaring rim above the ridge, characterizes a bell krater from Knossos (Coldstream and Catling, eds., 1996, 115, fig. 95:136), where it is categorized as an EG survival of a PG shape. The rim fragment (**I P2**) resembles LM IIIC kraters from the Vronda settlement (Day, Klein, and Turner 2009, 30, fig. 16:AE P18; 131, fig. 87:J1 P15), but it may also have come from a jar or necked pithos like those from Knossos of E (Coldstream and Catling, eds., 1996, 92, fig. 86:3) or EG date (Coldstream and Catling, eds., 1996, 170, fig. 121:129.5). The lekane (**I P3**) is similar to an example from the LM IIIC Vronda settlement (Day and Glowacki 2012, 97, fig. 86:O1 P13). Very little was recovered from the dromos beyond a fragment of a skyphos and several pithos sherds.

Objects

In Tholos I, Boyd discovered only one soapstone whorl, which could not be found in 1979.

Chronology

There is little evidence that would allow us to date this tomb. The bell skyphos (**I P1**) is probably of PG date, while the rim fragment (**I P2**) could have come from a LM IIIC krater or a PG–EG jar. The lekane (**I P3**) seems to be closest to LM IIIC examples from the settlement and elsewhere, but it may represent material from the settlement that came in with the soil. A date within SM–PG seems the most likely.

Catalog

Pottery

Fine Wares

I P1 (Fig. 9). Bell skyphos. Single fragment from rim and upper body, including handle attachment; at least two or as many as six additional body fragments may belong. Max. pres. h. 5.9; d. rim 16.0. Fine, reddish-yellow (5YR 7/8) fabric, worn and flaky surfaces. Traces of light red paint inside and out. Flaring rim, with collar below it; two round horizontal handles. *Bibliography*: Gesell, Day, and Coulson 1983, 397, fig. 4. *Comparanda*: Coldstream and Catling, eds., 1996, 50, fig. 72:106 (Knossos, LPG); Sackett, ed., 1992, pl. 51:GA2 (Knossos, LPG). *Date*: PG.

I P2 (Fig. 9). Krater or jar. Single fragment from rim. D. rim est. 20.0. Fine, reddish-yellow (5YR 7/8) fabric with flaky worn surfaces. Traces of streaky black paint inside and out. *Date*: PG?

Medium-Coarse Wares

I P3 (Fig. 9). Kalathos or lekane. Single fragment from rim. D. rim est. 26.1. Medium-coarse, reddish-yellow (5YR 7/8) fabric with pebble and clay inclusions. Some secondary burning on exterior. No traces of paint inside or out. *Comparanda*: Rethemiotakis and Englezou 2010, 44, fig. 23:45 (Eltyna, SM); Day and Glowacki 2012, fig. 85:O1 P13 (Vronda, LM IIIC). *Date*: LM IIIC or SM.

Vronda Tomb II (Boyd's Tomb 1)

Vronda II lies north of the LM IIIC settlement, west of Tomb I. Boyd reported that this tomb had partly collapsed (Boyd 1901, 132–133, pl. II; Gesell, Day, and Coulson 1983, 396–398). Although it was partially robbed, the tumble of several large blocks preserved a number of objects, some of which were pictured without further identification on plate II of Boyd's 1901 publication (Pl. 5A). The tomb was said to contain parts of three skeletons (including a skull), 13 nearly whole pots, two bronze rings, and two clay whorls (Boyd 1901, 132). The burial chamber was cleaned in 1981, and the stomion and pit that formed a pseudo-dromos in front of the tomb were excavated at that time, producing some additional sherds.

Architecture and Features

Tomb II is well preserved (Fig. 10). It stands five courses high to a maximum preserved height of 1.30 m. The *tsakali* bedrock was cut back when the tomb was constructed, particularly on the southeast (visible in the photo: Pl. 5B). The interior ground plan is a rough oval measuring 1.30 × 1.70 m. The tomb is constructed primarily of local breccia boulders, with smaller breccia and limestone blocks at the bottom. A dirt floor covered over a slight depression carved below the foundations of the walls into the bedrock. The stomion is on the northwest; it is an elaborately-constructed facade with a large lintel block of limestone and another course of limestone blocks with small stones as chinking above (Pl. 6A). The support for the lintel is made up of two courses of limestone blocks on either side. The stomion is 0.60 m high, 0.42 m wide, and 1.20 m deep. The floor of the stomion is made up of three flat paving stones, and it slopes downward from the opening toward the tomb chamber. There is no true dromos outside this stomion as in Vronda Tomb I or elsewhere (e.g., at Karphi: Pendlebury, Pendlebury, and Money-Coutts 1937–1938, 100–107, pls. 12, 13), but the projecting stones of the stomion form a pseudo-dromos. In front of the facade is a pit 1.20 m long and 1.60 m wide cut into the *tsakali*.

Stratigraphy

The tomb chamber was found filled with large stones, probably fallen from the upper part of the corbeling since Boyd's day. Some hard-packed light brown soil overlay the *tsakali* bedrock, and this was removed; it was probably the original floor of the chamber. It resembled the unexcavated soil in the stomion and pseudo-dromos, so it probably was not soil that had accumulated during the years the tomb lay open after Boyd's excavations. The stomion and pseudo-dromos had not been excavated and were cleared in 1981. The stomion was filled with hard-packed light brown soil (Level 2) with two very large, flat slabs of limestone and two smaller pieces of limestone above the soil (Pl. 6B). The pit in the pseudo-dromos had been dug down to the *tsaka-li*. After use, the pit was filled in with hard-packed light brown soil similar to that filling the stomion. At the level of the bottom of the lintel block, a layer of flat paving stones of limestone was placed in front of the stomion (Pl. 6C). Finally, the area was filled up with more soil (Level 1) and a layer of stones placed on top to form a sort of cairn or marker over the pit (Pl. 7A).

Burials

Boyd reported removing three human skeletons from the tomb (Boyd 1901, 133). Her excavation appears to have been quite thorough; during the cleaning only two pieces of human bone were recovered.

Burial 1
Type: disturbed inhumation
Age: adult
Sex: unknown

Fragments of adult human bone, a first metacarpal and a long bone shaft fragment, were recovered in the cleaning.

Faunal Remains

Two animal bones were recovered during the cleaning of this tholos (Table 2). The first, a single sheep or goat vertebra fragment, was eroded. A second bone fragment was unidentifiable as to animal or element represented. Two additional sheep or goat elements, possibly from Vronda Tomb II, were recovered on August 28, 1981. The distal portion of a left metatarsal came from an immature animal. An isolated first phalange was also recovered.

Pottery

Of the 13 vases mentioned by Boyd, only the lentoid flask (**II P1**) can be securely identified; others may be pictured in her plate II (1901; Pl. 5A). The lentoid flask is almost certainly of SM date and has parallels in the East Cretan repertoire of this period. Other fragments found in the cleaning were largely coarse wares, including pithos and cooking wares that may have been in the soil at the time of construction. The pottery from the pseudo-dromos produced a number of small fragments from fine drinking vessels and some possible oinochoe fragments, none of which is precisely datable. Vessel **II P2** is either a LM IIIC deep bowl or a SM–PG skyphos fragment, and the high placement of the handles suggests a LM IIIC date.

Objects

Boyd reported finding four objects in this tomb: two bronze rings and two clay whorls, none of which was located in the Herakleion museum in 1979. Of the two terracotta "whorls" or beads, one was plain with a diameter of 2.50 cm, while the other, with a diameter of 1.70 cm, had a "walnut" pattern (Boyd 1901, 132), probably similar to examples found in the cremation burials (**GR3 TC1**, **GR36 TC5**; this vol., Ch. 3). One of the bronze rings, with a diameter of 3.50 cm, had small hooked points, and it may have been an earring like the one found in Enclosure Grave 3. The other, with a diameter of 2.00 cm, also had hooks, but they were broken.

Chronology

There is very little material with which to date this tomb. The lentoid flask (**II P1**) suggests a SM date for at least one of the burials. Of the fragments recovered in cleaning, one may have come from a LM IIIC deep bowl (**II P2**), similar in shape to a very late LM IIIC example from the Vronda settlement (see below). Two drinking vessels (**II P3**, **II P4**) from the pseudo-dromos have rim profiles similar to LPG or LG cups, but they are much larger, indicating a LG date for the last burial.

Catalog of Finds from Chamber

Pottery

FINE DECORATED WARES

II P1 (HM 1972; Fig. 9; Pl. 7B). Lentoid flask. Intact, but worn and chipped at the rim. H. 15.6; d. rim 2.9; max. d. 12.3. Very soft, fine, very pale brown (10YR 8/3) fabric, reddish-yellow (5YR 7/6) where paint has worn off. Irregular lentoid body, more rounded on one face than the other, with short, slightly flaring neck. Rim beveled inside.

Upper handle attachment just below rim. Airhole below handle. Decoration worn, but traces of concentric circles on body, with large filled circle in center. Possible bands on neck. *Bibliography*: Gesell, Day, and Coulson 1983, 397, fig. 4:2, pl. 76:a; Tsipopoulou 2005, 79, pl. 32, fig. 144; Karageorghis et al. 2014, 97 (Creto-Cypriot juglet, SM). *Comparanda*: Catling 1968, 113, 115, fig. 5:21; Popham, Sackett, and Themelis 1979–1980, 331, pl. 126:8 (Lefkandi, LPG); Tsipopoulou 1997, 469, fig. 12 (Chamaizi Phatsi SM); 2005, 321, fig. 144:Σ3819 (Chamaizi, SM); Hayden 2003, 47, fig. 21:99 (Vrokastro, SM/PG). *Date*: SM.

Catalog of Finds from Pseudo-Dromos

Pottery

Fine Monochrome Wares

II P2 (Fig. 9). Deep bowl or skyphos. Single fragment from rim with handle attachment. D. rim est. 12.0. Fine, soft, pink (5YR 7/4) fabric. Red (2.5YR 4/6) paint. Monochrome inside and out. *Bibliography*: Gesell, Day, and Coulson 1983, 397, fig. 4:3 (emended). *Comparanda*: Day and Glowacki 2012, 13, fig. 16:E1 P96 (Vronda, late LM IIIC). *Date*: LM IIIC–PG.

II P3 (Fig. 9). Cup or skyphos. Two joining fragments and one nonjoining from rim. D. rim est. 15.0. Fine, soft, light red (2.5YR 6/6) fabric. Black to red (2.5YR 5/6) paint. Worn surfaces. Monochrome inside and out. *Comparanda*: **GR9 P13–GR9 P15**. *Date*: LG?

Medium-Coarse Wares

II P4 (Fig. 9). Cup or skyphos. Single fragment from rim. D. rim est. 14.0. Medium-coarse, reddish-yellow (5YR 6/6) fabric with phyllite inclusions. Creamy, heavy, red (2.5YR 4/6) to black paint. Worn and eroded surfaces. Monochrome inside and out. *Comparanda*: **GR9 P23**. *Date*: LG?

Vronda Tomb III (Boyd's Tomb B)

Vronda III, which was the best preserved of the tholos tombs excavated by Boyd, lay north of the settlement and southwest of Tomb II, but it could not be located in 1981 (Boyd 1901, 132). The tomb published by Eaby (2007, fig. 54) as Vronda III is actually Vronda Tomb VIII (see bleow). Boyd described the tomb as the best constructed of the eight she found, with the chamber made of large stones in fairly regular shapes, probably limestone. She reported that the chamber was square at the bottom to a height of 0.67 m, and then the corners rounded out and the corbeling began. What she called the dome was made of smaller, more irregular stones. The lintel block was broken in two pieces. The burial chamber had an estimated height of 2.00 m, while the ground plan was a square measuring 2.00 m on each side. The stomion was 0.80 m high, while the pseudo-dromos was 0.85 m wide. Boyd found nothing in this tomb.

Vronda Tomb IV (Boyd's Tomb 3)

Tomb IV lies to the northwest of the LM IIIC settlement, east of Tomb V. Boyd found this tomb intact, with four skeletons stretched out on the floor beside a pithos containing ash, and with 40 vases scattered around (Boyd 1901, 133–134, pl. I). A number of objects of bronze and iron were found, including five fibulae. Of the 40 vases mentioned by Boyd, only 19 can now be identified: 10 still preserved in the Herakleion museum in 1979 and another nine pictured in the original publication (Pl. 7C). Only five of the bronze objects could be found in the Herakleion museum in 1979: four fibulae and the bracelet. There was no trace of the pithos. During the 1981 cleaning, some sherds were recovered from inside the tomb and some from the area in front of the facade (Gesell, Day, and Coulson 1983, 397–399). A large number of fragments came from a dump just outside the tomb, which was cleaned in 1987 and 1988 when rainstorms revealed quantities of human bone in the scarp.

Architecture and Features

Vronda IV is of unusual plan, with a good facade and two walls defining a broad area in front of the stomion (Figs. 11, 12; Pls. 8A, 8B). It was built into the hillside, with the stomion facing west. The tomb chamber is preserved generally to a height of 1.60

m in seven courses, with one stone remaining of the eighth course in the south. It is roughly circular in shape, measuring 1.70 x 1.80 m, with the stomion off-center at the north end of the west side. The floor is bedrock.

The stomion floor slopes down to meet the floor of the chamber. The stomion is elaborately constructed with a large (0.96 x 0.26 m) limestone lintel block, a layer of small stones above it, and a third course of limestone blocks above that (Pl. 8B). The front of the tomb extends to a terrace wall on the north. This terrace wall projects some 1.45 m to the west, perpendicular to the stomion, forming a space in front of the tomb. An elaborate facade is thus created for the tomb, and this extends to the south. While there is no wall corresponding to the one projecting on the north, the facade extends at least to a line of stones running east that may mark the southern boundary of the tomb. The doorway itself is 0.86 m wide, 0.60–0.80 m high, and 0.70 m deep.

In front of the stomion, a small pit was cut into the bedrock and lined with two stones, breccia on the north and limestone on the south, to form a pseudo-dromos. The pit was 0.90 m long and 1.04 m wide. On the north, the terrace wall continues to the east of the tomb to mark out its boundary, while the line of stones on the south side may indicate the southern boundary. The presence of a sort of temenos wall around this tomb, along with the elaborate facade and the open area on the front, are unique features, not known at any of the other Kavousi tholoi and unparalleled elsewhere, although some of the Karphi tholoi at Ta Mnemata (Tombs 1, 2, and 5) have boundary walls around the outside (Pendlebury, Pendlebury, and Money-Coutts 1937–1938, pl. 12). It is possible that the area in front of the tomb was left open or was opened at the time of each burial for the enactment of a ritual. It is also interesting that one of the later Geometric cremation enclosures (Grave 3) was placed just downslope from Vronda IV and on a similar alignment (Fig. 12); it also had an unusual feature: a paving to the south of the grave that may also have been open for postfunerary rituals.

Stratigraphy

The tomb was found with stones and fill inside, and it was cleared out in 1981. The area in front of the stomion and over the pseudo-dromos was covered with stones (Pl. 8C). A layer of flat stones was found at the level of the lintel as in Tombs II and VII (cf. Pl. 6C). The stomion itself also was filled with flat stones and hard soil, like the other tholoi at Vronda (cf. Pl. 6B).

Burials

Boyd reported four skeletons lying in extended positions on the tomb floor, along with a pithos containing ash. This ash may represent the remains of a cremation burial, but no bones were recognized within; a broken fibula and three pieces of an iron blade accompanied the ash in the pithos. Although little bone was recovered from the tomb itself during cleaning, a quantity of human bone was uncovered in the dump adjacent to the tomb, which was found to contain the soil and discarded materials from Boyd's excavation. Boyd noted that three of the skulls were intact and the fourth was fragmentary (Boyd 1901, 134). The three intact skulls were apparently removed, but fragments of a single skull, possibly the broken one noted by Boyd, were recovered from the dump deposit. Eighty grams of cranial bone and 1,204.00 g of postcranial bone were found in the dump of Vronda IV.

In addition to the bone in the dump, assumed to be from the tomb itself, more human bone was found in the area in front of the tomb, which had not been excavated by Boyd. As Boyd indicated that the tomb contained intact skeletons, these remains may be from earlier burials in the tomb that were removed to make room for the later bodies. The bone from the area in front of the tomb comes from a minimum of two individuals, recorded here as Burials 5 and 6.

Burial 1

Type: disturbed inhumation
Age: mature adult
Sex: male

One of the partial skeletons found in Boyd's dump is an adult male of indeterminate age. The sex of this individual was determined on the basis of the morphology of the mandibular mental eminence (chin), the cranial fragments, and the sciatic notch. A total of six teeth were recovered from the dump, presumably from the fragmentary skull. The wear on the enamel of the molars and premolar suggests an older adult.

Burials 2 and 3
Type: disturbed inhumations
Age: adults
Sex: unknown

These burials consist of two fragmentary adult skeletons found commingled with the remains of Burials 1 and 4 in Boyd's dump. These additional adult burials are recognized on the basis of the presence of two left, two right, and one unsided talus, two left patellae, and 14 metacarpal shafts. A total of six adult teeth were recovered, probably from Burials 1, 2, and 3.

Burial 4
Type: disturbed inhumation
Age: juvenile, 6–12 years?
Sex: unknown

This burial from Boyd's dump is a juvenile of indeterminate age, probably between six and 12 years of age. The recovered bone includes fragments of the left ischium and unidentified long bones.

Burials 5 and 6
Type: disturbed inhumations
Age: adults
Sex: unknown

These two adult individuals were identified on the basis of two distinctly different sizes of the femur shaft fragments, not by a repetition of skeletal elements. Only postcranial bone fragments were found in the area in front of the tomb.

Faunal Remains

A single sheep or goat left mandibular condylar process was recovered during cleaning of Boyd's dump from this tholos (Table 2). A single dog cockle shell (*Glycymeris*) was also found (Table 3).

Pottery

Boyd reported that there was no regularity in the placing of the vases and that some of the smaller vessels were set inside larger ones (Boyd 1901, 134). Of the 40 vessels mentioned by Boyd, only 10 could still be located in the Herakleion Archaeological Museum in 1979. Others were pictured in a photograph in the report on the 1900 excavations (Pl. 7C; Boyd 1901, pl. I). While these could not be studied or cataloged, it is possible to distinguish a number of vessels and suggest dates for them.

One of the earliest vessels is the deep bowl pictured in the middle row in Plate 7C, second from the right, which resembles carinated LM IIIC types from Karphi (Day 2011b, 140–141, fig. 5.2:K61.1) and Chania (Hallager and Hallager, eds., 2000, pl. 35:71-P 0739), although the height of the base, which is almost a pedestal, suggests a later, perhaps SM, date. A bell skyphos (Pl. 7C: bottom row, third from right) is a type artifact for the SM–EPG period. It has the typical tall conical foot and dipped decoration that coats only the top of the vessel, and it has parallels at Knossos of SM (Brock 1957, 161, pl. 3:2) or PG (Brock 1957, 161, 17:208) date and at Karphi (Day 2011b, 228–229, fig. 7.4:M8.1). The broader shape of the Vronda skyphos puts it closer to the SM examples from Knossos (Coldstream 1996, 379).

The small cylindrical-mouthed jug decorated with multiple loops on the shoulder and bands below may also be early (Pl. 7C: bottom row, second from right); the decoration of pendant multiple loops is common in LM IIIC, although usually found on deep bowls (Day 2011b, 260–261; Day et al. 2016, 71). A PG oinochoe from the Chania area, however, is similar in shape and decoration (Andreadaki-Vlasaki 1991, 414, fig. 9), so this jug may be SM or PG. Three oinochoai pictured may be later. One, with a clear trefoil mouth (Pl. 7C: middle row, fourth from right), is similar to an oinochoe from Knossos of LM IIIC–SM date (Hood et al. 1958–1959, 248, 241, fig. 27:VII.9). Another oinochoe (Pl. 7C: middle row, left) resembles examples from LPG–PGB Knossos (Brock 1957, 156–157, pl. 26:351, 368) and MPG–LPG Hagios Ioannis (Boardman 1960, 130, pl. 35:I.40), although Desborough (1952, 268) suggested, with reservations, that this vessel might be Geometric. The final oinochoe (Pl. 7C: middle row, third from left) is larger and looks as though it may be of coarser fabric, with incised bands around the neck. Similar coarse oinochoai of PGB–EG date are found at Knossos (Coldstream and Catling 1996, eds., 5, pl. 47:8; 47, pl. 78:10; 256, pl. 233:3), but they also occur in a well deposit in the Unexplored Mansion at Knossos with material dating around 600 B.C. (Kotsonas 2012, 162, fig. 3). The coarse fabric of these vessels is similar to that of a type of small juglet that imitates Cypriot Black Slip ware, usually dated to PGB–EG, but which continues later into LG (Kotsonas 2012, 161–162).

The two pyxides shown (Pl. 7C: top row, second and third from left) are similar to a decorated example from Adromyloi of LG date (Droop 1905–1906, 45, fig. 22:3248; Tsipopoulou 2005, 215, fig. 60:AN 3246), and the right-hand pyxis also resembles an example of EG date from Eltyna (Rethemiotakis and Englezou 2010, 72, pl. 138:134e). The missing cup pictured in the bottom row of Plate 7C, second from the left, could date anywhere from the PG to LG periods; from the photograph, it would appear that the handle is round rather than flat, a feature that would place it toward the early (PG–G) end of the sequence of monochrome cups in the Kavousi area (cf. **IX P28, IX P29, IX P59**).

Finally, the pithos found in the tomb, which could not be located, was described by Boyd as 1.11 m in height with six handles, three above and three below (Boyd 1901, 134 n. 1). It was decorated with four raised bands, the three upper ones decorated with incised chevrons, the lowest with incised vertical lines. She mentions an "amulet" around the neck of the jar, although it is uncertain what this description may mean; possibly she refers to a raised ridge or a plastic decoration. The description of the vessel suggests it was similar to those found in the earlier settlement at Vronda (e.g., Day, Klein, and Turner 2009, figs. 24, 89). She also reported that there were three small square holes cut on one side of the vase, one above the other, in the spaces between the bands. These she interpreted as either spigot holes (if cut in when the pithos had a domestic function) or as holes for the run-off of decomposition liquids (if they were cut in for use as a funerary vessel). Reuse of LM IIIC pithoi in later periods is well attested on Crete (Haggis et al. 2004, 354; Whitley 2011, 27–31).

The preserved assemblage is unusual. There is a striking number of small-mouthed vessels for pouring: an askos (**IV P5**), a stirrup jar (**IV P4**), a flask (**IV P8**), two bird vases (**IV P6, IV P7**), two small pouring vessels, one a lekythos and the other a juglet (**IV P2, IV P3**), and four jugs/oinochoai that were not located. A number of storage vessels were also found: the neck-handled amphora **IV P10**, the necked jar **IV P9**, and the two pyxides pictured on Plate 7C. There was an unusual paucity of the drinking vessels generally found in the tombs: only two cups (**IV P1** and one not located), the deep bowl/skyphos, and the bell skyphos (the latter two pictured on Pl. 7C). A base of what might have been a cup or skyphos, however, found in the cleaning of the interior of the tomb (**IV P11**), suggests that a larger number of drinking vessels may once have existed.

From the dump came a large number of coarse vessels, including a krater, several pithoid jars, pithoi, and tripod cooking vessels. It is difficult to know if these were part of the tomb assemblage or remains from the LM IIIC settlement, which many of them closely resemble. In addition to the cup or skyphos (**IV P12**), the majority of the pottery fragments from the area in front of the tomb consists of large vessels: two or three kraters (**IV P13, IV P16, IV P17**), one with a pedestal base (**IV P16**), a kalathos (**IV P14**), and a jar (**IV P15**), possibly the remains of a funerary ritual involving feasting or drinking. One of the kraters (**IV P13**) is an unusual shape that finds a good parallel in a krater from the cemetery at Eleutherna (see below). The latter vessel, which is thought to be imported, possibly from Athens, bears a reserved panel decorated with a meander pattern and dates to Attic MG I, or roughly 850–800 B.C. The Vronda krater may suggest a late use for the tomb, perhaps from the time of the burial that included the decorated cup (**IV P1**).

Objects

Boyd found a number of metal objects in the tomb, seven of bronze and four of iron (Boyd 1901, 133 n. 2). She reports five fibulae, a ring, and a bracelet of bronze in the grave, in addition to fibula fragments and pieces of iron blades from within the pithos. Of the seven bronze objects found outside the pithos, five are still extant: four fibulae (**IV M1–IV M4**) and the bracelet (**IV M5**). Another broken bronze fibula and a ring measuring 2.00 cm in diameter are missing. The iron objects, including a spearhead with broad blade and another spear socket, as well as a sword handle and point measuring 14.00 cm in length, could not be found in the museum in 1979. It would appear, however, that there was at least one sword and one spearhead in the burial found by Boyd. Other objects were discovered in the course of cleaning the tomb. An iron fragment was picked up on the surface of VW 17100, just to the south of Tomb IV, but it is too fragmentary to identify or catalog. Two fragments of iron blades were found in the cleaning (**IV M8, IV M9**); both of these seem to have single edges and are probably knives. An iron horseshoe or tool found in the cleaning is modern (**IV M10**).

Boyd found a soapstone whorl with two holes, but this was not located in the museum in 1979. A fragment of a stone lid, however, was found in the area in front of the tomb (**IV S1**). From the dump came a fragment of an unusual stone bead with incised decoration (**IV S2**). She also found a clay whorl in the form of a truncated cylinder with two incised rings, measuring 1.80 cm in height and 2.00 cm in diameter, but it could not be located.

Chronology

The extant pottery is mixed in date, with vessels ranging from SM to LG, and it seems likely that this tholos was in use over a long period of time (although not necessarily continuously) from the late 11th to the 8th centuries. Of probable SM date are the askos (**IV P5**), two bird vases (**IV P6, IV P7**), and the flask (**IV P8**). The stirrup jar (**IV P4**) is of SM or EPG date. The lekythos (**IV P2**) is a well-known type at Knossos, beginning in PGB (Coldstream 1996, 356). The other juglet or aryballos (**IV P3**) is unusual, both in shape and decoration, but finds a parallel in a lekythos from Knossos of PGB date (Coldstream and Catling, eds., 1996, 142, pl. 142:55). Similarly, the large necked jar (**IV P9**) and neck-handled amphora (**IV P10**) find some parallels of LPG or PGB date. The cup (**IV P1**), however, is probably the latest vessel in the group, resembling LG cups, although its closest parallel in shape is a cup of PGB date at Knossos (Coldstream and Catling, eds., 1996, 6, fig. 56:35). The painted cross on the underside of the base, however, is a feature that appears on a number of LG cups and skyphoi, from the Plai tou Kastrou tomb at Kavousi (Tsipopoulou 2005, 102:H745, fig.115:H748, H749) and from other sites in East Crete (Tsipopoulou 2005, 180, fig. 89:Σ4030; 276, fig.115:AN1612; fig. 126:Σ3564); thus it suggests a LG date for this cup, although an example from Archanes (Sakellarakis 1986, 46, fig. 41) is of PGB–MG date.

While there are three vessels that may be late LM IIIC–SM in date, two of these are no longer extant, and the third is a fragment of a deep bowl from the cleaning (**IV P11**) that may have been in the soil and not part of the tomb assemblage. The majority of the vessels seem to be of SM or PG date, but the cup (**IV P1**) and the krater (**IV P13**) seem to be later, perhaps LG in date. It would appear that most of the four inhumations were made in the SM and EPG periods, with perhaps another in the later PG. It would be tempting to suggest that the LG cup was associated with a cremation burial in the pithos, if indeed that is what the ash found by Boyd represents.

Catalog of Finds within Chamber

Pottery

FINE WARES

IV P1 (HM 1971; Fig. 13; Pls. 7C, 9). Cup. Intact; pick mark on lower belly. H. 6.2; d. rim 9.0–10.0; d. base 3.5. Fine, hard, reddish-yellow (5YR 7/6) fabric. Washy, reddish-brown (2.5YR 4/4) paint, well preserved. Outturned rim has uneven diameter; rounded body, raised base, hollowed underneath. Band at rim; groups of vertical strokes just below rim band; bands on lower body; horizontal strokes on handle. Interior has broad bands, one below rim, one on lower body; short vertical strokes on interior of rim. Cross on underside of base. *Bibliography*: Boyd 1901, pl. I: middle row, right; Tsipopoulou 2005, 78, 427, fig. 126. *Comparanda*: Desborough 1952, 268, pl. 19:A 1472–A 1474 (possibly G); Tsipopoulou 2013, 152, 153, fig. 13:12309 (Piskokephalo, LG). *Date*: LG?

IV P2 (HM 1969; Fig. 13; Pls. 7C, 9). Lekythos. Intact but missing 75% of neck and rim. H. 10.5; max. d. 8.2; d. base 3.7. Fine, pink (7.5YR 7/4) fabric. Lustrous, thick, dark reddish-brown (5YR 2.5/2) paint. Worn surfaces. Wheelmade. Decoration of crosshatched triangles above narrow bands on shoulder. Horizontal strokes on handle top. *Bibliography*: Boyd 1901, pl. I: middle row, second from left; Tsipopoulou 2005, 78, 394, fig. 72 (LG). *Comparanda*: shape and decoration, Brock 1957, 157, pl. 26:355 (Knossos, PGB–MG); Coldstream and Catling, eds., 1996, 48, pl. 79:42 (Knossos, PGB). *Date*: LPG.

IV P3 (HM 1963; Fig. 13; Pls. 7C, 9). Juglet. Intact, though chipped at base and rim. H. 9.6; d. rim 2.9; d. base 3.7. Fine, rather soft, light red (2.5YR 6/6) fabric. Worn, light red (10R 6/8) paint. Traces of burning around lower handle attachment. Wheelmade. Bands on rim and base of neck. Decoration on shoulder: pendant triangle with multiple outlines and double outlined spiral with tail running from the top of the triangle and forming two double spirals; hatching in the space below the triangle. On lower body zone of alternating strokes; bands. Handle coated. Band on interior of rim. *Bibliography*: Boyd 1901, pl. I: middle row, fourth from left; Gesell, Day, and Coulson 1983, 397–399, fig. 4:7, pl. 76:e; Tsipopoulou 2005, 77, pl. 26 (PGB). *Comparanda*: for decoration, Coldstream and Catling, eds., 1996, 142, pl. 142:55 (Knossos, PGB); for shape, Coldstream and Catling eds., 1996, 47, pl. 78:11–13 (PGB). *Date*: PGB.

IV P4 (HM 1965; Fig. 13; Pls. 7C, 9). Stirrup jar. Intact. H. 13.7; max. d. 9.9; d. base 4.4. Fine, reddish-yellow (7.5YR 8/6) fabric. Paint entirely worn off, although shadow of decoration can still be seen. Spout leans to touch false neck; large knob on top of false spout. Crosshatched triangles on shoulder and three vertical lines that form part of another motif. Bands on spout and false spout; top of false spout painted; barred handles. Bands on lower body. *Bibliography*: Boyd 1901, pl. I: bottom row, left; Gesell, Day, and Coulson 1983, 396–397, fig. 4:6, pl. 76:d; Tsipopoulou 2005, 77, pl. 28 (SM). *Comparanda*: Hayden 2003, 36, fig. 11:61 (Vrokastro, SM/EPG). *Date*: SM–EPG.

IV P5 (HM 1966; Fig. 13; Pls. 7C, 9). Askos. Pres. h. 13.2; max. d. 10.7; d. base 4.2. Mended from seven fragments; missing spout. Fine, hard, very pale brown (10YR 7/3) fabric. Streaky, dull, very dark gray paint (10YR 3/1). Wheelmade. Hatched triangles with multiple outlines on shoulder, one on each side of vase. Wide and narrow bands on lower body. Vertical bands at base of spout; horizontal strokes on handle. Half of underside of base has paint. *Bibliography*: Boyd 1901, pl. I: bottom row, right; Gesell, Day, and Coulson 1983, 396–397, fig. 4:4, pl. 76:b; Tsipopoulou 2005, 78, pl. 29 (SM). *Comparanda*: Hayden 2003, 46, fig. 21:98 (Vrokastro, SM); Rethemiotakis and Englezou 2010, 46–47, fig. 24:47 (Eltyna, SM–EPG). *Date*: SM.

IV P6 (HM 1976; Fig. 13; Pls. 7C, 9). Bird askos. Restored from seven fragments; tip of tail, fragments of body missing. H. 9.7; L. 14.5. Hard, fine, pink (7.5YR 7/4) fabric and slip. Lustrous, red (2.5YR 4/6) paint, worn on one side. Handmade except for base. Hole pierced through top near front handle attachment. Decoration on body within double outlines: double triangles between vertical bands (three groups of triangles on one side, four on the other). Handle barred on top; band around foot. *Bibliography*: Boyd 1901, pl. I: middle row, third from right; Desborough 1972, 253, no. 37, pl. ΛΔ´1; Gesell, Day, and Coulson 1983, 396–397, fig. 4:5, pl. 76:c; Tsipopoulou 2005, 79 (SM). *Date*: SM.

IV P7 (HM 1975; Fig. 13; Pls. 7C, 9). Bird askos. Intact. H. 10.5; L. 16.0. Fine, hard, pink (7.5YR 7/4) fabric. Lustrous, dark reddish-brown (5YR 2/2) paint. Handmade. Tiny hole at base of handle attachment. On upper body, crosshatched triangles with multiple outlines, separated by vertical rows of dots. Swags on lower body with bands under belly and tail. Handle barred on top; neck coated. *Bibliography*: Boyd 1901, pl. I: top, second from right; Desborough 1972, 253, no. 36, pl. ΛΓ´4; Tsipopoulou 2005, 79, 439, fig. 143 (SM). *Comparanda*: Tsipopoulou 1997, 462, 470, fig. 5:4981 (Chamaizi Phatsi, SM); Day 2011b, 233–234, fig. 7.7:M11.2, pl. 26 (Karphi, SM). *Date*: SM.

IV P8 (HM 1962; Fig. 13; Pls. 7C, 9). Lentoid flask. Nearly complete; missing 75% of rim and 50% of neck and badly cracked. H. 19.8; max. d. 15.1. Fairly hard, fine, pink (7.5YR 7/4) fabric. Lustrous, red (2.5YR 4/8) to black paint. Lentoid body, with conical knob in center of one side. Decorated with concentric circles; bands on neck; stripe down top of handle. *Bibliography*: Boyd 1901, pl. I: bottom row, third from left; Tsipopoulou 2005, 76, fig. 144 (SM); Karageorghis et al. 2014, 97 (Creto-Cypriot flask, SM). *Comparanda*: **II P1, II-VII-VIII P1**; Gjerstad 1948, fig. III:2c. (Cyprus, White Painted I); Tsipopoulou 1997, 469, fig. 12 (Chamaizi Phatsi, SM). *Date*: SM.

MEDIUM-COARSE WARES

IV P9 (HM 1959; Fig. 14; Pls. 7C, 10). Large necked jar. About 70% preserved; missing 33% of shoulder and belly, part of rim. H. 25.5; d. rim. 11.0; d. base 13.0. Medium-coarse, rather soft, pink (5YR 8/4) fabric with stone and clay inclusions. Washy paint, very dark gray (5YR 3/1) on neck and interior, light red (2.5YR 6/6) below; worn on shoulder. Neck coated. On shoulder, large crosshatched lozenge slightly overlapping concentric circle. Groups of bands on lower body. Band across handles. Band on interior of rim. *Bibliography*: Boyd 1901, pl. I: top row, right. *Comparanda*: for shape, see Brock 1957, 24, pl. 14:206; 32, pl. 22:282 (Knossos, PG necked pithos); Sakellarakis 1986, 40–41, fig. 33 (Archanes, LPG); Coldstream and Catling, eds., 1996, 87, fig. 83:11 (Knossos, SM); 197, fig. 127:25 (SM); Tegou 2001, 130–131, figs. 23, 24 (Pantanassa, SM). *Date*: EPG.

IV P10 (HM 1961; Fig. 14; Pls. 7C, 10). Neck amphora. Intact. H. 21.3; d. rim. 11.0–12.0; d. base 7.5–8.0. Medium-coarse, reddish-yellow (5YR 7/6) fabric. Light red (2.5YR 6/6) paint. Worn and eroded surfaces. Uneven. Flaring rim and neck; ovoid body; flat base; flattened handle from rim to shoulder. Probably monochrome except at widest diameter, which bears a reserved band with three wavy lines separated by bands. *Bibliography*: Boyd 1901, pl. I: top row, left; Tsipopoulou 2005, 76, pl. 24 (PG; identified as from Tomb VII). *Comparanda*: Brock 1957, 16, pl. 8:122 (Knossos, PG); Popham, Sackett, and Themelis 1979–1980, 111, pl. 93:5.2 (Lefkandi, SPG); Coldstream and Catling, eds., 1996, 197, fig. 125:26 (Knossos, EPG); Rethemiotakis and Englezou 2010, 37, fig. 17:28 (EPG); for decoration: Popham, Sackett, and Themelis 1979–1980, 110, pl. 92:pyre 1 A1 (Lefkandi, EPG). *Date*: PG.

Metal

BRONZE

IV M1 (HM 519; Pl. 10). Fibula. Intact. L. 8.0; h. 5.0. Asymmetrical arched bow, rhomboidal in section, with bulges at either end. Two disks above bulge near catch plate. *Bibliography*: Boyd 1901, 136, fig. 2: bottom; Blinkenberg 1926, 74, fig. 58:type II.18.a; Sapouna-Sakellaraki 1978, 52, pl. 8:223 (type IIi). *Date*: SM–PG.

IV M2 (HM 520; Pl. 10). Fibula. Nearly complete; point broken. L. 6.9; h. 4.5. Arched bow, rectangular in section. Blinkenberg 1926, 63, fig. 33:type II.3.b; Sapouna-Sakellaraki 1978, 47, pl. 5:147 (type IIc). *Date*: SM–PG.

IV M3 (HM 521; Pl. 10). Fibula. Nearly complete; small section of catch plate missing. L. 5.2; h. 3.4. Arched bow, flat in section. *Bibliography*: Boyd 1901, 136, fig. 2 (top, right); Blinkenberg 1926, 64, types II.4e, II.4p; Sapouna-Sakellaraki 1978, 48, pl. 6:172 (type II d). *Date*: SM–PG.

IV M4 (HM 522; Pl. 10). Fibula. Intact. L. 5.8; h. 3.7. Arched spiral bow with square catch plate. *Bibliography*: Boyd 1901, 136, fig. 2 (top, left); Blinkenberg 1926, 66, fig. 42:types II.9a, II.9p; Sapouna-Sakellaraki 1978, 50, pl. 7:203 (type II f). *Date*: SM.

IV M5 (HM 523; Pl. 10). Bracelet. Complete, but bent. D. 7.0. Wire bracelet with twisted coils around ends. *Bibliography*: Boyd 1901 136, fig. 3. *Comparanda*: Effinger 1996, 151–152, pl. 25:b, c (Armenoi, LM IIIB).

Catalog of Finds from Tomb Cleaning

Pottery

FINE WARE

IV P11 (Fig. 14). Cup or skyphos. Two joining fragments preserving entire base. D. base 4.2. Fine, soft, light red (2.5YR 6/6) fabric, with very pale brown (10YR 8/3) surface. String marks on bottom of base. *Date*: PG?

Catalog of Finds from Area in Front of Tomb

Pottery

FINE WARES

IV P12 (Fig. 14). Cup or skyphos. Single fragment from rim. D. rim est. 12.1. Fine, soft, reddish-yellow (5YR 7/8) fabric, worn and encrusted. Light red (10R 6/8) paint. *Bibliography*: Gesell, Day, and Coulson 1983, 397–399, fig. 4:8 (emended). *Date*: LM IIIC?

IV P13 (Fig. 14). Krater. Partially mended from 35 fragments, preserving 25% of vessel, including one handle; missing base. D. rim est. 30.0. Fine, very soft and chalky, very pale brown (10YR 8/4) fabric. Traces of black paint on exterior. *Comparanda*: Coldstream and Catling, eds., 1996, 136, fig. 104:100.65 (Knossos LPG–PGB); Stampolides, ed., 2004, 242:267 (Eleutherna, Attic? MG I); Johnston 2005, 373–374, fig. 33:239 (Kommos, fifth or fourth century); Kotsonas 2008, 184–186, fig. 44:A 209 (Eleutherna, PGB–EG). *Date*: PG–EG.

IV P14 (Fig. 14). Kalathos. Single fragment from rim with part of excrescent cup. Soft, light red (2.5YR 6/8) fabric with worn surfaces, yellow (10YR 8/6) slip. Traces of black paint. *Comparanda*: Brock 1957, 162, pl. 78:1429 (Knossos, EPG); Coldstream and Catling, eds., 1996, 51, fig. 72:110; 198, pl. 185:36 (Knossos, EPG–MPG). *Date*: PG.

MEDIUM-COARSE WARES

IV P15 (Fig. 14). Jar. Two joining fragments from rim and single nonjoining fragment from round horizontal handle. D. rim est. 24.0–26.0. Medium-coarse, reddish-yellow (7.5YR 7/6) fabric with some pebble and clay inclusions. Pulled out rim; ridge at base of vertical neck. Monochrome black paint on exterior. Worn surfaces. *Comparanda*: Coldstream and Catling, eds., 1996, 92, fig. 86:6 (Knossos, EPG early). *Date*: PG.

IV P16 (Fig. 14). Pedestal base. Five joining and two nonjoining fragments preserving 25% of base. D. base 18.0. Medium-coarse, reddish-yellow (5YR 7/6) fabric with frequent tiny red phyllite inclusions; reddish-yellow (7.5YR 8/6) slip. Red (2.5YR 5/8) paint. Flaring base with simple rounded lip. Bands at base, wavy band above. Possibly from krater, oinochoe, or hydria. *Comparanda*: Coldstream and Catling, eds., 1996, 5, fig. 57:13 (Knossos, LPG); Tsipopoulou 2005, 115, fig. 81:H1954 (Skouriasmenos, LG–EO). *Date*: PG.

COARSE WARES

IV P17 (Fig. 14). Necked jar. Three fragments from rim, one fragment from round horizontal handle. D. rim 22.0. Coarse, reddish-yellow (5YR 6/6) fabric with phyllites and quartz. Reddish-brown (5YR 4/4) paint. Painted band on neck. *Date*: PG?

Stone

IV S1 (Fig. 14; Pl. 10). Lid. Half preserved, including knob in middle. D. 4.60; th. 0.70 (edge)–0.11 (middle). Serpentinite. Small, flat lid with small knob in center. *Comparanda*: Warren 1969, 68, 69, 259:27.D185; Day and Glowacki 2012, 145, fig. 119:L1 S1. *Date*: EM II–MM IB/II.

Catalog of Finds from Boyd's Dump

Pottery

MEDIUM-COARSE WARES

IV P18 (Fig. 15). Stirrup jar or amphoriskos. Single fragment preserving entire base. D. base 3.6. Medium-coarse, yellowish-red (5YR 4/6) fabric with mottled surface, like Kavousi Type IV (Haggis and Mook 1993), with some phyllites and white bits. *Comparanda*: Coldstream and Catling, eds., 1996, 50, fig. 72:107 (LPG bell skyphos); 69, fig. 76:19 (Knossos, SM–EPG stirrup jar). *Date*: PG.

Metals

BRONZE

IV M6 (IV dump 3, object 1; Fig. 15; Pl. 10). Pin. Single fragment; neither end preserved. Max. pres. L. 2.2; th. 0.2. Well preserved, although surface slightly corroded.

IV M7 (V88.144; IV dump 2, object 1; Fig. 15; Pl. 10). Ring. Intact. D. 1.90–2.00; d. wire 0.15. Single piece of bronze wire, bent and coming together to form ring. One end overlaps the other where they meet. Wire is round in section. Surfaces well preserved.

IRON

IV M8 (IV dump 4, object 1; Fig. 15). Iron knife. Single fragment from blade. Max. pres. L. 2.30; max. pres. w. 1.90; th. 0.19–0.21. Surface corroded.

IV M9 (IV dump 2, object 2; Fig. 15). Iron knife or sickle. Two joining fragments from blade. Max. pres. L. 3.10; max. pres. w. 1.50; th. 0.15–0.30. Blade has slight curve on inner edge to make it appear sickle-like. Corroded; no original surface left.

IV M10 (Fig. 15). Iron horseshoe. Single fragment preserving half of object. Max. pres. L. 7.5; max. pres. w. 3.0; th. 0.2. Large flat object, leaf shaped. Square holes along one edge at flat end. Surface well preserved. Probably modern; not much corrosion.

Stone

IV S2 (V88.151; IM 1009; IV, dump 3, object 4; Fig. 15; Pl. 10). Stone bead. Half of bead preserved, neatly sliced through middle. H. 1.4; w. est. 1.2; d. hole 0.3; wt. 2.0 g. Light brownish gray in color (2.5Y 6/2). Pyramidal in shape with square bottom and rounded corners. Incised decoration on four sides. Side A has outlined edges with X in center; side B has groups of oblique strokes. Sides C and D have possible triangles.

Vronda Tomb V (Boyd's Tomb C)

Boyd found this tomb entirely empty (Boyd 1901, 133). During cleaning in 1981 some pottery fragments were found, but no other objects or human bones were observed (Gesell, Day, and Coulson 1983, 401).

Architecture and Features

Vronda V is the best preserved of all the extant tombs, rising 1.74 m in six to seven courses almost to the keystone (Fig. 16; Pl. 11A); only one or two courses are missing. The floor plan is square, measuring 1.80 x 1.84 m (Fig. 17), and the corners begin to round out in the second or third course. The bottom course consists of very large stones, while those in the second course are both large and small; much limestone was used in these two lower courses. The upper courses are generally built of large breccia boulders, with some smaller stones used as chinking. The floor is *tsakali* bedrock. The stomion, which faces south, is well preserved, measuring 0.50 m in height, 0.68 m in width, and 0.80 m in depth. The large lintel block measures 0.83 x 0.26 m. The floor of the stomion slopes downward into the chamber. The facade of the stomion is made up largely of flat limestone blocks laid in three courses, with courses of small stones set between them, for a total of five courses. In front of the stomion and its facade, a pit was cut into the bedrock, and two stones from the facade project out to form a pseudo-dromos.

Stratigraphy

There were many large stones fallen into the chamber, two of which were so huge that they could not be easily removed and so were left in place. Neither the stomion nor the pseudo-dromos had been excavated. The stomion was found blocked with two large thin slabs and hard soil, as in the other tombs. The pseudo-dromos, which was a pit dug out of the bedrock, contained a few flat stones at the level of the lintel block. More soil had been laid above these, and finally a pile of stones was heaped over the pseudo-dromos, marking the location of the entrance.

Burials

Vronda V was empty when first discovered by Boyd. No human bone was recovered from this tomb by the Kavousi Project.

Faunal Remains

Two animal bones were recovered from the dromos: an immature sheep or goat lumbar vertebra, which had been split vertically through the vertebral body, and a second sheep or goat element, an unfused metapodial diaphysis segment from a young animal (Table 2).

Pottery and Chronology

Very little pottery was recovered that could help date the tomb or shed light on funerary customs. From the cleaning within the tomb came the deep bowl or skyphos (**V P1**). The handles on this vessel are set much higher than is customary with the SM or EPG bell skyphos; although this feature exists at Knossos in the EPG period (Coldstream and Catling, eds., 1996, 197, fig. 125:23), it is not common. The Vronda fragment may be from a LM IIIC deep bowl that belonged to the time of the original burials in the tomb, or it could have been an antique or a fragment that became embedded in the soil at the time of construction. The pithos fragment (**V P3**) is the latest vessel from this tomb, probably LG in date. Although the crosshatched lozenge chain is a common PG motif, the outlined solid lozenge chain seems to occur on LG–EO vessels from Knossos (Brock 1957, 173, motif 5ai). The other motif, alternating pendant and accumbent rectangles, may be a form of meander pattern, as the effect is of a reserved meander; a similar pattern can be seen on MG vessels from Knossos (Coldstream and Catling 1996, eds., 236, pls. 217:91; 269, 250:224). The use of a meander, even an unusual one, places the vessel in the Geometric period, and the lozenges suggest a LG date. Of the vessels from the pseudo-dromos, the pyxis is probably either an antique placed in the tomb or a fragment embedded in the soil at the time of construction. It is an unusual shape but has two parallels from the LM IIIC settlement, and it is probably LM IIIC in date. Some Byzantine fragments with incised wavy lines were also found.

Catalog of Finds from Interior of Tomb

Pottery

Fine Wares

V P1 (Fig. 18). Deep bowl or skyphos. Single fragment from rim and handle. D. rim est. 16.0. Fine, soft, reddish-yellow (5YR 7/6) fabric with small phyllites and some carbonates. Very light, yellowish-brown (10YR 6/4) slip. Traces of black paint. Very worn on exterior. Monochrome interior, paint on exterior. *Bibliography*: Gesell, Day, and Coulson 1983, 401, 402, fig. 6:V9. *Comparanda*: Day 2011b, 93–94, fig. 4.7:K23.34 (Karphi, LM IIIC); 201–202, fig. 6.16:K106.9 (Karphi, LM IIIC); Day and Glowacki 2012, 81, fig. 77:IC1 P8 (Vronda settlement, LM IIIC). *Date*: LM IIIC

V P2 (Fig. 18). Cup or deep bowl. Single fragment from rim. D. rim est. 14.0. Fine, reddish-yellow (5YR 7/6) fabric and slip. Black paint on interior and exterior. Monochrome. *Comparanda*: Day 2011b, 205–206, fig. 6.18:K115.2 (Karphi, late LM IIIC). *Date*: LM IIIC.

V P3 (Pl. 11B) Pithos. Large fragment from upper belly and shoulder represented by nine nonjoining body fragments. Max. pres. h. 12.0; max. pres. w. 2.6; th. 1.5. Well-fired, reddish-yellow (5YR 7/6) fabric with small pebble and clay inclusions. Reddish-yellow (5YR 7/6) slip. Black paint. Only slightly worn surfaces. Wheel ridging on interior. Decoration of black rectangles with thick bands above and below; framed and connected lozenges below this and thin bands. Other fragments (both from the tomb and the dromos) are monochrome black. *Bibliography*: Gesell, Day, and Coulson 1983, 401, pl. 76:f V10. *Comparanda*: Coldstream and Catling, eds., 1996, 36, fig. 68:11; 78, fig. 80:28.9 (Knossos, PGB). *Date*: LG.

Catalog of Finds from Pseudo-Dromos

Pottery

Medium-Coarse Ware

V P4 (Fig. 18). Pyxis. Single fragment from rim. D. rim est. 20.0. Fine, very pale brown (10YR 8/4) fabric, pale yellow (2.5Y 8/4) slip on exterior only. Washy light red (2.5YR 6/8) paint on exterior, perhaps crosshatched or piled triangles. No paint on interior. *Comparanda*: Day and Glowacki 2012, 91, fig. 83:IE P3; 97, fig. 86:O1 P17. *Date*: LM IIIC.

Vronda Tomb VI (Boyd's Tomb D)

Boyd also found Tomb VI empty (Boyd 1901, 133). During the cleaning and excavation of the stomion and pseudo-dromos (Gesell, Day, and Coulson 1983, 401), a few fragments of pottery and bones were recovered from the tomb and dromos.

Architecture and Features

Vronda VI has a chamber that is roughly circular in plan, with a diameter of 1.70–1.90 m, and is well preserved to a maximum height of 1.70 m, with four courses on the north and eight courses on the southeast (Fig. 19). The walls are constructed almost entirely of breccia, with little use of limestone except in the facade. Bedrock serves as the floor of the tomb. The stomion is on the west, with a large lintel block of limestone supported by an upright slab at each side, limestone on the south and breccia on the north (Pl. 11C). It measures 0.56 m in width, 0.50 m in height, and 0.80 m deep. The floor slopes down from the entrance of the stomion to the floor of the chamber. A pit, 0.90 m long, was cut into the *tsakali* bedrock in front of the stomion and served as a pseudo-dromos.

Stratigraphy

The stomion and pseudo-dromos had not been previously excavated. As with other tholoi at Vronda (Tombs I, II, and V), the stomion was blocked with stones, in this case three flat stones with hard-packed brown soil surrounding them. The pseudo-dromos was filled with a light brown soil with medium-sized stones, and in front of the stomion at the level of the bottom of the lintel were two large flat stones, like those found in Vronda II and V (Pl. 11D). Above this flat stone was more dirt and a pile of stones that marked the location of the entrance.

Faunal Remains

Twenty animal bones, a relatively large number, were recovered during cleaning of this tholos (Table 2). From a rabbit, there was a single front limb element, a left proximal ulna. Seventeen sheep or goat bones, primarily those of domestic goat (*Capra hircus*), included a goat left horn core segment, chopped through the base, and a right maxilla fragment with dentition that probably came from the same animal. Also identifiable as goat were a left distal humerus with cut marks on the medial diaphysis and a left metacarpal with a partially fused distal epiphysis. Additional skeletal elements from a young animal were four cervical vertebrae and two thoracic vertebrae, all with unfused articular plates, and a right proximal rib. There was also a left scapula, a left innominate portion, and two left proximal femur fragments. In addition, two domestic dog elements, a left proximal scapula fragment, and a left proximal humerus diaphysis segment were recovered from this area.

Pottery

Boyd found no pottery, objects, or bones in this tomb. A few sherds were recovered from the chamber, stomion, and pseudo-dromos. None of these vessels is closely identifiable or datable.

Vronda Tomb VII (Boyd's Tomb 4)

Tomb VII was poorly preserved and consisted only of a lintel and a few stones that formed the side of the dromos (Boyd 1901, 134). Boyd recovered 18 vases and a number of bronze and iron objects (Boyd 1901, 134–135). Four of the 18 vases, which she described as among the best pieces from Vronda, can be identified from the labels written on them; others may be pictured on Plate 5A (Boyd 1901, pl. II). Of the metal objects, only one fibula could be found. The tomb was not located in 1981, although its approximate position was clear from Boyd's plan. When Tomb XI was uncovered under a pile of stones in 1990, it was thought to be this missing tomb, and it was so labeled in the preliminary report (Gesell, Day, and Coulson 1995, 91–92). However, the good preservation of Tomb XI made it clear that it could not have been the remains of Boyd's tomb 4. A lintel block and two uprights built into a modern terrace was later observed just east of Tomb XI and may be all that was left of Tomb VII (Pl. 12A).

Pottery

Of the 18 vases reported by Boyd from this tomb, only four are extant; some of the vessels shown in her publication (Pl. 5A) also came from this tomb, but it is now impossible to determine which ones. The four preserved vessels include a bowl (**VII P1**), a jug (**VII P2**), a stirrup jar (**VII P3**) and a necked jar (**VII P4**). Stylistically, the bowl and jug seem to belong together, while the stirrup jar and necked jar appear earlier than the other two (Fig. 20).

Objects

Boyd found the following objects in this tomb: a bronze fibula, two bronze rings (one measuring 2.50 cm in diameter, with small hooked pins and a knob at the middle of the hoop, the other of the same size and with one hook broken), a broken bronze hairpin 7.20 cm in length, two bronze fragments shaped like fishhooks, three pieces of broken bronze plates with indented pattern and holes for fastening (cf. **GR9**

M5–GR9 M12; this vol., Ch. 3), other fragments of bronze and iron, and a soft soapstone whorl with a diameter of 2.00 cm. Only the fibula was found in the Herakleion museum in 1979 (**VII M1**; Pl. 12B).

Chronology

The pottery from Tomb VII is mixed in date, suggesting that it was used over a long period of time. The earliest vessel is the stirrup jar **VII P3**, which is SM in style. The necked jar **VII P4** is probably EPG, to judge from the decoration; while the wavy line is common enough on both SM and PG vessels, the compass-drawn circles are a sign of the PG style, and the hatched triangle is also found more in MPG–LPG pottery (Brock 1957, 171, motif 4j). The bowl **VII P1** is highly unusual, and no close parallels exist. At Knossos there are some similar vessels: a bowl of PGB–EO date (Coldstream and Catling, eds., 1996, 217, fig. 132:81), several skyphoi of PG date (Brock 1957, 165, pl. 62:1044; pl. 78:1539) and at least one cauldron-krater of PGB–EG date (Coldstream and Catling, eds., 1996, 21, fig. 62:117). The most likely stylistic date for this bowl would be later PG or G. The jug **VII P2** is also difficult to place chronologically; Metaxia Tsipopoulou dated it to PGB (2005, 78), but Coldstream (pers. comm.) suggested that it looked 7th century. Both the bowl and the jug are certainly later than the stirrup jar and necked jar; it is possible that they are the remains of a later postfunerary ritual left in the dromos of the tomb, perhaps when the Vronda site was again used extensively for burial in the late eighth or early seventh century.

Catalog

Pottery

FINE WARES

VII P1 (HM 3692; Fig. 20; Pls. 5A, 12B). Bowl. Intact, but cracked along one side. H. 9.1; d. rim 15.2; d. base 5.5. Soft, very pale brown (10YR 8/4) fabric, well fired. Worn paint; reddish-yellow (7.5YR 8/6) surface marks where black paint once was. Nearly horizontal rim rounds into conical body; two flat horizontal handles pinched out at widest diameter; flat base. Interior very uneven. Bands on body; short strokes on top of rim. Handles and interior coated. *Bibliography*: Boyd 1901, pl. II: bottom row, right; Gesell, Day, and Coulson 1983, 402–403, fig. 6:VII.18, pl. 77:a; Tsipopoulou 2005, 79, pl. 34 (LG). *Comparanda*: for shape, Coldstream 1972, 95, pl. 28:G101 (Knossos, EG–early MG); Rocchetti 1988–1989, 227–228, fig. 141:142 (Kourtes); Coldstream and Catling, eds., 1996, 217, fig. 132:81 (PGB–EG). *Date*: PG?

VII P2 (HM 1970; Fig. 20; Pl. 12B). Cylindrical-mouthed jug. Nearly complete, including lower handle attachment; missing handle. H. 12.0; max. d. 10.0; d. rim 3.5; d. base 3.4. Fine, hard, very pale brown (10YR 8/4) fabric. Paint almost entirely worn off. Vertical rim and short neck; globular body; single ovoid vertical handle; raised base, slightly hollowed underneath. Possible band at rim and base of neck. On shoulder: possible vertical panel of crosshatching and crosshatched triangle. Faintly preserved bands on lower body. *Bibliography*: Gesell, Day, and Coulson 1983, 401–402, fig. 6:V12, pl. 77:h; Tsipopoulou 2005, 78, pl. 30 (PGB). *Comparanda*: for shape, Platon 1955, 296, fig. 111α (third from left; Sphakia, PG); Rizza and Scrinari 1968, 16, fig. 25 (Gortyn, PG). *Date*: PGB–EO.

VII P3 (HM 1964; Fig. 20; Pls. 5A, 12B). Stirrup jar. Intact. H. 11.7; max. d. 11.0; d. base 4.3. Fine, rather soft, pink (7.5YR 7/4) fabric with dark inclusions, slipped. Lustrous, black (7.5YR 2/0) paint, now worn. Low false spout with knob on top; short spout with flaring rim, tipped back slightly to meet false spout; globular-ovoid body; ring base. Hole pierced through top of false spout. Bands on false spout, concentric circles on top. Handles solidly painted. Shoulder zone: groups of four piled triangles. Bands on lower body. *Bibliography*: Boyd 1901, pl. II: bottom row, second from right; Tsipopoulou 2005, 77, pl. 27 (SM). *Comparanda*: Catling 1968, 118–119, fig. 6:25 (SM–EPG); Coldstream and Catling, eds., 1996, 69, fig. 76:20 (Knossos, SM–EPG); 183, fig. 119:160.1 (SM). *Date*: SM.

VII P4 (HM 1960 bis; Fig. 20; Pls. 5A, 12B). Large necked jar. Restored; mended from 10 fragments; small section of rim missing. H. 14.1; d. rim 8.8; d. base. 6.3. Soft, reddish-yellow (5YR 7/6) fabric. Faded, light red (2.5YR 6/6) paint, very worn. Flaring rim and wide flaring neck; two round horizontal handles set high on shoulder; globular body; flat base, slightly hollowed underneath. Band at rim. On neck, hatched triangles above band. On shoulder, compass-drawn concentric circles above band. Wavy line on lower belly, band at base. Band on interior of rim. *Bibliography*: Boyd 1901, pl. II: bottom row, third from left; Gesell, Day, and Coulson 1983, 401–402, fig. 6:VII1.1, pl. 76:g; Tsipopoulou 2005, 76, pl. 23 (PGB). *Comparanda*: **GR28 P22**; Coldstream and Catling, eds., 1996, 87, fig. 83:11 (Knossos, SM). *Date*: PG.

Metal

BRONZE

VII M1 (HM 518; Pl. 12B) Fibula. Nearly complete; catch plate and point broken. L. 9.5; h. 5.2. Arched bow, flat in section. Blinkenberg, 1926, 63, type II.4c; Sapouna-Sakellaraki 1978, 47, pl. 5:149 (type II c). *Date*: SM.

Vronda Tomb VIII (Boyd's Tomb 2, Grave 18)

Boyd found only 10 vases and a few objects of metal in this poorly preserved structure (Boyd 1901, 133, pl. 2; Gesell, Day, and Coulson 1983, 401–403). Of the 10 vessels, only one can be identified; the others may be illustrated on Plate 5A. Tomb VIII was not located in 1981, but it was uncovered in the 1988 excavations in Building L-M (Gesell, Coulson, and Day 1991, 160–161). At that time it was labeled grave 18, but it was subsequently identified as Boyd's tomb 2. The tomb had apparently been refilled in the years following Boyd's excavations.

Architecture

Only the bottom two courses of the tomb walls were preserved to a height of 0.50 m (Fig. 21; Pl. 13A). At the base, the plan is nearly square, 2.00 m on each side, although the corners round out everywhere except on the southwest. Much of the lower part of the tomb was constructed of limestone blocks, with some breccia, while the upper preserved courses contain more breccia. The floor is of bedrock. The facade is not preserved, but the tomb has a wide stomion, 0.70–0.75 m wide and 0.75 m deep; only two courses are preserved, to a height of 0.55 m. The stomion was built of large, regularly shaped limestone blocks. No lintel block was preserved, but a single large, flat stone still remained from the blocking of the entrance. (Pl. 13B). A pit was cut into the bedrock in front of the door, extending in an oval about 0.83 m to the north, and this served as a pseudo-dromos. This tomb cut through the floor of Building L, Room L2 and may have disturbed other rooms as well. Building Complex L-M must have been out of use when the tholos tomb was constructed, and it is likely that the whole settlement had already been abandoned at that time.

Stratigraphy

A small amount of very hard soil still remained at the bottom of the tomb around the edges (V 7613.6), as well as in the stomion (V 7613.2, V 7614) and in the pit in front of the entrance (V 7617). In the stomion, a large flat stone was all that remained of the blocking (Pl. 13B). Behind this stone, articulated animal bones were uncovered. This material probably belongs to the blocking up of the doorway of the tomb during the last burial. The pit was filled with soil similar to that found in the stomion, and there were stones above the pit, as seen in the other tholoi (Pl. 13C). A crumbly, soft, loose brown soil with stones (yellowish brown, 10YR 5/4) was removed from the interior of the tomb (V 7102, V 7612, V 7613). Overlaying the tops of the walls of the tomb was the same sort of soil, but slightly harder (V 7601, V 7602, V 7603, V 7606). If we are correct in the identification of this tomb as Tomb VIII (Boyd's tomb 2), this soil represents filling in of the tomb subsequent to Boyd's excavation. It is likely that the soil initially removed from the tomb by Boyd and dumped nearby was thrown back in, perhaps with some other material from the surrounding area of Building L. Very little material was found that post-dates the LM IIIC settlement.

Burials

There were remains of four burials found in this tomb.

Burial 1

Type: disturbed inhumation
Age: juvenile, 1–2 years
Sex: unknown

Burial 1 is the scant remains of the skeleton of a very young child, aged one to two years old on the basis of fragmentary dentition.

Burial 2

Type: disturbed inhumation
Age: juvenile, 10–16 years
Sex: unknown

Burial 2 is a child or an adolescent aged less than 16 years, as indicated by the size of the bones and the unfused epiphyses on the iliac crest and proximal humerus.

Burials 3 and 4

Type: disturbed inhumations
Age: adults
Sex: male(?), unknown

Burials 3 and 4 are the commingled remains of two older adults, one of which was probably a male. The age estimation is based on cranial suture closure and one auricular surface, but no specific traits were preserved well enough to permit further evaluation.

Faunal Remains

The hard soil around the edges at the bottom of the interior (V 7613.6), in the stomion (V 7613.2, V 7614), and in the pseudo-dromos (V 7617) contained some animal bones that may have belonged with the burials (Table 2). Five sheep or goat bone fragments were recovered from the bottom of the tholos. A single right calcaneum could be further identified as coming from a domestic goat. Two isolated teeth (a right first molar and left deciduous fourth premolar), a left scapula proximal articular segment, and a left tibia proximal diaphysis segment were also recovered. Two intrusive rat elements, a right mandible with dentition and a right ilium, are likely to have been later than the other faunal remains.

The fill over the tomb contained remains of sheep/goat, pig, cattle, rabbit, and dog; these are likely to have come from the earlier settlement and were published with that material (Day and Glowacki 2012, 144, table 20). The fill in the pit in front of the stomion contained one limpet (*Patella*) shell (Table 3). Other shells in the fill of the tomb included two more limpets, a trough shell (*Mactra corallina*), and a topshell (*Phorcus*).

Pottery

Among the pottery from Tomb VIII is a stirrup jar, **VIII P1** (Fig. 22), which is of an unusual shape and may be the earliest vessel in the tomb. It is angular, but not as squat as the LM IIIB squat stirrup jar (Kanta 1980, 246–248), and it has a high foot. The decoration, however, looks LM IIIC or later. The decoration is similar to an example from Gypsades tomb V1A (Hood et al. 1958–1959, 247, 242, fig. 28:VIA 2) that was dated to LM IIIA:2, but similar decoration, although often more angular than in this case, can be found surviving into SM or even PG times. Stirrup jar **VIII P1** may date to the LM IIIC period, or it may represent an earlier vessel deposited with the dead; there is evidence for the use of earlier vessels, whether valuable family heirlooms or simply antiques, deposited in the later cremation burials (see below, pp. 348–350).

Very little pottery actually remained within the soil left in the tholos, and all of the extant material was in small fragments (Fig. 22). Most of the other pottery in the tomb was of LM IIIC date, and it may belong to the time of construction, or it could have been in the soil at the time the tholos was built. As the tomb clearly postdates the use of Building Complex L-M, because it cut into Building L, these fragments are more likely to have been material in the soil at the time of the construction. There were six deep bowl or cup fragments (**VIII P2, VIII P4–VIII P8**), a fragment from the foot or stem of a LM IIIC goblet or a later stemmed skyphos (**VIII P9**), a decorated kalathos (**VIII P3**), a fenestrated stand (**VIII P11**), and a cooking dish (**VIII P10**). None of the material except for the possible stemmed skyphos looks later than LM IIIC, although the kalathos (**VIII P3**) does not fit into the settlement material and may be later. This material was probably in the soil and does not represent the period of use of the tomb, as the tomb cuts through the walls and floor of Building L.

Objects

A number of metal artifacts were found by Boyd, including a bronze hairpin, a broken bronze fibula, a bronze fragment that was shaped like a fishhook but was probably the end of a pin or ring, an iron hilt, and fragments of an iron blade. None of these objects were located in the Herakleion museum in 1979. Several objects, however, were recovered in the 1988 excavations in the area of Building L-M. The bronze pin (**VIII M1**; Fig. 20) was probably left over from the burial. A fragment of an iron spear (**VIII M2**; Fig. 20) from the surface of V 7700 is likely to belong with this burial, and it may have been part of the iron hilt and blade found by Boyd. Fragments of a thin bronze band were also found in V 7613.7. Although these were not inventoried because they were very thin and poorly preserved, they may represent the remains of a band on a spear socket, as seen on **GR12 M26** (see below, p. 123). It is possible that both a spearhead and a sword or dirk were represented in the burial, or that all of the iron, including those items recovered by Boyd, belonged to the iron spearhead found in the 1988 excavations.

Chronology

The stirrup jar **VIII P1** is probably of LM IIIC date. Although it has the cone on top of the false spout that is usually considered a late feature, found in LM IIIC and later stirrup jars (Popham 1965, 320; Kanta 1980, 247; Hallager 2007, 190), the spout is not pulled back to meet the disk top, a feature that appears on SM and EPG examples but is not common in LM IIIC (Day 2011b, 291). The decoration, in which the top is divided into quadrants with filled triangles, can be found on LM IIIC, SM, and EPG pottery, but the later examples regularly have more rectilinear filling, not the curved loops found on the Vronda example. All the evidence points to a date in LM IIIC for this example. Because this tomb cuts into LM IIIC Building L, however, a building that was in use with the rest of the settlement in late LM IIIC (Day and Glowacki 2012, 161), it is likely that this stirrup jar was an earlier piece, possibly an antique or heirloom deposited in the tomb, and it should not be taken as an indication of the date of the burial, but only as a terminus post quem for the use of the tomb. All the other material found in the cleaning of the edges of the tomb and in the stomion is fragmentary and dates to LM IIIC. These fragments most likely represent pieces that were in the soil left over from the settlement and incorporated into the construction of the tomb.

Catalog of Finds from Interior of Tholos

Pottery

FINE WARE

VIII P1 (HM 1968; Fig. 22; Pls. 5A, 13D). Stirrup jar. Restored; fragments of body and rim of spout missing. H. 11.2; max. d. 12.0; d. base 4.3. Fine, soft, very pale brown (10YR 7/3) fabric. Very pale brown (10YR 7/3) slip. Worn, black (10YR 2/1) paint. Irregular in shape. Short spout; false spout with wide disk and knob on top; small hole pierced at base of false spout; globular-biconical body; raised base, hollowed underneath. Concentric circles on top of false spout; band around base of spout and vertical row of dots down front of spout. Shoulder divided into four areas, each with a triangle with concentric arcs in angles. Horizontal strokes on handles. Two groups of three or four bands on lower body. *Bibliography*: Boyd 1901, pl. II: middle, second from right; Gesell, Day, and Coulson 1983, 402–403, fig. 6:V14, pl. 77:b. *Comparanda*: for shape and decoration, Hood et al. 1958–1959, 242, 247, fig. 28:VIa.1 (Gypsades, LM IIIA:2); Kanta 1980, 246–248, fig. 125:11 (Episkopi, end of LM IIIB or beginning of LM IIIC). *Date*: LM IIIC.

Metal

BRONZE

VIII M1 (V88.140; V 7613.6, object 1; Fig. 22; Pl. 13D). Pin. Single fragment from bulb near end of pin. Missing both ends. Max. pres. L. 3.4; d. 0.2; d. bulb 0.6. Well preserved. Originally long straight pin with bulb near top. *Comparanda*: **GR12 M2**.

Catalog of Finds from Stomion (V 7613.2, V 7614) and Pseudo-Dromos (V 7617)

Pottery

FINE MONOCHROME WARE

VIII P2 (V 7614.3; Fig. 22). Deep bowl or cup. Single fragment from rim. D. rim est. 10.0–11.0. Fine, soft, pink (5YR 7/4) fabric with tiny red phyllite inclusions. Dark reddish-gray (5YR 4/2) paint. Very worn surfaces. *Comparanda*: Day, Klein, and Turner, 2009, 154, fig. 105:K4 P5 (LM IIIC). *Date*: LM IIIC.

MEDIUM-COARSE WARE

VIII P3 (V 7617.2; Fig. 22). Kalathos. Single fragment from rim. D. rim est. 32.0. Medium-coarse, soft, reddish-yellow (5YR 7/6) fabric with red phyllite inclusions. Very pale brown (10YR 8/4) slip. Red (2.5YR 4/6) paint. Worn surfaces. *Date*: LM IIIC or PG?

Catalog of Finds from Fill within Tomb

Pottery

FINE DARK-ON-LIGHT WARES

VIII P4 (V 7612.5; Fig. 22). Deep bowl or cup. Single fragment from rim. D. rim est. 13.0. Fine, soft, reddish-yellow (5YR 7/6) fabric. Very pale brown (10YR 8/4) slip. Dark reddish-brown (5YR 3/4) paint. Very worn surfaces. Traces of a curvilinear decoration. *Comparanda*: Day, Klein, and Turner 2009, 30, fig. 17:AE P24 (LM IIIC); Day and Glowacki 2012, 148, fig. 121:L2 P11 (LM IIIC). *Date*: LM IIIC.

VIII P5 (V 7613.7; Fig. 22). Deep bowl or cup. Single fragment from rim. D. rim est. 13.0–14.0. Fine, soft, reddish-yellow (7.5YR 7/6) fabric, gray (5Y 6/1) at core. Red (2.5 YR 4/8) paint. Very worn surfaces. *Comparanda*: Day and Glowacki 2012, 169, fig. 133:WS P4 (LM IIIC). *Date*: LM IIIC.

VIII P6 (V 7102.3; Fig. 22). Deep bowl or cup. Single fragment (two sherds) from rim. D. rim est. 11.0. Fine, soft, reddish-yellow (5YR 6/6) fabric with some red phyllites and quartzites. Creamy pink (7.5YR 8/4) slip. Red (2.5YR 4/6) paint over slip. Very worn surfaces. *Comparanda*: Day, Klein, and Turner, 2009, 154, fig. 105:K4 P5 (LM IIIC). *Date*: LM IIIC.

VIII P7 (V 7102.3; Fig. 22). Deep bowl or cup. Single fragment preserving entire base. D. base 4.0. Fine, soft, porous, pink (5YR 7/4) fabric. Very pale brown (10YR 8/2) slip. Worn surfaces. *Comparanda*: Day and Glowacki 2012, 169, fig. 133:WS P4. *Date*: LM IIIC.

VIII P8 (V 7102.3; Fig. 22). Deep bowl or cup. Single fragment preserving entire base. D. base 5.0. Fine, soft, porous, reddish-yellow (5YR 7/6) fabric. Very pale brown (10YR 8/2) slip. Traces of crackled black paint. Worn surfaces. *Comparanda*: Day, Klein, and Turner 2009, 44, fig. 26:B4 P13 (LM IIIC early). *Date*: LM IIIC.

VIII P9 (V 7102.1; Fig. 22). Goblet. Single fragment preserving entire stem. Max. pres. h. 2.6; d. stem 3.0. Fine, soft, reddish-yellow (5YR 7/6) fabric with tiny red phyllite inclusions. Very pale brown (10YR 8/4) slip. Worn surfaces. *Comparanda*: Popham 1992, pl. 43:12, 13 (Knossos, SM). *Date*: LM IIIC or SM?

Cooking Ware

VIII P10 (V 7612.1; Fig. 22). Cooking dish. Single fragment preserving nearly complete profile from rim to beginning of base. Max. pres. h. 6.6. Coarse, red (2.5YR 5/8), Kavousi Type IV fabric (Haggis and Mook 1993), gray (2.5YR 5/0) at core. *Comparanda*: Day, Klein, and Turner 2009, 46, fig. 30:B4 P41 (LM IIIC). *Date*: LM IIIC.

Coarse Painted Ware

VIII P11 (V 7102.3; Fig. 22). Fenestrated stand. Single fragment from rim, preserving edge of one fenestration. D. rim est. 26.0. Coarse, light reddish-brown (2.5YR 6/4), Type X/XI fabric. Very pale brown (10YR 8/2) slip. Red (2.5YR 5/8) paint. Very worn surfaces. Decoration of crosshatched panel. *Comparanda*: Day, Klein, and Turner 2009, 85, fig. 60:C2 P4; 138, fig. 96:J3 P10 (LM IIIC). *Date*: LM IIIC.

Metal

Iron

VIII M2 (V89.29; V 7702.2; Fig. 22). Spearhead. Single fragment from blade near socket attachment. Max. pres. L. 4.5; max. pres. w. 1.9; th. 1.0. Surfaces corroded and cracked. No preserved edge. Very thick fragment that must be from near the socket attachment.

Vronda Tombs II, VII, or VIII (Boyd's Tombs 1, 4, or 2)

The vessels that we have labeled with the prefix II-VII-VIII (Fig. 20; Pl. 13D) are illustrated by Boyd (1901, pl. II; Pl. 5A). They are recorded as coming from Tombs II, VII, or VIII, but they cannot be more specifically assigned. Some vessels on this photograph are clearly not from the tholos tombs at Vronda, especially those on the upper shelf. Of the vessels pictured on the top shelf in Plate 5A, the bowl at the far left came from Hagios Antonios (Boyd 1901, 131 n. 2), while the second and third vessels from the left are two halves of a lekythos from the Kastro (Gesell, Day, and Coulson 1985, 351, fig. 13). The second, third, and fourth vessels from the right include a teapot that looks earlier and may come from Hagios Antonios, and two jugs, the smaller of which resembles a jug from Knossos of PGB–MG date (Brock 1957, 157, pl. 38:597). The other vessels are without known parallels.

The missing vessels pictured on the middle shelf in Plate 5A, from left to right, include an amphoriskos, a cylindrical-mouthed jug, a bowl, a one-handled cup, and a bell skyphos. The shape of the amphoriskos resembles an example from the Plai tou Kastro tomb (HM 731) of SM or PG date and two krateriskoi of EPG date, one from Chamaizi Phatsi (Tsipopoulou 1997, 457–458, fig. 2:5051), and the other from Skopi Droggera (Tsipopoulou 1997, 482, 458, fig. 2:5055); its decoration of multiple pendant loops, however, is more reminiscent of the motif on LM IIIC deep bowls (Day 2011b, 260–261). The combination of the new shape and the old decoration suggests that it belongs to a transitional period between LM IIIC and EPG—that is, SM. The bell skyphos on the right is a good SM shape, with parallels at Knossos of SM (Popham 1992, 61, pl. 44:9, 10), SM–EPG (Boardman 1960, 130, 136, fig. 4:I.15, pl. 34:I.17, pl. 35:I.14, I.16, VI.3), or LPG (Coldstream and Catling, eds., 1996, 5, fig. 56:7) date; although it is difficult to tell from the photo, it may have been dipped. The jug or jar second from the left is an unusual shape, but it may be a thelastron or basket vase, such as the EO thelastra at Adromyloi (Tsipopoulou 2005, 209, fig. 142:H3210) and Dreros (Tsipopoulou 2005, 63, fig. 142:HΔ15) or the LG basket vase in one of the Vronda cremation burials (**GR9 P10**; this vol., Ch. 3).

The bowl with a ledge rim, third from the left in Plate 5A, resembles an example from Tomb IX (**IX P42**; see below) and another from Grave 9 in the later cremation burials at Vronda (**GR9 P23**; this vol., Ch. 3), both of which may be cups like a LPG example from Knossos (Coldstream and Catling 1996, eds., 186, fig. 119:16). The one-handled cup, third from the right, resembles an example from Vronda IX (**IX**

P60) of PG date and a cup from Praisos dated to the LG period (Tsipopoulou 2005, 288, fig. 124:AN8767). Heavy shallow cups like this one tend to be earlier in date than deeper, thin-walled cups, and this example is most likely to be PG–G in date as well as style.

The crude pyxis that appears second from the left on the bottom shelf in Plate 5A also probably comes from one of the tombs. It resembles a PGB example from Sklavoi (Tsipopoulou 2005, 304, fig. 56:Σ3974) and is probably PG.

Only two vessels can still be found in this group: the lentoid flask (**II-VII-VIII P1**), which has many parallels in SM deposits, and the oinochoe (**II-VII-VIII P2**). The pottery seems to be largely SM or PG, with a few possibly later pieces such as the cup.

Catalog of Extant Finds from II-VII-VIII

Pottery

Fine Wares

II-VII-VIII P1 (HM 3693; Fig. 20; Pls. 5A, 13D). Lentoid flask. Intact. H. 13.0; d. rim 3.8; max. d. 9.6. Soft, pinkish-white to pink (7.5YR 8/2–8/4) fabric with a reddish-yellow (5YR 7/6) core. Paint entirely worn off; surface lighter where it was. Narrow neck with flaring rim; single vertical rectangular handle from below rim to shoulder; irregular lentoid body, hole drilled at base of neck. Concentric circles on two flat sides of flask; possible stripes on handle. *Bibliography*: Boyd 1901, pl. II: top row, right; Gesell, Day, and Coulson 1983, 397, fig. 4:2, pl. 76:a; Tsipopoulou 2005, 121, fig. 144; Karageorghis et al. 2014, 97 (Creto-Cypriot juglet, SM). *Comparanda*: **II P1, IV P8, IX P11**; Tsipopoulou 1997, 469, fig. 12:4974 (Chamaizi Phatsi, SM); 2005, 110, fig. 145 (Kavousi, Plai tou Kastrou, PG). *Date*: SM.

II-VII-VIII P2 (HM 1019; Fig. 20; Pls. 5A, 13D). Oinochoe. Intact except for small part of upper neck and rim. H. 11.1; max. d. 7.9; d. base 3.4. Fine, soft, pink (5YR 7/4) fabric with small inclusions. Very dark gray (10YR 3/1) to weak red (7.5YR 5/4) paint. Trefoil mouth; narrow neck; single flattened handle from rim to shoulder; ovoid body; flat base, slightly hollowed underneath. Filled pendant triangles on shoulder and upper body; lower body solidly painted. Horizontal strokes on handle. String marks on underside of base. *Bibliography*: Boyd 1901, pl. II: bottom left; Tsipopoulou 2005, 75, pl. 21, fig. 85 (said to be from Vronda Tomb IV, PG). *Comparanda*: **IX P27**; Brock 1957, 37, pl. 26:352; 119, pl. 96:1376 (Knossos, PGB–MG); Tsipopoulou 2005, 92, pl. 51, fig. 73 (Kavousi, Plai tou Kastrou, PGB); 310, fig. 65:Σ4016 (Sklavoi, PG); for motif, Brock 1957, motif 4t (PGB–MG). *Date*: PG.

Vronda Tomb IX

Tomb IX was cleared by the local landowner, Giorgos Sekadakis, in 1951, and the whole vessels were taken to the Ierapetra museum at that time (Platon 1951, 445; another reference in Platon 1954 [p. 516], originally interpreted as referring to the same tomb, probably describes another tomb, as the number of vessels reported differs from that reported in 1951, and no sealstones were found in the Sekadakis tomb). There was no indication of the number of burials within the tomb. The number of pots was reported in 1951 as 23, though the landowner remembered 54, including one with painted decoration of an archer shooting a bird. Three rings were also reported to have been found in the tomb, and these have been identified as stone whorls. Of the pots, 20 can be securely identified from an unpublished photograph taken by the landowner just after excavation, and three more are listed in the Ierapetra museum as coming from the Sekadakis group from Vronda (**IX P6, IX P16, IX P21**). The tomb was cleaned in 1981 for drawing and photography (Fig. 23), and many sherds, bones, and fragments of iron blades were recovered, material that the landowner had thrown back into the tomb after recovering the whole vases. It was impossible to clean the tomb completely without damaging the olive tree that had been planted by the landowner, and some material was left in place. In 1987 more pottery was collected from the tomb and the immediate area.

Architecture

Only one corner and small sections of two walls of the tomb are preserved (Pl. 14A). The tomb is square or rectangular at the bottom course, but the corner begins to round out in the second course, about 0.30 m above the floor of the tomb. The maximum height of the wall is 1.30 m, preserved in seven courses. The maximum preserved length of the west wall is 0.90 m, and that of the east wall is 1.50 m. The lower two courses are built of roughly shaped rectangular blocks of limestone, while the upper courses are largely made of irregularly shaped breccia boulders. On the west side the tomb is built right into the local red clay. The entrance is not preserved.

Stratigraphy

All of the soil had been disturbed by the planting of the olive tree and the removal of the whole vases in 1951. Many later vessels (Medieval–Modern in date) that had probably been on the surface of the area were thrown back in along with the soil and the fragments of tomb pottery (**IX P57–IX P59**).

Burials

The landowner's son remembered that one of the skulls was actually in the dromos or stomion, but otherwise there is no information on the disposition of the bodies. During the cleaning of the tomb, remains of three individuals were recovered: two adults and one subadult.

Burial 1
Type: disturbed inhumation
Age: juvenile
Sex: unknown

The presence of a juvenile is indicated by very thin, child-like parietal fragments and small, extremely gracile long bone fragments.

Burials 2 and 3
Type: disturbed inhumations
Age: both adult, one 40–49 years
Sex: both male

The remains of Burials 2 and 3 consisted of fragmentary, commingled partial skeletons of two adult male individuals. One of the individuals was 40–49 years old at death. Both of these individuals had retained metopic sutures on the frontal bone of the cranium. One right and one left half of the frontal bones are preserved, but these two halves do not join at the suture, indicating that the bones come from two individuals. This trait is genetically based and suggests a probable family relationship.

Faunal Remains

No animal bones were recovered, but there were parts of two marine shells (Table 3), both dog cockles (*Glycymeris*).

Pottery

In total, 60 vessels have been cataloged from Vronda Tomb IX, including 22 whole vases in the Archaeological Collection of Ierapetra and 38 more fragmentary pots recovered from the cleaning. Fragments of other vessels have not been cataloged because their shapes were uncertain. These uncataloged vases included the bases of at least three fine closed vessels, probably jugs or oinochoai, along with numerous fragments from fine open vases including small rim fragments and a raised and hollowed base. There were, in addition, at least four bases in medium-coarse wares.

The cataloged pottery includes many vessels for drinking, probably the remains of a ritual undertaken during interment, but possibly deposited to slake the thirst of the dead in the afterlife. There are 14 cups (**IX P1, IX P2, IX P4, IX P28–IX P34, IX P50, IX P51, IX P59, IX P60**), two skyphoi (**IX P3, IX P35**), and four cups or skyphoi (**IX P37–IX P39, IX P52**). Other open vessels, such as the three bowls (**IX P5, IX P6, IX P42**), may also have been used for drinking, but they might also have contained offerings. The small necked jar (**IX P7**) and necked jar (**IX P8**), although coated on the interior, were probably used for storage because of their restricted mouths, as was the larger necked jar (**IX P9**). The bases **IX P40** and **IX P41** may be from footed krateriskoi, skyphoi, or cups. The large number of drinking vessels distinguishes Vronda IX from the other tholos tombs, where cups and skyphoi are rare, as in the unrobbed Vronda IV (see above). Large numbers of drinking vessels are, however, common in the later cremation burials on the summit and may indicate that at least some of the burials in this tholos tomb are closer in date to those in the cremation cemetery.

Closed vessels with narrow mouths are rather rare and include the stirrup jar (**IX P10**), flask (**IX P11**), bird askos (**IX P53**), jug (**IX P27**), juglets (**IX P12–IX P14**), and small oinochoai (**IX P16, IX P17, IX P44, IX P54**). These small vessels probably held valuable liquids, such as perfumed oil. The assemblage includes a large number of pouring vessels with less restricted mouths (12), whether jugs (**IX P15**) or oinochoai (**IX P18–IX P23, IX P46, IX P49**). Vessels **IX P24** and **IX P25** could be either jugs or oinochoai, but their rims are not preserved well enough to be certain. All of these vessels would have been used for pouring, possibly in the same rituals that included the cups. Other vessels were for storage, possibly for foods or liquids left as grave offerings: the pyxis (**IX P45**), three necked jars (**IX P7–IX P9**), and three amphorae (**IX P47, IX P48, IX P58**). The lid (**IX P43**) may have been used to seal one of these.

At least three of the vessels recovered during the cleaning belonged to a much later date (a small amphoriskos and two larger jars: **IX P55–IX P57**), either to the period of occupation of what may have been a Venetian farmstead at nearby Xerambela or to the Modern era. Five fragments of glazed ware were found, including a ring base with olive green glaze (5Y 5/4), a pierced rim fragment with light olive brown (2.5Y 5/6) glaze, and body fragments with yellow (2.5Y 7/8), pink (5YR 8/4), and red (2.5YR 5/8) glazes. Pithos sherds were found on the terrace just above the tomb, including one decorated with knobs and oblique incisions and another with dots and incised lines.

Objects

Four stone rings were reported (Platon 1951, 445), but these could not be located in 1979. They may have been stone beads or whorls. Many fragments of iron weapons and tools were found in the cleaning of the tomb. These included fragments from the socket and the blade of an iron spearhead (**IX M1**) and seven fragments that seem to come from iron knives of at least four different types (**IX M2–IX M8**).

Chronology

The flask (**IX P11**) and the bird askos (**IX P53**) are the earliest vessels from Tomb IX. The flask has many parallels in other tombs at Vronda (**II P1, IV P8, II-VII-VIII P1**; see above) as well as at other Cretan sites and is probably of SM date. The bird askos resembles other SM examples (**IV P6, IV P7**; Desborough 1972, 253, type IIb), but the shape and monochrome paint make it unusual, perhaps dating to the later SM–EPG era. Cup **IX P1** with its wavy line decoration may be SM, particularly if it had a high pedestal foot like SM cups from Knossos (Warren 1982–1983, 85, fig. 60:a, b). If it had a flat base, it may have been EPG, more like an example from Hagios Ioannis (Boardman 1960, 134, pl. 36:V.16). The footed cup **IX P34** is also probably EPG; it is top-heavy, with a rim diameter greater than its height, a feature that is found in early bell skyphoi on the Kastro (Mook 1993, 172). The other footed cup **IX P2** is also of early date, as can be seen from its dipped decoration and its shape that resembles the bell skyphos, except for the handle; it is not as early as **IX P34**, however, because the rim diameter is still smaller than its height. Although the shape is rare, similar examples of SM–EPG date can be found at Knossos.

The two-handled cup **IX P4**, with its dipped decoration, is unusual. The shape, aside from the handles, which may be a local variation, resembles krateriskoi from the Knossos area of SM–MPG date. The rim diameter is considerably smaller than the height on this vessel, suggesting that it could belong to the late end of this chronological span. Vessels **IX P3** and **IX P35** might have been of similar shape, although their feet are not preserved, and they may belong to the same chronological phase.

The stirrup jar (**IX P10**) is certainly of PG date, with both EPG and MPG parallels for its shape and decoration; the shape seems closest to those examples dated to the MPG period. Two oinochoai, **IX P22** and **IX P49**, resemble examples from the Knossos area of MPG date, but the scroll decoration of **IX P49** is more common on EPG jugs and amphorae. The decoration on **IX P22** looks like an upside-down variation of the moustache or tassel pattern also found on SM and EPG vessels (Coldstream and Catling, eds., 1996, 97, pl. 112:38, 39, Knossos, SM–EPG); it may be a later or a local version of the earlier motif. The small juglet **IX P13** has EPG and MPG parallels.

Several vessels seem to date to MPG–LPG, including four cups (**IX P28, IX P29, IX P50, IX P59**). Also of this date are jug **IX P15**, jug or oinochoe **IX P24**, and possibly amphora **IX P47**. A large number of vessels find parallels of LPG–PGB date from Central Crete, including cups **IX P30, IX P31, IX P33, IX P51**, and **IX P60**, necked jar **IX P8**, small juglets **IX P12** and **IX P16**, oinochoai **IX P18, IX P19**, and **IX P21**, and pyxis **IX P45**. The conical bases **IX P40** and **IX P41** may also belong to this ceramic phase or even later; they both show a circular depression on the underside of the base that is found primarily on MPG vessels at Knossos (Coldstream and Catling, eds., 1996, 32, fig. 66:L3; 198, fig. 126:48) and perhaps on even later examples from the Kastro (Mook 1993, 173–174). At Kommos this feature is attested on LPG vessels (Johnston 2000, 194, fig. 2:3, 4), although it also occurs on SM–PG closed vessels in Central Crete (Rethemiotakis and Englezou 2010,

91, fig. 51:126). Other vessels are probably also of PG date, including four cups (**IX P32, IX P37, IX P38, IX P52**) and krater **IX P36**.

A number of vessels are later than the PG period. On the basis of their parallels with Central Cretan pottery of LPG–MG date, oinochoe **IX P17**, jug **IX P27**, lid **IX P43**, and amphora or jug **IX P48** belong to the Geometric period, possibly LG. Three vessels are of PG–G date: bowl **IX P6**, small necked jar **IX P7**, and large necked jar **IX P9**. The remainder of vessels show a wider range of chronological possibilities. Cup **IX P33**, small necked jar **IX P7**, and oinochoe **IX P20** find parallels ranging from LPG to LG in date. Cup **IX P33** is similar to an example from one of the cremation burials (**GR9 P43**; see this vol., Ch. 3), and it may indicate that the two burials overlapped in time. Vessel **IX P7** is similar in shape to many small necked jars ranging in date from LPG to LG (see below, p. 39), but it seems to be coated on the interior, a fact that suggests its use as a drinking vessel. The decoration of a single metope on a dark-ground vessel bearing a crosshatched lozenge chain, however, is not otherwise found. One pyxis from Praisos has a similar decoration (Tsipopoulou 2005, 293, fig. 60:AN8788 [mistakenly labeled H8788]), although with bands on the lower body; the Tomb IX example may be earlier than the LG date assigned to the Praisos vessel. The small oinochoe **IX P20** is similar in shape to an example from Chamaizi Phatsi of early LG date (Tsipopoulou 1997, 471, fig. 13:4960), but the decorative scheme of triangles filled with hatching is probably earlier, as is the scheme of dark paint on a light background. The neck-handled amphora **IX P58** is of a shape that seems to be peculiar to East Crete (see parallels in catalog entry below, p. 44). It may be a local variation of the MG Atticizing amphora found in Central Crete (Coldstream 1996, 334–335). The meander pattern on the shoulder clearly marks this vessel as Geometric, and it is probably no earlier than the MG examples at Knossos and may be as late as LG. Bowl **IX P5** also dates to the Geometric period.

The pottery evidence from Tomb IX points to a date rather later than many of the tholoi, beginning in EPG with use later in PG and again in LG.

Finally, there is a large quantity of Venetian–modern pottery that was found during the cleaning of the grave. It was doubtless deposited there after the grave material had been removed by the local landowner.

Catalog

Pottery

Fine Dark-on-Light Wares

IX P1 (Fig. 24). Cup. One-third of upper profile preserved, including lower handle attachment; handle and base missing. Max. pres. h. 6.0; d. rim est. 10.0. Soft, reddish-yellow (5YR 7/8) fabric with some mica and white grits; heavy soil incrustation. Worn black paint. Wheel ridging on interior, wheel marks on exterior. Base may have been flat or pedestaled. Decoration of crude wavy line or scribble pattern with bands above and below. Bands on interior. *Comparanda*: Boardman 1960, 140–142, pl. 36:VIII.14 (Hagios Ioannis, EPG); Tsipopoulou 1997, 463, 479, fig. 6:4995, 5002 (Chamaizi Phatsi, PGA). *Date*: SM–PG.

IX P2 (IM 552; Fig. 24; Pl. 14B). Footed cup. Restored; tiny piece of rim missing. H. 11.7; d. rim 10.9; d. base 3.2. Fine, hard, pink (7.5YR 7/4) fabric. Dull, flaky paint, well preserved; mottled in color from light reddish-brown (5YR 6/4–5/4) to black on one spot in center. Profile S-curved; one round vertical handle from rim to shoulder; small conical stem, hollowed underneath; depression in center of interior. Dipped so that top is monochrome, bottom unpainted. Reserved band around base of exterior. Interior coated except for very center. *Comparanda*: Brock 1957, 166, pl. 3:19 (Knossos, SM–EPG); Coldstream 1972, 69–70, fig. 2:A25 (Knossos, SM–EPG). *Date*: PG.

IX P3 (Fig. 24) Skyphos. Six joining fragments from rim and one handle, one nonjoining handle fragment. Max. pres. h. 7.8; d. rim est. 11.0. Fine, soft, very porous, white (2.5YR 8/2) fabric and slip. Washy black paint. Very worn surfaces, heavily coated. May have been a bell skyphos with a conical foot. Bands at rim and below handle zone; handles coated. *Bibliography*: Boyd 1901, pl. II: middle row, right (Vronda, II, VII, or VIII). *Comparanda*: Boardman 1960, 132, 136, fig. 4:IV.3 (Hagios Ioannis, SM–MPG); Coldstream and Catling, eds., 1996, 19, fig. 60:77 (Knossos, PGB). *Date*: SM–PG.

IX P4 (IM 551; Fig. 24; Pl. 14B). Footed two-handled cup. Intact. H. 14.0; d. rim 12.0; d. base 4.0. Soft, reddish-yellow (5YR 7/6) fabric with some inclusions. Dull, washy, very dark gray (10YR 3/1) paint, worn. Flaring rim; deep, rounded body; two round, vertical handles from rim to body; low, conical stem with concave base. Handmade and uneven. Dipped so that top is monochrome coated, bottom is plain. Underside of base and bottom of interior reserved. Paint sloppily applied on interior, with drip marks. Soil incrustation on body. *Bibliography*: Gesell, Day, and Coulson 1983, 403–407, fig. 8:V.15, pl. 77:c. *Comparanda*: Desborough 1952, 102–103, pl. 12:2026 (Athens, LPG); Boardman 1960, 130, pl. 34:I.13; 132, 136, fig. 4:IV.3 (Hagios Ioannis, SM–MPG krateriskos). *Date*: SM–PG.

IX P5 (Fig. 24). Bowl. Mended from 10 fragments preserving 67% of rim, 30% of base and body; eight nonjoining fragments. H. 6.7; d. rim 15.0; d. base 6.0. Fine, rather hard, reddish-yellow (5YR 6/8) fabric. Black to red (2.5YR 5/8) paint. Worn surfaces. Possible traces of light red bands on exterior; monochrome interior. *Comparanda*: Tsipopoulou 1997, 463, 473, fig. 7:4975 (Chamaizi Phatsi, EG early); 2005, 315, fig. 132:AN1455 (Zou, LG); 2013, 153, fig. 13:12282 (Piskokephalo, LG). *Date*: PG–G.

IX P6 (IM 117; Fig. 24; Pl. 14B). Bowl. Complete; mended from six fragments. H. 7.5; d. rim 16.5; d. base 7.2. Fine, reddish-yellow (7.5YR 6/6) fabric with some fine inclusions, flaky surface. Worn, black (7.5YR N2.5) paint, but faded. Vertical rim, flattened on top; two horizontal lugs at rim; nearly conical body; flat base. Monochrome inside and out. Underside of base reserved; top of lugs decorated with stripes. *Comparanda*: Rocchetti 1967–1968, 207, fig. 49 (Phaistos, PG). *Date*: PG.

IX P7 (IM 154; Fig. 24; Pl. 14B). Small necked jar. Restored; top of one handle and part of another missing. H. 9.6; d. rim 8.1; d. base 5.5. Fine, soft, pink (7.5YR 8/4) fabric. Dark gray (5YR 4/1) paint faded to light red (2.5YR 6/8); badly worn. Wheelmade. Flaring rim; ovoid body; two round horizontal handles on shoulder; flat base. Painted inside and out, including underside of base, except for reserved band in handle zone with decoration of crosshatched lozenges between bands. Reserved band at base of rim. *Bibliography*: Gesell, Day, and Coulson 1983, 404–407, fig. 8:18, pl. 77:f. *Comparanda*: for shape, Brock 1957, 165, pl. 26:361 (Knossos, LPG); Coldstream and Catling, eds., 1996, 264, fig. 145:77 (Knossos, MG); Tsipopoulou 2005, 293, fig. 60:H8788 (Praisos, LG); 2013, 147, 149, fig. 11:12328 (Piskokephalo, LG); Rethemiotakis and Englezou 2010, 71, fig. 42:96 (Eltyna, MG); for decoration, Marinatos 1931–1932, 6, fig. 6:4 (Anavlochos, G); Platon 1955, 296, pl. 111:α (top right; Sphakia, PG); Brock 1957, 172, motif 5j (Knossos, PG). *Date*: PG–G.

IX P8 (Fig. 24). Large necked jar. Partly mended from 21 joining fragments preserving full profile, one handle; 25 nonjoining fragments, including more of base, rim, and other handle attachment. H. 17.1; d. rim 12.6; d. base 7.0. Fine, soft, very pale brown (10YR 7/4–8/4) fabric; worn and encrusted. Washy black paint, worn. Flaring rim; tall, wide neck; ovoid body with two round horizontal handles on shoulder; flat base. Coated black inside and out except for reserved band in handle zone with crosshatched triangles above bands. *Comparanda*: for decoration, Brock 1957, 171, motif 4l (Knossos, LPG). *Date*: PG.

IX P9 (Fig. 24). Large necked jar. Large fragment preserving 33% of profile; missing lower body and base, 75% of body and rim; three nonjoining rim fragments, fragment with stump of second handle, and five nonjoining body sherds. Max. pres. h. 13.5; d. rim 12.1. Fine, soft, reddish-yellow (5YR 7/6) fabric with some inclusions. Petrographic sample KAV 15/101: loner. Washy black paint, very worn. Surfaces worn and encrusted. Wheel ridging on interior. Flaring rim, wide short neck; two round horizontal handles on shoulder. Coated black on exterior except for reserved panel in handle zone with horizontal bands. Interior too worn to determine. *Comparanda*: Marinatos 1931–1932, 6, fig. 6:1 (Anavlochos, G); Platon 1955, 296, pl. 111:α (top, third from left; Sphakia, PG). *Date*: PG.

IX P10 (V98.43; Fig. 25; Pl. 14B). Stirrup jar. Mended from 22 fragments, preserving 75% of top, 27% of body, including both handles and entire base; missing top of false spout. Seven nonjoining fragments. Max. pres. h. 20.0; max. d. 13.8; d. base 5.0. Fine, soft, reddish-yellow (5YR 6/6) fabric with white grits. Petrographic sample KAV 15/103: Fabric Group 7. Very pale brown (10YR 8/4) slip. Worn black paint. Surfaces very worn and pocked. Spout leans back, probably touching false spout. Ovoid body, ridge on interior where top has been added as disk. Conical foot. Crosshatched triangles on shoulder; bands below. *Comparanda*: Brock 1957, 153, pls. 15:218, 219 (EPG?), 18:245 (Knossos, EPG?); Boardman 1960, 132, pl. 38:V.4 (Hagios Ioannis, SM–EPG); Coldstream and Catling, eds., 1996, 27, pl. 64:7 (Knossos, MPG); 29, fig. 66:J 55, pl. 66:55 (MPG); 186, pl. 177:29 (LPG); for shape, Coldstream and Catling, eds., 1996, 197, fig. 125:19 (SM–EPG); 28, pl. 64:16 (MPG); for decoration, Rethemiotakis and Englezou 2010, 31–32, fig. 13:18 (Eltyna, EPG). *Date*: EPG–MPG.

IX P11 (V98.44; Fig. 25; Pl. 14B). Lentoid flask. Mended from 18 fragments, preserving 75% of body; missing top of shoulder, neck, and handle. Max. pres. h. 12.3; max. d. 13.2; w. 8.7. Fine, hard, light reddish-brown (2.5YR 6/4) fabric. White (10YR 8/2) slip. Worn black paint. Round body, made in two halves and put together. Concentric circles on both sides. *Comparanda*: **II P1, II-VII-VIII P1, IV P8**; Tsipopoulou 1997, 469, fig. 12:4974 (Chamaizi Phatsi, SM). *Date*: SM.

IX P12 (IM 763; Fig. 25; Pl. 14B). Juglet. Intact. H. 8.8; max. d. 6.7; d. base 3.3. Fine, soft, reddish-yellow (7.5YR 7/6) fabric with some inclusions. Very pale brown (10YR 8/3) slip. Very dark gray (7.5YR N/3) paint, badly worn. Handmade. Slightly flaring rim, short narrow neck; ovoid body; single round vertical handle from rim to shoulder; flat base, slightly hollowed underneath. Upper body and shoulder has metopal panels with a frieze of hourglasses, divided by four vertical bands. Rest of body and handle coated. Top of rim painted, but not interior of neck. *Comparanda*: for shape, Kotsonas 2008, 174–175, 178, fig. 42:A 145β (Eleutherna, PGB aryballos); Tsipopoulou 2013, 139–140, fig. 5:12312 (Piskokephalo, LPG); for decoration, vertical version, Brock 1957, 168, motif 2f (Knossos, MG–LO). *Date*: PG.

IX P13 (IM 175; Fig. 25; Pl. 15). Juglet. Nearly complete except for small pieces of rim. H. 10.5; max. d. 8.9; d. base 3.6. Hard, rather fine, pinkish-white (7.5YR 8/2) fabric, with some small inclusions. Black (5YR 2.5/1) paint, badly worn. Wheelmade. Flaring rim; short neck; globular body; oval vertical handle from rim to shoulder; flat raised base. Possible wavy line on neck; groups of four short vertical strokes on shoulder; bands on lower belly. Rim possibly coated inside and out. Top of handle painted. *Comparanda*: Coldstream and Catling, eds., 1996, 42, pl. 77:29 (EPG); for decoration, Boardman 1960, 133, pl. 35:V.8 (Hagios Ioannis, MPG); Coldstream and Catling 1996, eds., 28, pl. 65:26 (Knossos, MPG); 186, pl. 179:31 (MPG); 247, pl. 227:97 (MPG); for shape, Brock 1957, 155, pl. 8:119 (Knossos, SM–EPG); Rizza and Scrinari 1968, 16, fig. 25 (Gortyn, PG). *Date*: MPG.

IX P14 (Fig. 25). Jug or flask. Single fragment from neck and rim. Max. pres. h. 4.3; d. rim 3.5. Fine, soft, light red (2.5 YR 6/8) fabric, worn and encrusted. Black paint on exterior.

IX P15 (Fig. 25). Cylindrical-mouthed jug. Partially mended into four large fragments from lower body and base (five sherds), lower body (six sherds), upper body (two sherds), and neck with handle (eight sherds); 20 nonjoining fragments. H. est. 22.0; d. rim est. 16.3; d. base 10.0. Rather fine, soft, reddish-yellow (5YR 6/6) fabric. Sampled KAV 15/100: Fabric Group 6. Very pale brown (10YR 8/3) slip. Black paint. Surfaces laminating and pocked. Flaring rim; short cylindrical neck; oval handle rises above rim to shoulder; ovoid body; flat base. Upper part painted; bands at middle of body. Stripes across handle. Interior of rim painted. *Comparanda*: for shape, Rethemiotakis and Englezou 2010, 38, fig. 18:30 (Eltyna, MPG–LPG). *Date*: PG.

IX P16 (IM 162; Fig. 25; Pl. 15). Small jug or oinochoe. Restored; rim and handle missing. Max. pres. h. 7.5; max. d. 7.1; d. base 3.5. Fine, soft, reddish-yellow (5YR 7/6) fabric. Black (5YR 2.5/1) paint; decoration clear, although surface is worn and encrusted. Narrow neck; single handle attached at shoulder; globular body; flat base. Multiple chevrons on shoulder; bands on lower body. *Comparanda*: Brock 1957, pl. 26:348, (Knossos, LPG–PGB); Rocchetti 1988–1989, 187–188, fig. 29 (Kourtes, PGA–PGB); 188–189, fig. 31:33 (Kourtes, PGB–MG); Coldstream and Catling, eds., 1996, 61, fig. 74:21 (Knossos, EG); 234, pl. 214:38 (PGB–EG); Rethemiotakis and Englezou 2010, 66, fig. 38:81 (Eltyna, PGB–EG); for decoration, see Brock 1957, 171, motif 4i (Knossos, PGB); Coldstream and Catling, eds., 1996, 48, pl. 79:32 (Knossos, PGB). *Date*: LPG–EG.

IX P17 (Fig. 25). Small oinochoe. Mended from three fragments, preserving entire base and part of shoulder; missing handle and three-quarters of shoulder and neck. Max pres. h. 9.5; d. base 3.0; max. d. 7.2. Fine, soft, reddish-yellow (7.5YR 7/6) fabric. Worn and pockmarked surfaces, encrusted. Traces of black paint. Trefoil mouth; tall, narrow neck; globular body; raised base, hollowed underneath. Bands on neck; shoulder decorated but too worn to determine motif; bottom coated, including underside of base. *Date*: PG.

IX P18 (IM 757; Fig. 25; Pl. 15). Oinochoe. Restored; 80% of rim missing and wrongly restored; hole worn through base. H. 10.8; max. d. 7.8; d. base 4.0. Soft, very pale brown (10YR 8/3) fabric with some small inclusions. Dark to very dark gray paint (10YR 4/1–3/1), badly worn. Trefoil mouth; flaring neck; depressed ovoid body; square handle from rim to shoulder; flat base, hollowed underneath. Crosshatched triangles on shoulder, with bands above and below; lower body painted. *Bibliography*: Gesell, Day, and Coulson 1983, 404, 407, fig. 8:V19 (emended); pl. 77:g. *Date*: PG.

IX P19 (IM 548; Fig. 25; Pl. 15). Oinochoe. Intact. H. 11.7; max. d. 9.3; d. base 4.5. Fine, soft, reddish-yellow (7.5YR 7/6) fabric. Dark reddish-brown to red paint (2.5YR 2.5/2–5/6). Trefoil mouth; short, flaring neck; ovoid body; flat raised base. Decoration on upper body and shoulder: bands alternating with wavy bands. Paint on top of handle. Bands begin dark at handle and gradually, moving clockwise, become fainter as the paint was used up. *Comparanda*: for shape, Brock 1957, 156, pl. 61:1033 (Knossos, LPG–PGB); Coldstream and Catling, eds., 1996, 185, pl. 177:7 (Knossos, EG); for decoration: Brock 1957, 174, motif 8a (Knossos, SM–PGB). *Date*: PG.

IX P20 (IM 546; Fig. 25; Pl. 15). Oinochoe. Restored; 25% of rim missing. H. 12.1; max. d. 10.1; d. base 4.5. Fine, soft, reddish-yellow (7.5YR 7/6) fabric with soft surface. Very faded red (2.5YR 5/8) paint, badly worn. Trefoil mouth; tall, flaring neck; biconical body; flat base. Bands on neck; framed crosshatched triangles (extent of crosshatching not clear) on shoulder; bands on lower body. Handle painted? *Comparanda*: for decoration, Brock 1957, 171, motif 4k (Knossos, PG–MG). *Date*: PG.

IX P21 (IM 549; Fig. 25; Pl. 15). Oinochoe. Restored; half of belly and base of handle missing. H. 15.0; max. d. 10.4; d. base 4.0. Fine, soft, reddish-yellow (5YR 7/6) fabric. Very worn red (2.5YR 4/8) paint. Handmade. Trefoil mouth, unevenly shaped; tall, wide neck; round vertical handle from rim to shoulder; biconical body with sharply offset shoulder; flat base. Neck coated; reserved band with crosshatched triangles on shoulder; two horizontal grooves around base of neck; lower body coated except for reserved band. Handle painted. *Comparanda*: for shape, Tsipopoulou 1997, 464, 470, fig. 8:4961 (Chamaizi Phatsi, MPG); 2005, 303, fig. 75:Σ3855 (Sklavoi, PGB); 2013, 137, 144, fig. 3:12322 (Piskokephalo, LG); 138, 140, fig. 5:12274; for decoration, Brock 1957, 154, pl. 62:1034 (Knossos, LPG). *Date*: LPG.

IX P22 (IM 592; Fig. 26; Pl. 15). Large oinochoe. Intact except for hole in underside of base. H. 29.4; max. d. 25.0; d. base 13.0. Fine, soft, reddish-yellow (7.5YR 8/6–7/6) fabric with small stone inclusions. Faded, very dark gray (7.5YR N/3) paint, worn on one side. Wheelmade, but irregular. Trefoil mouth, rather tall neck with collar at base; single flattened handle from rim to shoulder; ovoid body; flat base. Neck coated; on shoulder under central spout, but slightly off-center, curvilinear floral design or central vertical stroke with two curved strokes coming out of the bottom; alternating narrow and broad bands below; bands on lower body; handle painted. *Comparanda*: for shape, Rocchetti 1988–1989, 207–208, fig. 91 (MPG); Coldstream and Catling, eds., 1996, 186, pl. 179:31; for similar decoration: Coldstream 1972, 68, 74, fig. 1:C7 (Knossos, EPG–MPG); Popham 1992, 62, pl. 47d:2, 4 (Knossos, SM); Hayden 2003, 38–39, fig. 14:71 (Vrokastro, EPG–MPG). *Date*: EPG.

IX P23 (Fig. 26). Oinochoe. Five joining fragments preserving 75% of neck, including upper handle attachment; missing rim, body, base, handle. Max. pres. h. 7.6. Fine, soft, very pale brown (10YR 8/4) fabric with tiny black inclusions. Possible black paint. Worn surfaces. *Date*: PG.

IX P24 (V98.45; Fig. 26; Pl. 16). Jug or oinochoe. Nearly complete profile; missing one-third of body and neck, all of rim. Max. pres. h. 23.0; max. d. 15.2; d. base 5.8. Soft, reddish-yellow (5YR 7/8) fabric; encrusted. Worn black paint. Narrow neck; oval vertical handle from shoulder to rim; ovoid body; flat base. Lower body black with several reserved bands; decoration on shoulder and neck too worn to distinguish. *Comparanda*: Boardman 1960, 133, 136, fig. 4:V.8 (Hagios Ioannis, MPG): Coldstream and Catling, eds., 1996, 214, pl. 199:7 (PGB). *Date*: PG.

IX P25 (Fig. 26). Jug or oinochoe. Two joining fragments from handle and rim, preserving entire handle. Max. pres. h. 8.5. Fine, rather hard, reddish-yellow (7.5YR 7/6) fabric. Red (2.5YR 4/6) paint worn to shadow. Stripes on handle. *Date*: PG?

IX P26 (Fig. 26). Jar or pyxis. Partially mended from 13 fragments, preserving 80% of base, 85% of neck, including handle attachment; missing rim and handle. Max. pres. h. 10.0; max. d. 14.7; d. base 6.2. Fine, very soft, reddish-yellow (7.5YR 8/6) fabric. Black paint. Very worn surfaces. Neck thickens toward bottom as if made separately and added on with clay. Very thick toward base, with interior ridging. Decoration of four bands just at widest diameter and below. *Date*: PG?

FINE LIGHT-ON-DARK WARE

IX P27 (IM 759; Fig. 26; Pl. 16). Jug. Intact. H. 13.6; max. d. 10.8; d. base 4.2. Fine, soft, micaceous, reddish-yellow (5YR 6/6) fabric, with much spalling. Streaky, dark to light gray (5YR 4/1–5YR 6/1) paint, very worn. Possible burning or misfiring on one side. Flaring rim; tall cylindrical neck; square handle from rim to shoulder; raised base, hollowed underneath. Monochrome paint with decoration in added white: two bands on neck, pendant triangles on shoulder, plain band on lower body. Black band on interior of neck. Two broad horizontal incisions on neck. *Comparanda*: for shape, Rocchetti 1988–1989, 204–205, fig. 83 (Kourtes, but larger); for decoration, **II-VII-VIII P2**. *Date*: PG.

FINE MONOCHROME WARES

IX P28 (IM 789; Fig. 27; Pl. 16). Cup. Complete; mended from two fragments. H. 7.0; d. rim 11.5; d. base 5.2. Fine, soft, pink (7.5YR 7/4) fabric. Dull, very dark gray (7.5YR N/3) to red (10R 4/8) paint. Handmade; thick walls. Pointed rim; rounded bowl; flat base; round handle rises above rim to lower body. Monochrome inside and out, including handle. *Comparanda*: **IX P29, IX P50**; Boardman 1960, 140, pl. 36:VIII.12 (Hagios Ioannis, MPG); Tsipopoulou 1997, 464, 475, fig. 14:5025 (Chamaizi Phatsi, LPG); 473, 475, fig. 14:4945 (MPG). *Date*: PG.

IX P29 (IM 786; Fig. 27; Pl. 16). Cup. Intact. H. 6.8; d. rim 11.9; d. base 4.4. Fine, soft, reddish-yellow (5YR 7/6) fabric with some inclusions. Dull, flaky, reddish-yellow (5YR 6/6) to black (5YR 2.5/1) paint. Handmade; thick walls. Rim slightly beveled; shallow bowl; slightly raised base; round handle from inside rim to mid body. Monochrome inside and out, including handles. *Comparanda*: **IX P28, IX P50**; Boardman 1960, 140, pl. 36:VIII.12 (Hagios Ioannis, MPG); Tsipopoulou 1997, 464, 475, fig. 14:5025 (Chamaizi Phatsi, LPG). *Date*: PG.

IX P30 (Fig. 27). Cup. Half preserved, including half of handle, rim, base, and full profile. H. 7.2; d. rim 10.5; d. base 3.6. Fine, hard, light red (2.5YR 6/8) fabric. Petrographic sample KAV 15/94: Fabric Group 2. Streaky black paint on interior and exterior. Worn surfaces, with some soil incrustations on exterior. Outturned rim; flat handle; rounded bowl, tapering toward bottom; slightly raised base. String marks on underside of base. Monochrome. *Comparanda*: **GR9 P34, GR9 P43**; Coldstream and Catling, eds., 1996, 255, fig. 143:2 (Knossos, PGB); Tsipopoulou 2013, 141, 143, fig. 7:12301 (Piskokephalo, PGB). *Date*: PG.

IX P31 (Fig. 27). Cup. Mended from 11 fragments preserving one-third of upper and all of lower part of cup, entire handle, and complete profile; 10 nonjoining fragments. H. 8.7; d. rim 10.3; d. base 4.2. Fine, soft, reddish-yellow (7.5YR 7/6) fabric. Petrographic sample KAV 15/99: Fabric Group 7. Reddish-yellow (5YR 6/6) paint. Worn and pock-marked surfaces. Flaring rim; rectangular handle attached inside rim; deep bowl; raised base, hollowed underneath. String marks on base. Possibly monochrome inside and out. *Comparanda*: **GR28 P6, GR30 P7**; Kotsonas 2008, 200–204, fig. 50:A 254 (Eleutherna, LPG–PGB). *Date*: G–LG.

IX P32 (Fig. 27). Cup. Single fragment of base, one fragment of rim and handle, two fragments of rim and three body sherds. H. est. 7.8; d. rim 11.4; d. base 4.1. Fine, soft, reddish-yellow (7.5YR 8/6) fabric, with some white inclusions. Worn, red (2.5YR 4/8) paint on interior, exterior, and underside of base. Surfaces very worn and heavily encrusted. Offset rim; rectangular handle attached inside rim; rounded body; raised base. Monochrome interior and exterior. *Comparanda*: Tsipopoulou 2005, 106, pl. 94:H765 (Plai tou Kastrou, LG). *Date*: PG.

IX P33 (Fig. 27). Cup. Mended from 22 fragments, preserving full profile, entire handle, and half of upper body and rim. H. 7.3; d. rim 10.2; d. base 4.2. Fine, soft, reddish-yellow (5YR 7/6) fabric with clay pellets. Worn red (2.5YR 5/8) paint. Rim slightly outturned; round handle flattened on top attached on interior of rim; slightly rounded body; flat base. Monochrome on interior, exterior, and underside of base. *Comparanda*: **GR3 P19**. *Date*: PG–LG.

IX P34 (IM 812; Fig. 27; Pl. 16). Footed cup. Restored; small sections of rim and shoulder, 65% of base missing. H. 7.6; d. rim 7.9; d. base 3.6. Soft, very pale brown (10YR 8/4) fabric with some black inclusions. Light red (2.5YR 6/8) paint, very worn and encrusted. Handmade. Outturned rim; single round vertical handle rising above rim to body; deep bowl; low conical stem, hollowed underneath. Monochrome inside and out. *Bibliography*: Gesell, Day, and Coulson 1983, 404, 407, fig. 8:V16, pl. 77:d. *Comparanda*: Brock 1957, 166, pl. 3.19 (Knossos SM–EPG); Boardman 1960, 140–142, pl. 36:VIII.14 (Hagios Ioannis, EPG). *Date*: EPG.

IX P35 (Fig. 27). Skyphos. Four joining fragments of handle and body, three rim fragments; partial profile restored. Max. pres. h. 4.5; d. rim 8.8. Fine, soft, reddish-yellow (5YR 7/6) fabric. Red (10R 5/8) paint on inside, black on the outside. Worn surfaces. Bell skyphos. Monochrome. *Comparanda*: Boardman 1960, 130, pl. 34:I.17; 132, 136, fig. 4:IV.3 (Hagios Ioannis SM–MPG); Coldstream and Catling, eds., 1996, 19, fig. 60:77 (Knossos, PGB); 248, fig. 142:127 (LPG); Mook 2004, 171, fig. 12.7:A (Kastro, SM–EPG); Rethemiotakis and Englezou 2010, 39, fig. 19:34 (Eltyna, SM–EPG). *Date*: EPG–LPG.

IX P36 (Fig. 27). Krater. Single large rim fragment, one handle and body fragment, three more rim fragments, and 19 body sherds; missing base. Max. pres. h. 8.0; d. rim 20.0. Fine, soft reddish-yellow (7.5YR 7/6) fabric. Petrographic sample KAV 15/102: Fabric Subgroup 1c. Red (2.5YR 4/8) paint on interior and exterior. Surfaces very badly preserved. Offset rim with groove on interior of lip. Monochrome? *Comparanda*: Tsipopoulou 1997, 477, 482, fig. 16:5054 (Skopi Droggera, PGA); Rethemiotakis and Englezou 2010, 75, fig. 46:109 (Eltyna, PG). *Date*: PG.

IX P37 (Fig. 27). Cup or skyphos. Eight joining fragments from rim and body, two nonjoining fragments; missing handle(s) and base. Fine, soft, reddish-yellow (7.5YR 7/6) fabric with some red phyllites and white inclusions. Red (2.5 YR5/6) paint. Vertical rim. Monochrome on exterior and interior. Very worn surfaces. *Comparanda*: Boardman 1960, 140, pl. 36:VIII.13 (Hagios Ioannis, MPG). *Date*: PG.

IX P38 (Fig. 27). Cup or skyphos. Three joining fragments from rim. D. rim est. 12.0. Fine, soft, white (2.5Y 8/2) fabric. Outturned rim. Traces of black paint on interior and exterior. *Comparanda*: **GR9 P23**; Coldstream and Catling, eds., 1996, 27, fig. 65:12 (Knossos, MPG); Mook 2004, 171, fig. 12.7:E (Kavousi Kastro, SM/EPG); Tsipopoulou 2005, 286, fig. 124:AN8761 (Praisos, LG). *Date*: PG.

IX P39 (Fig. 27). Cup or skyphos. Four joining fragments from base, four body sherds, and lower handle attachment preserved. Max. pres. h. 5.3; d. base 5.0. Fine, soft, reddish-yellow (7.5YR 7/6) fabric. Possible traces of paint inside and out, but too worn or coated with sediment to be certain. *Date*: PG?

IX P40 (Fig. 27). Skyphos or cup. Single fragment preserving entire base. Max. pres. h. 4.5; d. 5.7. Fine, soft, very pale brown (10YR 8/4) fabric, worn and encrusted. Conical foot with circular depression at center of underside. Traces of black paint. *Comparanda*: Mook 1993, 173–174:P4.178 (Kavousi Kastro, PG–SubPG). *Date*: PG.

IX P41 (Fig. 27). Skyphos or cup. Max. pres. h. 4.1; d. 4.5. Soft, worn, very pale brown (10YR 8/4) fabric, encrusted. Conical foot with circular depression at center of underside. Traces of black paint. *Comparanda*: Mook 1993, 173–175:P4.178 (Kavousi Kastro PG–SubPG); Coldstream and Catling, eds., 1996, 50, fig. 72:106 (Knossos, LPG). *Date*: PG.

IX P42 (IM 767; Fig. 27; Pl. 16). Bowl. Intact except for two chips on rim. H. 5.4; d. rim 11.5–12.0. Soft, micaceous fabric with color varying from red (2.5YR 5/8) to reddish-yellow (5YR 7/8–7.5 YR 7/6). Red (2.5YR 5/8) to light red paint (2.5YR 6/8) paint. Small everted rim, flattened on top; conical body; raised base. Uneven diameter. Monochrome interior; exterior worn, but probably monochrome. *Date*: PG?

IX P43 (Fig. 28). Lid. Nine joining fragments from rim and four nonjoining, preserving 25% of rim. Max. pres. h. 5.4; d. rim 16.0. Fine, soft, white (5Y 8/2) fabric, encrusted. Badly worn black paint. Vertical rounded rim. One fragment has a hole in it near the rim. Monochrome on interior and exterior. *Comparanda*: Coldstream and Catling, eds., 1996, 157, fig. 111:162 (Knossos, EG–MG). *Date*: G.

IX P44 (Fig. 28). Oinochoe. Large fragment comprising rim and neck, most of handle, and small portion of shoulder; missing lower body and base. Max. pres. h. 7.0. Soft, reddish-yellow (5YR 7/8) fabric; worn, encrusted surfaces. Possible traces of black paint on exterior. Monochrome? *Date*: PG?

IX P45 (IM 685; Fig. 28; Pl. 16). Pyxis. Restored: missing 80% of rim. H. 7.8; d. rim 7.7. Fine, soft, pink (7.5YR 7/4) fabric with dark inclusions. Flaky, worn paint, black faded to yellowish red (5YR 5/6). Sharply outturned rim; squat globular body; raised base, hollowed underneath. Monochrome exterior; interior of rim and underside of base painted. *Comparanda*: Brock 1957, 165, pl. 78:1470 (Knossos, LPG); Coldstream and Catling, eds., 1996, 248, fig. 142:134 (Knossos, Corinthian LPG); Kotsonas 2008, 142–144, fig. 34:A327 (Eleutherna, LPG). *Date*: LPG.

Fine Decorated or Monochrome Wares

IX P46 (Fig. 28). Oinochoe. Two base fragments, three fragments of rim and complete handle, eight joining fragments from neck and shoulder. H. est. 23.5; d. base 5.5. Fine, soft, chalky, white (5Y 8/2) fabric with tiny black inclusions. Petrographic sample KAV 15/96: Fabric Subgroup 1c. Traces of black paint. Surfaces worn and encrusted. Trefoil mouth; flattened handle; flat base. *Date*: PG–G?

IX P47 (Fig. 28). Neck-handled amphora. Two joining fragments preserving 75% of base, two fragments preserving 20% of neck with all handle attachments; eight nonjoining fragments; missing rim. Max. pres. h. (top) 8.0; max. pres. h. (bottom) 5.0; d. base 6.0. Fine, soft, very pale brown (10YR 7/4) fabric, laminating and flaking. Petrographic sample KAV 15/104: Fabric Subgroup 1c. Surfaces almost entirely gone. Tall neck with two flattened vertical handles from neck to shoulder; ovoid body; slightly raised base. *Comparanda*: Coldstream and Catling, eds., 1996, 126, fig. 100:80.2 (Knossos, EPG). *Date*: EPG.

IX P48 (Fig. 28). Amphora or jug. Twenty joining fragments from neck, rim, and upper body preserving 10% of rim, 75% of neck with handle attachment, 30% of upper body, including one handle attachment; nonjoining base made up of four joining sherds, 40% preserved; 13 nonjoining fragments. Max. pres. h. 14.5; d. rim est. 9.8; d. base 5.2. Fine, soft, chalky, very pale brown (10YR 8/3) fabric. Traces of black paint on exterior, but surfaces too worn or coated to be certain. Tall wide neck with vertical rectangular handle; one fragment of similar shape, but slightly larger suggests a second handle. Attachment scar for handle on upper body. *Comparanda*: for similar manufacturing technique with added clay, Rethemiotakis and Englezou 2010, 65, fig. 80 (Eltyna, PGB–EG). *Date*: PG.

Medium-Coarse Decorated Ware

IX P49 (V98.46; Fig. 28). Oinochoe. Mended from many fragments, preserving 75%, including full profile and handle. H. 25.0; d. rim. 7.9; d. base 10.3. Medium-coarse, rather hard, reddish-yellow (5YR 6/6) fabric with fairly large white angular inclusions. Very pale brown (10YR 8/4) slip. Black paint, very worn. Surfaces eroded and pock-marked. Flaring rim, squared off; narrow neck; elliptical vertical handle from rim to shoulder; ovoid body; flat base. Shoulder has scroll design; bands on base of neck, at maximum diameter of body, and on base. Handle has vertical wavy line down center. *Comparanda*: **IX P22**; for shape, Brock 1957, 156, pl. 12:142 (Knossos, PGA); Tsipopoulou 2013, 141–142, fig. 6:12261 (Piskokephalo, PGB); for scroll decoration, Popham 1992, 62, pl. 47:d (Knossos, SM); Coldstream and Catling, eds., 1996, 97, pl. 112:38, 39 (Knossos, SM–EPG). *Date*: EPG–MPG.

Medium-Coarse Monochrome Wares

IX P50 (IM 788; Fig. 29; Pl. 16). Cup. Restored; handle missing except for lower attachment. H. 6.2; d. rim 11.4; d. base 4.0. Medium-coarse, soft, very pale brown (10YR 8/3) fabric, with black inclusions. Reddish-yellow (5YR 6/8) paint, worn, with heavy soil incrustation. Nearly vertical rim; round handle; rounded body; flat base. Rim and base uneven and slightly pushed in on one side. Circular depression at center of interior of base. Monochrome? *Bibliography*: Gesell, Day, and Coulson 1983, 404, 407, fig. 8:V17, pl. 77:e. *Comparanda*: **GR9 P42**; Brock 1957, 88, pl. 73:1011 (Knossos, PGB); Boardman 1960, 131, 137, fig. 5:I.47 (Hagios Ioannis, MPG–LPG); for base, Coldstream and Catling, eds., 1996, 236, fig. 138:105 (Knossos, PGB). *Date*: MPG–LPG.

IX P51 (Fig. 29). Cup. Mended from 16 fragments preserving 65% of body and lower handle attachment. H. 8.0; d. rim 11.0; d. base 4.5. Medium-coarse, soft, reddish-yellow (5YR 6/6) fabric with phyllites and hard red inclusions. Petrographic sample KAV 15/98: Fabric Group 2. Outturned rim; rounded body; thick, flat base. String marks on base. Monochrome paint, black on interior, worn to streaky red on exterior. *Comparanda*: **GR9 P41**; Coldstream and Catling, eds., 1996, 236, fig. 138:283.105 (Knossos, PGB); 255, fig. 143:287.6 (Knossos, LPG). *Date*: LPG.

IX P52 (Fig. 29). Cup or skyphos. Mended from seven fragments preserving 30% of profile; missing base and handle. Max. pres. h. 6.0; d. rim 11.0. Medium-coarse, soft, reddish-yellow (5YR 6/6–7.5YR 6/6) fabric with many small, hard white and greenstone inclusions. Sampled KAV 15/97: Fabric Group 3. Slightly outturned rim; rounded body. Very worn surfaces. Monochrome black paint. *Comparanda*: Tsipopoulou 2013, 152–153, fig. 13:12293 (Piskokephalo, LG). *Date*: PG?

IX P53 (IM 547; Fig. 29; Pl. 16). Bird askos. Restored from many fragments; tail and handle, body fragments missing. H. rest. 10.3; L. rest. 16.2; d. base 3.5. Medium-coarse, soft, very pale brown (10YR 7/3) fabric with large black inclusions. Dull and worn very dark gray (2.5YR N4) paint. Crudely made by hand, with irregularly-shaped spout; basket handle; conical foot. Monochrome. *Date*: SM–EPG.

IX P54 (Fig. 29). Small oinochoe. Single fragment preserving 80% of rim and neck, top of handle. Max. pres. h. 2.8. Medium-coarse, soft, reddish-yellow (5YR 6/8) fabric. *Date*: PG?

Medium-Coarse Slipped Wares

IX P55 (V81.1; Fig. 29). Amphoriskos. Restored. Complete profile preserved; missing half of rim and neck, one handle, most of base. H. 16.1; d. rim 8.2; d. base 5.0. Medium-coarse, hard, red (2.5YR 5/8) fabric. Worn, light red (2.5 YR 6/8) worn; white slip on exterior. Tall cylindrical neck with vertical rim; two flattened vertical handles from lower neck to shoulder; globular body; raised base. Broad band at rim with reserved band at lip, possible bands on shoulder and at lower handle attachment. Band on interior of rim. *Date*: Venetian.

IX P56 (Fig. 29). Pithos. Seven fragments preserving rim and half of one handle. Max. pres. h. 12.6; d. rim 18.1. Medium-coarse, hard, reddish-yellow (5YR 6/6) fabric. Burned on exterior in places. Vertical rim, flattened on top; rounded body; two round horizontal handles on shoulder. No paint visible on exterior, but traces of white glaze on exterior and red slip inside. Band of red slip on interior of rim. *Comparanda*: **IX P57**. *Date*: Venetian.

IX P57 (Fig. 30). Pithos. Large fragment mended from eight sherds from rim and upper body. Max. pres. h. 8.5; d. rim 22.0. Medium-coarse, hard, light red (10YR 6/8) fabric with hard red inclusions. Burned on places on the exterior. Red slip and white (10YR 8/2) glaze or paint. Vertical rim, flattened on top and slightly thickened inward. White paint or glaze on rim and from upper handle attachment down. Band of red slip on interior rim. *Comparanda*: **IX P56**. *Date*: Venetian.

Coarse Decorated Ware

IX P58 (IM 550; Fig. 30; Pl. 17). Neck-handled amphora. Restored; small fragments of rim missing. H. 25.5; d. rim 11.8; d. base 8.3. Coarse, soft, gritty, reddish-yellow (5YR 7/6) fabric with inclusions of small gray-blue stones. Flaky, black (7.5YR N2.5) paint, worn surfaces. Handmade, with very uneven rim and base. Tall neck with flaring rim; two round vertical handles from neck to shoulder; sharply offset shoulder; ovoid body; flat base. Monochrome except for panel on shoulder with meander pattern and reserved band on lower body. Interior of rim painted. *Comparanda*: for shape, Levi 1927–1929, 290, fig. 376 (Arkades, G); Coldstream and Catling, eds., 1996, 48, pl. 80:51 (Knossos, MG); 248, pl. 230:129 (Attic, LPG); 267, pl. 249:160 (MG); Tsipopoulou 2005, 203, fig. 17:H3183 (Adromyloi, LG); 284, fig. 17:AN8755 (Praisos, LG). *Date*: G–LG.

Coarse Monochrome Wares

IX P59 (IM 153; Fig. 30; Pl. 17) Cup. Complete; mended from two pieces. H. 6.5; d. rim 11.0–11.8; d. base 4.5. Coarse, soft, reddish-yellow (5YR 6/6) fabric, with black and white inclusions. Dark gray (5YR 4/1) paint, worn. Rounded rim pinched out to form a crude spout; round vertical handle from inside rim to shoulder; rounded body; flat base. Handmade. Monochrome inside and out; two incised grooves around body. *Comparanda*: **GR20 P9**; Coldstream and Catling, eds., 1996, 146, fig. 106:6 (Knossos, EG–MG). *Date*: PG.

IX P60 (Fig. 30). Cup. Twelve joining fragments preserving base and 30% of rim, entire profile; three nonjoining rim fragments, one with handle attachment. H. 6.0; d. rim 11.4; d. base 4.1. Coarse, soft, reddish-yellow (5YR 7/6) fabric with frequent greenstone inclusions; very worn surfaces, with heavy soil incrustation. Petrographic sample KAV 15/95: Fabric Group 3. Slightly outturned rim; rectangular handle from top of rim to lower body; rounded body; flat base, hollowed underneath. Wheel ridging on exterior. No traces of paint; may be plain or monochrome. *Comparanda*: Coldstream and Catling, eds., 1996, 78, fig. 78:10 (Knossos, LPG). *Date*: LPG?

Metal

Iron

IX M1 (Fig. 30; Pl. 17). Spearhead. Three nonjoining fragments, one from near top (a), two from socket (b, c), including end of socket (c); very tip of blade, lower blade, and much of socket missing. Max. pres. (a) L. 6.7, (b) 2.5, (c) 2.3; max. pres. w. (a) 2.1, (b) 1.6, (c), 2.1; th. (a) 0.2–0.6, (b) 0.15, (c) 0.3. Surfaces corroded and cracked.

IX M2 (Vronda IX dump; Fig. 30; Pl. 17). Knife. Two joining fragments from end of handle, with single rivet in center near end; point missing. Max. pres. L. 6.4; max. pres. w. 2.9; th. 0.3. Corroded, surfaces gone. Some traces of wood deposit from hilt on one side.

IX M3 (Vronda IX dump; Fig. 30; Pl. 17). Knife. Single fragment preserving area near end of handle, with traces of rivet hole at other edge. Blade and tip missing; very end of handle gone. Max. pres. L. 5.0; max. pres. w. 1.8; th. 0.25–0.30.

IX M4 (Vronda IX dump; Fig. 30; Pl. 17). Knife. Single fragment from blade. Max. pres. L. 4.8; max. pres. w. 2.1; th. 0.2. Corroded, surfaces gone. Traces of wood deposit on one side.

IX M5 (Vronda IX dump; Fig. 30; Pl. 17). Knife. Single fragment from tip. Max. pres. L. 5.0; max. pres. w. 1.9; th. 0.3. Tip points slightly up. Surfaces corroded.

IX M6 (Vronda IX, cleaning inside tomb from south; Fig. 30; Pl. 17). Knife. Single fragment preserving handle and beginning of blade. Max. pres. L. 4.2; max. pres. w. 1.8; th. 0.6. Surfaces corroded and cracked.

IX M7 (Vronda IX.2, object 2; Fig. 30; Pl. 17). Knife. Single fragment of knife blade from near handle end; half of rivet hole preserved. Max. pres. L. 2.5; max. pres. w. 1.7; th. 0.3. Badly corroded.

IX M8 (Vronda IX.3, object 6; Fig. 30). Blade. Single fragment from blade of knife or weapon, preserving one edge. Max. pres. L. 3.0; max. pres. w. 2.0; th. 0.045. Corroded and cracked.

Vronda Tomb X

This tomb was first identified and excavated in 1981 (Gesell, Day, and Coulson 1983, 405–409; Day 1984) on a lower terrace to the north of Boyd's tombs, but not as far north as Vronda IX (Fig. 6; Pl. 2). The tomb was placed at the edge of a terrace, with a modern terrace wall running across the top. There was thus a sharp drop in elevation from south to north (from 406.68 m asl in the southeast to 405.03 m asl in the northeast). The area around the tomb was also excavated. The tomb had been robbed and contained little of the original contents. A pit dug below the floor of the tomb was found filled with dog bones, stones, some fragmentary pottery, and a bronze pin fragment. Most of the pottery from the pit is nondiagnostic, but a few pieces date to the PG period and some to the Venetian era. Although the pit was originally thought to have been contemporary with the usage of the tomb (Gesell, Day, and Coulson 1983, 408–409; Day 1984, 21–22), it is now clear that the fill within it was deposited at some time in the Venetian or Ottoman periods.

Architecture

Tomb X is quite well preserved, with seven courses standing on the south, six on the west, and five on the east (Figs. 31, 32; Pls. 18A, 18B). It was constructed almost entirely of breccia boulders, with limestone employed only for the stomion. The ground plan is irregular, oval at the south but with square corners on the north to form a horseshoe shape (Fig. 31). It measures 1.60 m north–south x 1.30–1.36 m east–west. The stones were laid against the *tsakali* bedrock. The stomion is well built of limestone blocks and is unusually long. It measures 0.90–1.06 m in length and 0.70–0.74 m in width; the preserved height is 0.65 m. The lintel is no longer in place, but a large limestone block found just to the west of the stomion may once have served as the lintel. In front of the stomion, a pit that functioned as a sort of dromos had been dug into the *tsakali*. This pseudo-dromos measures 0.75 m north–south and 0.90 m east–west.

Stratigraphy

The tomb was built into the slope of the ridge, and some time after the walls were constructed a pit was dug beneath the floor into the *tsakali* bedrock (Fig. 32), undercutting the walls by as much as 0.10 m. At the bottom of the pit was a layer of fine, very pale brown (10YR 6/3) soil mixed with gravel (Level 8), possibly the surface upon which the fill above was thrown. The small amount of pottery recovered was SM or PG in date, including the spout of a stirrup jar or bird askos (**X P1**) and an open vessel with alternating pendant and accumbent loops (**X P2**). A number of stones at the very bottom appeared to resemble some sort of small structure, but no clear plan was discernible. The pit was 0.80 m deep and was filled up to the level of the bottom of the walls with a soft, light yellowish-brown (10YR 6/4) soil mixed with a large quantity of stones (110 *zembilia* of stones were removed) and animal bones, belonging mostly to dogs, including puppies (Level 7; Pl. 18C). Pottery from this fill was mostly coarse and included the pedestal base **X P4**.

At the top of the rubble fill was a hard-packed soil that was thought to represent the floor surface of the tomb. It was slightly lower (0.10–0.16 m) than the undisturbed floor level in the pseudo-dromos in front of the tomb. Above this hard surface, the tomb chamber was filled with more soil and rubble, with larger stones at the bottom (Level 6) and medium-sized stones amid hard soil (Level 5) at the top of the deposit. Pottery from this fill deposit was mixed, including fragments of two closed decorated vessels of SM or PG date (**X P5, X P6**) and the pedestaled base of a glazed bowl of Venetian date. The upper part of the interior was found filled with loose soil and stones (Level 4) and produced very little pottery. In the stomion and pseudo-dromos a hard soil was found overlying *tsakali* bedrock (Level 4) and above that was a harder-packed reddish-yellow (7.5YR 7/6) soil with a large number of fist-sized and smaller stones (Level 3). This layer produced the lid or skyphos of PG date (**X P3**), along with a handle fragment from a skyphos, several small, fine rims from cups or skyphoi, and a possible krater rim. It may represent undisturbed soil from the time of the use of the tomb. Above this was slope wash and topsoil (Levels 1 and 2).

On the south side of the tomb, a layer of hard clay-like soil with many stones lay over the tomb (Level 3), with slope wash and topsoil directly above (Levels 1 and 2). On the north side, because of the terrace wall, the tomb, the stomion, and the pseudo-dromos lay immediately below the topsoil, and there had been very little accumulation.

The pit below Tomb X is unique. Because it seems to have been dug below the walls of the tomb, it was thought to be contemporary with the tomb construction (Gesell, Day, and Coulson 1983, 400). The pottery that was found within the pit was almost entirely coarse and not diagnostic, and there was no recognizable later material within it, such as was found in the fill within the tomb chamber. Radiocarbon analysis of the dog bones in 1988, however, showed clearly that they were Medieval (A.D.

1300–1400), and so they could not have been contemporary with the use of the tomb (see below, p. 356).

Burials

No human bone was recovered from Vronda X, but two partially formed, adult human teeth were found inside the tomb. These teeth were found commingled with the dog burials from the pit beneath the original level of the tomb floor, and they are probably to be associated with the use of the tomb in the Early Iron Age.

Burial 1
Type: disturbed inhumation
Age: juvenile, 5–7 years
Sex: unknown

Two incompletely formed, human permanent molars were found, a mandibular first molar with the root one-half complete, and a maxillary first or second molar fragment. The developmental stage of the teeth indicates that they belonged to a child, five to seven years old.

Faunal Remains

Nearly 7,500 animal bones and bone fragments were recovered from the lower levels of Tholos X in 1981 (Table 2). For about 3,350 of these specimens the species were identifiable. The assemblage was dominated by the remains of as many as 12 domestic dog (NISP 2,942) and domestic cat (NISP 256) skeletons. With the exception of one isolated dog bone and three sheep or goat bone fragments, all the remaining faunal materials were found in the lowest levels of the tholos, Levels 6–8. The vast majority of this bone deposit (NISP 6,624) was recovered from Level 7, near the bottom of the pit that extended below the original floor of the tholos. Refits of broken bones and likely physical matches in size of recovered dog and cat skeletal elements between them suggest that all of this material represents a single deposit, probably a refuse deposit that accumulated following the robbing of the tholos in the Medieval–Modern period.

The 12 domestic dogs were represented by all parts of the animal skeleton, and they appear to have entered the deposit as complete bodies. They ranged in age from puppies, represented by mandibles with unerupted or deciduous dentition, to an older-aged individual, represented by a mandible with heavily worn and/or missing teeth. Four to eight of these animals were male, as four complete or nearly complete baccula and an additional four baccula fragments were recovered.

Measurement of a sample of complete adult long bones allowed estimation of the shoulder heights of the live animals (Harcourt 1974; Onar and Belli 2005). The estimates in height ranged from 35.80 to 70.90 cm (14.00 to 28.00 inches). The majority of the measured elements indicated animals ca. 60.00 to 65.00 cm in height, about the height of a modern Labrador retriever. A single smaller animal, about the size of beagle, and one larger animal, the size of a German shepherd, were also represented.

At least four domestic cats, both adult and kitten, were also present in the assemblage, represented by nearly complete skeletons, mandibles, and scattered elements. In sharp contrast to the faunal assemblage from the Late Minoan IIIC settlement at Vronda, common food animals—sheep, goat, pig, cow—were represented in the tholos by only a few scattered, isolated elements and element fragments. From Level 7 with the dogs and other animals came a single murex shell (*Hexaplex trunculus*; Table 3).

Pottery

The excavation of Tomb X produced 180 fragments of pottery weighing 2.97 kg. The largest amount of this material came from the pit within the tomb (60 fragments weighing 0.95 kg). Most of this pottery belonged to the time after the robbing of the tomb and was mixed, so it cannot tell us much about the date of the burials or the nature of the grave goods. The fragments from the very bottom of the tomb (Level 8), however, seem to have been undisturbed and included the spout of a bird askos or stirrup jar (**X P1**), probably of SM date, and a decorated fragment from an open vessel (**X P2**) that could be of any date from LM IIIC to EO. The pottery found in the soil over bedrock in the stomion should date the construction of the tomb, but unfortunately the small amount of material present was nondiagnostic. The undisturbed rocky harder fill in the stomion, which was probably deposited during the use of the tomb, produced some diagnostic vessels, including the lid or skyphos of PG date (**X P3**), a skyphos handle, a small cup base, and some cup or skyphos rims, perhaps the remains of a drinking ritual enacted at the time of the burial. Within the tomb itself, the material in the pit was mostly coarse and nondiagnostic, while that in the fill of the chamber above the floor level included PG closed vessels (**X P5**, **X P6**) and glazed wares of the Venetian period (**X P7**). Another skyphos (**X P8**) found in this deposit had a joining fragment from the surface and was also of PG date.

Objects

Only a single fragment of metal (**X M1**) was found in the fill in the pit below the tomb, apparently left behind after the robbing. This item is probably the pin of a bronze fibula similar to those found in the other tombs.

Chronology

A terminus post quem of SM is provided by the bird askos or stirrup jar spout (**X P1**) recovered from the undisturbed soil overlying bedrock. Vessels found in the fill in the tomb belong to the PG (**X P8**) or MG–LG (**X P5**) periods. The lid or skyphos (**X P3**) found in the stomion is more difficult to date; as a skyphos it may be PG, but as a lid it seems to have its closest parallels in MG Knossos. The tomb seems, then, to have been in use from SM until MG–LG times. The glazed wares found in the fill and the surface are Venetian (green and yellow glazed wares, **X P7**) or Ottoman–modern (reddish-brown glazed wares). The coarse pedestal base has LG parallels in East Crete, but its white slip suggests a Venetian date. It is most likely that this tomb was robbed before the 14th century and that the pit was dug to dispose of unwanted animals beginning in that period.

Catalog of Finds from Soil above Bedrock

Pottery

Fine Dark-on-Light Wares

X P1 (Level 8; Fig. 33). Stirrup jar or bird askos. Spout only. D. rim 2.2; max. pres. h. 3.7. Fine, light red (10R 6/8) fabric. Reddish-yellow (5YR 7/8) slip. Band of black paint on interior rim, traces of paint on exterior. *Date*: SM.

X P2 (Level 8; Fig. 33). Cup or skyphos/deep bowl. Single fragment from body. Th. 0.3. Fine, soft, reddish-yellow (5YR 7/8) fabric with soil encrustation. Traces of black paint on exterior and interior. Pendant and accumbent loops, possibly part of a guilloche pattern or S-pattern. *Comparanda*: Coldstream and Catling, eds., 1996, 81, fig. 76:36 (Knossos, LG). *Date*: SM–EO.

Catalog of Finds from Stomion

Pottery

Fine Dark-on-Light Ware

X P3 (Level 2; Fig. 33). Lid or skyphos. Two joining fragments from rim and upper body. D. rim 19.0. Soft, reddish-yellow (5YR 7/8) fabric. Streaky, black paint. Worn surfaces. Rounded rim. Monochrome on exterior and interior. *Comparanda*: for shape (skyphos), Coldstream and Catling 1996, eds., 197, fig. 125:12 (Knossos, MPG–LPG). *Date*: PG?

Catalog of Finds from Fill in Pit

Pottery

Coarse Ware

X P4 (Level 7; Fig. 33). Coarse pedestal base. D. base 10.2. Gritty, light red (10R 6/8) fabric. White slip on exterior. Solid pedestal base, slightly hollowed underneath. *Comparanda*: Tsipopoulou 2005, 272, fig. 109:AN1586 (Praisos, LG). *Date*: LG?

Metal

Bronze

X M1 (Level 7, south interior of tomb, object 27; Fig. 33; Pl. 19A). Pin or fibula. Single fragment, slightly bent at one end. Max. pres. L. 2.7; max. pres. w. 0.5; d. 0.2.

Catalog of Finds from Fill in Chamber

Pottery

Fine Dark-on-Light Wares

X P5 (Levels 1 and 5; Fig. 33). Closed vessel. Two joining fragments from body. Th. 0.8. Fine, soft, yellow (10YR 7/6) fabric. Black paint on exterior, none on interior. Crosshatched lozenges and triangles in rows.

Bibliography: Gesell, Day, and Coulson 1983, 407, fig. 8:20, pl. 77:h. *Comparanda*: Coldstream and Catling, eds., 1996, 167, pl. 166:7; 170, pl. 168:129.1 (Knossos, MG); 204, pl. 190:25 (LG); 205, pl. 191:33 (LG early); 206, pl. 193:57 (LG late). *Date*: MG–LG.

X P6 (Level 6; Fig. 33). Closed vessel. Single fragment from shoulder. Fine, soft, pink (5YR 7/4) fabric. Worn, black paint. Zigzag. *Date*: LM IIIC–G.

Glazed Ware

X P7 (Level 6; Fig. 33). Cup or bowl. D. base 5.8. Single fragment preserving entire base. Medium-coarse, reddish-yellow (7.5YR 7/6) fabric. Interior coated with yellow (2.5Y 7/8) glaze. Ring base. Incised X on underside of base. *Date*: Byzantine or Venetian.

Catalog of Finds from Topsoil and Slope Wash

Pottery

Fine Dark-on-Light Ware

X P8 (Levels 1 and 2; Fig. 33). Skyphos. Six joining fragments from handle and rim. Fine, soft, porous, reddish-yellow (7.5YR 7/6) fabric with white inclusions. Red (2.5YR 4/6) paint. Flaring rim; round horizontal handles. Monochrome coated outside except for reserved band in handle zone with oblique strokes. *Comparanda*: Brock 1957, 169, motif 2a (Knossos, SM); Coldstream and Catling, eds., 1996, 17, fig. 60:41 (Knossos, PGB–EG). *Date*: PG–EG.

Vronda Tomb XI

There was much excavation activity during the 1990 season in the area north of LM IIIC Building I-O-N, where Boyd had found a tholos (tomb 4; here Tomb VII) that was not located in the 1981 cleaning of the Vronda site (Fig. 4; Boyd 1901, 134). Although not much remains from the LM IIIC settlement in this area, aside from a possible retaining wall, a new tholos tomb was located (Tomb XI) to the west of the location of Boyd's tomb 4 (and was at first erroneously thought to be this tomb; see Gesell, Day, and Coulson 1995, 91–92).

Tomb XI is a built tholos tomb excavated in 1990 in Trenches VW 14000 and VW 15000. In 1991, during consolidation of the walls of the tomb, some hard soil left at the bottom around the edges of the tomb was removed as VW 14050. Showing on the surface of these trenches before excavation was a long stretch of terrace wall and a large, modern stone pile. When the stone pile was removed (VW 14000), and the stones were placed on the modern terrace wall to the west, a tholos tomb came to light. This tomb was first identified as Boyd's tomb 4 (Tomb VII). Later, closer reading of her description of the poor preservation of tomb 4, of which only a tiny bit of the doorway remained (Boyd 1901, 134), indicated that this tholos could not have been Boyd's tomb 4, but was a new one, subsequently labeled Tomb XI.

Tomb XI extended over two trenches, VW 14000 and VW 15000, but it was decided that for convenience the entire interior of the tomb would be dug as part of Trench VW 14000. Only the top of the tomb and the soil around it to the north were collected as part of VW 15000. The tomb was found filled with loose stones (VW 14001), some of them quite large, and it had been totally robbed, with only a small amount of hard soil containing bones and pottery clinging to the walls at the bottom (VW 14012, VW 14050). The pseudo-dromos and stomion of the tomb, however, had not been disturbed. After removal of the topsoil over the dromos (VW 14006), it was clear that a pit had been dug in front of the stomion. It was filled with rubble (VW 14007) that included fragments of fine cups and kraters, as found in the dromos deposits of the other tombs. A large flat stone had been placed in the pit in front of the doorway, and other large flat stones were found standing in the deposit at angles, possibly having slipped from their positions after being placed in front of the doorway. Below the stone "paving" and blocking stones (VW 14008) was a layer of clay (VW 14010, VW 14011) similar to the roofing clay found in the Vronda houses. This layer went down to bedrock.

Architecture

Tomb XI is a regular stone-built corbeled tomb, rectangular at the bottom (1.50–1.60 m east–west X 1.65–1.85 m north–south), with the stomion slightly off center (Fig. 34; Pl. 19B). The stomion is 0.70–0.80 m long and 0.57 m wide (Pls. 19C, 20A). In front of the stomion is a very irregular pit that probably represents a pseudo-dromos rather than a real dromos; it measures ca. 1.30 m in length and 0.72–0.88 m in width.

The tomb seems inferior in construction compared to the other tholoi at Vronda. It employs breccia boulders almost exclusively and lacks the limestone blocks found in other tholoi (Pl. 20B). The lintel is irregularly shaped, unlike the handsome squared lintels of the other tombs (e.g., Tomb II). The closest parallel in terms of construction is Vronda I. Much of the eastern interior wall has collapsed, and the lintel has partly fallen. Six irregular courses are preserved. The squared corners begin to round out for the corbeling in the second course on the northwest, the third course on the northeast, the fourth course on the southeast, and the fifth course on the southwest.

In addition to the tholos tomb, there is a terrace wall to the southeast. It is not certain whether this wall was constructed to hold back soil and wash from the tholos tomb or if it belongs with the LM IIIC settlement; it might also be part of a more recent structure.

Stratigraphy

Because it had been totally robbed, Tomb XI showed little stratigraphy. It was built on bedrock, and around the edges at the bottom was a small amount of very hard soil that must have come from the time of construction or use of the tomb (VW 14050). Otherwise, the tomb was found with a fill of loose soil amid large and small stones (VW 14000, VW 14001, VW 14012) that went from the bottom to the top of the tomb, about 1.45–1.60 m.

The area in and in front of the stomion, however, had not been cleared out prior to excavation. The doorway of the tomb was similar to that of the other tholos tombs; it was blocked first with clay, resembling the roofing clay used in the LM IIIC houses (VW 14011), and then with a large flat stone and more clay. The pit in front of the stomion had a layer of clay at the bottom (VW 14010.4) on the bedrock, but whether it was placed there deliberately or washed in during the partial collapse of the lintel is uncertain. A flat stone was placed above this clay layer, and several large stones were found above this clay layer (VW 14008, VW 14010.1). One large stone was probably originally set upright in front of the doorway, although it had later slipped despite the support of other stones behind it. More rubble had accumulated or had been thrown on top of these stones (VW 14007). This layer of rubble above the flat stones contained fragments of cups and kraters, as was also the case in several of the other tholos tombs.

Outside the tomb there was very little deposition. Overlying bedrock was a layer of rocky soil (VW 14005) that lay below a rocky, light yellowish-brown (10YR 6/4) soil, probably slope wash (VW 14004). Topsoil (VW 14002, VW 14003, VW 14006, VW 14009, VW 15000) lay immediately above this rocky layer. Excavation around wall VW 14013 near the top of the tholos revealed a harder surface just east of the tomb. Farther to the south, east of terrace wall VW 14013, the soil went deeper but was not fully excavated.

Burials

Remains of two individuals were recovered from the hard soil that lingered around the edges of the tomb (VW 14050).

Burials 1 and 2
Type: disturbed inhumations
Age: adults
Sex: possibly one male and one female

Fragmentary partial skeletons of a minimum of two adults, possibly one male and one female, came from Tomb XI. The remains include cranial and postcranial bone from one very robust, large individual and cranial bone from a small adult with a very gracile skull. The extreme wear on the preserved teeth, two lower central incisors, suggests that one of the individuals was an older adult and may also indicate use of the teeth in some nonmasticatory function.

Remarkably, the preserved bone included a single styloid process of the temporal bone, the only one preserved in any of the Kavousi inhumations. As the name indicates, this is a thin, elongated projection of bone found on the base of the skull, and it frequently breaks off and is lost.

Faunal Remains

Two sheep or goat elements, a left innominate fragment and a femur distal diaphysis segment, were recovered from the lower levels of the pit in front of the doorway of this tholos (Table 2). A left calcaneum fragment, possibly from a domestic cow, and a sheep or goat left mandible fragment were recovered from a deposit of stones over the pit.

Pottery

The pottery recovered from the area of the tholos is very fragmentary. In addition to the cataloged vessels, there were fragments from a small jug or lekythos, a fragment from the rim of an amphora or hydria, and a single fragment from the body of a skyphos of fine, hard fabric. None of the other material is closely datable, nor is it paralleled in the pottery from the other tholoi or cremation burials. Two of the cups or skyphoi (**XI P5**, **XI P6**) resemble monochrome cups from many of the graves and may be LG.

Only two vessels came from inside the tomb: a blue ware cup or skyphos (**XI P1**) and a monochrome cup or skyphos (**XI P2**). The similarity of **XI P1** to the LM IIIC blue ware from Karphi in shape and warping (Day 2011b, 254) suggests that it may be a LM IIIC vessel. The fabric of **XI P2** resembles that of cups from Vronda Tomb IX and may be PG.

Most of the pottery comes from the pseudo-dromos. The earliest and lowest are a krater fragment (**XI P4**) and a thick, heavy base from a vessel of uncertain shape and date (**XI P3**). These vessels were found in the soil and stones blocking the stomion. Above the flat stones in the pseudo-dromos and in the rubble thrown in to fill of the pit were conical cup **XI P10**, cups **XI P5** and **XI P6**, krater **XI P7**, and the LM IIIC cup base **XI P8**. The preponderance of drinking vessels above the level of the paver suggests the possibility that they may be left over from a post-funerary drinking ritual.

Chronology

The fragmentary nature of the material from the tomb makes dating difficult. One of the vessels found at the bottom of the tomb (**XI P1**) and a base from the blocking of the stomion (**XI P9**) are probably of LM IIIC date. These vessels may belong to the initial use of the tomb, but they may also represent "background noise" of LM IIIC, material that was in the soil and was left over from the use of the settlement; such material has been found in the cremation burials (see this vol., Ch. 3). The monochrome cup (**XI P2**), found in cleaning the tomb and therefore not from a secure contex, is of a later date, PG–G. The vessels found in the fill of the pseudo-dromos should give a date for the last use of the tomb, if indeed the entrances were opened during each burial event. These vases include the fine monochrome cups **XI P5** and **XI P6**, both of which resemble cups from the Geometric cremation burials at Vronda, and the body fragment from a fine skyphos that also looks late (not cataloged). The monochrome cup base **XI P8** also resembles material from the cemetery of enclosure burials. One krater rim, **XI P4**, may have belonged to a bell krater of SM–EPG date. The other krater, **XI P7**, is unusual and not similar to other vessels from either the settlement or the cemetery. The necked jar (**XI P11**) is similar to examples from Tomb IX and from the enclosure burials; it is certainly PG in style. In summary, the tomb, although it may have been constructed as early as LM IIIC, was certainly in use in the PG period, and it may have continued in use into the Geometric period.

Catalog of Finds from Hard Soil on Edges of Tomb Interior

Pottery

MEDIUM-COARSE MONOCHROME WARES

XI P1 (VW 14050.1; Fig. 35). Cup or skyphos. Large fragment (10 sherds) from rim. Max pres. h. 4.5. Medium-coarse, hard, gray (2.5YR 6/0) fabric with frequent small, white inclusions. Worn surfaces. Possible traces of paint on exterior. Warped and burned, probably misfired in kiln. *Date*: LM IIIC?

XI P2 (Tomb XI cleaning; Fig. 35). Cup or skyphos. Single large fragment from upper body near rim; missing rim, base, handle(s). Max. pres. h. 5.6. Medium-coarse, hard, reddish-yellow (5YR 6/6) to gray (5YR N/) fabric with gray phyllites, hard white angular inclusions, and some mica. Traces of black paint on exterior. Rather well-preserved surfaces on exterior. Ridging on interior. *Comparanda*: **GR3 P7**, **GR16 P8**, **GR28 P5**. *Date*: PG–G.

Catalog of Finds from Removal of Stomion Blocking

Pottery

FINE PLAIN WARE

XI P3 (VW 14010.2; Fig. 35). Cup or skyphos? Single fragment (two sherds) preserving 40% of base. Max. pres. h. 3.5; d. base 4.5. Fine, soft, light red (2.5YR 6/6) fabric. Very pale brown (10YR 7/3) slip. Well-preserved surfaces.

Raised flat base with string marks. *Comparanda*: **IX P32**. *Date*: PG.

Medium-Coarse Ware

XI P4 (VW 14010.2; Fig. 35). Krater. Single fragment from rim. D. rim est. 20.0. Medium-coarse, soft, light red (2.5YR 6/8) fabric with frequent phyllites and hard white inclusions. Red (2.5YR 5/8) paint. Well-preserved surfaces. *Comparanda*: Coldstream and Catling, eds., 1996, 96, fig. 89:6 (Knossos, SM–EPG); 197, fig. 125:23 (EPG); 246, fig. 137:285.60 (SM–EPG). *Date*: SM–EPG.

Catalog of Finds from Removal of Stones above Paving in Pseudo-Dromos

Pottery

Fine Monochrome Wares

XI P5 (VW 14007.1; Fig. 35). Cup or skyphos. Single fragment (four sherds) from rim. D. rim est. 10.0. Fine, soft, light red (2.5YR 6/6) fabric with gray (5Y 6/1) core. Red (2.5YR 5/6) paint. Worn surfaces. Four grooves below vertical rim. Monochrome. *Comparanda*: for rim, **GR20 P9**; Mook 2004, 175, fig. 12.10:G, I (Kavousi Kastro, G); for ridges, **GR16 P7**, **GR20 P11**; Tsipopoulou 2013, 141, 143, fig. 7:12301 (Piskokephalo, PGB). *Date*: LG?

XI P6 (VW 14007.1; Fig. 35). Cup or skyphos. Single fragment from rim. D. rim est. 12.0. Fine, medium-soft, reddish-yellow (7.5YR 7/6) fabric. Once black paint worn to shadow. Worn surfaces. *Comparanda*: **GR5 P7**, **GR13 P11**, **GR21 P3**. *Date*: LG?

XI P7 (VW 14007.1; Fig. 35). Krater. Single fragment (two sherds) from rim. D. rim est. 21.0. Fine, soft, porous, reddish-yellow (5YR 6/6) fabric. Red (2.5YR 4/6) paint. Worn surfaces. Small vertical rim. Monochrome. *Date*: G?

XI P8 (VW 14007.3; Fig. 35). Cup or skyphos. Single fragment preserving 30% of base. Max. pres. h. 2.8; d. base 5.0. Fine, soft, reddish-yellow (5YR 7/6) fabric with some red phyllite inclusions. Black to red (2.5YR 4/6) paint on interior, exterior, and underside of base. Well-preserved exterior surfaces, worn on interior. String marks on base. *Date*: PG.

XI P9 (VW 14010.1; Fig. 35). Cup or deep bowl. Single fragment preserving 30% of base. D. base 5.0. Fine, soft, light reddish-brown (5YR 6/4) fabric, with some tiny red phyllite inclusions. Red (2.5YR 4/6) paint. Worn surfaces. Raised base, hollowed underneath. Interior may have reserved disk or may be solidly painted. *Comparanda*: Day and Glowacki 2012, fig. 133:WS P4. *Date*: LM IIIC.

Fine Plain Ware

XI P10 (VW 14008.2; Fig. 35). Conical cup? Single fragment preserving 60% of base. Fine, soft, reddish-yellow (5YR 6/6) fabric. Very pale brown (10YR 8/3) slip. *Date*: LM IIIC–PG.

Catalog of Finds from Topsoil

Pottery

Medium-Coarse Decorated Ware

XI P11 (VW 14000.3 and 4, VW 14006.1, VW 14009.1; Fig. 35). Necked jar. One fragment (two sherds) preserving 75% of base, one handle fragment and attachment, one fragment from shoulder. Max. pres. h. 7.2; d. base 9.0. Medium-coarse, rather hard, light red (2.5YR 6/6) fabric with infrequent red and gray phyllites. Black paint worn to shadow. Worn surfaces. Round horizontal handles on middle of body; flat base. Crosshatched triangle(?) on shoulder. *Comparanda*: **IX P8**; Kotsonas 2008, 105, fig. 17:A143 (Eleutherna, EG, adhering to PG tradition). *Date*: PG.

Addendum: Other Vessels Possibly from Vronda Tholos Tombs

A number of vessels in the Herakleion museum are labeled in the museum catalog as coming from "Boyd Excavations 1900." These vessels could come from the Vronda tholos tombs, Chondrovolakes, the tholos tomb at Skouriasmenos, or the Kastro settlement. Four are consistent in date with those from the Vronda tholos tombs, and their shapes and decorative elements are similar to those from the other Vronda tholoi. For this reason, they are included here as an addendum. Others bearing the same label but of clearly earlier or later date are not discussed.

Of the cataloged vessels, the stirrup jar **Boyd P2** is the earliest. The shape is most commonly found in LM IIIC (Day 2011b, 291), but the Minoan flower decorating the top is a motif generally found on LM IIIB stirrup jars (e.g., Kanta 1980, figs. 10:7 [Knossos], 27:7 [Episkopi]; pl. 100:5, 6 [Enkomi]). However, it also appears as a motif on LM IIIC pottery, where it often has a multiple U-pattern on the interior (Day 2011b, 262). The juglet or oinochoe **Boyd P1** and the amphoriskos **Boyd P3** both find many parallels in EPG contexts; the amphoriskos is so similar to examples from the Plai tou Kastro tomb at Kavousi (Tsipopoulou 2005, 98, pl. 66; 99, pl. 70) that this type may be a popular local variation on the shape. The juglet **Boyd P4** could date as early as LM IIIC, but similar juglets also appear later, and the pendant crosshatched triangle would be appropriate on SM or EPG vessels.

Catalog

Pottery

Fine Decorated Wares

Boyd P1 (HM 1018; Fig. 36; Pl. 20C). Oinochoe or juglet. Restored; neck and much of rim missing. H. pres. 8.6; max. d. 7.5; d. base 3.2. Fine, soft, very pale brown (10YR 8/3) fabric. Worn, faded, reddish-yellow (5YR 7/6) paint. May have had a trefoil mouth; short neck; round, vertical handle from rim to shoulder; small conical foot. Blob decoration on body; band at base of neck; top of handle painted. *Bibliography*: Tsipopoulou 2005, 75, pl. 20 (PG). *Comparanda*: Boardman 1960, 133, pl. 35:V.10 (Hagios Ioannis, MPG); Coldstream and Catling, eds., 1996, 94, pl. 110:55.1 (Knossos, EPG); Rethemiotakis and Englezou 2010, 96, fig. 52:130 (Eltyna, EPG). *Date*: EPG.

Boyd P2 (HM 3696; Fig. 36; Pl. 20C) Stirrup jar. Restored; small fragments of handle and spout missing. H. 11.0; max. d. 10.8; d. base 3.9. Hard, pink (7.5YR 7/4) fabric and slip. Lustrous paint, weak to very dusky red (2.5YR 4/2–2/2), worn. Short false spout with slight knob on top; flaring spout nearly touches false spout; globular body; ring base. Decoration on shoulder: Minoan flower, multiple chevrons and concentric arcs (perhaps a debased Minoan flower); on either side of the spout, variations of multiple arcs. Concentric circles on top of false spout. Bands on lower body. *Comparanda*: for shape, Day 2011b, 291 (Karphi, LM IIIC); for decoration, Hatzaki 2007, 238, fig. 6.28:4 (Knossos, LM IIIB early). *Date*: LM IIIB late or IIIC early.

Boyd P3 (HM 1024; Fig. 36; Pl. 20C). Amphoriskos. Complete except for one-third of rim and half of base; cracked on one side. H. 10.7; d. rim 5.2; d. base 3.6. Fine, hard, pink to reddish-yellow (5YR 8/4–7/6) fabric. Very dark gray (7.5YR N3) paint, well preserved. Short outturned rim; ovoid body; two round horizontal handles on shoulder; high conical foot. String marks on base. Band at rim, zigzag in handle zone, three horizontal bands below. *Bibliography*: Tsipopoulou 2005, 75, pl. 22. *Comparanda*: Brock 1957, pl. 6:49, 60 (Knossos, EPG); Boardman 1960, pl. 37:IV.2 (Hagios Ioannis, EPG); Coldstream and Catling, eds., 1996, 27, pl. 64:J.6 (Knossos, EPG); Tsipopoulou 1997, 474, 478, fig. 17:5044 (Chamaizi Phatsi, SM); 2005, 98, pl. 66; 99, pl. 70 (Kavousi Plai tou Kastrou tomb, PG); Hayden 2003, 44, fig. 20:89 (Vrokastro, EPG). *Date*: SM–PG.

Medium-Coarse Decorated Ware

Boyd P4 (HM 3695; Fig. 36; Pl. 20C). Juglet. Mended; one-third of rim and section of handle missing. H. 9.3; max. d. 6.5; d. base 2.6. Medium-coarse, gritty, soft, reddish-yellow (7.5YR 8/6) fabric. Black to brown paint almost entirely worn off. Flaring rim; narrow cylindrical neck; rectangular handle from rim to shoulder; ovoid body; flat raised base. Neck coated; possible pendant crosshatched triangle on shoulder; handle coated; bands on lower body. Band on interior of rim. *Bibliography*: Tsipopoulou 2005, 121, pl. 126. *Comparanda*: for shape, Day 2011b, 55, fig. 3.5:K39.5 (Karphi, LM IIIC). *Date*: PG.

3

Enclosure Burials at Vronda

*Leslie Preston Day, Maria A. Liston, Kimberly Flint-Hamilton,
David S. Reese, and Lynn M. Snyder*

Grave 1

History and Details of Excavation

Grave 1, the first grave found in the settlement, lay on the southeast slope of the Vronda ridge, in the corner of what had been Room E3 of Building E East in the earlier LM IIIC settlement (Figs. 3, 4). It was discovered during the 1984 cleaning of Vronda in Trench V 800, and most of it was excavated as Locus V 805 (Day, Coulson, and Gesell 1986, 382–384). Some pottery from the burial had already been picked up in the surface collection, but most of the material came from Locus V 805 Level 2. Deposition was thicker in the northwest corner, the area protected by Walls V 802 and V 804, but grave material lay on or just below the surface toward the south and east (Pl. 21A). Some of the arrowheads, for example, were actually resting on the surface when excavation began (Pls. 21B, 21C). The trench was extended to the southwest (V 805 extension) to pick up more of the grave, and most of the arrowheads came from this area.

In 1987 the remainder of the grave was excavated in Trench V 300. Locus V 302 and Locus V 310 comprised the ashy soil from the cremation. The remainder of the grave material in the north balk of Trench V 300 was designated Locus V 337.

Architecture

Grave 1 had little preserved architecture (Fig. 37). Walls from Room E3 of LM IIIC Building E were used as boundaries for the cremation on the north (V 802) and west (V 804). Both walls V 802 and V 804 were preserved two courses high above a leveling course, and the limestone blocks in the walls were fissured from the heat of the fire (Pl. 21A). The burial space is estimated to have measured approximately 2.00 m north–south x 1.75 m east–west. Additional walls, perhaps consisting of a single row of stones, may originally have existed on the south and east, but no traces were encountered, perhaps because of the existence of a path on the modern surface in this area. The presence of the burned patch at the bottom of the grave and the fissuring of the limestone blocks of the walls indicate that the cremations took place in situ, and therefore Grave 1 was a cremation enclosure like many of the other graves on Vronda.

Stratigraphy

The stratigraphy in the burial was not complex. The cremation was made just above the clay that represents the collapsed roof of the LM IIIC Building E (V 805 Level 3). The upper part of this layer of clay was hard and pale brown (10YR 6/3) with a reddish patch, perhaps a result of burning from the pyre, and it was rather uneven (0.06–0.16 m), rising from 423.53 m asl in the southeast to 423.69 m asl in the corner. Above this surface on which the cremation was made lay the soft and ashy grave soil containing small stones and human bones (V 805.2 Level 2, V 805.3 Level 2, V 805.5 Level 2, V 302, V 310, V 337.2, V 337.4) up to the surface (V 800.1 Level 1). The depth of this cremation soil varied from 0.32–0.37 m along the north to 0.02–0.14 m in the south. Four vessels (**GR1 P1**, **GR1 P3**, **GR1 P4**, **GR1 P12**) were found smashed up against Wall V 802, the highest at 423.93 m asl (**GR1 P4**), and the lowest at 423.65 m asl (**GR1 P1**). A thin layer of surface soil lay above the cremation, in places so thin that artifacts were actually resting on the modern surface.

Burials

There were two commingled burials in the grave, both primary but disturbed. Because the bones lay so close to the surface, much skeletal material had been lost, and it is now impossible to distinguish the separate bodies. There is no evidence to indicate whether the burials were simultaneous or represent two different events. The bone is fully calcined, indicating a complete and thorough cremation. It was not possible to separate the remains of these two individuals.

Burial 1
Type: disturbed primary cremation
Age: adult, 20–40 years
Sex: male
Weight (combined skeletons): 1,572 g

The skeleton of Burial 1 is that of a young adult male, probably between 20 and 40 years old. The cranial fragments are very robust, particularly in the occipital region (Buikstra and Ubelaker, eds., 1994, 19–20). The bone is fully calcined, indicating a complete and thorough cremation. This cremation burial was commingled with Burial 2 in the enclosure.

Burial 2
Type: disturbed primary cremation
Age: older adult
Sex: unknown
Weight: see above, Burial 1

This cremation burial is an older adult, as indicated by the very heavily worn teeth. The wear pattern is typical of normal masticatory wear, not specialized use of the teeth as tools (Hillson 1996, 231–232). Two molars are worn down to the roots, with no enamel left. It was not possible to determine the sex of Burial 2 based on the preserved remains, which were commingled with those of Burial 1.

Faunal Remains

Nearly all the identifiable animal bone from Grave 1 appears to be from sheep or goat, and it is heavily burned or calcined and fragmentary (Table 4). In addition, nearly 200 small, unidentifiable bone fragments, also burned, were recovered from the flotation residue. The tiny size of these fragments and the total lack of diagnostic characteristics make further analysis impossible.

Identifiable burned or calcined sheep or goat elements were limited to the lower front and hind leg and included a single proximal metacarpal fragment, a left distal tibia fragment, an unsided metatarsal diaphysis fragments (see also below), and a single second phalange unfused proximal epiphysis fragment.

In addition, a fragmented, heavily burned or calcined metatarsal was recovered from the area of the concentration of arrowheads to the south and east. This element, although visibly shrunken and distorted by the heavy burning, shows the deep and sharply marked dorsal groove characteristic of deer, and is tentatively identified as Cervidae (likely fallow deer). A single large vermetid shell was also found (Table 5).

Pottery

Grave 1 produced some 894 fragments of pottery weighing approximately 6.05 kg. The pottery, except for the five nearly complete pots found along the walls, was fragmentary, and it is clear that much has been lost to erosion and surface activity. Thirty-three vessels have been cataloged, of which only 11 were substantially preserved; the others were in fragments, representing vessels that had been in the grave but were disturbed by later activity or surface erosion. Three other vessels that were represented by large numbers of fragments were not cataloged because they lacked diagnostic features. One large fragment (10 sherds and three nonjoining pieces) of fine ware clearly came from a single large vessel with a measurable interior diameter of 25.00 cm; the interior coating of red paint indicates that it was a krater. Two other vessels are represented by a large number of nondiagnostic fragments of soft, chalky fabrics: one of pale green fabric is made of 38 fragments (possibly representing more than one vessel), while 44 fragments, possibly from a closed vessel, have a pink fabric.

The five vessels found along the north wall of the grave belong to the last use of the feature. The small cup **GR1 P1** is of a shape that is found from the PG to EG periods at Knossos (Coldstream and Catling, eds., 1996, 134, fig. 103:30), but the chevron decoration is more common on MG and LG cups and skyphoi there (e.g., Coldstream and Catling, eds., 1996, 183–184, fig. 119:5; 218, fig. 131:99; 265, fig. 147:108), perhaps influenced by Attic MG II imports (Coldstream and Catling, eds., 1996, 264, fig. 145:70). The stemmed skyphos **GR1 P2** is one of a handful of this shape from the Vronda graves. The shape appears frequently in East Crete in the LG period; this example has close parallels in shape in vessels from Adromyloi (Tsipopoulou 2005, 211:H3223; 212, fig. 108:H3225), Hagios Georgios (Tsipopoulou 2005, 155, fig. 108:AN2319; 189, fig. 108:Σ4074), Zou (Tsipopoulou 2005, 315, fig. 108:AN1448), Praisos (Tsipopoulou 2005, 272, fig. 108:AN 1589), and Piskokephalo (Tsipopoulou 2013, 149–150, fig. 11:12284).

The wide-mouthed jug **GR1 P4** is also of an unusual shape, one that is sometimes included with cups but more often with jugs (Tsipopoulou 2005, 401). This shape has PGB–MG parallels at Fortetsa (Brock 1957, 38, 155, pl. 26:375), LG parallels at Sklavoi (Tsipopoulou 2005, 299, fig. 90:Σ3814), and EO parallels at Dreros (Tsipopoulou 2005, 61, fig. 89: HΔ26). The monochrome cup **GR1 P13** is paralleled at Knossos in the EG period (Coldstream and Catling, eds., 1996, 229, fig. 135:4), but its size suggests a date of MG or later. A cup or skyphos with grooves below the rim (**GR1 P18**) is similar to a decorated EO kotyle from Knossos (Coldstream and Catling, eds., 1996, 204, fig. 129:12).

The large monochrome skyphos **GR1 P17** is unusual in shape, with a nearly vertical plain rim and large flat base. It is somewhat similar to an EPG–MPG example from Knossos, where it is thought to imitate Cypriot antecedents (Coldstream and Catling, eds., 1996, 198, fig. 126:44). The amphora **GR1 P11** is of a type that is prevalent in the EPG material at Fortetsa but persists into the LPG period (Brock 1957, 19, 142, pl. 10:181; Coldstream and Catling, eds., 1996, 336). It is also found in graves of LPG date at Hagios Ioannis (Boardman 1960, 130, pl. 33:I3, I4); the shape at Knossos, however, goes into the EO period (Coldstream and Catling, eds., 1996, 263, pl. 237). The Grave 1 example (**GR1 P17**) is more elongated than the PG examples but not as narrow as the EO amphora (**GR1 P11**). The latter vessel may have stood as a marker over the grave as in the cases of the amphorae in Graves 9 and 12 (see below); it shows no evidence of burning, and some of the fragments were found in the surface soil.

The vessel **GR1 P10** is probably a small jar or a jug, but its similarity to pyxides of late PG date from Eleutherna (Kotsonas 2008, 142–144, fig. 34:A144ζ, A274) suggests that it may have been a pyxis. However, it might also have been a kantharos, similar to a PG example from Chamaizi (Tsipopoulou 2005, 322, fig. 110:Σ3824), if it had a second handle. The rims of the fragmentary cups are all similar to examples from other Vronda graves and are probably to be dated in general to the LG period.

Overall, the Grave 1 ceramic assemblage consists of at least 26 vessels for drinking, of which the majority (16) are monochrome cups or skyphoi. Closed vessels are rare: there are two small juglets and a strainer vessel of which only the base is preserved. The large amphorae may have been used for storage of goods in the grave, but it is more likely that they were used as markers for the two burials within, by analogy with some of the graves on top of the ridge.

Objects

Like the pottery described above, the remainder of the grave assemblage is also unusual. The bronze fibula **GR1 M1**, although of standard arched shape, differs from contemporary examples because of its large size and its flat rectangular section. A small piece of bronze found adhering to cremated human bone may have come from this fibula or from another bronze object that has disappeared. Arrowheads comprise nearly all of the iron artifacts. The 17 arrowheads are of three different types, determined by the form of the blade: most common is the elongated leaf-shaped blade without pronounced shoulders and with a simple flat tang (**GR1 M2, GR1 M4, GR1 M5, GR1 M7–GR1 M12, GR1 M16, GR1 M17**); another (**GR1 M6**) is similar but has triangular shoulders. Three examples (**GR1 M13–GR1 M15**) are not as elongated and are more triangular in shape. Two blades (**GR1 M3, GR1 M18**) have barbed ends, although **GR1 M18** may have had square shoulders like some of the spearhead blades from other graves. In addition to the cataloged arrowheads, there are fragments of others (Pl. 21D), an indication that there were originally more than 17 of these items. Arrowheads are unusual in the Vronda graves and only occur here and in Grave 12. A fragment of an iron awl (**GR1 M19**) found in the balk over Rooms 3 and 5, near the surface, probably came from Grave 1. A fragment of what may have been an iron sickle was found in V 310.1, but it was so fragmentary and corroded that it could not be drawn or inventoried.

The stone bead (**GR1 S1**) is made out of red and white carnelian, and it was clearly meant to function as an ornament. It is too tiny to have been a spindle whorl.

Chronology

Although there are some vessels with parallels in earlier periods, most of the pottery from Grave 1 is LG, with several possible examples of EO. It is likely that most of the burials in this enclosure were made in the the LG period, but the latest cremation(s) belongs to the EO period. The stemmed skyphos (**GR1 P2**) is a rare shape and only occurs in Graves 6, 19, and 28 (see below). Grave 1 may belong to the same phase as these graves.

Catalog

Pottery

Fine Decorated Wares

GR1 P1 (V84.77; V 805 Level 2, pot 1; Fig. 38; Pl. 21D). Cup. Restored from 12 fragments, 95% preserved, missing bit of rim and body. H. 5.0; d. rim 6.8–8.0; d. base 3.7. Fine, soft fabric with dark gray phyllite inclusions; pale brown (10YR 6/3), probably discolored from fire. Black paint, worn to brown. Worn surfaces. Chevrons in handle zone. *Bibliography*: Day, Coulson, and Gesell 1986, 383–384, fig. 14:42, pl. 84:h. *Comparanda*: for shape, Coldstream and Catling, eds., 1996, 146, fig. 106:6 (Knossos, EG–MG). *Date*: LG, imitating Attic MG.

GR1 P2 (V84.78; V 805 Level 2, pot 3; Fig. 38; Pl. 21D). Stemmed skyphos. Restored from 28 fragments, 90% preserved, including full profile; missing half of rim, part of one handle, small fragments of base and lower body. H. 11.5; d. rim 10.7–11.5; d. base 6.0. Fine, soft, porous, very pale brown (10YR 7/4) fabric with a few quartz inclusions. Thick and glossy black paint. Well-preserved surfaces. Possible traces of burning. "Running dog" or running loop pattern. *Bibliography*: Day, Coulson, and Gesell 1986, 383–384, fig. 14:39, pl. 84:f. *Comparanda*: Tsipopoulou 2005, 315, fig. 108:AN1448 (Stavromenos Zou, LG); for decoration, Brock 1957, 167, pl. 44:656 (Knossos, G). *Date*: LG.

GR1 P3 (V 805 Level 2, V 310.2, V 337.2; Fig. 38). Skyphos or cup. Partially mended into two large fragments, one from each side (four sherds each); four nonjoining fragments. Tiny piece of rim, 15% of upper body preserved; missing handle(s), lower body, and base. D. rim est. 13.6. Fine, soft, reddish-yellow (7.5YR 7/6) fabric. Reddish-yellow (7.5YR 8/6) slip. Black paint worn to brown shadow. Very worn surfaces. All but one fragment totally burned; slip has turned black, paint lighter (negative image). Side A has cable pattern; side B has metope of upright chevrons between vertical lines. *Date*: LG–EO.

GR1 P4 (V 805 Level 2, pot 4; Fig. 38). Wide-mouthed jug. Partially mended into two large fragments, one from base (16 sherds), one from rim (six sherds); seven nonjoining fragments. Vessel 75% preserved, including entire base and lower body, 35% of rim, both handle attachments. H. est. 9.9; d. rim 5.5; d. base 3.4. Fine, very soft, reddish-yellow (7.5YR 7/6) fabric with white quartz and black inclusions. Traces of brown paint, inside and out. Very worn surfaces. A few fragments burned. Foliate band on body. *Bibliography*: Day, Coulson, and Gesell 1986, 383–384, fig. 14:41, but redrawn. *Comparanda*: Tsipopoulou 2005, 61, fig. 89:HΔ26 (Dreros, EO). *Date*: LG–EO.

GR1 P5 (V 302.1; Fig. 38). Open vessel. Four fragments and three nonjoining fragments preserving nearly all of base and one decorated fragment from body.

D. base. 3.0. Fine, soft, light red (2.5YR 6/6) fabric. Traces of red paint. Very worn surfaces. No trace of burning. Decoration of concentric circles, semicircles, or loops. *Date*: LG?

GR1 P6 (V 805 Level 2; Fig. 39). Kalathos. Large fragment of body from near base to near rim, two nonjoining rim fragments. D. rim est. 20.0. Fine, soft, very pale brown (10YR 7/4) fabric, light gray (5Y 7/2) on surface, with some black and white inclusions. Very worn surfaces. Body and one rim fragment burned. *Date*: LPG (as suggested by size; see Coldstream 1996, 377).

GR1 P7 (V 302.1, V 337.2, V 337.4; Fig. 39). Kalathos. Four fragments from rim. D. rim est. 23.0. Fine, medium-soft, gray (5Y 7/2) fabric with gray (5Y 7/1) core, heavily burned. Groove on top of rim, ridge outside. Similar to **GR1 P6** but probably a different vessel. *Date*: LPG.

GR1 P8 (V 805 Level 2, V 337.2; Fig. 39). Small jug. Six joining fragments from base, four joining fragments from upper body, one fragment from neck, and 18 body sherds preserving 20% of entire vessel including 50% of base, lower handle attachment. D. rim est. 3.0; d. base 2.5. Fine, soft, pink (7.5YR 7/4) fabric. Black paint. Very worn surfaces. Most of fragments burned gray on interior. *Comparanda*: Tsipopoulou 2005, 163, fig. 87:AN2427 (Hagios Georgios, LG); Rethemiotakis and Englezou 2010, 38, fig. 18:31 (Eltyna, EPG). *Date*: LG.

GR1 P9 (V 805 Level 2; Fig. 39). Juglet. Single fragment from rim and neck. Max. pres. h. 1.4. Fine, soft fabric, burned to gray. Black paint. Very worn surfaces. *Date*: LG?

GR1 P10 (V 310.2, V 805 Levels 2 and 4; Fig. 39). Jug or jar. Ten joining and nine nonjoining fragments from rim and upper body and possibly a burned fragment of base (not drawn), preserving 35% of vessel, including nearly complete profile and one handle attachment. D. rim 6.9; d. base est. 4.0–5.0. Fine, soft, reddish-yellow (7.5YR 7/6) fabric with tiny white inclusions; base burned to gray. Red (2.5YR 4/6) paint. Very worn surfaces. Possible bands on exterior. *Date*: PG.

GR1 P11 (V 800, V 805 Levels 2 and 3, V 302.1, V 337.2, V 337.4; Fig. 39). Amphora. Seventeen joining fragments preserving 30% of rim and neck, including one handle attachment; four joining fragments from base; one fragment from elliptical vertical handle; 37 body fragments. H. est. 74.8; d. rim 22.5; d. base 17.0. Fine, soft, reddish-yellow (7.5YR 7/6) fabric with some quartz inclusions, increasing in frequency toward base. Petrographic sample KAV 15/45: Fabric Group 7. Pink (7.5YR 7/4) slip. Yellowish-red (5YR 5/6) paint. Worn surfaces. Handle attachment on neck and handle fragment indicates at least one vertical handle; a second would suggest an amphora. *Comparanda*: Lebessi 1970, 281, pl. 390α:40 (Mastambas, PGB); Rethemiotakis and Englezou 2010, 36, fig. 16:24 (Eltyna, EPG–MPG); 64, fig. 37:78 (LPG). *Date*: PG–EO.

GR1 P12 (V 800.1; Fig. 39). Amphora or large closed vessel. Single fragment from base. D. base 14.0–15.0. Fine, soft, reddish-yellow (7.5YR 7/6) fabric, with black and white inclusions. Worn surfaces. Date unknown.

FINE MONOCHROME WARES

GR1 P13 (V 805 Level 2, pot 2, V 337.2; Fig. 39). Cup. Partially mended from 25 joining fragments, 26 nonjoining fragments, preserving 75% of vessel, including most of base, full profile, part of handle. H. 8.1; d. rim 10.0; d. base 5.5. Fine, soft to medium-soft porous fabric, reddish yellow (7.5YR 7/6) at core, very pale brown (10YR 8/4) on surface; yellowish-red (5YR 5/6) paint. Worn surfaces. Many burned fragments join with unburned ones and thus were burned after breakage. Monochrome inside and out, including underside of base. *Bibliography*: Day, Coulson, and Gesell 1986, 383–384, fig. 14:43. *Comparanda*: **GR6 P9**. *Date*: LG.

GR1 P14 (V 337.4; Fig. 39). Cup. Single fragment from rim, preserving handle attachment on interior. Max. pres. h. 1.5. Fine, soft, reddish-yellow (5YR 7/6) fabric. Very pale brown (10YR 8/4) slip. Traces of red paint on exterior. Worn surfaces. *Date*: LG.

GR1 P15 (V 302.1, V 337.2, V 805 Level 2; Fig. 39). Cup. Seven nonjoining fragments from rim, including handle attachment. Max. pres. h. 2.1. Fine, soft fabric, burned various shades of gray. Black paint. Worn surfaces. Monochrome inside and out. *Date*: LG.

GR1 P16 (V 805 Level 2, pot 2; Fig. 40). Skyphos. Partially mended into two large fragments (five sherds, eight sherds) with seven nonjoining fragments, preserving 40% of rim, one handle; missing base and second handle, most of lower body. D. rim 13.5. Fine, soft, very pale brown (10YR 8/4) fabric with frequent small red and gray phyllite inclusions. Petrographic sample KAV 15/47: Fabric Group 7. Traces of red to black paint. Very worn surfaces. No burning. Monochrome. *Comparanda*: Haggis et al. 2007b, 261, fig. 14.6 (Azoria, LO). *Date*: EO.

GR1 P17 (V 805 Level 2; Fig. 40). Skyphos or kotyle. Partially mended from 39 fragments, preserving 60% of vessel, including full profile, all of base, one handle; missing second handle. H. 9.8; d. rim 16.0; d. base 7.0. Fine, very soft and chalky, micaceous, very pale brown (10YR 7/3) fabric. Red to black paint. Painted on interior, exterior, and underside of base. Very worn surfaces. Some fragments burned. *Bibliography*: Day, Coulson, and Gesell 1986, 383–384, fig. 14:40. *Date*: LG.

GR1 P18 (V 302.1, V 310.1, V 337.2, V 339.1, V 800.1; Fig. 40). Cup or skyphos. Partially mended from eight fragments from upper body and rim, 5% preserved; missing base, lower body, handle(s). D. rim est. 15.0. Fine, soft, pink (7.5YR 7/4) fabric. Traces of dark paint. Surfaces very worn. Two fragments totally burned. Monochrome. Grooves below rim. *Date*: LG.

GR1 P19 (V 337.2, V 805 Level 2; Fig. 40). Cup or skyphos. Large fragment (two sherds) from rim, nonjoining rim fragment; missing lower body, base, handle(s). D. rim est. 13.0. Fine, soft, light gray (2.5Y 7/2) fabric, totally burned and pitted. Black paint. Worn surfaces. Grooves on top of rim. Monochrome. *Date*: LG.

GR1 P20 (V 805 Level 2; Fig. 40). Cup or skyphos. Two joining and three nonjoining fragments from rim; missing lower body, base, handle(s). D. rim est. 12.0. Fine, porous, pale yellow (5Y 8/2) fabric, totally burned. Some small black inclusions. Very worn surfaces. Probably monochrome. *Date*: LG.

GR1 P21 (V 337.2, V 805 Level 2; Fig. 40). Cup or skyphos. Two nonjoining fragments from rim. Max. pres. h. 2.3. Fine, soft, light reddish-brown (5YR 6/4) fabric, very pale brown (10YR 8/4) slip. Very worn surfaces. Tall rim. *Date*: LG.

GR1 P22 (V 310.1; Fig. 40). Cup or skyphos. Single fragment from rim. Max. pres. h. 1.8. Fine, soft fabric, burned gray. Black paint. Worn surfaces. *Comparanda*: for rim type, **GR12 P6**, **GR20 P10**, **GR20 P12**, **GR28 P16**. *Date*: LG.

GR1 P23 (V 310.1, V 337.2, V 337.4; Fig. 40). Cup or skyphos. Three nonjoining fragments from rim. D. rim est. 12.0–15.0. Fine, soft fabric, burned gray. Black paint. Worn surfaces. Monochrome inside and out. *Date*: LG.

GR1 P24 (V 337.4; Fig. 40). Cup or skyphos. Two fragments from rim. Max. pres. h. 1.5. Fine, medium-soft fabric, burned to gray. Black paint. Worn surfaces. Monochrome inside and out. *Date*: LG.

GR1 P25 (V 310.1; Fig. 40). Cup or skyphos. Single fragment from rim. Max. pres. h. 1.6. Fine, soft, very pale brown (10YR 8/3) fabric. Worn surfaces. *Date*: LG.

GR1 P26 (V 805 Level 2; Fig. 40). Cup or skyphos. Single fragment from base. D. base 6.0. Fine, medium-soft, reddish-yellow (5YR 7/6) fabric. Very pale brown (10YR 8/3) surface. Black paint on exterior. *Date*: LG.

GR1 P27 (V 337.1, V 800.1; Fig. 40). Cup or skyphos. Two fragments from base. D. base 5.0–6.0. Fine, soft, reddish-brown (7.5YR 7/6) fabric. Very pale brown (10YR 8/4) slip. Very worn surfaces. Grooves around base on exterior. *Date*: LG.

GR1 P28 (V 302.1; Fig. 40). Cup or skyphos. Two fragments from base. D. base est. 5.0. Fine, soft fabric, burned gray. Black paint. Worn surfaces. String marks on base. Monochrome. *Date*: LG.

GR1 P29 (V 302.1; Fig. 40). Cup or skyphos. Two joining fragments from base. Max. pres. h. 2.0. Fine, soft, reddish-brown (7.5YR 7/6) fabric, with gray core. Black to brown paint. Well-preserved surfaces on interior, worn on exterior. Monochrome. *Date*: LG.

GR1 P30 (V 302.1; Fig. 40). Cup or skyphos. Two joining fragments preserving 65% of base. D. base 4.5. Fine, soft, light red (10R 6/6) fabric, very pale brown (10YR 7/3) on surface. Black paint. Worn surfaces. String marks on base. Monochrome. *Date*: LG.

GR1 P31 (V805 Level 2; Fig. 40). Strainer vessel. Three joining and two nonjoining fragments from base. D. base est. 6.0. Fine, soft, reddish-yellow (7.5YR 7/6) fabric, very pale brown (10YR 8/3) surface. Black paint on exterior. Worn surfaces. One fragment burned. Base pierced with holes. *Comparanda*: Hallager and Hallager, eds., 1997, 52, pl. 113:71-P 0798 (Chania, LG II?). *Date*: LG.

GR1 P32 (V 805 Level 2; Fig. 40). Closed vessel. Two joining fragments preserving entire base. D. base 4.5. Fine, soft, reddish-yellow (5YR 7/6) fabric with some dark inclusions. Worn surfaces, partly burned. Grooves around outside near base. *Date*: LG?

Medium-Coarse Ware

GR1 P33 (V 337.4, V 805 Level 2; Fig. 40). Cup. Fragment (four sherds) from lower body and base, one small fragment from rim, one handle attachment, and 19 body fragments. D. base 6.0–7.0. Medium-coarse, reddish-yellow (5YR 6/6–7.5YR 7/6) fabric with frequent phyllite inclusions. Petrographic sample KAV 15/46: small low-fired metamorphic group. Flaking surfaces. Rim coated with what looks like decomposed iron. *Date*: LG?

Metal

Bronze

GR1 M1 (V84.68; V 805.3 Level 2, object 1; Fig. 41; Pl. 21D). Bronze fibula. Mended from five fragments; complete except for tip of pin. Max. L. 8.8; max. w. 5.2; th. 0.2. Badly corroded. Arched. Flat catch plate; flattened bow, thin and rectangular in section, becoming thicker and square near core. Large pin, round in section. *Bibliography*: Day, Coulson, and Gesell 1986, 382, pl. 80:g. *Comparanda*: Sapouna-Sakellaraki 1978, 48–49, pl. 6:170 (type IId, 10th–9th century).

Iron

GR1 M2 (V84.64a, HNM 15729; V 805.5 Level 2, object 3; Fig. 41; Pl. 21D). Iron arrowhead. Nearly complete in two fragments. Max. pres. L. 7.3; max. w. 1.25; th. 0.5. Surfaces worn and corroded. Short (2.5) tang, leaf-shaped blade. *Bibliography*: Day, Coulson, and Gesell 1986, 382, pl. 80:j top.

GR1 M3 (V84.64c, HNM 15729; V 805.5 Level 2, object 3; Fig. 41; Pl. 21D). Iron arrowhead. Single fragment, nearly intact; missing end of tang, tip of barb, chip from blade. Max. pres. L. 4.3; max. w. 1.8; th. 0.5. Surfaces worn and corroded; some original surface on each side. Straight tang, short barbed blade. *Bibliography*: Day, Coulson, and Gesell 1986, 382, pl. 80:i (shown with tang that did not belong). *Comparanda*: Brock 1957, 54, 202, pl. 171:574 (Knossos).

GR1 M4 (V84.64b, HNM 15729; V 805.5 Level 2, object 3; Fig. 41; Pl. 21D). Iron arrowhead. Mended from two fragments; missing point. Max. pres. L. 5.1; max. w. 1.3; th. 0.5. Surfaces worn and corroded; some original surface on one side. Short (2.1) tang, leaf-shaped blade. *Bibliography*: Day, Coulson, and Gesell 1986, 382, pl. 80:j middle.

GR1 M5 (V84.64d, HNM 15729; V 805.5 Level 2, object 3; Fig. 41; Pl. 21D). Iron arrowhead. Complete in two fragments. Max. pres. L. 7.3; max. w. 1.6; th. 0.5. Very corroded. Long (2.9) tang, leaf-shaped blade. *Bibliography*: Day, Coulson, and Gesell 1986, 382, pl. 80:j bottom.

GR1 M6 (V84.65a, HNM 15730; V 805.5 Level 2, object 3; Fig. 41; Pl. 22A). Iron arrowhead. Single fragment of blade; missing tang. Max. pres. L. 4.6; max. w. 1.4, th. 0.3. Well-preserved surfaces. Long, almost triangular blade.

GR1 M7 (V84.65b, HNM 15730; V 805.5 Level 2, object 3; Fig. 41; Pl. 22A). Iron arrowhead. Nearly complete in two fragments; missing tip. Max. pres. L. 6.1; max. w. 1.5; th. 0.4. Corroded, but some original surface preserved. Short (2.2) tang, leaf-shaped blade. Tang was originally put on **GR1 M3**.

GR1 M8 (V84.65c, HNM 15730; V 805.5 Level 2, object 3; Fig. 41; Pl. 22A). Iron arrowhead. Complete in two fragments. L. 6.5; max. w. 1.3; th. 0.4. Very corroded; little of the original surface survives. Short (2.2) tang, narrow leaf-shaped blade.

GR1 M9 (V84.65d, HNM 15730; V 805.5 Level 2, object 3; Fig. 41; Pl. 22A). Iron arrowhead. Single fragment, missing tang and tip. Max. pres. L. 4.0; max. pres. w. 1.4; th. 0.5. Very corroded. Leaf-shaped blade.

GR1 M10 (V84.65e, HNM 15730; V 805.5 Level 2, object 3; Fig. 41; Pl. 22A). Iron arrowhead. Single fragment, missing tang, tip, and one tang. Max. pres. L. 3.6; max. pres. w. 1.5; th. 0.4. Corroded, but some preserved surfaces. Short, probably barbed blade.

GR1 M11 (V84.65f, HNM 15730; V 805.5 Level 2, object 3; Fig. 41; Pl. 22A). Iron arrowhead. Complete in three fragments. L. 6.5; max. w. 1.2; th 0.3. Very corroded; only a few surfaces remain. Short (2.2) tang, narrow leaf-shaped blade.

GR1 M12 (V84.65g, HNM 15730; V 805.5 Level 2, object 3; Fig. 41; Pl. 22A). Iron arrowhead. Single fragment; missing tang. Max. pres. L. 3.0; max. pres. w. 1.3; th. 0.3. Corroded, but with some original surfaces. Leaf-shaped blade.

GR1 M13 (V84.65h, HNM 15730; V 805.5 Level 2, object 3; Fig. 41; Pl. 22A). Iron arrowhead. Single fragment of blade, missing tang. Max. pres. L. 3.4; max. pres. w. 1.3; th. 0.3. Corroded, but with some original surfaces. Short, triangular-shaped blade.

GR1 M14 (V84.66a, HNM 15731; V 805.5 Level 2, object 3; Fig. 41; Pl. 22A). Iron arrowhead. Complete in two fragments. L. 5.1; max. w. 1.4; th. 0.5. Very corroded; some surface preserved on one side. Short (2.2) tang, short blade in shape of squat leaf. *Comparanda*: Courtois 1984, fig. 3:56, in bronze.

GR1 M15 (V84.66b+g, HNM 15731; V 805.5 Level 2, object 3; Fig. 41; Pl. 22A). Iron arrowhead. Complete in two fragments. L. 5.0; max. w. 1.4; th. 0.3. Corroded; little surface remains. Short (1.5), pointed tang, leaf-shaped blade.

GR1 M16 (V84.66c, HNM 15731; V 805.5 Level 2, object 3; Fig. 41; Pl. 22A). Iron arrowhead. Nearly complete in two fragments; missing tip of blade. Max. pres. L. 6.0; max. pres. w. 1.2; th. 0.5. Badly corroded. Short (2.4) tang, long, narrow, leaf-shaped blade.

GR1 M17 (V84.66d, HNM 15731; V 805.5 Level 2, object 3; Fig. 41; Pl. 22A). Iron arrowhead. Two joining fragments; missing tip of blade. Max. pres. L. 5.2; max. w. 1.3; th. 0.5. Very corroded. Longer (2.6) tang; narrow, leaf-shaped blade.

GR1 M18 (V84.66f; V 805.5 Level 2, object 3; Fig. 41; Pl. 22A). Iron arrowhead. Single fragment from tang and lower blade; missing upper blade and tip. Max. pres. L. 3.3; max. pres. w. 1.9; th. 0.4. Very corroded. Short (2.1) tang; blade comes out at right angles to tang; possibly originally barbed.

GR1 M19 (V 201.1, object 1; Fig. 41). Iron awl. Single fragment preserving pointed end and 50% of the tool; missing thicker end. Max. pres. L. 5.00; d. 0.04–1.00. Corroded and cracked.

Stone

GR1 S1 (V84.67, IM 1013; V 805.7 Level 3, object 4; Fig. 41; Pl. 22A). Stone bead. Intact, but cracked. H. 0.9; d. 1.1; d. hole 0.2; wt. 1.0 g. Mottled red and white stone, possibly carnelian. Biconical, though irregular in shape. *Bibliography*: Day, Coulson, and Gesell 1986, 382, pl. 80:h.

Grave 2

History and Details of Excavation

Grave 2 was uncovered during the 1984 cleaning in the corner of Trench V 12400 along the east wall of Room C2 of the earlier LM IIIC Building C (Figs. 3, 4). Here a large pile of stones mixed with ashy soil and burned bones was identified as Locus V 12402. The stone pile, with its accompanying deposit, was thick along the east where the house wall supported it, but it thinned out to the west and south where there had been serious erosion. None of the soil was removed for water sieving. In 1990 the north balk of Trench V 11900 (Locus V 11950) and the east balk of Trench V 12400 (Locus V 12452) were removed to see if more of the grave could be found, but only fragments of one cup remained from the burials.

Architecture

There was no architecture or any evidence for construction associated with the burials, but the existing house walls of Room C2 (V 11901, V 11902) and projecting spurs of bedrock on the north and southwest were apparently used as boundaries for the burial material (Fig. 42). The human remains were located along the east wall of C2, perhaps placed in a fissure in the bedrock. The area of ashy soil and stones extended 1.88 m north–south x 1.80 m east–west.

Stratigraphy

The deposit was uniform throughout, consisting of large quantities of stones with fine ashy soil (V 12402). It was difficult to distinguish the deposit from the wall tumble within the LM IIIC room. The stone tumble with bones began just below the surface at 425.38 m asl, and it continued down to the layer of roofing clay from the LM IIIC house at 424.87 m asl, a depth of 0.45–0.50 m. The deposit was deeper along the wall on the east but thinned out toward the west and north; much material may therefore have been lost to erosion.

Burials

Partial remains of a cremated adult were found in this grave. Because the soil was not kept for water sieving, some remains may have been lost, but the surviving fragments suggest that these were discard deposits of bone, possibly a dump from nearby Grave 5. There are, however, no joins between the bones or pottery in Graves 2 and 5 to prove a connection. Additional evidence that this was a discard deposit is the lack of any traces of burning in situ.

Burial 1
Type: cremation discard deposit
Age: adult
Sex: female
Weight: 667 g

The skeleton of Burial 1 is not completely calcined. The left side of the body appears to have been less thoroughly burned. The cranium is very gracile, with small mastoids and zygomatic arches and no brow ridge development, indicating a female (Buikstra and Ubelaker, eds., 1994, 19–20). The postcranial bones are small, with no apparent muscle markings. There were no pathological conditions noted on the bone.

There are a few fragments of another adult individual in this grave. The quantity of bone is so small that it supports the identification of this deposit as being part of another nearby grave.

Faunal Remains

Faunal materials from Grave 2 were limited to four isolated, unburned canid (dog) teeth, a number of unburned sheep or goat tooth fragments, and eight possible animal bone fragments, both burned and unburned (Table 4).

Pottery and Objects

Little pottery and no objects were found in the Grave 2 deposit, making it highly unusual. Of the 0.64 kg of pottery collected from the grave area, 18 fragments belonged to two vessels weighing 0.05 kg. Vessel **GR2 P1** is a monochrome cup or skyphos with rolled rim, similar to examples from other graves, especially skyphos **GR1 P16**. The other vessel (**GR2 P2**) represents a unique shape of uncertain type; it may be a skyphos, like an example from LG or EO Knossos (Coldstream 1972, 96, fig. 15:G100), or it may have served as a lid. Rough parallels for the shape are late. They include a wine strainer of Orientalizing date from Knossos (Coldstream 1973, 49, fig. 4:L5, pl. 18), and a lopas or cooking dish belonging to the third quarter of the third century from Knossos (Eiring 2001, 132, fig. 3.20:g). A fragment of a fine, round horizontal handle was also found, possibly from a skyphos. The rest of the pottery consisted of coarse body sherds and was discarded in 1984.

Chronology

There are no finds that would allow us to date this grave with certainty. It may represent a dump from Grave 5, as material from that grave was scattered as far as Trench V 2500 to the south. If there is an association with Grave 5, then this material should also date to LG. The cup or skyphos could be LG or EO, but the other vessel is unique and not datable.

Catalog

Pottery

FINE WARES

GR2 P1 (V 11950.1; Fig. 43). Cup or skyphos. Single fragment from rim. D. rim est. 14.0. Fine, soft, very pale brown (10YR 7/4) fabric. Worn surfaces. Monochrome black paint interior and exterior. *Comparanda*: **GR1 P15**, **GR16 P13**. *Date*: LG–EO.

MEDIUM-COARSE WARES

GR2 P2 (V 12402.4, V 12402.5 Levels 1 and 2; Fig. 43). Skyphos or lid. Seventeen fragments from rim and body; missing base, connection between rim and lower body, any handles. D. rim est. 14.0. Medium-coarse, brown (10YR 4/2) fabric with pink (7.5YR 7/4) surface and gold mica inclusions. Dark grayish-brown (7.5YR 4/4) paint. Worn surfaces. Burned. Unusual shape for a bowl or cup, so it may be a lid. Traces of paint on exterior near rim, on top of rim, and possibly on interior, but too worn to be certain. *Date*: LG?

Grave 3

History and Details of Excavation

Grave 3 is a stone-lined burial enclosure on the lower terrace to the northwest of the Vronda summit in the vicinity of three of the tholos tombs uncovered by Boyd in 1900 (Tombs IV–VI; Figs. 3, 4, 6). Investigation of this area began with a small mound that suggested the presence of another potential tholos tomb; it soon became apparent that the mound was not a tholos but an enclosure containing cremations, and it was excavated entirely in 1987 as Grave 3 (Gesell, Day, and Coulson 1988, 293–296). The grave was built up against a long northeast–southwest wall (VW 18103) that was at first thought to be the front of a tholos, with the chamber to the east (Pl. 22B). Once it became clear that no tholos existed east of Wall VW 18103, excavation moved to the western side of the wall where the enclosure began to appear just below the surface (Pl. 22C). The discovery of a deposit of pottery found set into stone tumble in the southeast corner marked the first indication of a grave in this location (Pl. 22D). Two broken cups were found and removed (**GR3 P2**, **GR3 P8**), and immediately below them were two intact vessels, a flask (**GR3 P18**) and a cup (**GR3 P19**; Pl. 22E). These cups seem to have been part of a postcremation ritual or offering for the second of the two burials.

The grave itself lies in two separate trenches, VW 18100 and VW 18200. The first attempt to excavate the parts of the grave separately in the two trenches proved impracticable because of the stone tumble and the disposition of the pottery and bones. The entire grave was thus dug as a single locus with dual designation: VW 18104/VW 18203. Unfortunately, the dual designation resulted in some confusion in recording that makes it difficult now to locate some of the pottery. Locus VW 18104/18203.1 was defined as the rock tumble in the grave, but a lower deposit that was almost devoid of stones in the northeast, which should have been given a new locus number, was excavated as VW 18104/18203.2. Finally, a second burial in ashy soil in the center and south of the grave was excavated as VW 18108/18204.

To the south of the grave was a platform paved with stones, which was excavated as VW 18201, VW 18202, VW 17201, and VW 17202. Some grave material was found scattered to the north in VW 18107 and VW 18108, to the east in VW 18102, and to the west in VW 18205.

Architecture

Grave 3 is a stone-lined burial enclosure, oriented northeast–southwest and measuring 1.00–1.07 m north–south x 1.75–1.87 m east–west (Fig. 44; Pl. 22E). The long eastern wall (VW 18103) is at least three courses high, and although it has more than one row of stones, the lack of a good eastern face shows that it functioned as a terrace wall. This terrace wall extends both north and south of Grave 3, so it seems most likely that it predated the construction of the grave. The row of stones, two to three courses high, which forms the east wall of Grave 3 was built up against the terrace wall, and these stones bond with those of the north wall. The north

(VW 18208), west (VW 18206), and south (VW 17207) walls of the grave consist of bedrock boulders in single rows, only one course high. The limestone blocks on the north wall are cracked from the heat of the pyre. Brecciating bedrock formed the floor of the enclosure.

To the south of the enclosure, along the wall VW 18103, was a platform with a stone paving that extended 2.90 m to the south (Pl. 22E), although it had eroded where not protected by VW 18103. In the midst of this paving, ca. 1.05 m from the southeast corner of the grave, a pot stand or base for a large object is preserved. It is composed of three upright stones in a rough circle; only three-quarters of the circle was preserved, and clearly another upright stone had disappeared. It may have held a grave marker, possibly an amphora like those in the graves on the summit, or a stone or other sort of marker. An appropriate large stone was found in the tumble at the surface in this area (Pl. 22E: stone is on lower left, cut off).

Stratigraphy

The total deposition in Grave 3 was 0.49 m on the east side of the grave and 0.42 m on the west where the modern surface sloped down. Above the brecciating bedrock floor of the grave in the north was the light yellowish-brown soil (10YR 6/4) of the original burial that had been pushed up by the later burial, especially into the northeast and northwest corners (VW 18104/18203.2). In the center and southern part of the enclosure was a layer of ashy soil and stones that had been burned on the underside (VW 18108/18204); this layer contained the second burial in the grave, and in some areas actually rested on top of the soil containing the bones of Burial 1. Above these two burials was a deposit of stones (VW 18104/18203.1; Pl. 22C), many of which had been burned, indicating that at least the last of the cremations took place within the enclosure. At the top of the stone layer in the southeast corner was a ceramic set consisting of a cup and flask (**GR3 P19**, **GR3 P18**; Pl. 22D) and a deposit of three drinking vessels above them that may have been part of a postcremation ritual for the grave (**GR3 P2**, **GR3 P4**, **GR3 P6**). A thin layer of topsoil lay above the stones. The stratigraphy in the graves was thus fairly simple, and it is possible to distinguish some of the objects from individual burials.

Associated Features

Aside from the stone platform and stand to the south of the grave, there were no features associated with Grave 3. Three tholos tombs (IV, V, and VI) lie very close, and Tomb IV may have influenced the location or alignment of Grave 3 (Figs. 3, 6).

Burials

Only two burials were made in the grave.

Burial 1

Type: disturbed primary cremation
Age: adult, 20–40 years
Sex: male
Weight: 550 g

Burial 1 is a disturbed primary cremation of an adult male, 40–60 years old. The skeleton shows differential burning on the cranium and postcranial bone. The cranium is only scorched and charred, although the inner and outer tables of the bone have completely separated, indicating exposure to high temperatures (Pl. 22F: bottom middle). While there is no reason to think that the soft tissues would not have been completely consumed by the fire, only the right temporal and portions of the right parietal show evidence of initial calcination, suggesting that this side of the head may have been turned down toward the flames while the rest was somewhat sheltered. The position of this cranium, face down in the northeast corner of the burial enclosure, suggests that the skull may have separated from the rest of the body during cremation and escaped more complete burning. In contrast, the postcranial bone is all completely calcined.

The cranium is quite robust and resembles other male crania from Kavousi, although the portions of bone with the more specific sexually dimorphic traits are missing. The postcranial skeleton appears to have been pushed to the north end of the grave when the second burial was cremated here. The cranial fragments were in relative anatomical order, suggesting that the cranium had remained undisturbed in this position subsequent to the cremation (Gesell, Coulson, and Day 1988, 293–294).

This individual exhibits clear evidence of healed or remodeled porotic hyperostosis (Aufderheide and Rodríguez-Martín 1998, 348–349). In addition, there is extensive porosity of the external cranial surfaces along the nuchal torus and above the right and left eye orbits on the frontal bone. This porosity of the exterior cranial vault is often associated with a variety of anemias, although other causes, including scurvy, are also possible (Lewis 2007, 111–115). There are extensive bone deposits on the internal surface of the frontal bone and the frontal sinuses, creating a scarred, ropy surface. These traits are consistent with hyperostosis frontalis interna, a condition of unknown etiology that occurs in older adults (Aufderheide and Rodríguez-Martín 1998, 419). It is more frequent in postmenopausal females and in males with hormonal deficiencies, including castrated males (She and Sakacs 2004, 207–208; Belcastro et al. 2011, 634–636). The presence of this condition suggests that some social quality of the deceased individual, an adult male who probably suffered from hormonal deficiency, may explain the anomalous location of the grave apart from the other enclosures.

Burial 2
Type: disturbed primary cremation
Age: adolescent, 16–20 years
Sex: female
Weight: 617 g

This partial cremated adult female skeleton was 16–20 years old at death. The cranial remains were found in the extreme southwest corner of the grave, and most of the associated postcranial bones were found in this end of the grave as well. Relatively little of Burial 2 was recovered, however. The cranial bone is quite gracile, and the long bones are small. The presence of a fused proximal humerus head confirms that the individual was older than 13–17 years of age (Scheuer and Black 2000, 286). A very young adult age is supported by the patterns of dental wear. The first maxillary incisor crown, which erupts at age six, shows very little wear, and mammelons (tubercles) on the surface of the preserved left central incisor are still present, also suggesting a very young age or malocclusion of the teeth.

There is fairly extensive evidence of pathology on this skeleton, although the bone lesions are nonspecific and do not suggest a specific diagnosis. There are a number of areas of periosteal bone formation on four long bone shaft fragments, suggesting an infectious or a metabolic disease such as scurvy (Ortner 2003, 88–89). Two of these bones are probably tibia shafts, and the other two are unidentified. Two areas of moderate activity appear to be associated with muscle attachments. The others are more diffuse lesions of minimal bone deposition.

Like Burial 1, this skeleton exhibits differential burning patterns. The cranium is bright blue and gray, indicating incomplete combustion of the bone, while the postcranial bone is completely calcined. Here again it appears that the skull was partially sheltered from the full effect of the cremation, possibly by its location on the pyre.

Pottery

The pottery from Grave 3 was composed of over 636 fragments weighing at least 4.17 kg. Most of these (87%) were fine or medium-coarse wares that were restored as 20 identifiable vessels; fragments of coarse, cooking, and pithos wares comprised the remainder, probably to be interpreted as "background noise"—that is, vessels that were in the soil or stones when the grave was constructed or filled in. The majority of the vessels can be associated with a particular burial, either because of their location or because of the presence or absence of burning. Burial 1 seems to have been richer in pottery, which included those vessels found along the north side and in the northwest corner: five cups (**GR3 P1**, **GR3 P3**, **GR3 P8**, **GR3 P11**, **GR3 P13**), three skyphoi (**GR3 P9**, **GR3 P10**, **GR3 P17**), a bowl (**GR3 P20**), a tray (**GR3 P16**), two aryballoi (**GR3 P14**, **GR3 P15**), a miniature jar (**GR3 P5**), and a bead (**GR3 TC1**). Many of these vessels show signs of burning after breaking, a fact that also supports their association with the earlier burial. The material from the deposit in the southeast corner belongs with the second cremation, including the cup (**GR3 P19**) and flask (**GR3 P18**), along with the drinking cups (**GR3 P2**, **GR3 P6**, **GR3 P7**) and wide-mouthed jug (**GR3 P4**) found above them; these two groups may represent two different ritual occasions. Other objects associated with this burial include a cup or skyphos (**GR3 P12**), a bronze pin (**GR3 M1**), a bronze earring (**GR3 M2**), and an iron pin (**GR3 M3**). In addition to the pottery associated with the burials, there were also some fragments of LM IIIC vessels from the period of the settlement, including a stand, a pithos base, a cooking dish rim, and the handle of a cooking pot.

Objects

Associated with Burial 1 was the terracotta incised bead (**GR3 TC1**). There were no other objects that belonged with the burial, and it is unusual to find a male burial without iron weapons or tools. This lack of weapons and tools may be a result of lower wealth or social status of the individual, or it may have to do with the social perception of this individual due to the possible hormone deficiencies and associated pathology. While beads would seem more appropriate to female rather than male burials, it does not seem to have been the case in the Vronda cemetery where beads are found with both male and female burials. Burial 2 was richer in metal objects, including the bronze pin (**GR3 M1**), iron pin (**GR3 M3**), and bronze earring (**GR3 M2**). Pins are often assumed to belong with female burials, and the evidence from this burial at least tends to support this association. The earring is similar to examples found by Boyd in Tholos VII (Boyd 1901, 136, fig. 3).

Chronology

Although in general the ceramic material from Grave 3 looks relatively early in the sequence of the enclosure burials, one vessel from the first burial (**GR3 P8**) finds parallels in the EO period, suggesting a date early in EO for the two burials. The pottery consists chiefly of cups, mostly undecorated, generally of the rather thick-walled variety found in Grave 9 (see below), but without the heavy bases found in that grave, a fact that suggests that Grave 3 was later than Grave 9. The pottery from Burial 1 includes the panel cup (**GR3 P3**), similar to examples in Graves 6 and 16, so some of the pottery from the first burial in this grave may belong to the same phase of the LG period. Although this shape has MPG parallels at Knossos, most of the vessels suggest a LG date. Mug-like cup **GR3 P1** is a most unusual shape, but there are general similarities in what are labeled wide-mouthed jugs from LG Hagios Georgios and those called cups with straight neck walls from EG Eleutherna; the decoration of dotted loops is common on LG pottery from other tombs in East Crete. The monochrome skyphos **GR3 P10** is similar in shape to LG examples from the Plai tou Kastrou tomb at Kavousi, while skyphos **GR3 P9** has parallels of both LG and EO date. One of the aryballoi (**GR3 P14**) resembles an EG example from Knossos but also LG aryballoi from East Crete and Eleutherna.

From the second burial, cup **GR3 P2** resembles monochrome cups from Knossos of MG date and from East Crete of LG date. The barred handle, however, has parallels at Knossos, where it first appears on an Attic MG I import and on other MG cups. The three cups deposited in the southeast corner are similar in shape and capacity. This second burial seems to have been made within the same pottery phase as Burial 1.

Catalog

Pottery

Fine Decorated Wares

GR3 P1 (V87.35, IM 963; VW 18104/18203.1, pot 5A; Fig. 45; Pl. 23). Mug-like cup. Restored from many fragments, with 80% preserved, including full profile, most of base and rim, and handle; missing bits of base, body, and rim. H. 9.5–10.0; d. rim 10.7; d. base 4.8. Fine, porous, chalky, pink (7.5YR 7/4–8/4) fabric with small gray and red phyllites. Red (2.5YR 5/8) paint. Surfaces very well preserved in places, worn in others. No burning, but edges worn near the handle. Decorated with vertical stripes on rim, upright dotted loops on body; handle barred; underside of base painted. *Bibliography*: Gesell, Day, and Coulson 1988, fig. 6:4. *Comparanda*: for shape, Tsipopoulou 2005, 133, fig. 90:AN2381 (Hagios Georgios, LG); Kotsonas 2008, 212–214, fig. 52:A169 (Eleutherna, EG); for decoration, Tsipopoulou 2005, 90, fig. 9 (Kavousi, LG); 189, fig. 108:Σ4074 (Hagios Georgios, LG). *Date*: LG.

GR3 P2 (V87.92; VW 18104/18203.1, pot 1B; Fig. 45). Cup. Partially mended from 12 fragments; two nonjoining fragments from rim. Preservation 50%, including full profile, entire base, half of rim, and handle; missing half of body and rim. H. 8.4; d. rim 12.0; d. base 5.2. Fine, hard, light red (10R 6/4) fabric. Brown (7.5YR 4/4) to black paint. Well-preserved surfaces, but worn paint. Some burned fragments. Handle decorated with oblique stripes. *Bibliography*: Gesell, Day, and Coulson 1988, 294–295, fig. 6:2, 3 (later joined). *Comparanda*: Coldstream 1972, 95–96, fig. 15:G105 (Knossos, MG); Tsipopoulou 2005, 181, fig. 125:Σ4037 (Hagios Georgios, LG); for barred handle, Coldstream 1972, 82–83, pl. 21:D30 (Knossos, MG); Coldstream and Catling, eds., 1996, 37, fig. 68:18 (Knossos, Attic MG I import). *Date*: LG.

GR3 P3 (VW 18104/18203.1, pot 5B; Fig. 45; Pl. 23). Cup. Partially mended from 10 fragments. Preservation 60%, including full profile, much of rim, and one handle; missing most of base. H. 7.2; d. rim 13.0; d. base est. 5.4. Fine, soft, rather porous, pink (7.5YR 7/6) fabric with black inclusions. Petrographic sample KAV 15/37:

Fabric Subgroup 1b. Very pale brown (10YR 8/2) slip. Red (2.5YR 5/6) paint. Some well-preserved surfaces, others very worn. Panel with zigzag. Horizontal stripes on handle. *Comparanda*: **GR16 P14**; Brock 1957, 58, pl. 38:622 (Knossos, EPG or MPG); Boardman 1960, 134, 137, fig. 5:V.20 (Hagios Ioannis, MPG). *Date*: G.

GR3 P4 (V87.92, IM 974; VW 18104/18203.1 pots 1C, 5, 6, VW 18108/18204.2; Fig. 45; Pl. 23). Wide-mouthed jug. Restored from 27 fragments. Preservation 70%, including full profile, most of base, 20% of rim, and handle; missing center of base, 80% of rim. H. 9.1; d. rim 5.0; d. base 4.6. Fine, very soft, pink (7.5YR 8/4) fabric with laminating surfaces; discolored from burning to light gray (10YR 7/1). Red (10R 5/6) paint. Rather worn surfaces. Oblique strokes on shoulder. Handle solidly coated. *Bibliography*: Gesell, Day, and Coulson 1988, 294–295, fig. 6:6. *Comparanda*: for decoration, Tsipopoulou 2005, 273, fig. 67:AN1595 (Praisos, LG). *Date*: LG.

GR3 P5 (V87.43, IM 926; VW 18104/18203.2 pot 8A, VW 18104/18203.1; Fig. 45; Pl. 23). Miniature necked jar. Restored from 15 fragments. Preservation 80%, including full profile, most of base, rim, and handles; missing large fragment of lower body. H. 6.5; d. rim 6.9; d. base 4.0. Fine, soft, reddish-yellow (5YR 7/6) to light gray (10YR 7/1) fabric with some soft inclusions. Shadow of black(?) paint. Very worn surfaces. Many fragments discolored from fire. Oblique strokes in handle zone. *Bibliography*: Gesell, Day, and Coulson 1988, 294–296, fig. 6:8. *Comparanda*: **GR36 P8**; **IX P7**; Coldstream and Catling, eds., 1996, 17, fig. 60:41 (Knossos, PGB–EG, for decoration); 48, fig. 71:52 (Knossos, LG); Tsipopoulou 2005, 309, fig. 62:Σ4013 (Sklavoi, LG). *Date*: LG.

Fine Monochrome Wares

GR3 P6 (V87.134, IM 975; VW 18104/18203.1 pots 6 and 1A, VW 18104/18203.1; Fig. 45; Pl. 23). Cup. Restored from 15 fragments. Preservation 40%, including most of upper body and rim, lower handle attachment; base restored, missing most of lower body and handle. H. 8.3–8.5; d. rim 12.5; d. base 6.0. Fine, rather hard, reddish-yellow (7.5YR 6/6) fabric. Thick, creamy, red (10R 4/6–2.5YR 4/8) paint. Well-preserved surfaces, worn in places. No burning. Heavy ridging on interior bottom. *Date*: LG.

GR3 P7 (VW 18102.1, VW 18104/18203.1 pots 1, 4, and 5, VW 18108/18204.2 pot 5; Fig. 45). Cup. Partially mended from 26 fragments; four nonjoining fragments. Preservation 55%, including full profile and handle; missing most of rim. H. 8.5; d. rim 11.0; d. base 6.2. Fine, soft, reddish-yellow (5YR 7/6) fabric with light greenish-gray (5GY 7/1) core. Red (2.5YR 5/8) paint. Worn surfaces. Some fragments burned. *Comparanda*: **GR5 P4**, **GR9 P16**; Brock 1957, 167, pl. 76:1131 (Knossos, LG–EO). *Date*: LG.

GR3 P8 (VW 18104/18203.1, VW 18104/18203.1 pots 5, 6, and 8, VW 18108/18204.1; Fig. 45). Cup. Thirty-five fragments from rim and body; possible handle fragment. Max. pres. h. 6.0; d. rim est. 10.0. Fine, very soft, chalky, white (10YR 8/1) fabric. Black paint. Very worn surfaces. Some fragments burned. *Comparanda*: **GR12 P32**; Brock 1957, 127, 167, pl. 103:1460 (Knossos, O); Tsipopoulou 2005, 245, fig. 130:H2005 (Praisos, EO). *Date*: LG–EO.

GR3 P9 (V87.36, IM 925; VW 18104/18203.1, VW 18104/18203.1 pot 5, VW 18104/18203.2 pot 8B, VW 18104/18203.3, VW 18108/18204.4; Fig. 45; Pl. 23). Skyphos. Restored from numerous fragments. Preservation 95%; missing a few bits from rim and body. H. 5.8–6.0; d. rim 12.5; d. base 5.5. Fine, soft, very pale brown (10YR 8/3) fabric, burned to gray (5Y 6/1). Black paint. Very worn surfaces. Burned. *Bibliography*: Gesell, Day, and Coulson 1988, fig. 6:5. *Comparanda*: Brock 1957, 66, pl.45:723 (Knossos, EO); Tsipopoulou 2005, 193, fig.114:Σ4097 (Hagios Georgios, LG). *Date*: LG.

GR3 P10 (VW 18104/18203.1, VW 18104/18203.1 pots 3, 4, 5, 6B, 8, VW 18104/18203 NW; Fig. 45; Pl. 23). Skyphos. Mended from 64 fragments. Preservation 80%–85%, including full profile, most of base, and both handles; missing parts of body, rim, and handles. H. 9.0; d. rim 14.4; d. base 5.8. Fine, soft, reddish-yellow (5YR 6/6) fabric. Petrographic sample KAV 15/36: Fabric Group 7. Red (2.5YR 5/8) paint. Painted interior, exterior, and underside of base. Worn surfaces. Burned and unburned fragments. *Comparanda*: Tsipopoulou 2005, 102, fig. 115:H748 (Kavousi, Plai tou Kastrou, LG). *Date*: LG.

GR3 P11 (VW 18102.1, VW 18104/18203.1 and 3, VW 18104/18203 NW, VW 18108/18204.1, VW 18108/18204.2 pot 5; Fig. 45). Cup or skyphos. Partially mended from 27 fragments, preserving 60% of rim and upper body; missing base and handle. Max. pres. h. 7.2; d. rim 14.0. Fine, soft, light reddish-brown (5YR 6/4) fabric. Black paint. Very worn surface. Discolored from burning. Ridge below rim. *Date*: LG.

GR3 P12 (VW 18108/18204.1, pot 4B; Fig. 45). Cup or skyphos. Partially mended from five fragments. Preservation 10% from rim and upper body; missing base and handle. Max. pres. h. 6.0; d. rim 13.3. Fine, soft, yellow (10YR 7/6) to gray (2.5Y 6/1) fabric. Black paint. Very worn surfaces. Burned, some fragments more than others. *Date*: LG.

GR3 P13 (VW 18104/18203.1, VW 18104/18203.1 pot 8; Fig. 45). Cup or skyphos. Three large fragments from rim and upper body (six sherds); missing base and handle. Max. pres. h. 5.7; d. rim 11.0. Fine, soft, pink (7.5YR 7/4) fabric with tiny red phyllite inclusions. Red (10R 4/6) paint. Very worn surfaces. Boss on shoulder. *Date*: LG.

Fine Plain Wares

GR3 P14 (VW 18104/18203.1, VW 18104/18203.1 pot 5; Fig. 46; Pl. 23). Aryballos. Partially mended from 23 fragments; four nonjoining fragments. Preservation 80%, including nearly full profile, entire base, handle; missing rim and much of neck. H. 6.7; d. base 3.2. Fine, soft, light brown (7.5YR 6/4) fabric, entirely burned. Very worn surfaces. *Comparanda*: Coldstream and Catling, eds., 1996, 254, pl. 231:286.1, 4 (Knossos, EG); Tsipopoulou 2005, 306, fig. 100:Σ3985 (Sklavoi, LG); Kotsonas 2008, 179–180, fig. 43:A98β (Eleutherna, LG). *Date*: LG.

GR3 P15 (VW 18104/18203.1, pot 9; Fig. 46; Pl. 23). Aryballos. Partially mended from 21 fragments. Preservation 85%, including base, rim, and handle; missing large fragment from body. H. 7.6; d. rim 2.2; d. base 3.3. Fine, soft, reddish-yellow (5YR 7/6) fabric. Very pale brown (10YR 8/2) slip. Very worn surfaces, much discolored. Interior uniform dark gray. Edges are very worn. Unusual ovoid shape. *Bibliography*: Gesell, Day, and Coulson 1988, 295–296, fig. 6:9. *Date*: LG.

Medium-Coarse Decorated Wares

GR3 P16 (V87.34, IM 924; VW 18104/18203.1 pot 5, VW 18104/18203 NW, VW 18104/18203.2 pot 6A; Fig. 46; Pl. 23). Small tray with reflex-type lugs. Restored from 12 fragments. Preservation 95%; missing tiny piece of base and tip of one handle. H. 3.4; d. rim (int.) 9.3–9.7; d. base 8.5. Medium-coarse, reddish-yellow (5YR 6/6) fabric with large phyllite inclusions. Very pale brown (10YR 8/3) slip. Brown (7.5YR 4/4) paint. Very worn surfaces. One handle with worn edges, surface flaked off. Oblique lines in metopal panel on side. *Bibliography*: Gesell, Day, and Coulson 1988, 295–296, fig. 6:7. *Comparanda*: Brock 1957, 81, pl. 58:890 (Knossos, LG); Kotsonas 2008, 222–224, fig. 55:A117β (Eleutherna, MG–LG). *Date*: LG.

GR3 P17 (VW 18102.1, VW 18104/18203.1 pots 1, 4, and 5, VW 18104/18203.1 NW, VW 18108/18204.2 pot 5; Fig. 46; Pl. 23). Skyphos. Partially mended from 16 fragments; three nonjoining fragments. Preservation 25%, including nearly complete profile and handle attachment; missing most of base and handle(s). H. 14.5; d. rim 17.5; d. base 6.0. Medium-coarse, reddish-yellow (5YR 7/6) to gray (5Y 6/1) fabric with red phyllites and quartz. Petrographic sample KAV 15/35: Fabric Subgroup 1a. Pink (7.5YR 7/4) slip. Dark reddish-brown (2.5YR 3/4) paint. Worn surfaces. Burned fragments join with unburned ones. Crosshatched butterfly motifs, four in preserved area. *Comparanda*: for shape, Coldstream and Catling, eds., 1996, 36, fig. 68:12 (Knossos, LPG–EG); Kotsonas 2008, 185–186, fig. 44:A209 (Eleutherna PGB–EG); for decoration, Hallager and Hallager, eds., 1997, 51, pl. 108:71-P 0242a (Chania, LG I early); Hayden 2003, 50, fig. 25:110 (Vrokastro, PG–LPG or later PGB); Tsipopoulou 2005, 87, fig. 104:H694 (Kavousi, Plai tou Kastrou, LG); this may be a more popular motif at Kavousi than elsewhere in Crete at this period. *Date*: LG.

GR3 P18 (V87.32, IM 874; VW 18104/18203.1, pot 3; Fig. 46; Pl. 24A). Flask. Restored. Nearly intact except for part of rim. H. 11.8; d. rim 3.5. Medium-coarse, rather porous, pink (7.5YR 7/4) fabric with hard white and black inclusions. Black paint. Worn and pocked surfaces. No burning. Horizontal bands on shoulder. Rounded bottom. *Bibliography*: Gesell, Day, and Coulson 1988, 294–295, fig. 6:10, pl. 81:d. *Comparanda*: Rethemiotakis and Englezou 2010, 43–44, fig. 22:41, 42 (Eltyna, MPG–LPG). *Date*: LG.

Medium-Coarse Monochrome Wares

GR3 P19 (V87.33, IM 875; VW 18104/18203.1, pot 2; Fig. 46; Pl. 24A). Cup. Intact except for chip in rim. H. 9.4; d. rim 13.2; d. base 5.7. Medium-coarse, soft, reddish-yellow (7.5YR 6/6) fabric with hard white, black, and red inclusions. Black paint fired to red on interior; underside of base painted. Worn surfaces. *Bibliography*: Gesell, Day, and Coulson 1988, 294–295, fig. 6:1, pl. 81:c. *Comparanda*: **IX P33**; Coldstream and Catling, eds., 1996, 29, fig. 65:48 (Knossos, LPG). *Date*: LG.

GR3 P20 (V87.135, IM 973; VW 18104/18203.1, pot 5B; Fig. 46; Pl. 24A). Conical bowl. Restored from two fragments. Preservation 25%, including full profile; missing handle(s). H. 7.75–8.00; d. rim 18.00; d. base 6.30. Medium-coarse, soft, dark reddish-yellow (7.5YR 7/8) fabric with small red phyllites. Black to red (2.5YR 5/8) paint. Very worn surfaces. No burning. *Comparanda*: **GR16 P22**; Tsipopoulou 2005, 293, pl. 470; fig. 132: AN8786 (Praisos, LG); 2013, 153, fig. 13:12282 (Piskokephalo, LG). *Date*: LG.

Metal

Bronze

GR3 M1 (V87.93, IM 899, HNM 15732; VW 18108/18204.2, object 1; Fig. 46; Pl. 24A). Bronze pin. Intact; missing top. L. 7.60; d. 0.03. Well preserved, but slightly bent toward end. Three globular beads near top. Tapers to point. *Bibliography*: Gesell, Day, and Coulson 1988, pl. 81:a.

GR3 M2 (V87.137, IM 978; VW 18108/18204, object 2; Fig. 46; Pl. 24A). Bronze earring. Complete in five fragments. D. 3.300; th. 0.015. Well preserved; ends slightly bent. Irregular loop of thin bronze wire, tapering at both ends. *Bibliography*: Gesell, Day, and Coulson 1988, pl. 81:b. *Comparanda*: Coldstream and Catling, eds., 1996, 218, fig. 167:219.f 21 (Knossos, PG–O).

Iron

GR3 M3 (V87.105, IM 945; VW 18108/18204, object 3; Fig. 46; Pl. 24A). Iron pin. Four joining fragments preserving the entire length. Max. pres. L. 12.0. Very corroded, with corrosion bubbles. Long pin with three globular swellings near top, separated by rings; the central swelling is the largest, the two on either side are smaller.

Stone

GR3 ST1 (V87.13, IM 852; VW 18104/18203.4). Possible tool. Cobble, oblong flat, fragment. L. 6.9; w. 4.1; th. 2.2. Wt. 125.0 g. Crystalline limestone, gray. Pecked one end?

Terracotta

GR3 TC1 (V87.21, IM 860; VW18014/18203, object 7; Fig. 46; Pl. 24A). Terracotta bead. Tall biconical. Intact except for a few chips. H. 2.1; max. d. 2.2; d. hole 0.5; wt. 6.0 g. Fine, rather hard, reddish-yellow (5YR 7/6) fabric. Very pale brown (10YR 8/3) slip. Burned on one side, surface cracked and melted. Incised decoration: incised strokes radiating from top and bottom to center. No wheel marks. Hole larger on one end than other. *Comparanda*: Hall 1914, 122, fig. 73 (Vrokastro); Brock 1957, 207, no. 109, pl. 173:e (Knossos, SM–EPG); Karageorghis 1983, fig. 165:T. 82:13 (Palaepaphos-*Skales*, CG IB–II); Sackett, ed., 1992, 412, pl. 329:12 (Knossos).

Grave 4

History and Details of Excavation

Grave 4 lies on the west side of the summit of the Vronda ridge in Room D3 of the LM IIIC Building D, very close to Grave 5 and the associated discard deposit known as Grave 11, and not far from Grave 36 (Figs. 3, 4; see below). It was one of the first graves encountered in the 1987 excavation season (Gesell, Day, and Coulson 1988, 283–285). Grave 4, along with Graves 5 and 11, was excavated in Trench V 4000. Much fine pottery was scattered in the upper layers of the trench (V 4001), and it belonged to both graves; assigning the fragments from the upper layers to the appropriate grave has been difficult because of disturbance in the area. After the walls of the LM IIIC Building C appeared just below the surface, they served to divide the material from the two graves; the west side of the LM IIIC house wall (V 4002/V 11901), first recognized as V 4003, contained Grave 4. Aside from some spills of material or dumps from the enclosure, all of Grave 4 was excavated in 1987.

Architecture

Grave 4 may once have been a rectangular enclosure, but the western boundary had eroded away without a trace because of the slope of the terrain. Considerable erosion or human activity had uncovered the area almost to bedrock. The burial space measured 0.75 m north–south × ca. 0.75–0.78 m east–west (Fig. 47). The cremators used existing house walls of the earlier Room D3 of LM IIIC Building D on the north, east, and south; they may have felt it unnecessary to add a fourth wall, especially if wall tumble served as a boundary on the west. The north wall (V 4504) stood four courses high, the east wall (V 4502/V 11901) three courses, and the south wall (V 4005/V 12401) two courses. One of the bedrock boulders on the east wall was calcined white from the heat of the pyre, and one of the boulders at the bottom was also calcined, suggesting that the pyre was placed on top of it. The floor of the grave was a layer of roofing clay from the earlier building, with some flat paving stones that probably also came from the collapse of its roof. The floor lay just above bedrock, and spurs of the bedrock projected through it.

Stratigraphy

Because of the slope of the hill and the protection afforded by the east wall of Buildings C and D, the deposition was greater than usual in parts of Grave 4. Along the east wall (V 4502), a spine wall that served as a house wall for the earlier Buildings C and D, the deposition measured approximately 0.70 m, thinning to 0.63 m toward the west, and at the far west it was only about 0.05 m. The builders dug down to a layer of roofing clay with small flat stones from the earlier building for the grave. The lowest layer (V 4011, V 4010), a layer of brown to yellowish-brown (10YR 5/3–5/4) soil, included grave objects but no human remains. The lowest burial remains were in V 4009, a layer of grayish-brown (10YR 5/2), ashy soil that contained fragments of all individuals in the grave. Above this layer was another layer of soft ashy soil with many snail shells and a few human bones, all from the same individuals (V 4004). Some human bones appeared also in V 4003, the stone tumble over the entire area west of the Building D house wall, and much pottery was found in this layer and the topsoil above it (V 4000, V 4001). Of particular interest were two cups, one large (**GR4 13**) and the other small (**GR4 17**), set in a niche or shelf in the east wall amid the stone tumble of V 4003.

There was little evidence of ancient disturbance in the lower levels of Grave 4, an unusual situation in comparison with other graves at Vronda. While it is possible that all of the individuals in the grave were placed there in a single burial event, a number of vessels show burning after breakage, suggesting that there were two burial events: a pregnant woman first, and then an infant. Some grave material spilled over the south wall into V 4006, and when Trench V 4500 was opened to the north of V 4000 in 1990, some remains from Grave 4 were also encountered in V 4502 and V 4506.2, but these probably represent surface disturbance postdating ancient times.

Associated Features

The niche in the east wall of the grave was used for the placement of two cups, probably after the cremation was over, as they show no sign of burning. Perhaps these cups are comparable to the cup and flask set in the tumble above Grave 3 (see above, p. 62). Aside from spills down the slope to the south, west, and north, there were no associated features, and there was no apparent dumping of material from the grave at a later time. As there were at most two burial events, the lack of dumping is not unexpected.

Burials

Grave 4 contained the skeletons of an adolescent to young adult female, a fetus, and an infant.

Burial 1

Type: disturbed primary cremation
Age: adolescent, 15–20 years
Sex: female
Weight: 606 g

Burial 1 is the fragmentary partial skeleton of an adolescent woman. The preserved epiphyseal fragments are fused, and the roots of the mandibular third molar are only half formed, indicating an age of 15–20 years at death (Scheuer and Black 2000, 159–161). There is an area of slight cribra orbitalia in the right eye orbit, probably reflecting anemia during childhood, but no other evidence of pathological conditions. The cremation of the bone is mixed, with most of the bone somewhat calcined and no evidence of differential burning between the cranial and postcranial bone.

Burial 2

Type: disturbed primary cremation
Age: fetus, 20 weeks
Sex: unknown
Weight: not recorded

This is a fragmentary partial skeleton of a fetus, approximately 20 weeks in utero (Pl. 24B). The remains are very limited, but portions of the cranial base are sufficiently preserved to allow estimation of age. The bone is nearly all calcined.

Burial 3

Type: disturbed primary cremation
Age: infant, 12–14 months
Sex: unknown
Weight: 91 g

This is a fragmentary skeleton of an infant, approximately one year of age (Pl. 24C). The age was determined on the basis of the size and development of the crypts for unerupted teeth in the right half of the mandible. These appear to be consistent with the dental development of an infant (Scheuer and Black 2000, 154). The bone is all white and completely calcined.

Faunal Remains

With the exception of four small, unidentifiable bone fragments from the lowest part of the grave (V 4009.1), none of the animal bone from the area of Grave 4 was burned or calcined (Table 4). Identifiable animal bones recovered include two very well-preserved and possibly modern, intrusive rabbit elements (a mandible and juvenile right tibia diaphysis segment), as well as a pig right proximal ulna segment that was unburned and showed root etching, indicating deposition near the surface. Lower limb bones of sheep or goat, also unburned, include a proximal metacarpal fragment, three hind limb elements, and a single proximal phalange (foot bone).

Pottery

Some 920 fragments of pottery weighing 3.53 kg were collected from within Grave 4, and an additional 70 fragments weighing 1.78 kg came from the area immediately to the west. Within the grave, fine and medium-coarse wares accounted for 99% of the fragments by count, while in the west they were only 56% of the total, a fact that probably reflects the greater amount of earlier material from the settlement mixed in on the west. The pottery from Grave 4 is highly unusual both in the large quantity of decorated fine ware and in the date of the pottery, which is nearly all Orientalizing. An unusually large number of small closed containers were found, including at least five aryballoi (possibly six) and three lekythoi. At least three of these aryballoi (**GR4 P4–GR4 P6**) were of the spherical type with concentric circles on the shoulder (Tsipopoulou 2005, 407, fig. 97:AN2365, H719, H720, H3199) and one (**GR4 P3**) was a Creto-Cypriot type of the EO period (Coldstream and Catling, eds., 1996, 446; Tsipopoulou 2005, 407, fig. 98:AN1410, AN1412). In addition to the cataloged pottery, there were also fragments of two more small jugs or aryballoi, one highly polished and the other of a soft gray fabric with thick red paint on the exterior. Fragments of another tiny aryballos seem to be of a different fabric from all the known examples. The aryballoi may have held perfumed oil, appropriate as grave offerings for a young woman and a child. The presence of the small cups may also be connected with the infant in the grave. The lekythos (**GR4 P20**) is of the Praisos type, common in LG–EO Knossos (Coldstream 1996, 355), and there are fragments of a possible second one of similar fabric.

There were probably two pyxides of almost identical shape (**GR4 P8**, **GR4 P9**), one decorated with concentric circles, the other perhaps with short vertical strokes. They are of similar shape and have parallels of EO and LO date at Knossos (Brock 1957, pl. 84:1257, 1264, 1267, 1270, 1278, 1294, 1328; Coldstream and Catling, eds., 1996, 8, pl. 48:9). The fact that the Knossos vessels have circles in added white on their broad black panels suggests that the panels on these pyxides may also once have been decorated with added white. Lid **GR4 P24**, with its decoration in added white, finds many parallels in the LG–EO periods at Knossos (see below). Lids seem to occur in graves with pyxides, and this lid may have fit over one of the two.

Of great interest are two unusual shapes: a large mug-like cup with tall rim (**GR4 P1**) and a krater (**GR4 P16**). While the rim diameter of **GR4 P16** makes it technically too small to be considered a krater, it is larger than any other drinking vessel found in the graves (5.375 L) and does not fit into any other category. It is a unique shape for the Vronda assemblage, with its rolled rim and two round vertical handles. It has a parallel from EO Arkades (Levi 1927–1929, 142, fig. 137); an oil separation jar from Azoria (Haggis et al. 2007b, 277, 279, fig. 26.1) of the Archaic period is also similar in shape, although not in function. The shape of the mug-like cup (**GR4 P1**) is reminiscent of EO cups from Knossos (Coldstream and Catling, eds., 1996, 71, fig. 76:3), but it is unusual for its decoration of leaves on the body. The leaves, however, have a parallel at Knossos of PGB–EG date (Coldstream and Catling, eds., 1996, 6, fig. 58:31). The large monochrome cup (**GR4 P13**) found in stones by the wall has a similar rim profile to the mug, and this rim type finds parallels at EO Knossos on a deeper monochrome cup with a taller lip (Coldstream and Catling, eds., 1996, 64, fig. 75:9).

The pithos fragments (**GR4 P25**) may belong with the grave assemblage. Although the Kavousi Type X/XI fabric is common in the LM IIIC settlement, the decoration of incised spirals on a raised band is not attested elsewhere at Vronda in LM IIIC. A good parallel can be found at Geometric Phaistos (Rocchetti 1974–1975, 252, fig. 114:9). Grave 36 also produced a pithos fragment with an incised tree pattern (**GR36 P18**; see below, p. 207), suggesting that such pieces, whether contemporary with the burial or fragments left over from earlier periods, may have been deposited deliberately with the dead.

Objects

There were few objects in the grave. The two bronze pins (**GR4 M1**, **GR4 M2**) were found close together and were probably a set used to hold together a garment or shroud for the deceased or for decoration. The bead (**GR4 TC1**) could have been decorative, or it may have functioned as a more utilitarian spindle whorl.

Chronology

The pottery suggests that Grave 4 is one of the latest on the Vronda site. Most of the vessels are EO in date, with few LG pieces, and some date to the LO period. The small aryballoi are certainly of EO date. The skyphos **GR4 P15** is similar to a LO kotyle at Knossos, a shape that first evolved in Corinth at the transition to LG and came to Crete later (Coldstream and Catling, eds., 1996, 384). The shapes of the cup (**GR4 P13**) and mug-like cup (**GR4 P1**), with crisply distinguished necks, are likely to be late in the seventh century. The skyphos **GR4 P2** may be an example of a so-called Ionian cup, a shape that began in the third quarter of the seventh century and continued into the Archaic period (Catling and Shipley 1989, 188–190, fig. 1a; Schlotzhauer 2000, 411–412, figs. 297, 298). The lack of much material of the LG period, along with the presence of shapes that can only belong at the earliest to the late seventh century, indicates that the burials were made in the LO period.

Catalog

Pottery

Fine Decorated Wares

GR4 P1 (V87.90; V 4001.5, V 4004.1 and 2, V 4004.4, V 4006.2, V 4009.1 and 2, V 4010.1, V 4011.2, V 4502.1; Fig. 48; Pl. 25). Mug-like cup. Restored from 80 fragments. Preservation 80%, including full profile, 85% of base, 95% of rim, handle; missing 30% of body. H. 14.8; d. rim 12.3; d. base 6.0. Fine, light reddish-brown (2.5YR 6/4) fabric, hard and clinky in some fragments, soft in others, slightly porous with some gold mica inclusions. Petrographic sample KAV 15/39: Fabric Group 7. Pink (7.5YR 7/4) slip. Dark brown (7.5YR 3/2) paint. Worn surfaces. Some fragments burned, with decoration turned to negative, the slip black and the paint light in color. Running quirk on neck, wavy line on shoulder, leaf pattern on upper body. Very crisp profile, with tall rim and torus ring base. *Bibliography*: Gesell, Day, and Coulson 1988, 284–285, fig. 2:8, emended. *Comparanda*: Rocchetti 1974–1975, 221–222, fig. 76:b (Phaistos, G); Callaghan and Johnston 2000, 237, pl. 4.10:241 (Kommos, EO); Tsipopoulou 2005, 179, pl. 264 (Hagios Georgios, LG). *Date*: EO.

GR4 P2 (V 4001.3, V 4002.1, V 4004.4; Fig. 48). Skyphos. Partially mended from 12 fragments, with two nonjoining. Preservation 10%, including parts of rim and both handles. Max. pres. h. 4.5; d. rim 18.0. Fine, rather hard, very pale brown (10YR 7/4) fabric. Black paint. Decoration of bands. *Comparanda*: Tsipopoulou 2004, 132, 139, fig. 6:01/133/9 (Chalasmenos, LG); 2005, 158, fig 119:AN1364 (Praisos, O). *Date*: LG–EO.

GR4 P3 (V87.69, IM 964; V 4009.1 object 1; Fig. 48). Creto-Cypriot lekythos or aryballos. Partially mended from a large fragment and several smaller ones. Preservation 25%, including entire base and 10% of body; missing rim, neck, and much of handle. Max. pres. h. 8.2; d. base 2.8. Fine, laminating, soft, porous, very pale brown (10YR 7/3–7/4) fabric. Very pale brown (10YR 8/4) slip. Black paint. Polished surface. Not burned, but rather overall gray in color. Concentric circles. *Bibliography*: Gesell, Day, and Coulson 1988, 284–285, fig. 2:5. *Comparanda*: **GR17 P2**; Lebessi 1970, 283, pl. 396γ:50 (Mastambas, EO); Tsipopoulou 2005, 265, fig. 98:AN 1410, AN1412 (Praisos, EO); Kotsonas 2008, 179, 181–182, fig. 43:A123α (Eleutherna, LG–EO). *Date*: EO.

GR4 P4 (V 4003.2, V 4004.1; Fig. 48). Aryballos. Partially mended from 17 fragments. Preservation 25%, including entire base, much of body, half of handle, and rim. H. est. 7.8; d. rim 2.4; d. base 3.2. Fine, porous, reddish-yellow (7.5YR 7/6) fabric with small voids. Very pale brown (10YR 8/3) slip. Fugitive paint, probably once red. Very worn surfaces. No burning. Small concentric circles on shoulder. *Bibliography*: Gesell, Day, and Coulson 1988, 284–285, fig. 2:3, emended. *Comparanda*: **GR4 P5, GR4 P6**; Coldstream and Catling, eds., 1996, 114, pl. 121:89, 90 (Knossos, EO); Tsipopoulou 2005, 96, fig. 97:H719 (Kavousi, Plai tou Kastro, LG–EO). *Date*: EO.

GR4 P5 (V 4004.2; Fig. 49). Aryballos. Partially mended from 15 fragments, with 15 tiny nonjoining fragments. Preservation 30%, including base and shoulder; missing rim and handle. Max. pres. h. 2.5; d. base 1.9. Very fine, porous, reddish-yellow (7.5YR 6/6) fabric. Pink (7.5YR 7/4) slip. Dark brown (7.5YR 3/2) paint. Fabric has laminated, and surface has flaked off. Some discoloration due to fire. Small concentric circles on shoulder. *Comparanda*: **GR4 P4, GR4 P6**; Tsipopoulou 2005, 96, fig. 97:H720 (Kavousi, Plai tou Kastrou, LG–EO); 156, fig. 97:AN2365 (Hagios Georgios, EO). *Date*: EO.

GR4 P6 (V 4004.1, 2; Fig. 49). Aryballos. Partially mended from seven fragments; five nonjoining fragments. Preservation 40%, including entire base, much of shoulder, and handle attachment; missing neck and rim. Max. pres. h. 5.7; d. base 2.8. Fine, soft, rather porous reddish-yellow (7.5YR 6/6) fabric. Reddish-yellow (7.5YR 7/6) slip. Dark brown (7.5YR 3/2) paint. Many fragments burned; one has worn edges. Small, twofold concentric circles on shoulder; two groups of three bands on body; bands at base. *Bibliography*: Gesell, Day, and Coulson 1998, 284–285, fig. 2:4, emended. *Comparanda*: **GR4 P4, GR4 P5**; Stampolides 1996, 65, fig. 125; 66, fig. 127 (Eleutherna LG–EO); Hayden 2003, 74, no. 205, fig. 47, pl. 31 (Vrokastro LG–EO); Tsipopoulou 2005, 96, fig. 97:H719 (Kavousi, Plai tou Kastrou, LG–EO). *Date*: EO.

GR4 P7 (V87.84, IM 966; V 4001.2, V 4003.2, V 4004.1 and 2; Fig. 49). Lekythos. Partially mended from five fragments of neck and five nonjoining body fragments; missing rim, handle, base, and most of body. Max. pres. h. 5.5. Fine, soft, rather porous, very pale brown (10YR 7/3) fabric with tiny black inclusions. Lustrous reddish-brown (5YR 4/4) paint. Well-preserved surfaces. Possibly a Praisos-type lekythos. Multiple zigzags on neck, concentric circles on shoulder. *Bibliography*: Gesell, Day, and Coulson 1988, 284–285, fig. 2:2, emended. *Date*: EO.

GR4 P8 (V 4001.1–5, V 4002.1, V 4003.2, V 4004.4, V 4006.2; Fig. 49; Pl. 25). Pyxis. Partially mended from 77 fragments. Preservation 20%, including fragment near base, rim, handles, and pieces of body; full profile can be restored but base and connections missing. Max. pres. h. 7.0; d. rim (int.) 9.0. Fine, soft, very pale brown (10YR 8/2) fabric with tiny phyllite inclusions. Petrographic sample KAV 15/38: Fabric Subgroup 1c. Very pale brown (10YR 8/2) slip. Crackled black paint faded to reddish brown (5YR 4/4). Well-preserved surfaces. Concentric circles with dots between; alternating broad bands with groups of narrow bands. *Comparanda*: **GR17 P4**; for decoration, Brock 1957, 176, pl. 324:36 (Knossos, PGB); Rocchetti 1974–1975, 241, fig. 99:38 (Phaistos); Coldstream and Catling, eds., 1996, 116, pl. 261:4, 8; 172, pl. 171:11(Knossos, EO); 236, pl. 218:100 (Knossos, LO); Kotsonas 2008, 248, 252, fig. 63:A97 (Eleutherna, EO). *Date*: EO.

GR4 P9 (V 4001.4 and 5, V 4002.1, V 4003.2, V 4004.2; Fig. 49). Pyxis. Partially mended from six fragments, with one possible nonjoining rim fragment. Max. pres. h. 8.2. Fine, soft, very pale brown (10YR 8/2) fabric. Very pale brown (10YR 8/2) slip. Crackled black paint faded to reddish brown (5YR 4/4). Well-preserved surfaces. Similar in shape to **GR4 P8**, but smaller. Broad bands alternating with groups of narrow bands. *Date*: EO.

GR4 P10 (V 4003.2; Fig. 49). Closed vessel, perhaps a jug. Single fragment (two sherds) from body. Max. pres. h. 5.4. Fine, rather soft, very pale brown (10YR 7/3) fabric. Black paint. Worn surfaces. Discolored as if slightly burned. Concentric circles with thick outer edges that overlap. Possibly same vessel as **GR4 P11**. *Date*: LG–EO.

GR4 P11 (V 4003.2; Fig. 49). Closed vessel, perhaps a jug. Single fragment from body. Max. pres. h. 5.0. Fine, rather soft, pink (7.5YR 7/4) fabric. Black paint. Well-preserved surfaces. Guilloche pattern. *Comparanda*: Tsipopoulou 2005, 127, fig. 40:H 7416 (Hagios Georgios, LG–EO). *Date*: EO.

Fine Monochrome Wares

GR4 P12 (V87.91; V 4004.4, V 4009.1 and 2, V 4010.2; Fig. 49). Cup. Partially mended from 26 fragments. Preservation 30%, including entire base, handle, 25% of rim; full profile can be restored. H. est. 5.6; d. rim 7.8; d. base 3.0. Fine, rather hard, reddish-yellow (5YR 7/6) fabric. Mottled black to yellowish-red (5YR 5/6) paint. Some well-preserved surfaces. *Bibliography*: Gesell, Day, and Coulson 1988, 284–285, fig. 2:6. *Comparanda*: Coldstream and Catling, eds., 1996, 134, fig. 103:28 (Knossos, PGB–EG). *Date*: LG.

GR4 P13 (V87.127, IM 968; V 4003.2, V 4004.1 and .2, V 4004.4, V 4009.1; Fig. 49; Pl. 25). Cup. Restored from 35 fragments. Preservation 95%. H. 9.3; d. rim 13.5; d. base 6.9. Fine, rather hard, very pale brown (10YR 7/4) fabric. Streaky, dark brown (7.5YR 3/2) to black paint. Painted on interior, exterior, and underside of base. Well-preserved surfaces. *Bibliography*: Gesell, Day, and Coulson 1988, 284–285, fig. 2:7, pl. 74:c. *Comparanda*: Coldstream and Catling, eds., 1996, 64, fig. 75:9, 17; 246, fig. 140:64 (Knossos EO, though deeper); Erickson 2010, 105–106, fig. 3.30:206 (Eleutherna, seventh or sixth century). *Date*: EO.

GR4 P14 (V 4502.1; Fig. 50). Cup. Partially mended from 25 fragments, 20% preserved, including nearly all of base, much of lower body, one fragment of handle; missing all of rim. Max. pres. h. 4.0; d. base 5.6. Fine, very soft and chalky, very pale brown (10YR 7/3) fabric. Black paint. Very worn surfaces, particularly on exterior. *Date*: LG?

GR4 P15 (V 4004.1–3; Fig. 50). Skyphos. Partially mended from 46 fragments, 70% preserved, including much of base, both handles, half of rim. Edges too worn and soft to mend. H. est. 10.0; d. rim est. 17.0; d. base 7.0. Fine, very soft, porous, very pale brown (10YR 8/4) fabric. Petrographic sample KAV 15/42: Fabric Subgroup 1b. Black paint. Worn surfaces, but well preserved in places. Some burning. *Comparanda*: Coldstream and Catling, eds., 1996, 116, fig. 96:158 (Knossos, LO); 141, fig. 104.28 (Knossos, EG–MG); 246, fig. 140:63 (Knossos, O kotyle). *Date*: EO.

GR4 P16 (V98.81; V 4001.5, V 4003.2, V 4004.1–4, V 4009.1 and 2, V 4010.1, V 4011.1–3, V 4502.1; Fig. 50; Pl. 25). Krater. Partially restored from 103 fragments; 82 nonjoining fragments. Preservation 75%, including full profile, almost all of base, 80% of rim, both handles (one not restored); missing chunks of body. H. 21.0; d. rim 18.0; d. base 7.8. Fine, fairly hard, reddish-yellow (5YR 6/6) fabric (soft in some fragments) with very pale brown (10YR 8/3) surface. Petrographic sample KAV 15/40: Fabric Subgroup 1b. Black paint, worn to brown shadow. Some worn, some well-preserved surfaces. No burning. *Comparanda*: Levi 1927–1929, 142, fig. 137 (Arkades, EO); Stampolides 1996, 46, fig. 85 (Eleutherna, LG). *Date*: EO.

Fine Plain Wares

GR4 P17 (V87.68, IM 965; V 4003.2 object 2, 4004.2; Fig. 50; Pl. 25). Cup. Mended from seven fragments. Preservation 80%, including full profile, entire base; missing 30% of rim and handle. H. 4.3; d. rim 5.8; d. base 2.9. Fine, soft, reddish-yellow (5YR 6/6) fabric with some tiny inclusions. Worn surfaces but no trace of paint. Traces of burning on underside and around rim. Crudely made; string marks on base. *Bibliography*: Gesell, Day, and Coulson 1988, 285, pl. 74:d. *Date*: G.

GR4 P18 (V 4001.3; Fig. 50). Jug or aryballos. Partially mended from five fragments, with four nonjoining fragments; half of base and lower body preserved. Max. pres. h. 3.0; d. base 3.0. Fine, soft, reddish-yellow (5YR 7/6) fabric, flaking and laminating. Very worn surfaces. *Date*: uncertain.

GR4 P19 (V 4001.6, V 4002.1; Fig. 50). Lekythos. Partially mended from three fragments, preserving nearly complete neck and rim, handle attachment; missing body, base, and handles. Max. pres. h. 4.0; d. rim 6.6.

Fine, soft, reddish-yellow (7.5YR 6/6) fabric. Funnel neck with ridges at bottom. *Date*: EO.

Medium-Coarse Decorated Wares

GR4 P20 (V87.89; V 4001.5, V 4003.2 and 4, V 4004.1 and 2 object 1, V 4004.5, V 4011.2; Fig. 51). Praisos-type lekythos. Partially mended and restored from 117 fragments. Preservation 50%–60%, including base, shoulder, much of neck, one handle attachment, one fragment of rim; full profile can be restored. H. est. 29.5; d. rim est. 10.0; d. base 8.0. Medium-coarse, soft, porous, light gray (10YR 7/1) fabric with granodiorite inclusions. Petrographic sample KAV 15/44: Fabric Group 4. Thick and glossy white (10YR 8/1) to very pale brown (10YR 8/2) slip. Black paint. Very worn surfaces. No burning. Vertical rim, deeply cut below; tall neck; ovoid body; groove around underside of base. Two registers of hatched leaves on neck; eight-pointed rosettes in circles on shoulder, two between handles, one set lower under handle. Circle and X-pattern painted on bottom. *Bibliography*: Gesell, Day, and Coulson 1988, 284–285, fig. 2:1, emended. *Comparanda*: Coldstream and Catling, eds., 1996, 264, fig. 146:89 (Knossos, LG–EO); 265, pl. 239:106; 268, fig. 149:193 (Knossos, LG); Callaghan and Johnston 2000, 228, pl. 4.7:157 (Kommos, PGB); Kotsonas 2008, 240, fig. 59:A134 (LG), A178 (LG–EO); 246, fig. 61:A244 (PGB) (Eleutherna); Rethemiotakis and Englezou 2010, 69–70, fig. 40:88, 40:90 (Eltyna, EG or MG–LG); for decoration, Coldstream and Catling, eds., 1996, 6, fig. 58:31 (Knossos, PGB–EG). *Date*: EO.

GR4 P21 (V 4002.1; Fig. 51). Lekythos. Single fragment from neck of lekythos like **GR4 P20**. Max. pres. h. 5.6. Medium-coarse, porous, pink (7.5YR 7/4) fabric with tiny black inclusions. Pale yellow (2.5Y 8/2) slip. Black paint worn to shadow. Worn surfaces. Double zigzag with dots between on neck. *Comparanda*: for dotted zigzag, see **GR26 P20**. *Date*: LG–EO.

Medium-Coarse Monochrome Wares

GR4 P22 (V 4004.2; Fig. 51). Cup. Partially mended from 18 fragments, 75% preserved, including full profile, entire base, 50% of rim, and part of handle. H. 6.8; d. rim 8.4; d. base 3.6. Medium-coarse, very soft, reddish-yellow (7.5YR 6/6) fabric with some large white and gray inclusions. Sampled KAV 15/41: Fabric Subgroup 1b. Yellowish-red (5YR 4/6) paint. Very worn surfaces and edges, making mending impossible. Many burned fragments. *Date*: PG?

GR4 P23 (V 4502.1; Fig. 51). Closed vessel. Partially mended from nine fragments. Most of base, 40% of lower body preserved; missing rim and handle(s). Max. pres. h. 8.0; d. base 9.0. Medium-coarse, very soft, reddish-yellow (5YR 6/6) fabric with large quartz inclusions. Black paint on exterior? Very worn surfaces. *Date*: uncertain.

Coarse Decorated Wares

GR4 P24 (V 4001.5, V 4002.1, V 4003.2, V 4008.1, V 4015.1; Fig. 51; Pl. 25). Lid. Partially mended from nine fragments, including bits of rim and top/base. H. est. 6.5; d. rim est. 20.0. Coarse, porous, rather hard, light gray (2.5Y 7/2) fabric, with frequent black inclusions. Sampled KAV 15/43: Fabric Subgroup 1b. Black to very dark grayish-brown or strong brown (10YR 3/2–7.5YR 5/6) paint, with decoration in added white. Very worn surfaces. Domed lid pierced near rim with at least two holes made before firing. *Comparanda*: Coldstream and Catling, eds., 1996, 24, 270, figs. 64:12, 149:240 (Knossos, LG–EO); Tsipopoulou 2005, 217, fig. 141:H3258 (Adromyloi, EO); Kotsonas 2008, 240, 242, fig. 59:A225 (Eleutherna, Knossian import, LG–EO). *Date*: EO.

GR4 P25 (V87.83; V 4009.1; Pl. 25). Pithos. Three non-joining body fragments. Th. 2.2. Coarse, pink (7.5YR 7/4), Kavousi Type X/XI fabric, light reddish brown (2.5YR 6/4) at core. Very pale brown (10YR 8/2) slip. Decorated with raised bands bearing incised running spirals. *Comparanda*: Rocchetti 1974–1975, 252, fig. 114:9 (Phaistos, LG). *Date*: LG?

Metal

Bronze

GR4 M1 (V87.94, IM 900, HNM 15733; V 4004.2, object 3; Fig. 51; Pl. 25). Bronze pin. Intact. L. 8.0. Well preserved. Long pin with conical knob on top above disk. Biconical swelling with four rings on either side near top. *Bibliography*: Gesell, Day, and Coulson 1988, 283, pl. 74:b; Day 1995, fig. 9. *Comparanda*: Catling 1996a, 555–556, type 5. *Date*: LG–EO.

GR4 M2 (V87.95, IM 901, HNM 15734; V 4004.2, object 4; Fig. 51; Pl. 25). Bronze pin. Mended from two fragments. Nearly complete; missing point. Max. pres L. 5.5. Surfaces well preserved. Bent. Conical knob on top, with disk below. Biconical swelling near top with two rings on either side. *Comparanda*: Catling 1996a, 555–556, type 5. *Date*: LG–EO.

Terracotta

GR4 TC1 (V87.14, IM 853; V 4004.2, object 1; Fig. 51; Pl. 25). Terracotta bead. Intact. H. 1.9; max. d. 2.5; d. hole. Wt. 8.00 g. Biconical. Fine, porous, medium-soft, very pale brown (10YR 8/3) fabric. Burned. No paint, no decoration. No wheel marks.

Graves 5 and 11

History and Details of Excavation

Grave 5 lies on the west central side of the top of the Vronda ridge in Room C4 of the earlier LM IIIC Building C, close to Graves 2 and 4 (Figs. 3, 4). This rectangular enclosure was fully excavated in 1987 in Trench V 4000 (Gesell, Day, and Coulson 1988, 285–286). Grave 11 was a pit located just to the southwest of Grave 5. First encountered at the end of the 1987 season in Trench V 4000, Grave 11 was fully excavated in 1988 during the removal of the north balk of V 3500; some part of the area had already been cleared, without recognition of grave material, during the cleaning in 1984. There was little human bone in the deposit, but a great deal of pottery, and subsequent study of the material revealed many joins with pottery from Grave 5. It seems likely, therefore, that Grave 11 was not an independent grave but rather a discard deposit of material from Grave 5, and the objects and bones from the two graves have been cataloged together.

As soon as human cranial fragments appeared immediately below the topsoil in the area east of the house/terrace wall V 4002 (V 4001), Grave 5 was excavated by biological anthropologists and labeled as burial 4. The latest burial in the enclosure was an inhumation (Pl. 26A), and during the excavation of this burial, the north balk of 4000 was removed (V 4007.3); from this point on, the area of the grave that lay in the north balk was excavated with the remainder of the grave. The skeleton rested on a layer of small, flat paving stones. Beneath the paving stones was a layer of ashy soil (V 4012) containing cremated remains of six individuals (labeled burials 7, 8); during the course of the excavation of this ashy soil, the trench was extended to the south into Trench 3500 to pick up the tiny bit of grave that lay in that area. Around the edges the soil became harder and was dark grayish brown in color. This soil was also found below V 4012, and it was removed as V 4016, down to bedrock and a patch of burned clay representing the hearth of the earlier LM IIIC room. In 1988 the bottom of the grave was cleaned as V 4019.

A small portion of Grave 11 was found at the end of the 1987 season. It was identified when human remains began to appear to the west of Grave 5 in V 4015. An area of dark ashy soil containing grave goods and some human bones was removed as V 4017. It was decided to leave the rest of the grave for excavation in the following season. In 1988, after the removal of the topsoil in the north balk of V 3500 (V3505, V 3506), more of the ashy soil was uncovered in V 3506.2. The dark ashy deposit with boulders was excavated as V 3509 and V 3510. Subsequent study of the material has shown that some part of the deposit of Grave 11 had been cleared in the cleaning of 1984 as V 3500.2 Level 2 and V 3504.7, 8, and 12 Level 2.

Architecture

Grave 5 is a rectangular stone-built enclosure measuring 2.00–2.05 m north–south x 1.08 m east–west and oriented northeast–southwest. It was constructed by digging into the debris of rock tumble and roofing that had collapsed from Room C4 of LM IIIC Building C. The grave diggers did not make use of existing house walls (Fig. 52; Pl. 26B). The builders went down to bedrock on the north end, but in the center they stopped at a burned patch of red clay that represents the hearth of the earlier building (Pl. 26C). The oval hearth extended beneath the east wall of the enclosure, and more of it was uncovered in clearing the floor of the building to the east, so it clearly belonged with the LM IIIC house and was not the result of the burning of the pyre. The builders apparently made a rectangular pit, then lined each side with a single row of boulders and filled up the space behind with additional stones and soil; the west wall had small chinking stones to level up the base of the blocks. The limestone blocks of the east (V 4025), west (V 4023), and south (V 4024) walls were fissured from the fire, particularly on the east and west sides.

Stratigraphy

It is now difficult to estimate the depth of deposition in Grave 5, as insufficient elevations were taken at the time of excavation. The tops of the walls of the enclosure lay 0.42–0.50 m above its floor, and this gives an approximate depth for the deposition found within. The bottom of the grave was the bedrock and clay floor of the earlier building, including the burned clay of the hearth. Above the bedrock and clay in the grave was a thin layer of rather hard dark grayish-brown soil (V 4016) that contained no cremated human bone. Above this, a thicker layer of soft, ashy gray soil (V 4012) contained remains of Burials 1–4 and some of Burial 6. A layer of small, flat paving stones appeared to separate this cremation layer from the inhumation above (V 4007.1 and 2, V 4007.4 and 5; Pl. 26D). The joins of pottery and bones suggest that there was no clear demarcation between the two sets of burials; some of the cremations (Burials 5 and 6) were picked up with the excavation of the inhumation (Burial 7), possibly because they were in the uppermost levels of the cremations. The ashy deposit associated with Burials 5 and 6 lay over the earlier cremations found at each end of the enclosure, indicating that these are the latest of the cremations in this enclosure and are stratigraphically distinct from the earlier burials (Gesell, Coulson, and Day 1988, 285–286). The soil accompanying the inhumation was dark brown (10YR 4/3–3/3) in color. Above the inhumation lay stones and topsoil over the entire trench, from which pottery from the burial was recovered (Pl. 26E).

Grave 11 seems to have been a pit either left in the roofing clay from the abandoned house or dug deliberately to contain the discard deposit dumped from Grave 5. The lowest level in this uneven pit consisted of ashy gray soil (V 3610) that filled in the crevices in the bedrock. Above this was similar dark gray soil with boulders (V 3506.2, V 3509, V 4017). Some material from Grave 11 was picked up in the topsoil that lay above (V 3505, V 4001).

Associated Features

The ashy discard deposit that was excavated as Grave 11 contained few human remains (11 g), but joins between the sherds found in the ashy soil and vessels from Grave 5 make it clear that the material collected as Grave 11 is debris from the cleaning of Grave 5. There were no features of the bones that could make it possible to associate them with a particular burial in Grave 5, and other than being identifiable as probably human, none of the bone fragments provided any additional information about the individuals buried in Grave 5.

The discard deposit of grave material was found scattered around the edges of Grave 5 (V 4008, V 4015). There is a possibility that the material from Grave 2, which lay to the south and over the house wall on the west, may have come from this burial as well. Grave 5 had been much disturbed. Some fragments of vessels from it were found as far away as Trench V 2500 to the south, so clearly the material spread along the west side of the summit.

Burials

There were seven burials in Grave 5: six cremations and one inhumation, although in preliminary reports it was described as having three cremations and one inhumation (Gesell, Day, and Coulson 1988, 285–286).

Burial 1
Type: disturbed primary cremation
Age: adult, 25–40 years
Sex: male
Weight: 1,264 g

Burial 1 is the fragmentary partial skeleton of an adult male, 25–40 years old at the time of death. The large quantity of bone associated with this skeleton suggests that very little was lost from the grave when the enclosure was reused. The cranium is very robust, with strong male features and a markedly protruding chin (Pl. 22F: bottom right). Portions of the sagittal suture are obliterated endocranially, and the coronal and lambdoid sutures were in the process of closing; these features support the estimation of age. The skeletal remains are unusually large and robust for the Vronda population.

The cranial bone from this burial shows considerably less thorough burning than the postcranium. The cranium is scorched and blackened, with only the exterior right parietal showing incipient calcination. The postcranial bone, on the other hand, is almost all completely calcined. Here again, as with the burials in Grave 3, the cranium appears to have been somewhat sheltered from the effects of the cremation pyre, and remained so during the subsequent cremations in the enclosure.

This skeleton has a number of interesting pathologies. The right parietal has a large, well-healed trepanation extending from the outer table through the diploë, the spongy bone found between the inner and outer layers of the bones that make up the cranial vault (Fig. 53; Liston and Day 2009, 64–65). There is no involvement of the inner table of bone. The preserved edges of this lesion are smooth and beveled and appear to be well healed, indicating that the patient survived the surgery. The lesion is approximately oval in shape, and extends from near the coronal suture toward the back of the skull for at least 4 cm. On the interior surface, the frontal bone is rough and pitted, particularly to the right of the frontal crest. This characteristic appears to represent another case of hyperostosis frontalis interna, similar to that seen in Grave 3, Burial 1. The headaches that at times are associated with this condition could potentially have been a reason for the surgery (She and Sakacs 2004, 207–208). There is also moderate healed cribra orbitalia in both eye orbits, indicating earlier anemia, probably during childhood.

There are a number of postcranial pathologies as well, including healed fractures on the anterior surface of an unsided patella fragment and on a long bone shaft fragment that is probably a humerus. The bone fragment was found in close association with other humerus fragments as well as a proximal ulna and metacarpals. The size and diameter of the bone is consistent with a humerus shaft as well, also indicating its identity, although the bone lacks any definitive identifying traits. Finally, there is pitting on the articular facets of several lumbar vertebrae as well as the first sacral vertebra, indicating osteoarthritis in these joints. Several unidentified vertebral bodies show evidence of osteophytic lipping, also indicative of joint disease (Ortner 2003, 555–558). Altogether, these pathologies suggest an individual with a rigorous, if not violent life, resulting in a number of healed injuries and cranial surgery, possibly to alleviate a cranial infection.

Burials 2 and 3
Type: disturbed cremations
Age: two adults, one older, perhaps 40–60 years
Sex: one male, one female(?)
Weight: 1,278 g

Two cremation burials were found against the north end of the enclosure, as though moved aside for later use of the mortuary feature. Burials 2 and 3 are both adults, and it is not possible to separate their bones. Also mingled with these burials were the cremated bones of Burial 4, an infant. The relationship of these burials with Burial 1 is uncertain, but no joins have been found between the skeletal material from either end of the enclosure. These two groups of disturbed burials appear to represent completely discrete mortuary events. The low weight of bone for two skeletons suggests that, unlike Burial 1, some of the bone was lost from the grave when the burial enclosure was prepared for later cremations.

The bone associated with these burials is almost all completely white and calcined. There is evidence of two cremation events on some of the cranial bone. The bone has the curved fractures and warping associated with the burning of fleshed, green bone. In addition, there is the "checked" network of cracks associated with dry burning. These finer cracks do not cross the larger cracks attributed to wet burning, confirming that they occurred subsequent to the fleshed cremation of the body. This pattern of cracking is probably the result of the body's having been cremated while fresh, with the bone again being subjected to heat during the cremation of the later burials in the grave.

One of the individuals in Burials 2 and 3 is an adult male with robust occipital and zygomatic bones as well as markedly large long bone shafts. The presence of some pitting and lipping on the vertebral facets as well as some other joint surface fragments indicates that this is not a very young adult. Two pathologies can be definitely associated with the larger, more robust individual. On the inner surface of the frontal bone, on both sides of the frontal crest, there is extensive pitting and striation of the bone, which potentially represent another case of hyperostosis frontalis interna, as seen in Grave 3. In addition, the frontal process of the left zygomatic has a healed oblique fracture. The fracture extends diagonally from the orbit margin near the frontozygomatic suture to the lateral edge of the frontal process, just above the temporal process. There is bony callous formation on the lateral surface of the frontal process. Above the fracture, there is some porosity and callous formation on the frontal bone above the orbit, possibly indicating that the trauma extended into this region. A final pathology cannot definitely be associated with either burial. Two fragments of broken ribs were found with these skeletons. The bone was actively healing at the time of death. Large deposits of unorganized bone tissue are present on both surfaces of the ribs, obscuring the breaks themselves.

The second skeleton is a much smaller individual, at least 18–20 years old and possibly female. There is no visible wear on the occlusal surface of the third molar, but the presence of a wear facet on the mesial surface indicates that the tooth had erupted.

Burial 4
Type: disturbed primary cremation
Age: infant, perinatal
Sex: unknown
Weight: 376 g

Burial 4 is a partial fragmentary skeleton of an infant, found commingled with the bone of Burials 2 and 3. There were no developing teeth recovered with this burial that would allow the determination of a more precise dental age, but the size of the sphenoid bone from the base of the skull suggests a 40-week, or perinatal, infant. The size and development of the bones are also consistent with other perinatal cremated remains from Vronda.

There are two cranial pathologies on the sphenoid associated with this infant. On the external surface of the greater wing of the sphenoid there is a layer of periosteal bone. On the broken edge of the fragment a distinct border between the periosteal bone and the normal bone beneath is apparent. On the lesser wing of the sphenoid there is a large lesion in which an area of bone is largely missing. The lesion is oval, 7.50 x 5.90 mm in size. The hole in the bone is bridged by thin spicules of bone. It is possible that this lesion is an anomaly in the ossification process by which the fetal membranous tissue is turned into bone (Barnes 1994, 30), but the associated inflammation suggests an infectious or inflammatory process. The periosteal bone suggests it was an active process at the time of the child's death.

Burial 5
Type: disturbed primary cremation
Age: juvenile, 9–12 years
Sex: unknown
Weight: 596 g

Burial 5 is a cremated juvenile with a dental age of 9 to 13 years. The bones were found in the middle of the burial enclosure, commingled with those of Burial 6, an infant. The skull is burned but, for the most part, not calcined; the postcranial bone is more thoroughly burned but also not totally calcined. There was no evidence of pathology or other anomalous condition on the bones.

Some additional cranial bone fragments were collected with this burial. These show incipient fusion of the posterior sagittal suture and pits for pacchionian bodies along the sagittal suture. These features indicate an older adult, not an adolescent. This bone is not associated with the cremated adults in Burials 1, 2 and 3, and therefore it represents another individual. There is, however, no other evidence for the adult except for the cranial fragments, unless the mandible fragment from Grave 2 comes from the same individual.

Burial 6
Type: disturbed primary cremation
Age: infant, 3–9 months
Sex: unknown
Weight: 108 g

This partial cremated skeleton of an infant has a dental age of three to nine months. The bone is minimally burned, showing only sooting on the exterior surfaces of the cranium. The only portion of the endocranium that appears to have been affected by the fire is along the temporal edge of the squamosal suture. The postcranial bones also were not strongly affected by cremation, although there are some signs of burning on most bones. The infant may have been cremated separately, with relatively little investment of fuel, or it was placed on the cremation pyre of one of the adults after the pyre had burned down somewhat, and there was insufficient fuel to completely cremate the infant.

Burial 7
Type: primary inhumation
Age: older adult, 60+ years
Sex: male
Weight: not recorded

Burial 7 is the poorly preserved skeleton of an adult male. This is an elderly individual, edentulous at death, and estimated to be more than 60 years old on the basis of the obliterated cranial sutures and the auricular surface of the left ilium (Meindl and Lovejoy 1989; Buikstra and Ublelaker, eds., 1994, 24–32). The cranium and long bones are quite robust, and the morphology of the pelvis fragments indicates the sex is male. The body had been placed in the enclosure rather carelessly, with the feet and lower legs crowded against the northeast corner of the enclosure, and the head just south of the middle of the enclosure (Pl. 26F). The left arm lay across the abdomen, and the right was flexed at the elbow, with the hand beside the head (Gesell, Coulson, and Day 1988, 286).

There is extensive evidence of osteoarthritis on most of the preserved joint surfaces, including the shoulders, hips, wrists, and ankles. Much of the cortical bone of the long bones is quite thin, ranging from 1.95 to 3.00 mm where it could be measured on the tibiae, indicating osteoporosis (Ortner 2003, 413–415). A distal phalanx on the right hand had been smashed and fractured long before death. On the left tibia, the soleus insertion is pitted and quite rough at the proximal end of the attachment, suggesting some prior injury to this muscle.

The most notable injury is the wound on the dorsal surface of the midshafts of the radius and ulna of the right arm. On the ulna there is a cloaca in the vicinity of the extensor pollicis longus insertion, between the posterior and interosseus borders of the shaft. This cloaca suggests the presence of posttraumatic osteomyelitis resulting from the infection of a wound on the arm (Ortner 2003, 199–204). There is a corresponding area of depressed bone and periosteal activity on the radius adjacent to the cloaca on the ulna. Both of these lesions appeared to be fairly localized and not active at the time of death, and therefore they are old, healed wounds.

Although the long bones were not sufficiently preserved to measure after excavation, measurements of the right ulna and femur in situ can be used to estimate a stature of 159–167 cm. This height is confirmed by the stature estimation from the complete left first metacarpal, which indicated a size of 164.00 + 5.49 cm. While metacarpals are not the best indicators of stature, together with the estimates taken from the long bones in situ, this evidence suggests that a stature estimation of perhaps 160–170 cm is probably accurate.

Faunal Remains

Animal bone from the area of Grave 5 and the associated discard deposit (Grave 11) is largely unburned and fragmentary (Table 4). Unburned fragments include one dog radius segment; isolated teeth, one mandible segment, and small skull fragments of sheep or goat; one cattle tooth; and three pig bones, including a maxilla fragment with third premolar, a distal fibia, and a calcaneum. Calcined fragments are almost entirely limited to tiny unidentifiable bone fragments from the area of the inhumation (V 4007.6) and the deposits of ashy soil in the dump (V 4017.2, V 3509.2). A single sheep or goat tarsal from a lower left hind limb was also recovered from the ashy soil below the paving stones that contained human cremations, Burials 1–4 and 6.

Pottery

Grave 5, together with the discard deposit called Grave 11, produced approximately 1,203 fragments of pottery weighing 4.48 kg. An additional 213 fragments, weighing 1.31 kg, which came from the bottom of the grave probably belonged to the floor deposit of Room C4 of LM IIIC Building C, as there were no associated human remains and a much smaller percentage of fine wares (2%) in comparison to the fine wares found within the grave and its dump (75%). Seventeen vessels have been cataloged from the grave. Because of the commingling of the burials by later disturbance, it is difficult to associate vessels with individual burials. Only one vessel could be firmly associated with a particular burial, and that was the small necked jar **GR5 P2** found with the inhumation, the last burial in the grave. This vessel is of a shape that began to appear in MG in the Knossian sequence (Coldstream and Catling, eds., 1996, 204, pl. 188:8; 264, fig. 145:77) but continued into LG (Coldstream and Catling, eds., 1996, 186, fig. 120:35; 115, pl. 124:148). In East Crete, it appears in the tholos tombs from Vronda (Tsipopoulou 2005, 76, fig. 61:H1960, not the one of the same number pictured on pl. 23), but also it seems to have been common in the transitional period between the LG and EO periods (Tsipopoulou 2005, 381), with similar examples from Hagios Stephanos (Tsipopoulou 2005, 199, fig. 61:Σ4531) and Hagios Georgios (Tsipopoulou 2005, 173, fig. 61:Σ3936). The decoration is a variation on the stacked zigzags found on Attic MG skyphoi (e.g., Coldstream 1968, pl.3:e), a design common to a number of imported Naxian MG skyphoi at Knossos (Coldstream 1990, 27, fig. 5); a similar misrepresentation of this design can also be found on a LG skyphos from Zou (Tsipopoulou 2005, 315, fig. 108:AN1448). The crisp profile of the Grave 5 example suggests that it is at least LG in date; it resembles a vessel from Grave 17 (see below), which contains some of the latest pottery in the graves.

No pottery or objects could be specifically attributed to any of the other burials. The material found in Grave 11 doubtless belonged to one of the earlier burials, but it is not clear to which. These vessels included a necked jar (**GR5 P3**), an amphora (**GR5 P13**), a ribbed jug (**GR5 P15**), and the base of a closed vessel (**GR5 P16**). The necked jar is similar in shape to **GR5 P2** but is larger and not as elegantly made. Although it resembles a SM shoulder-handled amphora from Knossos (Coldstream and Catling, eds., 1996, 87, fig. 83:11), the shape is reminiscent of necked jars from Eleutherna of EO date (Kotsonas 2008, 128–129, fig. 29:A342, A344). The ribbed coarse jug finds parallels for its shape in a fine jug of the EO period (Coldstream and Catling, eds., 1996, 236, pl. 218:77). The amphora (**GR5 P13**) has an unusual double handle; such handles are rare but at Knossos only appear on an amphora of MG date (Coldstream and Catling, eds., 1996, 187, pl. 182:55). The hatched zigzag or triangle on the neck of this example, however, finds parallels of PGB–LPG date at Eltyna (Rethemiotakis and Englezou 2010, 59, fig. 29:59) and of LG date at Adromyloi (Tsipopoulou 2005, 202, fig.13:H3182); these parallels provide a more likely date of LG for this piece.

The other pottery in the grave also supports a date of LG for the burials. A two-handled cup or kantharos (**GR5 P11**) is highly unusual for Crete. It may imitate the Attic kantharos, but without the stem or high swung handles. The kantharos appeared before Attic LPG and was imported into Crete but was not locally made (Coldstream and Catling, eds., 1996, 400). Several appeared in seventh century deposits at Kommos (Callaghan and Johnston 2000, 283, fig. 4.10:253), and one came from an eighth century context in Building Z at Kommos (Johnston 2000, 214–215, fig. 26.94). The aryballos **GR5 P12** finds its best parallels in LG–EO material (Coldstream and Catling, eds., 1996, 263, 265–266, pl. 241:47, 105, 107, 128, 131).

In addition to the cataloged pottery, Grave 5 produced a monochrome skyphos of very soft chalky fabric that could not be mended or drawn. There were also body fragments from a second aryballos. From Grave 11 came the base of a lekythos almost identical to the one in Grave 4 (**GR4 P20**), possibly part of the same vessel as the neck (**GR4 P21**).

Objects

A number of iron objects were found together in Grave 5. These included the following: three knives (**GR5 M7**–**GR5 M9**), a sickle-shaped knife (**GR5 M10**), five spearheads (**GR5 M2**–**GR5 M6**), a scraper (**GR5 M11**), a pair of tweezers (**GR5 M12**), and an obsidian blade (**GR5 ST1**). In addition to this hoard and the bronze pin associated with the inhumation (**GR5 M1**), there were fragments of at least two more iron pins. Other iron blade and socket fragments found in the grave probably belonged to one or more of the spearheads. There were, in addition, fragments of at least two iron rods that were rectangular in section (one 1.00 cm square, the other 0.50 cm) and a third that was rectangular on one end and flattened on the other. These were too poorly preserved to identify, but they could be remains of tools, iron rods, or spits. There were a great many iron tools and weapons along the southwest and northwest sides of the enclosure, but it was impossible to assign them to individual burials.

Chronology

The inhumation is clearly the latest burial in the grave, and the accompanying small necked jar is probably of LG date. Much of the pottery seems to belong to the LG period, but some vessels have EO parallels. The monochrome cups are not the heavier ones such as those found in Grave 9 (see below), but they also lack the thinness and crisp profiles of the EO and LO examples seen in Graves 4 and 30. A date early in the EO period seems likely.

Catalog

Pottery

Fine Decorated Wares

GR5 P1 (V 4012.5 object 4, V 4012.7, V 4016.3; Fig. 54). Skyphos or cup. Partially mended into three large fragments from 18 sherds; 27 nonjoining fragments. Preservation 70%, including entire base, 10% of rim; missing handle and most of rim. H. 7.2; d. rim 14.3; d. base 4.2. Fine, soft, reddish-yellow (7.5YR 7/6) fabric. Dark reddish-gray (10R 3/1) paint. Very worn surfaces. Pendant short vertical strokes below offset rim; underside of base painted. *Comparanda*: for decoration, Rocchetti 1988–1989, 226–227, fig. 137:138 (Kourtes, LG–EO). *Date*: LG.

GR5 P2 (V87.128, IM 969; V 4001.5, V 4007.2 object 3, V 4007.4; Fig. 54; Pl. 27). Small necked jar. Restored from 12 fragments, 95% preserved; missing parts or rim and neck. H. 11.9–12.2; d. rim 9.6; d. base 5.0. Fine, rather hard, reddish-yellow (5YR 7/6) fabric. Very pale brown (10YR 8/2) slip. Black, crackled paint. Very well-preserved surfaces. Stacked multiple triangles above narrow bands, four on one side, three on the other. Strokes on top of rim. *Bibliography*: Gesell, Day, and Coulson 1988, 286, pl. 74:f. *Comparanda*: **GR17 P3**; Tsipopoulou 2005, 226, 227, fig. 60:Σ3567, pl. 356 (Itanos, LG); 2013, 150–151, fig. 12:12278 (Piskokephalo, LG); Rethemiotakis and Englezou 2010, 71, fig. 42:95, 96 (Eltyna, MG); Englezou 2011, 293–297, 307, fig. 54: 71 (Ligortynos MG–LG). *Date*: LG.

GR5 P3 (V 3506.2, V 3509.1 and 2, V 3510.1 and 2, V 4001.3, V 4007.6, V 4008.1, V 4012.7, V 4015.2, V 4017.1, V 4019.1; Fig. 54). Necked jar. Partially mended from 94 fragments. Preservation 20%, including small bits of base, rim, both handles, and many body fragments; missing full profile, most of rim. H. est. 18.8; d. rim 10.0; d. base 8.0. Fine, soft, reddish-yellow (5YR 7/6) fabric with some clay pellets and chaff voids. Petrographic sample KAV 15/32: Fabric Group 7. Very pale brown (10YR 8/3) slip. Red (10R 4/8) to dusky red (5YR 3/4) paint. Very worn surfaces. A few well-preserved fragments have added white paint. Some fragments burned. Decoration too worn to make out; possibly alternating strokes or quatrefoil leaf; underside of base painted. *Comparanda*: Kotsonas 2008, 128–129, fig. 29:A342, 344 (Eleutherna, LPAR). *Date*: LG.

FINE MONOCHROME WARES

GR5 P4 (V 4012.3, V 4012.5; Fig. 54; Pl. 27). Cup. Mended from 62 fragments, 95% preserved, including handle; missing small fragments of rim and body. H. 9.0; d. rim 13.0; d. base 6.0. Fine, soft, reddish-yellow (7.5YR 6/6) fabric. Traces of brown paint. Very worn surfaces. Two fragments burned. *Comparanda*: **GR3 P7, GR5 P6, GR9 P16**; Gesell, Day, and Coulson 1995, 114–115, fig. 21:1 (Kavousi Kastro, LG); Coldstream and Catling, eds., 1996, 233, fig. 135:283.3 (PGB–EG). *Date*: LG.

GR5 P5 (V 4012.1–5, 7, and 8, V 4019.2, V 4011.1; Fig. 54; Pl. 27). Cup. Mended from 53 fragments. Preservation 80%, including full profile, most of base, 95% of rim; missing most of handle. H. 9.5; d. rim 13.0; d. base 4.5. Fine, soft, very pale brown (10YR 7/4) to gray (5Y 6/1) fabric with granodiorite inclusions. Black paint? Very worn surfaces. Almost entirely burned. *Date*: LG.

GR5 P6 (V 4012.1-7, V 4019.2; Fig. 54; Pl. 27). Cup. Mended from 46 fragments. Preservation 75%, including full profile, most of base, 75% of rim, part of handle; missing 25% of rim and upper body, rest of handle. H. 8.3; d. rim 13.3; d. base 4.8. Fine, soft, very pale brown (10YR 8/4) to grayish-brown (10YR 5/2) fabric. Traces of brown paint on interior, exterior, and underside of base. Very worn surfaces. Many fragments burned after breaking. *Comparanda*: Gesell, Day, and Coulson 1995, 114–115, fig. 21:1 (Kavousi Kastro, LG); Coldstream and Catling, eds., 1996, 233, fig. 135:283.3 (PGB–EG); Tsipopoulou 2013, 152–153, fig. 13:12308 (Piskokephalo, LG). *Date*: LG.

GR5 P7 (V 4012.1–6; Fig. 54). Cup. Partially mended into five large fragments (28 sherds); 11 nonjoining fragments. Preservation 50%, including half of base and rim, much of handle; missing full profile. Max. pres. h. 5.6; d. rim 12.2; d. base 5.5. Fine, soft, very pale brown (10YR 7/3) to gray (5YR 6/1) fabric. Black paint. Very worn surfaces. Entire cup very burned. *Date*: LG.

GR5 P8 (V 4012.5; Fig. 55). Cup. Represented by 57 fragments, too soft to mend. Preservation 65%, including much of base and lower body, some of rim and upper body, part of handle. Profile restored. H. est. 11.0; d. rim est. 14.5; d. base 6.0. Fine, very soft, chalky, pink (7.5YR 7/4) fabric. Surfaces very worn. No paint preserved. Bosses on body. *Date*: LG.

GR5 P9 (V 4007.1, V 4007.4, V 4012.5; Fig. 55). Cup. Three nonjoining fragments from rim and body with boss. Twelve more nonjoining fragments from same vessel. Max. pres. h. 3.5. Fine, very soft, chalky, very pale brown (10YR 8/4) fabric. Very worn surfaces. No paint preserved. Edges worn. No burning. Boss on body. *Date*: LG.

GR5 P10 (V 4007.4, V 4012.1; Fig. 55). Cup. Four joining fragments from rim and handle; other nonjoining fragments. Max. pres. h. 4.5; d. rim est. 13.0. Fine, very soft, chalky, very pale brown (10YR 8/3) fabric, micaceous and porous. Black paint. Very worn surfaces. No burning. *Date*: LG.

GR5 P11 (V 4001.4, V 4007.2 and 4, V 4012.1–5 and 8, V 4015.1 and 2, V 3506.2; Fig. 55; Pl. 27). Kantharos. Mended from 37 fragments; 19 nonjoining fragments. Preservation 75%, including entire base, 30% of rim, both handles. H. 9.5–9.7, d. rim 15.0; d. base 5.0. Fine, soft, reddish-yellow (5YR 7/6) fabric, very pale brown (10YR 8/4) on surface. Red (2.5YR 4/8) paint. Very worn surfaces. Some fragments burned. *Comparanda*: Müller-Karpe 1962, 124, fig. 18.8 (Athens Kerameikos, PG); Eustathiou 2001, 307, fig. 9 (Thera, G); Tsipopoulou 2005, 189, fig. 120:Σ4075 (Hagios Georgios, LG). *Date*: LG.

FINE PLAIN WARE

GR5 P12 (V 4012.5; Fig. 55; Pl. 27). Aryballos. Mended from 23 fragments, 90% preserved; missing part of rim, neck, and handle. H. est. 6.0; d. rim 1.9; d. base 2.5. Fine, soft, very pale brown (10YR 8/4) to gray (5Y 6/1) fabric, almost entirely burned. Very worn surfaces; no trace of paint. *Date*: LG–EO.

MEDIUM-COARSE DECORATED WARES

GR5 P13 (V 3506.1, V 3509.1–4, V 3510.1, V 4012.7, V 4015.1 and 2, V 4017.1; Fig. 55). Neck-handled amphora. Partially mended from eight fragments; nine nonjoining fragments from neck and three fragments from handles. Preservation 75% of rim and neck, including both handle attachments. No body or base. Max. pres. h. 12.2; d. rim

12.6. Medium-coarse, porous, rather hard, reddish-yellow (7.5YR 7/6) fabric with phyllite inclusions; some fragments very soft. Petrographic sample KAV 15/33: Fabric Subgroup 1b. Very pale brown (10YR 8/2) slip. Dark reddish-brown (5YR 2.5/2) paint. Rather well-preserved surfaces. Metopal panel on neck with hatched zigzags and simple zigzags below. Double rolled handles. *Date*: LG–EO.

GR5 P14 (V 4012.3, V 4012.7, V 2500; Fig. 55). Closed vessel. Ten fragments from near rim, near base, and body. Max. pres. h. 6.5. Medium-coarse, soft, porous, pink (7.5YR 7/4) fabric with black sand-sized inclusions. Very pale brown (10YR 8/2) slip. Brown (5YR 4/6) to black paint. Worn surfaces, but decoration preserved on some fragments. On shoulder: pendant loops with centers; hatching below. On body: twofold concentric circles. *Bibliography*: Day, Coulson, and Gesell 1986, 362, fig. 5:26. *Comparanda*: Mook 2004, 175, fig. 12.10:W (Kavousi Kastro, G); Tsipopoulou 2005, 116, fig. 18:H1957 (Kavousi Skouriasmenos, LG–EO); 129, fig. 20: H7420 (Hagios Georgios, LG). *Date*: LG.

Medium-Coarse Monochrome Wares

GR5 P15 (V 3500.2 Level 2, V 3504.7, V 3504.8, V3504.12 Level 2, V 3508.1, V 3509.1; Fig. 55). Jug. Partially mended from 40 fragments, 20% preserved, including part of rim and neck, some of body; missing base and handle. Max. pres. h. 11.3; d. rim 5.0. Medium-coarse, hard, gritty, reddish-yellow (5YR 7/6) fabric, with volcanic inclusions. Petrographic sample KAV 15/34: off-island import. Light reddish-brown (5YR 6/4) surface. Possible brown paint. Very worn surfaces. Some fragments burned. Exterior shows ridging. *Date*: LG–EO.

GR5 P16 (V 3505.1, V 3506.1 and 2, V 3507.1 and 2, V 4015.2; Fig. 55). Closed vessel. Partially mended from four fragments preserving 60% of base; 13 nonjoining fragments from body. Max. pres. h. 6.2; d. base 7.0. Medium-coarse, very soft, pink (7.5YR 8/4) to very pale brown (10YR 8/4) fabric with red phyllites, quartz, and gold mica. Red (2.5YR 5/8) paint. Very worn surfaces. *Date*: uncertain.

Coarse Decorated Ware

GR5 P17 (V 4007.6; Fig. 55). Amphora or pithos. Single fragment from neck. Max. pres. h. 6.0. Coarse, reddish-yellow (5YR 7/6) fabric with phyllites and infrequent inclusions and chaff voids. Very pale brown (10YR 8/3) slip. Crackled black paint. Worn surfaces, but shadow of decoration remains. Large hatched meander or meander hook. *Date*: LG.

Metal

Bronze

GR5 M1 (V87.138, IM 979; V 4007.2; Fig. 56 [drawn straight]; Pl. 27). Bronze pin. Two nonjoining fragments from head and body of pin; broken at top, missing knob and disk. Max. pres. L. (a) 2.5, (b) 1.1. Well preserved, but bent. Bulbous swelling with three rings on either side. *Comparanda*: Catling 1996a, 555–556, type 5 (Knossos, O). *Date*: LG–EO.

Iron

GR5 M2 (V87.98a, IM 938; V 4012.3, object 8; Fig. 56; Pl. 27). Iron spearhead. Mended from four fragments preserving full length; missing bits of socket. L. 25.2; max. w. 2.7; d. socket est. 1.8. Corroded and cracked. Short (6.5) socket, with no preserved hole. Sloping shoulders; no pronounced midrib. Short, narrow, leaf-shaped blade.

GR5 M3 (V87.98b, IM 938; V 4012.3, object 8; Fig. 56; Pl. 27). Iron spearhead. Mended from six fragments, preserving socket and most of blade; missing edges of blade toward tip. Max. pres. L. 22.5; max. pres. w. 2.2; d. socket 1.8. Very corroded and cracked. Long (9.0) socket with hole near end opposite edge. Sloping shoulders; no pronounced midrib.

GR5 M4 (V87.101, IM 941; V 4012.5, object 12; Fig. 56; Pl. 27). Iron spearhead. Two fragments preserving much of socket and beginning of blade; end of blade missing. Max. pres. L. 15.9; max. w. 2.3; d. socket 2.3. Corroded, but with some surviving surfaces. Long (10.5) socket without pierced hole. Worn blade, but apparently with midrib. Sloping shoulders.

GR5 M5 (V 4012.7; Fig. 56; Pl. 27). Iron spearhead. Three nonjoining fragments from socket, including beginning of blade and end of socket. Max. pres. L. 7.6; d. socket est. 1.6. Very corroded. Rounded socket.

GR5 M6 (V 4012.7; Fig. 56; Pl. 27). Iron spearhead. Large fragment from near end of socket to beginning of blade. Max. pres. L. 14.0; d. socket est. 2.0. Very corroded and laminated. Socket rounds into blade, but edges too laminated to determine shape.

GR5 M7 (V87.96/102, IM 936/942, HNM 15735; V 4012.1 object 1, V 4012.5 object 16; Fig. 56; Pl. 27). Iron knife. Nearly complete in three large fragments; missing end of handle. Max. pres. L. 25.8; max. w. 2.4. Very corroded; small bit of original surface near tip and near handle. Handle with two square copper alloy rivets leads directly into slightly curving blade, with cutting edge on inside of curve. *Comparanda*: Gjerstad 1948, 135, fig. 21:2a; Yon 1971, 18–19, type 3, pl. 15:36 (SM–PG); Coldstream and Catling, eds., 1996, 273, fig. 178:f66 (Knossos); Snodgrass 1996, 587, type D (SM–O); Rethemiotakis and Englezou 2010, 54, fig. 65:199 (Eltyna, SM–EPG).

GR5 M8 (V87.104, IM 944; V 4012.3 object 9, V 4012.5 object 14; Fig. 56; Pl. 27). Iron knife. Nearly complete in three fragments; missing very tip of blade. Max. pres. L. 13.2, max. w. 1.7; L. handle 5.0. Very corroded; some surviving surface on blade. Square end with two iron rivets in handle. Blade widens and curves slightly. *Bibliography*: Liston and Day 2009, 69, fig. 4.7:c. *Comparanda*: Gjerstadt 1948, 135, fig. 21:1a; Catling 1968,

94, fig. 3:9; Macdonald 1992, 63, fig. 9:13 (Amathus CG II); 67, fig. 10:22 (Amathus, CG–CA); Snodgrass 1996, 585–586, type A (Knossos, SM–O).

GR5 M9 (V87.103, IM 943; V 4012.5, object 11; Fig. 56; Pl. 27). Iron knife. Two nonjoining fragments from handle (a) and tip (b). Max. pres. L. (a) 4.0, (b) 3.8; max. pres. w. (a) 1.7, (b) 1.3. Corroded; some surviving surface on tip. Rather thick handle, rectangular in section, widening to blade. Very narrow, thin, and pointed tip. Possible rivet on handle. *Bibliography*: Gesell, Day, and Coulson 1988, 286, pl. 74:e, top left; Liston and Day 2009, 69, fig 4.7:d. *Comparanda*: Shaw and Harlan 2000, 364, 371, pl. 5.24:3 (Kommos, SM–PG).

GR5 M10 (V87.99, IM 939; V 4012.3, object 10; Fig. 56; Pl. 27). Iron sickle-shaped knife. Two joining fragments from blade; missing both ends. Max. pres. L. 5.2; max. pres. w. 2.0. Well-preserved surfaces; little corrosion. Fragment of curved blade near handle end. Half of rivet hole preserved, possible second rivet. Cutting edge on interior of curve. *Bibliography*: Gesell, Day, and Coulson 1988, 286, pl. 74:e, top right.

GR5 M11 (V87.97, IM 937; V 4012.3, object 4; Fig. 56; Pl. 27). Iron scraper. Nearly complete in two fragments; missing tip of handle. Max. pres. L. 9.3; max. pres. w. 2.5. Corroded, but with some surviving surfaces. Chisel-shaped object with broad end bent up. End broken, but looks as though the metal had been folded over another material. *Bibliography*: Liston and Day 2009, 68, figs. 4.4, 4.7:b.

GR5 M12 (V87.100, IM 940; V 4012.5, object 17; Fig. 56; Pl. 27). Iron tweezers. Two sets of joining fragments from the two sides of the tweezers; missing connection between two sides and ends. Max. pres. L. 5.7; max. w. 1.3. Corroded, but with some surviving surfaces. Two sides of tweezers. Thin strips of iron, widening from top to ends. *Bibliography*: Liston and Day 2009, 69, fig. 4.7:a.

Stone

GR5 ST1 (V87.80, IM 897; V 4012.3, object 7; Pl. 27). Obsidian blade, center section, two ridges. L. 2.0; w. 1.0; th. 0.3. Obsidian, black. Chipped on edges (use?).

Grave 6

History and Details of Excavation

Grave 6 lies on the southwest slope of the Vronda summit, between Building C-D on the west side of the summit and the shrine just below to the south (Figs. 3, 4). The rectangular, stone-lined burial enclosure was excavated in 1987 in Trench V 10800 (Gesell, Day, and Coulson 1988, 288–289). It should be noted that the grid points for Trench V 10800 were originally misplaced, and much of Grave 6 actually belongs in the next square to the west (V 10700); for convenience the erroneous designation for the trench as V 10800 has been retained, although the grave has been properly placed on the plan. Once the grave was recognized on the western edge of the trench, excavation was extended to the west by removing what was thought to be the east balk of Trench V 10700; this area was labeled the west balk of V 10800 (V 10806, V 10807) for the sake of convenience. After this extension, beginning with Locus V 10812, the entire grave was dug together. A small depression was recognized in the southeast and excavated separately (V 10813). During the course of excavation of the rock tumble (V 10812) a line of stones was observed in the middle of the tomb that seemed to divide the grave into northern and southern halves, and the excavator assigned separate locus numbers to the two halves of the grave down to just above bedrock. This division did not seem to be significant in terms of the history of the grave, but it is useful in helping to determine precisely where the objects came from.

The trench was later extended a second time to uncover the northwest corner of the grave in V 10823, V 10824, V 10825, and V 10826. At the end of the 1987 season, it was thought that more layers of cremations would be found below the pebbly layer at the bottom of the grave, and in 1988 the excavation of the grave continued. The pebbly surface (V 10827) turned out to be brecciating bedrock, which was cleaned as V 10828, and no more burials were found.

At the time of excavation, four burials were recognized. An infant was identified later from the residue from the water sieve. The four burials were originally given the identifying numbers 10–13; they were subsequently renumbered. Several clusters of pottery were identified and removed separately, so it is easy to determine where the various vessels were found in the grave. Finally, most of the iron tools and weapons found in the grave came from the south end of the enclosure (Pl. 28A). As the grave was on a steep slope, some material may have eroded and washed down the hill to the unexcavated area on the west. Fragments of grave vessels were found also to the south in V 10300.

Architecture

Grave 6 is a stone-lined, rectangular enclosure, oriented northwest–southeast and measuring 1.90 m north–south x 1.17–1.46 m east–west (Fig. 57; Pl. 28B). The east boundary wall (V 10810) is longer than the enclosure itself and has two good faces, as was the case with Grave 3, but there is no evidence that it preexisted the grave; there are no house remains in the area, and if the wall was built for the LM IIIC settlement, it must have served as a terrace or retaining wall for something higher to the east or for a road (Pl. 28C). This boundary wall is two to three courses high and has a good eastern face; it is similar in appearance, width, and construction techniques to the walls of the earlier houses. Many limestone blocks in the wall are fissured from the heat of the pyre. The north wall (V 10829) is two courses high, and it may have had two faces, although excavation has not been carried out to the north to make certain. It may have bonded with the east wall. The west (V 10830) and south (V 10831) walls were each constructed of a single row of limestone and bedrock boulders. The floor of the grave was brecciating bedrock that was calcined from the heat of the pyre.

Stratigraphy

The total deposition in Grave 6 was approximately 0.50 m in the south, where much erosion had occurred, and 0.70 m in the north. Although many different loci were identified in an attempt to keep material separate both horizontally and vertically, the stratigraphy was mixed. The builders of the grave founded the walls on bedrock and built their pyre directly on it, as is indicated by the calcination of the breccia bedrock. The earliest burial (Burial 1) was found in the lowest levels, primarily in the northern part of the enclosure, where it may have been swept during the course of subsequent burial events. Above the floor, except for a lens of ashy soil (V 10821, V 10822), the deposit was consistent, composed of rock tumble and soft, dark soil with snail shells, human cremated bone, and much fragmentary pottery (V 10814, V 10815, V 10817–10822, V 10824, V 10826). The earlier burials (Burials 1–3) tended to cluster toward the bottom, while the later ones were more toward the top, but no distinguishing feature separated them, nor was there any clear stratigraphic division. The final cremation (Burial 4) went all the way from the floor to the uppermost level of the grave deposit. The inhumation that was the last burial (Burial 5) seems to have been confined to the upper levels (V 10814, V 10815, V 10817, V 10818, V 10824) of stone tumble, and to a layer of cobbles and rather hard brown soil (V 10812) above it (Pl. 28D). For the most part, the pottery was found in all levels of the grave, although some of it was clustered in the south or the north. Above the stone cobbles over the last burial was topsoil (V 10800, V 10802, V 10806, V 10807, V 10823). Some pottery and bone were found east of wall V 10810 in Locus 10801, possibly thrown there during later disturbance of the enclosure.

Associated Features

There were no features definitively associated with Grave 6. Some material from the grave was found in the trench to the south (V 10300), having been deposited there either due to deliberate dumping or as the result of erosion downslope. The east wall of the grave extended to the south where there was a small enclosure that may have had some association with the grave, perhaps originally a paving like those associated with Graves 3, 26, and 27.

Burials

There were five burials in Grave 6: four cremations and an inhumation.

Burial 1

Type: disturbed primary cremation
Age: adult, 20–40 years
Sex: unknown
Weight: 791 g

Burial 1 consists of the partial cremated remains of an adult, probably 20 to 40 years old, as indicated by the endocranial suture closure. Most of the remains, consisting primarily of cranial bone, were found commingled with Burial 2 or crushed into the pebble layer at the bottom of the enclosure. The bone is all completely calcined and very fragmentary. There is evidence of strenuous use of muscles, as indicated by enthesopathies, pitting, and reactive bone on the areas of muscle attachments of the femur and ulna. In addition, the dorsal and ventral surfaces of a scapula fragment show signs of inflammation, with extensive periosteal bone deposits, particularly around the scapular spine. There is insufficient evidence to offer a suggested diagnosis of the cause of this new bone formation.

Burial 2

Type: disturbed primary cremation
Age: infant, perinatal
Sex: unknown
Weight: 35 g

Burial 2 is a partial cremated infant skeleton, entirely recovered from residue of the water sieve (Pl. 28E). The general size of the cranial bone, long bone fragments, and ribs corresponds to that of other perinatal infants from Vronda, but there is no evidence for a specific age. The bone is completely calcined and white in color.

Burial 3

Type: disturbed primary cremation
Age: adult, 20–40 years
Sex: unknown
Weight: 1,102 g

Burial 3 is a partial cremated skeleton of an adult of indeterminate sex, probably 20 to 40 years old. The cremated bone was found mixed with a large number of tools and weapons in a heap of debris that had been pushed to the south end of the burial enclosure when the grave was reused (Gesell, Day, and Coulson 1988, 288–289). There is some evidence for physical stress on the bones of the lower back and legs. The first sacral vertebra shows considerable lipping, and the linea aspera of the femur is very rough and flattened. Most of the bone is completely calcined, with the exception of the right humerus, an unsided radius shaft, and the anterior cranial vault. These bones are heavily scorched or burned, indicating that the skull and right arm were subject to less intensive burning.

Burial 4

Type: primary cremation
Age: adult, 50–60 years
Sex: male
Weight: 2,523 g

Burial 4 is the cremated skeleton of an adult, 50–60 years old, as determined on the basis of the morphology of a partial auricular surface fragment from the os coxa (Buikstra and Ubelaker, eds., 1994, 24–32). The age estimate is reinforced by the degree of tooth wear and the obliteration of the endocranial sutures. The morphology of the cranium and pelvis are clearly male. The lower legs of this burial were disturbed, but the rest of the skeleton remained in anatomical order at the time of excavation, indicating that this was a primary cremation burial. The body was placed with the head at the north end of the enclosure with one arm crossed over the abdomen. There is some compression of the lower thoracic and lumbar vertebra bodies, and the femora has very rough lineae asperae.

There is a definite differentiation in the degree of cremation between the upper and lower body. The cranium, pectoral girdle, humeri, right ulna, and cervical vertebrae are all very lightly burned, with only scorching or initial combustion of the organic elements of the bone. The thoracic vertebrae are somewhat more burned, while the lumbar vertebrae, legs, and innominates are completely calcined.

The weight of the postcranial bone is well beyond the expected weight for a single individual. Although no duplicated skeletal elements were identified, it is clear that some of this bone is associated with one or more of the earlier disturbed cremation burials in this enclosure.

Burial 5

Type: disturbed inhumation
Age: adult, 60+ years
Sex: unknown
Weight: 194 g

Burial 5, the last in Grave 6, is a fragmentary inhumation of an adult, possibly over 60 years in age. The remains consist of fragments of cranial bone, teeth, and the articulated feet and lower legs. Additional fragments of weathered human bone were found on the slope below the burial enclosure, indicating that the skeleton had washed out of the grave due to surface erosion. The preserved cranial vault sutures are completely obliterated. One tooth, a maxillary third molar, was recovered. This tooth shows extreme wear, with all of the enamel eroded from the occlusal surface and the sides of the tooth.

There is osteoarthritic breakdown of the joint surfaces of the ankle on both legs.

This burial was positioned with the head at the south end of the grave. The feet were crowded into the northeast corner of the enclosure. This fact may account for the articulation and preservation of these elements, while most of the rest of the skeleton had been washed out of the grave (Gesell, Coulson, and Day 1988, 288–289).

There is slight evidence of burning on some of the bone fragments from this grave. This burial lay near the modern surface before excavation. It has been shown that surface fires can affect the appearance of buried bone to a considerable depth below a fire (Asmussen 2009, 530). At the time of excavation, a localized area of recent burning was noted. It is likely that this area or earlier surface burning accounts for the scorching of the bone rather than the occurrence of a partial cremation in antiquity.

Faunal Remains

Within the area of Grave 6, both burned and unburned animal bone was recovered (Table 6). Identifiable unburned bones included a number of heavily eroded sheep or goat lower front and hind limb bones recovered from the rock tumble (V 10812.1), possibly associated with the inhumation and the ashy fill (V 10817.1, V 10820). A single pig right tibia diaphysis fragment from the fill was partially burned. Also found in the lower fill area and ashy lens above the floor were two heavily burned or calcined deer antler segments, one beam and one tine. Both segments appear to have been deliberately modified. The heavily burned or calcined beam segment from V 10819.4 retains one cut end and has been heavily scraped. The tine segment from V 10821.1, also calcined, appears to have been hollowed on the distal end.

Pottery

Grave 6 produced over 1,600 fragments of pottery, weighing 7.61 kg, which yielded 30 vessels after mending, with a high percentage of medium-coarse (23%) and coarse (7%) wares. The pottery assemblage from Grave 6 is also unusual in having fewer monochrome cups and more skyphoi among the recognizable drinking vessels than is typical in the Vronda graves. Most of the pottery comes from the southern part of the grave, including four skyphoi (**GR6 P2**–**GR6 P4**, **GR6 P23**), five cups (**GR6 P10**, **GR6 P14**, **GR6 P17**, **GR6 P22**, **GR6 P30**), a miniature amphora (**GR6 P5**), a juglet (**GR6 P6**), a jar (**GR6 P25**), and an oinochoe (**GR6 P29**). Those that come mostly from the north include cups **GR6 P16** and **GR6 P18**.

A few vessels can be associated with the lowest burials (Burials 1–3): **GR6 P8**, **GR6 P9**, **GR6 P15**, **GR6 P18**, **GR6 P21**, and **GR6 P24**. Most of these vessels are of LG date, but some look earlier, such as skyphos **GR6 P24** and cups **GR6 P9** and **GR6 P15**. One cup (**GR6 P18**), however, is quite deep, a sign of a date later in the LG period. The ring base **GR6 P21** may belong to a transport amphora, although it would seem to be from a more open shape, perhaps a pyxis; similar bases, usually belonging to the end of the seventh century but perhaps occurring earlier, appear at Kommos (Callaghan and Johnston 2000, 248–249, pl. 4.18:394). Comparable bases also appeared in Graves 9 and 19 (see below), neither of which produced pottery that is particularly late.

More vessels could be associated with Burial 4: **GR6 P5**, **GR6 P7**, **GR6 P10**, **GR6 P13**, **GR6 P14**, **GR6 P17**, **GR6 P19**, **GR6 P22**, **GR6 P23**, and **GR6 P29**. Monochrome cup **GR6 P10** is quite deep, with a slightly taller offset rim, suggesting a late LG date. A coarse skyphos (**GR6 P23**) that was misfired in a kiln also seems to have been associated with this burial. The large, coarse oinochoe with incised lines on the rim (**GR6 P29**), which is unique in the Vronda grave assemblages, seems to have no parallels elsewhere; the closest vessel is an oinochoe of PGB date from Gria Viglia, but this vessel lacks the incisions on the rim (Vasilakis 2004, 99, fig. 8). The miniature amphora (**GR6 P5**) may have been included for the infant burial; a similar miniature hydria of EO date that appears in one of the tombs at Knossos together with other miniature vessels may also be so interpreted (Coldstream and Catling, eds., 1996, 151, pl. 148:17).

Vessels associated with Burial 5 include a decorated cup (**GR6 P1**) and skyphoi (**GR6 P2**, **GR6 P3**), a monochrome cup (**GR6 P11**), a misfired cup (**GR6 P30**), a juglet (**GR6 P6**), a large jug (**GR6 P28**), and various closed vessels (**GR6 P20**, **GR6 P25**). Burial 5 had the largest number of decorated vessels of any burial in the grave. The skyphos **GR6 P2** is of a type that is common at late MG Knossos but has LG parallels in East Crete. An unusual feature of this vessel is the banding on the interior in place of the usual monochrome coating, but such banding can be found on skyphoi of EG date at Knossos (Coldstream and Catling, eds., 1996, 21, fig. 63:119) and of LG date at Hagios Georgios (Tsipopoulou 2005, 193, fig. 114:Σ4097). The stemmed skyphos **GR6 P3** is of a common type for East Crete in the LG period (Tsipopoulou 2005, fig. 108). The juglet **GR6 P6** is an unusual shape; although parallels are found at LPG–PGB Kommos (Callaghan and Johnston 2000, 223, pl. 4.3:96) and EG Eleutherna (Kotsonas 2008, 170–171, fig. 41:A153), it is closer to an example of White Painted I from Palaepaphos-*Skales* of CG IA (Karageorghis 1983, 296, fig. 175, T.85:41). The large white-slipped jug (**GR6 P28**) decorated with bands and pendant oblique strokes is unique in the Vronda grave assemblage, but comparable decoration may be seen on oinochoai from MPG Knossos (Coldstream and Catling, eds., 1996, 47, pl. 78:6; 247, pl. 229:96). Similar jugs with banded decoration come from Orientalizing Knossos (Brock 1957, pl. 93:1283, 1520) and EO Eleutherna (Kotsonas 2008, 252–253, fig. 63:A104).

Fragments of three vessels were found throughout the grave, and they could be associated with any of the burials: **GR6 P12**, **GR6 P16**, and **GR6 P27**. One of the two monochrome cups (**GR6 P12**) is of the deep variety found late in the LG period. The krater (**GR6 P27**) probably rested on the floor of the grave, as the base was recovered in the lowest levels, but parts of it were found on the surface as well. It is an unusual shape that is not paralleled elsewhere, although similar open vessels can be found in Graves 9 (**GR9 P34**) and 28 (**GR28 P21**; see below).

Objects

A large quantity of iron was found in Grave 6, most of it from a single deposit in the southern part of the grave at the bottom (Pl. 28A). It is unclear whether these objects gravitated to the bottom or whether they were all placed here together. This group included an axe (**GR6 M10**), a knife (**GR6 M9**), tongs (**GR6 M17**), a punch or hammer (**GR6 M14**), two chisels (**GR6 M11**, **GR6 M13**), a file (**GR6 M15**), two tools (**GR6 M12**, **GR6 M18**), "handles" (**GR6 M21**, **GR6 M22**), various tools with rectangular sections (**GR6 M19**, **GR6 M20**), a pin (**GR6 M1**), a fibula (**GR6 M4**), the dagger or dirk (**GR6 M8**), and all three spearheads (**GR6 M5**–**GR6 M7**). A terracotta bead (**GR6 TC1**) and only a few iron objects, including two pins or awls (**GR6 M2**, **GR6 M3**) and a second file (**GR6 M16**), came from elsewhere in the grave.

Although the weapons are customary, if few (three spearheads and a dagger or dirk), the quantity and variety of tools is unusual. It was initially thought that the tools might represent a specialist toolkit, perhaps for a metal worker because of the tongs and files. It is possible that the tools were included for the wealth represented by the metal and were not necessarily representative of the role played by the deceased in life, but the quantity of unusual tools suggests an association with a craft. While axeheads, flat chisels, files, and knives have been found in other tombs, unusual tools occur here for the only time at Vronda: a punch or hammer, a variety of long chisels or tools, and a pair of iron objects labeled handles. The last-mentioned items are probably not handles, but they are square in section and slightly curving like handles, with no known parallels. Two spearheads had the mineralized remains of textiles (**GR6 M5**, **GR6 M6**).

Grave 6 produced two objects made from modified deer antler. One (**GR6 B1**) was hollowed and may have been used as a handle for a tool (awl or knife). The other (**GR6 B2**) is less well preserved but is also hollowed so that it could have been used as a handle for a tool. The smoothed end of this tool has streaks of blue, different from the rest of the antler, and other pieces also have the same coloration. The blue color may have resulted from the cremation process, or it may represent deliberate decoration of the tool with blue pigment.

Chronology

It is difficult to date any of the burials in the grave precisely. While it seems that the monochrome cups from the bottom of the grave associated with the earlier burials (1–3) look earlier in LG than those from the upper levels (especially **GR6 P11**), it is difficult to pinpoint their precise phase, and at least one is large and deep like later LG examples (**GR6 P18**). The material associated with the last burial, particularly the skyphoi (**GR6 P2**, **GR6 P3**), have LG parallels; similar stemmed skyphoi appeared also in Graves 1, 19, and 28. The material all looks LG in date, that from the earlier burials early in the period and those from Burials 4 and 5 later. None of the pottery definitely continues into the seventh century.

Catalog

Pottery

FINE DECORATED WARES

GR6 P1 (V 10802.1, V 10814.2, V 10817.1; Fig. 58). Cup. Five fragments from rim, body and handle; missing base and most of handle. Max. pres. h. 4.8; d. rim est. 12.0. Fine, rather hard, pink (5YR 7/4) fabric. Glossy, very pale brown (10YR 8/3) slip. Black paint worn to shadow. Surfaces relatively well preserved, although paint fugitive. No burning. Crosshatched lozenges on shoulder. *Date*: LG.

GR6 P2 (V98.82; V 10801.1, V 10814.4 clusters 2 and 3, V 10817.1 and 2, V 10817.5; Fig. 58; Pl. 29). Skyphos. Partially restored from 14 fragments; one nonjoining fragment. Preservation 40%, including 75% of rim, one handle; missing base and other handle. Max. pres. h. 8.4; d. rim 14.0. Fine to medium-coarse, rather hard, light red (2.5YR 6/8) fabric. Petrographic sample KAV 15/26: Fabric Group 5. Creamy, very pale brown (10YR 7/4) slip. Red (2.5YR 5/8) paint. Very well-preserved surfaces. No burning. Metopal panel with zigzag; interior has bands rather than solid coating. *Bibliography*: Gesell, Day, and Coulson 1988, 288–289, pl. 77:f. *Comparanda*: Coldstream and Catling, eds., 1996, 114, fig. 95:94; 143–144, fig. 105:63, 95, 107 (Knossos, MG); Tsipopoulou 2005, 275, fig. 116:AN1603 (Praisos, LG). *Date*: LG.

GR6 P3 (V98.83; V 10807.2, V 10812.3, V 10814.1–3, V 10814.4 cluster 4, V 10817.1 and 2, V 10819.2 and 6; Fig. 58; Pl. 29). Stemmed skyphos. Restored from 34 fragments; six nonjoining fragments. Preservation 80%, including base, both handles, most of rim. H. 13.3; d. rim 11.0; d. base 5.0. Fine, soft, porous, very pale brown (10YR 8/4) fabric with tiny black inclusions. Petrographic sample KAV 15/25: Fabric Subgroup 1b. Black paint. Well-preserved surfaces, worn in some places. Metopal panel with S-pattern and zigzag. No obvious burning. *Bibliography*: Gesell, Day, and Coulson 1988, pl. 77:g. *Comparanda*: for shape, **GR1 P2**, **GR6 P4**, **GR28 P1**; Tsipopoulou 2005, 315, fig. 108:AN1448 (Zou, LG); 189, fig. 108:Σ4074 (Hagios Georgios, LG); for decoration, Coldstream and Catling, eds., 1996, 21, fig. 63:127 (Knossos, MG); Tsipopoulou 2005, 279, fig. 127:Σ3547; 287, fig. 127:AN8766 (Praisos, LG). *Date*: LG.

GR6 P4 (V 10801.1 and 2, V 10814.1–3, V 10817.1, V 10817.5 and 6, V 10819.3–6, V 10820.2–5, V 10821.1 and 2, V 10825.1; Fig. 58). Stemmed skyphos. Partially mended from 78 fragments (maybe more than one vessel represented), including rim, handles, base. H. est. 11.0; d. rim est. 12.0–13.0. Fine, soft, chalky, light gray (2.5Y 7/2) fabric. Black paint. Very worn surfaces. Once decorated, but too worn to determine. *Comparanda*: Tsipopoulou 2005, 157, fig. 108:AN 2369 (Hagios Georgios, LG). *Date*: LG.

GR6 P5 (V87.123, IM 929; V 10817.2; Fig. 58; Pl. 29). Miniature amphora. Intact, but missing one handle and rim. Max. pres. h. 6.8; d. base 3.6. Fine, soft, reddish-yellow (5YR 7/6) fabric with some small gray inclusions. Red (2.5YR 4/6) to black paint. Rather well-preserved surfaces on one side, worn on other. No burning. Parallel bands on neck, hatched triangles on shoulder, lower body and underside of base solidly painted. *Bibliography*: Gesell, Day, and Coulson 1988, 288–289, pl. 77:h. *Comparanda*: Rethemiotakis and Englezou 2010, 65, pl. 131:115δ (Eltyna, PGB–EG). *Date*: LG.

GR6 P6 (V 10814.2, V 10817.1 and 2; Fig. 58). Juglet. Partially mended from 29 fragments; eight nonjoining fragments. Preservation 60%, including base, most of body, rim, and handle; missing much of shoulder and all of lower neck. Max. pres. h. 8.2; h. est. 12.0; d. rim 4.0; d. base 5.0–6.0. Fine, soft, gritty, reddish-yellow (7.5YR 6/6) fabric. Yellowish-red (5YR 4/6) to black paint. Very worn surfaces. No burning. Bands below, vertical strokes on shoulder. *Date*: LG.

GR6 P7 (V 10819.4, V 10820.3, V 10812.3, V 10819.7, V 10822.1, V 10821.1; Fig. 58). Juglet. Partially mended from three fragments, preserving part of rim; missing body, handle, and base. Max. pres. h. 1.6; d. rim 6.0. Fine, soft, chalky, light gray (2.5Y 7/2) fabric. Dull, black paint. Well-preserved surfaces. *Date*: unknown.

GR6 P8 (V 10819.5, V 10819.7, V 10820.2 and 3, V 10821.1 and 2, V 10822.1, V 10825.1, V 10827.1, V 10828.1; Fig. 58). Pyxis or jar. Partially mended from 122 fragments, including base and rim. Max. pres. h. 10.0; d. rim est. 8.0; d. base 8.0–9.0. Fine, very soft, chalky, pale yellow (2.5Y 8/2) fabric. Black paint. Very worn surfaces. Once painted, but nothing remains. Edges worn and rounded and impossible to mend. *Comparanda*: Kotsonas 2008, 140–141, fig. 33:A105 (Eleutherna, LG–EO). *Date*: LG.

FINE MONOCHROME WARES

GR6 P9 (V 10818.1, V 10819.7, V 10821.1 and 2, V 10823.1; Fig. 58). Cup. Mended from 66 fragments, 60% preserved, including full profile, 75% of base, handle, 65% of rim; missing much of body. H. 7.3; d. rim 9.6; d. base 5.0. Fine, soft, pink to reddish-yellow (7.5YR 8/4–8/6) fabric. Traces of red to brown paint. Very worn surfaces. Many fragments burned and join to unburned fragments; some iron staining on base. *Comparanda*: **GR1 P13**; Coldstream and Catling, eds., 1996, 229, fig. 135:4 (Knossos, EG). *Date*: G.

GR6 P10 (V 10807.1, V 10812.1 and 3, V 10817.4–6, V 10819.4–6, V 10821.1 V 10823.1; Fig. 58). Cup. Mended from 25 fragments; 10 nonjoining fragments. Preservation 40%, including nearly full profile to close to base, top of handle; missing base. Max. pres. h. 10.0; d. rim 13.2. Fine, soft, reddish-yellow (5YR 7/6) fabric. Yellowish-red (5YR 5/6) paint. Rather well-preserved surfaces. Some fragments burned, including handle attachment. *Comparanda*: Coldstream 1972, 86, fig. 8:F17 (Knossos, LG–EO). *Date*: LG.

GR6 P11 (V 10801.2, V 10817.5, V 10823.1; Fig. 58). Cup. Partially mended from six fragments, 30%

preserved, including rim, base, and handle; full profile can be restored. Max. pres. h. 7.2; h. est. 9.0; d. rim 12.0; d. base 5.0. Fine, soft, porous, reddish-yellow (7.5YR 7/6) fabric with granodiorites and gold mica. Yellowish-red (5YR 5/8) paint. Worn surfaces, well-preserved in places. No burning. Exterior has pronounced ridges and wiping lines. *Comparanda*: Sakellarakis 1986, 48, fig. 45 (Archanes, LG); Tsipopoulou 2005, fig. 106:H762 (Kavousi, Plai tou Kastro, LG). *Date*: LG.

GR6 P12 (V 10800.1, V 10817.5, V 10818.1 and 2, V 10819.3–7, V 10820.2 and 3, V 10826.1, V 10828.1; Fig. 59). Cup. Partially mended from 58 fragments, 50% preserved, including half of base, rim, and handle; profile can be restored. H. est. 10.6; d. rim 13.0; d. base 7.0. Fine, soft, reddish-yellow (7.5YR 7/6) fabric. Red (2.5YR 4/8) paint. Worn surfaces. Almost totally burned; many edges worn. *Comparanda*: Lebessi 1970, 277, pl. 391γ:19 (Mastambas, LG); Gesell, Day, and Coulson 1995, 114–115, fig. 21:8 (Kavousi, Kastro, LG); Coldstream and Catling, eds., 1996, 147, fig. 106:32 (Knossos, LG); Kotsonas 2008, 208–209, fig. 51:A168 (Eleutherna, LG–EO). *Date*: LG.

GR6 P13 (V87.127, IM 968; V 10817.2, V 10817.5 and 6, V 10819.4–6, V 10821.1; Fig. 59). Cup. Partially mended from 20 fragments. Preservation 35%, including 80% of base, rim, and handle; profile can be restored. H. est. 8.0; d. rim 12.0; d. base 6.0. Fine, soft, reddish-yellow (7.5YR 7/6) fabric. Yellowish-red (5YR 5/6–4/6) paint. Painted on interior, exterior, and underside of base. Worn surfaces. Some fragments burned and join unburned fragments. Wheel ridging on interior, string marks on base. *Comparanda*: Gesell, Day, and Coulson 1995, 99, 115, fig. 21:5 (Kavousi Kastro, LG); Coldstream and Catling, eds., 1996, 21, fig. 63:131; 78, fig. 78:4 (Knossos, PGB–EG). *Date*: LG.

GR6 P14 (V 10812.2, V 10814.4, V 10814.6, V 10817.1 and 2, V 10817.4 cluster 2, V 10819.7, V 10820.3, V 10821.2; Fig. 59). Cup. Partially mended from 30 fragments, 30% preserved, including base, one fragment of rim, and handle; missing full profile. Max. pres. h. 5.0; h. est. 10.6; d. rim 13.0; d. base 5.0. Fine, very soft, chalky, very pale brown (10YR 7/3) fabric. Dull, streaky, reddish-brown (5YR 5/4) to black paint. Very worn surfaces and edges. No burning. *Date*: LG?

GR6 P15 (V 10305.2, V 10305.4, V 10821.1; Fig. 59). Cup or skyphos. Partially mended from 14 fragments; 10% of rim and upper body preserved; missing base and handle. Max. pres. h. 7.0; d. rim 13.0. Fine, rather hard, yellowish-red (5YR 5/6) fabric. Red (2.5YR 4/6) to reddish-brown (5YR 4/4) paint. Worn surfaces. No burning. *Comparanda*: Mook 2004, 175, fig. 12.10:P (Kastro, G). *Date*: G.

GR6 P16 (V 10801.1, V 10807.2, V 10812.1, V 10815.1, V 10818.2, V 10819.4, V 10824.1, V 10825.1; Fig. 59). Cup or skyphos. Partially mended from 18 fragments; 15% preserved; missing handle and base. Max. pres. h. 9.2; d. rim 14.0. Fine, soft, rather porous, reddish-yellow (5YR 6/6) fabric. Red (2.5YR 5/8) paint. Worn surfaces. No burning. *Comparanda*: Lebessi 1970, 278, pl. 391γ:26 (Mastambas, LG). *Date*: LG.

GR6 P17 (V 10817.2, V 10817.6, V 10819.4–7, V 10821.1; Fig. 59). Cup or skyphos. Partially mended from 16 fragments; 25% preserved; missing base and handle(s). Max. pres. h. 6.5; d. rim 11.0. Fine, soft, reddish-yellow (7.5YR 7/6) fabric. Red (2.5YR 5/8) paint. Well-preserved surfaces. One fragment burned. *Date*: LG.

GR6 P18 (V 10801.1 and 2, V 10803.1, V 10819.4 and 5, V 10819.7 and 8, V 10822.1, V 10823.1 and 2, V 10824.1, V 10827.1; Fig. 59). Cup or skyphos. Partially mended from 14 fragments; 16 nonjoining fragments. Preservation 25%, including base and rim fragments; missing handle; profile can be reconstructed. H. est. 8.9; d. rim 12.0; d. base 6.0. Fine, soft, rather porous, very pale brown (10YR 7/4) fabric. Traces of paint. Worn surfaces. Some fragments burned. *Date*: LG.

GR6 P19 (V 10802.1, V 10817.6, V 10819.3, V 10819.5 and 6, V 10821.1, V 10822.1; Fig. 59). Cup or skyphos. Partially mended from five fragments from rim and part of body; 15 nonjoining fragments. D. rim 12.2. Fine, soft, pink to reddish-yellow (7.5YR 7/4–7/6) fabric. Red (2.5YR 4/6) paint. Worn surfaces. Many fragments burned. *Date*: LG.

GR6 P20 (V 10800.1, V 10801.1, V 10802.1 and 2, V 10803.1, V 10807.2, V 10812.3 and 4; Fig. 59). Closed vessel. Partially mended from four fragments from base; 13 fragments may belong. Max. pres. h. 3.4; d. base est. 6.0. Fine, soft, pink (7.5YR 8/4) fabric. Red (2.5YR 4/6) paint. Worn surfaces. *Date*: uncertain.

GR6 P21 (V 10304.2; Fig. 59). Closed vessel. Single fragment preserving half of base. Max. pres. h. 4.0; d. base 13.0. Fine, soft, light gray (5Y 7/2) fabric. No paint preserved. Ring base. *Date*: LG.

Medium-Coarse Monochrome Wares

GR6 P22 (V 10802.1, V 10812.3 and 4, V 108114.1 object 2, V 10814.3, V 10817.2, V 10817.5, V 10819.3; Fig. 59). Cup. Partially mended from 19 fragments. Parts of rim, body, and handle preserved. Max. pres. h. 4.4; d. rim 12.0. Medium-coarse, soft, reddish-yellow (5YR 6/8) fabric with metamorphic inclusions. Petrographic sample KAV 15/28: off-island import? Gray (5Y 5/1) at core and on interior. Very worn surfaces. Burned. *Date*: LG.

GR6 P23 (V98.84; V 10801.1 and 2, V 10814.2, V 10817.1 and 2, V 10817.5 and 6, V 10819.1, V 10819.3–7, V 10820.2; Fig. 60; Pl. 29). Skyphos. Restored from 42 fragments, 90% preserved; missing small fragments of rim, body, and base. H. 8.6; d. rim 13.5–15.0; d. base 5.5. Coarse, soft, gray (5Y 5/1) fabric, reddish-yellow (5YR 6/6) where not burned, with frequent hard white and dark gray phyllite inclusions. Very worn surfaces. Totally burned and warped. *Comparanda*: Coldstream and Catling, eds., 1996, 143, fig. 105:95 (Knossos, late MG). *Date*: LG.

GR6 P24 (V 10801.1 and 2, V 10817.5, V 10819.4 and 5, V 10820.2 and 3, V 10820.5, V 10821.1 and 2, V 10822.1, V 10827.1; Fig. 60). Skyphos. Represented by 59 fragments from rim, base, and handle (may be more than one vessel). H. est. 10.0; d. rim 10.0–12.0; d. base 5.0–6.0. Medium-coarse, soft, porous, sandy, reddish-yellow (7.5YR 7/6) fabric, with some mica and clay pellets. Red (2.5YR 4/8) paint on interior, exterior, and underside of base. Very worn surfaces. Some fragments burned. *Comparanda*: Tsipopoulou 2005, 235, fig. 57:Σ4066 (Piskokephalo, PGB). *Date*: G.

GR6 P25 (V 10812.2, V 10814.2; Fig. 60). Jar. Partially mended from nine fragments from rim and body; 50% of rim preserved. Max. pres. h. 3.0; d. rim 15.0. Medium-coarse, soft, reddish-yellow (7.5YR 7/6) fabric with frequent red phyllites. Possibly slipped. Very worn surfaces. Some fragments burned. *Date*: LG.

Medium-Coarse Plain Ware

GR6 P26 (V 10818.1 and 2; Fig. 60). Cup or skyphos. Partially mended from 26 fragments. Preservation 30%, including 75% of rim, 40% of upper body; missing base and handle(s). Max. pres. h. 8.0; d. rim 16.0–18.0. Medium-coarse, reddish-yellow (5YR 6/6) fabric with phyllites, quartz, and much silver mica. Petrographic sample KAV 15/27: small low-fired metamorphic group. Surface smoothed and mottled (like certain Kavousi Type IV LM IIIC fabrics). Well-preserved surfaces. No burning. *Date*: LG.

Coarse Painted Wares

GR6 P27 (V 10800.1 and 2, V 10801.1 and 2, V 10802.1, V 10806.1, V 10807.2, V 10812.1, V 10812.3, V 10814.2, V 10814.4 and 5, V 10815.1, V 10816.1, V 10817.1–3, V 10817.5, V 10818.2, V 10819.1–5, V 10819.6, V 10820.2, V 10821.1, V 10823.1, V 10827.2; Fig. 60). Krater. Partially mended from 129 fragments, preserving 50% of rim, one handle, 30% of base. H. est. 36.0; d. rim 46.0; d. base 19.0–20.0. Coarse, reddish-yellow (7.5YR 7/6) fabric with gray siltstones and quartz. Petrographic sample KAV 15/29: Fabric Group 5. Very pale brown (10YR 8/3) slip. Traces of brown paint. Very worn surfaces. Some fragments burned. Bands on exterior. *Comparanda*: Coldstream and Catling, eds., 1996, 5, fig. 57:5 (Knossos, LPG). *Date*: LG.

GR6 P28 (V 10800.1, V 10801.1 and 2, V 10802.1, V 10806.1, V 10807.1 and 2, V 10809.1, V 10812.4, V 10814.7, V 10815.1, V 10817.5, V 10818.2, V 10819.1, V 10819.3–8, V 10820.2, V 10820.4, V 10821.1 and 2, V 10822.1, V 10823.2, V 10824.1, V 10826.1; Fig. 61). Jug. Partially mended from 100 fragments. Preservation 20%, including part of handle, neck, and rim; missing base and rest of handle; nearly complete profile can be restored. Max. pres. h. 34.0; d. rim 8.5. Coarse, soft, reddish-yellow (7.5YR 8/6) fabric with frequent red phyllite inclusions. Petrographic sample KAV 15/30: loner. Very pale brown (10YR 8/3) slip. Red (2.5YR 5/8) paint. Worn surfaces, with a few preserving slip and paint. Pendant oblique strokes at base of rim; bands on body. *Comparanda*: Papadaki and Galanaki 2012, 336, fig. 1 (Aitania, MPG). *Date*: LG.

Coarse Monochrome Ware

GR6 P29 (V98.85; V 10801.1 and 2, V 10814.1, V 10817.1, V 10817.2, V 10817.5, V 10817.6, V 10819.1, V 10819.3, V 10819.4–7, V 10820.2, V 10821.1; Fig. 61; Pl. 29). Oinochoe. Partially restored from 49 fragments; second large fragment from base; 54 nonjoining fragments. Preservation 75%, including half of base, much of upper body, entire neck, most of rim, and lower handle attachment; missing connection between base and body, top of handle, part of rim. Max. pres. h. 22.3; h. est. 31.5; d. base 11.8. Coarse, soft, reddish-yellow (5YR 7/6) fabric, reddish-yellow (7.5YR 7/6) at surface, with frequent black and white grits and calcareous matter. Petrographic sample KAV 15/31: Fabric Group 5. Red (2.5YR 5/8) paint. Very worn surfaces. Some fragments burned. Six incised lines around top of trefoil mouth. *Date*: LG.

Coarse Plain Ware

GR6 P30 (V 10801.2, V 10802.1, V 10807.2, V 10812.1, V 10812.4, V 10814.1–4, V 10817.1 and 2, V 10817.5, V 10819.2; Fig. 61). Cup. Partially mended from 37 fragments into four large fragments from rim and base. Preservation 60%, including nearly full profile, some of base, most of handle, much of rim. H. est. 10.8; d. rim 9.7–14.7; d. base est. 5.0. Coarse, rather hard, gray (5Y 5/1) fabric, reddish-yellow (5YR 6/6) where not burned. Very burned and warped. Very worn surfaces. *Date*: LG.

Metal

Iron

GR6 M1 (V 10821.1 object 2; Fig. 62). Iron pin. Two nonjoining fragments from pin, one near point, the other near end. Max. pres. L. (a) 2.5, (b) 1.9. Corroded and cracked. Head has swelling with two rings above it and two or three below.

GR6 M2 (V 10819.4; Fig. 62). Iron pin or awl. Two joining fragments from point. Max. pres. L. 5.2. Cracked and corroded.

GR6 M3 (V 10819.6 object 2; Fig. 62). Iron pin or awl. Single fragment from end of pin. Max. pres. L. 3.0. Cracked and corroded.

GR6 M4 (V87.106, IM 946; V 10821.1, object 5; Fig. 62; Pl. 29). Iron fibula. Four joining fragments preserving part of bow, pin, and catch plate; coil missing. Max. pres. L. 3.5. Corroded, but some surface still preserved. Simple arched fibula. *Comparanda*: Blinkenberg 1926, 63, type II: 4b, fig. 34 (Vrokastro); Sapouna-Sakellaraki 1978, 48, type IId, pl. 6:169.

GR6 M5 (V87.117, IM 957; V10821.2, object 16; Fig. 62; Pl. 29). Iron spearhead. Partially mended from five fragments; complete except for tip of blade. Max.

pres. L. 32.5; max. w. 2.4; d. socket 1.6. Well-preserved surface. One fragment showed remains of mineralized textiles on surface, but these were lost during conservation. Long (9.0) socket with hole-pierced opposite edges. Short, triangular midrib; long blade with sloping shoulders. *Bibliography*: Day 1995, fig. 7.

GR6 M6 (V87.119, IM 959; V 10821.2, object 9; Fig. 62; Pl. 29). Iron spearhead. Mended from five fragments; complete except for top of blade. Max. pres. L. 25.3; max. w. 2.2; d. socket 1.7. Surface corroded, with patches of original surface; textile and wood impressions on blade. Long (9.0) socket with hole-pierced opposite edges. Long blade with sloping shoulders and short, triangular midrib. *Bibliography*: Day 1995, fig. 7.

GR6 M7 (V87.111/120, IM 951/960; V 10821.1, object 4, V 10821.2 object 13; Fig. 62; Pl. 29). Iron spearhead. Three nonjoining fragments, preserving socket (a), blade (b), and tip (c). Max. pres. L. (a) 16.3, (b) 7.5, (c) 8.5; max. w. 2.7; d. socket 1.7. Well-preserved surfaces, especially at tip. Long (9.0) socket without pierced hole. Sloping shoulders; short, triangular midrib. *Bibliography*: Day 1995, fig. 7.

GR6 M8 (V87.107/109/110; IM 947/949/950; V 10821.1, objects 3 and 7, V 10820.5 object 1; Fig. 63; Pl. 29). Iron dagger or dirk. Mended from 15 fragments, including three rivets, two of bronze; seven nonjoining fragments. Nearly complete; missing tip of hilt and a few blade fragments. Max. pres. L. 36.5; max. w. 3.4. Well-preserved surfaces, especially near tip; corrosion bubble near end with small rivet(?), possibly remains of a hilt. Flange hilted, with three rivets to hold on handle. Long broad blade. *Bibliography*: Day 1995, fig. 7.

GR6 M9 (V87.140; V 10821.2, object 12; Fig. 63; Pl. 30). Iron knife. Partially mended from numerous fragments; many nonjoining fragments. Handle and part of blade preserved. Max. pres. L. 13.8; max. pres. w. 2.6; w. handle 1.3. Corroded and laminated. *Comparanda*: **GR12 M32**; Brock 1957, pl. 172:1611 (Knossos); Snodgrass 1996, 587, type E.

GR6 M10 (V87.108, IM 948, HNM 15737; V10821.1, object 6; Fig. 63; Pl. 30). Iron axe-head. Nearly intact. L. 15.8; max. w. 5.5. Corroded, but much of surface preserved. Polished and treated. Wide, flat blade, tapering slightly; tanged, with projecting horns or flanges at the end of the head, one now broken off. *Bibliography*: Gesell, Day, and Coulson 1988, 288, pl. 77:d; Day 1995, fig. 8. *Comparanda*: Pendlebury, Pendlebury, and Money-Coutts 1937–1938, pl. 29:2.455 (LM IIIC, bronze); Blegen 1952, 281, fig. 3:6; Karageorghis 1983, fig. 142:T. 76.131, pl. 143:T. 76.131 (bronze trunnion axe, Palaepaphos-*Skales*); Coldstream and Catling, eds., 1996, 120, fig. 175:f52, f53; Popham and Lemos 1996, pl. 128:T. 39.33 (LPG); pl. 128:pyre 13.2 (SPG II).

GR6 M11 (V87.121, IM 961, HNM 15741; V 10821.2, object 11; Fig. 63; Pl. 30). Iron chisel. Complete in three joining fragments. L. 10.5; max. w. 2.0. Corroded; few surviving surfaces. Flat chisel, with one broad end and one narrow end. *Bibliography*: Gesell, Day, and Coulson 1988, 288, pl. 77:c, top; Day 1995, fig. 8.

GR6 M12 (V87.141; V 10821.2, object 18; Fig. 63; Pl. 30). Iron awl or chisel. Complete in two fragments. L. 7.0; th. 0.6. Badly corroded, with corrosion bubble obscuring shape. Long, narrow object, flat in section at one end, square in section at other. *Comparanda*: Courtois 1984, fig. 4:53 (bronze).

GR6 M13 (V87.118, IM 958, HNM 15740; V 10821.2, object 14; Fig. 63; Pl. 30). Iron chisel. Mended from three fragments; complete. L. 9.50; max. w. 0.85. Corroded. Surface coated. Long, narrow object, rectangular in section on one end, flattened on other; possible slot on one side, but it does not appear to go through. *Bibliography*: Day 1995, fig. 8.

GR6 M14 (V87.113, IM 953, HNM 15738; V 10821.2, object 15; Fig. 63; Pl. 30). Iron hammer or punch. Complete in three fragments. L. 7.0; w. 1.0–1.5. Surfaces cracked but well preserved. Rectangular in section and slightly curving. Possible traces of slot for a handle in center, which may be a crack; if there is no place for the insertion of the handle, then this object might have been used as a hammer by hand or struck with a hammer like a punch. *Bibliography*: Day 1995, fig. 8.

GR6 M15 (V87.112, IM 952; V 10821.1, object 1; Fig. 63; Pl. 30). Iron file. Mended from three fragments; one end missing. Max. pres. L. 12.5; max. w. 1.0. Corroded, with cracks down center of each side. Surface coated. Four-sided object, square in section. One end tapers to a point, the other tapers to a smaller square. Grooves perpendicular to object on all four sides. *Bibliography*: Day 1995, fig. 8.

GR6 M16 (V87.144; V 10814.4, Cluster 1; Fig. 63; Pl. 30). Iron file. Mended from numerous fragments; both ends missing. Max. pres. L. 14.4; max. pres. w. 2.3. Corroded and split, with laminating surfaces; surface preserved on some fragments. Large, long object, round in section, with grooves perpendicular to length all around.

GR6 M17 (V87.114/116, IM 954/956, HNM 15739; V 10821.2, objects 10 and 17; Fig. 64; Pl. 30). Iron tongs. Complete in 17 fragments. L. 22.0; w. 1.2. Well preserved, with some surviving surfaces, though cracked and flaking. Round in section in center, tapering to flattened ends. *Bibliography*: Gesell, Day, and Coulson 1988, 288, pl. 77:e; Day 1995, fig. 8.

GR6 M18 (V87.115; IM 955; V 10821.2, object 8; Fig. 64; Pl. 30). Iron tool. Mended from three fragments; missing both ends. Max. pres. L. 12.3; max. pres. w. 1.9. Cracked and split. Surface coated. Rectangular in section, tapering to smaller rectangle at one end, open and four-sided at other.

GR6 M19 (V87.122a, IM 962; V 10821.3, object 19; Fig. 64; Pl. 31). Iron tool. Four fragments of iron, possibly from different tools. Max. pres. L. 3.0; max. pres. w. 1.1. Corroded. Square in section.

GR6 M20 (V87.122e, IM 962; V 10821.1, object 3; Fig. 64; Pl. 31). Iron tool, possibly an awl. Single fragment, square at one end, round at other. Max. pres. L. 4.1; max. pres. w. 0.7. Corroded.

GR6 M21 (V87.142a; V 10821.2, object 18; Fig. 64; Pl. 31). Iron object. Mended from many fragments. Nearly complete? Max. pres. L. 10.7; max. w. 2.4. Corroded and laminated, with solid center; some surfaces preserved. Square in section, tapering and curving at one end, square at other. Smoothed and beveled at tapered end as if for attachment of some other object. Of unknown use, but looks like a handle.

GR6 M22 (V87.142b; V 10821.2, object 18; Fig. 64; Pl. 31). Iron object. Mended from many fragments. Nearly complete? Max. pres. L. 11.2; max. w. 2.7. Corroded, cracked, and very laminated. Square in section, with a solid core. Similar in shape to **GR6 P21**, but possibly larger and more tapered.

Bone

GR6 B1 (V 10821.1; Pl. 31). Modified deer antler, unsided tine segment, hollowed? Two fragments, not joining, but probably from same antler. Both are curved, broken at one end and smoothed on the other. Max. pres. L. (a) 7.4, (b) 8.50; w. 1.10–1.40; d. interior 0.85. Calcined white and cracked. Together the pieces form a tube with an open end that has been worked and smoothed down. Possibly a handle for an awl or some other tool.

GR6 B2 (V 10819.4, object 1; Pl. 31). Modified deer antler. Unsided tine segment, hollowed? Four joining pieces, six nonjoining, preserving slightly tapering end of object. One end cut off, faceted, and scraped. Max. pres L. 6.5; w. 1.8–2.0. Calcined. Worked end has blue pigment, which may be seen as a triangular design; four other fragments show similar pigment. The pigment may possibly be decorative. Perhaps a handle for an awl or some other tool.

Stone

GR6 ST1 (V87.81; IM 898; V 10824.1, object 1; Pl. 31). Obsidian blade, center section, two ridges. L. 1.50; w. 0.80; th. 0.25. Obsidian, black. Marginal retouch on one edge, chipped on other edge.

Terracotta

GR6 TC1 (V87.64, IM 890; V 10819.4, object 1; Fig. 64; Pl. 31). Terracotta bead. Depressed globular. Intact, but surfaces worn. H. 1.2; d. 1.8; d. hole 0.3. Wt. 2.00 g. Fine, soft, reddish-yellow (7.5YR 7/6) fabric with some tiny black inclusions. Red (2.5YR 5/6) paint. Monochrome. No wheel marks.

Grave 8

History and Details of Excavation

Grave 8 lies in Room I2 of LM IIIC Building I on a terrace to the west of the Vronda ridge (Figs. 3, 4, 65). It was excavated in 1987 in Trench VW 9000, and a bit more of it was recovered in 1988. The grave was recognized by the presence of burned human bone, first in the topsoil (VW 9001.1) and later amid the rock tumble in Room I2 of Building I (VW 9003.1–3). There was no associated architecture, and the precise area of the grave was at first difficult to distinguish, but after further excavation it seemed to be limited to a roughly circular area with stones and pithos fragments, ca. 0.87 m north–south x 0.75 m east–west (VW 9006.1). There was no ash and very little associated material of any sort. The deposit was interpreted at the time as a secondary pithos burial, but the later examination of the fragments of pottery indicated that there was not a sufficient amount to postulate a pithos burial, so it was probably a pit burial. The circular area was cut into the red clay from the roof of the earlier building. In 1988, excavation continued in the room, and more fragments of bone appeared in the hard floor surface of the room (VW 9014.1, 3, and 4).

Architecture

There was no associated architecture. The grave was simply a roughly circular pit containing cremated human bones, and very little else.

Stratigraphy

The depth of deposition was 0.30–0.50 m. The grave was a pit that cut into the hard floor of Room I2 and the roofing debris above it. It was filled with the same sort of soil and rock tumble as was found in the rest of the room.

Burials

Two burials were made in the grave: an adult and a fetus that was recovered from the water sieve material. It is unclear what this burial represents. There is no evidence for in-situ burning, so it does not seem to have been a pyre site. It may simply be the remains of a discard deposit of a body cremated elsewhere and buried in a pit.

Burial 1

Type: secondary cremation deposit
Age: adult, 20–40 years?
Sex: female?
Weight: 346 g

Burial 1 consists of fragmentary skeletal remains that may be identified, on the basis of the dental development, as those of an adult at least 20 years old. It is not possible to determine the sex or specific age of the skeleton, although the commingled remains of a fetus suggest that it is probably a female who died during pregnancy. Despite a relatively young age, she may have suffered from a pathological bone loss, indicated by the unusually thin cortical bone of the humerus shafts, ranging from 1.10 to 2.05 mm in thickness. This degree of bone loss in a young woman is most unusual and much more severe than would be expected in common, age-related osteoporosis of an older woman (Ortner 2003, 411–413).

Burial 2

Type: secondary cremation deposit
Age: fetus, 16–20 weeks
Sex: unknown
Weight: 5 g

The second burial consists of the fragmentary remains of a fetus. The skeleton cannot be aged precisely, although there are recognizable cranial bone and long bone shaft fragments, a vertebral arch, and a fragment of an ilium. The frontal portion of the eye orbit is only 9.6 mm in length, suggesting that the age of the fetus was not more than 16–20 weeks (Fazekas and Kosa 1978; Schaefer, Black, and Scheuer 2009, 35–36).

Pottery

Grave 8 produced very little pottery: 70 fragments weighing 0.53 kg. Three vessels are represented, but none was preserved well enough to catalog. The first vessel is a fine cup, possibly monochrome, with a fairly tall offset rim and burned a uniform light gray. Some six fragments of this cup were found in V 9003.1. The second vessel is of fine, soft, chalky, reddish-yellow fabric, with edges that were totally smooth and a surface that was completely worn. It may have been a small jug or a cup, but only body fragments were preserved. Fragments of the same vessel were found in VW 9006.1. The third vessel, probably closed, is represented by body fragments of coarse fabric with painted decoration. This vessel appeared also in VW 9006.1 and VW 9001.1. One fragment may have come from the base of the vessel. None of this pottery is diagnostic, nor is it sufficiently preserved to estimate the shapes and decoration.

Objects

There is only one possible associated object: an obsidian chip from VW 9014, which may also have come from the floor of the LM IIIC building and has been cataloged with that building (Day and Glowacki 2012, 62).

Faunal Remains

The faunal materials found in this area are limited to three extremely small bone fragments recovered from flotation residue that were possibly burned (VW 9014.3), and two tooth enamel fragments, one of which comes from a sheep or goat (Table 6). These materials were located on the floor surface of the room in which the grave materials were deposited, and they are not likely to have been associated with the human remains.

Chronology

There are no finds that would allow us to date this burial except the cup, which may belong to LG.

Graves 9 and 14

History and Details of Excavation

Grave 9 is a stone-built burial enclosure that lies on the northeast side of the summit of the Vronda ridge in Room J1 of the earlier LM IIIC Building J (Figs. 3, 4). It was excavated entirely in 1988 in Trenches V 5300 and V 5400 (Gesell, Coulson, and Day 1991, 152–154). Grave 14 was identified as a scatter of human bones and associated Geometric pottery in a pit made in the gray roofing clay from the earlier building to the west of Grave 9 (Fig. 66). As there was little material and because some of the pottery joined with that in Grave 9, Grave 14 has been recognized as a discard deposit from Grave 9 and is considered associated.

The east end of Grave 9 was first recognized in Trench V 5400, immediately below the surface. When it became apparent from the soft ashy soil, stone tumble, snail shells, and human bones that there was a grave and that the majority of it lay in Trench V 5300, biological anthropologists dug the entire enclosure together as part of Trench V 5300. During the course of excavation, a linear accumulation running north to south across the middle of the grave caused the excavator to divide the enclosure into eastern and western sections, although the soft, black, ashy soil was similar in both halves. Study of the material has indicated that this linear accumulation was meaningless, similar to the one recognized in Grave 6 (see above, p. 81). Nevertheless, the division into two halves was continued almost down to the floor of the enclosure.

During excavation four burials were recognized in the enclosure and were labeled A–D; this count was later raised to seven individuals. Burial A was confined to Locus V 5312 on the east, and it later proved to consist of three individuals: a man, a woman, and an infant (here Burials 5–7). Burial B was found in V 5313 and V 5314 on the west (Burial 4), while burial C came from V 5315 and V 5319 on the east; it was later found to consist of a woman and a fetus (Burials 2 and 3). Finally, burial D was found at the bottom, in V 5320 (Burial 1).

Farther to the west, an area containing human bones and Geometric pottery was identified and dug as Grave 14 (V 5307). Bones from Grave 9 have been recorded also from V 5322, an area on the south side of the existing LM IIIC house wall that formed the southern boundary of Grave 9. On the north, there was considerable mingling of pottery from Graves 9 and 21 in the area that lay between them, and it was not always possible to determine to which grave the pottery belongs. More pottery from Grave 9 was found in all the loci of V 5400, where it had been scattered by the effects of erosion and gravity.

Architecture

Grave 9 is a stone-lined, built enclosure that measures 1.10–1.15 m north–south x 1.81–1.83 m east–west (Fig. 66; Pls. 32A, 32B). The builders of Grave 9 used an existing house wall from LM IIIC Building J as the southern boundary of their structure (Wall V 5303; Pl. 32A); it was three courses high. The north (V 5305), east (V 5404/V 5306), and west (V 5304) walls were each made up of single rows of limestone blocks (Pl. 32B). These blocks were badly fissured from the heat of the fire, while the blocks of bedrock in the house wall used as part of Grave 9 were calcined. The floor of the grave was clay roofing material collapsed from the earlier LM IIIC building rather than the bedrock that was common in other graves. The floor of the grave lay some 0.17 m above the floor of the house. There was a patch of very red clay on the floor of the grave that came from the firing of the roofing clay during cremation; this material was sampled in 1989 by Michael Evans (Day and Glowacki 2012, 179–181).

Stratigraphy

The total deposition in Grave 9 was only 0.30 m. At the bottom of the grave was a layer of hard brown soil (V 5320) that rose higher along the edges; the top of this layer may have been inadvertently cut into when upper layers were removed. This layer contained the earliest of the seven burials (Burial 1). Above this hard brown soil were successively lighter layers of gray ashy soil, and material from them all seems to have been intermingled. There was much disturbance for each burial event, and objects and pottery filtered down through gaps in the stones that were piled on the grave. Just above the hard brown soil of the first burial was a layer of dark gray ashy soil (on the west V 5314, on the east V 5319 and V 5315) that went up to a layer of flat stones on the east. Burials 2 and 3 were found below the flat stones on the east, while Burial 4 was found at this level and slightly higher in the west. There was, however, considerable mingling of pottery between V 5315 and the layer above it (V 5312). Above the very dark gray soil and the stone layer was another layer of slightly lighter gray dirt and tumble (on the west V 5313, on the east V 5312). Burials 5 and 6 were found in this layer on the east side of the enclosure. Burial 7 was found scattered in both of these dark ashy layers on both sides of the enclosure. Above this layer was another slightly lighter gray layer (on the west V 5311, on the east V 5310). The corners of the grave where the stones of the wall had been robbed out were excavated separately as V 5317 (northeast) and V 5318 (northwest). Finally, the top of the soft ashy deposit with stone tumble was V 5302 and V 5404, which lay just below the surface topsoil (V 5301, V 5401). There is thus no clear stratigraphy in the grave beyond the lowest deposit and the surface, but most of the material found in the lower levels was very burned and seems to have belonged with the earlier burials, while that at the top was unburned and may represent the latest burials. The metal objects, however, seem to have gravitated to the bottom of the grave, perhaps because of their weight, and their level in the grave may not be meaningful for determining which burial they accompanied. In general, most of the pottery was in the eastern half of the grave, while the metal objects were concentrated in the west (Pl. 32C).

Grave 14, to the west of the enclosure of Grave 9, represents a discard deposit of material dumped from the grave, probably the result of a cleanup in preparation for one of the later burials. It seems to represent a single event in which grave material was thrown into a natural pit in the roofing from the earlier building (V 5323). The soil was soft and dark, containing the stones that probably came from the grave; the lower layer (V 5316) was distinguished from the upper (V 5307) by the decrease in numbers of snail shells, but there was apparently no meaningful difference in the stratigraphy. Bones from Grave 9 have been recorded also from V 5322, an area on the other side of the existing LM IIIC house wall that formed the southern boundary of Grave 9. In addition, material from Grave 9 was collected immediately to the north in V 5324, and some even appeared in V 5346, which was excavated as part of Grave 21.

The enclosure lies at the edge of the east slope of the Vronda ridge, and natural erosion has taken away some of the material; both the northeast and southeast corners of the grave were robbed out, allowing for even more disturbance and for natural (or human) removal of material. Pottery from the grave was found scattered down the slope to the east over Trench V 5400. In addition, fragments of pottery from the grave have been found all over the area to the south in Trenches V 4800 and V 4900. There was considerable pottery from the area to the north between Grave 9 and Grave 21, and it is not always easy or possible to distinguish which objects came from which grave. Pottery from Loci V 5318, V 5324, and V 5346 joined with fragments from both graves.

Burials

Grave 9 contained at least seven cremations. The ashy discard deposit that was excavated as Grave 14 contained 280 g of human remains. Although there are no joins in the bones, the age, sex, and traces of healed pathology strongly suggest that the bone fragments are from the earliest burial in the grave, Burial 1.

Burial 1 (with Grave 14 Bones)

Type: disturbed primary cremation and discard deposit
Age: adult, 40–60 years
Sex: male?
Weight: 504 g (with 280 g from Grave 14)

Burial 1, the lowest burial in the grave, was found scattered across the bottom of the enclosure. It consists of a partial skeleton of an adult, probably male, 40–60 years old, and with closed and partially obliterated endocranial sutures. The auricular surface of the left ilium found with the disturbed material in Grave 14 indicates that this person was between 50 and 59 years old (Buikstra and Ubelaker, eds., 1994, 24–32). The bone collected in Grave 14 is not completely burned, and areas of the proximal femur and ilia, as well as some cranial fragments, are only heavily scorched. Subsequent burnings in the burial enclosure further burned the bone left inside the grave. The cranial fragments found inside the grave are distinguished by an unusual bright blue color, particularly on the interior surfaces of the cranial vault bones. This color is occasionally seen in small patches on other burials, apparently as a variant of deep gray. This is the only example from the Kavousi burials where the bone is a uniform blue. The cause of this color phenomenon is unknown.

This individual had suffered from anemia earlier in life, as exhibited by the extensive, but remodeled, porotic hyperostosis on his parietal bones. The underlying cause of the anemia is not known. There was some osteoarthritis in the spinal articulations, particularly in the thoracic region. In addition, he had suffered a broken toe that was completely healed at the time of his death. The only other pathology found on the skeleton appears on the humerus shaft. The bone cortex is very thin, ranging from 4.0 to 6.5 mm on a shaft segment with a circumference of 75.0 mm and a medio-lateral diameter of 22.5 mm. This feature is indicative of bone loss due to osteopenia or osteoporosis, which is somewhat unusual but not unknown in males of this age.

Burial 2
Type: disturbed primary cremation
Age: adult, 35–39 years
Sex: female?
Weight: 2,554 g

The fragmentary skeleton of Burial 2, belonging to an adult probably 35–39 years of age, was found concentrated in the east half of the grave. The weight of the postcranial bone is well beyond the expected weight for a single individual. Although no duplicated skeletal elements were identified, it is clear that some of this bone is associated with one or more of the earlier burials in Grave 9. The skeleton is completely calcined and shows evidence of two separate burning events. The bone is very warped and has the curved fractures characteristic of fleshed burning of bone. In addition, many of the pieces of bone have the checked pattern of cracks typical of dry burning of bone. It is likely that this second burning occurred when the later burials in the grave were cremated.

The age estimation is based on the morphology of the auricular surface, which indicates an age of 35–39 years. Also consistent with this age is the incipient closure of the cranial sutures, and the fact that the sacral vertebrae have only begun to fuse together. The skeleton is fairly robust, but there are feminine features on the skull. The fetal bone (Burial 3) found with this skeleton suggests that it is a female.

There are some pathologies on the skeleton. The outer table of the cranium is porous, particularly on the frontal bone above the orbits and high on the frontal squama. The porosity may be associated with an anemic condition, but the patterning is unusual for the more common iron-deficiency anemias. In addition, the femur shafts have very rough and flattened lineae asperae, suggesting unusual stress on the thigh muscles.

Burial 3
Type: disturbed primary cremation
Age: fetus, 20–24 weeks
Sex: unknown
Weight: 17 g

This partial skeleton of a fetus was found in sorting water sieve residue and was not recognized in the field. The bone is completely calcined, with the exception of the right femur shaft, which was only moderately scorched. The developmental stage of the long bones and the measurements of the femur suggest a body length of 20–30 cm, indicating a 20–24 week fetus (Fazekas and Kosa, 1978, 257, 309).

Burial 4
Type: disturbed primary cremation
Age: adult, 40–60 years
Sex: male
Weight: 2,407 g

This partial skeleton of an adult male 40 to 60 years old is the only burial collected primarily from the west end of the enclosure. The bone is very hard and for the most part completely calcined. There are a few portions that were more protected from the fire and are not calcined. These include some rib fragments, a sciatic notch, a femur shaft, and metatarsal fragments. Some charred soft tissue was found with this burial.

The teeth have extreme wear on the premolars and incisors. There is some evidence of cribra orbitalia and some lipping on the thoracic and lumbar vertebrae. The first metatarsal shows extreme lipping and an elevation of the plantar protuberance on the distal end, which would have resulted in discomfort and pain in this joint when walking. The distortion of the weight-bearing surfaces suggests that the individual walked with a limp.

Burial 5 and 6
Type: disturbed primary cremations
Age: adults (one older, one younger)
Sex: unknown
Weight: 2,063 g

These two cremated adults were found in the east end of the enclosure. There was also a cremated infant (Burial 7) whose bone was mixed with the two adult skeletons. The bone is all white and completely calcined, showing signs of having been burned repeatedly in subsequent uses of the burial enclosure for cremations. While it is clear that both of the skeletons are from adults, and one is probably considerably older than the other, neither of the skeletons can be individually aged or sexed. There is evidence that at least one of these individuals was involved in considerable physical activity and had developed osteoarthritis of the spine, elbow, hands, and knee. Some of the femur shaft fragments have a very rough, flattened linea aspera. There is pitting on the distal articulation of the right humerus, and the thoracic vertebrae facets have severe arthritic pitting, both indicative of degenerative joint disease. On the right patella there is a large bone spur on the surface of the medial facet, also indicating joint disease in this knee. In addition, remodeled porotic hyperostosis on the parietal bone fragments is evidence of earlier episodes of anemia, probably in childhood.

Burial 7
Type: disturbed commingled primary cremation
Age: infant, 0.5 to 2.0 years
Sex: unknown
Weight: 144 g

This fragmentary skeleton of an infant or young child was only recognized when sorting the residue from the water sieve. The bone is for the most part completely calcined, although some pieces are not completely white but retain a grayish color, indicating that the collagen has not been completely burned. The skeleton was found mingled with the two adult skeletons, Burials 5 and 6. The proximal epiphysis of the tibia is unfused, and a deciduous first molar with the crown between half and completely formed indicates that the infant was between 0.5 and 2.2 years old at death. There is slight cribra orbitalia in the eye orbits, suggesting that this juvenile suffered from anemia or scurvy even at this young age.

Faunal Remains

The faunal materials recovered from Grave 9 fall into two general categories (Table 6). Unburned rabbit or hare (*Lepus*) fragments, including segments of left and right mandible halves, were scattered throughout the deposit, although they were concentrated primarily in the upper levels (V 5302, V 5310, V 5311). The elements were unmodified, and their unburned condition suggests that they filtered into the disturbed burial deposits and were not associated with the burials themselves. In addition, numerous small rodent or insectivore (mouse, shrew) bones, all unmodified and unburned, were recovered from the deposit. These remains, too, are likely to represent natural accumulations of animals that inhabited the loose soil and stones matrix of the burial enclosure. An exception to this pattern is represented by several burned snake vertebrae (V 5319). These small and otherwise unmodified elements are most likely to have come from an animal inadvertently caught in the fire that burned the woman and fetus identified as Burials 2 and 3.

Burned and calcined sheep or goat bones were also recovered in association with the Grave 9 burials. In the area of Burials 5, 6, and 7, heavily burned fragments of a sheep or goat lower hind leg (patella and proximal sesamoid) were recovered. In addition, a heavily burned left astragalus identified as belonging to domestic sheep (*Ovis aries*) and a left innominate fragment suggest that a left hind limb was part of the apparent sacrifice associated with this burial group. A single unburned metapodial distal condyle fragment from an ovicaprid was also recovered in this context.

A second, calcined domestic sheep left astragalus, as well as a burned or calcined right astragalus, right distal tibia fragment, and right second and third carpal, identified more generally as sheep or goat, indicate that both front and hind limbs were included in the sacrificial meal or offering apparently associated with Burial 4 (V 5313, V 5314). A heavily burned right patella (V 5319) and right proximal tibia diaphysis fragment (V 5324) were recovered from the area of Burial 1. Because of the stratigraphic mixing of deposits with successive burial events in this enclosure, distinct sacrificial episodes cannot be delineated, but the distributions noted above are suggestive.

Botanical Remains

Botanical remains were recovered from Grave 9, including olive (*Olea europaea*), grape (*Vitis vinifera*), lentil (*Lens culinaris*), and fool's parsley (*Aethusa cynapium*). The olive fragments may have come from fuel on the pyre, but the large numbers of grape remains may represent offerings of grape or raisins on the pyre. The lentil may have been the remnant of a funeral meal, or it could represent provisions for the dead. Charred wood fragments found in the grave have been identified as olive wood.

Pottery

Grave 9 produced approximately 2,570 fragments of pottery, weighing some 23.00 kg, which yielded 58 cataloged vessels after conservation, the largest number of vessels found in any of the Vronda enclosure burials. Although many of these fragments were of fine fabric (46%), a greater percentage of medium-coarse (36%) and coarse (18%) wares were found than in the other enclosures. In addition, some 120 fragments weighing 2.30 kg came from the discard deposit (Grave 14); all but 30 fragments joined with vessels from Grave 9.

Chronologically, while the material is certainly Geometric in date, many vessels look earlier in that period, and only in the upper layers do later LG-EO types appear. Monochrome cups predominate (48% of the total vessels), and there are few cups with any decoration. Many of these monochrome cups (**GR9 P18–GR9 P20, GR9 P24, GR9 P25**) are of an unusual shallow, wide-based shape with ledge rims, a form that only appears in this grave and Grave 20 and may derive from Attic MG I shapes (Coldstream 1996, 386), although the Attic types do not have the ledge rim. Jugs are also common, and there are at least five different types, including a broad-based monochrome jug or oinochoe (**GR9 P37**) with a reserved band that may imitate Attic prototypes of MG date (Coldstream 1996, 396–397). Only one aryballos and a few skyphoi or lekythoi were found. The four large amphorae associated with the grave show no traces of burning, and fragments of at least two (**GR9 P38, GR9 P39**) were found scattered all over the northeast summit of the ridge, even into Trenches V 4800 and V 4900. They may have been set up as markers on the grave.

Judging from their find spots (V 5314, V 5315, and V 5319), certain vessels seem to be associated with earlier burials. There were only three fragments recovered from V 5320, so nothing can be attributed to Burial 1 with certainty; many of the vessels in the lower levels, however, particularly those that were extensively burned, are likely candidates for the earliest burials. This group includes nine cups from the east side (**GR9 P21, GR9 P25, GR9 P33, GR9 P34, GR9 P41–GR9 P44, GR9 P56**) and a skyphos (**GR9 P3**), as well as three cups from the west side (**GR9 P52, GR9 P55, GR9 P57**). Vessels that seem to have been in the middle to upper levels of the grave (V 5310, V 5311, V 5312) include: kalathos **GR9 P5**; juglet **GR9 P6**; cups **GR9 P13–GR9 P17, GR9 P19, GR9 P23, GR9 P26, GR9 P28, GR9 P30, GR9 P51, GR9 P53, GR9 P54**, and **GR9 P58**; wide-mouthed jug **GR9 P22**; and necked jar **GR9 P36**. Pottery from the upper levels of the grave and the surface includes: skyphos **GR9 P2**; kalathos **GR9 P4**; jugs **GR9 P7, GR9 P9, GR9 P48**, and **GR9 P49**; amphorae **GR9 P8, GR9 P38, GR9 P39**, and **GR9 P50**; cups **GR9 P18, GR9 P20, GR9 P24, GR9 P27, GR9 P29**, and **GR9 P40**; basket vase **GR9 P11**; aryballos **GR9 P31**; krater **GR9 P35**; and skyphos **GR9 P45**.

The following vessels from the grave had joining fragments from the discard deposit (Grave 14): jug **GR9 P7**; amphorae **GR9 P8** and **GR9 P39**; krater **GR9 P35**; necked jar **GR9 P36**; and jugs or oinochoai **GR9 P37** and **GR9 P49**. This pottery comes primarily from the upper levels of the grave, and these fragments may have been thrown out before the last burial. None show signs of burning, which suggests that they were disposed of by the next cremators using the grave. Possibly these vessels belonged to the next to last burial (possibly Burial 4, if Burials 5–7 represent a single event). Many of these same vessels also had joining fragments in Grave 21. The pottery from Grave 9 with joining fragments from Grave 21 included: basket vase **GR9 P11**, necked jar **GR9 P36**, jugs or oinochoai **GR9 P37** and **GR9 P49**, and amphorae **GR9 P38** and **GR9 P39**. It seems likely that when Grave 9 was cleaned out for the last burial, material was dumped to the west (Grave 14) and to the north (Grave 21, Locus V 5324). When the people came to bury in Grave 21, they cut through this material to make their own burial, and fragments of pottery became mixed in the grave soil. The upper burials in Grave 21 contain pottery later than anything in Grave 9, so it is less likely that Grave 21 was in use and the people burying in Grave 9 threw their dump on top.

A look at these three groups of pottery from the lower, middle, and upper sections of the grave shows some interesting patterns. The lower deposit contains a greater number of monochrome cups with heavy, slightly raised bases and handles that are round rather than flattened; many of these cups are in medium-coarse and coarse wares with thick walls, and they find parallels in PG and earlier Geometric contexts in the Vronda tholos tombs. The decorated cups have only simple decorations of wavy lines or bands. The cups in the middle levels of the grave tend to have thinner walls, with broad, flat bases and less rounded handles; more of the rims are taller and more sharply offset. In the upper levels of the grave, the ledge-rim cups predominate; ledge-rim cups appear one each in the lower and middle levels, but because these vessels did not come from stratigraphically distinguished layers and there had been a great deal of disturbance, any single piece could have been picked up from the lower levels or could have dropped down through the stones to earlier burials. The uppermost levels contained the greatest variety of shapes and much of the decorated pottery; most of the jugs and the amphorae came from this level. The amphorae were probably on the surface as markers, so their position cannot be used to determine their original context. There is a surprising amount of Attic influence on the pottery of Grave 9: the ledge-rim cups, the wide-based jug or oinochoe with reserved band, and even one of the amphorae (**GR9 P38**) show some Attic traits (Tsipopoulou 2005, 334), although they were made of Cretan fabrics.

Objects

Grave 9 produced an unusual number of metal artifacts, the most from any grave (55 cataloged objects). More bronze objects were recovered from this grave than any other, mostly in the form of sheeting with rivets (**GR9 M5–GR9 M12**). The sheeting is roughly rectangular, although no single piece was found intact. It is very thin and devoid of decoration, and the rivets or rivet holes are pierced along the edges. The pieces resemble patches, but there are so many sheets that it does not seem plausible that they were all used to patch a bronze vessel of which nothing survives. It is more likely that they were sheets of bronze attached to some other perishable material, such as wood. The rivets are approximately 1 cm long, suggesting that the walls of the object to which they were attached were about a centimeter thick. Such a thickness would seem to eliminate the possibility that these pieces of sheeting were stitched to leather, perhaps to form armor. It is more probable that they were attached to a wooden object, perhaps a box. Similar fragments of bronze sheeting have been identified at Knossos as plaques; these were rounded, with small stitch or rivet holes, and their function is uncertain (Coldstream and Catling, eds., 1996, 208–209, fig. 167:f3; Catling 1996a, 572–573). The fragments of bronze sheeting were found almost entirely in the northwest corner of the enclosure, suggesting that they all came from the same object; the one exception was **GR9 M11**, which was found along the south side of the enclosure.

Two nearly complete bronze fibulae were also found rather close to one another in the northeast corner. One (**GR9 M2**) is arched with moldings at either end of its asymmetric, swollen bow. This object is unusual because it has a coil made of iron. Apparently, the coil broke where the metal became thin, and there was no available bronze to repair the object, so a coil of iron was made and joined on with a tiny rivet. The other fibula (**GR9 M1**) is also an arched type but with a broader swelling and a profile shaped more like a half-moon.

Most of the metal objects are made of iron, and the majority are weapons or tools. Weapons are particularly plentiful, including at least 15 spearheads and five dirks or daggers. All iron two-edged socketed blades have been labeled spears, but some of these may have functioned as javelins, used for throwing rather than for thrusting. Distinguishing the function of these types of weapons, however, is difficult (Snodgrass 1964, 136–139; 1996, 580–581). Most of the spears can be classed with those of type A at Knossos (Snodgrass 1996, 580–581), particularly those of LG date. Those that are between 26 to 43 cm long are probably spearheads (**GR9 M14, GR9 M15, GR9 M17, GR9 M19–GR9 M21, GR9 M25, GR9 M27**). Javelins seem to be shorter, ranging in length from 18.0 to 25.0 cm, and they are broader, from 2.3–2.9 cm (**GR9 M18, GR9 M22–GR9 M24,** possibly **GR9 M16**). The other spearheads are too fragmentary to allow us to distinguish their type or function. One spearhead (**GR9 M20**) was found bent at a right angle in the middle; this must have been done deliberately, and a good parallel for this practice with a spearhead exists at PG Eltyna (Rethemiotakis and Englezou 2010, fig. 62:191). One example (**GR9 M29**) has a socket like a spear or javelin, but the end is rounded and has a small depression. This item was thought to be a possible spear butt, although there are no good parallels for it, and its function remains a mystery.

Find spots of the spearheads suggest possible associations, although the grave was so disturbed by successive burials that objects may well have traveled from their original locations, and it is impossible to associate any with particular burials. On the eastern edge of the enclosure were three spearheads (**GR9 M18–GR9 M20**). All three were of the type with sharp shoulders and pronounced midrib, two of them long and one short. In the area of the southeast corner, another trio of spearheads was found: two long examples with rounded shoulders and no midrib (**GR9 M21, GR9 M27**) and a third, shorter spearhead with pronounced shoulders and a central midrib (**GR9 M22**). From the northwest corner came seven spearheads: four of the long variety with sharp shoulders and pronounced midribs (**GR9 M14, GR9 M15, GR9 M17, GR9 M25**) and the others fragmentary (**GR9 M16, GR9 M26, GR9 M28**). In the southwest corner two additional short spears with pronounced midrib and rather sharp shoulders (**GR9 M23, GR9 M24**) were found, together with a fragment of one of the spears from the northwest corner (**GR9 M16**).

There were five dirks or daggers. Just as the distinction between spears and javelins is difficult, it is also hard to determine if a weapon was used for cutting and thrusting (a sword), or primarily for close thrusting (a dirk or dagger). Based on length, it would seem that in Grave 9 there are no true swords, and the daggers and dirks seem to have the same form, only differing in length. Three are probably dirks (**GR9 M31–GR9 M33**) with blades over 25.00 cm in length, while one is a dagger (**GR9 M30**); **GR9 M34** is probably also a dirk, but its full length is not preserved. These were all of the same type, Anthony Snodgrass's type IA (1964, 98–99): flange hilted with rivets for the attachment of some other material (bone, ivory, or wood) on the hilt; they differ only in length of blade and the amount of tapering. Two of these dirks were found in the middle near the northern boundary of the enclosure (**GR9 M33, GR9 M34**), and two more were found in the middle near the southern wall (**GR9 M31, GR9 M32**), while the dagger was found in the center toward the west (**GR9 M30**).

The iron tools are also plentiful. Among them are three different kinds of knives. One example, **GR9 M37**, is a simple straight-backed knife similar to type A at Knossos (Snodgrass 1996, 585–586). Another, **GR9 M35**, is of Snodgrass's type E, a straight, broad-blade knife with the tang continuing the line of the back but much narrower than the blade (1996, 587). There are also two sickle-like knives (**GR9 M38, GR9 M39**), on which both sides of the blade show pronounced curvature with the cutting edge on the inside of the curve (Snodgrass 1996, 587, type D). A fifth knife (**GR9 M36**) is known only from a fragment from the tip, and its shape is uncertain. Three were found in the northwest corner (**GR9 M35, GR9 M36, GR9 M39**), one in the southwest corner (**GR9 M38**), and the fifth near the northeast corner (**GR9 M37**), along with two fibulae and two dirks. Other tools include three axe-heads (**GR9 M40–GR9 M42**) from the southwest corner, in three sizes but of the same general shape, and a pointed chisel (**GR9 M45**) found with three spearheads in the southeast corner. The two scrapers (**GR9 M43, GR9 M44**) may have been used for a variety of tasks, including scraping wood, scraping hides for leather making, and even for surgical procedures (Liston and Day 2009), as perhaps was the small spatulate tool **GR9 M51**. Finally, a variety of small pointed tools or awls came from the grave (**GR9 M46, GR9 M47, GR9 M49, GR9 M50**). One fragmentary object (**GR9 M48**) may have come from an awl, some other tool, or even a spit. A number of small iron objects that are bent into peculiar shapes are probably fleshhooks (**GR9 M52–GR9 M55**), used for pulling meat out of a stew pot (Needham and Bowman 2005, 93); these items were all found at the west end of the enclosure. In addition to the cataloged objects, there was another rivet from a dirk or dagger (V88.182) or from bronze sheeting, as well as some 33 uncataloged bronze rivets or nails from daggers.

Chronology

Grave 9 seems to have been used earlier than the other graves in the area, and it may have been the earliest cremation enclosure on the site. Some of the material can be termed G, rather than LG, and the latest unburned vessels in the grave, while of LG date, hearken back to earlier styles of Geometric pottery. The cups from the bottom of the grave, with their heavy bases and thick walls often of medium or coarse fabrics, are similar to PG and G cups from tholos tombs at Vronda, especially Tomb IX, and to cups from Phase VII at the Kastro (Mook 2004, 175, fig. 12.10). Many others find close parallels in PG or EG times. Skyphos **GR9 P3** may be one of the earliest vessels. Its shape perhaps derives from the SM–PG amphoriskos. The two cups with conical profile (**GR9 P33, GR9 P55**) also have EPG–MPG parallels in the Knossos area. Cup **GR9 P51** is similar to much smaller examples of PGB date from Eleutherna. Several of the cups, however, look later, including **GR9 P21** and especially **GR9 P25**; the latter is a shallow, wide-bottomed cup that does not appear on Crete until the MG period (Coldstream 1996, 386). Two cups in this early group (**GR9 P34, GR9 P42**) have parallels at LG Chania (Hallager and Hallager, eds., 1997, 145, pl. 107:71-P 1449, 77-P 2155).

A date earlier in the LG period seems possible for the earliest burials in Grave 9, perhaps contemporary with Phase VII on the Kastro. The latest burials in the grave belong to the LG period, but a jug (**GR9 P9**) and an amphora (**GR9 P8**) may be of EO date. The basket vase (**GR9 P11**) finds parallels in vessels called "buckets" at Knossos in EO–LO deposits (Coldstream 1973, 41, pl. 14:H72, H73), but if it is a thelastron, the shape goes back into the PG period and cannot be used to support a seventh century date for the last burial in Grave 9.

Overall, many vessels show PG influence but have LG traits, such as the kalathos (**GR9 P4**), a shape that had gone out of use after the EG period in Central Crete (Coldstream 1996, 377), but they occur here with decoration that was popular into the LG period. The amphora (**GR9 P39**) is also a common PG–EG type. The ledge-rim cup that predominates in the latest two burials (that which was dumped in Grave 14 and in the area of Grave 21) imitates Attic MG I shapes and must postdate that period.

The jug or oinochoe (**GR9 P37**) also imitates Attic MG I types. Cup **GR9 P1**, which cannot be associated with any particular burial, has a deep, globular shape with a small rim and a very thick base that is reminiscent of LPG cups from Knossos (Coldstream and Catling, eds., 1996, 255, fig. 143:6); its striped handle, however, has parallels among Atticizing cups at EG–MG Knossos (Coldstream 1996, 386). The metal artifacts are not closely datable, but the two fibulae (**GR9 M1** and **GR9 M2**) support a LG date, although early in that period.

Catalog

Pottery

Fine Decorated Wares

GR9 P1 (V 5312.3, V 5312.4, V 5313.3, V 5315.5, V 5319.1; Fig. 67). Cup. Mended from 45 fragments. Preservation 30%, including full profile, entire base, handle and 50% of rim; missing much of body. H. 7.8; d. rim 8.4; d. base 5.0. Fine, soft, reddish-yellow (7.5YR 7/6) fabric. Black paint. Very worn surfaces. No burning. Monochrome inside and out, with vertical stripes on handle. *Bibliography*: Day 2011a, 755, fig. 5:4. *Comparanda*: for shape, **GR9 P42**; for striped handle, Coldstream and Catling, eds., 1996, 28, pl. 65:28, 29 (Knossos, Attic LPG). *Date*: G.

GR9 P2 (V 5301.2, V 5302.2 and 3, V 5311.1, V 5312.2; Fig. 67; Pl. 32D). Skyphos. Partially mended from 20 sherds into two large fragments. Preservation 45%, including half of rim and upper body, both handles; missing base. Max. pres. h. 8.5; d. rim 12.5. Fine, soft, porous, reddish-yellow (7.5YR 7/6) fabric with tiny black inclusions. Black paint. Well-preserved surfaces. No burning. Threefold concentric circles in handle zone, probably two on each side. *Bibliography*: Day 2011a, 755, fig. 5:15. *Comparanda*: Coldstream and Catling, eds., 1996, 61, fig. 74:11 (Knossos, EG?); for strap handle, Tsipopoulou 2005, 292, fig. 118:AN8784 (Praisos, LG). *Date*: LG.

GR9 P3 (V 5313.1, V 5319.1, V 5319.2, V 5319.4, V 5319.5, V 5319.7; Fig. 67; Pl. 32D). Skyphos. Mended from 57 fragments. Preservation 70%, including full profile, entire base, part of one handle; missing 75% of rim, other handle. H. 10.7; d. rim est. 10.0; d. base 5.3. Fine, very soft, reddish-yellow (7.5YR 7/6) fabric. Petrographic sample KAV 15/5: Fabric Subroup 1c. Black paint. Very worn surfaces. Burned lightly all over; many worn edges. Some possible bands with uncertain decoration above; may be vertical strokes. *Date*: SM–PG.

GR9 P4 (V 5301.1, V 5312.3, V 5315.1 and 2, V 5318.1, V 5404.3; Fig. 67; Pl. 32D). Kalathos. Ten fragments, 20% preserved, including half of base and fragments of rim. H.

10.0; d. rim est. 27.0; d. base 11.5. Fine, soft, reddish-yellow (7.5YR 7/6) fabric. Red (2.5YR 4/6) paint. Well-preserved surfaces. Some burning on interior and one of rim fragments. Alternating oblique strokes and checkerboard. *Bibliography*: Day 2011a, 755, fig. 5:12. *Comparanda*: for decoration, Coldstream and Catling, eds., 1996, 19, fig. 61:90 (Knossos, PGB); 198, fig. 127:42 (Knossos, Attic LPG); Tsipopoulou 2005, 222, fig. 116:Σ4526 (Zakro, LG); for shape, Coldstream and Catling, eds., 1996, 264, fig. 145:72 (Knossos, PGB); 47, fig. 71:24 (Knossos, PGB). *Date*: LG.

GR9 P5 (V 5310.2, V 5312.2 and 3, V 5319.5, V 5401.4; Fig. 68). Kalathos or lid. Nineteen fragments, including pieces of rim and both handles; base missing. D. rim est. 22.0. Fine, very soft, very pale brown (10YR 8/4–7/4) fabric. Black paint. Very worn surfaces. Much burning. Barred handles. *Comparanda*: Coldstream and Catling, eds., 1996, 41, fig. 70:5 (Knossos, kalathos or lid, EG). *Date*: G.

GR9 P6 (V88.84; V 5310.1 object 1, V 5310.2; Fig. 68; Pl. 32D). Miniature jug. Nearly complete in 11 fragments; missing 20% of rim and handle. H. 8.0; d. rim 4.5; d. base 3.0. Fine, rather hard, red (10R 5/6) fabric. Glossy, very pale brown (10YR 8/2) slip. Dark brown (7.5YR 3/2) paint. Very well-preserved surfaces. Crosshatched triangles on shoulder. *Bibliography*: Day 2011a, fig. 6:1. *Comparanda*: Brock 1957, 155, pl. 50:838 (Knossos, PGB–MG); Rocchetti 1988–1989, 200–202, fig. 75:577 (Kourtes); Coldstream and Catling, eds., 1996, 114, pl. 123:102 (Knossos, LG); 151, pl. 148:15 (Knossos, EO); 177, pl. 176:135.1 (Knossos, MG); Tsipopoulou 2005, 216, pl. 341:H3253 (Adromyloi, LG). *Date*: LG.

GR9 P7 (V 5301.1 and 2, V 5302.1 and 2, V 5303.1, V 5307.3, V 5310.1 and 2, V 5311.1, V 5312.1–3, V 5324.1, V 5401.1, V 5404.1, V 5404.3, V 4806.1; Fig. 68). Jug. Partially mended from 48 fragments, 10% preserved, including piece of rim, part of shoulder, body; missing base and handle. Max. pres. h. 12.3; d. rim 6.8. Fine, rather hard, reddish-yellow (7.5YR 6/6) fabric. Yellowish-red (5YR 5/6) to black paint. Worn surfaces. Bands? Neck made separately and joined onto body; extra clay added to strengthen joint. *Bibliography*: Day 2011a, 756, fig. 6:7. *Comparanda*: Rocchetti 1974–1975, 220–221, fig. 74:a (Phaistos). *Date*: LG.

GR9 P8 (V 5301.1, V 5302.2, V 5307.3, V 5310.2; Fig. 68). Amphora. Fragments from rim and neck. Max. pres. h. 9.5; d. rim est. 12.2. Fine, rather hard, reddish-yellow (7.5YR 7/6) fabric. Red (2.5YR 4/8) to black paint. Surfaces worn, but paint is distinguishable. Interlocking forward and backward S-pattern. *Bibliography*: Day 2011a, 756, fig. 6:3. *Comparanda*: Tsipopoulou 2005, fig. 16:H3841. *Date*: LG–EO.

GR9 P9 (V 5301.1, V 5302.2, V 5401.2, V 5404.3 and 4; Fig. 68; Pl. 32D). Jug. Partially mended from seven fragments. Entire neck and piece of rim preserved; missing base, body, handle(s). Max. pres. h. 7.2; d. rim est. 10.0. Fine, soft, porous, reddish-yellow (5YR 7/6) fabric with tiny black inclusions. Black paint. Well-preserved surfaces. No burning. Vertical guilloche pattern on neck. *Bibliography*: Day 2011a, 756, fig. 6:4. *Comparanda*: for decoration, Coldstream and Catling, eds., 1996, 263, pl. 237:44 (Knossos, EO). *Date*: LG–EO.

GR9 P10 (V5301.1, V 5307.3, V 5310.3, V 5311.1; Fig. 68). Stirrup jar. Four fragments preserving false spout, top, and two handles; missing spout, body, and base. Max. pres. h. 5.5. Fine, rather hard, pink (7.5YR 8/4) to reddish-yellow (7.5YR 6/6) fabric with tiny phyllite inclusions. Traces of paint. *Date*: SM–PG?

GR9 P11 (V 5301.2, V 5302.1 and 2, V 5304.3, V 5309.2, V 5310.2, V 5311.1 and 2, V 5312.2 and 3, V 5317.1, V 5401.5, V 5404.1, V 5408.7, V 5301.1, V 5346.2 and 3, V 5346.5; Fig. 68). Basket vase or feeding bottle. Partially mended from 31 fragments; five fragments from Grave 21. Preservation 15%, including part of base, half of handle with rim, and body fragments. H. est. 23.0; d. rim est. 11.0–12.0; d. base est. 7.0. Fine, rather hard, reddish-yellow (5YR 6/8) fabric with small phyllite inclusions. Brown (10YR 4/6) paint. Worn surfaces. No burning. Bands. *Bibliography*: Day 2011a, 756, fig. 6:5. *Comparanda*: **GR23 P2**; Rocchetti 1988–1989, 235–236, fig. 162 (Kourtes, SM–PG); Coldstream and Catling, eds., 1996, 4, fig. 56:B2 (Knossos, PGB); Tsipopoulou 2005, 63, fig. 142:HΔ15 (Dreros, EO); 209, fig. 142:H3210 (Adromyloi, LG); Rethemiotakis and Englezou 2010, 82, fig. 48:119 (Eltyna SM–EPG). *Date*: PG–G.

GR9 P12 (V 5309.3 and 4, V 5322.1; Fig. 68). Amphora. Partially mended from 12 fragments from body; missing base, handles, neck, and rim. Max. pres. h. 16.5. Fine, very soft, reddish-yellow (5YR 7/6) fabric. Very pale brown (10YR 8/2) slip. Red (2.5YR 3/4) paint. Fairly well-preserved surfaces. One fragment burned on edge after breaking. Metopal pattern with concentric circles and hatched lozenges or checkerboard. *Comparanda*: Coldstream and Catling, eds., 1996, 27, pl. 63:1; 48, pl. 81:62 (Knossos, MPG); Hayden 2003, 53–54, no. 123, fig. 30, pl. 19 (Vrokastro, PGB–EG). *Date*: PG–LG.

Fine Monochrome Wares

GR9 P13 (V98.90; V 5310.2, V 5312.1 and 2, V 5315.1 and 2; Fig. 68; Pl. 33). Cup. Mended from 50 fragments, 80% preserved, including full profile, most of base, handle, and 75% of rim. H. 10.0; d. rim 12.7; d. base 6.0. Fine, rather hard, very pale brown (10YR 7/4) fabric. Black paint. Very worn surfaces. One side burned. *Bibliography*: Day 2011a, 755, fig. 5:1. *Comparanda*: Mook 2004, 176, fig. 12.11:C (Kastro, LG). LG.

GR9 P14 (V98.91; V 5302.3, V 5310.2, V 5312.1 and 2; Fig. 68; Pl. 33). Cup. Mended from 40 fragments, 95% preserved; missing fragments of body. H. 9.4; d. rim 12.5; d. base 6.0. Fine, rather hard, reddish-yellow (5YR 7/6) fabric. Black paint. Worn surfaces. Some burning. Wheel ridging on interior. *Bibliography*: Day 2011a, 755, fig. 5:2. *Comparanda*: Rocchetti 1988–1989, 239, fig. 175 (Kourtes); Coldstream and Catling, eds., 1996, 205, fig. 130:46 (Knossos, MG late). *Date*: LG.

GR9 P15 (V98.92; V 5310.2, V 5312.1 and 2, V 5315.1; Fig. 69). Cup. Mended from 57 fragments. Preservation

75%, including full profile, entire base, handle, and much of rim. H. 9.8; d. rim 11.4; d. base 5.5. Fine, soft, reddish-yellow (5YR 7/6) fabric. Black paint. Very worn surfaces. Much burning. Spalling on interior. *Bibliography*: Day 2011a, 755, fig. 5:3. *Date*: LG.

GR9 P16 (V98.93; V 5310.2, V 5312.1 and 2; Fig. 69). Cup. Mended from 44 fragments, 80% preserved, including full profile, base, handle, and much of rim. H. 9.8; d. rim 11.5–13.0; d. base 5.8. Fine, soft, reddish-yellow (7.5YR 7/6) fabric with some hard inclusions. Petrographic sample KAV 15/18: Fabric Subgroup 1c. Black paint. Very worn surfaces. Very burned and warped. *Comparanda*: **GR3 P7, GR5 P4**; Coldstream and Catling, eds., 1996, 18, fig. 60:59 (PGB–EG). *Date*: LG.

GR9 P17 (V 5310.2, V 5312.1 and 2, V 5318.1, V 4903.1; Fig. 69). Cup. Mended from 49 fragments. Preservation 60%, including full profile, 30% of base, 50% of rim, half of handle. H. 9.0; d. rim 13.0; d. base 5.8. Fine, hard, reddish-yellow (5YR 7/6) fabric. Black paint. Very worn surfaces on exterior; well preserved on interior. Pronounced wheel ridging on interior. Very burned. *Comparanda*: Gesell, Day, and Coulson 1995, 115, fig. 21:4 (Kastro, LG); Coldstream and Catling, eds., 1996, 175, fig. 118:9 (LG–EO). *Date*: LG.

GR9 P18 (V 5302.1 and 2, V 5310.2 and 3, V 5311.1, V 5302.1 and 2, V 5312.2, V 5313.1, V 5404.3, V 4905.3; Fig. 69). Cup. Partially mended from 17 fragments; seven nonjoining fragments. Preservation 50%, including half of base, 60% of rim, and handle; missing half of body. H. est. 5.6; d. rim 11.0; d. base 7.7. Fine, soft, chalky reddish-yellow (7.5YR 6/6) fabric with some small red phyllites. Petrographic sample KAV 15/2: loner. Thick, glossy, red (2.5YR 5/6) paint. Ledge rim, torus base. *Bibliography*: Day 2011a, 755, fig. 5:13. *Comparanda*: **GR9 P19, GR9 P20, GR9 P24**; Coldstream and Catling, eds., 1996, 18–19, fig. 60:71, 74 (Knossos, Attic MG I); 37, fig. 68:18 (Knossos, Attic MG I). *Date*: LG.

GR9 P19 (V 5312.2 and 3, V 5317.1, V 5319.4; Fig. 69). Cup. Partially mended from 41 fragments, 65% preserved, including most of base, half of rim and handle; profile can be restored. H. est. 6.5; d. rim 11.2; d. base 8.4. Fine, soft, chalky, very pale brown (10YR 7/4) fabric with small black sandy inclusions. Black paint. Very worn surfaces. Half burned. Ledge rim, torus base. *Bibliography*: Day 2011a, 755, fig. 5:14. *Comparanda*: **GR9 P18, GR9 P20, GR9 P24**; Coldstream and Catling, eds., 1996, 18, fig. 60:71 (Attic MG I). *Date*: LG.

GR9 P20 (V 5301.2, V 5302.1, V 5311.1, V 5312.1 and 2, V 5401.1 and 2, V 5402.1, V 5404.1, V 5404.3, V 5408.5; Fig. 69). Cup. Partially mended from 44 fragments. Preservation 65%, including full profile, 65% of base, 50% of rim, handle attachments; missing handle, parts of body. H. 6.7; d. rim 11.0; d. base 8.5. Fine, soft, porous, very pale brown (10YR 7/4) fabric. Sampled KAV 15/1: Fabric Group 7. Thick red (2.5YR 4/6) to black paint. Worn surfaces. No burning. Ledge rim, torus base. *Comparanda*: **GR9 P18, GR9 P19, GR9 P24**; Coldstream and Catling, eds., 1996, 18, fig. 60:71 (Attic MG I). *Date*: LG.

GR9 P21 (V 5301.1, V 5310.2, V 5312.1 and 2, V 5315.1; Fig. 69). Cup. Partially mended from 46 fragments, 25% of rim and upper body and part of handle preserved; missing base. Max. pres. h. 7.3; d. rim 14.9. Fine, soft, reddish-yellow (5YR 6/6) fabric. Red (2.5YR 5/6) paint. Very worn surfaces. Some fragments burned. *Comparanda*: Coldstream and Catling, eds., 1996, 175, fig. 118:9 (Knossos, LG–EO). *Date*: LG.

GR9 P22 (V 5404.4, V 5310.1 and 2, V 5311.1, V 5312.1 and 2, V 5318.1; Fig. 69). Wide-mouthed jug. Mended from 33 fragments. Preservation 35%, including most of base, half of rim, handle; missing much of body. H. est. 10.5; d. rim 7.0; d. base 5.5. Fine, medium-soft, yellowish-red (5YR 5/6) fabric. Red (2.5YR 5/6) paint. Very worn surfaces. Some burned fragments. Foot made of disk to which the rest of the pot was added. *Bibliography*: Day 2011a, 755, fig. 5:10. *Comparanda*: Brock 1957, 155, pl. 26: 375 (Knossos, PGB–MG). *Date*: LG.

GR9 P23 (V 5301.1 and 2, V 5302.1, V 5311.1, V 5312.2 and 3; Fig. 69). Cup or skyphos. Mended from 16 fragments, 50% preserved, including full, profile, entire base, part of rim; missing handle. H. 7.0; d. rim 11.0; d. base 4.4. Fine, rather hard, yellow (10YR 7/6) fabric. Petrographic sample KAV 15/12: Fabric Subgroup 1c. Crackled and streaky black paint. Well-preserved surfaces. No burning. String marks on base. *Comparanda*: Coldstream and Catling, eds., 1996, 186, fig. 119:16 (Knossos, LPG); Tsipopoulou 2005, 286, fig. 124:AN8761 (Praisos, LG). *Date*: LPG–G.

GR9 P24 (V 5301.1 and 2, V 5302.1 and 2, V 5304.3, V 5311.1, V 5324.1 and 2, V 5408.5, V 5202.3; Fig. 69). Cup or skyphos. Partially mended from 23 fragments. Preservation 75%, including part of base, half of rim; missing handle(s). H. est. 6.4; d. rim 11.0; d. base 9.0. Fine, soft, chalky, reddish-yellow (7.5YR 7/6) fabric. Black paint. Rather well-preserved surfaces. No burning. Ledge rim. *Comparanda*: **GR9 P18–GR9 P20, GR9 P25**; Coldstream and Catling, eds., 1996, 18, fig. 60:71 (Attic MG I). *Date*: LG.

GR9 P25 (V 5315.1; Fig. 70). Cup or skyphos. Partially mended from five fragments of rim and body; missing base and handle(s). D. rim 12.0. Fine, soft, chalky, pink (7.5YR 7/3) to light brown (7.5YR 6/3) fabric. Black paint. Wheel ridging on interior and exterior. Much burning. Ledge rim. *Comparanda*: **GR9 P18–GR9 P20, GR9 P24**, Coldstream and Catling, eds., 1996, 18, fig. 60:71 (Attic MG I). *Date*: LG.

GR9 P26 (V 5311.1, V 5312.1 and 3; Fig. 70). Cup or skyphos. Partially mended from 10 fragments, 25% of rim and upper body preserved; missing base and handle(s). Max. pres. h. 9.0; d. rim 15.0. Fine, soft, light red (2.5YR 6/6) fabric. Brown paint. Surfaces very worn. No burning. *Date*: LG.

GR9 P27 (V 5305.8, V 5310.2, V 5315.1, V 5401.2, V 5405.8; Fig. 70). Cup or skyphos. Partially mended from seven fragments, 10% of rim and upper body preserved, one possible base fragment; missing handle(s). D. rim

12.0. Fine, soft, reddish-yellow (5YR 6/6) fabric with very pale brown (7.5YR 8/4) surface. Black monochrome paint on interior and exterior. Very worn surfaces. No burning. *Date*: LG.

GR9 P28 (V 5312.2 and 3, V 5309.2, V 5315.1, V 5409.2; Fig. 70). Cup or skyphos. Partially mended from 15 fragments, preserving 25% of rim and upper body; missing handle. Base fragment may belong, but does not join. D. rim 12.0. Fine, soft, reddish-yellow (5YR 7/6) fabric. Black to red (10R 4/6) paint. Small boss on shoulder. *Date*: LG.

GR9 P29 (V98.95; V 5301.1, V 5302.1, V 5324.1; Fig. 70). Cup. Half of base preserved in four fragments. D. base 6.0. Fine, rather hard, light reddish-brown (2.5YR 7/4–6/4) fabric. Yellowish-red (5YR 5/6) to black paint. Well-preserved surfaces. No burning. Pronounced wheel ridges on interior. *Date*: LG.

GR9 P30 (V 5310.2, V 5312.1–3; Fig. 70). Cup. Partially mended from 26 fragments, 50% of base and lower body preserved; missing rim and handle(s). Max. pres. h. 4.0; d. base 6.0. Fine, soft, reddish-yellow (7.5YR 8/6) fabric. Red (2.5YR 5/8) paint. Very worn surfaces. *Date*: LG.

FINE PLAIN WARE

GR9 P31 (V88.204; V 5301.2, V 5313.2, V 5312.2; Fig. 70; Pl. 33). Aryballos. Nearly complete; mended from 27 fragments; missing handle, 65% of rim. H. 8.0; d. rim est. 2.8; d. base 3.0. Fine, soft, very pale brown (10YR 7/4) fabric. Surface burnished or polished. Burned on one side, iron staining on neck. *Bibliography*: Day 2011a, 756, fig. 6:2. *Comparanda*: Coldstream and Catling, eds., 1996, 24, pl. 62:17 (Knossos, MG); 115, pl. 123:127 (LG–EO); 254, pl. 231:286.1 (EG); Johannowsky 2002, 64, pl. 64:402 (third quarter of seventh century); Kotsonas 2008, 179–180, fig. 43:98β (Eleutherna, LG). *Date*: LG.

FINE DECORATED, MONOCHROME, OR PLAIN WARE

GR9 P32 (V 5301.3; Fig. 70). Closed vessel of indeterminate shape. Large fragment preserving half of base and 18 other fragments. Max. pres. h. 6.5; d. base 12.0. Fine, soft, chalky, yellow (10YR 7/6) fabric. Very worn surfaces. No burning. *Comparanda*: This sort of rounded base with a ring on the bottom is found on transport amphorae of the end of the seventh century in Crete; see Callaghan and Johnston 2000, 248–249, pl. 4.18:386, 394 (Kommos); however, **GR9 P32** seems to be a more open vessel, possibly a pyxis. *Date*: LG?

MEDIUM-COARSE DECORATED WARES

GR9 P33 (V 5312.2, V 5312.5, V 5319.1, V 5319.5; Fig. 70). Cup. Partially mended from 23 fragments. Preservation 25%, including entire base, handle, and parts of rim; missing most of rim and upper body. H. 7.0; d. rim est. 13.0; d. base 4.0. Medium-coarse, soft, pink to light brown (7.5YR 7/4–6/4) fabric. Petrographic sample KAV 15/9: Fabric Subgroup 1a. Black paint. Very worn surfaces. Wavy band. *Bibliography*: Day 2011a, 755, fig. 5:5. *Comparanda*: Brock 1957, 58, pl. 38:622 (Knossos, EPG–MPG); Boardman 1960, 134, 137, fig. 5:V.20 (Hagios Ioannis, EPG). *Date*: LPG–G.

GR9 P34 (V 5312.2 and 3, V 5313.1, V 5319.4–7; Fig. 70). Cup. Mended from 35 fragments; 90% preserved, including full profile, entire base, handle. H. 7.0; d. rim 10.0; d. base 4.0. Medium-coarse, soft, very pale brown (10YR 7/4) fabric with tiny phyllite and carbonate inclusions. Petrographic sample KAV 15/10: Fabric Subgroup 1b. Black paint. Very worn surfaces, worn edges. Mostly burned. Two reserved bands at base of rim. *Comparanda*: for shape, **GR9 P42**, **IX P30**; for bands on rim or below, Coldstream and Catling, eds., 1996, 37, fig. 68:17 (PGB–EG); Hallager and Hallager, eds., 1997, 145, pl. 107:71-P 1449 (Chania, LG I import); Tsipopoulou 2005, 308, fig. 123:Σ4003 (Sklavoi, LG); 2013, 143, fig. 7:12301 (Piskokephalo, PGB); for shape and decoration, Tsipopoulou 2005, 175, fig. 123:Σ3942 (Hagios Georgios, LG). *Date*: LPG–G.

GR9 P35 (V 5301.1 and 2, V 5302.1 and 2, V 5302.4, V 5307.1, V 5308.4, V 5309.3 and 4, V 5310.1 and 2, V 5311.1, V 5324.1, V 5405.5, V 4800.1, V 4905.3; Fig. 70). Krater. Represented by 113 fragments, including rim, parts of both handles, and section near base. D. rim est. 24.0 (int.). Fine to medium-coarse, hard, light red (2.5YR 6/6) fabric. Petrographic sample KAV 15/15: Fabric Group 5. Very pale brown (10YR 8/4) slip. Reddish-brown (5YR 5/3) paint. Worn surfaces. Decorated, but too worn to determine pattern. *Bibliography*: Day 2011a, 755, fig. 5:16. *Date*: LG?

GR9 P36 (V98.86; V 5301.1 and 2, V 5302.1 and 2, V 5307.2, V 5310.2 and 3, V 5311.1, V 5312.2, V 5317.1, V 5324.1, V 5346.2–4, V 5348.2, V 5401.2, V 5404.3, V 5405.6 and 8; Fig. 71). Necked jar. Partially mended from 30 fragments; 25% of upper body and rim preserved, including both handles, and fragments of base. H. 17.5; d. rim 10.4; d. base 10.0. Medium-coarse, hard, light red (2.5YR 6/6) fabric with frequent inclusions. Petrographic sample KAV 15/14: Fabric Group 2. Pink (7.5YR 8/4) slip. Reddish-brown (5YR 4/4) to black paint. Worn surfaces. No burning. Hatched zigzag, chain. *Bibliography*: Day 2011a, 756, fig. 6.6. *Comparanda*: for shape, Tsipopoulou 2005, 149, fig. 60:AN1794; 153, fig. 59:AN1837 (Hagios Georgios, LG); for chain decoration, Tsipopoulou 2004, 132, 139, fig. 6:00/673 (Chalasmenos, LG); for decoration, Coldstream and Catling, eds., 1996, 76, fig. 77:26.2, 26:6 (Knossos, LG); for shape and decoration, Kotsonas 2008, 143, 145, fig. 34:A144 (Eleutherna, MG). *Date*: LG.

GR9 P37 (V98.87; V 5301.1 and 2, V 5302.1 and 2, V 5304.3, V 5307.3, V 5310.2 and 3, V 5311.1, V 5312.1 and 2, V 5313.1, V 5314.2, V 5346.2, V 5401.1, V 5403.2, V 5404.1–3, V 5404.5, V 5405.4; Fig. 71; Pl. 33). Jug or oinochoe. Partially mended from 64 fragments. Preservation 35%, including nearly complete profile, part of base and lower body, 25% of neck, and most of one handle.

Max. pres. h. 28.5; d. base 11.2. Medium-coarse, porous, reddish-yellow (7.5YR 7/6) to very pale brown (10YR 8/4) fabric with frequent small, dark inclusions. Petrographic sample KAV 15/21: Fabric Group 5. Red (2.5YR 5/6) to black paint. Well-preserved surfaces. No burning. Reserved horizontal band in center of body with traces of vertical strokes. *Bibliography*: Day 2011a, 756, fig. 6:9. *Comparanda*: Coldstream 1968, pl. 16:a (Corinth, EG); Coldstream and Catling, eds., 1996, 16, pl. 54:19 (Knossos, Attic MG I). *Date*: LG.

GR9 P38 (V88.59; V 5301.1 and 2, V 5302.1 and 2, V 5310.2 and 3, V 5324.1, V 5346.5, V 5400 surface, V 5401.2, V 5408.1 and 2; Fig. 71; Pl. 33). Amphora. Partially mended from 45 fragments. Preservation 10%, including large fragment of body, handle attachment, large fragment of neck, and 30% of rim; missing base and handles. Max. pres. h. 26.0; d. rim 22.5. Fine to medium-coarse, hard, reddish-yellow (5YR 6/6) fabric with tiny metamorphic and phyllitic inclusions. Petrographic sample KAV 15/24: Fabric Group 3. Very pale brown (10YR 8/3) slip. Black paint. Very well preserved surfaces. No burning. Vertical filled lozenge chain on neck under running S. On shoulder, sixfold concentric circles with hatching in outer and inner circles. In handle zone, solid lozenge chain with unfilled centers above rows of alternating oblique strokes, then fourfold concentric circles with hatching between and a small leaf-shaped object that may be a mistake or may represent an arrowhead or spearhead. Toward the base are meander hooks with rectangular crosshatching. *Bibliography*: Gesell, Coulson, and Day 1991, 154, pl. 59:d (identified as pithos); Day 1995, fig. 4; 2011a, 756, fig. 6:10. *Comparanda*: for decoration, see rectangular crosshatched meander, Brock 1957, 33, pl. 19:301 (Knossos, PGA–PGB); meander hooks, Tsipopoulou 2005, 102, fig. 114:H747 (Plai tou Kastro, LG); circles with strokes, Tsipopoulou 2005, 132, fig. 15:AN2379; 138, fig. 35:Π42; 154, fig. 33:AN1857 (Hagios Georgios, LG); for shape, Coldstream and Catling, eds., 1996, 49, pl. 81:63 (Cycladic EG I). *Date*: LG.

GR9 P39 (V98.88; V 5301.1 and 2, V 5302.1 and 2, V 5307.2, V 5309.2, V 5310.1-3, V 5311.1, V 5312.2 and 3, V 5313.2, V 5317.1, V 5319.7, V 5324.1, V 5346.5, V 5401.1, 2, 4, and 5, V 5402.3 and 4, V 5404.1, V 5404.3 and 4, V 5405.1, V 5405.4–6, V 5408.2, V 5408.5, V 5408.7, V 4800.1, V 4905.4; Fig. 71; Pl. 33). Amphora. Partially mended from 63 fragments, with 47 nonjoining fragments; 50% of base, 30% of rim and upper body preserved, along with both handles and much of neck and body. D. rim 23.0; d. base 17.0. Fine to medium-coarse, rather hard, light reddish-brown (2.5YR 6/4) fabric with black grits. Petrographic sample KAV 15/23: Fabric Group 6. Very pale brown (10YR 8/4) slip. Thick, glossy, black to reddish-brown (5YR 4/4) paint. Worn surfaces, laminated toward base. Handle zone has fourfold circles with solid center and reserved cross (cross-in-circle motif). Bucranium handles. *Bibliography*: Day 2011a, 756, fig. 6:11. *Comparanda*: Coldstream and Catling, eds., 1996, 15, pl. 49:3 (Knossos, Attic MG I); 49, pl. 81:63, 64 (Knossos, Cycladic EG, possibly Melian); 141, pl. 140:23 (Knossos, EG); 198, pl. 186:52 (Knossos, Attic EG I); Hayden 2003, 53, no. 122, fig. 29, pl. 19 (Vrokastro, PGB–EG); Kotsonas 2008, 95–96, fig. 14:A227 (Eleutherna, EG). *Date*: EG.

Medium-Coarse Monochrome Wares

GR9 P40 (V 5302.1 and 2, V 5310.2, V 5312.1 and 2, V 5317.1, V 5401.5, V 5404.3, V 5408.2, V 5408.5, V 5408.7; Fig. 72). Cup. Mended from 32 fragments, 50% preserved, including full profile, small piece of base, 75% of rim and upper body, handle. H. 9.5; d. rim 14.0; d. base est. 7.5. Medium-coarse, hard, light red (2.5YR 6/8) fabric with phyllite and quartz inclusions, dark gray (2.5YR 4/0) at core. Petrographic sample KAV 15/6: Fabric Group 2. Traces of black paint. Well-preserved surfaces. One fragment burned. Rim very uneven and possibly pinched out to form crude spout. May not be monochrome; surface may be slipped with slip having fired black. *Date*: LG.

GR9 P41 (V 5312.2–4, V 5319.7; Fig. 72). Cup. Partially mended from 46 fragments. Preservation 50%, including full profile, entire base, half of rim, and part of handle. H. 8.1; d. rim 11.0; d. base 4.0. Medium-coarse, rather soft, reddish-yellow (7.5YR 7/4) fabric with frequent inclusions. Petrographic sample KAV 15/11: Fabric Subgroup 1a. Black paint. Worn surfaces. *Bibliography*: Day 2011a, 755, fig. 5:8. *Comparanda*: **IX P51**; Coldstream and Catling, eds., 1996, 247, fig. 141:111 (Knossos, PGB–EG). *Date*: G.

GR9 P42 (V 5312.5, V 5315.1 and 2; Fig. 72). Cup. Represented by 48 fragments, preserving 20% of vessel, including entire base, handle, part of rim. H. est. 7.7; d. rim 14.0; d. base 4.0. Medium-coarse, soft, pink (7.5YR 7/4) fabric with small granodiorite inclusions. Very pale brown (10YR 8/4) slip. Reddish-brown (5YR 4/4) paint. Very worn surfaces. Some fragments burned. *Bibliography*: Day 2011a, 755, fig. 5:6. *Comparanda*: **IX P50**; Coldstream and Catling, eds., 1996, 215, fig. 132:27 (Knossos, MG). *Date*: G.

GR9 P43 (V 5312.4, V 5319.1, V 5319.5, V 5319.7; Fig. 72). Cup. Represented by 16 fragments, including parts of rim, base, and handle. H. est. 7.1; d. rim 10.0; d. base 4.0. Medium-coarse, soft, very pale brown (10YR 7/4) fabric. Petrographic sample KAV 15/8: Fabric Subgroup 1b. Black paint. Very worn surfaces. *Bibliography*: Day 2011a, 755, fig. 5:8. *Comparanda*: Coldstream and Catling, eds., 1996, 255, fig. 143:6 (Knossos, LPG). *Date*: G.

GR9 P44 (V 5315.1, V 5319.1, V 5319.5, V 5319.7; Fig. 72). Cup. Partially mended from 31 fragments; entire base preserved and 10% of rim, both handle attachments. D. rim est. 14.0; d. base 5.5. Medium-coarse, soft, reddish-yellow (7.5YR 7/6) fabric with frequent phyllite and quartz inclusions. Traces of black paint. Very worn surfaces. Some burning. Unusual shallow cup or possibly a lid. *Comparanda*: Tsipopoulou 2005, 213, fig. 122:H3230 (Adromyloi, PGB); Rethemiotakis and Englezou 2010, 63–64, pl. 36:76 (lid from Eltyna, PGB–EG). *Date*: G.

GR9 P45 (V 5302.2 and 3, V 5310.2, V 5311.1, V 5312.2; Fig. 72). Skyphos. Mended from six fragments, 15% preserved, including full profile, handle attachment. H. 7.0; d. rim 17.3; d. base est. 7.8. Medium-coarse, hard, reddish-yellow (7.5YR 6/6) fabric with large phyllite and carbonate inclusions, some quartz. Petrographic sample KAV 15/17: Fabric Subgroup 1a. Black paint. *Comparanda*: **GR9 P46**. *Date*: LG?

GR9 P46 (V 5302.2 and 3, V 5310.2 and 3, V 5404.1, V 5404.3 and 4; Fig. 72). Skyphos or basin. Mended from 18 fragments. Preservation 25%, including nearly complete profile and both handles. Max. pres. h. 8.0; d. rim 19.5. Medium-coarse, soft, light brown (7.5YR 6/4) fabric with large metamorphic inclusions. Petrographic sample KAV 15/16: Fabric Group 2. Black paint. Worn surfaces. No burning. *Comparanda*: **GR9 P45**; Tsipopoulou 2005, 222, fig. 116:Σ4524 (Zakro, LG); Kotsonas 2008, 226, 228, fig. 57:A346α (Eleutherna, LPAR); Rethemiotakis and Englezou 2010, 74, fig. 45:107 (Eltyna, PG–EG). *Date*: LG.

GR9 P47 (V 5302.1 and 2, V 5311.1, V 5312.2; Fig. 72). Base of closed vessel, probably jug. Partially mended from six fragments, preserving 35% of base and lower body; missing most of body, neck, rim, and handle(s). Max. pres. h. 5.0; d. base 7.0. Medium-coarse, soft, light yellowish-brown (10YR 6/4) fabric with frequent small quartz and phyllite inclusions. Reddish-yellow (5YR 6/8) to black paint. Worn surfaces. No burning. *Date*: G–LG.

Medium-Coarse Decorated, Monochrome, or Plain Ware

GR9 P48 (V 5301.4; Fig. 72). Juglet. Represented by 10 fragments, including part of handle and rim. Max. pres. h. 2.1. Medium-coarse, soft, reddish-yellow (7.5YR 7/6) fabric with large phyllite inclusions and carbonates. Very worn surfaces. *Date*: uncertain.

Coarse Decorated Wares

GR9 P49 (V 5301.1 and 2, V 5302.1 and 2, V 5307.3, V 5308.7, V 5309.2, V 5310.1 and 2, V 5311.1, V 5312.1 and 2, V 5324.1, V 5346.1, V 5347.1, V 5401.1 and 2, V 5404.3, V 5404.6, V 4800.2, V 4803.2, V 4806.1; Fig. 72). Jug. Partially mended from 53 fragments. Preservation 30%, including base, shoulder, neck attachment; missing handle. Max. pres. h. 15.5; d. base 8.0. Medium-coarse to coarse, hard, light yellowish-brown (10YR 6/4) fabric with frequent granodiorite inclusions. Petrographic sample KAV 15/20: Fabric Group 4. Very pale brown (10YR 8/3) slip. Dark reddish-brown (5YR 3/3) to black paint. Rather well-preserved surfaces. One fragment from base burned. Bands. Drip on interior of neck. *Bibliography*: Day 2011a, 756, fig. 6:8. *Date*: LG.

GR9 P50 (V 5301.1 and 2, V 5302.1 and 2, V 5310.1 and 2, V 5324.1, V 5301.1 and 2, V 5401.2, V 5402.4, V 5404.1, 3 and 4, V 5408.2, V 4800.5; Fig. 73). Amphora. Partially mended from 33 fragments, 18 nonjoining fragments, with 35% of rim and neck preserved, one fragment of base; missing most of body and handles. D. rim est. (int.) 20.0; d. base est. 16.0. Coarse, rather hard, reddish-yellow (5YR 7/6) fabric with gray phyllite inclusions and chaff voids. Petrographic sample KAV 15/22: Fabric Group 5. Very pale brown (10YR 8/4) slip. Black paint worn to shadow. Very worn surfaces. On neck, butterfly pattern on either side of vertical checkerboard with hatched motif. On shoulder, hatched chevrons(?). *Comparanda*: Brock 1957, 33, pl. 19:301 (Knossos, LPG–PGB); Coldstream and Catling, eds., 1996, 141, pl. 139:12 (Knossos, EG). *Date*: LG.

Coarse Monochrome Wares

GR9 P51 (V 5312.2; Fig. 73). Cup. Mended from 42 fragments, 35% preserved, including full profile, entire base, handle; missing most of body. H. 8.0; d. rim 13.0; d. base 6.0. Coarse, soft, reddish-yellow (7.5YR 6/6) fabric with phyllite, quartz, and silver mica inclusions. Petrographic sample KAV 15/4: small metamorphic group with mica. Very worn surfaces. Some burned fragments. *Bibliography*: Day 2011a, 755, fig. 5:7. *Comparanda*: Kotsonas 2008, 206, 209, fig. 51:A285 (Eleutherna, PGB). *Date*: PG–G.

GR9 P52 (V 5312.3 and 4, V 5314.7, V 5319.2, V 5319.5, V 5324.1; Fig. 73). Cup. Represented by 32 fragments, including entire base, 20% of rim, handle. H. est. 9.4; d. rim 12.0; d. base 5.0. Coarse, rather soft, light red (2.5YR 6/8) fabric with phyllites and tiny white carbonates. Petrographic sample KAV 15/19: Fabric Group 2. Black paint. Burned gray and warped. Very worn surfaces. *Date*: G.

GR9 P53 (V 5312.3; Fig. 73). Cup. Partially mended from seven fragments, 30% of rim and body preserved, with handle attachment; missing base. Max. pres. h. 8.7; d. rim 12.0. Coarse, medium-soft, reddish-yellow (5YR 7/8) fabric with phyllite, quartz, and carbonate inclusions and gray (5YR 5/1) core. Petrographic sample KAV 15/3: Fabric Group 2. Very worn surfaces; no paint preserved. *Date*: LG.

GR9 P54 (V 5312.3; Fig. 73). Cup. Partially mended from 50 fragments, 30% preserved, including parts of base, handle, and rim. H. est. 9.0; d. rim 13.0; d. base 3.7. Coarse, soft, red (2.5YR 5/6) fabric with phyllites and tiny secondary calcite inclusions and dark gray (5YR 4/1) core. Petrographic sample KAV 15/13: Fabric Group 2. Black paint. Very worn surfaces and edges. Some burning. *Date*: G.

GR9 P55 (V 5314.6; Fig. 73). Cup. Partially mended from 29 fragments. Preservation 30%, including entire base, handle, 25% of rim. H. est. 8.0; d. rim 12.0; d. base 4.0. Coarse, soft, reddish-yellow (5YR 6/8) fabric. Petrographic sample KAV 15/7: Fabric Subgroup 1a. Black paint. Very worn surfaces. Some burning. *Bibliography*: Day 2011a, 755, fig. 5:9. *Comparanda*: Brock 1957, 58, pl. 38:622 (Knossos, EPG–MPG); Boardman 1960, 134, 137, fig. 5:V.20 (Hagios Ioannis, EPG); Tsipopoulou 2013, 139–140, fig. 5:12297 (Piskokephalo, LPG). *Date*: EPG–LPG.

GR9 P56 (V 5319.5, V 5319.7; Fig. 73). Cup. Partially mended from 24 fragments, including 65% of base, piece of rim, and part of handle. Max. pres. h. 3.0; d. rim est. 12.0; d. base 6.0. Coarse, rather soft, gray (2.5YR 5/0) to reddish-brown (2.5YR 5/4) fabric with phyllites, quartz, and white calcareous inclusions. Very worn surfaces, but possible traces of monochrome paint. Warped and burned. *Date*: G.

GR9 P57 (V 5314.3, V 5314.7; Fig. 73). Cup or skyphos. Ten fragments from rim and body. Max. pres. h. 6.8; d. rim est. 8.0. Coarse fabric with phyllite and white carbonate inclusions. Totally burned gray. Surfaces entirely gone. *Date*: G.

GR9 P58 (V 5302.1, V 5312.3 and 4, V 5317.1, V 5401.5, V 5405.5, V 5408.2; Fig. 73). Skyphos or mug-like cup. Partially mended from 19 fragments, including entire base, 75% of lower body, a few rim; handle(s) missing. Max. pres. h. 5.2; d. rim est. 10.2; d. base 4.0. Coarse, soft, reddish-yellow (7.5YR 7/6) fabric with frequent small phyllite and quartz inclusions. Red (2.5YR 4/6) paint. Very worn surfaces. No burning. *Date*: LG.

Metal

Bronze

GR9 M1 (V88.158, IM 1176; V5312.2, object 2; Fig. 74; Pl. 34). Bronze fibula. Large fragment from top, bits of pin; missing catch plate and tip of pin. Max. pres. L. 2.4; max. pres. w. 2.0. Well preserved with little corrosion. Arched fibula. Square in section near coil, then bead, then rounded swelling with line down top. Narrows greatly, then has a small bead with rings on either side. *Bibliography*: Gesell, Coulson, and Day 1991, 153, pl. 59:c. *Comparanda*: Blinkenberg 1926, 69, type II.12; Sapouna-Sakellaraki 1978, 69, type IVb, pl. 19:604.

GR9 M2 (V88.130, IM 1184; V5312.4, object 3; Fig. 74; Pl. 34). Bronze fibula with iron coil. Four fragments, including catch plate; missing only pin parts. Max. pres. L. 5.2, w. 4.1. Well preserved, with little corrosion. Broken and mended in antiquity with iron coil and pin. Arched fibula. Swelling in center, with two rings at either end. *Bibliography*: Gesell, Coulson, and Day 1991, 153, pl. 59:a; Day 2011a, 756, fig. 7:10. *Comparanda*: Hall 1914, 144, fig. 85M; 165, fig. 100:A, C (Vrokastro, Bone Enclosure VI); pl. 20:C, D, F (Vrokastro, Bone Enclosure II); Blinkenberg 1926, 74–76, type II.19; Sapouna-Sakellaraki 1978, pl. 19:605 (Vrokastro); Popham, Sackett, and Themelis 1979–1980, 238, pl. 248.6 (Lefkandi, LPG); Coldstream and Catling, eds., 1996, 6, fig. 157:Df4 (Knossos).

GR9 M3 (V88.169, IM 1199; V 5312.3, object 4; Pl. 34). Bronze fibula. Single fragment of end with hook; missing body. Max. pres. L. 1.3. Corroded. Round in section and hollow.

GR9 M4 (V88.172; V 5312.3, object 5, V 5319.5; Pl. 34). Bronze awl or tool. Two fragments preserved; missing both ends. Max. pres. L. 2.0; max. pres. w. 0.4. Well preserved, with little corrosion. Small tool, rectangular in section. Cut marks on larger piece.

GR9 M5 (V88.210, IM 1219; V5314.3, object 6; Fig. 74; Pl. 34). Bronze sheeting. Two large nonjoining fragments, one from corner (a), one from along edge (b); 15 nonjoining bits, including rivets. Max. pres. L. (a) 2.5, (b) 7.5; max. pres. w. (a) 2.4, (b) 2.8; L. rivets 1.2–1.3, four additional rivets 1.1–1.4. Corner fragment well preserved, fragment b very worn and thin. Thin rectangular sheet of bronze with rivets along edge for attachment to some other material.

GR9 M6 (V88.211; V5314.3, object 7; Fig. 74; Pl. 34). Bronze sheeting. Two large nonjoining fragments, one from corner (a), one from edge, possibly at corner (b); six additional rivets and 13 nonjoining fragments. Max. pres. L. (a) 5.4, (b) 2.8; max. pres. w. (a) 3.8, (b) 2.5; L. rivets 0.7–1.3. Well preserved, with little corrosion. Fragment b is worn and thin and is also bent over. Thin rectangular sheet of bronze with rivets in corner and along edge for attachment. *Bibliography*: Gesell, Coulson, and Day 1991, 154, pl. 59:b; Day 2011a, 756, fig. 7:12.

GR9 M7 (V88.190; V 5214.8, object 8; Fig. 74; Pl. 34). Bronze sheeting. Four joining fragments from corner, preserving three good edges and three rivets; four additional rivets and 11 flakes of bronze. Max. pres. L. 6.2; max. w. 3.9; L. rivets 1.0. Corroded, but surface evident. Thin rectangular bronze sheet with rivet holes along edges. *Bibliography*: Day 2011a, 756, fig. 7:11.

GR9 M8 (V88.203/209, IM 1218; V 5314.3, object 9; Fig. 74; Pl. 34). Bronze sheeting. Two joining fragments from corner with rivet and four rivet holes. Max. pres. L. 4.0; max. pres. w. 1.8. Poorly preserved; warped, corroded, and worn thin. Corner of thin rectangular sheet of bronze with rivets or rivet holes for attachment to another material.

GR9 M9 (V88.208, IM 1217; V 5314.3, object 11; Fig. 74; Pl. 34). Bronze sheeting. Four joining fragments preserving corner, with one rivet. Max. pres. L. 3.3; max. pres. w. 2.6; L. rivet 1.3. Some warping and corrosion. Corner of thin rectangular sheet of bronze with rivets or rivet holes for attachment to another material.

GR9 M10 (V88.212, IM 1220; V 5314.6, object 12; Fig. 74; Pl. 34). Bronze sheeting. Two joining and two nonjoining fragments with three rivets; no preserved edges. Max. pres. L. 3.1; max. pres. w. 2.9. Slightly curved and corroded. Traces of unknown material attached to one side. Body fragment of rectangular sheet of bronze with rivets.

GR9 M11 (V88.207, IM 1216; V 5319.3, object 3; Fig. 74; Pl. 34). Bronze sheeting. Single fragment from body without preserved edges; six rivet holes, but no preserved rivets. Max. pres. L. 4.5; max. pres. w. 2.2. Very warped and corroded. Body fragment of rectangular sheet of bronze with rivets.

GR9 M12 (V88.252; V 5314.4, object 1; Fig. 74; Pl. 34). Bronze sheeting. Three large fragments and numerous nonjoining smaller ones, including nine rivets. Two fragments preserve edges. Max. pres. L. 3.4; max. pres. w. 2.5; L. rivets 0.9. Bent, corroded, and worn. Metal folded over on one edge. Body fragments of rectangular sheet of bronze with rivets.

Iron

GR9 M13 (V88.170, IM 1182; V 5312.3, object 2; Fig. 74; Pl. 34). Iron pin. Single fragment from center; both ends missing. Max. pres. L. 4.0; max. d. 0.3. Very corroded. Probably from pin because round in section.

GR9 M14 (V88.179, IM 1191; V 5314.1 objects 2 and 3, V 5314.2 object 3; Fig. 75; Pl. 35). Iron spearhead. Partially mended from five fragments. Nearly complete; missing end of socket. Max. pres. L. 33.5; max. w. 2.3; d. socket est. 1.6. Cracked and corroded, but some surfaces survive. Length of socket at least 5.6; no evidence for piercing, but may have been in missing part. Rectangular shoulders at right angle to blade. Pronounced midrib, ca. 16.0 up blade. Long, tapering blade. *Bibliography*: Day 2011a, 756, fig. 7.1.

GR9 M15 (V88.183, IM 1185; V 5314.1 objects 3 and 5, V 5314.2, object 2, V 5314.3 object 5, V 5314.4 object 4, V 5314.6 object 4; Fig. 75; Pl. 35). Iron spearhead. Mended from nine fragments. Nearly complete. L. 36.5; max. w. 2.5; d. socket est. 1.8. Corroded but some of original still preserved. Blade bent. Short (7.0) socket, pierced near top opposite edges. Rectangular shoulders at right angles to blade. Pronounced midrib nearly the length of blade. Long, tapering blade.

GR9 M16 (V88.217, IM 1214; V 5314.2 objects 1 and 4, V 5314.2 object 7; Fig. 75; Pl. 35). Iron spearhead. Partially mended from three large and many smaller nonjoining fragments. End of socket, much of blade, and end of blade preserved; missing tip of blade. Max. pres. L. (a) 6.3, (b) 10.5, (c) 6.8; max. pres. w. 2.9; d. socket 1.6–1.8. Very poorly preserved, laminated and corroded. Some surviving surfaces, but they have laminated off. Hole pierced in socket opposite edges. Blade lacks pronounced midrib and is very wide toward socket end.

GR9 M17 (V88.180, IM 1200; V 5314.3, objects 1 and 10; Fig. 76; Pl. 35). Iron spearhead. Complete in three fragments. L. 30.0; max. w. 2.2; d. socket 1.9. Surfaces worn and corroded, but well preserved. Rather short (7.8) socket, pierced toward end opposite edges. Socket not completely closed. Rectangular shoulders at right angles to blade. Pronounced midrib, extending 10.7 up blade. Rather short blade.

GR9 M18 (V88.157, IM 1201, HNM 15743; V5312.2, object 3; Fig. 76; Pl. 35). Iron spearhead. Intact. L. 22.3; max. w. 2.8; d. socket 1.9. Surface corroded and cracked. Short (7.5) socket, with hole pierced near end opposite edges. Blade comes out at right angles. Short blade with midrib. *Bibliography*: Gesell, Coulson, and Day 1991, 152–153, pl. 58:c; Day 2011a, 756, fig. 7:3. *Comparanda*: Blegen 1952, 281, fig. 3:2, 3, pl. 75:c (Athens).

GR9 M19 (V88.155, IM 1195, HNM 15742; V 5312.2, object 4; Fig. 76; Pl. 35). Iron spearhead. Restored. Nearly complete in three joining fragments; missing a few chips of edge. L. 41.2; max. w. 2.6; d. socket 1.6. Well preserved, though corroded and cracked, with some surviving surfaces. Blade slightly bent. Short (7.8) socket folded and no longer round. Hole pierced opposite folded edge. Rectangular shoulders at right angles to blade. Pronounced midrib, L. 15.0. *Bibliography*: Gesell, Coulson, and Day 1991, 152–153, pl. 58:a.

GR9 M20 (V88.156; V 5312.2 objects 5 and 6, V 5312.4 object 4, V 5319.5 object 4, V 5319.5 and 6; Fig. 76; Pl. 35). Iron spearhead. Mended from 11 fragments; nearly complete. Max. pres. L. 29.5; L. est. 36.0; max. pres. w. 2.3; d. socket 1.8. Very corroded, with large corrosion bubbles on blade. Some surviving surfaces on blade and socket. Metal has split at join of socket and blade. Blade bent at right angles; deliberately killed? Long (11.6) socket, pierced at end near one edge and not as usual on opposite edges. Rectangular shoulders at right angles to blade. Pronounced midrib, at least L. 15.0. Long, narrow blade.

GR9 M21 (V88.201, IM 1213, HNM 15749; V 5315.1 object 2, V 5312.2 object 1; Fig. 77; Pl. 35). Iron spearhead. Two joining fragments. Restored. Nearly complete; missing a few chips from edges and socket. L. 26.0; max. w. 1.9; d. socket 1.7. Corroded, cracked, and bent; little surviving surface. Metal folded and not hammered out, showing a different technology. Medium-long (8.5) socket, folded over and not pierced. Short blade rising in continuous curve from socket. No real midrib. *Bibliography*: Gesell, Coulson, and Day 1991, 152–153, pl. 58:b; Day 2011a, 756, fig. 7:2.

GR9 M22 (V88.173, IM 1188; V 5312.3, object 6; Fig. 77; Pl. 35). Iron spearhead. Mended from six fragments, nine nonjoining bits; nearly complete. L. 24.0; max. w. 2.5; d. socket 1.8–1.9. Very corroded, especially on edges. Some flat areas preserve original surfaces. Medium-long (8.0) socket without hole pierced in it. Rectangular shoulders at right angles to blade. Pronounced midrib, L. 7.0 from socket. Short, rather wide blade.

GR9 M23 (V88.199, IM 1206; V 5314.7, object 14; Fig. 77; Pl. 35). Iron spearhead. Two large fragments and numerous small chips and flakes, preserving socket, part of blade; missing tip of blade. Max. pres. L. 18.1; max. w. 2.3; d. socket 1.6–2.0. Socket well preserved, but corroded; socket end of blade flaked and laminated. No surviving surfaces. Medium-long (8.3) socket with hole pierced through end opposite edges; slightly flattened. Blade worn but appears to be leaf shaped with sloping shoulders. No pronounced midrib.

GR9 M24 (V88.195, IM 1192; V 5314.7, object 16; Fig. 77; Pl. 35). Iron spearhead. Three nonjoining fragments from socket (a), blade (b), and tip (c). Max. pres. L. (a) 12.2, (b) 5.7, (c) 3.1; max pres. w. 2.6; d. socket 1.9. Very corroded surfaces. Rather short (7.5) socket without pierced hole. Rectangular shoulders at right angles to blade; tapering midrib. Wide tip suggests that the blade was short.

GR9 M25 (V88.189/214, IM 1181/1211; V 5314.3 object 10, V 5314.7 object 9; Fig. 77; Pl. 35). Iron spearhead. Five joining fragments preserving nearly the entire length; missing a small portion between socket and blade. L. est. 28.2; max. w. 2.2; d. socket 1.8. Cracked and corroded, but some surviving surfaces. Socket L. at least 7.0, pierced near end at right angle to edges. Rectangular shoulders at right angles to blade; pronounced midrib that runs nearly the length of the blade. Long, narrow blade.

GR9 M26 (V88.174, IM 1189; V 5311.1 objects 1 and 3, V 5311.2 objects 1 and 2; Fig. 78; Pl. 35). Iron spearhead. Single fragment from socket made up of two joining pieces. Max. pres. L. 9.6; d. socket est. 1.9. Badly corroded. Long socket, apparently with continuous line into blade.

GR9 M27 (V88.191, IM 1178; V 5315.1, object 1; Fig. 78; Pl. 35). Iron spearhead. Four joining and one possibly joining fragments preserving entire socket and much of blade; missing edges and tip of blade. Max. pres. L. 23.0; max. pres. w. 1.7; d. socket 1.5–1.7. Very corroded with little preserved surface. Long (ca. 10.0) socket with possible hole pierced toward end. Leaf-shaped blade rises in continuous curve from socket. No midrib.

GR9 M28 (V88.188, IM 1180; V 5314.3, object 3; Fig. 78; Pl. 35). Iron spearhead. Three large fragments and many small ones: two joining fragments from end of blade (a), one nonjoining from socket (b); missing connections between blade and socket, much of socket, half of tip of blade. Max. pres. L. (a) 15.5, (b) 10.8; max. w. 2.1. Blade well preserved with some surviving surfaces; socket corroded, nonjoining fragment laminating. No indication of length of socket, how it connects to blade; no midrib.

GR9 M29 (V88.198, IM 1212; V 5314.7, object 15; Fig. 78; Pl. 35). Iron socketed weapon or tool. Single fragment and a few smaller ones preserving entire socket and end. Max. pres. L. 11.5; max. w. 2.2; d. socket 1.9. Very worn and corroded. Long (8.7) socket, pierced toward end opposite edges. In place of blade is a spoon-shaped oval with a slight depression on one side. May have melted on the pyre, but also possibly deliberately shaped. *Comparanda*: Catling 1964, 105–106, fig. 11:7–9 (socketed spatulae).

GR9 M30 (V88.178, IM 1198; V 5314.1 object 1, V 5314.6 object 2; Fig. 78; Pl. 36). Iron dagger. Six joining fragments preserving most of blade and one bronze rivet; missing fragments of blade, some edges, and tip. L. 21.8; max. w. 3.3. Cracked and corroded; some surviving surfaces. Flange hilted, tapering quickly to a short narrow blade.

GR9 M31 (V88.194, IM 1203; V 5319.4 object 4, V 5320.1 object 1; Fig. 78; Pl. 36). Iron dirk. Partially mended from 15 fragments; 12 joining, three join each other but not main fragment. Missing end of hilt, connection of hilt and blade, parts of blade, and rivets. L. est. 41.3; max. w. 3.3. Rather well preserved, laminated toward hilt. Flange hilted. Tapers to long narrow blade. Three small rivet holes, one on hilt, others at end of blade.

GR9 M32 (V88.193, IM 1204; V 5315.2 object 1, V 5319.2 object 1; Fig. 79; Pl. 36). Iron dirk or dagger. Three large fragments (made up of seven fragments) from tip (a), blade (b), and hilt (c), and 20 other fragments, including rivets; missing join of hilt and blade, blade fragments. Max. pres. L. (a) 16.6, (b) 9.4, (c) 5.6; max. w. 3.5. Corroded, but some surfaces survive on blade. Flange hilted; long, narrow blade, very wide near hilt, tapering to point. Bronze rivets found nearby may belong.

GR9 M33 (V88.186, IM 1194, HNM 15746; V 5319.5, object 5; Fig. 79; Pl. 36). Iron dirk. Partially mended from 11 fragments and two nonjoining fragments from tip; missing parts of blade and one tip of hilt. L. 38.6; max. w. 3.6. Well-preserved surfaces on hilt and upper blade, with many surviving surfaces. More corroded and cracked farther toward the tip. Flange hilted. Blade tapers to a narrow point. Three rivets of bronze in hilt and at attachment to blade, iron rivet higher in hilt. *Bibliography*: Gesell, Coulson, and Day 1991, 152–153, pl. 58:d; Day 2011a, 756, fig. 7:4. *Comparanda*: Karageorghis 1983, pl. 81:64.5 (bronze, Palaepaphos, 11th century).

GR9 M34 (V88.206, IM 1215; V 5312.4, object 1; Fig. 79; Pl. 36). Iron dirk or dagger. Five joining fragments from hilt and end of blade, plus 34 additional fragments; end of hilt and most of blade missing. Three bronze rivets preserved, one in hilt, one in blade. Max. pres. L. 17.7; max. w. 3.9. Some surviving surfaces; blade very corroded and laminated. Flange hilted.

GR9 M35 (V88.184, IM 1193, HNM 15744; V 5314.1 object 4, V 5314.4 objects 2 and 3, V 5314.7 object 3; Fig. 79; Pl. 36). Iron knife. Mended from numerous fragments; entire length and shape preserved. L. 17.5; max. w. 2.3. Surfaces well preserved, with little corrosion. Long (6.4), slightly curved handle, flat and rectangular in section. Blade hangs down from handle; very thin, with blunted end. *Bibliography*: Gesell, Coulson, and Day 1991, 153, pl. 58:f; Day 2011a, 756, fig. 7:6.

GR9 M36 (V88.216, IM 1207; V 5314.3 object 2, V 5314.5 and 6; Fig. 79; Pl. 36). Iron knife. Single fragment from tip of blade. Max. pres. L. 4.0; max. pres. w. 1.7. Just section laminated off from larger object; no preserved surfaces. Edges do not seem parallel, hence it has been identified as a knife; possible slight curve.

GR9 M37 (V88.213, IM 1208; V 5320.1, object 1; Fig. 79; Pl. 36). Iron knife. Two joining fragments from blade; missing end and tip of blade. Max. pres. L. 7.0; max. w. 1.2. Some surviving surfaces, though corroded. Small blade with iron rivet at one end, square in section. Blade curves slightly with cutting edge on interior of curve. *Bibliography*: Liston and Day 2009, 69, fig. 4.8:c. *Comparanda*: Karageorghis 1983, pl. 143:T. 76.133 (Palaepaphos, 11th century).

GR9 M38 (V88.187, IM 1196; V 5314.7, object 12; Fig. 79; Pl. 36). Iron sickle-shaped knife. Complete. L. 12.1; max. w. 1.8. Very corroded; only small bit of surface survives. Slightly curved blade, pierced for rivet at one end, and ending in oblique angle. Cutting edge on inside of curve, possibly serrated. Rounded tip. *Bibliography*: Day 2011a, 756, fig. 7:7. *Comparanda*: Karageorghis 1983, pl. 143:T. 76.26 (Palaepaphos, 11th century).

GR9 M39 (V88.175, IM 1190; V 5311.2 object 7, V 5311.2 object 4; Fig. 79; Pl. 36). Iron sickle-shaped knife. Two joining fragments preserving handle end with rivet hole; missing tip of blade. Max. pres. L. 8.3; max. w. 2.4. Corroded. Curved blade, rivet hole near end. End is at an oblique angle for attaching some other medium. Cutting edge on interior. *Comparanda*: Karageorghis 1983, pl. 143:T. 76.26 (Palaepaphos, 11th century).

GR9 M40 (V88.196, IM 1202, HNM 15747; V 5314.6, object 2; Fig. 79; Pl. 36). Iron axe-head. Mended from numerous fragments; nearly complete, except for chips. L. 10.1; max. w. 4.1. Some corrosion, but some well-preserved surfaces. Long (3.9) tang. Head joins at right angle and flares out gradually. *Bibliography*: Gesell, Coulson, and Day 1991, 152, pl. 58:e. *Comparanda*: Coldstream and Catling, eds., 1996, fig. 175:f 52, f 53; Popham and Lemos 1996, pl. 128:T. 39.33 (LPG); pl. 128:pyre 13.2 (SPG II); Snodgrass 1996, 588.

GR9 M41 (V88.202, IM 1205, HNM 15750; V 5319.4, object 2; Fig. 79; Pl. 36). Iron axe-head. Mended from numerous fragments; nearly complete except for chips. L. 12.8; max. w. 4.5. Cracked and very corroded, with some surviving surfaces. Long (4.3) tang. Head comes out at right angles and gradually widens. *Bibliography*: Day 2011a, 756, fig. 7:5. *Comparanda*: Coldstream and Catling, eds., 1996, fig. 175:f 52, f 53; Popham and Lemos 1996, pl. 128:T. 39.33 (LPG); pl. 128:pyre 13.2 (SPG II); Snodgrass 1996, 588.

GR9 M42 (V88.197, IM 1197, HNM 15748; V 5314.7, object 1; Fig. 80; Pl. 36). Iron axe-head. Mended from eight fragments. Nearly complete; missing chips and end of haft. L. 16.0; max. w. 6.2. Very corroded and splitting, but some surviving surfaces. Long (5.2) tang. Head comes out at right angles to haft and gradually widens. *Comparanda*: Coldstream and Catling, eds., 1996, fig. 175:f 52, f 53; Popham and Lemos 1996, pl. 128:T. 39.33 (LPG); pl. 128:pyre 13.2 (SPG II); Snodgrass 1996, 588.

GR9 M43 (V88.192, IM 1179; V 5319.4, object 1; Fig. 80; Pl. 37). Iron scraper. Complete except for chips. L. 10.1; max. w. 2.8. Very corroded and cracked; only a tiny bit of surviving surface. Narrow end bent under 1.5. Object is chisel shaped, widening to broad end, which is slightly bent up in opposite direction from the other end. *Bibliography*: Liston and Day 2009, 68–69, figs. 4.6, 4.8:e; Day 2011a, 756, fig. 7:9.

GR9 M44 (V88.181, IM 1177, HNM 15745; V 5314.5, object 1; Fig. 80; Pl. 37). Iron scraper. Nearly intact. L. 5.7; max. w. 2.3. Corroded. Flat, chisel-shaped object, widening from flat end to broad end. Broad end bent over. Possible slot through the body near the short end. *Bibliography*: Gesell, Coulson, and Day 1991, 153, pl. 58:g; Liston and Day 2009, 68–69, figs. 4.5, 4.8:d.

GR9 M45 (V88.159, IM 1187; V 5312.2, object 1; Fig. 80; Pl. 37). Iron chisel. Two joining fragments from one end, many other nonjoining fragments; missing other end. Max. pres. L. 11.5; max. w. 1.7. Very corroded and laminated. Flattened on one end, rectangular in section in middle. Other end may be pointed or flat.

GR9 M46 (V88.113, IM 1186; V 5314.5–7; Fig. 80). Iron awl. Intact. L. 2.9. Corroded, but some surviving surfaces. Short object, pointed at both ends, square in section in center.

GR9 M47 (V88.226, HNM 15751; V 5314.4, object 2; Fig. 80; Pl. 37). Iron awl. Mended from three fragments; nearly complete. L. 13.0; max. w. 0.6. Well preserved; little corrosion and good surfaces. Long tool, pointed at both ends and square in section in the middle. One end round and pointed, the other square and pointed. *Bibliography*: Liston and Day 2009, 69, fig. 4.8:a; Day 2011a, 756, fig. 7:8. *Comparanda*: Karageorghis 1983, 216, fig. 143:T. 76:27 (Palaepaphos-*Skales*, 11th century); Courtois 1984, 21:159, fig. 5:19 (bronze).

GR9 M48 (V88.171, IM 1183; V 5312.3, object 3; Fig. 80; Pl. 37). Iron awl. Single fragment preserving one end; other end missing. Max. pres. L. 8.7; max. w. 0.9. Cracked and corroded. Long tool, square in section, pointed at one end. Possibly a chisel or awl. *Comparanda*: Courtois 1984, 21, no. 158, fig. 5:15, 16 (bronze).

GR9 M49 (V88.200, IM 1210; V 5314.7, object 2; Fig. 80; Pl. 37). Iron awl. Intact. L. 3.4. Well-preserved surfaces. Short awl with points on both ends. Round in section and to one end; other end flattened before coming to a point.

GR9 M50 (V88.251; V 5312.3; Fig. 80; Pl. 37). Iron awl. Nearly complete in two joining fragments; missing tip of one end. Max. pres. L. 5.5. Well-preserved surfaces; little corrosion. Some wood adhering. Small tool, pointed at one end; round in section at one end, rectangular and flat at the other.

GR9 M51 (V88.215, IM 1209; V 5314.5 object 2, V 5314.6 object 1; Fig. 80; Pl. 37). Iron tool. Three joining fragments; missing both ends. Max. pres. L. 7.4. Corroded and cracked, but some well-preserved surfaces. Long thin object, rectangular in section, with one narrow end and one broad end. Narrow end may come to a point (a point is preserved but does not join). Originally thought to be the handle of a knife like **GR9 M35**. *Bibliography*: Liston and Day 2009, 69, fig. 4.8:b.

GR9 M52 (V88.227a; V 5314.3 object 4, V 5314.7 object 6; Fig. 80; Pl. 37). Iron fleshhook. Mended from five fragments. Nearly complete; missing one end. Max. pres. L. 14.7. Corroded but with small bits of surface. Long thin object, square in section and pointed at one end. Makes gentle S-curve. *Comparanda*: Dikaios 1969–1971, vols. II, IIIA, 776, pl. 178:20 (177) (Enkomi, bronze rod); **GR9 M53–GR9 M55**.

GR9 M53 (V88.227b; V 5314.3 object 4, V 5314.7 object 6; Fig. 80; Pl. 37). Iron fleshhook. Mended from four fragments. Nearly complete; missing one tip. L. 8.2, max. w. 4.4 (from side to side). Corroded but with some surfaces preserved. Long thin object, square in section, with two sharp bends at top to form the shape of a giant staple or wide tongs. One side pointed (L. 7.5), the other broken off. *Comparanda*: **GR9 M52**, **GR9 M54**, **GR9 M55**.

GR9 M54 (V88.228; V 5314.7, objects 11 and 13; Fig. 80; Pl. 37). Iron fleshhook. Three joining and three nonjoining fragments from near end up to bend in object, 50% preserved. Max. pres. L. 6.8; max. w. (at top) 2.3. Very corroded; interior core completely mineralized to yellow powder. Rectangular in section, making two right angle bends like top of a staple. *Comparanda*: **GR9 M52**, **GR9 M53**, **GR9 M55**.

GR9 M55 (V88.229; V5314.7 object 11, V 5314 water sieve; Fig. 80; Pl. 37). Iron fleshhook. Mended from seven fragments; nearly complete except for one tip. Max. pres. L. 8.6; max. w. (across top) 4.5. Surface and interior very corroded. Pointed at both ends; makes two right angles forming the shape of a staple, with pointed ends curved opposite to top. Square in section. *Comparanda*: **GR9 M52–GR9 M54**.

Stone

GR9 S1 (V88.77, IM 1004; V 5301.1; Fig. 80). Stone bead. Conical. Intact, but worn and with pocked surfaces. H. 1.30; max. d. 1.75; d. hole 0.40. Wt. 4.00 g. Soft, dark gray serpentinite with brown patches. Many deep grooves in hole and around edges of hole from use.

Grave 10

History and Details of Excavation

Grave 10 is located on the northeast summit of the Vronda ridge in Trench V 4800, close to Graves 12, 17, and 20 and built into Room J4 of the earlier LM IIIC Building J (Figs. 3, 4). In many respects it was an unusual grave: a single inhumation of a child within a pithos that was set in a stone-lined enclosure. It was entirely excavated during the 1988 season (Gesell, Day, and Coulson 1991, 154). The enclosure was recognized immediately below the surface; it was seen to continue into the north balk, which was promptly excavated along with the rest of the trench. Through a misunderstanding of the recording system, the excavator designated the entire enclosure Locus V 4804 while the pottery pails represent different areas or layers within the grave. After V 4804.2, a pithos appeared in the southern two-thirds of the enclosure, and this area was excavated as V 4804.3, while the area to the north was removed as V 4804.4. The pithos was smashed and lay on its side directly on the brecciating surface, with the base toward the north (Pls. 38A, 38B). There were no accompanying grave goods.

Architecture

The enclosure was long and rectangular, measuring 1.80–2.20 m north–south x 0.70–0.84 m east–west (Fig. 81; Pl. 38C). The north (continuation of V 4817), south (continuation of V 4803), and west (V 4802) walls are made of large single boulders with a few smaller stones between. The stones form a face on the interior of the enclosure, but there is no good outside face, except on the south wall, which may have been reused from LM IIIC Building J. The two stones of the northwest corner do not quite meet. The north wall was slightly different because the boulders were more widely spaced. The east wall (V 4801) is more regular in the positioning of the limestone blocks. This wall, like the south wall, may have been part of an earlier structure that was incorporated into the enclosure. All the walls were made up primarily of limestone blocks, with little breccia; the use of limestone gives the walls a more regular appearance. None of them shows the cracking or fissuring found on the limestone of other cremation enclosures, a fact that is not surprising, as the body within the grave was not burned. Within the enclosure was a brecciating bedrock surface upon which the pithos was laid, with a circle of small stones to support the vessel (Pl. 38B).

Associated Features

It is difficult to determine if there were any features associated with the grave but not actually within it. It was thought that the area to the east (V 4806), which contained soft, ashy soil and some grave objects (metal and pottery), might have been associated with Grave 10. The pottery was often burned, however, and there were joins with vessels in Grave 12, so the area probably contains a discard deposit from Grave 12 and has no direct association with Grave 10. To the north of the enclosure was a pit with dog bones, but these are modern and not associated with the burial.

Stratigraphy

Like others in this area, Grave 10 lay close to the modern surface, and the total deposition in the grave was 0.30 to 0.40 m. The walls and the pithos were placed immediately upon the bedrock, and the entire enclosure was filled with brown (10YR 4/3) soil that contained small and medium-sized stones and some snail shells (V 4804.2, V 4804.4). The topsoil (V 4804.1) lay just above this deposit.

Burials

Within the pithos was a single inhumation of a juvenile, aged five to six years old, with the head toward the north and the base of the pithos.

Burial 1
Type: inhumation
Age: juvenile, 5–6 years
Sex: unknown
Weight: dentition only, no weight recorded

This child's inhumation burial was placed inside a small pithos. Virtually no identifiable remains of this skeleton survived except for the teeth, and some of these were missing or fragmentary (Pl. 38D). When excavated, however, the teeth were found in approximately the correct arrangement, suggesting that the missing and fragmentary teeth are the result of microdisturbances inside the pithos, such as rodent activity. A dental age of five to six years was estimated on the basis of the development of the deciduous and permanent teeth. The permanent left maxillary incisors, left and right mandibular incisors, and the maxillary canines all have between one and three visible bands of linear enamel hypoplasias, probably formed during periods of illness or nutritional stress during infancy (Hillson 2008, 304–306).

Faunal Remains

The faunal materials recovered in association with the child's inhumation within a pithos are limited to unburned and generally unidentifiable bone fragments, many of which are likely to represent general site debris unassociated with the burial (Table 7). These included sheep or goat tooth enamel fragments, a single sheep or goat carpal, and scattered rabbit or hare bones and bone fragments.

Botanical Remains

A single pea (*Pisum* sp. *granula testa*) fragment was found in the grave.

Pottery

There was little associated pottery, aside from the pithos, and no objects were placed with the deceased. The pithos consisted of 219 fragments weighing 13.59 kg. Another 50 fragments of pottery weighing 1.62 kg were recovered from the grave, including part of one pyxis (**GR20 P5**; see below). The pyxis was originally identified as coming from the grave because of the three fragments found in the northern half of the enclosure, but it probably belongs to Grave 20, where many more fragments from the same vessel were found.

Chronology

It is difficult to date the construction of the grave because of the lack of associated pottery, but a LG date may be suggested because of the parallels between the pithos and material from the Kastro (pers. comm., M. Mook). A similar pithos fragment from Crete with stamped cross-rosettes is dated to the early seventh century (Boardman 1961, 114, 118, pl. 43:514). The layout of the three graves that use the existing house wall of Building J suggests the following sequence: Grave 12, Grave 10, and Grave 17. If Grave 20 already existed, it probably continued in use after Grave 10. The pyxis (**GR20 P5**), of which fragments were found in the northern half of Grave 10, may have been dumped there from Grave 20.

Catalog

Pottery

GR10 P1 (V98.89; V 4804.3, V 4804.1; Fig. 82; Pls. 38E, 38F). Pithos. Mended from 225 fragments and partially restored. Preservation 75%, including entire base; missing large section of body and about half of rim. H. 75.80; d. rim (int.) 2.04; d. rim (ext.) 29.00; d. base 25.00. Coarse, red (2.5 YR 5/6–5/8) fabric with phyllites, quartz, and greenstone. Petrographic samples PMD 98/17; KAV 15/92: Fabric Group 3. Decorated near base with applied band and stamped designs of circles with four wedges, a sort of windmill design. *Date*: G.

Grave 12

History and Details of Excavation

Grave 12 lies toward the northern end of the west side of the summit of the Vronda ridge in Room J4 of the earlier LM IIIC Building J (Figs. 3, 4). It was completely excavated in 1988 in Trench V 4800. The excavator identified the grave immediately below the surface and designated the whole grave as V 4805. Because of some confusion with the recording system, different areas of the grave and different soil layers within it were given pottery pail numbers rather than different locus designations. Hence, the pottery pail numbers serve to identify different loci within the grave, while the excavation dates of the pottery pails serve the function of pottery pail numbers in other graves. As soon as the walls of Graves 10 and 12 became apparent, the north balk of the trench was excavated as V 4800.4 and V 4800.5. Only the western two-thirds of Grave 12 was within the original 4 x 4 m boundaries of the trench; the east balk, which contained the eastern third of the enclosure, was excavated almost immediately so that the whole grave could be dug together. Excavation was conducted jointly by an archaeologist and a biological anthropologist who recorded the position of the bones and the objects within the grave.

The top layer of the grave (V 4805.1) contained stones, ash, snail shells, and some pottery, but no human bone. A circle of stones in the southeast, also extending over the southern wall of the grave, was excavated separately (V 4808), as was the area over the south wall (V 4803). After the opening of the east balk, all pottery from the circle of stones was collected with that from V 4805. As excavation continued, there was a gradual increase in the number of stones and the first appearance of burned human bone, and a great amount of pottery was found along the west wall of the grave and along the northwest edge. The soil became finer and darker beginning on the west (V 4805.3) but not continuing across the grave. A line of stones seemed to divide the grave into two, and the material from the two areas was kept separate as V 4805.3 (west) and V 4805.4 (east). Material from the northeast corner of the enclosure was also removed separately (V4805.5). Finally, the material just above the floor all over the grave was collected as V 4805.6.

During excavation three burials were distinguished and labeled burials A, B, and C; burial D was identified later during analysis. Subsequent study has shown that there were in fact eight burials, not quite corresponding to those identified in the ground (Burials 1–8); the fetus and infant were only identified in the residue from the water sieve. It is unclear how many cremation events occurred, but at least six of the bodies were found in V 4805.4 in the eastern part of the enclosure, including most of the skulls, and parts of these same individuals were found in V 4805.3 on the west. Perhaps during subsequent burials material was swept to both the east and the west sides of the grave. Parts of Burials 2 and 3 were found in the northeast corner in V 4805.5, so it would appear that that corner contained some material undisturbed by subsequent burials.

Study of the material has shown that there was a good deal of spillage or dumping from Grave 12. Grave 12 material has also been found in the area to the west in V 4806, to the east in V 4904, and to the north in V 4815. Some of the surface material became commingled with material from Grave 9 due to erosion or later human activity.

Architecture

Grave 12 is a large (0.93–1.00 m north–south x 1.88–1.93 m east–west) stone-lined enclosure (Fig. 81; Pl. 39A). On the south it was built up against an existing wall of the LM IIIC Building J (V 4803), but a new face of one to two courses was constructed from a line of stones set up against the wall. The east (V 4818), north (V 4820), and west (V 4819) walls consist of single rows of limestone blocks, each one course high, with chinking stones at the bottom to level up the blocks. The limestone blocks are badly fissured from the heat of the pyres, and one breccia boulder on the south wall has calcined from the burning. The breccia bedrock served as the floor of the grave, and it has disintegrated into what has been called a brecciating surface. A circle of stones was encountered in the southeast corner of the grave (V 4808); it extended over the top of the south wall, and it may have been deliberately constructed to contain pottery after one of the burials, likely the last.

Stratigraphy

The total depth of deposition in the grave was ca. 0.38 m. Although several different soils were distinguished within the enclosure, subsequent study of the bones and pottery shows joins among all of the different areas (pails and loci). As the brecciating surface at the bottom of the enclosure was white and calcined, it would appear that the pyre was laid directly upon it. Cleaning of this brecciating surface (V 4805.6) did not produce any pottery. Above the floor of the grave was a layer of dark brown (10YR 3/3) ashy soil in the eastern part of the enclosure (V 4805.4), a layer that contained remains of Burials 1–5 and some of 7 and 8. On the western side of the enclosure was a finer, very dark grayish-brown (10YR 3/2) soil layer (V 4805.3) that contained the bones of Burials 6, 7, and 8. A dark grayish-brown (10YR 4/2) layer of compacted soil with burned stones and charcoal was found in the northeast corner of the enclosure (V 4805.5); this layer contained most of the remains of Burials 2 and 3. Above these layers (V 4805.3, V 4805.4, V 4805.5) was another layer of similar soil that included more stones (V 4805.2) and some of Burial 6 with its fetus (Burial 7). Burials 6–8 were the last burials made in the grave, and the great amount of pottery found along the western wall of the grave and on the northwest edge may have accompanied them. The top layer of the grave (V 4805.1) contained stones, dark grayish-brown (10YR 4/2) ashy soil, snail shells, and some pottery, but no human bone. The topsoil over this area was very thin, and much grave material was found in it.

Grave material was also found outside the walls of the enclosure. Some of this may represent dumping when the grave was readied for subsequent burials, as was certainly the case in other Vronda graves. Some material from V 4806, the space between Graves 10 and 12, was possibly such a dump, or it could have been an open area for rituals and the display of grave markers. Another possible dump lay to the east of the enclosure in V 4904, later disturbed by a pit dug by the builders or inhabitants of Building R. Grave material recovered from the area to the north of Grave 12 (V 4815 and possibly V 4818) may also represent dumping or spillage. Finally, the material recovered from the walls of Grave 12, especially from the south wall (V 4803) and the circle of stones over the south wall and the southeast corner of the grave (V 4808), may represent a deposit made at the time of one of the latest burials in the enclosure, an interpretation that is supported by the lack of burning on much of this pottery.

Burials

Grave 12 contained the remains of eight cremation burials. The majority of the bodies were oriented with their heads at the east, but the skulls of Burials 6 and 8 lay at the west end of the enclosure.

Burial 1
Type: disturbed primary cremation
Age: adult
Sex: unknown
Weight: 18 g

Burial 1 is that of a cremated adult of unknown sex. Portions of the right temporal bone are the only bones that could definitely be assigned to this skeleton.

Burials 2 and 3
Type: disturbed primary cremations
Age: adults
Sex: unknown
Weight: 159 g

The skeletons of Burials 2 and 3 represent disturbed cremation burials found at the extreme east end of the enclosure, where they apparently had been pushed aside for the later burials. Both of the skeletons are of adults of unknown sex.

Burial 4
Type: disturbed primary cremation
Age: adult, 20–40 years
Sex: unknown
Weight: 2,921 g (combined with Burial 5; below)

Burial 4 is a disturbed adult cremation. The bone was commingled with that of Burial 5, and although it is not possible to separate the postcrania of the two burials, two partial crania could be reconstructed. The left mandibular second and third molars had been lost before death, suggesting that this burial was not a young adult, and the cranial suture closure suggests an age at the upper end of the 20–40 year range. The cranium has morphological features generally associated with male crania, including well-developed brow ridges and muscle attachments (Buikstra and Ubelaker, eds., 1994, 19–20). This cranium is much less burned than any of the other bone from the grave. The anterior cranium and upper face show very little evidence for burning, while the posterior cranial vault has burned to a dark gray color. The cranial base is completely calcined, suggesting that the skull had perhaps shifted away from the body, and the normally protected portions of the cranial base continued to be exposed to fire while the face and cranial vault were shielded. Alternatively, the cranial base may have been exposed to fire from later cremations in the enclosure, while the rest of the skull was protected in some manner. Some of the vertebral spines and one rib fragment from this burial also show only minimal exposure to burning. The bone is a distinctive blue color, similar to that seen in Grave 9, Burial 1. Some of the vertebral spines and one rib fragment from this burial show only minimal exposure to burning.

There is a retained metopic suture on the frontal bone of the skull. There are also interproximal grooves present on the preserved portions of two premolars and one maxillary and one mandibular molar. These marks are mechanically induced horizontal grooves between the teeth, indicating attempts to probe or dig into the teeth and gums, probably in response to some irritation (Ubelaker, Phenice, and Bass 1969, 145–147). A globule of melted bronze adheres to the left mastoid process. The position of the bronze suggests that it is the remains of an earring that was buried with the individual and became attached to the bone behind the ear. Other references to earrings with male burials have not been found, but the presence of this item of jewelry suggests caution regarding the common practice of sexing burials by the accompanying grave goods.

The retained metopic suture on this skull represents a cranial anomaly that normally is a genetic trait. This additional suture has been found in many individuals in graves in the area of the former Building Complex J-K and probably indicates a familial relationship among people buried here. In addition, this individual has a large number of sutural ossicles, extra bones that formed in the cranial sutures. These structures are normally benign and probably another indicator of a genetic tendency toward cranial developmental anomalies in individuals buried in the area of this building.

Burial 5
Type: disturbed primary cremation
Age: adult, 40–60 years
Sex: male
Weight: see above, Burial 4

Burial 5 is an adult male. The burial was a primary cremation lying with the head at the east end of the enclosure. The postcranial bone from this burial was commingled with part of the postcranial skeleton of Burial 4. This cranium is much less burned than any of the other bone from this grave (Pl. 22F: top left). The anterior cranium and upper face show very little evidence for burning, while the posterior cranial vault has burned to a dark gray color. The cranial base is completely calcined, suggesting that the skull had rolled away from the body, and the normally protected portions of the cranial base continued to be exposed to fire while the face and cranial vault were shielded.

The individual was probably 40 to 60 years old with extensive closure and incipient obliteration of the cranial vault sutures. The only pathological condition noted on the bone from this burial is some widespread porosity of the outer table of the cranial vault, probably indicative of anemia.

Burial 6
Type: primary cremation
Age: adult, 22–24 years
Sex: female
Weight: 1,767 g

Burial 6 is an adult female burial lying with the head at the west end of the enclosure. The postcranial bone from this burial was commingled with part of Burial 4. The weight indicates that most of the skeleton that survived cremation was recovered. All of the bone was completely calcined.

The identification of the sex is supported by the fetal bones that were found commingled with the skeleton. The pubic symphysis indicates an age of 20–24 years (Buikstra and Ubelaker, eds., 1994, 22–24). The cranial suture closure is also consistent with this age. The only observed pathologies or anomalies on this skeleton involve the lower legs and feet. There is a squatting facet on the distal left tibia (Pl. 39B), and the medial and distal phalanges of one toe are fused together. Together these features suggest a habitual posture of kneeling on the floor with the toes flexed under the feet. The fusion of the toe bones could be the result of habitual stress from this position, or trauma, presumably from kicking or stumbling over some object.

Burial 7
Type: primary cremation
Age: fetus, 22–34 weeks
Sex: unknown
Weight: 29 g

This burial is a cremated fetus, 22–34 weeks in utero, found commingled with the bones of the young adult female, Burial 6 (see above). The incomplete combustion of collagen in the bones, indicated by the dark gray color, supports the supposition that this was not a premature birth, but that Burials 6 and 7 represent a woman who died while pregnant and was cremated together with her fetus. This association in turn supports the identification of Burial 6 as a female, despite the lack of morphological evidence in the adult bones.

The age estimate is based on the developmental stage of the temporal bone and the presence of a single tooth bud that was not an incisor but was otherwise unidentifiable. The bone is calcined for the most part, but some areas of the cranium show little evidence of burning. A remarkable number of bones can be identified from this skeleton. The recovered bone includes portions of the frontal, parietal, temporal, and zygomatic bones of the cranium, as well as the coranoid process of the mandible. The postcranial bone includes the glenoid fossa of the left scapula, ribs, portions of two cervical vertebrae, several thoracic vertebral fragments, and long bone shafts.

Burial 8
Type: primary cremation
Age: juvenile, 5–6 years
Sex: unknown
Weight: 167 g

This burial is a juvenile cremation, possibly a primary burial, although the very fragmentary nature of the bone makes interpretation difficult. The fragmentary dental remains indicate that the child was around five years old at death. There were no pathological conditions noted on the bone.

Faunal Remains

The faunal materials from the area of Grave 12 are dominated by unburned and unidentifiable small bone fragments, along with unburned ovicaprid and pig elements that do not appear to represent associated limb elements or sacrificial inclusions (Table 7).

Among the more distinctive finds within the assemblage are several calcined fallow deer (Cervidae) antler beam segments from V 4805. One segment (**GR12 B1**) is cut at both ends, and possibly associated antler fragments show evidence of scraping or smoothing of their outer surfaces. Two additional fragments (**GR12 B2**) also appear to have been deliberately scraped and thinned. The presence of numerous metal tools, knives, and weapons in the grave suggest that these modified antler segments may represent raw materials for tool handles, handle fragments, or manufacturing debris.

In addition, a single deer left central and fourth tarsal and a fragmented left metatarsal (V 4805.2) are calcined. The metatarsal bears cut marks on the posterior diaphysis above the condyles, an indication that the lower hind leg was separated from the phalanges and hoof. These are likely to have been articulating elements and may represent sacrificial food remains.

Botanical Remains

Grave 12 produced few botanical remains: only one lentil (*Lens culinarius*) and an unidentified legume. These remains may represent offerings, sustenance for the dead, or remains of a funeral meal.

Pottery

Grave 12 produced a total of 1,769 fragments of pottery weighing 11.43 kg. An additional 775 fragments weighing nearly 9.00 kg came from dumps to the north, south, and east of the enclosure, and 761 fragments weighing 9.75 kg were found in the surface deposit over trench V 4800, many of them joining with vessels in Grave 12. Forty-four vessels have been cataloged from the enclosure. Many of these were found in the northwest corner, including **GR12 P2**, **GR12 P3**, **GR12 P6**, **GR12 P8**, **GR12 P16**, **GR12 P21**, and **GR12 P32**. Another group consists of pots with joining fragments from V 4808, over the wall near the southeast corner of the grave (**GR12 P11**, **GR12 P15**, **GR12 P20**, **GR12 P26**, **GR12 P36**, **GR12 P38**, **GR12 P42**, **GR12 P43**). Cup **GR12 P21** was found mostly in the northwest corner but had some joining fragments from V 4808 and from farther east in V 4900. Fragments of many pots were also found scattered on the surface in V 4800, including a large kalathos (**GR12 P10**), two kraters (**GR12 P11**, **GR12 P12**), an aryballos (**GR12 P13**)**,** three monochrome cups (**GR12 P20**, **GR12 P24**, **GR12 P26**), an oinochoe (**GR12 P35**), a large krater (**GR12 P41**), two amphorae (**GR12 P42**, **GR12 P43**), and a hydria (**GR12 P44**). These vessels had joining fragments from all loci of the grave itself as well as from the area to the east and north. Most fragments of the following vessels came from the east side of the grave (V 4805.4): aryballos **GR12 P29**, jug **GR12 P18**, oinochoe **GR12 P31**, and krater **GR12 P41**; most fragments of **GR12 P24** and **GR12 P25** were also found in the east. From the west side (V 4805.3) came wide-mouthed jugs **GR12 P4** and **GR12 P30**, skyphoi **GR12 P5** and **GR12 P7**, oinochoe **GR12 P14**, cup **GR12 P23**, and tray **GR12 P27**. Most of the other vessels came from upper levels of the grave (V 4805.2), where the largest number of fragments was found (**GR12 P12**, **GR12 P22**, **GR12 P33**, **GR12 P35**, **GR12 P39**, **GR12 P40**). Perhaps accompanying the latest burial are three cups found on the east side of the grave that were not burned: a decorated cup (**GR12 P1**), a monochrome cup (**GR12 P24**), and a skyphos (**GR12 P25**).

The large vessels from the grave were found on or close to the surface, and the amphorae (**GR12 P42**, **GR12 P43**) at least may have stood as grave markers; they show few signs of burning. Fragments of **GR12 P43** were scattered all over the northeast side of the summit, and it is difficult to know from which of the graves it originally came. About 40% of the fragments came from within the boundaries of Grave 12, while another 30% were recovered along the south side of the grave or within the possible pot stand (V 4808). A few fragments came from the area between Graves 9 and 12 and some from the area to the east of Grave 12. Only about 13% of the fragments came from the area of Grave 9, a few within the tumble over that grave (V 5302) and the rest mostly to the north (V 5305, V 5408) and east (V 5401) of it. These find spot percentages suggest that the vessel belongs with Grave 12, but they also attest to the great amount of disturbance of this area by later activity.

Another vessel that shows little burning and was scattered primarily on the surface is the large, pedestaled, coarse ovoid krater **GR12 P41**, only a small portion of which was found burned within the grave. This vessel is unique in shape to the site of Vronda and is certainly an import from elsewhere in Crete, although from where is still uncertain. The rosy phyllite fabric, which is very distinctive and does not occur in the Kavousi typology, may come from East Crete. The shape, with its shelf rim and pedestaled base, is also unusual in Greece. Some early pedestaled pithoi from Fortetsa (Brock 1957, 150, pls. 88:1454, 90:1350) have similar appearances, but the rim type is wholly unknown in Crete. Similarly shaped amphorae of LG date occur in Euboea, but these vases have tall rims and are unpainted on the interior (Blandin 2007, 34, pls. 53, 54). Because the vessel from Grave 12 is painted on the interior as well as the exterior, however, it would appear to be a krater rather than a closed vessel.

A higher percentage of the pottery is decorated (52% of the cataloged vessels) than in the other graves, and there is also a higher proportion of skyphoi, more wide-mouthed jugs, and fewer monochrome cups than usual (only 20% of the total number of vessels). Whether these statistics indicate a chronological or functional difference is not clear. The assemblage as a whole looks LG I in date, but several vessels are much earlier (**GR12 P11**, **GR12 P12**), and at least one, the small aryballos (**GR12 P13**), belongs to the EO period.

Objects

Most of the objects in this grave were scattered north to south across the center, not pushed up toward the sides as in Grave 9. The exception is a group of iron spearheads (**GR12 M25**–**GR12 M27**) found together in the northwest corner. Bronze objects were infrequent in Grave 12. Two of the pins (**GR12 M1**, **GR12 M2**) are similar in size and shape, and they may have been used on the shoulders of a garment or on a shroud; their size indicates that they were probably as much decorative as functional. The pin **GR12 M3** is much smaller, and it may have served a different function or belonged with a different burial. Pieces of another pin of similar size made of iron were also recovered from the water sieve but were too fragmentary to catalog; this iron pin may have formed one of a pair. There were also fragments of a bronze fibula, too poorly preserved to register, and some tiny bits of bronze sheeting (Pl. 39C). Finally, there was a fragment from a bronze awl(?), rectangular in section (**GR12 M4**).

Grave 12 is one of only two graves that produced arrowheads at Vronda. There were at least 20 iron arrowheads, most of the same sort as those found in Grave 1, but only 19 have been cataloged here. The remainder were too fragmentary to be inventoried or cataloged. It would seem likely that a group of arrows, possibly in a leather quiver, were placed in the grave, perhaps an indication that they were offered as possessions of the dead person rather than simply being included as a display of disposable wealth. Nearly all are similar in type, with a leaf-shaped blade and long tang; some have a rather more pronounced central rib. They are closest in shape to Snodgrass type B (1996, 584–585), which, however, has a tang that is square in section rather than the thin, rectangular variety seen here. Two examples of different types are also found: a barbed variety with a cylindrical section (**GR12 M9**) and another barbed variety with a pronounced midrib (**GR12 M19**). These objects may have served a specialized function.

Of the seven spearheads, three are short enough to have been javelins (**GR12 M24**–**GR12 M26**), one with square shoulders and a midrib and two with sloping or rounded shoulders and less pronounced midrib. Two have added bronze: **GR12 M26** has a bronze band around the end of the socket, perhaps for better attachment to the shaft, while **GR12 M24** has bronze on the blade, whether a patch or some sort of bronze sheeting or holder that was next to it in the grave. The bronze may have been added for decorative effect. The other four spearheads are possibly from spears, but all of them are broken, so it is difficult to tell their length or shape. Two (**GR12 M28, GR12 M29**) seem to have pronounced midribs and may be Snodgrass type A, while another (**GR12 M27**) has the sloping shoulders and flat profile that is most common at Vronda; **GR12 M30** is represented only by a small fragment of the socket. There is only a single short sword or dirk in the grave of the usual type (**GR12 M31**).

A variety of tools was found in the grave. Of the five knives, one is Snodgrass type E (**GR12 M32**), three are of type A (**GR12 M33**–**GR12 M35**), and one is a sickle-like knife of type D (**GR12 M36**) (Snodgrass 1996, 585–587). There is also a small serrated saw (**GR12 M37**). A number of other tools are also present, including a flat chisel (**GR12 M41**), a chisel or file (**GR12 M40**), a file (**GR12 M38**), a tool with spatulate end (**GR12 M43**), a tool with a chisel-like end and a tang (**GR12 M42**), and an awl (**GR12 M39**). In addition, there are two iron pieces that are probably fleshhooks (**GR12 M45, GR12 M46**); these objects are similar to fleshhooks found in Grave 9 (**GR9 M52**–**GR9 M55**) but nowhere else at Vronda. Finally, there is a single terracotta bead (**GR12 TC1**) of cylindrical shape with incised decoration: stamped circles around the center and strokes on the top and bottom. This type of bead is common in graves in the Knossos area from SM (Sackett, ed. 1992, 411, pl. 329.3), PG (Boardman 1960, 147, fig. 10:top left, pl. 39; Coldstream and Hatzaki 2003, 290–291, fig 5:B36), and MG–LG (Coldstream and Catling, eds., 1996, 279, fig. 187:294.f 8) times, as well as from Eltyna in the PG period (Rethemiotakis and Englezou 2010, fig. 55:143, 144).

Several pieces of modified deer antler came from this grave. One (**GR12 B1**) may have been used as a tool, while other fragments consisting of thin sheets (**GR12 B2**) may have served as decorative inlays on metal objects or may represent manufacturing debris.

Chronology

Architecturally, Grave 12 seems to be earlier than the other two graves in its immediate area (Graves 10 and 17). It is difficult to associate pottery with specific burials. Three vessels seem to belong with Burials 2 and 3 because of the number of fragments recovered from V 4805.5: kalathos **GR12 P9**, tray **GR12 P28**, and necked jar **GR12 P19**. While the kalathos could date as early as the PG period, the tray and jar look LG in date. The other pottery is mixed, and it may come from any of the earlier burials.

Two kraters have early features (**GR12 P12, GR12 P11**), but they may reflect the continuation of earlier styles or represent older pieces placed with the burials for symbolic or personal reasons. One of these vases, **GR12 P12**, may be a pedestaled krater similar to those at Knossos of PGB date (Coldstream and Catling, eds., 1996, 5, fig. 57:D13; 36, fig. 69:N2). Although Boardman (1960, 130) suggested that the shape and handles derived from the Attic PG period, he also thought that the stem was a later EG addition in the Attic sequence; similar examples can be found at Athens and Marmariana (Lemos 2002, 50, pls. 75, 76). A vessel similar both in shape and decoration of SubPG–G date came from nearby Azoria (Haggis et al. 2007a, 699, fig. 29). The other vessel (**GR12 P11**) represents an unusual variation on the bell krater; although the fabric looks identical, the two halves may not belong together. In shape, the top looks like a standard bell krater with horizontal handles, similar to those from MPG–LPG Knossos (Boardman 1960, 130, pl. 34:I.8; Coldstream and Catling, eds., 1996, 5, fig. 57:19; 8, fig. 59:1; 186, fig. 121:175.26) and Kommos (Callaghan and Johnston 2000, 218, pl. 4.6:40). The broad base, however, is unusual, and the overall shape is more like EPG–MPG jars in the Knossos area (Brock 1957, pl. 3.20; Boardman 1960, 134, no. V23, pl. 35). The decoration, however, is much later; dotted concentric circles do not seem to become popular until the EO period (Coldstream and Catling, eds., 1996, 286, pl. 261:4.8), but they appear on a LPG–EG vessel at Vrokastro, and Hayden reports that Coldstream thought the motif existed in PGB (Hayden 2003, 57, no. 137, fig. 33). Bell kraters did not disappear after the PG period but continued into the seventh century (Kotsonas 2008, 184). This example, then, could well be EO in date. The Mirabello fabric indicates that it originated in the Vrokastro area.

Other vessels in the grave are LG in date. The butterfly chain on decorated skyphos **GR12 P5** is also found on MG vases at Knossos imported from the Cyclades (Coldstream and Catling, eds., 1996, 236, pl. 217:91) and on other LG vessels; it may go back to Attic MG I prototypes (Kotsonas 2008, 266–267, fig. 65:A246). Another skyphos (**GR12 P7**) has a decoration of pendant multiple loops that may hark back to the earlier LPG–SubPG Euboean skyphos with concentric circles (Coldstream and Catling, eds., 1996, 21, 403, fig. 63:123, 124; Lemos 2002, 45–46, pl. 70), but this decoration could also be a survival of a motif popular in LM IIIC (e.g., Day et al. 2016, 75). Similar examples, however, appear as late as the LG period at Chalasmenos (Tsipopoulou 2004, 132, 139, fig. 6:00/668). Skyphos **GR12 P6**, which comes from the deposit in the northwest corner, has a metopal decoration of horizontal bands similar to examples from Graves 16, 19, and 36, as well as to LG vessels from East Crete (Tsipopoulou 2005, 420, fig. 117). Other vessels from the northwest corner find parallels in LG East Crete (**GR12 P2**, **GR12 P3**) or EO Knossos (**GR12 P8**, **GR12 P32**). The trays (**GR12 P27**, **GR12 P28**) are similar to examples from Graves 3, 26, and 36, and these graves may also be roughly contemporary with Grave 12.

Perhaps accompanying the latest burial are three unburned vessels found on the east side of the grave, two cups (**GR12 P1**, **GR12 P24**), a skyphos (**GR12 P25**), and an aryballos (**GR12 P13**). Cup **GR12 P1** is an unusual vessel; the tall carinated rim resembles EO cups found at Knossos (Coldstream and Catling, eds., 1996, 123, pl. 130:4; 208, fig. 131:126), but this cup is more shallow and the decoration is still LG. The aryballos **GR12 P13** finds many parallels of EO date at Knossos (Moignard 1996, 444, type B ii). To judge from the pottery, then, the earliest burials in Grave 12 seem to belong to the LG phase, while the latest burial(s) are EO in date (early 7th century).

Catalog

Pottery

Fine Dark-on-Light Wares

GR12 P1 (V 4805.1, V 4805.2, V 4505.4, V 4815.2, V 4904.4; Fig. 83). Cup. Partially mended from 15 fragments, with five additional fragments from rim. Preservation 50%, including half of base, 65% of lower body, both handle attachments, and parts of rim; missing handle and connection between rim and body. H. est. 7.7; d. rim est. 13.0; d. base 5.0. Fine, medium-soft, reddish-yellow (5YR 6/6) fabric. Pink (7.5YR 7/4) slip. Black paint worn to shadow. Well-preserved surfaces. No trace of burning. Decorated with hatched double zigzags on tall rim. *Comparanda*: for decoration, Brock 1957, 170, motif 3o (Knossos, LG–EO); for shape, Brock 1957, 167, pl. 58:886 (Knossos, O). *Date*: LG–EO.

GR12 P2 (V98.96; V 4805.2, V 4805.3; Fig. 83; Pl. 39C). Mug-like cup. Mended from 37 fragments; two nonjoining fragments. Preservation 90%, including full profile and handle; small pieces of rim, body, and base missing. H. 8.8; d. rim 8.0; d. base 4.5. Fine, soft, reddish-yellow (5YR 6/6) fabric, burned gray. Very pale brown (10YR 8/3) slip. Shadow of once black paint. Worn surfaces. Most of vessel burned slightly. Running quirk on shoulder above bands. *Comparanda*: for shape and decoration, Tsipopoulou 2005, 299, fig. 90:Σ3814 (Sklavoi, LG). *Date*: LG.

GR12 P3 (V 4805.2 object 1, V 4805.3, V 4805.4; Fig. 83). Mug-like cup. Partially mended from 33 fragments. Preservation 70%, including full profile, entire base, handle; missing 65% of rim, 35% of body. H. 11.0; d. rim 10.7; d. base 5.0. Fine, soft, reddish-yellow (5YR 7/6) fabric, gray where burned. Red (2.5YR 4/6) paint. Burned fragments join onto unburned ones, so pot was broken before burning. Metopal decoration with vertical strokes between bands above, horizontal bands below. Horizontal strokes on handle. *Comparanda*: for combination of strokes and horizontal bands, Tsipopoulou 2005, 163, fig. 30:2426 (Hagios Georgios, G). *Date*: LG.

GR12 P4 (V98.97; V 4805.2, V 4805.3, V 4805.4; Fig. 83; Pl. 39C). Wide-mouthed jug. Partially mended from 34 fragments, 85% preserved, including full profile; missing part of base and lower body. H. 10.5; d. rim 6.0; d. base 5.3. Fine, soft, reddish-yellow (7.5YR 7/6) fabric. Reddish-yellow (5YR 6/6) paint. Worn surfaces. All but three fragments and handle burned, the lower part of the vessel more than the upper. Metopal decoration of vertical strokes between bands above zigzag between bands. Horizontal strokes on handle. *Comparanda*: for shape and decoration, Brock 1957, 155, pl. 26:375 (Knossos, PGB–EG); for shape and handle decoration, Tsipopoulou 2005, 216, fig. 89:H3254 (Adromyloi, LG–EO); for combination of strokes and zigzag, Tsipopoulou 2005, 87, fig. 103:H693 (Kavousi, Plai tou Kastrou, LG); 153, fig. 59:AN1837 (Hagios Georgios, LG). *Date*: LG.

GR12 P5 (V98.99; V 4805.2, V 4805.3; Fig. 83; Pl. 39C). Skyphos. Mended from 32 fragments, 80% preserved, including full profile, 75% of rim, 95% of base, 80% of body, one handle, and the other handle attachment. H. 7.5; d. rim 10.0; d. base 4.0. Fine, medium-soft, reddish-yellow (7.5YR 8/6) fabric. Light gray (2.5Y 7/2) surface (burned). Black paint worn to shadow. Worn surfaces. Many fragments are burned but join with unburned fragments, thus burned after breaking. Decorated with butterfly pattern on shoulder, bands below. *Comparanda*: Rethemiotakis and Englezou 2010, 75, fig. 46:110 (Eltyna, EG); for decoration, Mook 2004, 176, fig. 12.11:L (Kavousi Kastro, LG); Kotsonas 2008, 140–141, fig. 33:A98 (Eleutherna, LG); for shape, Coldstream and Catling, eds., 1996, 183–184, fig. 119:5 (Knossos, LG). *Date*: LG.

GR12 P6 (V98.100; V 4805.2 pot 2, V 4805.3, V 4805.4; Fig. 83; Pl. 39C). Skyphos. Mended from 37 fragments, 90% preserved, including full profile, entire rim, both handles; missing two large pieces of body. H. 7.8; d. rim 8.0; d. base 5.5. Fine, soft, reddish-yellow (5YR 6/6) fabric. Very pale brown (10YR 8/3) slip. Shadow of paint. Worn surfaces. Metopal decoration with horizontal bands. *Comparanda*: **GR16 P15, GR19 P3, GR36 P2**; Tsipopoulou 2005, 139, fig. 117:Π79 (Hagios Georgios, LG); 277, fig. 117:Σ3805 (Praisos, LG); for decoration, Tsipopoulou 2013, 136, 152–153, fig 13:12309 (Piskokephalo, LG). *Date*: LG.

GR12 P7 (V98.101; V 4805.3, V 4805.4; Fig. 83; Pl. 39C). Skyphos. Mended from 46 fragments. Preservation 75%, including full profile, one and one-half handles; missing bits of base, rim, half of handle, and parts of body. H. 7.3; d. rim 12.0; d. base 5.8. Fine, medium-soft, reddish-yellow (7.5YR 7/6) fabric. Very pale brown (10YR 8/4) slip. Shadow of paint, once black. Very worn surfaces. Some fragments burned. Pendant multiple loops or semicircles on shoulder. Bands on interior with drips. *Comparanda*: for shape, Coldstream and Catling, eds., 1996, 21, fig. 63:118 (Knossos, EG); Kotsonas 2008, 195–196, fig. 47:A242β (Eleutherna, PGB); for decoration, Coldstream and Catling, eds., 1996, 28–29, fig. 65:31 (Knossos, MPG–LPG). *Date*: LG.

GR12 P8 (V 4805.2 pot 5; Fig. 83). Cup or skyphos. Partially mended from five fragments; a nonjoining rim fragment may belong to it. Preservation 20%; missing most of rim, handle(s). Max. pres. h. 7.3; d. rim est. 10.0; d. base est. 6.0. Fine, medium-soft, reddish-yellow (5YR 7/6) fabric. Very pale brown (10YR 8/3) slip. Shadow of paint. Very worn surfaces. No burning. Concentric circles on shoulder. *Comparanda*: Coldstream and Catling, eds., 1996, 51, fig. 72:109 (Knossos, EO). *Date*: LG–EO.

GR12 P9 (V 4805.3, V 4805.4, V 4805.5, V 4807.1; Fig. 83; Pl. 40). Kalathos. Partially mended from 187 fragments, 75% preserved, including full profile, half of base, and both handles. Base fragments have laminated. H. 17.0; d. rim (int.) 38.0; d. base 10.4. Fine, soft, reddish-yellow (7.5YR 7/6) fabric, very pale brown (10YR 8/3) to gray where burned. Red (2.5YR 5/8) paint on unburned sherds, black to brown where burned. Very worn surfaces. Most fragments burned. Hatched designs, probably zigzags. *Comparanda*: for shape, Coldstream 1992, 76, pl. 58:GH 7 (Knossos, LPG); Coldstream and Catling, eds., 1996, 29, fig. 65:37; 61, fig. 74:13 (Knossos, EPG–EG). *Date*: LG.

GR12 P10 (V 4800.1, V 4803.2, V 4804.4, V 4508.2, V 4805.3, V 4805.4, V 4808.2, V 4821.2; Fig. 83). Kalathos. Ten joining fragments from base, 10 other fragments from rim and body, including handle attachment. Two-thirds of base preserved. H. est. 17.4; d. rim est. 34.0 (int.); d. base 11.0. Fine, soft, light red (2.5YR 6/6) fabric. Petrographic sample KAV 15/53: Fabric Group 7. Very pale brown (10YR 8/4) slip. Dark paint worn to shadow. Most base fragments burned. Base has vertical grooves. Bands on lower body. Solid triangles on rim. *Comparanda*: **GR12 P9**; Coldstream and Catling, eds., 1996, 249, fig. 142:155 (Knossos, MPG). *Date*: LG.

GR12 P11 (V 4800.1, V 4803.1, V4805.2. V 4805.3, V 4805.4, V 4804.1; Fig. 84). Bell krater. Partially mended from 74 fragments. Preservation 20%, including fragments of base, body, part of one handle, and rim fragments. Base fragments do not join to rim. H. base fragment 14.4; h. rim fragment 18.5; d. rim est. 22.0–25.0; d.

base est. 18.0. Fine, medium-soft, reddish-yellow (5YR 6/6) fabric. Petrographic sample KAV 15/57: Fabric Group 4. Very pale brown (7.5YR 8/4) slip. Black to red (2.5YR 4/6) paint (almost looks bichrome). Possibly a bell krater, but it could also be a small pithos with vertical handles. Concentric circles with dots between every other pair. Bands below. *Comparanda*: for shape, Kanta and Davaras 2004, 152, fig. 5 (Krya, LM IIIC). *Date*: PG.

GR12 P12 (V 4800.3, V 4800.4, V 4806.2, V 4805.2; V4815.1, V 5321.2; Fig. 84). Krater. Fragments from rim, body, and one handle; missing base, second handle. D. rim est. (int.) 28.8. Fine, very soft, light red (2.5YR 6/6) fabric. Very pale brown (10YR 8/4) slip. Black paint, worn to shadow. Worn surfaces. One handle fragment burned. Bucranium handle. Concentric compass-drawn circles. *Date*: G.

GR12 P13 (V88.224; V 4800.4 object 1; Fig. 84; Pl. 40). Aryballos. Mended from 15 fragments, 95% preserved, including full profile, entire base, rim, and handle; missing fragment from lower body and small fragment from shoulder. H. 6.5; d. rim 1.6; d. base 1.5–1.6. Fine, soft, pink (7.5YR 8/4) fabric, badly burned. Black paint. Well-preserved surfaces. Four sets of concentric circles on shoulder; three sets of triple bands on body. *Comparanda*: Coldstream and Catling, eds., 1996, 264, pl. 238:88 (Knossos, EO); Coulson et al. 1997, 331, fig. 11 (Kastro, EO); Tsipopoulou 2005, 156, fig. 97:AN 2365 (Hagios Georgios, EO). *Date*: EO.

GR12 P14 (V 4803.1, V 4803.2, V 4805.1, V 4805.3, V 4805.4; Fig. 84). Oinochoe. Partly mended into two fragments, one from spout and shoulder (two sherds), one from base (five sherds); five nonjoining fragments. Preservation 30%, including entire base, entire neck and mouth, handle attachments. Max. pres. h. 5.6; d. base 3.0–3.2. Fine, medium-soft, reddish-yellow (5YR 7/6) fabric with some granodiorite inclusions. Petrographic sample KAV 15/50: Fabric Group 4. Very pale brown (10YR 8/3) slip. Black paint, now worn. *Comparanda*: Tsipopoulou 2005, 197, fig. 67:Σ3581 (Hagios Stephanos, PGB). *Date*: G.

GR12 P15 (V 4805.2, V 4805.3, V 4808.1; Fig. 85). Jug or oinochoe. Six joining fragments from carinated shoulder, including handle, and 15 nonjoining fragments. Preservation 15%; missing base and rim. Max. pres. h. 10.0. Fine, soft, sandy, pink (7.5YR 8/3) fabric. Very worn surfaces. *Comparanda*: Coldstream and Catling, eds., 1996, 152, pl. 150:40 (Knossos, EO); Tsipopoulou 2005, 208, fig. 77:H3204 (Adromyloi, LG); 252, fig. 77:H2060 (Praisos, EO); 297, fig. 78:AN1670 (Sklavoi, LG). *Date*: LG–EO.

GR12 P16 (V 4805.2, pot 4; Fig. 85). Oinochoe. Ninety-five fragments from rim, neck, base, and body. Preservation 20%, including handle fragments. Max. pres. h. 7.7; d. base 7.5. Fine, very soft, very pale brown (10YR 7/4) fabric with a few hard, sharp inclusions. Very pale brown (10YR 8/3) slip. Red (2.5YR 5/6) paint. Worn surfaces and edges. *Comparanda*: Coldstream and Catling, eds., 1996, 61, pl. 90:18 (Knossos, EG); 147, pl. 145:15 (EO); Tsipopoulou 2005, 316, fig. 67:Σ3826 (Zou, PGB). *Date*: LG.

GR12 P17 (V 4706.2, V 4805.3, V 4805.4, V 4805.5, V 4904.4; Fig. 85). Jug. Large fragment from neck and shoulder (10 sherds), 20 body fragments, base fragment. Preservation 30%, including nearly complete profile and handle; missing rim. Max pres. h. 25.2. Fine, medium-soft, reddish-yellow (5YR 7/6) fabric. Very pale brown (10YR 8/3) slip. Red (2.5YR 4/6) paint. Well-preserved surfaces. Handle and some of body fragments burned. Multiple triangles with dots between outer ones and checkerboard in center; vertical stripes on handle. *Comparanda*: Callaghan and Johnston 2000, 224, pl. 4.4:110; 227, pl. 4.5:145 (Kommos, PG); for decoration, Hall 1914, 164, fig. 99a; Popham and Lemos 1996, pl. 166:b (Lefkandi, LPG); Hayden 2003, 50, no. 112, fig. 26 (Vrokastro, PGB–EG). *Date*: G.

GR12 P18 (V 4805.2; Fig. 85). Jug or amphora. Two fragments from handle and seven possible body fragments. Max. pres. h. 11.0. Fine, soft, sandy, reddish-yellow (7.5YR 7/6) fabric with silver mica. Black to red (2.5YR 5/6) paint. Diagonal stripes on handle. *Date*: G?

GR12 P19 (V 4805.3, V 4805.4, V 4805.5; Fig. 85). Necked jar. Partially mended from 21 fragments; 29 additional fragments. Preservation 30%, including entire base, much of lower body, 25% of rim, and parts of both handles. H. est. 15.2; d. rim (int.) 8.0; d. rim (ext.) 10.8; d. base 10.0–11.0. Fine, very soft, pink (5YR 7/4) fabric. Petrographic sample KAV 15/48: Fabric Group 4. Pink (7.5YR 8/4) slip. Worn surfaces, only traces of paint. *Comparanda*: Coldstream and Catling, eds., 1996, 6, fig. 58:25 (Knossos, LPG); Tsipopoulou 2005, 290, fig. 60:AN8776 (Praisos, LG). *Date*: LG.

FINE MONOCHROME WARES

GR12 P20 (V98.94; V 4800.1, V 4805.2, V 4805.3, V 4808.8; Fig. 85; Pl. 40). Cup. Mended from 20 fragments. Preservation 90%, including full profile, most of base, and handle. H. 6.6–7.4; d. rim 9.0–12.2; d. base 7.0. Fine, medium-hard, reddish-yellow (7.5YR 7/6) fabric. Streaky, black to dusky, red (2.5YR 3/2) paint. Painted on interior, exterior, and underside of base. No burning. Irregular shape may be deliberate to create pouring vessel with round handle at right angle to crude spout. *Comparanda*: Coldstream and Catling, eds., 1996, 28, fig. 65:28 (Knossos, Attic LPG); Kotsonas 2008, 206, 209, fig. 51:A290, A250, A144δ (Eleutherna, PGB). *Date*: PG.

GR12 P21 (V 4805.2, V 4805.3, V 4808.1, V 4904.1; Fig. 86). Cup. Partially mended from 40 fragments. Preservation 25%, including full profile, half of base, and handle. H. 9.5; d. rim 14.0–14.5; d. base 7.2. Fine, medium-hard, light red (2.5YR 6/6) fabric. Black paint worn to brown shadow. Worn surfaces. Little burning. *Comparanda*: Mook 2004, 174, fig. 12.9:AA (Kastro, SubPG); Tsipopoulou 2005, 181, fig. 125:Σ4037 (Hagios Georgios, LG). *Date*: LG.

GR12 P22 (V 4805.2; Fig. 86). Wide-mouthed jug. Mended from 19 fragments. Preservation 30%, including full profile, entire base, part of one handle. H. 8.5; d. rim 6.0; d. base 3.6. Fine, soft, sandy, reddish-yellow (5YR 7/8–6/8) fabric. Thick, glossy, red (2.5YR 5/6) paint on interior and exterior. Well-preserved surfaces. No burning. *Date*: LG.

GR12 P23 (V 4805.2, V 4805.3; Fig. 86). Cup. Partially mended from 27 fragments. Preservation 60%, including full profile, entire base, two-thirds of rim, most of handle. H. 8.3; d. rim 13.0–14.0; d. base 5.0–5.7. Fine, very soft, reddish-yellow (5YR 7/6) fabric, very pale brown (10YR 8/2) on surface. Ridges below rim. Traces of shadow paint, very worn surfaces. Most of fragments burned, some have worn edges. *Date*: LG.

GR12 P24 (V 4800.1, V 4803.2, V 4805.4; Fig. 86). Cup. Eighteen fragments from rim and body, including lower handle attachment; missing base. D. rim est. 14.0. Fine, soft, porous, rather sandy, very pale brown (10YR 8/4) fabric. Worn black paint. *Date*: LG.

GR12 P25 (V 4803.2, V 4805.1, V 4805.2, V 4805.4, V 4805.5, V 4807.1, V 4900.2; Fig. 86). Skyphos. Partially mended from 29 fragments. Preservation 20%, including 40% of base and lower body, 10% of rim, one handle. Profile restored. Max. pres. h. 5.5; d. rim est. 10.0; d. base est. 6.0. Fine, soft, reddish-yellow (5YR 7/6) fabric; very pale brown (10YR 8/3) surface. Tall rim, deep ovoid body, base with two grooves around center. Shadow of paint inside and out, but worn surfaces. *Comparanda*: Coldstream and Catling, eds., 1996, 115, fig. 96:155 (Knossos, LO). *Date*: LO.

GR12 P26 (V 4800.2, V 4800.4, V 4805.2, V 4805.3, V 4806.2, V 4808.1; Fig. 86). Cup or skyphos. Partially mended from 23 fragments. Preservation 25%–30%, including two large fragments of base, assorted rim and body fragments; missing handles. Profile can be restored. H. 6.2; d. rim est. 12.0; d. base est. 5.5. Fine, soft, reddish-yellow (5YR 7/6) fabric with infrequent small phyllite inclusions. Red (2.5YR 5/8) paint. Worn surfaces. No burning. *Comparanda*: for shape, Tsipopoulou 2005, 302, fig. 126:Σ3852 (Sklavoi, LG); 321, fig. 126:Σ3820 (Chamaizi, PGB). *Date*: LG.

Fine Plain Wares

GR12 P27 (V88.242; V 4805.2, V 4805.3, V 4805.4; Fig. 86; Pl. 40). Tray with reflex-type lugs. Restored from 47 fragments; two nonjoining fragments. Preservation 95%; missing single fragments from base and body and tips of two lugs. H. 5.5, with handles 6.6; d. rim 14.7 (int.); d. base 14.0. Fine, soft, light reddish-brown (5YR 6/4) fabric. Highly burnished, very pale brown (10YR 7/3) surface. Many fragments burned after breaking. *Comparanda*: Sakellarakis 1986, 47, fig. 43, pls. 58, 59 (Archanes); Andreadaki-Vlasaki 1987, 311, 321, fig. 3:7 (Gavalomouri, LG–EO); Hayden 2003, 70, nos. 185, 186, fig. 44, pl. 29 (LG–O); Tsipopoulou 2005, 104–105, fig. 134:H756, 758 (Kavousi, Plai tou Kastrou, LG–EO); Kotsonas 2008, 218, 221, fig. 53:A140β (Eleutherna, EG). *Date*: LG.

GR12 P28 (V 4805.2, V 4805.3, V 4821.2, V 4901.5, V 4904.1; Fig. 86). Tray with reflex-type lugs. Large fragment from rim with one handle, one fragment with full profile, and over 100 laminated fragments from body and handles. H. 6.0; d. rim est. (int.) 17.0; d. base est. 12.0. Fine, soft, red (2.5YR 5/8) to dark gray fabric. Worn, burnished, very pale brown (10YR 8/3) surface. Much burning. *Comparanda*: **GR12 P27**; Coldstream and Catling, eds., 1996, 168, fig. 117:125.15 (MG); Tsipopoulou 2004, 134, fig. 8:00/254 (Chalasmenos, LG); Kotsonas 2008, 218, 221, fig. 53:A140β (Eleutherna, EG). *Date*: LG.

GR12 P29 (V 4805.4; Fig. 86). Aryballos. Large fragment (three sherds) from base and one rim fragment. Preservation 75% of base and 75% of rim. Max. pres. h. 2.0; d. rim 2.0; d. base 4.0. Fine, soft, light brown to pink (7.5YR 6/4–7/4) fabric. Base burned and laminating. No decoration. *Date*: LG.

Fine Decorated, Monochrome, or Plain Wares

GR12 P30 (V 4805.3; Fig. 86). Wide-mouthed jug. Fifteen fragments from rim, body, and handle; missing base. Max. pres. h. 3.5; d. rim est. 5.0. Fine, very soft, reddish-yellow (5YR 6/6) fabric with tiny white inclusions. Very worn surfaces. *Comparanda*: **GR12 P22**. *Date*: LG.

GR12 P31 (V 4805.4, V 4805.5; Fig. 86). Oinochoe. Eleven joining fragments preserving neck and rim. Max. pres. h. 5.5. Fine, very soft, sandy, very pale brown (10YR 7/4) fabric. Very worn surfaces, worn edges. *Date*: LG.

Medium-Coarse Decorated Wares

GR12 P32 (V 4805.2; Fig. 86). Cup. Partially mended from 15 joining and six nonjoining fragments. Preservation 75%, including full profile, entire base, and handle attachment; missing handle. H. 7.6; d. rim 7.6; d. base est. 4.5. Medium-coarse, light yellowish-brown (10YR 6/4) fabric with sand and phyllite inclusions. Pale yellow (2.5Y 8/2) slip. Very worn surfaces, mostly burned. Possible reserved bands at base of rim. *Comparanda*: Brock 1957, 127, 167, pl. 103:1460 (Knossos, O). *Date*: LG–EO.

GR12 P33 (V 4805.2, V 4805.3, V 4805.4, V 4805.5; Fig. 86). Skyphos or cup. Partially mended from 14 fragments from rim and body; missing base and handle(s). Max. pres. h. 5.0; d. rim est. 10.0. Medium-coarse, soft, reddish-yellow (5YR 6/6–7.5YR 7/6) fabric with quartz, greenstone, and phyllite inclusions. Red (2.5YR 4/8) paint. Worn surfaces. Bands and possible curvilinear motif. *Date*: LG?

GR12 P34 (V 4805.1, V 4805.2; Fig. 87). Jug or olpe. Partially mended from 11 fragments. Preservation 75% of base and lower body, including half of handle; missing neck, rim, and upper handle. Max. pres. h. 11.2; d. base est. 5.5. Medium-coarse, soft, reddish-yellow (7.5YR 6/6) fabric with greenstone inclusions. Petrographic sample KAV 15/52: Fabric Group 3. Very pale brown (10YR 8/3) slip. Possible traces of paint. Very worn surfaces. No burning. *Comparanda*: Brock 1957, 155, pl. 58:868

(Knossos, LG olpe); Coldstream and Catling, eds., 1996, 265, pl. 239:98 (Knossos, EG olpe), 121 (Knossos, MG olpe). *Date*: G.

GR12 P35 (V 4800.1, V 4805.2, V 4808.1; Fig. 87). Oinochoe. Partially mended from four fragments; two nonjoining fragments. Part of spout and 25% of neck and shoulder preserved; missing base, lower body, handle. Max. pres. h. 6.8. Medium-coarse, soft, reddish-yellow (7.5YR 6/6) fabric with frequent quartz and phyllite inclusions. Petrographic sample KAV 15/51: Fabric Group 3. Black paint worn to shadow. Very worn surfaces. No burning. Trefoil mouth. Stacked triangles on shoulder. *Comparanda*: **IX P16**; Tsipopoulou 2005, 310, fig. 67:Σ4017 (Sklavoi, PGB). *Date*: PG.

Medium-Coarse Monochrome Wares

GR12 P36 (V 4805.2, V 4805.3, V 4808.1; Fig. 87). Cup. Partially mended from 12 fragments. Preservation 30% of rim and handle; no base. Max. pres. h. 4.4; d. rim est. 10.0. Medium-coarse, medium-hard, reddish-yellow (5YR 6/6) fabric with frequent small granodiorite inclusions. Streaky red (10R 4/6) to black paint. Some worn, some well-preserved surfaces. No burning. *Comparanda*: Tsipopoulou 2005, 173, fig. 123:Σ3933 (Hagios Georgios, EO). *Date*: LG.

GR12 P37 (V 4803.2, V 4805.2, V 4805.4; Fig. 87). Cup. Sixteen fragments from base, handle attachment, and rim. Max. pres. h. 4.0; d. rim est. 14.0; d. base est. 6.0. Medium-coarse, medium-soft, reddish-yellow (5YR 6/6) fabric with phyllite inclusions. Some traces of brown to red paint. *Date*: LG.

GR12 P38 (V 4805.2, V 4805.3, V 4805.4, V 4808.1; Fig. 87). Cup or skyphos. Partially mended from 14 fragments. Preservation 30%–40%, including half of base and rim; missing handle. Profile can be restored. H. est. 9.5; d. rim est. 12.0; d. base est. 5.0. Medium-coarse, rather hard, reddish-yellow (5YR 6/8) fabric with frequent small phyllite and quartz inclusions and gray core. Traces of reddish paint. Very worn surfaces. *Comparanda*: **GR9 P12**; Mook 2004, 176, fig. 12.11:H (Kastro, LG). *Date*: LG.

GR12 P39 (V 4805.2, V 4805.3, V 4805.4; Fig. 87). Cup or skyphos. Nine fragments from rim and body; missing base and handle(s). Max. pres. h. 5.0; d. rim est. 14.0. Medium-coarse, soft, reddish-yellow (5YR 6/6) fabric with phyllite inclusions. Petrographic sample KAV 15/49: Fabric Group 2. Red (2.5YR 5/6) paint. Worn surfaces. No burning. *Date*: LG.

Medium-Coarse Plain Ware

GR12 P40 (V 4805.3; Fig. 87; Pl. 40). Handle of scuttle or ladle. Five fragments preserving entire handle. L. 15.0. Fine to medium-coarse, soft, reddish-yellow (5YR 6/6) fabric with quartz inclusions. Very pale brown (10YR 7/4) slip? Burned on one end. Long square handle, mostly horizontal but curving, like scuttle handle. Pierced at end. *Comparanda*: Andreadaki-Vlasaki 1987, 313, 334, fig. 4:1 (Gavalomouri, LG–EO). *Date*: LG?

Coarse Wares

GR12 P41 (V 4800.3, V 4800.4, V 4800.5, V 4805.2, V 4805.4, V 5300.1, V 5300.2, V 5321.2; Fig. 87). Pedestaled krater. Partially mended from 548 fragments. Large parts of rim and pedestal base preserved, along with body fragments with handle attachments. Max. pres. h. 9.0; d. rim est. 25.0–30.0. Coarse, soft, light red (2.5YR 6/6) fabric, like Kavousi Type IV with quartz and large phyllite inclusions. Petrographic sample KAV 15/56: low-fired metamorphic fabric. Traces of red (2.5YR 4/6) paint. Worn surfaces. Many fragments from grave burned. Painted on interior near rim and on sherd with handle attachment; possibly monochrome interior. May once have been painted on exterior. Almost certainly an import but from an unknown location. *Date*: LG?

GR12 P42 (V 4800.1, V 4803.1, V 4805.2, V 4805.3, V 4805.4, V 4808.1; Fig. 88). Amphora. Partially mended from 78 fragments, including rim fragments, neck and shoulder, and body fragments with handles; missing base. D. rim est. 25.0. Coarse, reddish-yellow (5YR 6/6) fabric with frequent quartz, phyllite, and greenstone inclusions. Petrographic sample KAV 15/54: Fabric Group 3. Black crackled paint. Very worn surfaces. Stacked triangles on neck, shoulder, and body. *Comparanda*: Coldstream and Catling, eds., 1996, 27, pl. 63:1 (Knossos, MPG); 141, pl. 139:12 (Knossos, EG). *Date*: G.

GR12 P43 (V 4800.2, V 4805.2, V 4805.3, V 4805.4, V 4805.5, V 4806.1, V 4808.1, V 5301.1, V 5302.1, V 5302.3, V 5305.4, V 5309.3, V 5401.2, V 5408.7; Fig. 88). Amphora. Represented by 88 fragments from rim, neck, shoulder, and handles; missing base and lower body. D. rim est. 19.0. Rather coarse, reddish-yellow (5YR 6/8) fabric with quartz and large metamorphic inclusions. Petrographic sample KAV 15/55: Fabric Group 2. Black paint. Most surfaces very worn; fabric is laminating. No burning. Bucranium handles on shoulder. Concentric circles on neck and shoulder. *Comparanda*: for shape, Coldstream and Catling, eds., 1996, 141, pl. 140:23 (EG); Tsipopoulou 2005, 312, fig. 26:Σ4084 (Sklavoi, LG); for decoration, Brock 1957, 146, pl. 9:157 (Knossos, PGA); Callaghan and Johnston 2000, 237, fig. 4.10:250 (Kommos, EO). *Date*: LG.

GR12 P44 (V 4800.2, V 4805.2, V 4805.3, V 4805.4, V 4805.5; Fig. 88). Hydria. Twenty fragments, including bits of rim, neck, body, and two handles (one horizontal, one vertical). D. rim est. 14.0. Rather coarse, reddish-yellow (7.5YR 7/6) fabric with large brown phyllite inclusions. Red (2.5YR 4/6) paint. Crosshatching, possibly a meander. Bands. *Date*: LG?

Metal

Bronze

GR12 M1 (V88.136, HNM 15763; V 4805.3; Fig. 89; Pl. 40). Bronze pin. Intact, but slightly bent. L. 12.0; d. bulb 0.9; d. disk 0.6. Well preserved, with little corrosion. Long pin, round in section, with bulb and small disk at top. *Bibliography*: Gesell, Coulson, and Day 1991, 155, pl. 60:b. *Comparanda*: Coldstream and Catling, eds., 1996, 209, fig. 167:f18; 251, fig. 169:f36, f37 (Knossos, MPG–LPG).

GR12 M2 (V88.145, HNM 15764; V 4805.3, object 12; Fig. 89; Pl. 40). Bronze pin. Complete, but bent near point. L. 9.1; d. bulb 0.9; d. disk 0.3. Well-preserved surfaces. Long pin, round in section. Bulb near one end, small disk at top, smaller than **GR12 M1**. *Bibliography*: Gesell, Coulson, and Day 1991, 155, pl. 60:c. *Comparanda*: see above **GR12 M1**.

GR12 M3 (V88.255; V 4805.5 watersieve; Fig. 89; Pl. 40). Bronze pin. Mended from four joining fragments, preserving all but the point; bent. Max. pres. L. 3.4; d. swelling 0.3; d. disk 0.3. Well-preserved surfaces. Short pin with two rings on either side of a biconical swelling toward top; flat disk on top.

GR12 M4 (V88.141; V 4805.4, object 1; Fig. 89; Pl. 41). Bronze tool. Single fragment from end. Max. pres. L. 3.6; max. w. 0.3. Well-preserved surfaces. Pin-like, but rectangular in section. Tapers to one end. Possibly an awl.

Iron

GR12 M5 (V88.89, HNM 15753; V 4805.4, object 28A; Fig. 89; Pl. 41). Iron arrowhead. Nearly intact; missing end of tang. Max. pres. L. 8.3; max. w. 1.6. Very well preserved, including most of surface. Medium tang (2.6), leaf-shaped blade. *Bibliography*: Gesell, Coulson, and Day 1991, 155, pl. 59:e. *Comparanda*: Dikaios 1969–1971, vol. IIIA, pl. 163:28, 29 (Enkomi, bronze).

GR12 M6 (V88.90, HNM 15754; V 4805.4, object 28B; Fig. 89; Pl. 41). Iron arrowhead. Nearly complete; missing point and very end of tang. Max. pres. L. 7.2; max. w. 1.5. Surface preserved only on half; rest corroded. Short (1.8) tang, leaf-shaped blade. *Bibliography*: Gesell, Coulson, and Day 1991, 155, pl. 59:f.

GR12 M7 (V88.108, HNM 15759; V 4805.4, object 18; Fig. 89; Pl. 41). Iron arrowhead. Nearly intact; missing end of tang. Max. pres. L. 7.7; max. w. 1.4. Corroded and missing much of surface. Short (2.1) tang, leaf-shaped blade.

GR12 M8 (V88.121, HNM 15761; V 4805.4 object 20, V 4805.4 object 14; Fig. 89; Pl. 41). Iron arrowhead. Mended from three fragments. Nearly complete; missing tip and end of tang. Max. pres. L. 7.7; max. w. 1.4. Surfaces corroded and worn. Medium (2.3) tang, leaf-shaped blade.

GR12 M9 (V88.109, HNM 15760; V 4805.3, object 29; Fig. 89; Pl. 41). Iron arrowhead. Mended from five fragments. Nearly complete; missing tip of one barb. L. 9.7; max. w. 1.5. Corroded and splitting; much of surface gone except near point. Short (0.9) tang, round in section. Barbed blade. *Comparanda*: Levi 1927–1929, pl. 7 (Arkades, Tomb L, Orientalizing, bronze); Snodgrass 1964, 142, 144–145, type I, fig. 9:a.4 (Anatolian type, from Kavousi, Skouriasmenos); Dikaios 1969–1971, vol. II, 674; vol. IIIA, pl. 163:36 (557):type II (barbed and tanged from Enkomi, bronze).

GR12 M10 (V88.105, HNM 15756; V 4805.4 object 18, V 4805.5; Fig. 89; Pl. 41). Iron arrowhead. Mended from two fragments. Blade complete; missing tang. Max. pres. L. 6.5; max. w. 1.5. Corroded, with a few traces of surface. Rather triangular, leaf-shaped blade.

GR12 M11 (V88.107, HNM 15758; V 4805.4, object 18; Fig. 89; Pl. 41). Iron arrowhead. Intact, except for missing tang. Max. pres. L. 5.6; max. w. 1.5. Well preserved, with many original surfaces. Rather triangular, leaf-shaped blade.

GR12 M12 (V88.116; V 4805.4, object 10; Fig. 89; Pl. 41). Iron arrowhead. Mended from two fragments; missing tang. Max. pres. L. 5.5; max. w. 1.4. Very corroded and worn. Leaf-shaped blade.

GR12 M13 (V88.110; V 4805.3 object 3, V 4805.4 object 17; Fig. 89; Pl. 41). Iron arrowhead. Mended from two fragments; missing most of tang and tip. Max. pres. L. 4.8; max. w. 1.3. Worn and corroded. Leaf-shaped blade.

GR12 M14 (V88.129; V 4805.3, object 26; Fig. 89; Pl. 41). Iron arrowhead. Nearly intact; missing tip and tang. Max. pres. L. 5.4; max. w. 1.7. Well-preserved surfaces. Thick, leaf-shaped blade.

GR12 M15 (V88.124; V 4805.4; Fig. 89; Pl. 41). Iron arrowhead. Mended from two fragments; missing tip and tang. Max. pres. L. 3.1; max. w. 1.0. Worn and corroded; no original surfaces. Leaf-shaped blade.

GR12 M16 (V88.123; V 4805.3; Fig. 89; Pl. 41). Iron arrowhead. Mended from two fragments; missing tip and tang. Max. pres. L. 3.0; max. w. 1.2. Worn and corroded; tiny piece of original surface. Leaf-shaped blade.

GR12 M17 (V88.122; V 4805.4, V 4805.5; Fig. 89; Pl. 41). Iron arrowhead. Mended from two fragments; two nonjoining fragments of tang. Max. pres. L. 3.1; max. w. 1.2. Well-preserved surfaces. Leaf-shaped blade.

GR12 M18 (V88.131a; V 4805.4, object 33; Pl. 41). Iron arrowhead. Two joining fragments from tip and blade. Max. pres. L. 3.2; max. w. 1.3. Well-preserved surfaces. Leaf-shaped blade.

GR12 M19 (V88.131b; V 4805.4 object 33, V 4805.4 object 14; Fig. 89; Pl. 41). Iron arrowhead. Single fragment from tip. Max. pres. L. 3.7; max. w. 0.8. Corroded. Possibly barbed, like **GR12 M8**. *Comparanda*: Courtois 1984, 14, no. 78, fig. 3:48, 49 (Enkomi, LB–EIA, bronze).

GR12 M20 (V88.106, HNM 15757; V 4805.4, object 18; Pl. 41). Iron arrowhead. Single fragment; missing point and tang. Max. pres. L. 5.1; max. w. 1.8. Well preserved, with original surfaces. Leaf-shaped blade.

GR12 M21 (V88.101; V 4805.3, object 23; Pl. 41). Iron arrowhead. Two nonjoining fragments, one from body, one from tang; missing tip. Max. pres. L. 2.4; max. w. 1.2. Very worn and corroded. Leaf-shaped blade.

GR12 M22 (V88.112; V 4805.4, object 16; Pl. 41). Iron arrowhead. Only tang preserved. Max. pres. L. 3.3. Some surface preserved. Long (2.4) tang.

GR12 M23 (V88.127; V 4805.4, object 14; Pl. 41). Iron arrowhead. Single fragment from tang and end of blade. Max. pres. L. 3.3; max. w. 1.4. Corroded, but with some surviving surfaces on one side. Short tang and leaf-shaped blade.

GR12 M24 (V88.95; V 4805.3, object 21; Fig. 90; Pl. 42). Iron spearhead. Partially mended from eight fragments; three more fragments from near tip and tip. L. est. 23.0; max. w. 2.1; d. socket 1.5–2.0. Well-preserved socket. Parts of blade corroded; some sections still have original surface. Long (10.0) socket, pierced near end opposite edges. Blade comes out at right angles to socket and has pronounced midrib. Surface of one side of blade has bronze plate adhering, held on by four rivets (holes visible in X-ray). Apparently patched or decorated with bronze.

GR12 M25 (V88.97; V 4805.3 object 2, V 4805.3; Fig. 90; Pl. 42). Iron spearhead. Mended from numerous fragments; full length preserved. L. 26.0; max. w. 2.5; d. socket 1.8. Very corroded and laminated; some original surface at each end. Long (8.5) socket, pierced opposite edges near end. Leaf-shaped blade with no pronounced shoulders. Midrib going partly up blade.

GR12 M26 (V88.98; V 4805.3, object 3; Fig. 90; Pl. 42). Iron spearhead. Mended from 42 fragments, large nonjoining fragment from blade. L. 24.0; max. w. 2.7; d. socket 2.4. Very corroded and laminated. Long (9.5) socket, not pierced. Short, leaf-shaped blade without pronounced shoulders. No pronounced midrib. Bronze band around end of socket, held in place by two pins or rivets (holes visible in X-ray).

GR12 M27 (V88.96; V 4805.3, object 2; Fig. 90; Pl. 42). Iron spearhead. Partially mended from 38 fragments into three large fragments; end of socket missing. Can be reconstructed on paper. Max. pres. L. 9.5; max. w. 2.1; d. socket est. 1.6. Very fragmentary and corroded. Angular shoulders, no midrib.

GR12 M28 (V88.93; V 4805.3, object 24; Fig. 90; Pl. 42). Iron spearhead. Mended from seven fragments; 18 other nonjoining bits. One nonjoining socket fragment. Max. pres. L. 23.0; max. w. 2.1. Well-preserved blade with some surviving surface. Shoulders missing. Pronounced midrib one-third of way up blade.

GR12 M29 (V88.114; V 4805.3, object 11; Fig. 90; Pl. 42). Iron spearhead. Partially mended from 28 fragments; one large fragment from tip of blade to near socket; tiny fragment of socket. Max. pres. L. 14.4; max. w. 1.6. Cracked and laminated, particularly around socket. Pronounced midrib toward socket end.

GR12 M30 (V88.133; V 4805.3, object 19; Pl. 42). Iron spearhead. Single fragment from socket, broken at both ends. Max. pres. L. 2.6; d. est. 1.6. Corroded and splitting, with some surviving surfaces. Round socket. May go with **GR12 M26** or **GR12 M27**.

GR12 M31 (V88.92, HNM 15755; V 4805.4, object 16; Fig. 91; Pl. 42). Iron dirk. Restored from 12 fragments. Nearly complete; missing part of upper blade tip. L. restored 35.3; L. blade 26.0; max. w. 3.5. Well-preserved surfaces. Flange hilted with knob at end. Two of three rivets preserved, one of bronze.

GR12 M32 (V88.111; V 4805.3 object 32, V 4805.5 object 35; Fig. 91; Pl. 42). Iron knife. Two nonjoining fragments, one from blade, one from handle. Max. pres. L. 4.0; max. pres. w. 1.8. Corroded and laminated, but with some surviving surfaces. Top of blade curves slightly. Blade makes right angle with handle. *Comparanda*: Snodgrass 1996, 587, type E (Knossos, PG–EG).

GR12 M33 (V88.117; V 4805.4, objects 16, 17; Fig. 91; Pl. 42). Iron knife. Single fragment (other piece inventoried with it belongs to a tool) preserving tip and end of blade; missing handle. Max. pres. L. 13.0; max. w. 1.8. Cracked and corroded, but with some surviving surfaces. Single edge. *Comparanda*: Snodgrass 1996, 585–586, type A (Knossos, SM–O).

GR12 M34 (V88.118; V 4805.4, object 6; Fig. 91; Pl. 42). Iron knife. Mended from five fragments; missing tip of blade and handle. Max. pres. L. 8.7; max. w. 1.5. Poorly preserved; just one layer laminated off larger object. Single edge.

GR12 M35 (V88.100; V 4805.3, object 30; Pl. 43). Iron knife. Small fragment of blade; six other nonjoining fragments. Max. pres. L. 3.1; max. w. 2.0. Corroded, but some surviving surface. Single edge.

GR12 M36 (V88.134, HNM 15762; V 4805.3, object 5; Fig. 91; Pl. 43). Iron sickle-shaped knife. Restored from five fragments, with nine other flakes left over. Nearly complete; missing much of one end. L. 13.8 (across curve); max. w. 2.0. Laminating, but some surviving surfaces on one side. Curved blade with single edge on inside of curve. *Comparanda*: Gjerstad 1948, 135, fig. 21:6 (bronze); Snodgrass 1996, 587, type D (Knossos, SM–O).

GR12 M37 (V88.86, HNM 15752; V 4805.3, object 9; Fig. 91; Pl. 43). Iron saw. Mended from five fragments; one nonjoining fragment from end. Nearly complete; missing one chunk from body and bit connecting end. Max. pres. L. 13.0; max. w. 2.5. Corroded, but some surviving surfaces on both sides. Thin, flat blade, serrated on one side; rounded tip. *Bibliography*: Gesell, Coulson, and Day 1991, 155, pl. 60:a. *Comparanda*: Karageorghis 1983, 285, fig. 167:T. 83.71 (bronze, Palaepaphos-*Skales*).

GR12 M38 (V88.126a; V 4805.4, object 14; Fig. 91; Pl. 43). Iron file. Partially mended from five fragments preserving one end; five nonjoining fragments. Two fragments from V 4805.4 may represent other end. Max. pres. L. 15.7; max. w. 1.2. Badly corroded, cracked, and exploded; little surviving surface, but some pieces with striations of file. Long tool, rectangular in section, with striations on four sides.

GR12 M39 (V88.132a; V 4805.4, object 27; Fig. 91; Pl. 43). Iron tool, possibly awl. Single fragment, broken at both ends. Pin-shaped fragment may belong. Max. pres. L. 5.3; max. w. 1.0. Corroded and cracked. Long tool, square in section, tapering toward both ends.

GR12 M40 (V88.126b; V 4805.4, object 14; Fig. 92; Pl. 43). Iron chisel or file. Mended from two fragments, close to one end. Fragments from V88.117 and V 4805.4 object 16 may be from same object. Max. pres. L. 7.8; max. w. 1.1. Corroded. Square in section. May be part of file (**GR12 M36**), but no striations are visible on any fragments.

GR12 M41 (V88.128; V 4805.4, object 17; Fig. 92; Pl. 43). Iron flat chisel. Single large fragment, nearly intact; missing chips. L. 8.7; max. w. 2.0. Worn and corroded surfaces; thin at one end. Narrow at one end, broad and rounded at other.

GR12 M42 (V88.115; V 4805.3, object 13; Fig. 92; Pl. 43). Iron tool. Complete in two fragments. L. 25.0; max. w. 1.7. Corroded, with corrosion bubble on body; some surviving surfaces. Long, thin, rectangular tool, rectangular in section, with tang for insertion into wood.

GR12 M43 (V88.135; V 4805.3, object 31; Fig. 92; Pl. 43). Iron spatulate tool. Mended from four fragments; nearly complete. L. 12.3; max. w. 1.0. Badly corroded; some surviving surfaces on flat end. Small, thin tool, pointed at one end, rectangular in section in middle, spatulate on other end. *Comparanda*: Courtois 1984, 24, no. 211, fig. 5:20 (bronze; Enkomi, LC III or EIA I).

GR12 M44 (V88.132b; V 4805.4, object 27; Fig. 92; Pl. 43). Iron tool. Single fragment from rounded end. Max. pres. L. 2.1; max. w. 0.5. Well-preserved surfaces. End of tool, possibly spatulate on one end and pointed on the other, like those from Graves 5 and 9?

GR12 M45 (V88.249; V 4805.3, V 4805.5 object 35; Fig. 92; Pl. 44A). Iron fleshhook. Half preserved in five fragments. L. 7.0; max. w. 0.7. Cracked and corroded surfaces. Bent at end(s) to catch pieces of meat. Long tool, square in section, tapering at both ends. One end bent at right angles to the rest. *Comparanda*: **GR9 M63–GR9 M66**.

GR12 M46 (V88.250; V 4805.3, V 4805.4; Fig. 92; Pl. 44A). Iron fleshhook. Five joining fragments preserving one end of object. Max. pres. L. 5.50; max w. 0.55. Cracked and corroded, a few surviving surfaces. Long, pin-like object, but square in section. Possibly like **GR12 M45**.

Bone

GR12 B1 (V 4805.3; Pl. 44A). Modified antler beam. Single large fragment, three nonjoining fragments. Max. pres. L. 8.35; w. 1.20–1.60. Possibly worked at both ends. One end is cut, scraped, and hollowed; the other is scraped and smoothed to a point.

GR12 B2 (V 4805.4; Pl. 44A). Possibly modified palmate portions of antler. Five small, nonjoining fragments. Max. pres. L. 3.10; max. pres. w. 1.45. Thin pieces, no discernible shape. Perhaps modified on the edges and burned.

Terracotta

GR12 TC1 (V88.74, IM 1003; V 4805.4 object 7; Fig. 92; Pl. 44A). Terracotta bead. Nearly intact; a few chips missing. H. 1.20–1.50; d. 2.10; d. hole 0.55. Wt. 5.00 g. Rather hard, medium-coarse, reddish-yellow (5YR 6/6) fabric with infrequent but large black and red inclusions. Some burning. Depressed globular, but irregular; one side is higher than other. Hole has same diameter on both top and bottom. Incised decoration: stamped circles around middle, with incised horizontal bands on either side. Top and bottom have short strokes radiating from central hole.

Grave 13

History and Details of Excavation

Grave 13 is a cremation burial excavated in 1988 on the north slope of the Vronda ridge in Trench VN 200 (Figs. 3, 4; Gesell, Coulson, and Day 1991, 160; Day and Glowacki 2012, 174–175). There was no associated architecture, just an irregular pit in what appeared to be roofing debris very close to the modern surface (Fig. 93). After the removal of the topsoil some stones were encountered, along with roofing debris and a patch of dark, ashy soil with snail shells and remains of cremated human bone. Along the north side of the trench other areas were distinguished, several with traces of burning but no human remains.

The grave is unusual for its total lack of architecture. It was initially interpreted as a pyre site, from which the majority of bones and objects had been removed for disposal elsewhere. There is ample evidence for burning in situ, as much carbon was found, and the roofing clay had fired hard, with a bright red color. The roofing clay suggests the presence of a building in an earlier phase, but no traces now remain, perhaps because of erosion or removal by human activity. If so, much of the grave material may have suffered the same fate.

Architecture

There is no associated architecture. The cremations were apparently made in an irregular pit dug into the roofing clay. If any enclosure once existed, it had vanished before excavation began.

Stratigraphy

Above the bedrock and brecciating surface (VN 211) over most of the trench was a deposit of roofing clay (VN 205, V 208). The soft, dark, ashy soil with snail shells and cremated bone seems to have been confined to an irregular pit in this clay (VN 206); part of this soft, dark, ashy soil was removed with roofing clay in VN 202 and VN 203. The plan shows two major areas containing cremated remains, of which the eastern (0.75 m north–south x 0.55 m east–west) was encountered earlier and showed signs of actual burning; there was some carbonized wood, and the roofing clay into which the pit had been dug was fired red. To the west was another area, discovered slightly later, which measured 0.88 m north–south x 1.10 m east–west; it was characterized by the presence of ashy soil, bones, and some pottery. Both deposits belonged to the grave, but their precise relationship is unclear; the eastern pit seems to have been the site of actual burning, but the western area may represent a dump from the east or the site of a second cremation. Evidently, there was a great deal of disturbance in this area, both from natural erosion and from human activity that may have been related to the removal of the bones for burial elsewhere. The topsoil (VN 200, VN 201) lay directly on top of the roofing debris and the grave soil.

The stratigraphy in the northern part of the trench, particularly in the northeast corner, was different from the rest of the area. Here, above the bedrock and the brecciating surface of the bedrock (VN 211), lay a deposit with patches of black carbonized material, possibly associated with the cremation or perhaps with some earlier industrial or domestic fire (VN 210). Over this burned deposit was a layer of loose soil with cobbles (VN 209) that lay under the roofing (VN 205). Farther to the west, toward the center of the trench, was a rather hard reddish-brown layer, possibly caused by burning (VN 207). This layer lays below a lighter layer of soil not found in the rest of the trench (VN 204).

Burials

Grave 13 contained two commingled burials.

Burials 1 and 2

Type: cremation pyre
Age: adults
Sex: unknown
Weight: 198 g

The feature excavated as Grave 13 was apparently used as a pyre site at which remains were not buried in situ but were collected for deposition elsewhere. The small amount of bone collected from this feature represents a minimum of two individuals, as attested by the presence of two mandibular symphyses (chins). The collected bone includes small cranial fragments, a large number of tooth root fragments, many rib fragments, and a few unidentifiable long bone shaft fragments. All of the pieces are quite small and somewhat weathered. A third molar with complete root tips indicates that one individual is an adult, and the lack of any immature bone suggests that both burials are adults. The bone is partially or completely calcined, with no clear pattern of differential burning. The condition of the bone and the almost complete absence of uncalcined remains suggest that this burial, found almost at the surface, may have been significantly affected by freezing, which differentially fragments incompletely burned bone (M. Liston and F. Toth, unpublished research).

Faunal Remains

The fragmentary, unburned, and eroded animal bone debris found in the area of Grave 13 does not appear to be associated with this pyre site (Table 7).

Pottery

Grave 13 produced 227 pottery fragments weighing 1.88 kg. Fourteen vessels were cataloged, composed of 75 fragments weighing 0.54 kg; the rest was material from the LM IIIC settlement. Because so little pottery came from the grave, and not much that is paralleled elsewhere, it is difficult to date Grave 13. The cups are fragmentary but seem to be rather shallow, suggesting a date early in the LG period. Cataloged items **GR13 P1** and **GR13 P2** may belong to the same vessel, and if so, it may have been a straight-sided pyxis or alabastron. In addition to the cataloged vessels, there are fragments of a hard, burned vessel (blue ware) and a cup rim and handle that may belong with one of the cataloged cups or skyphoi. There is also a small, round, horizontal handle, suggesting that at least one of the cataloged vessels is a skyphos.

The fabrics of the vessels from this grave are much harder than those found in graves elsewhere on the site. This difference in fabrics may be due to soil conditions that diverge from the areas on top of the ridge or on the west slope, or it may indicate a different source or a chronological difference. Some of the fabrics resemble those from Tomb IX, the SM–EG tholos located farther down the hill to the north. If so, then Grave 13 may be a pyre site for one of the tholos tombs, or it may also be one of the early cremations on the site. The assemblage, with its large numbers of monochrome cups, resembles those of the other graves as well as that of Tomb IX.

Objects

No objects were cataloged from the grave. A few bits of corroded iron appeared in the residue from the water sieve, and one of the bones had iron rusted on it, suggesting that iron objects originally accompanied the burial.

Chronology

As there are few parallels between the scanty material from Grave 13 and that in the other graves or elsewhere in Crete, it is difficult to date the grave and the burials. The shallowness of the monochrome cups may suggest a date early in LG. The possible straight-sided pyxis or alabastron may be earlier, perhaps PG, and not early in that period.

Catalog

Pottery

Fine Decorated Wares

GR13 P1 (VN 206.3, VN 206.5 and 6; Fig. 94). Jar or straight-sided alabastron. Partially mended from three fragments from rim and carination; one nonjoining rim fragment, three body fragments. Max. pres. h. 3.6; d. rim 5.0. Fine, soft, pink (7.5YR 7/4) fabric. Black paint. Very worn surfaces. Almost totally burned. *Comparanda*: Karageorghis 1983, fig. 40:110, pl. 17:110 (Palaepaphos-*Skales*, CG I) *Date*: PG–G.

GR13 P2 (VN 205.3, VN 206.5; Fig. 94). Closed vessel, possibly straight-sided pyxis or alabastron. Partially mended from 10 fragments preserving 25% of base and part of lower body. Max. pres. h. 4.5; d. base 7.5. Fine, soft, porous, micaceous, pink (7.5YR 7/4) fabric. Very pale brown (10YR 8/2) slip. Black paint. Well-preserved surfaces. Most of fragments burned. Multiple upright triangles with hatching between some of lines. *Date*: PG–G.

GR13 P3 (VN 201.1, VN 202.1, VN 203.1; Fig. 94). Wide-mouthed jug. Partially mended from 10 fragments, including one from rim and four joining fragments from base of neck and upper body. D. rim 10.0. Fine, hard, light red (2.5YR 6/6) fabric. Very pale brown (10YR 8/2) slip. Very worn surfaces. Black paint worn to shadow on interior. No burning. *Comparanda*: Tsipopoulou 2005, 150, fig. 90:AN1797 (Hagios Georgios, LG). *Date*: LG.

GR13 P4 (VN 205.3, VN 206.6; Fig. 94). Wide-mouthed jug. Single fragment from rim and neck, three body fragments. D. rim est. 8.0. Fine, soft, reddish-yellow (5YR 7/6) fabric. Black paint worn to shadow on exterior. Very worn surfaces; fabric exfoliating. No burning. *Comparanda*: Tsipopoulou 2005, 216, fig. 89:H3254 (Adromyloi, LG–EO). *Date*: LG.

Fine Monochrome Wares

GR13 P5 (VN 201.1 and 4, VN 202.1, VN 203.3 and 5, VN 206.3 and 6, VN 206.3; Fig. 94). Cup. Partially mended from eight fragments. Preservation 10%, including rim fragments with upper handle attachment, large fragment from base. D. rim 14.3; d. base 6.0. Fine, medium-soft, light reddish-brown (5YR 6/4) fabric, very pale brown (10YR 8/2) on surface. Black paint. Very worn surfaces. No burning. *Comparanda*: **GR12 P24**. *Date*: LG.

GR13 P6 (VN 202.1; Fig. 94). Cup. Two fragments preserving part of rim and one handle. D. rim est. 12.0. Soft, rather chalky, very pale brown (10YR 8/4) fabric with small red phyllite inclusions. Dark red (2.5YR 3/6) paint on interior and exterior. *Date*: G.

GR13 P7 (VN 202.1, VN 206.3 and 7; Fig. 94). Cup or skyphos. Partially mended from eight fragments. Preservation 20%, including 30% of rim and upper body, fragments of base; missing handle(s). Max. pres. H. 6.6; d. rim 11.0. Fine, hard, light reddish-brown (2.5YR 6/4) fabric. Black paint. Well-preserved surfaces. No burning. *Comparanda*: Mook 2004, 175, fig. 12.10:E (Kastro, G). *Date*: G.

GR13 P8 (VN 202.1, VN 203.5; Fig. 94). Cup or skyphos. Partially mended from four fragments; two fragments from base may belong. Preservation 20%; missing full profile and handle(s). D. rim 13.0; d. base 6.0. Fine, soft, light reddish-brown (2.5YR 6/4) fabric. Red (2.5YR 4/8) paint. Rather well-preserved surfaces. Slight burning on one side. *Date*: G.

GR13 P9 (VN 206.6; Fig. 94). Cup or skyphos. Two joining rim fragments. D. rim est. 12.0. Fine, soft, light reddish-brown (5YR 6/4) fabric with a few phyllite inclusions and voids. Very pale brown (10YR 8/2) on surface. Black(?) paint. Very worn surfaces. *Date*: G.

GR13 P10 (VN 202.1, VN 206.7, VN 211.1; Fig. 94). Cup or skyphos. Two joining fragments from rim, very chipped; two more possible nonjoining fragments. Max. pres. h. 5.0; d. rim est. 12.0. Fine, soft, light red (2.5YR 6/6) fabric. Red (2.5YR 4/8) paint. Worn surfaces. No burning. *Date*: G.

GR13 P11 (VN 203.5; Fig. 94). Cup or skyphos. Single fragment from rim. D. rim est. 12.0. Fine, soft, reddish-yellow (7.5YR 6/6) fabric. Yellowish-red (5YR 5/6) paint. Worn surfaces. *Date*: G.

GR13 P12 (VN 200.1, VN 201.1, VN 202.1, VN 203.1; Fig. 94). Cup or skyphos. Two joining fragments from base; five nonjoining fragments. Max. pres. h. 2.3; d. base 6.0. Fine, soft, reddish-yellow (5YR 7/6) fabric, greenish gray (5G 5/1) at core. Dark red (2.5YR 3/6) paint. Worn surfaces. Some burning. *Date*: G.

GR13 P13 (VN 201.1 and 4, VN 202.1; Fig. 94). Closed vessel. Single fragment preserving 30% of base and four nonjoining fragments of body. D. base 7.0. Fine, rather hard, light red (2.5YR 6/6) fabric with some red phyllites. Pink (7.5YR 8/4) surfaces, perhaps slip. No paint. Worn surfaces. No burning. *Date*: G.

MEDIUM-COARSE DECORATED OR MONOCHROME WARE

GR13 P14 (VN 202.1; Fig. 94). Wide-mouthed jug. Two joining fragments from rim and shoulder; three nonjoining fragments. D. rim 8.0. Medium-coarse, rather hard, light red (2.5YR 6/6) fabric with hard angular black and small hard white inclusions. Black paint. Well-preserved surfaces. No burning. *Comparanda*: Tsipopoulou 2005, 61, fig. 91:HΔ28 (Dreros, LG); 173, fig. 90:Σ3935 (Hagios Georgios, LG). *Date*: LG.

Grave 15

History and Details of Excavation

Grave 15 lies on the western slope of the Vronda ridge, in the doorway that led from the courtyard into Room I4 of Building I in LM IIIC (Figs. 3, 4). It was first discovered in 1988, and most of the grave was excavated at the end of that season in Trench VW 10000 (VW 10006, VW 10008, VW 10012). A small portion of the grave on the west went over the house wall on the west side of the doorway into Room I4 in Trench VW 10100 (VW 10102), and that portion was excavated at the same time. Excavation was not completed because the grave was found so late in the season, and digging continued in 1989 (VW 10015). Finally, in 1990, the small remaining patch of dark grave soil in this area was dug as VW 10021. Only a single burial was recognized during excavation (A), but two more were distinguished during further study, and a fetus (Burial 3) was found in the residue from the water sieve.

Architecture

Grave 15 was placed in the doorway that entered the earlier Building I, Room I4 (Fig. 95), possibly because the stones of the wall to the east (VW 10007) were still standing at the time of burial. The ashy soil went over the wall on the western side of the doorway (VW 10106), so clearly that wall was not still standing above ground at the time of burial. Additional stones were placed on the northeast and the south to form a roughly circular space for the burial, measuring ca. 1.22 m north–south x 1.15–1.20 m east–west (Pl. 44B). There may have been more architectural features, possibly even walls forming a rectangular enclosure, but the grave was close to the surface and badly disturbed. There were no visible signs of burning except for the ashy gray soil containing the bones and pottery.

Stratigraphy

The depth of deposition was only 0.20–0.30 m, and the stones that seem to make up the boundaries did not rise much higher. The grave was placed directly upon the pebbly surface of the Building I courtyard, and the soil within the burial area was uniformly dark gray and ashy (VW 10012, VW 10015, VW 10102). It had been badly disturbed, and not much remained within it. A few fragments of pottery from the burial were picked up from the slope wash (VW 10006; Day and Glowacki 2012, 71) and cobble layer (VW 10008; Day and Glowacki 2012, 80).

Associated Features

Grave 35 to the north and west (see below) may have been associated with Grave 15, possibly as a discard deposit from it.

Burials

Four burials were found in Grave 15, all close to the surface and disturbed. The first two burials extended all the way from the floor of the grave to the top of the deposit in VW 10006. The fetus was localized in VW 10012. The final burial was not in anatomical order, indicating that it was disturbed; it had spilled over the west side of the doorway in VW 10102 and even into VW 10103.

Burials 1 and 2
Type: disturbed primary cremations
Age: adults
Sex: unknown
Weight: 1,424 g

Burials 1 and 2 were distinguished by the presence of two fragmentary crania located near the east end of the burial deposit. All of the bone is completely calcined and white in color. One person is an adult, possibly 40 to 60 years old. The other appears to be somewhat younger. One of the individuals was very petite, possibly a female.

Burial 3
Type: disturbed primary cremation
Age: fetus, 16–32 weeks
Sex: unknown
Weight: 13 g

The fetal bone of Burial 3 was found commingled with the remains of Burials 1 and 2. The bone is from a fetus between 16 and 32 weeks in utero, as indicated by the presence of an unfused petrous portion of the temporal bone. The recovered bone includes portions of the cranium, the scapula, ribs, vertebrae, long bones, and one manual phalanx.

Burial 4
Type: disturbed primary cremation
Age: adult
Sex: unknown
Weight: 623 g

Burial 4 is the cremation burial of an adult of unknown sex, identified by the presence of a concentration of cranial bone located near the west end of the burial deposit. Virtually all of the bone is completely calcined. Only the thoracic and lumbar spines and a few cranial vault fragments retain any gray color.

Faunal Remains

The few sheep or goat bone fragments found in the area of Grave 15 were unburned, eroded, and leached, and they are likely to represent general site debris, unassociated with the burials (Table 7). A single topshell (*Phorcus*) also came from this grave (Table 5).

Botanical Remains

Only three types of botanical remains were recovered: grape (*Vitis vinifera*), fool's parsley (*Aethusa cynapium*), and medick (*Medicago* sp.).

Pottery

Grave 15 produced some 360 fragments of pottery weighing 1.80 kg. Only four vessels were sufficiently well preserved to be cataloged. There were remains of another vessel of soft, chalky fabric, but the edges and surfaces of the fragments were so soft that it was impossible to reconstruct. Other pottery found with the soil in the burials, including several fine deep bowl fragments, came from the LM IIIC building; this material was dealt with in the publication of the building (Day and Glowacki 2012, 71–72).

Find spots suggest that the skyphos (**GR15 P1**), the cup (**GR15 P2**), and the lekythos or jug (**GR15 P4**) should be associated with Burial 4. They were scattered over the wall to the west of the door and into VW 10103. Skyphos **GR15 P1** is heavily burned, and it may have been thrown out at the time of the last burial.

Chronology

There is very little material with which to date this grave. The skyphos (**GR15 P1**) has an offset rim that looks late, and both this vessel and the jug (**GR15 P3**) have grooving on the bottom of the base, a feature that is unusual before the late seventh century (pers. comm., A. Kotsonas; cf. Erickson 2010, 130, fig. 4.7; 313, fig. 8.10). The monochrome cup resembles LG examples from the Kastro. The last burial seems to date to the late seventh century.

Catalog

Pottery

Fine Monochrome Wares

GR15 P1 (VW 10102.1 and 2, VW 10103.2, VW 10012.2, VW 10008.4; Fig. 96). Skyphos. Partially mended from 48 fragments. Preservation 50%, including most of base, 30% of rim, both handles. Max. pres. h. 4.0; h. est. 8.2; d. rim 11.0; d. base 4.8. Fine, very soft, pink (7.5YR 7/4) fabric. Black paint. Very worn surfaces. Groove around underside of base. Many fragments burned. *Date*: LO.

GR15 P2 (VW 10103.2; Fig. 96). Cup or skyphos. Partially mended from 35 fragments, including several from rim; missing base and handle. Max. pres. h. 4.0; d. rim 11.6. Fine, soft, reddish-yellow (7.5YR 7/6) fabric. Red (10R 4/6) paint. Very worn surfaces. No burning. *Comparanda*: Mook 2004, 176, fig. 12.11:H (Kastro, LG). *Date*: LG.

Fine Decorated, Monochrome, or Plain Wares

GR15 P3 (VW 10006.2, VW 10008.4, VW 10012.1; Fig. 96). Jug? Partially mended from 20 fragments, preserving entire base, part of lower body, and handle; missing upper body, neck, and rim. Max. pres. h. 2.4; d. base 3.5. Fine, very hard, greenish-gray (5BG 5/1) fabric, burned so hard that the interior has vitrified. Surfaces very worn. Groove around underside of base. *Date*: LO?

GR15 P4 (VW 10103.3; Fig. 96). Lekythos. Single fragment from neck. Max. pres. h. 2.4; d. 1.6–1.8. Fine, soft, very pale brown (10YR 8/3) fabric and slip. Possibly burned slightly. *Date*: LG–EO?

Grave 16

History and Details of Excavation

Grave 16 is a stone-built enclosure located on the north side of the summit of the Vronda ridge, set into Room K1 of LM IIIC Building K (Figs. 3, 4). It was excavated in 1988 in Trench V 6200; the southeast corner was actually in Trench V 6300, but the entire grave was dug as a single entity in V 6200 (Gesell, Coulson, and Day 1991, 157–160). Immediately below the topsoil over the entire trench (V 6200) was a layer of brown wash or fill (V 6201) that covered the grave and the earlier room in which it had been built. A large quantity of pottery was discovered in the center of the locus, which, together with the snail shells and dark ashy soil, indicated the presence of a burial. The excavation was undertaken by the trench supervisor with advice from the physical anthropologists. During the excavation of this locus the tops of the walls of the enclosure were uncovered, while the east wall, which lay primarily in Trench V 6300, was excavated later. Within the enclosure, the upper layer of rubble was excavated as V 6203, while a lower layer of stones was distinguished as V 6204. A small circle of stones in the east end of the enclosure was uncovered with a great deal of pottery (V 6204.1). The lowest level (V 6205) was a layer of harder soil burned black to brown. Only one individual was recognized in the course of excavation, but the remains of two were identified during study.

Architecture

The grave is a rectangular enclosure oriented east–west and measuring 0.78–0.95 m north–south x 2.10 m east–west (Fig. 97; Pl. 44C). It was constructed in the midst of the rubble from the collapsed walls of Building K, Room K1, and it did not abut an existing house wall. The builders dug down to bedrock to construct the walls. The north (V 6206; w. 0.7–0.8 m) and west (V 6213; w. 0.83–0.98 m) walls have two good faces, while the south (V 6212) and east (V 6321) walls were each constructed of a single row of boulders (Pl. 44D). The west and south walls have one course of stones, occasionally with a second course formed by a single stone. All of the walls contain stones, largely breccia boulders with a few limestone blocks, which were burned and fissured, except in the east wall. A shelf of bedrock on the east end held a small circle of stones that surrounded a pottery deposit containing a large amphora (**GR16 P20**), which was very fragmentary and may have stood there as a marker, as has also been suggested for vases associated with Graves 9, 12, and 20.

Stratigraphy

The total deposition in the grave was 0.25–0.35 m. Within the grave, three layers were distinguished. The first, very thin layer was directly on bedrock and consisted of hard, dark brown–black soil (V 6205).

The first burial came from the lower parts of this layer exclusively (V 6205.4 and V 6205.5). Above this layer was rubble with soft, dark soil (V 6204) that contained the remains of the second burial, although some of the bones were also recovered in the lowest level (V 6205.1–3). A second rubble layer above it (V 6203) contained no human bones and probably represents the stones piled on top of the cremation after it was completed. The wash that lay over the entire area covered over the rubble in the grave (V 6201).

Associated Features

An area of soft burned soil was found just to the north of the grave (V 6207.6 and 7), possibly a dump of material from the first of the two burials made at the time of the second. There were no other associated features.

Burials

The grave contained two commingled cremated individuals.

Burial 1
Type: primary cremation
Age: young adult, 13–20 years
Sex: unknown
Weight: 839 g (combined with Burial 2; see below)

The first burial in this enclosure is an older juvenile or young adult, probably 13–20 years old. The proximal epiphysis of the humerus had very recently fused onto the bone shaft (Scheuer and Black 2000, 285). The open cranial sutures are consistent with this age estimation. The sex is indeterminate. The preserved bone is almost entirely calcined and white in color. While most of the major regions of the axial skeleton and limbs are represented, it is not possible to specifically identify most of the fragments.

Burial 2
Type: primary cremation
Age: adult, 30–40 years
Sex: unknown
Weight: 839 g (see above, Burial 1)

This commingled cremation burial is an adult, probably 20–40 years of age, as suggested by the suture closure and dental wear. There is no indication of the sex of the individual from the skeletal remains. There is some evidence for osteoarthritis in the spine, and the anterior teeth exhibit extreme wear, possibly indicating some nonmasticatory use of the dentition. The degree of wear is unlikely to have occurred in a younger adult. The only pathology noted on the bone is some slight periosteal activity of unknown cause on the tibia shaft fragments.

Faunal Remains

Although a number of fragments of animal bone that were partially burned or calcined were recovered from the area of Grave 16, identifiable elements were limited to one rabbit or hare femur diaphysis segment. This bone was unburned, and it is more likely to have been an accidental inclusion than an item associated with the burial ritual (Table 7).

Pottery

Grave 16 produced 1,005 fragments of pottery weighing 9.86 kg, and more fragments were recovered from the surface. An additional 397 fragments weighing 4.29 kg came from a dump north of the grave in V 6207; at least some of these fragments were probably were thrown out from the first burial at the time of the second cremation, including cup **GR16 P7** and cup/skyphos **GR16 P10**, fragments of which came from the west end of the grave as well. It is likely also that any vessels that were seriously burned (as opposed to having a slight discoloration from fire, perhaps caused by placing the pottery on the pyre before the fire was entirely out) should also belong with the first burial. These vessels include an aryballos (**GR16 P5**), two cups (**GR16 P12**, **GR16 P13**), and a mug-like cup (**GR16 P4**). Cup **GR16 P1** also came from the west side.

Another group of vessels came from the circle of stones at the east end of the grave, where they were probably placed at the time of the second cremation after the pyre had died out, although it is possible that they were placed there with the first burial and not disturbed by the second. The large amphora **GR16 P20** may have stood there as a marker for the grave; it shows no sign of burning, and it was too large to have fitted comfortably into the grave. The majority of the fragments, which presumably had lain on the surface, have disappeared. Also in this group were the following: cup **GR16 P6**, skyphoi **GR16 P2** and **GR16 P16**, and mug-like cup **GR16 P3**.

Finally, two small amphorae (**GR16 P17**, **GR16 P18**) were located at the west end of the enclosure; they probably belong with the last burial, as they were found so close to the surface and show no signs of burning.

Objects

There were very few objects found in the grave. The presence of an iron pin (**GR16 M2**) and another of bronze (**GR16 M1**) might indicate that one of the burials was a female. A dirk (**GR16 M6**) and the two spearheads (**GR16 M4**, **GR16 M5**), which are quite similar in size and shape, suggest a male burial. The spearheads are both short with rounded or slightly sloping shoulders. A dirk is of common flange-hilted variety with iron rivets. The needle **GR16 M3** and the chisel or scraper **GR16 M7** may come from a leather worker's toolkit. The obsidian blade **GR16 ST1** may have been deposited by chance with the stones and rubble in the grave, a leftover from an earlier use of the Vronda site. The presence of such blades in other graves (**GR5 ST1**, **GR6 ST1**; see above), however, suggests that obsidian was still used in the eighth century, and thus **GR16 ST1** may have been deliberately left in the grave.

Chronology

The grave can be dated entirely to the LG period, even though several pieces are of PG style (**GR16 P14**, **GR16 P19**, **GR16 P20**). Of the vessels perhaps belonging to the first burial, the mug-like cup **GR16 P4** resembles examples of East Cretan LG date (Tsipopoulou 2005, 133, fig. 90:AN2381; 179, fig. 89:Σ3966) that might have derived from Knossian prototypes of MG date (Coldstream and Catling, eds., 1996, 177, pl. 176:135.1; 262, pl. 239:18). The monochrome cup or skyphos **GR16 P10** is very deep, suggesting a date late in the LG period.

The pottery in the eastern part of the enclosure, perhaps associated with the second burial, is also of LG date. The mug-like cup with meander hooks **GR16 P3** is LG, with close parallels for decoration in a skyphos from Plai tou Kastrou at Kavousi (Tsipopoulou 2005, 102, fig. 114:H747). Coldstream (1968, 260) uses the meander hook motif to show the influence of Attic MG II on East Cretan Eteocretan Geometric, although it appears earlier at Knossos; apparently the motif of crosshatched meander or meander hooks is particularly popular at Kavousi (see also Tsipopoulou 2005, 89, fig. 51:H697). The skyphos **GR16 P16** is of a well-known type that imitates the MG skyphoi at Knossos, which in turn derive from Attic MG examples (Coldstream and Catling, eds., 1996, 42, fig. 70:O.20; 114, fig. 95:94; 143–144, fig. 105:63). The aryballos **GR16 P5** has parallels in the LG period. The amphora, however, seems to be of PG style (**GR16 P20**), possibly an antique that was used as a marker for this grave. The amphorae from the west end (**GR16 P17**, **GR16 P18**) have many parallels in the LG period, but they may derive from a Euboean SubPG type (Popham, Sackett, and Themelis 1979–1980, 50, pl. 28:70/P2, pl. 35). The panel cup **GR16 P14**, found in the upper rubble within the grave, is similar to one in Grave 3, with parallels of EPG and MPG date, and the skyphos (**GR16 P15**) found in the lower stone rubble has parallels of MG date at Knossos and of LG date in East Crete. It is similar to examples in Graves 12, 19, and 36, none of which is particularly early or late in the Vronda grave sequence. At least two vessels that seem to be associated with the upper burial have close parallels in the earlier burial in Grave 3 (**GR16 P14**, **GR16 P22**).

Catalog

Pottery

FINE DECORATED WARES

GR16 P1 (V 6205.1; Fig. 98). Cup. Single fragment (two sherds) from rim, with beginning of handle attachment; missing base and handle. Max. pres. h. 6.5; d. rim est. 10.0. Fine, soft, light red (2.5YR 6/6) fabric. Very pale brown (10YR 7/4) slip. Dull black paint. Very worn surfaces. No burning. Zigzag and panel of crosshatching. Interior unpainted except for band at rim and drips. *Comparanda*: Stampolides 1990, 387, fig. 16 (Eleutherna, LG); Coldstream and Catling, eds., 1996, 47–48, fig. 71:26, 35 (Knossos, PGB); 173, fig. 118:32 (Knossos, LG late). *Date*: LG.

GR16 P2 (V88.58; V 6204.1, object 7; Fig. 98; Pl. 45). Skyphos. Mended from 42 fragments. Preservation 95%; missing fragments of base, body, and rim. H. 9.2; d. rim 13.0–15.7; d. base 5.0. Fine, soft, reddish-yellow (7.5YR 8/6) fabric. Very pale brown (10YR 8/3) slip. Red (2.5YR 5/8) paint. Worn surfaces. No burning. Metopal arrangement with horizontal bands and groups of three short strokes hanging from rim band. *Bibliography*: Gesell, Coulson, and Day 1991, 159, pl. 63:b. *Comparanda*: Coldstream and Catling, eds., 1996, 141, fig. 104:28

(Knossos, Atticizing EG); Kotsonas 2008, 195–196, fig. 47:A308 (Eleutherna, LPG). *Date*: LG.

GR16 P3 (V88.57/68; V 6204.1 object 4, V 6204.1; Fig. 98; Pl. 45). Mug-like cup. Mended from 29 fragments. Preservation 75%, including full profile, entire base, most of lower body, 50% of rim, most of handle; missing part of handle and half of upper body. H. 10.0; d. rim 8.5; d. base 6.0. Fine, soft, reddish-yellow (5YR 7/6) fabric. Very pale brown (10YR 8/3) slip. Red (2.5YR 4/6) paint. Some well-preserved surfaces. No burning. Crosshatched meander hook. Broad bands on interior. *Bibliography*: Gesell, Coulson, and Day 1991, 159, fig. 4:3, emended; Day 1995, fig. 6:3, emended. *Comparanda*: Coldstream 1968, pl. 61:c (East Greek LG); Tsipopoulou 2005, 102, fig. 114:H747 (Kavousi, Plai tou Kastrou, LG). *Date*: LG.

GR16 P4 (V98.105; V 6204.2 and 3, V 6205.1–3; Fig. 98; Pl. 45). Mug-like cup. Mended from 50 fragments. Preservation 60%, including full profile, entire base, handle, and 80% of rim. H. 10.2; d. rim 9.3; d. base 5.0. Fine, soft, reddish-yellow (5YR 7/6) fabric. Very pale brown (10YR 8/4) slip. Red (2.5YR 4/8) paint. Very worn surfaces. Burned and warped. Crosshatched pendant triangle. Vertical stripes on handle. *Date*: LG.

GR16 P5 (V98.107; V 6204.1; Fig. 98). Aryballos. Mended from 26 fragments. Preservation 90%, including full profile; missing fragment of shoulder, handle, and half of rim. H. 7.0; d. rim 2.7; d. base 3.0. Fine, rather hard, light reddish-brown (5YR 6/3) fabric, dark gray on interior. Polished. Very worn surfaces; fugitive traces of paint. Bands; possibly a motif on shoulder, but no longer discernible. *Bibliography*: Gesell, Coulson, and Day 1991, 158–159, fig. 4:5, emended; Day 1995, fig. 6:5, emended. *Comparanda*: Tsipopoulou 2005, 162, fig. 99:AN2423 (Hagios Georgios, LG); Kotsonas 2008, 175, 178, fig. 42:A180γ (Eleutherna, PGB). *Date*: LG.

FINE MONOCHROME WARES

GR16 P6 (V88.70; V 6204.1, object 6; Fig. 98; Pl. 45). Cup. Mended from 30 fragments. Preservation 95%; missing piece of base and chips from rim and body. H. 10.0; d. rim 14.0; d. base 6.0. Fine, soft, very pale brown (10YR 7/3) fabric. Red (2.5YR 4/6) paint. Very worn surfaces. No burning. *Bibliography*: Gesell, Coulson, and Day 1991, 157, pl. 63:a. *Date*: LG.

GR16 P7 (V98.106; V 6204.1–3, V 6205.1–3, V 6207.6; Fig. 98). Cup. Mended from 45 fragments, 90% preserved; missing parts of body. H. 8.3; d. rim 11.8; d. base 4.6. Fine, soft, reddish-yellow (5YR 7/6) fabric, very pale brown (10YR 8/3) on surface. Red (2.5YR 4/8) paint. Many fragments burned and warped. Grooves on rim. *Comparanda*: Mook 2004, 174, fig. 12.9:AA (Kastro, SubPG). *Date*: G.

GR16 P8 (V 6201.1 and 2, V 6204.1–3, V 6205.1 and 2; Fig. 98). Cup. Partially mended from 19 fragments. Preservation 50%, including half of base and 85% of rim; missing handle, although unattached handle from V 6205.3 probably belongs to it. Profile can be restored. H. est. 9.0; d. rim 12.0; d. base 6.0. Fine, soft, reddish-yellow (5YR 6/6) fabric. Red (2.5YR 5/8) paint. Very worn surfaces. Some burning. String marks on base. *Date*: G.

GR16 P9 (V 6201.1, V 6201.4, V 6204.2; Fig. 98). Cup. Partially mended. Preservation 30%–40% in 17 fragments, including 50% of rim and part of handle; missing base and lower body. Max. pres. h. 5.0; d. rim 12.0. Fine, hard, pink to reddish-yellow (5YR 7/4–7/6) fabric. Black paint. Worn surfaces on some fragments, well preserved on others. No burning. *Comparanda*: Coldstream and Catling, eds., 1996, 157, fig. 111:163 (Knossos, PGB–EG). *Date*: G.

GR16 P10 (V 6204.3, V 6205.1, V 6207.6; Fig. 98). Cup or skyphos. Partially mended from 12 fragments from base and rim. H. est. 9.5; d. rim 13.0; d. base est. 5.2. Fine, soft, reddish-yellow (7.5YR 7/6) fabric. Black paint worn to shadow. Very worn surfaces. No burning. String marks on base. *Date*: LG.

GR16 P11 (V 6201.6 and 7; Fig. 98). Cup or skyphos. Two joining fragments preserving 25% of rim; no base or handle. Max. pres. h. 4.0; d. rim 11.0. Fine, rather hard, reddish-yellow (5YR 7/6) fabric. Black paint. Interior surfaces well preserved; exterior surfaces worn. No burning. *Date*: LG.

GR16 P12 (V 6204.1–3, V 6205.1 and 2; Fig. 98). Cup or skyphos. Partially mended from 11 fragments preserving entire base; some rim and body fragments from V 6204 and V 6205 may belong. Max. pres. h. 3.0; d. base 5.4. Fine, very soft fabric, reddish yellow (5YR 7/6), very pale brown (10YR 7/3), or light brownish gray (2.5Y 6/2), depending on degree of burning. Traces of red paint. Very worn surfaces. Some fragments burned after breaking. *Date*: G.

GR16 P13 (V 6204.2; Fig. 99). Cup or skyphos. Partially mended from 20 fragments. Preservation 10%, including entire base, handle, and 35% of rim; missing much of body. D. rim est. 14.0; d. base 6.0. Fine, soft, sandy, reddish-yellow (5YR 7/6) fabric. Traces of red paint. Very worn surfaces and edges, making mending impossible. Most fragments burned. *Date*: LG.

MEDIUM-COARSE DECORATED WARES

GR16 P14 (V88.55; V 6203.1; Fig. 99; Pl. 45). Cup. Mended from 19 fragments, with five nonjoining fragments. Preservation 60%, including full profile, entire base, handle; missing half of rim. H. 6.9; d. rim 12.3; d. base 4.5. Medium-coarse, soft, sandy, light gray (5Y 7/2) fabric. Black paint. Some well-preserved surfaces, some totally gone. Reserved panel may have oblique or vertical strokes. Horizontal strokes on handle. *Bibliography*: Gesell, Coulson, and Day 1991, 158–159, fig. 4:4; Day 1995, fig. 6:4, emended. *Comparanda*: **GR3 P3**; Brock 1957, 167, pl. 38:622 (Knossos, PGA); Boardman 1960, 134, 137, fig. 5:V.20 (Hagios Ioannis, EPG). *Date*: PG.

GR16 P15 (V88.71; V 6204.2, object 8; Fig. 99). Skyphos. Mended from 21 fragments; 24 nonjoining fragments. Preservation 75%, including full profile, entire base, both handles, and 50% of rim. H. 9.2; d. rim 12.0; d. base 6.0. Medium-coarse, soft, pale yellow (2.5Y 8/2) fabric with frequent tiny black inclusions. Black paint. Worn surfaces. No burning. Metopal panel with horizontal thin bands. *Bibliography*: Gesell, Coulson, and Day 1991, 158–159, fig. 4:6; Day 1995, fig. 6:6, emended. *Comparanda*: **GR12 P6**, **GR36 P2**; for shape, Coldstream and Catling, eds., 1996, 33, fig. 67:M5 (Knossos, MG); for decoration, Tsipopoulou 2005, 134, fig. 117:AN2385 (Hagios Georgios, LG). *Date*: LG.

GR16 P16 (V 6204.1; Fig. 99). Skyphos. Partially mended from 14 fragments. Preservation 25% of rim, including one handle attachment; missing base, lower body. Max. pres. h. 5.6; d. rim 12.0. Medium-coarse, slightly gritty, reddish-yellow (7.5YR 7/6) fabric. Dark brown (7.5YR 3/2) paint. Well-preserved surfaces. No burning. Metopal panel with zigzag. *Comparanda*: **GR6 P2**. *Date*: LG.

GR16 P17 (V98.103; V 6200.2, V 6201.2, V 6201.4 object 2, V 6201.6, V 6203.1, V 6204.2; Fig. 99; Pl. 45). Neck-handled amphora. Partially mended from 21 fragments. Preservation 25%, including base, much of lower body, shoulder and part of one handle, piece of neck; missing rim and second handle. Profile can be restored. H. est. 27.8; d. rim 9.0; d. base 6.5. Medium-coarse to fine, gritty, pink (7.5YR 7/4) fabric. Petrographic sample KAV 15/60: Fabric Subgroup 1b. Pale yellow (2.5Y 8/2) slip. Black paint. Worn surfaces, but some paint well preserved. Decorated with S-pattern on neck, crosshatched panel on shoulder, alternating hatched triangles on upper body, wavy line below. Horizontal strokes on handles. Neck made separately and added, with additional ridge of clay to strengthen joint. *Bibliography*: Gesell, Coulson, and Day 1991, 158–159, fig. 4:2, emended; Day 1995, fig. 6:2, emended. *Comparanda*: for shape, Coldstream and Catling, eds., 1996, 142, pl. 142:58 (Knossos, LG); Tsipopoulou 2005, 147, fig. 13:AN1789 (Hagios Georgios, LG); 291, fig. 16:AN8778 (Praisos, LG). For decoration, Tsipopoulou 2005, 190, fig. 19:Σ4077 (Hagios Georgios, EO). *Date*: LG.

GR16 P18 (V98.104; V 6201.4 object 1, V 6201.6 and 7; Fig. 99). Amphora. Partially mended from 41 fragments. Preservation 60%, including entire base, both handles, 30% of neck and rim, and large part of body. H. est. 32.8; d. rim 13.5; d. base 8.5. Medium-coarse, gritty, reddish-yellow (7.5YR 7/6) to yellow (10YR 7/6) fabric with granodiorite inclusions. Black paint. Worn surfaces, but decoration clear. Base burned. Neck has oblique strokes, zigzag, and S-pattern. Shoulder has alternating curved strokes. Horizontal strokes on handles. *Bibliography*: Gesell, Coulson, and Day 1991, 158–159, fig. 4:1, emended; Day 1995, fig. 6:1, emended. *Comparanda*: Coldstream and Catling, eds., 1996, 141, pl. 141:27 (Knossos, LG); Tsipopoulou 2005, 147, fig. 13:AN1789 (Hagios Georgios, LG); 314, fig. 15:AN1445 (Stavromenos Zou, LG). *Date*: LG.

Medium-Coarse Monochrome Ware

GR16 P19 (V 6200.1, V 6201.4, V 6204.1 and 2, V 6205.1; Fig. 100). Cup or skyphos. Partially mended from 15 fragments. Preservation 25% of rim; missing base and handle. Max. pres. h. 6.8; d. rim 12.0. Medium-coarse, soft, sandy, reddish-yellow (5YR 6/6) fabric with white inclusions and spalling. Black paint. Very worn surfaces on exterior; better preserved on interior. *Comparanda*: Coldstream and Catling, eds., 1996, 28, fig. 65:28 (Knossos, Attic LPG skyphos); Callaghan and Johnston 2000, 227, pl. 4.5:150 (Kommos, ninth century). *Date*: LPG?

Coarse Decorated Ware

GR16 P20 (V 6201.6, V 6203.1, V 6204.1, V 6204.3, V 6205.2 and 3, V 6212.1; Fig. 100). Large neck-handled amphora, 25 fragments from neck and shoulder, including rim and part of one handle. Missing lower body, base, and rest of handles. D. rim 14.5. Coarse, rather hard, reddish-yellow (5YR 7/6) fabric with frequent large phyllite inclusions and some carbonates. Petrographic sample KAV 15/61: Fabric Group 6. Very pale brown (10YR 7/4) slip. Brown (7.5YR 4/2) paint. Well-preserved surfaces. No burning. Pendant multiple triangles with drips. *Comparanda*: Brock 1957, 146, pl. 10:186 (Knossos, PGA); Coldstream and Catling, eds., 1996, 80, pl. 101:4 (PG); 92, pl. 108:8, 9 (EPG); 101, pl. 114:5 (EPG). *Date*: PG–G.

Coarse Monochrome Wares

GR16 P21 (V 6204.3, V 6205.1–3; Fig. 100). Cup. Partially mended from 44 fragments. Preservation 50%, including entire base, handle, 25% of rim; missing connection between rim and base. H. est. 10.3; d. rim 16.0; d. base 6.2. Coarse, very soft, yellowish-red (5YR 5/8) fabric with phyllites, quartz, and greenstone. Petrographic sample KAV 15/59: Fabric Group 3. Thick red (10R 4/6) paint. Very worn surfaces. No burning. *Date*: LG.

GR16 P22 (V 6204.2; Fig. 100). Bowl. Partially mended from 15 fragments. Preservation 20%, including entire base, fragments of rim; missing upper body and handle(s). D. rim est. 21.0; max. pres. h. 5.0; d. base 7.2. Very coarse, soft, reddish-yellow (5YR 6/8) fabric with mica inclusions. Petrographic sample KAV 15/58: small metamorphic group with mica. Thick red (10R 4/6) paint. Burned. *Comparanda*: **GR3 P20**. *Date*: LG.

Metal

Bronze

GR16 M1 (V88.223; V 6205.2; Fig. 100; Pl. 45). Bronze pin. Two fragments preserving end and shaft. L. (a) 2.40, (b) 0.07. Well preserved. Head broken off. Biconical swelling with two or three rings on either side.

Iron

GR16 M2 (V88.91; V 6204.2 object 3, V 6205.2 object 3; Fig. 100; Pl. 45). Iron pin. Mended from two fragments; complete. L. 11.3; d. disk 0.8. Swollen and cracked but well preserved. Thick cylindrical disk with broken knob on top, then two rings, a space, three rings, a long swelling, three rings, a space, and two rings. Tapers to point.

GR16 M3 (V88.87; V6205.2, object 5; Fig. 100; Pl. 45). Iron needle. Three joining fragments from head of needle; missing point. Max. pres. L. 5.1; L. est. (if straight) 7.0. Corroded and cracked. Head is flattened with hole pierced through it.

GR16 M4 (V88.119a; V 6205.2, object 2; Fig. 101; Pl. 45). Iron spearhead. Fragments preserving socket and parts of blade up to near tip. L. est. 23.6; d. socket 2.0. Very corroded and laminated. Long (8.0) socket, pierced opposite edges. Length of blade and shape indeterminable.

GR16 M5 (V88.119b; V 6205.2, object 2; Fig. 101; Pl. 45). Iron spearhead. Three joining fragments preserving socket to near tip. L. est. 23.5; max. w. 1.8; d. socket est. 2.0. Very corroded and laminated. Long (8.0) socket with hole pierced near end opposite edges. Blade comes out in continuous curve, with a slight short midrib.

GR16 M6 (V88.85; V 6204.4 object 2, V 6205.2 object 4; Fig. 101; Pl. 45). Iron dirk. Nearly complete in eight fragments; missing projections of hilt. L. 37.0; max. w. 4.0. Well preserved, although cracked some and corroded. Flange hilted, with rivet hole near end and two at attachment of blade; two iron rivets preserved, L. 1.2–1.4. Wide, long (27.0), tapering blade.

GR16 M7 (V88.88; V6204.1, object 1; Fig. 101; Pl. 45). Iron scraper or chisel. Nearly complete in single fragment, with several chips; missing wide end. Max. pres. L. 5.7; max. w. 1.8. Very corroded, without any surviving surfaces.

Stone

GR16 ST1 (V88.4; V6205.1, object 1; Pl. 45). Obsidian blade. Single fragment; missing both ends. Max. pres. L. 1.4; max. w. 0.6. Blade with two parallel edges and a dorsal ridge. Triangular in section.

Grave 17

History and Details of Excavation

Grave 17 lies on the north end of the top of the Vronda ridge in Room J4 of the earlier LM IIIC Building J, and it shares a wall (originally part of Building J) with Graves 10 and 12 (Figs. 3, 4; Pls. 46A–46C). It was excavated entirely in 1988 as Locus V 4809 (Gesell, Coulson, and Day 1991, 155–156). This disturbed enclosure lay even closer to the surface than neighboring Grave 12, and there were marks on the bedrock floor of the grave toward the south that may have been caused by deep plowing. The southern half of the enclosure has disappeared because of these later disturbances, and all that remains are three walls on the north, east, and west. During excavation, a linear accumulation in the center of the grave naturally divided it up into two sections; the rubble layer of the east half was excavated as V 4809.1, while the west half was removed as V 4809.2. A small area just south of these two loci was cleared as V 4809.3. The area had been much disturbed by the Venetian Building R and by modern agriculture, and it is also possible that there was some mixing of material from Graves 10 and 12.

Architecture

Three of the original four walls of the rectangular enclosure remain (Fig. 81; Pl. 46B). The enclosure measures 1.88–2.15 m east–west, and the grave material was found in an area that extended 0.85–1.00 m south of the north wall. The north wall (V 4803) was reused from LM IIIC Building J. The west wall (V 4821) is composed of three stones not aligned at a right angle to the north wall; although an irregular face exists on the east of this wall, the wall is not very well built. The eastern wall (V 4811) is better constructed, with two faces and rubble fill between. It may also have been used as part of Venetian Building R (Pl. 46A). The floor is bedrock. One limestone block on the north and one on the east wall are fissured, and the breccia boulders are calcined from the heat of the fire.

Associated Features

There are no certain features associated with Grave 17; the material from V 4806, a small space that lies between Graves 10 and 12 and over the wall north of Grave 17, is probably associated with Grave 12.

Stratigraphy

The total depth of deposition in Grave 17 was 0.12–0.13 m. The pyre(s) were laid directly on the bedrock floor, and material was deposited on top of it. The deposit was uniform throughout, with gray ashy soil and stones. A linear accumulation seemed to divide the enclosure into two halves (V 4809.1 on the east, V 4809.2 on the west), but objects and bones joined across this accumulation. It is impossible to determine how many cremation events occurred in the grave, but much of the pottery is lightly burned, suggesting few burning events. The layer of ashy soil and stones was thin on the south (V 4809.3) and lay just below the surface soil.

Burials

There were remains of three cremations in the enclosure. They were found in both east and west halves of the grave, and the infant lay in the southern part of the grave (V 4809.3). All show evidence of having been disturbed, and the final burial in the grave may have disappeared through erosion or human activity.

Burial 1

Type: disturbed primary cremation
Age: adult, 40–60 years
Sex: male
Weight: 2,065 g

A total of 2,065 g of adult bone was recovered from Burial 1. Compared to the quantities of bone collected from other burials at Vronda, this is a very high total for a single skeleton. Although there is no duplication of elements to indicate the presence of a second individual, it is likely that some of the bone belongs to the teenager identified as Burial 2 (see below). Although that individual had not yet finished growing, many portions of the skeleton already have the structure of mature bone, and the size difference is not great enough to distinguish the smaller fragments. However, as an indicator of the remarkably complete preservation, Burial 1 has the only vomer bone from the entire Kavousi population. This bone, which makes up part of the nasal septum, is very fragile and rarely survives cremation.

Burial 1 is a robust adult male (Pl. 22F: top right). The cranial bone of this individual was concentrated in the east end of the enclosure, but there was very little other evidence for the position of the body. The cranium is much less thoroughly burned than the postcranium. Much of the right side of the cranium is only scorched, although there is initial calcination of some areas. Portions of the femur and tibia shafts are also only scorched, while the rest of the bones are partially to completely calcined.

This individual was between 40 and 60 years old. The cranial sutures are obliterated endocranially, and there are pits along the sagittal suture accommodating arachnoid granulations, small pits that increase in size and number as an individual ages (Grossman and Potts 1974, 95–96). These pits are associated with older individuals. There is evidence of porotic hyperostosis on the parietal bones, suggesting anemia at some point earlier in life. The bone cortex is porous, and the diploë appears to be expanded where it is visible along breaks in the bone. The upper surfaces of the eye orbits also exhibit cribra orbitalia. Both of these traits are associated with anemia, although the exact cause cannot be determined.

Burial 2

Type: disturbed primary cremation
Age: juvenile, 15–17 years
Sex: unknown
Weight: 138 g

The bones associated with Burial 2 belonged to a juvenile individual. The bone is all completely calcined and very fragmentary, and it was commingled with the bone of Burials 1 and 3. While the presence of at least two individuals was recognized in the field, it was not possible to separate the bone until it was sorted in the lab, and it was recognized that one of the individuals was a juvenile. The individual was 15–17 years old. This age has been determined on the basis of the unfused distal epiphysis of the radius and the femur head and the active fusion of the lesser trochanter of the femur.

Burial 3

Type: disturbed primary cremation
Age: infant
Sex: unknown
Weight: 20 g

This burial is an infant of unknown age discovered in the water sieve residue from Grave 17. The bone is completely calcined. The bone is large enough to belong to a young infant, but no features that could be used to assign a specific age were recovered. Most parts of the skeleton are represented in the recovered bones, which included cranial vault fragments, mandible and maxilla fragments, portions of both clavicles and scapulae, ribs, vertebral arches, one tibia shaft, and other unidentifiable long bone shaft fragments.

Faunal Remains

A few possible animal bone fragments were recovered from this badly disturbed context (Table 7). These remains were unburned and unidentifiable, with the exception of a single deciduous incisor from a domestic pig (*Sus*).

Botanical Remains

Only a few botanical remains were recovered from Grave 17, including a lentil (*Lens culinarius*) and fool's parsley (*Aethusa cynapium*).

Pottery

Grave 17 produced 956 fragments of pottery weighing 2.41 kg. Eleven vessels could be identified, nearly all fine wares (82%). Most of the pottery came from the east side of the grave, including a decorated cup (**GR17 P1**), two aryballoi (**GR17 P2, GR17 P7**), a small necked jar (**GR17 P3**), a monochrome cup (**GR17 P9**)**,** a skyphos (**GR17 P6**), and a hydria (**GR17 P8**). One monochrome skyphos (**GR17 P5**) was scattered over the east end and the south side. Only a pyxis (**GR17 P4**) and a coarse bowl (**GR17 P10**) were found on the west side. None of the material can be associated with a particular burial.

The large coarse basin **GR17 P11** probably belongs to this grave. Some fragments of it actually were found within the Grave 17 in V 4809.2 (the west half of the grave), while the majority was found outside the grave, first in V 4707 and then in V 4752, the area just to the west between Graves 10 and 17 and Grave 20. It was initially cataloged with Grave 20, but the fact that a large part of the base was actually found in Grave 17 not at a surface level has led us to consider it part of the assemblage of Grave 17.

The coarse bowl **GR17 P10** is likely to date to the Final Neolithic period, although it could be a crude handmade vessel of the Early Iron Age. The base and pinched rim make it look Neolithic, however,

and it may have been in a crevice in the bedrock and picked up with the grave pottery; there are other FN remains on the site of Vronda, although they are not plentiful (Day et al. 2016, 199).

In addition to the cataloged pottery, there are fragments of a thin-walled juglet of very hard, fine fabric decorated with bands that was not inventoried because of a lack of diagnostic features. There were many fragments from a large, soft, tan vessel for which no shape or decoration can be distinguished. Additionally, there is a fragment from the center of a large lid without any rim, handle, or preserved decoration. Many fragments listed as coming from the hydria (**GR17 P8**) may have been from a smaller vessel of the same fabric, as some fragments are thinner than those that belonged to the hydria.

Objects

There was a surprising amount of metal in the grave considering the depth of the deposit. In addition to the cataloged iron objects, there was a fragment of a knife or spear (V88.102) and uninventoried fragments that may have come from a blade (V 4809.1 object 5); these objects were too poorly preserved to be cataloged. Two bronze (**GR17 M1, GR17 M2**) and two iron pins (**GR17 M4, GR17 M5**) are of similar size and types; they are probably matched pairs. The javelin head **GR17 M6** has a very short blade with rounded shoulders, and it is too short to have been a spear. The sickle-shaped knife **GR17 M7** is similar to other curved blades in the Vronda graves, although its handle is larger than those seen on others.

Chronology

The aryballos **GR17 P2**, a Creto-Cypriot type of the EO period, gives an EO date for the grave. While such aryballoi became standard in the LG period at Knossos, the use of circles as fillers rather than chevrons is more common at the transition to the EO period (Coldstream 1996, 354–355). This example seems to be of the less globular and more ovoid shape of the Orientalizing period (Moignard 1996, 441). The other aryballos (**GR17 P7**) is of an unusual ovoid shape without good parallels except for an example from Grave 19 (**GR19 P14**). The skyphos **GR17 P5** has an articulated base, perhaps a disk base, a feature that is uncommon on drinking vessels earlier than the seventh century (pers. comm., A. Kotsonas). Probably also of EO date is the pyxis **GR17 P4**. An unusual shape with no close parallels, it resembles a squat straight-sided pyxis, but the upper body is more globular. The straight-sided pyxis disappeared in the Knossian repertoire after the EG period, but it did enjoy popularity in later times elsewhere in Crete (Coldstream 2001, 27). The decoration of circles on the shoulder, however, finds many parallels in the EO assemblages at the North Cemetery at Knossos and occurs at EPAR Eleutherna. The use of alternating broad and narrow black bands can be seen on neckless pithoi from Knossos as early as the EG period, but the amount of blank space between the bands is unusual and looks like a later feature here. The pyxis **GR17 P4** and the Creto-Cypriot aryballos **GR17 P2** are similar to examples from Grave 4, and they may indicate that the latest material from Grave 17 is synchronous with that from Grave 4. Grave 17 would thus be among the very latest burial features in the cemetery. The cup **GR17 P1** and the small necked jar **GR17 P3** are of earlier style, dating to the LG period. The decoration on the cup is like that on **GR20 P1** and resembles LG examples from Knossos (see below); the small necked jar is similar to an example from Grave 5 (**GR5 P2**).

Catalog

Pottery

Fine Decorated Wares

GR17 P1 (V 4809.1, V 4809.2; Fig. 102). Cup. Partially mended into two large fragments, one from base (19 sherds) and one from rim with handle attachment (five sherds); 23 nonjoining fragments. Preservation 50%, including entire base and most of shoulder, part of rim and most of handle. Profile can be restored. H. est. 7.8; d. rim 9.0; d. base 3.4. Fine, soft, pale yellow (5Y 8/2) fabric, probably lightly burned. Black paint. Very worn surfaces. Vertical stripes on body at point of lower handle attachment. *Comparanda*: **GR20 P1**; Coldstream and Catling, eds., 1996, 24, fig. 64:24 (Knossos, EO). *Date*: LG–EO.

GR17 P2 (V88.66; V 4809.1, object 2; Fig. 102). Creto-Cypriot lekythos or aryballos. Partially mended; nine joining fragments from base and lower body, three from neck and rim, 12 nonjoining body fragments. Preservation 50%, including entire base and lower body, parts of shoulder, neck, and rim; missing handle. Max. pres. h. 8.0; h. est. 11.6; d. rim est. 3.2; d. base 2.6. Fine, soft, reddish-yellow (7.5YR 7/6) fabric. Black paint worn to shadow. Worn surfaces. Many fragments burned. Concentric circles on each side, row of small double circles on front. *Comparanda*: Brock 1957, 159, pl. 45:687 (Knossos, EO); Coldstream and Catling, eds., 1996, 118, pl. 129:213; 152, pls. 148:33, 34, 150:43 (Knossos, EO); Tsipopoulou 2005, 265, fig. 98:AN1410, AN1412 (Praisos, EO). *Date*: EO.

GR17 P3 (V88.56; V 4809.1, object 1; Fig. 102; Pl. 46D). Small necked jar. Mended from 29 fragments; five nonjoining fragments. Preservation 85%, including complete profile, entire base and lower body, most of rim and neck, parts of both handles; missing bits of shoulder and parts of handles. H. 11.3; d. rim 7.0–8.0; d. base 5.5. Fine, soft, very pale brown (10YR 8/4) fabric; many fragments lightly burned to pale gray. Dusky red (10R 3/4) paint. Very worn surfaces. Metopal panel with double zigzag between vertical stripes on shoulder. Bands below. *Bibliography*: Gesell, Coulson, and Day 1991, 155, pl. 60:d. *Comparanda*: **GR5 P2**; Coldstream and Catling, eds., 1996, 115, pl. 124:148 (Knossos, LG); 264, fig. 145:77 (MG); Tsipopoulou 2005, 226, pl. 356:AN1381; 227, fig. 60:Σ3567 (Itanos, LG); 2013, 150–151, fig. 12:12278 (Piskokephalo, LG); Rethemiotakis and Englezou 2010, 71, fig. 42:95, 96 (Eltyna, MG); Englezou 2011, 293–297, 307, fig. 54:71 (Ligortynos, MG–LG). *Date*: LG.

GR17 P4 (V 4809.1, V 4809.2; Fig. 102). Pyxis. Partially mended from 93 fragments into large fragments of base, lower body, and shoulder. Preservation 30%, including nearly full profile; missing one handle, much of rim. H. est. 17.8; d. rim est. 8.0–9.0; d. base est. 7.0. Fine, medium-soft, reddish-yellow (5YR 6/6) fabric. Very pale brown (10YR 8/3) slip. Crackled black paint, worn to shadow. Well-preserved surfaces, although paint gone. No burning. Holes pierced through body of vessel where mended in antiquity; three preserved. Fivefold concentric circles on shoulder. Groups of bands on body, broad bands alternating with groups of three narrow bands. *Comparanda*: **GR4 P8**, **GR4 P9**; Kotsonas 2008, 140–141, fig. 33:A126 (Eleutherna, EPAR); for decoration, Coldstream and Catling, eds., 1996, 151, pl. 149:6, 12, 13 (EO–LO); 278, pl. 255:59 (OR); for shape, Coldstream and Catling, eds., 1996, 114, fig. 97:110 (EG); Kotsonas 2008, 134–135, fig. 32:A213 (EG). *Date*: EO.

Fine Monochrome Wares

GR17 P5 (V 4809.1, V 4809.3; Fig. 102). Skyphos. Partially mended into four large fragments: base (11 sherds), rim (five sherds), rim and body (nine sherds), and body (three sherds); 21 nonjoining fragments. Preservation 45%, including nearly full profile, part of one handle; missing second handle. H. est. 10.0; d. rim 14.0; d. base 6.4. Fine, soft, reddish-yellow (7.5YR 7/6) fabric, very pale brown (10YR 8/4) surface. Reddish-brown (5YR 4/4) paint. Worn surfaces. Some fragments burned, and some edges very worn. Articulated base. *Comparanda*: Coldstream 1972, 82, fig. 7:D24 (Knossos, early LG); Coldstream and Catling, eds., 1996, 147, fig. 106:32 (Knossos, LG). *Date*: EO.

GR17 P6 (V 4809.1; Fig. 102). Skyphos. Partially mended from 79 fragments. Preservation 20%, including much of base and rim, one handle; missing one handle. Max. pres. h. rim 5.5; d. rim est. 12.0–14.0; d. base est. 6.0–7.0. Fine, soft, very pale brown (10YR 8/4) fabric. Traces of reddish-brown paint. Very worn surfaces. Many fragments burned. Small ring base is unusual and is probably a late feature. *Comparanda*: Coldstream and Catling, eds., 1996, 71, fig. 76:19.5 (Knossos, EO). *Date*: EO.

Decorated or Monochrome Fine Wares

GR17 P7 (V88.60; V 4809.1; Fig. 102). Aryballos. Mended from 13 fragments; one nonjoining sherd. Preservation 85%, including full profile; missing handle and part of neck and rim. H. 6.8; d. rim 3.1; d. base 1.8. Fine, soft, reddish-yellow (7.5YR 7/6) fabric, dark gray on interior. Traces of brown (7.5YR 4/4) paint. Very worn surface. Burned. *Comparanda*: **GR19 P14**. *Date*: LG.

GR17 P8 (V 4809.1; Fig. 102). Hydria. Represented by 51 fragments; 224 fragments of similar fabric may belong to it. Preservation 20%, including rim, lower neck with handle attachment, two round horizontal handles, base fragments. Max. pres. h. 5.5; d. rim est. 10.0–12.0; d. base est. 12.2. Fine, very soft and chalky, pale yellow (2.5Y 8/2) fabric. Black paint. Very worn surfaces. *Comparanda*: Brock 1957, 36, pl. 25:340, 342, 349 (Knossos, PGB); Tsipopoulou 2005, 163, fig. 43:AN2428 (Hagios Georgios, LG–EO); 159, fig. 49:AN2413 (Hagios Georgios, EO). *Date*: LG–EO.

Medium-Coarse Ware

GR17 P9 (V 4809.1; Fig. 103). Cup. Partially mended from 72 fragments. Fragments of rim and base preserved, plus three fragments of one handle. Max. pres. h. (rim) 3.0, (base) 2.5; d. rim est. 13.0–14.0; d. base est. 7.0–8.0. Medium-coarse, very soft, reddish-yellow (5YR 6/6) fabric with tiny white inclusions. Petrographic sample KAV 15/63: Fabric Group 2. Black paint? Very worn surfaces. Many fragments burned. LG.

Coarse Wares

GR17 P10 (V 4809.2; Fig. 103). Bowl. Two joining fragments from base, three fragments from rim, five nonjoining fragments. Max. pres. h. 7.5 (rim); d. rim est. 13.0; d. base est. 10.0. Coarse, light brown (7.5YR 6/4) fabric with frequent silvery inclusions; many holes where inclusions have burned out. Petrographic sample KAV 15/91: Fabric Subgroup 1a. Possibly slipped? Handmade. *Date*: FN–EM?

GR17 P11 (V 4809.2, V 4707.1, V 4752.2; Fig. 103). Basin. Partially mended into two large fragments, one from the base (six fragments) and one from the rim and handle (eight fragments); 86 other fragments, including second handle and rim fragments. Preservation: 24% of base and 50% of rim; missing most of middle body. Max. pres. h. 15.5; d. rim est. 30.0; d. base est. 16.0. Coarse, reddish-yellow (7.5YR 6/6) fabric, light red (2.5YR 6/8) on interior, gray at core; like Kavousi Type IV with phyllite and quartz inclusions. Petrographic sample KAV 15/62: small low-fired metamorphic group. Interior shows spalling. Worn surfaces with black mottling like the cookpots of this fabric from LM IIIC. Some burning. Interior is very rough. *Date*: LG.

Metal

Bronze

GR17 M1 (V88.139; V 4809.1, object 2; Fig. 103; Pl. 46D). Bronze pin. Three fragments preserving nearly full length, missing point. Max. pres. L. 8.7; d. disk 0.7. Corroded; biconical swelling has exploded. Long straight pin with biconical swelling surrounded by three rings; large disk with conical knob at top. *Date*: EO.

GR17 M2 (V88.222; V 4809.1; Fig. 103; Pl. 46D). Bronze pin. Complete in three fragments. L. 8.3; d. disk 0.6. Well-preserved surfaces; little corrosion. Long, straight pin with biconical swelling surrounded by three rings; large disk with conical knob at top. *Date*: EO.

GR17 M3 (V88.137; V 4809.1; Fig. 103; Pl. 46D). Bronze sheeting. Single fragment preserving three, possibly four, edges; no rivets. Max. pres. L. 3.6; max. pres. w. 2.2. One edge very corroded. Bent and worn. Roughly rectangular, with four holes for attaching to some other medium. *Comparanda*: **GR9 M5–GR9 M12**.

Iron

GR17 M4 (V88.99; V 4809.1, object 1; Fig. 103; Pl. 46D). Iron pin. Nearly complete in two joining fragments; missing disk and knob. Max. pres. L. 7.0. Corroded. Long pin; biconical swelling near top, with three rings on either side. *Date*: EO.

GR17 M5 (V88.104; V 4809.1, objects 3 and 7; Fig. 103; Pl. 46D). Iron pin. Nearly complete in two fragments; missing point. Max. pres. L. 7.9; d. disk 0.7. Corroded. Long pin; biconical swelling with three rings on either side. Disk and conical knob on top. *Date*: EO.

GR17 M6 (V88.94; V 4809.1, object 6; Fig. 104; Pl. 46D). Iron spearhead. Two nonjoining fragments, one (two joining and four nonjoining fragments) from socket, the other preserving the entire blade. Max. pres. L. (socket) 6.2, (blade) 9.7; d. socket 1.9. Corroded, but some surviving surfaces. Short (6.2) socket, with hole pierced opposite edges near end. Very short blade, possibly a javelin.

GR17 M7 (V88.103, HNM 15765; V 4809.2, object 9; Fig. 104; Pl. 46D). Iron sickle-shaped knife. Complete in four fragments; missing small chips from blade. L. 15.3; max. w. 1.9. Well-preserved surfaces with some corrosion. Curved blade with single edge on interior. Rounded end with one rivet hole pierced 2.0 cm from end and a possible second rivet on the rounded end. *Comparanda*: Snodgrass 1996, 587, type D.

Grave 19

History and Details of Excavation

Grave 19 is a stone-lined burial enclosure that lies on the southwest slope of the Vronda ridge within Room G1 of the LM IIIC shrine (Figs. 3, 4). It was excavated in 1988 and 1989 in Trench V 9400 (Gesell, Coulson, and Day 1991, 163). The grave appeared in the topsoil only 4 cm below the modern surface (V 9400). Excavation was made more difficult by large roots from a nearby tree that grew through the enclosure (Pl. 47A) and had clearly disturbed it. The enclosure lacked the soft, dark, ashy soil with stones found in most of the cremation burials but was distinguished by the presence of burned human bone and a large quantity of fine pottery. The pottery was collected in five clusters in the north and south ends of the grave: cluster 1 toward the southeast corner, cluster 2 in the north, cluster 3 in the northwest corner, cluster 4 in the northeast corner, and cluster 5 in the southwest corner. Because the burials were not found in anatomical order and all of the pottery showed signs of burning, it seems likely that the upper layers of the grave were disturbed by human activity or erosion, leaving only remains of the first four burials. Only two burials were recognized during excavation (A and B); a third was identified when the bones were washed and studied, while the remains of the fetus appeared in the residue from the water sieve in 1991.

In 1989 the north balk of V 9400 was removed, and more grave material appeared in V 9408 and V 9409. The grave was then dismantled in an attempt to find any undisturbed material from the earlier shrine; the south wall was removed as V 9411, the north wall (V 9413) was removed as V 9409.3, and the west wall (V 9414) was removed without any locus designation as there was no associated material. The bench from the LM IIIC shrine used in the grave was left in place.

Material from the grave was found in pockets on the bench (V 9404, V 9405), scattered to the south in Locus V 9403, and to the west in Trench V 9300. Fragments of pottery that joined to vessels found in the grave appeared on the surface to the southwest in V 9308, perhaps as a result of natural erosion down the slope, and in the north balk of V 9300 in V 9309 and V 9310 to the southwest and west of Grave 19.

Architecture

Grave 19 was a stone-lined burial enclosure oriented north–south and measuring 1.40–1.50 m north–south x 1.00–1.20 m east–west (Fig. 105). The grave made use of the bedrock face and the bench (V 9402) from the earlier shrine for its east side, and the burial continued to the east wall and over the bench. The north (V 9413), south (V 9411), and west (V 9414) walls consisted of single rows of boulders. The north wall of the grave was not the north wall of Room G1 of Building G, as was originally thought, but it lay south of the shrine wall. There had been much disturbance in the area before excavation began.

Stratigraphy

Grave 19 lay very close to the modern surface, and it had suffered considerable disturbance. It was very shallow; the total deposition was 0.20 m. It is probable that what was found represents the earliest burials in the grave, with all the later burials having been disturbed. Everything was found mixed up in the grave, although great care was taken to remove the pottery in clusters. Within the enclosure, the stratigraphy was simple. The grave was constructed on top of the clay from the collapsed roof of Room G1. At the bottom of the grave was a layer of cobbles that went below the west wall of the grave (V 9410, V 9412) but contained human bone. Above these cobbles was a layer that lay below the level of the bench along the east (V 9406) and was distinguished by its color, which was slightly lighter than the layer above it. From the level of the top of the bench to the surface, the soil was the same: dark yellowish brown (10YR 3/4) to dark brown (10YR 4/3) in color and crumbly with cobbles (V 9401, V 9408, V 9409), very unlike the usual dark ashy grave soil but not too different from the topsoil encountered all over the trench (V 9400, V 9407). Pottery came almost entirely in clusters in this crumbly soil (V 9401). In the northeast corner at the bottom was a patch of hard red clay, probably fired from the heat of the pyre, and above this patch was a lens of dark soft soil below cluster 4; it did not extend beyond the corner.

Associated Features

Pottery found in the area to the south of the shrine and Grave 19 in Trench V 8900 may have been dumped from Grave 19 during later burial events. The whole area had been disturbed by several other graves (Graves 26, 27, and 32) and by Venetian habitation. Fragments of Geometric pottery like the material from Grave 19 (but without joins) were found in V 8900, V 8902–V 8905, and especially V 8906. While V 8903 was a late terrace wall, the other loci preserved a disturbed layer of cobbles and boulders that may represent the same depositional layer as the rock tumble layer to the west and northwest. Fragments of a large decorated amphora (**GR19 P23**) found on the surface in V 8800 could have come from Grave 19. It is possible that this amphora stood as a marker for the grave, like the vessels associated with Graves 9, 12, 16, and 20. The pottery from the dump is cataloged separately following the catalog of finds from within Grave 19 below.

Burials

Four cremations were found in Grave 19. None was in anatomical order, suggesting that the last burial(s) had eroded away or been disturbed.

Burials 1 and 2

Type: disturbed primary cremations
Age: two adults, one 20–40 years
Sex: one unknown, one female?
Weight: 1,833 g

Burial 1 and Burial 2 were found commingled with their heads at the north end of the enclosure. An olive tree had grown into the grave, sending roots through the deposit and contributing to the fragmentation of the bones, to the point that very few pieces could even be identified. Some of the postcranial bone exhibits signs of having been burned twice. There are the curved, transverse cracks and warping associated with the burning of fleshed bodies. Over these cracks and breaks there is a network of checked cracks more indicative of dry bone burning (Fairgrieve 2008, 51–52; Symes et al. 2008, 42–46). As with Burials 2 and 3 from Grave 5, these patterns suggest that this bone was burned twice, once while the body was being cremated and again when a later cremation took place in the enclosure.

One of the individuals is a young adult, probably aged 20–40 years. The other is so fragmentary that no age estimation can be made. Neither skeleton could be sexed, although the presence of fetal bone (Burial 3, below) suggests that one is probably a female. One premolar recovered with these burials has three roots instead of the usual fused two. Other than this no remarkable features were noted on the bone.

Burial 3

Type: disturbed primary cremation
Age: fetus, 22–36 weeks
Sex: unknown
Weight: 10 g

This burial is a fetus, found in association with Burials 1 and 2. All of the fetal bone was found in the water sieve residue, and nearly all of it is completely calcined. The developmental age is between 20 and 32 weeks in utero.

Burial 4

Type: disturbed primary cremation
Age: adult, 60+ years
Sex: male
Weight: 1,218 g

Burial 4 is an older adult male. The bone from this burial is much less burned than that of Burials 1 and 2. Both the cranium and the postcranial elements are only discolored or scorched in some areas, while others show the dark gray color of initial calcination.

This man was probably quite elderly for the time, in excess of 60 years old, as indicated by the morphology of the auricular surface of the ilium. The lambdoid suture is almost completely obliterated, and the posterior dentition was missing antemortem from the preserved right maxilla. There was extensive periodontal disease and a dental abscess under the right maxillary canine as well.

Botanical Remains

One fragment of grass (*Gramineae*) and one wild buckwheat seed (*Polygonum convolvulus*) were found in Grave 19.

Pottery

Grave 19 yielded 962 fragments of pottery weighing 6.96 kg, of which only 2.68 kg represented pottery deposited in the grave; the rest was material in the soil from the shrine. An additional 50 fragments weighing 0.40 kg were recognized as possibly coming from this grave, although found downslope from Grave 19 to the south; these have been cataloged separately from the grave material. There seems to have been no meaningful pattern to the location of the pottery within the grave; joins were made between fragments found in clusters both in the north and south. It would appear that all of the material had been pushed aside to the north and south ends of the grave to make way for a later burial of which little now remains. None of the pottery can be associated with any specific burial, as the bones were also found pushed to the two ends of the grave. Fragments of two cups (**GR19 P7**, **GR19 P8**) were found in the very lowest levels of the grave, and they may belong to the earliest burial(s).

The assemblage is unusual for the number of aryballoi found in it. Only Grave 4 has a greater number. At least one aryballos (**GR19 P15**) has parallels in EG and MG Knossos (see below). Also unusual in shape are the wide-mouthed jugs (**GR19 P5**, **GR19 P6**). There were few traces of the large vessels that were found in and around the graves on the summit of the hill.

Objects

The only object found in the grave was a terracotta bead or spindle whorl (**GR19 TC1**).

Chronology

It is difficult to date the full range of use for this grave as the latest burial(s) may have disappeared. The three decorated skyphoi are helpful, however, in dating the assemblage. The shape of skyphos **GR19 P2** is typical of late MG Attic forms, and because of the lag in the adoption of Attic styles on Crete it cannot be earlier than the LG period. The decoration of skyphos **GR19 P3**, which is similar to that of **GR16 P15**, is common in LG East Crete (Tsipopoulou 2005, 134, fig. 117). The stemmed skyphos is also similar to other examples in the graves at Vronda (**GR1 P2, GR6 P2, GR6 P3, GR28 P1**), and its shape, too, is typical of LG East Crete (Tsipopoulou 2005, 412–413). One of the aryballoi (**GR19 P14**) is similar to an example from Grave 17, which is very late in the Vronda sequence. The monochrome cups may be earlier. Cups **GR19 P7** and **GR19 P8** both come from the lowest levels of the grave, and although they are similar to PGB–EG cups at Knossos, they are rather deep for that period and are more likely to be EG–MG, like examples from Eleutherna (Kotsonas 2008, 208–211). Cup **GR19 P16** is similar to Attic LPG shapes, but again, it is probably too deep for that date. These cups may have been manufactured in the Geometric period, but they may have been antiques. The burials in Grave 19 seem to belong to the LG period, but they may contain material that is earlier.

Catalog of Finds from Grave 19

Pottery

FINE DECORATED WARES

GR19 P1 (V 9400.5, V 9401.2 objects 1–3, V 9401.4–6; Fig. 106). Cup. Partially mended from 55 fragments. Preservation 30%, including 75% of base, 65% of rim, and most of handle; profile can be restored. H. 9.3; d. rim 11.0–12.0; d. base 5.5–6.0. Fine, soft, reddish-yellow (7.5YR 6/6) fabric. Red (2.5YR 5/6) paint. Worn surfaces. Some fragments burned. Vertical strokes on rim; underside of base painted. *Date*: LG.

GR19 P2 (V98.109; V 9401.2 object 3, V 9401.5; Fig. 106; Pl. 47C). Skyphos. Mended from 41 fragments. Preservation 75%, including full profile, most of base and lower body, 75% of upper body, and both handles; missing bits of one handle. H. 8.5; d. rim 13.7; d. base 6.2. Fine, soft, porous, very pale brown (10YR 7/3) fabric. Black to dark yellowish-brown (10YR 4/4) paint. Some well-preserved surfaces, others very worn. Some fragments burned. Metopal panel with dotted zigzag between bands; underside painted. *Bibliography*: Gesell, Coulson, and Day 1991, 163, pl. 63:h. *Comparanda*: Hayden 2003, 61–62, fig. 37:156, pl. 24 (Vrokastro, MG–LG); for shape, Coldstream and Catling, eds., 1996, 147, fig. 106:30 (Attic MG II); for the dotted zigzag, Brock 1957, 35, 38, pl. 26:361 (Knossos, PGB). *Date*: LG.

GR19 P3 (V98.108; V 9401.2 objects 2 and 3, V 9401.4–6; Fig. 106; Pl. 47C). Skyphos. Restored from 57 fragments; six nonjoining fragments. Preservation 95%; missing only a few bits of body and base. H. 8.5; d. rim 9.0; d. base 5.0. Fine, rather hard, reddish-yellow (5YR 7/6) fabric. Very pale brown (10YR 8/2) slip. Very worn surfaces; paint only appears as faint shadow. Many burned fragments, joining to unburned ones; a few places on body where vessel is flattened or scored. Metopal panel with thin horizontal bands. *Comparanda*: **GR16 P15**; Tsipopoulou 2005, 134, fig. 117:AN2385 (Hagios Georgios, LG). *Date*: LG.

GR19 P4 (V 9401.1, V 9401.2 SE, V 9401.2 objects 2–4, V 9401.4 object 5, V 9401.3 and 5, V 9409.1; Fig. 106). Stemmed skyphos. Partially mended from 48 fragments into three fragments: one from base, two from rim and handle. Preservation 40%, including full profile, most of base, 30% of rim, and both handles. H. 11.7; d. rim 11.4; d. base 4.9. Fine, very soft, porous, light gray (5Y 7/1) to very pale brown (10YR 8/3) fabric with many voids and some tiny white inclusions. Black paint. Very worn surfaces. Much burning. Metopal panel with horizontal bands and oblique strokes. *Comparanda*: **GR6 P3, GR6 P4, GR28 P1**; Tsipopoulou 2005, 189, fig. 108:Σ4074 (Hagios Georgios, LG); 315, fig. 108:AN1448 (Zou, LG); 155, fig. 108:AN2319 (Hagios Georgios, LG). *Date*: LG.

GR19 P5 (V98.112; V 9401.2 object 3, V 9401.1, V 9401.4 object 5; Fig. 106; Pl. 47C). Wide-mouthed jug. Mended from 40 fragments. Preservation 90%; missing bits of rim and body. H. 12.0; d. rim 7.9; d. base 5.5. Fine, soft, chalky, pink (7.5YR 8/4) fabric. Black paint. Very worn surfaces. Many fragments burned or discolored. Horizontal bands on shoulder? Rather irregular in shape. *Comparanda*: Brock 1957, 155, pl. 34:449 (Knossos, PGB–MG); Sakellarakis 1986, 45–46, fig. 41, pls. 55, 56 (Archanes, PGB–MG); Coldstream and Catling, eds., 1996, 184, fig. 119:6 (Knossos, LG); 262, pl. 239:18 (MG); Tsipopoulou 2005, 180, fig. 89:Σ4030 (Hagios Georgios, LG). *Date*: LG.

GR19 P6 (V 9401.2 objects 2 and 3, V 9401.4–6; Fig. 106). Wide-mouthed jug. Partially mended from 39 fragments. Preservation 25%, including bits of base, shoulder, rim, and large part of handle and shoulder; missing full profile and upper handle. H. est. 16.7; d. rim est. 10.0; d. base est. 6.9. Fine, soft, porous, very pale brown (10YR 7/4) fabric. Red (2.5YR 4/6) paint. Very worn surfaces. Surface cracked, flaking, and almost vitrified. On shoulder: large central vertical strokes surrounded by smaller ones. *Comparanda*: Coldstream and Catling, eds., 1996, 143, fig. 105:81 (MG–LG); Tsipopoulou 2005, 150, 173, fig. 90:AN1797, Σ3935 (Hagios Georgios, LG). *Date*: LG.

Fine Monochrome Wares

GR19 P7 (V98.110; V 9401.2 objects 2 and 3, V 9401.2 SE, V 9401.3 object 4, V 9401.5 and 6, V 9406.2 V 9409.1; Fig. 106; Pl. 47C). Cup. Mended from 45 fragments. Preservation 85%, including full profile, 50% of base, most of rim and handle; missing half of base, bits of rim, lower handle attachment. H. 8.3; d. rim 12.3; d. base 4.9. Fine, rather hard, reddish-yellow (5YR 7/6) fabric. Black paint on interior, exterior, and underside of base. Surfaces very worn. Most fragments burned or discolored by fire. Groove on exterior of rim. *Comparanda*: Coldstream and Catling, eds., 1996, 233, fig. 135:283.3 (Knossos, PGB–EG). *Date*: G.

GR19 P8 (V98.111; V 9401.2 objects 2–4; V 9401.4 object 5, V 9401.5, V 9401.8, V 9406.2; Fig. 106; Pl. 47C). Cup. Mended from 50 fragments, 85% preserved; missing 25% of base, part of lower body, and lower part of handle. H. 8.7; d. rim 13.3; d. base 6.2. Fine, rather hard, reddish-yellow (5YR 7/6) fabric. Black paint on interior, exterior, and underside of base. Very worn surfaces. A few burned fragments. *Date*: G.

GR19 P9 (V 9401.2 objects 2 and 3, V 9401.2A, V 9401.4 object 5, V 9401.5, V 9401.7, V 9408.1; Fig. 106). Cup. Partially mended from 21 fragments into five large fragments from rim and body; missing base and most of handle. Max. pres. h. 7.0; d. rim 14.0. Fine, soft, reddish-yellow (7.5YR 7/6) fabric with very pale brown (10YR 8/3) surface. Traces of brown paint. Very worn surfaces. Many fragments burned, joining to unburned pieces. *Date*: G.

GR19 P10 (V 9400.1, V 9401.1, V 9401.4, V 9409.2, V 9308.4, V 9310.4, V 9309.1 V 8906.2; Fig. 107). Cup or skyphos. Partially mended from 12 fragments from near rim to near base; two rim fragments probably do not belong. Max. pres. h. 8.0. Fine, soft, light red (2.5YR 6/6) fabric. Black paint, worn to brown shadow. Very worn surfaces. No burning. *Date*: G.

GR19 P11 (V 9401.2 object 1, V 9401.4 object 5, V 9401.5 object 2, V 9309.1; Fig. 107). Cup or skyphos. Partially mended from six fragments from rim and base; missing full profile and handle(s). Max. pres. h. 3.5; d. rim est. 13.0; d. base est. 6.0. Fine, soft, reddish-yellow (5YR 7/6) fabric. Red (2.5YR 5/8) paint. *Date*: LG.

GR19 P12 (V 9401.2, object 3; Fig. 107). Open vessel, possibly cup or skyphos. Six fragments preserving entire base. D. base 6.0. Fine, very soft and chalky, yellow (10YR 8/6) fabric. Washy red (2.5YR 5/6) paint. Some fragments burned. *Date*: uncertain.

Fine Plain Wares

GR19 P13 (V98.114; V 9401.2 object 1, V 9401.4 SW; Fig. 107). Aryballos. Mended from 26 fragments. Preservation 90%, including entire body; missing neck, rim, and handle. H. est. 5.3; d. base 2.2. Fine, rather hard, light gray (5Y 7/1) fabric, gray (5YR 6/1) on interior. Well-preserved, polished surfaces. Totally burned. *Comparanda*: Coldstream and Catling, eds., 1996, 113, pl. 123:86 (Knossos, MG). *Date*: LG.

GR19 P14 (V 9401.2 object 1, V 9401.3, V 9401.4; Fig. 107). Aryballos. Partially mended from nine fragments. Preservation 30%, including profile from base to neck with handle attachment and bit of rim; missing most of handle and neck. Max. pres. h. 5.0; d. base 2.0. Fine, soft, light gray (5Y 7/1) to gray (2.5Y 5/0) fabric. Worn surfaces, but some polishing preserved. Totally burned. *Comparanda*: **GR17 P7**; for shape, Kotsonas 2008, 175, 178, fig. 42:A145β (Eleutherna, PGB). *Date*: LG.

GR19 P15 (V98.113; V 9401.2; Fig. 107). Aryballos. Partially mended from 25 fragments. Preservation 90%, including full profile, handle, and base; missing rim. Max. pres. h. (with handle) 6.4; d. base 2.5. Fine, soft fabric, light gray (5Y 7/1) on interior, reddish yellow (5YR 6/6) on exterior. Pinkish-white (7.5YR 8/2) slip. Very worn surfaces. No burning. *Comparanda*: Coldstream and Catling, eds., 1996, 236, pl. 218:85 (Knossos, MG); 254, pl. 231:286.4 (Knossos, EG); Tsipopoulou 2005, 170, fig. 100:Σ3921 (Hagios Georgios, LG). *Date*: LG.

Medium-Coarse Monochrome Wares

GR19 P16 (V 9401.2 objects 2 and 3, V 9401.4 object 5, V 9401.4; Fig. 107). Cup. Mended from 31 fragments. Preservation 30%, including full profile, entire base, 25% of upper body and rim, part of handle. H. 8.4; d. rim 10.3; d. base 4.8. Medium-coarse, porous, very pale brown (10YR 7/3) fabric with tiny black inclusions. Black paint. Worn surfaces. Some fragments burned. *Comparanda*: **GR4 P22**, **GR9 P42**; Coldstream and Catling, eds., 1996, 29, fig. 65:47 (Knossos, Attic LPG); Kotsonas 2008, 201, 204, fig. 50: 209δ (Eleutherna, PGB–EG). *Date*: G.

GR19 P17 (V 9401.3 object 4, V 9401.2 objects 2 and 3, V 9401.5; Fig. 107). Cup. Partially mended from 40 fragments. Preservation 75% of base, 25% of rim, and two handle fragments; base and rim may not be from same vessel. Max. pres. h. 6.3; d. rim 13.4; d. base 5.8. Medium-coarse, reddish-yellow (7.5YR 7/6) fabric with mica and clay pellets. Petrographic sample KAV 15/64: off-island import? Black paint. Very worn surfaces, especially on base. A few fragments burned. *Comparanda*: Coldstream 1972, 87, fig. 8:F18 (Knossos, LG–EO). *Date*: LG.

GR19 P18 (V 9400, V 9401.1, V 9401.2, V 9401.3 object 4, V 9401.4, V 9409.7; Fig. 107). Cup or skyphos. Partially mended from 10 fragments, preserving half of base and bits of rim and body. Max. pres. h. 6.6; d. rim 13.7; d. base 8.6. Medium-coarse, reddish-yellow (5YR 6/6) fabric with phyllites, carbonates, and hard white bits. Some places burned gray. Black paint? *Date*: LG.

GR19 P19 (V 9401.2 objects 2 and 3, V 9401.5; Fig. 107). Cup or skyphos. Partially mended from 18 fragments. Entire base preserved and a piece of rim; missing handle. Max. pres. h. 4.5; d. rim 13.0; d. base 5.3. Medium-coarse, soft, reddish-yellow (5YR 7/6–7.5YR 7/6) fabric with phyllites and hard gray inclusions. Red (2.5YR 4/6) paint. Worn surfaces. One fragment from base burned. *Date*: LG.

Terracotta

GR19 TC1 (V88.76, IM 1005; V 9401.2, object 2; Fig. 107; Pl. 47C). Terracotta bead. Biconical. Intact. H. 1.9; max. d. 2.9; d. hole 0.4. Wt. 11.00 g. Fine, soft, porous, pink (7.5YR 7/4) fabric with some tiny inclusions. Possible traces of very pale brown slip. Gray from burning on one side. Worn surfaces. Hole on one side slightly larger where instrument pushed through from inside.

Catalog of Finds from the Dump

Pottery

Fine Decorated Wares

GR19 P20 (V 8906.1, V 8906.4 and 5, V 8902.2, V 8903.1, V 8905.4; Fig. 107). Cup. Partially mended from 15 fragments. Preservation 75% of base, entire handle, four fragments from shelf, and one rim fragment. Max. pres. h. 3.0; d. rim 13.0; d. base 7.0. Fine, soft, porous, light reddish-brown (5YR 6/4) fabric with tiny, black inclusions and voids. Black paint worn to shadow. Worn surfaces. Uncertain date.

Medium-Coarse Decorated

GR19 P21 (V 8900.1, V 8901.1 V 8906.1; Fig. 107). Lid. Large fragment from rim; one nonjoining rim fragment. Max. pres. h. 2.6; d. rim (int.) 14.4. Medium-coarse, porous, chalky, reddish-yellow (7.5YR 8/6–7/6) fabric with phyllites and mica. Dark brown (7.5YR 3/2) paint. Very worn surfaces. *Comparanda*: Tsipopoulou 2005, 186, fig. 141:Σ4059 (Hagios Georgios, EO). *Date*: LG–EO.

GR19 P22 (V 8900.1, V 8903.1, V 8906.1 and 2, V 8907.2, V 8910.1, V 8724.1; Fig. 107). Jug or amphora. Represented by 32 fragments from rim, base, and body of large closed vessel. Preservation 20% of base and 10% of rim and neck. Max. pres. h. 6.2; d. rim 12.0; d. base est. 8.0. Medium-coarse, soft, chalky, porous, light brown (7.5YR 6/4) to reddish-yellow (7.5YR 7/6) fabric with frequent silver mica inclusions. Black paint. Very worn surfaces. Petrographic sample PMD 98/50. Shape uncertain; ring base, closed neck and mouth; handle attachment for horizontal handle. *Date*: LG–EO.

GR19 P23 (V 8900 surface; Fig. 107). Amphora or pithos. Two large fragments (seven sherds) from body. Max. pres. h. 6.3; max. pres. th. 1.8. Medium-coarse, soft, reddish-yellow (5YR 7/6) fabric with infrequent large red phyllite inclusions and chaff voids. Very pale brown (10YR 8/3) slip. Black paint worn to shadow. Worn surfaces. Hatched upright bars (possibly a meander), butterfly between uprights, hatched zigzag, possible checkerboard. *Comparanda*: for the butterfly, see Coldstream and Catling, eds., 1996, 19, pl. 58:83 (Knossos, Attic MG I); for the hatched zigzag or triangle, see Tsipopoulou 2005, 202, fig.13:H3182 (Adromyloi, LG); Rethemiotakis and Englezou 2010, 59, fig. 29:59 (Eltyna, PGB–LPG). *Date*: LG.

Grave 20

History and Details of Excavation

Grave 20 lies on the northern summit of the Vronda ridge, just to the west of Graves 10 and 17 and between LM IIIC Buildings J and C (Figs. 3, 4; Gesell, Coulson, and Day 1991, 156). It was excavated in 1988 in Trench V 4700. Grave 20 was a built rectangular enclosure that was identifiable immediately below the surface on the basis of the soft, dark, ashy soil with stone rubble and snail shells that characterize the cremation burials, particularly on the summit of the Vronda ridge. There was little deposition on top of the hill, and the grave was much disturbed; the southwest corner was almost entirely eroded away. Much associated pottery was actually found outside the grave, particularly to the west and south where the walls had disappeared and so did not contain the material within the enclosure. After the removal of the layer of stones over the grave (V 4701), it was excavated by anthropological assistants in three sections: the dark brown soil on the south (V 4703), the very black soil in the middle (V 4704), and the dark brown soil on the north (V 4705), similar to that found on the south. Another layer of harder dark brown soil was excavated underneath these three areas (V 4709) down to bedrock, although there was some mixing with the soil from V 4703 and V 4705. Four burials were recognized at the time of excavation, labeled A–D; subsequent study has identified a total of seven individuals. The areas around the grave were also excavated and produced grave material: the western and southern part of the trench (V 4702), the west wall (V 4708), the east wall (V 4706), and the area beyond this wall to the east (V 4707).

In 1992 the east balk of this trench was removed (V 4750), and much material was recovered between Graves 20 and 10 (V 4752). Some of this material seems to have come from Grave 20, while at least one vessel has joins with Grave 17. The area was much disturbed, and it is difficult to separate out the various different burial activities here.

Architecture

Grave 20 is a stone-lined rectangular burial enclosure, oriented north–south and measuring 1.75–1.88 m north–south x 0.93–1.08 m east–west (Fig. 108; Pl. 47B). It used an existing wall from LM IIIC Building J as its eastern boundary (V 4706), but the other walls seem to have been constructed for its use as a burial site. The north wall (V 4710) was originally thought to have been an earlier house wall as well, but it is not oriented with either Building C or Building J and is more likely to have been constructed for the burial; it rises two to three courses high. The east wall (V 4706), only a single course high, has two good faces. The west (V 4708) and south (V 4711) walls are each made up of a single row of boulders.

The north wall is different from the others and the usual walls of the burial enclosures. The actual wall is formed by a row of small limestone blocks, and there is a large breccia boulder to the north of them. The space between the enclosure face and the boulder is filled with flat cobbles. The boulder may have formed part of the wall; the east wall of the enclosure seems to end at the north side of the boulder. If so, then this wall was a very thick, some 1.25 m wide. The southwest corner of the enclosure is missing, and a spur of bedrock runs through the area. The stones of all the walls are fissured or calcined from the intense heat of the cremation fire.

Stratigraphy

There was little deposition because of erosion and later disturbance. The bottom of the grave lay within 0.40 m of the surface in the northeast and along the east, and the grave was shallower in the south and west. The walls and the first burial(s) were made directly on the bedrock. Burials 1–3 were found in the hard brown soil that represents the lowest level of the grave (V 4709) and also in very black soil in the center of the grave (V 4704). Subsequent burials (Burials 4 and 5) were later pushed to the north and south (V 4705) or to the south (Burial 6; V 4703) in dark brown soil. The final burial (Burial 7) was found in the center of the grave in the soft, black, ashy soil (V 4704). Above these burial remains was a layer of stones (V 4701), with topsoil above (V 4700) and a modern rock pile.

Associated Features

The area immediately to the east of Grave 20 produced a good deal of material from several graves, including Grave 20. The soil in the area (V 4707, V 4752) was dark and soft with many stones, and it looked like dumped material from one or possibly several of the graves. No human remains were recovered from this deposit. Pottery may have been displayed here, as large vessels were prominent among the finds.

Burials

Seven burials were made in the enclosure. All lay close to the surface and were very disturbed.

Burials 1, 2, and 3

Type: disturbed primary cremations
Age: adults
Sex: male, male(?), female
Weight: 1,461 g

The three cremated individuals designated Burials 1–3 were found commingled at the bottom of the enclosure. All of the postcranial bone is completely calcined and white. Two of the crania, the two males, are much less thoroughly cremated. The third cranium is completely calcined.

The cranium of one individual was found at the center of the north end of the enclosure, and portions of the mandible, the right half of the pectoral girdle, the cervical and thoracic vertebrae, and the left and right ribs were found articulated, resting on the bottom of the tomb in ashy soil. There was no other articulation preserved, and the rest of this skeleton presumably was disturbed by subsequent burials. It is unusual at Vronda for any but the latest cremation in an enclosure to preserve articulated or anatomically arranged bone. When the bone collected with this burial was inventoried, it proved to contain a minimum of three individuals. The association of these other individuals with the articulated skeleton is unknown. All of these individuals were adults, one definite male, one possible male, and one very small female. One of the males was quite elderly, 60 or more years old. The cranial vault sutures are obliterated, and all of the anterior maxillary teeth were missing before death.

There are some pathological conditions on these skeletons. One of the crania has extensive porosity on the parietals and occipital, suggesting an earlier bout of anemia. A right mandibular condyle with lipping on the joint surface indicates that one of the individuals suffered from temporo-mandibular joint (TMJ) problems. Above the left orbit of one of the crania there are a total of six supraorbital foramina. This is an unusual anomaly, but probably not pathological.

Burial 4

Type: disturbed primary cremation
Age: fetus, 18–22 weeks
Sex: unknown
Weight: 14 g

Burial 4 is a cremated fetus found in the water sieve residue from Grave 20. The bone is completely calcined, with the exception of the preserved fibula shaft, which is barely scorched and provides the best estimation of age. The size of the bone is consistent with an 18–22-week-old fetus. In addition to the fibula shaft, cranial vault fragments, a petrous portion of the temporal bone, the greater wing of the sphenoid, ribs, and the dens of the second cervical vertebra were identified.

Burial 5

Type: disturbed primary cremation
Age: adult, 60+
Sex: male
Weight: 376 g

Burial 5 is an adult male with a rugged cranium with well-developed muscle markings and a projecting glabella (Buikstra and Ubelaker, eds,. 1994, 24–32). The head of this burial was found in the north end of the enclosure. The cranial vault is mottled and only slightly burned, but the facial bones are completely calcined. The postcranial bones are more thoroughly burned, but not completely calcined. This individual was probably 60 or more years old, based on the obliteration of the cranial vault sutures and the numerous teeth missing antemortem. There is evidence of periodontal disease on the maxilla and mandibula and extensive porosity of the outer table of the skull. The inner and outer tables of the skull had separated during cremation, and it was not possible to tell if there was any associated thickening of the cranial bone, as may occur in severe anemia. There are large pores present on the inner table of the frontal bone. The articular tubercle of the left zygomatic arch is also quite porous. The most likely cause of this porosity is some form of anemia, but metabolic disease such as scurvy is also possible. The appearance of the bone suggests that there has been remodeling since the condition occurred, suggesting that it was a transient stress from which the individual recovered.

Burial 6

Type: disturbed primary cremation
Age: adult
Sex: male
Weight: 1,715 g

This burial is a disturbed primary cremation of an adult male. It is not possible to estimate an age for the skeleton. The cremation is mixed, from completely calcined to barely scorched. The only anomaly on the skeleton is a very large frontal crest, 6.10 mm high at its base on the interior side of the frontal bone. The significance of this, if any, is unknown.

Burial 7

Type: disturbed primary cremation
Age: adult, 45–50 years
Sex: male
Weight: 1,855 g

Burial 7 is an adult male. The appearance of the skeleton is mottled, with no definite patterns of burning. The right temporal bone is much less burned than the left. A fragment of the pubic symphysis exhibits the morphology of individuals 45–50 years old. There is periosteal bone on the tibia shafts, probably associated with a systemic bacterial infection. Pitting on the anterior facet of the atlas vertebrae, as well as other vertebral facets, indicates extensive, but typical, osteoarthritis, which would be expected in an individual of this age.

Faunal Remains

The scattered animal bone fragments recovered from the area of Grave 20 appear to represent both possible sacrificial remains and intrusive general site debris (Table 8). Sheep or goat remains include both cranial and postcranial fragments. Burned fragments that might be remains of sacrificial deposits include part of a right distal humerus and an isolated incisor, both from a young animal. In addition, a left patella represents a possible hind limb segment.

Unburned elements, which may or may not represent deliberately deposited remains, include fragments of four hind limb elements and a fragment of a left distal humerus epiphysis. The presence of both juvenile and adult sheep or goat elements, along with one burned and one unburned second and third carpal, indicate that a minimum of at least three animals are represented. In addition, two domestic pig femur diaphysis fragments, one burned and one unburned, and two unburned rabbit or hare elements were recovered.

Botanical Remains

Grave 20 produced a large number of botanical remains, including olive (*Olea europaea*), grape (*Vitis vinifera*), pistachio (*Pistacia vera*), *Vicia/Lathyrus*, legume, fool's parsley (*Aethusa cymapium*), and small medick (*Medicago* sp.). The olive may have been used as fuel, while the grape seeds may have come from grave offerings of grapes or raisins. The legume and pistachio may be part of a funeral meal or provisions for the dead. The fool's parsley and medick may have been placed on the grave for their medicinal properties or for their flowers, or perhaps they represent weeds present on the cremation site.

Pottery

Grave 20 produced approximately 2,000 fragments of pottery weighing 27.60 kg, in addition to sherds collected from the surface and in spills to the east and west (465 fragments weighing 11.85 kg). In all, 21 vessels, mended from 928 fragments weighing 9.79 kg, were identified as coming from this grave; the amphora **GR20 P7** made up 60% of these vessels by count and 73% by weight. It is difficult to associate pottery with individual burials in Grave 20 because of the disturbance. No vessels can be assigned with certainty to the first three burials. A few vessels recovered in V 4704 may have belonged with one of these burials, as there was some mingling of bones from Burials 1–3 and Burial 7 in this locus. Vessels that show signs of burning may have come from the earlier burials, including skyphos **GR20 P2**, cups **GR20 P10** and **GR20 P12**, and lid **GR20 P4**.

Pottery that came primarily from this locus but was not burned may have belonged with Burial 7, including monochrome cups **GR20 P9** and possibly **GR20 P15**. Vessels possibly to be associated with Burial 5 (i.e., found at least in part in V 4705) include a small krater **GR20 P11** and a wide-mouthed jug **GR20 P16**. Cup **GR20 P13** and lid **GR20 P18** came from the upper level of the grave but were burned, and they may have been connected with Burials 5 or 6. A large amphora (**GR20 P7**) was found in the southeast corner of the grave, although fragments were spread throughout the area; this vessel may have belonged with Burials 5 or 6.

Pots found scattered outside the grave may have come from any of the first six burials, including two necked jars (**GR20 P5**, **GR20 P6**), a kalathos (**GR20 P17**), and two closed vessels (**GR20 P20**, **GR20 P21**). Pots that can be associated with the last burial in the grave, those found in the upper rock fill of the grave and not burned, include several cups (**GR20 P1**, **GR20 P3**, **GR20 P9**) and a possible jug (**GR20 P8**).

Cup **GR20 P1** was recognized as one of the few definite imports into Vronda, with many parallels in the early LG phase at Knossos (Brock 1957, 45, pl. 35:420; Coldstream 1972, 94, pl. 28:G87; Coldstream and Catling, eds., 1996, 114, fig. 95:112; 143, fig. 105:96; 176, pl. 173:40). A similar cup also appeared in Grave 27 (**GR27 P1**; see below). The petrographic analysis suggests, however, that it came from the south coast area rather than Knossos. Two ledge-rim cups or skyphoi (**GR20 P12, GR20 P15**) are similar to cups from the upper burials in Grave 9 (**GR9 P17–GR9 P19**) and possibly imitate Attic MG I types (Coldstream and Catling, eds., 1996, 18–19, fig. 60:71, 74; 37, fig. 68:18).

Of the two necked jars, one (**GR20 P5**) is of an early shape with LPG parallels at Knossos (Coldstream and Catling, eds., 1996, 42–43, fig. 69:O37) and others of EG date (Coldstream and Catling, eds., 1996, 34, pl. 69:19; 170, fig. 121:129.5). There are also PGB examples from East Crete (Tsipopoulou 2005, 89, fig.1:H698; 349, fig. 1:H1937). The other necked jar (**GR20 P6**), while similar, is closer to MG and LG types (see below). A closed vessel of uncertain shape (**GR20 P20**) is decorated with a band of upright concentric semicircles that imitates an earlier PG form of decoration (Coldstream and Catling, eds., 1996, 6, fig. 58:26, 27; 32, pl. 67:7; 215, pl. 199:18; 248, pl. 228:141; Callaghan and Johnston 2000, 225, pl. 4.5:129).

The amphora **GR20 P7** is irregular in shape, but it is similar to MPG–EG examples from Knossos, MG examples from Vrokastro, and LG specimens from East Crete (see below). The shape does not give a precise date, but the only example with simple handles comes from EG Knossos. The decoration is unfortunately not well enough preserved to help with the dating. The mend holes on the neck suggest that this vessel was already old enough to require repair when used in the grave. The lid **GR20 P18**, with its S-pattern, has parallels at MG and early LG Knossos (Coldstream and Catling, eds., 1996, 115, pl. 124:138, 140; 156, pl. 159:132).

In addition to the cataloged pottery, there were fragments of other vessels within the grave and outside it, particularly in the area just to the east of the grave (V 4750–V 4752). There were rim fragments of a large but fine-walled pyxis or krater, along with many other fragments of large fine or medium-coarse vessels that may have come from one of the large pots in Grave 20 or Grave 17. The surfaces of these vessels are so soft that it is impossible to make out any decoration, and there are few diagnostic fragments.

Objects

There were few objects considering the number of burials in Grave 20, but others may have disappeared because of its proximity to the surface. Most of the metal objects were found at the north end of the grave, where the depth of deposition was greater. The two fibulae (**GR20 M1, GR20 M2**) are of the twisted bow type, which is generally early SM–EPG. Catling (1996a, 551) dates this type of simple arch-bow fibula, whether twisted or plain, to the SM period, although Efi Sapouna-Sakellaraki (1978, 51) suggests that it continues into LG times. Of the two examples of bronze sheeting, **GR20 M3** is very similar to those in Grave 9, while **GR20 M4** is unique at Vronda; it may have served as a facing for a rectangular or leaf-shaped object, possibly the handle of a knife or other tool. The two iron pins are of similar size and shape (**GR20 M5, GR20 M6**) and are probably a matched pair. The two iron spearheads (**GR20 M7, GR20 M8**) are short and have the rounded shoulders often found on javelins, although both have a more pronounced midrib than is usual for the Kavousi leaf-shaped javelins. Of the two knives, one (**GR20 M9**) is of Snodgrass type A (1996, 585–586), while the other (**GR20 M10**) is Snodgrass type D (1996, 586). One possible awl was cataloged (**GR20 M11**).

In addition to the cataloged metal objects, there were several fragments of possible pins, at least two of bronze (these may also have come from one of the fibulae) and one or two of iron. There were also other fragments of what might have been awls or some sort of iron tools, but these were not cataloged as they were small, fragmentary, and had few if any preserved edges.

Other objects found in the grave include two beads. A bead of bone or ivory (**GR20 B1**) is very badly burned. A tiny disk-shaped bead of stone (**GR20 S1**) found in the water-sieved material is probably one of many that once made up a necklace.

Chronology

Cup **GR20 P1**, set in a niche on top of the north wall of the enclosure, gives a good early LG date for one of the burials in the grave, but it is uncertain if the cup belongs with Burial 5 or 7. The amphora **GR20**

P7 is of EG–MG style at Knossos, but the evidence for repair suggests it may be an older piece reused in the burial. Much of the other pottery from all areas of the grave is of PG style, but because of the lag in adopting Geometric styles at Kavousi, it may still date to the later eighth century. The flaring rim of **GR20 P10** is similar to LPG–PGB dipped cups at Knossos (Coldstream and Catling, eds., 1996, 18, fig. 60:67) and Eleutherna (Kotsonas 2008, 198, 202, fig. 48). Grave 20, then, is certainly earlier than Grave 17 and possibly earlier than Grave 12. Its relationship to Grave 10 is uncertain, but it would appear that the walls of Grave 10 rest on fill containing pottery from Grave 20, suggesting that Grave 20 was in use before Grave 10. The presence of the ledge-rim cups suggests that Grave 20 dates to the same phase as the later burials in Grave 9. There is some general similarity in assemblages between Graves 9 and 20 (the ledge-rim cups, the amphorae, the bronze sheeting), but it is difficult to know whether this similarity is indicative of date or whether it suggests social standing or kinship.

Of the other objects, the fibulae with twisted bows (**GR20 M1**, **GR20 M2**) are generally early, of SM or EPG date, but they may be antiques or heirloom pieces, as nothing that early has been found in the ceramic assemblage from the grave.

Catalog

Pottery

Fine Light-on-Dark Wares

GR20 P1 (V98.116; V 4700.1, V 4701.1 and 2, 4705.1 and 2, 4752.2–4; Fig. 109). Cup. Mended into two large fragments from rim (13 sherds); 18 nonjoining sherds. Preservation 50%, including one handle; missing base. Max. pres. h. 8.0; d. rim 12.0. Fine, rather hard, reddish-yellow (5YR 7/6) fabric; some fragments soft. Petrographic sample KAV 15/66: Fabric Group 6. Thick, glossy paint, reddish brown (5YR 4/4) to yellowish red (5YR 4/6) to black. Very well-preserved surfaces. In handle zone vertical strokes, alternating three narrow and one broad, in a triglyph-metope arrangement. Reserved band on interior of rim. *Bibliography*: Gesell, Coulson, and Day 1991, 156, pl. 60:f. *Date*: LG.

GR20 P2 (V 4701.1 and 2, V 4702.3, V 4704.2 and 3, V 4705.2; Fig. 109). Skyphos. Partially mended into two large fragments, one from base and rim (10 sherds), the other from rim and handle (eight sherds); three nonjoining fragments. Preservation 75%, including full profile, entire base, 75% of rim, and both handles. H. 7.0; d. rim 8.4; d. base 4.5. Fine, soft, reddish-yellow (5YR 7/6) fabric. Black paint. Very worn surfaces. Mostly burned. Short pendant strokes from rim, horizontal bands below. Decoration only preserved where burning has turned slip black and paint white. *Comparanda*: for shape, Coldstream and Catling, eds., 1996, 21, fig. 63:126 (Knossos, EG). *Date*: LG.

GR20 P3 (V 4700.1; Fig. 109). Cup or skyphos. Single fragment preserving entire base. D. base 5.5. Fine, soft reddish-yellow (7.5YR 8/6) fabric and slip. Red (2.5YR 5/8) to black paint. Horizontal bands. *Date*: LG.

GR20 P4 (V 4701.2, V 4706.2, V 4707.2, V 4752.2–4; Fig. 109). Lid. Partially mended from eight fragments; 13 nonjoining fragments, including top. Preservation includes 20% of rim, a bit of top; missing handle. Max. pres. h. 6.5; d. rim 19.0. Fine, soft, reddish-yellow (7.5YR 7/6) fabric. Reddish-yellow (7.5YR 8/6) slip. Black paint worn to shadow. Very worn surfaces. Many fragments burned. Strokes on rim. Curvilinear motif on top. *Comparanda*: Tsipopoulou 2005, 151, fig. 141:AN1808 (Hagios Georgios, EO). *Date*: LG.

GR20 P5 (V 4700.1, V 4701.1 and 2, V 4702.1, V 4702.3, V 4703.1 and 2, V 4804.4, V 5201.1B; Fig. 110). Necked jar. Partially mended, 30% preserved, including 25% of base, 50% of rim, one handle and most of another, assorted body fragments. H. est. 27.0; d. rim (int.) 11.2; d. base 16.0. Fine, rather hard, pink (5YR 7/4) fabric with infrequent dark gray inclusions. Pale yellow (2.5Y 8/2) slip. Black paint. Worn surfaces. No burning. Wheel ridging on interior. Concentric circles on shoulder. Bands below. *Comparanda*: for shape and decoration, Brock 1957, 24, pl. 14:206 (Knossos, MPG); Sakellarakis 1986, 19, fig. 3, pl. 9 (Archanes, EPG–MG); for shape, Coldstream and Catling, eds., 1996, 16, pl. 52:12; 227, fig. 133:229.18 (Knossos, EG); Kotsonas 2008, 105–106, fig. 17:A143 (Eleutherna, EG); Rethemiotakis and Englezou 2010, 97, fig. 52:131 (Eltyna, EPG). *Date*: G.

GR20 P6 (V 4700.1, V 4701.2, V 4702.3, V 4752.4; Fig. 110). Necked jar. Represented by 16 fragments from rim, shoulder, handle, and part of lower body; missing one handle and base. D. rim (int.) 11.4. Fine, rather hard, reddish-yellow (5YR 7/6) fabric with light reddish-brown (5YR 6/4) core. Crackled black paint. Well-preserved surfaces. No burning. Small concentric circles on shoulder. Band in added white on lower body. No burning. *Comparanda*: **GR20 P5**; Callaghan and Johnston 2000, 239, pl. 4.10:262 (Kommos, MG); Kotsonas 2008, 112, 115, fig. 20:A118, A133 (Eleutherna, LG). *Date*: G.

GR20 P7 (V98.115; V 4701.1 and 2, V 4703.1–3, V 4800.4, V 5321, V 5309; Fig. 110; Pl. 48). Amphora. Restored from 553 fragments. Preservation 75%, including full profile, most of base and rim, both handles; missing fragments of neck and body. Many other fragments from V 4707 and V 4752 may belong. H. 68.0; d. rim (int.) 24.0; d. base 16.5. Fine, very soft, reddish-yellow (5YR 7/6) fabric (needed consolidation so edges would hold together). Petrographic sample KAV 15/65: Fabric Subgroup 1b. Pink (7.5YR 8/4) to very pale brown (10YR

8/2) slip. Shadow of once black paint. Very worn surfaces. Many fragments burned, but joining to unburned ones. Restored shape very uneven, partially because of difficulties in restoration, but also in its original state. Drill holes in neck indicate mending in antiquity. Vertical strokes on neck. Checkerboard on body. *Comparanda*: Hood and Boardman 1961, 72, pl. 9:3 (Knossos, EG); Hayden 2003, 63, no. 160, fig. 38 (Vrokastro, MG); Coldstream and Catling, eds., 1996, 5, fig. 58:14 (Knossos, PGB); 15, pl. 50:4, 5 (EG); 27, pl. 63:1 (MPG); 141, pl. 139:12 (EG); 141, pl. 140:23 (EG); 198, pl. 186:52 (Attic EG I); Kotsonas 2008, 94–96, fig. 13:A164, A161 (Eleutherna LPG and PGB). *Date*: G.

GR20 P8 (V 4700.1, V 4701.1, V 4812.1; Fig. 111). Closed vessel, probably jug. Four decorated body fragments, and one more possibly from surface just east of Grave 17. Max. pres. h. 3.8. Fine, rather sandy, reddish-yellow (7.5YR 7/6) fabric. Pink (7.5YR 8/4) slip. Streaky black paint. Well-preserved surfaces. No burning. Groups of narrow bands between broad bands. *Date*: uncertain.

Fine Monochrome Wares

GR20 P9 (V 4701.1 and 2, V 4702.1–3, V 4704.2; Fig. 111). Cup. Partially mended from 45 fragments. Preservation 75% of base, plus fragments of rim and handle. H. est. 6.5; d. rim est. 12.0; d. base est. 6.0. Fine, soft, rather porous, very pale brown (10YR 8/4) fabric. Dull, thick, crackled black paint. Worn surfaces. No burning. Groove at base of rim. *Comparanda*: Coldstream and Catling, eds., 1996, 146, fig. 106:6 (Knossos, EG–MG); Mook 2004, 175, fig. 12.10:P (Kastro, G). *Date*: LG.

GR20 P10 (V 4701.1, V 4702.1, V 4704.1, V 4704.3; Fig. 111). Cup. Partially mended from 22 fragments preserving part of rim, 25% of base, most of one handle. H. est. 6.5; d. rim 12.0; d. base 6.0. Fine, soft fabric, uniformly burned gray. Traces of black paint. Nearly all burned and warped. *Date*: G.

GR20 P11 (V 4701.2, V 4702.3, V 4704.2, V 4705.2, V 4707.2; Fig. 111). Krater. Seven fragments from rim and body, including handle attachment. D. rim est. 20.0. Fine, soft, pink (7.5YR 7/4) to very pale brown (10YR 7/4) fabric with some phyllite inclusions and tiny silver mica. Traces of reddish-brown paint. Very worn surfaces. Half of fragments burned. Grooves at base of rim. *Date*: LG.

GR20 P12 (V 4700.1, V 4701.1 and 2, V 4702.1, V 4704.2; Fig. 111). Cup or skyphos. Partially mended from 13 fragments, including two from rim. D. rim est. 12.0. Fine, soft, porous, very pale brown (10YR 8/4) fabric. Dull, thick, crackled, black paint. Worn surfaces. Some fragments burned. Probably ledge-rim cup. *Comparanda*: Coldstream and Catling, eds., 1996, 197, fig. 124:13 (Attic LPG). *Date*: LG.

GR20 P13 (V 4700.1, V 4701.1 and 2, V 4702.2 and 3, V 4704.1 and 2, V 4707.2; Fig. 111). Cup or skyphos. Represented by 25 fragments, including rim; missing handle. D. rim est. 10.0. Fine, soft, reddish-yellow (7.5YR 8/6) fabric. Red (2.5YR 5/6) paint. Worn surfaces. One fragment burned. *Date*: G.

GR20 P14 (V 4701.2, V 4702.1, V 4702.3, V 4703.1 and 2, V 4704.2–4, V 4705.3; Fig. 111). Cup or skyphos. Eleven fragments from rim and body; missing base and handle(s). D. rim est. 13.0. Fine, soft, chalky, very pale brown (10YR 8/2) fabric. Black paint. Some fragments burned. Worn surfaces. Probably ledge-rim cup. *Comparanda*: Coldstream and Catling, eds., 1996, 197, fig. 124:13 (Attic LPG). *Date*: G.

GR20 P15 (V 4701.2, V 4704.2, V 4707.2; Fig. 111). Cup or skyphos. Five fragments preserving 25% of base; no rim, no handle(s). D. base 5.0. Fine, soft pink (7.5YR 8/4) fabric. Traces of reddish paint. Very worn surfaces. No burning. *Date*: uncertain.

GR20 P16 (V 4701.2, V 4702.3, V 4705.2, V 4706.1; Fig. 111). Wide-mouthed jug. Fifteen fragments preserving 25% of base, parts of rim, handle, and body. H. est. 9.0; d. rim est. 9.0; d. base 5.0. Fine, soft, porous, very pale brown (10YR 8/3) fabric. Red (2.5YR 5/6) paint. Very worn surfaces. All fragments lightly burned. *Comparanda*: Tsipopoulou 2005, 133, fig. 90:AN2381 (Hagios Georgios, LG). *Date*: LG.

Medium-Coarse Decorated Wares

GR20 P17 (V 4752.2, V 4752.3; Fig. 111). Kalathos. Six fragments from rim, one from handle, and 12 body fragments. Similar to closed vessel **GR20 P21**, and some fragments assigned to that vessel may have belonged to this one. D. rim est. 40.0. Medium-coarse, soft, reddish-yellow (5YR 7/6) fabric with some red phyllites. Red (2.5YR 5/8) to black paint. Very worn surfaces. No burning. Filled triangles on rim. Crosshatched lozenge on body. *Comparanda*: Brock 1957, 20, pl. 11:162 (Knossos, PG); Coldstream and Catling, eds., 1996, 61, fig. 74:13 (Knossos, EG); 199, fig. 127:59 (Knossos, MPG); for decoration on rim, Coldstream and Catling, eds., 1996, 249, fig. 142:155 (Knossos, MPG). *Date*: PG.

GR20 P18 (V 4701.1 and 2, V 4702.2 and 3, V 4703.2, V 4704.2, V 4706.1; Fig. 111). Conical lid. Represented by 19 fragments from rim, seven from body. Preservation 30% of rim; missing top/base, handle. D. est. 16.0. Medium-coarse, reddish-yellow (7.5YR 8/6) fabric with tiny black and hard white inclusions. Black paint. Very worn surfaces. Many fragments burned. Running S-pattern or quirk. *Comparanda*: Brock 1957, 179, motif 11q (Knossos, G lids); Kotsonas 2008, 150, 152, fig. 36:A105α (Eleutherna, LG–EPAR). *Date*: LG.

GR20 P19 (V 4704.2, V 4752.1, V 4752.4; Fig. 111). Small necked jar. Partially mended from six fragments. Entire base preserved and one fragment of rim; missing handle. H. est. 8.0; d. rim est. 7.0; d. base est. 5.5. Medium-coarse, reddish-yellow (5YR 7/6) fabric with frequent small phyllite and hard black inclusions. Very worn surfaces. No burning. *Date*: LG?

GR20 P20 (V 4752.2 and 3; Fig. 111). Amphora or necked jar. Six nonjoining body fragments. Other fragments from surrounding loci may belong. Max. pres. h. 14.0; max. pres. d. 25.0. Medium-coarse, very soft, pink (7.5YR 8/4–7/4) fabric with phyllite inclusions. Petrographic sample KAV 15/67: Fabric Subgroup 1b. Red (2.5YR 4/6) to black paint. Very worn surfaces, except one fragment. No burning. Concentric upright semicircles. *Comparanda*: Coldstream and Catling, eds., 1996, 215, fig. 131:18 (Knossos, LPG–PGB). *Date*: LG.

GR20 P21 (V 4707.1, V 4752.2–4; Fig. 111). Closed vessel. Represented by 28 body fragments, two from handle attachments. Possibly more than one vessel represented; some may belong with **GR20 P17**, others have thinner walls and may come from a smaller closed vessel. Medium-coarse, soft, reddish-yellow (5YR 7/6) fabric with frequent red phyllites. Red (2.5YR 5/8) to black paint. Very worn surfaces. No burning. Concentric circles with filled triangles at edge. *Comparanda*: for decoration, Callaghan and Johnson 2000, 229, fig. 4.12:166 (Kommos, PGB). *Date*: G.

Metal

Bronze

GR20 M1 (V88.237; V 4704.5, object 3; Fig. 112; Pl. 48). Bronze fibula. Three nonjoining fragments, including part of twisted bow, catch plate, coil, and pin; missing end of pin. L. est. 5.4, w. est. 2.8. Rather corroded. Twisted arched fibula with rectangular catch plate. *Comparanda*: Blinkenberg 1926, 65–66, types II.7 and II.8; Sapouna-Sakellaraki 1978, 49–51, pl. 7:197–215 (esp. 202) (type IIf; SM–PG). *Date*: SM–PG.

GR20 M2 (V88.238; V 4704.5 object 2, V 4701.1, V 4704.5; Fig. 112; Pl. 48). Bronze fibula. Four nonjoining fragments, including catch plate, pieces of twisted bow, coil; missing pin. L. est. 3.5; w. est. 1.5. Little corrosion. Twisted arched fibula with rectangular catch plate. *Comparanda*: Blinkenberg 1926, 65–66, types II.7 and II.8; Sapouna-Sakellaraki 1978, 49–51, pl. 7:197–215 (esp. 202) (type IIf; SM–PG). *Date*: SM–PG.

GR20 M3 (V88.236; V 4709.2 object 3, V 4705.2 object 4; Fig. 112; Pl. 48). Bronze sheeting. Mended from eight fragments into large rectangle; no preserved edges. Max. pres. L. 7.3; max. pres. w. 3.9. Very corroded and warped. Rectangular sheet with six rivet holes and five rivets around edges.

GR20 M4 (V88.235; V 4704.5, object 4; Fig. 112; Pl. 48). Bronze sheeting. Three joining fragments with rivets, possibly with edges preserved. Max. pres. L. 4.0; max. pres. w. 1.4; th. 0.9. Badly corroded. Leaf-shaped object made of two sheets held in place by two rivets.

Iron

GR20 M5 (V88.253; V 4705.2, V 4709.2; Fig. 112; Pl. 48). Iron pin. Partially mended from two fragments at tip; nonjoining fragment from end with disk. Max. pres. L. 2.1. Well-preserved surfaces. Long pin, hollow inside, with disk and conical knob at top.

GR20 M6 (V88.254; V 4705.2, V 4709.2; Fig. 112; Pl. 48). Iron pin. Two joining fragments from point and one nonjoining fragment from end with part of disk; no knob. Max. pres. L. 2.6. Badly corroded. Long pin with swelling (too corroded to distinguish shape) surrounded by three rings.

GR20 M7 (V88.232, IM 1223; V 4705.1 object 6, V 4705.3 object 3; Fig. 112; Pl. 48). Iron spearhead. Two large nonjoining fragments; nearly complete. L. est. 21.0; max. pres. w. 2.1; d. socket 1.7. Badly corroded, particularly at attachment of blade and socket. Some surviving surfaces on blade. Long (8.2) socket with hole pierced opposite edges near end. Blade slightly offset from socket. Midrib. Broad, short blade.

GR20 M8 (V88.230, IM 1221; V 4709.2, object 2; Fig. 112; Pl. 48). Iron spearhead. Mended from 11 fragments; nearly complete but missing edges of socket. L. 23.6; max. w. 2.0; d. socket est. 2.0. Badly corroded. Long (8.2) socket with hole pierced near end. Leaf-shaped blade. Short midrib.

GR20 M9 (V88.231, IM 1222, HNM 15736; V 4705.2, object 1; Fig. 112; Pl. 48). Iron knife. Mended from three fragments. Nearly complete, including two bronze rivets; missing tip of blade. L. 18.5; max. w. 1.6. Cracked and corroded; some surviving surfaces. *Comparanda*: Catling 1968, 94, fig. 3:9; Snodgrass 1996, 585–586, type A.

GR20 M10 (V88.233; V 4705.2, object 3; Fig. 112; Pl. 48). Iron knife. Partially mended from numerous fragments. L. est. 16.0; max. w. 1.5. Very poorly preserved. Badly corroded and laminating. *Comparanda*: **GR20 M9**; Snodgrass 1996, 587, type D; Rethemiotakis and Englezou 2010, fig. 65:199.

GR20 M11 (V 4709.2; Fig. 112). Iron awl or tool. Single fragment from near flat end; missing both ends. Max. pres. L. 4.4. Corroded. Tool is round at one end, square in section in middle, and seems to come to a flat edge at other end.

Bone or Ivory

GR20 B1 (V88.150, IM 1008; V 4709.2, object 5; Fig. 112; Pl. 48). Bead. Biconical. Preservation 75%; missing much of one side. Max. d. 1.1; d. hole 0.2. Ivory or very compact bone. Surfaces cracked and burned. Larger hole on top where there is a concavity. *Bibliography*: Gesell, Coulson, and Day 1991, 156, pl. 60:e.

Stone

GR20 S1 (V88.241; V 4709.2; Fig. 112; Pl. 48). Stone bead. Disk. Intact. H. 0.20; d. 0.70; d. hole 0.18. Black, soft serpentinite? No decoration. *Comparanda*: Rethemiotakis and Englezou 2010, 83 fig. 58:161 (Eltyna PG).

Graves 21 and 22

History and Details of Excavation

Grave 21 is a partial enclosure that lies on the northeast side of the Vronda summit, just north of Grave 9 in Room J1 of LM IIIC Building J (Figs. 3, 4, 66). It was excavated in 1989 during the removal of the north balk of Trench V 5300 (Gesell, Day, and Coulson 1995, 75–76). The area was much disturbed by a small tree in the center (see Pls. 49A–49C). In the topsoil over the area (Locus V 5346), a hoard of fine pottery was found, and soon after, the usual ashy soil with stones, snail shells, and human bones (V 5347) indicated another burial. The grave was then excavated by a team of archaeologists and physical anthropologists. Although the southern and western boundaries were clear in the lines of large rectangular limestone blocks, it was difficult to define the northern and eastern boundaries of the burial area (Pl. 49B). Below the rubble of V 5347, a fine, ashy soil of even darker color appeared (V 5348; Pl. 49C). When large quantities of pithos fragments appeared on the east, this area was given a new locus designation of V 5349, from which the upper part of the pithos was removed. The pithos was complete, lying on its side with the top still covered with a stone lid (Pl. 49D), and it contained another set of burials excavated as V 5350 (Pls. 49E, 49F). When the pithos was removed, the stone packing around it was excavated as V 5351. Six burials were recognized during the course of excavation, three in the pithos (C) and three above it in the enclosure, lying side by side in anatomical order (A and B); a fetus representing the seventh burial was discovered in the residue from the water sieve.

West of the limestone blocks that formed the western boundary of the enclosure just below topsoil, more soft, dark, ashy soil with snail shells, human bone, and Geometric pottery was encountered (V 5353). This area was initially labeled Grave 22, but there was little deposition, few bones and artifacts, and no associated features, so it was determined that it was a discard deposit from Grave 21. This deposit continued down to a layer of roofing clay (V 5357), the top of which still had some pockets containing grave material.

Architecture

Grave 21 was probably an enclosure, oriented east–west and measuring at least 1.13–1.25 m north–south x 1.88–2.25 m east–west, but only the south and west walls were well preserved (Fig. 66; Pl. 49A). Both walls were built of large rectangular blocks of limestone, disturbed in the southwest corner by a wild olive tree. The south wall (V 5355) is a row of five large stones that rests on gray and red roof collapse; it continues west of the grave but does not extend the full length to the east. The short west wall (V 5356) consists of only two or three stones resting on irregular rubble, roofing material, and a possible hearth. The east wall may have eroded downslope to the east, like other remains in so much of this area. A sort of northern boundary wall was made by an irregular curving line of cobbles and stones, different from the blocks that made up the other walls; it may have been created for the pithos burial. The area to the north and east has suffered from erosion; any blocks similar to those on the south and west may well have disappeared before excavation began. The boulders of the south wall are fissured from the heat of the cremation fire.

The pithos burial, which is the earliest feature in the grave, consisted of a large pithos set in a circle of stones ca. 0.50 m in diameter, with the base at the east and the top at the west. The builders dug a pit through some of the earlier roofing clay to construct the grave. It is not clear if the pithos burial predates the construction of the enclosure, or whether the enclosure was built to house the pithos burial, as with Grave 10, and then was later used for a pyre. Because the northern and eastern edges of the enclosure are rather curvilinear, following the outlines of the pithos, and because these wall-like structures respect the two short walls of the enclosure, it seems likely that the entire enclosure should be associated with this lower pithos burial. Most of the north and east walls were removed during excavation, and nothing remains of the enclosure today.

Stratigraphy

The total deposition in Grave 21 was 0.53 m from the bottom of the pit dug for the pithos to the surface; of this, only about 0.20 m was actually in the grave over the pithos and below the surface soil. There was little stratigraphy. A pit was dug to support the pithos and its burial (V 5350), and a ring of stones was set in to hold the pithos in place (V 5351). The enclosure may also have been constructed at the same time. Above the pithos was soft, ashy, gray soil (V 5349) with a darker and moister layer above in which the stones showed signs of burning (V 5348). A third layer of grave soil, which contained a greater number of stones and snail shells (V 5347) and probably represented the pile of stones over the grave, lay just below the surface soil (V 5346). Grave 21 material was also recovered from the area to the south of Grave 21, between it and Grave 9 (V 5324), as well as from the topsoil to the north and northeast of the grave in V 5354 and V 5818. The 0.12 m deep deposit of soft, ashy soil recognized as Grave 22 (V 5353) contained no joining pottery or human bones.

Associated Features

A pit to the northwest of Grave 21 contained dark soil, animal bones, and some possible Geometric pottery (V 5357.2, V5357. 3, V 5359). It may be associated with the burials, possibly as a discard deposit from Grave 21, just as Grave 14 was material discarded from Grave 9.

Burials

There were seven burials in the grave, six cremations and an inhumation. The preliminary publication (Gesell, Day, and Coulson 1995, 75–76) lists six individuals; the seventh individual, a fetus, was recovered after excavation from the water sieve residue. The three earliest burials were made within the pithos, while the remaining four cremations were found on top of the pithos.

It is likely that there were only two burial events in Grave 21: the pithos burial with the cremated adults and inhumed child, and the later, more typical cremation burials of three individuals, possibly using the already existing enclosure or, less likely, constructing a new one. The three cremations on top were all in some anatomical order, suggesting that they were all placed on the same pyre at the same time. The presence of unfused metopic sutures on both the male in the pithos and on one of the three cremations on top suggests that some of the individuals could be related.

Burial 1

Type: inhumation
Age: juvenile, 3–4 years
Sex: unknown
Weight: 29 g

Burial 1 in Grave 21 is an inhumed juvenile found in the bottom of the deposits in the pithos, mingled with the small pots and on top of the iron weapons (Pl. 50A). The bone is badly preserved, and little is identifiable except the teeth. The dental age of this child is around three to four years (Scheuer and Black 2000, 156–157).

Burials 2 and 3

Type: commingled secondary cremation deposit
Age: adults
Sex: one male, one female
Weight: 2,284 g

Above the child's bones, the cremated remains of two adults were placed in the pithos. It was not possible to separate the postcrania of these two burials, but portions of the calvaria could be reassembled. On the basis of the cranial morphology, it may be suggested that one of the individuals is probably a female, and the other probably a male. Two left pubic symphyses were found, one of which belonged to a person 45 to 50 years of age. The other individual was slightly older, probably 50 years or more. Fragments of the right auricular surface could be examined from both individuals. One resembled the morphology of a 50- to 59-year-old individual, and the other a 45- to 49-year-old individual (Buikstra and Ubelaker, eds., 1994, 24–32). The cranial sutures on the various fragments likewise suggest that both individuals were in the 40–60-year age group.

There are a number of pathological conditions visible on the bone that support the age estimation of these individuals. There is moderate to severe osteoarthritis on the vertebral facets, with eburnation on some of the joints. In addition, there is a dental abscess on the right side of one mandible, probably at the location of the first molar.

There is an anomaly, probably a fracture, on the superior dorsal surface of a right patella. There is slight cribra orbitalia on the right orbit of the possible female, suggesting that she may have suffered from some form of anemia earlier in life. Finally, the frontal bone of the female cranium has a retained metopic suture. This burial is one of two adults from this grave that possess this trait, which is a benign, genetic-based anomaly that may indicate a familial relationship between these adults.

The bone from these two burials was somewhat better preserved than that of many cremations at Vronda. This is probably the result of the protection from crushing provided by the pithos. The cremation of the bone does not differ from that of the bone in other burial enclosures. The bone that can be associated with the female skeleton appears to be marginally less burned than that of the male, but both skeletons show a range of burning. There are very strong variations in the degree of burning on the same unbroken pieces of bone. One example, a parietal fragment, exhibits complete calcination, apparently unburned bone, and an intermediate stage, all in an area less than 5 cm across.

Burials 4, 5, and 6
Type: commingled primary cremations
Age: adults
Sex: male, male(?), female(?)
Weight: 2,877 g (includes bone collected as Grave 22)

The commingled remains of three adults were found in the grave (Pl. 22F: bottom, left), with the crania in the west end of the enclosure and the feet at the east, beyond the base of the pithos. The cranial bone of Burials 5 and 6 is much less burned than the postcranial material. The cranium of Burial 4, however, is completely calcined and hard to the point of being brittle. The postcranial bone from all of these burials is generally completely calcined. Some postcranial bones, particularly from the thoracic area and neck, are less completely burned. The burials were disturbed by the olive tree planted at the west end of the enclosure, and they could not be separated with any degree of confidence, but various portions of the bodies remained articulated. The pectoral girdle of one individual was recognizable below the crania, and several sections of vertebrae were found in their expected order, with rib fragments on either side. Remains of two pelvises were found at the end of the vertebral columns, with leg bone and foot fragments found in anatomical progression extending to the east end of the enclosure.

On the basis of these remains, a tentative reconstruction of the three cremated skeletons is possible. The arms and legs all show the flexion typical of the Vronda cremations.

Of the two individuals in Burials 5 and 6, one is an adult, probably 40–60 years old, and at least one, possibly both, of the individuals is male. The third cranium, associated with Burial 4, is of unknown sex and age but may be female if associated with the fetus of Burial 7. This individual has a retained metopic suture and two large accessory bones at lambda. There is extensive osteoarthritis on many of the vertebral facets found in the grave. The thoracic and cervical vertebrae have pitting and osteophytes on the facets, indicating degenerative joint disease of the articular facets. The crania of Burials 4 and 6 both have evidence of cribra orbitalia on the upper surface of the eye orbits. The left mandible of one of the burials has evidence of TMJ problems.

Burial 7
Type: disturbed primary cremation
Age: fetus, 20–24 weeks
Sex: unknown
Weight: 11 g

Burial 7 consists of a preterm fetus. The bone is quite small, and very little was recovered from the grave. However, portions of the cranial vault, ribs, vertebrae, and upper and lower arm bones are all identifiable in the fragments. That these bones are all sufficiently ossified to permit their identification makes it likely that the development of the fetus had reached the later part of the middle trimester (20–24 weeks), and the small size suggests that the fetus was probably not older than this (Scheuer and Black 2000, 101, 193, 238, 291).

Faunal Remains

Animal bone recovered from Grave 21 consists predominately of scattered, unburned fragments of domestic pig and sheep or goat, along with a number of isolated teeth and a single femur diaphysis fragment from domestic dog (Table 8). Burned bones include a right tibia diaphysis segment.

Calcined bone, which is more likely to be associated with the burials in the enclosure, is limited to a single deer (Cervidae) antler beam fragment with one cut end, which is heavily burned and calcined (V 5348.3). A second probable deer bone fragment, a burned left innominate pubis segment, was recovered from the stone packing around the pithos (V 5351.1).

Botanical Remains

A rather large number of botanical remains were found in Grave 21, including olive (*Olea europaea*), grape (*Vitis vinifera*), pistachio (*Pistacia vera*), bitter vetch (*Vicia ervilia*), Vicia/Lathyrus, legumes, barley (*Hordeum vulgare*), and medick (*Medicago* sp.). A good deal of grape was found within the pithos, perhaps an offering to the dead that may have been placed in the kalathos (see below). The pithos also contained a fragment of pistachio.

Pottery

Grave 21 produced 1,267 fragments of pottery weighing 6.35 kg. These were mended into 13 smaller vessels and the burial pithos. Four vessels were found within the pithos: a kalathos (**GR21 P8**), a cup (**GR21 P12**), and two jugs or oinochoai (**GR21 P9**), one of which was too worn and soft to restore or draw. The pithos itself (**GR21 P13**) is an unusual shape, without parallels elsewhere on Crete but similar to **GR10 P1** and, to a lesser extent, to an example from the Kastro (Coulson et al. 1997, 327, fig. 7). The low-fired metamorphic fabric suggests an origin in northeast Crete.

The pottery from the enclosure that belonged with the later cremations includes seven cups (one decorated [**GR21 P1**] and six monochrome [**GR21 P3–GR21 P7**, **GR21 P11**]), an amphora (**GR21 P10**), and a necked jar (**GR21 P2**), all of which appear to be of LG date.

Objects

Within the pithos were three metal objects: a dirk (**GR21 M2**) and two small lead tubes (**GR21 M3**). The dirk is of the usual flange-hilted type, with bronze rivets. The precise function of the lead tubes is uncertain; somewhat similar lead objects found at Knossos are identified as lead strip weights or hinges. The stone lid (**GR21 S1**) was a flat slab of sandstone that was roughly chipped to form a lid for the pithos burial.

Only a single spearhead (**GR21 M1**) was found in the enclosure above the pithos. This spearhead is too poorly preserved to distinguish its type or function; it may have been a shorter javelin. There was also a fragment of a modified deer antler in this deposit (**GR21 B1**).

Chronology

Grave 21 appears to have been constructed after Grave 9. It was certainly in use after the last burial in Grave 9, to judge from the few pots found in the upper levels. The pithos burial contains chiefly pottery from the PG period, with EPG–PGB parallels. The kalathos (**GR21 P8**) resembles late PG or PGB examples from Knossos (Coldstream and Catling, eds., 1996, 134, fig. 102:4; 264, fig. 145:72) and Eleutherna (Kotsonas 2008, 217–218, fig. 53:A163), although the metopal arrangement is not common in Central Crete. The jug or oinochoe (**GR21 P9**) also appears to have a PG shape, but the metopal panel with thin horizontal bands is later and resembles decoration on a number of skyphoi from Vronda of LG date (**GR12 P6**, **GR16 P15**, **GR19 P2**, **GR36 P2**). The monochrome cup (**GR21 P12**), however, resembles MG cups at Knossos. A date around the middle of the eighth century for the first use of the grave seems possible.

The other cremations in the enclosure are later, nearly all belonging to the LG–EO periods. The shape of the decorated cup or skyphos (**GR21 P1**) has a close parallel from Knossos broadly dated to the PG–G periods, but it is from a mixed context (Hayes 1983, 138, no. 231, pl. 6). The design of the cross-hatched checkerboard is rare but can be found at LG Knossos (Coldstream and Catling, eds., 1996, 117, fig. 98:202); it is, however, usually confined to large MPG amphorae there (Coldstream and Catling, eds., 1996, 27, pl. 63:1). It is also found on LG examples at Chania (Hallager and Hallager, eds., 1997, 145, pl. 112:71-P 1452/1512 with hatching instead of cross-hatching). The neck-handled amphora (**GR21 P10**) finds close LG parallels in East Crete (Tsipopoulou 2005, figs. 14, 15), perhaps imitating amphorae from Knossos of MG–LG date (Coldstream and Catling, eds., 1996, 141, pl. 141:27; 142, pl. 142:58; 267, pl. 249:160). The shape may derive from a Euboean type of amphora of SubPG date (Popham, Sackett, and Themelis 1979–1980, 50, 337–338, pl. 28:70/P2, pl. 35). Cup **GR21 P7** is a ledge-rimmed variety similar to those found in Grave 9. The other monochrome cups are deep although lacking in the high rims that become prevalent in the EO period; they should date late in the LG sequence.

A few vessels seem to be later, dating to the LG–EO periods. Cup **GR21 P5** is thicker-walled than similar examples from the EO period (e.g., **GR30 P6**) and, although similar to LO cups from Knossos (Coldstream and Catling, eds., 1996, 244, fig. 138:21; 263, fig. 145:55), it does not have a rim as sharply offset as those later examples; it is probably of LG–EO date. Cup **GR21 P11**, a deep variety of the monochrome cup, has parallels in Grave 26 (**GR26 P7**) and in vessels of Orientalizing date at Knossos (Coldstream and Catling, eds., 1996, 88–89, pl. 107:39; 247, fig. 141:112). A very late LG or EO date for this upper grave seems likely.

Catalog

Pottery

Fine Decorated Wares

GR21 P1 (V 5346.1 and 2, 4, 5; Fig. 113). Cup. Partially mended from five fragments, 10% preserved, including rim and upper body and one fragment of lower body; missing base and handle. Max. pres. h. 7.5; d. rim 12.0. Fine, medium soft, reddish-yellow (5YR 6/6) fabric. Very pale brown (10YR 8/2) slip. Red (2.5YR 4/6) paint. Well-preserved surfaces. No burning. Vertical strokes on rim. Checkerboard with cross hatching instead of solid fill; vertical strokes and bands on lower body. *Comparanda*: for shape, Tsipopoulou 2005, 172, fig. 128:Σ3927 (Hagios Georgios, LG); for decoration, Brock 1957, 169, motif 1w, pl. 70:987 (Knossos, LG–EO); Tsipopoulou 2005, 173, fig. 61:Σ3936 (Hagios Georgios, LG); 222, fig. 116:Σ4526 (Zakro, LG). *Date*: LG.

GR21 P2 (V 5346.2 and 3, 5, 6, V 5354.1, V 5818.1, V 5360.1; Fig. 113). Necked jar. Partially mended from 24 fragments. Preservation 35%, including nearly complete profile, 30% of rim; missing much of base, handles. H. est. 16.2; d. rim est. 9.4; d. base est. 10. Fine, rather soft, reddish-yellow (5YR 7/6) fabric with much spalling. Pink (7.5YR 8/4) slip. Black paint. Surfaces very worn. Interior surface has laminated off. No burning. Vertical strokes on shoulder. *Comparanda*: for shape, Kotsonas 2008, 121, 125, fig. 25:A48 (Eleutherna, EPAR); 127, 129, fig. 28:A51 (Eleutherna, LPAR); for decorative scheme, Tsipopoulou 2005, 76, fig. 61:H1960 (Vronda, PGB); Kotsonas 2008, 121, 125, fig. 25:A30 (Eleutherna, EPAR). *Date*: LG.

Fine Monochrome Wares

GR21 P3 (V 5301.1, V 5324.1, V 5346.3, V 5346.5 and 6, V 5349.2; Fig. 113). Cup. Mended from 42 fragments. Preservation 50%, including full profile, most of base and lower body, half of rim, half of handle; missing bottom half of handle. H. 9.0; d. rim 12.0; d. base 6.0. Fine, very soft, reddish-yellow (7.5YR 7/6) fabric, very pale brown (10YR 8/3) on surface. Black paint. Very worn surfaces. String marks on base. No burning. *Date*: LG.

GR21 P4 (V 5346.5, V 5348.2 and 4, V 5349.1 and 2, V 5350.5; Fig. 113). Mug-like cup. Mended from 21 fragments. Preservation 60%, including full profile, 30% of base, 50% of rim, lower half of handle; missing top half of handle. H. 9.0; d. rim 11.5; d. base est. 6.0. Fine, soft, reddish-yellow (5YR 7/6) fabric, very pale brown (10YR 8/3) on surface. Black paint. Surfaces very smooth and worn. Many fragments burned, including base, after breaking. *Date*: LG.

GR21 P5 (V 5346.1 and 2, V 5346.4 and 5, V 5347.1, V 5348.2, V 5348.4 and 5, V 5349.1 and 2, V 5350.2, V 5818.1; Fig. 113). Cup. Partially mended from 43 fragments. Preservation 50%, including complete profile, tiny bit of base, 75% of rim, handle; missing most of base and lower body. H. 10.8; d. rim 13.5; d. base est. 6.0. Fine, soft, reddish-yellow (7.5YR 7/6) fabric. Yellowish-red (5YR 5/6) paint. Well-preserved surfaces and paint. No burning. Grooves at top and bottom of rim. *Comparanda*: Lembessi 1970, 278, fig. 392β:28; 288, fig. 392β:66 (Mastambas, OR). *Date*: LG–EO.

GR21 P6 (V 5346.3 and 5, V 5347.1, V 5348.2, V 5350.1; Fig. 113). Cup. Eleven fragments from rim and handle; missing base and lower half of handle. D. rim. est. 12.5. Fine, soft, reddish-yellow (5YR 7/6) fabric. Red (2.5YR 4/6) to black paint. Very worn surfaces. Many fragments burned badly. *Comparanda*: **GR21 P11**. *Date*: LG.

GR21 P7 (V 5346.1 and 2, V 5354.1; Fig. 113). Cup or skyphos. Large fragment from rim. Missing base and handle(s). Max. pres. h. 5.0; d. rim 14.0. Fine, soft, chalky, reddish-yellow (7.5YR 8/6) fabric. Black to red (10R 5/8) paint. Well-preserved surfaces. No burning. Ledge rim. *Comparanda*: **GR20 P13**; Coldstream and Catling, eds., 1996, 197, fig. 124:13 (Attic LPG). *Date*: LG.

Medium-Coarse Decorated Wares

GR21 P8 (V89.68, IM 1249; V 5350.4; Fig. 113; Pl. 50B). Kalathos. Restored from 14 fragments, with four nonjoining fragments from rim and body. Preservation 90%; missing section of rim. H. 6.6–7.0; d. rim 15.6 (int.); d. base 6.8. Medium-coarse, soft, reddish-yellow (5YR 6/6) fabric with frequent small white inclusions. Thick, glossy, red (2.5YR 5/8) paint. Some well-preserved surfaces, some worn. No burning. Wavy line between bands above handles, groove on rim. Underside has circle with a crude X-pattern. *Bibliography*: Gesell, Day, and Coulson 1995, pl. 21:b. *Comparanda*: for underside of base, Coldstream and Catling, eds., 1996, 6, fig. 56:24 (Knossos, EG); for decoration, Coldstream 2001, 57–59, fig. 1.20:h (Hagios Ioannis, SM); for shape and decoration, Kotsonas 2008, 217–218, fig. 53:A163 (Eleutherna, PGB). *Date*: G.

GR21 P9 (V89.56, IM 1243; V 5350.6; Fig. 113; Pl. 50B). Jug or oinochoe. Partially mended from many fragments. Preservation 85%, including most of base and lower body, handle, and bits of neck; missing rim. Max. pres. h. 8.5; h. est. 11.3; d. base 4.4. Medium-coarse, very soft, pale yellow

(2.5Y 8/4) clay. Black paint. Very worn surfaces. Warped from fire. Metopal panel on shoulder with horizontal bands. May have had trefoil mouth. *Bibliography*: Gesell, Day, and Coulson 1995, pl. 21:a. *Comparanda*: for shape, Coldstream and Catling, eds., 1996, 17, pl. 54:24 (Knossos, PGB); for shape and decoration, Tsipopoulou 2013, 144–145, fig. 8:12314 (Piskokephalo, LG). *Date*: G.

GR21 P10 (V 5346.2, V 5346.3, V 5346.5, V 5818.1; Fig. 113). Amphora. Partially mended into several large fragments preserving part of neck and lower body, bit of rim, and one handle. Missing most of rim, much of body. Round, horizontal handle found with it probably does not belong. H. est. 27.0; d. rim est. 10.0; d. base 7.0. Medium-coarse, soft, chalky, reddish-yellow (7.5YR 7/6) fabric with frequent sandy white inclusions and carbonates. Very pale brown (10YR 8/3) slip. Black paint. Very worn surfaces. Horizontal thin bands on neck, groups of oblique strokes on shoulder; alternating thick and groups of thin bands on lower body. *Comparanda*: for shape, Tsipopoulou 2005, 291, fig. 14:AN8780 (Praisos, LG); for decoration, Tsipopoulou 2005, 291, fig. 14:AN8779 (mislabeled 8789; Praisos, LG); 284, fig. 14:AN8754 (Praisos, LG). *Date*: LG.

Medium-Coarse Monochrome Wares

GR21 P11 (V89.37, IM 1244; V 5346.3, pot B; Fig. 114). Cup. Mended from 23 fragments. Preservation 75%, including entire base, 65% of body, 25% of rim, and handle. H. 10.8; d. rim est. 12.0; d. base 4.5. Medium-coarse, reddish-yellow (5YR 6/6) clay with tiny black and white inclusions. Black paint. *Date*: LG–EO.

GR21 P12 (V89.57, IM 1240; V 5350.5; Fig. 114). Cup. Mended from 16 fragments. Preservation 50%, including full profile, entire base, 30% of rim and upper body, and lower handle attachment; missing handle. H. 7.7; d. rim 11.5; d. base 4.0. Medium-coarse, soft, chalky, reddish-yellow (7.5YR 6/6) fabric with frequent phyllite, granodiorite, and gold mica inclusions. Traces of red paint. Very worn surfaces. *Date*: G.

Plain Coarse Wares

GR21 P13 (V98.71; V 5350; Fig. 114; Pl. 50B). Pithos. Restored from numerous fragments (two crates). Preservation 95%. H. 80.0; d. rim 36.4; d. base 22.7. Coarse, red (2.5YR 5/6–5/8) fabric with frequent metamorphic inclusions (Kavousi Type XVI) and reddish-yellow (7.5YR 6/6) surface. Petrographic sample PMD 98/35; KAV 15/93: small low-fired metamorphic group. Surface smoothed and has many cracks. *Bibliography*: Day 1995, fig. 13. *Date*: LG.

Metal

Iron

GR21 M1 (V89.93; V 5347.1; Fig. 114; Pl. 50B). Iron spearhead. Partially mended. Most of socket and beginning of blade preserved; missing most of blade, including all edges. Max. pres. L. 14.8; max. pres. w. 2.1; d. socket 2.3. Corroded, cracked, and laminated; no surviving surfaces. Long (8.6) socket, only half a circle; hole pierced near end opposite edges. Blade has sloping shoulders and pronounced midrib.

GR21 M2 (V89.94; V 5350.2, V 5350.5, V 5350.6; Fig. 114; Pl. 50B). Iron dirk or short sword. Three large nonjoining fragments from hilt (a), middle of blade (b), and end of blade (c), including two bronze rivets preserved. Missing tip of hilt. Max. pres. L. (a) 9.0, (b) 7.2, (c) 22.8; L. est. 41.5; max. pres. w. 3.0. Very corroded and laminated except at tip, where some surfaces survive. Flange hilted, with rivets at juncture of hilt and blade. Long, tapering blade.

Lead

GR21 M3 (V89.92; V 5350.2; Fig. 114; Pl. 50B). Lead tubes. Two cylindrical fragments without evident join, but similar in size and shape. Max. pres. L. (a) 1.9, (b) 2.5; d. (a) 1.9, (b) 0.9. Well preserved but fragmentary; little corrosion. Cylindrical tube(s) of uncertain function. *Comparanda*: Coldstream and Catling, eds., 1996, 257, fig. 193:287.f5; 271, fig. 193:292.f10a (lead strip weight or hinge).

Bone

GR21 B1 (V 5348.3; Pl. 50B). Modified deer antler. Single fragment of antler beam. Max. pres. L. 3.4; max. pres. w. 1.55. One end cut and scraped. Burned and blackened.

Stone

GR21 S1 (V89.28; V5350.7, object 7; Pl. 50B). Stone lid. Intact. D. 35.0–38.0; th. 2.5–5.3. Flat slab of light gray sandstone chipped slightly around edges to form crude lid, oval in shape. Served as lid for pithos burial.

Grave 23

History and Details of Excavation

Grave 23 is a stone-lined burial enclosure on the south edge of the terrace that supports LM IIIC Building I-O-N on the western slope of the Vronda ridge (Figs. 3, 4). It lies just south of Grave 24 and west of Grave 30 and the associated discard deposits known as Graves 33 and 7. The grave itself was excavated in 1989 (Gesell, Day, and Coulson 1995,

88–89), while some of the surrounding areas were uncovered in 1990. The grave lies at the intersection of four trenches: VW 8100, VW 8200, VW 9100, and VW 9200. It was initially encountered in the surface and upper levels in all four trenches (VW 8101, VW 8201, VW 9101, VW 9104, VW 9111, VW 9201), but after the enclosure was clearly defined, it was excavated as a single unit labeled locus VW 8104. Two burials were recognized during excavation (A and B), but subsequent study showed that there were actually four individuals in the grave. Material from the grave was scattered over all four trenches, and many of the fragments came to light in the areas to the west (VW 8226, VW 9225), southeast (VW 8102), east (VW 8111), and north (VW 9202, VW 9205) in 1989 and 1990. In 1990 the north wall of the enclosure (VW 9116) was removed to locate the original wall of Building O, Room O1.

Architecture

Grave 23 is a burial enclosure, oriented northwest–southeast and measuring 1.55 m north–south x 0.95–1.05 m east–west (Fig. 115). It was one of the most irregular burial enclosures on the site, and the interior space was more oval than rectangular (Pl. 51A). The enclosure was set into the packing for the south terrace that supported the southern rooms of the LM IIIC Building I-O-N. Rather than using the house wall of Room O1 (VW 9119), the builders of the enclosure modified the wall and constructed a new northern wall (VW 9116), perhaps to make the grave longer. This north wall had two roughly regular faces, while the other walls of the grave (VW 8282, VW 8116, VW 8117) consisted of single rows of boulders, mostly of local breccia. The limestone boulders on the east side (VW 8116) showed some signs of fracturing from the heat of the pyre. The bedrock on the bottom of the enclosure at the time of excavation showed calcination from the fire, but after several years this feature was no longer evident. The walls are not well preserved, having suffered extensively from water drainage and erosion.

Stratigraphy

The amount of deposition in Grave 23 was not great, and there was much disturbance and erosion. At its deepest, the grave deposit was only 0.32 m. The builders cut into the terrace packing for Building I-O-N to construct the enclosure, at some places coming down to bedrock and cutting into the south wall of Room O1 (VW 9119). The pyre was laid directly on the bedrock surface, and some of the burned beams were still preserved at the time of excavation. One of the beams was identified by Peter Kuniholm as oak. The soil within the enclosure was soft, dark, and ashy (VW 8104), and there were no other soil types recognized within the deposit. Above the ashy, dark grave soil was a layer of stone cobbles (VW 9111), slope wash (VW 9104), and topsoil (VW 8101, VW 8201, VW 9101, VW 9201). Stone tumble to the north (VW 9202, VW 9205, VW 9116), east (VW 8111), southeast (VW 8102), and west (VW 8226, VW 9225) contained dump or spillage from Grave 23. One joining piece of pottery found to the north in the area of Grave 24 was probably deposited there as a result of disturbance from Grave 23.

Associated Features

Grave 24 may have been associated with Grave 23. The child in Grave 24 was apparently thrown into the space where it was found before the construction of Grave 23.

Burials

Four burials were made in the grave, three cremations and an inhumation. The inhumation (Burial 4) was found in approximate anatomical order throughout the levels of the grave, surrounded by cremation deposits. Great disturbance by water drainage made it difficult to determine if this burial had been the first or the last, but it seems more likely that it was the latest burial in the grave.

Burial 1

Type: disturbed primary cremation
Age: infant, perinatal
Sex: unknown
Weight: 186 g

The presence of this infant burial was not recognized until the cremations were inventoried in the laboratory. The infant bone was found in bone bags and water sieve residue from both the north and south ends of the enclosure. Most of the bone is completely calcined, although a few pieces, including the petrous portion of the right temporal bone, are not completely burned. While an exact age could not be determined for this skeleton, it is likely that it was a full-term perinatal infant.

Burials 2 and 3
Type: disturbed primary cremations
Age: adults
Sex: unknown
Weight: 852 g

Burials 2 and 3 were found commingled in the grave. Both of the crania were found in the south end of the enclosure. Only the crania could be reconstructed sufficiently to distinguish between the two burials. The rest of the skeletons are irretrievably mixed. The postcranial bone was divided arbitrarily on the basis of the degree of cremation. One set of bones, assigned to Burial 2, is completely calcined and uniformly white. The other set, assigned to Burial 3, is hardened and somewhat scorched by the fire.

Burial 2 was an inhumation of an adult of indeterminate sex. Very few fragments of cranial sutures are preserved, so it is not possible to assign an age even on the basis of this criterion. On fragments of the left and right parietals there are small foci of lytic lesions—circumscribed areas of antemortem bone destruction—on the internal surface of the bones. These lesions are concentrated along the grooves for the middle meningeal arteries. A potential cause of this phenomenon has been identified as streptococcal meningitis secondary to a chronic ear infection (Ortner and Putschar 1985, 121, fig. 164).

The bone from Burial 3 belongs to a mature adult. The cranial sutures around the bregma are obliterated endocranially. The sex of this individual cannot be determined. No pathological conditions were noted on the bone.

Burial 4
Type: primary inhumation
Age: adult, 40–60 years?
Sex: unknown
Weight: 148 g

This burial is a partial skeleton of an adult. It was not possible to determine the age or sex of the individual, although the heavy wear on the teeth probably indicates an individual in the 40- to 60-year age group. The bone is heavily decayed, resembling the inhumations found in the tholos tombs at Vronda and near the Kastro at Aloni (Skala; see Fig. 2). In addition to the decay, there is extensive root damage and possibly rodent gnawing on the bone. Very little of the original bone surface remains intact. The inhumed bone was surrounded by the cremation deposits of Burials 1–3. Some of the bone from Burial 4 appears to have been scorched by fire, possibly the result of surface fires or a very minimal degree of cremation.

The maxillary central incisors from this burial show extensive and unusual wear. On the lingual surface, the enamel is completely worn away, and the dentine is exposed nearly to the cementoenamel junction. The incisive edge, however, shows almost no evidence of wear. This degree and pattern of wear is not associated with mastication, but with the use of the teeth as tools. The anterior teeth were used to grip or scrape some object in such a way that the outer surface of the lower teeth was worn, without grinding, down the cutting edge of the teeth. The occlusal surface of the preserved canines, premolars, and molars is heavily worn as well. Both mandibular canine teeth have two distinct, well-developed, enamel hypoplasias on each tooth indicating at least two episodes of dietary or disease stress during childhood. The only pathology noted on the bone was an area of excessive porosity on both tibia shafts. The bone surface was missing, but this porosity continued well into the bone cortex, perhaps indicating a prolonged and severe disease process in the bone.

Faunal Remains

Minimal amounts of animal bone were recovered from Grave 23 (Table 8). The single identifiable sheep or goat element, a right scapula from a juvenile animal, was unburned, and its association with the burials is uncertain.

Botanical Remains

A number of botanical remains were found associated with Grave 23, including olive (*Olea europaea*), grape (*Vitis vinifera*), grass pea (*Lathyrus cicera*), fool's parsley (*Aethusa cynapium*), corn gromwell (*Lithospermum arvense*), and medick (*Medicago* sp). The olive may represent an offering or remains from fuel for the pyre. The grape probably comes from offerings of grapes or raisins or remains of a funeral meal. Grass pea is a food source that might have been deposited as an offering, or it could have been part of a funeral meal. The other remains might have been included for their medicinal value or as floral offerings placed on the pyre. Charred fragments of wood from this grave have been identified as oak.

Pottery

Grave 23 produced 60 fragments of pottery weighing 0.37 kg; an additional 347 fragments weighing 5.62 kg were recovered from dumps to the east, southeast, north, and west of the grave. Only eight vessels were recognized from the grave, and some of the cataloged pots were found in the vicinity of the grave rather than within it. Those found mostly in the grave included a krater stem (**GR23 P3**) and cup or skyphos (**GR23 P6**, parts of which were also found to the east). Those vessels whose pieces were primarily in the tumble, slope wash, or topsoil include a cup or skyphos (**GR23 P1**), a basket vase or thelastron (**GR23 P2**), a soft, decorated closed vessel (**GR23 P4**), and a cup (**GR23 P5**). Parts of cup **GR23 P1** were found west of the grave, and a jug or oinochoe (**GR23 P8**) was found to the north, with some pieces coming from the area of Grave 24 (VW 9208). Most of the pottery is unburned, suggesting that it belonged to the last cremation or the inhumation.

In addition to the cataloged pottery, there were many fragments from the body of a soft, chalky, reddish-yellow fabric with red paint, and a number of coarse pieces that had been thoroughly burned.

Objects

The metal and iron objects all came from within the enclosure, and most of them came from the northern half, associated with the cranium of Burial 2. One of the two bronze fibulae (**GR23 M2**), a bronze pin (**GR23 M1**), and an iron needle (**GR23 M4**) were all found close together, and the second fibula (**GR23 M3**), two beads (**GR23 S1, GR23 S2**), and a millstone (**GR23 ST1**) were found slightly to the west. The two fibulae may have been a matched pair, as they are very similar, and no other examples of this type were found in the Vronda graves. The millstone may have been simply one of many stones piled on the grave, but it might also have been an offering or deliberately placed with the burial.

Chronology

Grave 23 was constructed after the body from Grave 24 was dumped into Room O1 of the earlier settlement. The basket vase (**GR23 P2**) may date the construction of the grave because fragments of it were recovered during the removal of the north wall of the enclosure. There are no precise parallels for the shape outside of Grave 9 (**GR9 P11**), although two thelastra, one from PGB Knossos (Coldstream and Catling, eds., 1996, 4, fig. 56:2) and another from EO Dreros (Tsipopoulou 2005, 63, fig. 142:HΔ15), are similar. With regard to the decoration, the cross-hatched lozenge chain is an early motif, appearing in the PG period (Brock 1957, 172, motif 5j) but continuing later in East Crete; an example of PG–MG date can be found at Vrokastro (Hayden 2003, 51, no. 115, fig. 26) and another at LG Praisos (Tsipopoulou 2005, 293, fig. 60:AN8788). The pedestaled krater (**GR23 P3**) has parallels of MG date at Knossos (Coldstream and Catling, eds., 1996, 167, fig. 117:125.6); the ribbed pedestal can also be found on the mainland, particularly in MG II Eretria (Blandin 2007, 17–19, pl. 23.2). The cups, especially **GR23 P5** and **GR23 P6** with tall offset rims and thin walls, look late in the seventh century; the rims are too tall to be of LG date. The disk foot with stepped profile on **GR23 P7** is very late, common in the Archaic period, with some parallels of LO date from Knossos (Erickson 2010, 128), but none appear before the end of the seventh century (pers. comm., A. Kotsonas). The pottery indicates the use of the grave in the seventh century, with the last burial at the very end of that time.

The fibulae and the pin support this dating. Although the fibulae are of an east island type known in Rhodes and Crete, first appearing in the MG period and continuing into the early Archaic (Sapouna-Sakellaraki 1978, 63–65, type IIIe), at Knossos this form seems to be primarily of EO date (Catling 1996a, 552, type 9). The pin is of the most common type found in the North Cemetery at Knossos and is generally Orientalizing in date (Catling 1996a, 555–556, type 5). In general, Grave 23 is similar in date to Graves 30 and 4, with the last burial occurring toward the end of the seventh century.

Catalog

Pottery

FINE DECORATED WARES

GR23 P1 (VW 9225.2; Fig. 116). Cup or skyphos. Two joining fragments from rim, two body fragments;

missing base and handle(s). D. rim 11.0. Fine, soft, reddish-yellow (5YR 6/6) fabric with small phyllite inclusions. Very pale brown (10YR 8/4) slip. Red (2.5YR 5/6) paint. Very worn surfaces. Panel with crosshatching. *Date*: LG–EO.

GR23 P2 (V98.102; VW 8101.1, VW 8104.2, VW 8201.1, VW 9104.1, VW 9104.4, VW 9116.1, VW 9201.1, VW 9202.2; Fig. 116; Pl. 51B). Basket vase, possibly a thelastron. Partially mended from 38 fragments; eight nonjoining fragments. Preservation 65%, including full profile, entire base, 75% of handle; missing most of rim and rest of handle. H. 11.2; h. with handle est. 17.5; d. rim 11.2; d. base 4.0. Fine, rather hard, reddish-yellow (5YR 7/6) fabric. Very pale brown (10YR 8/4) slip. Yellowish-red (5YR 5/6) paint. Well-preserved surfaces. Some discoloration from fire on one side. Crosshatched lozenge chain with zigzag above. *Comparanda*: **GR9 P10**; Rocchetti 1988–1989, 234–236, fig. 157 (Kourtes). *Date*: LG.

GR23 P3 (V89.39, IM 1239; VW 8104.1, object 1; Fig. 116; Pl. 51B). Pedestaled krater. Partially mended from 14 fragments. Preservation 75% of pedestal; missing body, rim, and handles. Max. pres. h. 10.6; d. base 11.0. Fine, soft, slightly porous, reddish-yellow (5YR 7/6) fabric with tiny black inclusions. Reddish-yellow (7.5YR 7/6) slip. Black (7.5YR 3/0) to dark reddish-brown (2.5YR 2.5/4) paint, bands. Well-preserved surfaces. No burning. *Comparanda*: Mook 1993, 220, fig. 68:P1.99 (Kastro, LG). *Date*: LG.

GR23 P4 (VW 8101.1 and 2; Fig. 116). Closed vessel. Fragments of base and body. D. base 7.0. Fine, very soft, chalky, very pale brown (10YR 8/4) fabric and slip. Strong brown (7.5YR 4/6) paint. Very worn surfaces. One fragment possibly discolored from fire. Narrow bands with oblique strokes above and below. *Date*: LG.

FINE MONOCHROME WARES

GR23 P5 (VW 8101.4, VW 8104.1 and 2, VW 8201.1, VW 9104.1, VW 9111.1, VW 9202.1; Fig. 117). Cup. Partially mended from 21 fragments. Preservation 30% from rim and upper body; missing base and handle(s). Max. pres. h. 7.0; d. rim est. 9.5. Fine, soft, light red (2.5YR 6/6) fabric. Red (2.5YR 5/6) paint. Rather well-preserved surfaces. No burning. Incised lines on rim. *Comparanda*: Brock 1957, 89, pl. 73:959; 104, 127, 133, pl. 103:1198, 1460, 1547 (Knossos, LO); Andreadaki-Vlasaki 2004, 31, fig. 15:K 10/8 (Chania, LG–EO). *Date*: LO.

GR23 P6 (VW 8101.4, VW 8104.1–3, VW 8111.1, VW 9205.1; Fig. 117). Cup or skyphos. Mended from four fragments from rim and body. Preservation 10%; missing base, lower body, and handle(s). Max. pres. h. 4.0; d. rim 12.0. Fine, soft, rather porous, very pale brown (10YR 7/4) fabric. Black paint. Worn surfaces. No burning. *Comparanda*: Brock 1957, 106, pl. 103:1226 (Knossos, LO); Andreadaki-Vlasaki 2004, 31, fig. 15:K 10/8 (Chania, LG–EO). *Date*: LO.

GR23 P7 (VW 8102.1; Fig. 117). Cup or skyphos. Partially mended from four fragments. Preservation 75% of base; missing upper body, rim, and handle(s). Max. pres. h. 2.7; d. base 6.0. Fine, soft, reddish-yellow (7.5YR 7/6) fabric. Black paint. Disk foot with stepped profile. *Comparanda*: Erickson 2010, 130, fig. 4.7 (Knossos, sixth century); 213, fig. 8.10 (Praisos, sixth century). *Date*: LO.

MEDIUM-COARSE MONOCHROME WARES

GR23 P8 (VW 9202.1 and 2, VW 9205.1 and 2, VW 9208; Fig. 117). Jug or oinochoe. Partially mended from 22 fragments. Preservation 20%, including 75% of shoulder, handle, and part of neck and rim; missing base and most of rim. Max. pres. h. 9.0; d. rim est. 4.0. Medium-coarse, soft, reddish-yellow (5YR 6/6) fabric with metamorphic (gray schist) inclusions. Petrographic sample KAV 15/68: small metamorphic group with mica. Dark red (2.5YR 3/6) paint. Worn surfaces. No burning. May be trefoil mouthed, as rim seems uneven. *Date*: EO.

Metal

BRONZE

GR23 M1 (V89.74; VW 8104.2, object 3; Fig. 117; Pl. 51B). Bronze pin. Nearly complete in two fragments; missing point. Max. pres. L. 3.5; d. disk 0.4. Corroded at bottom, well preserved at head. Small straight pin. Knob on top and disk. Biconical swelling with three rings on either side. Tapers to point. *Comparanda*: Catling 1996a, 555–556, type 5 (Knossos, O). *Date*: O.

GR23 M2 (V89.73; VW 9111.1, object 1; Fig. 117; Pl. 51B). Bronze fibula. Single fragment preserving part of catch plate, bow, and coil; missing pin. Max. pres. L. 3.5; max. th. 0.5. Very well-preserved surfaces. Flat catch plate, probably square or rectangular. Beaded fibula with ovoid swelling having two smaller biconical swellings on either side. Round in section, but flattens toward coil. Double coil of beaten bronze. *Bibliography*: Gesell, Day, and Coulson 1995, pl. 27:c; Day 1995, fig. 11 (EO). *Comparanda*: Blinkenberg 1926, 99–101, type IV.11; Sapouna-Sakellaraki 1978, 63–65, type IIIe, pl. 15:467–469 (MG–Archaic); Catling 1996a, 552, type 9 (Knossos, EO).

GR23 M3 (V89.76; VW 8104.3, object 7; Fig. 117; Pl. 51B). Bronze fibula. Single fragment from bow; missing catch plate, coil, and pin. Max. pres. L. 2.3; max. th. 0.6. Well preserved. Beaded fibula, with large biconical swelling in center and two pairs of smaller biconical swellings on either side. *Comparanda*: **GR23 M2**. *Date*: EO.

IRON

GR23 M4 (V89.96; VW 8104.3, object 6; Fig. 117; Pl. 51B). Iron needle. Mended from three fragments; complete except for point. End flattened, with hole pierced through it. Max. pres. L. 4.5; d. 0.3. Very corroded. *Comparanda*: **GR16 M3**, **GR30 M11**.

Stone

GR23 S1 (V89.26, IM 1001; VW 8104.2, object 4; Fig. 117; Pl. 51B). Stone bead. Disk. Intact except for one chip.

H. 1.10; d. 2.25; d. hole 0.65. Wt. 8.00 g. Dark gray, soft, burned serpentinite.

GR23 S2 (V89.27, IM 1002; VW 8104.3, object 8; Fig. 117; Pl. 51B). Stone bead. Disk. Intact. H. 0.9; d. 1.65; d. hole 0.6. Wt. 4.00 g. Soft, bluish-gray limestone. Hole larger on one end than other.

GR23 ST1 (V89.48; VW 8104.2 object 5). Quern. Slab, oblong narrow, fragment. L. 15.5; w. 21.2; th. 7.5. Wt. 3,180.00 g. Sandstone, shelly, white. Abraded surface. Quern, Type 15.

Grave 24

History and Details of Excavation

Grave 24 is the designation given to a scatter of bones found in LM IIIC Building O, Room O1 on the western slope of the Vronda ridge (Figs. 3, 4). The burial was excavated in 1989 and 1990 in Trenches VW 9100 and VW 9200 (Gesell, Day, and Coulson 1995, 84; Day and Glowacki 2012, 94–95). There was no built enclosure, just a scatter of uncremated bone in stone tumble on top of roofing clay (Fig. 118). The body appears to have been deposited very carelessly, either when originally buried or after some disturbance of the area. There was no clearly defined burial area, and the limits of the grave were determined by the presence of human bone, usually in soft dark soil. In 1989 the bones were first recognized in Locus VW 9205, and the grave in this trench was excavated as VW 9208. The scatter extended to the north into Trench VW 9100, and the burial was excavated as VW 9112. In 1990 more excavation was conducted in Room O1 in VW 9116 and VW 9118, and more bones and soft soil appeared under the north wall of Grave 23, which was removed in order to find the original wall of the room.

Architecture

There was no associated architecture. The body appears to have been thrown into this area and perhaps covered with stones.

Stratigraphy

The bones lay on top of a red roofing material from the collapsed roof of the Late Minoan IIIC building and within a matrix of soft dark soil and rock tumble (VW 9205, VW 9208, VW 9112, VW 9116, VW 9118). Occasionally the bones were found outside the area of soft dark soil.

Associated Features

Grave 23 is very close and almost contiguous, and this burial may be related to it in some way. There is no indication that the body in Grave 24 was discarded from Grave 23, which seems to have been constructed after the deposition of the body in Grave 24. The two burials appear to be discrete.

Burials

A single burial is represented in Grave 24: the disarticulated inhumation of a child six to seven years old, who suffered from some disease causing lytic destructive lesions—circumscribed areas of ante mortem bone destruction—on the cranial bone.

Burial 1
Type: inhumation
Age: juvenile, 6–7 years
Sex: unknown
Weight: 174 g

The bones of Burial 1 are those of a juvenile with a dental age of six to seven years. The bone preservation was quite poor. The bone surfaces are heavily eroded, and the long bone shafts are laminating. Even the tooth enamel is etched in places. A number of the cranial bone fragments have lytic lesions apparently originating in the inner spongy diploë and extending through the inner or outer table of the bone. Radiographs show an area of sclerosis around the lesions. In contrast to the cranial fragments of Burial 2 in Grave 23, which also displayed lytic lesions, the appearance and location of the lesions in this case indicate a probable diagnosis of histiocytosis rather than menningitis. Histiocytosis is a disease that produces lesions in multiple organs including the skeleton and can be fatal or relatively benign, depending on the patient (Ortner 2003, 361–363).

Faunal Remains

With the exception of one unidentifiable burned bone fragment, the animal bones recovered from the area designated Grave 24 are fragmentary, unburned, and generally extremely eroded (Table 8). Identifiable elements include isolated domestic pig and sheep or goat teeth and several limb bone fragments. All appear to be the remains of general building debris from the LM IIIC building and are probably not associated with burial activities.

Botanical Remains

Some fragments of fool's parsley (*Aethusa cynapium*) were recovered from the area of Grave 24.

Pottery

There was no pottery associated with Grave 24. All the material that was found in the soil with the bones belonged to the LM IIIC occupation of the building (Day and Glowacki 2012, 94–95).

Objects

There were no objects clearly associated with the burial in Grave 24.

Chronology

There are no finds in Grave 24 that would allow dating. From the associated pottery the burial could even belong to the LM IIIC period, as all of the pottery in the locus dated from that time. Stratigraphically, however, there are some indications of date (for a detailed analysis of the stratigraphy, see Day and Glowacki 2012, 94–95). The child was thrown in on top of the roofing clay of the building. That means that the burial must have occurred at some time after the building collapsed, and other evidence points to the abandonment of the settlement before the middle of the 11th century. That provides a terminus post quem for the burial. At the other end, a terminus ante quem is provided by the construction of Grave 23. When the wall of Grave 23 was removed in excavation to find the original house wall, it was discovered that the wall of Grave 23 went over the dark ashy soil containing some bones from Grave 24. Grave 24, then, at least predates the construction of the north wall of Grave 23.

Grave 26

History and Details of Excavation

Grave 26 is a built burial enclosure that lies on the southwest slope of the Vronda ridge, just west of the LM IIIC shrine and in line with Graves 27 and 32 (Figs. 3, 4). While the area to the east was dug in 1988, the grave itself was excavated in 1989 and 1990 in Trench V 8700, uncovered during exploration of the LM IIIC shrine and its surroundings (Gesell, Day, and Coulson 1995, 81, pl. 24:a, b). The area had been badly disturbed in the Venetian and modern periods by the construction of a terrace wall, agriculture, and activities associated with Building F to the east, including the digging of rubbish pits.

The eastern half of Trench V 8700 up to a modern terrace wall was excavated in 1988, and some material discarded from the grave came from the two major layers that overlay the grave: an upper layer of cobbles and pebbles (V 8702, V 8709) and a lower layer of stone tumble (V 8703, V 8710). In 1989 the modern terrace wall was removed (V 8713) and the same layer of cobbles and pebbles was traced over this area (V 8715, V 8716, V 8717, V8718, V 8719, V 8722) with stone tumble below it (V 8723, V 8724). Grave 26 was identified and distinguished from the rock tumble above it by the soft, ashy soil that contained quantities of snail shells and some human bones. A burial in a smashed amphora was uncovered in V 8727 in the northwest corner of the enclosure, and a test below this layer to the south (V8730, V 8731) revealed more burials. The lower part of the grave was excavated in 1990 as V 8732.

Two burials were recognized in the field, and subsequent study showed that there were three individuals, one in the amphora (**GR26 P22**) higher up in the northwest corner and two in the lower part of the grave. The walls of the grave were only one to two courses deep, and the grave itself was a large pit below the walls cut into a red clay layer that seems to have been laid down earlier, perhaps in Middle Minoan times. At the bottom of the pit were the remains of five carbonized beams running east to west across the enclosure. The most northerly beam was 0.50 m long and 0.12–0.18 m wide; the southern beam was 0.10 m wide. The beams and the hard red clay of the sides of the pit demonstrate clearly that some of the cremations occurred in situ.

Architecture

Grave 26 was a built, stone-lined burial enclosure, oriented north–south and measuring 1.98 m north–south x 1.14 m east–west (Fig. 119; Pls. 52A, 52B). The west wall was not preserved, making the east–west dimensions uncertain. The east wall (V 8728) was originally thought to be an earlier terrace wall, perhaps built to support the LM IIIC shrine to the west above it, but as it bonds with the south wall of the grave, this interpretation now seems unlikely, and it seems best to consider it part of the original grave structure. The east wall was one to two courses high, with a good western face but no eastern face. The south wall (V 8729), which bonds with the east wall, is wide, with two good faces and two courses, but it ends in a jagged edge on the west, as if cut off later. The north wall is a single row of stones only one course high. Between the row of stones of the north wall and the massive wall that bounds a platform south of Grave 27 was a stone paving, perhaps forming a platform (V 9260) similar to the one associated with Grave 3. Most of the walls are constructed of limestone blocks, and there is little use of the breccia found in many of the other graves. None of the walls goes down to the bottom of the grave, which was dug into the red clay. The bottom of the east wall is 0.44 m above the floor of the pit; the bottom of the north wall is 0.64 m above the floor; and the bottom of the south wall is 0.38 m above the floor of the pit (Pl. 52C).

Stratigraphy

The total deposition in Grave 26 from the bottom of the stone tumble that went over it to the bottom of the pit was 0.63 m. The amphora burial in the northwest corner was high up in the deposit (Pls. 52D, 52E). The bottom of this burial was 0.17 m higher than the floor of the pit.

Although the grave was a stone-lined enclosure, the bottom of the grave was actually a large oval pit cut out of the red clay-like soil. The pyre was laid directly on the floor of the pit, and five beams from the pyre were still visible at the time of excavation. The two lower burials may have belonged to a single burial event, as they were both in the center of the pit and there was no evidence that one pushed the other aside during a second cremation. The fact that so much of the pottery was burned, however, suggests that there were at least two events. Perhaps the individual in the amphora was cremated in the enclosure, and then the bones were removed, placed in the amphora, and deposited back in the enclosure. The grave was filled with soft, dark, ashy soil (10YR 6/3 pale brown) with cobbles, bones, and burned ceramics (V 8732, V 8730, V 8731).

A layer of small pebbles and flat stones seems to have segregated the lower burials from the upper layer containing the amphora burial (V 8727; Pl. 52B), but otherwise the two deposits were similar. A layer of large stones or rock tumble overlay the entire grave, its walls, and the area to the east (V 8723, V 8724, V 8703, V 8710), and this tumble contained some grave material perhaps thrown out when the amphora burial was put in. Above the rock tumble was a layer of smaller cobbles and pebbles (V 8702, V 8722, V 8715, V 8716, V 8717, V 8718, V 8719, V 8709) in which a few fragments of grave material appeared. This layer had been disturbed by a pit (V 8711, V 8720): a circle of dark soil that may have been from an olive tree. It contained nothing from the grave nor was it a dump from any of the graves in the area. The modern surface soil lay just above the layer of cobbles and pebbles (V 8700, V 8701, V 8707, V 8708, V 8712). To the west of Grave 26, west of the modern terrace wall, was more rock tumble that contained material from Grave 26 (V 8726).

Associated Features

The grave may have had some association with the other graves in the area; Graves 26, 27, and 32 are roughly in a line. The paved area or platform north of Grave 26 may have been used for a postfuneral ritual or event; it butted up against a similar but more massive paved platform that lay to the south of Grave 27.

Burials

Three burials were found in Grave 26: two adults and a juvenile. One of the adults and the juvenile are disturbed primary cremations, while the second adult is a secondary cremation in an amphora set in the north end of the enclosure.

Burials 1 and 2

Type: disturbed commingled primary cremations
Age: adult and juvenile, 16–18 years
Sex: unknown
Weight: 1,632 g

Burials 1 and 2 are disturbed primary cremations. While there was very little anatomical arrangement to the bone, and the two individuals were so commingled that it was not possible to distinguish the two burials, there is ample evidence that extensive burning took place in the grave. There probably were two separate cremation pyres, but the evidence from the bones is not definitive. The bone is completely calcined and in very fragmentary condition. There were two clusters of cranial bone. One lay at the north end of the enclosure, and the other against the west side at about the midpoint.

The skeletons represent one older adult, at least 40–60 years old, and one juvenile, probably an older child or teenager. The material is too fragmentary to make precise age or sex determinations. There is an unfused femoral epiphysis, indicating that the juvenile was somewhat less than 18–20 years old (Steele and Bramblett 1988, 219). There are no pathologies or anomalies found on this bone. Only 15 g of bone could definitely be assigned to the juvenile. No joins were found between this skeletal material and that of Burial 3, the amphora burial.

Burial 3

Type: secondary cremation deposit in amphora
Age: adult
Sex: unknown
Weight: 9 g

Burial 3 consists of the partial remains of a cremated adult, deposited in a G amphora (**GR26 P22**). Only a few skeletal elements were found in the amphora, including some cranial material and a single radius shaft segment, probably constituting a culturally significant token representation of the individual. A similar pattern of element selection was recognized in Grave 28, Burials 6 and 7 (see below; Liston 2007, 58, 61). The bone is nearly all calcined.

Faunal Remains

The sheep or goat bones recovered from the lower levels (V 8731.1–5) of this enclosure may represent the complete body of an animal that was probably burned in situ (Table 9). All portions of the animal carcass are represented, with fragments from the skull and mandibles, the vertebra and axial elements, and both front and hind limbs having been identified. Articular joint units from front and back limbs are represented by distal long bones (radius and ulna) and associated carpals. Evidence of the apparent burning of a whole animal is unique in the Vronda cemetery assemblage.

Botanical Remains

A rather large number of botanical remains were recovered from the lower part of the grave. These include a large quantity of grapes (*Vitis vinifera*), two peas (*Pisum* sp., *Pisum* sp. *Granular testa*), an unidentified legume, and fool's parsley (*Aethusa cynapium*). The grapes are possibly offerings placed on the grave, while the peas and legumes may be the remains of funerary meals or provisions for the dead. The fool's parsley may have had medicinal significance, or it could simply represent a weed in the area at the time of cremation. At least five charred beams were noted running east–west across the grave at the bottom.

Pottery

Grave 26 produced some 1,085 fragments of pottery weighing 4.75 kg. Twenty-three vessels were reconstructed from these fragments and from fragments found in the rubble and cobble layers above. Several pieces could be associated with the amphora burial, including the amphora itself (**GR26 P22**), a skyphos (**GR26 P13**), which was found in the smashed center of the amphora, and a second skyphos (**GR26 P1**). Other vessels that were picked up in the rock tumble above may also have come from this burial, although they could have been thrown out when the amphora burial was made. These vessels include mug or jug **GR26 P3**, cup **GR26 P7**, necked jar **GR26 P21**, and oinochoe **GR26 P23**; parts of the oinochoe were also found in the rock tumble to the west. It is possible that some of the pottery found in the tumble was used in postfunerary rituals, although the considerable disturbance in the upper levels of this area during the Venetian occupation of Building F, especially a hole dug for planting a tree or disposing of rubbish, makes it impossible to be sure.

Within the grave itself, two trays (**GR26 P4**, **GR26 P5**), two lids (**GR26 P6**, **GR26 P17**), two skyphoi (**GR26 P9**, **GR26 P10**), a pyxis (**GR26 P11**), a kalathos (**GR26 P15**), a hydria (**GR26 P20**), and a jug (**GR26 P18**) were found in clusters on the north and west sides. Skyphos **GR26 P8** was also found on the west side and kalathos **GR26 P16** on the north.

The assemblage is unusual for its number of skyphoi and kalathoi and the scarcity of cups; it is similar in character to Grave 36. An unusual number of large pouring vessels is represented: an oinochoe (**GR26 P23**), a hydria (**GR26 P20**), and a jug (**GR26 P18**). There are also more lids than are usually found. In addition to the three small lids that might have sealed the pouring vessels (**GR26 P6**, **GR26 P12**, **GR26 P17**), many of the skyphoi and kalathoi may also have been used as lids (especially **GR26 P16**). One of the trays (**GR26 P4**) is unique in having only one flat triangular lug; the other (**GR26 P5**) is of the usual type with two lug handles. A fragment of another lid, bowl, or cup similar in shape to **GR28 P18** and **GR32 P11** was found in V 8732.1.

The oinochoe (**GR26 P23**), hydria (**GR26 P20**), and amphora (**GR26 P22**) are unusual shapes in the Vronda graves, although not uncommon in East Crete. The shape of the belly-handled amphora with handles set high on the shoulder (**GR26 P22**) has parallels at LG Hagios Georgios (Tsipopoulou 2005, 152, fig. 28:AN1813) and EO Eleutherna (Kotsonas 2008, 99–100, fig. 15:A15), while several of the decorative motifs appear on a LG vessel from Vrokastro (Hayden 2003, 67, no. 172, fig. 42, pl. 29). The hydria (**GR26 P20**) is similar to examples of LG–EO date from Hagios Georgios (Tsipopoulou 2005, 148, fig. 46:AN1791; 159, fig. 49:AN2413; 163, fig. 43:AN2428), as well as earlier PGB hydriai from Knossos (Coldstream and Catling, eds., 1996, 36, pl. 72:3) and LPG–EG Fortetsa (Brock 1957, 36, 147, pl. 25:340, 342, 349). The decoration of dotted zigzag has parallels at LG Hagios Georgios (Tsipopoulou 2005, 180, fig. 89:Σ4030) and at Knossos in an earlier PGB–EG vessel (Coldstream and Catling, eds., 1996, 154, fig. 110:105). The oinochoe (**GR26 P23**) was made in a highly unusual coarse fabric that was uniformly burned gray, as if to imitate a metal (silver?) prototype. Its shape is unique in Crete but has parallels in an oinochoe of CG II–III date from Palaepaphos-*Skales* on Cyprus (Karageorghis 1983, 148, fig. 119:T. 631, 2) and in a gray oinochoe possibly imported from Phrygia and found at Eleutherna (Kotsonas 2008, 282–285, fig. 70). Petrographic analysis, however, indicates that it was manufactured on the north coast of East Crete, and it may be an imitation of a Cypriot shape or Phrygian technique.

Objects

The metal objects and terracotta bead from Grave 26 all seem to belong with the earlier two burials in the enclosure. The two spearheads and dirk suggest that the adult burial in the grave was male; children in the Vronda burial population were not generally provided with many gifts, but weapons, especially pairs of spearheads (**GR26 M2**, **GR26 M3**) and a dagger or dirk (**GR26 M4**) as seen here, often seem to accompany adult male burials. The two spearheads are similar in shape, with sloped shoulders and no pronounced midrib, but one of them is longer than the other; one (**GR26 M3**) may have been a spear, the other (**GR26 M2**) a javelin. The dirk is of the same type as found in other Vronda burials. The fibula (**GR26 M1**) is a simple arched type but is unusual in having a double coil. Finally, the bead (**GR26 TC1**) is an unusual variety, both in shape (flat cylindrical) and in its elaborate incised decoration and polished surface.

Chronology

Dating the grave is difficult. The three vessels that can be assigned to the last burial all seem to be of LG date. The rest of the material from the north and west sides that may belong with the earlier burials also seems to be of LG date, with a few pieces of an earlier style mixed in and a few that are of LG–EO date. The grave seems to have been in use, then, over a relatively short time during the later part of the LG period. The material from Grave 26 has many similarities to that from Grave 36, and perhaps the two graves were contemporary, but their similarities could, alternatively, be functional rather than chronological.

Catalog

Pottery

Fine Decorated Wares

GR26 P1 (V 8727.1, V 8730.1; Fig. 120). Skyphos. Partially mended from 22 fragments. Preservation 25%, including 75% of base, one handle, and bits of rim. Max. pres. h. 5.4; d. rim 11.0; d. base 4.0. Fine, soft, reddish-yellow (5YR 6/6) fabric with many voids. Red (2.5YR 5/8) paint. Very worn surfaces. Metopal panel with horizontal bands and uncertain curvilinear ornament, probably S-pattern. *Comparanda*: Kotsonas 2008, 195–196, fig. 47:A283, A308 (Eleutherna, LGB–PGB). *Date*: LG.

GR26 P2 (V 8727.1; Fig. 120). Mug or jug. Two joining fragments from rim with handle attachment. Max. pres. h. 4.2; d. rim 7.0. Fine, soft, reddish-yellow (5YR 7/6) fabric with some small phyllites, hard white inclusions, and gold mica. Black paint. Very worn surfaces on exterior, but well preserved on interior. Band on rim and in handle zone. Shape uncertain. May be a jug or mug. Possibly same vessel as **GR26 P3**. *Date*: LG?

GR26 P3 (V 8723.2, V 8724.2, V 8727.1, V 8730.1, V 8731.1; Fig. 120). Mug or jug. Partially mended from 27 fragments. Preservation 25%, including entire base and lower body. Max. pres. h. 7.0; d. base 4.4. Fine, soft, light reddish-brown (5YR 6/4) to pink (5YR 7/4) fabric with a few phyllites, some carbonates, and gold mica, like **GR26 P2**. Worn surfaces. Streaky black paint. Horizontal bands. *Comparanda*: possibly an imitation of a Corinthian LG kotyle, like Coldstream 1968, pl. 19:f, h, k, l; Mook 1993, 232, fig. 67:P191 (Kavousi Kastro, Corinthianizing). If **GR23 P2** and **GR23 P3** go together, shape like Tsipopoulou 2005, 181, fig. 88:Σ4034 (Hagios Georgios, LG, jug). *Date*: LG?

GR26 P4 (V98.121; V 8732.1–4, V 8732.4 W, V 8732.5 N; Fig. 120; Pl. 53). Tray with reflex-type lug. Restored from 60 fragments. Preservation 75%, including full profile, entire base, 85% of rim, and lug. H. 6.7 (with lug 8.5); d. rim 17.2–20.2; d. base 13.5–14.0. Fine, soft, reddish-yellow (5YR 7/6) fabric. Black paint. Surface mostly polished, with paint preserved on underside of lug. Worn surfaces. Many fragments burned. Ledge under inturned rim. Uneven. Only one lug, which is not flat but at an angle from rim. Strokes on top and underside of lug. *Comparanda*: Hayden 2003, 70, nos. 185, 186, fig. 44 (Vrokastro, LG–O?). *Date*: LG.

GR26 P5 (V98.209; V 8732.1–5, V 8732.4 W, V 8732.5 N; Fig. 120; Pl. 53). Tray with reflex-type lugs. Restored from 30 fragments; 27 nonjoining fragments. Preservation 50%, including full profile, 25% of base, 40% of rim, one entire lug and parts of another. H. 6.3 (with lug 8.5); d. rim 17.3; d. base 14.2. Fine, soft, reddish-yellow (5YR 7/6) fabric. Black paint. Very worn surfaces, once polished. One fragment of rim entirely coated with oxidation from iron dagger **GR26 M4**. Many fragments burned. Lug not flat but at angle from rim. Strokes on top of lug. *Comparanda*: Coldstream and Catling, eds., 1996, 117, fig. 98:208 (Knossos, O); 168, fig. 117:125.15 (Knossos, MG); Hayden 2003, 70, nos. 185, 186, fig. 44 (LG–O?); Tsipopoulou 2004, 134, 140, fig. 8:00/254 (Chalasmenos, LG); 2005, 104–105, fig. 134:H756, 758 (Kavousi, Plai tou Kastrou, LG–EO); Kotsonas 2008, 222, 224, fig. 55:A117β (Eleutherna, MG–LG). *Date*: LG.

GR26 P6 (V98.213; V 8732.2–4, V 8732.4 W, V 8732.5 N; Fig. 120; Pl. 53). Lid. Restored from 11 fragments; three nonjoining fragments. Preservation 45%, including 60% of rim and body; missing top. Max. pres. h. 3.4; d. rim 11.0. Fine, soft, pale brown (10YR 6/3) to light brownish-gray (10YR 6/2) fabric. Black paint? Very worn surfaces. All fragments burned. Possibly decorated with crosshatching. Domed lid, pierced near rim. *Comparanda*: Coldstream and Catling, eds., 1996, 92, fig. 85:48.12 (Knossos, MG); Tsipopoulou 2004, 135, 141, fig. 10:00/656 (Chalasmenos, LG). *Date*: LG.

Fine Monochrome Wares

GR26 P7 (V98.204; V 8703.3, V 8723.2, V 8724.1, V 8727.1, V 8730.1, V 8731.2; Fig. 120; Pl. 53). Cup. Restored from 29 fragments; 29 nonjoining fragments. Preservation 60%, including most of base, entire handle, much of rim. H. 10.0; d. rim 12.0; d. base 6.0. Fine, soft, light gray (5Y 7/1) fabric, reddish-yellow (5YR 7/6) on surface, with tiny white, chalky inclusions; some fragments seem very hard. Thick, glossy black paint. *Comparanda*: Coldstream and Catling, eds., 1996, 247, fig. 141:112 (EO); Mook 2004, 176, fig. 12.11:E (Kastro, LG); Tsipopoulou 2004, 132, 139, fig. 6:01/1077 (Chalasmenos, LG). *Date*: LG.

GR26 P8 (V98.205; V 8724.1, V 8732.2 and 3, V 8732.4 W; Fig. 120; Pl. 53). Skyphos. Restored from 36 fragments. Preservation 75%, including full profile, entire base, half of rim and body, both handles. H. 6.2; d. rim 7.2; d. base 4.6. Fine, soft, reddish-yellow (5YR 7/6) fabric with many voids and small carbonate inclusions. Very worn surfaces. Many fragments burned. *Comparanda*: Coldstream 1972, 81–82, fig. 7:D23 (Knossos, MG); 98, fig. 9:G138 (LG). *Date*: LG.

GR26 P9 (V98.206; V 8732.1–4, V 8732.4 W, V 8732.4 N, V 8732.5 N; Fig. 120; Pl. 53). Skyphos. Restored from 19 fragments; three nonjoining fragments. Preservation 35%, including full profile, both handles. H. 6.4; d. rim 10.0; d. base 3.5. Fine, soft, rather porous, reddish-yellow (5YR 7/6) fabric. Very pale brown (10YR 8/4) slip. Very worn surfaces. Many burned fragments, joining to unburned ones. Several fragments stained with iron oxide. *Comparanda*: Coldstream 1972, 82, fig. 7:D28 (Knossos, MG or early LG); Tsipopoulou 2005, 103, fig. 115:H749 (Kavousi, Plai tou Kastrou, LG). *Date*: LG.

GR26 P10 (V98.207; V 8703.2, V 8732.2–5, V 8732.4 W, V 8732.4 N, V 8732.4 E, V 8732.5 N; Fig. 120; Pl. 53). Skyphos. Restored from 15 fragments; 12 nonjoining fragments. Preservation 50%, including full profile, 90% of base, 20% of rim, and one handle. H. 5.6; d. rim 10.3; d.

base 4.8. Fine, very soft, reddish-yellow (5YR 7/6) fabric, soapy to touch. Very pale brown (10YR 8/2) slip. Very worn surfaces. A few burned fragments. *Comparanda*: **GR26 P13**; Brock 1957, 56, 166, pl. 38:587 (Knossos, LG–EO); Coldstream and Catling, eds., 1996, 214, pl. 199:4; 262, fig. 144:6 (Knossos, EO kotyle). *Date*: LG.

GR26 P11 (V98.208; V 8732.2–4, V 8732.4 W, V 8732.5 N; Fig. 120). Pyxis. Partially mended from 26 fragments. Preservation 40%, including 75% of base, 30% of rim, both handles. Max. pres. h. 4.0; h. est. 8.2; d. rim 8.3; d. base 5.5. Fine, soft, reddish-yellow (5YR 7/6) fabric, very smooth to touch. Very worn surfaces. Some burned fragments. *Date*: LG.

GR26 P12 (V98.212; V 8732.1–3; Fig. 121; Pl. 53). Strainer lid. Restored from nine fragments. Preservation 40%, including full profile. H. 2.0; d. rim 9.1. Fine, soft, reddish-yellow (5YR 7/6) fabric. Dark reddish-brown (5YR 3/4) paint. Worn surfaces. Some fragments burned. Two rows of holes pierced from outside to interior. *Comparanda*: Coldstream and Catling, eds., 1996, 270, pl. 248:229 (Knossos, MG). *Date*: LG.

Fine Plain Wares

Some pieces of the fine plain wares may have had decoration, but their surfaces are too worn to determine whether it was present or not.

GR26 P13 (V89.38, IM 1237; V 8732.2, V 8732.4, V 8732.4 W; Fig. 121; Pl. 53). Skyphos. Restored from 25 fragments. Preservation 90%, including full profile, entire base, 25% of rim and both handles. H. 5.6; d. rim 9.3; d. base 4.7. Fine, very soft, chalky reddish-yellow (5YR 6/6) fabric. Pink (7.5YR 8/4) slip or surface. Very worn surfaces. Some fragments burned. String marks on base. *Comparanda*: **GR26 P10**; Brock 1957, 56, pl. 38:587 (Knossos, LG–EO); Coldstream and Catling, eds., 1996, 214, pl. 199:4; 262, fig. 144:6 (Knossos, EO kotyle). *Date*: LG.

GR26 P14 (V98.210; V 8727.1, V 8732.2–5, V 8732.4 W; Fig. 121; Pl. 53). Kalathos. Restored from 38 fragments. Preservation 50%, including full profile and one handle. H. 7.0; d. rim 16.0; d. base 5.1. Fine, soft, reddish-yellow (5YR 7/6) fabric. White (10YR 8/1) slip. Very worn surfaces. Some fragments burned. Three grooves on rim. *Comparanda*: Coldstream and Catling, eds., 1996, 116, fig. 98:181 (Knossos, LO). *Date*: LG.

GR26 P15 (V98.211; V 8732.1–5, V 8732.4 W, V 8732.5 N; Fig. 121; Pl. 54). Kalathos. Restored from 31 fragments, 60% preserved, including full profile, both handles. H. 7.0–7.5; d. rim 15.0; d. base 6.0. Fine, soft, rather porous, reddish-yellow (7.5YR 7/6) fabric. Very pale brown (10YR 8/3) slip. Very worn surfaces. Many burned fragments joining to unburned ones. *Date*: LG.

GR26 P16 (V 8732.3 and 4, V 8732.5 N; Fig. 121). Kalathos or lid. Partially mended from 13 fragments. Preservation 25% of rim and upper body, along with one handle; missing base. Max. pres. h. 4.8; d. rim 15.0. Fine, soft, reddish-yellow (5YR 7/6) fabric. Very pale brown (10YR 8/3) slip or surface. Very worn surfaces. Many burned fragments. *Comparanda*: Coldstream and Catling, eds., 1996, 41, fig. 70:5 (Knossos, EG). *Date*: LG.

GR26 P17 (V98.214; V 8732.2–4, V 8732.4 W, V 8732.5 N; Fig. 121; Pl. 54). Conical lid. Restored from 12 fragments. Preservation 30%, including full profile, two holes. H. 2.9; d. rim 9.5. Fine, soft, reddish-yellow (7.5YR 7/6) fabric. Very pale brown (10YR 8/3) slip. Very worn surfaces. Nearly all fragments burned. Grooves around top; two holes pierced near rim. *Comparanda*: Coldstream and Catling, eds., 1996, 57, fig. 73:1.6 (Knossos, LG–EO); Tsipopoulou 2004, 135, 141, fig. 10:00/656 (Chalasmenos, LG). *Date*: LG.

GR26 P18 (V 8732.2–4, V 8732.4 W, V 8732.5 N; Fig. 121). Jug. Partially mended from 25 fragments of base, 19 from neck and rim. Preservation 30% of base and bit of rim; not certain that the two halves go together. Max. pres. h. 6.2; d. rim 4.6; d. base 8.6. Fine, soft, reddish-yellow (7.5YR 7/6) fabric. Very pale brown (10YR 8/3) slip. Very worn surfaces and smooth edges. Many fragments burned. Very crudely made base, with bits of clay added around edge of base. Interior of neck has striations that spiral up from shoulder to rim. *Date*: LG.

GR26 P19 (V 8732.4; Fig. 121). Aryballos. Single fragment from rim and neck; missing base, body, and handle. Max. pres. h. 1.7. Fine, soft, reddish-yellow (7.5YR 7/6) fabric. Pink (7.5YR 7/4) slip. Worn surfaces. No burning. *Date*: LG?

Medium-Coarse Decorated Wares

GR26 P20 (V98.122; V 8732.2–4, V 8732.4 W, V 8732.4 N, V 8732.5 N, V 9259.1; Fig. 121; Pl. 54). Hydria. Restored from 143 fragments. Preservation 80%, including full profile, two handles; missing parts of neck, rim, body, base, and part of vertical handle. H. 30.8; d. rim 8.5; d. base 9.0. Medium-coarse, rather soft, reddish-yellow (5YR 7/6) fabric with dark gray siltstones. Petrographic sample KAV 15/69: Fabric Group 5. Pale yellow (2.5Y 8/2) slip. Black paint worn to shadow. Worn surfaces. Many fragments burned but joining with unburned ones. Vertical rim, flattened on top and pierced twice. Concave upper neck to ridge. Ridge at base of neck. Ovoid body, ring base. Dotted zigzag(?) on neck. Double row of dotted zigzag on shoulder. *Date*: LG.

GR26 P21 (V 8702.1; Fig. 122). Necked jar. Partially mended from 82 fragments. Preservation entire base, 20% of rim and one handle; profile can be restored. H. est. 13.5; d. rim 9.0; d. base 6.0. Medium-coarse, very soft, gritty, reddish-yellow (7.5YR 7/6) fabric with phyllites and carbonates. Traces of red paint on exterior and underside of vessel. Very worn surfaces. No burning. *Comparanda*: Coldstream and Catling, eds., 1996, 43, pl. 77:P1 (Knossos, LPG–PGB); Tsipopoulou 2005, 254, fig. 59:H6233 (Praisos, LG); 290, fig. 60:AN8776 (Praisos, LG); Kotsonas 2008, 103–104, fig. 16:A192 (Eleutherna, EG). *Date*: LG.

GR26 P22 (V98.124; V 8726.2, V 8727.2 and 3, V 8730.1; Fig. 122; Pl. 54). Belly-handled amphora. Restored from numerous fragments. Preservation 85%; missing bits of body, base, and much of rim. H. 39.0; d. rim 13.0; d. base 11.5. Medium-coarse, soft, very chalky, reddish-yellow (7.5YR 7/4) fabric. Black paint worn to shadow. Very worn surfaces and edges; consolidation was required before it could be restored. Tall, flaring neck; ovoid body; bucranium handles, raised flat base. Extra clay used on interior at neck attachment. Concentric circles on neck, possibly on lower body. Hatched and crosshatched designs on shoulder and body. *Date*: LG.

Medium-Coarse Monochrome Ware

GR26 P23 (V98.123; V 8702.1, V 8710.2, V 8719.1, V 8723.2, V 8726.2, V 8727.1 and 2; Fig. 122; Pl. 54). Trefoil-mouthed oinochoe. Restored from 24 fragments; 11 nonjoining fragments. Preservation 75%, including full profile, entire base, 25% of body, entire rim. H. 18.2; d. base 7.0. Medium-coarse, rather hard, gray to dark gray (N5/0–7.5YR 4/0) fabric with phyllites, hard white inclusions and some softer ivory-colored bits. Petrographic sample KAV 15/70: Fabric Subgroup 1b. Black paint. Very worn surfaces. Uniformly burned. Four grooves at base of neck. *Comparanda*: for shape, Brock 1957, 154, pl. 38:583 (Knossos, LG–EO); Sakellarakis 1986, 32–33, fig. 22, pls. 35, 36 (Archanes, LG–EO). *Date*: LG.

Metal

Bronze

GR26 M1 (V90.136; V 8732.3, object 4; Fig. 123; Pl. 54). Bronze fibula. One large fragment from bow and four fragments of pin and coil; missing catch plate. Max. pres. L. 3.5; max. w. 2.3; d. 0.3. Well-preserved bow, corroded pin. Simple arched bow, round in section, slightly flattened toward catch plate. Double coil. *Comparanda*: Blinkenberg 1926, 60–62, types II.1, II.2; Sapouna-Sakellaraki 1978, 42–45, pl. 3:51A, B (type IIa). *Date*: SM–PG.

Iron

GR26 M2 (V90.137; V 8732.2, object 1; Fig. 123; Pl. 54). Iron spearhead. Complete in four fragments. L. 28.3; max. w. 1.9; d. socket 1.4. Very corroded. Long (9.3) socket, wrapped very tightly without great diameter. No visible hole pierced in socket. Sloping shoulders. No midrib. Narrow blade.

GR26 M3 (V90.135; V 8732.3, object 3; Fig. 123; Pl. 54). Iron spearhead. Complete in two fragments, but bent. L. est. (unbent) 34.0; max. w. 2.3; d. socket 1.8. Socket and blade corroded, but well-preserved surfaces on one side of blade. Long (11.5) socket, folded tightly. No visible hole pierced in socket, but corrosion worst where hole should be. Long, narrow blade with curving shoulders. No midrib.

GR26 M4 (V90.138a; V 8732.3, object 2; Fig. 123; Pl. 54). Iron dirk. Nearly complete in five fragments; missing tip of hilt and tip of blade. Slightly bent. Max. pres. L. 36.2; L. est. 39.0; max. w. 3.6. Very corroded, with pottery fragment from **GR21 P4** stuck to blade. Long hilt, with rivet at top and another halfway down. No rivets at top of blade. Flange hilted. Long broad blade.

Terracotta

GR26 TC1 (V90.50, IM 996; V 8732.3, object 5; Fig. 123; Pl. 54). Terracotta bead. Disk. Intact. H. 1.0; d. 2.1; d. hole 0.4. Wt. 6.00 g. Fine, hard, red (2.5YR 4/6) fabric. Burnished red to black surface, possibly burned. Well-preserved surfaces. Incised decoration on all surfaces. On top are short stokes radiating from hole. On bottom are three groups of three strokes radiating from center hole. Horizontal bands with oblique strokes between on side. Hole larger on the bottom than on the top.

Grave 27

History and Details of Excavation

Grave 27 is a stone-lined burial enclosure lying on the southwestern slope of the Vronda ridge, in line with Graves 26 and 32 and west of the LM IIIC Shrine (Figs. 3, 4). It was excavated in 1989 in the north balk of Trench V 9200; the surrounding area was excavated in 1988 and 1990 (Gesell, Day, and Coulson 1995, 81). The grave had been robbed and was found almost entirely empty. After the removal of a modern terrace wall, the enclosure appeared, and it was cleared of a filling of loose boulders and soft soil that went down to the floor of the grave. A small amount of grave material was found within the enclosure, but most of the associated pottery and objects were recovered from the surface and stone tumble to the north, east, and west.

Architecture

Although the grave had been robbed, it was the most architecturally interesting of the graves in the area and one of the most elaborately constructed on Vronda. It was a built enclosure grave, oriented north–south and measuring 2.08 m north–south x 1.23–1.32 m east–west (Fig. 124; Pl. 55A). The east boundary (V 9253) is a terrace wall with a good western face only, preserved two courses high; it was built chiefly of limestone blocks, using little of the breccia bedrock (Pl. 55B). The south wall is massive, 1.25–1.05 m wide, with two good faces (V 9251, V 9258), and it was built of large, rectangular limestone blocks (Pl. 55C). It is the largest wall found associated with any of the graves, and it may have served as a paved platform for postfunerary rituals, as inferred for structures associated with Graves 3 and 26. The west wall (V 9252) is simply a row of stones, with two faces that were not of very good quality (Pl. 55D). Another single row of boulders to the north and west may have belonged to it (V 9271), but the boulders seem to have slipped out of position. The north wall is gone, but in the northeast corner two stones bonded into the east wall project out and show the original line of the north wall (Pl. 55B). Like the east wall, it was constructed of two courses. All walls show fracturing or calcination from the heat of the funeral pyre.

Stratigraphy

As the grave had been robbed, there was no stratigraphy. The floor of the grave was brecciating bedrock mixed with dirt. From the floor to the tops of the walls (V 9255), the enclosure was filled with loose, dry, crumbly pale brown (10YR 6/3) soil and loose rubble, some 0.45 m deep. Above the enclosure a modern terrace wall had been constructed. The area around the grave produced human bones, grave pottery, and objects. To the east, grave pottery was found in layers of stone tumble (V 9201, V 9204) and cobbles (V 9202, V 9203), as well as in the topsoil (V 9200). Fragments were also recovered from layers of rock tumble in Trench V 9700 (V 9702, V 9703). To the north, pottery and bones appeared in a layer of pale brown (10YR 6/3) soil (V 9257) and the rock tumble (V 9254) that lay over it. North and east, some grave material was collected in the topsoil of V 9280. To the west, more grave material appeared in stone tumble (V 9259) and in the cleaning of the single row of stones on the northwest (V 9261). On the south, material from Grave 27 appeared in V 9256 and V 9260, between Graves 26 and 27. In short, the people who robbed out the grave spread the material all over the surrounding areas.

Associated Features

The platform to the south seems to have been associated with Grave 27, perhaps functioning like the platforms to the south of Grave 3 and north of Grave 26.

Burials

Only the remains of a single individual, an adult(?) disturbed cremation, were recovered scattered around the area of the enclosure.

Burial 1

Type: disturbed primary cremation
Age: adult?
Sex: unknown
Weight: 66 g

Because of the robbing, very little human bone was recovered from in and around Grave 27. The burial remains appear to belong to a disturbed primary cremation, as there is extensive evidence of burning on the walls of the burial enclosure. The surviving bone is thoroughly calcined and includes fragments of both cranial and postcranial bone, but almost none of the fragments can be identified specifically. The bone is probably from an adult, but even this is not certain.

Faunal Remains

Few animal bones were collected from the area (Table 9). A burned sheep or goat tibia fragment was found, as well as a cervid antler fragment (**GR27 B1**), which was scraped and thinned and had a hole bored into it.

Pottery

The rubble from within the robbed grave produced only 102 fragments of pottery weighing 0.40 kg. Most of the pottery that can be associated with Grave 27 came from the surrounding areas. Thirteen vessels could be identified. The pottery assemblage is unusual in the number of decorated vessels present. A krater (**GR27 P4**), two or three amphorae (**GR27 P11**–**GR27 P13**), and a cup (**GR27 P1**) had unusually elaborate decoration; even the monochrome cups are of different fabrics or have uncommon decoration, like the painted base of **GR27 P2** or the bosses on cup **GR27 P8**.

The large decorated krater **GR27 P4** is unique to Vronda. The shape derives from the Attic MG II style (Coldstream and Catling, eds., 1996, 248, fig. 137:285.153), and it was much imitated at Knossos in the MG or early LG periods (Coldstream and Catling, eds., 1996, 114, pl. 123:117; 167, fig. 117:125.6; 175, fig. 122:134.25). A similar vessel also appears at MG II Vrokastro (Hayden 2003, 62, no. 159, fig. 37, pl. 25) and at the Kastro at Kavousi (pers. comm., M.S. Mook). In part, the decoration is also similar to that found on large vessels at Knossos of LG–EO date, such as the dotted meander (Coldstream and Catling, eds., 1996, 113, pl. 120:68; 151, pl. 148:8; 153, pl. 151:59), which is also found in East Crete (Hayden 2003, 69, no. 183, fig. 44, pl. 29; Tsipopoulou 2005, 145, fig. 51:AN1786), and the circles connected by tangents (Hayden 2003, 63, no. 160, fig. 38, pl. 25; 71, fig. 46:191), which are also particularly common at LG and SubLG Thera (Coldstream 1968, pl. 40:c–e). The curving parallel bands that rise from the bottom around and over the handles, however, are a peculiarity; they have parallels on Cypriot jugs or their imitations belonging to the CA I period. Combined with the unusual bichrome color of the paint on this vessel, this feature suggests a local imitation of both Knossian and Cypriot forms.

Much of the material, including the krater, was made of very soft, chalky fabrics with thick and glossy paints reminiscent of those from Grave 9. In addition to the cataloged pottery, there were fragments of at least seven more cups or skyphoi, one with a boss. Another medium-coarse vessel is represented only in body fragments decorated with horizontal bands and short vertical strokes between them.

Objects

In addition to the one cataloged fragment of iron (**GR27 M1**), which may come from a tool or a spit, there was also a fragment from a spear socket and another iron blade fragment. It is likely that at least one spearhead was buried with the individual(s) in the grave. Fragments of modified deer antler (**GR27 B1**) came from the area, possibly remains of inlay on a metal object.

Chronology

The large pedestaled krater **GR27 P4** dates in the EO period. Cup **GR27 P1** is similar to, but not exactly like, examples from Knossos or the cup from Grave 20 (**GR20 P1**); these vessels date to the early LG period at Knossos (Brock 1957, 45, pl. 35:420; Coldstream 1972, 94, pl. 28:G87; Coldstream and Catling, eds., 1996, 114, fig. 95:112; 143, fig. 105:96; 176, pl. 173:40). The other cups look to be of LG date but lack the fine-walled, crisp profiles found at the end of that period. For most of the pottery, a LG date, perhaps of the same phase as Grave 20, would not be inappropriate; a few pieces belong to the EO period.

Catalog

Pottery

Fine Decorated Wares

GR27 P1 (V 9250.3, V 9255.1, V 9256.1, V 9259.2 and 5; Fig. 125). Cup. Partially mended from nine fragments; three nonjoining fragments. Preservation 20%, including full profile and entire base; missing handle. H. 8.0; d. rim 9.8; d. base 4.4. Fine, rather hard, pink (7.5YR 7/4) to reddish-yellow (7.5YR 7/6) fabric. Very pale brown (10YR 8/2) slip. Black to reddish-brown (5YR 4/4) paint. Well-preserved surfaces. No burning. Panel in handle zone decorated with thick and thin vertical lines; horizontal stripes on rim. *Comparanda*: **GR20 P1**. *Date*: LG.

GR27 P2 (V 9250.4, V 9261.1–3; Fig. 125). Cup. Partially mended from 30 fragments. Preservation 25%, including 50% of base, full profile, lower handle attachment; missing handle. H. 8.7; d. rim 11.2; d. base 6.3. Fine, very soft, chalky, pink (7.5YR 8/4) to very pale brown (10YR 8/4) fabric. Petrographic sample KAV 15/73: Fabric Subgroup 1b. Black to light red (2.5YR 6/8) paint (on same fragment; caused by firing). Rather well-preserved surfaces. Monochrome. Bottom of base has parallel oblique strokes possibly on either side of a central circle. *Date*: LG.

GR27 P3 (V 9250.2 and 3, V 9254.1 and 2, V 9255.1, V 9257.1; Fig. 125). Cup or skyphos. Partially mended from six fragments; 32 nonjoining fragments. Preservation 20% of base and part of lower body; missing rim and handle(s). Max. pres. 7.0; d. base 6.0. Fine, soft, light reddish-brown (5YR 6/4) fabric. Black paint worn to brown shadow. Worn surfaces. Broad bands alternating with groups of narrow bands. *Comparanda*: Mook 2004, 177, fig. 12.12:A (Kastro, OR). *Date*: LG.

GR27 P4 (V 9200.2, V 9201.1 and 2, V 9250.4 and 5, V 9257.1, V 9261.1 and 3, V 9262.1, V 9280.1; Frontispiece; Fig. 126; Pl. 55E). Pedestaled krater. Partially mended from 66 fragments into three large rim and handle fragments; fragments of base and body do not join. Preservation 40%–45%, including most of stem, both handles; missing bottom rim of stem. Max. pres. h. 27.3; d. rim 22.8. Fine, very soft, chalky, very pale brown (10YR 8/4) fabric. Petrographic sample KAV 15/72: Fabric Subgroup 1b. Dark reddish-brown (2.5YR 3/4), red (2.5YR 5/8), and black paint. Worn surfaces. No burning. Horizontal bands on rim. Below rim are two zones of double circles connected with tangents above and below a dotted meander pattern. On lower body, fourfold circles with stars in center and pendant and upright dotted loops between them. At base of bowl are three zigzag lines. Large curving band of multiple lines, narrow bands between two broad, curve down from handle zone over other patterns and divide up the surface of the vessel into decorative areas; this curving band finds parallels on Cypriot jugs or their imitations. *Bibliography*: Gesell, Day, and Coulson 1995, pl. 24:c. *Comparanda*: for shape, Marinatos 1931–1932, 5, fig. 5 (Anavlochos, LG); Coldstream and Catling, eds., 1996, 175, fig. 122:134.25 (Knossos, MG–early LG); Blandin 2007, 22–23, pl. 34:1 (Eretria, MG II); for decoration, Brock 1957, 82, pl. 58:904. *Date*: EO.

GR27 P5 (V 9261.1 and 3; Fig. 126). Lekythos. Four joining fragments from rim and neck; five nonjoining fragments. Max. pres. h. 2.6; d. rim 7.0. Fine, soft, chalky, pale yellow (2.5Y 8/2) fabric. Black paint. Horizontal bands on rim and neck. *Comparanda*: **GR4 P20**. *Date*: LG–EO.

Fine Monochrome Wares

GR27 P6 (V 9200.2, V 9250.3, V 9259.2 and 5; Fig. 126). Cup. Partially mended from 26 fragments; 10 nonjoining fragments. Preservation 60%, including full profile, 65% of base, part of handle, and two large rim fragments. H. 9.8; d. rim 13.0; d. base 5.8. Fine, soft, reddish-yellow (7.5YR 7/6) fabric with some small phyllites, hard white bits, and voids. Black to dark reddish-brown (5YR 3/3) paint on interior, exterior, and underside of base. Worn surfaces. No burning. *Comparanda*: Mook 1993, 216, 465, fig. 160:P7.73 (Kavousi Kastro, LG). *Date*: LG.

GR27 P7 (V 9703.2, 3, 5, and 6, V 9280.2; Fig. 126; Pl. 55E). Cup. Partially mended from 35 fragments; 11 nonjoining fragments including handle. Preservation 60%, including full profile, 90% of base, 20% of rim; missing handle attachments. H. 8.5; d. rim 12.2; d. base 5.2. Fine, soft, red (2.5YR 5/6) fabric with reddish-yellow (7.5YR 7/6) surface and small dark gray inclusions. Black to brown (7.5YR 4/2) paint. Very worn exterior surfaces; better preserved inside. A few fragments discolored from fire. *Date*: LG.

GR27 P8 (V 9202.1, V 9261.1–3; Fig. 126). Cup. Partially mended from 15 fragments; four nonjoining fragments. Preservation 45%, including nearly full profile, 60% of base, and lower handle attachment, two bosses; missing rim and handle. Max. pres. h. 7.7; d. base 6.0. Fine, very soft and chalky, very pale brown (10YR 8/3) fabric with small red phyllites. Black paint on interior, exterior, and underside of base. Surfaces very worn except where paint preserved. Two bosses in handle zone. *Comparanda*: for the bosses, Tsipopoulou 2005, 86, fig. 128:H681 (Kavousi, Plai tou Kastrou, LG). *Date*: LG.

GR27 P9 (V 9250.3, V 9257.1; Fig. 126). Cup. Two nonjoining fragments from rim, including upper handle attachment. Max. pres. h. 3.5, d. rim 15.0. Fine, soft, very pale brown (10YR 7/3) fabric. Black(?) paint. Very worn surfaces. One fragment burned, the other not. *Date*: LG.

GR27 P10 (V 9250.3, V 9254.1; Fig. 126). Cup or skyphos. Partially mended from four fragments; two nonjoining fragments. Large fragment from rim; missing base, lower body, handle(s). Max. pres. h. 2.0; d. rim 11.0. Fine, soft, very pale brown (10YR 7/3) fabric. Black(?) paint. Very worn surfaces. Most fragments burned. Monochrome. *Date*: LG.

Medium-Coarse Decorated Wares

GR27 P11 (V 9254.2, V 9703.3, V 9703.5, V 9703.7; Fig. 127). Amphora or hydria. Three fragments from rim, one fragment from neck and shoulder, one body fragment, one base fragment. D. rim 16.0; d. base 13.0. Medium-coarse, soft, chalky, reddish-yellow (7.5YR 7/4) fabric with red phyllites. Petrographic sample KAV 15/71: Fabric Subgroup 1b. Black to red (2.5YR 4/8) paint. Very worn surfaces. Some fragments burned. Single zigzag and double zigzag. *Comparanda*: for decoration, Tsipopoulou 2005, 102, fig. 114:H746 (Plai tou Kastrou, LG). *Date*: LG.

GR27 P12 (V 9250.1–3; Fig. 127). Amphora or hydria. Two fragments, one from neck, one from base. Max. pres. h. (neck) 7.5; d. base 13.5. Medium-coarse, rather hard, reddish-yellow (7.5YR 7/6) fabric. Petrographic sample KAV 15/74: Fabric Subgroup 1b. Surfaces worn on base, well preserved on neck. *Date*: LG.

Coarse Decorated Wares

GR27 P13 (V 9201.2, V 9257.1, V 9280.1, V 9703.3 and 6; Fig. 127). Closed vessel, perhaps an amphora. Three nonjoining fragments, two from body, one preserving half of base. D. base 11.5. Fine, soft, chalky, very pale brown (10YR 8/3) fabric with frequent red phyllites. Petrographic sample KAV 15/75: Fabric Subgroup 1b. Yellowish-red (5YR 5/6) to black paint. Concentric circles, spirals, or guilloche. *Comparanda*: Tsipopoulou 2005, 116, fig. 18:H1957 (Skouriasmenos, LG–EO). *Date*: LG–EO.

Metal

GR27 M1 (V89.95; V 9250.3, object 2; Fig. 127; Pl. 55E). Iron tool or spit. Two joining fragments, possibly from blunt end of object. Max. pres. L. 4.4; max. d. 1.0. Corroded and cracked. Cylindrical object, round in section, possibly a spit or tool.

Bone

GR27 B1 (V 9254.1; Pl. 55E). Worked deer antler. Single fragment of antler; broken on all sides. Max. pres. L. 2.9; max. pres. w. 1.1; d. hole 0.4–0.5. Scraped and thinned, possibly faceted. Pierced with single hole. Calcined white. Possibly an inlay for iron sword or knife.

Grave 28

History and Details of Excavation

Grave 28 is a stone-lined burial enclosure that lies on the western slope of the Vronda ridge, in the area of the earlier LM IIIC Building O, Room O3 (Figs. 3, 4, 95). The enclosure was entirely excavated in 1989 in Trench VW 11100 (Gesell, Day, and Coulson 1995, 84–87, figs. 5, 6, pls. 26, 27; Day and Glowacki 2012, 101–103). In 1990, exploration of the areas to the west and north of the grave in Trenches VW 11100, VW 11200, and VW 12200 produced material that had been dumped from the burials during repeated use; this material included only pottery, and no human bones or other artifacts were found outside the enclosure.

After the removal of the surface soil over the entire trench, the grave began to appear as a terrace with rock tumble. During the cleaning of this tumble the first human bones were found. From this point, the grave was dug in many different loci, each with a different soil type and each containing a separate burial; eight burials were identified during excavation, and further study confirmed that there were eight individuals, six in the enclosure and two in vessels (**GR28 P3**, **GR28 P22**) in the southeast corner of the grave. These burials initially were given letter designations (Burials A–H) in the order in which they were recognized and removed. Later, these letters were changed to numbers to indicate the order in which the burials were thought to have occurred, and these ideas were refined as study continued and it became clear that the two pot burials were placed in the enclosure before the last cremation. Thus, in earlier reports the two pot burials were labeled burials 7 and 8 and the last cremation burial 6 (e.g., Day and Glowacki 2012, fig. 79, shows the last cremation as burial 6). The new numbers replaced the older letter designations as follows: Burial 1 = Burial G; Burial 2 = Burial H; Burial 3 = Burial E; Burial 4 = Burial D; Burial 5 = Burial B; Burial 6 (the amphora) = Burial F; Burial 7 (the necked jar) = Burial C; and Burial 8 = Burial A.

The rock tumble with rather soft soil (VW 11110) was excavated first. The cranial fragments of at least two burials appeared in the south (Burials 1 and 5) and in the center (Burial 8). In the southeast corner of the enclosure (VW 11110.2), packed in tightly among stones, two vessels appeared, each sealed with a cup or lid, with a large flat stone lid over the top of one (Pls. 56A–56C); each vessel contained the remains of a single individual (Burials 6 and 7).

Once these pot burials were removed, the looser rock tumble elsewhere in the enclosure was excavated, and the deposit within contained remains of different burials and soils that were kept separate by pails. Loci VW 11110.3, 6, and 9 contained the soft ashy soil of Burial 8, which was placed in a large pit that went quite deep and had cut into the lower deposits. This burial was recognized as being in anatomical order and was removed before the excavation of the lower levels proceeded. Locus VW 11110.5 lay along the western wall of the enclosure and contained no bones and very little other material. Locus VW 11110.7 on the south contained parts of Burial 5, while VW 11110.4 and 8 lay on the north within the area of Burial 4.

Many different stratigraphic features appeared after the removal of the stone tumble. Along the east wall was more tumble, very tightly packed together (VW 11111). In the center and south under this tumble was a layer of dark, dirty, brown soil (VW 11112), which overlay another cremation that was in anatomical order, Burial 3 (VW 11115). More of Burial 5 was removed in the southwest corner in VW 11113, while more of Burial 4 was recovered in VW 11114 in the northwest corner. After the removal of VW 11115, with its articulated cremation, two more cremations appeared. One (Burial 1) began in a soft, dark layer (VW 11116) but occurred primarily in a compact, reddish-brown layer in the south (VW 11119); some of this burial may have been pushed to the north into VW 11118. Along the north, in a similar compacted layer of soil and cobbles, another burial was recognized (Burial 2) in VW 11118 and VW 11120. At all times the excavators endeavored to remove the different stratigraphic units separately. For this reason, it is easier to reconstruct the sequence of burials and deposition in this grave than in any of the others.

In 1990 the area to the west of Grave 28 was uncovered to reveal more rooms of LM IIIC Building N. The area of Room N1 was found to be covered with a deep deposit of dark soil and large stones that was similar to grave soil (Day and Glowacki 2012, 108–110). No human bones appeared, however, so it was not given a grave designation. Subsequent study of the pottery indicates that this deposit was dumped from Grave 28, perhaps at the time the pit for Burial 8 was dug. Other dumps of material from Grave 28 were uncovered immediately to the north of the grave, and some fragments of pottery appeared just to the south.

Architecture

Grave 28 is a stone-lined enclosure measuring 1.76 m north–south x 1.60 m east–west (1.05 m to the edge of the bench in the earliest levels) and oriented northeast–southwest (Fig. 95; Pl. 56D). It made use of an existing terrace wall from one of the LM IIIC houses, the wall that supported the courtyard of Building I and served as the eastern boundary for Building O (VW 11015). Constructed primarily of bedrock boulders, it stood two courses high and had two good faces (Pl. 56E). The three other walls were built for the grave, but they are unusual in that they were real walls with two good faces rather than the rows of boulders commonly found in the graves. The south wall (VW 11123) was built for the enclosure on top of stone tumble from the collapsed Building O, tumble that fell directly on the roofing clay that overlay the floor of the building (Pl. 56E). A similar situation seems to have existed also on the north. The south wall is unusually thick (0.78–1.10 m) and abuts the terrace wall on the east; it was constructed largely of crude bedrock boulders without proper coursing, but sometimes two layers deep. The north wall (VW 11122) also has two good faces and measures 0.95–1.18 m; it merely abuts the east wall but bonds with the west wall at the corner.

The west wall (VW 11107) has a good outside face, but its inner face exists only in the single lower course of stones, labeled a bench (VW 11117) during excavation (Pl. 56F). Some of the later burials (4, 5, and 8) went over this addition to the wall, and it looks as though the grave was enlarged to the west when used for the last burials. This expansion may have allowed the builders to increase the size of the grave horizontally, and as a result those using the enclosure for Burials 4–8 did not dig deeper and disturb the first three burials. The original width of the west wall was 1.13–1.22 m, but after Burial 3 it measured only 0.50–0.63 m. All four walls show bedrock boulders calcined from the heat of the fire, and a sample taken from the west wall by soil scientists confirmed that the breccia had been burned. The floor of the grave was a surface of red and black mottled soil.

The grave is unusual for its preservation and depth and also for its walls, which were carefully constructed with two faces and were not just rows of boulders. The care used in construction may indicate the status of the individual initially buried in the enclosure.

Stratigraphy

Grave 28 had an unusual depth of deposition and complex stratigraphy that was excavated by each layer observed (Figs. 128, 129). Along the east, where the walls were highest, the deposit was 0.50–0.56 m deep; in the west it was 0.18–0.38 m deep. The builders went down to the floor level of Building O3 in the north, and bedrock in the south. Above this floor surface the first burial was made in the tomb, Burial 1. Most of the bones from this initial burial were found in a compact reddish-brown soil on the south (VW 11119), probably pushed there during the second cremation, but some skeletal remains were recovered from a softer dark soil in the southwest (VW 11116), and possibly along the north in VW 11118. Associated with this layer (VW 11119) were nearly all of the iron objects (Pl. 57A), including two spearheads (**GR28 M2, GR28 M3**), an axehead (**GR28 M5**), and a tool (**GR28 M6**), along with five monochrome cups (**GR28 P5–GR28 P9**) and a mug-like cup (**GR28 P11**).

On the north side of the grave were two soil layers containing the remains of Burial 2: a mottled black and red layer at the bottom (VW 11120) and a compact reddish-brown soil with dense cobbles (VW 11118) just above it. The iron knife (**GR28 M4**) was at the top of this layer; however, as iron objects tend to settle toward the bottom of a deposit, it may belong with Burial 4 in VW 11114 above it.

Burial 3 was an articulated cremation that had not been much disturbed by the later burial activity in the grave. The remains from this burial lay primarily in a soft, dark, ashy soil (VW 11115), although some bones were found in a mottled brown soil just above (VW 11112). The ashy soil contained a good deal of carbon, possibly from the beams used in the cremation; the wood grain of this carbon ran parallel to the long east wall of the enclosure. The remains of Burial 3 went over the bench that represents part of the west wall. When the pit that contained Burial 8 was made later, it scraped the top of Burial 3, and pottery from Burial 3 was apparently thrown out with the soil to the west; fragments of a large krater (**GR28 P25**) were found in both VW 11115 and in the dark ashy soil over Building N, Room N1 (VW 11201, VW 11205, VW 11212, VW 11213, VW 11215). Except for the scraping by Burial 8, Burial 3 was left undisturbed; subsequent burials (4 and 5) seem to have spread out horizontally over the top of the bench and did not go so deep in the grave.

Burial 4 was found along the north side of the grave where it had been pushed by the subsequent Burial 5. Some of the remains were found in a yellowish-brown soil with small cobbles in the northwest corner (VW 11114), and others were picked up in rock tumble in the northeast (VW 11110.4 and 8). The knife (**GR28 M4**) found at the top of VW 11118 may have been associated with Burial 4.

Burial 5 was found spread over much of the grave, except in the center, where the digging of the pit for Burial 8 resulted in its removal. Remains of this burial come from the rock tumble. In the southwest corner the bones appeared with brown soil and burned boulders in VW 11113 and above it in VW 11110.7. Some remains had also been pushed to the north and were picked up with Burial 4 from VW 11110.8. Along the east side of the grave remains of Burial 5 were found in a layer of densely packed tumble (VW 11111). Some remains were also picked up amid the rock tumble at the top of the grave in VW 11108.3.

Although it was difficult to distinguish the stratigraphic position of the pot burials, Burial 6 and Burial 7, they seem to have been made after Burial 5 but before Burial 8. The two vessels were wedged tightly into the southeast corner of the enclosure (VW 11110.2), with a circle of stones to support them (Pl. 56C). This tightly packed cobble layer was similar to VW 11111 to the north along the east wall of the enclosure, and it looks as though this layer had been cut into so the vessels could be wedged in tightly. The softer soil with cobbles from the pit of Burial 8 went over VW 11111, and it is likely that the vessels were put in first and Burial 8 was made later. Each of the two vessels contained a single individual, and the two pots, despite the chronological difference in style, were wedged in together very tightly and must have belonged to the same burial event. The northernmost jar (Burial 7; **GR28 P22**) was covered by a monochrome cup (**GR28 P4**) set upside down over its mouth. The mouth of the southern amphora (Burial 6; **GR28 P3**) had a lid (**GR28 P19**) set into it top down, and the whole group was covered by a large flat stone lid (**GR28 S1**; Pl. 57B).

The final burial in the grave appears to have been Burial 8, which was unusual. Instead of cleaning the enclosure out and creating a rectangular space for the pyre, the builders dug out a large pit in the center of the grave and cremated the individual in it. When this pit was dug, pottery from Burials 3, 4, and 5 was thrown out to the west. Burial 8 was found in the center of the enclosure in soft dark soil with cobbles (VW 11110.3, 6, and 9), and it went down to the top of Burial 3 in VW 11112. Associated with this burial were a bronze fibula (**GR28 M1**), a miniature jug (**GR28 P2**), a krater base (**GR28 P27**), and possibly a stemmed skyphos (**GR28 P1**).

Associated Features

Dumps of pottery and dark grave soil were found to the north of the grave (VW 11109, VW 11150), to the south (VW 10109, VW 10121, VW 10122), to the southwest (VW 10248), immediately to the west (VW 11103, VW 11106), and farther to the west in a massive deposit over LM IIIC Building N, Room N1 (VW 11201, VW 11212, VW 11213, VW 11214, VW 11215, VW 11218, VW 11220, VW 12200).

Burials

Eight burials were made in Grave 28, six primary cremations in the enclosure and two secondary cremations in vessels in the southeast corner of the grave. Two of the burials (Burials 3 and 8) were undisturbed primary cremations.

Burial 1

Type: disturbed primary cremation
Age: adult, 40–60 years
Sex: male
Weight: 1,350 g

Burial 1, the cremation burial of an adult male, is one of the earliest burials in the enclosure. The burial had been pushed to the south half of the grave together with a mass of pottery, probably at the time of the later cremations. The bone shows differential burning between the cranial bone and the postcranium, which is completely calcined. The exterior surface of the cranium is more burned than the interior. The skeleton is probably a male, between 40 and 60 years old, as is indicated by the cranial suture closure and further supported by the general condition of the joints, vertebral bodies, and dental wear. The preserved dentition includes a premolar in which the entire tooth crown was destroyed by a large caries. Other fragments of teeth show considerable wear, generally with destruction of the entire tooth crown. This wear suggests that the age of this man was probably in the later part of the 40–60-year range. Much of the skeleton is missing, presumably due to later activity in the enclosure.

Burial 2
Type: disturbed primary cremation
Age: juvenile, 7–14 years
Sex: unknown
Weight: 487 g

This burial was found scattered throughout the bottom of Grave 28. The burial is that of a juvenile, determined to have been between seven to 14 years old on the basis of the fused anterior arch of the atlas vertebrae. There is moderate porotic hyperostosis on the left and right parietals of the cranium associated with this burial, suggesting that the juvenile suffered from an anemic condition of unknown cause at the time of death. All of the bone is completely calcined and white in color.

Burial 3
Type: primary cremation
Age: adult, 20–40 years
Sex: female?
Weight: 1,351 g

Grave 28 is unusual among the Vronda enclosures in that it has two undisturbed primary cremation burials. The first, Burial 3, lay along the east side of the enclosure. The skeleton lay in anatomical order and was semiflexed, a position typical of cremated bodies due to contraction of the muscles during burning.

Burial 3 is an adult female, probably 20 to 40 years old, as determined on the basis of the cranial suture closure and degree of dental wear. The skeleton was not completely calcined, with the exception of the right leg. The rest of the skeleton was less thoroughly burned, with the ribs, vertebrae, and scapulae being unusually well preserved and complete. These portions of the skeleton are usually fragmented if not completely consumed during cremation.

The internal surface of the cranium has a number of clusters of lytic lesions, 1–3 mm in diameter, most located along the middle meningeal arteries. These lesions penetrate into the diploë of the cranium but not the outer table of the cranial bone. Such lesions are often associated with bacterial meningitis. Pitting on the endocranial surface of the petrous portions of the left and right temporal bones suggests that this could have been secondary to a middle ear infection (otitis media). The condition may ultimately have caused the woman's death.

Burial 4
Type: disturbed primary cremation
Age: adult, 60+ years
Sex: male?
Weight: 302 g

This burial is an older adult, possibly a male. The remains are white and completely calcined. Like Burials 1 and 3, much of the bone associated with this burial has been lost. The bone was found at the north end of the grave. Some periosteal bone formation on the left side of the frontal bone above the eye orbit suggests a localized lesion or trauma. There was a dental abscess in the right mandible around the roots of the canine and first premolar. Otherwise, there were no pathologies noted on the bone.

Burial 5
Type: disturbed primary cremation
Age: adult, 20–40 years
Sex: unknown
Weight: 242 g

Burial 5 is a disturbed cremation of an adult. The bone is all completely calcined and very fragmentary. It was collected from the south end of the enclosure, where it had apparently been pushed to make room for later burials. The individual is an adult, probably 20–40 years old, as indicated by the degree of closure of the cranial sutures.

Burial 6
Type: secondary cremation deposit
Age: adult
Sex: unknown
Weight: 19 g

This burial was contained in a Late Geometric amphora (**GR28 P3**) covered with a lid (**GR28 P19**) and sealed with a flat stone (**GR28 S1**). The bone is mottled white and gray, indicating incomplete cremation. The bone belonged to an adult of unknown sex. The preserved bone includes some cranial fragments, portions of the right scapula, and the right radius shaft (Liston 2007, 62, labeled burial 8).

Burial 7
Type: secondary cremation deposit
Age: adult
Sex: unknown
Weight: 14 g

The northern of the two pot burials, this burial was contained in a PG necked jar (**GR28 P22**) closed with an inverted cup (**GR28 P4**). The cremation produced a mottled coloration of the bone ranging from black and gray to the white of completely calcined bone. The bone belongs to an adult of unknown sex. Both cranial and postcranial bone are represented in the jar, and the postcranial bone includes an unsided radius fragment (Liston 2007, 62, labeled burial 7).

Burial 8
Type: primary cremation
Age: adult, 60+ years
Sex: male
Weight: 2,134 g

This burial is the second primary cremation in the grave. The bone was found in anatomical order, with the limbs flexed and the body slumping down into a pit in the center of the tomb that had apparently been dug before the pyre was constructed. This burial is a large, robust, adult male. The reconstructed femur has a midshaft diameter of 101.00 mm. By comparison, any circumference over 86.00 mm is normally a male individual. The cremation shows the frequently seen pattern of more complete cremation on the postcranium than on the cranium. The skeleton is an older man, probably more than 60 years. The mandible is edentulous, and the cranial sutures are completely obliterated. There is lipping and porosity on the preserved vertebral facets. On the cranial bone there is extensive but moderate porotic hyperostosis of the outer surfaces of the parietals, extending down as far as the supramastoid crests. In addition, the cortices of the long bone shafts are quite thin, 3.50 to 5.00 mm on the tibia and 4 to 7 mm on the femur shaft. This thinness suggests he had lost considerable bone mass either due to age-related osteopenia or some pathological process.

Faunal Remains

The two vessels containing the secondary burials were filled with loose soil apparently deposited gradually in the vessels, which contained, in addition to the human remains, the skeletons of dozens of tiny rodents. These animals were mostly shrews that presumably took up residence in the amphora over the millennia. There is no evidence that the rodents were grave offerings. A single worn murex shell was found in the rock tumble at the top of the grave (Table 5).

Botanical Remains

Botanical remains collected from Grave 28 include grape (*Vitis vinifera*), two legume fragments, and fool's parsley (*Aethusa cynapium*). Charred wood from the enclosure has been identified as oak (*Quercus coccifera*).

Pottery

Grave 28 produced some 795 fragments of pottery weighing 4.00 kg, as well as six complete vessels (**GR28 P2–GR28 P4, GR28 P19, GR28 P22**). In addition, much pottery discarded from the grave was found scattered widely to the west, and a few fragments were found to the south and north of the enclosure.

Some of the pottery can be associated with specific burials. Five monochrome cups (**GR28 P5–GR28 P9**) and a mug-like cup (**GR28 P11**) belong with the earliest burial in the grave, and they were all found together in the southeast corner, possibly associated with a burial ritual—a toast or libation. The large krater (**GR28 P25**) found scattered all over to the west of the grave and with Burial 3 probably goes with that burial, which was disturbed by Burial 8. The jug (**GR28 P20**) and possibly the aryballos (**GR28 P17**) may belong with Burial 5, as most of their fragments came from the loci associated with that burial.

The pottery found to the north and west of the grave—cups **GR28 P10**, **GR28 P12**, and **GR28 P13**, cups or skyphoi **GR28 P14–GR28 P16**, vessel **GR28 P18**, kraters **GR28 P21** and **GR28 P24**, and jar **GR28 P28**—are all part of the dump made at the time of Burial 8, and they could go with Burials 3, 4, or 5. Krater **GR28 P24** is an unusual piece that has a close parallel in shape and decoration in a Spartan PG vessel (Coldstream 1968, pl. 46:a), and in decoration on lekanai from LG Chalasmenos (Tsipopoulou 2004, 134, 140, fig. 8:01/189/3, 00/663). Krater **GR28 P21** is an unusual shape that is more open than closed, but it is not painted on the interior. The shape resembles a large skyphos from Knossos (Coldstream 1972, 82, 84, fig. 7:E1), but farther afield it is similar to Argive LG II kraters (Coldstream 1968, pls. 28:e, 29:d). However early the shape might appear, the decoration of zones of concentric circles is common on large open vessels of LG date from East Crete (Tsipopoulou 2013, 144) and can also be found on LG amphorae at Hagios Georgios (Tsipopoulou 2005, 129, fig. 20:H7420; 152, fig. 28:AN1813; 153, fig. 29:AN1815). A larger version of the krater is represented by **GR28 P25**, which was associated with Burial 3. The two-handled jar **GR28 P28** is an unusual type without parallels at Vronda. Similar coarse jars of PG–G date have been found at Phaistos (Rocchetti 1974–1975, 219, fig. 71:a), where the shape is called an amphoriskos (or kantharos). Coarse jars occur particularly in PG East Crete (Tsipopoulou 2005, 189, fig. 110:Σ4076B; 322, fig. 110:Σ3824), where they are identified as amphoroid kraters.

The vessels in the southeast corner held Burials 6 and 7, and they present an interesting picture. The southern amphora **GR28 P3** is probably of late LG date because of the running dog motif on its shoulder (Tsipopoulou 2005, 279, fig. 16:Σ3811). Although the shape does not find good parallels in any period, it resembles an EPG amphora at Knossos (Coldstream and Catling, eds., 1996, 32, pl. 67:7), which has higher-set handles, but it is also a more globular and elegant version of the crude East Cretan LG belly-handled amphorae (Tsipopoulou 2005, 153, fig. 29:AN1815). The northern necked jar **GR28 P22**, however, is very crude, and although it lacks good parallels, it seems to date much earlier, perhaps to the PG period. It is likely to have been an antique or heirloom piece, but the two burials were made at the same time and were contemporary. The other two vessels (**GR28 P4**, **GR28 P19**) used as lids for these vessels look LG in date. Finally, three pots can be associated with Burial 8, the latest of the primary cremations in the grave:

skyphos **GR28 P1**, miniature jug **GR28 P2**, and krater base **GR28 P27**. The stemmed skyphos is a peculiarly East Cretan shape (Tsipopoulou 2005, fig. 108) and belongs to the LG period.

Objects

Few objects were found in the grave, and most of them were associated with the first cremation. The two spear or javelin heads (**GR28 M2**, **GR28 M3**) are unusual because they are extraordinarily short, and the similarity between the two suggests that they formed a set. The axe-head (**GR28 M5**) is similar to those from Graves 6 and 9, and tool (**GR28 M6**) is probably a chisel. The knife (**GR28 M4**) may be associated with Burial 4 and is similar to examples from Graves 5 and 20. The fibula (**GR28 M1**) is of a type rare at Vronda; only one other example is known from Grave 32 (**GR32 M1**). The type is common elsewhere, however, from the middle of the eighth century until about 600 B.C. (Sapouna-Sakellaraki 1978, 94–97, type VIIa), and it occurs frequently in East Greece in the LG period (Boardman 1961, 36–37), so it should not date much later than 700 B.C.

History and Chronology

A brief history of Grave 28 is as follows. The grave was built for Burial 1, a male of 40–60 years. The care involved in constructing the grave, with three new, good walls built instead of the usual row of boulders, suggests a high status for this individual. He was buried with two spear or javelin heads (**GR28 M2**, **GR28 M3**), an axe-head (**GR28 M5**), and a tool **GR28 M6**, as well as five monochrome cups (**GR28 P5**–**GR28 P9**) and a mug-like cup (**GR28 P11**). This burial was later pushed to the south when Burial 2, a child 7–14 years of age, was made. In turn, Burial 2 was moved aside for Burial 3, a woman aged 20–40 years. Only one vessel can be associated with Burial 3, krater **GR28 P25**, although other vessels found dumped outside the grave may have belonged with this burial. When Burial 4 was made, the grave was extended over the eastern part of the west wall, and the cremators did not go down deep enough to disturb Burial 3; the iron knife (**GR28 M4**) may be associated with this burial. Burial 4 was later pushed to the north when Burial 5 was made. When the stones were placed over Burial 5 at the end of the cremation, some of them were tightly packed along the east wall. Burials 6 and 7 were made in this densely packed cobble layer after Burial 5, and they were not disturbed by the final burial. Burial 8 was made in a pit that disturbed the earlier burials and went down to the upper levels of Burial 3. The decorated stemmed skyphos **GR28 P1**, the jug **GR28 P2**, and the fibula **GR28 M1** are associated with this male burial of 60+ years. The pottery found to the west of Grave 28 should be associated with Burials 3, 4, or 5.

The earliest burial in the grave can be dated by the deposit of cups in the southeast corner (**GR28 P5–GR28 P9**). While comparable shapes dated to LPG or EG can be found, the Grave 28 cups are tall (h. 9–10 cm) and thin-walled, with large capacities, similar to those of LG date; such tall cups do not appear in Crete before the eighth century (Kotsonas 2011a, 948). A date in the LG period seems appropriate for the first burial. The latest burial (8) can also be dated to the LG period by the associated stemmed skyphos (**GR28 P1**), which is similar in date and style to the examples from Graves 1 and 6. The entire use of the grave seems to belong to the LG period.

Catalog

Pottery

Fine Decorated Wares

GR28 P1 (VW 11101.1, VW 11110.4 and 6, VW 11111.1, VW 11112.1, VW 11118.2; Fig. 130; Pl. 57C). Stemmed skyphos. Partially restored from 15 fragments; 25 nonjoining fragments. Preservation 40%, including full profile, entire base and stem, 30% of rim and body, both handles; missing much of upper body and rim. H. 10.6; d. rim 11.0; d. base 4.6. Fine, soft, chalky, porous, reddish-yellow (5YR 7/6) fabric. Very pale brown (10YR 8/3) slip. Red (2.5YR 4/6–4/8) paint, fired black in places. Well-preserved lower surfaces, but upper surfaces very eroded. No burning. Metopal panel with two rows of oblique strokes. *Comparanda*: **GR6 P3**, **GR6 P4**, **GR19 P4**; Coldstream 1968, pl. 57:d, e (Eteocretan Geometric); for shape, Tsipopoulou 2005, 315, fig. 108:AN1448 (Stavromenos Zou, LG). *Date*: LG.

GR28 P2 (V89.30, IM 1242; VW 11101.3, object 3; Fig. 130; Pl. 57C). Miniature jug. Intact except for missing handle. H. 6.3; d. rim 4.5; d. base 3.6. Fine, rather soft, reddish-yellow (7.5YR 8/6) fabric. Very pale brown (10YR 8/2) slip. Brown shadow of paint. Very worn surfaces. Metopal panel in front with vertical stripes. *Comparanda*: **GR9 P6**; Brock 1957, 155, pl. 50:838 (Knossos, PGB–MG); Coldstream and Catling, eds., 1996, 114, pl. 123:102 (Knossos, LG); 151, pl. 148:15 (Knossos, EO); 177, pl. 176, 135:1 (Knossos, MG); Tsipopoulou 2005, 216, pl. 341:H3253 (Adromyloi, LG). *Date*: LG.

GR28 P3 (V89.65, IM 1245; VW 11110.2, object 2; Fig. 130; Pls. 57B, Pl. 57C). Amphora. Restored from numerous fragments. Preservation 80%, including full profile, entire base, both handles, 60% of rim and neck; missing 30% of rim and neck. H. 31.0; d. rim 13.0; d. base 9.7. Fine, soft, reddish-yellow (7.5YR 7/6) fabric with some small dark inclusions. Very pale brown (7.5YR 8/4) slip. Red (2.5YR 5/6) to dusky red (2.5YR 3/2) paint. Very worn surfaces. Two registers of zigzag on neck; two registers of running dog in metopal panel on upper body. *Bibliography*: Gesell, Day, and Coulson 1995, 86–87, fig. 6:2, pl. 27:b; Day 1995, fig. 5. *Date*: LG.

Fine Monochrome Wares

GR28 P4 (V89.53, IM 1248; VW 1110.2, object 4; Fig. 130; Pls. 57B, 57C). Cup. Mended from 15 fragments. Preservation 99%; missing one small fragment of rim. H. 10.0; d. rim 11.5–12.5; d. base 5.0. Fine, soft, pink (10YR 7/4) fabric. Black paint. Worn surfaces on exterior, better condition on interior. Wheel ridging on interior. Handle has pinched in rim where attached. *Bibliography*: Gesell, Day, and Coulson 1995, 86–87, fig. 6:3, pl. 27:b; Day 1995, fig. 5. *Comparanda*: Tsipopoulou 2005, 85, pl. 36 (Kavousi, Plai tou Kastrou, LG–EO). *Date*: LG.

GR28 P5 (V89.84; VW 11119.1 and 2; Fig. 130; Pl. 57C). Cup. Mended from ca. 110 fragments. Preservation 80%, including full profile, entire base, 95% of rim and handle; missing part of upper body. The rim opposite the handle mended from many tiny fragments. H. 10.0; d. rim 11.5–13.5; d. base 5.2. Fine, soft, reddish-yellow (5YR 6/6) fabric. Petrographic sample KAV 15/80: Fabric Group 2. Red (2.5YR 4/6) paint. Worn surfaces. Burned gray on one side. Rim very uneven, either because side opposite handle pulled out to make a wide spout or from warping in fire. *Bibliography*: Gesell, Day, and Coulson 1995, 85–86, fig. 5:1. *Comparanda*: Coldstream and Catling, eds., 1996, 141, fig. 104:5 (Knossos, LG). *Date*: LG.

GR28 P6 (V89.85; VW 11119.1; Fig. 130; Pl. 58). Cup. Mended from 45 fragments. Preservation 99%; missing chips from rim and body. H. 9.0–10.0; d. rim 13.0–14.0; d. base 4.2. Fine, soft, reddish-yellow (7.5YR 7/6) fabric. Petrographic sample KAV 15/81: Fabric Subgroup 1c. Dark reddish-brown (2.5YR 3/4) paint. Worn surfaces. Part of handle burned after breaking. Irregular in shape. *Bibliography*: Gesell, Day, and Coulson 1995, 85–86, fig. 5:3. *Comparanda*: Tsipopoulou 2013, 152–153, fig. 13:12308 (Piskokephalo, LG). *Date*: LG.

GR28 P7 (V89.81; VW 11119.1; Fig. 130; Pl. 58). Cup. Mended from 42 fragments. Preservation 99%; missing one chip. H. 9.8; d. rim 12.0–13.0; d. base 5.3. Fine, soft, very pale brown (10YR 7/3) fabric. Yellowish-red (5YR 5/6) paint. Worn surfaces. Burning under handle toward bottom. *Bibliography*: Gesell, Day, and Coulson 1995, 85–86, fig. 5:4. *Comparanda*: Mook 2004, 176, fig. 12.11:C (Kastro, LG). *Date*: LG.

GR28 P8 (V89.86; VW 11119.1; Fig. 130; Pl. 58). Cup. Mended from 48 fragments. Preservation 95%; missing chips from body. H. 10.5; d. rim 13.2, d. base 5.2. Fine, soft, reddish-yellow (7.5YR 7/6) fabric. Red (2.5YR 4/6) paint. Worn surfaces. Burning on rim. Wheel ridging on interior. *Bibliography*: Gesell, Day, and Coulson 1995, 85–86, fig. 5:5. *Date*: LG.

GR28 P9 (V89.79; VW 11119.1; Fig. 131; Pl. 58). Cup. Mended from 33 fragments. Complete. H. 8.5–10.5; d. rim 12.5–13.0; d. base 5.6. Fine, soft, very pale brown (10YR 8/3) fabric. Reddish-brown (5YR 4/3) paint. Very worn surfaces. Burning on one side. Irregular in shape. *Bibliography*: Gesell, Day, and Coulson 1995, 85–86, fig. 5:6. *Comparanda*: Coldstream and Catling, eds., 1996, 281, fig. 151:17 (Knossos, MG); Rethemiotakis and Englezou 2010, 75–76, fig. 46:112 (Eltyna, PGB–EG). *Date*: LG.

GR28 P10 (VW 11100 cleaning, VW 11109.1, VW 11150.1; Fig. 131). Cup. Partially mended from 24 fragments; seven nonjoining fragments. Preservation 75%, including full profile, 80% of base, handle, 75% of rim. H. 9.6; d. rim 14.0; d. base 5.6. Fine, soft, reddish-yellow (5YR 7/6) fabric, reddish-yellow (7.5YR 7/6) on surface. Base has central bulge on interior. Black paint. Very worn surfaces, a few well preserved. No burning. *Comparanda*: for base, Coldstream and Catling, eds., 1996, 186, fig. 119:18 (Knossos, PGB–EG). *Date*: LG.

GR28 P11 (V89.82; VW 11119.1 and 2; Fig. 131; Pl. 58). Mug-like cup. Mended from 40 fragments. Preservation 99%; missing chip from rim. H. 9.4; d. rim 8.2; d. base 5.0. Fine, soft, very pale brown (10YR 7/3) fabric. Petrographic sample KAV 15/82: Fabric Subgroup 1c. Traces of reddish paint on interior, probably also on exterior. Very worn surfaces. Burned inside and out. Incised lines on rim. *Bibliography*: Gesell, Day, and Coulson 1995, 85–86, fig. 5:2. *Comparanda*: Coldstream and Catling, eds., 1996, 18, fig. 60:68 (Knossos, PG–EG); Tsipopoulou 2005, 61, fig. 89:HΔ26 (Dreros, EO); 131, fig. 2005:H7427 (Hagios Georgios, LG–EO). *Date*: LG.

GR28 P12 (VW 10109.1; Fig. 131). Mug-like cup. Partially mended from six fragments. Preservation 80% of base, handle, and one fragment from rim. Max. pres. h. 3.5; d. rim 10.0; d. base 5.2. Fine, soft, reddish-yellow (7.5YR 7/6) fabric, light greenish gray (5GY 7/1) at core. Red (2.5YR 4/8) paint. Very worn surfaces. *Comparanda*: Coldstream and Catling, eds., 1996, 131, fig. 101:8 (Knossos, LG–EO). *Date*: LG.

GR28 P13 (VW 11215.1 and 2; Fig. 131). Cup. Partially mended from five fragments. Preservation part of rim and most of handle; missing base and body. Max. pres. h. 4.0; d. rim 16.0. Fine, medium-soft, pink (5YR 7/4) fabric. Black crackled paint. Very worn surfaces. *Date*: LG.

GR28 P14 (VW 11103.1, VW 11205.1–3, VW 11213.1, VW 10248.4 and 6; Fig. 131). Cup or skyphos. Partially mended from 13 fragments. Preservation 20%, including base and parts of rim; missing handle(s). H. est. 8.3; d. rim 14.0; d. base 5.3. Fine, soft, porous, very pale brown (10YR 8/3) fabric. Black paint. Very worn surfaces. Some burning on rim. *Comparanda*: Coldstream and Catling, eds., 1996, 233, fig. 135:283.3 (Knossos, PGB–EG). *Date*: LG.

GR28 P15 (VW 11212.1, VW 11213.1, VW 11214.1; Fig. 131). Cup or skyphos. Partially mended from 16 fragments. Preservation 15%, including most of base and part of rim; missing handle. H. est. 9.3; d. rim 12.0; d. base 5.0. Fine, rather soft, pink (5YR 7/4) fabric with very pale brown (10YR 8/3) surface. Traces of brown paint. Very worn surfaces. Some burning. *Comparanda*: Coldstream and Catling, eds., 1996, 157, fig. 111:163 (Knossos, PGB–EG). *Date*: LG.

GR28 P16 (VW 11201.1, VW 11212.1; Fig. 131). Cup or skyphos. Represented by 16 fragments from base and body, one from rim; missing handle(s). Max. pres. h. 2.4; d. rim 12.2; d. base 6.0. Fine, soft, reddish-yellow (7.5YR 7/6) fabric with tiny red phyllites, very pale brown (10YR 8/3) surface. Traces of black to brown paint. Very worn surfaces. Wheel ridging on interior. *Comparanda*: Mook 2004, 174, fig. 12.9:AA (SubPG). *Date*: LG.

GR28 P17 (VW 11108.1 and 3; Fig. 131). Aryballos. Partially mended from six fragments. Preservation 40%, including entire base, much of lower body; missing most of neck, all of rim, and handle. Max. pres. h. 4.7; d. base 2.2. Fine, soft, light red (2.5YR 6/6) fabric. Pink (7.5YR 8/4) slip. Badly worn surfaces. Possible band below neck, other paint below. May be decorated or monochrome. No burning. *Date*: LG.

Fine Plain Ware

GR28 P18 (VW 11215.1 and 2; Fig. 131). Lid, cup, or kalathos. Single fragment from rim and body. Max. pres. h. 4.3; d. rim 12.0. Fine, soft, reddish-yellow (5YR 7/6) fabric. Thick, creamy, very pale brown (10YR 8/3) slip, possibly polished. No burning. *Date*: LG.

Medium-Coarse Decorated Wares

GR28 P19 (V89.55, IM 1241; VW 11110.2, object 1; Fig. 131; Pls. 57B, 58). Conical lid. Intact except for chips in rim and base. H. 7.7; d. rim 13.2; d. base 5.0. Medium-coarse, reddish-yellow (7.5YR 7/6) to yellow (10YR 7/6) micaceous fabric. Very pale brown (10YR 8/4) slip. Black paint. Worn surfaces, except on one side, where well preserved. Upright dotted leaves. *Bibliography*: Gesell, Day, and Coulson 1995, 86–87, fig. 6:4, pl. 27:b; Day 1995, fig. 5. *Comparanda*: Coldstream and Catling, eds., 1996, 64, fig. 75:5 (Knossos, EO); for shape, Coldstream and Catling, eds., 1996, 187, fig. 120:44 (Knossos, MG); for decoration, Rethemiotakis and Englezou 2010, 62, fig. 34:70 (Eltyna, MG). *Date*: LG.

GR28 P20 (VW 11103.1, VW 11108.3 object 1, VW 11108.4, VW 11109.1, VW 10121.1; Fig. 131). Jug. Partially mended from 24 fragments. Preservation 80%, including full profile, entire base and lower body, handle, and half of neck and rim. H. 13.0; d. rim 6.0; d. base 6.0. Medium-coarse, reddish-yellow (5YR 6/6) fabric, gray at core, with red phyllite inclusions. Petrographic sample KAV 15/77: Fabric Group 2. Reddish-yellow (7.5YR 7/6) slip. Traces of red to brown paint. Very worn surfaces. No burning. *Comparanda*: Callaghan and Johnston 2000, 225, pl. 4.4:126 (Kommos, LPG–PGB); 227, fig. 4.5:145 (PG); Tsipopoulou 2005, 299, fig. 84:Σ3815 (Sklavoi, LG). *Date*: LG.

GR28 P21 (VW 11205, VW 11218.1, VW 12200.1 and 2; Fig. 132). Krater. Partially mended from 20 fragments from rim, handle, and body; eight nonjoining fragments. Max. pres. h. 10.0; d. rim 22.0. Medium-coarse, rather hard, reddish-yellow (7.5YR 7/6) fabric with gray phyllites. Black paint. Very worn surfaces. Some fragments burned. Two registers of concentric circles. *Comparanda*: Tsipopoulou 2013, 145–146, fig. 8:12281 (Piskokephalo, LG); for shape, Coldstream 1972, 82, 84, fig. 7:E1; Rethemiotakis and Englezou 2010, 75, fig. 45:108 (Eltyna, MPG–LPG Atticizing stemmed krater); for decoration, Coldstream and Catling, eds., 1996, 262, pl. 235:29 (Knossos, LO); Tsipopoulou 2005, 129, fig. 20:H7420; 152, fig. 28:AN1813; 153, fig. 29:AN1815 (Hagios Georgios, LG). *Date*: LG.

GR28 P22 (V89.54, IM 1246; VW 11110.2, object 3; Fig. 132; Pls. 57B, 58). Necked jar. Intact, except for chips from rim and handle. H. 16.6; d. rim 11.0; d. base 9.5. Medium-coarse to coarse, reddish-yellow (7.5YR 7/6) fabric with large inclusions. Black paint. Rather worn surfaces. No burning. Crude decoration of large double wavy line on one side, figure-of-eight on other. Very crudely made and uneven. *Bibliography*: Day 1995, fig. 5; Gesell, Day, and Coulson 1995, fig. 6:1, pl. 27:b. *Comparanda*: for shape, **VII P4**; Coldstream and Catling, eds., 1996, 62, pl. 91:31 (Knossos, PGB–EG). *Date*: PG.

MEDIUM-COARSE MONOCHROME WARE

GR28 P23 (VW 11212.1, VW 11213.1, VW 11214.1; Fig. 132). Closed vessel. Partially mended from five fragments, preserving entire base; missing upper body, rim, and handle(s). Max. pres. h. 4.7; d. base 8.0. Medium-coarse, reddish-yellow (7.5YR 7/6) to yellow (10YR 7/6) fabric with dark gray phyllites and quartz. Black paint. Very worn surfaces. No burning. Paint visible that may be decorated or monochrome. *Date*: uncertain.

COARSE DECORATED WARE

GR28 P24 (VW 10248.1, VW 10122.3, VW 11201.11, VW 11205, VW 11214.1; Fig. 132). Krater. Partially mended from 21 fragments. Preservation 25% of rim, one handle attachment; missing base, lower body, and handle. Max. pres. h. 6.5; d. rim 20.0. Coarse, soft, reddish-yellow (5YR 7/6) fabric with small red phyllites. Petrographic sample KAV 15/76: Fabric Subgroup 1a. Red (2.5YR 4/6) paint. Worn surfaces. Some fragments burned. Cross-hatched butterfly; incisions on rim. *Date*: LG.

COARSE MONOCHROME WARE

GR28 P25 (VW 11103.2, VW 11106.1, VW 11108.3, VW 11110.7 and 9, VW 11115.1, VW 11205, VW 11215.4, VW 11218.1, VW 12200.1; Fig. 133). Krater. Partially mended from 43 fragments; 103 nonjoining fragments. Preservation 15%, including entire base, both handles, some rim. Max. pres. h. 10.5; d. rim 32.0 d. base 15.0. Coarse, very soft, reddish-yellow (5YR 7/6) fabric with light gray core and red phyllite inclusions. Petrographic sample KAV 15/78: Fabric Subgroup 1a. Reddish-yellow (7.5YR 7/6) surface. Black to red (2.5YR 4/6) paint. Very worn surfaces. No burning. Grooves around lower body. *Date*: LG.

COARSE PLAIN WARES

GR28 P26 (V89.52, IM 1238; VW 11108.1, object 1; Fig. 133). Closed vessel. Partially mended from 22 fragments; four nonjoining fragments. Entire base preserved; missing upper body, rim, and handle(s). Max. pres. h. 7.0; d. base 6.0. Coarse, strong brown (7.5YR 5/6) fabric with frequent small inclusions. Very worn and laminating surfaces. *Date*: uncertain.

GR28 P27 (VW 11101.2 object 2; Fig. 133). Pedestal base, possibly from krater. Single fragment preserving 20% of base. H. 3.6; d. base 12.0. Coarse, reddish-yellow (5YR 7/8) fabric with gray core and red phyllites. Very worn surfaces. No burning. *Date*: LG.

GR28 P28 (VW 11215.4, VW 11218.2, VW 12200.2; Fig. 133). Two-handled jar. Partially mended from eight fragments; nine nonjoining fragments. Preservation 40%, including entire base, much of lower body, both handles, and one fragment of rim. H. est. 14.0; d. rim est. 10.7; d. base 5.3. Very coarse reddish-yellow (7.5YR 7/6) to very dark grayish-brown (10YR 3/2) fabric with frequent inclusions of white marble (calcite). Petrographic sampled KAV 15/79: Fabric Subgroup 1b. Gray at core. Surfaces very worn. *Date*: PG–G.

Metal

BRONZE

GR28 M1 (V89.78; VW 11110.9, object 5; Fig. 134; Pl. 58). Bronze fibula. Single fragment preserving spring, bow, and catch plate; missing pin. Max. pres. L. 3.6; max. pres. w. 2.5. Well-preserved surfaces. Square or rectangular catch plate, flat in section. Bow round in section, swelling at center with knob at top, and rounding out again toward coil. *Bibliography*: Gesell, Day, and Coulson 1995, pl. 26:c; Day 1995, fig. 10. *Comparanda*: **GR32 M1**; Sapouna-Sakellaraki 1978, 94–97, pl. 37:1271, 1272 (mid eighth century to ca. 600).

IRON

GR28 M2 (V89.97; VW 11119.1, object 2; Fig. 134; Pl. 59A). Iron javelin or spear. Nearly complete; missing chips. L. 15.4; max. w. 2.1; d. socket 2.5. Very corroded; both faces of blade preserved, but interior gone. Long (8.4) socket, spread wide and very open (half circle around). Hole pierced near end opposite socket. Very short blade with rounded shoulders. Midrib. *Comparanda*: Karageorghis 1983, 9–10, fig. 69:T. 42:4 (Palaepaphos-*Skales*, CA I); Snodgrass 1996, 583, type B.

GR28 M3 (V89.98; VW 11119.3, object 4; Fig. 134; Pl. 59A). Iron javelin or spear. Mended from two large fragments, one from socket, one from blade; numerous nonjoining bits. L. 16.1; max w. 1.8; d. socket 2.0. Very corroded and laminated. Long (8.0) socket, open, only rolled around a half circle. Two holes pierced near end. Rounded shoulders. *Comparanda*: Karageorghis 1983, 9–10, fig. 69:T.42:4; (Palaepaphos-*Skales*, CA I); Snodgrass 1996, 583, type B.

GR28 M4 (V89.91; VW 11118.1; Fig. 134; Pl. 59A). Iron knife. Mended from three fragments. Nearly complete; missing chips and surface. L. 14.4; max. w. 1.6. Very corroded. Surfaces completely gone. Flat rectangular end. Possibly one rivet toward beginning of blade, but corrosion bubbles make it difficult to tell. Slightly curving blade with cutting edge on interior of blade. *Comparanda*: Karageorghis 1983, 95–96, fig. 98.52:1A, C (Palaepaphos-*Skales*, CG III); 155, fig. 120.64:8 (CG II); Snodgrass 1996, 587, type D.

GR28 M5 (V89.66; VW 11119.1, object 3; Fig. 134; Pl. 59A). Iron axe-head. Intact. L. 10.8; max. w. 3.6. Very corroded and laminating. Squared off end, long (5.0) haft with small projecting tangs at end where head comes out. Slightly flaring head. *Comparanda*: **GR6 M9**, **GR9 M40–GR9 M42**; Blegen 1952, 281, fig. 3:6; Karageorghis 1983, 230, fig. 142:T.76.131 (Palaepaphos-*Skales*, CG I).

GR28 M6 (V89.67; VW 11119.1, object 1; Fig. 134; Pl. 59A). Iron tool, possibly chisel. Intact. L. 14.0; max. w. 1.2; th. 0.9. Surface corroded. Long tool, rectangular in section. One end flattened and squared off, the other rounded and flattened. *Comparanda*: Courtois 1984, 37, no. 321, fig. 12:2 (Enkomi, bronze).

Stone

GR28 S1 (V89.46; VW 11110.2, object 3; Pl. 57B). Stone lid. Intact. L. 22.7; w. 16.7; th. 3.3. Shale. Covered with incrustation, except where top of vessel left circle. Roughly ovoid in shape and possibly chipped to form lid. *Bibliography*: Gesell, Day, and Coulson 1995, 86, pl. 27:b; Day 1995, fig. 5.

Grave 29

History and Details of Excavation

Grave 29 lies on a terrace on the northern edge of the west slope of the Vronda ridge in Trench V 14400 (Figs. 3, 4). It was first recognized as a deposit of dark, soft, ashy soil containing human remains at the end of the 1989 season, and excavation was completed in 1990 (Gesell, Day, and Coulson 1995, 77). The area had been much disturbed by modern activity, particularly a recent terrace wall (V 14401). Human bone appeared in the surface soil of the trench (V 14402), but there was no associated architecture, and it was difficult to isolate the deposit. Originally it was thought to be a burial enclosure, as it was bounded by a number of large boulders and apparently covered with stones like other burial enclosures. The surrounding stones, however, were not in any regular pattern, nor did they form an enclosure of any type; rather, they were outcroppings of bedrock. The ashy deposit extended beyond the stones (Fig. 135), and it continued well below the ancient surface into a large pit.

Immediately below the surface, a layer of rather hard, yellowish-brown soil (V 14403) that became darker along the east was encountered, and along the south were clumps of what appeared to be roofing material (V 14407) and brecciating bedrock (V 14406). Along the east and west sides of a high spur of bedrock was a deposit of soft, dark, ashy soil that contained human bone (V 14404, V 14408). This deposit seems to have been an irregular pit, but all attempts to follow the outline or keep the material separate from that in the surrounding harder, yellowish-brown soil (V 14409, 14410) were unsuccessful. There was very little grave material, and it is likely that this deposit represents a dump from a grave elsewhere. It is unlikely that there had ever been a burial enclosure here, as the grave material was found on the surface and there was no evidence of any burning in situ. Much of the earlier material from the LM IIIC settlement also seems to have been discarded together with the grave goods, and it is possible that this area represents a refuse pit used in the Geometric period, possibly as a result of cleaning in the area of the burials and their associated rituals.

Architecture

Only one ancient wall (V 14413) was identified in the trench (Fig. 135); it served as the base for the modern terrace wall (V 14401). It is aligned with the LM IIIC Building D on the terrace above to the southeast, and it is unlikely to have any connection with the grave. The irregular area of dark, ashy soil measured approximately 1.13 m north–south x 2.00 m east–west toward the bottom (excavated in 1990) and spread out to 2.30–2.60 m north–south x 1.40 m east–west.

Stratigraphy

The deposit of soft, dark brown soil (V 14404, V 14408) containing human bone and Geometric pottery was irregular in shape and ca. 0.75 m deep. Most of the pottery from the grave, however, was found in V 14403, the slope wash below surface soil. The deposit containing cremated bone was surrounded on all sides by a deposit of harder yellowish-brown soil (V 14409, V 14410, V 14411) that in turn lay over roofing (V 14412) or brecciating bedrock (V 14406). The slope wash (V 14403) lay over both the Grave 29 material and the harder yellowish-brown soil, with surface soil just above (V 14402); some of the grave material began to appear immediately on the surface as well as in the slope wash. All of the material may have been dumped, some from a LM IIIC building and some from a grave.

Burials

Although there is little human bone, the remains probably come from just one cremated individual.

Burial 1

Type: cremation discard deposit
Age: adult?
Sex: undetermined
Weight: 94 g

Burial 1 is probably an adult, but the very small quantity of bone makes this determination uncertain. The bone is for the most part calcined, although some cranial fragments are dark gray, indicating incomplete combustion of some of the bone collagen. One fragment of bone, a tibia shaft segment, was probably part of the body but escaped obvious burning. Sections of unburned bone have been observed in forensic cremations that are otherwise partially or completely calcined (Symes et al. 2008, 30–33).

Faunal Remains

The animal bone debris recovered from this context, a dump of materials from elsewhere, is limited to apparent discarded village food and/or butchering debris, consisting primarily of unidentifiable bone fragments of domestic animals (Table 9). Identifiable remains include pig, cow, and sheep or goat tooth fragments, along with one sheep or goat mandible fragment and three long bone diaphysis fragments, none of which show any human modification. Many of the small unidentified bone fragments are heavily eroded, and a number appear to have been heated, heavily burned, or calcined, probably by proximity to a pyre or grave installation.

Pottery

Although a few pieces of Geometric pottery were found in the upper parts of this area, the remainder of the 1,100 fragments weighing 13.22 kg belonged to the LM IIIC settlement and have been discussed elsewhere (Day and Glowacki 2012, 168). Only one vessel was well enough preserved to catalog: a jug, amphora, or hydria that had a running S-pattern on the neck (**GR29 P1**). Other identifiable vessels, found only in small fragments, included a monochrome cup with a ledge rim, perhaps like those from Graves 9 and 20 (**GR9 P18, GR9 P19, GR9 P24, GR9 P25, GR20 P12, GR20 P14**), and a base of a closed vessel of soft, chalky fabric with black paint, rather like the amphorae in Grave 16 (**GR16 P17, GR16 P18**) or the jug in Grave 9 (**GR9 P37**).

Objects

A lead button (**GR29 M1**) was found in the surface soil. Such an artifact is more likely to have belonged with the grave than the settlement and is cataloged here. It has parallels at the Kastro in LM IIIC (Mook 1993, 291–292, fig. 54:79), in the Psychro cave (Boardman 1961, 54, fig. 26:237), and in the SM–PG tholos tomb at nearby Vasiliki (Tsipopoulou, Vagnetti, and Liston 2003, 104, 108, fig. 11:42). Those lead buttons for which the weights have been provided show a marked similarity to the Vronda weight of 15.10 g: the Vasiliki bead weighs 14.1 g, while that from the Kastro, which is not complete, weighs 11.0 g.

Chronology

It is difficult, given the limited amount of pottery, to date the grave. The S-pattern on the neck of the jug (**GR29 P1**) suggests a LG date. The cup with possible shelf rim may place the burial in the same chronological phase as Grave 9.

Catalog

Pottery

COARSE DECORATED WARE

GR29 P1 (V 14402.1, V 14403.2 and 3; Fig. 136). Jug, amphora, or hydria. Single fragment from base, one from neck and shoulder, nine body fragments. D. base 15.0. Coarse, gritty, light red (2.5YR 6/6) fabric, like Kavousi Type XXII. Pink (7.5YR 8/4) slip. Red (2.5YR 4/6) paint. On lower neck, S-pattern; bands on body. Base has holes pierced near bottom. *Comparanda*: Tsipopoulou 2005, 283, fig. 14:AN8751 (Praisos, LG). *Date*: LG.

Metal Object

GR29 M1 (V89.71; V 14402.1; Fig. 136; Pl. 59B). Lead bead or button. Intact. H. 0.1; d. base 2.2; d. top 0.9; d. hole 0.5 (top)–1.0 (bottom). Wt. 15.10 g. Well preserved. Worn on top. Two incised circles on top of base. Pierced with hole that is larger on bottom than on top.

Graves 30, 33, and 7

History and Details of Excavation

Grave 30 is a large, stone-lined enclosure grave on the south edge of the terrace supporting LM IIIC Building I-O-N on the west slope of the Vronda ridge (Figs. 3, 4). It is close to Graves 23 and 8. It was excavated in 1990 in Trench VW 8000 (Gesell, Day, and Coulson 1995, 88, pl. 27:d). The east wall of the enclosure was actually in Trench V 10500, which was also excavated in 1990. Two other deposits of cremated bone that were identified as burials have been shown to belong with Grave 30, either as spills of material from upslope or as discard deposits made when later cremations demanded space. Subsequent study of the pottery from Grave 30 has shown that Grave 33, just down the slope to the west, contained material from Grave 30. Dumps of grave material were also picked up to the north of Grave 30, and Grave 7, excavated in 1987 (Gesell, Day, and Coulson 1988, 293), can now understood as a discard deposit from Grave 30.

Grave 30 was recognized as an enclosure grave almost from the surface, as human bones were encountered in the topsoil (VW 8001) and the slope wash over the grave (VW 8003, VW 8006). The soft, ashy grave soil with cobbles was removed as VW 8008, and beneath this layer a pebbly soil was identified in the center (VW 8010), while a more compact brown soil was present around the edges of the grave (VW 8011). The actual pebbly floor of the grave was cleaned off as VW 8015. During the course of excavation, six burials were identified (A, A2, B–E), including an infant (Burial B). Subsequent study has shown that remains identified as two bodies belong to a single individual (Burials C and D).

Grave 33 was also excavated in 1990. It lies downslope from Grave 30 on the next terrace below in Room O1 of the LM IIIC Building O (Day and Glowacki 2012, 75). Human bones were encountered in an area of rock tumble (VW 8009) that appeared just below the surface, and grave material was also later found to the west in VW 8107.1 and VW 8108.1. Dark ashy soil with cobbles and bones (VW 8012) appeared below VW 8009 and lay immediately on top of the collapsed roofing from the earlier Building O. Joins of pottery between this grave and Grave 30 show that Grave 33 was a discard deposit from Grave 30.

There was also much evidence of dumping activity north of Grave 30 (see Day and Glowacki 2012, 58–60). Pits of dark ashy soil without any human bones had been encountered in 1989 in the clearing of the southeast corner of Building I, Room I2 (V 11000; Day and Glowacki 2012, 90), and similar deposits were found just north of Grave 30 in VW 8002 (Day and Glowacki 2012, 90) and east of the grave in V 10500 (Day and Glowacki 2012, 163, 165). All of this material is similar to or joins with that in Grave 30 and is most likely to represent dumping from the grave.

Finally, north of Grave 30 another grave (Grave 7) had been identified in 1987 (Day and Glowacki 2012, 59–61). This amorphous area of dark ashy soil with human bone (VW 9007, VW 9008) was below rock tumble (VW 9003). Some of the same material also appeared in VW 9009, just to the west of the area distinguished as Grave 7. Again, joins of pottery between Grave 7 and 30 suggest that Grave 7 was also a discard deposit from Grave 30.

Architecture

Grave 30 is a rectangular, stone-lined enclosure oriented northwest–southeast and measuring 1.09 m north–south x 1.91 m east–west (Fig. 137; Pl. 59C). It was built into the packing for the terrace wall constructed to support Building I-O-N, but it did not use existing walls from the LM IIIC building for its sides. It lies at an oblique angle to Building I, a fact that suggests that the walls of the earlier building were no longer visible at the time of burial. The south wall of the grave (VW 8007) was built directly on the edge of the terrace wall; it consists of a single row of boulders. The north (VW 8004) and east (VW 8016) walls are very wide, with two good faces but preserved only one course high. The east wall measures 1.25 m wide and is bonded with the north wall. The north wall (VW 8017) is narrower (1.00 m wide) and one course high. These walls resemble those in Grave 16 on top of the summit. The west wall was difficult to define until it was cleaned for consolidation in 1991. There was a row of three small stones, one going under the north wall (seen in Pl. 59C, but not in Fig. 137). The north, east, and south walls show fracturing of limestone and calcination of breccia boulders, but the west wall shows no signs of burning. There were no architectural features associated with Graves 7 or 33.

Stratigraphy

Because Grave 30 lay very close to the modern surface and was on a slope, erosion caused much damage. The depth of deposition varied greatly according to the slope: 0.38 m in the north and 0.18 m in the south.

On top of the brecciating surface of the grave (VW 8015) two different soils were distinguished. The lowest was a pebbly layer, chiefly in the center of the grave (VW 8010), which contained remains of Burials 2, 3, and 5. Around the edges of the grave a more compact brown soil (VW 8011) perhaps represents material from the original burial swept to the sides of the grave to make way for Burial 2. Bones from Burial 1 were found in this layer and in higher levels, and the deposits around the edges may have risen higher, but they were not distinguished during excavation. Most of the grave was filled with a dark, ashy soil with cobbles (VW 8008), in which all the burials were found mixed. The entire area seems to have been disturbed by the final burial event, a woman (Burial 5) and infant (Burial 4) found in anatomical order at the top. Above the burials was a yellowish-brown soil, probably slope wash, which went over the north wall of the enclosure (VW 8003, VW 8006). Topsoil lay above this layer (VW 8001), and a modern terrace wall ran across it.

Grave 33, the discard deposit to the west, was an irregular patch of dark, ashy soil with cobbles and bones (VW 8012) that lay directly on top of the roofing clay collapsed from the LM IIIC building (VW 8013). Above it was a layer of rock tumble with bones (VW 8009) that lay just below the surface soil (VW 8001). The depth of deposition varied greatly because of the slope of the hill down to the south and to the west. The deposit was deepest in the northeast at 0.48 m, but it sloped down to 0.32 m on the northwest; on the southeast it was 0.21 m deep and on the southwest it was only 0.10 m. The grave seems to represent a single dumping event from Grave 30, one contemporary with the discard deposit represented by Grave 7.

Grave 7, a discard deposit to the north of Grave 30, was a pit in the roofing clay that contained ashy soil and human bones (VW 9008). Next to this pit was an area of red soil with pithos fragments (VW 9009) that contained some grave material. Above the pit was a broader area of ashy soil mixed with cobbles (VW 9007) and a layer of rock tumble with bone and evidence of burning (VW 9003). Topsoil appeared above this rock tumble (VW 9001). The total depth of deposition for the pit of Grave 7 was only 0.13 m.

The other dumps of material were similar, recognizable by their dark, soft, ashy soil. The dump in V 10502 was 0.23 m deep, as was also its continuation in V 11002.

Associated Features

The various ash dumps to the north (Grave 7), east (V 10500), and west (Grave 33) were associated with Grave 30.

Burials

Five burials were made within the enclosure of Grave 30, although at the time of excavation there were thought to be six. The human bones originally identified as burials from Grave 7 and Grave 33 are included in the following discussion. The 468 g of bone from Grave 7 included both cranial and postcranial bones. The age and large size of the bones suggests they are most likely to have come from Grave 30, Burial 2, an adult male, 40–60 years old. The material from Grave 33 is from an adult, but it is so limited that it does not offer any indications of age or sex and might be associated with any of the adults from this grave. Only 25 bone fragments weighing 36 g were found scattered in this ashy discard deposit. The degree of cremation ranges from little observable exposure to complete calcination, in no apparent pattern.

Burial 1
Type: disturbed primary cremation
Age: adult, 20–40 years
Sex: male?
Weight: 597 g

Burial 1 is a disturbed primary cremation of an adult. The bone is mottled, but it is largely calcined and very fragmentary. Most of the material associated with Burial 1 was collected near the east end of the enclosure, and it and appears to have been pushed aside to this end when the grave was used for subsequent burials. There are, however, joins with bone found in the west end of the enclosure as well, indicating that the skeleton was pushed to both ends of the grave. There was no evidence of articulation in the cremated bone. The skeleton is an adult, 20–40 years old, as indicated by the closure of the cranial sutures. Cranial bone found in the west end of the enclosure suggests that the skeleton is a male, although this identification is not definitive.

Burial 2
Type: disturbed primary cremation
Age: adult, 40–60 years
Sex: male
Weight: 1,128 g (includes 468 g from Grave 7)

Burial 2 is a disturbed cremation burial found on the south side of the enclosure toward the west end, and it extended over the deposit containing Burial 1. The combined weight of bone for this burial from within the enclosure and from the disturbed material excavated as Grave 7 indicates that a large portion of the skeleton has been recovered. The recovered bone shows the common pattern of differential cremation, with the cranium only scorched and the postcranium more thoroughly burned. Portions of the postcranial bones, including parts of the femur, tibia, and humerus shafts, were also relatively protected from the fire. There is some minor evidence of articulation of the bone, although most of the skeletal material was disturbed. The cranium was found against the south wall near the west end of the enclosure.

The skeleton is that of an adult male with a robust skull and very large postcranial bones. This man was very large, to judge from the skeletal remains. Cranial suture closure suggests a mature adult, probably 40–60 years old. This assessment is supported by the presence of degenerative joint disease in the postcranial skeleton. There is arthritis on the metacarpal-phalangeal joint of the thumb. The lumbar vertebrae facets are pitted, also indicating joint disease, and the insertions of the gluteus maximus muscles on the proximal right and left femora are damaged and scarred, suggesting heavy labor during his lifetime.

Burial 3
Type: disturbed primary cremation
Age: adult, 20–40 years
Sex: unknown
Weight: 772 g

Burial 3 is a disturbed primary cremation of an adult, mixed in the deposit from which the remains of a primary adult cremation (Burial 5; see below) were excavated. The presence of this burial was not suspected until the bones of the primary cremation were washed and inventoried. It is possible to distinguish the bones of the two burials on the basis of the degree of cremation. The bone of Burial 3 is partially or completely calcined. The skeleton is an adult, probably 20 to 40 years old. It was not possible to determine the sex of the skeleton.

Burial 4
Type: primary cremation
Age: infant
Sex: unknown
Weight: 116 g

The skeleton of Burial 4 was found along the north side of the enclosure. The bone is completely calcined. This burial is one of only three juvenile cremation burials recognized during the excavation of the Vronda graves. The bone is very fragmentary, but that which could be identified in the field was in anatomical order. In spite of its being recognized during excavation, a large quantity of additional bone was recovered from the water sieve residue. The skeleton is of an infant, probably some weeks postnatal, but no specific age could be determined.

Burial 5
Type: primary cremation
Age: Adult, 35–39 years
Sex: female
Weight: 1,918 g

The well-preserved skeleton of Burial 5 is that of an adult. Most of the bone shows little evidence of burning, although portions are heavily scorched. The body was found with the head toward the east, in a flexed position with the knees splayed. The position of the legs was somewhat distorted by the presence of a very large stone that had fallen between the upper legs and was resting partially on the left femur and tibia. The arms were flexed against the chest, with the hands near the head. The skeleton is a female, with a wide sciatic notch and a gracile cranium. The degree of cranial suture closure shows that this individual was between 20 and 40 years old at death. A more precise age of 35 to 39 years is estimated on the basis of the morphology of the auricular surface of the right ilium.

There are a number of pathologies on this skeleton. The most notable is a fracture of the left ulna at the elbow. There is a diagonal fracture from the base of the olecranon process, extending distally across the shaft of the bone (Pl. 60A). The upper part of the olecranon process was not recovered. The radial notch has been displaced distally. There is a large amount of bony callous formation, and the shaft of the ulna is atrophied, indicating that the woman probably did not have full use of the arm after this injury. Other pathologies include a deeply pitted insertion of the gluteus maximus in the right femur (the corresponding section of the left femur was not recovered). Finally, there is an area of periosteal bone on the maxillary alveolus above the right second incisor and canine. The teeth are missing, so it is not possible to determine if this is associated with a dental pathology; other possible causes include scurvy.

Faunal Remains

The animal bone fragments recovered from this area are nearly all heavily burned and/or calcined (Table 9). Nevertheless, although both front and back limb element fragments and isolated tooth fragments were identified, these scattered and fragmentary remains of sheep or goat, domestic pig, and possibly domestic cattle (tentative identification based on size) do not appear to represent the more common sacrificial remains recognized in other parts of Vronda cemetery (for example, lower legs and feet, articulated limb units). One limpet shell was recovered from the area excavated as Grave 7 (Table 5).

Botanical Remains

No botanical remains were recovered from Grave 30, although some grape (*Vitis vinifera*) came from the modern terrace wall that ran over the top of the grave (VW 8000), and it may have been associated with one of the burials.

Pottery

Grave 30 produced a total of 1,567 fragments of pottery weighing 6.40 kg from within the enclosure. An additional 204 fragments weighing 1.99 kg came from the area called Grave 7, and 86 fragments weighing 1.20 kg were found in the discard deposit (Grave 33). Overall, the pottery presents an unusual assemblage in the Vronda graves. The large number of monochrome cups and skyphoi is typical, but the two large pyxides (**GR30 P5**, **GR30 P28**) with their lids represent uncommon shapes for the Vronda enclosure burials. Only Grave 32 produced similar pyxides (**GR32 P2–GR32 P4**). Two decorated open vessels (**GR30 P24**, **GR30 P25**) are also unusual for their elaborate decoration.

It was difficult to associate pottery with any individual burial, even the last. Much of the pottery left with the burials had been removed, and it is not clear when the act of discarding took place or if it occurred on more than one occasion. It is possible that those vessels that come from VW 8011 (the brown soil of Burial 1 pushed to the sides by Burial 2) belong with the first burial; many show joins with VW 8008.6 and 7 from the east side of the grave. These vessels include cup **GR30 P7**, which was greatly burned, cup **GR30 P12**, lekythos **GR30 P31**, and lid **GR30 P3**. Vessels found toward the bottom in the center in VW 8010 may be associated with Burial 2, including aryballos **GR30 P2** and jug base **GR30 P23**. Cups **GR30 P8**, **GR30 P9**, and **GR30 P16**, along with pyxis **GR30 P28**, may also belong to that burial, as fragments from these vessels were found in VW 8010. Vessels that were dumped in Grave 33 probably came from one or more of the first three burials, including pyxides **GR30 P5** and **GR30 P28**, cups **GR30 P6** and **GR30 P8**, and skyphos **GR30 P29**, which was found entirely in Grave 33. The only fragments found in the Grave 7 dump came from pyxis **GR30 P5**.

Dumped to the north and east, possibly when Burial 3 and remains of the earlier burials were discarded to make way for the final burial of the woman and infant, were the following vessels: a decorated cup (**GR30 P1**), a lid handle (**GR30 P4**; possibly LM IIIC), a skyphos **GR30 P13**, a cup/skyphos **GR30 P14**, and cup bases **GR30 P19**–**GR30 P21**. Pithos fragment **GR30 P33** was found near the surface in Trench VW 8101.3, southwest of the enclosure of Grave 30 and east of Grave 23. It may have belonged with either grave, but it was marginally closer to Grave 30, and so it has been included here. If the entire vessel once stood in or near the area of Graves 23 and 30, it must have been on the surface and thus would have served as a marker; it would have been far too large to have been placed in either of these enclosures. As both graves are late and probably in use at the same time, this pithos may have served as a marker for both graves, standing somewhere in between the two. It must be remembered, however, that only a single fragment was found, and it may have traveled from elsewhere and not been associated with the burials at all.

Objects

A large number of metal objects came from Grave 30, and it is certainly the richest grave found on the west slope. Most of the iron objects were found at the bottom of the grave, although it is uncertain whether their positions resulted from the effects of gravity or their association with the earliest burials. Those in VW 8011, possibly belonging with Burial 1, a male 20–40 years of age, include a bronze fibula (**GR30 M1**), an iron pin (**GR30 M3**), and perhaps a dagger or dirk (**GR30 M10**). Objects associated with VW 8010 and hence with the second or third burial (a male aged 40–60 years and another individual aged 20–40) include three pins (**GR30 M4**, **GR30 M5**, **GR30 M7**), two spearheads (**GR30 M8**, **GR30 M9**), and a needle (**GR30 M11**). Bronze sheeting (**GR30 M2**), a sickle-shaped knife (**GR30 M12**), an axe (**GR30 M13**), and a tool (**GR30 M15**), along with one pin (**GR30 M6**), are possibly associated with the last burial event, but they may also belong with earlier burials; the sheeting was found quite close to the infant (Burial 4), and in the field the excavators thought it accompanied that burial.

The grave is unusual for the number of iron pins buried with the dead; five pins were cataloged, but there were enough fragments to suggest the presence of at least one more. There seem to be three types of pins. Two (**GR30 M3**, **GR30 M4**) are of the usual type with disk head and rings on either side of a biconical swelling. Two more (**GR30 M6**, **GR30 M7**) have spherical rather than biconical swellings. A third type is represented by **GR30 M5**, which may have rings and no biconical swelling. The fibula **GR30 M1** is of an unusual type for Vronda, an Attico-Boeotian form that is generally found in the LG–EO period.

Chronology

Although there is material of LG date in Grave 30, including most of the monochrome cups, the pottery overall looks very late, and it is possible that this burial feature was among the latest in the sequence of Vronda graves. Even the early burials in the grave were accompanied by pottery that was in use until the end of the seventh century. Burial 1 may be dated by cup **GR30 P7**, which is probably of LG date. The lower burials can be dated by the material thrown out of the grave, including the lid **GR30 P3**, which is paralleled in decoration by an imported Attic MG I lid at Knossos (Coldstream and Catling, eds., 1996, 266, pl. 243:143); the shape is a common one at the LG Plai tou Kastrou tomb at Kavousi (Tsipopoulou 2005, 109, fig. 140:H775 A, H775B). Perhaps also from the lower burials is the cup with high offset rim (**GR30 P6**), which has parallels in a MO cup at Knossos (Coldstream and Catling, eds., 1996, 244, fig. 139:32) and in LG–EO cups at Chania (Andreadaki-Vlasaki 2004, 31, fig. 15), although that date may be too early (pers. comm., A. Kotsonas); and the skyphos **GR30 P29**, which has the offset rim and ring base usually found on LG–EO skyphoi, with a particularly close parallel from the Kastro of Orientalizing date (Mook 2004, 177, fig. 12.12:H). The pyxis (**GR30 P28**), although paralleled in MG–LG material, is decorated with bands that could be of seventh century date (pers. comm., A. Kotsonas). However, there are no EO aryballoi and lekythoi like those found in Graves 4 and 17, the latest of the burials on the site.

The relief pithos **GR30 P33** certainly belongs to the seventh century, as portrayals of centaurs brandishing branches do not appear until 670–660 B.C. (Simantoni-Bournia 2004, 25). Its closest parallels are of late seventh to early sixth century date from Vrokastro (Hayden 2005, 41, fig. 86:2139, pl. 21) and Orientalizing Azoria (Haggis et al. 2007b, 282, fig. 29:10). A surface find from the terrace south of Grave 30, the pithos cannot be associated with any particular burial within this grave, but it represents the latest LO vessel from Vronda. Thus, although there is not much evidence for the earliest burial in the grave, there is nothing to suggest a date earlier than the LG period, and some of the early pottery is of EO date. At least one of Burials 1–3 belonged to the early to mid-seventh century, a date in keeping with the unusual fibula (**GR30 M1**), and the burial event that included Burials 4 and 5 must have occurred later than that.

Catalog

Pottery

Fine Decorated Wares

GR30 P1 (VW 8003.2; Fig. 138). Cup. Single fragment from rim. D. rim est. 12.0. Fine, soft, reddish-yellow (7.5YR 7/6) fabric. Very pale brown (10YR 8/3) slip. Red (2.5YR 4/8) paint. Worn surfaces. No burning. Crosshatched lozenge chain. *Comparanda*: **GR6 P1**; for decoration, Tsipopoulou 2004, 134, 140, fig. 8:01/189/3, 00/663. *Date*: LG.

GR30 P2 (VW 8008.4, VW 8008.6, VW 8008.8, VW 8010.1 and 2, VW 8011.1; Fig. 138). Aryballos. Partially mended from 45 fragments. Preservation 75%, including 75% of base and body, half of neck, and handle; missing rim. Max pres. h. 5.8; d. base 3.2. Fine, soft, reddish-yellow (5YR 7/6) fabric. Very pale brown (10YR 8/4) slip. Black to red (2.5YR 5/6) paint. Very worn surfaces. Some fragments burned, including handle. Crosshatched upright triangles on shoulder. *Comparanda*: Brock 1957, 158, pls. 61:991, 96:1528 (Knossos, LG–EO); Sakellarakis 1986, 35–36, fig. 27, pl. 40 (Archanes, EO); Coldstream and Catling, eds., 1996, 183, pl. 176:1, 4 (Knossos, LG); Tsipopoulou 2005, 96, fig. 97:H722 (Kavousi, Plai tou Kastrou, LG–EO); 264, fig. 97:AN1409 (Praisos, LG–EO); Kotsonas 2008, 256, 261, fig. 64:A312 (Eleutherna, Corinthian import, mid-ninth century). *Date*: LG–EO.

GR30 P3 (VW 8008.6, VW 8011.1 and 2; Fig. 138; Pl. 60B). Lid. Partially mended from 13 fragments; 24 nonjoining fragments. Preservation 35%, including full profile, parts of rim, both handle ends; missing top of handle. Max. pres. h. 5.8; d. rim 15.0. Fine, soft, chalky, porous, light gray (5Y 7/2) fabric. Black paint. Surfaces worn. Possibly decoration in added white. Bands and dots. *Date*: LG.

GR30 P4 (V 10502.7; Fig. 138). Lid. Single fragment preserving entire ring handle. Max. pres. h. 3.3. Fine, very soft, reddish-yellow (5YR 6/6) fabric. Black paint. *Comparanda*: Day and Glowacki 2012, fig. 102:N3 P4. *Date*: uncertain.

GR30 P5 (V98.120; VW 8000, VW 8001.1–4, VW 8008.4, VW 8009.1, VW 9009.1; Fig. 138). Pyxis. Partially mended from 33 sherds into three large fragments. Preservation 20%, including half of base, full upper profile, 75% of handle; missing most of lower body. Max. pres. h. 12.2; d. rim 14.0; d. base 11.4. Fine, soft, chalky, very pale brown (10YR 8/2) fabric. Petrographic sample KAV 15/84: Fabric Subgroup 1b. Very pale brown (10YR 8/2) slip, once lustrous. Black to yellowish-red (5YR 4/6) paint. Worn surfaces. Two fragments slightly burned. Chevron bands between vertical thin bands. *Comparanda*: for shape, Coldstream and Catling, eds., 1996, 76, fig. 77:26.6 (Knossos, LG); 205, pl. 193:50 (Knossos, EG); 215–216, pl. 202:42 (Knossos, Attic MG II); Hayden 2003, 70–71, no. 188, fig. 45, pl. 29 (Vrokastro, LG–EO); for decoration, Coldstream and Catling, eds., 1996, 18, pl. 55:46 (Knossos, PGB–EG); Tsipopoulou 2005, 155, fig. 108:AN2319 (Hagios Georgios, LG); Kotsonas 2008, 258, 261, fig. 64:A184 (Eleutherna, LG Corinthian import). *Date*: LG.

Fine Monochrome Wares

GR30 P6 (V98.117; VW 8001.1, VW 8001.3A, VW 8009.1; Fig. 138; Pl. 60B). Cup. Mended from 36 fragments; eight nonjoining fragments. Preservation 65%, including full profile, entire base, much of rim, and handle; missing parts of body and bits of rim. H. 10.0; d. rim 11.8; d. base 5.2. Fine, rather hard, reddish-yellow (5YR 7/6) fabric. Black paint worn to mottled reddish brown (5YR 4/4). Very worn surfaces. *Comparanda*: Gesell, Coulson, and Day 1991, 174–175, fig. 12:1 (Kastro, O). *Date*: LO.

GR30 P7 (V98.118; VW 8008.6 and 7, VW 8011.2 VW 8015.1; Fig. 138). Cup. Mended from 75 fragments. Preservation 90%; missing section of rim and upper body, lower part of handle. H. 9.4; d. rim 11.0–12.0; d.

base 4.8. Fine, medium-soft, reddish-yellow (5YR 7/6) fabric. Red (2.5YR 4/8) paint. Worn surfaces. Many fragments burned. Comparanda: **GR28 P8**. *Date*: LG.

GR30 P8 (VW 8008.7–9, VW 8009.1, VW 8010.1 and 2; Fig. 138). Cup. Partially mended from 31 fragments. Preservation 65%, including entire base and handle, 50% of rim and upper body; missing part of body. H. 9.3; d. rim 12.5; d. base 4.5. Fine, medium-soft, pink (7.5YR 7/4) fabric. Black paint. Very worn surfaces. *Comparanda*: **GR28 P7**. *Date*: LG.

GR30 P9 (VW 8006.1, VW 8008.1, VW 8008.4, VW 8008.6 and 7, VW 8010.1; Fig. 138). Cup. Partially mended from seven fragments; three nonjoining. Preservation of 25% of rim and upper body, including upper handle attachment; missing base and handle. Max. pres. h. 5.3; d. rim 13.2. Fine, rather hard, reddish-yellow (5YR 7/6) fabric. Black paint. Worn surfaces. Some fragments burned. *Date*: LG.

GR30 P10 (VW 8008.4; Fig. 138). Cup. Partially mended from 32 fragments. Preservation 50%; profile can be reconstructed. H. est. 10.2; d. rim 11.4; d. base 5.2. Fine, soft, reddish-yellow (5YR 7/6) fabric with red phyllites. Red (2.5YR 4/6–4/8) paint. Surfaces eroding and exfoliating, but some well preserved. Handle burned. *Comparanda*: **GR30 P16**; Tsipopoulou 2004, 132, 139, fig. 6:01/1077 (Chalasmenos, LG). *Date*: LG.

GR30 P11 (VW 8001.1; Fig. 138). Cup. Six fragments from rim and handle. Max. pres. h. 4.6; d. rim est. 11.0. Fine, hard, pink (5YR 7/4) fabric. Dark reddish-brown (5YR 3/3) paint. Well-preserved surfaces. *Date*: LG.

GR30 P12 (VW 8008.6; Fig. 138). Cup. Fragments from rim and body, including upper handle attachment; no base or lower body. Max. pres. h. 3.2; d. rim est. 12.5. Fine, soft, chalky, pale yellow (5Y 8/2) fabric. Black paint. Very worn surfaces. *Date*: LG.

GR30 P13 (VW 8006.1 and 2, VW 8008.1 and 4, V 10502.5; Fig. 138). Skyphos. Partially mended from 15 fragments; 12 others may belong. Preservation 50%, including much of rim and upper body, handle attachment; missing base and both handles. Max. pres. h. 5.5; d. rim 12.5. Fine, soft, reddish-yellow (7.5YR 7/6) fabric with red phyllites. Red (2.5YR 4/8) paint. Worn surfaces. *Comparanda*: Mook 1993, 214, fig. 139:P3.180 (Kastro, LG); Tsipopoulou 2005, 269, fig. 119:AN1364 (Praisos, O). *Date*: LG–EO.

GR30 P14 (VW 8001.1, VW 8003.1 and 2, VW 8006.1 and 2; Fig. 138). Cup or skyphos. Represented by 30 fragments from rim and body; missing base and handle(s). D. rim est. 12.2. Fine, soft, pink (5YR 7/4) to light gray (5Y 7/1) fabric. Thick, fine, black paint. Well-preserved surfaces. *Comparanda*: **GR30 P29**; Mook 2004, 177, fig. 12.12:H (Kastro, O). *Date*: LG–EO.

GR30 P15 (VW 8001.1; Fig. 138). Cup or skyphos. Three joining fragments from rim; rim chipped. Max. pres. h. 4.4; d. rim 12.5. Fine, hard, reddish-yellow (5YR 6/6) fabric. Black paint. Worn surfaces; mottled where paint worn off. *Date*: LG.

GR30 P16 (VW 8008.1, VW 8008.4, VW 8008.6, VW 8010.1; Fig. 139). Cup or skyphos. Partially mended from seven fragments. Profile can be reconstructed; missing handle(s). H. est. 10.1; d. rim 11.5; d. base 6.0. Fine, soft, reddish-yellow (5YR 7/6) fabric. Red (2.5YR 4/8) paint. Worn surfaces. Many fragments burned; some have very worn edges. *Comparanda*: **GR30 P10**; Tsipopoulou 2004, 132, 139, fig. 6:01/1077 (Chalasmenos, LG). *Date*: LG–EO.

GR30 P17 (VW 8008.1; Fig. 139). Cup or skyphos. Two joining fragments from base, two from body. Max. pres. h. 2.4; d. base 5.8. Fine, soft, reddish-yellow (5YR 7/6) fabric. Black paint, worn to surface mottling, on interior, exterior, and underside of base. Worn surfaces. *Date*: LG.

GR30 P18 (VW 8008.4; Fig. 139). Cup or skyphos. Three joining fragments from base and lower body. Max. pres. h. 4.8; d. base 5.0. Fine, soft, light red (2.5YR 6/6) fabric with light gray (5Y 7/1) core. Traces of red paint. One fragment burned. Worn surfaces. *Date*: LG.

GR30 P19 (V 10502.3; Fig. 139). Cup or skyphos. Two fragments from base. Max. pres. h. 1.7; d. base 4.5. Fine, rather hard, reddish-yellow (5YR 6/6) fabric, very pale brown (10YR 8/3) on surface. Black paint. Very worn surfaces. *Date*: LG.

GR30 P20 (V 10502.3; Fig. 139). Cup or skyphos. Single fragment preserving 75% of base. Max. pres. h. 1.7; d. base 5.0. Fine, soft, reddish-yellow (5YR 7/6) fabric with tiny white inclusions. Red (2.5YR 4/8) paint. Ring base. *Date*: EO.

GR30 P21 (VW 8003.2; Fig. 139). Cup or skyphos. Two fragments from base. Max. pres. h. 5.2; d. base 5.0. Fine, soft, reddish-yellow (7.5YR 7/6) fabric. Very pale brown (10YR 8/2) slip or surface. *Date*: LG.

GR30 P22 (VW 8006.1, VW 8008.1 and 2; Fig. 139). Juglet. Partially mended from 12 fragments. Preservation 85% of rim and neck; missing lower body, handle, base. Max. pres. h. 3.5; d. rim 2.8. Fine, soft, slightly porous, light brown (7.5YR 6/4) fabric. Black paint. Very worn surfaces, mottled where paint has come off. *Date*: LG.

Fine Plain Wares

GR30 P23 (VW 8010.2; Fig. 139). Cup or jug. Single fragment preserving half of base. Max. pres. h. 3.0; d. base 3.3. Fine, soft, reddish-yellow (5YR 7/6) fabric. Very pale brown (10YR 8/3) slip. *Date*: uncertain.

Medium-Coarse Decorated Wares

GR30 P24 (VW 8001.2, VW 8008.4; Fig. 139). Open vessel, possibly a krater. Partially mended from nine fragments, preserving large section of lower body. Max. pres. h. 6.0. Medium-coarse, porous, reddish-yellow (7.5YR 7/6) fabric with phyllite inclusions. Petrographic sample KAV 15/86: Fabric Subgroup 1b. Light red (2.5YR 6/6) to black paint. Zones of alternating multiple triangles with dotted lozenge above. *Comparanda*: Coldstream and Catling, eds., 1996, 156, fig. 110:134 (Knossos, Attic MG II); Tsipopoulou 2005, 157, fig. 108:AN2369 (Hagios Georgios, LG). *Date*: LG.

GR30 P25 (VW 8001.1, VW 8001.3 and 4; VW 8008.2–4; Fig. 139). Skyphos or cup. Partially mended from 18 fragments from rim, carination, and body; no base, no handle. Max. pres. h. 10.0; d. rim est. 17.8. Medium-coarse, porous, reddish-yellow (7.5YR 7/6) fabric. Petrographic sample KAV 15/87: Fabric Subgroup 1a. Black to reddish-brown (5YR 5/4) paint. Interlocking spirals with strokes as filler above. Drips on interior. Well-preserved surfaces. *Comparanda*: Tsipopoulou 2005, 116, fig. 18:H1957 (Kavousi Skouriasmenos, LG–EO). *Date*: LG–EO.

GR30 P26 (VW 8001.3A, VW 8008.4; Fig. 139). Conical bowl, possibly a lid. Six fragments from rim. Max. pres. h. 6.6; d. rim 14.7. Medium-coarse, soft, light red (2.5YR 6/6) fabric with gray phyllites. Very pale brown (10YR 8/2) slip. Dark reddish-brown (5YR 3/2) paint. Worn surfaces. *Date*: LG.

GR30 P27 (VW 8001.1 and 2, VW 8008.1–4, VW 8011.3; Fig. 139). Lid. Partially mended from 21 fragments, preserving profile from rim to near handle; missing handle. Max. pres. h. 4.5; d. rim 22.0. Medium-coarse reddish-yellow (7.5YR 7/6) to light gray (2.5Y 7/2) fabric with black sand-sized inclusions. Thick, glossy, very pale brown (10YR 8/2) slip. Black paint. Very worn surfaces. Elaborately decorated with panel of chevrons, hatched curvilinear motif (possibly a bird), circles, and multiple lines. *Comparanda*: for shape, Coldstream and Catling, eds., 1996, 57, fig. 73:1.6 (LG–EO); Kotsonas 2008, 150, 152, fig. 36:A105a (Eleutherna, LG–EPAR). *Date*: LG–EO.

GR30 P28 (V98.119; VW 8000.3, VW 8001.1–4, VW 8008.3 and 4, VW 8009.1, VW 8011.3; Fig. 139). Pyxis. Partially mended from 72 sherds into two large fragments, one from rim and handle, the other from handle and body; 40% of base also preserved. Max. pres. h. (with handles) 21.0; d. rim 10.5; d. base 12.0. Medium-coarse, hard, light red (2.5YR 6/6) fabric with frequent but small phyllites and hard, white inclusions. Petrographic sampled KAV 15/83: Fabric Group 6. Pink (7.5YR 8/4) slip. Red (2.5YR 4/6–4/8) paint. Well-preserved surfaces. Several pieces burned. Bands below; possible metopal panel on shoulder but surfaces too worn to tell. *Comparanda*: Coldstream and Catling, eds., 1996, 245, pl. 224:39 (Knossos, late MG); Hayden 2003, 63, no. 161, fig. 39 (Vrokastro, MG–LG). *Date*: LG.

Medium-Coarse Monochrome Wares

GR30 P29 (VW 8009.1; Fig. 140). Skyphos. Partially mended from 26 fragments. Preservation 30%, including full profile, bit of base, one handle, rim; missing much of body and rim. H. 11.1; d. rim 13.4; d. base 6.7. Medium-coarse, soft, reddish-yellow (7.5YR 7/6) fabric with dark metamorphosized phyllites. Petrographic sample KAV 15/85: Fabric Subgroup 1a. Black paint on interior, exterior, and underside of base. Very worn surfaces. *Comparanda*: Mook 2004, 177, fig. 12.12:H (Kastro, O). *Date*: EO.

GR30 P30 (VW 8000.3, VW 8001.1, VW 8008.1–3; Fig. 140). Cup or skyphos. Four joining fragments preserving 85% of base; four nonjoining body fragments. Max. pres. h. 3.2; d. base 5.0. Medium-coarse, rather hard, reddish-yellow (5YR 6/6) fabric with phyllites and voids where inclusions have fired out. Crackled black paint on interior, exterior, and underside of base. Very worn surfaces. One fragment burned. *Date*: LG.

GR30 P31 (VW 8008.6; Fig. 140). Jug or lekythos. Partially mended from numerous fragments into base (two sherds) and neck (12 sherds); other fragments from neck preserved, but they do not join. D. base 3.7; d. neck 3.2. Medium-coarse, very soft, chalky, pink (7.5YR 8/4) to light gray (2.5Y 7/2) fabric. Red (2.5YR 4/8) paint. Surfaces very worn. Many fragments burned. Neck is much taller than illustrated, but fabric is so soft and edges so worn that joins are impossible to make. *Date*: LG–EO.

GR30 P32 (VW 8001.4; Fig. 140). Cup. Two joining fragments from rim. Max. pres. h. 4.5; d. rim 14.0. Medium-coarse, rather hard, dark gray (5Y 4/1) fabric with frequent hard white inclusions. Possible fugitive pale yellow (2.5Y 8/2) slip on exterior. *Date*: uncertain.

Coarse Decorated Wares

GR30 P33 (V89.87; VW 8101.3, object 1; Fig. 140; Pl. 60B). Relief pithos. Single fragment from body. Max. pres. w. 9.4; max. pres. h. 6.2; th. 1.8–2.0; max. pres. d. est. 56.0. Coarse, medium-hard, light red (2.5YR 6/8) to red (2.5YR 5/8), Kavousi Type IV fabric with dark reddish-brown (5YR 3/2) darkening or discoloration on exterior. Very worn. Stamped decoration in two zones, separated by a flat horizontal band. Upper zone preserves two legs of figure in running (*knielauf*) position, to left. In front of figure, to left, is a worn, slightly raised vertical stroke that does not extend below ankle level of the running figure. Lower zone preserves the top part of a guilloche or cable pattern with pendant triangles above. Running figure probably represents a centaur or, less likely, a hoplite. The preserved legs are identical to centaur figures on a stamped pithos in similar fabric from Azoria (and possibly identical to a stamped pithos from the Vrokastro survey, but on different fabric). By analogy with the Azoria pithos, the short vertical line in front of the figure may represent the tail of the leading centaur to left. The guilloche pattern in the lower band is also paralleled on the Azoria pithos (but not on the Vrokastro survey pithos). *Comparanda*: Simantoni-Bournia 2004, pl. 2:4 (Kastri, Siteia after 670 B.C.); Hayden 2005, 41, fig. 86:2139, pl. 21 (Vrokastro, late seventh–early sixth); Haggis et al. 2007b, 282, fig. 29:10 (Azoria, O). *Date*: LO.

Metal

Bronze

GR30 M1 (V90.143; VW 8010.2, object 3; Fig. 140; Pl. 60B). Bronze fibula. Large fragment from ellipsoid bow of fibula preserving the top of the catch plate to the coil; second fragment of coil, and tiny fragment of pin. Max. pres. L. 4.1; max. pres. w. 1.7. Very well preserved, with little corrosion. Flat catch plate. Narrow biconical swelling and band. Ellipsoid rises from band like umbrella; top edges have three bands. Seven incised parallel bands along the axis of the bow. Another band and ridge, then rectangular in section to coil. Double coil. *Comparanda*: Blinkenberg 1926, 169–172, type VIII.5; Sapouna-Sakellaraki 1978, 105–106, fig. 43:1489, 1494 (type IXa, LG–EO); Coldstream and Catling, eds., 1996, 272, fig. 171:292.f 41, 292.f 42.

GR30 M2 (V90.146; VW 8008.2, object 2; Fig. 140; Pl. 60B). Bronze sheeting. Two large sheets of bronze mended from six fragments; another nonjoining fragment. Max. pres. L. (a) 5.1, (b) 3.6; max. pres. w. (a) 3.5, (b) 2.9. Well preserved. Very thin bronze sheets, both with slight curve. Second fragment has preserved rivet holes, and one bronze rivet found in grave may belong.

IRON

GR30 M3 (V90.144, HNM 15766; VW 8011.1, object 4; Fig. 140; Pl. 60B). Iron pin. Intact. L. 8.0; d. disk 0.9. Very well preserved; almost no corrosion. Conical knob, large disk. Biconical swelling with three rings on either side. *Comparanda*: Coldstream and Catling, eds., 1996, 121, fig. 175:75.f 61 (Knossos, MG?). *Date*: LG–EO.

GR30 M4 (V90.141; VW 8010.1 object 3; Fig. 140; Pl. 60B). Iron pin. Single fragment from head and body; missing tip. Max. pres. L. 5.0; d. disk 0.8. Very corroded. Small knob, thick disk. Biconical swelling with four rings on one side, three on other. *Date*: LG–EO.

GR30 M5 (V90.156; VW 8010.1; Fig. 140; Pl. 60B). Iron pin. Two nonjoining fragments from head (a) and point (b). Max. pres. L. (a) 3.0, (b) 2.0; d. disk 0.7. Corroded. Knob at end, thick disk made of two rings. Three rings above what may be a biconical swelling, with single ring below swelling. *Date*: LG–EO.

GR30 M6 (V90.145; VW 8008.7, objects 10 and 12; Fig. 140; Pl. 60B). Iron pin. Mended from two fragments; missing head and tip of pin. Max. pres. L. 7.2. Corroded. Large spherical swelling with three rings on one side, two or three on the other.

GR30 M7 (V90.148; VW 8010.1, object 4; Fig. 140; Pl. 60B). Iron pin. Three nonjoining fragments from head (a), middle (b), and point (c). Max. pres. L. (a) 2.4, (b) 1.3, (c) 1.5. Very corroded. Spherical swelling near head with at least two rings on either side.

GR30 M8 (V90.140; VW 8010.1, object 5; Fig. 141; Pl. 61). Iron javelin or spearhead. Three joining fragments from socket end of spear; missing end of socket and tip of spear. Max. pres. L. 18.4; max w. 2.2; d. socket est. 1.8. Very corroded. Long (at least 9.5) socket. End missing, but pierced near end opposite edges. Rounded shoulders. Pronounced midrib.

GR30 M9 (V92.52; VW 8008.5, VW 9010.1, VW 8010.1 object 5; Fig. 141; Pl. 61). Iron spearhead. Nine joining fragments from socket (a) and one large fragment of blade (b); many other flakes from blade. Max. pres. L. (a) 11.8, (b) 10.0; d. socket 1.6. Corroded, but some original surfaces survive. Long (at least 11.8) socket, with hole pierced near end opposite edges. No apparent midrib.

GR30 M10 (V90.138b; VW 8010.1 object 5, VW 8011.1 object 1; Fig. 141; Pl. 61). Iron dagger or dirk. Large fragment from hilt and blade (a), smaller one from tip of blade (b); missing end of hilt, rivets, and upper part of blade. Max. pres. L. (a) 22.7, (b) 4.2; max. pres. w. 3.7. Cracked and corroded. Some original surfaces preserved. Long flanged hilt, rivet hole near top, and two rivet holes at attachment of blade. Broad blade.

GR30 M11 (V90.149; VW 8010.1, object 6; Fig. 141; Pl. 61). Iron needle. Two joining fragments from head with eye; missing point. Max. pres. L. 1.80; max. w. 0.35. Some corrosion. Flattened head pierced with hole.

GR30 M12 (V90.139; VW 8008.4, object 4; Fig. 141; Pl. 61). Iron sickle-shaped knife. Mended from five fragments preserving most of blade; missing tip of blade. Max. pres. L. 18.3; max. w. 2.5; th. 0.7. Very corroded; no surviving surfaces. End at oblique angle to blade; rivet hole near end. Blade curves with cutting edge on inner side. No indication of serration.

GR30 M13 (VW 8008.6, object 9; Fig. 141; Pl. 61). Iron axe-head. Partially mended into four large fragments from tang and end of head; numerous nonjoining fragments and flakes. Max. pres. L. (a) 10.5, (b) 6.5, (c) 8.5, (d) 5.4; max. pres. w. (a) 1.9, (b) 3.0, (c) 2.6, (d) 1.8. Very corroded, laminated, and exploded. Long (at least 5.6) haft. Head comes out at right angles to it.

GR30 M14 (V90.142; VW 8010.2, object 14; Fig. 141; Pl. 61). Iron chisel. Single fragment preserving use edge; handle end missing. Max. pres. L. 5.5; max. w. 2.5; th. 0.8. Corroded; no surviving surfaces. Narrow handle, widening to sharp angular cutting edge. *Comparanda*: Coldstream and Catling, eds., 1996, 120, fig. 175:f36.

GR30 M15 (V90.147; VW 8008.4, object 6; Fig. 141; Pl. 61). Iron tool, possibly a chisel. Mended from two fragments; missing one end. Max. pres. L. 6.8; max. w. 0.8. Corroded, but with some surviving surfaces. Pointed at one end; square in section in center, tapering to other end, becoming rectangular in section.

Terracotta

GR30 TC1 (V90.37, IM 989; VW 8008.6, object 8; Fig. 141; Pl. 61). Terracotta bead. Globular. Intact, but worn. H. 1.95; d. 2.30; d. hole 0.40. Wt. 10.00 g. Fine, soft, light red (2.5YR 6/6) fabric with tiny phyllites and mica inclusions. Incised decoration: vertical/oblique slashes on sides; horizontal slash around center. No wheelmarks. Hole is irregular, pulled out into an oval on one side. Inside the hole there appears to be another hole, as if the maker inserted a pointed instrument, started to make the hole, then pulled it out and pushed it back in at a slightly different angle (perhaps it was going too far off center), and finally pulled the instrument a bit to make the hole larger.

GR30 TC2 (V90.39, IM 983; VW 8010.2, object 12; Fig. 141; Pl. 61). Terracotta bead. Biconical. Intact except for one missing chip. H. 1.8; d. 2.5; d. hole 0.3–0.4. Wt. 8.00 g. Fine, medium-hard, reddish-yellow (5YR 6/6) fabric. Traces of brown to black paint. Cracked and burned. Monochrome painted. No decoration. No wheelmarks.

Grave 31

History and Details of Excavation

Grave 31 is a possible pyre site lying on the northwest summit of the Vronda ridge, in the center of what had been Room D1 of Building D in the LM IIIC settlement (Figs. 3, 4). It was excavated in 1990 and consisted of a pit in the roofing material from the earlier building (Gesell, Day, and Coulson 1995, 73; Day, Klein, and Turner 2009, 97). The lack of architectural features made it difficult to define. During the course of the excavation of a large stone tumble over the southeast corner of the room in Locus V 4512, a patch of burned soil with human bones was encountered. Again, during excavation of the area adjacent to the west in V 4513, another patch of similar burned soil and bones was found. The area of soft dark soil was more clearly defined, and the material was removed as V 4514. Below the dark, soft soil was a layer of harder, dark, burned soil with much organic material in it (V 4519), and a third layer of dark soil lay beneath (V 4524).

Also in 1990, the north balk of adjacent Trench V 4600 was removed, and a small amount of dark ashy soil (V 4650) that contained a few human bones associated with Grave 31 was found.

The presence of burned human bone, however fragmentary, indicates some cremation activity at this site, but the grave is unlike the usual Vronda cremation areas because of its lack of architectural features and accompanying grave goods. There were no objects or pottery found with the bones except for the usual numbers of earlier fragments that one would expect as background noise. It seems likely that Grave 31 represents a pyre site from which the majority of bones was removed for secondary burial elsewhere, unlike the more common pattern of leaving the dead on the pyre, placing funeral goods there, and piling stones over the burial. Secondary burial in amphorae or pithoi are not unknown at Vronda (e.g., Graves 21, 26, 28), and this area may be a place where an original cremation occurred.

Architecture

Grave 31 had no architectural features (Fig. 142). It was an irregular pit dug into the collapsed roofing clay and rock tumble from the earlier LM IIIC house. The area of the grave was roughly oval, measuring 1.55 m northeast–southwest x 0.60 m northwest–southeast.

Stratigraphy

There were three levels of burned soil in the grave, all together 0.15–0.20 m thick. The lowest layer (V 4524) was soft and dark, and above it was very compacted, burned soil containing much organic material (resembling straw; V 4519). This material may be the remains of something that was used as fuel for the funeral pyre. Soft ashy soil with burned bones (V 4514) lay above this compacted layer, with rock tumble over the entire area that could not be easily distinguished from the rock tumble over the grave (V 4512, V 4513).

Associated Features

There was another pit in the roofing debris and tumble to the southwest of Grave 31 that may be associated with the burial (V 4517, V 4518, V 4528, V 4536). This pit was filled with a deposit of ca. 0.20 m of soft ashy soil, similar to that found in Grave 31. As with Grave 31, there were no associated objects and very little pottery.

Burials

There was a single individual represented in the skeletal remains from Grave 31. The bone was disturbed, with no evidence of articulation. The deposit appears to be a cremation site, with most of the bone removed, perhaps for deposit elsewhere.

Burial 1
Type: disturbed primary cremation
Age: adult
Sex: female
Weight: 424.00 g

The gracile cranium and wide sciatic notch of Burial 1 indicate that the remains belonged to an adult female. The recovered bone was unevenly cremated, resulting in a range of conditions varying from scorched and blackened bone to completely calcined material. The completely formed tips of all of the recovered tooth roots and the generally mature morphology of the skeletal elements show that this individual was an adult. There is no evidence of unfused or partially fused epiphyses on the long bones or other skeletal elements.

Faunal Remains

The single identifiable animal bone recovered from Grave 31 was a single first cervical vertebra (atlas) that was fragmented and burned (Table 9). Based on its robust character and size but fragmented condition, it could only be identified as Bovidae (i.e., ovicaprid or domestic cattle) or deer. Five other unidentifiable fragments were also heavily burned and calcined.

Pottery

While 344 fragments of pottery weighing 19.86 kg were recovered from the grave, there were no whole or nearly complete pots. Most of the sherds came from pithoi and scrappy coarse vessels of LM IIIC date, consistent with the pottery from the roofing debris and rock tumble from the walls of the earlier Building D. There was not a single fragment of identifiable Geometric pottery. Grave 31 thus differs completely from the other graves in the Vronda cemetery.

Chronology

There is no material with which to date the pyre in Grave 31, as there were no accompanying grave goods or any stray finds left behind by the cremators.

Graves 32 and 25

History and Details of Excavation

Grave 32 is a stone-lined enclosure that lies on the southwest slope of the Vronda ridge, the southernmost in a line of three enclosure graves (27, 26, 32) situated just west and southwest of the earlier LM IIIC shrine (Figs. 3, 4, 119). It was excavated in 1990 in Trench V 8200, although the surrounding area had been uncovered in 1988 and 1989, and the surface soil was removed in 1989 (Gesell, Day, and Coulson 1995, 80–81). The grave had been much disturbed, not only by a large olive tree immediately to the east of the enclosure but also by Venetian activity and a modern terrace wall. Because of these disturbances, the material within the grave was scanty and joined with pottery excavated in the immediately surrounding areas (Trench V 8300, around the olive tree, and Trench V 8800). Although pottery of the Geometric period was also found high up to the east in V 8900, this material has been attributed to episodes of dumping from Grave 19 (see above, p. 140).

The grave lay beneath a layer of stone tumble (V 8205; Pl. 62A) that may belong to the same layer encountered in V 8800 (V 8812), and it lay below a layer of wash (V 8202, V 8203) that appeared immediately below topsoil (V 8201). The walls were defined during the excavation of V 8206, which was inside the enclosure along the west wall (Pl. 62B). Once the grave was defined, it was excavated as V 8209, a shallow deposit without the usual concentrations of pottery or cremations in anatomical order. At the base of the enclosure was a burned pebbly surface with calcined bedrock pebbles and burned red clay. Only one burial was recognized during excavation, but subsequent study has shown that there were three. An intact aryballos (**GR32 P1**) was found in the northwest corner, as was an iron pin fragment.

Grave 25 was identified and excavated in 1989 (Pls. 62A, 62B). Beneath a layer of rock tumble that also went over Grave 26 to the north (V 8723, V 8724, V

8703), a deposit of dark (10YR 7/3, very pale brown), moist soil (V 8725) containing a small amount of human bone was discovered in what appeared to be an enclosure oriented east–west, but with walls on three sides only. This deposit was not deep and did not look like a primary cremation. Subsequent study of the material shows some joins of pottery with Grave 32, and it seems likely that the area labeled Grave 25 was simply a spillover or discard deposit from Grave 32. A fibula (**GR32 M1**) was found just to the west of Grave 25 during sweeping for photography in V 8731; because of its proximity to Graves 25 and 32, it has been cataloged with Grave 32. Bones from Grave 32 (associated with Grave 25) were also found in the rock tumble (V 8205) northeast of the olive tree, in the cobble layer above the tumble (V 8702), in the layer of red clay wash that went over the cobble layer (V 8204), and in the area immediately to the west of Graves 26 and 32 (V8726). When the discarding of material into the area of Grave 25 occurred is uncertain. The location of the other material from Grave 32, however, suggests that it was deposited when the olive tree was planted.

Architecture

Grave 32 is a stone-lined, built enclosure grave, oriented north–south and measuring 2.29 m north–south x ca. 0.80 m east–west (Fig. 119; Pls. 62A, 62B). Because of the disturbance of the olive tree, no east wall survives. The enclosure is longer than was customary. The west boundary wall (V 8207) has two faces, neither of them good. The south wall (V 8208) is formed by a single row of three stones. The north wall (V 8734) is composed of a large boulder separating Grave 32 from the space called Grave 25; this limestone block is fissured from the heat of the fire. The floor of the enclosure shows burning, both in the calcined pebbles and in the fired clay at the bottom.

Grave 25, however, is not a built enclosure, nor does it show any evidence of burning. The good wall on the north is actually the south wall of Grave 26, while the west wall (V 8733) is a single row of stones that continues the line of the west wall of Grave 32. These stones are bonded into the south wall, which was the northern boundary of Grave 32. No east wall has been preserved. There was no evidence of burning, and the deposit was shallow, so it seems to have been a discard deposit from Grave 32.

Stratigraphy

Within the enclosure, the stratigraphy is simple and straightforward, but the scattered pattern of pottery joins shows massive later disturbance. The total deposition in the grave was only about 0.24 m. Soft, ashy, dark yellowish-brown (10YR 4/2) soil (V 8209, V 8206) lay above the floor of the grave. This layer continued all the way up to the tops of the walls. Above the level of the walls of the enclosure was a large, deep area of stone tumble that was also found in Trenches V 8300, V 8700, and V 8800 (V 8205, V 8305, V 8306, V 8703, V 8710, V 8723, V 8724, V 8812, V 8814; Pl. 62A). A layer containing smaller cobbles and rather more compact soil was found over the stone tumble (V8203, V 8302, V 8810, V 8811, V 8702, V 722, V 8715–V 8719, V 8709); it also contained some Venetian pottery and was probably deposited during the occupation of Building F to the east. Slope wash (V 8202) was deposited above this layer just below topsoil (V 8201).

Grave 25 was simply a deposit of dark, soft, moist, very pale brown (10YR 7/3) soil with human bones and snail shells (V 8725) in the space created between Graves 26 and 32. It was quite shallow, only 0.135 m deep, and it did not contain and notable quantity of pottery or articulated bones. The deposit lay directly below the rock tumble of V 8723 and V 8724.

Associated Features

Grave 25 was associated with Grave 32 as a discard deposit. Other strata and deposits in the area containing Grave 32 material probably result from disturbance in the Venetian and modern periods.

Burials

Two burials were recovered from within Grave 32, both female, one 40–60 years of age and the second a younger 20–40. The bones from Grave 25 included an adult and a perinatal infant. The characteristics of the adult are consistent with the remains of one of the two individuals in Grave 32. It was probably the younger woman who was buried with her infant.

Grave 32, Burials 1 and 2, and Grave 25
Type: disturbed primary cremations
Age: two adults, one 40–60 years, another 20–40 years
Sex: female

Weight: 1,365 g (including 208 g from Grave 25)

The grave held the cremated remains of two adults. The original grave deposits in Grave 32 were disturbed, resulting in the deposits initially identified as Grave 25. The disturbance made it impossible to distinguish between the bones of the two adult individuals in the grave. That there are two individuals is clear because of the duplication of cranial elements, including two mandibular symphyses and three superior margins of the eye orbit. Two right scapular spines were found, indicating duplication in the postcranial bones as well. One of the women is older, perhaps 40–60 years, with obliterated cranial sutures and antemortem tooth loss. The other appears to be younger based on the lack of cranial suture closure and the lack of age-related changes on the joints. The presence of a possibly perinatal infant (Burial 3; below) also supports a younger age for one of the women. The cranium of the older woman was only scorched by the cremation pyre, while the younger cranium, like the postcrania, is completely calcined. There is some slight periosteal bone formation on the tibia shafts of one individual. This condition is sometimes associated with systemic infections or scurvy in adults. Otherwise the bones were unremarkable.

Burial 3
Type: disturbed primary cremation
Age: perinatal infant
Sex: unknown
Weight: 7 g

A third skeleton belonging to a possibly perinatal infant was recovered from the water sieve residue of the soils from both inside the enclosure and in the discard deposit (Grave 25). As the total weight of the perinatal bone is only 7 g, any specific age attribution is impossible. Both cranial and multiple postcranial skeletal elements were identified. All of the bone is completely calcined.

Faunal Remains

The few possible animal bone fragments found in this area, while burned, do not appear to be directly associated with the burials (Table 9). The only specimens for which the elements are identifiable include a possible sheep or goat metapodial diaphysis fragment and a domestic pig scapula fragment. The pig scapula fragment is burned.

Pottery

The pottery from Grave 32 is scant. Only a few vessels were found within the grave itself, while others were found in the rock tumble above and in the surrounding trenches, a result of the later disturbance. A total of 238 fragments of pottery weighing 1.25 kg was collected from within the grave itself, and another 140 fragments weighing 0.82 kg came from the area first labeled Grave 25. It has been assumed that most of the pottery in V 8300 (around the olive tree) came from Grave 32, but some pottery may have rolled down from where it was discarded from Grave 19 above to the northeast. Many vessels joined to fragments in the rock tumble above the grave and immediately to the north. Pottery from the area farther to the east (in V 8900), which came from a higher level, is assumed to have been dumped from Grave 19.

Those vessels that were actually found within the grave include an aryballos (**GR32 P1**), one of three pyxides (**GR32 P4**), a lid (**GR32 P5**), and a lekanis (**GR32 P7**), which, however, was also scattered over the area to the north and to the east. Vessels found outside the grave may have been discarded when the second cremation was made in the enclosure or as a result of the later disturbances in Venetian and modern times. A hydria (**GR32 P9**) was found in the rock tumble over Grave 32, as well as in tumble to the east; it was probably disturbed when the olive tree was planted, but the presence of some fragments farther north and east in Trench V 8900 allows for the possibility that it came from Grave 19. The rock tumble to the north of the grave produced fragments of the other two pyxides (**GR32 P2**, **GR32 P3**) and a cup (**GR32 P10**), while the tumble to the east yielded a cup (**GR32 P6**), a juglet (**GR32 P8**), and a bowl (**GR32 P11**). Fragments of **GR32 P2** were found in the area called Grave 25, and they may have been dumped there from the earlier burial.

The pottery is highly unusual. There were at least three pyxides, one similar in shape to an example from Grave 17 (**GR32 P4**), and the other two with triangular handles reminiscent of the pyxides in Grave 30 (**GR32 P2**, **GR32 P3**). Pyxis **GR32 P2** is an unusual shape, very squat with a broad flat base.

Except for the presence of the handles, perhaps added in deference to local taste (Coldstream 2001, 37), it is more like the Attic flat pyxis of MG II date and may be imitating this form (Coldstream and Catling, eds., 1996, 215, pl. 202:23). The globular pyxis with no lip is common in Siteia (Tsipopoulou 2013, 146), and the shape and decoration resemble an Early Protocorinthian pyxis from Thera (Coldstream 1968, pl. 21:g). The crosshatched lozenge chain motif is common as a filler on Geometric pottery of all phases and appears on an EO pyxis from Eleutherna (Kotsonas 2008, 140–141, fig. 33:A60), but as the major decoration it is paralleled by many LG vessels from East Crete, such as a hydria from Hagios Georgios of LG–EO date (Tsipopoulou 2005, 163, fig. 43:AN2428). The lekanis with reflex handles (**GR32 P7**) is an unusual shape at Vronda, found only in this grave.

Other vessels from the grave have not been cataloged because they were too fragmentary. A large closed vessel with a round handle is represented in 32 fragments from the grave itself (V8206, V 8209) and from the cobble layer above (V 8205), the stone tumble to the northeast (V 8812), and the area to the west (V 8726). A tiny fragment of an aryballos with concentric circles on the side, possibly a Creto-Cypriot type like those in Graves 4 and 17, was found in V 8206. Another pyxis of pale green fabric like **GR32 P4** was found in V 8205, as was a coarse, basin-like bowl (**GR32 P11**), and a single fragment of a decorated cup with a concentric circle or spiral appeared in V 8305.

Finally, there were many fragments of a fine, closed vessel of soft, very pale brown fabric found in V 8812. It is uncertain whether this vessel was an earlier piece or a discard from the grave. Not enough is preserved to recognize a shape, but it shows some interesting techniques of manufacture. The top of the vessel (or possibly the bottom) is a circular disk, to which were added the sides of the vessel with additional clay to make the joint secure. This technique is common on LM IIIC stirrup jars, and this vessel could be a stirrup jar. There is a large spout like a stirrup jar spout as well. Three fragments have a large hole (d. 1.7 cm) pierced through them from the inside out, perhaps where the spout was put onto the stirrup jar.

Objects

There were few objects found in the grave. The fibula found to the west of Grave 25 (**GR32 M1**) probably belongs with the earlier burial in this grave; it can be dated to the second half of the eighth century. The iron fragments could not be identified, but their presence suggests that there were iron objects in the grave, perhaps including a pin. A possible glass bead (**GR32 G1**) was also found. It is noteworthy that the grave contained no male burials and no weapons.

Chronology

Grave 32 is late in the Vronda sequence. Latest of all is the aryballos **GR32 P1**, with a close parallel from Knossos of LO date (Coldstream and Catling, eds., 1996, 111, fig. 94:24). The base of **GR32 P10**, with its sharply beveled edge, is highly unusual and may also be a late feature. Its profile resembles Archaic bases, except that it is flat. Similar pyxides appear in Graves 17 and 30, both of which are among the latest in the sequence, belonging to the EO period. The lekanis with reflex handles (**GR32 P7**) also has close parallels at EO Knossos, where they are called lekanides (Coldstream and Catling, eds., 1996, 64, pl. 93:20; 72, pl. 97:28), and there are other examples of LG–EPAR date at Eleutherna (Kotsonas 2008, 222, 224, fig. 55:A137α). Although apparently monochrome, it may have had decoration in added white. It is likely that the grave is later, then, than nearby Graves 26 or 27 and contemporary with Graves 4, 15, 17, 23, and 30.

Catalog

Pottery

FINE DECORATED WARES

GR32 P1 (V90.58, IM 1231; V 8209.1, object 1; Fig. 143; Pl. 62C). Aryballos. Intact except for a few chips. H. 5.4; h. with handle 5.6; d. rim 2.9; d. base 2.8. Fine, soft, reddish-yellow (7.5YR 8/6) fabric with tiny phyllite inclusions. Very pale brown (10YR 8/3) slip. Red (2.5YR 4/8) paint. Surface pocked and worn. Traces of discoloration from fire on rim, one side, base. Tongue pattern. *Bibliography*: Gesell, Day, and Coulson 1995, 81, pl. 24:d. *Date*: LO.

GR32 P2 (V98.125; V 8206.4, V 8205.1, V 8302.2, V 8305.1 V 8703.2, V 8725.1, V 8807.2 and 3, V 8810.1–4, V 8812.1 and 2, V 8812.4, V 8812.6–8, V 8811.2, V 8814.2; Fig. 143). Pyxis. Partially mended from 49 fragments. Preservation 60%, including full profile, 75% of base and lower body, and two fragments from rim and handles. Another 29 fragments may belong to this pyxis or **GR32 P3**. H. est. 14.0; h. with handles 16.3; d. rim 11.8; d. base 14.4. Fine, soft, reddish-yellow (5YR 7/6) fabric. Glossy, white (10YR 8/1) to very pale brown (10YR 8/2) slip. Shadow of red(?) paint. Very worn surfaces. Some fragments burned, preserving negative image of design. Crosshatched lozenge chain above narrow bands. *Comparanda*: Coldstream and Catling, eds., 1996, 76, fig. 77:6 (Knossos, LG); 277, fig. 151:41 (Knossos, MG); for decoration, Coldstream 2001, pls. 8:d (Knossos, MG), 10:c (Knossos, LG); Tsipopoulou 2005, 202, fig. 25:H3183 (Adromyloi, LG); 293, fig. 60:AN8788 (Praisos, LG); Tsipopoulou 2013, 145–146, fig. 8:12280 (Piskokephalo, LG). *Date*: LG.

GR32 P3 (V 8206.1 and 2, V 8302.2, V 8305.1 V 8703.2, V 8725.1, V 8807.2 and 3, V 8810.1–4, V 8812.1 and 2, V 8812.4, V 8812.6–8, V 8811.2, V 8814.2; Fig. 143). Pyxis. Fragments of two more handles of pyxis like **GR32 P2**, rim and body fragments. Max. pres. h. (with handles) 6.5; d. rim 12.0. Fine, soft, reddish-yellow (5YR 7/6) fabric. Glossy, white (10YR 8/1) to very pale brown (10YR 8/2) slip. Shadow of red(?) paint. Very worn surfaces. Some fragments burned. Crosshatched lozenge chain above narrow bands. *Comparanda*: **GR32 P2**. *Date*: LG.

GR32 P4 (V 8206.2, V 8206.4, V 8209.1, V 8305.2 and 3, V 8306.1, V 8703.1, V 8726.1; Fig. 143). Pyxis. Partially mended from 43 fragments. Max. pres. h. 7.2; d. rim 8.7; d. base 5.5. Fine, soft, porous, pale yellow (2.5Y 8/2) fabric with tiny black inclusions. Black paint. Very worn surfaces. No burning. Bands on lower body, but too worn to see design on shoulder; underside of base painted. *Comparanda*: **GR4 P8**, **GR4 P9**, **GR17 P4**; Coldstream and Catling, eds., 1996, 281, pl. 259:13 (LG); Tsipopoulou 2005, 117, fig. 64:H1958 (Kavousi, Plai tou Kastrou, LG–EO); 138, fig. 64:Π4 (Hagios Georgios, EO). *Date*: LG–EO.

GR32 P5 (V 8209.1; Fig. 143). Domed lid. Three fragments of rim and two of body. D. rim est. 20.0. Fine, soft, very pale brown (10YR 7/4) fabric, mostly burned. Black paint worn to shadow. Very worn surfaces and edges. Pierced on rim. *Date*: LG–EO.

Fine Monochrome Wares

GR32 P6 (V 8305.1; Fig. 143). Cup or skyphos. Large fragment (three sherds) from rim and upper body. D. rim 9.5. Fine, soft, light brownish-gray (2.5Y 6/2) fabric. Black paint. Burned. Surface mottled where paint has worn off. Very thin walls. *Date*: LG.

GR32 P7 (V 8206.2–4, V 8209.1 and 2, V 8702.1 and 5, V 8703.1; Fig. 143). Lekanis with reflex handles. Partially mended from 57 fragments into two large fragments from base and rim. Preservation 30%, including parts of both handles and horned projections; profile can be restored. H. est. 7.6; d. rim 16.0; d. base 11.0. Fine, soft, rather chalky, yellow (10YR 7/6) fabric. Black paint on exterior and underside of base. Very worn surfaces. Possibly once decorated in added white. Some base fragments gray from burning and some edges worn. *Date*: EO.

Fine Plain, Monochrome, or Decorated Ware

GR32 P8 (V 8302.2, V 8305.3; Fig. 143). Juglet. Partially mended into two large fragments, one from body (six sherds), one from neck (seven sherds). Max. pres. h. 5.8; d. neck 2.8. Fine, soft, pink (7.5YR 7/4) to reddish-yellow (7.5YR 7/6) fabric. Very worn surfaces. *Date*: LG.

Medium-Coarse Decorated Ware

GR32 P9 (V 8201.1, V 8303.1, V 8305.1 and 2, V 8702.2 and 3, V 8703.1, V 8703.1 and 8, V 8909.4; Fig. 143). Hydria. Represented by 34 fragments from rim, handles, and body of large hydria. D. rim 12.0. Medium-coarse, pale yellow (2.5Y 8/2) fabric with small black inclusions and some chaff voids. Black paint. Very worn surfaces. *Date*: LG?

Medium-Coarse Monochrome Ware

GR32 P10 (V 8812.1; Fig. 143). Cup or skyphos. Two joining fragments preserving 75% of base; two non-joining body fragments. Max. pres. h. 3.6; d. base 6.0. Medium-coarse, reddish-yellow (5YR 7/6) to light gray (2.5Y 7/2) fabric with many calcareous inclusions. Black paint on interior, exterior, and underside of base. Rather well-preserved surfaces. *Date*: LG.

Coarse Ware

GR32 P11 (V 8305.3; Fig. 143). Bowl. Nine fragments from base and rim. D. rim 17.0; d. base 10.0. Coarse, reddish-brown (5YR 4/4) fabric, like Kavousi Type IV, but with many hard white inclusions. Worn surfaces. Many fragments burned. *Date*: uncertain.

Metal

GR32 M1 (V89.77; V8731, object 1; Fig. 143; Pl. 62C). Bronze fibula. Single fragment from bow; missing catch plate, coil, and pin. Max. pres. L. 2.8; max. pres. w. 1.4; th. 0.3–0.7. Well preserved. Knobbed fibula. One side flattens out near catch plates. Swelling in center with small flat knob on top. Tapers to spring. Round in section. *Comparanda*: **GR28 M1**; Boardman 1961, 36–37; Sapouna-Sakellaraki 1978, 94–97, pl. 37:1271, 1272 (type VIIa). *Date*: 750–700 B.C.

Glass

GR32 G1 (V90.134; V 8209.1; Fig. 143; Pl. 62C). Glass bead? Fragment. H. 1.3. Black vitrified material, with some organic looking striations. Staining from iron.

Grave 34

History and Details of Excavation

Grave 34 is an enclosure grave lying on the western slope of the Vronda ridge in Room O4, the northernmost room of the earlier LM IIIC Building O, and just north of Grave 28 (Figs. 3, 4). It was excavated in 1990 in Trench VW 12000 (Gesell, Day, and Coulson 1995, 88; Day and Glowacki 2012, 105). Because of its position on a steep slope of the ridge, the grave had suffered greatly from erosion, and it was found close to the surface. The western boundary wall had disappeared, and there were few artifacts within the grave.

At the time excavation began, the terrace or house wall from the LM IIIC settlement (VW 12003) was already visible on the surface, and the area to the west of the wall, where Grave 34 lay, was excavated as VW 12004. Almost immediately bones from the burial appeared in rock tumble, along with soft black soil. The black soil with bone was excavated as VW 12005 until the three surviving walls of the enclosure were fully defined, and then it was dug as VW 12012. Under the feet of the burial in the southeast, a layer of reddish-brown soil appeared, and it was excavated as VW 12013. Just below the top of this layer a bench or low wall appeared along the south. The center of the grave continued to be excavated as VW 12014. When the ashy grave soil had been removed, there was a layer of yellowish-brown soil with stones that was removed as VW 12015; this layer went down to the roofing material from the LM IIIC building and contained no bones or grave pottery.

Architecture

Grave 34 is a stone-lined enclosure measuring 1.50–1.60 m north–south x ca. 1.13 east–west (Fig. 144; Pl. 62D). It used existing walls from the LM IIIC building on the east and south. The east wall (VW 12003) was constructed of large bedrock boulders with a bench or platform of small cobbles along it, similar to those found in LM IIIC Building N, Room N2, to the south. The south wall (VW 11130) was also built of large boulders. The north wall (VW 12016) was apparently constructed for the grave; it consisted of a line of large boulders with a line of cobbles on either side, possibly benches like those on the east wall. No western boundary wall was found, and it probably eroded down the slope to the west. There was no sign of burning in the grave or on its walls.

Stratigraphy

The depth of deposition in the grave was 0.40 m at the center along the east and 0.30 m down the slope to the west. The grave was built on top of red clay roofing debris from the earlier LM IIIC building. At the bottom was a layer of compact yellowish-brown soil (VW 12015) that may represent slope wash over the roofing debris; it and was probably there before the construction of Grave 34. This layer rose higher in the southeast corner over the bench, and the feet of Burial 1 rested directly upon it. The burial was all in a dark, ashy soil (VW 12005, VW 12012, VW 12014) that continued up to the surface (VW 12004).

Associated Features

There were no associated features. Grave 34 was close to Grave 28 and may have been deliberately placed near it. Some of the material collected farther to the west in Trenches VW 12100 and VW 12200 may have come from Grave 34, probably having been deposited there as a result of erosion rather than deliberate dumping.

Burials

Two burials were recovered from Grave 34, and there is evidence that these individuals may have been cremated together.

Burial 1

Type: primary cremation
Age: adult, 35–40 years
Sex: female?
Weight: 1,639 g

The skeleton of Burial 1, an adult female, is only partially calcined, but the vertebrae are more thoroughly burned than the rest of the body. One femur and tibia, as well as a talus fragment, have almost no evidence of burning. The cranium and the rest of the postcranium are dark gray or partially calcined. The body was found in a semiflexed position with the head to the north. The position was typical for the Vronda primary cremation deposits, with both arms flexed, in this case angled toward the left side of the body, and the legs partially flexed.

The skeleton is that of an adult, but the cranial sutures are not closed. A small fragment of the auricular surface that was preserved indicates that the woman was about 35–40 years old. The very gracile cranium and long bones indicate that the individual was a female. The only pathology that was noted is some porotic hyperostosis. The external surface of the cranial bone is porous, and there is some expansion of the diploë visible in the breaks in the cranial bone, suggesting an anemic condition, although the cause cannot be determined.

Burial 2
Type: primary cremation
Age: juvenile, 2–8 years
Sex: unknown
Weight: 139 g

Burial 2 is the skeleton of a small child. Most of the bone is completely calcined, with the exception of the left distal humerus. This bone is only scorched and is black in color. Most of the bone from this burial was found in the abdominal and thoracic area of Burial 1, the adult female. It was originally thought that the bones might be a fetus because of their position, but eventually it became obvious that this child was older, probably placed on the woman's body and cremated together with her. The age assessment is based on the dental development. A fragment of a deciduous maxillary first molar was found, with the roots at least one-half formed. The tip of the root was broken and could not be evaluated. On the basis of this tooth, the child may be assigned an age probably between two and eight years.

Faunal Remains

Identified faunal materials from this grave include one heavily burned and calcined ovicaprine or cervid metatarsal diaphysis, a sheep or goat first phalange distal fragment, a sheep or goat left distal tibia with cut marks on the medial face, and a second left tibia proximal/anterior diaphysis fragment (Table 10).

The heavily burned metapodial fragment is consistent with burned or calcined sheep, goat, or deer lower limb elements found in other Vronda graves. The unburned tibia fragments, one bearing cut marks, may represent grave offerings that were not touched by the pyre fire or more general cast-off food debris, intrusive to the grave context. There were also 42 unidentifiable animal bone fragments from this context, 16 of which were heavily burned or calcined.

Botanical Remains

The only botanical remains from Grave 24 came from fool's parsley (*Aethusa cynapium*).

Pottery

Grave 34 produced very little pottery, only 138 fragments weighing 1.44 kg, and none of the fragments could be mended into whole or nearly complete vessels. Two rim fragments from monochrome cups of the sort found in other graves (**GR34 P1**, **GR34 P2**) appeared high up in the deposit (VW 12004). One of them (**GR34 P2**) has a profile like LM IIIC deep bowls, but its paint and fabric are like the LG material from the graves, and it was discolored from fire. A lekythos or juglet (**GR34 P3**) was also certainly from the grave, but the two other vessels (jar **GR34 P4** and basin **GR34 P5**) may equally well have been material left there from the LM IIIC period. Whatever additional pottery accompanied the dead, it seems to have been close to the surface, and it must have slipped down the slope to the west.

Objects

The only object recovered from the grave was a broken kylix stem that had been turned into a bead or spindle whorl (**GR34 TC1**). This object may have been contemporary with the grave, but it is more likely to have come from the LM IIIC debris in the area, as kylix stems cut down into spindle whorls are common in the settlement and at LM IIIC sites in general (Day et al. 2016, 156–157).

Chronology

There is no material that would allow us to date this grave. The one certain vessel from the deposit, **GR34 P1**, is of the thin-walled fine variety found in the LG period, but it is not more closely datable.

Catalog

Pottery

Fine Monochrome Wares

GR34 P1 (VW 12004.1; Fig. 145). Cup or skyphos. Single fragment from rim. D. rim est. 11.0–12.0. Fine, soft, pink (5YR 7/4) fabric. Traces of red to brown paint. Very worn surfaces. *Date*: LG.

GR34 P2 (VW 12004.1; Fig. 145). Cup or skyphos. Two joining fragments from rim. D. rim est. 16.0. Fine, soft, reddish-yellow (5YR 7/6) fabric. Traces of brown paint. Worn surfaces. Slightly burned to light gray. Profile looks LM IIIC, fabric and paint look LG. *Date*: uncertain.

Fine Plain or Monochrome Ware

GR34 P3 (VW 12012.2; Fig. 145). Lekythos or juglet. Partially mended from four fragments from neck; missing rim, body, and handle. Max. pres. h. 2.3. Fine, very soft, reddish-yellow (5YR 7/6) fabric. Very worn surfaces and edges. *Date*: LG?

Medium-Coarse Plain Wares

GR34 P4 (VW 12005.1, VW 12012.1, VW 12014.2; Fig. 145). Closed vessel, possibly a jar. Partially mended from 14 fragments. Preservation 20% of base, fragment with handle attachment, and tiny piece of rim of same fragment. Max. pres. h. 5.0; d. base 16.2. Medium-coarse, soft, chalky, reddish-yellow (5YR 6/8) fabric with phyllites, gold mica, quartz, and chaff voids. Very pale brown (10YR 8/2) slip. Possibly black paint. Very worn surfaces. *Date*: uncertain; may be from LM IIIC settlement.

GR34 P5 (VW 12005.1; Fig. 145). Basin. Single fragment from rim. D. rim 29.0. Medium-coarse, hard, reddish-yellow (5YR 6/6) fabric, gray at core, with phyllite inclusions. Very pale brown (10YR 8/3) slip. Reddish-yellow (5YR 6/6) paint. *Date*: uncertain.

Terracotta

GR34 TC1 (VW 12014.1; Fig. 145). Terracotta spindle whorl made from stem of pierced kylix. Intact. H. 1.3–1.7; d. 1.4–1.6; d. hole 0.5. Wt. 12.00 g. Fine, soft, reddish-yellow (7.5YR 7/6) fabric. Very pale brown (10YR 8/2) slip. Red (10R 4/8) paint. Worn surfaces. Bands on stem. *Date*: LM IIIC, reworked.

Grave 35

History and Details of Excavation

Grave 35 lies on the west slope of the Vronda summit, just next to Grave 15 and above the LM IIIC house wall that formed the eastern boundary of Grave 28 (Figs. 3, 4, 95). It was recognized in 1990 in Trench VW 10000 as a scatter of unburned human bones in the courtyard of the earlier Building I (Gesell, Day, and Coulson 1995, 82; Day and Glowacki 2012, 78–79). Human cranial bones were first recognized in an area of cobble tumble over the surface of the courtyard (VW 10027) and then excavated in a lower layer of the same tumble (VW 10029). There was nothing more than a scatter of bones, however, and no architecture or grave offerings were associated with Grave 35. The deposit may be related to Grave 15, which lies just to the southeast, or to Grave 28, to the northwest.

Architecture

There was no associated architecture. The space in which the bones were found measured roughly 1.75 m north–south x 1.35–2.20 m east–west (Fig. 95). The boundary of the space on the west was provided by the terrace wall that served as the eastern wall of Room O2 of the earlier Building O (VW 10105). To the north are two rows of single stones, either linear accumulations or more probably two faces of a wall or bench (VW 11011) separating work areas in the LM IIIC courtyard. To the east is a block of bedrock that may have been tumble or may have served as a limit to the north. On the south are a number of stones that may have had some definition (Pl. 63A).

Stratigraphy

The deposition in the area was very shallow, and all the finds lay just 0.20 m below the modern surface. The bones were in the upper levels of a deposit of cobble tumble (VW 10027, VW 10029) that lay on top of the pebbly surface or floor of the courtyard. There was none of the soft, ashy soil usually associated with cremations, nor any sign of burning as would be found at a pyre site.

Associated Features

Grave 15 is very close to the southeast and may be related to Grave 35. It was thought that the remains from Grave 35 might represent a discard deposit from Grave 15 or from Grave 28 below to the northwest, but as neither of these graves contained inhumations, this explanation does not seem likely.

Burials

Only a single individual was recognized in Grave 35.

Burial 1
Type: disturbed inhumation
Age: adult
Sex: unknown
Weight: 26 g

The material collected as Burial 1 of Grave 35 consists of four fragments of unburned adult human cranial bone. The bone is from an adult with fused cranial sutures. It was found in a pit with a deposit of animal bone. The bone is unquestionably human, but no other information could be derived from it.

Faunal Remains

There were no animal bones definitely associated with the human remains. Those found in Loci VW 10027 and VW 10029 were discussed with the other animal bones in the cobble layer of the courtyard (Day and Glowacki 2012, 80).

Pottery

There was no associated pottery. The stone tumble that contained the bones produced some 280 fragments of pottery weighing 3 kg, but all of the sherds belonged to the LM IIIC occupation of the area, and there was nothing demonstrably later (Day and Glowacki 2012, 79–80).

Chronology

There is nothing associated with this scatter of bones that would allow us to date the burial.

Grave 36

History and Details of Excavation

Grave 36 is a stone-lined burial enclosure on the west edge of the summit of the Vronda ridge, just west of Room D2 of LM IIIC Building D (Figs. 3, 4). It was excavated in Trench V 12800 in 1990 (Gesell, Day, and Coulson 1995, 74–75), although at least one vessel probably from this grave had been recovered in the cleaning of a wall in the area in 1984. The grave had been disturbed when a modern terrace wall was constructed and its northwest corner was robbed out. Concentrations of fine ware appeared just below the surface in V 12802.4 amid cobble-sized stones and snail shells, as did the tops of the walls of the enclosure. Once the grave was identified, it was excavated as V 12803 by biological anthropologists in conjunction with the trench supervisor, until the snail shells and cobbles ran out. During the removal of this layer, material from the north and south halves of the grave were kept separate. The grave was then dug as V 12806 to the bottom, where carbonized beams were found running across the grave. The removal of these beams, along with a different soil, was recorded as Locus V 12807. Additional grave material was identified to the south and southeast of the grave in Loci V 12801 and V 12805.

Three burials were recognized during excavation and labeled A–C. Subsequent study showed that there were actually seven burials; two infants and a child were not recognized in the field but were recovered in the water sieve residue, and the three recognized burials were identified as a total of four adults based on duplicated vault fragments.

Architecture

Grave 36 is a built enclosure, oriented northeast–southwest and measuring 1.80–1.95 m north–south × 1.08–1.15 m east–west (Fig. 146; Pl. 63B). It made use of existing house walls from Building D of the LM IIIC settlement for its north and east boundaries. The north wall consists of a row of stones (V 12801) backed up against house wall V 12920. It stands three courses high and is built of breccia with a few limestone boulders, one of which was fractured from the heat of the fire. The east wall (V 12904) also stands three courses high and is built mainly of limestone with a few breccia cobbles; the limestone blocks are fractured at the north and south ends (Pl. 63C). The south wall (V 12809) is built of two rough courses but has only a good inner face; it seems to bond with the west wall, and the limestone blocks are fissured. The west wall (V 12808) also has two good faces of breccia and limestone, although the inner face is poor, without regular courses. It seems to have been built on tumble or on an earlier wall. There has been much disturbance from a modern terrace wall, and the northwest and southeast corners are missing. The preservation of the walls is much higher than is usual for the Vronda enclosures.

Stratigraphy

The total deposition in the grave was approximately 0.63 m. On the bedrock surface were laid the beams of wood for the pyre, with the grain going down the grave from north to south. These beams were removed with a lighter and rather hard-packed soil (V 12807) during the excavation. The first two burials, both infants, were found in this layer, as were parts of commingled Burials 3 and 4. Above the beams was a layer of dark brown, ashy soil containing a considerable quantity of human bone and grave goods but few stones (V 12806). This layer yielded the remains of nearly all of the individuals buried in the grave: Burials 3 and 4 to the south and Burials 5 and 6 to the north. Remains of charred beams running across the grave from east to west were recovered in this locus near the east wall. The layer (V 12803) above V 12806 was similar in color and consistency but had fewer human bones and more cobble-sized stones and snail shells. This layer may represent the stones placed over the grave at the last burial. Most of Burial 7 was found here (some parts of it were found in the level below), and some bones from Burials 5 and 6 were also recovered in this layer, possibly from the top of the lower layer of cremation material. Finally, there was a layer of topsoil (V 12802).

Associated Features

There were no associated features. The small juglet (**GR36 P14**) found set in between the stones in the top of a house wall to the south and east of Grave 36 may have been a deliberate offering placed there after the burials, but it was a surface find made before excavation uncovered the grave, and its relation to the grave is uncertain.

Burials

All seven burials in the Grave 36 enclosure were disturbed. The location of the grave just below a terrace wall probably resulted in a great deal of drainage through the deposits within. There is a considerable amount of commingling among the bones of the four adults and three children recovered.

It is interesting that the skeletons in this enclosure can be divided into two groups, each containing a 40–60-year-old adult, another adult with a retained metopic suture, and one or two juveniles, including one with a retained metopic suture. Each group was buried with an unusual number of items of jewelry. The northern group (Burials 5, 6, and 7) was found with a set of five clay beads (**GR36 TC1–GR36 TC5**), arranged so as to suggest that they were strung together; this is the largest set of beads found at Vronda. A rock crystal bead (**GR36 S1**) was found with the group of burials at the south end of the enclosure (Burials 1–4). It is unfortunate that the drainage disturbance in this grave does not allow for a more detailed reconstruction of the exact sequence of the cremations, because the patterning of the individuals is unusual for the Vronda cremations.

Burials 1 and 2

Type: disturbed primary cremations
Age: infants
Sex: unknown
Weight: 26 g

Burials 1 and 2, located in the south end of the enclosure, are disturbed cremations of two very young infants. The presence of these individuals was not recognized during excavation, but four (two left and two right) infant-sized frontal bones with eye orbit upper margins were found in the water sieve residue. The size of the orbit margins is similar, suggesting that the infants may have been about the same age, possibly even twins. The single developing tooth crown that was recovered with the bone suggests an age around the time of full-term birth (Scheuer and Black 2000, 156). The bone is all completely calcined and white. The frontal bone of one child has a retained metopic suture, open for the entire length of the frontal bone (Scheuer and Black 2000, 107). While in a newborn infant it is more common for the metopic suture to remain unfused, this example is one of four of this anomaly from Grave 36 and may indicate some familial relationship among the adults and juveniles.

Burials 3 and 4
Type: disturbed primary cremations
Age: adults, 20–40 and 18–20 years
Sex: unknown
Weight: 1,207 g

Burials 3 and 4, cremation burials of two young adults, were found in the south end of the enclosure near the south wall. The rock crystal bead (**GR36 S1**) was found with these two skeletons. Most of the bone from the two burials is completely calcined. Both of the individuals were adults. Based on the cranial sutures, one was probably a young adult, 20–40 years old, and the other younger less than 19–20 years based on the presence of an unfused epiphysis of the distal ulna (Scheuer and Black 2000, 303–304). The sex could not be determined for either skeleton. One of the adults has a retained metopic suture, but it is unclear with which of the two this frontal bone belongs. The outer table of this frontal bone is quite porous, particularly over and within the orbits. There is also extensive porosity of the external surface of the cranium, without any expansion of the diploë. This characteristic suggests the individual may have suffered from scurvy or anemia (Brickley and Ives 2008, 61–62).

Burial 5
Type: disturbed primary cremation
Age: juvenile, 2–4 years
Sex: unknown
Weight: 55 g

Burial 5, found in the north half of the enclosure, is a young juvenile. As with Burials 1 and 2, the presence of this child was not recognized until the bone was inventoried in the laboratory. The bone was commingled with the adult Burials 6 and 7. The bone of Burial 5 is completely calcined. A deciduous molar root with the tip complete indicates that this child was more than two years old and less than four (Hillson 1996, 124–125). In addition, a proximal epiphysis of the proximal phalanx of the hand was found. These epiphyses appear between 10 months and two years of age and form earlier in females than males (Scheuer and Black 2000, 337). The frontal bone has a retained metopic suture. There is fairly severe cribra orbitalia in the preserved left eye orbit, possibly indicating an anemia of unknown cause.

Burials 6 and 7
Type: disturbed primary cremations
Age: adults, one 40–60 years
Sex: one male, one unknown
Weight: 1,775 g

The adult Burials 6 and 7 were found commingled in the northern half of the enclosure. It was possible to reconstruct much of the cranium of the individual designated Burial 7. The total weight of the bone from the two burials is low enough to suggest that a considerable amount of the bone has been lost even from these burials, which were apparently the latest in the enclosure.

The cranium of Burial 6 is that of an adult, but not enough remains to sex this individual. The completely open cranial sutures and the presence of adult long bones with fused epiphyses but no evidence of age-related changes indicate that this individual was a younger adult, probably less than 40 years of age at death. There is a retained metopic suture on the frontal bone but no other visible pathologies or anomalies. The cranial bone of this burial is completely calcined, with the exception of the mid-frontal region around the metopic suture, which shows somewhat less damage from the flames.

The cranium of Burial 7 is that of an adult male, probably 40–60 years old. At least one molar was lost antemortem, and the cranial sutures are obliterated endocranially. This cranium shows various degrees of cremation. The frontal bone above the orbits shows little evidence of burning, while higher on the frontal and parietals there is heavy scorching and some calcination of the bone.

Faunal Remains

The small assemblage of possible animal bone recovered from Grave 36 consists primarily of unidentifiable bone fragments (Table 10). Many of these fragments that came from the area above and among the burned beams at the bottom of the feature are heavily burned and/or calcined, but none of the small fragments are further identifiable.

Two domestic pig element fragments, a left scapula blade fragment and a possibly associated, left humerus diaphysis segment from higher in the stratigraphic sequence (V 12803.3), are unburned and show heavy surface erosion. Their relationship to the burials is uncertain. A limpet (*Patella*) shell was also recovered from the topsoil in this grave (Table 5).

Botanical Remains

A few botanical remains were recovered from Grave 36. These included several fragments of grape (*Vita vinifera*), possibly from grave offerings, and one fragment of fool's parsley (*Aethusa cynapium*).

Pottery

Grave 36 produced a total of 1,111 fragments of pottery weighing 7.27 kg. The majority of the fragments (848) could be mended into 17 recognizable vessels, in addition to another that was picked up on the surface in 1984. The pottery represents an unusual assemblage. There were few monochrome cups but a large number of decorated skyphoi and kalathoi, some of which may have served as lids rather than bowls. The number of necked jars of various sizes was also unusual.

Many of the vessels in the grave have markings on the bottoms of their bases. Most of these appear to have been made before firing, as they are rather broad and deep, often with doughy edges. These may represent potter's marks, perhaps incised to identify a group of vessels made by a certain potter or for a particular consumer. If so, they may belong together. Two kalathoi (**GR36 P4**, **GR36 P5**), however, have marks that were scratched on later, and these may be graffiti that had meaning for the burial(s) with which they were associated. Seven vessels have marks on the bottom: **GR36 P3–GR36 P5**, **GR36 P7**, **GR36 P9**, **GR36 P10**, and **GR36 P17**. One necked jar (**GR36 P10**) has a single line running across the base. Two vessels, a tray (**GR36 P7**) and a necked jar (**GR36 P9**), have a single X, either gouged across the bottom (**GR36 P9**) or made simply in the center of the base (**GR36 P7**). One skyphos (**GR36 P3**) has five small strokes on the edge of the base, and juglet **GR36 P17** has a single small mark on the base. Two kalathoi (**GR36 P4**, **GR36 P5**) have multiple incised strokes; **GR36 P4** is marked with an X and four other strokes, while **GR36 P5** has a series of small X marks (seven in number) and a few other strokes, including one that looks like a modern angular P (rho). In addition, a pithos fragment of LM IIIC fabric (**GR36 P18**) with a tree incised on it after firing was also found in the grave; this sherd may have some significance within the LG grave, perhaps having been picked up, incised, and then placed in the grave. The precise meaning of any of these marks is not certain.

Because the materials from the northern and southern halves of the grave were kept separate during excavation, it is possible to locate the end from which most of the pottery came. Those vessels found chiefly in the northern part of the grave, possibly associated with Burials 5, 6, or 7, include cups **GR36 P12** and **GR36 P13**, skyphoi **GR36 P2** and **GR36 P3**, kalathos **GR36 P5**, trays **GR36 P6** and **GR36 P7**, and necked jars **GR36 P9** and **GR36 P10**. Those vessels made of fragments from the south of the grave, perhaps associated with Burials 3 and 4, are fewer but include skyphos **GR36 P1**, kalathos **GR36 P4**, and possibly cup **GR36 P15** and skyphos **GR36 P16**. The other pottery was found in both sections and perhaps came from the center of the grave or was pushed there from the north and south when later pyres were laid. Those vessels that were recovered from the lowest levels of the grave may be associated with the infant Burials 1 and 2 and adult Burials 3 and 4. These vessels include lekythos **GR36 P11** and small necked jar **GR36 P8**, but fragments of **GR36 P3**, **GR36 P4**, **GR36 P9**, **GR36 P12**, and **GR36 P17** were also found at the bottom. The following vessels with fragments found dumped outside the grave to the south must have come from one of the earlier burials: skyphos **GR36 P1**, lekythos **GR36 P11**, cup **GR36 P15**, and juglet **GR36 P17**.

Objects

Grave 36 also produced an unusual assemblage of other burial goods. There was very little metal, except for the three iron pins **GR36 M1–GR36 M3**; other nonjoining fragments of iron pins suggest that there may have been a fourth, now lost or destroyed by corrosion. There were a few poorly preserved fragments of bronze sheeting, the largest 1.9 cm long, along with three fragments of bronze rivets found in the cleaning of the floor of the grave. The number of beads and the variety of materials they are made from, however, is highly unusual. In addition to the five terracotta beads (more than were found in any other grave), there was a unique rock crystal bead (**GR36 S1**), an ivory or bone bead (**GR36 B1**), and a glass bead (**GR36 G1**), the last two badly damaged by fire. Although found in different parts of the grave, these beads are small and might easily have slipped into lower levels through small holes in the stones, so specific find spots might not indicate their original location. Together they may have formed a necklace. The rock crystal bead (**GR36 S1**) was found at the bottom of the grave, and it is probably associated with Burials 3 or 4. Necklaces of mixed materials were found at the North Cemetery at Knossos, with the stone as the focal point for the object (Evely 1996, 622).

The stone tool (**GR36 ST1**) came from the surface soil. It has been cataloged with the grave material, but it may well have come from the LM IIIC Building D.

Chronology

It is uncertain how many burial events occurred in the grave and for how long a period it was in use. It is also difficult to associate pottery and objects with individual burials, even the last burial, because of the disturbance. Of the pottery that was found in the lowest levels of the grave (V 12807), the small necked jar (**GR36 P8**) has parallels in the LPG–MG period at Knossos (Brock 1957, 52–53, pl. 35:534; 61, pl. 45:643; Coldstream and Catling, eds., 1996, 186, fig. 120:24), but the shape continues into the LO period at Knossos (Coldstream and Sackett 1978, 56, fig. 8:27) and Eleutherna (Kotsonas 2008, 145–146, fig. 34:Mon/A10/87). The Vronda example bears a closer resemblance to examples of EG and MG date. The twisted handle on the lekythos (**GR36 P11**) is a feature that appears chiefly on oinochoai found outside Crete in the MG and LG periods (e.g., Coldstream 1968, pls. 5:a, 29:a). A close parallel for this lekythos, however, can be seen in an oinochoe from Piskokephalo; although the shape of its body imitates MPG finds from Central Crete, the vessel is dated to the LPG period (Tsipopoulou 2013, 138:12271, 140, fig. 5).

There was no pottery that belonged definitely to the upper levels of the grave, and there was very little that had not been heavily burned. It is possible that the material from the latest burial had been removed or eroded away. Overall, many of the vessels from the grave appear to be of PG style. The two kalathoi (**GR36 P4**, **GR36 P5**) have close parallels at PGB Knossos, and the shape disappeared at Knossos after the EG period. Nevertheless, the metopal arrangement seen on one side of **GR36 P4** is not attested at Knossos and may indicate a later date, and kalathoi continued later in East Crete. Many of the vessels, however, are of LG date. The decoration of skyphos **GR36 P2**, for example, is popular in other enclosures at Vronda and in LG contexts in East Crete in general. Monochrome cup **GR36 P15** is very deep, a feature that belongs to the later LG period. A LG date for the material from this grave seems likely. The entire assemblage resembles that in Grave 26, with its large number of skyphoi and kalathoi and a pair of trays; this similarity may suggest a chronological or a functional link.

Catalog

Pottery

FINE DECORATED WARES

GR36 P1 (V98.127; V 12802.4, V 12803.1–3, V 12805.1, V 12806.2; Fig. 147; Pl. 63D). Skyphos. Restored from 51 fragments. Preservation 80%, including full profile, 75% of base, both handles, entire rim. H. 9.7; d. rim 12.4–13.2; d. base 9.5. Fine, soft, reddish-yellow (5YR 6/6) fabric. Very pale brown (10YR 8/3) slip. Reddish-brown (2.5YR 4/4) paint. Very worn surfaces. Some burning on one side; edges scored and worn, some warping. Hatched triangles? *Comparanda*: Coldstream and Catling, eds., 1996, 27, fig. 65:11 (MPG); 126, fig. 99:79.8 (Knossos, LG). *Date*: LG.

GR36 P2 (V98.131; V 12806.1N, V 12806.2S; Fig. 147; Pl. 63D). Skyphos. Restored from 39 fragments; 17 nonjoining fragments. Preservation 95%; missing body fragments. H. 6.5–7.0; d. rim 11.0; d. base 5.0. Fine, soft, very pale brown (10YR 8/4) fabric with small phyllite inclusions. Traces of red to black paint. Very worn surfaces. Some fragments burned. Irregular in shape. Narrow horizontal bands in metopal panel in handle zone. *Comparanda*: for decoration, Tsipopoulou 2005, 277, fig. 117:Σ3805 (Praisos, LG); for shape, Sakellarakis 1986, 37–38, fig. 29 (Archanes); Coldstream and Catling, eds., 1996, 264, fig. 145:70 (Knossos, Attic MG II). *Date*: LG.

GR36 P3 (V 12803.1, V 12803.3N, V 12803.3S, V 12806.1N, V 12806.2S, V 12807.2; Fig. 147; Pl. 63D). Skyphos. Mended into two large fragments from 51 sherds. Preservation 65%, including full profile, base, both handles. H. 8.7; d. rim 13.4; d. base 5.8. Fine, soft, reddish-yellow (7.5YR 6/6) fabric. Red (2.5YR 4/6) paint. Very worn surfaces. Many fragments burned. Metopal panel with crosshatched motifs, only visible on a few fragments. Base has five strokes gouged on edge of bottom before firing. *Comparanda*: Coldstream and Catling, eds., 1996, 17, fig. 60:41 (Knossos, PGB–EG). *Date*: G.

GR36 P4 (V98.128; V 12803.1, V 12803.3, V 12806.1N, V 12806.2S, V 12807.2; Fig. 147; Pl. 64). Kalathos. Mended from 40 fragments. Preservation 99%; missing only a few small fragments. H. 6.2–6.7; d. rim 15.0; d. base 5.3. Fine, soft, reddish-yellow (5YR 6/6) fabric. Very pale brown (10YR 8/3) slip. Red (2.5YR 4/6) paint. Very worn surfaces. Many fragments burned with melted surface. Side A has X-pattern between vertical strokes in handle zone. Side B has in handle zone vertical strokes with occasional horizontal strokes between, and on lower body hatched multiple loops. Base has thin, shallow marks, incised after firing. *Comparanda*: **GR26 P14**; for shape, Coldstream and Catling, eds., 1996, 47, fig. 70:14 (Knossos, PGB); 48, fig. 71:43 (Knossos, PGB); 115, fig. 96:144 (Knossos, PGB); 170, fig. 117:129.6 (Knossos, EG); Tsipopoulou 2005, 276, fig. 118:Σ3800 (Praisos, LG); Rethemiotakis and Englezou 2010, 73, fig. 43:100, 101 (Eltyna, LPG–PGB); 74, fig. 44:105 (EG); for decoration, Kourou 1999, 10, fig. 3:AK8 MN453 (Naxos, MG I–II). *Date*: PGB–EG.

GR36 P5 (V98.129; V 12803.2 and 3, V 12806.1N; Fig. 148; Pl. 64). Kalathos. Mended from 48 fragments. Preservation 95%; missing only a few body sherds. H. 6.8–7.2; d. rim 14.2–15.2; d. base 5.4. Fine, soft, pink (7.5YR 7/4) to light brownish-gray (10YR 6/2) fabric. Traces of brown paint. Very worn surfaces. Nearly every fragment burned, some more than others. Oblique strokes below rim. Seven thin, shallow X marks and other marks on bottom of base, incised after firing. *Comparanda*: Tsipopoulou 2005, 276, fig. 118:Σ3800 (Praisos, LG). *Date*: PGB–LG.

GR36 P6 (V98.126; V 12803.3 N and S, V 12806.1 N, V 12806.2; Fig. 148; Pl. 64). Tray with reflex-type lugs. Restored from 56 fragments. Preservation 90%, including both lug handles; missing small fragments from body and base H. 5.5; d. rim 20.6; d. base 15.3. Fine, soft, reddish-yellow (5YR 7/6) fabric. Very pale brown (10YR 8/3) slip. Traces of brown paint. Surfaces once polished, now very worn. One side badly burned. Groups of strokes on handles. In center of interior is a large knob or omphalos. *Comparanda*: Coldstream and Catling, eds., 1996, 168, fig. 117:125.15 (Knossos, MG); Hayden 2003, 70, no. 186, fig. 44 (LG–O); Tsipopoulou 2005, 104, fig. 134:H756 (Kavousi, Plai tou Kastrou, LG–EO). *Date*: LG.

GR36 P7 (V 12803.3, V 12806.1N; Fig. 148). Tray with reflex-type lugs. Partially mended from five fragments, 30 nonjoining fragments. Preservation 10%, including nearly complete profile, part of one handle; missing most of base, second handle. H. 6.0; d. rim 16.0; d. base est. 12.4. Fine, soft, reddish-yellow (7.5YR 6/6) fabric. Very pale brown (10YR 8/3) slip. Traces of brown paint. Surfaces once polished, now very worn. Many fragments burned, with melted edges and pocked surfaces. underside of base gouged with X-pattern before firing. *Comparanda*: Hayden 2003, 70, nos. 185, 186, fig. 44 (LG–O). *Date*: LG.

GR36 P8 (V98.132; V 12803.2, V 12803.3S, V 12806.2, V 12807.2; Fig. 148; Pl. 64). Small necked jar. Mended from 33 fragments. Preservation 95%; missing small parts of body and rim. H. 7.6; d. rim 5.0; d. base 3.4. Fine, soft, reddish-yellow (5YR 7/6) fabric with tiny phyllite inclusions. Pink (7.5YR 8/4) slip. Shadow of black(?) paint. Very worn surfaces. In handle zone: oblique strokes with oblique hatching between. *Date*: PGB–MG.

GR36 P9 (V98.130; V 12803.1 V 12803.3, V 12803.3, V 12808.6N, V 12806.4, V 12807.1N, 12807.1S, V 12807.2; Fig. 148; Pl. 64). Necked jar. Restored from 98 fragments. Preservation 85%, including full profile, entire base, most of both handles, most of rim; missing part of one handle, body fragments. H. 15.3–15.5; d. rim 9.0–9.5; d. base 7.5. Fine, soft, light red (2.5YR 6/6) fabric with red phyllite inclusions. Shadow of paint. Very worn surfaces. Large sections burned. Metopal panel in handle zone with vertical strokes and oblique hatching. Large X gouged on bottom of base before firing. Very irregular shape. *Comparanda*: Coldstream and Catling, eds., 1996, 50, fig. 72:98 (Knossos, PGB); Tsipopoulou 2013, 139, 142, fig. 6:12326, 12327 (Piskokephalo, PGB); 146, fig. 9:12329 (Piskokephalo, LG). *Date*: LG.

GR36 P10 (V 12801.1, V 12803.3N, V 12806.1, V 12806.2N; Fig. 148). Necked jar. Mended from 15 joining fragments; 38 nonjoining fragments. Preservation 30%, including entire base, both handles, and some of rim; profile can be reconstructed. H. 16.5; d. rim 8.2; d. base 7.0. Fine, soft, chalky, very pale brown (10YR 8/4) fabric with some white inclusions. Petrographic sample KAV 15/90: Fabric Subgroup 1c. Brown (7.5YR 4/4) paint. Very worn surfaces; decoration is uncertain. Edges scored and worn. Burning on one side. Line gouged across bottom before firing. *Comparanda*: Tsipopoulou 2005, 149, pl. 175:AN1795 (Hagios Georgios, LG–EO); 149, fig. 60:AN1794 (Hagios Georgios, LG). *Date*: LG.

GR36 P11 (V 12802.2, V 12803.2 and 3, V 12804.1, V 12805.1 and 2, V 12806.2S, V 12807.2; Fig. 149). Lekythos. Partially mended from 87 fragments. Preservation 40%, including part of base, entire neck and handle, part of rim; profile can be reconstructed. H. 23.6; d. rim 6.0; d. base 11.4. Fine to medium-coarse, soft, reddish-yellow (5YR 7/6) fabric with small red inclusions. Petrographic sample KAV 15/89: Fabric Group 6. Pink (7.5YR 8/4) slip. Red (2.5YR 4/6) paint. Very worn surfaces. Bands on neck. Rope-twisted handle. *Comparanda*: Tsipopoulou 2005, 155, fig. 70:AN2320 (Hagios Georgios, EO); 2013, 138, 140, fig. 5:12271 (Piskokephalo, LPG). *Date*: LG.

Fine Monochrome Wares

GR36 P12 (V 12803.3, V 12803.3N, V 12806. N, V 12807.1S; Fig. 149). Cup. Mended from 52 fragments. Preservation 85%, including full profile, base, handle, most of rim; missing top of handle and body fragments. H. 9.0; d. rim 10.3; d. base 5.0. Fine, soft, reddish-yellow (7.5YR 7/6) fabric. Black paint worn to strong brown (7.5YR 4/6). Very worn surfaces. Many individual fragments burned. Wheel marks on bottom. *Comparanda*: Coldstream and Catling, eds., 1996, 247, fig. 141:112 (Knossos, EO). *Date*: LG.

GR36 P13 (V 12801.1, V 12803.3N, V 12803.3S, V 12806.1N, V 12806.2S, V 12807.2; Fig. 149; Pl. 64). Cup. Mended from 66 fragments. Preservation 85%, including full profile, half of base, handle, all of rim; missing half of base and fragments of body. H. 8.5; d. rim 12.7; d. base 5.5. Fine, soft, reddish-yellow (7.5YR 7/6) fabric, light greenish gray (5GY 6/1) at core. Yellowish-red (5YR 4/6) paint. Worn surfaces. Many fragments burned. *Comparanda*: Coldstream and Catling, eds., 1996, 5, fig. 56:3 (Knossos, PGB). *Date*: LG.

FINE PLAIN WARE

GR36 P14 (V84.71; V 12900 surface; Fig. 149; Pl. 64). Juglet. Partially restored from six fragments. Preservation 90%, including lower handle attachment; missing rim and handle. Max. pres. h. 7.5; d. base 3.8. Fine, soft, reddish-yellow (7.5YR 8/6) fabric. Very worn surfaces; no trace of paint. No burning. Surface very uneven, as if handmade. *Comparanda*: Coldstream and Sackett 1978, 57, fig. 9:36 (Knossos, LO); Coldstream and Catling, eds., 1996, 48, pl. 80:49 (Knossos, PGB). *Date*: LG.

MEDIUM-COARSE MONOCHROME WARES

GR36 P15 (V 12803.2 and 3, V 12806.2, V 12805.1; Fig. 149). Cup. Partially mended from 38 fragments. Preservation 30%, including entire base, handle, and one fragment of rim; missing full profile. H. est. 12.2; d. rim 12.6; d. base 5.0–5.2. Medium-coarse, very soft, reddish-yellow (5YR 6/8) fabric with hard white inclusions. Petrographic sample KAV 15/88: Fabric Group 2. Dark brown (10YR 3/3) paint. Very worn surfaces and edges; fragments cannot be joined together. Burned on handle side. *Comparanda*: Coldstream and Catling, eds., 1996, 71, fig. 76:3 (Knossos, EO); Mook 2004, 176, fig. 12.11:H (Kastro, LG). *Date*: LG.

GR36 P16 (V 12803.2, V 12803.3S, V 12806.2S; Fig. 149). Skyphos. Partially mended from 67 fragments. Preservation 50%, including full profile, 75% of base, both handles, 50% of rim. H. 10.0; d. rim 14.0–18.0; d. base 5.2. Medium-coarse, hard, gray (2.5Y 5/0–6/0) fabric with phyllite, quartz, and mica inclusions, some carbonates. Very worn surfaces and edges; may have been monochrome painted. Very warped from burning, but perhaps rim was pulled out to form a spout. Wheelmarks on bottom. *Comparanda*: **GR6 P23**. *Date*: LG.

MEDIUM-COARSE PLAIN WARE

GR36 P17 (V 12803.2, V 12808.1, V 12807.2S; Fig. 149). Juglet. Partially mended: 12 fragments from base, lower body, and handle. Max. pres. h. 6.2; d. base 5.0. Medium-coarse, soft, yellow (10YR 7/6) fabric, burned gray on interior, with tiny inclusions of gold and silver mica. Very worn surfaces. Some fragments burned on exterior. Small short mark gouged on bottom before firing. *Date*: G.

COARSE DECORATED WARE

GR36 P18 (V 12802.1; Pl. 65). Pithos. Single fragment (two sherds) of large pithos. Max. pres. L. 15.0; max. pres. w. 10.0; th. 2.0. Coarse, reddish-yellow (7.5YR 7/6) Type X/XI fabric, very pale brown (10YR 8/3) on surface. Incised design made after firing. Crude tree? LM IIIC fragment, but incision may belong chronologically with grave and other incised marks.

Metal

IRON

GR36 M1 (V90.153; V12806.2, object 4; Fig. 150; Pl. 65). Iron pin. Three nonjoining fragments preserving head (a), middle (b), and tip (c). Max. pres. L. (a) 2.5, (b) 1.4, (c) 1.7; d. disk 0.4. Corroded. Small conical knob and small disk. Biconical swelling near head with two rings on top of it, three below. Tapers to point.

GR36 M2 (V90.154; V 12806.2, object 4; Fig. 150; Pl. 65). Iron pin. Two joining fragments preserving part of head and body to point; missing disk and knob. Max. pres. L. 7.5. Very corroded. Swelling near head with three rings below. Tapers to point.

GR36 M3 (V90.155; V 12807.2; Fig. 150; Pl. 65). Iron pin. Three fragments preserving point (a) and part of head (b); missing disk. Max. pres. L. (a) 1.7, (b) 1.7. Very corroded. Biconical swelling with three rings on either side. Tapers to point.

Bone or Ivory

GR36 B1 (V90.123, IM 987; V 12807.2; Fig. 150; Pl. 65). Ivory of bone bead. Globular. Preservation 70%; chipped in three places. D 1.8; d. hole 0.2. Wt. <1.00 g. Ivory or compact bone. Cracked and burned. Hole larger on one side than other.

Glass

GR36 G1 (V90.126; V 12806.1; Fig. 150; Pl. 65). Glass bead. Spherical. Intact, but missing a few chips. D. 1.0; d. hole 0.4. Wt. <1.00 g. Translucent, light greenish-gray (5GY 6/1) glass with irridescent surface. Worn and pitted. *Comparanda*: Coldstream and Catling, eds., 1996, 52, fig. 157:Q.f18; 120, fig. 182:75.f33c; 230, fig. 183: 280.f1.

Stone

GR36 S1 (V90.55, IM 986; V 12807.1, object 1; Fig. 150; Pl. 65). Rock crystal bead. Depressed globular. Intact, but cracked. H. 1.45; d. 2.00; d. hole 0.50. Wt. 8.00 g. *Bibliography*: Day 1995, fig. 12. *Comparanda*: Coldstream and Catling, eds., 1996, 250, pl. 303:285.f 19a.

GR36 ST1 (V90.85; V 12802.3, object 1). Whetstone. Cobble, rectangular, complete. L. 8.5; w. 7.8; th. 2.2. Wt. 290.00 g. Quartzite (grainy), dark grayish brown.

Abraded smooth one face; shaped edges. Whetstone Type 7 (Dierckx 2016, 141).

Terracotta

GR36 TC1 (V90.116, IM 991; V 12803.3; Fig. 150; Pl. 65). Terracotta bead. Biconical. Intact except for a few chips. H. 1.8; d. 2.2; d. hole 0.5. Wt. 10.00 g. Medium-coarse, rather hard, red (2.5YR 5/6) fabric. Burned black and surface cracked. No traces of paint. No decoration. No wheelmarks.

GR36 TC2 (V90.117, IM 992; V 12803.3; Fig. 150; Pl. 65). Terracotta bead. Globular. Intact. H. 1.5; d. 1.8; d. hole 0.4. Wt. 4.00 g. Fine, rather hard, light red fabric (2.5YR 6/8), burned gray all over. Black paint. Monochrome painted. No decoration. No wheelmarks. Hole slightly off center, and worn at one end (from use?).

GR36 TC3 (V90.118, IM 990; V 12806.1; Fig. 150; Pl. 65). Terracotta bead. Depressed globular. Intact, but worn surfaces. H. 1.9; d. 2.1; d. hole 0.6. Wt. 10.00 g. Fine, rather hard fabric, burned gray all over. Black paint. Painted and decorated with stamped or incised circles. No traces of use of wheel. Hole has some oblique slashes inside, from use? *Comparanda*: Boardman 1960, 147, fig. 10, top left (Hagios Ioannis, PG).

GR36 TC4 (V90.119, IM 993; V 12806.1; Fig. 150; Pl. 65). Terracotta bead. Globular. Intact. H. 1.8; d. 2.1; d. hole 0.4. Wt. 6.00 g. Fine, rather hard, light red (2.5YR 6/8) fabric. Black paint. Monochrome painted. No wheelmarks. Hole slightly off center; one end pushed out.

GR36 TC5 (V90.120, IM 994; V 12806.1; Fig. 150; Pl. 65). Terracotta bead. Biconical. Preservation 40%. H. 2.2; max. d. 2.2; d. hole est. 0.4. Wt. 4.00 g. Fine, medium-soft, reddish-yellow (5YR 6/6) fabric without inclusions. Surface looks melted. Incised decoration: slashes on top of each cone. No paint. No wheelmarks. *Comparanda*: Boardman 1960, 147, fig. 10 (bottom left), pl. 39 (PG).

Grave 37

History and Details of Excavation

Grave 37 was identified in Trench V 1200 when a cremated fragment of a human cranium was found on the southeast edge of the Vronda summit in 1992 during the cleaning of the southwest corner of Room 7 of Building B (Fig. 3). No attempt was made to explore the area and locate the grave, which probably lies just above this wall to the west. Some fragments of Geometric monochrome cups found in the rock tumble in Room E1 of Building E below this area and to the south may have fallen in from this grave.

Stratigraphy

Surface cleaning revealed additional cremated bone fragments near the surface in a layer of stones above the south wall of Room B7 of Building B.

Burials

Only a small amount of cremated bone was found in the surface cleaning, probably indicating the presence of an unexcavated cremation grave. The cranial fragment belonged to an adult, but the sex of the individual is unknown. The weight was not recorded.

Pottery

There was no associated pottery. Two monochrome cups found in the rock tumble in Room E1 of Building E may have fallen in from this grave (Day and Glowacki 2012, 6).

Chronology

There is no material that would permit us to date this grave with certainty. The monochrome cups found in E1 are not particularly distinctive. One of them is very globular with a very pronounced rim. Neither of them are of the early heavy variety, nor are they of the very late thin-walled variety with crisp profile. A LG date is indicated.

Catalog

Pottery

Fine Monochrome Wares

GR37 P1 (V 751.1; Fig. 151). Cup. Large fragment from rim and handle. D. rim est. 11.0. Fine, fairly hard, reddish-yellow (7.5YR 7/6) fabric. Brown (7.5YR 4/4) paint. Worn surfaces. Monochrome. *Date*: LG.

GR37 P2 (V 751.1; Fig. 151). Cup. Large fragment from rim. D. rim est. 13.0. Fine, soft, yellow (10YR 7/6) fabric. Black paint. Very worn surfaces. Monochrome. *Date*: LG.

Other Possible Enclosure Burials

Hoard of Metals Found by Boyd

Boyd found a hoard of metal artifacts on top of the Vronda ridge in 1900, in what she identified as one room in the large house on the summit (1901, 132)—that is, Building A-B. She listed the following iron objects: one pick, one axe-head, a sword (complete in seven pieces), and numerous fragments. Such iron objects are not in keeping with the material from the LM IIIC settlement but are similar to the tools and weapons found in the enclosure burials (Day, Klein, and Turner 2009, 17). The room in which Boyd's workmen found the objects may have been that originally labeled Room 9 (Day, Klein, and Turner 2009, 17), a corner of Room A1 where a linear accumulation of stones west of the house wall created a rough rectangle measuring 1.65 m east-west x ca. 2.60 m north-south.

Catalog

GR M1 (HM 12; Pl. 66A). Short iron sword or dirk. Three nonjoining fragments preserving nearly complete blade; end of handle missing. L. 45.30; max. w. 3.10; L. handle 14.20; max. w. handle 3.40; L. blade 2.31; th. blade 0.70; th. handle 1.20. Worn and corroded. Blade uneven with pointed midrib. Flange hilted; one side of handle is flat, the other side is too corroded to determine shape, but it has the stem of a rivet driven into it. Naue II type sword. *Comparanda*: Boyd 1901, 137, fig. 4; Levi 1927–1929, 465, fig. 589:6; Snodgrass, 1964, 98, 108, 110 (type Ia:l).

Catalog of Grave Material Not Associated with Any Particular Grave

Pottery

Fine Ware

GR P1 (V 3800.1, level 1; Fig. 151). Decorated vessel. Two nonjoining fragments from body. Fine, well-levigated, light red (2.5YR 6/8) fabric, with small pebble inclusions. Yellow (10YR 8/6) slip. Worn surfaces. Decoration in black, now gone; all that is left are the ridges of the compass marks for the concentric circles. Interior very worn; no original surface preserved. *Bibliography*: Day, Coulson, and Gesell 1986, 360–362, fig. 5:2a, 2b. *Date*: LG.

Medium-Coarse Ware

GR P2 (V 5201.1B; Fig. 151). Closed vessel. Single fragment from body. Th. 0.09. Medium-coarse, yellow (10YR 7/6) fabric with mudstone and phyllite inclusions. Decoration of small concentric circles in a row; each circle has three rings around central point.

Finds from Chondrovolakes

On the lower slopes of the ridge, between the modern village and the area of the Vronda settlement and tombs, Boyd excavated four of what she termed shaft graves in 1900 (Boyd 1901, 154–155). There were four graves of rectangular shape measuring 2.60 x 0.70 m with walls ca. 0.50 m wide and preserved to a height of 0.35 m. These walls were filled with black powdery soil that contained no bones or metal objects. Edith Hall, in her publication of the bone enclosures at Vrokastro (1914, 154), said that the ones she found were identical to the graves at Chondrovolakes. From this evidence it would appear that these four graves, which lay north of the Vronda ridge (Fig. 2), were enclosures of the same sort found in the cemetery over the earlier Vronda settlement. Three complete and five broken vessels of a "late stage of Geometric" were found (Boyd 1901, 154), only one of which can be securely identified: an aryballos of EO date. Cornelis Neeft (1987, 238) would put this aryballos into his category of ovoid aryballoi, list XCII, subgroup H (with simple motif on shoulder, bands, and rays at the base). The closest parallels for the shape and decoration date to 660–655 B.C. (Neeft 1987, 344, 379).

Pottery

Chondrovolakes 1 (HM 1977; Fig. 151; Pl. 66A). Aryballos. Mended; small piece of shoulder, section of handle, and large part of rim missing. H. 7.5; max. d. 5.0; d. base 1.8. Fine, soft, rather flaky, very pale brown (10YR 8/3) fabric. Very dark gray (10R 8/3) to red (7.5YR 5/5) paint. Well-preserved surfaces. Bent-over rim, flat on top; short neck; ovoid body; single flat vertical handle from rim to shoulder; tiny ring base. Band on top and sides of rim and at base of neck; rosettes of dots on shoulder; vertical stripes down handle at edges; alternating red and black bands on body; rays around base. *Bibliography*: Tsipopoulou 2005, 118, pl. 118. *Comparanda*: Brock 1957, 131, pl. 109:1517 (Fortetsa, Protocorinthian SubG). *Date*: LO.

4

Cremation Process

Maria A. Liston

Excavation

The analysis of the cremated skeletons from Vronda began in the field with the excavation of the graves. Starting with the first full-scale excavation season in 1987, the excavation of all graves within the Late Minoan IIIC village at Vronda was conducted or supervised by a biological anthropologist. In addition to the artifacts and contextual information, each piece of bone that could be identified in the field was plotted on a plan when it was lifted from the grave. When the plots of successive days of excavation were later combined, the arrangement of skeletal remains in anatomical relationships could be discerned. On the basis of these plots, reconstructions of the skeletons were then drawn (Figs. 152–154). These plots were used both to reconstruct the cremation process and to evaluate the position of the body and any subsequent disturbance. It was rarely possible to discern an entire cremated skeleton as it lay in the grave. Various sections of the skeleton, such as vertebral bodies, were sometimes recognizable in situ as being in anatomical order, but in general, it was necessary to rely on the excavation plots to recover body position (Pl. 66B).

Beginning in 1988, all of the soil from the graves was saved for water sieving to ensure complete recovery of the skeletal material. Samples of the soil from the graves were saved from the earlier 1987 season as well, and 100% of the residue was sorted for bone fragments and other material. This ensured nearly total recovery of the preserved cremated bone.

Inventory and Measurement

After excavation and cleaning, the skeletal material was inventoried using a specialized form developed for this project (Fig. 155). A simple listing of entire bones, or even designations such as proximal and distal, does not have any real meaning when applied to cremated bone, as the fragments produced in cremation differ markedly from those of mechanically broken or decayed unburned bone (Curtin 2008, 201, 204–205). Using this inventory form, it was possible to produce a more complete catalog of the preserved bone from the site and to evaluate the frequency of various portions of bone or groups of similar bones such as ribs and vertebrae that generally were recovered only as small fragments.

Each burial was weighed as well as inventoried. It has been shown that the weight of cremated remains is useful for distinguishing primary cremations from secondary depositions, for evaluating the completeness of the recovered bone, and for distinguishing single and multiple burials (Reinhard and Fink 1982; Bass and Jantz 2004; Holck 2008; Ubelaker and Rife 2008, 118–120). At times two or three burials were commingled in a single deposit but separate from the other burials in the grave. These commingled burials had to be inventoried and weighed together, and it was assumed that equal amounts of bone and identifiable elements could be assigned to each burial. While this assumption introduced some inaccuracy, it provided a view of the degree of preservation in the grave as a whole relative to the number of individuals identified in the remains (Table 11).

Reconstructing the Cremation Process

There are a number of problems associated with the interpretation of the Kavousi cremation graves. Later images of cremations on pottery provide some information about this mode of funerary practice, as do literary references to cremation, but these sources do not provide enough information to reconstruct the cremation process at Vronda with confidence. For example, it is not clear whether a pyre small enough to fit within the enclosure graves would have been sufficient to burn bone to the degree found in the completely calcined skeletons at Kavousi. Another question is whether a body placed on top of a pyre could be deposited on the ground as an articulated skeleton at the end of a cremation. Finally, we cannot say whether the stone enclosure had a functional purpose or whether it served only as some ritual or symbolic delineation of a grave.

In the Roman world, a professional cremation technician or pyre builder, an *ustor*, was needed to ensure that a funerary pyre was sufficient to accomplish the task of cremating the dead. In EIA Crete, it is likely that a village community would have had one or more persons who were particularly skilled at constructing adequately large pyres, but we have no textual information about their techniques and practices. In an attempt to answer some of our questions specific to the Kavousi site, we undertook a series of replicative cremation experiments to imitate as closely as possible the conditions of Iron Age cremations. A pig was used as a substitute for a human body. In addition, cremations of human bodies were observed at a mortuary crematorium in an attempt to address problems specific to human cremations (Fig. 156).

Construction and Fuel Requirements of an Experimental Pyre

In our first attempt at reconstructing the process of cremation on a wooden pyre, a 95 kg female pig was used as a substitute for a human body. The use of animals, particularly pigs, in experimental cremations is common practice (Shipman, Foster, and Schoeninger 1984; Buikstra and Swegle 1989; Fairgrieve 2008, 72–75). A grave enclosure similar to the Kavousi graves was built to contain the cremation pyre. The enclosure walls of uncut bedrock or limestone blocks were built directly on the ground surface after the ground cover was removed. The walls consisted of one or two courses of stone, depending on the size of the rock, and rose to a height of approximately 0.30 m on each side. The area within the enclosure was 1.90 m long and 0.85 to 0.90 m wide.

Air-dried wood from two standing dead ash trees (family Oleaceae, genus *Fraxinus*) was used to build the cremation pyre. The pyre was modeled on evidence preserved by the charred remains of logs in Vronda Grave 26. It was built on a base of four large logs spaced evenly across the short axis of the enclosure. Kindling was distributed between the logs to facilitate igniting the larger logs and to support the weight of the pig. The pyre was built up to a height of one meter in alternating rows of ash logs 0.75 and 1.80 m long. A higher pyre would have been too unstable to support the body of the pig. The resulting volume of wood used was approximately 1.35 cubic meters. Some additional logs were reserved for later use as the pyre burned down.

Per Holck (2008, 27–35) has calculated that approximately 490,000 kcal of heat from fuel are required for complete cremation of an ostensibly average body weighing 70 kg. In addition, approximately 134,060 kcal of heat are given off by the combustion of the body itself. Using Holck's calculations for the heat energy available from a European ash species, *Fraxinus excelsior*, approximately 1.84 m^3 of ash wood would be required to burn a 70 kg body. Because much of the heat supplied by the combustion of a body itself comes from the burning of fat, and pigs have a larger percentage of fat per unit of body weight than the average human, a pig should be somewhat easier to cremate. Among modern practitioners of cremation, it is known that large, obese bodies burn hotter and are easier to cremate than those of people who have died after a wasting illness (Holck 2008, 31).

Process and Results of the First Cremation Experiment

The pig in the original experiment had been dead for several days and was refrigerated but not frozen before cremation. The body was removed from refrigeration nearly 24 hours before cremation and was allowed to warm to air temperature. There was no evidence of rigor mortis. The complete cremation of the 95 kg carcass was accomplished in six and one-half hours (Fig. 156:a). Due to shifting winds, it was not possible to position a pyrometer to monitor the temperature of the pyre. The pyre was tended for an additional half hour after the soft tissues were consumed in an attempt to completely burn the stomach contents. Unburned abdominal tissues are a common feature observed in forensic fire investigations (Fairgrieve 2008, 66–69).

After the fire died down, the pyre was left undisturbed for nine days, and then the enclosure was completely excavated using techniques identical to those practiced in the Vronda excavations. The identifiable bone was plotted, and the ashes were screened in order to recover all bone, charcoal, and charred flesh. In subsequent cremation experiments the pyre site was excavated the next day. This often required dousing the remains with water in order to lower the temperature sufficiently to handle the remains. Ancient writers refer to pyres being drenched with wine or water, which would have been essential in order to collect the bones on the same day as the cremation (e.g., Hom. *Il.* 23.239–240; McKinley 2006, 85).

The cremation experiment demonstrated that an articulated skeleton could be deposited at ground level after placement and burning on top of the pyre (Fig. 156:b). Unless the pyre was disturbed through efforts to completely consume the body, in all subsequent cremations the bones also remained in anatomical order, visible on top of the pyre. Moreover, the time allocation of six and one-half hours of burning on an open pyre was sufficient to produce a thoroughly calcined cremation. The bones of the pig were nearly all completely calcined by the pyre and showed warping and cracking typical of bone burned while covered with flesh. A similar process and results have been reported in numerous sources (e.g., Shipman, Foster, and Schoeninger 1984; Buikstra and Swegle 1989; Symes et al. 2008).

Insights from Subsequent Cremation Experiments

Subsequent cremations of pig carcasses have confirmed the findings from the original experiment. An assortment of young pigs that died of natural causes were obtained from local farmers and cremated as part of a course exercise at the University of Waterloo. In two cases the pigs were quite young, approximately the size of a human infant (2.0 kg and 3.5 kg). In addition, a large young adult pig of unknown weight was cremated at the Corinth excavation house as part of a short course on cremation burial organized by the Wiener Laboratory at the American School of Classical Studies. In each case the pig was placed on the pyre, lying on its side with its head near one end of the pyre (Pl. 66C). When possible, a foreleg was extended cranially. This was done in order to see if the original position of the limbs was reflected in the final deposition of bone. The other legs remained perpendicular to the axis of the body. Regardless of initial position, in each case the limbs were rapidly contracted against the body when burning commenced.

In the cremation of an adult pig at Corinth, the availability of fuel was limited, and the major source consisted of wooden pallets. Despite the quantity used, the thin wooden slats were insufficient to cremate the body, and a large quantity of firewood intended for winter heating was eventually added to the pyre. The pyre lacked a stone enclosure and collapsed rapidly, spreading burning wood across a large area. The initial failure of this cremation experiment provided a number of useful insights into the difficulties of achieving a complete cremation.

Overall, the experiments clarified a number of the problems associated with the interpretation of the Kavousi cremation enclosure graves. They also illustrated the problems associated with completing a successful cremation that have also been noted in Roman literature (Noy 2000, 191–193). The appearance and distribution of the cremated bone in the experiments was analogous to that of the human bone from the primary cremations at Kavousi. Nevertheless, the condition of the bones after the cremation experiment at Corinth, where additional wood had to be piled on top of the body in order to burn it fully, suggested a mechanism that could have produced the disordered and disarticulated remains that were found in some of the Kavousi graves. The juvenile pigs were much less ordered at the end of the cremation experiment, and in two cases no observable anatomical arrangement was preserved. This observation, too, is pertinent to the condition of infant and young children's remains excavated at Vronda. With one exception (Grave 30, Burial 6), the bones of the very young were not recognized during excavation; instead, they were found in sorting the water sieve residue.

The function of the enclosure walls also became apparent during the process of the experimental cremations. When the pyre was constructed inside an enclosure, the low stone walls did not significantly impede the flow of air to the pyre, but they provided stability to the pyre structure. The pyre grows less stable as the logs are burned from the bottom, and it tends to shift or tilt. When the lower half of the pyre has burned, the structure, with the corpse on top, becomes top-heavy and unstable. The presence of low walls, however, tends to contain the logs and prevent the burning corpse from falling off of the pyre if the structure shifts. When, in three experimental cremations, no stone enclosure was constructed, keeping the bodies of the pigs on the pyre was challenging. In the experiment conducted at Corinth, where inadequate fuel burned very quickly, the body of the pig ended up on the ground as the pyre structure collapsed. In the end, it took almost twice as long, and a great deal more wood, to cremate that pig than any of the others in the experimental pyres. These problems were not unknown in antiquity; inadequate fuel sources and falling corpses are well documented in Roman accounts, and the half-burned corpse was an object of particular horror (Noy 2000, 188–191). Also, although the walls of the enclosure did not prevent the surrounding ground cover from being scorched by flames from the pyre, they were sufficient to retain the falling logs, lessening the chance that the fire would spread uncontrollably.

Having descended from a height of one meter to ground level, the bones of most of the pig skeletons remained in approximate anatomical order, with only minor scattering of the feet and tail bones. The limbs were drawn toward the body, despite having been extended at the beginning of the cremation. At Kavousi, the presence of scattered bone fragments, particularly phalanges and metacarpals or metatarsals, has been noted outside the enclosure graves. As the pyre collapsed, these fragments must have been thrown aside, landing outside the area eventually occupied by most of the skeleton; some even fell outside the walls of the grave enclosure. The occurrence of such fragments does not necessarily indicate later disturbance. However, the major limb bones and bones of the axial skeleton remained within the enclosure and were not likely to occur outside the area of the pyre unless they were removed deliberately.

The collapse of the experimental pyre in a downwind direction may also explain the tendency of the Kavousi skeletons to be located toward one side of the enclosures rather than in the center. Plots of articulated bone reveal that the vertebral column and ribs, indicating the position of the trunk, were asymmetrically located in burials in Graves 12, 21, 28, 30, and 34 (see Figs. 152–154). On many days in Crete strong winds blow from the north or south. This phenomenon would tend to make one side of a pyre burn faster than the other, producing just such an asymmetrical deposit.

Classification of Cremation Burials

Only one certain pyre located outside of a burial enclosure was identified at Vronda (Grave 31), along with one possible example (Grave 13), suggesting that the normal practice in this community was to cremate the bodies within the rectangular enclosure, which typically became the place of deposition as well. Nonetheless, the cremated skeletons within the enclosures represent at least four depositional types. One category is that of primary cremations, in which portions of the body remained in anatomical or articulated order, thus indicating that the bone had not been deliberately moved since it was originally deposited during cremation. A second category is that of disturbed cremation deposits, which remained in the original place of cremation, the grave enclosure, but were deliberately moved aside for reuse of the grave, disturbed during the cremation itself, or affected by other postdepositional processes. Unfortunately, it is rarely possible to distinguish between burial-related disturbance and other cultural or taphonomic processes. A third category is that of secondary cremation deposits, in which the bone was gathered for deposition away from the pyre site, generally in vessels placed in an enclosure. A fourth category is that of discard deposits, in which bones were dumped outside and nearby the enclosures. Still other deposits include dumps containing only grave goods and few or no associated human remains. The total weight of the recovered bone and the number of identifiable elements, as well as the location of the bones, was helpful in classifying these burials. The bone from pyre sites outside of grave enclosures is considered separately because it represents what was left behind, inadvertently or not, rather than the bone that was selected for burial elsewhere.

Primary Cremations

The first indication during early excavations at Vronda that cremation had taken place in situ in the enclosure graves was the presence of burned stones, apparently placed on the remains while the pyre was still hot, along with the evidence for burning on the sides and floors of the enclosure. In later seasons, the soil scientists associated with the project confirmed that the soil, bedrock, and stones used in construction had indeed been exposed to fire. Subsequently, anatomically arranged skeletal elements were identified by plotting bone fragments as they were found. This pattern of bone deposition indicated that the enclosures contained primary cremation burials, not secondary depositions of gathered ashes as had been previously assumed.

The primary cremations were identified by the presence of anatomically ordered but completely calcined skeletons found in the ashy soil that filled the enclosures. It was not until the excavation of Grave 6 that evidence for the articulation of skeletal remains was found. In this grave, only the upper half of the skeleton was preserved in articulation, with the arms folded across the chest area. The lower portions of the pelvis and legs had been disturbed by later activity, as the tomb lay very close to the surface. Excavations ultimately revealed complete or partial articulated skeletons in Graves 6, 9, 12, 16, 17, 20, 28, 30, 34, and 36.

The plotting of the cremated fragments revealed that the skeletons were not neatly arranged in extended or flexed positions. The crania were generally located near one end of the grave, and the bodies were more or less parallel to the long axis of the grave. The legs and arms were irregularly arranged, although almost always somewhat flexed, despite the fact that the enclosure graves were long enough for an extended burial. Scattered bone, particularly of the ankles, feet, and hands, was often found outside the enclosure, similar to the pattern seen in the experimental pig cremation.

Forensic literature, as well as observation of commercial cremations (Fig. 156:b), indicates that the body position revealed in the reconstructions of the Vronda graves is similar to the positions of the bone remaining after a fleshed body has been cremated, either accidentally, as in a house or car fire, or deliberately in a crematorium (e.g., Rathbun and Buikstra 1984; Symes et al. 2008, 31–35). When heated by fire the muscles shrink, flexing the joints and pulling the limbs toward the body in a characteristic pugilistic posture. Regardless of the original position of the body on the pyre, the arms and legs will bend at the elbows, wrists, knees, and ankles, unless free movement of the limbs is obstructed in some way. Each of the articulated skeletons at Kavousi demonstrated this semiflexed, pugilistic posture, with a few exceptions where a single limb appears to have been restrained in some way on the pyre (e.g., Grave 34, Burial 1; Fig. 154:b). The result at the end of cremation is a skeleton that occupies only part of the available space in the enclosures, which were built to accommodate the extended length of adults.

Cremation Process at Vronda

As a result of careful excavation and the experimental cremations that have enabled us to evaluate our hypotheses about the cremation process, we can now confidently reconstruct the activities that produced the burial remains found in the enclosure graves at Vronda. A cremation enclosure was initially prepared in or adjacent to one of the abandoned houses at Vronda. It is clear that the enclosures were constructed before the initial cremation pyre at the grave, as the walls were not built on top of pyre debris but directly on the floor of the house or the surface dug into the floor. Often the stone socles of two house walls meeting at a corner were used to form two sides of the grave. The fill from collapsed roofing material was cleared from a rectangular area, and one or two additional walls were constructed, using uncut stones similar to those found in the house walls. In some cases, the fill was cleared from the center of the room and the entire grave enclosure was built for the purpose of the cremation and burial. The grave enclosures varied somewhat in size but averaged 1.90 m in length and 1.02 m in width. The house walls generally preserved no more than two courses of stone up to 0.30 m high. Walls built expressly for the enclosure were more variable. In some cases, such as Graves 16 and 28, the grave walls were quite substantial. In others, such as Graves 23 and 30, no more than a single row of stones was used. The variation in the wall construction suggests that the stone walls were not intended to support the wood of the pyre in the initial preparation for cremation.

The pyre was built inside the area enclosed by the walls. In some cases, sufficient charred wood was preserved to give an indication of the actual pyre structure, and it was possible to identify the species of woods used, generally olive or oak. The base of the pyre consisted of moderately large logs, probably 0.10 to 0.15 m in diameter. These were sometimes (as in Grave 26) placed to run across the short axis of the enclosure, with gaps between the logs that would have facilitated air flow and provided space for smaller kindling, which has not survived. In Grave 36, however, the first layer of logs was placed running down the long axis of the enclosure. The rest of the pyre was constructed in layers of wood that alternately ran across the length of the grave and the short axis. The pyres were large enough to accomplish the efficient and complete cremation of the soft tissue and bones. Given the horizontal dimensions of the grave enclosure, most pyres would have needed to be nearly one meter in height to provide adequate fuel for the cremation process.

The body was placed on the pyre in an extended position. Bronze pins were frequently present, perhaps associated with clothing or a shroud, although in many cases they do not appear to have been burned. Grave offerings, including portions of meat and plant foods such as grapes, olives, pistachio, legumes, and grains, were at times placed on the pyre. Most of the ceramics were put on the pyre after the cremation, and iron and bronze jewelry, tools, and weapons were arrayed around the body as well. Many of the offerings may have been placed in the grave after burning, but subsequent cremations then burned these, making it difficult to distinguish between gifts placed on the pyre and those added after burning was complete (see below, this vol., Ch. 11, pp. 340–242).

The pyres would have been lit in the spaces at the base of the wood stack to enable the rising flames to ignite the upper layers of fuel. Within 20 to 30 minutes the body itself would have begun to burn. The pyre would have required continuous tending to prevent the fire from spreading uncontrollably and to ensure that the pyre remained upright. On windy days this task would have been particularly difficult. After approximately four to five hours the pyre would have burned down to a level that was largely enclosed by the walls surrounding it. After two to three more hours, only embers and charred bone and tissue would have remained. A layer of cobbles was then placed over the enclosure.

When the graves were reused, the sealing layer of cobbles was removed. Adhering pieces of bone, ash, and ceramics were sometimes removed from the grave in this process. Often the remains of previous burials were pushed to one end of the grave, and a pit was created in the center. Then the process of building the pyre was begun again.

5

Human Remains

Maria A. Liston

The 123 skeletons excavated during the Kavousi Project include 86 adults and 39 nonadults (individuals younger than ca. 20 years) found in a total of 38 graves containing human remains (Table 11). Nine of a total of 11 tholos tombs were excavated or cleaned, producing remains of 18 individuals. The cemetery of intrusive enclosure graves at Vronda contained 105 individuals in 30 numbered graves. Six funerary deposits that were initially assigned grave numbers later turned out to be discarded deposits of ash, bone, and pottery from adjacent enclosure graves. One numbered structure, Grave 18, was later identified as Vronda Tholos VIII.

Tholos Tombs: Demography, Health, and Pathology

The 11 tholos tombs at Vronda comprise the earliest burial group at the site. Of these 11 tombs, one of the eight excavated by Boyd (Tomb III) was not found, and three (Tombs V, VI, VII) had no human remains associated with them when they were excavated by the Kavousi Project. Four tholos tombs excavated by Boyd and three others that were investigated by the Kavousi Project had a total of 18 individuals represented among the skeletal remains.

Due to the small sample size, little meaningful demographic analysis of these burials can be conducted. It is clear, however, that both adults and children were buried in the Vronda tholos tombs. Children were found in four of the tombs: IV, VIII, IX, and X (in which the only remains recovered were from a five- to seven-year-old child). These juvenile remains included an infant less than two years old and three older children between five and 16 years of age. Adult remains were found in all of the tombs except Tomb X, with a minimum of 13 individuals represented. Five could be identified as probable males, one of whom was 40–49 years old. Only one possible female was identified, from Tomb XI.

The inhumation burials from the tholos tombs are too poorly preserved to make any reasonable estimations of overall health of the burying groups, but there are indications of the more common generalized pathologies, namely periosteal bone formation and joint disease. Bone with identifiable pathological conditions was found in three of the tholos tombs. One adult in Vronda IV had mild periosteal bone deposits on the tibia shafts, indicating either an infectious or inflammatory process or a vascular insufficiency (Ortner 2003, 206–207; Resnick and Niwayama 1995, 4434–4435). Joint disease in the spine was observed in an adult, also from Vronda IV, with osteoarthritic pitting on the facets of two vertebral fragments. It is not clear if the bones displaying these pathologies belonged to the same individual.

Enclosure Graves: Demography, Health, and Pathology

The burials in the enclosure graves at Vronda represent a different set of mortuary practices from those which may be inferred, however scantily, from the tholos tombs. Most of the enclosures were built into and among the structures of the village houses after the buildings had been abandoned. These intrusive graves were used primarily for cremation burials, but a few contained inhumations.

Of the 105 burials in the 30 enclosure graves at Vronda, seven are inhumations, and the remaining 98 are cremations (Table 11). The inhumations in the enclosure graves are primary burials, but they are often in worse condition than bones of the disturbed inhumations from the earlier tholos tombs due to the very shallow deposition of sediments above the graves and later agricultural use of the site. Only one skeleton, Grave 5, Burial 7, is largely complete, but the articular ends of the long bones are nearly all missing. The condition of the inhumed bone from the Vronda enclosure graves is consistent with inhumed bone from other sites in Crete. The material is very fragmentary, and the surfaces of the bone are heavily eroded. Very few epiphyseal ends or other cancellous bone remains. The majority of the surviving pieces are cranial vault sections and long bone shaft fragments. Demographic and paleopathological analysis of the sample is severely limited by the condition of the bones.

The 98 cremated skeletons from Vronda are generally in better condition than the inhumations. Often the last cremation burial in an enclosure preserved the bones in anatomical order, while earlier cremations were disturbed or deliberately pushed to one or both ends of the graves. While the bone is very fragmented, the burning process paradoxically prevents further decay by destroying the organic collagen while leaving behind the inorganic mineral matrix. This process preserves the surface structures and shape of the bone, although it is reduced in size by ca. 20%–30%. As a result, while metric analyses are not useful, pathological conditions and indicators of age and sex may be preserved better than in the inhumations.

Evaluating Population Structure, Health, and Disease at Vronda

The evaluation of biological categories such as age, sex, and ancestry depends primarily on the well-preserved morphology of the skull and pelvis. Supplementary information may be available from other parts of the skeleton, particularly in children. The elicitation of other biological information, such as stature and evidence for disease, requires intact long bones (for size measurements) and the preservation of diverse areas of the skeleton (for the evaluation of the distribution pattern of skeletal lesions). Unfortunately, cremation produces fragmentary remains and the destruction of critical areas of the pelvis, so that these requirements are not fulfilled. Attempts at metric analysis rarely produce useful results (Agelarakis 2005, 44–48). The preservation of unburned remains in the shallow graves at Vronda is even worse because of the detrimental effects of alternating wet winters and dry summers. Problems of preservation have plagued biological anthropologists from the earliest days of analysis. In his 1942 dissertation on Greek skeletal material from all over the country, J. Lawrence Angel has a section in his first chapter called "Reasons for Paucity of Material" (1942, 25–27).

Despite these difficulties, it has been possible to collect a reasonably detailed data set on the age, sex, and health status of the individuals buried at Vronda. Every effort was made to achieve a complete collection of the skeletal remains. The graves were excavated either by the skeletal biologist (Liston) or under her direct supervision. In the first year, large samples of the grave soils were water sieved, and the enhanced recovery of bone material associated with this practice dictated the change to 100% sieving in subsequent seasons. Considerable effort was expended in the reconstruction of the skeletal remains, and in many cases the resulting portions of the skull and pelvis proved more than adequate for the determination of biological characteristics.

Although some authors have argued that it is not possible to determine biological information, particularly sex, from cremated remains (Young 1949, 282–283 n. 23; Musgrave 1996, 680; 2005, 250), relevant skeletal portions are often preserved and can be evaluated using the same methodologies employed in inhumations. The inconsistent degree of shrinkage caused by burning means that morphoscopic methods, rather than metric analyses, are more likely to be useful in analyzing cremated bones (Agelarakis 2005, 32–33; Fairgrieve 2008, 108). Our experience with these and other cremated remains indicates that it is entirely possible to evaluate age and sex with confidence. The present author was also able to test the commonly used methods of age and sex determination on a small sample of modern crematory remains of known age and sex, and the evaluations proved to be consistently accurate.

Population Structure

Demographic analysis of cemetery populations can be a powerful tool for evaluating the health and social conditions of the living populations from which they derived. However, such analyses are subject to many confounding variables, and they rely first and foremost on the accurate estimation of age (Jackes 2000, 417–421; Larsen 2015, 418–421). Such accuracy is not attainable in cremated or poorly preserved remains. As a result, the discussion presented here is not a true demographic analysis; there are no life tables or models of mortality. Nevertheless, it is still important to record and consider patterns of sex and age at death, even if the resulting image of society is produced with very broad strokes.

Patterns of sex distribution and age at death speak to fundamental issues of how well individuals respond to their biological and cultural environments (Milner, Wood, and Boldsen 2000, 471–472). The relative frequency of infant and juvenile deaths in poorly preserved remains may not give us an accurate estimation of the risk of death at birth and beyond, but it can suggest whether or not status level was acquired at birth, and if any or most children were accorded the same privileges in death as the adults in the society. It may not be possible to calculate an accurate average age at death or to know what percentage of the population survived to old age, but at Vronda, at least, it is possible to observe that while some individuals survived beyond 60 years of age, none of those individuals were female.

Age at Death

Age for the skeletons was estimated using a variety of methods. Because of the fragmented condition of cremation burials, it was not possible to use the same method on every skeleton or to privilege one method over another. Any skeletal portion that could be evaluated for age was scored, using as many methods as possible. In many cases, it was only possible to determine if the individual was an adult, juvenile, or infant/fetus. Adults were identified both by the size of the bones and the absence of any indicators of incomplete growth, such as unfused or incompletely fused epiphyses and developing dentition (Buikstra and Ubelaker, eds., 1994, 40–43; Ubelaker 1999, 64; Schaefer, Black, and Scheuer 2009, 351–355) or the presence of age-related skeletal changes such as osteoarthritis and severe dental wear (Buikstra and Ubelaker, eds., 1994, 52–53; 121–122). Juveniles and infants were identified both by size and the presence of immature cortical bone, as well as the presence of unfused epiphyses and developing dentition.

Age estimations, particularly when using broad categories, are difficult to interpret. Cultural practices intersect with biology to give meaning to age designations. Every individual has at least four age identities: their biological age, chronological age, and cultural or social age. A fourth category distinguishing juvenile from adult is sexual maturity. While we can evaluate the biological indicators, skeletal age estimations always have some degree of inaccuracy, and some individuals will fall outside of the most likely range of estimated age.

Skeletal age is based on patterns of development and maturation in juveniles and patterns of bone renewal, breakdown, and degeneration in adults. A skeletal adult is an individual whose epiphyses have all fused, joining the ends and joint surfaces to various bones, and whose third molars (wisdom teeth) have erupted. The last epiphysis of the skeleton to fuse is normally the medial end of the clavicle, at the point where it articulates with the top of the sternum. This process may begin as early as the age of 16 years, and occasionally it may drag on as late as 33 years. In many modern individuals with verified ages, the process commences and ends between about 17 and 25 years in females and 18 and 28 years in males. By the age of 21, more than 75% of individuals will have at least partial union of the epiphysis (Webb and Suchey 1985, 463). The formation and eruption of the third molars is even more variable. The median age of eruption of the third molars is 17 to 18 years in males and females, but the actual range can extend into the 30s or later (various data summarized in Schaefer, Black, and Scheuer 2009, 93–95). At Vronda third molars with nearly or completely formed root tips were assumed to have erupted, because root formation continues for a short period after a tooth erupts through the gums. A third marker of skeletal adulthood, the fusion of the basilar suture on the base of the skull, was almost never preserved in the Vronda cremations. At Vronda, an individual with an age estimation of 20 years or more was assigned to the category of adult; individuals with any one marker of skeletal immaturity were assumed to be less than 20 years of age and were termed juveniles or adolescents (the latter if they were in their late teens and presumably had attained sexual maturity).

An individual's biological age may not always reflect actual chronological age. Just as some individuals retain a youthful appearance while others age rapidly, some individuals may retain youthful-looking bones while others, in rare instances, appear older than their chronological age. Many cultures place little or no importance on specific chronological age in years. Instead they group together individuals born within a few years of each other, or they mark progression through life stages by indications of sexual maturation such as the growth of breasts, menarche, growth of facial hair, or pregnancy. Other events such as the achievement of a particular task—a first kill in hunting, for example—may also define progressions in maturity.

We have some information about the cultural meaning of age in later historic Greece, particularly in Athens, but we have no knowledge of how age affected the lives of prehistoric peoples in Crete or when they would have been considered adults in the society. It is likely that some of the older juveniles, in the range of 16–20 years, would have been considered adults in their social roles, particularly the females who were found with neonatal infants or fetuses. In the absence of any verifiable knowledge of cultural norms, however, all individuals who have not achieved full skeletal maturity are classified as biological juveniles in the Vronda analysis.

For adults, the most accurate aging methods normally involve either of two joint surfaces of the pelvis, the pubic symphysis, where the right and left halves of the pelvis join (Todd 1920, 1921; Brooks and Suchey 1990), and the auricular surface of the ilium, where the sacrum articulates with the os coxae (Lovejoy et al. 1985). Unfortunately, these surfaces rarely survive cremation and subsequent burial. In cremations, the most frequently preserved skeletal elements that exhibit consistent age changes are the cranial sutures, joints between the various bony plates of the skull. The most accurate methods of cranial suture aging rely on scoring specific areas of multiple sutures to provide a composite score and age range (Buikstra and Ubelaker, eds., 1994, 32–38). This was rarely possible at Vronda because of the incomplete preservation of the cranial vaults. As a result, many adults were assigned to broad age categories on the basis of cranial suture closure at limited sites and the presence or absence of osteoarthritic changes in the vertebrae and hands or feet. The vault sutures were evaluated using protocols for cremated remains (Holck 2008, 64–67). These categories were young adults (20–39 years), mature adults (40–59 years), and older adults (60+ years). Juveniles were given specific ages where possible based on dental development and epiphysis closure (summarized in Schafer, Black, and Scheuer 2009, 351–355). Measurements of long bones for estimating skeletal age could rarely be made due to the fragmentary nature of the remains.

Vronda Population

All age groups are represented among the 105 individuals identified in the Vronda enclosures and other associated intrusive graves. Only one of the individuals in the tholos tombs could be aged beyond broad categories, so the tholos burials are not included in this discussion. Thirty four (34%) of the burials in the graves were nonadults (including fetuses) under the age of 20, and 71 (98%) were adults (Chart 1). The total percentage of juveniles is somewhat lower than expected, as in nonindustrialized modern populations juvenile deaths are consistently around 20% of live births, and in premodern populations it is well established that up to 30% of infants died in their first year and up to 50% of children died before age 10 (Parkin 1992, 92–93). In a broad survey of Mediterranean cultures, Angel (1975, table 1, between 182–183) estimated that 10.5 juveniles died for every 10 living adults in Early Iron Age Greece. Likewise, by the early Roman Empire, when sanitation conditions may have improved relative to earlier periods but urban density had increased, the infant mortality rate was around 300/1000, although more recent estimates suggest this could be somewhat exaggerated (Parkin 1992, 93; 2013, 47–49). High numbers of infants dying at birth or by the end of their first week are the norm in premodern societies and were a recognized phenomenon in antiquity. Aristotle comments, "the majority of deaths in infancy occur before the child is a week old" (Arist. *Hist. An.* 7:588a8).

The Vronda enclosures are not unique among the Kavousi cemeteries in having a high proportion of infant and juvenile burials. Among the 11 tholos tombs at Vronda and three at nearby Aloni, despite the fact that every grave had been emptied prior to modern excavations, remains of six juveniles were recovered from five tombs that contained any human bone at all (pers. obs.). Six of the 21 inhumed individuals (29%) in the tholos tombs in the Kavousi area were children or infants. This is exactly the same percentage of juveniles found in the much less disturbed cremations in the enclosures. At Kavousi Kastro, the partial remains of one fetus and one neonatal infant recovered in domestic dump contexts probably indicate the disposal practices for some of the potentially missing infants from Vronda. In these two cremation deposits at the Kastro, remains of both adults and children were recovered (Liston 1993, 50–51).

At Vronda, for the recovered burials within the juvenile age range, the patterns of age at death are also similar to those observed at other sites of ancient Greece and elsewhere. Fetal and infant mortality was high, reflecting both intrinsic failures of development and the perils of birth. Juvenile mortality climbed again after age two, probably reflecting increasing exposure to environmental pathogens and loss of maternal antibodies after weaning. Older children have a very low risk of death, but adults begin to die in greater numbers as they age. The years after puberty through about 40 were probably particularly dangerous for women, as pregnancy and childbirth would bring new stresses and a great potential for death from infection and hemorrhage.

Age at Death by Sex

In the enclosure burials at Vronda, male and female patterns of mortality differed markedly. A total of 34 individuals (44%) could be both aged and sexed (Chart 2). This includes three older juveniles who were sexed as female on the basis of both pelvic morphology and the presence of fetal bone commingled with the remains. Ten out of 12 (83%) of these females died before age 40, and none survived into the oldest category of 60+ years. Age could not be determined for an additional six (33% of the total number) of female burials. In contrast, among the 22 burials identified as male that could be aged, none died as late teenagers, and only four (18%) died between 20 and 39 years of age. Twelve (56%) died between 40 and 59 years, and six (27%) survived into extreme old age, defined here as over 60 years. Age could not be determined for an additional three (12% of the total number of male burials). Sex could not be determined for 31 (43%) of the 72 adult skeletons. Age could not be estimated for 18 (25%) of these adults of indeterminate sex.

Sex Distribution

Sex is a term with enormous cultural baggage, and gender, a term often incorrectly used interchangeably with sex, is even more laden with cultural meaning.

It refers to the culturally learned expressions of behavior associated with a given sex. Genders can be much more fluid and numerous than the simple binary of male and female. In the complete absence of any knowledge of gender expression in Early Iron Age Crete, however, we are limited to the identification and discussion of the primary biological sexes, male and female.

Biological sex refers to the expression of normal chromosomal differences, either two X chromosomes (XX) for females or an X and Y chromosome (XY) for males, in the 23rd pair of chromosomes. This chromosomal difference spurs the production of differing relative amounts of sex hormones at various life stages, resulting in differences in the size and morphology of the bones, particularly in the skull and pelvis. There are variants of the sex chromosomes, usually trisomies, in which an individual has three chromosomes rather than the usual two in a given pair. Like other major mutations, extra chromosomes are often fatal early in the fetal period, but individuals with an extra sex chromosome may survive, although they are usually infertile. For skeletal studies, the presence of a Y chromosome, either singular or plural (XYY), still results in the production of male hormone ratios during development, and the skeleton will normally appear as male (Kumar, Abbas, and Fausto 2005, 170, 175–180).

Cremation and poor preservation of inhumed bones preclude attempts to identify sex in the Vronda burials using DNA analysis. Estimation of sex was based, therefore, on the standard features of the skull and pelvis, which reflect the greater robusticity and larger faces of males and the broader pelvic dimensions of females (Buikstra and Ubelaker, eds., 1994, 16–21). Because of the fragmentation of the remains, no metric evaluations of sex were possible, either for the skull and pelvis or for long bone dimensions. As in the determination of age, the same methods could not be used on every individual due to differential preservation. Every skeletal feature that reliably exhibits sexual dimorphism was evaluated.

Of the 78 adolescent and adult skeletons identified in the enclosure graves at Vronda, 43 (55%) could be sexed. Of these, 25 were males (58%) and 18 (42%) were females. In a population in which there is no artificial selection for one sex or the other, expressed through infanticide or differential neglect, it is expected that the sex ratio will approximate 1:1. Because sex could not be determined for 35 adult and adolescent individuals, it is impossible to determine if there was a real sex bias. For the inhumed bone in the intrusive graves at Vronda, preservation in general was particularly poor, and of the preserved adult remains, only the relatively complete primary inhumation in Grave 5, a male, could be sexed.

Skeletons identified as males consistently outnumber females in samples from archaeological sites all over Greece, and among these, skewed sex ratios are evident at Bronze Age sites where preservation is poor on both Crete and the mainland (Angel 1942, 1971; Halstead 1977). However, at Lerna in the Peloponnese and in the Athenian Agora, where preservation is better, the numbers of male and female skeletons are more nearly equal (Halstead 1977; pers. obs.). At Vronda, the mortuary sample is too small and the burials are spread across too long a period of time to establish whether there was an actual imbalance in the sex ratio of the living population.

Children in the Vronda Graves

The presence of children in the cremation graves is particularly interesting. Previous excavations of Geometric cremation cemeteries in Greece rarely recovered cremated children and infants (Kurtz and Boardman 1971; Garland 1985; Morris 1987; Musgrave 2005, 251). Pliny the Elder (Plin. *HN* 7.72) notes that children were not cremated before they developed teeth. Much speculation on the possible reasons for this has been published, and many theories about the social structure of the Early Iron Age have been based on the absence of children from the cemeteries (summarized in Morris 1987, 57–62). The presence of cremated children in the graves at Vronda, found through water sieving, and the fact that the most careful excavation techniques could not reveal their presence while in the field, suggests that earlier excavations did not find children in cremation graves because recovery techniques were not sufficiently meticulous, not because children were not present. Since the Kavousi excavations were completed, newer projects and reexamination of the skeletons from earlier projects in Athens have shown that earlier interpretations of burial practices for children are flawed (Liston 2017, 515–519;

unpublished data from the excavations for the new Acropolis Museum on the south side of the Acropolis of Athens).

It has been argued elsewhere that children in Greece, particularly infants, having made little contribution to society, were not honored with much effort or expense at their death (Garland 1985, 78–80; Morris 1987, 61–62). Cheap or reused vessels were used to contain inhumations of children. Cremation of juveniles is almost unknown with the exception of a few instances in one quarter of the Athenian Agora (Liston 2017, 518). Only occasionally were children buried with substantial grave gifts of the sort offered in honor of the adult dead. Grave gifts, when present in children's burials, were instead the usual possessions of children (Garland 1985, 83–84). At Kavousi, however, children were buried in the same manner as adults or in well-made, and in one case decorated, pithoi. The postuse taphonomy of the cremation graves makes it difficult to associate ceramics and metal objects with particular burials, but there is no clear evidence that children in the enclosure graves were denied grave goods. Moreover, in one case (Grave 21), an iron weapon was found with a child's inhumation in a pithos. While there were also two cremated adults in the vessel, the weapons were under the bones of the child, the first burial in the pithos.

In every time period represented in the Kavousi sample, and in every type of mortuary disposal, children are represented. The excavation of the Kavousi graves has shown that formal burial was not reserved exclusively for adults, nor were juveniles being buried in archaeologically invisible ways. The mortuary treatment of children shows some variability, but the variations coincide with the different types of adult burial found at the site as well. The variation is not necessarily related to family status, as fetal and infant cremations are found in the tholos tombs, discard deposits, and in the richer and more elaborate enclosure graves. In addition, as mentioned earlier, children are found in all of the undisturbed enclosure graves on the site.

While juveniles are well represented in the cremation graves, it is not likely that their numbers completely reflect the population from which they are derived. Differential burial of infants in the ancient Greek world is a well-documented phenomenon (Hillson 2009, 138; Liston and Rotroff 2013, 63). The clearly visible settlement of the Kastro could have been the home of the Vronda burying population, but the half-hour walk to Vronda may explain why some individuals, particularly children, were not transported there for burial.

Health and Disease at Vronda

The poor preservation of skeletal materials at Vronda, either from decay of inhumed burials or from cremation of the majority of remains, impedes the evaluation of the health status of the people, a problem that also plagues other studies of EIA cemeteries in Crete (Musgrave 1996, 682–685). The problem is not that pathologies are not preserved. There are many examples of both common and rare conditions that provide insight into the lives of individuals, but it is nearly impossible to look at overall incidence of any disease or condition because the representation of skeletal elements varies so widely among the graves. Individual cases can be described, but there is little information on how common the disease was in the Vronda burial population. The individual case studies indicate, nonetheless, that the residents of Vronda suffered from most of the same diseases that plagued other ancient peoples and that some individuals in the population developed rarer conditions.

Despite the cremation of most of the skeletons associated with the eighth and seventh century graves at Vronda, a number of pathological conditions can be identified on the bone (Table 12; Chart 3). In fact, the tendency for cremated bone to resist decay better than inhumed remains in Greece suggests that the Vronda sample should offer a better picture of overall health than the remains from inhumation cemeteries.

Anemias

The most common pathological conditions on the Kavousi bone from the LG and EO graves at Vronda are represented by porous bone in the cranial vault, known as porotic hyperostosis, and porous lesions on the superior surface of the eye orbits, termed cribra orbitalia. The etiology of these conditions is currently the subject of considerable debate. It was once accepted that they were associated with systemic genetic anemias. Angel initially attributed the porotic changes on skulls from various Greek sites to thalassemia, the most common genetic anemia in the Mediterranean, but later attributed it to either dietary or parasitic stresses causing iron deficiency (Angel 1971, 1978; Angel and Bisel 1986). The iron deficiency hypothesis has been challenged, however, as has the assumption that cribra orbitalia and porotic hyperostosis have the same underlying pathological cause (Walker et al. 2009; Rivera and Lahr 2017). For now, it seems clear that the lesions indicate some form of stress involving the production of blood cells in the cranium, but the underlying causes may be more complex than previously believed.

The cranial vault bones were consistently the best-preserved bones in the cremated skeletons at Vronda. As a result, for this pathology alone, the number of observed cases probably reflects the actual prevalence of the condition. Twenty-six adults and children (25%) showed some form of cranial vault or orbital porosity, with accompanying expansion of the diploë (Table 12; Chart 3). In most cases the pathology was extensively remodeled, indicating that the condition was not active at the time of death. This is similar to the incidence of 20.4% found by Angel in an early study of the Middle Bronze Age skeletons at Lerna (1971), although in a later article he reported a range of 0%–36% across various eastern Mediterranean sites, and only 12% at Lerna (1966, 761). In more recent studies, it has been observed that the condition was much more frequent in the Neolithic period, affecting 12% to 60% of the mortuary populations, and it was also quite high, ranging from 29% to 59%, at various Bronze Age sites, including Lerna (Papathanasiou 2005, 382; Stravopodi et al. 2009, 263). In Crete, the condition continued to be common through the Byzantine period, with frequencies of up to 85% (Bourbou 2010, 113–115). However, EIA skeletons in the Athenian Agora show remarkably low rates of porotic hyperostosis and cribra orbitalia, with no active cases and only a few remodeled lesions (Liston 2017, 523).

Osteopenia/Osteoporosis

Age-related bone loss is an inevitable part of the life course for both men and women, and postmenopausal women experience additional loss of bone mass due to the effects of reduced estrogen. Loss of cortical bone and reduction of trabecular (spongy) bone mass both occur and can be observed directly as well as through radiographs. Osteoporosis leaves individuals vulnerable to fractures of weight-bearing bones, such as vertebral bodies and the femur neck, and to increased risk of fracture in accidents. The degree to which an individual is at risk for osteoporosis varies with genetics, environment, diet, and activity levels, but age is the most consistent risk factor for osteoporosis and fractures (Ortner 2003, 410–415; Glencross 2011, 399–401; Larsen 2015, 57–59).

Four cremated individuals (Grave 8, Burial 1: female, 20–40 years; Grave 9, Burial 1: male(?), 40–60; Grave 28, Burials 4 and 6: adult, unknown age) and one inhumed skeleton (Grave 5, Burial 7: male 60+) had extremely thin cortical bone (1–3 mm) on the long bone shafts of the humerus, femur, and tibia. This thinning of the bone cortex is indicative of senile osteoporosis in the elderly individuals. In the younger woman it could reflect the impact of pregnancies on her bone mass.

Joint Disease

Osteoarthritis, or degenerative joint disease, is an almost inevitable result of aging in humans, with mild manifestations found in nearly everyone over the age of 50. Changes to the bones that remain visible after the soft tissue has decayed are less common but still among the most frequently observed skeletal pathologies in archaeological remains. Osteoarthritis was also a common pathology on the Kavousi skeletons at Vronda. A total of 15 adults were found to have osteoarthritic changes in various joints (Chart 3). The actual rate of occurrence of osteoarthritis was probably higher, but cremation consistently destroys articular ends of bone, thus eliminating most joints from evaluation. The most commonly recorded location for this pathology was on the articular facets of the vertebrae. Pitting and lipping were frequently found, indicating disease of the synovial joints on the articular facets (Pl. 67A). The cartilaginous joints between the vertebral bodies normally exhibit more arthritic changes than the articular facets, and these also occasionally showed marginal osteophytes, but as vertebral bodies were not preserved consistently in the cremations, their frequency cannot be evaluated. In total, 8 adults (11%), including six males, three females, and one unsexed adult, had osteoarthritic changes on one or more vertebrae. This proportion is considerably lower than Angel's (1954) estimation of a 70% occurrence of osteoarthritis of the spine in prehistoric Greece; more recent data from other studies in Greece suggest that a frequency of 12%–40% is more realistic than his estimate (see Papathanasiou

2001, 37; Fox 2005, 75–76; Iezzi 2005, 167; Liston 2017, 523–525).

Trauma

Trauma is an important marker of the level of health in society. Traumatic injuries are relatively common, less subject to misidentification than other lesions, and provide some insight into the conditions that produced the visible evidence. In addition, because of the well-documented process of fracture healing, it is possible to estimate broadly the amount of time elapsed between the trauma and death (Walker 2001, 575–578). Cranial fractures are often an indicator of interpersonal violence, and the patterns can tell us who was at risk. Other fractures can reveal dangerous occupations or living conditions. In addition, enthesopathies, strains, and tears where tendons and ligaments attach to bone also can indicate physical stress from occupations or other activities.

Traumatic injuries were present at Vronda, but most were relatively minor. A total of 11 individuals (15% of adults) suffered traumas that resulted in visible damage to bone (Chart 3). Enthesopathies, or lesions of muscle attachments, were the most common traumatic injury. These occur as the result of normal activity levels and not trauma, but when there is evidence for major tearing or distortion of the attachment, more acute injury may be represented. Enthesopathies are found either around the joint capsules of bones or on the diaphysis (bone shafts) in areas where muscles attach to the bone through fibrous connective tissues. Visible changes occur in response to micro- and macrotrauma, normal physical activities, and age-related change (Villotte and Knüsel 2013, 136–139). Evaluation of enthesopathies is complex, but major osseous changes normally indicate trauma or significant physical activity. The major enthesopathies seen on the Vronda skeletons probably represent the injuries that might be expected in an agricultural, pastoral population living in a rural area of rugged terrain.

The most common enthesopathies occurred on the posterior surface of the femora in an area called the linea aspera. This location is where some of the major muscles associated with locomotion are attached (Abrahams, Marks, and Hutchings 2003, 298), and nearly all of the Vronda skeletons exhibited very well-developed muscle attachments in this area. In some adult individuals (Grave 6 Burial 1, Grave 9 Burial 5, Grave 30 Burial 3), however, the proximal linea aspera was disrupted or displaced, indicating a significant injury to the attached muscles (Pl. 67B). The rough, mountainous terrain of the Kavousi area may have contributed to these injuries, as well as nonlocomotor activities or accidents. Grave 6 Burial 1, a young adult, possibly female, with a femoral enthesopathy, also had a large enthesopathy on the proximal ulna at the elbow in the area of the supinator muscle (Pl. 67C). This muscle, along with the biceps, rotates the forearm. Isolated supinator muscle injuries are rare but often occur together with biceps tendon injuries. Forceful throwing motions (e.g., pitching a baseball) and lifting heavy objects are two of the more common causes of these injuries seen in modern clinical practice. Either could have been a cause of the injury seen on this individual (Stone and Stone 1990, 134; Nayyar et al. 2011).

Another injury possibly associated with activity or locomotion is a single case of osteochondritis dessicans in the patella of an adult, Burial 2 in Grave 21. This is the result of traumatic injury to articular cartilage and underlying bone, where the underlying bone is damaged and resorbed. It is most commonly found in the knee joint and often appears in adolescents and young adults (Ortner 2003, 351–352).

Fractures are another category of trauma that may have useful implications for activity patterns. Fractures can result from accidents or deliberate violence, and the patterns of injury across a population may differ depending on the cause. At Vronda, six healed fractures were identified in the skeletal remains. The most common fracture was associated with the distal segment of the fourth or fifth toe, found in two individuals (Grave 9, Burial 4, an adult male, 40–60 years of age; Grave 12, Burial 6, an adult female in her early 20s). This fracture is one of the most common in humans, as the toes are particularly vulnerable to impacts (Galloway, ed., 1999, 222–223). The sites of Vronda and Kastro are built on rough bedrock, sometimes leveled but often projecting above the level of the floors of the houses. A potential source of these broken toes is easily identified: more than one excavator also suffered from impacts with this bedrock.

More severe fractures of arm bones were found in two individuals. Grave 5, Burial 1, an adult male probably in his 30s, had a well-healed fracture of the humerus shaft. It is not clear if the fracture was complete or partial, but it was a significant injury. Humeral shaft fractures can result from either deliberate violence or accident, and falls are a common cause of these injuries. This individual also had a healed superior patella fracture. These fractures usually occur when the quadriceps muscle contracts violently in a stumbling fall (Galloway, ed., 1999, 125–126, 186–187). In addition, this man's skull had the only evidence for surgery at Kavousi, a well-healed trepanation on the right parietal bone (see below, pp. 231–232).

Burial 5 in Grave 30, an adult female, experienced a more debilitating arm fracture. The olecranon process of the ulna, which articulates around the distal humerus, allowing the arm to flex at the elbow, was completely fractured (Pl. 67D). This fracture had failed to heal and formed a pseudarthrosis, a false joint. This feature suggests that the arm was not immobilized after the injury, and the fragments failed to unite. If they had united, the fractured portions could have ankylosed with the distal humerus, locking the joint permanently. Nevertheless, it appears that the woman would have retained the ability to flex her arm at the elbow, although there would have been some impact on the strength and stability of the joint (pers. comm., J. Santangelo).

There are two traumatic injuries that can potentially be attributed to deliberate conflict. The first is found on an elderly adult male inhumation (Grave 5, Burial 7). There is a remodeled a depression on the midshaft of the right radius and a wound with a cloaca on the corresponding area of the right ulna on the arm (Pl. 67E). The cloaca is indicative of osteomyelitis, an infection of the inner bone that resulted in a draining wound. The wounds on both bones appear to be largely healed, with very little evidence of active infection at the time of death. The location of the injuries, in the distal half of the lower arm, is consistent with so-called parry injuries, which occur when the arm is raised with the palm outward to ward off a blow, putting the ulna on the upper surface. Parry fractures are commonly interpreted as indications of interpersonal violence (Larsen 2015, 122). While there is no visible fracture, the evidence for bone infection suggests this man sustained a significant injury to the soft tissue that also involved the ulna and radius. This individual also suffered extensive osteoarthritis in the joints of both shoulders and elbows, suggesting a habitually active life.

A second individual, an adult of unknown sex (Grave 5, Burial 2 or 3), suffered a fracture of the orbital rim involving the frontal process of the zygomatic bone, with slight inward displacement (Pl. 67F). The commingling of the remains of Burials 2 and 3 in this grave make it impossible to determine if this fragment of bone is from a male or female, as a member of each sex is represented in the bones. This type of fracture commonly results from direct trauma with a focused point of impact such as a fist or club. The impact would have caused extensive hemorrhaging around the eye and possibly sensory nerve damage and anesthesia (numbness) of the cheek, nose, and upper lip (Banks and Brown 2001, 47–50). It was well healed at the time of death, indicating the injury was several years old. Facial fracture patterning has strong cultural influences and varies by sex and age as well as choice of weapon, but blows to the face are a common element of interpersonal violence in many populations due to the pain and disability that immediately follow the injury (Larsen 2015, 172–173).

Periosteal Bone Deposits or Infectious Disease

Infectious disease was the greatest threat to people in antiquity after the development of agriculture and permanent settlements. Yet most infectious diseases affect only soft tissues or have a rapid course, and the patient either recovers or dies before there is any chance of skeletal involvement. Diseases that affect the skeleton tend to be chronic diseases that may diminish the quality of life but do not cause death. As a result, the evidence for infectious disease at archaeological sites tends to be limited. It is most often seen in periosteal bone deposits, formed when the periosteal membrane that surrounds most cortical bone has been activated, producing new bone deposits on the external surfaces of the bones (Ortner 2003, 180–181).

Periosteal bone deposits on long bones are most likely to be associated with inflammation or infection and may or may not be associated with trauma (Ortner 2003, 206–207). The most commonly identified site for periosteal bone formation in the Kavousi sample was the tibia shaft, primarily on the anterior surface of the tibia, or shin bone. Three individuals at Vronda had periosteal bone deposits on their tibiae (Grave 3, Burial 2: juvenile female, 16–20 years; Grave 16, Burial 2: adult 30–40, unknown sex; Grave 20, Burial 7: adult male, 45–50). Another individual, one of the three commingled adults in Grave 21, Burials 4–6, had mild periosteal bone deposits on the femur shaft. In addition, the cremated infant in Grave 23, Burial 1, also showed periosteal bone on the long bone fragments, including an instance on a tibia (Pl. 68A). Periosteal bone on multiple bones in a neonatal infant can be the result of normal growth or a pathological process (Lewis 2007, 131–132). The fragmentary cremated remains of this infant make it impossible to evaluate this condition. Finally, there were also cases of individuals having periosteal bone formation on the maxilla and mandible, a phenomenon associated with dental abscesses and periodontal disease, as noted below in the section on dental disease.

Dental Disease

The dentition can provide valuable information on the health status of individuals and populations. In cremations, however, the dental enamel nearly always separates from the tooth roots and is so fragmented that recovery is nearly impossible, even with water sieving. Intact teeth are rare and appear nearly always as isolated finds in a burial, not as part of a set of teeth. There are no complete sets of dentition among the cremations and very few fragments of maxillae or mandibles that preserve associated teeth. As a result, the information on dental health is very limited at Vronda. However, isolated examples of dental pathologies make it clear that the inhabitants of the village suffered from the expected types of dental problems, even though it is impossible to estimate the rate of occurrence of any type of disease.

Dental Attrition and Abrasion

While dental attrition is the inevitable consequence of using the teeth for normal food mastication, the degree of wear may have important implications for evaluating diet. Extreme attrition and abrasion, particularly in younger individuals, can indicate either a diet with a high amount of grit, often from processing grains with stone grinders, or nonmasticatory use of the teeth as tools in processing other materials (Burnett 2016, 415–419).

Two individuals from Vronda (Grave 6 Burial 5; Grave 9 Burial 4) exhibited extreme dental attrition, with the incisors worn down into the roots.

Both of these individuals were older, 40–60 and 60+ years, but the degree of tooth loss was extreme even for these ages. This degree of wear on anterior teeth is unusual, and suggests the use of the teeth in processing or working with materials, not simple masticatory wear. Ironically, the loss of nearly all tooth enamel through wear resulted in preservation of the tooth morphology during cremation, as there was no enamel to break off during burning.

Caries

Caries, or tooth decay, is the most common form of dental disease in most populations. Rates of caries are, to some extent, inversely related to rates of dental attrition. They are also impacted by diet, occurring more frequently in populations consuming foods that are high in sugars and other carbohydrates (Hillson 2008, 313; Larsen 2015, 67–68). Unfortunately, the destruction of tooth enamel during cremation also destroyed the evidence for most of these lesions. Enough cases are preserved, however, to indicate that this common pathology was present at Vronda. In two individuals (Grave 26, Burial 1, an adult of unknown age and sex; Grave 30, Burial 5, a female of 35–39 years) a molar and a premolar were sufficiently preserved to show large caries destroying most of the tooth crowns. A third individual (Grave 21, Burial 3) had caries in three teeth, a mandibular molar and two maxillary incisors, probably a first and second incisor, in which the caries formed on the contiguous surfaces of the adjacent teeth at the joint between the crown and root. The location indicates that the gum tissue had receded, exposing this area of the tooth to bacteria. Caries in the incisors are unusual, generally indicative of particularly poor dental health (Hillson 2008, 313–314).

Peridontal Disease and Antemortem Tooth Loss

Dental disease involves not only the teeth themselves but also the surrounding soft tissues and bones. Poor oral health is manifested in the reduction first of the gums and then of the alveolar bone anchoring the teeth. This process can be followed by antemortem tooth loss, with or without associated dental caries (Hillson 1996, 263–265). Teeth can also be lost through deliberate or accidental trauma. The loss of teeth, whether to decay or trauma, is an important indicator of dental health. When teeth are lost during life, the supporting bone, the alveolus, quickly responds first by filling in the resulting hole where the tooth root was anchored, and then by resorbing, closing off the hole and creating a depression in the affected tooth row. As a result, it is readily apparent if a tooth was lost before death because of changes to the alveolar bone. The cremation of the bodies at Vronda damaged the facial bones and teeth severely. Two individuals showed clear evidence of periodontal disease. The alveolar bone of the maxilla and mandible of one individual (Grave 20, Burial 5) and the maxilla of another (Grave 30, Burial 5) had periosteal bone around tooth sockets, also indicating periodontal disease. Although very few skulls preserved evidence of antemortem tooth loss, one exception was that of an adult male over 60 years (Grave 28, Burial 8) from which more than half of a mandible was recovered. The preserved portion was completely edentulous, with extensive resorption of the alveolar bone, indicating that the man had been toothless for a considerable period of time before death.

Dental Abscess and Granulomata
Another manifestation of poor dental health is the presence of cists or cavities in the jaws. These normally form at the tips of the tooth roots either in response to inflammation due to periodontal disease or as a result of bacterial infection and caries in the tooth or surrounding tissues (Hillson 2008, 322–323). Three examples of periodontal disease appear at Vronda (Grave 19, Burial 4; Grave 20, Burial 5; Grave 28, Burial 6), and two of these (Grave 19, Burial 4; Grave 28, Burial 6) have dental abscesses (Pl. 68B). There is periosteal reactive bone around the lesions, indicating an active infection or inflammation at the time of death in both individuals.

Linear Enamel Hypoplasia
Teeth preserve a record of growth in infancy and early childhood. Because teeth do not remodel over a lifetime, they preserve their structure as initially created during the formation of the tooth. When this tooth formation process is interrupted by illness or stress, it can result in visible flaws in the tooth enamel. The flaws provide a record of the health events that lasts as long as the tooth survives. These growth interruptions take the form of thinner enamel, seen as horizontal grooves or rows of pits in the tooth crown, and are termed linear enamel hypoplasias (LEH; Hillson 2008, 302–303).

Here again at Vronda, the destruction of tooth enamel during the cremation process leaves a limited record of LEH. One neonatal infant cremation (Grave 23, Burial 1) preserves an unusual LEH on a deciduous tooth, which forms during pregnancy. This condition indicates a severe stress in maternal health that was passed on to the developing child. The fact that the infant died at around the time of full-term birth may be associated with this earlier stress. Another case involving multiple examples of LEH was preserved in the teeth of a five- to six-year-old child (Grave 10, Burial 1, an inhumation burial in a pithos). Very little of the skeleton was preserved, but the deciduous and permanent tooth crowns survived. A total of eight anterior teeth of the maxilla and mandible were affected, including all four mandibular incisors, the two left maxillary incisors, and both maxillary canines. The incisors begin forming around the time of birth and are complete by about three years. The canines begin forming at around 18 months and are complete by about five years (Schaefer, Black, and Scheuer 2009, 82–95). The locations of the LEH on this child's dentition suggest multiple health stresses before death occurred.

Hyperostosis Frontalis Interna
The Vronda population preserves evidence of other less common types of pathology. One condition that is not extremely rare but is not commonly noted in the archaeological literature is known as hyperostosis frontalis interna. The condition manifests as the irregular thickening of the internal surface of the frontal bone, which makes up the forehead and the upper portion of the eye orbits. The appearance can range from small smooth lumps to extensive ropy projections extending across the entire frontal squama. In modern clinical practice the disease is diagnosed most often in postmenopausal women. It is rare in men unless there is some hormonal anomaly. It has also been found in archaeological skeletal remains of men who were castrated. There are few clinical symptoms except for severe headaches in some individuals (Barber, Watt, and Rogers 1997, 158–162; She and Szakacs 2004, 207–208; Belcastro et al. 2011, 635–636).

Two cases of hyperostosis frontalis (Grave 3, Burial 1; Grave 5, Burial 1) have been observed. The skeleton from Grave 3 was an adult male, 20–40 years old at death (Pl. 68C). The identification of sex in this individual is secure, having been determined on the basis of the well-preserved but fragmentary cranium. The clear presentation of a case of HFI that can be scored as severe is remarkable. The disease is rare in men in the absence of a disruption of the normal male hormones, particularly androgen. In modern clinical practice, 58% of males undergoing a treatment for prostate cancer that includes a complete androgen block developed HFI, while the disease was found only in its mildest form in a healthy control group (May et al. 2010, 1334–1336). The presence of the disease may indicate that this individual suffered from hormonal anomalies. There were no other skeletal indicators, however, that would suggest he had been castrated (Belcastro et al. 2011, 633–634).

Remarkably, the second case of HFI identified at Vronda is also associated with an adult male, Grave 5 Burial 1. This man was 25–40 years old when he died, probably at the upper end of the age range. He had a milder case of HFI, but it is extensive on the right side of the frontal bone. This individual also has the only evidence of surgical intervention at Vronda. On the right side of his skull there is evidence for a trepanation.

Trepanation

The trepanation on the skull of Grave 5 Burial 1 is located high on the right parietal bone, behind the coronal suture. The surgery was accomplished using the scraping method, producing an oval depression 6.5 x 2.0 cm in size (Fig. 53). The incision was placed high on the parietal bone, avoiding both the temporal muscles and the cranial sutures, which have major blood vessels passing through them (for full description, see this vol., Ch. 3, pp. 74–75; Liston and Day 2009). If this man suffered from headaches as a result of his HFI (Bavazzano et al. 1970), the trepanation may have been an attempt to alleviate his discomfort. Alternatively, if the androgen deficiency that precipitated the HFI was caused by some other pathology that left no skeletal evidence, the trepanation may have been an attempt to treat that disease. The skeletal remains do not provide the answers.

Juvenile Bone Pathologies

The paleopathology of juvenile bone is somewhat more complicated than that of adults. It is difficult to distinguish normally growing immature bone from pathological immature bone, and the most common causes of infant and child mortality, such as viral or bacterial infections causing fever, respiratory distress, and diarrhea, leave no evidence on the bone. Nevertheless, the ascertainment of juvenile morbidity and mortality are critical factors in investigating the health of a population (Lewis 2007, 133–134; 2018, 2–10). Here again, cremation has further complicated the analyses, because small immature bones are less likely than those of adults to survive in identifiable form after burning and subsequent disturbance of graves through reuse. All but one of the infants and many of the older juveniles were not recognized during excavation, but only in sorting the residue from the water sieving. Cranial vault bone and long bone shafts were most likely to be recovered, while the bones that are made up primarily of trabecular bone, such as vertebral bodies and pelvic bones, were unlikely to survive. Regardless, two juveniles, one cremated and one inhumed, preserved unusual significant pathologies.

An infant (Grave 5, Burial 4), probably a full-term (40 weeks) neonate, has a lesion of unknown origin on the greater wing of the sphenoid (Pl. 68D). The lesion is oval, ca. 7 x 5 mm. The bone in this area is completely destroyed, with only bony spicules radiating out from the center of the lesion remaining. There is periosteal bone on other areas of the sphenoid fragment as well, suggesting either a comorbidity with an infectious disease or a process with both bone lysis and proliferation. Lacunae in the cranial vault of infants may originate either through anomalies in bone formation or through lytic processes destroying the bone. This lesion appears to be a failure of ossification of the membrane precursor of the sphenoid greater wing. There are a number of possible causes, including infantile myofibromatosis and Langerhans cell histiocytosis (LCH; Lewis 2018, 238–239, 267), the latter having also been identified in a second child at Vronda.

The second juvenile is an inhumed partial skeleton of a child with a dental age of six to seven years, the only burial in Grave 24. The cranial bones of the child have a number of lesions on the inner and outer tables of the bone, penetrating the diploë (Pl. 68E). In one lesion, located on a postmortem break, the entire thickness of the cranial bone has been destroyed. The lesions are located on both parietals, the frontal squama, and the upper surface of one eye orbit. In addition, there is extensive porosity of the inner and outer tables of the cranial bones.

Radiographs of these lesions were taken in Athens. The radiographs depict round or oval punched-out lesions, with little or no surrounding sclerosis of the bone. There are no visible lesions on the postcranial bone. This punched-out effect is seen in lesions associated with multiple myeloma and metastatic skull lesions. These, however, are much more common in adults than in young children. The appearance of the lesions on the Kavousi child, combined with the young age of the individual, may suggest a case of histiocytosis.

Langerhans cell histiocytosis develops when large numbers of Langerhans histiocyte cells aggregate in other tissues. When this occurs, the histiocytes are surrounded by an area of inflammation. Virtually any bone may be involved, but the most common sites are the cranial vault, the mandible, ribs, vertebrae, and the shafts of the femur and humerus. Radiographically, the lesions appear as sharply defined, round, radiolucent areas with a punched-out appearance. The lesions in LCH may affect the skin, liver, spleen, lung, and pituitary gland, as well as bone and marrow. In both conditions prognosis is ultimately poor, and in more severe forms death occurs before the age of one year (Khung et al. 2013, 569–571; Lewis 2018, 238–239). The radiographic and macroscopic appearance of the bone lesions of the child in Vronda Grave 24 resembles those of LCH. The disease does not appear to be inherited but is caused by somatic cell mutations—that is, mutations that occur after conception in the developing fetus or child. The possible presence of the disease in two juveniles at Vronda is noteworthy, but not impossible, as it is one of the most commonly identified pathologies in juvenile remains.

Family Groups

The cremated remains from Vronda provide very little opportunity to explore family groupings or relatedness among the population represented in the graves. Teeth generally provide the best chance of preserving DNA, but the teeth are shattered during cremation. Cremated bone can preserve DNA but only at combustion temperatures lower than those indicated by the calcined bone of most of the Vronda cremations (Wahl 2008, 152). Ancient DNA analyses were more aspiration than reality when the material was excavated and, as a result, the bones were handled by many people, ensuring that any DNA is probably thoroughly contaminated.

A group of morphological features with genetic bases, however, may offer some glimpse of patterning among the burials at Vronda. Nonmetric traits (also called morphoscopic traits) are normal variants of bone, particularly in the skull, that are thought to be heritable traits, although they may be influenced to some extent by environmental conditions including deliberate or unintentional cranial deformation (Konigsberg, Kohn, and Cheverud 1993, 43–44; Del Papa and Perez 2007, 257–258). Because these traits offer no known selective advantage, they are not subject to natural selection but are passed on from generation to generation. The traits exhibit patterning associated with ancestry, both in terms of major population groups and, potentially, of subgroups within a population (DiGangi and Hefner 2013, 136–137).

Nonmetric traits include variations in surface morphology (pits or notches), holes through the bone (foramina), the shape and orientation of endocranial features, and, most notably at Vronda, the presence of an extra suture, the metopic suture (Pl. 68F). The metopic suture is an inheritable cranial anomaly occurring in many populations, although there is definite geographic variation. The condition consists of the retention into adulthood of the medio-frontal suture, which normally disappears between birth and the age of two years. (Scheuer and Black 2000, 105). These nonmetric traits from Vronda were analyzed to see if there were patterns of expression among individual graves. The incomplete preservation and fragmentary nature of the crania made it impossible to score all of the traits on many crania. Too many cells in the data set are empty to allow us to produce a robust analysis of the distribution, so we can only point out some broad patterns in the data.

A grave-by-grave analysis exposed no patterns across the cemetery. However, when the graves were clustered by the houses within or adjacent to which they were located, a striking pattern emerged. Three of the traits occurred in over 50% of individuals in building cluster J-K. One trait was the presence above the ear of the suprameatal pit/spine, occurring on 10 of 17 individuals, or 59% (Pl. 68G). A second trait was the endocranial sagittal sulcus turning left (instead of right, as is normal) on eight of 11 individuals, or 73%. A third trait was the presence of the metopic suture on the frontal bone on 13 of 17 individuals, or 76%. Metopic sutures were also found, at much lower percentages, in both building complexes C-D (three of 17 individuals, or 18%) and I-O-N (one of 17 individuals, or 6%). All of the other traits found at such high levels in J-K were absent, or present in only a single individual, from the other building clusters. Only one other trait was rare in J-K but common in other building clusters: the presence of a supraorbital notch (instead of a foramen), which occurred in five out of 13 (38%) individuals from I-O-N but in only three of 13 individuals (23%) from J-K. The most commonly expressed trait in J-K, the metopic suture, was also found on two adults from the Vronda IX tholos tomb.

None of these traits are particularly rare in Europeans, but the cluster of traits in the graves found in the abandoned Buildings J and K, which share common walls, suggests that the persons buried here may have shared some common ancestry. As J-K is the cluster of buildings located at the top of the Vronda hill, and the associated graves were consistently richer in grave goods than other enclosures at Vronda, it seems likely that these were the burial places of an elite kinship group that retained possession or use of this building cluster long after the Vronda hilltop had been abandoned as a place of habitation. It is probably not too great a leap of interpretation to assume that other kinship groups likewise reused their former family house structures to bury their dead at Vronda. These other groups appear to have been less isolated genetically, sharing similar frequencies of the nonmetric traits.

Summary

The attributes of population structure and the pathological conditions observed among the Vronda skeletons give a remarkably detailed picture of the health status and lives of the people who were buried at the site. The village had a fairly typical age and sex distribution. Children were fragile, especially in their early years, and many families must have experienced the loss of one or more children, most often in infancy. Pregnancy, childbirth, and nursing were stressful for young women, and many died before reaching late middle age; few would have experienced menopause. Men generally had longer lives, with many more surviving past the age of 40, and there were a few who lived to be quite elderly. Most people were quite active, and many experienced injuries to their muscles and ligaments that would have been painful and temporarily limiting. However, the majority of these injuries probably did not result in permanent disability. Some people survived more extreme accidents that resulted in major fractures, but this degree of injury was rare. The medical care that was available provided sufficient treatment for broken bones to heal well, with few permanent effects. Conflict between individuals was also rare, or at least it seldom escalated to violence that caused broken bones.

If people lived long enough, they experienced the typical pains and conditions associated with advancing age. Joints became painful and inflamed, in the back, the hands, and other joints. Many people experienced dental decay and tooth loss. Some developed swollen, tender areas in their jaws, often at the base of teeth that had large cavities. These sores would occasionally have burst unpleasantly, but afterward the pain would have been less. One man, perhaps after suffering severe headaches, underwent an unusual surgery in which his skull was carefully scraped away across a large area. Whether this helped alleviate his symptoms is unclear, but he survived for many years after the surgery, probably with a significant scar on the side of his head. Although life at Vronda would have seemed precarious and unpleasant to many modern people, all in all the members of the population were well adapted to their environment, reasonably well nourished, and no more vulnerable to disease and injury than earlier or later villages in Greece.

6

Faunal and Botanical Remains

Lynn M. Snyder, David S. Reese, and Kimberly Flint-Hamilton

Animal Bones

Lynn M. Snyder

Approximately 3,400 animal bones (excluding those from the discard pit under Tomb X) and bone and tooth fragments were recovered from grave contexts, both tholos tombs (Table 2) and enclosure graves (Tables 4, 6–10), during the cleaning and excavation seasons at Vronda. Because of special water-sieving procedures instituted whenever a grave or pyre was encountered, nearly 90% of the remains, by count alone, consisted of tiny, unidentifiable bone and tooth fragments recovered from the water-sieving residue screens.

In both recovery and processing, faunal materials were treated somewhat differently than the remains recovered from nonmortuary related settlement habitation contexts. As with all excavations at Vronda, animal bones and teeth recognized during excavation were segregated and bagged separately in small paper bags labeled with date, excavator, and provenience information. These bags were then processed in the usual procedure for faunal materials (for details see Snyder 2016, 169–172).

Due to natural soil conditions and other environmental factors, the faunal assemblages from Vronda were in general moderately to severely eroded and broken, often masking evidence of human handling of the food remains from which they came. The shallow nature of the soil deposition on the Vronda ridge also contributed to bone breakage and erosion. Controlled screening tests in two areas of the excavated settlement confirmed that, as might be expected under such soil and depositional conditions, water sieving in the village context added little to the recovery of identifiable faunal materials (Lyman 1987; Snyder and Klippel 2000).

Identifiable bone and teeth elements were limited to some 340 specimens, nearly all of which were found during hand excavation. The tiny bone fragments captured in the water sieving residue screens were first examined by the physical anthropology team for recognizable human bone fragments. The remainder, all tiny, unidentifiable bone or tooth fragments, were presumed to be animal in origin and were counted, but they were not otherwise informative.

Of the identifiable materials, just over 65% came from domestic sheep (*Ovis aries*) or goats (*Capra hircus*). Possible domestic cattle bone fragments were recovered, and domestic pig (*Sus scrofa*) was represented by 32 specimens. Eleven fragments of domestic dog (*Canis familiaris*) bones or teeth were also recovered. The scattered remains of a number of native or commensal animals were noted, including small rodents or insectivores, rabbit or hare, a single bird bone, and several small vertebrae of a nonpoisonous snake. All these small animals were likely site visitors or intruders, and their presence was not directly related to the actions of the village inhabitants. The remains of fallow deer (*Dama dama*), nearly all heavily burned and calcined, represent a separate instance of direct association with burial contexts and practices.

Intrusive or Commensal Animals and General Village Debris

This category consists primarily of scattered, sometimes eroded, and generally unburned bones, as well as bone fragments and teeth of small animals and species not usually considered human food. In an archaeological context, a number of animals (snakes, small reptiles, small rodents) are identified as "commensal" (Reitz and Wing 1999, 115), that is, occurring naturally in the village or near the village environment and not brought to the assemblage by deliberate human actions such as hunting or harvesting of a domestic food resource (Reitz and Wing 1999, 113).

In addition, at a site such as Vronda that was occupied over an extended period of time, human actions such as food processing, consumption, and discard, as well as possible tool- and weapon-making processes, directly affected the distribution of animal bone debris. After the abandonment of the LM IIIC settlement, later human action, such as intrusive excavation and rebuilding associated with cemetery installations, later terrace building, and agricultural use, along with eventual natural slope and soil erosion, further affected the distribution of lost or discarded occupational debris.

The physical characteristics of the animal bones, teeth, and bone fragments from the graves that may indicate how this faunal material came to be incorporated in the mortuary context include physical location, lack of evidence of deliberate human modification in the form of cut or chop marks or burning, surface erosion due to exposure on the ground surface, trampling, rodent and small carnivore gnawing, and even root etching that takes place as plant roots draw nourishment from the bone itself (Hesse and Wapnish 1985, 23–26). Conversely, in some instances, extremely well-preserved bone surfaces may indicate more recent deposition by burrowing rodents or small predators.

Snake Species

Remains of a snake were recovered from the soil matrix of Grave 9 (V 5319.2, V 5319.4/5). Fourteen vertebrae, all heavily burned or calcined, were found in the flotation residue, and they probably belonged to one animal. The size and the absence of a hymal spine on these complete vertebrae indicate that the remains probably belonged to a small, nonpoisonous snake species. Multiple small rodent and insectivore remains were also found in the flotation residue from Grave 9 (V 5310.3, V 5312.1, V 5312.3, V 5312.4/5, V 5319.2). It is possible that the snake and numerous mice or shrews were drawn to the coolness of the stone enclosure and the voids between the stones. They may have been inadvertently burned by the cremation.

Small Rodents: Mice or Shrews

In addition to more than 400 small rodent bones found in the flotation residue from Grave 9 (V 5310.3, V 5312.1, V 5312.3, V 5312.4/5, V 5319.2), an unburned mouse mandible was recovered from Grave 12 (V 4505.3), and an isolated mouse or shrew long bone (a humerus) was recovered from Grave 36 (V 12807.2). Because of a lack of comparative materials during study seasons and the likelihood that these remains represented unassociated intruders, these specimens were noted and returned to the bone storage bags for potential later analyses.

The recovery of small rodent and insectivore remains from voids within stone-built structures, as well as in the interior of buried ceramic or metal containers, is not unusual. These remains are most likely to represent natural deaths or small predator prey naturally accumulating within the archaeological context.

Bird (Aves *Species*)

Bird remains are rare at Vronda (Snyder 2016, 175), and from the cemetery context only one bone fragment, an otherwise unidentifiable third phalange or talon fragment, was recovered. It came from the area of Grave 12 (V 4305.5). Ground birds, songbirds, and various small and large birds of prey frequent the area of the Vronda hill today. The origins of this single, unmodified fragment are unknown.

Domestic Dog (Canis familiaris)

Twelve domestic dog elements or element fragments (10 isolated teeth and two long bone fragments) were recovered from grave contexts. Individual isolated teeth, without associated cranial materials, were found in the areas of Graves 2 (V 12400.1), 13 (VN 205.10), and 21 (V 5348.4; V 5351.2). None of these isolated teeth or bone fragments show any signs of modification and were unburned. A single dog femur diaphysis fragment was also recovered from the area of Grave 21 (V 5349.2), and a segment of a right radius (front limb) was found in the area of Grave 5/11 (V 4016.1).

While a few dog bones bearing cut marks have been found at the nearby settlement sites of Kastro (Snyder and Klippel 2003) and Azoria (Haggis et al. 2004, 384; 2011a, 27; 2011b, 442, 448), they are rare, and there is no consistent evidence that dogs were a regular food source for any of the three closely associated villages. Multiple complete or nearly complete dog skeletons were recovered, however, from the fill of Tholos Tomb X at Vronda, a tomb that was robbed in antiquity and appears to have become the repository of discarded dog carcasses (Day 1984; see this vol., Ch. 2, p. 46). It seems likely that the scattered and unmodified dog remains from the Vronda cemetery are random fragments of redeposited village refuse or debris.

Hare or Rabbit (Leporidae)

Remains of rabbits were found in five grave contexts: Graves 4, 9, 10, 16, and 20. None of the recovered remains were burned or showed any evidence of human modification. The lack of burning and the mix of scattered cranial and limb bones within the graves suggests that these remains, too, most likely represent naturally occurring animals that were mixed into the grave either during the disturbance of building the pyre enclosure or use or cleaning of the enclosure, or, alternatively, by other actions of small predators at the site (but see discussion of Grave 10 below).

In three of the graves (Graves 4, 9, and 10) cranial tooth-bearing elements (maxilla or mandible) were present, along with postcranial limb bones. In Grave 9 a left mandible segment (V 5302.2) and right mandible segment (V 5310.1) that articulated (i.e., they came from the same animal) were found, as well as one right distal humerus (V 5312.2) and one left proximal ulna diaphysis segment (V 5324.1). Although scattered and minimal, the presence of articulating mandible segments, in addition to two front limb bone fragments, suggests that the scattered remains of a single whole animal may be represented. In Grave 4 a single right mandible (V 4009.1), which was very well preserved and appeared to be possibly a modern intrusion, and a single tibia (hind limb) diaphysis segment from an immature animal (V 4009.1 and 2) were recovered. In Grave 10 (V 4804.2 and 3) a partial left maxilla (upper tooth row) fragment and one additional cranial fragment, along with femur and tibia diaphysis fragments (hind limb), two metapodials and one phalange (foot element), were recovered. While such scattered elements do not necessarily indicate that the animal was originally whole, the two major hind limb element fragments and foot elements suggest that the remains of a rabbit hind leg, possibly food or food debris, may have been deposited or discarded in this area.

A single rabbit femur diaphysis segment (V 6204.1) was the only identifiable animal bone recovered from the small assemblage of animal bone from Grave 16. In Grave 20 two rabbit bones were found: one right proximal scapula (shoulder bone) fragment (V 4701.2) and a single second phalange, or toe bone (V 4709.2).

Domestic Animals: Pig, Cow, Sheep, and Goat

The remains of domestic animals occur in both settlement and cemetery contexts at Vronda. The bones and teeth of domestic pigs are relatively few but widespread throughout the cemetery. Interpretation of their possible importance in the Vronda graves, however, is not straightforward. Bone fragments tentatively identified as domestic cattle are rare and generally problematic. Sheep and/or goat are the most abundant taxa found in both settlement and cemetery deposits, and there are clear indications that at least some of these remains were deliberately placed in the cemetery context.

Domestic Pig (Sus scrofa)

The remains of domestic pig are widespread, although not abundant, in the Vronda graves, occurring in 12 grave assemblages. Their direct association with burial practices and ritual, however, is in many cases problematic. All parts of the pig skeleton are represented, with cranial materials and teeth accounting for nearly half the identified materials.

The majority of identified pig bones and teeth (28 specimens) are unburned, and a number (11 specimens) show erosion and/or root etching, suggesting either long term exposure on the ground surface or near surface burial (Hesse and Wapnish 1985, 24). Eight specimens, one tooth, one maxillary fragment, and six limb bone fragments are partially or heavily burned.

Of the eight heated or burned elements, one tooth fragment and a right maxilla/frontal fragment were recovered from Grave 12. Additional unburned teeth and tooth fragments from the same grave assemblage may belong to this same cranial element. One humerus diaphysis segment, unburned, was also recovered from this grave. Other burned limb elements were recovered from Grave 6 (a right tibia diaphysis segment), Grave 20 (a burned femur diaphysis fragment), Grave 21 (one juvenile femur diaphysis fragment), Grave 30 (fragments of a right distal humerus and left distal radius), and Grave 32/25 (a left proximal scapula fragment).

If the burned and some of the unburned pig elements are associated with cemetery activities, the predominance of bones representing meaty upper limb bone elements (fourteen specimens) over lower limb and foot elements (six specimens), along with the lack of a clear preference for one body side over the other, suggests that in scattered instances individual meal portions, rather than whole animals, whole limbs, or major limb segments, were thrown or placed in the graves.

The presence of scattered cranial elements and teeth (16 specimens), together with surface erosion and root etching on many of the identified pig specimens, seems to indicate that some of the pig remains may simply be part of general settlement refuse debris that inadvertently became part of the grave fill deposits.

Domestic Cow (Bos taurus)

As in the Vronda settlement faunal assemblages, the remains of domestic cow are very rare, and in the cemetery context there is no clear evidence that food or body portions of this animal were part of the burial ritual. Two isolated cow teeth were recovered during excavation of the Vronda burials. A lower fourth premolar was found in the ashy soil (V 4012.4) of Grave 5/11, and a left upper second molar (V 10801.1) was found in Grave 6. The remaining five bone fragments tentatively identified as cow were so fragmentary that in all instances the identification was characterized as *Sus/Bos*, Cervidae/*Bos*, or *Bos*? to indicate that the fragment was identifiable to body element and recognized as coming from an animal of medium to large body size. These bone fragments came from Grave 21 (an innominate fragment), Grave 24 (a metapodial condyle fragment), Grave 30 (a solitary distal humerus epiphysis and one humerus diaphysis fragment), and Grave 31 (one atlas, or first vertebra, fragment).

The limb bone elements identified in Graves 21 and 30 and the vertebra fragment in Grave 31 were burned or calcined, and in these three cases it could be argued that the burning indicates direct association with the burial or ritual process. However, their tentative identification as domestic cow could be inaccurate, and these broken and burned fragments could represent the remains of a large ram, buck goat, or fallow deer.

Sheep (Ovis aries) and Goat (Capra hircus)

By far the most commonly occurring animal bone remains in both the Vronda LM IIIC settlement (Snyder 2016) and the grave assemblages are those of domestic sheep and goats. Sheep and goats were herded by Cretan villagers throughout the Minoan and post-Minoan periods in the area, providing both food (meat, milk) and raw materials for textile and tool production (wool, hair, hides, and bone). In the Vronda cemetery context, however, these animals appear in some cases to have served an additional purpose, that is, as ritual meals or offerings placed in the graves or on the pyres.

Because of the great similarity in body size and skeletal morphology between sheep and goats, it is often difficult to distinguish individual skeletal elements as either one or the other, particularly when the recovered archaeological remains have become fragmented and/or eroded by either human activities (butchery, cooking, and disposal) or postdiscard burial and weathering (taphonomic processes). Furthermore, extreme temperatures such as those commonly reached in pyre or cremation burials (Holck 2008, 30–31) further reduce the bone matrix, leading to shrinkage, cracking, splintering, and warping or distortion of the original bone shape and structure. Thus, nearly all sheep or goat bones and bone and tooth fragments recovered from grave contexts at the Vronda cremation cemetery were identified simply as sheep/goat. In only two instances, both in Grave 9, could a more exact identification, that of domestic sheep, be made. All parts of the sheep or goat skeleton are at least minimally represented in the faunal assemblages associated with the Vronda cemetery. In some cases, bones and bone fragments that are scattered, unburned, and sometimes heavily eroded, leached, and root etched appear to be simply the remains of scattered settlement debris, with no deliberate association with the pyres or burials.

In a number of the Vronda graves, however, two aspects of the bones suggest a direct ritual association with the burial context: burning or charring and the representation of body parts. Both burned and unburned sheep or goat bones were recovered from grave contexts. It is notable that in these contexts the high temperatures produced by the fires left the bones heavily burned and calcined, a condition which, while causing cracking and distortion, also contributed to the preservation of the bones, including their surfaces. In many cases the apparent annealing of the bone structure made the surviving fragments nearly impervious to the corrosive effects of soil chemistry and ground water leaching (Holck 2008, 112–113).

In general, burned and unburned sheep or goat bones were recovered from grave contexts in approximately even proportions. Excluding isolated teeth and occasional rib and vertebra fragments that could not be identified to specific animal species and were unquantifiable for element or animal count, unburned bones and bone fragments (71 specimens) slightly outnumbered those showing complete or partial burning or heating (61 specimens). The number of unburned specimens must surely include some bones present simply as unassociated village debris. It is likely, however, that heavy burning and calcification of sheep and goat bones is a strong indicator of direct association with pyre burning and burial events, and therefore the number of burned bones from these contexts seems highly significant and interpretable.

One aspect of ritual meals and offerings that has been shown to have strong patterning is the body portion of the sacrificial animal chosen for offering to the gods or to the deceased (Ekroth 2017, 15). In the Vronda grave assemblages, disregarding isolated teeth, rib, and vertebra fragments, lower limb elements greatly outnumber upper limb and cranial elements. There were 12 specimens of cranial fragments and 17 specimens of upper limb elements or fragments, compared with 85 examples of lower front and hind limbs and 16 specimens of hooves.

These patterns of sacrifice and/or offerings are illustrated in several grave and pyre contexts. In Grave 1 nearly all identified sheep or goat bone was heavily burned and calcined, and the remains were dominated by bones of the lower hind limb (distal tibia, metatarsal, phalanges), accompanied by one element fragment (proximal metacarpal) from the lower front limb. Further evidence of deliberate grave offerings in Grave 1 can be seen in a single deer metatarsal (see discussion of Cervidae, below). Although not burned, the sheep or goat bones from Grave 4 are limited to one fragment from a lower front limb and several fragmentary elements from the lower back limbs of a young sheep or goat. While the majority of animal bone recovered in association with the badly disturbed Grave 5 was unburned, a single burned lower hind limb element, a central and fourth tarsal, was found in the lower ashy soil. Grave 6 yielded unburned fragments of both lower front and hind limbs, along with fragments of deer antler that showed evidence of deliberate modification (see Cervidae, below).

Grave 9 shows perhaps the clearest patterning in the recovered sheep or goat remains. From the area of Burials 5, 6, and 7 a heavily burned lower leg is represented by a left astragalus from a sheep (*Ovis aries*) in addition to a patella (knee joint) and proximal sesamoid (foot bone). In addition, a burned left innominate (pelvis) fragment indicates the possibility that at least part of the upper portion of this hind limb was also included in the grave. A second calcined left astragalus, also identifiable as coming from a sheep, and a burned right astragalus, a right distal tibia fragment, and a right second and third carpal, identified more generally as sheep or goat, indicate that at least two and probably three animals are represented in the sacrificial meal or offering associated with Burial 4 (V 5313, V 5314). A heavily burned right patella and right proximal tibia diaphysis fragment, indicating portions of a lower right hind leg, were recovered from the area of Burial 1.

Grave 12 produced the heavily burned/calcined bones of both deer (see discussion below) and sheep or goat. Both upper and lower portions of the front limb are represented by a single scapula fragment, one humerus diaphysis fragment, one radius fragment, and one proximal metacarpal fragment, all unburned. Hind limb elements include unburned innominate fragments and fragments of a femur, a distal tibia, and a calcaneum. In addition, concentrated in the area of V 4805.3 and V 4805.5 were burned or partially burned lower leg elements including fragments of a distal tibia, left and right calcanea, and a left proximal metatarsal. This area also produced a heavily burned central and fourth deer tarsal and associated left metatarsal (V 4805.2), along with humanly modified deer antler and beam segments (see below).

Both burned and unburned sheep or goat bones were recovered from the matrix of Grave 20. Other than one proximal humerus fragment that was unburned, all the remaining front limb bone fragments represent the lower part of the leg: right distal humerus and left second and third carpal, both burned, and another unburned left second and third carpal. Recovered lower hind limb elements include a right calcaneum, right and left patellae (knee joint)—one burned, one unburned—and unburned fragments of a right calcaneum and a proximal metatarsal.

The animal bone assemblage recovered from the lower levels of Grave 26 (V 8731) is unusual in that a whole sheep or goat carcass that was partially burned appears to have been deposited in the area. Left and right elements of both front and hind limbs were recovered, along with cranial elements and rib and vertebra fragments. Some of these remains were heavily burned, others were partially burned or heated, and some showed no signs of burning (Pls. 69A, 69B). Articulating front left leg fragments (distal radius and associated carpals) show partial burning, with the heavier burning toward the proximal end of the radius. The distal end of this element and the associated carpals show little or no burning or heating. Whether these remains represent an animal sacrifice is unclear. The apparent burning of a whole animal in this instance is unique in the Vronda cemetery assemblages.

There is little animal bone from Grave 27, but a single sheep or goat proximal tibia fragment (knee joint area) that is heavily burned and calcined may represent a lower left leg. This grave also produced one humanly modified deer antler fragment (see below). Grave 34 produced one heavily burned sheep or goat metatarsal diaphysis fragment, along with one first phalange fragment and two tibia fragments, all of which were unburned. The distal tibia diaphysis fragment shows cut marks on its medial face, indicating the removal of the lower portion of the leg, and it is possible that these fragments, although unburned, are part of a lower leg segment placed in the grave but only partially consumed by the pyre fire.

Nondomesticated Animals

Fallow Deer (Dama dama)

Remains of fallow deer are rare in the Vronda cemetery assemblage, occurring in only five graves (Graves 1, 6, 12, 21, and 27). Within these graves, fallow deer are represented exclusively by antler beam, tine, and palmate antler fragments, with two exceptions (Graves 1 and 12). The presence of antler fragments, most showing evidence of modification in the form of cutting, scraping, hollowing, and piercing, suggests that the majority of these remains represent either broken tools or tool handles, possible decorative plating, or manufacturing debris.

The fallow deer is represented on Crete by modern populations in the area of Chania. They also appear in prehistoric archaeological remains recovered from a variety of sites on the island, for example, in Neolithic levels at Knossos and, more frequently, in Bronze and Early Iron Age assemblages near Chania (Moody 2012, 243–246), Mochlos

(Reese 2004), Kavousi Kastro (Snyder and Klippel 2003), and also Azoria in the Archaic period (Dibble 2017). Modern research suggests that while never domesticated, these animals were introduced to Crete at least twice as animals that were most likely released and hunted—in the Neolithic and again in the Late Bronze and Early Iron Ages (Moody 2012, 245).

The majority of deer remains in the graves come from the antlers, and the presence of antler fragments might be taken as evidence of hunting by the inhabitants of the area. Alternatively, because antlers are shed by males each year (Hesse and Wapnish 1985, 75), the antlers could have been recovered rather than hunted, collected for use as raw material for tools, tool handles, decorative plating, or other purposes. The presence of a fragmented metatarsal and several additional, heavily burned and calcined lower limb element fragments in one grave, together with one complete but fragmentary metatarsal in another (Graves 1 and 12), however, indicates that live animals were present in the area (or traded across the island) and were perhaps sometimes taken either by hunting or natural death.

A single left proximal metatarsal, heavily burned and fragmented, was recovered from the area of Grave 1 (V 805.2/3, V 805.3). Further fragments from the left lower limb (distal tibia, distal metapodial) and one left proximal metacarpal fragment—all heavily calcined and burned—may also be from the same animal. The extensive breakage and distortion of the bone fragments from the high temperatures of the pyre make more exact identifications impossible, and although these fragments were identified tentatively as deer, they also may be sheep or goat.

Antler fragments recovered from Grave 6 include an unsided beam segment (V 10819.4) that had been cut at one end, faceted, and scraped. Additional fitting and nonrefitting fragments of antler were also recovered with this heavily calcined segment. Another tine segment (V 10821.1) that was also heavily burned and appears to have been hollowed may also have been a handle fragment.

Grave 12 contained both beam and palmate antler fragments. A single large beam segment has been shaped by faceting on one end and possibly cut and smoothed at the other. Three additional, nonjoining segments do not show obvious modification and have broken edges. The flatter and wider palmate portions of antler also do not show obvious evidence of modification, but their deliberate placement in the grave seems obvious. Finally, in this grave a nearly complete deer left metatarsal, with one associated/articulating central and fourth tarsal is heavily burned and calcined (Pl. 69C). This element shows clear cut marks above the distal condyles on the dorsal surface, probably indicating separation of the lower back limb just above the phalanges and hoof. As with the palmate antler fragments, the ritual meaning of inclusion in the grave is unclear, but it is possible that these fragments represent raw materials associated with tool and/or tool handle production by one of the individuals placed in the grave.

A single antler beam segment from Grave 21 shows one cut and scraped or worn end and may be part of a bone handle or possibly a burnishing or shaping tool used in pottery production. A very fragmentary left pubis fragment (from a left innominate or hip bone) was tentatively identified, based on size and general morphology, as Cervidae or *Bos* and may also be from a fallow deer.

A single antler beam fragment, broken on all edges and possibly split, was recovered from Grave 27. This element is pierced by one large, very symmetrical round hole, approximately 0.5 cm in diameter. Similar tools, more often made from large ungulate rib shaft segments, are commonly found in North American Plains Indian archeological and ethnological contexts, often with multiple well-worn holes placed at intervals along the shaft. Historically, these bison rib tools were used as arrow shaft straighteners to smooth small irregularities from wooden arrow shafts. The specimen from Grave 27, however, could also have been a fragment of inlay for a sword or knife handle.

Marine Shells

David S. Reese

Ten shells were found in the tholos tombs (Table 3). Among those recovered were three limpets (*Patella*), four dog cockles *(Glycymeris)*, one murex (*Hexaplex*), one topshell (*Phorcus*), and one trough shell (*Mactra*). The six shells from the enclosure burials come from badly disturbed deposits and are probably chance items, although three could have been strung as ornaments (Table 5). The shells are: two *Patella*, one *Hexaplex*, one *Phorcus*, and one vermetid (which could be strung). Shells have been found in other burials of the EIA on Crete, but they are not plentiful. At Knossos, the LPG Tomb XI at Fortetsa produced a cockle covered in gold foil (Brock 1957, 18, 197, pl. 13; Reese 2000, 630). Several tombs in the North Cemetery contained marine shells: *Spondylus* in Tomb 40 (Evely 1996, 635–636; Reese 2000, 638), *Patella* in Tomb 60 (Evely 1996, 635; Reese 2000, 624), *Hexaplex* in Tombs 75 and 104 (Evely 1996, 635; Reese 2000, 626), *Dentalium* in Tomb 100 (Evely 1996, 635–636; Reese 2000, 639), *Lima* in Tomb 107 (Evely 1996, 635–636; Reese 2000, 638), a cockle in Tomb 132 (Evely 1996, 636; Reese 2000, 630), and a *Glycymeris* in Tomb 294 (Evely 1996, 636; Reese 2000, 627).

Palaeobotanical Remains

Kimberly Flint-Hamilton

General observations on the palaeoethnobotany of Vronda have been included in the discussion of the LM IIIC settlement (Flint-Hamilton 2016), but some observations can be made about the botanical remains from the cremation enclosures on the site (Table 13). The botanical remains from the cremations were plentiful for several reasons. The carbonization from the burning preserved more remains, and although later disturbed, the enclosures were covered over and did not remain open in the way the LM IIIC abandoned houses did. Finally, all of the soil from the enclosures was run through a flotation device, resulting in a larger sample than was found within the houses. Species encountered include most commonly arboreal seeds and fruits (grape and olive, with occasional wild pistachio), legumes (lentil, bitter vetch, grass pea, pea, and unidentified legumes), grains (barley and undetermined grain), as well as wild species (fool's parsley, wild buckwheat, corn or field gromwell, and small medick).

Arboreal Seeds and Fruits

Grape (Vitis vinifera)

Grapes comprise the most plentiful botanical remains, with 120 examples from eight graves (Graves 9, 15, 20, 21, 23, 26, 28, and 36). Twenty-five of these were whole or nearly whole pips, 12 were fragments of the pips, 82 were fragments of the fruits, and one was a fragment of the stem.

Olive (Olea europaea)

Olive is the second most common of the botanical remains. Four graves (Graves 9, 20, 21, and 23) produced 12 examples (one in nine fragments), of which only the one from Grave 23 was nearly whole.

Pistachio (Pistacia vera)

Two whole wild pistachios were found, one in Grave 20, the other in Grave 21.

Gramineae

Grains were uncommon in the graves, appearing in only two enclosures. Grave 21 produced a whole barley caryopsis (*Hordeum vulgare* s.l.), while a spikelet fragment of unidentifiable grain came from Grave 19.

Legumes

Legumes were somewhat more common than grains, appearing in nine graves (Graves 9, 10, 12, 17, 20, 21, 23, 26, and 28). Nine of these were unidentifiable legumes, three were peas, four were lentils, one was bitter vetch, one was vetch, and another was grass pea. The peas and lentils would have been foodstuffs, while the vetches and grass pea were used more commonly for animal fodder.

Wild Species

Wild plant species occurred in eleven graves (Graves 9, 15, 17, 19, 20, 21, 23, 24, 26, 28, 34). Fool's parsley (*Aethusa cynapium* L.) is the most common of the wild species, and forty-eight examples were found. Fool's parsley is not edible by humans or animals, but it may have a homeopathic use (Flint-Hamilton 2016, 192). Small medick (*Medicago* sp.) appeared in four of the graves; it may have been used for animal fodder (Flint-Hamilton 2016, 191–192), but in the grave context its occurrence is probably not deliberate. A single example of wild buckwheat (*Polygonum convolvulus* L.) and one of field gromwell (*Lithospermum arvense* L.) occurred in Graves 19 and 23, respectively (Flint-Hamilton 2016, 191); these are most likely to have been weeds that came into the graves accidentally.

Discussion

Many of the species found in the cremations may have been present there by chance. This is true particularly of the wild species, which may have grown in the vicinity of the Vronda ridge. The olives found within the graves may have been deliberate offerings for the deceased, possibly contained within some of the associated storage vessels, or they could represent remains of the funeral meal. It is also possible that they were contained within the fuel for the pyre; olive wood has been identified in some of the enclosures, and, in addition, the olive jift may have been added to the fire. The olive fruit might thus have been added with the fuel accidentally. The most common species found in the graves was grape. Grapes may have been deposited either fresh or dried as offerings to the deceased or divinities in bowls or storage vessels, or they may have constituted remains of the funeral meal. The same can be said of the other edible species (pistachio, legumes, and grains).

There is little evidence for plant remains in burials of EIA Crete or in the Aegean generally, largely because most graves were excavated before flotation and sieving became common archaeological practices. The North Cemetery at Knossos produced some olive pips and fruit, some possible grains, and a large number of fenugreek seeds (Evely 1996, 635–636); the majority of these were found in later tombs and may represent a change in burial customs at that cemetery. Early Iron Age burials in Athens produced figs and grapes that have been interpreted as part of a funeral meal or as offerings (Papadopoulos and Smithson 2017, 683–684). More species were recovered from the EIA graves at Torone, including *prunus spinosa*, grapes, barley and other cereals, and pulses such as lentil, broad bean, and bitter vetch (Papadopoulos 2005, 339–342). These have been interpreted as grave goods.

7

Funerary Architecture

Leslie Preston Day

The cemeteries at Vronda include two different types of built tombs, beehive-shaped tholoi and stone-lined enclosures. The two forms overlapped in use but probably not in construction. The tholos tombs were earlier and contained a good deal of SM and EPG material. As most of them did not encroach upon the buildings of the LM IIIC settlement, some might have been contemporary with it, but there was one clear exception to this placement, Tholos VIII, which was constructed into the remains of Building L (Fig. 4). The tholos tombs continued to be used sporadically into the LG period, with some burials overlapping chronologically with the earlier enclosure graves. The earliest material in the enclosure graves, however, belongs to the PG period, although most of the enclosures seem to be of LG date and later. The latest burials in the enclosure graves were made in the LO period. The enclosures were built directly on top of or even within the LM IIIC buildings.

Tholos Tombs

The 11 known tholos tombs at Vronda lie scattered around the edges of the ridge to the north and west of the LM IIIC settlement and farther away to the north (Fig. 4). Five tombs are west of the settlement (IV–VII, and XI), and with two exceptions (VII, XI) they are situated well beyond its known limits. On the north, one tomb cuts into Building L-M (VIII), while five more lie to the north (I–III, IX, X), two of them (IX, X) at a considerable distance (Fig. 6; Pl. 2). They appear in clusters or groups: Tombs I, II, and probably III (which was not located) are all on a terrace between 414 and 416 m asl. Although Tomb VIII is some distance from these and higher (420–421 m asl), it may belong to the same cluster. Another cluster on the west includes Tombs IV, V, VI, XI, and possibly VII; Tombs V and VI are between 414 and 415 m asl, while IV and XI are on the 417 m asl contour line (416–418 m asl). Tomb X is apparently a singleton, located ca. 60 m north of Tombs I and II at 405–406 m asl, while Tomb IX is farthest away (150 m north of Tomb X) at 381–382 m asl (Fig. 6).

All of the tombs are similar in size, date, and construction (Table 14). All belong to the small type of tholos found on Crete (Eaby 2007, 201–202), particularly in the eastern part of the island, and there are no examples of the larger type, which is known in the Kavousi area only at Skouriasmenos and possibly Aloni (Boyd 1901, 143–148; Gesell, Day, and Coulson 1983, 412–413). Although not located, from Boyd's description and measurements Tomb III seems to have been much like the others at Vronda. None of the extant tombs were fully preserved. Tomb V was the most complete, with a preserved height of 1.74 m in six to seven courses. Of the tombs whose chambers were still preserved, Tomb VIII showed the poorest preservation, measuring only 0.50 m high in two courses. This tholos was further disturbed and filled in after Boyd's time for dwellings or as a result of agricultural activities. The bottom measurements of the chambers of the tombs ranged in length and width from 1.30 to 2.00 m.

None of the tholos tombs were freestanding. They were constructed by digging into the slopes of the ridge, and as almost all were built at least partly into the hillside, they lie on major contour lines. Only Tomb V was dug into a level area. Often the tombs were cut into the local marl, called *tsakali*, which is soft and easy to dig. Its white color shows clearly against the brown of the soils within and around the tombs. Stones were used to lay out the ground plan, which could be square (Tombs III, V, VIII, IX, XI), oval (II, IV, VI), round (I), or even horseshoe-shaped, that is, with one oval end and a squared side near the entrance (X; Fig. 157). Limestone was the preferred building material for the lowest courses, particularly around the entrances. The vault was then built up in rough courses, using primarily local breccia (brecciated dolomite; see Klein and Glowacki 2016, 2–3) but also some limestone, with small amounts of mud mortar to keep the stones in place (Fig. 158). When the ground plan of a tomb was rectilinear (V, IX), the builders began to round out the corners for the vault in the second course. Each course was set inward from the one below until the diameter was small enough to be closed with a either a capstone or a large, flat stone. Because none of the tombs were preserved up to the top, it is unclear which form of roofing was used. In Tomb V, the courses rose to a level surface that, when closed off, could have served as a pavement, possibly for a postfunerary ritual or to hold a marker. None of the other tombs are well enough preserved to determine if this was a regular feature at Vronda.

The floors of the tomb chambers were simple: earth laid over the *tsakali* or breccia bedrock. No paving was found in any of them. The floors of the entranceways or stomia could, however, be paved with flat stones, as in Tombs I and II. The floor of the stomion was often higher than that in the tomb and sloped down into it, as in Tombs II, IV, V, and VI, but it could also be at the same level (I, VIII, X).

All of the tombs were provided with an entranceway or stomion, each with an elaborately constructed facade on the exterior. Some of the tombs have their entrances parallel to the slopes of the terraces on which they rest (Tombs I, V, VI, XI), but the entrances of others run perpendicular to the slopes (II, IV, VII, VIII, X); at least two of these tombs are dug deeply into the hillside (IV, X). There is no clear pattern in the orientation of the stomia. There were two examples each facing west, northwest, southwest, or north; none of the preserved examples, however, faced east. The stomia ranged in length from 0.64 to 1.14 m, in width from 0.56 to 0.86 m, and in height from 0.50 to 0.60 m, although Boyd gives a height of 0.80 for the stomion of the now missing Tomb III. The lintel of the stomion was generally one or more large flat slabs of limestone, ranging in width from 0.75 to 1.04 m. The entranceways, which were not disturbed or removed by Boyd, had been filled and sealed with soil and two or three large, flat slabs.

Most of the tombs had elaborate facades (Tombs II, IV, V, VI, XI). Three facades had at least one course of stones above the lintel blocks (II, VI, XI), but the other two were more elaborate. Tomb V had a tall facade with three courses of limestone blocks above the lintel. Tomb IV had at least two courses of mixed breccia and limestone that stood above the lintel and continued north of the stomion to meet a wall built on the north side of the tholos, which created a small court in front of the tomb. These facades could have served as a form of display, an indicator of real or desired social status or wealth (Eaby 2007, 211), and they may have stayed uncovered or visible not only during the burial but also for postfunerary rituals.

Although the dromos was common on tholos tombs elsewhere on Crete (Eaby 2007, 211), none of the Vronda tombs has a true dromos. Tomb I has an entryway with a stone lining, which runs about 1.5 m west of the stomion. Eaby (2007, 212) considers this feature an extended stomion rather than a true dromos; if it were an extended stomion, however, then it would have been covered with roofing slabs, for which there is now no evidence. Instead of a dromos, each of the tombs is provided with a small pit dug into the soil or down to bedrock in front of the stomion, and we have labeled this a pseudo-dromos (Tombs I, II, IV–VI, VIII, XI). These pseudo-dromoi are generally slightly wider than the stomia and of varying lengths (Table 14). They vary in shape, depending on the soil conditions and the contours of the bedrock. They can be roughly rectangular or oval, measuring 0.63–1.60 m in length and 0.63–1.22 m in width. Such a pit was needed to allow for entrance into the tomb. The bottoms of these pits were generally at the same level as the floor of the stomion.

The pseudo-dromoi of many of the tombs had not been disturbed or excavated prior to the work of the Kavousi Project, and they share a common feature. They had been filled in with earth, then large stones were placed in them fairly flat and at the level of the bottom of the lintel (e.g., Pls. 6C, 11D), creating a sort of paved surface. It is possible that the pits were left open at this level for a period of time, perhaps for postfunerary rituals. The fill above these flat stones often contained fragments of drinking vessels and kraters, which may have been the remains of such rituals. It is also possible that the pottery was simply in the soil with which the pits were later filled, as suggested by the fragmentary nature of the pottery and its early date. Most of the fragments resemble material from the LM IIIC settlement rather than the pottery recovered from within the tombs. The pit was eventually filled in completely, and a pile of stones was placed over its top, marking the location of the entrance to the tomb.

The tombs were generally used on more than one occasion for what appear to have been family burials, as can be seen from the number of individuals found (one to six), their ages and sexes (both sexes and all ages, including children), and the long range of dates of the pottery (SM to G) found in them.

The tombs must have been opened for later burials, but it is not certain if the pits in front and the doorways were opened on each occasion. It has been suggested that the entrances are too small to allow for the introduction of a body (Eaby 2007, 209), and the burials may have been made by removing the capstone or covering slab and dropping the body within, as was clearly the case at nearby Azoria (pers. comm., M. Liston). Nevertheless, the pits do provide sufficient space for individuals to enter through the doorway or for bodies to be introduced, although it would be a tight squeeze. The facades may have been uncovered for each burial to serve as an impressive backdrop for the burial ritual.

There has been much scholarly debate over the origin of this small Cretan tholos tomb type (for the arguments, see Eaby 2007, 197–202; Day et al. 2016, 229). Tholoi were, of course, common in the EM and MM periods on Crete, particularly in the south part of the island. These early tombs were large, constructed above ground, and had low doorways like those of the Vronda tholoi; not all of them were certainly vaulted (Eaby 2007, 198). The Mycenaean form of tholos, which may have derived from or been influenced by the earlier Cretan type, was also large, but was cut into a hillside, corbeled, and provided with a long dromos and tall stomion. The postpalatial and EIA tholos tombs on Crete are more similar to mainland types. The EIA tholoi are generally smaller, although a larger type exists (Eaby 2007, 201–202). Some of the small tholoi (e.g., at Karphi) are provided with dromoi, as seen with the mainland tombs, but they are generally short and do not incline inward toward the top. Although there are some mainland features in the architecture of the Vronda tholoi (the elaborate entrance, the corbeling), their size and form suggest quite different burial rituals from those practiced on the mainland (Boyd 2016). The Mycenaean tholoi, with their long dromoi, were arranged for the procession of participants into the tomb, while the Cretan EIA tombs did not allow for rituals within the chamber, which was too small to accommodate more than one or two individuals at a time. Instead, the Vronda tholoi were set up with facades that did not facilitate entry and allowed only viewing of ceremonies conducted outside the tomb itself.

Enclosure Graves

Of the 36 graves recognized as containing human remains during the 1984 cleaning and 1987–1992 excavations at Vronda (Table 15), 22 are stone-lined enclosures, six can be identified as dumps from a nearby enclosure (Graves 7, 11, 14, 22, 25, 33), two are possible pyre sites (Graves 13, 31), one is a circular pit (Grave 8), one was simply a body dumped into the remains of an earlier building without accompanying grave goods (Grave 24), another seems to be a dump of material from a grave elsewhere (Grave 29), and three contained human remains with no associated architecture (Graves 2, 35, 37) and may represent discard deposits. In addition, Boyd may have uncovered another grave on top of the summit in the area of Building A-B, possibly the same remains labeled Grave 37 or perhaps a different burial.

The enclosure burials were made in stone-lined structures that served both to contain the pyre and to serve as the final resting place for the dead. These enclosures are generally rectangular, with the exception of Grave 23, which is more oval than rectangular, and Grave 15, which is roughly circular (Fig. 4). The rectangular enclosures are remarkably consistent in size and proportions, the majority measuring 1.50–2.00 m in length and 0.95–1.25 m in width. In general the width measures 50% to 70% of the length. Most of the graves that cluster within LM IIIC Buildings C-D and J-K have widths that are 50%–60% of their lengths. Grave 10, which was used for the burial of a child in a pithos, is extraordinarily narrow for its length, possibly because it did not contain a pyre.

Two graves (19 and 28), both of which lie on the western slope of the ridge, are unusually wide for their length. The configuration of Grave 19 may have been influenced by the presence of a bench along the east wall of Room G1 of the LM IIIC shrine. The builders may have expanded the grave to the west to use the bench as the west wall of the enclosure, but as the lower levels filled with burial remains, some of the later pyres were placed over the bench as well, making the grave extraordinarily wide. Grave 28, however, originally measured 1.76 m in length and 1.05 m in width; that is, its width was 59% of its length, similar to the other enclosures. The western wall was extremely wide, and later burials encroached over the eastern side of the wall. When the grave was expanded after Burial 3, its width expanded to 1.60 m, which is 91% of its length. It was the largest enclosure on the site at 2.82 m². The next largest is Grave 27, with a total space of 2.65 m².

Seven other graves enclose a space of 2.05–2.50 m² (Graves 5, 6, 9, 21, 26, 30, 36). Five of these are on or near the summit (Graves 5, 6, 9, 21, 36) and held large numbers of burials with rich grave goods. Two of the largest group lie in a row to the west of the shrine (Graves 26, 27), and one of them (Grave 27) also shows architectural refinements that might indicate the burial of an individual or group with higher status. Grave 32, which seems to have been constructed as part of the same group, but is later in date, may also have been very large. Its length is extraordinary, and the width was greater than what has been preserved, as the east wall was lacking.

Eight more graves enclose a total space of 1.53–1.87 m² (Graves 3, 10, 12, 16, 19, 20, 23, 34). Those on top of the ridge are at the larger end of this group (1.81–1.85 m²), with the exception of Grave 10, which encloses an area of 1.54 m². The smallest grave (Grave 15), which is a circle rather than a rectangle, encloses a space of only 1.43 m².

Walls

The builders of the enclosures most often incorporated standing house walls from the LM IIIC settlement for one (Graves 9, 12, 17, 19, 20, 28, 34, 35), two (Graves 1, 15, 36), or three (Grave 4) of the grave walls. Grave 3 was constructed against a terrace wall that may have existed previously to support Tomb IV. Only in Graves 5, 16, 21, 23, 26, 27, 30, and 32 were all four of the walls new, often having been dug into the middle of an earlier room (Graves 5, 16, 21) or terrace (Graves 23, 30) down to the floor. The walls of the houses that were used stood 0.25–0.85 m high in one to four courses, the majority of them 0.50–0.80 m high. They varied in width from 0.50 to 0.90 m, although the terrace wall for Grave 3 was larger at 1.00–1.25 m. The width of the wall was probably less important in the construction of the enclosure than the preserved height, and in several instances (Graves 3 and 36) the builders made a narrow wall of their own against a standing LM IIIC wall. This structure may have served to help support the wood of the pyre, which could be laid across the narrow wall.

The other walls of the enclosures were of two kinds. Generally, the builders laid down a single row of large stones (often limestone), one course high, with only a single face on the interior. Smaller stones were sometimes set in to fill the gaps between the stones. Occasionally, walls were constructed with two good faces, as in Graves 16, 26, 27, 28, 30, and 32. A single two-faced wall was sometimes constructed (Graves 26, 27, 32), but two such walls appear in Graves 16 and 30 and three walls in Grave 28. These walls were usually quite thick, measuring 0.78–1.22 m. Graves that did not incorporate house walls were generally less deep than the others, with maximum preserved wall heights of 0.40–0.77 m. The new walls were constructed chiefly of limestone, although Graves 16 and 28 incorporated a larger amount of local breccia than the others.

Floors

The floors of the graves are simple, consisting either of bedrock or soil, often representing the floors of the original houses. When the floor is the brecciating bedrock, it often appears to be made of pebbles (as suggested for Grave 6 in preliminary reports: Gesell, Day, and Coulson 1988, 288), but its consistency probably resulted from a natural process rather than human decision. Some of the graves were constructed on top of the collapsed roofing material from the LM IIIC houses (Graves 1, 4, 9, 19, 28, 34). Grave 5 was built on top of bedrock and the remains of a LM IIIC hearth. Cremation occurred within the enclosure, as can be seen from the fracturing of the limestone blocks, the calcination of the breccia boulders, and the anatomical order of the bones from the last burial. Stones were piled on top of the enclosures at the end of each burial event; these were removed for each subsequent burial.

Pavements

Occasionally the enclosures were provided with additional architectural features in the form of platforms or pot stands (Fig. 159). Several graves are accompanied by paved areas along one of the short sides (Table 16). The best-preserved example of these comes from Grave 3, which has a paved area to the south that was level with the top of the south wall (Pl. 22E). The area of small flat stones, rather broken up in places, measures approximately 2.50 m north–south x 1.50 m east–west (measuring from the inner edge of the enclosure wall, the top of which may have served as part of the pavement) and incorporates an area of 3.75 m². Toward the southern end, a small stand made up of stones set around an open area possibly held a marker (a stone or a vessel); a large stone found in the vicinity could have served that function.

The graves on the southwest slope near the earlier shrine are also provided with paved areas. These graves show greater sophistication in their organization: three are lined up in a row (Graves 26, 27, 32), and Graves 26 and 27 have pavements on one of their short sides (Fig. 159). Grave 27 has a large paved area to the south that measures 1.35–1.50 m north–south x 2.25 m east–west, incorporating a space of 3.22 m². It has small flat stones between the south wall of the enclosure and a large wall made of massive stones on the south. The pavement associated with Grave 26 lies on the north of the enclosure and abuts the pavement for Grave 27, which must have existed when Grave 26 was constructed. It extends from the massive wall marking the south boundary of the Grave 27 pavement to the north wall of the enclosure. The space, which has eroded on the east, measures ca. 1.25 m north–south x 1.75 m east–west, with an area of 2.19 m². It consists of small flat paving stones, somewhat smaller than those making up the enclosure walls. Although the pavement associated with Grave 27 is slightly higher than that belonging to Grave 26 (by 0.10–0.20 m) the two graves may have shared the entire paved area between them for funerary or postfunerary rituals.

Other graves may originally have had similar features (Table 16). Because Graves 26 and 27 in the shrine area are provided with pavements, it is not unlikely that Grave 32, the third and latest in the same line, also had one. The logical place for this would have been just to the north of Grave 32 in the space labeled Grave 25 (Fig. 159). The area was covered with rock tumble, some of which may have belonged to disturbed pavement. The area measures ca. 1.00 m north–south x 1.50 m east–west, for a total area of 1.50 m²—somewhat smaller than the other platforms. Another possible platform may have existed to the south of Grave 6 (Fig. 159). The eastern wall of Grave 6 extends south of the enclosure itself, and as in the case of Grave 3, this bounded area may once have been paved. It measures ca. 1.75 m east–west x 2.30 m north–south, or 4.03 m². Similarly, the area between Graves 10 and 12 and north of Grave 17 may also have been filled in and was possibly once paved. There were stones at about the same level as the top of the west wall of Grave 12 (Fig. 159). This area measures ca. 1.60 m north–south x 1.60 m east–west, with a total area of 3.20 m² (or, if the area is measured between Grave 17 to the outer edge of the wall on the north, then the north–south dimension would measure 2.75 m, and the overall area would be 4.40 m²). The space could have been used for burial rituals or for supporting one or more of the large amphorae that may have served as markers for the graves in this area.

Pot Stands

Circles of stones that may have supported pots are associated with a small number of enclosure graves. The pithoi in both Graves 10 and 21 were uncovered resting in ovals made of stones that supported the vessels (Pls. 69D, 69E). A circle of stones was recognized within the enclosure on the southeastern side of Grave 12, and among other pottery found within were two large amphorae. Grave 16 produced a similar circle filled with fragments of a large amphora and other vessels on the eastern side of Grave 16. In both these cases it is possible that these circles surrounded by cobbles supported large markers that stood above the mound of stones covering the graves. Finally, outside the enclosure of Grave 3 in the pavement to the south of the enclosure was a rough circle supported by large slabs of stone that may have served to support a marker, whether a large vessel or a stone marker (Fig. 159).

Other Types of Burials without Architectural Features

Other types of burials are not well represented at Vronda. One possible pit burial may be identified in Grave 8, but it was poorly preserved and disturbed. The burial was a small, circular pit with fragments of pithoi and the cremated bones of two individuals without any accompanying grave goods. It may have been a secondary burial in a container set in a pit, but the remains are too few to be certain. Pit burials may be characterized as holes cut into the ground or bedrock with a single burial, inhumation or cremation, usually in a pithos or amphora (Eaby 2007, 305–309). They were relatively common in EIA Crete, and particularly in the LG period (Eaby 2007, 309). They were often used for child or infant burials; interestingly, however, Grave 8 contained the remains of a woman and a fetus.

Two other types of burials are known: pyre sites and discard deposits of bodies or dumps of material from earlier burials in the enclosure. Two pyre sites can be tentatively identified (Graves 13, 31). These had no architectural remains and seem to have been simple pits dug into the soil or roofing clay for a cremation, after which the bodies were removed for secondary burial elsewhere. There were many more dumps of cremation material. Most of these can be associated with a particular enclosure through pottery joins. When the enclosure became full with burials but was still in use, the ashes, bones, and objects accompanying earlier burials were removed to a location nearby. These deposits were assigned grave numbers at the time of excavation, but it became clear from their locations and from joins of pottery that they came from one of the enclosures (Grave 11 from Grave 5, Grave 14 from Grave 9, Grave 22 from Grave 21, Graves 7 and 33 from Grave 30, Grave 25 from Grave 32). Several ash dumps were found in the vicinity of Grave 28, but as these contained objects but no human bones, they were not assigned numbers. Occasionally, dumped material was found without an excavated associated grave (Graves 29, 37). Finally, one body of a child was apparently placed into one of the abandoned rooms of Building O and possibly covered with stones (Grave 24); there were no grave goods or associated architectural features.

Unlike the tholos tombs, which were substantial structures placed around the former settlement, the enclosure burials were rather simple structures situated in such a way as to interact with the earlier architectural remains. These enclosures were almost all placed within rooms of the former settlement and made use of existing walls and structures in their construction. Seen from above (for example, on the path to the Kastro) the grave enclosures formed an integral part of the visible remains of the earlier village (Pl. 69F) and sent a clear message of a deep connection between the burying population and the former inhabitants.

8

Early Iron Age Pottery

Leslie Preston Day

The EIA pottery from both the tholos tombs and the enclosure graves is analyzed here by shape. The vessels from the tholos tombs tend to be earlier in date, beginning in the SM period, but in most cases, particularly that of Tomb IX, some of the pottery may be dated to the LG period. Vessels from the enclosure graves are generally later. Although they are mostly of LG date, lingering PG styles are evident in some of the material. The earliest of the enclosures (Grave 9) produced a large quantity of pottery of PG style, while the latest (Graves 4, 17, 23, 30, 32) contained vessels of LO date amid a majority of LG and EO pottery. It is thus possible to see a diachronic development in the production and consumption of pottery over this period of time. The pottery for the most part is similar to that found in the Kastro settlement, suggesting that it was not produced exclusively for funerary purposes but played a role in the life of the community and was then deposited in the burials. One exception to this pattern can be seen in the bird askoi, which are not found in settlement contexts at Kavousi or other sites on Crete and may have been manufactured for funerary use. There is, however, one example found in a ritual context in the Spring Chamber at Knossos (Evans 1928, 136, fig. 69).

In the following discussion open shapes are treated first, then closed shapes. Within the broader categories of open and closed shapes, smaller vessels are presented before the larger types. When pertinent, features such as decoration (or lack thereof), fabric (fine, medium coarse, or coarse), or date will be considered.

Discussion by Shape

Open Shapes

Cup

Cups are common on Crete from the time when the dipped, flat-bottomed cup entered the Knossian ceramic repertoire through imports from Athens and the Cyclades in the MPG period (Coldstream 1996, 386; 2001, 55). Dipped cups became most popular in the LPG period, gradually displacing the bell skyphos as the primary drinking vessel by the EG at Knossos (Coldstream 2001, 55). Despite the popularity of the dipped cup in Central Crete, however, few examples have been found at Kavousi, and there are no certain examples at Vronda. Rim fragments that appear monochrome, however, may well have come from dipped cups.

Cups are rare in the tholos tombs at Vronda, with the exception of Tomb IX, but they represent the most common vessel shape in the enclosure graves. The numbers of cups in the enclosures suggest that they were used by the participants in the funerary ritual rather than being intended for the dead. Usually made of fine clay, they also appear in coarser fabrics, particularly in Tholos Tomb IX and Grave 9. Three groups can be distinguished: decorated, monochrome, and plain.

Decorated Cups

Only a single decorated cup (**IV P1**) was found in the tholos tombs. This small cup (Fig. 160:a) is low and globular, with an extra small capacity (see Glowacki, this vol., App. A, pp. 376–377). Its greatest diameter lies just below the top of the lower handle attachment. It has a small everted rim, a flat rectangular handle, and a raised and slightly concave base. The shoulder bears groups of vertical strokes between bands, while the lower body has multiple bands. It has been assigned a LG date by Tsipopoulou (2005, 78), but it may well be earlier. Cup **IX P1** may have been similar if it had a flat base. The shape is similar to cups of Type 3 from the enclosures (see below).

In the enclosure graves decorated cups are also comparatively rare. They tend to be smaller than the more common monochrome cups, with slightly over half of their capacities in the extra small to small range (see Glowacki, this vol., App. A, p. 376). Four types have been recognized.

The Type 1 decorated cup (**GR3 P3** [Fig. 160:b], **GR9 P33**, **GR16 P14**) has a conical body and a plain rounded vertical lip, similar to PG cups from Hagios Ioannis (Boardman 1960, 134, 137, fig. 5:V.16, V.20). Although the shape is PG, these cups have reserved panels with simple decoration consisting of a wavy line, zigzag, or strokes. The metopal arrangement of **GR3 P3** and **GR16 P14** suggests that they date to the LG period; metopes on cups begin in the MG at Knossos as window panels opposite the handles but spread toward the handle in LG examples (Coldstream 2001, 57). This type of cup is rare at Vronda, as elsewhere on Crete.

Type 2 decorated cups are deep and monochrome coated but with simple decoration on the handle (**GR3 P2** [Fig. 160:c], **GR9 P1**), rim (**GR9 P34**, **GR19 P1**), or base (**GR27 P2**). The coated cup with decorated handle bearing stripes or bars, imitating Attic LPG styles, can be found at Knossos (Coldstream and Catling, eds., 1996, 28, fig. 65:28, 29). Cup **GR3 P2** bears the closest resemblance to the Knossos examples, and it is also similar to several of the Type 3 monochrome cups (**GR16 P7**, **GR19 P7**). Cup **GR9 P1**, however, looks earlier. It has a smaller rim diameter in relation to its height (H/DR ratio 0.93), and it has a small, only slightly everted rim and a heavy base; in shape it is a small version of monochrome cup **GR19 P16**. The handle bears vertical stripes rather than bars. Cups **GR3 P2** and **GR9 P1** are much deeper than those found at Knossos. Cup **GR19 P1** is very deep, and the handle is attached inside the rim at the top and pushes into the body on the bottom. In shape it resembles monochrome cups such as **GR28 P4**. The decoration consists of a reserved band on the lip with two grooves below; two vertical strokes on the reserved band are all that can be seen of the decoration. Cup **GR9 P34** is small, with a slightly outturned rim and a small raised base. Decoration consists of two reserved bands at the base of the rim. Bands on or below the rim can be found on cups of PGB–EG and LG date in central and eastern Crete. Finally, **GR27 P2** is an unusual deep monochrome cup with a rather tall offset rim and a disk base. It bears a possible reserved band on the lower body, and the underside of the base has a painted design. It is difficult to know if this qualifies as decoration that would be seen when someone drained the cup or if it should be classified as a potter's mark; it is here considered decoration.

Type 3 decorated cups are the most common in the enclosure graves at Vronda. These are rounded, bellied cups with rather pronounced offset rims. Few of the examples preserve full profiles, but they have similar upper bodies. Because the handles are missing on most examples, some could be skyphoi, but the similarities among them have led to their categorization as cups. They bear a wide variety of designs on the upper body. Two of these cups (**GR1 P1** [Fig. 160:d], **GR12 P33**) are small and rather shallow. Cup **GR1 P1** is the smallest and is similar in shape to an even smaller cup of PGB–EG date from Knossos (Coldstream and Catling, eds., 1996, 134, fig. 103:30). The chevron decoration is found on a cup of MG date from Knossos (Coldstream and Catling, eds., 1996, 265, fig. 147:108), although the motif is most common on skyphoi (Coldstream 1996, 383). Cup **GR12 P33** is another small cup; although the handle is not preserved, in shape it is too small and thick walled to have been a skyphos. It bears banded decoration and some undetermined curvilinear motif. The others (**GR1 P3, GR6 P1, GR16 P1, GR17 P1, GR20 P1, GR21 P1, GR27 P1, GR30 P1**) are larger and deeper. Rim diameters of these larger cups range from 9.00 to 13.60 cm. Three cups (**GR17 P1, GR20 P1, GR27 P1**) have the same decoration: groups of thick and thin vertical bands that resemble a triglyph-metope pattern. This is a common pattern on LG cups at Knossos, where it may have antecedents in LG Attica and the Argolid (Coldstream 1996, 389). Cup **GR20 P1** is an import, probably from the south coast area. Cup **GR16 P1** has banded decoration (zigzag, crosshatching) while **GR6 P1** has crosshatched lozenges. The other possible cups are similar in size and shape and are decorated with a guilloche pattern and a panel of vertical chevrons (**GR1 P3**), crosshatched lozenges (**GR30 P1**), or crosshatched checkerboard (**GR21 P1**). While these fragments may come from skyphoi, their resemblance to known cups makes their identification as cups likely.

The Type 4 cup is characterized by a tall offset rim. Only a single example is known for certain (**GR12 P1**; Fig. 160:e), but four others without handles may come from similar though deeper cups (**GR3 P8, GR12 P8, GR12 P32, GR23 P1**). Cup **GR12 P1** is of unusual shape, with a tall rim that flares from a shallow rounded body and a slightly concave base. The handle is attached inside the rim. A reserved band on the rim carries hatched zigzags. The shape has a parallel from the tholos tomb at Skouriasmenos (Tsipopoulou 2005, 120, pl. 121:H1978), dating to the Orientalizing period, possibly LO. Of the deeper cups, only one has a fully preserved profile (**GR12 P32**) and traces of a handle. This cup has a high concave rim, rising from the widest part of the body in an almost carinated profile, and a small disk base. The proportions are unusual, particularly the ratio of height to rim diameter, which is 1:1. It is monochrome but has two narrow reserved bands at the bottom of the rim. Although only the rim and upper body of **GR3 P8** is preserved, it appears to have a similar profile, with a slightly higher rim and a ledge where the concave rim meets the curving body. The lower body of this cup may have once been decorated. Cup **GR23 P1** is similar to the other two, although its rim is shorter and there is no carination where it meets the body; it is decorated with a crosshatched design. Cup **GR12 P8** has a nearly complete profile, although the rim does not join the body. It is decorated with double concentric circles over bands. This shape of cup resembles EO examples in Central Crete, although the decorations clearly seem to belong to the LG period.

Finally, an unusual cup comes from Grave 19 (**GR19 P20**). It lacks a complete profile but has a small offset rim, an elliptical handle, and an almost carinated lower body with a shelf at the lower handle attachment. It is decorated with narrow bands on the lower body. Nothing like it is known from other sites.

Monochrome Cups

Monochrome cups, also called coated cups (Coldstream 1996; Kotsonas 2008), black cups (Coldstream 2001) or black glaze or black gloss cups (Callaghan and Johnston 2000), like their decorated counterparts, were apparently modeled on Attic MG I shallow flat-based cups (Coldstream 1996, 386; 2001, 55). Once established, they became the most common vessels in EIA Crete (Kotsonas 2008, 205) and the chief drinking vessels, replacing the skyphos by the LG period (Coldstream 2001, 55).

Among the tholos tombs, only Tomb IX produced monochrome cups (**IX P28–IX P33** [Fig. 160:f, g], **IX P50–IX P52, IX P59, IX P60**), although two cups that appear in the 1901 photographs of the tomb assemblages appear to be monochrome, one from Tomb IV (Pl. 7C bottom, second from left), the other from Tombs II, VII, or VIII (Pl. 5A middle, third from right). For the most part, the examples from Tomb IX look earlier than those found in the later enclosure burials at Vronda. Their short height, thick walls, heavy bases and handles, and small rims mark them as being of PG date.

The monochrome cups are rather small, although the two missing cups appear to have been larger; heights range from 6.00 to 8.70 cm (average 7.15 cm), rim diameters from 10.20 to 11.90 cm (average 11.13 cm), and base diameters from 4.00 to 5.20 cm (average 4.28 cm). The cups are predominantly shallow; although the ratio of height to rim diameter averages 0.65, for most cups it falls between 0.53 and 0.72. In general, this means that these cups are more shallow and have smaller bases than the monochrome cups found in the enclosure graves. They also have smaller capacities, generally extra small and small, with the exception of **IX P31**, which is deeper, with a H/DR ratio of 0.84 and medium capacity (Glowacki, this vol., App. A, p. 376). Most (76%) of the cups have small everted rims, with single examples of incurved, vertical, and offset rims. Bases are generally flat (55%), but they may be be raised (18%), concave underneath (18%), or raised and concave (9%). Cup **IX P32** has a genuine disk base. Often the bases are thick and heavy (**IX P29, IX P33, IX P51, IX P60**), and some show string marks (**IX P30, IX P31, IX P51**). Handles are variably rectangular with squared edges (45%), round (33%), or elliptical (22%). All of the handles are attached inside the rim. Missing are the thinner strap handles found in the enclosure graves. A few of the cups are heavy, with thick walls (**IX P28, IX P29, IX P59**), and they may have been handmade.

One cup (**IX P50**) has a conical body with a very small everted rim. Although precise parallels are lacking, its shape resembles that of cups of MPG–LPG date in sites around Knossos (see above, p. 43), and it is similar to several decorated (**GR3 P3, GR9 P33, GR16 P14**) and monochrome (**GR9 P42**) cups in the enclosure graves, although those lack the everted rim. Three cups in Tholos IX (**IX P30–P32**) look later than the others. Cup **IX P30** has thin walls, a small rounded rim with two grooves below, similar to those of PG date from the Kastro (Mook 1993, 201), a flat rectangular handle, and a raised base. Cup **IX P31** has a pronounced S-curve with a tapering lower body, and it is much deeper than any of the other cups. Cups become progressively deeper in the Geometric period, and this example resembles Type 3c, discussed below in this section, from the enclosure graves. Finally, **IX P32** is a thin-walled, bellied cup with a high center of gravity, an offset rim, and a disk base. While all three of these cups show later features, the thickness of the walls and the heaviness of the handles suggest that they belong within the PG–G time frame; they may date to the same era as the earliest cups from enclosure Grave 9.

The monochrome cup is the most frequent vessel in the Vronda enclosure grave assemblages. Despite its ubiquity, the shape is surprisingly difficult to date within the EIA, perhaps because most examples come from graves that have pottery of mixed dates, and few vessels have been found in stratified deposits. The sequence on the Kastro is very useful in this regard, providing monochrome cups that can be dated to phases VI (SubPG), VII (G), VIII (LG), and O (Mook 2004, 169–178). Unfortunately, the amount of published material is still limited, and whole shapes are not plentiful.

In the enclosure graves at Vronda, four types of monochrome cup have been identified, based on the shape and depth of their bodies and their capacities. Type 1 monochrome cups have a conical profile like Type 1 decorated cups. They are found only twice, with both examples coming from the lowest deposits in Grave 9 (**GR9 P42, GR9 P55**; Fig. 160:h). Cup **GR9 P55** is deeper than the decorated examples. Cup **GR9 P42** has a more rounded profile with a small offset rim and a raised base. The capacities of these vessels are either medium or large (Glowacki, this vol., App. A, p. 376). The shape is known from examples of EPG–LPG date from the Knossos area (Boardman 1960, 134, fig. 5:V.16; 140, pl. 36:VIII.12) and from East Crete (Tsipopoulou 2005, 423, type στ), and this type is certainly PG in style. The type is also one of the earliest at Vronda.

Type 2 monochrome cups are unusually shallow. Two subtypes can be distinguished. Type 2a cups have two distinguishing features: a concave rim separated from the body by a ledge and a broad disk base (**GR9 P18–GR9 P20** [Fig. 160:i], **GR9 P24, GR9 P25, GR20 P12, GR20 P14, GR21 P7**). They occur in three graves only, all clustered within the boundaries of the earlier Building J: Graves 9, 20, and 21. These ledge-rim cups are usually made of very soft fabric and are coated with a thick black paint. A similar shape is known from Knossos, where it is seen as an imitation of imported Attic MG I cups (Coldstream 1996, 386), although the Knossian examples lack the ledge rim. The ledge rim itself is a feature of Euboean MG II skyphoi (Blandin 2007, 16, pl. 20:1). Ledge-rim cups are also found on the Kastro in the SubPG phase (Mook 1993, 198, fig. 156:P7.29). Like the Knossian examples, these cups have H/DR ratios of 0.50–0.61, but the Vronda examples are generally deeper than the Knossian cups, with heights of 5.60–6.70 cm. The capacities are usually small but can be medium or even medium large (Glowacki, this vol., App. A, p. 376). They cannot date any earlier than 850 B.C., the date of the beginning of Attic MG I, and they are almost certainly later than that. Cups of this type were probably imported into Knossos first, after which they spread to other parts of the island. One was found in the lowest levels of Grave 9, but most of the others were found higher up in the grave with LG pottery, suggesting a date in the early part of the LG period. Of the two that were analyzed petrographically, one may have come from the area of the south coast (**GR9 P20**), the other more generally from Central Crete (**GR9 P18**; see this vol., Ch. 9, p. 302).

Type 2b shows a greater variety of shapes, but all examples are very shallow, with heights in the range of 4.00–6.50 cm and H/DR ratios of 0.29–0.54 (**GR9 P44, GR20 P9, GR20 P10**). The only example that was well enough preserved to measure has a medium capacity (Glowacki, this vol., App. A, p. 376). One is bellied, with an offset rim that is convex with a groove at the base (**GR20 P9**), and the two others have more flaring rims. The handle on **GR20 P10** is attached on the interior of the rim, while the handle on **GR9 P44** is unusually attached at the base. They all have flat or slightly raised bases. As with the ledge-rim cups, they are only found in one cluster of graves, including Grave 9 and Grave 20.

Type 3 cups are the most common. They are deep and bellied, with offset rims and flat or slightly concave bases. We can distinguish three subtypes within Type 3 based on the heights of the vessels and the ratios of height to rim diameter, and it is possible that these subtypes represent a chronological development, probably within the LG period.

Type 3a cups are deep with a height of 8.00–9.60 cm and H/DR ratios of 0.60–0.70. Two variations of this type have been identified on the basis of the shape of the lower body. Either the cup has a hemispherical body, rounded toward the base (**GR3 P6, GR4 P13, GR6 P13** [Fig. 160:j], **GR9 P17, GR9 P40, GR12 P21, GR12 P23, GR19 P8, GR27 P7, GR28 P10**) or the lower body tapers (**GR5 P4, GR5 P6, GR16 P7, GR19 P7, GR28 P6, GR36 P13**; Fig. 160:k). One example (**GR9 P54**) tapers to a small raised base, while another (**GR27 P8**) tapers to a disk base. Rims are usually sharply offset (11 examples); the rim on **GR4 P13** has a particularly sharp offset and is unusually tall, features that mark it as EO in date. Most of these cups have a maximum diameter above the midpoint of the vessel, but at least two have their maximum diameters at the rim (**GR5 P6, GR12 P23**). Handles can be elliptical, rectangular, or strap. Eleven have handles attached inside the rim, and only three have the handle attached at the rim. Several have grooves on the rim (**GR16 P7, GR19 P7**), below the rim (**GR12 P23**), or on the body (**GR28 P10**). Bases are generally flat, but a few are slightly raised, and several are concave underneath.

The capacities of Type 3a cups are large: 82% are large or extra large (70% large, 12% extra large; Glowacki, this vol., App. A, p. 376). Smaller versions of Type 3a also occur (**GR9 P23, GR12 P20, GR21 P12**); these have heights of 7.0–7.7 cm and the same H/DR ratios as their larger counterparts. One cup, although its handle is not preserved (**GR9 P23**), has an unusual profile with wide flaring rim and small raised base; its widest diameter is the rim. Cup **GR12 P20** is also unusual; its irregular shape, with a small rim, heavy round handle, and wide flat base, suggests a PG date. Cup **GR21 P12** is a small version of the standard type like **GR28 P10**, although its profile has more of an S-curve and its base is heavier than usual. Type 3a is similar to Knossos type Dii of LPG–MG date (Coldstream 1996, 386), type Biii at Eleutherna of MG date (Kotsonas 2008, 207), or type γ in East Crete of LG date (Tsipopoulou 2005, 423); it probably dates to the LG period.

Type 3b cups are deeper, with a height of 8.1–10.8 cm and H/DR ratios of 0.7–0.8. As with Type 3a, two variations of this type exist, one with a hemispherical body (**GR3 P19, GR6 P11, GR9 P13, GR9 P14** [Fig. 160:l], **GR16 P8, GR28 P7, GR30 P8**), the other with a tapering lower body (**GR3 P7** [Fig. 160:m],

GR5 P5, GR5 P8, GR6 P18, GR9 P16, GR9 P41, GR9 P52, GR12 P38, GR16 P6, GR16 P10, GR19 P17, GR21 P3, GR27 P6, GR28 P8, GR28 P9). Cup **GR9 P43** tapers to a small, heavy, raised base. Rims can be small or large. The rims are generally slightly offset, but five are sharply offset (**GR3 P7, GR5 P5, GR6 P11, GR9 P16, GR21 P3**). The widest diameter is above the middle, except in the cases of **GR5 P5** and **GR16 P10**, which have their widest diameters at the rim. Handles are generally elliptical in section but can be rectangular (**GR3 P7**) or strap (**GR9 P13, GR21 P3, GR28 P8**); one example (**GR9 P41**) has a round handle. Handles are regularly attached at the rim (10 examples) but can be attached within the rim (eight examples). Bases are generally flat, but they may be slightly concave underneath; **GR19 P17** has a low disk base.

On one Type 3b cup grooves appear at the base of the rim (**GR9 P16**). Another (**GR5 P8**) has a pair of what have been called bosses (Coldstream 2001, 57), nipples (Brock 1957, 188; Coldstream 1972, 83–84), or mastoi (Papadopoulos and Smithson 2017, 818); the first term is preferred here. Several other cups also bear bosses of this sort, although they are not well enough preserved to determine into which category of cup they fall (**GR3 P13, GR5 P9, GR9 P28, GR27 P8**). Coldstream (1972, 83) suggests that large cups with bosses were an invention of the Attic EG but died out after that period, then they were adopted in the Argolid, Cyclades, and Crete. He believed that the earliest cups with bosses belong to the MG period on Crete and continued into the LG (Coldstream 1972, 84).

In general, cups of the Type 3b subgroup have larger capacities than those of Type 3a; 83% are of the two largest categories, 53% large and 30% extra large (Glowacki, this vol., App. A, p. 376). A few small versions of this type of cup exist (**GR4 P12, GR6 P9**), with heights of 5.60–7.30 cm and H/DR ratios of 0.72–0.76. Type 3b cups are similar to the earlier cups of type Diii at Knossos of MG–LG date (Coldstream 1996, 387) and type Biv of LG–EO date at Eleutherna (Kotsonas 2008, 207); they belong to Tsipopoulou's LG type γ cups in East Crete (2005, 423).

Type 3c cups are deep, with a height of 8.10–10.60 cm and H/DR of 0.80–0.87. The same two variations of this type exist as with the other subtypes, one with a hemispherical body (**GR6 P12, GR9 P15** [Fig 160:n], **GR19 P16, GR28 P5, GR36 P12**), the other with a tapering lower body (**GR1 P13, GR21 P5, GR26 P7** [Fig 160:o], **GR28 P4, GR30 P7**). Rims are generally small and slightly offset, although at least one rim is more sharply offset (**GR30 P7**). One cup (**GR21 P5**) has a particularly tall rim with grooves both on the rim itself and at its base. The maximum diameter is usually above midway, but two have the widest diameter at the middle (**GR6 P12, GR21 P5**). Strap handles are most common, but elliptical handles occasionally occur (**GR1 P13, GR19 P16, GR36 P12**), and one cup has a rectangular handle (**GR21 P5**). Handles are attached inside the rim (eight examples) or on the rim (three examples). Bases are flat or slightly concave; **GR21 P5** has a low disk base. One cup has a very heavy base that may indicate an early date (**GR19 P16**). Cups of this type have large capacities, but not as large as those of Types 3a and 3b; 37% are large, 27% are extra large, and 9% are medium large, with comparatively high percentages of medium (18%) and small (9%) capacities (Glowacki, this vol., App. A, p. 376). A small version of Type 3c can be seen in **GR4 P22**, which has a height of 6.80 cm and a H/DR ratio of 0.81. Cups of Type 3c resemble the later (LG–EO) type Diii cups at Knossos (Coldstream 1996, 387) and type Bv cups of LG–EO date at Eleutherna (Kotsonas 2008, 208); many of them fall into Tsipopoulou's (2005, 423) type γ of LG–EO date.

Type 3d cups are deep, with heights over 10.00 cm and H/DR ratios of 0.85–0.90. These cups show greater variation in shape. Cups **GR21 P11** (Fig 160:p), **GR30 P10**, and **GR30 P16** are deep, with offset rims, strap handles, and lower bodies tapering to flat bases. They have large and extra large capacities (Glowacki, this vol., App. A, p. 376).

The Type 4 cup is represented only by a single example, **GR30 P6** (Fig. 160:q). It has the same proportions as the Type 3d monochrome cup, but it has a tall, sharply offset rim, a body tapering to a concave raised base, and a strap handle. It has a large capacity (Glowacki, this vol., App. A, p. 376). This cup is much later than most of the other monochrome cups, with parallels in the EO and LO periods; it belongs to Tsipopoulou's type ζ of Orientalizing date (2005, 424). Others cups that may belong to this category include **GR23 P5** and **GR23 P6**; **GR23 P5** is a cup with incised lines on its tall rim, while **GR23 P6** has the tall rim but no handles preserved to indicate that it is a cup rather than a skyphos.

Type 5 cups have only a single example, **GR9 P51** (Fig. 160:r). This shallow cup has a rounded vertical rim and a large, slightly raised base. The elliptical handle is attached on top of the rim. The maximum diameters are both at the rim and at the place of the lower handle attachment. The height of the cup is 8.00 cm, and the H/DR ratio is 0.62. It has a large capacity (Glowacki, this vol., App. A, p. 376). Its profile appears similar to earlier cups from the LM IIIC settlement, although the base is wider than was customary in that period. The Type 5 cup can be paralleled by cups of LG type στ in East Crete (Tsipopoulou 2005, 423), although the Vronda example is more shallow with thinner walls. Similar but much smaller cups of PGB date were found at Eleutherna (Kotsonas 2008, 206, 209, fig. 51:A285).

Other monochrome cups found in the graves are fragmentary, without full profiles, and they cannot easily be placed within the typology (**GR1 P14, GR1 P15, GR5 P7, GR5 P9, GR5 P10, GR6 P10, GR6 P14, GR6 P15, GR6 P16, GR6 P17, GR9 P21, GR9 P26, GR9 P27, GR12 P24, GR12 P36, GR12 P37, GR13 P5, GR13 P6, GR16 P9, GR16 P13, GR17 P9, GR19 P9, GR21 P6, GR27 P9, GR28 P12, GR28 P13, GR30 P9, GR30 P11, GR30 P12, GR36 P15, GR37 P1**).

Dating of the monochrome cups in the Vronda enclosure graves can be made stratigraphically and also stylistically on the basis of the size and depth of the vessels. The earliest monochrome cups in the enclosures, particularly those from the lowest burials in Grave 9 (see above, p. 96), have parallels in Tholos Tomb IX, which generally has material earlier than the cremation enclosures but includes some Geometric pottery. Although there may have been some intrusions from the later burials (e.g., cups **GR9 P20** and **GR9 P24**; see above, p. 96) many of the cups in Grave 9 show similarities. First of all, these cups tend to be made of medium-coarse and coarse fabrics, with heavier walls than the cups from the later burials in this grave and in other enclosures on the site. They are generally more shallow than the later varieties of cup, as are the PG cups from the tholos tombs and elsewhere on Crete (Coldstream 2001, 55). Many have heavy bases (e.g., **GR9 P34, GR9 P41, GR9 P43, GR9 P54**), similar to cups **IX P37** and **IX P60** from Vronda Tomb IX, on which the bases are often also uneven (e.g., **IX P52**). The rims are smaller and less pronounced in the earlier cups from Grave 9, as is also the case with the cups in the tholos tombs. At least two cups have conical profiles and no pronounced rim (**GR9 P42, GR9 P55**). Finally, the handles tend to be more rounded, contrasting with the flat strap handles found in later burials or graves (e.g., **GR9 P41–GR9 P43, GR9 P55**). Only **GR9 P20** has a real strap handle, and it is possibly intrusive from later burials. These cups are larger than those found in the earlier tholos tombs, even most of those from Vronda Tomb IX, a fact that suggests they are eighth century in date, and thus later than the cups in the tholos tombs, many of which may date to the late ninth century (PG) to early eighth century (G).

While the earliest monochrome cups in the cremations are recognizable, dating the later ones is more difficult, except for those that belong to the seventh century. At the Kastro, where monochrome cups can be dated stratigraphically, the rims of the SubPG cups are generally wider in diameter than their bodies or have the same diameter as the bodies (Mook 2004, 174, fig. 12.9), while those of G Phase VII have small rims that are not as wide as the bodies (Mook 2004, 175, fig. 12.10). The LG cups of Phase VIII are deeper, with taller, almost carinated rims, and generally the bases are concave underneath (Mook 2004, fig. 176, 12.11), while those of EO date have even deeper rims, sometimes also convex, and ring bases (Mook 2004, 177, fig. 12.12). In general, the monochrome cups from the Vronda enclosure graves show development along similar lines. If Type 1 cups date to the mid eighth century, as seems likely both stratigraphically and stylistically, the other types fall within the late eighth century (LG), although it is difficult to place any individual cup within the chronological sequence. Type 2 cups, particularly the ledge-rim cups, are probably early in the LG sequence. The Type 3 cups are all LG with the exception of Type 3d, which is EO. In general, the deeper the cup, the later the date seems to be. The capacities of these cups increase in size throughout time, at least until the end of the LG period. It is difficult to determine stratigraphically the dates of all but the earliest and latest vessels in the graves because of the disturbance, so dating individual monochrome cups in the graves to a particular burial or to a phase of the LG period cannot be done with any certainty.

Elsewhere on Crete, the earliest cups were small and shallow, often poorly made, with irregular bases, thick handles, and small rims (Coldstream 2001, 55). By the LG period the cups became very deep (Coldstream 2001, 57). Even within the LG period, the cups became progressively deeper. At the North Cemetery at Knossos their H/DR ratio increased from 0.6–0.7 in the MG period to 0.7–0.9 in LG–EO (Coldstream 1996, 387). At Knossos, then, the height and H/DR ratio are rough chronological indicators. The same can be said at Eleutherna (Kotsonas 2008, 207).

The gradual increase in the size of monochrome cups has been noted elsewhere, but the reasons for this "supersizing" are unknown. That size was important can be seen from the fact that undersized cups were often associated with children and infants (Kotsonas 2011a, 949). The LG cups were designed to hold larger quantities of liquid, reflecting a change in consumption patterns. Cups may have held more because of an increase in the amount of water mixed with the wine. It is clear from Homer that mixing water and wine had become a regular feature of social life by the mid eighth century, whenever that custom originated; one only has to look at the Cyclops episode in the *Odyssey* to see this (Hom. *Od.* 9.347–363). The change may reflect a new consumption pattern in which each individual mixed water and wine to his own taste in his own cup, rather than having a shared krater in which the wine was mixed, as the decline in the numbers of kraters in many of the graves at Eleutherna may suggest (Kotsonas 2011a, 949). Social custom may also have changed so that cups were shared among a number of individuals in gatherings, rather than holding liquid for a single person. Cups from both graves and settlements on Crete show this increase, and therefore the increase was not due to a specifically funerary reason.

Plain Cup

A few examples of plain cups were found in the enclosure graves, apparently without any coating or decoration, although the surface preservation is so poor that any traces of paint may have been removed during cleaning (**GR1 P33, GR4 P17, GR6 P30, GR6 P22, GR9 P53, GR9 P56, GR9 P57, GR16 P21**). Six of these cups (**GR1 P33, GR6 P22, GR6 P30, GR9 P53, GR9 P57, GR16 P21**) are of medium-coarse or coarse fabrics, and at least four of them are burned. None of these vessels has a complete profile, but all appear to be deep cups. The seventh (**GR4 P17**), a very small cup with a height of 4.30 cm and a H/DR ratio of 0.74, is made in fine ware; it has a small offset rim, a deep body and a small base, slightly concave underneath, with string marks on the bottom. Finally, **GR28 P18**, with a concave lip over its slightly rounded body, possibly belongs to a type of cup of EO date recognized at Knossos (Coldstream 2001, 57, fig. 1.19:n), although it lacks a handle. Like the example from Knossos, its plain surface is slipped and polished. It may also represent a bowl or a lid.

Mug-Like Cup or Cup with Very Tall Neck

There are a number of vessels that are similar to cups but deeper, with narrower mouths; these we have called mug-like cups. They also resemble a type of wide-mouthed jug (see below, p. 278). They are nearly always decorated. Mug-like cups do not appear in the tholos tombs. In the enclosure graves they come in two types. The first type (1) only occurs in a single example. It is straight sided into a rounded bottom with a handle attached from the vertical rim to just above the place where the body rounds out, and the base is flat (**GR3 P1**; Fig. 161:a). It is decorated with a panel of vertical strokes on the rim and another of dotted loops in the handle zone. This mug-like cup shape, while not common, can also be found at LG Hagios Georgios (Tsipopoulou 2005, 133, 402, fig. 90:AN 2381) and at Eleutherna, where vessels of this shape are called cups with straight neck walls and belong to the EG period (Kotsonas 2008, 212–214, fig. 52:A169). The mug-like cup may be a local adaptation of the MG II Attic mug shape (Kotsonas 2008, 212), like one imported into Knossos (Coldstream and Catling, eds., 1996, 276, fig. 151:294.12).

The second type (2) has a more rounded body with a definite neck (**GR4 P1**) or a pronounced rim (**GR12 P2, GR12 P3** [Fig. 161:b], **GR16 P3, GR16 P4, GR21 P4, GR28 P11**). Although these mug-like cups are more similar to cups, their mouths are more restricted, and they tend to have a greater H/DR ratio (0.83–0.97) than other cups. Rims can be tall (**GR4 P1, GR12 P3, GR16 P4, GR28 P11**) or short (**GR12 P2, GR16 P3, GR21 P4**), and the vessels have rectangular or strap handles attached from the rim, or occasionally inside the rim, to the widest diameter. Some are entirely coated on the interior (**GR12 P2, GR21 P4, GR28 P11**) like the cups, but others have a simple rim band (**GR4 P1**, **GR16 P4**) or are coated on the rim and lower body (**GR16 P3**). Decorative arrangements vary, but most mug-like cups carry their major motifs on the upper body. On **GR4 P1** there is an overlapping horizontal S-pattern on the rim above a zigzag and some sort of curvilinear hatched motif on the body, and the bottom is dark. On **GR12 P2** there is an overlapping horizontal S-pattern just below the rim, with banding below. A crosshatched pendant triangle hangs from bands on the rim of **GR16 P4**, which is painted dark on the lower body. On **GR12 P3** and **GR16 P3** decorative motifs appear in panels: groups of bands with vertical strokes between the upper register of bands, and hatched or crosshatched meander hooks, respectively. Vessel **GR28 P11** is adorned with grooves on the rim.

Mug-like cups have been found at Eleutherna (Kotsonas 2008, 212–213) and also in East Crete, where they are called wide-mouthed oinochoai (Tsipopoulou 2005, 401–403). Their function is not clear; the coating on the interior of many of them suggests that they are drinking vessels, but their rather closed mouths would also make them suitable for pouring liquids. Their capacities are similar to those of cups (Glowacki, this vol., App. A, p. 376).

FOOTED CUP

Footed cups belong almost exclusively to the tholos tombs. Three cups (and possibly another) with high conical feet were found in Tomb IX. Two of these cups had single handles (**IX P2** [Fig. 161:c], **IX P34**), while the third had an unusual configuration of two vertical handles (**IX P4**) and may be a precursor of the kantharos. Two of the cups were dipped (**IX P2**, **IX P4**), and one was monochrome painted (**IX P34**). The fourth cup (**IX P1**), which may or may not have had a conical foot, is decorated with a scribble or wavy line between two bands and spaced bands on the interior. It has parallels for shape and decoration in SM footed cups at Knossos (Coldstream and Catling, eds., 1996, 88, fig. 83:19).

Although not as common as the bell skyphos, similar footed cups have been found in the SM–EPG periods at Knossos (Coldstream 1996, 385), and the Vronda examples are probably of EPG date. Like the bell skyphoi, they are almost certainly drinking vessels.

TWO-HANDLED CUP OR KANTHAROS

The two-handled cup or kantharos is known only from a single example from the enclosure graves (**GR5 P11**; Fig. 161:d). It is similar to the monochrome cup but has two handles instead of one. The rim is carinated and represents the greatest diameter of the vessel, a feature that marks it out as different from the cups, a majority of which have rims whose diameters are less than those of the bodies. It is difficult to know how to classify this vessel, but a similar example can be found at Kommos, where it is labeled a kantharos (Johnston 2000, 214–215, fig. 26:94) although it lacks the high-swung handles generally associated with the kantharos shape. The kantharos was popular in Attica and on the mainland (Lemos 2002, 54–55, 93), but it rarely appears on Crete and never with the high-swung handles typical of mainland kantharoi (Tsipopoulou 2005, 422). The kantharos shape derives from Attic and Cycladic prototypes and does not appear on the island until the advanced LG period. The handles on the Vronda example are vertical strap handles rather than the round horizontal handle found on the skyphos. Whatever it is called, it seems to have been a drinking vessel, and its unusual form may indicate that it was used in circumstances different from those in which one-handled cups or skyphoi were deployed, much as the later Greek kantharos was used in drinking rituals.

Skyphos

The skyphos is an open vessel with two horizontal handles, usually round, that was used for drinking and possibly for eating (Kotsonas 2008, 187). It can be decorated, monochrome, or plain. At Knossos (Coldstream 1996, 378–384; 2001, 51–55) and Eleutherna (Kotsonas 2008, 187–197) three different types belonging to the Early Iron Age were recognized: the bell skyphos, the shallow skyphos descended from cauldron shapes, and various mainland types with low bases or high feet (treated here as stemmed skyphoi). The bell skyphos, which is limited chronologically to the PG period, is not found in the cremation burials at Vronda, but several examples were found in the tholos tombs. The other types are common and are here labeled low-based skyphoi.

BELL SKYPHOS

There are two similar shapes that have deep bowls, two handles, and conical bases. These have been labeled either skyphoi or amphoriskoi. The skyphos is an open shape probably used for drinking, while the amphoriskos, as its name implies, served as a wide-mouthed storage vessel. It is often difficult to distinguish between the two on the basis of shape. Here those vessels with very wide mouths and an S-curved body are categorized as skyphoi. They are most often coated on the interior. Amphoriskoi, in contrast, have narrower mouths with a clearly articulated neck separating the body from the rim, and they have only a band of paint on the interior of the rim (see below, p. 284).

The bell skyphos, so common elsewhere in Crete in the SM–PG periods, is rare in the tholos tombs at Vronda and does not occur in the enclosure graves at all. Two bell skyphoi are pictured in Boyd's publication but have not been located: one came from Tomb IV (Pl. 7C: bottom row, third from right), the other from Tomb II, VII, or VIII (Pl. 5A: middle row, right). Both are of the standard PG dipped variety (Coldstream 1996, 379). The preserved bell skyphoi are fragmentary, preserving either the upper body (**I P1**, **IX P3**, **IX P35**) or the conical base (**IX P40**, **IX P41**). It is difficult to discern their decorative schemes. One of those, of which only the top is preserved (**IX P3**), has a band on the belly, while the other two appear to be monochrome; the bases are not preserved, making it impossible to tell if they were dipped. The dipped bell skyphoi were found most commonly in the LPG period at Knossos, but from the PGB period onward, they were most often monochrome (Brock 1957, 187). The two Vronda bases are plain, so they probably come from dipped bell skyphoi. Of those of which only the tops are preserved, one is large, with a rim diameter of 16 cm (**I P1**), while the other two are small, with rim diameters of 10.5–11.0 cm (**IX P3**, **IX P35**).

LOW-BASED SKYPHOS

Only one skyphos (**X P8**) has been identified in the tholos tombs. The remnants of this vessel may come from a flat-based skyphos, perhaps similar to a SM–EPG example from Knossos (Coldstream and Catling, eds., 1996, 131, pl. 133:9), although the profile of the Vronda example has more of an S-curve. Other possible skyphoi are more likely to be fragments from deep bowls of LM IIIC date that may have been in the soil when the tombs were constructed (**II P2**, **V P1**). The rims on both these vessels are only slightly everted, and their profiles are too straight and the handles set too high for them to be skyphoi.

Skyphoi, however, frequently appear in the enclosure burials. They can be either decorated or plain. Decorated skyphoi are quite common (**GR4 P2, GR5 P1, GR6 P2, GR9 P2, GR9 P3, GR12 P5–GR12 P7, GR16 P2, GR16 P15, GR16 P16, GR19 P2, GR19 P3, GR20 P2, GR26 P1, GR36 P1–GR36 P3**). One example (**GR20 P2**) is much smaller than the others. These skyphoi are generally hemispherical in shape but may have tapering lower bodies, as on **GR16 P2**, **GR16 P15**, and **GR36 P3**. Several have an S-curve from rim to body (**GR12 P5**; Fig. 161:e), while others have offset rims (**GR36 P2**). At least one (**GR19 P2**; Fig. 161:f) has an almost vertical rim. Handles are generally round, and they are set pointing upward at the widest point on the body, not rising above the rim. One has horizontal strap handles set horizontally on the body (**GR9 P2**). Bases, when preserved, are flat, often concave underneath. A few raised bases exist (**GR12 P6, GR16 P15**), and two skyphoi have ring bases (**GR5 P1, GR36 P1**). Heights of skyphoi are generally 6.80–9.70 cm, rim diameters 8.00–14.00 cm, and the H/DR ratio falls in the range of 0.60–0.80. Three skyphoi are considerably deeper (**GR12 P6, GR19 P3** [Fig. 161:g], **GR20 P2**), with H/DR ratios of 0.80–0.98. Skyphos **GR9 P3** has a height greater than its rim diameter. One possible skyphos (it lacks handles) is more shallow (**GR5 P1**), with a H/DR ratio of 0.50; it is similar in shape to **GR4 P2**, but deeper. In terms of capacities (Glowacki, this vol., App. A, p. 377), decorated skyphoi can be divided into small (0.28 L), medium (0.38–0.48 L), large (0.57–0.79 L), and extra-large (0.95–1.05 L) size groups, of which the medium and large categories are most common.

The decoration of these skyphoi is usually confined to a metope in the handle zone. The remainder of the vessel may be coated or banded. Skyphos **GR5 P1** is unusual in having a thin reserved band with upright strokes just below the rim. The most common motif within a metope is a series of three to five horizontal lines (**GR12 P6, GR16 P15, GR19 P3, GR36 P2**), a type of decoration that is common on skyphoi in the Siteia area (Tsipopoulou 2005, 420, fig. 117), although it is not found in the central part of the island. Zigzags are also common, usually between bands (**GR6 P2, GR16 P16**), and on one example with dots (**GR19 P2**). Zigzags are common motifs on skyphoi of MG II late date at Knossos (Coldstream 1996, 383, type Ciif). Other motifs found on single examples include compass-drawn circles, pendant semicircles or loops, butterfly pattern, crosshatched triangles or squares, and groups of pendant strokes, sometimes curving, hanging from the rim. Interiors are mostly coated, but at least two examples have bands (**GR6 P2, GR12 P7**). Skyphos **GR12 P6** does not appear to be painted on the interior. Two examples have paint on their undersides (**GR5 P1, GR19 P2**), a feature that is more common on the monochrome skyphoi.

One decorated skyphos is considerably larger than the others (rim d. 17.5 cm), approaching the size of the krater (**GR3 P17**). It has an everted rim that is thickened outwardly and flattened on top, with a ridge below the rim, a shape that is possibly a late development from the PG bell krater. It has a hemispherical body, round horizontal handles set below the ridge, and a flat base. It is elaborately decorated with a band of crosshatched butterfly motifs in the handle zone and bands on the lower body, and is clearly coated on the interior. Its shape is similar to a pyxis of LPG–EG date from Knossos (Coldstream and Catling, eds., 1996, 36, fig. 68:12). Another open vessel may also be a large skyphos (**GR30 P25**). This vessel has a slightly everted rim with a diameter of 17.8 cm and a body that is almost carinated, similar in many ways to krater **GR28 P24**. The decoration is elaborate, with groups of vertical strokes below the rim and, on the lower body, interlocking running spirals with oblique strokes above.

Skyphos **GR9 P3** is an unusual vessel that looks like a krateriskos but was probably a skyphos because it has interior paint. It has a tall flaring rim, globular body, and slightly raised flat base, and its handles are set below the rim. It shows traces of decoration, but they are too badly preserved to be described. This vessel does not quite fit into the category of skyphos, however, because it is deeper than usual, with a height greater than the rim diameter. For this reason, it might also be a krateriskos.

Another unusual vessel is **GR4 P2**, with its widely flaring rim and shallow body. Although it has a few Cretan parallels from LG Chalasmenos and EO Praisos, its shape recalls nothing so much as the so-called Ionian cup of the late seventh century (Catling and Shipley 1989, 188–190, fig. 1:a; Cook 1998; Schlotzhauer 2000, 411–412, figs. 297, 298). It may thus be the latest skyphos found in the enclosure graves.

Monochrome skyphoi are also found (**GR1 P16, GR1 P17, GR3 P10, GR4 P15, GR6 P24, GR9 P45, GR9 P46, GR15 P1, GR17 P5, GR17 P6, GR26 P9–GR26 P11, GR26 P13, GR30 P13, GR30 P29**, and possibly **GR26 P8**). Some of these are Orientalizing in date (**GR4 P15, GR12 P25, GR15 P1, GR17 P5, GR17 P6, GR30 P29**) and may once have born decoration in added white. These monochrome skyphoi can be either shallow (H/DR ratio 0.47–0.64) or deep (H/DR ratio 0.71–0.86). The shallow varieties have heights of 5.60–6.40 cm and rim diameters of 9.30–12.50 cm, while the deeper skyphoi have heights of 9.00–11.10 cm and rim diameters of 13.40–17.00 cm. Capacities run from 0.24 to 1.25 L, with the majority falling between 0.33 and 0.79 L.

Rim treatments of the monochrome skyphoi show great variation. Two have flaring rims on S-shaped bodies (**GR17 P6, GR26 P9**; Fig. 161:h). Several have offset rims that either turn outward (**GR3 P10, GR15 P1, GR30 P13**) or are vertical (**GR30 P29**). A few have almost no articulated rim at all (**GR3 P9, GR9 P46, GR26 P10, GR26 P13**; Fig. 161:i) or a small rim that is rounded and thickened outward (**GR1 P16, GR26 P8**; Fig. 161:j). One has a tiny rim, which may be a late feature (**GR4 P15**; Fig. 161:k). Two have conical bodies with nearly vertical rims (**GR1 P17, GR9 P45**); the former is close to a kotyle shape.

Bodies can be hemispherical or conical. Handles are generally attached below the rim, often at the widest diameter; they are usually round but can be elliptical or flat, as on **GR26 P10** and **GR26 P13**. Bases are generally flat (four examples) or slightly concave underneath (three examples), but they can be raised (one example). Four skyphoi have ring bases (**GR15 P1, GR17 P5, GR17 P6, GR30 P29**; Fig. 161:l); this seems to be a late feature, found on vases of Orientalizing date. It is not uncommon to find the bases, when they are preserved, coated on their undersides.

Among the monochrome skyphoi with unusual shapes are **GR26 P8** and **GR12 P25**. The mouth of **GR26 P8** is more restricted than usual, and it may have served a function different from the other skyphoi. Skyphos **GR12 P25** is distinguished by its deeper shape, resembling the earlier amphoriskos. It is unclear whether this vessel is monochrome or decorated on the exterior, but it is certainly monochrome within. The tall rim and the base with two concentric grooves suggest a LO date for this vessel.

Only two complete plain skyphoi are known (**GR6 P23, GR36 P16**). These are coarse or medium-coarse in fabric and show signs of burning. They may once have been monochrome, but the surfaces are so poorly preserved that it is impossible to determine their treatment. Both are large, fairly deep (H/DR ratio 0.6), and have offset rims and flat bases, one slightly concave underneath.

While a greater percentage of skyphoi than cups are decorated, in general cups outnumber skyphoi in the graves. Cups also tend to be larger than skyphoi in the LG period, although a slightly larger percentage of the skyphoi are around or over one liter in capacity (Glowacki, this vol., App. A, p. 377). Nearly all of the skyphoi are of the type identified at Knossos (Coldstream 1996, 380–384; 2001, 53–55) and Eleutherna (Kotsonas 2008, 196–197) as imitating low-based Attic and Cycladic shapes. The Vronda examples, like others from East Crete, seem to follow their own path, both in shape and decoration. The majority of skyphoi, whether decorated, monochrome, or plain, have bodies with an S-curved profile. There are no certain chronological indicators before the seventh century. Kotsonas (2008, 197) has suggested that the development of the skyphos can best be seen in the growth of the lip, and at Vronda the two skyphoi with the tallest lips (**GR17 P6, GR30 P29**) both come from graves with significant amounts of EO and LO material in them. The bases may also be used to determine seventh-century date; ring bases seem to be a late feature, and bases with grooves on the underside may date to the later part of the seventh century.

STEMMED SKYPHOS

Peculiar to the eastern part of Crete is the appearance of a stemmed skyphos in the LG period (**GR1 P2, GR6 P3** [Fig. 161:m], **GR6 P4, GR19 P4, GR28 P1**). This type appears only in the enclosure graves and is not known from the tholos tombs. Stemmed skyphoi are generally decorated; **GR6 P4** may have been decorated or monochrome, but the surface is too worn to be certain. The shape is a deep hemispherical bowl with two round horizontal handles and a low, flaring foot. The rim is not articulated and can be vertical or slightly incurving. The foot is small, with a low stem spreading into a flat base that is hollow underneath. Decoration appears in a metope that is generally divided horizontally into two or three zones by bands. Each zone carries a simple linear motif such as zigzag, S-pattern, or oblique strokes, but it can also have horizontal lines or be blank. Skyphos **GR1 P2** is unusual in that it has a metope that runs almost to the handles, and instead of zones of decoration, it bears a single "running dog" motif, which appears late in the LG period (Tsipopoulou 2005, 485).

It is uncertain whether this shape derives directly from the PG bell skyphos, as Tsipopoulou (2005, 412) has suggested, or from the mainland stemmed types, as can be seen at Knossos (Coldstream 1996, 380–381; 2001, 53–54). The Vronda vessels have real stems rather than high conical feet, a feature that perhaps came from the mainland. Although at Kavousi there are two mainland types from the tombs around the Kastro (Tsipopoulou 2005, 99, fig. 108:H733, pl. 71), at Vronda only the late hemispherical type appears. The decoration of these vessels, along with the elegant but nonfunctional stem, suggests that these were high status vessels used on social occasions.

CUP OR SKYPHOS

A number of rim fragments from both the tholos tombs and the enclosure graves could come either from cups or skyphoi, but as the handles are not preserved, it is impossible to be certain. Several of the rim fragments from the tholos tombs are more likely to have come from LM IIIC cups or deep bowls, as the rims are reminiscent of those from the settlement (**IV P2, V P2, VIII P2, VIII P4–VIII P6, XI P1**). There are also bases that belong on LM IIIC open vessels (**VIII P7, VIII P8**).

Krateriskos

A krateriskos from Boyd's 1900 excavations (**Boyd P3**) may come from one of the Vronda tholos tombs. With its flaring rim, deep ovoid body, and conical base, and shoulder decoration of crude zigzag, it is a type common in the EPG period (see above, this vol., Ch. 2, p. 52).

Bowl

Open vessels that do not belong to other categories of open shapes are here classified as bowls. Generally, they are larger than cups or skyphoi but smaller than kraters, and they usually show no evidence of having had handles. Four bowls came from the tholos tombs, and they are quite different from one another (**VII P1** [Fig. 161:o], **IX P5** [Fig. 161:n], **IX P6, IX P42**). Two are without handles (**IX P5, IX P42**), one has horizontal lugs at the rim (**IX P6**), and the last is carinated, with an incurving rim and two horizontal strap handles at the carination (**VII P1**). Three are decorated, two with bands, one with striped lugs, and one (**IX P42**) is monochrome. Three of these bowls come from Tomb IX and have large rim diameters (15.00–16.50 cm). The simplest is **IX P5**, which has a conical body with a slight convex curve rising to a vertical rim, a raised base that is slightly concave underneath, and decoration of horizontal bands. Parallels suggest a wide range of dates from the EG to the LG periods (see above, pp. 38–39). Another simple bowl (**IX P42**), rather more shallow than the others, has a broad disk base, a rounded body, and a wide, flat, everted rim. It appears to be monochrome. No good parallels can be found for this shape. Bowl **IX P6** has a simple deep rounded body rising from a broad flat base. The rim is slightly thickened on the exterior. Two small lug handles are set at the rim on opposite sides of the vessel. The bowl itself is monochrome, but the lug handles are decorated with strokes.

The last bowl (**VII P1**) is unique. While it is similar in shape to larger kraters and smaller skyphoi that at Knossos and Eleutherna are seen as imitating the tripod cauldron (Coldstream 1996, 380; Kotsonas 2008, 194–96), the deeply incurved rim of the Vronda example is not found on those shapes. At Knossos, the skyphoi are generally decorated with stripes on the lower body, and they sometimes have similar strokes on the rim (e.g., Coldstream and Catling, eds., 1996, 156, fig. 110:119), but they almost always have other ornaments on the upper body, a feature that is lacking on the Vronda example. At Knossos, the form is most common in the EG period (Coldstream 1996, 380). Incurved rims are generally found on pyxides, and it is possible that this vessel functioned as a pyxis rather than a bowl.

Three conical bowls were found in the enclosure graves: **GR3 P20** (Fig. 161:p), **GR16 P22**, and **GR30 P26**. These are similar in shape to bowl **IX P5**, and they are large, with rim diameters of 14.70–21.00 cm. They are made of coarse or medium-coarse fabric, and their conical bodies have simple rounded rims, and the preserved bases are raised, one with a flat, another with a concave bottom. They show traces of paint on both interior and exterior. Bowl **GR30 P26** has a rim band on the exterior, **GR16 P22** is monochrome, and **GR3 P20** has a poorly preserved surface that shows only a few traces of paint. Another bowl (**GR32 P11**) is similar in shape and size (rim diameter 17.00 cm) but has a slightly more rounded body, a slightly offset rim, and a flat base. It is of coarse fabric and is apparently plain. It bears some resemblance to an uncataloged example from Grave 26, as well as a possible cup from Grave 28 (**GR28 P18**).

Bowls like these are not common in other parts of Crete. Handleless bowls are known from East Crete (Tsipopoulou 2005, 430), but these examples are smaller. Bowls may have been used to hold food or other offerings at the grave. All of these bowls could have been used for serving or consuming liquids or solid foods, although the rims on **IX P42** and **VII P1** would have made drinking difficult.

Tray

Four enclosure graves produced unusual trays with shallow bowls and large tricornerd lug handles of a reflex type (**GR3 P16, GR12 P27** [Fig. 162:a], **GR12 P28, GR26 P4, GR26 P5, GR36 P6, GR36 P7**). This shape is peculiarly Cretan, and it has been called a tray with reflex lugs (Coldstream 1996, 391), a lekanis with three-cornered lugs (Moignard 1996, 452), and a basin (Kotsonas 2008, 217). The Vronda examples vary in height from shallow (2.3 cm) to relatively deep (6.3 cm), but most fall within the 5.5–6.0 cm range. They have large (8.5–15.3 cm) flat bases, and the sides rise in a straight or slightly convex line to a flattened (**GR12 P27, GR12 P28, GR26 P4, GR26 P5, GR36 P7**) or vertical (**GR3 P16, GR36 P6**) rim with a diameter that is larger (9.5–20.6 cm) than that of the base. Attached on the rim are two large, flat, three-cornered lug handles that are horizontal (**GR3 P16, GR12 P28, GR36 P6, GR36 P7**) but may be bent slightly up above the level of the rim (**GR12 P27, GR26 P4, GR26 P5**). One example (**GR26 P4**) has only a single lug handle, and the body is oval rather than round on top. One of the handles on each vessel has one (**GR3 P16, GR36 P6**) or two (**GR12 P28**) holes pierced vertically through the central point of the lug. The lug on the one-handled tray (**GR26 P4**) has no hole; the single preserved handles on the others show no piercing. **GR36 P6** has a unique feature: a large raised knob or omphalos on the center of the interior.

The trays are made from well-levigated fine clay, and their surfaces are generally polished or burnished. Burning has sometimes destroyed all traces of the finish, as on **GR26 P5**. Tray **GR3 P16**, which is unusual also because of its small size, was not polished but was entirely coated with paint except for a reserved metope on the side decorated with oblique lines. The lug handles of several of the vessels were decorated, generally on top (**GR26 P4, GR26 P5, GR36 P6**), but also on the bottom (**GR26 P4**). The others may once have had decorated lugs, or they may have been left entirely plain, like fragmentary examples from the Kastro settlement, where they are usually burnished and without decoration (Mook 1993, 179), and like a vessel from a grave at Aitania (Papadaki and Galanaki 2012, 336, fig. 1).

Until recently it has been difficult to know how to date these trays. Examples from Vrokastro, for example, are given a wide range of dates from the PG through the EO periods (Hayden 2003, 70). On the Kastro, the shape was introduced in the PG period and reached its greatest popularity in LG (Mook 1993, 181). Three trays found at nearby Chalasmenos have been assigned securely to the third quarter of the eighth century by the excavator (Tsipopoulou 2004, 134). Trays with reflex-type lugs were not common at Knossos, where a more shallow, more rounded tray with reflex handles was usual in the Geometric period (Coldstream 1996, 391–392). A few trays of EO date, however, are similar to the Kavousi examples; they are plain and burnished, with tricornered lugs but more rounded flaring profiles (Coldstream and Catling, eds., 1996, 391, fig. 64:14). At Eleutherna trays similar to the Kavousi examples were more common, and these began to occur in the EG period (Kotsonas 2008, 220) and continued into the EO period. The development of some features helps to date the Eleutherna trays: the curve of the side, the shape of the handles, and the piercing of the lugs (Kotsonas 2008, 221–222). The EG–MG examples there have more convex sides, while the later trays are straighter. The handles became vestigial by the EO period, and by LG–EO times only one or none of the handles was pierced. It would appear that the Vronda trays are most likely to belong to the late eighth century (LG) on the basis of the well-developed lugs, the piercing of only one handle, and the preference for the plain polished surfaces that became common in the EO period.

Trays appear in domestic contexts (Mook 1993, 179–181) but are more common in graves, usually in pairs, as at Knossos (Brock 1957, 165; Coldstream 1996, 390). The Vronda trays are nearly always in pairs (Graves 12, 26, 36). Only **GR3 P16** was a singleton, and it is unusual for its small size. The shape may originally have been intended as a tray or serving bowl, but the piercing of the lugs suggests that in the funerary context these objects functioned as lids. In the Mastambas tomb, one of these trays was actually found upside down as a lid on a stemmed pithos of LG–EO date (Lebessi 1970, 288, pls. 388:α, 401:α, β:63), and at Aphrati they were found still in use as lids for cremation urns (Levi 1927–1929, 180, fig. 85; 116, fig. 95).

The decoration of the undersides of some of the trays makes sense if they were meant to be used as lids, but it has also been suggested that they were ornaments to be hung on walls (Droop 1905–1906, 38–39). The decoration can be painted, as on examples from the Plai tou Kastrou tomb at Kavousi (Tsipopoulou 2005, 104, fig. 134:H756), or it may consist of molded patterns, as seen at Eleutherna (Kotsonas 2008, 218–221, fig. 53:A140β) and in the area of Hagios Nikolaos (Droop 1905–1906, 37–39, figs. 15, 16). The undecorated examples, however, would not have made very good ornamental hangings.

One of the Vronda trays (**GR36 P6**) has a large knob in the center, a feature characteristic of the later mesomphalos phiale, a shape that came into Greece from Assyria and was used for Greek libation rituals (Luschey 1939; Schütte-Maischatz 2011). The Cretan tray in no way resembles the later phiale, which is a shallow, rounded, handleless bowl with a knob in the center pressed out from the bottom and creating a depression on the underside to make it easier to pour with one hand. The phiale was certainly known to the Cretans in the EIA, and several imported bronze examples came from the Eleutherna burials (Stampolides 2008, 152, fig. 107:b; 156, fig. 114). While the Vronda tray is of a different shape and is much larger and heavier than the imported bronze phiales, the interior knob ties it to those vessels. The presence of the knob in **GR36 P6** might suggest that it had a ritual function, perhaps related to funerary rites. The knob may also have served as a sort of stopper if this vessel were used as a lid for a vessel with a much smaller mouth.

As with many other shapes of pottery, the tray may have served a variety of functions, depending on the circumstances. In the graves in particular, they might potentially have been used as serving dishes for a funeral meal, as offering bowls, as libation vessels, or as lids. Contextual associations, fortunately, can tell us something about their use. There are no vessels that require a lid in Grave 3, and the only vessels **GR3 P16** could fit were cups. In Grave 12, the trays could have served as lids for only one of the three amphorae. Similarly, in Grave 26, either of the trays might have served as a lid for the amphora, but there are no other vessels that would have required a lid. Finally, in Grave 36, the trays are too large to seal any vessel found within. It would seem that whatever use these vessels had elsewhere, in the Vronda graves they did not function as lids. The one-handled tray (**GR26 P4**) and the large tray with the knob (**GR36 P6**) may have had a ritual function, but the other trays are most likely to have been used for serving or storing food, either for a funeral meal (after which they would have been placed on the grave) or to hold sustenance for the dead.

Related to the trays with reflex-type tricornered lugs is a vessel from Grave 32 with reflex handles instead of lugs (**GR32 P7**; Fig. 162:b). The shape has been termed a basin at Eleutherna (Kotsonas 2008, 222–226) and a lekanis at Knossos (Moignard 1996, 452). Because it is deeper than the tray and has reflex handles rather than lugs, it is here termed a lekanis. At Vronda this shape is rare, appearing only once, and at Knossos it was also rare in the cemeteries (Moignard 1996, 452). However, it was more common at Eleutherna, where it seems to represent a later development of what is here called the tray (Kotsonas 2008, 222). Both at Knossos and Eleutherna, the shape is of EO date. The Knossos examples are elaborately decorated all over, including the underside, a fact that suggests they were meant to be hung, like the even more elaborately decorated example from Arkades (Levi 1927–1929, 289, fig. 374; 307, fig. 407). The Vronda lekanis, however, is almost totally monochrome, although perhaps it was once decorated with white paint.

Kalathos

Kalathoi are large or medium-sized vessels that generally have a flaring profile and a large rim in relation to the base. Only a single fragment from a kalathos is preserved from the tholos tombs, although the shape is common in SM–EG tombs elsewhere on Crete (e.g., at Knossos: Coldstream 1996, 377–378; 2001, 57), where they were often used as lids for cremation urns. The fragment **IV P14** is from the rim of an unusual kalathos with an excrescent cup, similar to EPG–MPG examples from Knossos (Coldstream 1996, 376–377). More kalathoi occur in the enclosure graves at Vronda, although they are not common. They are quite distinctive, however, and they occur in two types.

The Type 1 kalathos is large, with a flattened rim, nearly concave profile, and heavy base (**GR1 P6, GR1 P7, GR9 P4, GR9 P5, GR12 P9** [Fig. 162:c], **GR12 P10, GR20 P17, GR21 P8**). Rim diameters range from 20.00 to 40.00 cm, while bases are 6.80–11.00 cm in diameter. The ratio of height to rim in these vessels is 0.37–0.45, and the ratio of base to rim is 0.27–0.44. Most kalathoi have flaring, nearly concave profiles, but one seems to be straight in profile (**GR12 P10**), and another is concave toward the bottom and convex at the top (**GR9 P4**). Rims are flattened on top, and sometimes the top is decorated with grooves (**GR21 P8**) or painted patterns, such as alternating dark and light triangles (**GR12 P10**). Handles are round and set either near the rim or at the middle of the body. Bases are thick and heavy, often beveled (**GR9 P4, GR12 P10**) or grooved (**GR12 P9**); the base on **GR12 P10** has vertical grooves on the beveled edge.

Kalathoi of Type 1 occur in fine or medium-coarse fabrics, and their bodies are often decorated. Kalathos **GR21 P8** is monochrome with a reserved metope bearing a wavy line between pairs of horizontal lines. The underside of the base is decorated with an X-pattern with a circle in the center. Another vessel, **GR9 P4**, has horizontal zones of decoration: oblique strokes, checkerboard, and two more zones of oblique strokes. Other motifs include hatched zigzag (**GR12 P9**) and a possible cross-hatched lozenge (**GR20 P17**). On **GR9 P5** the handles are decorated with stripes. This type of kalathos is known from other EIA sites on Crete (e.g., Coldstream 2001, 57–59).

The Type 2 kalathos is much smaller than the Type 1 examples, with a straighter profile and a base that is less heavy (**GR26 P14–GR26 P16, GR36 P4** [Fig. 162:d], **GR36 P5**). Vessels of this type are not dissimilar to the skyphoi, but they have neither the S-curved profiles nor the articulated rims of the skyphoi. The rim is simple and rounded, the handles are flattened or round and attached just below the lip, and the bases are flat, or, on one example, raised. Rim diameters range from 14.70 to 16.00 cm, heights from 6.50 to 7.20 cm, and base diameters from 5.10 to 6.00 cm. The height-to-rim ratios are 0.43–0.48, and the base-to-rim diameters are 0.32–0.40.

All the recognizable examples of the Type 2 kalathoi are made in fine wares, and they can be either plain and slipped (**GR26 P14–GR26 P16**) or decorated. They may be decorated with simple oblique strokes, as on **GR36 P5**, or more complex designs. On one side, **GR36 P4** has a zone of metopes with X-patterns in each metope above bands, and on the other side it has a complicated pattern of groups of vertical strokes and a hatched pattern in a zone below the lip, along with a hatched curvilinear motif and hatched leaf on the lower body. Both kalathoi from Grave 36 have incised marks on the underside of the base (see below, pp. 294–296).

Although kalathoi belong to the EPG–EG period in Central Crete (Coldstream 1996, 376–378), they lasted longer in the eastern part of the island (Tsipopoulou 2005, 411). Some of those from the Vronda graves may be antiques that were buried with the dead. For example, **GR21 P8** seems to be considerably earlier than the other vessels in the pithos burial in Grave 21, and its decorated base also suggests that it is early, as decorated bases began in the LPG period at Knossos (Coldstream 1996, 378). Very large kalathoi like Vronda Type 1 tend to be of EPG to MPG date at Knossos (Coldstream 1996, 377). The smaller Type 2 kalathoi also have parallels at Knossos from LPG–EG (see above, pp. 167, 206). Either the shape continued to be popular at Vronda and East Cretan potters kept manufacturing kalathoi, or older vessels were regularly placed in the graves.

The function of kalathoi is uncertain, but they were probably multifunctional. Some of the larger ones may have been used as bowls to hold foodstuffs or other offerings at the funeral ritual, whether for the participants or their deities or as sustenance for the dead. In Central Crete, kalathoi were used as lids for cremation urns or pithoi from the LPG period onward. At Vronda, where the bodies were left within the enclosure, such cremation vessels did not exist for the most part, but the kalathoi may nonetheless have been used as lids over jars or smaller pyxides. The angle of the handles on both **GR9 P5** and **GR26 P16** suggests that these vessels were manufactured to serve as lids. The decorated bottom of **GR21 P8** suggests an intended use as a lid, but in the context of the burial it did not function that way, as it was found with other vessels within a pithos that had a stone lid in place. It is likely that kalathoi were manufactured to be used in domestic settings (Rethemiotakis and Englezou 2010, 153–154), some as bowls, others as lids, and that they were placed in the graves with offerings.

Krater

Kraters are large open vessels probably used, as in later Greek times, for the mixing of water and wine. They come in a variety of shapes and sizes, but most of them have a rim diameter of 20 cm or more. The exception is **GR4 P16**, which has a rim diameter of only 18 cm, but a capacity close to that of the kraters (Glowacki, this vol., App. A, p. 377).

Kraters are rare in the tholos tombs, and only five possible examples exist, all fragmentary (**I P2, IV P13, IX P36, XI P4, XI P7**). At least three of these five vessels have minimum rim diameters of 20 cm, and they may have functioned as large skyphoi, used for communal drinking rather than for mixing liquids. One of these is a rim fragment with handles (**IX P36**) that may have come from a PG bell krater. Two other rim fragments (**I P2, XI P4**) show less of a curve but are similar to SM–EPG examples from Knossos (see above, pp. 17, 51). Finally, the area in front of Tomb IV produced two kraters. A very large krater with a rim diameter of 30 cm (**IV P13**) has unusual flattened handles, but otherwise it is similar to examples of LPG–EG date at Knossos and Eleutherna (see above, p. 26). Only a single fragment comes from what may be a footed krater. A wide, flaring foot decorated with a wavy band (**IV P16**) may have been attached to a krater, although it could also have come from a larger closed vessel, such as the hydriai from the LG–EO Skouriasmenos tomb at Kavousi (Tsipopoulou 2005, 114, fig. 42:H1952; 115, fig. 81:H1954).

Kraters are not common in the cremation graves, but several different types are represented. Only a single example of the bell krater, so common on other Cretan sites, has been found in the cremation burials (**GR12 P11**; Fig. 163:a). The top part of this vessel is similar to examples from Knossos (Coldstream 1996, 368–372; 2001, 47) and Eleutherna (Kotsonas 2008, 183–184), but the bottom is different, with a wider base. The vessel is fragmentary, and it is possible that the reconstruction is not correct or that the base belonged to another similar vessel; at any rate, there is no join between the upper and lower halves. Krater **GR12 P11** has a wide flaring rim that is outwardly thickened, with no ridge below it. The handles are not preserved except for the lower attachment on one side. The base is beveled but poorly preserved. The decoration below the coated lip consists of sixfold concentric circles, with dots between the outermost, the third, and the fifth pairs; two upright bands are all that remain of what was once probably a central decorated panel. The lower body is decorated with bands. The decoration conforms to the regular arrangements on Knossian bell kraters with concentric circles flanking a central panel with rectilinear motifs (Coldstream 1996, 368; 2001, 47), although the dotted circles are an unusual feature. This dotted circle motif is not common until the EO period, although it may have existed earlier (see above, p. 117). The shape is similar to a famous krater of LPG date from Knossos (Sackett and Musgrave 1976, 121, fig. 4:3), but it lacks the ridge below the rim common to the large examples from the North Cemetery.

There are no examples from the enclosure graves of the type of krater imitating cauldrons that were common at Knossos (Coldstream 1996, 372–374) and Eleutherna (Kotsonas 2008, 185–187). Most of the Vronda kraters are of types that imitate mainland styles or have no good parallels elsewhere. Of the kraters recognized at Knossos as being influenced by mainland styles, **GR12 P12** (Fig. 163:b) probably belongs to Coldstream's first type, an Atticizing krater with a high conical foot, overhanging rim, concave lip with a ridge below, and bucranium handles (Coldstream 1996, 374–375). Although only the top of the Vronda example is preserved and the vessel's foot is lost, the other features are similar. The decorative scheme of **GR12 P12**, with its concentric circles in the handle zone, is closest to kraters of this type of MPG date (Coldstream and Catling, eds., 1996, 186, pl. 178:27, 28). Possibly also of this mainland type is **GR28 P21**, although its base is missing. It has simple horizontal round handles rather than bucranium handles. It may also be a later version of the type, as is suggested by the decoration of two zones of concentric circles separated by parallel bands, a motif that is common on East Cretan amphorae of LG date (Tsipopoulou 2005, 493) and on Orientalizing jars at Knossos (Moignard 1996, 422–423).

Two kraters of Coldstream's Type Cii (1996, 375), with tall ribbed pedestals, are also found in the cremation burials (**GR23 P3**, **GR27 P4**; Fig. 163:c). Only the stem of **GR23 P3** is preserved, and it has banded decoration and grooves only at the top and bottom. Krater **GR27 P4**, however, is quite similar in shape to examples from Knossos, which are based on Attic Type II kraters (Coldstream 1996, 375; 2001, 51) both in shape and decoration. The vessel has a deep hemispherical body with a short vertical rim and stirrup handles, not the bucranium handles common at Knossos. The pedestal is tall and ribbed. The decoration also bears some similarity to that on the kraters from Knossos, which generally have a central meander. The rest of the decorative scheme, however, is most unlike other pedestaled kraters on Crete or elsewhere. The meander pattern is dotted, a feature that is found in the LG period at Knossos and in East Crete (see above, p. 170). Above and below the meander are zones of circles connected by tangents, which are particularly common also in Theran LG and SubLG material (e.g., Coldstream 1968, pl. 40:c–e), suggesting Cycladic influence. The decoration on the lower zone of fourfold circles with stars in the center is unique (visible on Pl. 55E). Finally, the large bands of multiple lines, narrow ones between two broad ones, which curve down from handle zone over other patterns and divide up the surface of the vessel into decorative areas, have parallels on jugs that imitate Cypriot Black-on-Red ware of LG and LO date at Knossos (Coldstream and Catling, eds., 1996, 88, pl. 107:29; 102, pl. 115:22), on imported jugs of Cypriot Black-on-Red II (Coldstream and Catling, eds., 1996, 265, fig. 146:94), and on White Painted IV ware from Knossos (Coldstream and Catling, eds., 1996, 227, pl. 208:11). Combined with the peculiar bichrome color of the paint on this vessel, this decorative feature suggests that it may have been a local product of combined Knossian, Cycladic, and Cypriot forms. Because of the use of multiple brushes, however, it is possible that the vessel was made for the local market by an itinerant Cypriot potter, as suggested by Kotsonas (2011b, 142). It dates to the EO period.

An unusual pedestaled ovoid krater, **GR12 P41** (Fig. 163:d), is certainly an import. Its shape is not known at Vronda, and good parallels from anywhere are lacking. The shape resembles some early pedestaled pithoi from Knossos (Brock 1957, 150, pls. 88:1454, 90:1350), but the traces of paint on the interior suggest that it was an open vessel. The rim is different from anything found on Crete, and parallels are lacking from other areas of Greece or the eastern Mediterranean. Similar shelf rims occur on Early Iron Age cooking pots from the Levant (Zimhoni 1997, 19, fig. 1.4:1; 37, fig. 2.4:1; 126, fig. 3.40:1; Spagnoli 2010, 162–163, pl. 34:393; 240–241, pl. 73:776; 276–277, pl. 91:1001), and a close example comes from Megiddo (Finkelstein, Ussishkin, and Halpern, eds., 2000, 270, fig. 11.19:3). No matter how much the rim might resemble those on Levantine cooking pots, however, the overall shape is unknown in the eastern Mediterranean, the fabric is not suitable for cooking, and the pedestal base seems inappropriate for a cooking pot. Although several of the pieces of this vessel are badly burned, it would appear that the burning occurred after breaking in the pyre rather than from use in cooking, as the burned fragments join onto unburned pieces. Petrographic analysis indicates that this krater originated in northeastern Crete.

Smaller kraters that are probably more like those of type Ciii at Knossos (Coldstream 1996, 376) are also found (**GR20 P11**, **GR28 P24**, **GR30 P24**). These vessels are all known only from their rims or bodies, so it is uncertain if they had the flat bases found at Knossos. Generally, their rim diameters measure 20 cm, so they may also be considered as very large skyphoi. Krater **GR28 P24** has an everted triangular rim that is scored with deep grooves and a round horizontal handle at the widest diameter. It carries in the handle zone a frieze of crosshatched butterflies. Only a large fragment of the lower body of **GR30 P24** is preserved; it has zones of motifs of oblique lines, alternating in their directions to form triangles, and a dotted lozenge chain above. It is clearly an open vessel and may have been large enough to have functioned as a krater. Krater **GR20 P11** in particular resembles a large skyphos, with an everted rim that is thickened on the outside and has grooves at the base. It has a round horizontal handle below the rim. The vessel is probably monochrome, and it is uncertain if it should be categorized as an overly large skyphos or a krater.

One monochrome vessel that is technically too small to be classified as a krater is larger than any other drinking vessels, with a rim diameter of 18 cm and a height of 21 cm (**GR4 P16**; Fig. 163:e). Because of its size it may have functioned as a krater rather than a drinking vessel. This vessel has a large offset rim that is outwardly thickened and a deep ovoid body. Its unusual handles are round but vertical, rather than horizontal; they are mounted below the rim to the widest part of the body. It has a low ring base.

There are three vessels for which few if any parallels exist. They are large, rather open shapes that may have functioned as kraters although they are not painted on the interior (**GR6 P27** [Fig. 163:f], **GR9 P35**, **GR17 P11**, **GR28 P25**). With the exception of **GR9 P35**, these vessels are all coarse. Two vessels (**GR9 P35**, **GR28 P25**) have somewhat restricted mouths with flaring lips; they resemble necked jars but have much wider mouths. The smaller (**GR9 P35**) has a flaring mouth with an almost triangular lip and a rim diameter of 24 cm. The body curves to its widest diameter where the round horizontal handles are attached, then runs straight down toward the missing base. It is decorated with bands on the neck and upper body and has an undetermined motif in the handle zone. Krater **GR28 P25** is of similar shape, but larger, with a rim diameter of 32 cm. The mouth is flaring but the rim is simple and rounded. The body curves out further than **GR9 P35**, but the lower body is similar. It has a slightly raised flat base, and traces of paint remain on the lower body. Krater **GR6 P27** has a rim similar to **GR12 P12** but without the ridge. The round horizontal handles are attached below the rim. The lower body tends toward a conical profile. With a rim diameter of 46 cm, this is the largest open vessel found in the burial enclosures, and it looks as though it might be a local adaptation of the bell skyphos. It is decorated, but only bands can still be seen. Krater **GR17 P11** may be identified better as a basin and is discussed below.

The relative paucity of kraters in the Vronda burials is in keeping with a pattern observed throughout Greece in this period (Papadopoulos and Smithson 2017, 824), although kraters are relatively more common in eastern and central Crete. Elsewhere in the eighth and seventh centuries this vessel type almost disappeared in tombs on Crete, if not in settlements or sanctuaries (Kotsonas 2011a, 944–946). Kraters are not as rare in the Vronda enclosure graves as Kotsonas has suggested based on the preliminary reports (2011a, 944), but they are not common; only 13 vessels can be identified tentatively as kraters. In most cases, only a single krater is found in an enclosure, while three to 17 drinking vessels appear. In two instances, Graves 12 and 28, more than one krater occurs in an enclosure, but these do not necessarily belong to the same burial event. In Grave 12, three kraters were identified, along with 19 drinking vessels. Two of these kraters, however, appear to be earlier than the rest of the pottery from the burials, the bell krater **GR12 P11** and **GR12 P12**. These vessels may have been heirloom pieces or antiques deposited in the grave. The third vessel that may have been a krater (**GR12 P41**) has a unique fabric and shape; whether it was used as a krater or made as a krater is not clear. Grave 28 had two kraters that were both so small that they may have been used for drinking, along with 15 other vessels. It is clear that the regular grave assemblages rarely included kraters and that certainly not all burials were accompanied by a krater.

Kotsonas has connected the demise of the krater with the rise of the large cup, suggesting a change in social habits (Kotsonas 2011a, 948–949). Instead of using a krater for mixing wine and water and serving individuals their portions in smaller cups, people began using larger cups in which they could mix their own wine and water to their own taste. Kotsonas suggests that in the funerary context, drinking rituals centered on a krater were replaced by those using a number of drinking vessels for individual use. At Vronda, however, kraters are rare even in the earlier tholos tombs; only Tombs IV and IX definitely produced kraters. Thus, no major change seems to have occurred in the use of kraters from the SM to LG periods. The idea proposed by Kotsonas that the change is a sign of the social movements leading to the rise of the polis cannot be confirmed by the evidence from Vronda.

Whatever their social use in domestic contexts, kraters in funerary settings may have had a specialized function. Many of those at Vronda are very large, and they may have stood outside the grave as markers or for use in postfunerary rituals. It is interesting to note that the largest kraters come from enclosures that seem to have had areas for display associated with them (Graves 6, 12, 27) or other evidence for the use of grave markers (Grave 9).

Basin

Two larger vessels that may be categorized as basins came from the tholos tombs (**I P3, V P4**). Basin **I P3** resembles the LM IIIC lekane (Day et al. 2016, 77, 92–93) and may belong to that period. It might have been a fragment that was in the soil when the tomb was built, although similar examples occur in SM tombs (Rethemiotakis and Englezou 2010, 44, fig. 23:45). The vessel **V P4** also looks early and may come from a LM IIIC pyxis rather than a basin (Day et al. 2016, 80).

Only a single large, deep basin (**GR17 P11**), apparently made of cooking ware fabric, was found in the enclosure graves. It has an offset rim that is outwardly thickened and flattened on top and a ridge at the base of the rim. The rim measures 30 cm in diameter. Two round horizontal handles are attached at the widest diameter. The base, which does not join, is flat. The surface of this vessel may have been slipped and slightly polished. The evidence for burning might reflect its use as a cooking pot, or it may have been burned by the cremation fires. It is possible that this vessel was used as a krater, but because it is coarse and undecorated, it is more likely to have been used for cooking or was set near the pyre to quench the fire.

Closed Shapes

Aryballos

The aryballos is a small pouring vessel with a round mouth, handle from rim to shoulder, and a short, narrow neck. Inspired by Corinthian imports, the aryballos entered the Cretan repertoire in the PG period (Coldstream 1996, 356), and it continued into the LO period with many local variations. The shape is common in the enclosure graves at Vronda. Aryballoi are generally divided into types based on their surface treatment, including unpainted, painted, and coated or monochrome varieties (Coldstream 1996, 356–358; 2001, 44; Kotsonas 2008, 174–183).

Decorated varieties are common (**GR4 P4–GR4 P6, GR12 P13, GR16 P5, GR30 P2, GR32 P1**). Most bear groups of bands on the lower body and small concentric circles on the shoulder (**GR4 P4–GR4 P6, GR12 P13**; Fig. 162:e). This is a type that is well known at other Cretan sites and belongs to the EO period (Moignard 1996, 444, type Bii; Coldstream 2001, 44). These aryballoi range in height from 5.4 to 7.8 cm. Necks are generally short, and rims can be flaring or vertical. Handles are round or elliptical. The bases on two examples are flat, and two others have ring bases. Decoration on the shoulders consists of small concentric circles, ranging from a singlefold circle around a large central dot to fourfold circles. Groups of two to four narrow bands are placed at the lower handle attachment, while groups of two to three bands adorn the lower body and the base. Another aryballos (**GR30 P2**; Fig. 162:f) has crosshatched triangles on the shoulder in metopal panels, with a dark-coated bottom. The shape is depressed globular with an elliptical handle and flat base. It resembles other aryballoi of LG–EO date from East Crete (Tsipopoulou 2005, 406, fig. 97). Aryballos **GR32 P1** (Fig. 162:g) is of a type that is unique at Vronda: it is decorated with tongue pattern on the shoulder and banding below. Such aryballoi are known at Knossos, where they are of LO date (Coldstream 2001, 45, fig. 1.12:d). The Vronda example has a globular body that tapers toward the bottom, a short neck, and a flaring lip. The rectangular handle has two vertical stripes, one on each side. The tongue pattern is common in the LO period, and the banding on the lower body may be in imitation of Corinthian aryballoi (Moignard 1996, 445). Aryballos **GR16 P5** has bands on the lower body but no preserved decoration on the shoulder. Finally, aryballos **GR28 P17** may be decorated, as it bears a band below the neck; paint appears on other parts of the body, either from decoration or because it is monochrome.

The unpainted variety is also quite common in the enclosures (**GR3 P14, GR3 P15, GR5 P12, GR9 P31, GR12 P29, GR17 P7, GR19 P13–GR19 P15**, and possibly **GR26 P19**, of which only the rim and neck survive). Aryballoi of this type are made in fine fabrics that are usually self slipped and polished, although most of them are badly burned. They are small, with heights of 6 to 8 cm. The most common type (Type 1; **GR9 P31**; Fig. 162:h) is depressed globular in shape, with a short neck, flaring rim, and an elliptical handle from rim to shoulder; bases are generally flat but can be slightly concave underneath. Aryballos **GR5 P12** has a slightly different shape: globular but with a more tapering lower body, like examples from Eleutherna (Kotsonas 2008, 180). Aryballos **GR3 P15** is a different shape (Type 2; Fig. 162:i), more ovoid with a tapering body. Type 3 is represented by **GR17 P7** (Fig. 162:j) and **GR19 P14**; like **GR3 P15**, these examples are ovoid but do not taper toward the bottom, and they have widely flaring rims. Their shape is closest to a decorated example from Eleutherna of PGB date (Kotsonas 2008, 174). Although the parallel suggests an early date for these two aryballoi, **GR17 P7** was found in a tomb containing much EO pottery, so it may be later, or it could be an early vessel placed in a later enclosure.

The aryballos is generally assumed to have functioned as an unguent vessel, perhaps for perfumed oil. Many of the examples from the Vronda cremations have been badly burned, suggesting that they once contained oil that permeated the vessels and made them burn more completely, whether placed on the pyre with the dead before burning or simply burned during subsequent cremations in the enclosure. Such oil vessels from later Greek times have been associated with athletes, but they may also have contained perfumed oils as part of a woman's toilette. Interestingly, only one group of aryballoi can certainly be associated with an adult male burial (**GR3 P14, GR3 P15**). The others came from graves that had young people or children (Graves 16, 19) or female burials together with children (Graves 4, 17, 30, 32). Two graves that contained only women and children produced a large number of the aryballoi (Graves 4, 32). It is possible that aryballoi were associated with women's lives and thus formed part of their burial goods. It is also possible that the aryballoi were associated with children.

Juglet

Four small pouring vessels from the tholos tombs that are too large to be called aryballoi are here termed juglets (**IV P3** [Fig. 162:k], **IX P12** [Fig. 162:l], **IX P13** [Fig. 162:m], **Boyd P4**). Three of these (**IV P3, IX P12, Boyd P4**) have restricted necks and mouths that suggest a use for oil or unguents; the other (**IX P13**) has a less restricted mouth. These vessels have heights of 8.8–10.5 cm, with low centers of gravity. They have slightly flaring lips, short necks, and globular (**IV P3, IX P13**) to ovoid (**IX P12**) bodies. Handles are round to elliptical. Bases vary; one (**IX P12**) is flat and concave, two are slightly raised (**IX P13, Boyd P4**), and

IV P3 has an articulated raised base. Decoration also varies. Most elaborate is **IV P3**, which has on the shoulder a pendant hatched triangle and double outlined spiral with tail running from the top of the triangle and forming two double spirals; there is hatching in the space below the triangle. Groups of alternating strokes lie in a zone below the shoulder, and the lower body has narrow bands. Bands also decorate the neck and rim, as well as the interior of the rim. Juglet **IX P13** has the simplest decoration; it has bands on the lower body and groups of four bars hanging from a band at the base of the neck. Juglet **IX P12** is coated, with a metopal arrangement on the body featuring an hourglass pattern between vertical strokes. Juglet **Boyd P4** has a pendent crosshatched triangle.

Askos

No askoi were found in the enclosure burials, but a single example of a true askos came from Tholos Tomb IV (**IV P5**). This is a rare shape that is similar to a stirrup jar but has a basket handle in place of the false spout and stirrup handles. The askos **IV P5** has a globular to ovoid body with an elliptical basket handle on top and a high conical foot. The spout is missing. It is decorated on each side of the shoulder with a triangle with multiple outlines; within the triangle are two groups of oblique strokes that are perpendicular to each other, possibly in imitation of a common decoration on stirrup jars where the triangle has strokes filling each of the angles (e.g., Coldstream and Catling, eds., 1996, 131, fig. 101:10, of SM date). Below the shoulder is a broad band with two narrow bands on each side, and there is another combination of broad and narrow bands on the lower body. The handle is barred, and the foot is coated. This is a shape that possibly derives from Cyprus (Karageorghis 1975, 54–55, pl. 78:K.1; Rethemiotakis and Englezou 2010, 126–127) and was probably used to hold some precious liquid or unguent (Rethemiotakis and Englezou 2010, 126).

Bird Askos

The bird askos or bird vase is a shape that is typical of the SM period, although some forms do continue into PG as well. Three certain examples are known from the Vronda tholos tombs (**IV P6**, **IV P7** [Fig. 162:n], **IX P53** [Fig. 162:n, o]), and another spout may have come from a similar vessel (**X P1**). These examples are all of Desborough's type IIb: vases with spouts instead of bird heads, bodies resting on a conical or pedestal foot (1972, 247), a type that is rare and limited to the SM period. Two of the bird askoi come from Tomb IV (**IV P6**, **IV P7**). They are similar in shape, with a small spout in place of a head, a round basket handle on the top of the body, and a high conical foot. Both have small airholes on the body beneath the front handle attachment. They are both decorated with triangular motifs. Askos **IV P6** has three double triangles divided from one another by vertical strokes, while **IV P7** has three crosshatched triangles with multiple outlines separated by vertical columns of dots. Both have barred handles. Askos **IV P6** has a band around the top of the foot, while **IV P7** has bars all the way to the spout and two groups of lines around the body: one group toward the spout, the other toward the tail. Askos **IX P53** is quite different, both in shape and decoration. The spout is larger, and the body has a real tail. It has a round basket handle and a tall raised base, flat on the bottom. It is monochrome painted. This vessel looks less elegant and less naturalistic than those from Tomb IV, and it may be of later date. The fragment **X P1** is simply a spout, but it looks very similar to **IV P7** and is more likely to have come from a bird askos than a stirrup jar.

The bird askos has been thoroughly discussed by Desborough (1972) and also more recently by Irene Lemos (1994) and Coldstream (1996, 366–367). Desborough recognized two major types: those with bird heads and those with spouts in place of the bird head. He further categorized them by the treatment of the feet, depending on whether they stood on struts, had bases, or were without a formal base. The preference on Crete in the SM period was for the bird askos with spout, and struts were more common than the conical base found on all three of the Vronda examples (Desborough 1972, 261–262).

The origins of the shape are still unclear. Desborough thought it might have originated on Cyprus, but earlier LH IIIC examples exist on the mainland and in the Dodecanese islands (Lemos 1994, 230). It would appear that the bird askos was reintroduced into the Aegean in the SM period, probably from Cyprus. The type with a spout, however, seems to have developed on Crete. Whatever the dynamics of influences, bird askoi indicate connections between Crete and Cyprus in the 11th and

10th centuries (Desborough 1972, 275). Later bird askoi of LPG and EG date were more commonly characterized by a bird head at the front and three legs or struts. This was a reintroduction of the Cypriot shape long after it had gone out of use on Crete and indicates contact between the two islands also in the ninth century. There are no examples of this type at Vronda.

The function of the bird askos is uncertain, but because of its restricted mouth, it was probably used like the later lekythos for the pouring of small quantities of liquid (Desborough 1972, 273–275), possibly perfumed oil. It might have served a ritual function, both in burials and in religious contexts, as examples have been found only in cemeteries and in the Spring Chamber at Knossos. Lemos (1994, 234) suggested that the shape might have been associated with child burials. At Vronda, all three bird askoi came from tombs with children, and one possible spout came from Tomb X, which also contained a child. The association, however, is not certain, as the tombs were used for multiple burials.

Stirrup Jar

Only four stirrup jars can be definitely ascribed to the tholos tombs. All of them are quite different in shape (**IV P4** [Fig. 164:b], **VII P3**, **VIII P1** [Fig. 164:a], **IX P10** [Fig. 164:c]). A fifth stirrup jar from Boyd's 1900 excavations may also come from the Vronda tholos tombs (**Boyd P2**), and it is similar to **VIII P1** in shape. Three of these jars were 11–14 cm in height, while **IX P10** was much larger, with a height over 20 cm. Two of the four (**IV P4**, **VII P3**) have spouts that lean back and touch the top of the false spout; **IX P10** may also have had this feature, but the false spout is not preserved. Three of the four have knobs on top of the false spout, a feature that is common from later LM IIIC into PG times; **IX P10** is missing its false spout but may also have had a knob. One of the stirrup jars (**VII P3**) has a hole pierced through the top of the false spout, but none of them have airholes. Two of the stirrup jars have almost biconical bodies (**VII P3**, **VIII P1**), while the other two are ovoid in shape (**IV P4**, **IX P10**). Three of the vessels have rather tall raised bases that are hollowed underneath, while **IX P10** has a true conical base. In three of the stirrup jars, the maximum diameter is below the middle of the vase, but on **VIII P1** the maximum diameter is at precisely the midpoint in the height of the vessel, an indication that it is of earlier date than the others. Hector Catling has suggested that the ratio of maximum diameter to height is a useful indicator of type, and he recognizes three groups (1996d, 297). The stirrup jars from the tholoi also break down into three groups. One group has a ratio of 93% (**VII P3**, **VIII P1**), corresponding most closely to Catling's second group. Stirrup jar **IV P4** has a ratio of 72%, closest to Catling's first group, and **IX P10** has an estimated ratio of 57% (based on an estimated height of 24.50), close to Catling's third group, which is datable to the PG period.

The main decorative zone is the shoulder, and all of these jars show variations on triangles. There are triangles with arc fillers in corners (**VIII P1**), stacked triangles (**VII P3**), or crosshatched triangles (**IV P4**, **IX P10**). Stirrup jar **Boyd P2** has a Minoan flower on multiple stems next to a panel of upright stacked chevrons. Other areas of the top bear decoration. The top of the false spout can have circles (**VII P3**, **VIII P1**, **Boyd P2**) or can be solidly coated (**IV P4**). The false spout can be banded (**IV P4**, **VII P3**) or solid (**VIII P1**), while the spout can be banded (**IV P4**) or solid (**VIII P1**). The handles are barred (**IV P4**, **VIII P1**), solidly painted (**VII P3**), or apparently plain (**IX P10**). The bodies show banding: pairs or groups of narrow bands (**IV P4**, **VIII P1**, **Boyd P2**), broad bands (**IX P10**), or combinations of narrow and broad bands (**VII P3**). The foot is coated on all of them.

A single fragment of a stirrup jar was found in one of the enclosure burials (**GR9 P10**). Only the top with the false spout and both handles was preserved. The false spout has a pronounced conical shape, a feature that suggests a SM–PG date, as with **IV P4**. The top, with the false spout and handles, was made as a separate disk and attached to the body. This feature manifests itself in the raised ridge of clay at the joint between the disk and the body itself, and it is one of the hallmarks of LM IIIC stirrup jars at Vronda (Day et al. 2016, 77–78). The stirrup jar may have formed part of the grave assemblage, in which case it would have been an antique or heirloom, but it may also have been a fragment worked into the soil from Building J, Room J1, into which the grave was dug.

The stirrup jar is a typical Late Minoan shape that survived into the EIA but not beyond the PG period. At Knossos there was a tendency toward less globular (often more ovoid) bodies and increasing height of feet until a real conical foot appeared. It would seem that the Vronda examples form a series from the LM IIIC period through PG times, with **VIII P1** and **Boyd P2** the earliest, then **VII P3** (SM–EPG), **IV P4** (SM–PG), and finally **IX P10** (EPG–MPG). After this time its function, to hold aromatics or oils, was fulfilled by the lekythos.

Flask

Four lentoid flasks were found in the tholos tombs (**II P1** [Fig. 164:d], **II-VII-VIII P1**, **IV P8** [Fig. 164:e], **IX P11**). These are all similar in size, shape, and decoration, although with some variety. All of the examples are lentoid in shape, usually with one side flatter than the other, as on **II P1** and **II-VII-VIII P1**. Flasks **IV P8** and **IX P11** have symmetrical halves, although one side of **IV P8** has a knob in the center. The rims flare somewhat from a short neck, and **II P1** has a slightly beveled rim. The single handle joins the short neck either just below the lip (**II P1**, **II-VII-VIII P1**) or in the center of the neck (**IV P8**). The handles can be round (**II P1**) or rectangular (**II-VII-VIII P1**, **IV P8**). An airhole is often found below the handle (**II P1**, **II-VII-VIII P1**). Because **IX P11** is fragmentary, it shows how these vessels were constructed. The two halves of the body were thrown on a wheel, then were joined together, and the neck and handle were added. The decoration on all of the lentoid flasks consists of large concentric circles on each side, but with some variation. Flask **II P1** seems to have a large circle in the center, surrounded by three others. Its neck was coated or banded, and the interior of the rim was painted. Flask **IV P8** has three groups of two concentric circles with space between the groups. The neck is banded, and there are stripes down the handle. Flask **II-VII-VIII P1** has two groups of circles: three around a central dot and four more around the outer edge. It has possible stripes on the handle, but any decoration on the neck is too worn to be determined. Flask **IX P11** has four concentric circles evenly spaced around the body, apparently without a central dot.

Lentoid flasks are not common on Crete, and at Knossos they are limited to the LPG–EG periods (Coldstream 1996, 365–366; 2001, 46). The later examples generally have a trefoil mouth. In East Crete, however, the shape appears in the SM period and continues into the LG period (Tsipopoulou 2005, 439–440). The Vronda examples, with their simple decoration of concentric circles, probably belong to the SM period. The shape is thought to have derived from the Levant (Desborough, 1979–1980, 353) and is also found on Cyprus, where the lentoid versions generally are provided with two handles, while the single-handled flasks tend to be more globular (Coldstream 1996, 365). The shape seems to have been adapted on Crete (Coldstream 1996, 365). These flasks have small and restricted mouths and may have functioned much like the later lekythos.

A single vessel that might be termed a flask was found in Grave 3 (**GR3 P18**; Fig. 164:f). The flask is similar to a lekythos in having a flaring mouth, narrow neck, and handle running from below the rim to the shoulder. The body, however, is rounded, though not spherical, with a rounded bottom. The shape is reminiscent of the lentoid flask, but the body is less rounded. The decoration of parallel horizontal bands resembles other LG vessels found in the Vronda cremation burials. It was found together with a monochrome cup set into the stones over the enclosure, indicating that it was part of a postfunerary ritual, probably a libation.

Lekythos

The lekythos is a closed vessel with a round mouth and a tall narrow neck that has a vertical handle attached midway up the neck (Coldstream 1996, 351). Only a single example of the lekythos was found in the tholos tombs (**IV P2**; Fig. 164:g). It is a small vessel that could be called an aryballos or a juglet, were it not for the handle, which is attached on the neck, well below the rim. Kotsonas uses the term "lekythion" for this shape (2008, 168–171). The rim flares from a rather tall neck, the body is depressed globular, and the base is slightly raised; the handle is rectangular. Decoration consists of hatched triangles on the shoulder above horizontal bands, with a band at the base. The handle is barred. Vessels that are similar both in shape and decoration are known from LPG–EG Knossos (Coldstream 1996, 352; 2001, 42, 43, fig. 1.11:c), where they are called aryballoi. A vessel with such a small mouth would probably have been used for pouring valuable liquids such as oil, and this shape seems to be transitional between the stirrup jars and flasks of the SM period and the later lekythos or aryballos.

Lekythoi are more common in the enclosure burials. A few examples were found, all fragmentary (**GR4 P3, GR4 P7, GR4 P19–GR4 P21, GR17 P2**,

GR26 P2, GR27 P5, GR36 P11, and possibly **GR6 P7, GR15 P4, GR30 P31, GR34 P3**). They come in a variety of sizes and types.

There are several examples of what is called the Creto-Cypriot type of lekythos (Coldstream 1996, 354; 2001, 42; Moignard 1996, 440–441) or aryballos (Tsipopoulou 2005, 406; Kotsonas 2008, 181–182). These vessels are small enough to be categorized as aryballoi, but because their handles are attached halfway up the neck, they have here been categorized as lekythoi. The type begins as an imitation of Cypriot shapes but develops on Crete. Two examples (**GR4 P3, GR17 P2** [Fig. 164:h]) are of the evolved type found in the LG or LG–EO periods at Knossos (Coldstream 1996, 354). Neither of these two is complete, but both have spherical bodies on elegant raised bases. Lekythos **GR17 P2** has a tall neck with a ridge where the now missing handle once attached and a flaring rim. Lekythos **GR4 P3** has a round handle, but the neck and rim are missing. Both have large, multifold concentric circles on each side of the vase, and **GR17 P2** has groups of small doublefold concentric circles on the sides. This type of Creto-Cypriot aryballos is common in the EO period (Moignard 1996, 446).

At least one lekythos (**GR4 P20**; Fig. 164:j) and possibly two others (**GR4 P21, GR27 P5**) are of the Praisos type, a tall ovoid vessel with a ridge on the neck at the attachment of the handle, decorated in dark paint on a light background (Coldstream 1996, 355, type Dii). Lekythos **GR4 P20** is the best preserved. It has a molded lip, tall neck with a small ridge, elliptical handle from the middle of the neck to the shoulder, ovoid body, and raised base with an incised circle around the bottom creating a false ring base, as seen at Knossos. The decoration is confined to the shoulder and neck, with the lower body divided up by groups of three or more thin bands. On the neck are two zones of hatched upright leaves, separated by broad and narrow bands at the ridge. The shoulder bears double concentric circles with eight-petaled rosettes in the center; small circles with dotted centers, either singly or in pairs, lie in the empty spaces at the top between the large circles with rosettes. The decoration is more complex than the simple motifs found on similar vessels at Knossos. Another lekythos (**GR4 P21**), of which only part of the neck is preserved, is of similar fabric, with a more pronounced ridge and with a dotted zigzag motif below the ridge. The fragment **GR27 P5** is a molded lip similar to that found on **GR4 P20** and may come from a similar vessel. This type of lekythos comes from a non-Atticizing tradition at Knossos (Coldstream 1996, 355), where it seems to belong to the LG period, but examples from eastern Crete date to the LG–EO periods (Tsipopoulou 2005, 404). Petrographic analysis suggests that the Mirabello fabric is from the Vrokastro area.

Lekythos **GR4 P7** may be an earlier variation of the Praisos type. It has the neck ridge with handle attachment, but instead of the flaring lip, it seems to have a short, almost vertical lip. It is possible that the lip of this piece was broken (perhaps in antiquity) and smoothed down, after which the vessel continued in use, as there are no parallels for this type of mouth. The decoration is clearly Geometric, rather than imitating Cypriot models. On the neck are triple zigzags with vertical strokes connecting them to the ridge, and there are concentric circles on the shoulder. Concentric circles are common on the shoulders of this type of vessel at Knossos, but the zigzag motif with strokes is not. It appears on vessels of MG I date at Corinth (Coldstream 1968, pl. 17:d) and suggests that this vessel is of LG date.

A fragment from the lip and upper neck of another lekythos, **GR4 P19**, is unusual in having a ridge at the base of the lip rather than farther down the neck, and there is a raised band above the ridge. It has no decoration. No parallels are known, but the presence of the ridge and the flaring lip suggest that it may have been a variation of the Creto-Cypriot type of lekythos. It may be an import.

Lekythos **GR36 P11** (Fig. 164:i) is a most unusual vessel for which no good parallels exist. It is considerably larger than most of the other lekythoi, resembling a jug more than a lekythos. Nevertheless, it does have the handle attached below the rim and the tall neck typical of the lekythos. The lip is outturned, with grooves at the base. The neck is tall and cylindrical, and the handle is rope twisted, a feature that is found on jugs and oinochoai of MG II date from the Athens and of LG II date from Argos (Coldstream 1968, pls. 5:a, 29:a). The neck is decorated with bands.

The lekythos is a pouring vessel with a restricted mouth that was probably used, like the aryballos, for oil, perhaps perfumed oil. The shape may have replaced the lentoid flask or the stirrup jar used in earlier periods in Crete (Coldstream 2001, 42). Lekythoi may have been used to hold offerings for the dead, or they may have been used in the funerary ritual. It is interesting to note that these vessels, which are all larger than the aryballoi, are never burned as thoroughly as the aryballoi.

Jug

Jugs with cylindrical mouths and handles attached at the rim (Coldstream 1996, 347) are comparatively rare in the tholos tombs, where there are only three full-sized jugs: **VII P2** (Fig. 165:c), **IX P15** (Fig. 165:b), and **IX P27** (Fig. 165:a). These examples range in height from 12.10–22.00 cm and come in a variety of shapes. Jug **IX P27** has a tall, narrow neck that resembles a lekythos, but the handle attaches at the rim rather than on the neck, so it must be categorized as a jug. It may have served a function similar to that of the lekythos, however, before the lekythos became established in the repertoire of Cretan pottery. It has an outturned lip, square handle, squat globular body, and raised concave base. The decoration is dark ground with added white: bands on the neck, pendant triangles on the shoulder, and another band on the lower body. The largest jug is **IX P15**, which has a wider neck and flaring rim, elliptical handle, globular body, and flat base. The decoration is worn, but as in the case of **IX P27**, it may be dark ground; the shoulder and lower neck, at least is black, while the rest is too worn to be certain. Jug **VII P2** is quite different from the other jugs and looks much later, LG–EO in date. It has a short cylindrical neck with an only slightly flaring rim and a flat elliptical handle. The body is globular, with a slightly raised concave base. The decoration is worn, particularly on the shoulder, where only a single vertical band can be seen. The neck and lower body are decorated with bands, wide ones on the neck, narrower bands on the bottom, and narrow bands between bands at the widest diameter. The shape was common at PG Knossos, after which it died out until it enjoyed a renewed popularity in the EO period (Coldstream 2001, 39, pl. 16:a–c). The shape and banded decoration appear to date to the EO period.

In contrast to their infrequency in the tholoi, jugs represent the most common pouring vessels in the Vronda cremation burials. They can have restricted mouths (**GR 1 P8, GR1 P9, GR5 P15, GR6 P6, GR6 P28, GR9 P7, GR9 P9, GR23 P8, GR26 P18, GR28 P20, GR36 P17**), or they can be wide mouthed (**GR1 P4, GR3 P4, GR9 P6, GR9 P22, GR12 P4, GR12 P22, GR12 P30, GR13 P4, GR13 P14, GR19 P5, GR19 P6, GR20 P16, GR28 P2, GR36 P14**).

Jugs with Restricted Mouths

Although jugs with restricted mouths are generally large, there is a single example of a small juglet with restricted mouth (**GR6 P6**; Fig. 165:d), and it is similar to **IV P3** from Tholos Tomb IV. It has a short flaring neck, squat globular body, elliptical handle attached at the rim, and short conical base. Decoration consists of a solidly coated neck, strokes in the shoulder zone, and broad bands at mid body and foot; the interior of the rim is painted. This form is of LPG or EG style, similar to examples from Eleutherna and Kommos that are identified as lekythoi. The vessel was probably used for oils and unguents, like the lekythoi, aryballoi, and small oinochoai. Jug **GR1 P8** is similar in size, but it has a short, cylindrical neck. Jugs **GR30 P22** and **GR32 P8** may be comparable in shape, but their handles and bases are missing. Their necks are more cylindrical.

Larger jugs with restricted mouths are more common. The majority of these (**GR5 P15, GR6 P28, GR9 P7, GR23 P8, GR26 P18, GR28 P20**; Fig. 165:e) have short, rather narrow cylindrical necks, generally not well articulated from the shoulder, and slightly flaring rims. Where preserved, bodies are globular (**GR5 P15, GR28 P20**), ovoid (**GR9 P7, GR6 P28**), or biconical (**GR23 P8**). The few surviving handles are elliptical. Bases are rarely present, but when preserved they are generally flat or concave underneath. Several are coarse or medium-coarse (**GR5 P15, GR6 P28, GR23 P8, GR28 P20**). Jug **GR5 P15** has been identified by petrographic analysis as an import from outside Crete. A number of the jugs appear to be undecorated, while the remainder have simple bands. The neck is often coated, with banding on the rest of the vessel. Jug **GR6 P28** has groups of bands at the base of the neck, bottom of the shoulder, and lower body. Short strokes hang from the neck bands, a motif that is common on oinochoai of LPG–LG date.

A jug with a taller neck and more flaring lip, **GR9 P9** is close to LG jugs and amphorae from East Crete. The neck is dark coated, with bands below the rim and a panel of vertical guilloche pattern that may mark this vessel as being of EO date.

Jug **GR26 P2** represents a different type, with a jug-like mouth but a handle attached below the rim. Only the neck is preserved, and it has banding toward the bottom of the fragment, while the interior is coated. Similar in fabric and paint to **GR26 P3**, it may belong to the same vessel, which despite having interior paint seems to be a jug. The handle attaching below the rim is usually associated with lekythoi, but the neck of this vessel is too unrestricted to be termed a lekythos. It is most likely to be a jug, similar to LG jugs from eastern Crete, on which the handle attaches on the neck (Tsipopoulou 2005, 163, fig. 87:AN2427). The decoration of narrow bands suggests that it may be a Corinthian imitation.

Wide-Mouthed Jug

Wide-mouthed jugs are also common, and they are similar in shape to the drinking vessels known as mugs (see above, pp. 260–261). At Knossos and in East Crete (Coldstream 1996, 348; 2001, 39; Tsipopoulou 2005, 401–402), the wide-mouthed jug shape includes those vessels that are categorized as mug-like cups here, but at Eleutherna the jugs have been distinguished from mugs (Kotsonas 2008, 157–158, 211–214). At Vronda, the difference between the wide-necked jugs and the mugs can be seen in the neck and mouth: the jugs have more restricted mouths than the mugs and generally are unpainted on the interior. Wide-mouthed jugs also tend to have smaller capacities than mugs; the average capacity for the larger jugs is 0.36 L, while the average for the mugs is 0.55 L.

Small or miniature versions of this shape occur (**GR9 P6** [Fig. 165:f], **GR 28 P2**, **GR36 P14**). These vessels have short, almost cylindrical necks with slightly flaring rims, round handles, globular or ovoid bodies, and flat or slightly concave bases. They range from 6 to 8 cm in height. One (**GR36 P14**) is plain and probably handmade, but the other two are decorated. Jug **GR9 P9** has its main decoration on the shoulder below a coated neck; it consists of crosshatched triangles above three bands. Banding also occurs on the lower body. Jug **GR28 P2** is monochrome painted, with a metopal panel opposite the handle that bears vertical stripes. The graves from which these three vessels came all had infant or child burials, suggesting that the miniature form of the wide-mouthed jug may have been associated with children.

Larger wide-mouthed jugs occur more frequently. These jugs can be decorated (**GR1 P4**, **GR3 P4** [Fig. 165:g], **GR12 P4**, **GR13 P4**, **GR19 P5**, and possibly **GR13 P3**) or monochrome (**GR9 P22**, **GR12 P22**, **GR12 P30**, **GR13 P14**, **GR20 P16**). The decorated jugs are generally characterized by a dark ground with motifs on the shoulder or upper body. Three have short necks: **GR1 P4**, **GR3 P4**, and **GR12 P4**. The handles on these vessels are rectangular or strap in form, the bodies are squat globular or ovoid, and the bases are flat or slightly concave underneath. Decorative motifs include double foliate bands, oblique strokes, and combined vertical strokes and zigzags; **GR12 P4** has its decoration in a metopal arrangement opposite the handle. Jugs **GR19 P5** and **GR13 P4** have taller necks; the neck of **GR13 P4** is more articulated and flaring than that on **GR19 P5**, which is more vertical. On both jugs the handles are rectangular, and their bodies are ovoid with flat bases. Jug **GR19 P5** is decorated in dark ground, with a reserved panel on the shoulder bearing horizontal bands. Three of the monochrome examples (**GR9 P22**, **GR12 P22**, **GR12 P30**) have small, restricted necks in comparison to other examples of wide-mouthed jugs, while the necks on **GR13 P14** and **GR20 P16** are wider. Handles are elliptical, and the bodies are globular or ovoid, with flat bases.

A larger jug (**GR19 P6**) has a more restricted neck that places it closer to the cylindrical types. It has a short, wide neck with flaring rim, an elliptical handle, and an ovoid body. The neck is coated except for a reserved band below the lip, and the main decoration on the shoulder consists of narrow vertical strokes with a wider vertical band in a triglyph-metope arrangement. Below this design are bands. The handle is barred at the bottom, and toward the top it has vertical bars in addition.

Jugs are not as common as oinochoai in EIA Crete (Coldstream 1996, 347–349) but are more common at Vronda. They must have been used for a variety of purposes, chiefly pouring, but also possibly ladling, drinking, or feeding. The narrow-mouthed variety seems to be the most ordinary and utilitarian of the pouring vessels, as vessels of this type are often made in medium-coarse or coarse fabrics and not as elaborately decorated as the wide-mouthed jugs or oinochoai. The smaller examples of this type are likely to have functioned like the aryballos and lekythos for oils or unguents. The wide-mouthed variety could have been used for pouring and/or drinking, perhaps in the funerary context for both toasting and pouring liquid on the pyre to put out the fire.

Oinochoe

The oinochoe is a pouring vessel like the jug but with a trefoil mouth. There are two distinct varieties: the small oinochoe, 15 cm in height or less, and the large oinochoe, greater than 15 cm in height. The two sizes of vessels may indicate that they served very different functions. Both types are represented in the tholos tombs and in the enclosure graves.

In the tholos tombs, the oinochoe is a more common pouring vessel than the jug. A large number of these are the small version (**II-VII-VIII P2, IX P16–IX P21** [Fig. 165:h–j], **IX P44, IX P54, Boyd P1**). All of the preserved examples except **Boyd P1** come from Tholos Tomb IX, although at least three oinochoai (two small and one larger coarse example) are pictured as coming from Tomb IV (Pl. 7C), and a larger example appears on the photograph of pottery from Tombs II, VII, and VIII (Pl. 5A).

Small oinochoai in the tholos tombs generally have rather short necks (**IX P16, IX P19, IX P20**), but occasionally the necks are tall and narrow (**II-VII-VIII P2, IX P17, IX P18, IX P21**). The bodies are globular, sometimes with a low center of gravity, as on **II-VII-VIII P2, IX P17** and **IX P18**; the exceptions are **IX P19** and **IX P20**, which have carinated bodies. Handles are elliptical or square. Bases are generally flat and concave but may be raised (**IX P19**) or raised and concave (**II-VII-VIII P2, IX P17**). Decoration is restricted to the shoulders, and motifs include stacked triangles, wavy lines, multiple triangles with fillers, crosshatched triangles, filled triangles, and bands. Necks may have banded decoration. Handles may be coated or have vertical lines running down. Lower bodies are either banded or solidly coated. One oinochoe seems to be monochrome (**IX P44**). The vessel designated **Boyd P1**, which has no good provenience, should probably be considered an oinochoe, in view of its similarity to vessels from Knossos and Eltyna (see above, p. 52).

Small oinochoai are much rarer in the enclosure graves, and only three have been identified with certainty (**GR12 P14** [Fig. 165:k], **GR12 P16, GR12 P35**). Oinochoe **GR12 P14** is under 6.00 cm in height, with a flaring rim, short neck, strap handle, ovoid body, and raised concave base. It is decorated with simple bands on neck and body. Only the top of **GR12 P35** is preserved, but it has a short neck and a wider, more globular body. It has a motif of stacked triangles on the shoulder and is similar in shape and decoration to PG examples from East Crete. This type of small oinochoe is generally PG in style. Oinochoe **GR12 P16** is larger but so fragmentary that it is difficult to determine its measurements or to discern the full profile or decoration. It has a taller and narrower neck than the smaller oinochoai. Only the neck and part of the rim of **GR12 P31** is preserved, but it also seems to have had a tall and narrow neck; it may have been a lekythos. Possibly **GR21 P9** is also a small oinochoe, but its rim is too badly damaged to be certain. Its similarity to PG oinochoai elsewhere makes identification as an oinochoe most likely (for parallels, see above, p. 156). It has a rather short neck, elliptical handle, globular body, and slightly raised base. The decorative scheme is dark ground, with a metopal panel in the shoulder zone bearing horizontal bands. Such decoration suggests a Geometric date for the piece.

The larger oinochoai are rarer than the smaller examples in the tholos tombs (**IX P21–IX P23** [Fig. 166:a], **IX P46, IX P49** [Fig. 166:b]), and they are varied in shape and decoration. Oinochoai **IX P22** and **IX P49** are similar to one another in shape, with short necks, elliptical handles, globular to ovoid bodies, and flat bases. Both bear their main decoration on the shoulder, and they have simple curvilinear motifs. Oinochoe **IX P49** has a scroll pattern, common on amphorae and hydriai from Knossos (see above, p. 43), while **IX P22** bears a sort of vegetal flower pattern, with a vertical stamen and two curvilinear leaves rising out of the stamen or stem (for the design, see Fig. 26). Oinochoe **IX P22** has a solidly coated handle and neck with a ridge, while **IX P49** has a wavy line down the handle and banding at the base of the neck. Both show banding on the lower body. Oinochoai **IX P23** and **IX P46** are poorly preserved but seem to resemble the other large oinochoai, although their necks are more restricted.

In the enclosure graves only two certain examples of the large oinochoai have been recognized (**GR6 P29, GR26 P23**; Fig. 166:c). These are both unusual and without close parallels. Oinochoe **GR6 P29** has a trefoil lip, rather tall, wide neck, ovoid body, and flat base. It is made of a coarse fabric and has traces of red paint, particularly well preserved on the interior of the rim, and incised lines around the rim and upper part of the neck. Oinochoe **GR26 P23** is smaller and made of a coarse gray fabric. It is without close parallels on Crete, although its fabric suggests it was manufactured in the northeastern part of the island. It has a pronounced trefoil lip, a short wide neck, round handle, ovoid body, and flat base. The only decoration consists of a series of incised bands at the base of the neck. Large oinochoai may have been used for pouring both wine and water.

The oinochoe began on Crete in EPG times and continued in popularity into the Geometric period. It became less common in LG–EO times (Coldstream 1996, 342–347; 2001, 39–40). It was the most popular vessel type in graves of the PGB period and the transition to the EG period (Kaiser 2013, 62). The large oinochoai from the Vronda tholos tombs are similar to full-sized PG examples from Knossos (Coldstream 1996, 342). The small oinochoe seems to have been designed for a purpose different from the large one. Its small size and restricted neck would have been useful for dispensing unguents and oils, and it may have been similar in function to that of the small juglets, bird askoi, flasks, and stirrup jars of the earlier SM period. Like the jug, the oinochoe is a pouring vessel, but because of the trefoil mouth, the stream of liquid can be directed more accurately. Oinochoai are usually decorated with painted designs or incisions, and they may have been used in more formal domestic situations than the jugs. Jugs could be used to ladle water or wine from a large container, while oinochoai are more suited to pouring liquids into drinking vessels during ritual occasions at the burials.

Jug or Oinochoe

A number of vessels with missing rims from the enclosure graves may be either jugs or oinochoai (**GR9 P37, GR9 P49, GR12 P15, GR12 P17, GR12 P18, GR12 P34**). Of particular interest is **GR9 P37** (Fig. 166:d), probably a large oinochoe that may imitate mainland types. It has a rather tall neck, strap handle, ovoid body, and broad ring base. The decorative scheme is dark ground with a reserved band at the middle of the body bearing an uncertain motif, a reserved band at the base, and a reserved triangle on the handle. The shape resembles Attic MG I or MG II oinochoai (Coldstream 1996, 396–397), but it lacks the decorated reserved panel found on the neck of the Attic examples. Flat-based oinochoai of PGB date can be found at Eleutherna (Kotsonas 2008, 164–165, fig. 40:A235). The simple reserved band decorating the body is found on earlier oinochoai from Corinth (for parallels, see above, p. 103). Although the fabric of this vessel is rather soft, it has been coated with a thick black paint, similar to that found on so many of the accompanying ledge-rim cups and perhaps imitating the fine glaze of the Attic originals or their Knossian copies.

Another jug or oinochoe, **GR12 P17**, is well preserved except for its neck and rim. It has a rather tall neck, an elliptical handle flattened on top, and an ovoid body with a broad flat base, concave underneath. Bands decorate the neck and the lower body, with the bottom of the vessel coated in dark paint. The main decoration is on the shoulder: a triangle with checkerboard pattern and multiple outlines, with dots between the outermost outlines. The handle has vertical stripes, and the area around the handle is coated.

Among the other pouring vessels without preserved rims is **GR12 P15**, which is carinated at the shoulder. This unusual shape has parallels of LG–EO date at Knossos and various sites in East Crete (see above, p. 119). Another poorly preserved vessel may be a small olpe (**GR12 P34**), the only example of this shape in the Vronda burials. The olpe is rare on Crete, but EG–LG examples exist at Knossos (Coldstream 1996, 349; 2001, 39).

Hydria

The hydria is not found in the assemblages from the tholos tombs, and the shape is rare in the enclosure burials. Only four certain examples are known (**GR12 P44, GR17 P8, GR26 P20** [Fig. 166:e], **GR32 P9**). The best-preserved example is **GR26 P20**, which has many PGB parallels for shape at Knossos and LG parallels for both shape and decoration in East Crete (see above, p. 165). Petrographic analysis suggests that this vessel comes from the south coast of the island. It has a tall neck with a ridge below the rim. The rim flares outward before becoming vertical, and it is pierced. The vertical handle is elliptical and attached at the ridge. Another ridge is found at the juncture between the neck and ovoid body. The round handles are set low on the body at its widest diameter, and the body rests on a raised concave base that is almost a ring base. The decoration is confined to the neck and shoulder, although there may have been some motif on the lower body. The ridges are emphasized with bands, as is the foot. The neck bears what is probably a large double zigzag with dots between, and on the shoulder there are two pairs of double dotted zigzags.

Among the other hydriai is **GR17 P8**, which, in comparison to **GR26 P20**, is larger, with a taller neck and a similar lip arrangement. The vertical handle is attached on the neck and shoulder. It has a more globular body, and the round handles are also placed very low. The vessel has a broad ring base. Fragments of lip, neck, handles, and body of **GR32 P9** are preserved. This vessel has a slightly flaring neck and is decorated, although the decoration cannot be discerned except for the presence of a possible cross-hatched motif. Finally, another fragmentary vessel, **GR12 P44**, may be a hydria, as it has both horizontal and vertical handles.

The paucity of hydriai in the enclosures is striking, particularly when compared with the rich series of this shape from the tombs around the Kastro. There are six examples from the Plai tou Kastrou tomb and two from the Skouriasmenos tomb (Tsipopoulou 2005, 371–379). In general, in East Crete hydriai comprise one of the most frequent shapes found (Tsipopoulou 2005, 371). The ovoid shape of the body, low round handles, and vertical lips place the best-preserved examples from Vronda with those from the LG period in East Crete. The shape is also found in the Knossos domestic assemblages and in the tombs in PG and EG times (Coldstream 1996, 340). Hydriai are rarer at Eleutherna (Kotsonas 2008, 153–157), where development in the shape can be seen from the LPG to LG periods. The vessel type is by definition a water jar, but it could certainly have been used for pouring, carrying, and storing other liquids. The hydria is common in domestic assemblages in the Kastro settlement, and it would appear that the vessel shape was not generally used in the funerary rituals practiced at the Vronda cremations, nor was it deemed appropriate to leave in the enclosure, whether for the dead or the living.

Amphora
Amphorae are storage jars with two handles opposite one another. Two types accompany the Vronda burials: neck-handled amphorae and belly-handled amphorae. There are no certain belly-handled amphorae from the tholos tombs, although it is possible that the very fragmentary **XI P11** belongs to this category. The neck amphorae, however, are represented in the tholoi by three certain examples: **IV P10** (Fig. 167:a), **IX P47**, and **IX P58** (Fig. 167:b), all of which are quite different from one another.

Amphora **IV P10** is unusual in having vertical handles from the rim to the shoulder and a rather wide, flaring neck. The shape is similar to the amphoriskos of SM–PG date (Brock 1957, 161, pl. 11:164; Rocchetti 1988–1989, 221–223, nos. 126, 128) and also to examples from Lefkandi of early ninth century date (see above, p. 25). The decoration of alternating wavy and straight lines in a reserved area on the belly suggests an EPG date. At Lefkandi reserved panels with scribbles are typical of that period (Popham, Sackett, and Themelis 1979–1980, 330).

Another neck-handled amphora from the tholos tombs, **IX P58**, has a very tall neck with a flaring rim and handles that are attached below the rim and on top of the pronounced shoulder. Its shape derives from the Attic LPG type (Coldstream 1996, 332–334), and it was common in East Crete in the LG period. The crude meander pattern on the shoulder marks this example as Geometric. The third neck amphora is a small fragmentary one from Tomb IX (**IX P47**), similar to one of EPG date from Knossos (see above, p. 43). Yet another fragmentary vessel, **IX P49**, may be a similar amphora, although it could also be a hydria, as one body fragment has a handle attachment that may be from a round horizontal handle or a vertical handle. Like **IX P58**, however, its rectangular handles are attached on the neck below the rim. Both **IX P47** and **IX P58** have restricted mouths and could have served for storage of liquids or food. In contrast, **IV P10** has a much wider mouth and may have served a different function. Its shape could represent a development from the amphoriskos observed at Knossos.

In the enclosure burials, both neck-handled and belly-handled amphorae occur in small or large versions, the small examples 25.0–40.0 cm in height, the larger ones closer to 70.0 cm in height. Of the two varieties, the neck-handled amphora is slightly more common, usually in the small version (**GR5 P13, GR16 P17, GR16 P18** [Fig. 167:c], **GR16 P20, GR21 P10, GR27 P12**), while there is only a single example of the large variety (**GR1 P11**). Small neck-handled amphorae have rim diameters of 9.0–14.5 cm and are 27.0–32.0 cm in height. They generally have tall necks with flaring rims. Handles are attached at the middle of the neck and at the shoulder, and they are generally elliptical or rectangular. One amphora (**GR5 P13**), however, has a double rolled handle. Bodies are generally ovoid, although **GR21 P10** is ovoid-biconical. Two amphorae have rather high conical feet (**GR16 P17, GR16 P18**), while two others (**GR21 P10, GR27 P12**) have flat bases.

The neck-handled amphorae are elaborately decorated on the neck, shoulder, and the handles, and occasionally on the body as well, but the decorative schemes are different. Neck decoration can be in bands, as on **GR16 P18**; motifs include the S-pattern, parallel bands, and zigzag. The amphora **GR16 P17** may also have bands of motifs, but only the large S-pattern is preserved, with some parallel bands below the rim. Parallel bands below a coated rim are found on **GR21 P10**. Amphora **GR5 P13** bears a metopal panel with a double zigzag filled with oblique strokes and a small band of zigzag below. Shoulder patterns on the amphorae include rows of curved strokes, groups of curved strokes alternating in bands, crosshatching, and pendant triangles with multiple outlines. The lower body of **GR16 P17** also has decoration: a band of alternating strokes and a band of zigzag. Other amphorae have bands on the body and solid coating at the bottom of the vessels, including the foot. Handles are decorated with horizontal or vertical bars.

The smaller neck amphorae, while common in East Crete in the LG period (Tsipopoulou 2005, 356–364), are rarer at Knossos, where a great deal of Attic influence can be seen. There they occur more often in the Protogeometric than the Geometric period. The LG amphorae tend to be smaller than earlier varieties of the shape (Coldstream 1996, 332–335; 2001, 23).

The single example of a large neck-handled amphora comes from Grave 1 (**GR1 P11**). This vessel has a tall neck with an angular lip, a tall ovoid body, and a flat base. The neck has added clay on the interior at the attachment to the body. Only a small fragment of a vertical strap handle was found. The amphora has an estimated height of about 75.00 cm. The decoration is light ground, with a creamy pink slip, a band at the lip, and bands at the lower body. The handle has a series of vertical strokes, possibly above a pair of X motifs. Shape and decoration place this amphora within a large class of PG amphorae from Knossos and Eltyna, particularly those of LPG date (Coldstream and Catling, eds., 1996, 5, 336, pl. 47:15) with the angular lip and panels with diagonal cross pattern decorating the neck. The vessel type at Knossos is thought to show Attic influence (Coldstream 2001, 23), and the Grave 1 example is similar. Petrographic analysis suggests that it was an import from the south coast area.

The smaller neck-handled amphorae would have been used for storage, perhaps of wine. The contents may have been intended for sustenance of the dead in the afterlife, or they could have been used to hold the wine used in the funeral rituals, then left within the enclosure before it was covered with stones. The large version, however, may have served as a marker, like those found in the cluster of Graves 9, 12, and 20 in the former Building J.

Belly-handled amphorae are slightly less common in the enclosure burials and may have served functions different from those of the neck-handled amphorae. Only two examples of what might be called smaller belly-handled amphorae were found (**GR26 P22, GR28 P3**; Fig. 167:d), and there was one miniature example (**GR6 P5**). Although the two small amphorae differ from one another, they are both unusual in having handles set above the widest diameter. This shape, with its higher handles, is called an amphora with horizontal handles (Tsipopoulou 2005, 365–370; Kaiser 2013, 53–54) or a belly-handled amphora (Kotsonas 2008, 92–100). Of the two examples, **GR28 P3** is the smaller, with a height of 31 cm and rim diameter of 13 cm. It has a rather short neck with a rim that is thickened outward and bent over at an angle. The body is globular-ovoid, with simple round handles rising on the shoulder and a wide ring base. Decoration is dark ground, with reserved panels decorated with various motifs: two rows of zigzags on the neck, two rows of running dog pattern on the upper body with narrow bands above, below, and between, and narrow bands on the lower body. The interior of the neck is coated. The second small amphora (**GR26 P22**) is taller, nearly 40 cm high, with a rim diameter of 13 cm. It has a rather tall neck with a flaring lip; extra clay has been added for strength on the interior where the neck joins the body. The body is tall and ovoid, with double-arched or bucranium handles on the shoulder. The base is raised and slightly concave underneath. The decoration is worn but is clearly light ground, with bands and concentric circles on the neck, hatched panels and bands on the shoulder, and hatched panels on the lower body below three bands. Both of these amphorae were used for the same purpose: holding the bones of a cremation.

The miniature version from Grave 6 (**GR6 P5**) may have been deposited with the infant burial in that enclosure. As preserved it is only 6.8 cm in height, and it may not have been much taller originally. It has a moderate narrow neck and a globular body with a flat, almost rounded base. The handles are attached at its widest point. It is decorated in dark ground, with two metopal panels: the panel on the neck has horizontal lines, while that on the shoulder has crude hatched triangles.

The larger belly-handled amphorae, with heights closer to 70 cm and rim diameters of 19–25 cm (**GR9 P38** [Fig. 168:a], **GR9 P39** [Fig. 168:b], **GR9 P50**, **GR12 P42**, **GR12 P43**, **GR20 P7** [Fig. 168:c]), are more comparable to the full-sized examples from Knossos (Coldstream 1996, 336–338; 2001, 23–24). They are generally fragmentary, making it difficult to construct whole profiles; only one (**GR20 P7**) can be completely reconstructed. These vessels have tall necks with flaring rims, some with lips that angle outward (**GR9 P39**, **GR9 P50**, **GR20 P7**). At least two of them have reinforcing ridges below the rim (**GR9 P39**, **GR9 P50**). This feature is similar to examples from Kommos (Johnston 2000, 200–201, fig. 6:26, 28), and petrographic analysis suggests that these two amphorae come from the south coast area (Nodarou, this vol., Ch. 9, p. 301). Bodies are ovoid or globular-ovoid. Where preserved, the lower bodies are straight or slightly concave. The simple round or double-arched bucranium handles may be attached near the shoulder or at the maximum diameter. Bases are flat or beveled.

The large belly-handled amphorae are elaborately decorated on the neck and body. Two basic schemes seem to exist: a dark ground (**GR9 P38**, **GR9 P39**) and a light ground. In the dark ground, the majority of the surface is black, with reserved bands (**GR9 P39**) or panels (**GR9 P38**). Amphora **GR9 P39** has its major decoration in a band at the handle attachment, with dark bands above and below. A secondary panel may once have existed on the neck and/or shoulder. The motifs in the handle zone are cross-in-circle, a decoration common at Knossos on MPG and EG amphorae, reflecting strong Attic influence (Coldstream 1996, 337). Amphora **GR9 P38**, however, has a large metopal panel on the shoulder and body with five zones of motifs: sixfold concentric circles with hatching in outer and inner circles, a solid lozenge chain with unfilled centers above rows of alternating oblique strokes, fourfold concentric circles with hatching between, and meander hooks with rectangular crosshatching; a small leaf-shaped object among the lower concentric circles may represent a weapon or leaf, or it may be accidental. On the neck is a vertical filled lozenge chain between upright lines and a horizontal S-pattern. Such a variety of motifs all over the body is in keeping with the eclectic Cretan style (Coldstream 1996, 337). An unusual feature of this amphora is the decoration of strokes on top of the rim. The other amphorae are basically light ground, with designs on the neck and body. Neck designs include solid butterflies between strokes (**GR9 P50**), a vertical panel of checkerboard (**GR9 P50**), alternating strokes (**GR12 P42**), concentric circles (**GR12 P43**), and vertical strokes (**GR20 P7**). Body motifs are more difficult to determine because of poor preservation but include checkerboard, alternating oblique strokes, and concentric circles.

Belly-handled amphorae are well known on Crete and show heavy Attic influence that persisted into the ninth century in Central Crete (Coldstream 1996, 336). They lost popularity at Knossos in the EG period but continued in use in the eastern part of the island (Tsipopoulou 2005, 365–367). Among the Kavousi examples, the ophiolitic fabric of **GR9 P39** suggests that it came from the south coast, and it may have been highly influenced by Attic and Cycladic EG types. Amphora **GR9 P50** is also made of a south coast fabric. The other examples seem to have been locally produced in East Crete. A good example of the East Cretan type may be seen in **GR20 P7**, which is rather poorly made but perhaps not so carelessly as examples from farther east.

The small amphorae, whatever their original function, were used to hold the cremated remains in a secondary burial. The larger amphorae may have served as markers over the enclosure graves. They appear in three graves only, all of which belonged to the same cluster: Graves 9, 12, and 20. The fragments were found scattered over the entire area, often on the surface, and they generally show little sign of burning. At least one of them (**GR20 P7**) has evidence of ancient repair on the upper neck. This fact suggests one of two possibilities: either the vessel was broken and reused as a marker, its date of manufacture perhaps long predating its use in a funerary context, or it was broken while standing as a marker and mended. All of the amphorae appear to be earlier in date than their contexts would suggest, and it is possible that the burying population deliberately chose large, older vessels as markers for symbolic reasons, perhaps related to familial connections.

A number of other fragments from the enclosure burials may come from amphorae, but it is difficult to tell their shape precisely. Possibly from small amphorae are **GR9 P8**, **GR19 P22**, **GR27 P11**, and **GR27 P13**, while **GR9 P12** seems to come from a large amphora. The fragment **GR9 P8** preserves only the neck, without handles. The rather short neck has a flaring lip and a ridge at the base of the neck. It is decorated with an interlocking S-pattern. It may be the neck of a jug, but it is larger than any jugs. The fabric of **GR19 P22** is coarse and micaceous, and in shape it is characterized by a narrow neck that flares out and a low pedestal base. Another vessel, **GR27 P11**, has a tall narrow neck with a flaring lip and a ring base. It probably has dark ground decoration; the neck and rim are coated, while a large body fragment preserves a reserved band bearing a zigzag and a double row of zigzags. A ring base is also found on **GR27 P13**, which has body decoration of curvilinear motifs, possibly a spiral or guilloche pattern with triangles below. The large body fragment **GR9 P12** appears to be from a large amphora with an ovoid body. It is decorated with concentric circles to the side of a vertical panel of hatched or crosshatched checkerboard. All of these fragmentary vessels have parallels in their decorative motifs in the tombs around Kavousi. Two other ring bases may also come from amphorae, although they could also be from hydriai (**GR6 P21**, **GR9 P32**).

Amphoriskos

Only a single certain example of this shape is known to have come from the Vronda tombs. A decorated amphoriskos is pictured (Pl. 5A, middle row, left) as coming from Tholos Tomb II, VII, or VIII, but it could not be located in 1979. It is adorned with groups of pendent multiple loops. No amphoriskoi were found in the enclosure graves.

Necked Jar

The next two categories of pottery, here called the necked jar and the pyxis, are difficult to define, and pottery experts of the period disagree on the terminology (Kotsonas 2008, 100–101). At Knossos, size is the main consideration. The large cremation urns are termed pithoi (Coldstream 2001, 24), and smaller vessels of similar shape are considered pyxides (Coldstream 2001, 35–37). The same terminology has been adopted for East Cretan vessels by Tsipopoulou (2005, 349–355, 379–386) and for Eltyna vessels by Rethemiotakis and Englezou (2010, 111–114, 146–149). These authors classify a pithos as being 25.00–55.00 cm high, while a pyxis is less than 25.00 cm in height. Kotsonas, however, in his analysis of the pottery from Eleutherna, finds neither term quite sufficient. He suggests instead that size should be the determining factor in identification: large vessels of this shape should be called jars, whether necked or neckless, while smaller examples are termed pyxides (Kotsonas 2008, 100–141, 142–146). In this analysis, the term pyxis will be used only for neckless jars, whether large or small (see Kotsonas 2008, 136–146). The term necked jar is applied to jars with restricted necks, whether large or small, even though the small necked jars were probably used like pyxides to store small items.

The necked jar is a closed vessel used for storage. There are two distinct types based on size. The small version is less than 12 cm in height and may have been used like a pyxis for small-scale storage. The large version is a jar that is over 13 cm high. The small versions of this shape are elsewhere called pyxides (Coldstream 1996, 361; 2001, 35–37; Tsipopoulou 2005, 379–386), but that term has also been used of vessels of quite different shape and possibly function. The larger ones are also known as necked jars or necked pithoi (Coldstream 1996, 313; Kotsonas 2008, 100–101), shoulder-handled amphorae (Catling 1996d, 303), amphorae with horizontal handles (Tsipopoulou 2005, 365–370), pithamphora (Sakellarakis 1986, 40–41), or simply pithoi (Tsipopoulou 2005, 349–351). Here we will identify the shape with ovoid body, large neck, and horizontal handles on the shoulder as a necked jar, whether large or small.

Necked jars are found frequently in both the tholos tombs and the enclosure graves. A single example of the small necked jar appears in Tholos Tomb IX (**IX P7**; Fig. 169:a). This jar has a short flaring neck, globular body, round horizontal handles, and wide, flat base. The shape is a common one at EG-LG/EO Knossos (Coldstream 1996, 361; 2001, 37), and **IX P7** resembles especially MG types. The decoration of the vessel is dark ground with a reserved band at the base of the neck and a reserved panel with a crosshatched lozenge chain in the handle zone. The interior is coated, and, like the pyxis, it may have served for small-scale storage.

There are a number of small necked jars in the enclosure graves (**GR3 P5**, **GR5 P2** [Fig. 169:b], **GR17 P3**, **GR20 P19**, **GR36 P8**). They resemble necked jars of greater size but may have functioned as containers for the storage of small items. Two are very small indeed, almost miniature (**GR3 P5** [Fig. 169:c], **GR36 P8**), with heights of 6.5–7.6 cm and rim diameters of 5.0–6.9 cm. These two vessels are similar in shape, with slightly flaring lips, round horizontal handles on the shoulder, and flat bases, hollowed underneath. Of the two, **GR36 P8** is the more globular in profile, and its handles rise above the lip. Both are decorated with linear patterns of oblique strokes. The other two small jars (**GR5 P2**, **GR17 P3**) are larger and similar to one another, ranging from 11.3 to 12.0 cm in height, with rim diameters of 7.5–9.6 cm. Both have slightly flaring necks with lips that are flattened on top and round handles set horizontally on the shoulder. They are ovoid in shape with bases that are flat or hollowed underneath. Both are decorated with bands, with a panel of decoration above the handle zone. The bands on **GR17 P3** are more regular, while those on **GR5 P2** are more varied in size, with many wide bands giving an impression of a black surface. The panels contain similar motifs of multiple zigzags or alternating strokes. These two jars are certainly LG in date. The very small vessel **GR20 P19**, with a flaring lip, has no handles preserved, so it is not certain that it fits into this category.

This type of small jar is well known on Crete, although its antecedents are debated. Coldstream (1996, 361; 2001, 35–37) thinks vessels of this shape (Type Bv) derived from the straight-sided pyxis, which itself had Bronze Age antecedents, under possible influence from Cypriot pottery. Tsipopoulou (2005, 379) suggests that the shape derived from the SM amphoriskos, and indeed it has some resemblance to that shape. Wherever the inspiration came from, the small necked jar is a typical Geometric shape. At Knossos in the LG period it most often has a taller and narrower neck than other types and is decorated with bands (Coldstream 1996, 361).

The more common large necked jars are found in three tholos tombs (IV, VII, and IX). They are represented by jars **IV P9** (Fig. 169:e), **VII P4** (Fig. 169:f), **IX P8** (Fig. 169:d), **IX P9**, and possibly **IV P15**, **IV P17**. Jar **IV P9** has a small neck and a wide, flat base; the handles are high on the shoulder. A similar shape is found at Knossos as early as the SM period, where, like **IV P9**, it is characterized by a solidly painted neck and a group of bands below the handles (Catling 1996d, 303). Unlike **IV P9**, however, the decoration on the shoulder of these Knossian vessels is always an elongated S, whereas the Vronda jar bears a concentric circle and overlapping crosshatched lozenge, motifs that suggest a later date, probably EPG. A second necked jar comes from Tomb VII (**VII P4**). This is a smaller jar with a proportionally tall flaring neck, a short, wide body, a flat concave base, and handles that rise up and flare out on the shoulder. It is decorated with a hatched triangle on the neck and concentric circles on the shoulder. The shape of this jar is unusual; it has a close parallel in Grave 28 of the cremation cemetery (**GR28 P22**) but not elsewhere, although it does bear some resemblance to a pyxis from Praisos (Tsipopoulou 2005, 245, fig. 61:H2003). The decoration suggests a LPG date for this shape. The third large necked jar (**IX P9**) has a rather wide flaring neck, globular body, and small elliptical horizontal handles on the shoulder. Its base is missing. The decoration is entirely dark ground except for a reserved panel in the handle zone bearing horizontal lines. Finally, **IX P8** has a wide flaring neck, ovoid body, elliptical horizontal handles, and a flat base. This vessel has the least restricted mouth of the necked jars, and the interior is painted, suggesting that it may have served a function different from that of the other jars. Its decoration is entirely dark ground with a reserved panel in the handle zone bearing crosshatched triangles above a pair of lines. The two large rims from the area in front of Tomb IV (**IV P15**, **IV P17**) may also be from large necked jars.

The larger necked jars from the enclosure graves show greater variation than those from the tholos tombs. Some, here identified as Type 1, are similar in shape to their smaller counterparts (**GR5 P3**, **GR9 P36**, **GR20 P5**, **GR20 P6**, **GR21 P2**, **GR28 P22**, **GR36 P9**, **GR36 P10**), while others (Type 2) have different features (**GR6 P8**, **GR12 P19**, **GR26 P21**). Those similar to the smaller necked jars can be divided into two subtypes, Type 1a with a tall neck, Type 1b with a short neck. The tall-necked Type 1a variety is represented by two examples (**GR5 P3** [Fig. 169:g], **GR28 P22** [Fig. 169:h]). Jar **GR5 P3** has a tall neck with flaring rim, slightly flattened on top, and round handles set on the shoulder. The body is ovoid, with a flat base. Decoration in the handle zone seems to consist of alternating strokes above three narrow bands, although it is poorly preserved; a second zone of decoration below this is possible. The lower body is coated, with bands above and traces of added white paint. A similar style of decoration with lower body painted and one or two zones of decoration on and below the shoulder can be found on necked jars of MG date from Eleutherna (Kotsonas 2008, 106–110). The shape, however, goes back to the SM period (e.g., Coldstream and Catling, eds., 1996, 87, fig. 83:11) and continues into the seventh century at Eleutherna (e.g., Kotsonas 2008, 128–129, fig. 29:A342, 344). The second example with a tall neck is **GR28 P22**, a vessel that might almost fit into the category of amphora, and it was so was labeled in preliminary reports (Gesell, Day, and Coulson 1995, 86–87). The shape is not unlike **VII P4**. It has a tall neck with flaring rim that was set off from the globular body with a groove; there are tall handles on the shoulder, and the base is flat. Decoration is confined to the shoulder between a large band on the neck and another large band below the handles; there are large wavy lines on one side, wavy lines creating circles or a figure-of-eight on the other.

The necked jars with shorter necks (Type 1b) fall into two subtypes: those with a straight, almost vertical rim (**GR9 P36** [Fig. 169:i], **GR21 P2**, **GR36 P10**) and the others with a more flaring rim (**GR20 P5**, **GR20 P6**, **GR26 P21**, **GR36 P9** [Fig. 169:j]). The two examples with a short straight rim differ from one another in shape and decoration. One of these, **GR9 P36**, has a baggy ovoid body with its largest diameter below the middle of the vessel. It has a short vertical rim, two round handles on the shoulder, and a wide flat base. Decoration is probably confined to the shoulder and handle zone, with at least one band on the lower body. The decoration on the upper body consists of a metope with hatched zigzag over bands (possibly with hatching between) and a chain below. A second vessel, **GR36 P10**, has a rather more elegant ovoid body, with a short neck flattened on top, round horizontal handles set high on the shoulder, and a flat base. Its decoration is dark ground, possibly monochrome, but it has at least one broad reserved band on the lower body.

More common are the Type 1b necked jars with flaring necks. One has a simple flaring rim with rounded lip (**GR36 P9**). It is ovoid in shape, with round horizontal handles on the shoulder and a flat base. The decoration of **GR36 P9** is dark ground, with a metopal panel in the handle zone and a reserved area below with narrow bands. The panel is decorated with hatched motifs, possibly rectangles. Two other examples have flaring necks with lips that are flattened and thickened outward (**GR20 P5**, **GR20 P6**). Jar **GR20 P5** has a globular shape with handles set on the shoulder and a flat base, hollowed underneath, while **GR20 P6** seems to have a more ovoid body and the handles are set lower. Decoration on **GR20 P5** is basically light ground, with bands at rim, base, and mid body, and concentric circles on the shoulder. Jar **GR20 P6** looks later, with dark ground decoration, reserved bands on the lower body, and a decorated panel on the shoulder with small concentric circles.

Type 2 necked jars are less homogeneous than those of Type 1, but they have in common short necks and deep rounded bodies (**GR6 P8**, **GR12 P19**, **GR26 P21**). Jar **GR12 P19** (Fig. 169:k) is unusual in shape and resembles a pyxis, but it is without the inturned rim. It has a flattened and outward-thickened rim, a globular body with handles set rather low on the shoulder, and a wide ring base. Decoration on the upper body is no longer preserved, but broad bands adorn the lower body. This shape is thought by Coldstream (1996, 360) to represent a modification of the Attic PG globular pyxis. Necked jar **GR6 P8** is close in shape to a pyxis. It has no handles, and the full profile is not preserved. Its estimated height is 13.2 cm, placing it among the small jars, but its rather globular profile and small rim means that it had a greater capacity than most of the other small jars. The neck is vertical and slightly concave, the body globular, and it has a ring base. Although it was once painted, no decoration can now be discerned. Finally, **GR26 P21** has an unusual short outturned rim. The vessel is ovoid in shape with round horizontal handles on the shoulder and a flat base, hollowed underneath. The decoration of **GR26 P21** is too worn to distinguish, except for the underside, which was painted.

Another unusual jar, **GR28 P28**, appeared in Grave 28. It is made of very coarse, calcite-tempered clay, similar to fabrics common in the EM period. The shape, however, is unlike anything of EM I or EM II, but it has parallels in the EIA. It might be called an amphora, in having two vertical handles from neck to body, but it lacks the tall neck seen on most amphorae.

The large necked jars seem to have been made for storage, as they have somewhat restricted mouths, and the larger shape would be useful for foodstuffs. Because of its interior paint and wide mouth, however, **IX P8** may have served to hold liquids that could have been ladled out. At Knossos such vessels held cremated bones, but elsewhere they may have been used to store other goods. At Vronda only one was used for bones (**GR28 P22**), while the others must have held other materials, perhaps food or drink used in rituals during and after the cremation or for the sustenance of the dead in the afterlife.

Pyxis

The pyxis is a small neckless vessel that can be closed with a lid. It served for small-scale storage. The shape is not well represented in the tholos tombs, and only **IX P45** is preserved (Fig. 170:a). Pyxis **IX P45** is of an unusual type, lacking handles. It has a short, very flaring neck, a squat globular body, and a raised base that is concave underneath. It is entirely monochrome coated. The shape is similar to Coldstream's type Bi or Bii of MPG–EG date (Coldstream 1996, 360), although it is much squatter than most of the Knossos examples.

Three vessels from the tholos tombs are not pyxides, but they resemble pots categorized as pyxides by others, and they do not fit into the categories either of bowls or necked jars. These vessels are published in Boyd's photographs but are now lost, one from Tomb IV and two others from Tomb II, VII, or VIII. The example from Tomb IV has a small lip, squat globular body, and wide flat base; the handles are attached at the widest diameter. It was decorated, but all that can be said for certain is that it had a broad band below the handle zone. Both of the other so-called pyxides from the tombs are similar. One is of squat globular shape with a short rim, handles that are set high, and a wide flat base. The other is smaller and less squat, with a narrower base, but otherwise it has similar features. These vessels are similar to Coldstream's pyxis type Biv of LPG–PGB date at Knossos (Coldstream 1996, 361).

There are seven examples of the pyxis from the enclosure graves, all rather large in size, decorated, and with incurved rims (**GR4 P8, GR17 P4, GR30 P5, GR30 P28, GR32 P2–GR32 P4**). Another large body fragment (**GR4 P9**) probably comes from a pyxis, but its mouth and base are not preserved; the similarity to **GR4 P8**, however, indicates that it was a pyxis, and it may have been of similar shape. Rarely is the full height preserved, but the two with full profiles have heights of 14.0 and 17.8 cm (without the handles). Three pyxides have incurved rims that are thickened on the interior (**GR4 P8, GR17 P4** [Fig. 170:b], **GR32 P4**), two of them with a wide groove below the rim for holding a lid. These are called Type 1. The handles on these pyxides do not rise above the level of the rim. The other four have simpler incurved rims that are nearly horizontal, with a pointed or rounded lip (Type 2). On three of them (**GR30 P28** [Fig. 170:c], **GR32 P2** [Fig. 170:d], **GR32 P3**) the handles rise high above the rim; on the fourth (**GR30 P5**), the handles are set lower on the body. Handles are generally elliptical (four examples), but two of the type with thickened rim have round handles (**GR17 P4, GR32 P4**). Bodies are ovoid (**GR4 P8, GR17 P4, GR30 P28, GR32 P4**) or globular (**GR30 P5, GR32 P2**). Of the five pyxides whose bases are preserved, one has a raised base hollowed underneath, three have ring bases, and one has a flat base that is hollowed underneath.

Pyxides are elaborately decorated, although rarely is the decoration well preserved. The main decoration generally lies in a shoulder panel, with banding below, although on one pyxis (**GR30 P5**) the decoration covers the entire upper body. Decorative motifs include concentric circles with or without dots (**GR4 P8, GR17 P4**), crosshatched lozenges (**GR32 P2, GR32 P3**), and chevron bands (**GR30 P5**). The bands on the lower bodies vary a great deal: simple narrow bands (**GR30 P5, GR32 P2**), pairs of narrow bands (**GR30 P28**), or broad bands alternating with groups of narrow bands (**GR4 P8, GR4 P9, GR17 P4, GR32 P4**).

In two graves the pyxides occur in pairs, sometimes with similar shape and decoration (**GR4 P8, GR4 P9; GR32 P2, GR32 P3**), sometimes different (**GR30 P5, GR30 P28**). They also occur exclusively in the latest graves on the site: Graves 4, 17, 30, and 32, so their popularity is a late feature. One of the pyxides (**GR17 P4**) shows signs of an ancient repair, suggesting that these vessels had some value at the time they were used, prompting the repair, or that faulty vessels (older or repaired ones) were deemed suitable for use in burials.

The origins of the form are still debated. Some believe that the shape may go back to the Bronze

Age barrel-shaped pithos (Christakis 2005, 17, form 95), revived in the PGB period (Kotsonas 2008, 137), while others (Coldstream 1996, 317–318) suggest that they developed from Attic MG imports, possibly those that had been damaged and reshaped (J. Papadopoulos 1998). Whatever the origins, the Vronda examples of this shape seem to have been inspired by Knossian examples in the LG and EO periods. It is possible that **GR30 P5** imitates Corinthian styles.

The function of the pyxis is uncertain. At Knossos this vessel type was used for holding cremated remains and was regularly accompanied by a covering lid. The cremations in the enclosure burials were left in situ, and the bones were not regularly collected and placed in a container, except in rare instances where an amphora or necked jar was used. The presence of the pyxis must indicate that such vessels served another function, probably some sort of storage.

Straight-Sided Alabastron

Two fragments of a possible straight-sided alabastron were found in Grave 13 (**GR13 P1, GR13 P2**). Its precise shape is uncertain, and the top and bottom do not join. The straight-sided pyxis is known at Knossos in the SM and PG periods (Coldstream 1996, 359; 2001, 35) but is not common. It probably developed from the straight-sided alabastron of LM IIIB and LM IIIC (Coldstream 1996, 359; 2001, 35). If these fragments belong to this shape, they represent an early example (similar to the SM and EPG vessels from Knossos) and one with unusually elaborate decoration. It is also possible that this vessel is a variation on the Cypriot White Painted I amphoriskos, a shape that may have been inspired by the Canaanite jar and was common in CG I (Karageorghis 1983, 355 and parallels cited there), although it is smaller than the Cypriot versions and lacks the elaborate base.

Basket Vase

Two examples of a small jar or cup with a basket or bucket handle have been found in the enclosures (**GR9 P11** [Fig. 170:e], **GR23 P2**). These are similar to the shape known as a thelastron or feeding bottle (Coldstream 1996, 349–350; Tsipopoulou 2005, 437–438), but no spouts have been identified as belonging to them, and so they are termed basket vases here. The smaller of the two examples, **GR23 P2**, measures 11.2 cm in height (17.5 cm with the handle). It has a wide mouth with outturned rim, a globular body, and a flat base that is slightly concave on the bottom. The large round basket handle rises over the rim and is attached on two sides of the rim. The decoration is dark ground with a reserved panel bearing a zigzag below the lip and a crosshatched lozenge chain on the shoulder above bands. The interior is coated, so it would appear to be an open vessel, although it would not be possible to drink from it because of the handle. The larger vessel, **GR9 P11**, measures 17.0 cm in height (an estimated 23.0 cm with handle). It has a narrower mouth, almost a neck, and the body is ovoid; the base is flat. The single round basket handle rises above the lip. It is decorated with bands.

Jars with basket handles appear in the Khaniale Tekke tombs at Knossos (Hutchinson and Boardman 1954, 223, 225, pl. 24:33, 34, 36–38). These vessels are of LG date and differ from the Vronda examples in having tall and narrow restrictive necks.

The thelastron shape, also called a feeding bottle or drinking jar (Coldstream and Catling, eds., 1996, 4), is probably a survival from the LM III period (Kanta 1980, 281). The shape can be found, although never in great quantities, in LM IIIC (Day 2011b, 294–296; Day et al. 2016, 79), SM (Catling 1996d, 302), and PG deposits, where it is generally dipped or plain (Rocchetti 1988–1989, 237). The earlier shape has a more closed mouth and is usually smaller than the two examples from Vronda. There is no consensus about the function of these spouted vessels; they may have been used for feeding infants or the elderly or infirm. The Vronda examples, however, because of their size and their open mouths, would not have been useful for feeding liquids, even if the vessels had spouts. Their function remains unknown.

Lid

A number of lids were found in the graves, and most of them seem to have been made independently of a particular closed vessel (a pyxis or necked jar). Lids in Cretan cemeteries are either conical with a knob or domed without a knob (Coldstream 2001, 31). Two possible lids were found in the tholos tombs (**IX P43, X P3**), although **X P3** may be a skyphos. Both of these are of the domed variety, and both are large (with rim diameters of 16 and 19 cm, respectively). The lid **IX P43** has a straight rim that was pierced near the lip, while **X P3** has a slightly outturned lip. Both are monochrome.

The lids from the enclosure graves belong to both the conical and domed types. The more numerous domed lids can be either large (**GR4 P24, GR19 P21, GR20 P4, GR20 P18, GR32 P5**), with a diameter of 15.00 cm or more (Coldstream 2001, 31; Kotsonas 2008, 146), or small (**GR26 P6, GR26 P12, GR26 P17**), with a diameter of under 13.00 cm (Kotsonas 2008, 149). There is one certain small conical lid (**GR28 P19**) and two larger examples that may be from conical lids (**GR30 P3, GR30 P27**).

Among the large domed lids, the best preserved is **GR4 P24** (Fig. 170:f), which has the offset lip generally found on this type of vessel. It is pierced just above the lip, and the body has a rather deep dome. It is decorated in dark ground, with bands and curvilinear motifs above the lip in added white. The interior is also coated. Similar to this, but smaller, is **GR19 P21**, which has the same sort of lip but a more shallow dome. Its decoration is also dark ground, and it is painted on the interior, but if there was any decoration in white, it has now disappeared. Domed lids of dark ground and white decoration are common in the Knossos cemeteries, where they occur in the LG period (Coldstream 1996, 329–330; 2001, 33–35). Probably belonging to the category of domed lid but with a light ground decoration is the very fragmentary **GR32 P5**, of which only the lip survives. It has as offset lip like the two previous examples, and the lip itself is pierced. It has some rectilinear decoration in dark paint on a clay ground, and the interior is coated. Lid **GR20 P18** has a simple domed body with a slightly pointed rim that is pierced. It is decorated with an S-pattern or quirk above a band, and the interior is coated. The top is not preserved, so it is not possible to tell if it had a knob or handle. Finally, **GR20 P4** (Fig. 170:g) is probably a type of domed lid, although it is an unusual variant. It has an inturned lip that is flattened on top and a conical body. The lip is decorated with bars and the body with bands and curvilinear motifs; the interior is coated. The top is not preserved, so it is uncertain whether the lid was domed; it may have had a knob or a handle.

One probable conical lid from Grave 30 (**GR30 P3** [Fig. 170:h]), with a diameter of 15 cm, is the smallest of the large lids. It is of an unusual type not found in Central Crete. The lip is vertical and then bends into a somewhat convex side. This body shape has parallels in the Plai tou Kastrou tomb of LG date near the Kastro at Kavousi (Tsipopoulou 2005, 108, fig. 136:H771, 772), although those examples have birds in place of knobs. Instead of a knob, the Vronda lid has a round horizontal basket handle on top, which is also common on other lids from the Plai tou Kastrou tomb (Tsipopoulou 2005, 108–109, figs. 138:H773, H774; 140:H775A, H775B). This variation may be a local development. The decoration is in bands, with dots between two pairs of bands, a decorative scheme that may imitate Attic MG I models, like one imported to Knossos (Coldstream 1996, 398). Lid **GR30 P27** is of a similar shape, but the rim is not so vertical. It once had a knob or possibly an animal figure, as can be seen from the circles painted at the center, although the knob itself is missing. The lid is decorated with an elaborate pattern of stacked chevrons and curvilinear patterns that may represent some sort of bird or animal. Most of the large conical lids seem to have simple handles or knobs, and the elaborate knobs found on lids elsewhere, including those with animal heads or birds in the Plai tou Kastrou tombs at Kavousi, are missing in the enclosure burials.

As for the small lids, only one conical lid appeared in the graves (**GR28 P19**; Fig. 170:i), and it was found sealing the amphora in Grave 28 that held the secondary remains of a cremation (**GR28 P3**). This lid resembles a pedestaled bowl, with a rounded lip, conical body, and an inverted conical knob on top. The rim and the knob are coated, while the body is decorated with dotted upright leaves. The shape and decoration have good parallels in MG and EO Central Crete (see above, p. 179).

The other three small lids are probably domed. Two of them have complete profiles (**GR26 P12, GR26 P17**; Fig. 170:j), and there is no trace of a handle or knob. The top of the third (**GR26 P6**) is not preserved, but there seems to be no indication of a handle. All three of these lids came from the same grave, and all are about the same size, 8–11 cm in diameter. Lid **GR26 P17** has a simple pointed lip that is pierced. The dome rises almost to a point and is much thicker than the rest of the vessel. It is undecorated except for grooves running around the vessel near the top of the dome. Although **GR26 P6** is larger and the walls of the lid are thicker, it has the same basic profile and the rim is pierced; however, no incised grooves are found on it. In comparison with the other two lids, **GR26 P12** shows less of a dome. It has a nearly vertical rim, then a rounded shape that is pierced. It is clearly a strainer lid, which is unusual, although parallels exist (see above, p. 167).

There is a paucity of lids in the Vronda enclosure graves in comparison to the wide variety found in graves elsewhere, even in the Kavousi area. The Plai tou Kastrou tomb, in particular, produced a large number and variety of lids. In part, this disparity stems from the fact that the cremations at Vronda were primary; the bones were not removed and stored in a container in a tomb, so there is no large quantity of burial pithoi and jars that needed to be sealed. Elsewhere on Crete, conical lids were made to accompany a burial pithos or pyxis, while domed lids were made independently of the storage vessel (Coldstream 1996, 325, 327).

When lids occur in the Vronda enclosures, they are often found in pairs or groups (two each in Graves 20 and 30, three in Grave 26). Only one lid was certainly used to seal a vessel containing a secondary cremation burial: **GR28 P19** was found resting in the mouth of one of the two burial vessels in Grave 28, and it was found upside down, with the knob down in the neck of the amphora. Clearly, the lid was not made to go with the amphora, and it could not cover its rim, so it was set upside down into it, and a large stone was placed over the top. The other burial vessel, a necked jar, was covered with a monochrome cup set upside down over the mouth.

The amphora in Grave 26 had been smashed, and thus it was not found with a vessel sealing the mouth. Although this grave contained three lids, they were all too small to fit the mouth of the amphora. If the amphora was ever sealed, perhaps one of the kalathoi was used. Two of the small lids from Grave 26 are the right size to seal the hydria (**GR26 P20**) or the necked jar (**GR26 P21**), while the third one could not have sealed anything because it was perforated; it was doubtless some sort of strainer.

The two lids in Grave 20 do not seem to fit any of the closed vessels. Lid **GR20 P4** is too large for either of the two necked jars (**GR20 P5**, **GR20 P6**) but too small to fit over the mouth of the amphora **GR20 P7**. Lid **GR20 P18**, however, could have fit over either of the two necked jars.

We are better able to attribute the lids to closed vessels in Grave 30. The smaller lid (**GR30 P3**) could have fit on either of the two pyxides (**GR30 P5**, **GR30 P28**). The larger lid (**GR20 P27**), however, is too large for **GR30 P5** but could have been set over **GR30 P28**. It seems best to conclude that each of these two pyxides was provided with its own lid: **GR30 P5** with **GR30 P3** and **GR30 P28** with **GR30 P27**.

There is little certainty about the lids found singly in the graves. Lid **GR4 P24** could have fit on either of the two pyxides (**GR4 P8**, **GR4 P9**), although not resting on the incurved rim. Lid **GR19 P21** may have sealed the hydria **GR19 P22**. Finally, **GR32 P5** is too large to fit onto any of the other vessels in the grave, and the high handles of the three pyxides (**GR32 P2**–**GR32 P4**) would have prevented its use.

Conical lids, whether small or large, seem to have developed to fit pyxides or cremation urns (Coldstream 2001, 31; Kotsonas 2008, 146). The domed lid developed independently. In East Crete, a variation of the Minoan type with a round horizontal handle continued into the eighth century (Tsipopoulou 2005, 434).

Lids were used in domestic contexts to cover closed vessels and keep their contents safe from predation by insects or animals. In the funerary context, however, their purpose seems to have been to seal the contents or to protect the living from the remains of the dead inside. Both of these functions appear in the Vronda cremations: the sealing of vessels containing secondary burials and the protection of food or drink used in the funerary ritual or deposited for the use of the dead in the afterlife. The domed lid may also have had an additional symbolic meaning. It has been suggested that domed lids are made in imitation of shields (Coldstream 2001, 33), which would have offered a symbolic protection in addition to a real one.

Pithos

Only three large storage vessels were found in the Vronda enclosure graves (**GR10 P1**, **GR21 P13**, **GR30 P33**). Two (**GR10 P1**, **GR21 P13**) served as containers for bodies, **GR10 P1** for an inhumed child, **GR21 P13** for an inhumed child and two cremated adults. Both vessels are tall (75.8–80.0 cm) and coarse; both have wide (29.0–36.4 cm) mouths and small (22.7–25.0 cm) bases. Pithos **GR10 P1** is ovoid in shape, with a tall neck and vertical rim that was flattened and thickened outwardly. It has round horizontal handles placed on the shoulder and a torus base. The body has raised bands, which were possibly a form of decoration but also perhaps a reflection of its construction techniques; the bands may have strengthened the walls of the vessel where individual sections were pieced together, as on earlier pithoi from the settlement (Day et al. 2016, 103). The lowest band has an impressed design of quatrefoils or windmills.

Pithos **GR21 P13** is similar in shape to **GR10 P1**. It is larger, however, and its neck is shorter, the handles are placed higher, the lower body tapers more, and the base is smaller and less articulated. The rim is slightly flaring and rounded. The body is ovoid but tapers toward the bottom to become almost concave. The base is small with a slight bevel. The vessel was made in four sections: the rim, two body cylinders, and the base. The joins are clearly visible in the section. The vessel is undecorated, lacking even the bands found on **GR10 P1** and earlier large pithoi from the site. Pithos **GR21 P13** was identified as Kavousi fabric type XVI (Mook and Day 2009, 165–166), and more recently its fabric has been recognized as one of a small group of low-fired metamorphic fabrics probably coming from northeastern Crete (see below, p. 300).

Pithoi are not well known in EIA Crete, as much of the material of the period comes from graves and there are few domestic assemblages. These two pithoi are similar to one another, but different from the Bronze Age types known from the Vronda settlement and from pithoi found at other EIA sites.

The third pithos from the cemetery is represented by a single body fragment (**GR30 P33**). This piece is so similar in decoration and fabric (Type IV) to an Orientalizing pithos from Azoria (Haggis et al. 2007b, 282, fig. 29:10) that it could have been made by the same potter using the same stamp. Because it is so fragmentary, however, it is just possible that the decoration consisted of running hoplites, as seen on a similar Orientalizing vessel from Vrokastro (Hayden 2005, 41, fig. 86:2139, pl. 21).

General Observations about the Pottery

Wares

The Vronda burial features produced a large quantity of fine wares but relatively few medium-coarse or coarse wares. The tholos tombs overall had 79% fine, 16% medium-coarse, and 5% coarse wares (Table 17). Of the two tombs that were found intact, both had small quantities of coarse wares (Tomb IV, 6%; Tomb IX, 5%). Tomb IX, however, had greater amounts of fine ware (84%) and less medium-coarse ware (11%) than Tomb IV (65% fine, 29% medium coarse).

In the enclosure graves, the coarse wares, although similar in quantity to those found in the tholoi, often came from vessels belonging to the LM IIIC settlement that were part of the soil matrix of the site. The proportion of fine wares is completely different from what has been found in earlier domestic contexts at Vronda and contemporary domestic contexts on the Kastro (pers. comm., M. Mook). In the majority of the enclosure graves, fine wares accounted for 65%–80% of the cataloged vessels (Table 18). Some enclosures had smaller percentages of 50%–64% (Graves 2, 9, 16, 21, 28, and 34), and a few had percentages over 80% (Graves 1, 13, 15, 23, 26, and 37). Medium-coarse wares accounted for 15%–27% of the total number of vessels, with lesser proportions in several graves (Graves 1, 8, 10, 13, 15, 17, 23, 29, and 37) and greater proportions in a few (Graves 19, 21, and 34). Coarse wares were most uncommon, accounting generally for less than 10% of the total vessels. A few graves had greater percentages (13%–18% in Graves 6, 9, 16, 17, and 28; more than 30% in Graves 8 and 29). Grave 10 had only a single coarse pithos. There seems to be no topographical pattern to the quality of the pottery (measured by coarseness), but there may be a chronological pattern: there is a tendency for the graves with late pottery (EO–LO) to have lower quantities of coarse and medium-coarse wares.

Fabrics

It is difficult to distinguish different fabrics found in the graves. Those vessels from the tholos tombs uncovered by Boyd are the best preserved, but they have been mended and restored, and it was difficult to examine the fabrics even macroscopically. The fragments recovered from the cleaning of the tholos tombs and from Tomb IX are poorly preserved.

The fabrics of these vessels are mostly soft and were found coated with soil that was not easy to remove without also removing the surfaces. The majority of the fine fabrics were soft, often with some small inclusions. The fabric color was most often reddish yellow (5YR 6/6–7/8; 7.5YR 7/6) but sometimes very pale brown (10YR 7/3, 7/4, 8/3, 8/4), pink (5YR 7/4; 7.5YR 7/3–8/4), or light red (2.5YR 6/6, 6/8). A few of the soft fabrics were quite different in color, either pinkish white (2.5YR 8/2) or pale yellow (5Y 8/2).

A second, smaller group of fine fabrics was harder, with colors most commonly pink (7.5YR 7/4) and reddish yellow (5YR 6/6, 6/8, 7/6; 7.5YR 7/6), but with a few light red (2.5YR 6/4, 6/8), light reddish brown (2.5YR 6/4), very pale brown (10YR 7/4), or pinkish white (7.5YR 8/2). The hardness of the fabrics may be the result of different soil conditions in the tholos tombs found by Boyd, but both hard fabrics and soft fabrics were found together in Tomb IX. It is possible that the harder fabrics are not local, but at least one of the vessels from Tomb IX (**IX P30**) proved to be from the same area on the northeast coast as many of the soft fabrics. Medium-coarse fabrics were also generally soft and similar in color to the fine wares, with more examples that were red (2.5YR 4/6, 5/8) or light red (2.5YR 6/6–7/6). Coarse fabrics were also soft and reddish yellow in color (5YR 6/6–7/6).

Petrographic analysis was limited only to vessels from Tomb IX (see this vol., Ch. 9). All of the sampled pottery comes from within Crete, and most was locally produced in East Crete. From northeast Crete, there are three examples of Fabric Group 1, three of Fabric Group 2, three of Fabric Group 3, and a loner sample linked to Fabric Groups 2 and 3. From the south coast there is one example of Fabric Group 6 and two of Fabric Group 7.

It was even more difficult to distinguish fabric groups macroscopically in the pottery from the enclosure graves. The preservation of the ceramics was poor and inconsistent, depending on the soil conditions, and fragments of the same vessel from different parts of the grave could have fabrics that appeared very different from one another. A good example is **GR20 P1**, a cup of which part was found near the surface close to the north wall of the enclosure while the rest was recovered elsewhere. The single sherd found near the wall on the surface was in excellent condition: hard fabric with well-preserved surfaces. The other fragments, however, were of soft fabric and very worn, yet at least one joined onto the hard sherd. In addition, vessels from these graves also suffered from exposure to the fires within, which changed not only the color but also affected the consistency of the fabric; joining fragments from the same vessel could have wholly different color and fabric descriptions.

In general, the fabrics from the enclosure burials are very soft to soft and reddish yellow (5YR 6/6–7/8, 7.5YR 6/6–8/6) in color with pink or very pale brown surfaces or slips. A smaller number are very pale brown (10YR 7/3–8/4), pink (5YR 7/4, 7.5YR 7/3–8/4), or light red (2.5YR 6/6–6/8) in color. When analyzed petrographically, most of these were from Fabric Groups 1 and 2 located in the northeast part of the island. Another common group has very soft and chalky fabrics, generally very pale brown (10YR 7/3–8/4), reddish yellow (5YR 6/6, 7/6; 7.5YR 6/6–8/6), or pink (7.5YR 7/3–8/4) in color, with some yellow (10YR 7/6, 2.5Y 8/1–8/2) or white (10YR 8/1) fabrics. Most of these belong to Fabric Group 1 (northeast coast), but several come from Fabric Groups 5 and 7 (south coast). A third group has very soft, porous fabrics, very pale brown (10YR 7/3–8/4) in color, with some reddish yellow (5YR 7/6, 7.5YR 7/6) and pale yellow (2.5Y 8/2). These also came from Fabric Groups 1 (northeast coast) and 7 (south coast). Similar in fabric and color to the porous and chalky fabrics are two groups, one that is sandy and another that is micaceous. A small group, very soft like the others, contains many tiny white inclusions, similar to a fabric that appeared in the LM IIIC settlement (Day, Klein, and Turner 2009, 12). One of these was analyzed and identified as a member of Fabric Group 2 (northeast coast). Finally, there are a few harder fabrics. These tend to be reddish yellow (5YR 6/6, 7/6; 7.5YR 6/6, 7/6) or light red (2.5YR 6/6) in color, with some very pale brown (10YR 7/4), light reddish brown (2.5YR 6/3–7/4), red to pale red (10YR 5/6, 6/4; 2.5YR 4/8), or pink (5YR 7/4, 7.5YR 8/4) fabrics. These came from a variety of places, belonging mostly to Fabric Groups 1–3 (northeast coast), 5 and 6 (south coast), but with one from Fabric Group 7 (south coast).

Petrographic analysis has helped to distinguish different fabrics and their provenance. The majority of vessels both from the tholos tombs and the enclosure graves seem to be manufactured in the area of northeast Crete (Nodarou, this vol., Ch. 9, pp. 303–304). Nevertheless, a few samples came from vessels made on the south coast of the island. The pottery from the later enclosure graves is generally from East Crete, specifically from the northeast (Fabric Groups 1–3) or the Vrokastro area (Fabric Group 4), from the southern coastal area from Myrtos to the Mesara (Fabric Group 5), or from South-Central or North-Central Crete (Fabric Groups 6 and 7; Nodarou, this vol., Ch. 9, pp. 301–302). The majority of the pottery from the enclosure graves was probably produced locally, but it is impossible currently to distinguish vessels made at Kavousi from those produced at other sites in northeast Crete.

The variety of imported fabrics, even in such mundane vessels as monochrome cups, however, is unexpected. Surprisingly, exchange with Central Crete was rather limited, despite the importance of Knossos in the eighth century. Some of the material from the enclosures seems to show Attic stylistic influence, particularly the vessels from Grave 9, but the fabrics indicate Cretan production, and the influence may have been filtered through the south coast or Knossos. One vessel from Grave 20 (**GR20 P1**) closely resembles Knossian examples, but the fabric places its manufacture on the south coast.

The fabrics sampled for petrographic analysis do not resemble those found in the earlier LM IIIC settlement, nor those from the Kastro, in part because only coarse wares were sampled from those settlements. The fabrics showed wide variation within a limited area of Crete.

Shapes

In general, the Vronda burials were accompanied by more open than closed vessels (Chart 4). In this discussion and related charts, the shapes have been grouped according to their functions. Open shapes include vessels for drinking (cups and skyphoi) and mixing or serving (bowls, trays, kalathoi, kraters, and basins), while closed shapes refer to vessels for pouring, both those with restricted mouths (aryballoi, juglets, askoi, stirrup jars, flasks, and lekythoi) and those with wider mouths (jugs, oinochoai, basket vases, and hydriae). The closed category also includes vessels for storage (amphorae, amphoriskoi, necked jars, pyxides, and pithoi). Lids belong to a separate category of coverings.

In both the tholos tombs and the enclosures (Charts 5, 6), cups predominate. They comprise 27% of the total in the enclosures, while they amount to 15% in the tholoi. Skyphoi are rarer, comprising 9% of the total in the enclosures, but only 4% in the tholos tombs. Those drinking vessels that cannot be identified include 17% of the total in the enclosures and 21% in the tholos tombs. Pouring vessels are more common in the tholos tombs (oinochoai 11%, jugs 6%) than in the enclosures (oinochoai 1%, jugs 5%) as are necked jars (7% in the tholoi, 3% in the enclosures). Of the other shapes in the tholoi, none makes up more than 5% of the total, including shapes not generally found in the enclosures, such as bird askoi, flasks, and stirrup jars. The enclosures, in contrast, produced large numbers of aryballoi (5%) and amphorae (5%), as well as undetermined closed vessels (5%). Shapes from the enclosures that were not found in the tholos tombs include trays, hydriai, and basket vases.

The shapes found in the tholos tombs are similar to those known from other SM–PG tholos tombs, such as Chamaizi Phatsi (Tsipopoulou 1997), and the styles are consistent with those from Central Crete. The vessels from the enclosures, however, while resembling the shapes found in other contemporary graves, are quite different from those encountered at Knossos and in Central Crete. The potters of East Crete during the LG–LO period seem to have been conservative in their adoption of new shapes, and many of the closed vessels would have been deemed to date to the PG period if not for their decoration or context. In both tholoi and enclosures many of the vessels are irregular and poorly made, perhaps due to the lack of skill among potters of the area. Some of the vessels from the enclosures seem to imitate Attic shapes or those from other mainland centers, probably filtered through Central Crete, where they appear earlier. Shapes include cups (particularly the ledge-rim cups), skyphoi, kraters, oinochoai, amphorae, and pyxides.

Decoration

Nearly all of the pottery from the graves was painted, either with a design or with monochrome coating, the latter perhaps in imitation of metal vessels. Decorated vessels are more common than dipped or monochrome ones in the preserved material from the tholos tombs, but the two types of decoration occur in about equal numbers in the enclosures. In the tholos tombs, the most popular motif is the crosshatched triangle or lozenge, but concentric circles (primarily on flasks), wavy lines, and bands are also common (Chart 7). Stacked or filled triangles appear on stirrup jars and askoi. Two motifs that are Geometric in date are found on a jug (hourglass) and amphora (meander) from Tomb IX (**IX P12, IX P58**).

The pottery from the enclosure burials tends to have a dark ground, with decoration restricted to articulated areas such as handle zones, necks, and shoulders. Even when the entire body is not coated, the lower portions are generally covered in broad bands, which give the overall look of a dark ground. Decoration is often in metopal panels. The motifs found on the decorated pottery from the enclosure graves (Chart 8) are more varied and are quite different from those on the generally earlier pottery from the tholos tombs. The most common motif on all shapes consists of horizontal bands, either as the main decoration (often in metopes on skyphoi or jugs) or as a major decorative element, particularly on the lower parts of bodies of larger vessels. When the bands are on the lower part of the vessels, they are more often broad bands or pairs of broad bands with narrow bands between. Occasionally, the lower bodies are decorated with multiple narrow bands, but such syntax tends to belong to vessels of EO date. Oblique or vertical strokes are also popular, as are concentric circles; the latter are the most frequent motif on aryballoi. Crosshatched triangles, lozenges, and panels constitute another popular form of decoration. Zigzags are also found, either as the main motif (particularly on skyphoi) or as secondary decoration; they also occur in pairs with filling of hatching or dots between. Other common motifs include butterfly (if horizontal) or hourglass (if vertical), checkerboard, meander and meander hook, S-pattern, triangles, and running dog.

The pottery from the graves at Vronda seems for the most part to have been produced regionally, and much of it fits with pottery from other East Cretan burial sites. While the earlier pottery from the tholos tombs is similar in style and development with ceramic trends in Central Crete, the later PG pottery enjoyed a longer lasting popularity in the east, and the new mainland styles were slower to appear than elsewhere on the island until the LG period. By EO times, the Kavousi area seems to have followed the styles found in Central Crete, although perhaps local potters lagged in picking them up. While much of the pottery found in the graves has counterparts at the Kastro in the LG–O periods (see Mook 1993), the types reflect the specific needs of the burial rituals. Nevertheless, the pottery from the enclosure graves is similar to that from domestic assemblages on the Kastro in terms of shapes and decorations, and it would appear that none of the vessels were manufactured specifically for funerary use.

Potters' Marks and Graffiti

Painted or incised marks on pottery that are not part of the surface decorative pattern are generally identified as potters' marks. They are rare at Vronda, where they appear only on the underside of bases.

Painted marks on bases are likely to have been decorative in nature. They occur on vessels both in the tholos tombs and in the enclosure graves, and a variety of patterns are represented. Only one example of a painted mark appears in the tholos tombs: a cross on the base of a cup from Tomb IV (**IV P1**). The enclosure graves produced only three examples of painted marks. A cross in a circle adorns the base of an EO lekythos from Grave 4 (**GR4 P20**), and this might have been seen when the vessel was used for pouring. A set of parallel lines perhaps with a dot in the center appears on the base of a monochrome cup from Grave 27 (**GR27 P2**), but this may also be a decorative feature meant to be seen when the cup was drained. One kalathos (**GR21 P8**) also bears a painted decoration on the underside: a cross with a large dot in the center. As kalathoi are regularly decorated on their undersides, perhaps for use as lids, it is best to consider this a form of decoration rather than a mark.

Incised marks are also uncommon at Vronda and are only found in a single cremation enclosure, Grave 36. Seven of the vessels from this grave are marked on their undersides, a skyphos (**GR36 P3**), two kalathoi (**GR36 P4, GR36 P5**), a tray with reflex lugs (**GR36 P7**), two necked jars (**GR36 P9, GR36 P10**), and a small jug (**GR36 P17**). The incisions on the two kalathoi were apparently scratched in after firing, and they are therefore graffiti, but the marks on all the other vessels were made prior to firing when the clay was still malleable. The marks that were made before firing are simple. Strokes appear on two vessels: a single stroke on the base of the juglet **GR36 P17** (Pl. 70) and five small strokes (only three of which are easily visible) at the edge of the skyphos base **GR36 P3** (Fig. 147; Pl. 70). A single line bisects the base of the necked jar **GR36 P10** (Fig. 148; Pl. 70). The other necked jar, **GR36 P9** (Fig. 148; Pl. 70), and the tray **GR36 P7** (Fig. 148; Pl. 70) both have a single large, incised X-pattern. The graffiti on the two kalathoi are more complex. The vessel **GR36 P5** has a series of small X marks scratched all over the underside, along with another symbol that is made up of a vertical stroke with a small triangle running off it to one side (Fig. 148; Pl. 70). Kalathos **GR36 P4** has an X-pattern and a series of other strokes that run across it (Fig. 147; Pl. 70). In neither case do the marks appear to be alphabetic.

Potters' marks appear on pottery of all periods in Greece, from the Bronze Age through the Hellenistic periods. In preliterate periods, such marks were nonalphabetic but later were replaced by Linear A and B signs that could be painted or incised on the vessels. In the EIA, marks were again nonalphabetic, as was the case with the Vronda examples. Although vessels marked with painted, incised, or stamped signs are common on later Greek pottery (Johnston 1979, 2006), they occur less frequently on EIA pottery and are particularly rare on Crete. Papadopoulos (1994, 457) lists only two examples, both from the Fortetsa cemetery at Knossos, and later publications of EIA cemeteries and settlements on Crete have identified only a few more (Kotsonas 2008, 63; Papadopoulos 2017, 65–66), mostly painted and generally found on the eastern end of the island (Tsipopoulou 2005, 519).

East Crete has provided many examples of painted decoration on the bases of cups and skyphoi, five of them from the Kavousi tombs near the Kastro. Crosses are the most common form of painted marks on Crete, and they are found primarily on LG cup and skyphos bases from East Crete. Parallel lines, without the central dot found on **GR27 P2**, can also be found on two LG wide-mouthed jugs, one from Sklavoi (Tsipopoulou 2005, 299, fig. 90:Σ3814), the other from Hagios Georgios (Tsipopoulou 2005, 150, fig. 90:AN1797). Other painted marks found at East Cretan LG sites, but missing at Vronda, include single lines (Tsipopoulou 2005, 321, fig. 126:Σ3820), crosshatching (Tsipopoulou 2005, 105, fig. 126:H761), and a reserved triangle (Tsipopoulou 2005, 302, fig. 126:Σ3852). More elaborate designs appear on oinochoai or jugs from East Crete (Tsipopoulou 2005, 268, fig. 78:AN1357; 274, fig. 79:AN1600; 297, fig. 78:AN1670; 314, fig. 79:AN1446; 2013, 147–148, fig. 10:12270; 149, fig. 11:12325).

Incised marks on the undersides of vessels are rare, but eight have been found in East Cretan sites, seven from the Siteia area and one from Kavousi. Four marks appear on skyphoi, three on oinochoai, and one on a cup (Tsipopoulou 2005, 519). Most of the patterns are simple and include three small oblique lines on the edge made before firing (Tsipopoulou 2005, 132, pl. 138:AN2378), lines (Tsipopoulou 2005, 314, fig. 117:AN1447), circles or concentric circles (Tsipopoulou 2005, 134, fig. 117:AN2385; 120, fig. 83:H1967), and two parallel lines cut by an arc (Tsipopoulou 2005, 212, fig. 122:AN3227). A few patterns are more complex, possibly alphabetic, including what looks like a capital lambda (Tsipopoulou 2005, 284, fig. 75:AN8753), another with a possible kappa (Tsipopoulou 2005, 283, fig. 75:AN8752), and a third with three letters (Tsipopoulou 2005, 269, fig. 119:AN1364). Two of the marked oinochoai come from the same tomb at Praisos (AN 8752, AN8753), and two of the skyphoi come from a single tomb at Hagios Georgios (AN 2378, AN2385; Tsipopoulou 2005, 519).

Potters' marks are known from Azoria from the eighth–fifth centuries (West 2015), including an incised one on a LG monochrome cup (Haggis et al. 2007a, 705, fig. 34:5). The EIA temples at Kommos also produced potters' marks and inscriptions (Csapo, Johnston, and Geagan 2000), but most of these are alphabetic and only rarely inscribed on the bottoms of pots. A late seventh-century vessel has an inscribed X like those on **GR36 P7** and **GR36 P9** (Csapo, Johnston, and Geagan 2000, 124–125, pl. 2.4:72); X is the most common single mark (Csapo, Johnston, and Geagan 2000, 103). Another vessel of similar date bears a design called a star, which appears similar to the scratchings on **GR36 P4** (Csapo, Johnston, and Geagan 2000, 124, pl. 2.4:65).

There has been much discussion about the function of potters' marks on vessels of the Bronze Age through Classical periods in Greece and in Cyprus (see most recently Papadopoulos 2005, 541–552; 2017, 88–96). Aliki Bikaki (1984, 42–43) suggested possible functions for the potters' marks at Bronze Age Keos on Hagia Eirene: to identify the maker, the capacity of the vessel, its provenance, or its destination. She rejected the idea, however, that the marks were made for a particular individual consumer because the sudden explosion of marking pots points to a general demand, not individual needs (Bikaki 1984, 43). Papadopoulos (2005, 544) has suggested but rejected the idea that they could indicate commodities. He also rejected the idea that these marks indicated a capacity or ownership unless put on after firing (1994, 480–481; 2005, 544–551; 2017, 88–89). He suggests that they may be symbols denoting a preordered or prepaid group of vessels or a reserved set of pots. If, indeed, the firing of pots was seasonal and they were in high demand, the potter might have marked vessels in a particular firing that were produced for a special client or for export (Papadopoulos 1994, 481). Such marked pots might also have been made as dedications to the gods (1994, 486) or for a tomb (1994, 490). Most recently, Papadopoulos (2017, 91) has suggested that these marks may be a sort of signature by the potter.

What is to be made, then, of the marks on the vessels from Vronda? The painted marks are all on drinking vessels or kalathoi. As kalathoi were commonly turned over and used as lids, it makes sense that the bottoms would have been decorated, however simply. Marking the underside of cups may also have been a form of simple decoration, meant to be seen when the user emptied the vessel. The set of vessels in Grave 36, however, represents something quite different. These are the only vessels in all of the tombs that are marked with incisions, and they belong together. Of the seven marked vessels (two kalathoi, a skyphos, a tray, two necked jars, and a juglet) five were marked before firing, while the two kalathoi were incised afterward. It seems likely that the five marked vessels in this tomb were made as a special commission, perhaps for a single particular family, whether for domestic use or for burial. Why each vessel had a different mark is uncertain. Most of the marked vessels, including the skyphos, one of the kalathoi (**GR36 P5**), the tray (**GR36 P7**), and both of the necked jars, can be associated with the last three burials in the tomb, a child and two adults buried in the north side of the enclosure. The other kalathos (**GR36 P4**) and the juglet (**GR36 P17**) seem to go with the earlier four burials of two infants and two young adults. It would appear, then, that the majority of marked vessels in this grave come from one particular group of burials, although we do not know if these were made at the same time or were sequential, nor can we associate any pottery with any individual within the grave. It seems most likely that the pot marks made on the vessels before firing identified them as being for a particular individual or family. Such marks were not commonly made, so we cannot say that marks were generally put on pottery intended for burials or funerary ritual. As we cannot identify for certain the settlement in which the burying population lived, we also cannot say if the marks were generally made for a particular kinship group.

The two kalathoi that were inscribed after firing represent something different. It is interesting that the incisions were made only on this shape, and they could have been made by the potter, the owner, or someone else during the burial event. If these kalathoi were used as lids, then someone may have given them decoration on the bottom when they were placed over one of the jars. If they were drinking vessels, the incisions may have been made purely as decoration, perhaps during the funerary ritual. A large fragment from a LM IIIC pithos incised with a tree graffito also appeared in this tomb, attesting to the interest in scratched symbols among this burying population.

9

Petrographic Analysis of the Grave Ceramic Assemblage

Eleni Nodarou

Kavousi Fabrics and the Aim of the Study

Ceramic studies in East Crete have been enhanced greatly over the years by the application of both macroscopic and microscopic analyses. The detailed macroscopic classification of the fabrics from the Kavousi-Thriphti survey (Haggis and Mook 1993) has provided a valuable tool for dating and quantifying the poorly preserved survey pottery, and it has also demonstrated the potential of applying this type of analysis to coarse utilitarian wares. An integrated fabric approach combining macroscopic and archaeometric analysis has been applied to pottery from the area of Kavousi in two instances: the FN–EM pottery from various contexts of the Kavousi-Thriphti survey (Day et al. 2005) and the ritual sets from the LM IIIC shrine at Kavousi Vronda (Day et al. 2006). There cannot, however, be any direct comparison of the assemblage from the Geometric cemetery discussed here with the two Kavousi assemblages previously analyzed because of the chronological distance between them and the differential representation of pottery shapes and fabric types. The FN–EM material from the Kavousi-Thriphti survey is part of a larger program of analysis of Prepalatial pottery, and the shapes and wares sampled do not represent the entire assemblage. Among the survey material there are only a few vessels from Vronda, and they belong to a single and very specific pottery style, the Vasiliki Ware of the EM IIB period. The LM IIIC assemblage from the excavation of the Vronda shrine is chronologically closer to the assemblage discussed here, but it includes only the ritual equipment of the shrine and cannot provide an accurate account of the various fabrics in use within the settlement. Nevertheless, despite these limitations, these earlier studies have shown that in the Kavousi area there are three main categories of fabrics, made with raw materials from three different sources, which persist diachronically: (a) coarse fabrics containing low-grade metamorphic rocks related to the Phyllite-Quartzite series; (b) granitic-dioritic fabrics originating from the area of

Gournia-Kalo Chorio; and (c) coarse fabrics with sand inclusions connected with the Ophiolite series of the south coast of Crete.

A total of 104 pottery samples from the cemetery at Kavousi Vronda were selected for petrographic analysis (for the concordance between samples and fabric groups, see Table 19). The vessel shapes comprise primarily semi-fine to fine drinking and serving vases, along with a few larger vessels, mainly semi-coarse transport amphorae and two burial pithoi. The number of small vessels in the analysis is dictated by their overall predominance relative to larger domestic shapes in the overall burial assemblage. The dates of the pottery range from the Geometric to Early Orientalizing periods. The aim of the analysis is twofold: to characterize the pottery fabrics of the cemetery in terms of the raw materials and clay recipes used, and to make inferences about the possible provenance of the pottery that was deposited in the cemetery. This approach will allow an investigation of continuities and discontinuities in the fabrics used at Kavousi through time as well as potential contacts with other areas in East Crete or farther afield at the onset of the historical period.

Analytical Results

The petrographic analysis has demonstrated that the majority of the samples from the cemetery at Kavousi Vronda are related to a metamorphic environment connected with the Phyllite-Quartzite series outcropping in Northeast Crete (Fabric Groups 1–3). This finding did not come as a surprise: metamorphic fabrics were also recorded in the previous analyses of the pottery from the Kavousi survey and the LM IIIC ritual assemblage in more than one fabric group and as early as the EM period. When the assemblages from the survey and LM IIIC Kavousi are published in their entirety, it will be important to compare the percentages of the metamorphic versus other fabrics because at the cemetery the former constitute by far the predominant component. The other fabrics, namely, the one containing granitic-dioritic rocks deriving from the western part of the Mirabello area (Fabric Group 4) and those connected with the Ophiolite series outcropping on the south coast of East Crete (Fabric Groups 5 and 6), are encountered in smaller percentages. For an overview of the main petrographic groups, see Table 20. All references to color in the following discussion are based on observations under crossed polarized light (XPL).

Fabric Groups with Metamorphic Rock Fragments

Fabric Group 1: Brown Metamorphic

Fabric Subgroup 1a: Semi-Coarse

Samples: KAV 15/7 (**GR9 P55**), 15/9 (**GR9 P33**), 15/11 (**GR9 P41**), 15/17 (**GR9 P45**), 15/35 (**GR3 P17**), 15/76 (**GR28 P24**), 15/78 (**GR28 P25**), 15/85 (**GR30 P29**), 15/87 (**GR30 P25**), 15/91 (**GR17 P10**)

Fabric Subgroup 1b: Semi-Fine

Samples: KAV 15/8 (**GR9 P43**), 15/10 (**GR9 P34**), 15/25 (**GR6 P3**), 15/33 (**GR5 P13**), 15/37 (**GR3 P3**), 15/40 (**GR4 P16**), 15/41 (**GR4 P22**), 15/42 (**GR4 P15**), 15/43 (**GR4 P24**), 15/60 (**GR16 P17**), 15/65 (**GR20 P7**), 15/67 (**GR20 P20**), 15/70 (**GR26 P23**), 15/71 (**GR27 P11**), 15/72 (**GR27 P4**), 15/73 (**GR27 P2**), 15/74 (**GR27 P12**), 15/75 (**GR27 P13**), 15/79 (**GR28 P28**), 15/84 (**GR30 P5**), 15/86 (**GR30 P24**)

Fabric Subgroup 1c: Fine

Samples: KAV 15/5 (**GR9 P3**), 15/12 (**GR9 P23**), 15/18 (**GR9 P16**), 15/38 (**GR4 P8**), 15/81 (**GR28 P6**), 15/82 (**GR28 P11**), 15/90 (**GR36 P10**), 15/96 (**IX P46**), 15/102 (**IX P36**), 15/104 (**IX P47**)

Fabric Group 1 predominates in the assemblage, with a total of 41 of the 104 petrographic samples. It is encountered in three granulometries (Fabric Subgroups 1a–1c) ranging from semi-coarse to fine (Pls. 71A–71C). It is characterized by a brown firing matrix that is optically inactive. The optical activity of the matrix relates to the firing temperature: an optically active matrix indicates low firing temperature, whereas an optically inactive matrix reflects high firing temperature.

The nonplastic inclusions are rather sparsely distributed in the clay matrix and consist primarily of small quartz and metamorphic rock fragments (dark phyllite and, to a lesser extent, schist and quartzite) and occasionally some micritic limestone and rare microfossils. In some samples quartz is the predominant component, in others there are more metamorphics. In the fine fraction there are quartz fragments and occasionally some biotite mica. A bright red mineral (or clay pellets) encountered in the fine fraction is rather characteristic; it occurs in small quantities but regularly in the samples of this group. Overall, it is a homogeneous fabric in terms of composition and texture and seems to represent the production of a small number of workshops (if not a single one). The vessels represented are mainly drinking and serving shapes such as cups, skyphoi, bowls, kraters, and a few oinochoai, as well as lesser numbers of containers for transport and/or small-scale storage of liquids, such as jars and amphorae.

Parallels for Fabric Group 1 occur at the LM IB site of Papadiokampos (Pl. 71D) and at Neopalatial Petras, but they do not represent strictly local production at these sites. A similar fabric in both a coarser and a finer version has been described in the FN–EM material from the Kavousi-Thriphti survey (Day et al. 2005, 191–193, descriptions 7 and 8) with parallels from Prepalatial sites on the south coast (Myrtos Phournou Koriphi) and elsewhere in northeast Crete (Mochlos, Petras). The color of the matrix and the mineralogical composition are almost identical with those of Fabric Group 1 from Kavousi Vronda. The presence of the bright red mineral leaves no doubt that it is the same fabric, but its provenance cannot be determined on mineralogical grounds. Peter Day and colleagues (Day et al. 2005, 192) associate this fabric tentatively with the northern part of the isthmus of Ierapetra, but there are no parallels in the comparative material from the LM IIIC sites of Chalasmenos and Vasiliki Kephala (pers. obs.). On the contrary, most of the comparative examples derive from farther east on the north coast of Crete. Therefore, there is a possibility that this fabric relates to the Phyllite-Quartzite series outcropping in northeast Crete and could be connected to an alluvium containing quartz and metamorphic rocks.

Fabric Group 2: Red Metamorphic, Coarse to Semi-Coarse

Samples: KAV 15/3 (**GR9 P53**), 15/6 (**GR9 P40**), 15/13 (**GR9 P54**), 15/14 (**GR9 P36**), 15/16 (**GR9 P46**), 15/19 (**GR9 P52**), 15/49 (**GR12 P39**), 15/55 (**GR12 P43**), 15/63 (**GR17 P9**), 15/77 (**GR28 P20**), 15/80 (**GR28 P5**), 15/88 (**GR36 P15**), 15/94 (**IX P30**), 15/98 (**IX P51**)

The metamorphic fabrics encountered in East Crete usually contain a multitude of rock fragments, namely phyllites, quartzites, and slates ranging from finer to coarser grained (e.g., Nodarou 2010). The phyllites in particular display variability in color (brown, red brown, silvery, golden yellow) and composition, containing biotite or muscovite mica and small quartz fragments. Fabric Group 2 is coarse to semi-coarse with a dark red to dark brown firing matrix that is optically inactive (Pl. 71E). It displays a homogeneity in the nonplastic inclusions, which consist mainly of a single type of metamorphic rock, a brown or reddish-brown fine-grained elongate phyllite, in contrast to the variability of the metamorphic components usually seen in the East Cretan fabrics. The secondary nonplastic components include rare micritic limestone, quartzite, sandstone, chert, and a few sparse quartz fragments. In the clay base there are frequent biotite mica laths. The packing of the nonplastics depends on the coarseness of the samples—that is, the fragments are larger and denser in the coarser samples. The vessels represented are mainly forms used for drinking, with fewer serving shapes. Close parallels for Fabric Group 2 are encountered in the Neopalatial pottery from Papadiokampos (Pl. 71F), but at that site there is no evidence for local production with metamorphic materials (see also Fabric Group 1). In terms of origin this fabric can be broadly assigned to the Phyllite-Quartzite series outcropping in northeast Crete.

Fabric Group 3: Metamorphic with Greenstone

Samples: KAV 15/24 (**GR9 P38**), 15/54 (**GR12 P42**), 15/92 (**GR10 P1**), 15/95 (**IX P60**) (coarser); KAV 15/51 (**GR12 P35**), 15/52 (**GR12 P34**), 15/59 (**GR16 P21**), 15/97 (**IX P52**) (finer)

This fabric has several characteristics in common with Fabric Group 2. The matrix ranges from reddish brown to dark brown and is optically inactive. The nonplastic inclusions consist of metamorphic rock fragments, namely fine-grained brown phyllites, a few quartzite and quartz fragments, and rare pyroxene (Pl. 72A). The clay matrix contains frequent biotite mica laths. The most characteristic component, though, is the green altered rock (possibly of igneous nature) that is present in all the samples. Although it does not occur in large quantities (sample KAV 15/24, with frequent greenstones, is the exception rather than the norm), it is a rather consistent component, and its occurrence indicates a common origin for all the samples. The vessels represented belong to the same repertoire as those of Fabric Group 2, with shapes related to small-scale storage or transport, serving, and consumption of liquids. Sample KAV 15/92 should be singled out as it is a burial pithos and one of the few large vessels of the cemetery, showing us what the recipe for large domestic vessels might have been. The gap in our knowledge on the composition of domestic vessels against vessels of special use can be filled only with data from settlement sites, when published. Parallels for Fabric Group 3 exist in the Minoan assemblages of Petras and Papadiokampos.

Comment on Fabric Groups 2 and 3
Fabric Groups 2 and 3 display considerable compositional similarity. Both have a clay base that fires in a dark reddish-brown color and contains frequent biotite mica laths, and they are also characterized by the presence of the same type of metamorphic materials (fine-grained brown phyllite). In a geological environment with rather variable metamorphics, the similarity between these two groups indicates that most likely they share a common origin. The presence in Fabric Group 3 of the altered greenstone may or may not be crucial for provenance assignment; its significance remains to be investigated through further sampling of archaeological and geological materials. An observation that may prove significant in the discussion of East Cretan raw materials comes from modern clay samples acquired in the areas of Mochlos and Chamaizi: they contain all the components encountered in Fabric Groups 2 and 3—that is, fine-grained brown phyllite, greenstone, pyroxene, and biotite mica schist (Pl. 72B). Following the discussion of Fabric Group 1, it appears that the pottery from Kavousi Vronda connected with metamorphic raw materials derives from the broader area of Mochlos-Chamaizi. Further sampling of archaeological material and clay sources in the area is required, however, and until this hypothesis is confirmed, Fabric Groups 2 and 3 should be considered broadly East Cretan.

Small Metamorphic Groups

Samples: KAV 15/4 (**GR9 P51**), 15/58 (**GR16 P22**), 15/68 (**GR23 P8**)

This fabric is coarse and characterized by a dark brown and optically inactive matrix (Pl. 72C). The nonplastic inclusions are of metamorphic nature and consist of micaceous phyllite, quartz-mica schist, and quartzite. There are also sparse fragments of quartz. The base clay contains frequent biotite and muscovite mica laths. The amount of mica present in this fabric gives the vessels a shiny appearance and differentiates it from the rest of the metamorphic groups. A raw material offering a close parallel for this fabric comes from the area of Chamaizi (Pl. 72B), where clays containing biotite mica have been sampled. Considering that the entire metamorphic series identified at Kavousi presents similarities with other East Cretan fabrics, it is likely that this small micaceous group originates from the broader area of Chamaizi. The vessels represented are a cup, a bowl, and a jug or oinochoe.

Samples: KAV 15/27 (**GR6 P26**), 15/46 (**GR1 P33**), 15/56 (**GR12 P41**), 15/62 (**GR17 P11**), 15/93 (**GR21 P13**)

This fabric is rather coarse, characterized by an orangish-brown firing matrix ranging from optically active to moderately active (Pl. 72D). It is mineralogically connected to Fabric Group 2, which has the same fine-grained brown phyllites. The main difference is the optical activity of the clay matrix, indicating a lower firing temperature. A close parallel exists in the Neopalatial assemblage of Papadiokampos, corroborating the similarity of these samples with Fabric Group 2, as well as the broader connection with East Crete. With the exception of two cups, the vessels represented are larger than the usual liquid containers; one is a burial pithos.

Sample KAV 15/101 (**IX P9**)

This fabric is semi-coarse and characterized by a dark brown and optically inactive matrix, which in parts displays greenish mottling due to the high firing temperature (Pl. 72E). The nonplastic inclusions consist of very fine-grained red metamorphic rocks that are consistent with those seen in Fabric Groups 2 and 3. The presence of microfossils and the greenish tinge of the matrix, however, indicate the use of a calcareous raw material that differentiates this sample from the other metamorphic groups. An exact parallel for the fabric of this necked jar is encountered in the Neopalatial assemblage of Papadiokampos, though, again linking this sample with Fabric Groups 2 and 3 and the broader area of East Crete (Pl. 72F).

Fabric Group Connected with Granitic-Dioritic Raw Materials

Fabric Group 4: Fine with Granitic-Dioritic Rock Fragments

Samples: KAV 15/20 (**GR9 P49**), 15/44 (**GR4 P20**), 15/48 (**GR12 P19**), 15/50 (**GR12 P14**), 15/57 (**GR12 P11**)

Fabric Group 4, containing granitic-dioritic rock fragments, has been described macroscopically (Haggis and Mook 1993; Haggis 2005, 169) and microscopically in many instances (for bibliographic overview, see Betancourt 2008, 30–31; Nodarou and Moody 2014, 91). Its provenance is connected with the intrusive granitic-dioritic rocks in the Cretaceous limestones outcropping in the central and western part of the Gulf of Mirabello (I.G.S.R. 1959; Dierckx and Tsikouras 2007). The few samples from the Vronda cemetery are characterized by a very fine, brown firing matrix (Pl. 73A), and the nonplastic inclusions consist of very few to rare small fragments of granitic-dioritic rocks. The shapes represented are all small containers for liquids

In East Crete the granitic-dioritic fabrics are rather common from the Prepalatial to Late Minoan periods and Hellenistic to Roman times. At Kavousi they are present in the material from the survey (Day et al. 2005, 179–180) and also in the ritual assemblage from the LM IIIC shrine (Day et al. 2006, 146–148). In the broader area they are very common in the LM IIIC assemblage from Chalasmenos, where they occur in both the ritual as well as the domestic assemblage (for the former, cf. Chlouveraki et al. 2010), and in the contemporary assemblage from Vasiliki Kephala, albeit in smaller percentages (Nodarou, work in progress). Thus, the small amount of granitic-dioritic pottery in the Kavousi Vronda cemetery presents a sharp contrast with the slightly earlier LM IIIC assemblages from Kavousi, Chalasmenos, and Vasiliki. It is difficult to know, however, whether this disparity is the result of chronological differences, changes in ceramic production, or shifting patterns in the distribution and consumption of granitic-dioritic pottery in the Geometric and Archaic period in this area of the isthmus.

Fabric Groups Connected with the South Coast

Fabric Group 5: Gray Siltstone, Coarse to Semi-Coarse

Samples: KAV 15/15 (**GR9 P35**), 15/21 (**GR9 P37**), 15/22 (**GR9 P50**), 15/26 (**GR6 P2**), 15/29 (**GR6 P27**), 15/31 (**GR6 P29**), 15/69 (**GR26 P20**)

This coarse to semi-coarse fabric is characterized by a very fine dark reddish-brown firing matrix that is optically inactive (Pl. 73B). In some samples the matrix displays discolorations in the form of mottling as a result of the high firing temperature. The nonplastic inclusions consist primarily of dark gray elongate and rounded siltstones that are more or less densely packed in the clay base. There are also very few to rare fragments of sedimentary rocks (fine-grained sandstones), metamorphics (phyllite, quartzite, quartzite-schist), and small fragments of quartz. The matrix contains a few biotite mica laths and very small quartz fragments. In some samples there are also dark reddish-brown textural concentration features (clay pellets). The fineness of the matrix and the size and rounded shape of the inclusions indicate that the raw material has been sieved and that sand was added as temper in the clay mix. Fabric Group 5 is rather homogeneous in terms of composition and texture. The shapes represented are all containers for liquids. The provenance of this fabric should be sought in the Ophiolite series of the south coast of East Crete or in South-Central Crete.

Fabric Group 6: Ophiolitic Fabric, Semi-Fine to Fine

Samples: KAV 15/23 (**GR9 P39**), 15/61 (**GR16 P20**), 15/66 (**GR20 P1**), 15/83 (**GR30 P28**), 15/89 (**GR36 P11**), 15/100 (**IX P15**)

This semi-fine to fine group is characterized by the same matrix as Fabric Group 5 (Pl. 73C). The nonplastic inclusions are small and rather scarce, consisting of rounded fragments of sedimentary (fine-grained sandstone and siltstone) and metamorphic rocks (fine-grained phyllite and a small amount of quartzite), very few to absent basic volcanic rock fragments (basalt), and rare quartz. This rock and mineral suite is compatible with the Ophiolite series. The shapes represented, including one pyxis and one cup, are also containers for liquids.

Comment on Fabric Groups 5 and 6

The geology of the South Cretan coast is characterized by the Ophiolite series and the Flysch mélange, consisting of a mixture of metamorphic, sedimentary, and volcanic rocks, rounded in shape. When encountered in the pottery, this composition signals an area of production in the part of the island extending from Myrtos to the western Mesara (see Nodarou 2022). The absence of an adequate number of publications of south coast fabrics presumed to be local prevents a more specific and secure assignment of provenance within the south coast region. From the southeastern part of the island, such fabrics have been reported from Myrtos Phournou Koriphi (Whitelaw et al. 1997), Symi Viannou (Nodarou and Rathossi 2008), the Kavousi-Thriphti survey (Day et al. 2005, 187–189), LM IIIC Chalasmenos (Chlouveraki et al. 2010), and Vasiliki Kephala (pers. obs.). Similar fabrics (but not exact parallels), however, have been encountered in the EIA assemblage from Knossos, where there is also doubt regarding their origin, that is, whether they are strictly local or from the Mesara (Boileau and Whitley 2010, Fabric Group 5). The Ophiolite series extends over a large area in South or South-Central Crete; its geology is rather complex and repetitive, and the provenance of pottery made from associated raw material sources cannot be securely defined on petrographic or mineralogical criteria alone. For the Kavousi material, the closest source for this fabric is the south coast and the broader area of Ierapetra, with the isthmus ensuring easy circulation of products on a north–south axis.

Other Fabric Groups and Loners

Fabric Group 7: Fine Fabric with Clay Pellets

Samples: KAV 15/1 (**GR9 P20**), 15/32 (**GR5 P3**), 15/36 (**GR3 P10**), 15/39 (**GR4 P1**), 15/45 (**GR1 P11**), 15/47 (**GR1 P16**), 15/53 (**GR12 P10**), 15/99 (**IX P31**), 15/103 (**IX P10**)

This very fine fabric is characterized by the same dark reddish-brown and optically inactive matrix (Pl. 73D) that has been described for the south coast fabrics. Most samples are completely devoid of nonplastic inclusions, while in some there are rare small quartz fragments and very rare to absent fine-grained sandstones. The component that links the samples of this group is the regular presence of biotite mica in the base clay and clay pellets. Although the mineralogical composition is not diagnostic of origin, this group is rather homogeneous, and the clay pellets in all the samples are indicative of a common practice of manufacture. The fine mica laths in the base clay lead to the identification of this group as the fine version of the south coast fabrics. The shapes represented are all connected to the storage/transport and consumption of liquids.

Loners

Sample KAV 15/30 (**GR6 P28**)

This very fine fabric is characterized by a dark reddish-brown firing matrix that ranges from optically active near the margin to inactive in the center of the section (Pl. 73E). It contains very few sedimentary rocks and clay pellets. This sample, from a jug, seems to represent a slightly coarser version of Fabric Group 7.

Sample KAV 15/2 (**GR9 P18**)

This rather fine fabric is characterized by a dark brown firing matrix that is optically inactive, and it contains sparse inclusions of fine-grained sedimentary rocks (sandstones; Pl. 73F). The fine fraction consists of very fine biotite mica laths, rare quartz fragments, and very rare metamorphics. The composition is very close to Fabric Group 7, but it differs in two textural aspects: the clay pellets are a brighter red color, and they are more numerous and rather discordant with the micromass; moreover, there are clay striations not seen in Fabric Group 7. Also, the application of a thick layer of red slip on the surface makes this sample stand out from the vessels of Fabric Group 7. The mineralogical composition points toward the Ophiolite series, which, as discussed above, has rather complex and repetitive geology. Therefore, this sample may be connected with a different area, and considering the rarity in the Vronda assemblage of the ledge-rim cup from which it derives, its origin might be sought in North-Central or South-Central Crete.

Sample KAV 15/34 (**GR5 P15**)

This sample has no parallel in the Vronda assemblage. It is semi-coarse with a dark brown firing matrix that is optically inactive (Pl. 74A). The nonplastic inclusions consist of medium- to small-sized volcanic rock fragments (basalt and trachyte) and a few fragments of mono- and polycrystalline quartz. The fine fraction consists mainly of muscovite mica and plagioclase/sanidine laths. There are also dark brown and almost mottled clay pellets, which are indicative of a high firing temperature. The vessel represented is a jug, and it is an off-island import. Its composition, with volcanic rocks, could be compatible with an origin on the islands of the east Aegean (possibly the southern part of Kos?) or the coast of Asia Minor, but the few published fabrics from these areas do not provide convincing parallels.

Sample KAV 15/28 (**GR6 P22**)

This sample is characterized by a dark brown firing matrix with a dark reddish-brown outer margin (Pl. 74B). The micromass is optically inactive. The coarse fraction is rather silty with mono- and polycrystalline quartz and a few fragments of metamorphic rocks, mainly fine-grained phyllite. Some very rare fragments of plagioclase (rarely in intergrowth with chlorite) and volcanic rocks, as well as the presence of rather abundant elongate fine mica laths in the fine fraction, point toward an off-island origin for this cup. This geology of metamorphic rocks with a volcanic component has been described in the Hellenistic stamped amphorae from Kos (Whitbread 1995, 90–93), but there cannot be any secure provenance assignment for this sample on the basis of the present evidence.

Sample KAV 15/64 (**GR19 P17**)

This sample is characterized by a dark brown firing matrix that is optically inactive (Pl. 74C). The nonplastic inclusions consist of very few fragments of metamorphic rocks, namely muscovite-mica schist and fine-grained phyllite, some mono- and polycrystalline quartz, and rare fragments of epidote. The matrix contains abundant muscovite mica laths. This composition is not diagnostic of origin, but the amount of mica in the matrix may be indicative of an off-island origin. The stylistic study has demonstrated that this monochrome cup has no exact parallels in the Vronda assemblage, which might support the proposition that it is an import.

Provenance and Consumption Patterns

Ceramic assemblages from funerary contexts are highly selective and should always be treated with caution, as they usually comprise special types of vases that are not representative of the domestic pottery used in everyday activities in the settlement. Nevertheless, the petrographic analysis of the pottery from the cemetery at Kavousi Vronda contributes to our knowledge in two ways: first, it shows the diachronic and continuous use of certain ceramic fabrics in the area of Kavousi from the prehistoric to the early historic periods, and second, it is the first time that material of the LG–EO period from East Crete has been analyzed, thus establishing a useful body of data to be used comparatively in the future.

The analysis has resulted in the establishment of five fabric groups for the semi-coarse and semi-fine wares connected with three different geological environments. Three fabric groups (1–3) are related to the Phyllite-Quartzite series of the north coast of East Crete, possibly originating in the Mochlos-Chamaizi area, one (Fabric Group 4) to the granitic-dioritic outcrops of the Mirabello area, and two (Fabric Groups 5 and 6) to the Ophiolite series possibly, at least for some of the vessels, from the south coast if not farther afield. The fine wares are concentrated in the fine variant of Fabric Group 1 and in Fabric Group 7, the latter also connected with ophiolitic raw materials.

The number of samples is representative of the assemblage in terms of shapes, wares, and macroscopic fabrics, and the quantification within the fabric groups allows for certain observations regarding the quantification of the fabrics within the assemblage. Unlike the FN–EM pottery from the Kavousi-Thriphti survey (Day et al. 2005) and the LM IIIC material from Chalasmenos and Vasiliki Kephala, in which the granitic-dioritic fabrics occur in significant quantities, at Kavousi Vronda the majority of the pottery is manufactured in metamorphic fabrics, and the percentage of granitic-dioritic and south coast fabrics is significantly lower.

One might argue that at least for the granitic-dioritic pottery the limited quantity is due to the overall absence of cooking wares in the cemetery. Indeed, at most sites around the Gulf of Mirabello (such as Chrysokamino and Mochlos) and even further east (Petras), the cooking vessels are in their majority manufactured with granitic-dioritic raw materials. At Vronda, the low occurrence of granitic-dioritic fabrics extends also to the transport and storage vessels as well as to the ritual objects. The same is the case with the fabrics related to production of the south coast: their representation is quite significant at the settlement sites of Chalasmenos and Vasiliki Kephala and rather low at Kavousi Vronda, where they were used primarily for transport/storage vessels and ritual implements.

The limited number of Mirabello and south coast products at the Kavousi Vronda cemetery inevitably raises the question of whether there was a decrease of ceramic production at these potting centers or a shift of interest in exchange networks and consumption patterns. The former may be excluded, at least for the granitic-dioritic pottery, as the Vrokastro survey has arguably demonstrated the continuous use of such materials for the production of various shapes in the EIA (Hayden, Moody, and Rackham 1992; Hayden and Risser 2005). Albeit restricted in number, the imports from the Mirabello area and the south coast that are present at Kavousi show that the contacts of the Vronda community with the western and southern part of the isthmus of Ierapetra were not broken after the LM IIIC period. The predominance of metamorphic fabrics originating from the Mochlos-Chamaizi area, however, shows a clear shift in the consumption patterns of the community toward the products of the eastern part of north Crete, possibly due to the political, economic, social, and cultural changes taking place at the end of the Bronze Age.

Last but not least, a comment should be made on the few samples considered to be off-island imports. Although they were not numerous, the presence of non-Cretan pottery in the material culture that reached the Vronda cemetery indicates long-distance contacts, possibly with the islands of the eastern Aegean and most likely via a major center on the north coast of Crete. A recent discussion of the Cretan EIA (Kotsonas 2017, with examples from Central Crete) has demonstrated that the island was neither isolated nor inert during this period and that a multiscalar approach is needed to investigate intraregional movement as well as the role of Crete in the eastern Mediterranean.

An East Cretan Assemblage—An East Cretan Community?

The predilection of the Kavousi population to consume ceramic products from the eastern part of the island should be viewed within a broader scheme of community choices and possibly of geographical (and ethnic?) commonality. The Vronda community's choice of vases may point toward a conscious effort to establish and maintain affiliations with other East Cretan sites rather than with those in the areas to the west and the south. A recent study of G–A material from the North Necropolis at Itanos shows similarities with the pottery fabrics from the Vronda burial assemblage. Unfortunately, analytical evidence for the G–O period is still scarce, especially from sites that lie between the two cemeteries, such as Mouliana, Chamaizi Liopetra, and Myrsini, which might provide interesting comparatives for Kavousi in the future. If the preliminary evidence for the resemblances between Kavousi and Itanos is confirmed by further analyses, however, a new picture of the East Cretan communities, with shared elements of material culture and possibly other common cultural traits, may emerge.

10

Finds Other than Pottery

Leslie Preston Day

with a contribution by Julie Unruh

This chapter is concerned with the many finds from the burials that do not qualify as pottery, including objects of metal, stone, bone or ivory, glass, and terracotta. These objects represent personal adornments, weapons, and tools.

Metal

Three types of metal have been encountered in the graves: bronze, iron, and lead. Objects of bronze and iron came from the tholos tombs, but because so many of the tombs had been plundered, few objects were found within them, and some of those recovered by Boyd could not be located. Most of the metal objects were made of bronze, with only a few of iron. In the enclosure graves more of the artifacts were made of iron (182 objects in total from all graves), with considerably fewer bronze objects (38) and only two of lead.

Bronze

Boyd reported that the tholos tombs produced bronze hairpins, fishhooks, and sheeting with holes for rivets, in addition to the jewelry discussed below. None of these items could be found in the Herakleion museum in 1979. Bronze objects were found in the enclosure graves, but they were scarcer than those made of iron. Generally, in the enclosure graves, bronze was used for items of personal adornment, such as pins and fibulae. This paucity probably reflects a real scarcity of bronze and/or its constituent parts. Evidence for this lack of materials lies in the signs of ancient repair on at least one of the bronze objects. Fibula **GR9 M2** shows clear evidence of having been repaired. The bronze toward the coil wore very thin and clearly broke, and a new coil and pin of iron was joined onto it. X-ray radiography (Pl. 34) revealed a single metallic phase throughout. Effie Photos-Jones' metallographic/SEM-EDAX analysis (see this vol., App. B, p. 383) highlighted the corrosion free, single alloy nature of the object (Pl. 34; see also Pl. 82A), as well as areas where two metals (iron and the bronze alloy) coexisted (see Pl. 82D); the extensively corroded iron envelops the bronze perhaps in an attempt to mend the bronze pin. Object **GR12 M2** may also have been repaired. It is bent toward the tip, as if the end had been joined back on after breaking or wearing, but the mender could not get it straight or did not care to do so. It would seem that the people who buried their dead in the Vronda enclosures did not have sufficient quantities of bronze even to repair a fibula, or the cost of the repair in bronze may have been prohibitive. It is also possible that the metals being deposited in the graves did not have to be in excellent repair or still fully functional; the discard of the valuable material would have been sufficient to demonstrate the wealth and status of the family. Bronze was used most commonly for jewelry in the Vronda enclosures, never for entire weapons, and there is only one possible tool. Bronze sheeting that once covered an object of a different material was also found, including a series of flat sheets from Grave 9 that possibly came from a box or even a shield and several curved sheets. Strips of bronze could also be added to the sockets or to the lower blades of spearheads (**GR12 M24**, **GR12 M26**), and bronze rivets were used in swords and daggers.

Pins

Only two certain pin fragments are known from the tholos tombs, suggesting that straight pins were less popular among the burying population than fibulae. Pin **VIII M1** is a fragment of an elongated bulb, probably from near the top of the pin. Pins with spherical bulbs appear early in the sequence of pins, dating chiefly to the SM period (Jacobsthal 1956, 1–2), while those rare examples with elongated bulbs seem to belong to the Orientalizing period (Jacobsthal 1956, 24, although the contexts are not always certain). A close parallel for the Vronda example can be found at Knossos (Coldstream and Catling, eds., 1996, fig. 158:26.f3). The Knossos pin is thought to be a SM type that continued into the PG period (Catling 1996a, 554). A fragment of the body of another pin without either end preserved was found in the cleaning of Tholos IV (**IV M6**). A third pin-like object from Tholos X (**X M1**) could be the bent bottom half of a pin or a needle, but it could also have come from a fibula.

Although rare in the tholos tombs, straight pins made of bronze or iron are very common in the enclosure graves (for the iron pins, see below, p. 311). There are 11 bronze examples from seven graves. In Graves 4 and 17 the pins come in pairs (**GR4 M1** and **GR4 M2**, **GR17 M1** and **GR17 M2**), while in Grave 12 there are three (**GR12 M1**–**GR12 M3**), although another uncataloged fragmentary pin made of iron is similar in size to **GR12 M3** and may have made a pair with the bronze pin. Other bronze pins were singletons (**GR3 M1**, **GR5 M1**, **GR16 M1**, **GR23 M1**), but in two instances (Graves 3 and 16) each of the bronze pins was accompanied by an iron pin, as suggested in the case of Grave 12. The bronze pins come in three types.

Type 1 includes pins with a small nail-like head and a globular swelling just below it (Fig. 171:a). Only two examples are known from Vronda (**GR12 M1**, **GR12 M2**). Pins of this type are similar to Catling's type 2, which were in use on Crete from the PG to the EO periods (Catling 1996a, 555). They have been found on the mainland in Submycenaean and PG contexts and represent the earliest type of pins in Greece (Jacobsthal 1956, 1–4; Popham, Sackett, and Themelis 1979–1980, 246, pl. 140:23.16, 23.17; Kilian-Dirlmeier 1984, 69–71, type B1; Lemos 2002, 104–105; Papadopoulos and Smithson 2017, 918–921). The Vronda examples are probably early. They seem to have been cast in one piece, which is a feature of the SM types (Jacobsthal 1956, 2), although they have larger globes than is usual for SM examples. They also lack the knob-like projection on top of the disk, which seems to come into style on the mainland in LPG times (Jacobsthal 1956, 2). An early PG date of manufacture would seem likely. Pins of this type may have been antiques when placed in the graves.

Type 2, the most common pin form, has a disk head with a small finial on top and a biconical boss with moldings on either side (Fig. 171:b). Pin **GR12 M3** probably belongs to this category; it apparently has no finial on top, but its preservation makes it difficult to be certain. Four examples have three moldings on either side of the boss (**GR5 M1**, **GR17 M1**, **GR17 M2**, **GR23 M1**), while two examples (**GR4 M2**, **GR12 M3**) have only two moldings. Pin **GR4 M1** seems to have four moldings, while **GR16 M1** may have four on one side and one or two on the other, but it is too small and badly preserved to be certain. This type is also the most common among iron pins. It corresponds to Hector Catling's type 5, which he dates to the Orientalizing period (1996a, 555–556). Paul Jacobsthal (1956, 17–18) ascribes the type to the Subgeometric period and comments on how the Cretan examples differ from those found on the mainland. The type probably belongs to the EO period.

Type 3 has two round swellings or small bosses (Fig. 171:c). It has only a single example (**GR3 M1**), and the top of the head is broken, making it impossible to determine whether it had a disk head. This pin does not seem to conform to any of the known types, although it may be similar to Jacobsthal's group 3 of Subgeometric date (1956, 12, no. 34). A pin of similar appearance found at Arkades has four swellings at the top, and it does not seem to have been broken (Levi 1927–1929, pl. 7:P98, top center).

Bronze pins can occur in the same enclosures with iron pins (Graves 3, 16, 17), and they are nearly always found in graves that contain female and/or child burials. They may have been used for fastening a garment. Sinclair Hood suggested that pairs of pins may have been used to fasten the shoulders of a peplos on a female burial, while a single pin may have fastened the cloak of a male burial (Coldstream and Hood 1968, 215; but see the warning about this interpretation in Papadopoulos and Smithson 2017, 915–917). The two pins that were found in Grave 4 may have fastened a woman's garment at the shoulders, as may also have been the case with the pair in Grave 12 (**GR12 M1, GR12 M2**). The pair of bronze pins and a second pair of iron pins in Grave 17 seem to have accompanied the children, who might have worn a garment that required pinning at the shoulders, regardless of sex; in Classical times, children were often not differentiated in dress by gender (Lawton 2007, 50). Similarly, two pins, one of bronze and one of iron, accompanied a female burial in Grave 3 (**GR3 M1, GR3 M3**) and possibly a child burial in Grave 16 (**GR16 M1, GR16 M2**). Pins may also have been used to fasten a shroud, but Catling's idea that pins were used to secure the cloth that held the bones after they were removed from the pyre (Catling 1996a, 555) cannot pertain to the Vronda burials, as the bones were not removed from the pyre. At least some of these pins may have been used for the hair (for the use of hairpins, see Coldstream and Hood 1968, 214).

Fibulae

Fibulae were common in the tholos tombs. Five fibulae are still preserved: four from Tomb IV and one from Tomb VII. At least one other fibula was found in Tomb IV, but it can no longer be located. All of these fibulae are of the arched type, but they show variations. Two are of Efi Sapouna-Sakellaraki's type IId (1978, 48–49), a flat "sheet" fibula with a tongue-shaped catch plate (**IV M3, VII M1**), which she dates to the EPG period on the basis of an example from one of the Fortetsa tombs. Her type IId is the same as type Ib in the Vronda enclosure graves. Fibula **IV M2** is type IIc of SM–PG date (Sapouna-Sakellaraki 1978, 47–48). No similar examples appeared in the enclosure graves. Fibula **IV M4** has a spiral bow of type IIf, a type that begins in SM and lasted into the LG–EO periods (Sapouna-Sakellaraki 1978, 50–51). Two similar examples, categorized as type Ic, can be found in the enclosure burials (**GR20 M1, GR20 M2**). Fibula **IV M1** is Sapouna-Sakellaraki's type IIi, with a rhomboidal section and two swellings at either end, which can be dated to the 11th–9th centuries (1978, 52). No examples of this type appear in the enclosure graves.

Fibulae are not particularly common in the Vronda enclosure graves; only 11 were found in eight graves, occasionally in pairs of the same type (**GR20 M1** and **GR20 M2, GR23 M2** and **GR23 M3**; possibly **GR9 M1** and **GR9 M2**), but more often singly. Five different types of fibulae can be identified from the enclosure graves.

Type 1 is a simple arched-bow fibula (**GR1 M1, GR20 M1, GR20 M2, GR26 M1**), like those in the tholos tombs. The largest number of fibulae can be placed in this type, but the type can be broken down into three subcategories.

The first subtype (Type 1a) has a simple arched bow, round in section, slightly flattened toward the catch plate (Fig. 171:d). Such fibulae belong to Efi Sapouna-Sakellaraki's type IIa (1978, 42–45) and Christian Blinkenberg's type II.1, 2 (1926, 60–62). Only one example (**GR26 M1**) was found in the Vronda graves. This type of fibula is very early, found primarily in SM–PG contexts in Crete (Sapouna-Sakellaraki 1978, 44). Catling (1996b, 525–526) suggests a Cypriot origin for this type.

The second subcategory (Type 1b) is the simple fibula with flat bow (Fig. 171:e), which belongs to Sapouna-Sakellaraki's type IId (1978, 48–49) and

Blinkenberg's type II.4 (1926, 63–64). There is a single very large example (**GR1 M1**) that is similar to many other fibulae from Crete, particularly East Crete, including several from the tholos tombs at Vronda (**IV M3, VII M1**; Sapouna-Sakellaraki 1978, fig. 6:169–174). The type was common in the PG period but continued later in the Dodecanese and went into the EG period in Athens (Sapouna-Sakellaraki 1978, 49).

The third subgroup (Type 1c; Fig. 171:f) is characterized by a twisted bow, as seen on **IV M4** (Pl. 10), and belongs to Sapouna-Sakellaraki's type IIf (1978, 49–51) and Blinkenberg's type II.7 and II.8 (1926, 65–66). A pair of fibulae of this type was found in Grave 20 (**GR20 M1, GR20 M2**). Such fibulae are generally considered to be of SM date (Catling 1996a, 551), although they persisted into the LG–EO period (Sapouna-Sakellaraki 1978, 51).

Type 2 fibulae are arched, with moldings at either end of an asymmetric swollen bow (**GR9 M1, GR9 M2**; Fig. 171:g). A pair of fibulae of differing sizes from Grave 9 belong to a type that was popular in Crete from the PG to the EG periods, and similar examples come from Vrokastro, Teke Tomb D at Knossos (Coldstream and Catling, eds., 1996, 6, fig. 157:D.f4) and Lefkandi (Catling 1996a, 551, Type 3; Lemos 2002, 111–112). The type may have originated in Athens in the SM period and spread around the Aegean (Sapouna-Sakellaraki 1978, 72–73), but it may also have developed earlier in Cyprus (Lemos 2002, 111). The type continued to be popular from the PG period into the Archaic period.

Type 3 fibulae are similar in shape to Type 2 but with a disk finial on the bow (**GR28 M1** [Fig. 171:h], **GR32 M1**). Two examples of this type, Sapouna-Sakellaraki's type VIIa (1978, 94–97), came from different graves, but they are nearly identical. The type was in use from the mid eighth century down to ca. 600 B.C. (Sapouna-Sakellaraki 1978, 97), although at Knossos it seems to have occurred earlier in the LPG period (Catling 1996a, 551, type 5).

Type 4 is a fibula of the arched-bow type but with a large, central, biconical boss and collars on either side (**GR23 M2** [Fig. 171:i], **GR 23 M3**). A matched set of fibulae of this type was found in and around Grave 23. This type is Sapouna-Sakellaraki's type IIIe (1978, 63–65) and Blinkenberg's type IV.11 (1926, 99–101). Such fibulae are found chiefly in the eastern islands, especially Rhodes, but they also occur on the mainland and in Crete. They belong to the Geometric and Orientalizing periods (Sapouna-Sakellaraki 1978, 65). Two examples from Knossos are probably of EO date (Catling 1996a, 552, type 9).

Type 5 is a fibula with a "navicella" bow, amygdaloid in shape, often referred to as the Attico-Boeotian type (**GR30 M1**; Fig. 171:j). A single example of this type, Sapouna-Sakellaraki's type IXa (1978, 105–106), Blinkenberg's types VIII.3 and VIII.4 (1926, 160–169), and Catling's type 11 (1996a, 552) appeared in Grave 30, one of the latest of the Vronda cremations. Like many such fibulae, this one has incised decoration on the swollen amygdaloid bow. The catch plate is broken off, so it is difficult to reconstruct its size or decoration. This Attico-Boeotian form (Blinkenberg 1926, 169–172) is found primarily in the southern islands, and it seems to date to the LG period (Sapouna-Sakellaraki 1978, 106); at Knossos it comes from graves dated from the PG to the EO periods (Catling 1996a, 552).

As at Knossos (Catling 1996a, 554), the fibulae in the Vronda enclosure graves represent a large number of types, a fact that suggests they were not the products of a local workshop but were imported to the site, probably over a considerable period of time. The fact that one was repaired (**GR9 M2**) suggests that they were kept for a long time, and many of them may have been antiques. The variety of types contrasts with the relative homogeneity of the bronze pins, which are nearly as numerous, but generally conform to a single type, with a few exceptions. All of the fibulae have parallels in other Cretan graves, as well as outside Crete, particularly in Rhodes and Asia Minor. None of the fibulae can be certainly associated with the earliest enclosure burials on Vronda, but a number were found in the graves containing the latest material (Graves 23, 30, 32). Of the eight graves in which fibulae were found, six contained female burials, five of these with infants or fetuses and one with a child. The other two graves (Graves 1 and 26) had at least one body that could not be sexed. It would seem possible, then, that fibulae are associated with female burials, and the pairs of fibulae in Graves 9, 20, and 23 may have fastened some sort of garment. It is likely that these objects were placed in the grave after the cremation was complete rather than fastening the shroud or garment, as they do not show evidence of burning.

Ring

A single bronze ring was found in the cleaning of Tomb IV (**IV M7**; Fig. 15; Pl. 10). It is a simple round wire bent into a circle, with overlapping terminals. Such rings are not common but are found in SM–PG graves at Knossos (Coldstream and Catling, eds., 1996, 218, fig. 167:219.f21; 250, fig. 169:285.f23), Eltyna (Rethemiotakis and Englezou 2010, 171, fig. 59:173–175), and Lefkandi (Popham, Sackett, and Themelis 1979–1980, 248).

Bracelets

A single bracelet was found in Tomb IV (**IV M5**; Pl. 10). While apparently a simple ring of bronze, with some bronze wire spiraling around it toward the ends, it has in fact a complicated arrangement for closure, although its workings are obscured by corrosion and by the inventory number painted on it. The bracelet itself is a loop of thick bronze wire that is round in section. The two ends are apparently looped together, possibly to form eyelets or a clasp of some sort. At each of the ends of the loop two flattened wires, possibly the ends of the original wire, have been wound around the loop in spirals, either to make the joining of the ends more secure or for decoration.

Bracelets of bronze are rare in any period, and few have been found on Crete. Bracelet **IV M5** is unique at Kavousi, but it has a close parallel from Chamber Tomb 17 at Armenoi of LM IIIB date (Effinger 1996, 78, 151–152, pl. 25:b, c), on which the ends are certainly bent to form eyelets that were joined together, and the remaining wire was twisted back around the bracelet (Godart and Tzedakis 1992, pl. 142:1, 2). The wires are thus more decorative than functional. Bracelets of gold and silver are more common than those of bronze (Effinger 1996, 78), but still rare. This type seems to be of Late Minoan date, suggesting that the Vronda bracelet might have been an antique or a family heirloom.

Earring

One earring was found in enclosure Grave 3 (**GR3 M2**; Fig. 46; Pl. 24A). It is made of a single wire of bronze, bent in a hoop, without ornament and with pointed terminals. With a diameter of 3.3 cm, it is too large to have been a ring and too small to have served as a bracelet, although both these types of object are similar. An earring seems to be the most reasonable identification. Catling suggested the same for a hoop from Tomb 219 in the Knossos North Cemetery (Catling 1996a, 557). Grave 12, Burial 4 produced a mastoid process with a glob of bronze still adhering to it (inventoried as V88.219), which may have come from what was once an earring. If so, then some jewelry was apparently left in place and cremated with the individual (in this case, a male).

Sheeting

Of indeterminate function are the small thin plates of bronze with rivets or holes that were found in four of the enclosure graves (**GR9 M5–GR9 M12, GR17 M3, GR20 M3, GR20 M4, GR30 M2**). The variations in the sheets suggest that they did not all serve the same function. Grave 9 produced the largest number of these; eight of them from roughly the same area of the enclosure (the northwest corner) were cataloged (**GR9 M5–GR9 M12**), and other fragments and rivets came from all over the grave. The sheets are all thin, flat, possibly rectangular pieces of bronze of various sizes with rivet holes along the edges and often with the bronze rivets still lodged within (Fig. 171:k). Several of the pieces are from corners, with rivets on two or three sides, suggesting a rectangular shape (**GR9 M6, GR9 M7, GR9 M9**). The rivets are all similar: round in section with slightly flattened tops but no real heads. The rivets range from 0.7–1.3 cm in length, and the fact that they are hollow suggests they were manufactured as rolls of bronze.

Although the pieces of bronze sheeting look as though they might have served as patches for metal vessels, no traces of such bronze objects were found in the grave, and it is hard to imagine the necessity for so many patches. The bronze sheets may have served as reinforcement for an object made of another material, such as a quiver or scabbard, as they have been interpreted at the Knossos North Cemetery (Catling 1996a, 572), but it is unlikely that the Vronda examples were attached to leather or fabric because of the length of the rivets. These sheets are most likely to have been attached to some other perishable material, such as wood, perhaps adornment for a wooden box. Although unlikely, they may alternatively represent the remains of greaves or a shield. Some of the earliest Greek greaves were found in the Skouriasmenos tomb at Kavousi, and another votive pair came from Praisos (Snodgrass 1964, 87), so the presence of this type of armor in the contemporary tombs at Vronda is within the realm of possibility. Similarly, a shield boss came from the Plai tou Kastrou tomb (Boardman 1971, 5–6), a find which raises the possibility that the Vronda fragments were attached to the wooden frame of a shield. The fragments of bronze plate found by Boyd in the Skouriasmenos tomb (1901, 147–148), however, are quite different. Those fragments are decorated and have no trace of holes or rivets.

The large fragment of sheeting from Grave 30 (**GR30 M2**; Fig. 171:l) lacks holes and rivets, and it is not flat, but slightly curving. It may have been placed over some part of the body or some large object in the grave. A second fragment, however, does have rivet holes and a single preserved rivet. The small patch of sheeting from Grave 17 (**GR17 M3**; Fig. 171:m) has holes but no rivets, and it is also curved. It, too, may have been attached to another object in the grave. It could have decorated the socket of one of the spearheads, for example, or have been attached to something rounded, made of wood or leather, that is now lost. One of the two pieces of sheeting in Grave 20 (**GR20 M3**) is flat with holes, like the sheeting from Grave 9, and part of one rivet is preserved; it probably served a function similar to fragments in Grave 9. The second piece of sheeting, however, is unusual (**GR20 M4**; Fig. 171:n). It seems to have a different shape, almost leaf-like, and there are two sheets of bronze held together by a rivet with empty space between the two sheets. This object looks as though it may have been a bronze facing for a small rectangular or leaf-shaped object, such as the handle of a knife (two were found in the grave).

Tools

A single bronze object from Grave 12 (**GR12 M4**; Fig. 89; Pl. 41) has been identified as a tool. It looks very much like a bronze pin, but it is rectangular in section. It may have been an awl or a composite tool with one pointed end. Another pointed bronze object from Grave 1 (**GR1 M19**; Fig. 41) may be an awl; it is round in section instead of square.

Iron

Iron is much more plentiful than bronze in the graves, but it is not as well preserved. Nevertheless, it was often possible to clean iron objects of their corrosion enough to recover their shapes and even some of their original surfaces. Whenever possible, the drawings of these objects attempt to portray their original appearance, while the photos show their actual state.

The objects have been divided into three general categories: jewelry, weapons, and tools. Jewelry includes objects of personal adornment. Iron was not used much for jewelry, which was more often made out of bronze. Nevertheless, iron pins are common, and there is at least one iron fibula in the enclosure graves. Weapons include those objects that were used primarily for offensive or defensive purposes (Macdonald 1992, 43), such as arrowheads, short swords, daggers, and spearheads. These were not necessarily always used in battle, as they are also appropriate for hunting. Other objects could have been used as weapons, such as axes and knives, and they are so categorized by some scholars. Colin Macdonald (1992, 43, 52) and Anthony Snodgrass (1964, 66–67) include axes in the category of weapons, with some reservations. Snodgrass, however, does not consider knives as weapons, although Macdonald does (Macdonald 1992, 48–50). As both axes and knives, although useful as weapons, probably had a primary use as tools, they are categorized here as tools. Tools include objects with an agricultural, industrial, or domestic function, such as knives, chisels, awls, scrapers, tweezers, tongs, hammers or punches, spatulas, and fleshhooks.

Bimetallic objects are rare in the Vronda assemblages. Iron dirks and daggers from the enclosures most regularly have bronze rivets that attached bone, ivory, or wood to the hilts, but a few have iron (**GR16 M6**) or mixed iron and bronze (**GR9 M33**) rivets. Occasionally, a bronze band was used on spearheads, once at the end of the socket (**GR12 M26**), once at the beginning of the blade (**GR12 M24**). Knives, too, occasionally have bronze rivets (**GR5 M7, GR5 M9, GR20 M9**), although they can also have iron rivets (**GR5 M8, GR9 M37, GR28 M4**). Knives with bronze rivets appear in the same graves as knives with iron ones. While bimetallic objects are generally thought to be earlier than those made entirely of iron (Macdonald 1992, 52–53), objects of both types occur in the same graves at Vronda. The use of bronze details may have been primarily decorative.

Appendix B, by Photos-Jones, delves into the iron objects from the enclosure graves at Vronda and the bloom/billet/smithing hearth bottom(?) fragments from Kastro. Examined together, they give rare insight into the entire iron-making process, from raw material (iron bloom at Kastro) to final object (axes/arrowheads/daggers) at Vronda. Based on present evidence, she suggests that the Cretan smith may have been intentionally adapting the level of carburization to suit the intended function of the artifact to be manufactured.

Pins

No iron pins were reported from the tholos tombs, but 16 iron pins were inventoried from the enclosure graves, and other small, pin-like iron objects found in many of the graves may have belonged to additional pins. Because of the corrosion, it is often difficult to recover the original appearance of these pins and to distinguish different types. Few were found intact, but it is clear that they were made in a variety of sizes, from large (**GR3 M3**, preserved length of 12 cm) to small (**GR30 M3**, length 8 cm). Most of the examples seem to fall into one of two types, with a third represented by a single pin.

Type 1 pins have a round or oval boss with moldings or rings on either side (Fig. 171:o). Although the tops are preserved on none of them, they may have had disks with finials. Those with a round boss have three rings on either side of it (**GR30 M6**, **GR36 M3**) or three rings above and two below (**GR30 M7**). The pin with an oval boss has three rings on either side, with a fourth pair of rings separated from the others by a gap (**GR16 M2**).

Type 2 is more common and corresponds to Type 2 bronze pins (Fig. 171:p). This type has a disk head with finial and a biconical boss with rings on either side of it. The number of rings varies; three examples have three rings on either side of the boss (**GR17 M4**, **GR30 M3**, **GR36 M1**), and another two have three below and four (**GR17 M5**) or five (**GR30 M4**) above. The type is equivalent to type 5 at Fortetsa (Brock 1957, 195) and either type B or C at Knossos (Snodgrass 1996, 594–595).

A third type may be represented by **GR3 M3** (Fig. 171:q). It has a central oval boss with single rings on either side and smaller round bosses with another ring above and below it. This pin has no corresponding type at Knossos.

Other pins are too poorly preserved for their types to be determined. Pin **GR36 M2** has a boss of some sort with three rings on each side of it, but it is impossible to tell if the boss is round or biconical. Pin **GR20 M6** also has a swelling with three rings, but the shape of the swelling is indistinguishable. Pin **GR30 M5** seems to have only a series of rings, but the corrosion may make it impossible to distinguish a boss in the center. Finally, there is too little of **GR6 M1**, **GR6 M2**, and **GR20 M5** to determine their types.

Iron pins were found in pairs (**GR6 M1** and **GR6 M2**, **GR17 M4** and **GR17 M5**, **GR20 M5** and **GR20 M6**) or in larger numbers. Five were found in Grave 30 (**GR30 M3–GR30 M7**), with fragments that may have come from a sixth, while there were three in Grave 36 (**GR36 M1–GR36 M3**), with fragments of what may have been a fourth. In the two cases where a single iron pin was found (**GR3 M3**, **GR16 M2**), the burial was also accompanied by a bronze pin; in the case of Grave 16 the iron pin was one of the largest found on the site, while the bronze pin was the smallest. The iron pins, then, generally appear to have been placed with the dead in pairs or paired with a bronze pin. They seem to accompany female burials, as there are identifiable women in all the graves with iron pins except Graves 16 and 36 (both of which have a number of unidentified skeletons that may have been female). There is also a high correlation of the occurrence of pins with infant or child burials, but whether these infants or children usually accompanied women who wore pins or whether pins accompanied the infants is not certain. These pins probably held together some sort of garment, possibly a peplos; an iron pin from Archanes still had the remains of woven wool cloth adhering to it (Sakellarakis 1986, pls. 1–5). They may also have fastened a shroud.

The situation with pins in the Vronda graves, if one considers both bronze and iron examples together, is similar to that observed in the Knossos North Cemetery: there is one dominant type, with a few examples of others (Catling 1996a, 554). This fact would suggest that most of the pins were manufactured locally on Crete, rather than being imported from a variety of centers as the fibulae were.

Fibulae

Only a single iron fibula was found at Vronda, coming from Grave 6 (**GR6 M4**; Fig. 62; Pl. 29). It is a simple arched-bow fibula with flat bow, similar to the bronze fibula found in Grave 1 (**GR1 M1**) but smaller. Iron fibulae are rare in general; some were found at Knossos, but they were few and fragmentary (Snodgrass 1996, 595). One also occurred at Vrokastro (Hall 1914, 140, no. 4, pl. 19:D).

Arrowheads

Arrowheads were found in only two of the graves, and in both contexts they occurred in large groups. There were at least 17 in Grave 1 (**GR1 M2–GR1 18**) and 20 in Grave 12 (**GR12 M5–GR12 M23**). The concentration of arrowheads in such large quantities is exceptional for Crete. The arrowheads are remarkably uniform in shape, with little variation. Three types are distinguishable.

Type 1 has a leaf-shaped blade with a thin tang. Most of the arrows of this type have rounded shoulders (Type 1a; Fig. 172:a), while a few (Type 1b; Fig. 172:b) have more angular shoulders, producing a lozenge-shaped blade. Of these, Type 1a is the most common, with 26 examples (**GR1 M2, GR1 M4, GR1 M5, GR1 M7–GR1 M12, GR1 M16, GR1 M17, GR12 M5, GR12 M7, GR12 M8, GR12 M10, GR12 M12–GR12 M18, GR12 M20–GR12 M23**), while only three examples of Type 1b exist (**GR1 M6, GR12 M6, GR12 M11**).

Type 1a has a long history in bronze on Crete and in the Aegean, but iron examples have been found more rarely in later contexts. The type can be equated with type VIIa of Hans-Günter Buchholz's classification of arrowheads (1962, 11, fig. 7; 22, fig. 13), a largely Cretan type that Buchholz identified as initially having had an eastern, non-Aegean origin. It also corresponds to Robert Avila's type 2f (1983, 112–113, fig. 28:766–769). This type is the most common found in LC graves (Catling 1964, 130), and it may have persisted even into the 11th century (e.g., Yon 1971, 17–18, pl. 15:31–34) on Cyprus, where there is evidence for local manufacture (Catling 1996b, 522). On Crete the type continued into the SM period, and several examples of that date, made in bronze, were found in Tomb 201 at the North Cemetery at Knossos (Catling 1996b, 521), although no iron examples of this common type were recognized there (Snodgrass 1996, 584–585). Bronze examples of SM–G date also appear at Kommos (Shaw and Harlan 2000, 364, pl. 5:26, 1, 4). It seems that this iron arrowhead type found at Vronda imitates an earlier Cretan bronze type that itself may have derived from Cyprus, and perhaps it continued in popularity in East Crete long after newer shapes became prevalent elsewhere. Type Ib similarly finds earlier parallels in bronze in Cyprus (Courtois 1984, 13, no. 51, fig. 3:16).

A solitary example of Type 1c, a single fragment of an arrow, probably of the leaf shape and having a pronounced midrib, was found in Grave 12 (**GR12 M19**; Fig. 172:c). Because the lower portion is not preserved, it is not clear whether it was barbed. If it was not barbed, then this is a variation of the leaf-shaped blade (Type 1), but one that has a midrib like Cypriot bronze examples (Gjerstad 1948, 139, fig. 23:5; Courtois 1984, 15, no. 84, fig. 3:51). If barbed, it constitutes a different type and resembles a bronze arrow from SM Tomb 201 at the North Cemetery at Knossos (Coldstream and Catling, eds., 1996, 194, fig. 163:f2; Catling 1996b, 521–522).

Type 2 has a short, triangular blade with a short, thin tang (Fig. 172:d). It is represented by only three examples, all from Grave 1 (**GR1 M13–GR1 M15**). Vronda Type 2 is not similar to any known types in Greece, although close parallels can be found in Bronze Age Cyprus (Courtois 1984, 15, no. 90, fig. 3:56) and Iron Age Lachish (Tufnell 1953, 385, pl. 60:52), where an example was found together with many leaf-shaped types.

Type 3 is a thin blade, barbed, and with a flat tang (Fig. 172:e). Only two examples exist, both from Grave 1 (**GR1 M3, GR1 M18**). Vronda Type 3 resembles Catling's type c bronze arrowhead (1964, 131, fig. 16:9) and perhaps ultimately derives from the common Mycenaean type (Buchholz 1962, 26, fig. 12, type VI; Avila 1983, 108–110, fig. 28:738–750, type 2c). It does occur in later iron examples (Avila 1983, 146–147, fig. 54); one of a group of bronze arrowheads found in Toumba Tomb 79 at Lefkandi provides a close parallel (Popham and Lemos 1996, 152–153, figs. 4, 5).

Type 4 is also barbed and has a pronounced midrib (Fig. 172:f). Its tang is round in section and must have fitted into a circular slot carved in the top of the wooden shaft. Only a single example exists of this round-tanged barbed arrowhead with central midrib (**GR12 M9**), which is very rare in the Aegean. Two almost identical examples in bronze of Orientalizing date came from Tomb L at Arkades

(Levi 1927–1929, pl. 7:TL) and the Skouriasmenos tomb at Kavousi (Snodgrass 1964, 145, fig. 9:a5). Two similar examples with round tang but no barbs may appear at Kommos (Shaw and Harlan 2000, 365, pl. 5.26:10, 11), but they are so corroded that it is difficult to be certain of their form. Otherwise the type is not attested. Joseph Shaw has suggested that this type may have functioned as a small spear or javelin (Shaw and Harlan 2000, 369).

Interestingly, the arrowheads at Vronda differ from iron arrows found in other Geometric Cretan cemeteries. Most of the Vronda examples derive from bronze types prevalent on Cyprus in the Bronze and Early Iron Ages. The three types of iron arrowheads encountered at Knossos (Snodgrass 1996, 584–585) do not seem to be the same as those from the Vronda cremations. At the Knossos North Cemetery, iron arrowheads are rare, and no more than one was found in a single grave, perhaps an indication that their presence had more to do with the value of the metal than with their function. At Vronda, however, it is clear that groups of arrowheads were placed together in the graves, perhaps in a quiver of leather or some other perishable material. Such a group is rare in the Aegean; only Toumba Tomb 79 at Lefkandi produced a similar group of arrowheads, 35 in number (Popham and Lemos 1996, 152–153).

The differing types of arrowheads may represent a difference in function. Although generally discussed as weapons of war (Snodgrass 1964, 141) arrows would also have been useful for hunting. It is possible, as suggested by modern bow hunters, that if you are shooting at an animal, you want to make sure the arrow does not come out, so a barbed arrowhead is preferred. If, however, arrows are being used in war, it may be preferable to retrieve them more easily for reuse, so the leaf-shaped arrowhead, being easier to pull out, would be more appropriate. It may be, however, that both types of arrowheads were used for both hunting and war and that different types were often used together because they were expendable and frequently lost (Fortenberry 1990, 226).

Spears and Javelins

Weapons in general were uncommon in the tholos tombs. The two unplundered tholoi (Tombs IV and IX) produced spearheads. The example from Tomb IV was reported by Boyd (1901, 133), and another was found in Tomb IX (**IX M1**). In addition, blade fragments from Tomb VIII (**VIII M2**) may have come from a spear. Poorly preserved fragments of a thin bronze band found in Tholos VIII may belong to the end of a spear socket like the one from Grave 12 (**GR12 M26**). Only the fragmentary spear from Tomb IX is well enough preserved for determination of its general shape. The two fragments of the socket that are preserved suggest that it was long, and the blade does not seem to have a pronounced midrib.

Spears or javelins represent the most common type of iron weapon found in the Vronda graves (Table 21). These objects have generally been categorized as spearheads because of the difficulties in distinguishing spears (used for thrusting) from javelins (used for throwing) and their possible overlap in function. Whether spears or javelins, all have a two-sided blade, tapering to a point, often with a strengthening midrib, as well as a cylindrical socket that is folded over and contains a hole for a pin that would have secured the socket to a wooden handle. In form, there are four major types of spearheads represented in the Vronda assemblages, all with long sockets; short and long variants exist within each type.

Type 1 is the most common, with its long narrow blade, and it can be subdivided into two subtypes. Type 1a has a very narrow blade that rises in a curve from the socket without any shoulders (Fig. 172:g, h). It has no pronounced midrib, and it occurs in a variety of lengths, from 16.1 to 32.5 cm, but most frequently in the range of 23.0–26.0 cm (**GR5 M5, GR6 M5, GR6 M6, GR9 M21, GR9 M27, GR12 M25, GR12 M26, GR16 M4, GR16 M5, GR17 M6, GR20 M7, GR20 M8, GR28 M3, GR30 M8**). This type, designated type P by Snodgrass (1964, 129–130), seems to derive from Bronze Age examples, particularly on Crete (e.g., Höckmann 1980, 58, fig. 12:H10, type H). One specimen of this type (**GR9 M21**) is made in a different way. The lower part of the flat blade was beaten around the shaft to form a rough socket, and the two sides overlap, making the object somewhat similar to Snodgrass's type K (1964, 126, fig. 7j), although not as small as that type. Another example (**GR12 M26**) has a band of bronze around the bottom of the socket held in place by two bronze pins. Perhaps the bronze served as a decorative feature or enabled the tightening of the socket onto the wooden shaft. Such collars have also been noted at Athens and Lefkandi (Lemos

2002, 121–122). Type 1b has a similar narrow blade, but the socket is nipped in at the top and the blade rises with shoulders (**GR9 M23, GR12 M27, GR26 M2, GR26 M3** [Fig. 172:i]). The few preserved examples range from 28.0 to 34.0 cm in length.

Type 2 has wider, sloping shoulders and a more tapering blade, and it occurs in a variety of lengths, from 15.4 to 25.2 cm (**GR5 M2–GR5 M4** [Fig. 172:j], **GR6 M7, GR9 M16, GR28 M2**). This type also has Bronze Age prototypes (Höckmann 1980, 45, fig. 8, type F), and similar examples appear in the EIA (Snodgrass 1964, 127–128, fig. 8:b, type M). A particularly close parallel can be found at Vrokastro (Hall 1914, pl. 21:H).

Type 3 has rectangular shoulders and a pronounced midrib that runs nearly to the tip (**GR9 M14** [Fig. 172:k], **GR9 M15, GR9 M17, GR9 M19, GR9 M20, GR9 M22, GR9 M25, GR12 M24**). This type, too, varies in length from 21.0 to 41.2 cm, but it is generally longer than Types 1 and 2. This is Snodgrass's type V, for which he suggests a Cypriot origin, possibly a development of the "sigynna" type (1964, 131–132, fig. 8:k). Some close parallels also exist in Stratum VI at Megiddo (Harrison 2004, pl. 35:3, 4). With one exception in Grave 12, this type is confined to Grave 9.

Type 4 is characterized by square shoulders, like Type 3, but the socket continues up into the blade, tapering sharply away and leaving a blade that is of elliptical section (Fig. 172:l). It is rare in the Vronda enclosures, with only two certain examples (**GR9 M18, GR9 M24**). This form is Snodgrass's type L (1964, 126–127, fig. 8:a), and it is the dominant type in the North Cemetery at Knossos (type A). Snodgrass (1996, 581) suggests that it is peculiarly Cretan. One example of this type (**GR12 M24**) has a bronze band at the bottom of the head, just above the socket, that is held in place by four bronze pins. It is unclear what function this band might have served; it may have been purely decorative.

The other examples of spearheads are too fragmentary to classify. Spearheads **GR12 M28** and **GR12 M29** both have flattened midribs that do not extend to the tip of the blade. The iron object **GR9 M29** is highly unusual. It is socketed like a spearhead, but instead of a blade it has a rounded head with a depression in the center. It is unclear if this object was a spear whose blade had been damaged and melted, or if it was some sort of weapon attached like a spearhead to a wooden shaft, perhaps a spear butt. It may also have served as a tool of some sort, although its precise function is unknown.

The function of these spearheads is much debated. There is no consensus on how to distinguish whether an individual object was meant to be used as a spear (for thrusting) or as a javelin (for throwing) as differentiated by Snodgrass (1964, 136–139). In studies of Bronze Age spears and javelins by Olaf Höckmann (1980) and Robert Avila (1983), numerous types have been recognized, but the authors disagree on which of the types were used for throwing and which for thrusting. Cheryl Fortenberry (1990, 197), in discussing the differing ideas about determining the functions of Mycenaean spearheads, has suggested that the length of spearheads is 20 cm and above, while javelins measure 8–20 cm. In the material from the North Cemetery at Knossos, Snodgrass makes the distinction between the types on the basis of width, length, and shape. He identifies the longer objects (37.80–49.50 cm) with wider blades (ca. 3.40 cm), squared shoulders, and pronounced midribs as spears, while javelins are shorter, with lengths of 25.40–39.80 cm and an average width of 2.75 cm (Snodgrass 1996, 580–581).

These distinctions do not match the weapons at Vronda, however. Few of the spearheads are long enough to meet his criteria for spears, and there is very little differentiation among them in width; the longer weapons are not substantially wider than the shorter examples. Many weapons that are of the correct shape for what Snodgrass identifies as spears are short and should fall into the category of javelin. Of the 23 examples of weapons of this class that are well enough preserved to estimate length, only two are less than 20 cm long (**GR28 M2, GR28 M3**), and they could be javelins, if they are not spear butts. The fragmentary object **GR17 M6** may also belong in the javelin category. Five examples measure 30–39 cm in length (**GR6 M5, GR9 M15, GR9 M17, GR9 M20, GR26 M3**), and **GR9 M19** is over 40 cm; these objects are surely to be classed as spears, especially as many of them have rather short sockets in proportion to their total length. The length of the socket is a feature that Snodgrass has suggested may determine whether a weapon was intended for throwing or for thrusting, as a socket that is longer in proportion to the entire head is more efficient for throwing (1964, 137). The remaining 15 heads fall between 20 and

29 cm (**GR5 M2, GR5 M3, GR6 M6, GR9 M18, GR9 M21, GR9 M22, GR9 M24, GR9 M25, GR12 M24–GR12 M26, GR16 M4, GR16 M5, GR20 M8, GR26 M2**), and these could have functioned either as spears or javelins. The presence of proportionally long sockets on **GR5 M3, GR12 M24, GR12 M26** suggests they may have been javelins. The form, length, and size of the blade suggest that **GR9 M14** was a spear. The function of all of the others is unclear. In the catalog, these weapons are called spears or javelins if the identification seems likely, and otherwise they are simply referred to as spearheads. It may be that most of the weapons were meant to be multipurpose, for thrusting or throwing, depending on circumstances.

Spearheads seem to have accompanied male burials. In all graves containing spearheads where some of the human remains could be sexed, there is at least one male burial. Usually the spearheads occurred in multiples in the graves. It is generally believed that ancient Greek warriors carried two spears or a spear and a javelin (Snodgrass 1964, 115), but these weapons are not always found in pairs in graves. Snodgrass (1964, 137) suggests that a large and small spearhead occurring together in a grave suggests that the individual carried both a spear and a javelin; however, if the spearheads are of the same size, they may simply have indicated the wealth and status of the buried individual. At Vronda spears occurred in pairs in Graves 16, 20, 26, 28, and 30. When in pairs, the spearheads seem to be similar in shape and size, although often one of them is slightly larger. Nevertheless, there are no clear examples of a javelin and a spear being placed together in the same grave. Spearheads also occur in uneven numbers in many of the graves. Single spearheads were found in two graves (17 and 21). Grave 6 contained three spears, one larger than another and a third that was fragmentary. Graves 5 and 12 produced five spearheads each, in both cases with the majority of the well-preserved examples being of average length. Finally, Grave 9 produced an extraordinary total of 15 spearheads. Of these, eight are of Type 3, including six long spears and two shorter examples that are possibly javelins. There are also three spears of Type 1, one of Type 2, and one of Type 4 in this enclosure, and two more are of uncertain type because of their fragmentary shape.

Short Swords and Daggers

A few swords came from the tholos tombs. Boyd reported a sword handle and point from Tomb IV, as well as fragments of an iron blade with the ash in the pithos (Boyd 1901, 134). An iron hilt was found in Tomb VIII, and fragments of an iron blade that may have come from a sword or dagger (Boyd 1901, 133). No certain sword or dagger was found in the cleaning of the tombs, although fragments of iron may have come from such a weapon. It is interesting to note that in both Tombs IV and IX metal remains included a spear and a sword or dagger.

Short swords (dirks) and daggers were found in some of the enclosure burials (Table 22). They can be differentiated from spearheads because they lack the cylindrical socket; rather, they have a flanged hilt. The blades, although similar to those on spears, do not generally have the strengthening midrib.

Just as it is difficult to distinguish between spears and javelins, it is also hard to determine if a weapon was a sword, used for cutting and thrusting, or a dagger or short sword (dirk), primarily used for close thrusting. While it is clear that swords are the longest of the three and daggers the shortest, it is not so easy to determine the difference between a dagger and a dirk or a dirk and a sword. Most scholars use the length of the blade as an indication of function (D'Onofrio 2011, 650), but they do not agree on the parameters for the categories. Snodgrass (1964, 104) considers a weapon to be a dagger if its length is 35.5 cm or less, a dirk if its length is 35.5 to 45.0 cm, and a sword if it is longer than 45.0 cm. According to Thanasis Papadopoulos (1998, 2–3), who reviews various scholarly opinions on distinguishing the dagger from the sword or dirk, the length for a dagger ranges from 25.0 to 39.0 cm. Fortenberry (1990, 143), however, has suggested that a dagger measures less than 30.0 cm, a dirk is 30.0–45.0 cm in length, and a sword is more than 45.0 cm long.

No matter which measurements are used, nothing that could be categorized as a long sword was found in the Vronda graves, a fact that is in keeping generally with what we know about Crete, where there is a preference for the short sword (Snodgrass 1964, 110; 1996, 577). In all, 11 of these weapons have been found in the Vronda enclosures. Seven of them have an actual or estimated length of 36.5–41.5 cm and are probably short swords or dirks (**GR6 M8**, **GR9 M31**, **GR9 M33**, **GR12 M31**, **GR16 M6**, **GR21 M2**, **GR26 M4**). One example, with a length of 21.8 cm, is certainly a dagger (**GR9 M30**). Two others have estimated lengths of 30.5–31.6+ cm (**GR9 M32**, **GR30 M10**); these may be short swords or daggers, but in view of the size of their upper parts, they are more likely to have been short swords. The weapon **GR9 M34** is only half preserved, but its large size suggests that it also is a short sword.

Whether short swords or daggers, all the weapons were of the cut-and-thrust Naue II type (for a discussion of this type of sword, see Snodgrass 1964, Catling and Catling 1979–1980, and Kilian-Dirlmeier 1993), which was introduced from central Europe in the Bronze Age (Catling and Catling 1979–1980, 253) and became common in iron in the EIA. The typology of bronze swords cannot be applied to their iron counterparts because of corrosion (Lemos 2002, 117–120). The Naue II type has a hilt with flanges to hold in place a handgrip of some other material, whether bone, ivory, or wood. The hilt was secured on the Vronda weapons by three rivets: a single rivet near the center top and a pair of rivets where the base of the hilt meets the blade. Although the placement of the rivets is similar in all of the weapons, **GR26 M4** is unusual in having an additional hole much higher on the hilt, near the pommel attachment. The rivets are sometimes missing, but the holes are clear (**GR9 M31**, **GR30 M10**). The preserved rivets are most commonly made of bronze (**GR6 M8**, **GR9 M30**, **GR9 M34**, **GR12 M31**), but occasionally some (**GR9 M33**, **GR 26 M4**) or all (**GR16 M6**) are made of iron.

A fragment of a bone or ivory hilt inlay found on the Kastro is certainly of the same type used on the Vronda weapons (pers. comm., L.A. Turner). The hilt has two pommel ears projecting out to the sides at the top, and a pommel would have rested on these ears secured by a tab at the top. Sword **GR12 M31** has a pommel attachment that may be bronze; visual examination suggests that it is of iron, but X-ray images show some other material.

All the daggers and short swords belong to Snodgrass's type IA (1964, 98–99) or his type A at Knossos (1996, 578–579) and to Kilian-Dirlmeier's type 3 (1993, 107–109), which is Cretan. They differ from one another only in the length of the blade, amount of tapering, and the number and material of the rivets (Table 22). Most of the short swords (six examples) are rounded in a continuous curve from the hilt to the blade (Fig. 173:a). Four of them, however, have angular shoulders (Fig. 173:b); the one certain dagger also has angular shoulders (Fig. 173:c). Only one weapon, from Grave 30 (**GR30 M10**), has a slightly convex edge to the blade, while the rest of the daggers and dirks are tapered, the daggers more than the dirks.

Except in Grave 9, which has five examples, short swords or daggers are singletons in the graves, and all but two short swords were found in graves that contained definite male burials. The two burials in Grave 16 could not be sexed, but one or both may have been males, and none of the burials in Grave 26 could be sexed but may have included males. One short sword (**GR21 M2**) was broken, possibly deliberately, although it is more likely to have been broken by postdepositional activities. As is the case with spearheads, Grave 9 has an extraordinary number of daggers and short swords. Some of the three probable male burials may have been accompanied by both a dagger and a sword, although the possibility exists that either a dagger or a short sword was placed in the grave with every adult, perhaps the daggers with female burials, the swords with males.

Swords and daggers are often found in the same graves as spearheads (Graves 6, 9, 12, 16, 21, 26, 30), a fact that suggests the presence of "warrior" burials (see below, pp. 369–370). Grave 12 had 17 arrowheads in addition. Except for Graves 6 and 16, all of these graves had identifiable male burials. No additional accoutrements of elite warrior graves (spits, firedogs, shields, armor) accompanied these burials.

One-Edged Knives

The most common tool type recognized in the grave assemblages is the one-edged knife. Knives are multifunctional tools (Evely 1993, 20) for agricultural or domestic purposes, although certain types of knives may have been used as weapons. Knives at Vronda come in a variety of different shapes, but most have blades that curve so that the cutting edge is concave. The tips regularly curve upward slightly. Some blades are curved almost in a semicircle, resembling sickles used for agriculture, and these are termed sickle-shaped knives. They are small and were not necessarily used only for agricultural field work. Most of the Vronda knives would not have been suitable for chopping because of the curve of the blade. Handles of different materials (wood or bone/ivory) were attached opposite the point, and one or two rivets or rivet holes are preserved. One example (**GR28 M4**) is flanged for the insertion of another material at the end. One type of knife (Type 4, see description of types below) actually has a thin handle that may have been inserted into a wooden shaft.

Iron knives seem to be common in the tholos tombs. Fragments of knives were found in Tombs IV and IX. Little can be said about the shapes of those from Tomb IV (**IV M8**, **IV M9**), except that **IV M9** seems to have been a sickle-shaped knife, with the cutting edge on the interior concave edge. The knives from Tomb IX, however, are better preserved, and at least four distinct types are represented, all of which can be found in the later cremation burials. One type has an almost straight blade (**IX M2**) like Type 3 in the enclosures. Another has a small handle with rectangular section (**IX M6**), similar to Type 4 in the enclosure graves. A knife of Type 5 may be represented by **IX M5** and possibly **IX M3**; this type is characterized by a blade with the cutting edge on the lower, convex side of the knife, with its end pointing upward. Finally, **IX M4**, **IX M7**, and **IX M8** seem to be fragments of sickle-shaped knives, or Type 2 in the later cremations.

The knives from the enclosure graves come in five major types, many of them paralleled by knives from Knossos (Brock 1957, 202; Snodgrass 1996, 585–587). Type 1 has a concave cutting edge (Fig. 173:d); it is characterized by a blade that moves directly from the handle and makes a marked bend somewhere along its length (**GR5 M7**, **GR17 M7**, **GR28 M4**). This is similar to Snodgrass's type D (1996, 587). Knife **GR5 M7** may be an iron version of a Cypriot bronze type (Karageorghis 1974, pl. 168:T.9.49). Two examples may be flanged (**GR5 M7**, **GR28 M4**), like earlier bronze types (Sandars 1955, 177–179, class 1b), but they are too corroded to be certain of their form. Attachment to a wooden or bone handle is made with one or two rivets; where preserved, the rivets are either of bronze (**GR5 M7**) or iron (**GR28 M4**).

Type 2 is the sickle-shaped knife, and it is the most popular. It is distinguished from Type 1 by the continuous curve of the blade and by the absence of a tip that curves upward at the end. It comes in two subcategories based on the depth of the curve of the blade. Type 2a has a deep curve (**GR5 M10**, **GR9 M39**, **GR12 M36**, **GR30 M12** [Fig. 173:e]), while the less common Type 2b has a more shallow curve (**GR9 M38** [Fig. 173:f], **GR20 M10**). Those with preserved ends have at least one rivet hole for attachment of a handle (**GR9 M38**, **GR30 M12**). There seem to be no similar types in the Knossos cemeteries, but the shape is popular elsewhere, particularly in EIA tombs at Palaepaphos-Skales on Cyprus (Karageorghis 1983, figs. 142.T.76:26, 156.80:44). Jean Deshayes (1960, 335) categorizes this type of blade as a sickle, but suggests that the difference between a sickle and a knife is arbitrary and based on whether the blade has a concave cutting edge.

Type 3 exists in only three examples (**GR5 M8**, **GR12 M33**, **GR20 M9** [Fig. 173:g]). This type has an almost straight blade with only a slight concavity to the cutting edge. The hilt extends the line of the blade and has one or two rivets, which are either bronze (**GR20 M9**) or iron (**GR5 M8**). These knives do not correspond to any of Snodgrass's types but are similar to one of the examples from Fortetsa (Brock 1957, pl. 172:1594).

Type 4 is a knife with a handle or tang that is narrower than the blade and rectangular or square in section (Fig. 173:h). This type is represented by only three examples (**GR6 M9**, **GR9 M35**, **GR12 M32**). Similar knives were also found in tombs at Knossos (Brock 1957, pl. 172:1611; Snodgrass 1996, 587, type E). One of the Vronda examples (**GR12 M32**) is slightly different from the other two; although it has a similar handle, the upper curve of the knife is convex, rather than concave, like a LPG example from Lefkandi (Popham and Lemos 1996, pl. 127).

Type 5 is another knife with a thin handle or tang, similar to Snodgrass's type B (1996, 586), which is rare at Knossos, as at Vronda, where only one exists (**GR5 M9**) in the cremation burials (Fig. 173:i). The blade curves upward at the end, and the cutting edge is convex, rather than concave, while the back is concave. A similar blade comes from Tholos IX at Vronda (**IX M5**). In addition to the blades mentioned by Snodgrass, a knife from Kommos probably also belongs to this type (Shaw and Harlan 2000, 364, pl. 5.24:3). The type is also known in Athens (Papadopoulos and Smithson 2017, 115–117, T13–11) and Cyprus (Macdonald 1992, 50).

A surprising number of knives in the Vronda assemblages have concave cutting edges, a fact that suggests their function. They would not have been useful as weapons but probably were employed in activities that involved cutting, especially gathering grains and pruning trees and bushes. Except for Type 4, most would not have been good for chopping, but it is possible that they were used for other activities such as paring, whittling, sawing, scraping, carving, and piercing.

Saw

Only a single example of a saw, recovered from Grave 12, was found among the Vronda burials (**GR12 M37**; Fig. 91; Pl. 43). It is a small and simple type, similar to earlier Cypriot examples in bronze (Catling 1964, 94, type b). It has a straight, toothed cutting edge and a wide, rounded tip. The handle end is short and narrows slightly. X-rays clearly show the teeth on the cutting edge (Pl. 74D) and reveal possible carburization of the edge. Small saws such as this one would have been used for precision tasks in the working of wood, metals, stone, and bone or ivory (Evely 1993, 34).

Axes

Only a single type of axe-head is represented in the enclosure graves at Vronda, the so-called trunnion axe (Catling 1964, 87–88; Evely 1993, 58–60). This type of axe is a rectangle with a slightly smaller butt, which may be separated from the blade by horned or knobbed projections. Only six examples have been found (**GR6 M10** [Fig. 173:j], **GR9 M40**–**GR9 M42** [Fig. 173:k], **GR28 M5**, **GR30 M13**). Two of these have horned projections (**GR6 M10, GR28 M5**), while the others have square shoulders.

Trunnion axes are not common in Late Bronze or Early Iron Age Crete, and Doniert Evely (1993, 58) catalogs only four examples. Several appeared in the Lefkandi tombs, one of LPG date, the other SPG II (Popham and Lemos 1996, pl. 128:T39.33, P13.2). A number were found in the Cape Gelidonya shipwreck, which dates to about 1200 B.C. (Bass 1961, 273, fig. 25, pl. 88; 1967, 97–98, figs. 109, 110). Partly because the known number of these axe-heads is small, their function has become a matter of controversy. Jean Deshayes (1960, 128) thought that they were actually adzes, set at right angles to the wooden haft, not parallel to it, and George Bass has accepted this usage (Bass 1967, 99, fig. 111). Catling (1964, 87), however, identified them as axes, and Evely (1993, 58) seems to lean toward this interpretation, but suggests that whether axes or adzes, they "would be of service to agricultural workers, woodworkers,

or anyone requiring a general purpose chopping or perhaps digging implement" (Evely 1993, 60). These axes could also have been used as weapons.

Chisels

Chisels are common in the enclosure graves and come in two major types. The first type is a broad chisel, a flat slab of iron, rectangular in section, tapering slightly at one end (Evely 1993, 8–10, type 3). This type is the most common found in bronze in Minoan times, where it is found with either one bevel (**GR6 M11**; Fig. 174:a) or two (**GR12 M41** [Fig. 174:b], **GR30 M14**) and either a flat or a rounded cutting edge (Evely 1993, 13). The difference between these chisels and the trunnion axe is not great, and there has been some question about whether they are chisels or axes (Evely 1993, 13; Snodgrass 1996, 588); Deshayes, for instance, illustrates a number of examples of axes that look like the Vronda flat chisels, but these are generally much earlier than the Vronda examples (Deshayes 1960, figs. 3:15, 5:4). The Vronda examples are simple, without definite markings on their butt ends (for the terminology of parts of the chisel, see Evely 1993, 4, fig. 2).

The second type is a narrower rectangle of metal, square in section, that tapers slightly at one or both ends (**GR6 M13, GR6 M18, GR12 M40, GR28 M6** [Fig. 174:c], **GR30 M15**). Although neither end is preserved, **GR6 M18** and **GR9 M51** may also belong to this type, which corresponds to Evely's types 1 and 2 (1993, 12). Evely distinguishes type 2 from type 1 by the evidence for striking on the butt end of the chisel: those with undamaged butts are of type 1, while those with strike marks belong to his type 2. Only one of the Vronda examples, **GR6 M13**, shows signs of a damaged butt. One chisel (**GR9 M45**) is hexagonal in section, perhaps corresponding to Evely's type 5 (1993, 14). Finally, there is a unique chisel that has sharp shoulders and a small tang on the butt end (**GR12 M42**); there are only two parallels for this type of chisel, one from Anatolia dated to the end of the third millennium (Deshayes 1960, 95, fig. 11:22), the other from Gaza dated to the Hyksos period (Deshayes 1960, 90, fig. 9:22).

Some smaller tools that have one flat or beveled end and a sharp point at the other are similar to some of the Bronze Age chisels, but they have been discussed below with awls (**GR6 M12, GR20 M11**). Chisels were doubtless used for a variety of tasks.

The larger flat chisels could be used in the shaping of wood and stone. The smaller thin chisels could also be used in fine work on wood, stone, metal, or bone.

Scrapers

Examples of a tool that resembles a flat chisel, but which has a bent-up end, were found in Graves 5, 9, and possibly 16 (**GR5 M11, GR9 M43** [Fig. 174:d], **GR9 M44, GR16 M7**). These objects have been labeled scrapers. The best preserved (**GR9 M43**) is a relatively flat slab of iron, wider at one end than the other. The wide end, which seems to have been the primary use end of the implement, has been bent up slightly. The narrow end of this scraper is also bent, but in the opposite direction to the use end. The other scraper from Grave 9 (**GR9 M44**) is shorter and smaller, but its use end is also bent up; the narrower end is not bent at all. The third scraper (**GR5 M11**) is similar to **GR9 M43**, but the narrow end has been broken, making it impossible to tell if it also was bent under. Finally, **GR16 M7** can be recognized as a possible scraper. This tool, which is broken at the wide end, was originally thought to be a flat chisel, but a slight curve can be seen just where it is broken off.

The function of these tools is uncertain, and they have not been reported elsewhere. As the curvature of the sharpened edge resembles that of chipped stone scrapers, they may have been used for working wood or leather. They would also have been appropriate as surgical instruments, perhaps for scraped trepanation of the sort found on one of the skeletons in Grave 5 (Liston and Day 2009, 68).

Files

Three files were found in the enclosure graves (**GR6 M15** [Fig. 174:e], **GR6 M16, GR12 M38**). These resemble some of the chisels, but remains of the serrations on the sides show that they functioned as files or rasps. Two of the examples are square in section (**GR6 M15, GR12 M38**), while the third is larger and more round in section (**GR6 M16**). No other files are known on Crete in the Bronze or Early Iron Ages. Files may have been used in working metals, wood, or even leather.

Spatulate Tools

Several tools from the enclosure graves look like awls, with one pointed end, but the other end has been flattened to form a small spatula (**GR12 M43** [Fig. 174:f], possibly **GR9 M51**). These objects may have had a variety of uses. They may have been tools for personal adornment, including the preparation of cosmetics on the spatulate end. Medical uses are also a possibility; the pointed end could have served as a probe for wounds, while the spatulate end may have held a dose of medicine or herbs. No similar tools are known; one spatulate tool from Lapithos (Catling 1964, 75, pl. 2:f) has a suspension ring on one end instead of a point, but its function is uncertain.

Awls and Punches

A number of small tools from the enclosure graves can be identified as awls (pointed and meant for piercing) or punches (blunted and used for percussion). Evely (1993, 86) points to the difficulty in distinguishing the two different types because of their great variety of shapes and sizes. Such tools are common in the Vronda graves. Those that have been identified as awls (**GR6 M12, GR9 M46–GR9 M50** [Fig. 174:g], **GR12 M39, GR20 M11**) are pointed, often at both ends, and they are generally very short (less than 10 cm). Only one example (**GR9 M47**), at 13 cm, is of medium length (10–20 cm). Some of the objects identified as possible iron or bronze pins may also have been awls (iron: **GR6 M2, GR6 M3**; bronze: **GR9 M4, GR12 M4**). Awls were probably used in a variety of ways, including working in leather, metals, or wood. They could be used in leatherworking to punch holes in the material to allow the needle to pass through (Evely 1993, 86). In dealing with wood, bone, ivory, metals, and some softer stones, the point of an awl could be used to scratch on guidelines (Evely 1993, 86). Along with scrapers, some of these pointed tools may also have served as surgical probes (Liston and Day 2009, 69).

Small tools that are square in section and not pointed on the end are identified here as punches, although this identification is not certain (**GR6 M19** [Fig. 174:h], **GR6 M20, GR12 M44, GR27 M1**). The object **GR6 M14** may also have been a punch, if it had no means of attachment to a wooden handle. Punches can be used with a hammer to drill holes in metal (Evely 1993, 86).

Hammer or Punch

What appears to be a small hammer or a punch was found in Grave 6 (**GR6 M14**; Fig. 63; Pl. 30). It is short (7 cm), with two blunt ends that show signs of having been used for pounding. There is a trace of what may have been a perforated slot passing through the object near one end, although this may also be a crack. If it is a slot, then it might have accommodated a thin handle, although metal hammers were often held in the palm of the hand (Evely 1993, 97). Otherwise, the object may have functioned as a punch that was struck with a stone or a hammer.

Tongs and Tweezers

Tweezers and tongs are considered together here, as their usage is similar. Both were designed to hold other objects by pinching, tweezers for fine work and personal grooming and tongs for larger industrial jobs. Only one set of tweezers (**GR5 M12**; Fig. 56; Pl. 27) and one set of tongs (**GR6 M17**; Fig. 64; Pl. 30) were found in the enclosure graves. The tweezers are of a type that is common in the Bronze Age and even in the Early Iron Age, although they are usually found in bronze (Catling 1964, 227–229; 1996a, 557–558). The Vronda examples are of the open coil type, with a pinched round coil.

The tongs are unusual. They are of a very simple form, consisting of a single iron rod bent over in the middle to form a U shape. The sides are square to rectangular in section, while the loop is round and the ends have been flattened. Several sets of tongs are known from Late Bronze Age Cyprus (Catling 1964, 99), but they have a much more elaborate top, with a collar and shoulders. Tongs would have been used in metalworking.

Needles

Three needles were found in the Vronda enclosure graves (**GR16 M3** [Fig. 174:i], **GR23 M4**, **GR30 M11**). These objects resemble pins, but instead of the elaborately decorated shank and head, they have been flattened toward the top, and a hole was pierced through the flattened section. None is entirely preserved. Only the single type is represented, while the other common type attested in the Bronze Age, the so-called wrap-over type, was not found (Catling 1964, 105). Needles would have been used in textile manufacturing and leatherworking, as well as for making baskets, mats, and nets (Evely 1993, 86).

Fleshhooks

Enclosure Graves 9 and 12 produced several objects of iron that can be identified as fleshhooks. These are small, rectangular in section, and have two pointed ends. They are bent in a variety of ways, the best preserved (**GR9 M55**) in a ⊓ shape (Fig. 174:j). Another (**GR12 M45**) has one end bent at right angles to the pointed end (Fig. 174:k). Bronze objects identified as fleshhooks appear as early as the Early Bronze Age at Poliochni, Troy, Malia, and Levkas, where they are generally round in section (Branigan 1974, 30, pl. 15:1181, 1184). Similar examples appear in Middle Cypriot I tombs at Lapithos, but they are square in section and the points go opposite the loop (Catling 1964, 65–66, fig. 4:8). These objects have been interpreted as hooks for extracting pieces of meat from a cauldron in which the meat was boiled or stewed, and they are seen as personal items that males, possibly warriors, would have taken with them to a feast (Hamilakis and Sherratt 2012, 197). They have also been identified as implements for retrieving sacrificial offerings for the priest from the cooking pot mentioned in Biblical texts (Needham and Bowman 2005, 93). Similar objects of bronze and iron from northern Europe and the British isles have been published as fleshhooks (Bouzek 1994, 227, fig. 8; Needham and Bowman 2005, 96, fig. 1; Bowman and Needham 2007, 56, fig. 3). They are seen as deriving from the southeast, possibly disseminated in the Early Iron Age, perhaps through the Phoenicians (Bouzek 1997, 216). A "meat catcher" was identified in Grave 11 at Eltyna (Rethemiotakis and Englezou 2010, 85, fig. 67:206, pl. 174:242), and it is possible that some of the fragments come from a larger object like this. The graves at Eltyna also produced a number of iron spits. It is interesting that in the Vronda graves no certain spits and no firedogs have been identified, although firedogs and spits are included in the material from tholos tombs around the Kastro (Boardman 1971). The fleshhooks perhaps indicate the validation of a different type of feasting practice on Vronda, removing pieces of meat from a (possibly metal) cauldron with a hook, rather than pulling meat from the spit, as was practiced by the burying population around the Kastro.

Other Tools

Two objects from enclosure Grave 6 look like handles (**GR6 M21, GR6 M22**; Fig. 64; Pl. 31), but no parallels for them have been found. They are similar in size, and both are slightly curving toward the smaller end. In both cases the broader end is finished, while the smaller end at the curve is broken off. These tools are rectangular in section, and both show signs of the same sort of manufacture. The outside is a rectangle, which at the smaller end is hollow, but the larger finished end has a filling of two or four sheets of iron. It is possible that these objects were used as sleeves for another tool, probably an awl, drill, or chisel.

Lead

Only two objects of lead appeared in the enclosure graves. One was a lead button or weight (**GR29 M1**; Fig. 136; Pl. 59B). The other consists of two hollow tubes, probably from the same object (**GR21 M3**; Fig. 114; Pl. 50B). The button or weight finds close parallels in the Northwest Building on the Kastro (Mook 1993, 291–292, fig. 54:79), the tholos tomb at Vasiliki (Tsipopoulou, Vagnetti, and Liston 2003, 104, 108, fig. 11:42), and the Psychro Cave (Boardman 1961, 54, fig. 26:237). Where weights are ascertainable, these lead objects are remarkably similar, weighing from 11 to 15 g, and they have been interpreted as possible evidence for the use of conical beads as dress weights (Tsipopoulou, Vagnetti, and Liston 2003, 108). They could also have functioned in spinning wool, as they are within the parameters for spindle whorls, both in weight and size of the suspension hole. Any weight below 10 g is ineffectual as a spindle whorl (Carington Smith 1975, 80–81; Barber 1991, 52; Evely 2000, 488). Also important for determining function is the size of the suspension hole, which in a spindle whorl should be at least 3–10 mm in diameter and not off center (Barber 1991, 52). This lead bead has a hole that is 5–10 mm wide. The lead tubes are similar to examples from Tombs 285 and 292 in the Knossos North Cemetery, where they are interpreted as lead strip weights or hinges (Coldstream and Catling, eds., 1996, 271, fig. 193:292.f10a, 287.f5).

Ivory or Bone

Two beads of bone or ivory have been recovered from the enclosure graves. One bead (**GR20 B1**; Fig. 112; Pl. 48) is a spherical to biconical shape, with a string hole larger on the top than the bottom and with a concavity on the top. The other (**GR36 B1**; Fig. 150; Pl. 65) is tiny and roughly spherical; it accompanied five terracotta beads, a rock crystal bead, and a glass bead. Whether these beads are made of ivory or bone, they were probably meant to be seen as ivory and thus represent display items.

Several of the graves produced worked bone, particularly the antlers of deer. Several antlers seem to have been modified to serve as handles for metal tools, possibly awls (**GR6 B1**, **GR6 B2**, **GR12 B1**, **GR21 B1**). Others are present in very thin sheets. The object **GR27 B1** has a hole pierced through it, while the fragments of **GR12 B2** are similar, but plain. These flat pieces of antler may have been used for inlay on the handle of a knife or sword/dagger, or they could represent manufacturing debris. The deliberate inclusion of a unique material like this may show that the deceased was recognized as a hunter, warrior, or manufacturer of antler tools.

Glass

Only two objects that can be identified as glass appeared in the enclosure graves. One (**GR36 G1**; Fig. 150; Pl. 65) is a subglobular bead of translucent greenish glass, similar to two of the types found in the North Cemetery at Knossos (Webb 1996, 600–601). One type, which is thought to mimic transparent stones such as rock crystal, begins in the PGB period and continues throughout the Geometric period there; it is often corroded with lamination around the string hole. The other type is found at many sites in the Aegean, Italy, and possibly the Near East (Webb 1996, 602); it has a join line running down one side. Bead **GR36 G1** is corroded and lacks the join line. It probably belongs to the first type. Similar beads came from a cremation burial on Ialysos on Rhodes, where they are assumed to have originated from workshops in north Syria, Phoenicia, western Asia, and north Mesopotamia (Stampolides and Karageorghis, eds., 2003, 522, no. 1019). The other glass object (**GR32 G1**) is of uncertain shape and material. It obviously was present in the heat of the cremation pyre, as it has melted and burned. Its original shape cannot be recognized. It may have been a bead, as it is roughly spherical, but there is no evidence for a string hole.

Stone

Beads

Stone objects include beads, lids, and tools, and they were found in both the tholos tombs and the enclosure graves. From Tomb IV came a unique rectangular bead with incised decoration (**IV S2**). Although it is broken, it was probably pyramidal in shape, with a flat bottom bearing an X pattern and incised patterns on the sides. No parallels could be found for this bead. Boyd found a bead in Tholos IV, a "soapstone whorl with two holes" in Tholos VIII, and another with a single hole in Tholos VII (Boyd 1901, 133–135).

Stone beads are found in the enclosure graves, but they are rarer than beads in terracotta. There are only six examples (Table 23). Three are disks (**GR20 S1** [Fig. 174:l], **GR23 S1**, **GR23 S2**), of which the example from Grave 20 is a tiny disk that may imitate faience disks, such as those at Knossos North Cemetery (e.g., Coldstream and Catling, eds., 1996, fig. 183). The two from Grave 23 are almost a matched pair. Two beads are roughly spherical (**GR1 S1**, **GR36 S1** [Fig. 174:m]), and there is only a single example of a conical bead or whorl (**GR9 S1**; Fig. 174:n). Three beads (50%) are made out of serpentinite (**GR9 S1**, **GR20 S1**, **GR23 S1**), one is limestone (**GR23 S2**), one is a red and white stone that may be carnelian (**GR1 S1**), and one is rock crystal (**GR36 S1**). The rock crystal bead accompanied the glass, ivory, and terracotta beads in Grave 36 and probably came from a necklace. Rock crystal is a prized material, whether locally available on Crete or imported from the East (Evely 1996, 623), and it must have formed the centerpiece of this elaborate necklace. It is likely that these beads were all used for personal adornment, as with the terracotta beads described below, and while they were often found in burials that contained women or subadults, there is no certain correlation of stone beads with either sex or any age group.

Lid

A single stone lid was found in the area in front of Tholos IV (**IV S1**). It is a small knobbed lid with a diameter of 4.60 cm, probably an antique or heirloom. Similar lids are EM II–MM IB/II in date.

From the enclosure burials, two crude stone lids were found in connection with vessel burials (**GR21 S1**, **GR28 S1**). Both were made of local stone. Lid **GR21 S1** may have been crudely shaped, and it covered and sealed the burial pithos (as seen in Pls. 49E, 49F, 57B). Lid **GR28 S1** was irregular in shape and was set on top of the lid that sealed the amphora of Burial 6.

Tools

Fragments of obsidian blades were found in three of the enclosure graves (**GR5 ST1**, **GR6 ST1**, **GR16 ST10**). It is likely these were simply objects that were in the soil from earlier periods at Vronda, as they are typical of the Minoan parallel-sided blades found on other Bronze Age sites (pers. comm., H. Dierckx). Nevertheless, they could still have been used in the EIA, as may have been the case at the North Cemetery at Knossos (Evely 1996, 626).

A few ground stone tools were uncovered in the graves, including a whetstone (**GR36 ST1**), a millstone (**GR23 ST1**), and a possible tool (**GR3 ST1**). These were probably thrown in with other stones to cover over the pyre, although it is possible that they might have been included as tools belonging to the deceased.

Terracotta

The only terracotta objects found in the graves were beads or spindle whorls. Boyd found two clay whorls, one plain and one with a "walnut" pattern, in Tomb II (Boyd 1901, 132). She also reported one in Tomb VIII (Boyd 1901, 133) and one in Tomb IV (Boyd 1901, 134). The bead or whorl from Tomb VIII was in the shape of a truncated cylinder with incised rings, but the object was missing in 1979 and cannot be described further.

The enclosure graves produced 14 examples of beads or whorls (Table 24). All but two were made in fine wares; **GR12 TC1** and **GR36 TC1** were made in medium-coarse fabrics. The beads or whorls come in a variety of shapes and have different types of decoration. The beads, in the majority (six examples, 43%), are biconical in shape and usually undecorated (**GR4 TC1, GR19 TC1, GR36 TC1**) or monochrome painted (**GR30 TC2**; Fig. 174:o), but two examples have melon-incised decoration (**GR3 TC1** [Fig. 174:p], **GR36 TC5**). Three beads are globular or spherical; of these two are monochrome painted (**GR36 TC2** [Fig. 174:q], **GR36 TC4**) and one has melon-incised decoration (**GR30 TC1**; Fig. 174:r). Three more are depressed globular or subglobular; one is monochrome painted (**GR6 TC1**), and two have incised decoration and stamped small circles (**GR12 TC1, GR36 TC3**). Of these, **GR36 TC3** is irregular in shape and has stamped circles placed randomly on the surface (Fig. 174:s). Object **GR12 TC1** is unusual in decoration (Fig. 174:t); the bead is divided into three zones with rays on top and bottom and a row of small, stamped circles between horizontal bands around the center. Such decoration is found on several of a large group of coarse incised beads from the Hagios Ioannis cemetery dated to the PG period (Boardman 1960, 147), but the type continues into MG–LG times at Knossos (Coldstream and Catling, eds., 1996, 279, fig. 187:294.f 8). One bead (**GR26 TC1**; Fig. 174:u) is unique in shape, surface treatment, and decoration; it is a disk that appears to have been highly burnished. It carries incised decoration on all surfaces: on the top a series of short strokes that surround the central hole like rays, on the bottom three groupings of three rays that run from the central hole to the edge, and on the sides oblique slashes between horizontal lines. No parallels for this bead have been found. Finally, **GR34 TC1** is a LM IIIC kylix stem that was cut down and then served as a whorl. This type is very common in the LM IIIC settlement (see Day et al. 2016, 156–157). The whorl may simply have been lying in the area rather than deliberately placed with the dead, although it may also have been an antique. To summarize, in terms of decoration most beads are plain or monochrome painted (seven), while the rest have incised decoration (three with melon decoration, two with stamped circles, one with a variety of different patterns). The modified kylix stem has the bands that had been painted on when it was part of a vessel.

In general, beads appear singly in the graves. Only in two instances do they occur in multiples, either in pairs (**GR30 TC1, GR30 TC2**) or in a group (**GR36 TC1–GR36 TC5**). The group from Grave 36 was found in association with beads of other materials: one of rock crystal (**GR36 S1**), one of glass (**GR36 G1**), and one of ivory or bone (**GR36 B1**), and together they may well have formed a necklace. At the North Cemetery at Knossos, Tomb J produced a group that may also have been a necklace (Evely 1996, 626–627). Often terracotta beads accompanied beads or pendants of other materials, such as faience, glass, rock crystal, and other forms of stone (Evely 1996, 622). Possibly the rock crystal, ivory, and glass served as a focal point for this necklace.

The function of the other terracotta beads is not so clear. They are generally called beads or whorls, as some of them, at least, might have served a utilitarian purpose in spinning. Those that weigh 10.00 g or more may have been functional for spinning (**GR19 TC1, GR30 TC1, GR34 TC1, GR36 TC1, GR36 TC3**), while those weighing less that 10.00 g (**GR3 TC1, GR4 TC1, GR6 TC1, GR12 TC1, GR26 TC1, GR30 TC2, GR36 TC2, GR36 TC4, GR36 TC5**) are too light to have served as spindle whorls (Barber 1991, 52; Evely 2000, 488). If the recut kylix stem is a LM IIIC survival and the two heavier beads or whorls from Grave 36 were, as their context suggests, part of a necklace, then only two of the beads are heavy enough to have served as spindle whorls (**GR19 TC1, GR30 TC1**). The majority, then, would have been used for personal adornment. Perhaps they were strung around the neck or wrist of the deceased, or they may have been sewn onto a garment in some way. It is tempting to associate the beads with female burials, especially if some of them functioned as spindle whorls, as spinning would have been women's work.

Nevertheless, correlations are not clear. The bead in Grave 3 is associated with the first burial, which has been identified as an older man, although with some skeletal features that suggest he was castrated or had hormonal irregularities. All but three (Graves 6, 26, 36) of the graves with beads or whorls have identifiable female burials, and in at least two cases the fetuses indicate that these women were pregnant (Graves 12, 19). It is likely that some of the unsexed burials in the other three graves were also female. All but two of the graves (3, 26) had neonates, infants, or children. A correlation of beads with subadults or with female burials is possible but not certain.

Beads or whorls appear on nearly all Cretan sites of the EIA, usually singly or in pairs, but occasionally in groups (Evely 1996, 627). They are found in the North Cemetery at Knossos (Evely 1996, 626–628) in all periods and at a variety of other sites, settlements, sanctuaries, and tombs (Evely 1996, 627 n. 1392). Although they occur in all periods, they are most frequent in the PG period. Most types are not closely datable, but the coarse, elaborately incised beads like **GR12 TC1** are certainly PG in date. Scholars have proposed an Attic origin for these beads (Boardman 1960, 147–148; Smithson 1961, 170–173), and some have looked even farther afield to the north (Bouzek 1974, 48). They occur in many areas outside of Crete (e.g., at Lefkandi: Popham, Sackett, and Themelis 1979–1980, 83, pl. 214:a) in the PG period.

Textile Remains

Two textile remains in the corrosion products of iron spearheads from Grave 6 were recognized in the cremation enclosures. These are the positive replacements of cloth, created when the iron oxidized and corrosion products replaced the textile fabrics, leaving a mineral version of the original fabric (Cocking 1996, 613). One spearhead (**GR6 M6**) has extensive textile remains as well as mineralized wood (Pl. 75A); the wood remains go over the textile. The fabric appears to have a tabby weave. The remains on the second spearhead (**GR6 M5**) were probably similar but were removed during cleaning and conservation.

Textile remains oxidized onto metal are not unknown in this period (Cocking 1996). In the case of Vronda, the textile impressions indicate that the spearheads were in contact with cloth, either lying on cloth in the grave, wrapped in cloth, or placed in some sort of woven bag. The absence of other textile impressions suggests that metal objects were not all wrapped. The fact that the impressions exist on these spearheads indicates that the spearheads were placed in the grave after the cremation was complete; otherwise, the cloth would have burned with the body and it could not have oxidized into the iron. It is interesting that some wooden object was placed in the enclosure on top of the iron spearheads. Possibly the shafts of the wooden spears were laid on top of or next to the wrapped spears.

Analysis of Textiles

Julie Unruh

In several locations the textile weave seen on **GR6 M6** (Pl. 75A) appears to be a plain weave, woven at ca. 25 threads/cm in both warp and weft. In one system of the weave, the yarns seem to be two ply, [z?]-S (i.e., spun z, plied S). The yarn diameters average 0.30–0.40 mm; the ply diameters average 0.15–0.20 mm.

The second system also seems to be composed of S-twisted elements but with slightly smaller yarn diameters between about 0.20–0.30 mm. There is inconsistent evidence that yarns in this system are single ply rather than two ply. Tentatively, they are identified as single ply, but this identification is not definite.

A series of closely spaced yarns are incorporated into the textile diagonally to the weave structure, spaced approximately 0.70–1.00 mm apart. The yarns are approximately 0.20–0.30 mm in diameter, and in several locations they appear to be two ply, z-S. They do not appear to be woven into the textile, but they run both over and through the weave; in other words, they appear to be small stitches. An interpretation of them as embroidery stitches seems more consistent with their configuration rather than an interpretation of them as a seam. In the small area in which they were seen, no decorative pattern was discerned other than consistent spacing in parallel. An isolated feature near the edge of the blade also runs over and through the weave structure, but it is not on the same diagonal as the possible embroidery yarns. If it is a yarn, it may be two ply, about 0.35 mm diameter. It may be an embroidery element not aligned with the others, or else it is one stitch of a seam.

11

Burial Customs

Leslie Preston Day

The burials at Vronda included two different types that can be distinguished by date: inhumations in stone-built tholos tombs that took place in the SM and PG periods and cremations (with a few inhumations) in stone-lined enclosures that occurred from the LG to LO periods. While there is some chronological overlap between the latest burials in the tholoi and the earliest use of the enclosure graves, these two mortuary types represent distinctly different sets of burial customs.

We do not know for certain where the communities practicing either type of burial lived. It is likely that the inhabitants of the LM IIIC settlement at Vronda moved to the Kastro in the 11th century, when Vronda was abandoned and the Kastro grew in size (see below, this vol., Ch. 12, p. 359). Thus, the burying population may have come from the Kastro, depositing their dead at Vronda first in the tholos tombs, then in the enclosures.

With both types of burial, bodies had to be brought from a considerable distance (Fig. 2). That means that any traces of activities that took place in homes or within the communities before burial or cremation have not been preserved or recognized at Vronda. We know from later Greek culture that the prothesis or laying out of the body was an important element of funerary ritual (Kurtz and Boardman 1971, 58–61; Garland 1985, 23–31). Even the Gortyn Code presumes a law requiring the laying out of the corpse (Gagarin and Perlman 2016, 286). To bring a body to Vronda for burial thereafter would have entailed a lengthy procession. Such processions are now regarded as an important feature of mortuary activity in the Late Bronze Age, particularly on the Greek mainland (Boyd 2016). They also formed part of the burial process in later Greek times (Kurtz and Boardman 1971, 58–61; Garland 1985, 31–34), although these earlier and later examples generally did not cover so great a distance as would likely have been traversed in the Kavousi area. The Gortyn Code, indeed, seems to specify that a landowner had to allow those bearing a corpse to a rural site to cross his land if there was no road to the site, suggesting that there were burials in rural places and communal cemeteries (Gagarin and Perlman 2016, 317–318) as represented at Vronda. There are no traces of any special mortuary buildings or chapels on Vronda such as those that have been found at nearby Anavlochos, Dreros, and Vrokastro (Gaignerot-Driessen 2016, 133) or farther away at Eleutherna (Eaby 2007, 181). Thus, all activities and rituals must have been centered on the graves themselves, and the goods needed for the ceremonies were brought from the settlement for each burial. It is possible that for the cremations wood was gathered from all over the area and taken to Vronda before the funeral, but those carrying the wood may have formed part of the funeral procession.

Tholos Tombs

Burial customs in the tholos tombs are difficult to reconstruct because nearly all of the tombs had been partially (Tombs II, VII, VIII) or completely looted (I, III, V, VI, X, XI). Neither of the two that had not been robbed (IV and IX) was excavated using modern archaeological methods. Tomb IV was uncovered by Boyd in 1900, and only a brief description of it appeared in her publication, where some of the pottery and metals were pictured. The local landowner removed the whole vessels from Tomb IX in 1951, and the rest of the material that he threw back into it was excavated in 1981 and 1988. The remaining evidence for burial customs comes mainly from the surviving architecture and finds. The tholos tombs were constructed around the periphery of the former settlement and, with one exception, the builders avoided using the space occupied by the former inhabitants (Figs. 3, 4). The walls and even the roofs of the settlement buildings were probably still standing to some height when the tombs were constructed. Tomb VIII is unique in having cut into the earlier Building L; Tombs VII and XI are close to the buildings of the settlement but did not encroach upon them. Some of the tholoi are clustered together: Tombs I and II are close to one another, and Tombs III and VIII may also have been near them, to judge from Boyd's plan; Tomb III, however, could not be located. Tombs IV–VI, XI, and possibly VII form another cluster. Tombs X and IX are singletons and were found at quite a distance from the settlement on the ridge (for location, see Fig. 6; Pl. 2).

The tombs apparently contained only inhumations, although a pithos with ash that might represent the remains of a secondary cremation was found in Tomb IV. As the contents of the pithos were not examined and are no longer preserved, it is impossible to know its use. The tombs were constructed for the first of several burials, then reused.

Tomb IV yielded the largest number of bodies recovered from the tombs, with a total of six. Four were found within the chamber, and two more were recovered in the pseudo-dromos, where they were probably discarded during one of the later uses of the chamber. At least during the first burial(s), the stomion and pseudo-dromos were open and visible, providing a theatrical backdrop for the interment and its accompanying rituals. The bodies may have been introduced into the tomb through the doorways, but because the openings are very narrow (0.42–0.86 m in width, 0.50–0.65 m in height), it would have been difficult to move the deceased through them. The stomion may thus have served a function that was more symbolic than practical, and the dead may have been deposited through the top of the chamber by removing the capstone. Boyd (1901, 134) observed that the pithos found in Tomb IV at Vronda was too large to have been inserted through the doorway and must have been lowered in from above. There is evidence from tholos tombs elsewhere that the capstone was removed and the bodies lowered into the chamber, particularly at nearby Azoria (Liston, cited in Eaby 2010, 172).

After the body was placed in the chamber, grave goods were deposited within, including jewelry, weapons, and vessels for drinking, pouring, and storage. The doorway was then blocked with large, flat stones and soil. The pseudo-dromos was partially filled up to the level of the bottom of the lintel. At this point a few flat paving stones were generally placed in the pseudo-dromos, possibly to serve as a surface for a postfunerary ritual. Fragmentary pieces of drinking and mixing vessels found in the fill above these stones may represent the remains of such rituals. How long the pseudo-dromos remained open is unknown, but it was finally covered with soil, and a mound of stones was placed over it to mark its location. The tombs, then, were visible as a pile of stones or even two piles, one marking the top of the tholos (possibly flat on top, as with Tomb V), the other indicating the entrance to the chamber.

It is probable but not certain that the same sequence of events was followed during later burials. The stones and soil may have been removed from above the pseudo-dromos, allowing the doorway to be opened. The opening of the area in front of the tomb is suggested by the presence of human remains within the area in front of Tomb IV. These bones may have been thrown out of the tomb at the time of subsequent burials, whether they were removed through the open doorway or through the opening in the roof after removal of the capstone. The fact that the pseudo-dromoi were opened again, even if the entrances were left blocked, suggests a ritual enactment of some sort in front of the tomb at the time of each burial, for which the entrances formed a backdrop. The same postfunerary rituals may have occurred after each burial as well.

Skeletal Remains

Because only two tombs were found unlooted, information on the human remains from the Vronda tholoi is limited (Table 11). Tholos IV produced four complete skeletons, but these were not scientifically studied and are now largely lost. Bones from four individuals remained in Boyd's dump, and fragments of two others were collected from the previously unexcavated area in front of the tomb. Tholos IX had at least three bodies, but they had been discarded by the local landowner, and only fragments were found in the cleaning of this and other tombs. In all, there were 20 individuals represented from the tholos tombs, of which two mentioned by Boyd as having come from Tholos II have been lost. Of the 18 individuals for which remains are now preserved, thirteen (72%) were adults and five (28%) were children. Few adults could be sexed, but those that were sexed were predominately male. There were five identifiable males (86%) and only a single possible female (14%). One child was 1–2 years old, one 5–6 years, one 6–12 years, and one 10–16 years; the fifth child could not be aged. It would appear that both sexes and all ages are represented, but the evidence is too scanty to make any further analysis possible.

Grave Goods

It is difficult to identify complete ceramic assemblages in the tholoi because so few tombs have been found with their contents intact, and no detailed account of the disposition of the goods within the tombs is available. Nevertheless, we can get some idea of assemblages from Tombs IV and IX. Overall, the most common types of ceramic vessels deposited in the tombs were those used for drinking (39%) and relatively small vessels with restricted mouths used for pouring (32%). The latter are often described as oil flasks and were probably used for unguents. Storage jars (14%) and large open vessels (10%) were also found (Chart 5).

Tomb IV, with four burials in the chamber (three adults, one of them male, and a child), produced five drinking vessels, 11 vessels for pouring, and four storage containers. The area in front of the tomb, which contained the bones of two more adults, produced two or three kraters, a kalathos, and a jar. Of the 28 extant vessels from the whole tomb (among the 40 mentioned by Boyd), 21% were for drinking, 7% for pouring, 32% for storing and pouring of unguents, and 25% for storage; the other 14% came from large open vessels or from those of uncertain function (Chart 9). Most of the pouring vessels were small, and at least some of them were probably used in libations, perhaps during the burial rituals. The small vessels with restricted mouths probably contained oil, possibly perfumed oil, which may have been used to anoint the body, accompany the dead, or serve as offerings. The presence of kraters in the area in front of the tomb suggests that these vessels were used in the performance of funerary or postfunerary rituals.

Tholos IX, which contained at least three burials (two adult males and a child), contained 22 vessels for drinking, 15 vessels for pouring, eight unguent vessels, and seven storage jars, one provided with a lid. Of the 57 vessels belonging to the burials in Tomb IX (i.e, excluding the three Medieval–Modern jars collected with the material), drinking vessels made up 39%, pouring vessels 26%, unguent vessels 14%, storage vessels 12%, and other types 9% (Chart 9). It is clear that the pottery assemblage from Tomb IX contained a greater number of drinking vessels than Tomb IV and more pouring vessels in general, often much larger ones.

Tomb IX, however, contained fewer oil flasks and storage vessels.

If the drinking vessels were part of the burial rituals used for toasts or libations, then the funeral ceremonies associated with the burials in Tomb IX included more mourners or more drinking than those taking place in the case of Tomb IV, where only a single cup seems to have accompanied each burial. This disparity suggests that the cups in Tomb IV may have been deposited to accompany the dead in the afterlife or the journey to it, or that drinking was not as important a part of the burial ritual for the users of Tomb IV as it was for those of Tomb IX. Alternatively, it is possible that fewer participants in the ceremony took part in drinking for the burials in Tomb IV.

With its drinking ceremonies that included a larger number of participants, Tomb IX displays a similarity in burial rituals with those practiced in the later enclosures. Indeed, the final burial in Tomb IX seems to be closer in date to the enclosures than most of the burials in Tomb IV. We may be witnessing a gradual change in burial customs, one that began while the tholos tombs were still being used, that involved the participation of a greater number of funeral attendees in drinking rituals. It is also possible, however, that the evidence from Tomb IX represents a new type of burial ritual that began when the tholoi were reused in the eighth century, after a possible gap of at least a hundred years, and which was common practice in the cremation burials.

It is also noteworthy that the percentage of storage vessels in the assemblage from Tomb IX shows a decline in comparison to the percentage in Tomb IV. Perhaps new beliefs about what happened to the individual after death came into play. The idea that the dead needed some perishable goods kept in storage vessels may have become less important, as was also the case in the later cremation burials. It might be suggested that the rapid consumption of the flesh of the deceased in a cremation meant that fewer stored goods were required.

The assemblages from both Tombs IV and IX show the importance of small unguent vessels, including lekythoi, juglets, small oinochoai, flasks, stirrup jars, bird askoi, and askoi. In everyday activity, these small vessels may have been used as containers for oil or perfumed oil. In the burial context, however, they may have been utilized for pouring small amounts of liquid, perhaps for a series of libations during the burial ritual or for anointing the dead. It is also possible that they accompanied the dead to sustain the individual in the afterlife. If perfumed, they may have served to counteract the odors of decaying flesh. Whatever their function, there are certainly more of them than were found in most of the later cremation burials. It is unfortunate that more nearly complete assemblages were not recovered from the tholoi. With only two of the eleven tombs represented, it is unclear if the differences in the assemblages are random or if they form a significant pattern.

The tholos tombs produced some metal objects, especially jewelry and weapons (Chart 10). Bronze jewelry predominated, with fibulae being the most common type (six in Tomb IV, one each in Tombs VII, VIII, and X). Bronze rings were found in three tombs (two in Tomb II, one in Tomb IV, and two in Tomb VII), and bronze hairpins or fishhooks appeared in two (three in Tomb VII, one in VIII). Tomb VIII produced a bronze pin, and Tomb IV yielded a bronze bracelet. Fragments of bronze sheeting came from Tombs VII and VIII. Iron weapons were also found, but they were less common. One spear (or possibly two) and a short sword were recovered from Tomb IV, a spear and a sword from Tomb VIII, and a spear from Tomb IX. Knives also accompanied the dead, with two having been found in Tomb IV and nine in Tomb IX. Both Tombs IV and IX had at least one spear, one sword, and a number of knives. Tomb IV seems to have had a good deal of bronze jewelry, as did Tombs VII and VIII. In general, metal objects from the tholoi outnumber the stone and terracotta objects by a ratio of 3:1. Of the metal objects, bronze jewelry (pins, fibulae, bracelets, earrings) accounts for 49% of the total, while iron weapons (14%) and tools (26%) make up most of the other finds.

Aside from the metal jewelry, weapons, and tools, the most common objects recovered from the tholos tombs were beads or whorls of stone or terracotta. Terracotta beads were found in only two tombs, two in Tomb II, another in Tomb IV. Boyd mentions finding "soapstone whorls," probably stone beads, in Tombs IV and VII, and three stone rings that may have been stone beads were reported from Tomb IX. There were over twice as many beads of stone as there were of terracotta. A single stone lid was also found. In terms of the number of objects, the tholos tombs seem to have been poorer than the later enclosure burials.

Although few animal bones and no plant remains were recovered from the excavation of the tholos tombs, some faunal remains were found in the cleaning of the hard soil around the edges of the tombs or in the entrances and pits in front of them. All of the tholoi produced sheep or goat bones, but not in large numbers; an articulated portion of a sheep or goat, however, came from the stomion of Tomb VIII. Other species were rare but included cattle (Tomb XI), dog (Tomb VI), and rabbit or hare (Tomb VI). The many dog and cat bones found in the pit below Tomb X have been analyzed, and they produced radiocarbon dates falling within the 14th century of the present era. Therefore, they belong to the use of the tomb after it was robbed, and the pit was dug to dispose of unwanted animals, especially dogs (see this vol., Ch. 12, p. 356).

Ten marine shells were recovered during the cleaning of the tholos tombs (Table 3). Species represented include dog cockle (*Glycymeris*) in three tombs, limpet (*Patella*), and one each of murex (*Hexaplex*), topshell (*Phorcus*), and trough shell (*Mactra*). One of the dog cockles from Tholos IV had a natural hole and might have been used as a pendant. The other shells are most likely to have been food debris, or they may have carried some symbolic meaning.

There is little evidence, unfortunately, to help us understand the role of animal remains in the burial practices associated with the tholos tombs of EIA Crete. Many of these tombs were excavated early in the last century, when bones and shells were not observed or commented on in excavation reports unless they represented an extraordinary occurrence. In the final report on the excavations at Karphi, for example, mention was made of a conch shell (possibly a triton shell or *Charonia*) in Ta Mnemata Tomb 8 (Pendlebury, Pendlebury, and Money-Coutts 1937–1938, 133). Otherwise, only occasional references were made to animal bones in the tombs there (some animal teeth in Tomb M 11; dog, sheep/goat, and ox in M 16; horse, ox, sheep/goat in M 17). Faunal remains have been noted in a few other EIA tholoi: animal bones were recorded at the Skouriasmenos Tomb at Kavousi (Boyd 1901, 145), sheep/goat and a pig jaw were found in Eltyna Tholos Tomb 10 (Rethemiotakis and Englezou 2010, 56), and pig and cattle were mentioned in association with Tombs A and B at Arkades (Eaby 2007, 242). There are almost no references to shells; in addition to the triton shell in M 8 at Karphi, another is recorded from Praisos, Tomb A, and an oyster shell was noted at Hagios Georgios (Eaby 2007, 252).

Enclosure Burials

The enclosure burials differ from the tholos tombs in date, architecture, arrangement, method of disposal of the dead, and burial customs. The builders of the tholoi respected the area of the former settlement, whereas the people who used the enclosures placed them within the abandoned buildings, often utilizing earlier walls in their construction (Fig. 4). The enclosures do not lie near the tholos tombs, with one exception. Grave 3 is aligned with Tomb IV and is also close to Tombs V and VI and, to a lesser extent, Tombs VII and XI. Even more than the tholoi, the enclosures are clearly arranged in clusters around the summit and slopes of the ridge. The enclosure burials are for the most part later than those within the tholos tombs; the earliest use of Grave 9 may have occurred around the middle of the eighth century, but most of the burials occurred from 750 to 670 B.C., within the Late Geometric and Early Orientalizing periods, with some taking place in the later seventh century.

Twenty-one of the 37 labeled graves held what we have called primary cremations, meaning that the enclosure not only held the pyre but also served as the final resting place for the dead. The bones were not removed for interment elsewhere. In addition to primary cremations, the enclosures included several secondary cremations that were placed in vessels, as well as some inhumations, including the remains of two children interred in pithoi. The enclosures were used on multiple occasions, so earlier burials were usually disturbed by later ones. Sometimes ash, bones, and pottery were thrown out of the enclosures, as attested by the discard deposits identified as Graves 7, 11, 14, 22, 25, 33 and possibly Graves 2, 29, and 35. Grave 10 was an enclosure that was not a pyre site but contained an inhumation of a child in a pithos.

There were also a few graves that were not enclosures. Grave 8 was a pit. Grave 31 and possibly Grave 13 may have been pyre sites from which most of the human remains were removed. Grave 24 was a feature containing the remains of a child who was not cremated but apparently placed in one of the abandoned rooms of the earlier settlement. Finally, Grave 37 was only recognizable from the presence of a single cremated skull fragment and two monochrome drinking vessels; the form of this grave is not certain.

Construction and Form of the Enclosures

The construction and form of the enclosures are quite simple, but they vary in the extent to which remains of the LM IIIC settlement were incorporated into the structure. Many enclosures utilized the visible walls of the LM IIIC buildings for one or more of their boundaries, as with Graves 1, 4, 9, 10, 12, 17, 19, 28, 34, 36, and possibly 15. Others were dug into the debris of the buildings (Graves 5, 16, 20, 21). Sometimes they were constructed near former buildings (Graves 26, 27, and 32 near the shrine), on the slopes of the ridge (Graves 3, 6), or on ancient terraces (Graves 23, 30). These enclosures either followed an orientation similar to the buildings or terraces in which they were set (Graves 5, 16, 20, 30) or they took advantage of topographical contours.

The actual construction of the enclosures required little effort on the part of the builders. Their task involved only the digging of a rectangular trench, measuring roughly 1 x 2 m, either up against a surviving wall (or walls) or in the collapsed debris of the buildings, then lining the remaining edges with large stones, usually limestone. Removing the collapsed debris from the LM IIIC walls and roofs would have involved some heavy digging and lifting, but only for a short time, as the graves were shallow and the stones in the debris were not large enough to cause difficulty in removal. Subsequent burials would have necessitated the removal of the stones placed on top of the enclosure, but as we know from excavation, the ashy soil is very soft and the stones loosely packed. The stones could have been easily removed, and the ashy soil was pushed to the side or thrown over the edges.

The construction of the enclosures, then, did not involve the same effort and expense as the building of the tholos tombs, nor did it result in the same kind of permanent visible monument. The tholos tombs, however, were probably only visible at the time of burial, because the entranceways were sealed and the pseudo-dromoi filled in. At most, there was a flat circle of stones like a pavement (particularly visible in Tomb V) on top of the tomb, on which offerings, remains of rituals, or even markers (the pithos in Tomb V, for example) might have stood, along with a heap of stones marking the location of the tomb entrances. When the burial occurred in one of the tholos tombs, the entrance was opened and provided a theatrical backdrop for the funerary rituals, particularly in the case of Tomb IV, which had an elaborate facade. The body was then interred, and after postfunerary rituals, the tomb was closed up again until the next use.

The enclosure burials represent something entirely different. While the construction of these enclosures was simple, the expense came in procuring sufficient wood for the pyre, and the spectacle, rather than relying on an elaborate architectural setting, came from the burning of the body on the pyre, with flames and smoke rising for some six to eight hours. The sight and sound of the burning pyre and the body being consumed upon it, along with the smell of meat cooking for a funeral banquet, created an experience for those attending the funeral that was totally different from an interment in a tholos tomb. The burials in the enclosures took longer, allowing for more rituals that might have involved feasting, dancing, music, storytelling, and other activities. Furthermore, the smoke and flames could be seen for a great distance, certainly from both the Kastro and Azoria, but also perhaps as far away as Vrokastro. At night the flames would have been dramatic, and during the day the smoke would have been visible for miles, particularly if green wood was added to the pyre, perhaps deliberately for this effect. Thus, the cremation burials offered dramatic, long-lasting, and widely visible rituals, despite the lack of permanent monumental architecture. Afterward, markers such as amphorae or pithoi would have been set up throughout the area, with heaps of stones delineating the actual enclosures.

Scholars have tried to trace the origins of rectangular burial enclosures in Crete since the first examples were brought to light at Vrokastro, and many have suggested that they derive from the house tombs or ossuaries of the Early Minoan and Middle

Minoan periods (Hall 1914, 155; Pendlebury 1939, 308; Stampolides 1990, 395; Eaby 2007, 326). Tsipopoulou (1984, 243–244), however, thinks that there is unlikely to be a direct relationship between them, and she is probably right. It is interesting that all of the enclosures of EIA Crete contain cremations (Gaignerot-Driessen 2016, 131). Liston's experimental cremations show that the enclosure walls were important in keeping the burning material from collapsing and rolling away (this vol., Ch. 4, p. 214). It seems most likely that we should seek the reasons for the form of the rectangular enclosures not in a thousand-year-old past, but in the practical realm: enclosures contained the burning material and allowed for a safer and tidier event. They were rectangular because the pyre itself was usually rectangular in shape (long beams alternating with short beams at right angles), and their size and shape were appropriate to the scale of the human body.

Enclosure cremations are known but not common on Crete and in the ancient Greek world in general. Enclosures are of two types. One type served as a pyre site from which the majority of the bones were removed, and this may be termed a crematorium. The other type was also a pyre site, but the bones were not removed for burial; this type we have called a primary cremation enclosure at Vronda. The latter have also been labeled simple cremations by American excavators in the Agora (Papadopoulos and Smithson 2017, 609). It can be difficult to distinguish between the two types archaeologically, as both produce burned bones and ashy soil, but the crematoria ought to have fewer bones and ash than the primary cremation structures, and the bones in the crematoria would not be in anatomical order as they were when the body was left in the enclosure. The occurrence of later disturbances and the early excavation of most of the enclosures in Greece, however, have made it difficult to distinguish the two types. In general, it would appear that the use of enclosures for crematoria was more common than for primary cremations.

On Crete enclosures seemed to have been used for both practices, but the primary cremations may be particularly typical of East Crete (Eaby 2007, 326). Enclosures similar to those at Vronda have been found at nearby Vrokastro, where they were labeled bone enclosures (Hall 1914, 154–172; Velho 2008). Hall found 12 bone enclosures, seven of which seem to have been used for primary cremations (Bone Enclosures I, III, IV, IX, X, XI, and possibly VIII). These were similar in size and shape to the Vronda graves and contained fragmentary LG–EO pottery, along with bronze jewelry and iron tools and weapons. Like Vronda Graves 26 and 28, Bone Enclosure III also had an amphora with a secondary cremation. Of the other enclosures at Vrokastro, II, V, and VI had burned bone, but little of it, and may have been crematoria; they were notable for having rooms that were not well organized and of irregular shapes. Such crematoria were not found at Vronda. Enclosures VI and VIII at Vrokastro also contained pithos burials, in both cases holding an inhumed child, as observed in the pithos burials found in Vronda Graves 10 and 21.

Elsewhere in East Crete enclosure graves have been found at Anavlochos, Dreros, and Praisos, but the earlier excavated Anavlochos graves had no bones, and the Praisos graves are simply described as like Dreros, so it is difficult to be certain of the category to which they belong (Eaby 2007, 88). Recent excavations at Anavlochos have revealed a large tumulus containing enclosure graves with LG material (Gaignerot-Driessen et al. 2020, 1–13), including one primary cremation like those at Vronda. An unexcavated enclosure was identified at Meseleroi (Hayden 1995, 104–105, 124). Enclosure burials are known at Aphrati farther to the west, but they are probably crematoria (Eaby 2007, 115). At Prinias in Central Crete, rectangular and trapezoidal enclosures containing many pithos and urn burials were added to a large tumulus and may have served as crematoria (Eaby 2007, 107). Finally, the cemetery at Eleutherna contained many enclosures, most of them crematoria (Stampolides 1990, 381–388; 1996, 27–91; 2004, 125–129; Stampolides 2001, 189–195). One enclosure, however, was apparently used for a primary cremation. Tomb ΛΛ, dating to ca. 700 B.C., contained the cremated bodies of man and a woman, with a third, partially cremated man on the edge, and it may be comparable to the Vronda enclosures.

Primary cremations are known to occur outside Crete but generally not in stone-built enclosures. Rectangular pits identified as primary cremations have been recognized in PG–EG Athens (Papadopoulos and Smithson 2017, 609–613), but they do not appear to have surrounding walls. Papadopoulos (Papadopoulos and Smithson 2017, 613–617) discusses LG primary cremation pits in Attica, as well as LPG–SPG II examples at Lefkandi and EIA to Archaic cremations from other areas of the Greek world. As with the Athenian examples, however, these were dug into the ground and not lined with stones. Thus, stone-lined enclosures with primary cremations seem to be Cretan, and predominantly a feature of East Crete.

Enclosure Clusters

The enclosures are arranged in clusters around the Vronda ridge, and these clusters may have had significance for the burying population (Fig. 4). While the presence of the earlier walls may have been a factor in the location of the earliest graves, it would appear that later graves were placed in association with existing enclosures. The largest cluster occupies the area of the LM IIIC building complex J-K and includes Graves 9, 10, 12, 17, 20, 21, and probably 16. Another cluster is in the former building complex C-D (Graves 2, 4, 5, 36), and there is a pyre site associated with this group (Grave 31). To the southwest of the summit lies a cluster in the area of the former shrine (Graves 19, 26, 27, 32). The final cluster lies to the west of the summit in the area of the building complex I-O-N (Graves 8, 15, 23, 28, 30, 34, 35). Other enclosures seem to be singletons, not part of clusters. Grave 1 is alone on the southeast side of the ridge in the area of Building E. Grave 37 lies somewhere on the southeast side of the summit in the area of Building A-B; the metal hoard found by Boyd (Boyd 1901, 132) may have come from a grave in this same area. Grave 6 lies on the southwest slope between the cluster in the building complex C-D and the cluster in the shrine; although its elevation is closer to that of the graves on the summit, it is physically nearer to the shrine cluster, and it may belong with either group. Grave 29 is a dump of material on the northeast slope of the ridge; its original location was elsewhere. Several of the graves that are not in clusters are in the vicinity of the earlier tholos tombs. Grave 13 lies to the north of the summit, not far from Tholos Tomb VIII, and Grave 3 is on a terrace west of the summit by itself, although it is close to other tholos tombs (IV–VII and XI).

Each cluster of graves has one enclosure that seems to have been earlier than the others. The cluster with the earliest material is that in the ruins of building complex J-K on the summit of the ridge, and the earliest enclosure there is Grave 9, which may have been the first of the cremation enclosures built on the Vronda site. It contained not only the earliest but also the richest burials, both in terms of pottery and of objects. Fifty-eight ceramic vessels, 54 metal objects, and a stone bead were found in this grave, in which seven individuals were cremated, including one fetus. The metal finds included an extraordinarily large number of weapons: 15 spearheads and five small swords or daggers. The earliest burial seems to have been that of an adult male, 40–60 years old, certainly an important member of the community; other burials, probably of family members, followed. Graves 10, 17, 20, and 21 were constructed after Grave 9 and in its vicinity. They may perhaps have been used for members of the extended kinship group of those buried in Grave 9, or possibly by families seeking status by burying their dead near such an important grave. A number of the individuals shared genetic traits that indicate common ancestry.

All of the enclosures in this area on the summit are particularly rich, and they are distinguished by the presence of large numbers of amphorae that might have served as grave markers. Grave 12 had 44 vessels, 48 metal objects, and a terracotta bead for eight burials, including a fetus. In addition to bronze sheeting, numerous tools, and some jewelry, the metals included many weapons: 20 arrowheads, seven spearheads, and a short sword. At least two amphorae and three large kraters associated with this grave may have stood as markers over it. Grave 10 is an enclosure containing an inhumation of a child in a pithos without any accompanying goods. Grave 17, which had been disturbed by plowing, had at least three cremations and produced 11 vessels and seven metal objects, including four pins and a single spearhead. It also had the latest material found in the cluster and must have been the last used in its group. Grave 20 held seven burials, including a fetus, and produced 21 vessels, 11 metal objects, and two beads, one each of stone and bone or ivory. The metal objects included two spearheads. A very large amphora may have served as a marker.

The enclosure of Grave 21 had two distinct phases of use, both of them postdating Grave 9. Belonging to the first phase is a pithos burial with an inhumed child and two cremated individuals. In the second phase, four more cremations took place on top of the pithos, including one of a fetus. The pithos burial was accompanied by four pottery vessels, a short sword, and lead tubes. The cremations above it produced nine vessels and an iron spearhead. Grave 16 was probably part of this group, but it lies at a slightly lower elevation from the others and is removed from them. The two burials within it were provided with 22 vessels, seven metal objects, and an obsidian blade. The metal finds include two spearheads and a short sword. A large amphora may have stood as a marker. Most of the graves in this cluster (Graves 9, 12, 16, 20) could be considered "warrior graves" because of the number of iron weapons that accompanied them (see this vol., Ch. 12, pp. 369–370). Two of the graves contained inhumations or a combination of inhumation and cremations in pithoi (Graves 10, 21), the only inhumations in vessels found on the site.

The graves clustered in building complex C-D were smaller in number and not as rich in goods as those associated with building complex J-K, and their use began somewhat later. There is no evidence for amphorae or other large vessels being used as markers in this group. Judging from the style of the pottery, Grave 36 seems to have been the earliest enclosure. Accompanying the seven burials, including three of children, which took place in this grave were 18 vessels, three metal pins, and eight beads (five of terracotta, and one each of stone, bone or ivory, and glass). Grave 5 held six cremations (three of which were children) and an inhumation. Grave 2 may have been an additional dump of material from this enclosure. Grave goods from Grave 5 included 17 vessels, 12 metal objects (including five weapons), and an obsidian blade. Grave 4 was the latest used of these enclosures, and most of the pottery was of EO date. The grave held three individuals, a young woman, a fetus, and an infant. The grave goods included 25 vessels, two bronze pins, and a terracotta bead. No weapons or tools accompanied these burials. A genetic trait—unfused metopic sutures—was found on several individuals in this group.

The shrine (Building G) cluster has no grave that was clearly the first one constructed. The earliest pottery comes from Grave 19, and for that reason it may have been the earliest in use. This enclosure was heavily disturbed by erosion and an olive tree, and it held at least four cremations, including a fetus. The latest burials may have been removed by erosion or human activity before excavation began. The pottery included 18 vessels and a terracotta bead, as well as four more pots found outside the enclosure; there were no metal artifacts. Grave 27 was architecturally the most elaborate enclosure, and if the earliest grave in each cluster belonged to the most important person buried there, then it may have been the first in the area on the basis of its architecture. Unfortunately, it was completely empty, and its contents were found scattered on the surrounding slopes, so the date of the original burial is uncertain. At least one individual was buried there, along with 13 vessels and three metal objects, including a spearhead. The pottery, although fragmentary, was of high quality, with a large quantity of decorated LG vessels, one of which was an elaborate stemmed krater. Grave 26 held three cremations, the last a secondary burial in an amphora. Accompanying goods included 23 vessels, three metal weapons (two spearheads and a short sword), and a terracotta bead. Grave 32 was the last-used enclosure in this group. Two women and an infant were buried there, and the grave goods included 11 vessels of EO–LO date, a bronze fibula, and a possible glass bead.

The final cluster on the west in the area of the building complex I-O-N includes a large number of graves, but because many of them had been seriously disturbed (Graves 8, 15, 23, 34, 35), it is difficult to know which of the graves was the earliest. Grave 28 is the most elaborately constructed grave and contains some of the earliest pottery in this area, so it may have been the first. It also held the largest number of burials on the site: six primary cremations and two secondary cremations in vessels that were sealed with lids. The six primary cremations produced 24 vessels and six metal objects, including two weapons. No grave goods accompanied the secondary cremations except the vessels that held them and the lids that sealed them. Grave 34 produced the remains of an adult and child that seem to belong to a single burial event. Two or three vessels accompanied the burial, but most of the material appears to have come from a domestic deposit of LM IIIC date that was cut into by the grave diggers. Among the finds was a kylix stem cut into a spindle whorl, a type which was common in the LM IIIC period (Day et al. 2016, 156–157). If any other goods accompanied this burial, they had eroded away down the slope before excavation. Grave 8 was a pit grave containing the remains of an adult and a fetus. It produced only three vessels and no objects.

Grave 35 was so close to the modern surface and so badly disturbed that little material remained except the bones of a single individual. Any walls or accompanying objects or pottery were gone. It is possible that the grave was a dump from Grave 15 or Grave 28. Graves 15, 23, and 30 all contained late material, indicating that they continued in use into the second half of the seventh century.

While each of the clusters had at least one grave that shows such late use (Grave 4 in the C–D cluster, Grave 17 in the J–K cluster, Grave 32 in the shrine cluster), the western cluster is unusual in the number of graves (three) that continued into the LO period. Grave 15 was a small, shallow enclosure that contained four burials, including a fetus. Only four vessels survived from this grave, and there were no other objects. Grave 23 was also badly disturbed. It contained three cremations and an inhumation. Eight vessels, three bronze objects (a pin and two fibulae), an iron needle, and two stone beads came from this grave. No weapons accompanied these burials. Finally, Grave 30 is another large enclosure with dumps identified as Graves 7 and 33. Five burials were found associated with this enclosure. There were 33 vessels, many of them of EO–LO date, probably the latest pottery on the Vronda site. The grave was also rich in objects, with 15 metal finds and two terracotta beads. Five of the metal objects were pins, but there were also iron weapons (two spearheads and a short sword) and tools. The fragment of a large relief pithos found nearby may have come from a vessel, which, like the amphorae from the graves on top of the ridge, could have served as a marker for this grave.

Of the single enclosure graves that are not in one of the four clusters, two are in the vicinity of groups of earlier tholos tombs. Grave 3 was positioned in front of Tomb IV and near Tombs V and VI, and Grave 13 lay not far from Tomb VIII and possibly near the missing Tomb III. It is likely that at least some of these tholoi were still visible above the surface, and the cremation enclosures may have been deliberately placed in their vicinity. Perhaps the families who buried in these two graves had kinship ties to the users of the tholoi. Alternatively, they may have wanted to establish themselves with the people buried in the tholos tombs, or perhaps they saw some meaning with which they wished to be connected (see below, pp. 360–362). Grave 3 is in alignment with the front of Tholos IV, and it is close to it. This enclosure contained only two cremations, which were accompanied by 20 vessels, three metal objects (two pins and an earring), and a terracotta bead. Grave 13 was badly disturbed, and it is likely to have been a pyre site rather than an enclosure. Remains of one or two cremation burials and 14 vessels were associated with it.

The remaining graves are singletons, not attached to any cluster or near earlier tholos tombs. In general, they were not as rich as the graves within the clusters. Grave 1 lies below the summit of the ridge to the southeast. It was found close to the surface and was therefore much disturbed, but it yielded the remains of two burials, along with 33 vessels, 17 arrowheads, a bronze fibula, and a stone bead. Grave 37, the precise location of which is not certain, is known from a cremated bone from a single individual and two monochrome cups. The grave may be the same one uncovered by Boyd in 1900, which produced iron weapons (a sword) and tools, or it may be a different grave. Grave 6 lies close to both the C–D cluster and the shrine cluster, but it cannot be demonstrated to belong to either. This enclosure held four cremations and an inhumation, with 30 vessels, 22 metal objects, a terracotta bead, and an obsidian blade accompanying them. The assemblage was noteworthy for the number of iron tools (14 in all, including knives and an axe-head); there were also four weapons (three iron spearheads and a dagger). Finally, Grave 29, on the west slope of the summit, is material from a dump discarded from an unknown cremation. Remains of one person, three vessels, and a lead button were found in this feature.

In summary, it would appear that each enclosure represents a family burial plot, to judge from the presence of all ages, both sexes, and a few nonmetric genetic traits that are evident within the skeletal material (Liston, this vol., Ch. 5, pp. 232–233). The clusters of graves may indicate that members of the same kinship groups buried their dead in proximity to one another. The earlier settlement shows a similar pattern, with the houses of nuclear families set within larger clusters of extended kinship groups (Glowacki 2007; Glowacki and Klein 2011; Day et al. 2016, 220–221; Day 2017), and this arrangement may have continued into the eighth century. As in the earlier settlement, the presence of grave clusters may indicate the importance of both nuclear families and larger kinship groups. After an initial cremation enclosure was constructed, others not in the immediate family, but possibly in the extended family, placed their enclosures nearby. It is also possible that the initial graves represent the burials of particularly prominent individuals or families, and that other members of the community built their enclosures and burned their dead nearby to suggest connections with that person or group.

Grave 9 was probably the first enclosure grave established on Vronda, then other enclosures were built and used nearby. This cluster may have belonged to families of higher status and/or wealth than those who buried elsewhere on the site, as suggested by the numbers of vessels and metal objects, as well as the presence of grave markers. Other families chose to be buried in a cluster slightly to the west but still on the summit, and these graves also showed wealth, although they were not as rich as Grave 9 and others clustered with it. The burials in the cluster on the southwest in the area of the former shrine seem to have been of lesser wealth or status, although it should be noted that the graves were disturbed by habitation in the area in the Venetian period, and much information about them has been lost. Finally, the graves in the area of building complex I-O-N were the poorest of the graves. In only two of them (Graves 28 and 30) were large quantities of goods deposited with the dead. The pottery and other finds, however, were not as plentiful or as varied as what was found in the graves on the summit; in particular, there were fewer weapons.

All of the clusters continued to be used into the later seventh century. Most of the graves in the northeast cluster associated with building complex J-K and Grave 9 went out of use, except for Grave 17. The northwest cluster found with building complex C-D on the summit went out of use except for Grave 4, which was only used in the LO period. Graves in the shrine cluster were used throughout the LG to EO periods, but by LO times only Grave 32 continued in use. The use of graves in the I-O-N cluster began a bit later than on the summit, but at least three of these remained in use into LO times. Thus it would appear that at the end of the cemetery's use more burials were being made on the west than on the summit.

For the most part, primary cremations formed the largest percentage of the burial types in the enclosures: 79% in the I-O-N cluster to 88% in the C-D cluster. This number includes the fetuses. The J-K cluster produced the only examples of child inhumations in pithoi and the largest number of pregnant women with fetuses. The I-O-N cluster had the greatest variety of burials, including a pit burial (Grave 8), two inhumations (Graves 23, 24), and two secondary cremations curated in vessels (Grave 28), and several of these burials seem to be later in date. It is possible that this growing variety of types indicates an increasing complexity in society.

Disposal of the Dead

Primary cremation was the most common method of disposal in the enclosures. This treatment was accorded to 89% of the dead, including fetuses and the remains from two possible pyre sites, Graves 13 and 31, from which some of the bones were removed for burial elsewhere. Nevertheless, the enclosures show some variation in the method of disposal of the dead. Secondary cremation burials occurred, making up 5% of the treatments observed: two in Grave 21, one in Grave 26, and two in Grave 28. In all five cases, the body had been cremated elsewhere, and the bones and ashes were collected, with a preferential selection of head and forearm bones from the right side of the body (Liston 2007, 69). All of these were burials of adults, but not enough of the skeletons was preserved to determine the sex or age of the individuals.

Inhumation burials made up 6% of the mortuary treatments. Grave 10 had a pithos burial of a child of five to six years old. The earlier pithos burial in Grave 21 contained the remains of an inhumed child of three to four years of age, along with the cremated bones of two older adults. It is possible that the pithos originally contained only the child, but at a later date the two secondary cremations were added (the child's remains were at the bottom), although it is equally possible that all three were deposited at the same time. If the cremated adults were added later, they might have been the parents of the child. If they were placed in the pithos at the same time as the child, however, they were too old to be the parents, but they could have been the grandparents. In both examples of the pithos burials, the pithos was placed in an enclosure, with the vessel resting on its side and a stone slab covering the opening. Inhumations that were not contained in pithoi include the last burials in Graves 5, 6, 23, and 35, as well as the remains of a six- to seven-year-old child in

Grave 24, which was not even a proper enclosure. The body of the child was deposited on top of the roofing material in one of the rooms of an abandoned LM IIIC house and covered over with stones. The child had suffered from a disfiguring and fatal disease, which may have prompted his or her treatment as a "deviant" burial (Murphy, ed., 2008), a category that includes both immature individuals and those suffering from disease (e.g., Weiss-Krejci 2008, 178–179, 183–185).

Because the enclosure was both pyre and final resting place, despite later disturbances more of the skeletal remains are present in the primary cremations than is usually the case when the cremated bones are collected, curated in a vessel, and placed in a tomb. Thus, despite the warning made by scholars working with other cremations in the Greek world that it is impossible to determine the sex of cremated remains (e.g., Musgrave 1996, 680; 2005, 250), many of the individuals cremated at Vronda could be aged and/or sexed, allowing us to recognize some social patterns among the burials.

It is unfortunate, nonetheless, that we cannot determine the sex of the children found in the enclosures. Gender may have played a significant role in the decisions made about how children should be treated and what goods were appropriate for deposition with them. It is also difficult to interpret attitudes of the burying population toward the unborn fetuses found in Graves 4, 8, 9, 12, 15, and 19–21. On the one hand, these fetuses may have been recognized as individuals and given the same rites and grave goods as other children. On the other hand, they may not have been seen as people at all, because they had not yet been born. Due to our lack of knowledge about the role of children in society in general, they have been excluded from our analysis of patterns of social treatment in the cremations.

Of the 105 individuals recovered from the cemetery of enclosure burials (including the discard deposits and other types of burials), eight were unborn children or fetuses (Table 11). Eighty-five (81%) came from primary cremations, seven (7%) were inhumations (two in pithoi), five (5%) were secondary cremations in amphorae or jars, and three (3%) were from pyre sites. The treatments of the rest (4%) were uncertain.

All ages and both sexes are represented among the individuals from the enclosures. Seventy-eight individuals could be aged (74% of the total). Of these, adults made up 56%, adolescents 9%, children and infants 25%, and fetuses 10%. Of the 44 adults that could be aged, slightly more died between the ages of 20 and 40 (48%) than between 40 and 60 (36%), and 16% of the adults that could be aged were over the age of 60. Children could be aged, but not sexed. Of the 35 nonadults recovered, eight were fetuses (23%), 11 were infants, that is, less than two years of age (31%), eight were juveniles, 2–14 years old (23%), and eight were adolescents or teenagers (23%). While the majority of the nonadults were cremated (86%), including all of the fetuses, infants, and adolescents, three of the juveniles were inhumed (14%). Two were placed in pithoi, and the third child was not given a formal burial (Grave 24). Of particular interest is the presence of cremated children, as it has often been assumed that children were not cremated (Liston, this vol., Ch. 5, pp. 224–225). Twenty-one children were cremated, accounting for 22% of the primary cremations, in comparison to 65 adults (69%) and 8 fetuses (9%).

No group seems to have been selected for a particular type of burial. It is true that both pithos burials (Graves 10 and 21) contained inhumations of children, but children are also well attested in the cremations, and some adults were also buried rather than cremated. The child in Grave 24 may have been marked for special burial because of a disfiguring disease. Otherwise, there seem to be no exceptional burials for any identifiable group. These facts, together with some nonmetric genetic traits observed within graves or clusters, have led us to the interpretation that the enclosures represent family burials.

The last burials in each enclosure, particularly those used over a long period of time, are often remarkable in some way. In at least three enclosures the final burials were inhumations (Graves 5, 6, 23). The final burial in Grave 26 is a secondary cremation in an amphora. The last burials in Grave 28 are also unusual. The second to last burials, apparently placed there in a single event, comprised two individuals in vessels, while the final burial was made by digging a pit in the enclosure and placing the pyre within it, rather than using the entire enclosure. In Grave 21 the last burials were also made in a single event that included four individuals (three adults and a fetus) who were laid on the pyre together, as indicated by the fact that the remains of all three of the adults were still in anatomical order. If each enclosure was used by a single family over several generations, these final burials may represent the last members of their lineage group. Perhaps the lack of surviving family members meant that the canonical burial rituals could not be undertaken, and some other, perhaps simpler, mode of disposal was employed: a communal cremation pyre, an inurned burial from a secondary cremation, or an inhumation.

Often the latest burials in the cemetery, those of LO date, are also unusual. Grave 4 contained the cremated remains of a pregnant woman and an infant in what might have been a single ceremony or two closely spaced events. Grave 32 was used only for two women and a child. Grave 15 was not a proper rectangular enclosure but was instead of an irregular shape. Only Graves 17 and 30 showed the same mixture of ages and sexes, the same method of disposal of the dead, and the same types of metal and ceramic objects accompanying the dead as were found in the earlier burials. Perhaps these variations reflect larger social changes, changes that led to the abandonment of the Kastro and the re-inhabitation and reorganization of the community at Azoria.

The enclosures were used repeatedly for burials, and the earlier material was either pushed to the sides or discarded nearby. We have designated material found outside the enclosure as discard deposits when it included human bone. If there was no bone, only pottery and other cultural material (often with joins to material from within the enclosure), we have labeled the deposits as dumps. When a new cremation was to be made, the stones that had been piled on top of the extinguished pyre were removed and deposited nearby. It is unclear if pits were dug to hold the debris or if natural pits or depressions were used. The discard deposits called Graves 7 and 11 may have been dug deliberately, while a natural depression seems to have been used for Grave 14.

Discard deposits containing grave material were recognized by the presence of ashy soil mixed with stones that produced human skeletal remains, pottery, and often large quantities of shells from land snails (Graves 11, 14, 22, 25). Apparently, the loose stones that were heaped over the pyres provided a natural habitat for these snails. This discarded material may simply represent what was taken off the top of the enclosure when the grave was opened for a subsequent burial, with some broken bones and pottery having been accidentally included in it. Although the skeleton of the deceased was probably recognizable as such when the cremation ended, the piling of stones over the top would have broken up the body and the pottery, so that the remains of the bodies were no longer easily identifiable. As a result, pieces of human bone were thrown out along with broken bits of pottery. During excavation, when the stones over the graves were removed, bits of bone were often found adhering to their bottoms, suggesting that some of the bones found in the discard deposits may have been tossed out accidentally.

Discard deposits were made very close to the enclosure, usually adjacent to it. In general, there seems to have been a tendency to try to keep material from former cremations within the enclosure, as there was not a great deal of grave material within the discard deposits. There is ample evidence that much earlier material was swept to the sides of the enclosure when the next cremation occurred. Only in three instances were large discard deposits of material encountered in the vicinity of an enclosure. In Grave 5, the discard deposit labeled Grave 11 was adjacent and to the south of the enclosure, but Grave 2 may well have been an earlier discard deposit, and there is much ceramic grave material spread across the area to the south. Grave 30 had discard deposits to the north (Grave 7) and west (Grave 33) that contained both skeletal and ceramic material, but there were also areas of dark soil with grave pottery but no bones for a considerable distance to the northeast. Finally, there were dumps of dark ashy soil to the north and ceramic material to the west, north, and south of Grave 28, the grave with the largest number of burials within (Day and Glowacki 2012, 110). Grave 35 may also represent a discard deposit from this grave, but it could equally well have come from Grave 15 above and to the southeast of Grave 28.

What is unusual about the dumps from Grave 28 is that they contained few human remains, only pottery. This would seem to indicate that while the burying population tried to keep as much of the earlier material in the grave as possible, they did not always recognize that material for what it was and threw it out. Many of the dumps and discard deposits contained stones that were burned on one side, an indication that the stones had been placed on top of the grave at the end of the burial before the fire was completely out, then removed during a later burial. The discard deposits from other graves, particularly those in the I-O-N cluster, seem to have contained more of the contents of the graves, a possible indication of carelessness on the part of that burying population. For the most part, however, the people reusing the enclosure were careful to keep material within it, and they pushed it to the sides. The care with which the grave material was curated within the enclosures suggests some reverence for the dead even after the ceremonies were completed.

Grave Goods

The category of grave goods includes all of the material beyond the human remains found in the enclosures. These goods consist of cultural materials, namely, pottery and objects of metal, ivory or bone, glass, stone, and terracotta, along with nonartifactual materials, such as animal bones, shells, and botanical remains, which accompanied the burials. This material was deposited in the graves for a variety of reasons. Some goods probably represent objects that accompanied the body, personal possessions of the deceased used during life. It seems likely that objects of personal adornment decorated the clothing and/or shrouds of the dead, particularly metal jewelry such as pins and fibulae. Rings, earrings, and bracelets probably were worn by the dead. In the charts, these items are all considered jewelry. Other objects, such as beads of terracotta, stone, bone/ivory, or glass, may have served as jewelry, but also may have had other functions, so they are placed in a separate category of personal adornment. Also included in this category are the fragments of bronze sheeting that may have adorned objects placed with the bodies. Metal tools and weapons may have been both personal items used in life and status markers for the individual (e.g., warrior, hunter, craftsman). Weapons, in particular, may have had symbolic meaning for the burying community or family as well as for the deceased. They may have been placed in the graves as a form of status display, showing that the family had enough wealth to remove valuable items from circulation. Other goods present in the enclosures may have been offerings made to sustain the dead person in the afterlife or on the journey to the underworld, and still others may have been votives for the dead person or offerings to divinities. Finally, some objects, such as pottery, along with foodstuffs, may represent the remains of funerary meals or postfunerary rituals in which members of the living community participated.

Because the enclosures were used repeatedly, they form a palimpsest of objects that can be difficult to read. Rarely can we associate specific objects or vessels with particular burials. Thus, it is difficult to see any patterns in the deposition of specific objects and pottery according to gender, age, or status; it is also difficult to see changes in complements of grave goods through time. Nevertheless, some information can be gained from the existing evidence, as discussed in the following sections.

Deposition of Grave Goods

Grave goods found in the enclosures (Chart 11) are similar to those in the tholos tombs (Chart 10). They seem to differ only in date and in quantity. For the most part the number of grave goods found in the enclosures was larger than in the tholoi.

It is not clear which objects, if any, accompanied the dead on the pyre and which were placed on the grave after the cremation was finished. It is likely that personal items, such as jewelry or beads, adorned the bodies when they were cremated. A few examples of heavily melted bronze, including at least one probable earring still adhering to the petrous portion of the skull, suggest that some bronze jewelry adorned the body during the cremation. The melting point of bronze is generally around 1,000°C or a little less (Papadimitriou 2008, 276). The temperature varies according to the alloy, with arsenical bronze melting at a higher temperature than tin bronze. In turn, bronze that is 10% tin and 90% copper melts six times more efficiently than pure copper (Kaufman and Scott 2015, 1018). Theoretically, while wood pyres like those at Vronda could have reached a high enough temperature to melt bronze pins, they would rarely have become that hot in a situation of open burning. The addition of a body to the fire lowers the temperature somewhat because it absorbs heat, and moving air currents carry the heat away too quickly for the fire to reach temperatures adequate for melting bronze.

One set of experiments in which pig carcasses were burned using 10.00 cm cut beams, evenly spaced, created nearly ideal cremation conditions, but in repeated experiments with different amounts of wood, the temperature only occasionally spiked to near 1,000°C, and only in one trial did the temperature exceed that value (Yermán et al. 2018, 65–70). Another set of experimental pyres produced similar results. These experiments were designed to investigate the conditions needed to cremate animal carcasses and to produce calcined bone. The temperatures on outdoor pyres ranged from 600°C to 900°C (Snoek, Lee-Thorp, and Schulting 2014, 56).

Thus, while it is possible for bronze to have melted occasionally, probably after collapse of the pyre when charcoal from the inner logs was producing more heat, it is likely that jewelry put on the body before burning would have survived unscathed, although very high tin content in the bronze would have increased the chances of melting. In the Vronda graves, the presence of some melted bronze indicates that bronze jewelry accompanied the body, but the other bronze objects may have been placed in the enclosure either before or after the cremation.

The determination of when iron objects were placed with the bodies is even more difficult. The melting point of iron is 1,538°C, and thus it could not have melted in the normal process of cremation. Nevertheless, two spearheads from Grave 26 show nitriding of the surface that may be evidence for their inclusion on the pyre during cremation, although other explanations are possible (Photos-Jones, this vol., App. B, p. 383). One piece of evidence, however, suggests that weapons were at least occasionally placed in the grave after the fire was out and before the enclosure was heaped with stones. Two spearheads from Grave 6 show textile impressions in their surface corrosion, and it is impossible that textiles would have survived the fire to leave impressions on the oxidizing spears. Rather, these two spearheads must have been deposited after the cremation was finished, wrapped in cloth or placed in a cloth bag (possibly one with embroidered patterns) along with other tools and weapons found in the vicinity. Textile impressions found in the North Cemetery at Knossos have been interpreted as an indication that the body was wrapped before burning (Musgrave 1996, 690), but they might also have come from the wrapping of weapons placed on the grave or with the dead. Whether this practice was customary or whether the metal objects were generally placed on the pyre with the deceased at the time of cremation is unknown.

Iron tools and weapons may have been affected by the heat of the pyre but not completely transformed, and there is no evidence from the objects themselves as to whether they went through the cremation process or not. In northern European contexts, weapons always accompanied the corpse on the fire (Gräslund 1994, 16). At Knossos, the presence of small finds and potsherds at the pyre sites shows that some grave goods were burned with the bodies and care was taken to collect the objects and vessels along with the bones (Cavanagh 1996, 667), but it is unclear whether iron weapons and tools were included in this practice. At Vronda the evidence for deposition of metal objects with the deceased on the pyre is ambiguous; some metals may have accompanied the dead, but others clearly were placed in the enclosures afterward.

The enclosure burials produced some examples of beads, not only of terracotta and stone but also of bone or ivory and glass. The terracotta beads nearly all show burning. Ten of the 14 examples (a figure that includes the earlier spindle whorl picked up in Grave 34) are burned either slightly or considerably. Their condition suggests that they accompanied the body during the cremation, although some may have been burned in subsequent cremations (especially **GR19 TC1**, which is only burned on one side). Grave 30 produced two terracotta beads, one of which is burned (**GR30 TC2**) and the other not (**GR30 TC1**). This fact suggests either that one was burned with the body and the other was not, or that neither was on the body and one suffered some burning during one of the later cremations in the grave. At least two terracotta beads show severe burning that cracked and almost melted the objects (**GR3 TC1**, **GR36 TC5**); they may have accompanied the body on the pyre. The two beads made of bone or ivory are severely burned and cracked, suggesting that they were also placed with the bodies on the pyre. Of the two glass beads, the one from Grave 36 (**GR36 G1**) shows no sign of burning, while that from Grave 32 (**GR32 G1**) was heavily damaged by fire. The stone beads do not appear to have been burned, with the exception of **GR23 S1**. They may not generally have accompanied the body on the pyre, or perhaps they were present but impervious to the effects of the fire. In short, the evidence is not entirely clear for the placing of beads with the body on the pyre, but the burning suggests that at least some may have adorned or accompanied the deceased when they were cremated.

For the pottery we have more direct evidence concerning deposition. That not all the pottery was placed on the pyre before or during the cremation can be deduced from the burning patterns on the vessels. Many pots showed no signs of burning, some were slightly gray from proximity to burning or smoke, some were partially burned after breaking (that is, burned fragments joined onto unburned sherds), and others were totally charred. The ceramic vessels that are unburned were certainly placed on the grave after the pyre was extinguished. Some patterns of light burning or smoking may have developed if the vessel was placed in the enclosure after the cremation was complete but before the embers were entirely extinguished. Those vessels with variegated patterns of burning, particularly joining fragments from the same pot, some of which are burned and some not (e.g., Pls. 23:**GR3 P10, GR3 P17**, 39C:**GR12 P5**), suggest that the vessel was broken, and then some fragments were exposed to later fires while others were not. The best explanation for this phenomenon is that the vessels were placed on the pyre after cremation was complete, and then were broken, perhaps deliberately, as at Anavlochos (Gaignerot-Driessen et al. 2020, 6), or possibly when the stones were piled on top of the enclosure (for deliberate breaking of pottery as part of funerary ritual, see Boyd 2015, 156; Driessen 2015). When the enclosure was opened and used for subsequent burials, some pieces of pottery were protected from the effects of the fire, while others in the heart of the pyre were burned. Those vessels that are thoroughly charred, particularly those found toward the bottom of the enclosures, seem to have been exposed to repeated cremation fires.

At least one vessel type, the aryballos, may have accompanied the dead on the pyre. Many of the aryballoi found in the graves had been completely burned: 35% were totally burned, 30% show discoloration, burning on one side or on several fragments, and 35% show no trace of burning. Most of the aryballoi that were unburned were of the decorated variety and of EO date; the three from Grave 4 were deposited after the cremation was over, the one from Grave 32 was also placed in the enclosure after the fire was out, and **GR12 P1**, found on top of one of the enclosure walls in Grave 12, may have been a postfunerary deposition. Such practices have been noted elsewhere on Crete; at Arkades, for example, an unburned EO aryballos was placed within an urn with the secondary cremation remains (Levi 1927–1929, 215, fig. 239, showing the vessel with the bones in the urn). Aryballoi that were discolored or partially burned may also have been deposited after the cremation event but were then exposed to the fire of subsequent pyres; in Grave 4, one of the aryballoi (**GR4 P6**) showed some burning and may have been placed on the pyre when the fire was still hot. The seven aryballoi that were totally burned were generally undecorated and of LG date, and these vessels probably accompanied the dead on the pyre. They almost certainly contained oil, perhaps perfumed oil, which apparently caused the small vessels to burn more completely. The fact that most of the decorated EO aryballoi were not burned, while the earlier and undecorated examples were, may suggest a change in burial customs; aryballoi that once were placed with the dead as personal belongings were later deposited after the cremation was over, perhaps as part of a ritual or as offerings. The perfumed oil may have been used to anoint the dead before the cremation.

At Vronda, then, there is evidence that some objects (pottery and beads, as well as metal jewelry and some tools and weapons) were regularly placed on the pyres with the deceased to be cremated, but the lack of burning on some of the pottery and the textile impressions on some of the iron objects suggest that not all of the objects accompanied the dead on the pyre and that some were placed in the enclosure afterward.

Pottery

The pottery found in the graves may have been placed there for a variety of reasons that are now difficult to reconstruct. Vessels may have been put in the enclosures to be used by the deceased in the afterlife or on the journey to the underworld, they may have held foodstuffs to sustain the deceased, or they may have been remains of rituals, including the funeral banquet or toasting. The pots and/or their contents may have constituted offerings to the dead or to divinities. Occasionally vessels were found that seem to belong to a postfunerary ritual. The larger vessels, such as the amphorae found in Graves 9, 12, 16, and 20, as well as some particularly large kraters or basins (Graves 6, 12, 17, 20, 28) may also have served as markers on top of the graves, perhaps after use during the funerary rituals; they often show little or no sign of burning.

Overall, the proportions of functional types of pottery in the ceramic assemblages from the enclosure graves show a good deal of uniformity. The majority of vessels (55%) were used for drinking; this functional category includes cups, mug-like cups, and skyphoi (Chart 6). Other open shapes, generally larger vessels such as bowls, kalathoi, kraters, basins, and trays, make up another 8% of the overall pottery assemblage. Small oil flasks with restricted necks, including aryballoi, lekythoi, juglets, stirrup jars, and a flask, comprise 12% of the total. Wide-mouthed pouring vessels, among which there are jugs, oinochoai, and hydriai, make up another 6% of the assemblage. Storage vessels of various sizes, including amphorae, pyxides, necked jars, and pithoi, constitute a slightly larger percentage (11%). Lids, probably used on some of the storage vessels, comprise only 3% of the total. Finally, other vases of unknown function, including basket vases, make up the remaining 5%.

None of the vessel types can be definitively associated with a particular age group or gender because of the mixing of burials and later disturbances. There are no vessels that can be clearly associated with male burials. In the three graves that contained only women and children, however, some patterns can be observed that might be applicable to other burials. The three graves contained a larger than normal number of aryballoi and pyxides, and these vessel types may have been deposited specifically either with female or infant burials. Seven aryballoi accompanied the pregnant woman and infant in Grave 4. Two were found with the two women and the infant in Grave 32. An aryballos may have been present in Grave 34, with its remains of a woman and child, although the pottery is too fragmentary to permit a certain identification. Of the 27 aryballoi recovered in the excavations, 10 (37%) were found in these three graves with women and children, and nearly all of these were of the decorated variety. Overall, 22 aryballoi were found in graves with identifiable female burials (82%), and 20 came from graves with children (74%). These figures suggest a correlation between the occurrence of female burials and/or children with the presence of aryballoi. If they accompanied women, the vessels may have been personal possessions of perfumed oil. Their small size may have made them suitable offerings for children, as well. Of the two types of aryballoi, the decorated variety seems to be most common in the later graves of the EO period, including Graves 4 and 32.

Of the 12 pyxides found in the cremation cemetery, 10 came from graves with infants or young children (83%), so there may be a correlation between the occurrence of infant burials and pyxides. Nine of the pyxides, however, belong to the EO period, and their deposition may reflect the date rather than the age or gender of the individuals with whom they were buried. It is possible that pyxides came to be deposited with infant burials toward the end of the cemetery's use.

The very few miniature vessels found in the graves may have accompanied the burials of infants and children. Only eight examples of miniature vessels are known: a cup from Grave 4, a tray from Grave 3, an amphora from Grave 6, wide-mouthed jugs from Graves 9 and 28, a juglet from Grave 36, and two necked jars from Graves 3 and 36. All of these graves, except for Grave 3, contained remains of infants or children. An adolescent female was found in Grave 3, and the miniature tray and jar seem to have been associated with this burial. No other evidence for special vessels for specific groups of people could be identified.

The large number of drinking vessels is remarkable and may have resulted from the deposition at the end of the funeral of vessels used in toasting, libations, or other drinking rituals (Cavanagh 1996, 674). The burning patterns on these vessels indicate that most were not placed on the pyres before or during the cremation. Rather, they were deposited on the grave after the fire was out. This fact suggests that they were part of the funerary ritual, instead of offerings to the dead. Because the cremations took so long to complete, it is possible that the time was used for elaborate drinking rituals, at the end of which the vessels involved (drinking vessels as well as mixing bowls or kraters) were deposited on the grave, and possibly deliberately smashed, before it was covered over. Some fragments may have even been removed by the participants as mementos (Driessen 2015, 16).

Some of the drinking vessels may have been associated with postfunerary rituals. Grave 3 produced a flask and cup in the rubble deposited in the grave after the cremation, and their position in the grave and lack of burning indicate a postfunerary ceremony, although there is no evidence to suggest how long after the covering of the grave such an event occurred. Cups in niches created between the stones covering the grave and the tops of the walls in Graves 4 and 20 may represent similar postfunerary deposits. The aryballos in Grave 12, also set into the top of the rubble, may have been deposited after a postfunerary libation. Such postfunerary deposits may have existed in other enclosures, but because of the later disturbance of the graves for subsequent pyres, the evidence is no longer clear. Thus, many of the cups and even some of the smaller pouring vessels or oil flasks may have been deposited at some time after the cremation, after which they were disturbed when a new cremation was made. The paved areas next to Graves 3, 26, and 27 suggest that the enclosures were provided with areas for rituals after the burial rites, and markers seem to have been set up in these areas, as indicated by the pot stand in the pavement south of Grave 3.

Other types of vessels may also have been used in funerary rituals. Among these are serving vessels such as kraters, bowls, trays, and kalathoi, as well as pouring vessels including aryballoi, jugs, juglets, lekythoi, oinochoai, and hydriai. Some vessels, particularly cups and kraters, may have held water or wine that was poured on the embers of the pyre at times when the fire got out of hand or at the end of the cremation (Cavanagh 1996, 667), as was done for the cremations of both Patroklos (Hom. *Il.* 23.237–238) and Hector (Hom. *Il.* 24. 291–292) in the *Iliad*. The few kraters and large bowls may also have been used for mixing wine with water, but they could perhaps have held water for ritual cleansing or fire control. Bowls, kalathoi, and trays may have held food for a funerary banquet or for offerings. That the pouring vessels were used in conjunction with the drinking vessels is suggested by the combination of the flask and cup set into Grave 3. The occurrence of sets including one or two drinking vessels with each pouring vessel, as seen at Knossos (Cavanagh 1996, 672), was not characteristic, however, of the Vronda cemetery, where the ratio of drinking vessels to pouring vessels was anywhere from 2:1 to 19:1 (average 7:1), and many graves contained no jugs or oinochoai at all. Pouring vessels may also have been used to make libations of oil, wine, or water.

The presence of kraters in some of the enclosures is interesting. The krater was almost certainly used for mixing water in wine at feasts or drinking parties on the mainland at least from the time when the Mycenaean palaces began (Sherratt 2004, 325–326), and the wide use of kraters in LM III Crete attests to the preparation of mixed wine on the island by that period, if not earlier, continuing into the EIA.

Although in general the number of kraters on Crete seems to have declined from a peak in the PG period, they still occurred in small numbers in eighth-century tombs (Cavanagh 1996, 672). Kraters have been seen as indicators of elite self-representation, particularly in conjunction with the weapons that marked masculine identity (Whitley 2009, 285–286; Rabinowitz 2014, 95–114). Only eight (or possibly nine, if the large open vessel in Grave 17 was used as a krater) graves contained kraters. Those burying groups that did not have kraters may have made up for the lack by providing numerous very large cups in which water and wine could have been mixed individually (Kotsonas 2011a, 949; see this vol., Ch. 8, pp. 259–260) and perhaps drunk from communally.

Of the few graves that did have kraters (32% of the 25 graves that contained pottery), most also had weapons and human remains that could be sexed as male. There is a direct correlation between male burials with the occurrence of weapons and kraters. Of the 13 graves that contained identifiable males, eight (62%) have both weapons and at least one vessel that may have served as a krater (Table 25). Even in the two tholos tombs that have the most complete assemblages (IV and IX) there is a correlation between identifiable male burials and the presence of weapons and kraters. Of nine enclosure graves with male burials and both weapons and kraters, five (56%) are in the former Building J, which seems to have housed the richest burials. The two graves in the I-O-N cluster that have kraters, weapons, and male burials (Graves 28, 30) are the only graves in that cluster that could be considered rich. In cases where males were buried with weapons but not kraters (as in Graves 5, 16, and the pithos burial in Grave 21), perhaps the participants provided their own drink and mixed it in their own large cups. In other cases where kraters were not found (Graves 4, 23, 27), it is possible they were absent because there were only female burials with children or infants; the adults in Graves 23 and 27 cannot be sexed, but females may have been present. Grave 26 contained weapons but no identifiable male burials and no kraters; however, one of the unsexed bodies in Grave 26 might have been male. Finally, Grave 36 had at least one male burial, but there are neither weapons nor a krater; three of the burials in this grave were infants or children, and the other three could not be sexed.

Some of the vessels found in the graves may have been left as offerings to the dead, whether or not they also played a role in funerary rituals. At least some of the pottery may have been included for use by the deceased in the afterlife. Storage vessels and other pottery placed on the pyre with the dead may have contained foodstuffs for the journey, perhaps during the period before the flesh was entirely consumed and the person was thought to have completed the transition from living to dead. Grape pips found in several of the graves (Graves 9, 15, 20, 21, 23, 26, 28, 30, 36) indicate that food offerings were placed with the dead, probably during the cremation, as they were preserved by burning. Alternatively, some offerings may have been made to divinities, rather than providing for the dead, or certain vessels may have been used in rituals to deities, then deposited in the enclosures before or after the cremation.

Large vessels that show little or no burning may have stood as markers over or beside the enclosures. These are generally amphorae but they might include kraters, such as the ones associated with Grave 6, 9, 12, and 28. Large, elaborately decorated amphorae are almost entirely restricted to the graves on the northeast side of the summit of the ridge in the area of former Building J-K (Graves 9, 12, 16, 20); the one exception is Grave 1 in the area of Building E southeast of the summit, which contained a large amphora of early date. Smaller amphorae were used to contain secondary cremations (Graves 26, 28) or for storage (Graves 5, 16, 20, 21, 27). Thus, the pottery found in the graves may have been placed there for a variety of reasons.

Objects Other than Pottery

The enclosure graves produced grave goods similar to those found in the tholos tombs but in seemingly greater quantity: metal jewelry, weapons, and tools, along with beads of stone, bone or ivory, glass, and terracotta that may have served as adornment for the dead or their possessions. A large number of tools were found in the enclosures but not in the tholoi, and weapons were also more plentiful in the enclosures. Some of these objects may have been personal belongings. Others may have been placed with the deceased by members of their burying group as remembrances of their identities in life, and/or as symbols of their place in the communities of the living or the dead.

Jewelry was an item of personal possession, and its display may have played an important role in the establishment of the identity and status of the deceased and the family of the dead person. Some pieces may have been placed on the body before the pyre was lit, but others may have been removed during cremation and placed in the grave after the body was consumed. If put on the grave afterward, such jewelry was probably placed approximately where it would have been worn, to judge from the find spots of some of the pins and fibulae in relation to the semiarticulated bones (i.e., near the shoulders, where these objects would originally have pinned a garment). Jewelry was usually of bronze, and altogether 11 fibulae, 18 straight pins, and at least one earring were found.

Fibulae appear in a variety of types, and only in three instances (Graves 9, 20, 23) do they appear to have been deposited in pairs of the same type. Three fibulae were found in Grave 9, an enclosure that held a large number of burials. Otherwise fibulae were singletons. It has been suggested that a single fibula was used to fasten a cloak (Shepherd 2013, 547) and therefore should be associated with male burials, but there is no certain correlation between the gender of the individuals in the graves and the presence of fibulae. The fibulae may have served the function of closing garments, including shrouds, but they could simply have been adornments to the clothing of men and women.

Pins appear in both bronze and iron, and the iron pins are common and similar to the bronze examples, which show little variation in type. The presence of so many pins, whether of bronze or iron, contrasts with their rarity in the earlier tholos tombs. Pins are often found in pairs and were probably attached at the shoulders, where they would have held together pieces of a garment, possibly a peplos (Shepherd, 2013, 547). Indeed, in some of the graves (e.g., Grave 12) the pins lie in the area of the shoulders of the last cremation, perhaps adorning the clothes of the deceased or having been placed in the appropriate area after the cremation was complete. In the burial context, they might also have held together a shroud.

Pins are often associated with female burials. Grave 4, for example, in which a pregnant woman and an infant were cremated, produced two pins. The two pins and earring found in Grave 3 accompanied the female burial. The greatest number of pins (five), however, was found in Grave 30, in which only one woman was identified. Other graves with female burials that produced pins include Graves 5, 12, 20, and 36. Several graves without identifiable female burials, however, also produced a number of pins (Graves 6, 16, 17, 23). Either there is no necessary correlation between the presence of female burials and pins or at least some of the individuals whose sex could not be determined on the basis of the bones in those graves were actually female. As with the fibulae, these pins may have accompanied the body on the pyre, whether as fastenings or for display of family wealth (or both), or they might have been placed on the bones after cremation.

Weapons appear in both the tholos tombs and the enclosure graves (Charts 10–12), but they are more frequent in the enclosures. In the tholoi 10% of the objects were weapons, in comparison to 35% in the enclosures. Iron weapons consist of spearheads, daggers or short swords, and arrowheads. Some objects, such as axes and knives, might have functioned as weapons but are more likely to have been used primarily as tools.

Spearheads are the most common weapons. They were often found in pairs (Graves 16, 20, 26, 28, 30) but could appear singly (Graves 17, 21) or in multiples: three in Grave 6, five in Grave 5, seven in Grave 12, and 15 in Grave 9. In several graves, spears were accompanied by short swords or daggers (Graves 6, 9, 12, 16, 26, 30). Of the total of 42 spearheads, over half (22) came from Graves 9 and 12. Dirks or daggers were less common, with just 10 examples, appearing in only seven enclosures (Graves 6, 9, 12, 16, 21, 26, 30). Only the short sword within the pithos burial in Grave 21 was not accompanied by at least one spearhead. The short swords or daggers in all of the other graves were singletons, but in Grave 9 there were five.

Only Graves 1 and 12 produced arrowheads. In both cases there were large numbers (17–20), suggesting that the arrows were buried as a group of weapons, possibly in a leather quiver accompanied by a wooden bow that has not survived. There are no instances of a single arrowhead in a grave, either deposited as a token weapon or actually lodged in a body.

We deduce that weapons were generally associated with male burials inasmuch as graves with only female burials, often accompanied by infants or children (whose sex is undeterminable), did not contain any weapons (Graves 4, 32, 34). Spearheads, in particular, seem to have accompanied male burials. In all graves containing spearheads where some of the human remains could be sexed, there was at least one male burial. Only Graves 16 and 26 lack an identifiable male body, although one or more of the burials in each grave was undetermined. Grave 5, with five spearheads, has two males, along with a possible female and three children; an inhumation of a male was the last burial. Grave 12, with the remains of a male, two females, a child, a fetus, and four unidentified adults, also contained five spearheads. Grave 9, with its large number of spearheads (15), has only three identifiable males, but two others are only tentatively sexed as female.

We do not know that individuals buried with weapons were truly warriors in life, but the role of warrior may have been a masculine ideal for the burying population (Whitley 2002, 219; see this vol., Ch. 12, pp. 368–370). It is possible that male children were also buried with weapons. The pithos burial in Grave 21, for example, contained the unburned body of a child that could not be sexed and may have been a boy; the dagger or short sword in this grave probably belonged with the child rather than the cremated adult male, as it was found beneath the child's bones. Grave 16 has the unsexed remains of an adult 30 to 40 years of age and of an adolescent aged 13 to 20 years, and the short sword may have belonged with either burial. Similarly, the short sword in Grave 26 may have belonged either to an unsexed adult or an adolescent (16–18 years old), but from its location the sword could not have accompanied the third adult, a secondary cremation in an amphora.

In at least one of the burials with weapons (Grave 9), three of the spearheads were deliberately bent or "killed" (**GR9 M15, GR9 M19, GR9 M20**). Another damaged spearhead came from Grave 26. Killed weapons, usually swords but occasionally spearheads, have been identified in Bronze and Early Iron Age graves (Åström 1987; Blandin 2007; D'Onofrio 2011; Harrell 2015; Lloyd 2015). In Cretan burials one bent spear was found in a cremation burial at Pantanassa (Tegou 2001, 135, fig. 34), another occurred in a PG grave at Eltyna (Rethemiotakis and Englezou 2010, 40, 173, pl. 219), and others are mentioned as having been found in graves at Prinias (Lloyd 2015, 20). The recent excavation of graves at

Anavlochos produced a bent spearhead (Gaignerot-Driessen et al. 2020, fig. 6).

Much attention has been paid to these killed weapons, although they are relatively uncommon anywhere in the Aegean. We do not know why they were destroyed. To bend a spearhead or sword so completely would require great force. It could not be done accidentally, even in the heat of a cremation, but would require premeditation. Many explanations for the deliberate damaging of weapons have been suggested, and they generally fall into three categories. The first is a pragmatic explanation, namely that the weapons were bent to fit into the grave (Smithson 1974, 341; Catling 1996b, 518; Lloyd 2015, 21). This cannot have been the case at Vronda, however, because the size of the enclosures was ample for the length of the weapons. In another interpretation, the damaging of weapons is considered part of a more general pattern of the destruction of grave goods (Grinsell 1961; Åström 1987). This practice is not generally apparent at Vronda. Damage to objects other than the few killed weapons seems to have resulted from the piling of stones on the enclosure at the close of the cremation and may have been accidental rather than deliberate. Finally, some scholars focus on the connection between the weapon and the buried individual. They propose that fear, either of the deceased returning armed to haunt the living or of pollution, repugnance at reusing the weapon of a loved one, or respect for the accomplishments and authority of the deceased played a role in the act of destruction (Grinsell 1961, 476–478; Blandin 2007, 113–114; D'Onofrio 2011, 651).

Weapons, especially swords but also spears, were personal objects, perhaps made to order for the individual. As only a small segment of the population possessed them, it would have made sense to bury them with the dead, although we still have no explanation for why they were destroyed. What is interesting is that most known examples of killed weapons are associated with cremation burials (Lloyd 2015, 17). Perhaps the weapon had to be transformed in the same way that the body of the deceased was transformed—not destroyed entirely, but rendered into something other than it had been (a bent weapon, a few bones and ashes).

Whatever the reasons behind this funerary ritual, the killing of weapons was at all times and in all places restricted and limited (Lloyd 2015, 28). That is particularly so at Vronda, where only four possible examples of killed spearheads have been found. Three of these killed weapons came from Grave 9, which produced the largest number of grave goods and which was probably the earliest of the enclosure burials on the site. The killing of these weapons may be another indication of the social prominence of the family that used Grave 9.

Tools also commonly accompanied the dead, both in the tholos tombs and in the enclosures, although they are not as widely distributed as other types of objects. Only 10 enclosure graves had tools, and the number of tools in a grave ranged from 1–23. The location of the graves with tools is interesting; half were clustered on the summit of the ridge in the ruins of building complex J-K. This group also had the largest number of tools per grave: 23 tools in Grave 9, 16 in Grave 12, three in Grave 20, two in Grave 16, and one in Grave 17. In the ruins of building complex C-D, only Grave 5 produced tools, six in number. Grave 6, which did not lie in any of the buildings but was close to the summit, yielded sixteen tools. The graves in the area of former building complex I-O-N generally produced few tools. One came from Grave 23, three from Grave 28, and five from Grave 30. None of the graves in the area of the former shrine produced tools.

In general, the three graves with the largest number of tools (Graves 6, 9, and 12) averaged between three and four tools per person (assuming that the fetuses were not considered persons in terms of burial goods). Graves 5, 16, and 30 averaged one per person (not counting the inhumation in Grave 5, which seems to have been provided with no objects beyond a single ceramic vessel). For all the other graves there were fewer tools per person: one for every two persons in Graves 20 and 28, one for every three persons in Grave 17, and one for every four persons in Grave 23. Grave 17 is interesting, as it had only one adult burial, along with a child and an infant, and only a single tool. It may be that tools only accompanied adult burials, in which case the statistics change; the average rises to 4.5 tools per adult in Grave 9, four per adult in Grave 6, 3.2 per adult in Grave 12, three per adult in Grave 5, 1.5 per adult in Grave 30, one per adult in Grave 16, and less than one in the other graves. There seems to be no correlation between the occurrence of tools and particular gender or age groups.

Tools are most likely to have been personal possessions of the deceased, although it is possible that some may have served a symbolic function, idealizing the deceased as a craftsman or farmer. The group of tools in Grave 6, for example, may have been a metalworker's toolkit. It included many types of tools not regularly encountered in the graves, such as tongs, rasps or files, a possible hammer or punch, and the two strange, curved iron objects that are here called handles for lack of a secure identification. Slags and blooms from the Kastro attest to ironworking there in the LG period, so we know that metalworkers comprised part of the population in the area (see Photos-Jones, this vol., App. B).

Knives were probably everyday objects carried by most people, and they could have served a variety of purposes. Many of them, including sickles and curved knives, the small hand saw, and axes, were used in agricultural activities. Chisels, awls, scrapers, and needles were likely to have been used in various crafts (stoneworking, woodworking, leatherworking, sewing), and some might even have been used as surgical instruments (Liston and Day 2009, 67–70). The tweezers in Grave 5 may have been used for personal grooming. No tool seems to have been associated with a specific gender; needles may have been buried with women, but this association is not certain, as only one grave with a needle had an identifiable female burial.

The fleshhooks were dining implements, designed to remove meat or other large solids from a vessel containing food. Fleshhooks appear in only two of the graves (9 and 12), which were among the richest and which produced large quantities of weapons and other tools. These may have served a function parallel to that of the ship firedogs and spits found in the tholos tombs around the Kastro (Boardman 1971). The spits and firedogs are thought to have been used at the funeral meal, which would have included meat cooked over an open fire. If the fleshhooks were used for the funeral meals at Vronda, then those meals must have included stewed dishes. Such foods would have been suitable for a cremation funeral as they generally take time to cook, and the rituals associated with a cremation would have lasted many hours. An inhumation, however, would have been a much shorter event, for which the grilling of food on spits over spit stands and an open fire would have been more appropriate. This type of cooking may also have carried more status value.

Tools, then, were placed in the graves for a variety of reasons: as personal possessions, social markers, leftovers from funerary ceremonies, and possibly even gifts or offerings.

The enclosure burials produced some examples of beads, not only of terracotta and stone, but also of bone or ivory and glass. These were probably some form of adornment, and they generally appeared as singletons. Occasionally, however, they came in pairs (Grave 30) or even in groups; in Grave 36 they may have formed part of a necklace with rock crystal, glass, and ivory or bone beads. A few of the single terracotta beads could have been used as spindle whorls, in which case they may have been personal possessions placed in the grave with the deceased.

Antiques and Heirlooms

It has been assumed that most of the pottery and objects deposited with the dead in the tombs were contemporary with the burials, but there are instances where earlier vessels and objects accompanied the deceased. The definition of curated objects and their importance have been the subject of several recent studies (Whitley 2002, 2016; Crowe 2019; Dabney 2019; Davis et al. 2019). Such earlier pieces preserved, stimulated, or transmitted memories, whether collective or personal, although their specific meanings varied with the circumstances (Davis et al. 2019, 435). Brent Davis and colleagues have identified different categories of such objects. They could be heirlooms (objects passed down from one generation to another), mementos (reminders of specific events or people), entangled objects (foreign or exotic items that show social status and access to international trade networks), antiquities (objects already ancient when acquired and indicating a connection with the distant past), companion objects (utilitarian objects passed down, perhaps to indicate inherited technical knowledge or skills), or found objects (discovered by chance from earlier occupation when digging for construction or in gardens or fields and repurposed). Found objects may also have derived from tomb looting (Crielaard, 1998, 190).

All these objects were meant to invoke memory, and in one way or another they had a symbolic meaning beyond their status as grave goods. They are often difficult to recognize, but Bronze Age objects are not unknown in EIA burials in Crete (Crowe 2019). The boar's tusk helmet found in SM Tomb 201 in the North Cemetery at Knossos (Catling 1996b, 534; Crowe 2019, 484) is a good example, as are the Minoan larnakes from PGB–O tombs in the same cemetery (Coldstream 1996, 392–393; Crowe 2019, 485).

Jewelry and pottery, which can be rather closely dated, show that heirlooms and antiques were also buried with the dead at Vronda. Among the finds from the tholos tombs, there were several early pieces, including a Bronze Age stone lid (probably of EM II–MM II date) from Tomb IV (**IV S1**), a LM III bronze bracelet (**IV M6**), also from Tomb IV, and a stirrup jar of LM IIIB or LM IIIC date from Tomb VIII (**VIII P1**). A stirrup jar with no good provenience (**Boyd 2**) may also have been an earlier piece. The stone lid may have been an antiquity, an object perhaps kicked up in the soil from an earlier use of the site that was found to be useful or perhaps was seen as an object from an earlier, possibly legendary time. The bracelet, however, may have been a family heirloom, passed down from generation to generation.

The enclosures also contained items that seem to have belonged to earlier periods. With the pottery it is difficult to be certain because during the ninth and early eighth centuries earlier PG styles continued to be manufactured, but some of the jewelry is clearly of earlier date than the burials. The fibulae of the arched-bow type, whether simple or twisted, that appear in several of the cremations (Graves 1, 20, 26) belong to the SM or EPG periods, not the eighth to seventh centuries to which much of the material in the tombs belongs. One fibula from Grave 9 (**GR9 M2**), probably of slightly later date, had apparently been worn through just above the coil and was repaired with a tiny pin. Perhaps the fibula was a personal possession dear to the deceased or a family heirloom so prized that it had been mended, and was later placed in the grave as an expression of sentiment, status, or both. Alternatively, because the fibula was so damaged, it may have been readily discarded with the burial because it had little worth.

Other broken and mended objects from the enclosures at Vronda may represent curated objects. At least two vessels from the graves have drill holes indicating that the pots were broken and mended before deposition, probably using lead clamps that are now lost. The LO date of the mended pyxis from Grave 17 (**GR17 P4**), which was contemporary with the latest material from that enclosure, indicates that it was not an heirloom or an antique, so either it was considered appropriate for discarding in the grave or it had value and was worth mending, whether as a cherished object of the deceased or the family or for symbolic reasons (Dooijes and Nieuwenhuyse 2007, Nadalini 2007). Grave 17 was one of the last enclosures used in its very rich cluster, and the presence of a mended vessel there could perhaps indicate the breakdown of the traditional burial rites. The amphora from Grave 20 (**GR20 P7**) was also mended. Although the grave in which it was found was in the same cluster as Grave 17, the material from it was earlier, and the amphora may have stood over the enclosure as a marker. The tall neck was mended near the rim, but the body of the vessel seems to have been intact, so it could have been repurposed for funerary use. Possibly this vessel was not originally broken but suffered damage and was repaired during the later use of the grave. In either case, it may have been a curated object.

The repair of vessels is rare in EIA Crete. Drilled holes for mending with metal clamps have been found mostly on imported vessels from Kommos (Johnston 2005, 388) and on pottery from graves at Knossos (Coldstream and Catling, eds., 1996, 256, pl. 232:15), Hagios Georgios (Tsipopoulou 2005, 519), and Eleutherna (Kotsonas 2008, 60).

There is no direct evidence for other curated vessels among the pottery found in the enclosures. Because of the continuation of Protogeometric styles well into the eighth century in East Crete and the reuse of the enclosures, it is impossible to say whether any particular vessel represents a curated object. Nevertheless, a good case can be made for the use of an heirloom vessel in Grave 28. There, two pots of greatly different stylistic dates were deposited together, each containing a secondary cremation. The amphora (**GR28 P3**) is clearly LG in date, while the necked jar (**GR28 P22**) finds its best parallels in the EPG period, indicating that it was an heirloom or antique.

The evidence from Vronda seems to indicate that heirlooms or other curated objects were occasionally deposited with the dead, but the practice does not appear to have been widespread. Nevertheless, the use of curated objects may attest to an interest in establishing connections with people of earlier generations, an interest that can also be seen in the decision to locate the cemeteries in the area of the former Vronda settlement.

Flora and Fauna

Many faunal remains were recovered from the enclosures. While a good deal of the faunal material was unburned and much of it seems to have been intrusive or disturbed, there is some evidence that animals or parts of animals were placed deliberately on the pyre to accompany the dead (see this vol., Ch. 6, pp. 238–240). The most common remains belong to sheep or goats, as was also the case at Ortho Petri, Eleutherna (Agelarakis 2005, 38, 65). In most cases, the burned ovicaprid bones come from the lower legs of the animal (as in Graves 9, 20, and 34) and may represent offerings or remains of sacrificial meals. Grave 26, however, produced bones from a complete animal, suggesting that the sheep or goat was placed on the pyre with the deceased, possibly at the edge of the fire, as some of the bones are less burned or show no burning at all. In several cases, individual meat portions of pig were thrown or placed in the graves. Occasionally, as in Graves 1, 12, and 21, calcined lower limbs of deer were also encountered, suggesting that venison was also part of the menu for the funeral banquet, or it may have been left as an offering to the deceased or to deities. It is of great interest that two of the graves with deer metatarsals (Graves 1, 12) also produced large groups of arrowheads. As bow and arrows are often hunting weapons, it is possible that deer remains were placed in the graves as tokens of the hunting prowess of the deceased. Animal remains in burials of the Early Iron Age are well attested throughout the Greek world, and they seem to have been a regular part of burial rituals (Ruscillo 2017, 569–573). Whether the faunal bones represent offerings or remains of funerary feasting is not clear elsewhere, but at Vronda, on some occasions at least, animals were burned as offerings on the pyre with the deceased, while other bones are more likely to have been the remains of funerary meals.

Very few marine shells were found in the enclosure graves. Five specimens were identified, including two limpets (*Patella*), a murex (*Hexaplex trunculus*), a topshell (*Phorcus*), and a vermetid. There is no sign that any of these were strung as ornaments, and most were probably deposited as food residue; the vermetid, however, could have been used as an ornament. There are fewer shells in the enclosures than in the tholos tombs, where nine shells were recovered. No shells have been reported with cremations at Knossos, Eleutherna, or Vrokastro, but burned marine shells and crustaceans were found in the cremation burial deposits in the tomb of Orthi Petra at Eleutherna (Agelarakis 2005, 58). It would appear that Cretans did not regularly deposit shells when the cremation rite was practiced, although it happened occasionally. The small number from Cretan sites contrasts with the large quantity of marine shells found in contemporary burials in coastal areas of Greece, as, for example, at Torone (Ruscillo 2005). It is likely that the shells found in the Vronda tombs represent personal items or a personal offering from someone close to the deceased, as has been suggested at Torone (Papadopoulos 2005, 334).

Some botanical remains were recovered from the enclosure burials. Most common were olive and grape. Olive was found in Graves 9, 20, 21, and 23, while grape occurred in Graves 9, 15, 20, 21, 23, 26, 28, 30, and 36 (for counts, see Table 13). These plant remains may have been offerings, sustenance for the dead, or discarded parts of the funeral meal. The olive pits could also have been included as fuel for the pyre. The grapes may have been placed on the pyre as fresh fruit or dried raisins. Other edible remains include pistachio, lentil, legumes, peas, hulled barley, and other grains.

Comparison of Burial Customs in Tholos Tombs and Enclosures

The tholos and enclosure cemeteries at Vronda are separated by topography, chronology, and burial rites. With a few exceptions (Tholos VIII, Graves 3, 13), the tholos tombs lie on the periphery of the former settlement, while the enclosures were constructed within the earlier buildings. The SM–PG tholos tombs are earlier than the LG enclosures, although several of the tholos tombs were apparently used again in the LG period, and the earliest enclosures may have overlapped with the late use of the tholoi. The tholos tombs contained inhumations (with the exception of a possible secondary cremation in Tholos IV), whereas the enclosures were largely used for primary cremations, with a few inhumations and secondary cremations.

The cremation enclosures placed within the decayed buildings of the LM IIIC settlement represent a new type of burial for the Kavousi area, one that is unusual for EIA Crete and not common elsewhere in Greece (see this vol., Ch. 12, pp. 363–364). Although cremation burials had been normal in Central Crete since at least the 11th century, they were rare in the east of the island until the eighth century. The customary type of cremation on Crete included the removal of some bones and ashes for burial in a vessel within tombs, and few examples exist of enclosures that served as both the pyre site and the final resting place for multiple burials (Eaby 2007, 325–336; Wallace 2010, 301–302). The type of cremation practiced at Vronda is highly unusual and represents a break both with earlier traditions of inhumation and with contemporary methods of cremation.

The assemblages in the enclosures are more completely preserved than those from the tholos tombs. The graves, however, suffered disturbances during multiple episodes of use, and some of the material close to the surface had disappeared or was scattered. Even so, important differences in burial customs may be discerned through the comparison of grave goods recovered from the tholoi and the enclosures.

The most prominent feature of the enclosure grave assemblages at Vronda is the large quantity of cups. On average, drinking vessels constitute 55% of the ceramic assemblages (Charts 4–6), with slightly over three cups or skyphoi out of the average of six vessels for each buried individual (excluding Graves 8, 10, 24, 31, and 35, which produced no accompanying pottery). In contrast, drinking vessels were less numerous (39%) in the tholos tombs. Pouring vessels with restricted mouths were fewer in the enclosures (12%) than in the tholos tombs (32%), and the aryballos and lekythos replaced the bird vases, flasks, and stirrup jars of the earlier tombs. As in the tholoi, storage vessels associated with the enclosures included amphorae and jars, but there were more pyxides for small-scale storage accompanying the cremations, and some of the large amphorae may have stood as markers over the graves rather than serving as actual storage vessels.

Jewelry (pins, fibulae, earrings, bracelets) was less common in the enclosures than in the tholos tombs (16% of the objects in the enclosures, 40% in the tholoi), but iron weapons and tools were especially plentiful, more so than in the tholoi (Charts 10–12). Weapons account for 35% of the objects in the enclosures, but only 19% in the tholoi, and tools amount to 31% of the objects in the enclosures, but only 19% in the tholoi. Personal adornments are generally thought to be associated with female burials, and weapons or tools with men, and thus there may have been a difference in the sex ratios present in the enclosures and the tholos tombs. Of the 43 individuals from the enclosures that could be sexed, 58% are male and 42% are female. In the tholos tombs, of the five individuals that could be sexed, 80% are male and 20% female. The number of sexed individuals in the tholos tombs, however, is so small that the differing proportions are not statistically meaningful.

Beads are more plentiful in the tholos tombs (15%) than the enclosures (9%), but the beads found in the cremations represent a greater variety of materials (stone, terracotta, ivory or bone, glass, lead) than are found in the tholoi (stone and terracotta). A few stone lids appeared in both. Small obsidian blades occurred in several of the enclosures, but it is not certain if these were deliberately deposited grave goods or small pieces that had been left behind in the soil from the LM IIIC settlement.

It would appear that although the range of grave goods in the tholos tombs and enclosure graves are similar, the amounts of any given type of object are not the same (Charts 4, 12). Such differences probably reflect changes in burial rituals and/or beliefs and perhaps also wider transformations in society. The larger quantity of drinking vessels found with the cremations, for example, may be indicative of the longer rituals involved with that rite, but it could also be due to a change in sympotic behavior among the burying community (Węcowski 2012). Similarly, the greater richness of the metal objects in the enclosure graves may result from greater wealth of the burying population, changes in what was considered appropriate to mark the persona of the deceased, or changes in the makeup of society.

Reconstructing the Burial Rituals

As we do not know for certain where the members of the population that buried their dead at Vronda resided (although the Kastro is a likely location), and as such rituals generally leave no traces in the archaeological record, there is no evidence for the initial stages of the burial rituals, whether the deceased was interred in a tholos tomb or cremated in an enclosure. Much of the preliminary ritual, including the washing and laying out of the body, doubtless occurred in the home or village of the deceased; there is no evidence for any mortuary buildings on Vronda that might have been used for the preparation of the body. The deceased would have been dressed appropriately, but unfortunately no traces of the funeral clothing were preserved with any of the dead, whether they were inhumed or cremated. It is possible that at some point the body was covered with a shroud that might have been closed with pins or fibulae. The body had to be transported to Vronda for burial, and there is likely to have been a lengthy procession accompanying the remains from the deceased's home. Although many aspects of the early stages of the funerary rituals still remain unknown, the archaeological remains from the tombs and graves provide more information about the burial practices that were undertaken once the bodies of the dead arrived at Vronda.

In the case of the tholos tombs, the rituals began with the construction of a new tomb or the opening of an older one. Apparently the front of the tomb, with its pseudo-dromos and stomion, was uncovered to serve as a backdrop for the ceremony; the tombs are too small to have accommodated any of the participants. The body was brought into the tomb through the doorway, or the capstone was removed and the body was lowered in from above. Grave goods were placed around the corpse, some of them possibly having been used for libations or toasts during the ceremony. Goods that were intended to accompany the dead on the journey to the underworld or in the afterlife may have been displayed during the ceremonies. Other rituals, for which no physical evidence remains, may also have taken place at this time, including laments, remarks upon the deceased, recitation of tales, music, dancing, drinking, and the preparation and consumption of funerary meals. Finally, the doorway was closed and the tomb was sealed. The area in front was left open, however, and flat paving stones were put in place to serve for postfunerary rituals. We do not know how long the postfunerary events continued or what they entailed, but when the prescribed time had elapsed, the pseudo-dromos was filled in and a heap of stones was piled there to mark its place. Funerary markers of some sort may have stood over the tomb. The top of Tomb V was flattened so that the capstone formed part of a pavement. A large, decorated pithos found in pieces in and around the tomb may have stood on this paving, at least after the last burial.

The rituals surrounding the cremation burials were somewhat different from those accompanying the burials in the tholos tombs. First of all, an enclosure had to be constructed or opened up and cleaned. Also, a good deal of wood for the pyre must have been gathered for the cremation (Liston, this vol., Ch. 4, pp. 212–213). The depiction of cremations in the *Iliad* demonstrate this clearly. The description of the cutting of wood for the pyre of Patroklos is lengthy (Hom. *Il*. 23.110–128), and it is stated that the collection of wood for Hector's pyre took nine days (Hom. *Il*. 24.784).

The fuel would have included some large logs or beams, as well as kindling and bushes. Graves 26 and 36 produced evidence of the beams at the bottom of the enclosures. In Grave 26, the charred remains of five beams were found lying perpendicular to the long axis of the enclosure, running from east to west. Grave 36, however, produced two possible layers of beams, the lowest running down the long axis of the enclosure from north to south, the upper going across the short axis from east to west. It would appear that at least in this grave, the longer beams were placed first, then the shorter ones were set on top and perpendicular to them. This alternation of beams accords well with later Greek depictions of funeral pyres, for example on the amphora by Myson, now in the Louvre (G 197), depicting King Croesus on the pyre (Denoyelle 1994, 120). It is probable that there were alternating rows of beams with kindling distributed between them, rising to at least a meter in height. Types of wood recognized in the graves include oak (Graves 23, 28) and olive (Grave 9). Jift from olive pressing may also have been used as fuel, a practice that may account for the large number of olive pits found in the enclosures. Charcoal might have been used as well.

Once the construction of the pyre was completed, the body was placed upon it, usually alone, but occasionally with others, as observed in Graves 4, 21, and 34. Other multiple cremations may have occurred, but because of later disturbances it is impossible to be certain. Concurrent deaths and cremations of women and their children, particularly neonates and infants, may have been frequent. Some personal possessions, such as jewelry, tools, or weapons, were included with the bodies on the pyre.

At last the fire was lit, and the flesh was consumed by flames. The cremation would have taken at least six to eight hours to complete. During this time the body underwent visual transformations, accompanied by sounds and odors. As the body burned, it contracted, giving the impression that the corpse had agency. This spectacle doubtless affected the experience and actions of the mourners and evoked memories of the past while creating others for the future (Williams 2004, 265). Meanwhile, it is likely that many rituals occurred that left no trace in the archaeological record, including sacrifices, libations, drinking, eating, singing, dancing, and storytelling. The numerous cups found in the graves may be remnants of the drinking rituals performed during the cremations. Animal bones in some of the graves suggest that sheep or goats were sacrificed; in one instance an animal was even placed on or close to the pyre. It is possible that pig and deer limbs were also placed with the dead. People may also have wandered around the Vronda site looking at other graves and the remains of the earlier settlement, reactivating memories of past events and funerals. When the cremation was finished, it is possible that the embers were extinguished by pouring water or wine on the pyre.

Grave goods, some of which may have been set near the pyre during the cremation, were placed in the enclosures, including some of the metal weapons and tools and much pottery, pieces used in the rituals, vessels containing food and drink for the gods, or pottery that held sustenance for the dead in the afterlife. Stones were piled over the enclosure before the heat or flames had been entirely extinguished, as indicated by the traces of burning found on the bottoms of many of the stones. Perhaps at this time markers were placed on some of the graves, particularly large amphorae that were found with the graves on the summit. The stone stand in the pavement associated with Grave 3, whether used to hold a large vessel or another stone (a limestone slab was found in the debris associated with this grave), provides further evidence for the use of grave markers.

Remains found at the top of the enclosures in Graves 3, 4, 12, and 20 suggest the practice of post-funerary rituals. Usually these involved cups (Graves 3, 4, 20) and/or a flask (Grave 3) or aryballos (Grave 12). We cannot determine how long after the cremation such rituals occurred, but probably they happened during the sealing of the enclosure or soon afterward. Rituals may also have occurred at intervals thereafter, but they left no certain physical remains.

In general the enclosure graves were used repeatedly, but there were a few exceptions. Grave 10 held a single inhumation of a child in a pithos. Grave 34 contained a woman and a child who were cremated together, and Grave 4, too, may represent a single event or two closely spaced events. The three adults in Grave 21 may also have been cremated simultaneously. Otherwise, the enclosures were used for two to eight burial events, assuming that each fetus was cremated with its mother. There were two events in Graves 1, 3, 16 and 32, two or three in Grave 21, three in Graves 15, 17, 19, and 26, four in Grave 23, five in Graves 6 and 30, six in Graves 9 and 20, and seven in Graves 5, 12, 28, and 36. During reuse, the stones were removed from the grave, and some bones and pottery probably came out with them. This material was usually deposited close to the enclosure, and the stones may have been used again for the next burial. Most of the ashes, bones, and objects from earlier burials were pushed to the sides of the enclosures. The remainder of the burial was performed as for the initial cremation, unless there was an inhumation or a secondary cremation instead.

For the secondary cremations, the rituals were probably the same as for the primary cremations, at least until the pyre had burned out. Then some of the bones and ashes were gathered and placed into a vessel. Cranial and forearm fragments were collected, with a preference for bones from the right side (Liston 2007). No pottery or objects accompanied the remains in the vessels, although they were provided with lids, generally cups or skyphoi that may also have been used in the burial rituals. In one instance (Grave 8), the bodies (a woman and fetus) were placed not in a container; instead they were deposited in a pit dug into the roofing material from the earlier building.

The inhumations were quite different, as they involved the burial of the body rather than cremation on a pyre. Whatever rituals accompanied these inhumations, they left behind little evidence. Often the latest burials in an enclosure, the inhumations seem to have been made shallowly, with stones piled above to protect the bodies. They were, thus, open to weathering and predation from animals. Only in Grave 5 was the burial well preserved, with the body stretched out in an extended position diagonally across the enclosure. Aside from a small jar, there were no accompanying grave goods. This burial would have taken a shorter time to complete, and the rituals must have been less extensive and time consuming.

12

History and Society in the Vronda Graves

Leslie Preston Day

History of Mortuary Use of the Vronda Ridge

The chronology of the EIA in East Crete is still not fully established, making the dating of the Vronda burial events problematic. The dating for this period on Crete is based upon the ceramic sequence, which is reasonably clear for Knossos and Central Crete (Coldstream 2001, 22; Kotsonas 2008, 31–35; see this vol., Ch. 1, p. 11) but not for the eastern part of the island, where the inhabitants seem to have been slower to accept the new Protogeometric and Geometric styles of pottery developing on the mainland (Tsipopoulou 2005, 346–347; Kotsonas 2008, 35–37).

Three major problems affect our understanding of the ceramic sequence of the eastern part of the island and specifically of the Vronda burials. First, all of the mortuary features were used over a long period of time, particularly the tholos tombs, and there is no way to associate individual vessels with particular burials because of later disturbances, whether they resulted from continuing burial events or subsequent depredations. Second, many of the vessels placed within the graves may have been antiques or heirlooms and were not contemporary with the time of the burials (see this vol., Ch. 11, pp. 348–350). It would be helpful if we could assume that the first use of each grave is datable according to the earliest pottery found within it, but that is not the case, because we know that in some cases vessels earlier than the time of burial were deposited in the graves. This can be demonstrated most effectively by the two vessels containing the secondary cremations in Grave 28. These vessels were wedged tightly together in the corner of the enclosure and must represent a single burial event. One of them (**GR28 P22**) is of PG style, while the other (**GR28 P3**) is of LG date. The individuals whose remains were placed within the amphorae were also nearly the last burials in the grave, and the deposit of cups found at the bottom of the enclosure and below the two vessels certainly belong to the LG period. Thus, it appears that the use of this enclosure took place entirely within the LG period, despite the presence of earlier pottery, and this phenomenon may have been characteristic of other graves as well. Some people may have been buried with older pottery because it had symbolic value, possibly expressing a connection between the living buriers and the deceased or between them and the older generations that the deceased was joining.

The third problem is that few correlations exist between the pottery found at Vronda and the ceramics from other parts of Crete. There are few certain imports at Vronda from Central Crete or from outside the island. While some of the earliest material (SM–EPG) from the tholos tombs is similar to that found at Knossos and other Central Cretan sites, there is no way of determining whether the use of the tholos tombs was contemporary with those periods in Central Crete. Earlier styles may have lingered in the eastern part of the island for some period of time after the later PG styles became popular at Knossos and elsewhere. Probably the tholos tombs were first constructed and used soon after the abandonment of the Vronda settlement, but the precise dates of the later burials are difficult to determine because PG styles were still in circulation in the eighth century at Kavousi. The long life of the PG style is not limited to the graves at Vronda but can also be seen in the houses on the Kastro (Mook 2004, 169–173). The tholos tombs were used sporadically into the middle of the eighth century, but there may have been long periods of disuse.

In the case of the enclosure graves, the dating of the burial remains is somewhat less problematic, because the Vronda pottery is similar to that of the Knossian LG period. There is, however, no certainty that the LG style appeared in East Crete immediately. As in so many periods, the adoption of the new style may have occurred later than in other parts of the island. Most of the enclosure graves were in use in the LG period, that is, the second half of the eighth century, but their use may have begun later than the start of that period in Central Crete and ended later as well. The EO styles found in a number of the enclosures may also have been introduced at Kavousi later than in Central Crete. It is clear, however, that the last usage of the enclosure graves occurred during or after the third quarter of the seventh century.

Other forms of dating have provided little help. From the twelfth to the tenth centuries few linkages exist between the Aegean and eastern Mediterranean cultures and Egypt that might help to establish secure dates (Knapp and Manning 2016, 116–117). Greek imports in the Levant have played a major role in determining the absolute chronology of the Aegean down to the late eighth century, but controversy about dating the phases of Levantine sites continues (e.g., Fantalkin 2001; Fantalkin, Finkelstein, and Piasetzky 2011; Finkelstein and Piasetzky 2011; Mazar 2011; Toffolo et al. 2013). The flattening of the radiocarbon calibration curve between 800 B.C. and 400 B.C. and the lack of substantial timber samples for dendrochronology means that in general it is difficult to obtain absolute dates for the time period (Papadopoulos 2014, 184).

At Vronda, carbon samples from the burial features have provided some C^{14} dates, but they are not useful. For the tholos tombs, C^{14} dates were derived in 1988 from samples taken from Tombs IX and X by Erle Nelson of Simon Fraser University. Samples of human remains came from Tomb IX. As this tomb was uncovered by a local landowner, who threw the bones and broken pottery back into it after removing the whole vessels, the possibility for contamination of the samples is great. In addition, the pottery suggests that the tomb was in use intermittently in the SM/EPG, PG, and Geometric periods, and it is impossible to know to which of these periods the bones belonged. One of the samples came from a skull, the other from a limb bone. These produced two dates, ca. 800–400 B.C. and A.D. 0 ± 100 years. Three samples of dog bones from Tomb X were also analyzed, but they proved to be Medieval in date (A.D. 1298 ± 85, 1408 ± 80, 1418 ± 85).

For the enclosure burials, two C^{14} dates were obtained from burned wood from the pyres and analyzed by Beta Analytic (Day et al. 2016, 199, 237–239). One sample from Grave 3 produced a date of 970 ± 140 B.C, while a charred beam from the bottom of Grave 26 gave a date of 794 ± 122 B.C. Both of these graves have been dated stylistically to the LG period, that is, 750–700 B.C. in terms of the traditional absolute chronology for Crete, so the dates are either too high or too broad to be useful, placing Grave 3 in the LM IIIC–PGB ceramic phases and Grave 26 in the MPG–EO phases, whereas the pottery suggests that they are roughly contemporary in the LG period. The high dates may be a result of "old wood" effects (Weninger and Jung 2009, 374–375), caused by the use or reuse of wood cut down long before it was placed on the pyre. It is also likely that the low resolution of the dates stems from the flattening out of the radiocarbon curve from 800 to 400 B.C.

Despite the problems with ceramic sequence and absolute dating, we can reconstruct a general history of mortuary activity (Table 26). The use of the Vronda ridge for burial began soon after the abandonment of the LM IIIC settlement (around the middle of the 11th century), probably within 50 years. Although some of the tholos tombs may have been constructed and in use during the life of the settlement, most of the material found within them is later, and the enclosure burials certainly postdate the settlement by about 300 years. The abandonment of the Vronda settlement was the result of the population either dying out or moving elsewhere, as there is no sign of intentional destruction (war) or natural disasters, such as earthquake or fire. People took with them precious objects, such as metal tools, as well as pottery and other objects of daily life (Day et al. 2016, 214–215). At about the same time the settlement at Azoria also seems to have been abandoned (Haggis and Mook 2015, 18–19). It is likely that at least some of the surviving population of the Vronda settlement moved up to the Kastro (Pl. 1A), as no other habitations of the Early Iron Age have been found in the immediate area, despite extensive field survey (Haggis 2005), and there is evidence for an increase in settlement size on the Kastro in the PG period (Mook 2004, 169).

The burials in the tholos tombs on Vronda belong to the period after the abandonment of the settlement. The tombs were arranged around the periphery of the former village, outside its recognizable boundaries, which could still be seen because the walls and even some of the roofs remained standing (Figs. 3, 4). Although the use of the tombs after the abandonment of the settlement is clear, the date of their construction is uncertain, and the precise dates of the various burials cannot be ascertained. Most of the nearly complete vessels that were recovered are later than the pottery left behind in the abandoned settlement, with the exception of a stirrup jar from Tomb VIII, another from Tomb II, VII, or VIII, and possibly several vessels from Tomb IV that are now missing. While the stirrup jar from Tomb VIII may indicate an early use of that tholos, it is more likely to have been an antique or heirloom, because Tomb VIII cut through the LM IIIC Building L. Therefore, it must postdate the abandonment of that building, which, as indicated by the ceramic evidence, occurred at the same time as the rest of the settlement.

Nevertheless, during the cleaning of nearly all of the tholos tombs on the ridge, fragments of LM IIIC pottery were found embedded in the floors and in the entrances and areas in front. This evidence can be interpreted in several ways. The fragments of LM IIIC pottery may simply represent background noise from material that was left in the soil from the period of the settlement's use. It is also possible that the tombs were constructed at the very end of the occupation when some LM IIIC pottery was still in use. Perhaps the tholoi were needed to bury a large number of people who died from an illness, after which the community was no longer viable, thus making it necessary for the survivors to move to another site. The inhabitants of the settlement might also have tried to establish their rights to the territory as they departed by burying their dead in the vicinity. That the inhabitants would go to the trouble of constructing such large and elaborate tombs under stressful conditions at the time of their departure, however, does not seem likely.

Another possibility is that at least some of the tholoi were built and used by the inhabitants of the earlier settlement, but all of the goods and human remains left in them were removed except for small fragments ground into the floors and around the edges. In favor of this interpretation is the fact that no graves have been found that clearly belong with the LM IIIC settlement, although tholoi contemporary with their settlements are known at other LM IIIC sites in East Crete, for example at Karphi (Day 2011b, 221–242) and Chalasmenos (Coulson and Tsipopoulou 1994, 83–91). In both of these cases, the tombs were built well outside the limits of the settlement and not as close as at Vronda. Evidence for the removal of material from earlier burials can be seen in the tholos tomb at nearby Azoria, where the earliest pottery, found primarily in fragments but including one intact stirrup jar, belonged to the LM IIIC period, while the majority of vessels were of SM–PG date (Eaby 2010, 173).

If the Vronda tombs were built in LM IIIC, it is hard to know why later people removed all traces of the earlier burials so completely, but there are several possibilities. One is that the material from the earlier burials might have been removed and shared among members of the community (Williams 2005, 254). The fact that some artifacts and human remains belonging to earlier interments were still left in tholos tombs at Vronda and elsewhere (e.g., Chalasmenos, Karphi, Plai tou Kastrou), however, argues against such an interpretation. Possibly the removal of the earlier remains is an indication of hostility on the part of the burying population toward the earlier inhabitants, prompting a deliberate forgetting of those previously buried there. In that case, perhaps the tholoi were taken over by different kinship or corporate groups who tried to rid themselves of the outsiders represented by the earlier remains. The burying population may have been different from the people who had lived in the settlement at Vronda and may have been staking a claim on the site and its associations after the original inhabitants had left. In this case they may have tried to obliterate all traces of the former residents. The complete removal of all but fragmentary traces of earlier burials, however, does not seem in keeping with the burial practices observed elsewhere on the island. For example, the idea that earlier graves were cleaned out before reuse has been rejected with regard to the tombs of the North Cemetery at Knossos (Catling 1996c, 639; Wallace 2010, 294–295).

The most probable explanation is that the former residents of Vronda came back and constructed tholos tombs around the periphery of the former settlement, which was gradually decaying as its roofs and walls collapsed. A similar situation occurs at the North Cemetery at Knossos, where the tombs are not believed to have been constructed before the SM period, although the burying population may have been imitating earlier tomb types (Catling 1996c, 639). Although most of the Vronda tholos tombs had been robbed, it would appear from the extant pottery that they were in use primarily in the SM and EPG periods, then again later in the PG period. Some Geometric and even LG pottery, however, was found in several tholoi (Tombs IV, V, VII, IX). It seems likely that the tombs were not used continuously from the SM through the LG periods. They were probably used first in the SM–EPG period (ca. 1050–920 B.C.), then again in the mid to late ninth century, and finally in the eighth century, about the same time as use of the enclosure graves began.

The enclosures can be more securely dated to a much shorter period of time, from the middle of the eighth century (LG) into the late seventh century (LO). The earlier enclosures overlapped with the latest uses of the tholos tombs. Most of the graves belong to the LG period. At least six continued in use in the LO period or were constructed in the seventh century.

Burying Population and Location of Cemeteries

A consideration of the Vronda cemeteries raises several questions. First, who was burying in these graves? Second, why was the site of the abandoned settlement used as a burial ground? Third, why were there two quite different cemeteries, and how did they relate to one another and to the tombs around the Kastro?

Burying Population

With regard to the first question, we have little direct evidence to determine where the burying population lived. Much of the skeletal material from the tholos tombs at Vronda and the tombs around the Kastro has been lost, and most of the bone from the enclosure burials is totally burned, so no samples for DNA analysis can be recovered. It is almost certain, however, that the burying population lived in the Kavousi area. Azoria and the Kastro are the only two sites identified in the vicinity of Vronda that were occupied after its abandonment (Fig. 2).

Although originally thought to have been inhabited continuously from the LM IIIC period to the Archaic period (Haggis 2005, 132), the settlement at Azoria now seems likely to have been abandoned around the same time as Vronda (Haggis and Mook 2015, 18–19). It is unclear if Azoria was inhabited in the Geometric period; while there is evidence for activity on the site at that time, it is not enough to suggest inhabitation (pers. comm., M. Mook). As at Vronda, the site was used for burial in the PG period; one tholos tomb has been found dating to this time (Haggis et al. 2007a, 697; 2011b, 458; Eaby, 2010, 173). Azoria, then, could neither have been the home of those burying in the Vronda tholos tombs nor the home of those using the cremation enclosures.

After both Vronda and Azoria were abandoned, the settlement on the Kastro expanded and continued in use from the PG through the EO periods (Mook 2011, 480). Population increase and settlement nucleation may have resulted in the construction of new cemeteries, as happened elsewhere in the Greek world, in which groups of people could express their collective identities and establish links with their ancestral past (Papadimitriou 2016, 340). The Kastro buildings have been interpreted as family dwellings arranged in clusters belonging to kinship groups (Mook 2011, 480), and the same sort of grouping by family and kinship groups can be seen in the organization of the cemeteries both around the Kastro and at Vronda. It is therefore most likely that those who buried in the tholoi, both at Vronda and Azoria, as well as those who used the enclosures on Vronda, were living on the Kastro.

At the same time that the cremation enclosures were in use on Vronda, so, too, were the tholos tombs with inhumation burials found around the periphery of the Kastro. These tholoi were located at Aloni (Skala), Plai tou Kastrou, and Skouriasmenos (Fig. 2; Boyd 1901, 143–148; 1904, 15–17; Gesell, Day, and Coulson 1983, 410–413). Although most of these tombs had been plundered, enough evidence remains to indicate they held wealthy elite burials, with gold objects, armor, weapons, jewelry, ship firedogs and spits, and imported metalwork and pottery (Boardman 1971; Tsipopoulou 2005, 81–117). Although the continuing practice of inhumations in tholoi might seem to suggest that the residents of the Kastro and the people who burned their dead on Vronda belonged to different communities, it is possible that the new method of disposal of the dead (i.e., cremation) was related to status distinctions, expressions of kin group affiliation, or other factors.

It is clear that the tombs around the Kastro were used for elite burials, probably made by competing kinship groups (Wallace 2010, 287; Mook 2011, 480–481) like those recognized in contemporary Cretan sites (Wallace 2010, 295–296). Ship firedogs and spits are thought to have been particularly high-status feasting equipment (Maran 2012, 130), and the armor and imported goods recovered from the tombs are also indicative of elite status. The Kastro must also have been home to people of lower social classes, as well as people from differing kinship or corporate groups who may have chosen or been forced to cremate on Vronda rather than bury their dead in built tombs near the Kastro or were excluded from burial there. It is true that the Vronda enclosures contained large numbers of weapons and tools, but they lacked both the armor (shields, greaves), the ship firedogs and spits (in place of these are fleshhooks, used for pulling chunks of meat out of a cooking pot), and imported or exotic materials that may have served as important elite markers (Prent 2014). The Vronda cremations that are contemporary with the Kastro tholos tombs appear to have been undertaken by people who were wealthy, but perhaps not as rich and (presumably) powerful as those who buried their dead in the tholos tombs above Vronda.

The use of the tombs around the Kastro peak seems to have been restricted to the elite, although we do not know enough about the circumstances of burial. Perhaps we could call the people who were interred there aristocrats to distinguish them from other less powerful elites (for the distinction between aristocrats and elites, see Rabinowitz 2014, 95). It is possible that those who were not aristocrats chose to bury on Vronda, or were excluded from doing so, perhaps revealing fissures in the community or rivalry between competing elite kinship groups. If the aristocrats continued their traditional way of burial near the town, other elites may have decided to place their dead at Vronda, using a new method of burial that usually involved cremation. The Late Geometric period witnessed the beginnings of polis formation in Greece and on Crete, and we might see in this cemetery the assertion of a new group claiming some of the power previously held only by the aristocrats. In the Kavousi area, within a hundred years a new form of social organization was established at Azoria, and this cemetery might represent the beginning of that social change.

Those who buried their dead in the tholos tombs on Vronda may have been the children or grandchildren of the inhabitants of the LM IIIC settlement. These people would have had a real connection to the site through their own memories or those of their older relatives. Those who cremated their dead on Vronda some 300 years after the settlement was abandoned could not have had the same kind of real attachment to the site, but they may have tried to claim it nevertheless.

Memory, Landscape, and Burial

Why was Vronda chosen for this new type of burial? As Saro Wallace (2010, 322) points out, the Vronda ridge is not visually striking or memorable, except that it commands an excellent view of the Kastro. Nevertheless, that view may have been an important consideration, especially in the siting of the enclosure burials (Pls. 1A, 1B, 69F, 75B, 75C). The choice of Vronda for burial may well have been the result of social memory and the establishment of group identity. The ruined walls of the LM IIIC settlement would have been visible to people of the Kastro, especially as they made their way down to the spring near the site. There has been much discussion in recent years about the effect of site remains and found or curated objects on the location of later sites and in the establishment of the identity of local groups and communities (e.g., Rowlands 1993; Chesson, ed., 2001; Alcock 2002; Bradley 2002; Van Dyke and Alcock, eds., 2003; Jones 2007; Williams 2013; Dakouri-Hild and Boyd, eds., 2016; Borgna et al., eds., 2019). At least since Early Minoan times at Vronda, the remains of earlier dwellings that were visible may have played a role in the location of important buildings in the settlement; some were even reused by later inhabitants. The people who built the Protopalatial structures on the ridge perhaps had some knowledge of the Prepalatial settlement, although no architectural remains of that period have yet been found in the excavations. The Neopalatial inhabitants built their massive building next to and possibly directly over the large Protopalatial structure on the summit, while those who constructed the LM IIIC settlement also built on top of and incorporated walls from the Neopalatial structures, particularly in the case of the large Building A-B (see Day et al. 2016, 199–205, 208). The decision to locate EIA burials around or within the abandoned settlement may represent a similar expression of continuity or connection with the past.

As the tholos tombs began to be used within 50 years of the abandonment of the settlement, those who buried in the tholoi probably had real memories of the former village. They may even have been descendants of the former inhabitants. The reuse of Vronda as a burial site is an example of communicative memory, which is informally created out of the personal experiences of living people. It is often shared through social interaction and stories, and it generally lasts only three or four generations (Maggidis 2019, 165). Studies centered on ancient Egypt, where the past is better documented than in prehistoric Greece, have suggested that communicative memory is forgotten even after two generations (Meskell 2003, 37). The early use of the Vronda tholoi fits well within this period of time, as it is likely that the burying population at first had direct memory of the earlier settlement. The same situation seems to have existed at Karphi (Day 2011b, 327).

When the nucleation of settlement occurred in the Kavousi area after the middle of the 11th century and the inhabitants of both Vronda and Azoria moved up to the Kastro peak, people from the three sites now merged and resided together. Nevertheless, groups may still have wished to mark their own separate identities by stressing their connections to their ancestors who had lived at Vronda or Azoria. A good way of expressing these connections was to bury their dead near the places they identified as their former family homes. Thus, burial at the site of Vronda may have been an expression of their identity, separate from that of the people who had been living on the Kastro peak when the nucleation occurred and from that of the former inhabitants of Azoria.

The later use of the tholoi and the new cremation enclosures in the eighth century seem to represent something different, a form of cultural or social memory that connected the present with a remote or mythical past through social interaction and rituals that built a collective and communicative identity (Maggidis 2019, 165; Panagiotopoulos 2019, 363). Reuse of earlier structures in the EIA is well attested on Crete (Prent 2003; 2014; Wallace 2010, 312–322; Labrude 2016). There is evidence for ritual activities involving ceremonial consumption of meat and wine within monumental Minoan buildings at major palace sites (Prent 2003, 2014). These rites attest to a renewed interest in a heroic past, whether real or invented (Prent 2014, 655). In the isthmus of Ierapetra, however, it was not the palatial past that excited interest, but rather the remains of more recent times when settlement shifted to defensible mountain sites (Wallace 2010, 288; Gaignerot-Driessen 2019, 69). For example, a possible elite feasting building of the LG era was constructed in the ruins of one of the abandoned LM

IIIC houses at Chalasmenos (Tsipopoulou 2004), and the ruins of the LM IIIC village at Vronda became the site of funerary rituals. By the eighth century, any actual memories of the former settlements would have been lost, but that need not have prevented people from inventing histories and stories about the former inhabitants.

People saw ruins and tried to explain them. Ruins have the power to stimulate imagination, from which good stories often emerge. A textual example of this process can be found in the *Iliad*, on the occasion when, prior to the chariot race in the funeral games for Patroklos, Nestor points out the course to his son (Hom. *Il.* 23.326–333). He mentions a marker composed of a stump and two stones that is to serve as the turning post for the chariot race and suggests that it represents either the grave marker of someone who died long ago or a goal post for a racecourse belonging to people who used to live in the area. This passage is a good example of the way in which people interpreted the remains of the past that were such common features of the landscape in ancient Greece. Although it is not the only such reference in Homer (Grethlein 2008), this example is of particular interest because the term used for the marker (σῆμα) is a word that is used not only for a sign or marker in general, but also, more specifically, for a grave marker (Nagy 1983, 46). Ruins were often interpreted as tombs.

The Vronda ruins would have been viewed as belonging to ancient people, and the burying population most likely interpreted them as the remains of their ancestors and constructed narratives about them in the absence of any written records. These stories would have given symbolic power to the site, and the local people would have incorporated them into the construction of their identity. More than that, we may see here deliberately invented traditions, new practices that were designed to promote specific cultural values and norms of behavior by claiming them to have been in force at some particular point in the historic or prehistoric past. Such invented traditions often develop during periods of rapid change and transformation when existing social patterns have been weakened or destroyed (Tsipopoulou and Rupp 2019, 87). Elite groups or political authorities may have deliberately made connections with Vronda, using burial rituals to create collective mnemonic experiences that would forge communal identity and affirm social hierarchy (Maggidis 2019, 165). The physical remains of the walls and the tholoi were tangible objects that prompted and guided the course of memory. As Susan Alcock suggests, monuments constitute "inscribed" memorial practices (2002, 28). The mortuary landscape, then, is bound up with memory and with stories, although the memory and the stories may have had little or nothing to do with the real history of the Vronda settlement, as was the case with the turning post in the *Iliad*. Thus, we need to investigate the memory landscape of Vronda.

We cannot know how the local people in the eighth century interpreted the remains of the settlement or the tholos tombs, but it is clear that they were aware of them. Many of the walls of the 12th century houses were still standing at least 50–75 cm high, as can be seen from the south wall of Room J1 (Building J) that was used for Grave 9, or the south wall of Room J4 with which Graves 10, 12, and 17 were associated. People could see the ruins from the mountains above or view them more closely when visiting the spring near Vronda, cultivating local terraces, or pasturing flocks. They doubtless created narratives about the ruins. They may have thought the whole area was an ancient burial ground, as occurred in Egypt, when poor houses for the workers on the pyramids were interpreted in Roman times as tombs (Meskell 2003, 51–52). Local people may have recognized the remains as houses and associated them with earlier members of their own group, their ancestors. Burying in these ruins literally returned the dead to the ancestors. That knowledge of the original functions of the specialized buildings had been lost can be seen from the fact that tombs were built indiscriminately in both the shrine and the houses. There is no certain grave located in the most important building of the settlement, Building A-B, but the iron hoard found by Boyd probably represents a grave in this building, and the remains identified as Grave 37 were also found nearby.

The tholos tombs themselves may also have attracted those who began cremating their dead on Vronda. These tombs were still visible, or at least their tops, which may have held markers, could still be seen, along with the piles of stones over their entrances. Florence Gaignerot-Driessen (2016, 131–133) has suggested that a major determinant in the placement of LG–EO cemeteries on Crete was the presence of earlier tholos tombs. At Vronda, the tholos tombs may also have been reused in the eighth century, in one case (Tomb IV) perhaps even to hold the secondary remains of a cremation. One of the enclosures (Grave 3) was located within a cluster of tholos tombs (Tombs IV–VII, XI), and the fact that its orientation is aligned with the front facade of Tholos IV suggests that this was a deliberate placement. Perhaps the kinship group who used Grave 3 was asserting ties to those who had buried in Tholos IV, although after several hundred years, this association may have been more fictive than real. Vronda, then, conforms to the pattern observed in the Mirabello region in the LG period of placing graves in the vicinity of tholos tombs with which the burying population may have claimed ties. As the majority of the enclosure burials, however, were made within the ruined buildings of the LM IIIC site, it would seem likely that it was those settlement remains, more than the tholos tombs, that attracted the burying population. Once the Vronda ridge was used for cremations, it became fixed as the burial place for a particular group of people.

Monuments and remains, however, do not provide the only way of activating memories. "Incorporated" memorial practices are equally important (Alcock 2002, 28). These consist of performative ceremonies that generate sensory and emotional experiences, such as the "performance" of the cremation burial ritual. Cremation is a highly theatrical method of burial, one that would long be remembered by the onlookers, and these memories would have been reactivated every time a cremation took place. The Vronda ridge was thus transformed from being simply a place of legend related to people of the past, to being the site of remembered spectacular funerals that helped define the burying population as well.

Memory was entangled with the burials at Vronda in a variety of ways. First, the ruins themselves attracted burials. Second, the burial ritual itself created memory on the part of the participants. Third, the burial ritual celebrated the memory of the individual(s) buried there. During the ceremony the body itself and the grave goods accompanying it would have signified important social attributes of the immediate family, the larger kinship group, or the community overall. The material goods, such as the clothing, tools, weapons, and jewelry, would have been part of the sensory experience, but they also spoke to the role that the deceased had played within society or the role that society valued. The inclusion of antique objects or family heirlooms among the grave goods may also have expressed connections with the ancestors. Memory, then, probably played a powerful role in the location of the cremation cemetery at Vronda, in connecting with earlier populations, in constructing local identity, and in defining family and personal identity within the community.

The use of Vronda for cremation burials came at a time of social upheaval, when Crete was opening up to new ideas and influences from the Aegean and eastern Mediterranean. Contact with new ideas, cultures, and people may have pushed the residents of the Kavousi area to assert their own identity in the face of other competing communities. It may also have been a factor in the decisions to establish their connections to their own past through the practice of funerary rituals and burial at Vronda.

Introduction of Cremation

The important question of why a new type of mortuary practice, cremation, was introduced into the Kavousi area in the middle of the eighth century remains to be addressed. The advent of cremation represents a profound transformation in burial customs, and its adoption can be interpreted in several ways. Earlier archaeologists often viewed major changes in burial customs as being linked to ethnicity (Wallace 2010, 286; 2018, 16), and the introduction of cremation was widely ascribed to the arrival of Dorian Greeks on Crete (for a history of this idea, see Hall 1997, 116–117; Wallace 2018, 313). The introduction and use of cremation in the Aegean has been long studied (see, most recently, Lochner and Ruppenstein, eds., 2013), and it is now clear that during the Bronze Age cremation took place both on mainland Greece and Crete as a minority rite, but it became more widely practiced in the EIA (Melas 1984; Cavanagh 1996, 675; Cavanagh and Mee 1998, 93; Kanta 2001; Whitley 2016, 219–220).

Although cremation may have been practiced first in East Crete (Whitley 2016, 219–220), it certainly became the dominant practice in Central Crete from the 11th century onward. In the eastern part of the island, however, the majority of people still continued to practice Bronze Age types of collective inhumation in tholos tombs (Eaby 2011, 182). At Vrokastro, near Kavousi, cremations became popular in the PG period (Hayden 2003, 12–13; 2004, 156–158).

The adoption of the cremation rite at Vronda in the later eighth century may have been spurred by local changes in rites associated with stronger ties to Central Crete and the mainland. Along with the beginning of cremation in the earliest and richest enclosure graves on Vronda comes a slight increase in ceramic influences from Central Crete and Athens, the latter perhaps filtered through Knossos. Certain cups (especially those with ledge rims), mugs, amphorae, and pyxides suggest an awareness of Attic styles, as does the use of amphorae as grave markers. Increased contact with Central Crete, mainland Greece, and the wider Mediterranean world would have exposed the inhabitants of the Kavousi area to new and different customs and objects. Indeed, the tholoi around the Kastro, contemporary with the Vronda enclosure burials, provide ample evidence for outside contacts with Knossos (pottery at Skouriasmenos), Cyprus (pottery at Aloni), North Syria (bronze work at Skouriasmenos), and Sicily or South Italy (a fibula at Aloni). William Cavanagh (1996, 675) has suggested that the widespread adoption of cremation in the 11th and 10th centuries on Crete indicates a "community of custom and belief, linking Crete and Knossos with much of central Greece."

The use of cremation, however, does not necessarily imply a new people at Vronda, nor can it be linked to Dorian Greeks. For one thing, the type of primary cremation in which the enclosure functioned as both the pyre and the final resting place for the deceased is highly unusual on Crete as elsewhere in the Greek world (see above, Ch. 11, pp. 333–334). If this type of cremation was brought by a new group from the outside, it is difficult to discern any origin for these people. It is possible that the idea of cremation came to the people of Kavousi through contact with other sites with earlier attested cremations, such as nearby Vrokastro, or sites in Central Crete. There are, however, no certain earlier cremations in which the remains were left in situ, which seems to have been a local adaptation.

It is possible that the bone enclosures at Vrokastro also had such cremations, but because they were excavated at a time when skeletal remains were of little interest and no anthropologist was involved in their excavation, there can be no definitive evidence one way or the other. Some of the Vrokastro bone enclosures seem similar to those at Vronda, as they contained masses of burned bones along with LG pottery and metals (Hall 1914, 154–172), but some of the compartments had few bones or objects and may have served as crematoria from which the skeletal remains were removed for secondary burial. The Vrokastro enclosures also produced different types of burials that resemble the pattern at Vronda: secondary cremations (Hall 1914, 159–160) and inhumations of children in pithoi (Hall 1914, 163–165). The oddity of the Vronda cremations might be an indication that the people of Kavousi did not fully understand the cremation rite as it was practiced in other places in the Greek world and on Crete; thus they only took over the dramatic part of the ritual—burning on the pyre—not the collection of the bones for burial in a tomb. There may, however, be other complex and compelling reasons for the change in burial customs.

One common theory, namely, that cremation was a cheaper funerary option than building a tomb, is certainly not true for Crete (McKinley 2006, 81). Although at first glance it might appear that building a tholos tomb requires a greater expenditure of energy and resources, that is not entirely so. The building material for the tholos tombs (stone) is plentiful on Crete. Once the tomb was constructed, it could be (and was) reused for a number of burials. The only work to be done was to uncover the entrance for subsequent burials, and little labor and no new resources were required. The cremation enclosures were even easier to build, involving some digging and the use of walls that were already there, a single line of stones no more than one or two courses high, or a combination of both. Like the tholoi, the enclosures, once constructed, could be (and were) reused repeatedly. The resources (stones, preexisting walls) were readily at hand, and the structure required little labor to build. The cremation itself, however, required a great deal of wood, a commodity that was not abundant on the island. The difficulties of obtaining sufficient wood for cremation are noted in ancient literature: for example, Homer made much of the gathering of the wood for the funeral pyres of Patroklos and Hector in the *Iliad*. In the case of Hector, this task took nine days (see above, Ch. 11, p. 353). Thus, procuring the fuel for the cremation required the investment of a great deal of time and labor. Economics alone, then, cannot account for the change in burial custom.

The reasons behind the change may lie in the nature of the cremation process itself (Thompson 2015). Death is a transition. With inhumation, that transition is slow, involving the gradual decay of the body out of sight underground and/or in a tomb. Cremation, in contrast, provides an immediate and visible transition of the body from its fleshed state into bones and ashes. The Vronda cremations may reflect changes in eschatological beliefs, beliefs that now favored an acceleration of the deceased's transition to whatever afterlife was anticipated. The body no longer underwent a long putrefaction process over months or years; rather, it was consumed in a period of hours.

The introduction of cremation (which, as we have seen, would not have been a new idea to the area) may have been tied to cultural ideas of pollution—pollution in a spiritual, rather than a physical sense (Farnham 2016). Modern attitudes toward cremation, when positive, tend to see it as cleaner and more sanitary (Sørensen and Bille 2008, 260–261), but those attitudes cannot be cast back into antiquity. The notion of fire as ritual purification from the pollution of death (either for the dead or the living) is a plausible explanation, but not the idea that it was more hygienic. Cremation may have been tied to the idea that the dead person was a danger to the community until the flesh was gone. Beliefs that the spirit of the dead lingered until the body was reduced to bone are common enough (Metcalf and Huntington 1991, 79–85). That some danger was perceived from the decaying body can be seen from the fact that in the tholos tombs the doorways were sealed up with stones and soil and the pseudo-dromoi filled in. Although this procedure in part may have been a way of keeping the odors of decay within, it also served to seal in the spirits of the dead. With cremation, the flesh was seen to be totally consumed, and the spirit released, as in the contemporary accounts in the *Iliad* (Hom. 23.69–74).

Sudden and remarkable changes in mortuary behavior may have been linked to physical expressions of competition, display, and hierarchy (Manning 1998, 40; Janes 2014, 573). In this regard, the change in burial practices may have been connected to intergroup rivalry between elite clans, either within the burying population or between the burying population and those of other towns or settlements. The social organization on Crete in the later part of the eighth century is generally thought to have been characterized by competitive clans (Wallace 2010, 287). It is possible that the adoption of a new and sensational type of burial was undertaken by one of the elite groups in the area, perhaps one whose members identified themselves as the descendants of the former inhabitants of Vronda and also wished to assert their social ties to the even richer elites of Central Crete or mainland Greece. Additionally, it is possible that cremation was adopted in part to support a territorial claim (Renfrew 1976, 205–208; McKinley 2006, 86; Wright 2013, 406; Rizzotto 2015, 102), perhaps in contention with other groups on the Kastro, or to counter the expansion of yet another community into the Kavousi area. Burying at Vronda would have demonstrated the group's control over the site and its past associations, as well as its claim to nearby resources of water, arable land, and pasturage. The long-lasting visibility and the unprecedented spectacle of the cremations would have affirmed this claim in a particularly theatrical way (Day 2011a).

Cremation represented not just a novel form of disposal of the dead but an entirely new sensory experience. It may be more important to think about the impact that such an event would have had on the people who witnessed it than it is to try to trace either the origins of the cremation practice in the burying community or the reasons for its adoption. In comparison to earlier funerals involving inhumations in tholoi (see above, Ch. 11, p. 352), cremation ceremonies would have been far more dramatic. For at least six to eight hours, the burning of the body on the pyre would have engaged nearly all the senses of everyone present (Williams 2004, 271–273; Hamilakis 2013, 131–143). The mourners would have seen the transformation of the body as the burning of the shroud or clothing revealed the hair, skin, fat, muscles, organs, and bones of the deceased. They must have felt the heat of the flames and smoke rising from the pyre, heard the crackling and snapping of the fuel, and watched, perhaps in horror, the bursting forth of liquids from the burning body. Meanwhile, they may have marveled at the appearance of the beautiful grave goods (pottery and metals), some of which were perhaps displayed before being placed in the burial enclosure at the cremation's end. The funeral participants may also have engaged in rituals that involved dancing, mourning gestures, lamentations, music, and the recitation of stories while the cremation was underway. Toasting, eating, pouring libations, and all the time hearing the cries of sacrificial animals and the roaring of the pyre would have added to the sensory experience. And even as the air became suffused with the smell of roasting human flesh, there must have been other, more pleasurable odors from the meat being cooked for the funeral meal and the perfumes that helped to cover the stench of the cremation, all mingling with the natural scents of local vegetation—the thyme, sage, and oregano that grew wild on the mountain slopes.

Because the cremation took so long, there was ample opportunity for feasting and drinking, activities that are attested by the drinking vessels and kraters and the possible remains of the funeral meals (animal bones, botanical remains) associated with the cremation enclosures. And even for those who were not in attendance, the spectacle of the cremation would have been more widely visible than an inhumation. The smoke from the fire and the flames, particularly at night, could have been seen by anyone on the Kastro or anywhere on the northern part of the isthmus. To everyone in the vicinity, both rival elite groups on the Kastro and members of other nearby communities, the cremation of the dead made a visible claim to the Vronda ridge.

Social Structure and Burial

Although we are limited by the lack of settlement evidence for the people who buried their dead on Vronda, we can nevertheless make some inferences about their life and socioeconomic organization from their mortuary practices.

The interpretation of burials has long played an important role in archaeology (for good discussions of the history of interpretations of burials, see Carr 1995; Gillespie 2001, 73–84; Keswani 2004, 6–21; Papadopoulos 2005, 345–354; Chapman 2013). In the early days of the discipline, burials were seen as direct reflections of the lives and social positions of the buried individuals and were analyzed accordingly. Since the 1960s, however, burials have been interpreted according to shifting theoretical viewpoints. Processualists connected variations in mortuary treatment with differences in status within burying groups, focusing on grave goods, location of burials, possible costs evinced in the construction of burial facilities, and the distribution of graves within and among cemeteries (Saxe 1970; Binford 1971; Brown, ed., 1971; Peebles 1971; Goldstein 1976; Tainter 1978; Brown 1981, 1995; Chapman, Kinnes, and Randsborg, eds., 1981; O'Shea 1981, 1984). In short, they saw burials as directly reflecting the organization of societies and used mortuary data to reconstruct that organization. Their focus was on an evolutionary development of sociopolitical structures, and they classified societies in terms of specific political types, for example, egalitarian or hierarchical.

Postprocessualists, however, have critiqued these ideas in a variety of ways, insisting that mortuary behaviors are affected by many complex factors that have been recognized in a growing corpus of anthropological studies. They have suggested that the mortuary record is not an exact representation of the living society but is instead the product of religious and social practices that can actually mask or distort the reality of social relationships and identities within societies (Hodder 1982; Pader 1982; Parker Pearson 1982, 1984, 1993, 1999; Shanks and Tilley 1982; Morris 1987, 1992; Metcalf and Huntington 1991). Some have focused on the social identity of the individual rather than the sociopolitical structures (Gillespie 2001, 81). According to the postprocessualist view the material record represented by the burial is not straightforward but should be seen as the remains of rituals through which the survivors negotiated their relationships with the dead and the ancestors and inscribed the dead into social memory (Gillespie 2001, 78).

These theoretical viewpoints and many others come into play with mortuary analysis. It is necessary to investigate all aspects of burials, including their locations and relationships to other burials or structures; the quantity, quality, and nature of all grave goods (Ekengren 2013); the age, gender, and social position of the deceased; and any evidence for rituals that may have been performed during and after the funeral. In the present analysis, we will try to elicit some understanding of the society of EIA Kavousi not by using a single theoretical approach, but by employing, more pragmatically, a variety of theoretical viewpoints.

The interpretation of burial remains presents many problems, and it is even more difficult when dealing with multiple burials in the same grave and the commingling of several generations of burial events. Cremation burials present their own set of difficulties due to the damage caused by the burning of the bodies and grave goods. Nevertheless, the Vronda burials present an unusual opportunity to understand burial practices because the bones and grave goods were not formally removed, curated, and placed elsewhere. Although they were often disturbed by subsequent burial events, they remained within the enclosures or were dumped nearby.

We now turn to the question of what we can learn about the social organization of the burying population and the lives of the individuals who were laid to rest on Vronda from their burial remains.

Kinship

The importance of the family and larger kinship groups is clear from the evidence of the Vronda graves, both in terms of their contents and location. Smaller household groups are represented by the individual tholoi or enclosures, and larger extended families or clans are attested by the clustered groupings of the graves. The tholoi and the enclosures alike contain multiple burials of individuals of all ages and both sexes, indicating that these graves were used by multigenerational families. While the groupings might indicate different corporate groups that were not organized by kinship, a few genetically linked traits in the enclosures, in particular the unfused metopic sutures that were found not only on skeletons within the same graves but also within the same cluster of graves (Liston, this vol., Ch. 5, pp. 232–233) seems to show that kinship was the determining factor in burial. The location of the enclosures, and to a lesser extent of the tholoi, in clusters further supports the interpretation that the graves were arranged according to larger kinship groups, a pattern one can also see in the LM IIIC settlement at Vronda and at the Kastro in the LG period (Mook 2011, 480–483).

That these families or clans may have been in competition with one another is suggested by the evidence of theatrical burials, either in front of the backdrop of a tholos tomb or in the highly dramatic and visible cremations in the enclosures. In general, the social organization of Cretan communities of the SM–EO periods is thought to have been characterized by competing elites belonging to different extended families or clans (Wallace 2010, 287; Gaignerot-Driessen 2016, 155–156). This interpretation is based partly on the analysis of settlement plans but mostly on funerary evidence, namely, large graves that are rich in metal goods, particularly those with weapons (the so-called Warrior Graves—see below, pp. 369–370) and imported or exotic objects (Gaignerot-Driessen 2016, 132). Certainly the burials in the Kavousi area support this model of social structure (individual families in graves, extended kinship groups in clusters), as do the burials made close to the Kastro.

Social Differentiation

Although the limited preservation of the grave goods makes it difficult to identify hierarchical distinctions among the burials in the tholos tombs, there is some evidence for social differentiation within the enclosure burials. Some graves and groups of graves have more pottery and objects than others. One cluster of graves located in the ruins of building complex J-K seems to have been the richest in view of the number of metal objects found; six graves (out of a total of seven in the cluster) produced 63% of all of the metal objects found in the enclosures. The cluster of three graves in the former building complex C-D produced only 8% of the metal finds overall. Three of the seven graves in the I-O-N cluster yielded 11% of the metal finds, and three of the four graves in the shrine cluster produced only 3%. Graves that were not associated with any particular cluster account for the remaining 15% of the metal goods. Such disparity between groups, namely, the wealth of the J-K cluster in comparison to all the others, suggests some level of social differentiation among groups within the population. It is interesting that the J-K cluster was also the group in which the earliest cremation enclosure, Grave 9, was found. Other graves in the cluster were arranged around it, suggesting that their users wished to identify or associate themselves with the deceased in Grave 9. Two of the clusters (building complexes J-K and C-D) lay on top of the ridge, where the cremations could be seen most clearly. Perhaps wide local visibility was another indication of the higher status of the groups burying there.

At the same time, it is important to remember that those burying on Vronda were probably only part of a larger community, many of whom continued to inhume their dead in tholos tombs around the Kastro. The tholos tombs near the Kastro settlement have yielded evidence of groups that had wider contact with the outside world and even greater wealth than the people who used the cremation enclosures on Vronda. In comparison to the Vronda graves, these tombs contained more valuable goods made of gold and bronze as well as iron. The Plai tou Kastrou tomb, whose contents were acquired by Arthur Evans on one of his trips to eastern Crete, included iron weapons and a bronze shield boss, a possible helmet, and feasting equipment of iron spits and ship firedogs (Boardman 1971). The spits and firedogs can be interpreted as remains of the implements used at funerary banquets such as those described in the Homeric poems. A bronze wheel and lotus cauldron handles represent exotic objects indicating connections with the eastern Mediterranean. Some of the pottery from the Plai tou Kastrou tomb was imported from Cyprus, the Cyclades, and the Greek mainland.

Other tholos tomb burials near the Kastro were also provided with rich and exotic goods. The tombs at Aloni (Skala) produced a strainer vessel that may have been made in Cyprus (Gesell, Day, and Coulson 1983, 411, pl. 78:b) and a horse fibula that suggests contact with South Italy or Sicily (Boyd 1904, 17, fig. 8). The occurrence of the latter object is not surprising in the period leading up to the Greek colonization of Sicily, in which some Cretans took part. The LG–EO tomb at Skouriasmenos, which had been largely plundered of its contents by the time it was explored by Harriet Boyd, produced a pair of bronze greaves, along with swords, spearheads, axe-heads, and bronze arrowheads.

The imported decorated bronze plate with griffins found at Skouriasmenos may have been imported from Syria or made by Syrian artists in Crete (Reed 1976, 366, 371), while the gold and faience objects may be further evidence for connections with the Near East. In addition, the tomb contained pottery imported from Knossos (Gesell, Day, and Coulson 1983, 412, fig. 78:d) and possibly Euboea (Tsipopoulou 2005, 109, pl. 105), as well as imitations of Cypriot vessels.

The assemblages from these tholos tombs differ from those of the Vronda tombs in the presence of defensive armor, feasting equipment, and exotica (foreign or foreign-inspired pottery and objects). These goods have generally been associated with competing elites (Crielaard 1998; Panagiotopoulos 2012; Prent 2014). Other Cretan cemeteries, especially Knossos, Aphrati, Prinias, and Eleutherna, have yielded a range of prestige objects not found at Vronda, including precious metals, bronze vessels, and off-island pottery. Exotic goods, as well as antiques or heirlooms, could be used by elites to enhance their prestige. The inclusion of foreign objects in graves became an active ingredient in the process of social differentiation (Prent 2014, 658), and as exchange intensified in the Mediterranean in the eighth century, more objects became available, particularly on Crete, which was a locus of interaction for Mediterranean people and for the exchange of goods. The material from the tholos tombs around the Kastro reflects this situation.

The Vronda graves do not show the same patterns so clearly. Although there is some pottery in the tholos tombs that suggests interaction with Cyprus (flasks and bird askoi), within the enclosures there is very little material that is not of local Cretan manufacture. The pins and some of the fibulae may have come from beyond the Kavousi area, but petrographic analyses have shown that the pottery is mostly East Cretan, with some vessels from southern and central sites on the island. Some of the pottery displays the potters' awareness of stylistic developments in distant places such as Attica or Cyprus, like the Creto-Cypriot lekythoi or the krater resembling Cypriot bichrome from Grave 27, but there are few if any actual imports. The lack of exotic items might indicate that there was not as much active social differentiation within the burying group on Vronda as there was among those burying at the Kastro. Nevertheless, these are certainly not poor burials, as indicated by the amount of metal found in them and by the expensive and theatrical funerals represented by the cremations. These burying groups were elites, even if they were not as prominent as the elites burying around the Kastro. Thus, we seem to have evidence for a hierarchical society, and the fact that some of the population chose to bury in a spectacular fashion at Vronda suggests competition between differently ranked elite groups.

Social Identity

In addition to providing evidence for the social structure of the burial community, burial remains may also tell us something about the deceased individuals (Gillespie 2001). The concept of personhood has been used by archaeologists to reconstruct the people of the past (Chesson 2001, 4–5; Gillespie 2001, 75). While the "individual" may be an anachronistic label that comes from western concepts, the idea of personhood can be seen as a complex of relationships enacted within social groups (Gillespie 2001, 83). Thus, observation of burial practices and grave goods can tell us something about the persons buried in a cemetery and their relationship with the community. Unfortunately, because the graves at Vronda were nearly all disturbed by later activity that mingled or destroyed the remains, the undertaking of such an approach presents difficulties. Nevertheless, a few deductions can be made about the persons buried at Vronda.

Association with a kinship group was apparently very important. Where one was buried seems to have been determined by kinship, and people were cremated within a family enclosure that was clustered near enclosures of a larger kinship group. Some of the graves that lie slightly removed from the more closely clustered graves may represent families that were only marginally related to those in the rest of the cluster or those who were asserting a connection to the kinship groups who buried within the cluster. At any rate, individual identity or personhood was tied up with family connections.

The objects found in the graves may also tell us something about the lives of the deceased, although these goods were deposited for a variety of reasons, not all of them having to do with the identity of the dead. For example, most of the ceramic vessels found in the enclosures seem to have been associated with drinking rituals at the funeral. A few vessels, such as aryballoi, may have been personal objects buried with the dead; two of the three graves holding the remains only of women and children contained aryballoi. These two graves also produced pins or fibulae, which probably belonged to the deceased in life. Other graves contained beads that may have served as jewelry. There were no other objects that could be certainly associated with women's lives and activities, nor were there any toys or other objects that might have belonged to children, although miniature vessels (a tray and a necked jar in Grave 3, a cup in Grave 4, an amphora in Grave 6, small wide-mouthed jugs in Graves 9 and 28, a jar and a jug from Grave 36) were almost exclusively found in graves with infants or children. Thus, we have little evidence of how these two groups of persons, women and children, lived their lives, except that their remains suggest they both experienced high mortality rates.

We have more information about aspects of personhood among men, although none of the graves contained only male burials. Burying men with weapons seems to have been a regular practice at Vronda; 77% of the weapons came from graves with identifiable male burials, and only three graves (23%) with identifiable males lacked weapons (Graves 3, 19, 36). As at Knossos and other Cretan sites (Wallace 2010, 300), the deceased males were celebrated as warriors or hunters; spears, arrows, and even swords and daggers were weapons for the hunt as well as for war. It is interesting that the two graves that produced arrowheads (Graves 1, 12) also contained cervid bones, particularly metapodials, not just antler fragments that might have been part of tools or inlays. As deer were not domesticated but probably hunted, the hunting skills of the deceased may have been celebrated in these two graves.

The weapons and tools deposited in the enclosures may show us the roles for which men were valorized in burial (being fighters and hunters), and/or they may represent the wealth of the person or family. It is also possible, however, that some of these objects were personal possessions of value to the individual's identity. Knives, particularly the sickle-shaped ones, may have been part of an agricultural toolkit for farmers or pastoralists. The tongs, hammer, chisels, files, and other tools from Grave 6 may have belonged to a metalworker. Fleshhooks may have been the personal eating utensils for some of the men buried in Graves 9 and 12.

It has been suggested that the presence of kraters in some of the graves may reflect the social identity of the deceased, particularly when viewed in conjunction with the weapons that marked masculine identity (Whitley 2009, 285–286; Rabinowitz 2014, 95–114; see above, Ch. 11, p. 344). Kraters were found primarily in the wealthiest graves (Graves 6, 9, 12, 17, 20, 28, 30, possibly 27), generally together with weapons; only two come from graves without weapons (Graves 4, 23). Kraters may symbolize patronage exercised in rituals of communal drinking among male elites, and Adam Rabinowitz has argued that the krater expresses the dominance of the host over the guests. In burial contexts the krater would have formed part of the drinking equipment that accompanied the funerary rituals, and the wine was perhaps distributed by the family of the deceased, thus stressing the role of the dead person as provider of sympotic events. Weapons, in turn, reflect the claim to participate in communal, elite, male activities such as warfare or hunting. During the funeral, these weapons may have symbolized the participation of the deceased in these activities, with a focus on personal achievement or personal qualities rather than an emphasis on the social status of the deceased among his peers (Rabinowitz 2014, 95). Neither weapons nor kraters alone can indicate the structure of society, particularly whether it was composed of competitive elites or more egalitarian groups. The association of kraters with weapons in burials, however, marks two aspects of the self-identity of the person: as a warrior or hunter (communal and egalitarian pursuits) and as a host (communal and competitive activities). These two aspects of the persona are not mutually exclusive and may hint at the structure of society.

It is likely that the funerals associated with the cremations at Vronda were occasions for expressing the identity and status of the associated kin group as much as the personhood of the deceased. All of the enclosure graves have numerous drinking vessels that are probably the remains of funerary rituals. The funeral ritual involved drinking, and the family of the deceased may have provided the wine as well as food for the funerary banquet. An observed decline in the numbers of kraters in Greek burials in the eighth century might have been related to a change from an elite sponsorship of drinking to one in which there was greater sharing among the participants, an indication perhaps of the growth of a more egalitarian society.

It is also possible, however, that the increased number of cups in the Vronda enclosures had nothing to do with status but reflects the change in funerary rituals necessitated by the introduction of cremation. Cremations were by nature several hours long, with rituals probably performed throughout, along with singing, dancing, recitation (possibly tales of earlier people buried there or the ancestors), eating (as attested by the butchered animal bones), and especially drinking. The funeral became a sympotic event in ways that the earlier burials in tholos tombs could not be, and this development may account for the large number of drinking vessels deposited in the graves.

Because the enclosures contained so many weapons, they have some claim to be labeled "warrior graves," a common class of burials identified in the Late Bronze and Early Iron Age Aegean (Catling 1995; Crielaard 1998; Whitley 2002; Kanta 2003; Dickinson 2006, 73, 157–158, 192–194; Wallace 2010, 157–161, 300; D'Onofrio 2011; Molloy 2012, 119–122; Lloyd 2015; Kotsonas 2018). Such graves appeared in Crete in the LM II–LM IIIA periods (Whitley 2002, 219–223) then disappeared for a time until the SM period when they reappeared, particularly in the North Cemetery at Knossos (Catling 1995; 1996c, 646–648; Whitley 2002, 226–227). Much has been made of such burials in reconstructing the history of EIA Athens and other sites on the mainland.

The term "warrior graves," however, is misleading, as it suggests that we know that the deceased actually engaged in combat. Rarely does the evidence support this idea; only occasionally have burials with weapons been associated with bodies showing wounds that might have come from combat. It is quite possible that these weapons were more regularly used in hunting, particularly the spears and arrows. Thus, as James Whitley (2002, 218) has suggested, these "warrior graves" should be instead be termed simply "burials with weapons."

At Vronda, burials with weapons are certainly found in the enclosures, and they were probably present in the tholoi. The two unplundered tholos tombs (IV, IX) produced iron objects that can certainly be identified as spearheads, but the blade fragments found by Boyd in Tomb VIII may also have come from a spearhead or sword or dagger. Many weapons appeared in the enclosure graves, but they were particularly plentiful in Graves 9 and 12. In addition to the weapons, both graves held a large number of tools, some of which may also have functioned as weapons (knives and axes).

These two graves were also used on many occasions, more often than most of the enclosures. There were six burials and a fetus in Grave 9 and seven burials and a fetus in Grave 12. Of the six burials in Grave 9, two could be identified as male (both 40–60 years old, one of them the first burial in the enclosure), one as female, and the others (two adults and an infant) were unsexed. The weapons came in multiples of five, suggesting that five of the burials were accompanied by weapons. Even if the two unsexed adults were males, either the woman or the infant was also apparently provided with weapons. Unfortunately, fewer of the burials in Grave 12 could be sexed, but there was at least one male (40–60 years old) and one female, along with four adults and a child. Some of the unsexed bodies were probably male, and some of the weapons may have accompanied them, but it is still possible that one of the females or the child was provided with weapons. Graves in which there were no adult male burials (such as Graves 4, 32, and 34) did not produce any weapons, so it is unlikely that weapons accompanied the women; some of the children, who could not be sexed, may have been male and provided with weapons, such as the inhumed child in the pithos in Grave 21. All members of the families who used these enclosures may have been socially identified as warriors, regardless of age and perhaps of gender.

Of particular interest is the presence of large numbers of arrowheads in the enclosure graves 1 and 12. It is highly unusual to find more than a few arrowheads in EIA graves, even in Crete where the ancient inhabitants were noted for their archery. These objects may identify the dead as an archer, whether as a warrior or a hunter. The fact that both graves contained remains of deer suggests that the identity of the deceased as a hunter was stronger than that of a warrior, although the symbolism may be multivalent and both identities are possible.

There is no indication on the bones that any of the individuals cremated at Vronda were involved in warfare. No wounds were identified on any of the bodies. The inhumation in Grave 5 (Burial 7), however, did show healed wounds on the right arm, defensive wounds that seem to have resulted from violence. Although we cannot be certain, it would appear that none of the weapons found in this grave (five spearheads) accompanied this individual; they belonged instead with one or more of the six cremations made within the enclosure. Thus, there are two graves (9, 12) with what could qualify as warrior burials on the basis of the weapons present, but there was no evidence of wounds on the bones of the deceased, and there was one grave with an individual whose bones displayed long-healed wounds but had no accompanying weapons. It would appear, then, that the people in the enclosures were buried with weapons to indicate an ideal or symbolic association with warrior or hunter status, not merely to show the regular activities of the deceased in life.

Although burials with weapons appear throughout the Greek world in the EIA, they were never frequent except on Crete, where there are numerous examples (Lloyd 2015, 16). Few Cretan cemeteries have been fully published, but from Fortetsa, Knossos North Cemetery, and Eltyna we have sufficient data to compare with the Vronda assemblage (Table 27). At the Knossos North Cemetery 190 weapons were found in 32 tombs (Cavanagh 1996, 672); this means that 27% of the total number of excavated tombs contained weapons, and 39% of the smaller number of tombs that had any objects at all had weapons (based on data published in Coldstream and Catling, eds., 1996). At Fortetsa, of the 22 excavated graves, seven produced weapons (32%), and of the graves with objects, 39% had weapons (based on evidence presented in Brock 1957). Of the 16 graves at Eltyna, eight produced weapons (50%), while 67% of the graves with objects had weapons (Rethemiotakis and Englezou 2010), an unusually high number. The Vronda enclosures are also rich in weapons. Twelve of the 36 (33%) recognized graves produced weapons, and of the 20 graves in which objects were found, 12 had weapons (60%). Thus, the frequency of metal weapons in the Vronda assemblage is relatively high, especially in comparison to Knossos North Cemetery and Fortetsa.

Other Aspects of Society

Economy

The objects found in the Vronda burials suggest something about the economic life of the burying population(s). All of the evidence from graves and settlement points to an agricultural and pastoral base for the local economy. There is only a small amount of evidence for trade or exchange, composed chiefly of metal objects and imported pottery or pottery imitating foreign types.

Much of the pottery sampled for petrographic analysis from the tholos tombs (limited to vessels from Tomb IX) comes from within Crete and was locally produced in East Crete. Nevertheless, a few samples came from the south coast of the island. Such evidence indicates that the community participated in exchange within the island, but it is difficult to determine the scale of that activity. Contact with areas off the island can be seen in certain types of pottery, but the evidence for such long-distance interaction is even more limited. It is clear that there was an awareness of styles in the eastern Mediterranean, particularly in Cyprus and the southern Levant. Two vessel types were connected with the east: lentoid flasks and bird askoi. The lentoid flask is generally thought to be of Levantine origin (Desborough 1979–1980, 353; Coldstream 1996, 365). The bird askos shows contact between Cyprus and Crete, and the particular type found at Kavousi is thought to have been Cretan in origin and to have influenced some of the Cypriot types (Desborough 1972, 269). These two vessel types clearly indicate that there was some contact between Crete and the eastern Mediterranean in the later 11th and early 10th centuries, certainly more than during the time of the LM IIIC settlement.

The majority of the pottery from the later enclosure burials also seems to have been locally or regionally produced. At the moment we cannot distinguish the local from the regional. The variety of fabrics imported from outside Kavousi, even in such mundane vessels as monochrome cups, however, is surprising. The fabrics sampled for petrographic analysis do not resemble those found in the earlier LM IIIC settlement, nor those from the Kastro, in part because only coarse wares were sampled from those settlements. The fabrics show wide variation within a limited area of Crete.

The pottery from the enclosures is generally from East Crete, specifically from the northeast (Fabric Groups 1–3) or the Vrokastro area (Fabric Group 4), or less commonly from the southern coastal area from Myrtos to the Mesara (Fabric Group 5) or from South or South-Central Crete (Fabric Groups 6 and 7; see Nodarou, this vol., Ch. 9, pp. 303–304). Surprisingly, exchange with Central Crete was rather limited, despite the importance of Knossos in the eighth century. Some of the material from the enclosures seems to show Attic stylistic influence, particularly the vessels from Grave 9, but the fabrics indicate Cretan production, and the influence may have been filtered through the south coast or Knossos. One vessel from Grave 20 (**GR20 P1**) closely resembles Knossian examples, but the fabric places its manufacture on the south coast.

There is even less evidence in the enclosures for exchange with the Aegean or the eastern Mediterranean. Small aryballoi with crosshatched triangles on the shoulder, for example, are probably influenced by Corinthian MG prototypes and are similar to those found at Knossos (Coldstream 2001, 44). Other aryballoi are made in shapes that are also derived from Corinthian prototypes, but the common decoration of small concentric circles is more reminiscent of lekythoi of Cypriot origin (Coldstream 2001, 42).

In addition to the ceramic influence of Athens and Corinth, there is evidence of continuing contact with Cyprus. Several examples of the so-called Creto-Cypriot lekythos or aryballos show the adaptation of Cypriot forms to local tastes in the EO period. The elaborately decorated krater from Grave 27 (**GR27 P4**) attests to multiple influences from Crete, the Aegean, and the eastern Mediterranean. It seems to be a local imitation of Cypriot bichrome ware, and it also displays the concentric circles often found on Cypriot pottery. The shape, however, is indicative of Attic influence, and some of the other decorative motifs are common in the Cyclades and Central Crete. The analysis of the pottery suggests that although there was a limited exchange network between Vronda and the Aegean and the rest of the Mediterranean world, it was more complex than previously suspected. It also suggests that the imported vessels used in the burial rituals and/or deposited with the dead may have been of greater value than was originally thought.

Metals, rather than ceramics, formed the most important category of exchange, whether as raw materials or as finished products. The raw materials were almost certainly imported. Neither the copper nor the tin used for making bronze can be found on the island. Although iron sources are known in Crete today, there is no indication that they were exploited in antiquity, and there is some question about whether the iron from these sources would have been useful because of its high phosphorus content (Muhly and Kassianidou 2012, 124). Certainly, there is no evidence for iron resources in the Kavousi area, and the metals must have been procured from more distant places, possibly from Cyprus, which may also have served as the source for the technology of ironworking (Muhly and Kassianidou 2012, 126). The bronze and iron objects, however, may have been manufactured locally. A stone mold for a bronze knife came from the Kastro, albeit from a disturbed context of fill (Mook 1993, 294–295, fig. 56), and iron slags and blooms also from the Kastro indicate that ironworking occurred there (Photos-Jones, this vol., App. B, pp. 382–383). Nevertheless, at least some of the metal objects may have been imported from elsewhere on Crete or outside the island.

The jewelry found in both the tholoi and the enclosures is generally made of bronze, as is the sheeting that once was attached to some other material. A fibula from one of the enclosure burials (Grave 9) was repaired with iron, suggesting difficulties in obtaining the raw materials. The presence of iron pins in addition to bronze examples in the enclosures suggests that bronze was also difficult to acquire. The uniformity of the pin types indicates that most of them were manufactured on Crete. The mostly bronze fibulae from the enclosures, however, show great variety in types, suggesting that the objects themselves, rather than the raw materials, were actually acquired through exchange. Many of these are of types that come from the mainland or the Cyclades, and all types were common on Crete. It is uncertain what the people of the Kavousi area exchanged for these objects or materials; they may have offered agricultural or pastoral products or woven goods, as Cretan pottery is rarely exported.

Imported pottery and exotic goods from a wider variety of places on Crete, the Aegean, and the Mediterranean were present in the settlement and tholos tombs of the Kastro at the same time that the Vronda enclosures were in use. It is clear that some of the inhabitants of the Kavousi area were engaged in the exchange of exotic goods and pottery, but those who buried at Vronda were not. The elite population buried at Vronda, whose status may be inferred from the numerous metal objects found with the cremations, did not have the same level of contact with outside areas or chose not to display exotic objects in the funerary context.

What was the nature of the contact with the Aegean and the eastern Mediterranean represented by these ceramic and metal objects? In the 11th and 10th centuries, when the tholos tombs at Vronda were in use, contact with the eastern Mediterranean is thought to have been limited to small-scale, regional intercommunications among local elites that resulted in the exchange of metal objects and raw materials (Crielaard 1998, 199). It is unlikely that the people of Vronda in this period had physical contact with outsiders, but they clearly had networks of exchange within the island (seen in the ceramics) that may have given them access to exotic objects.

In the late eighth to late seventh centuries, when the enclosure burials on Vronda were in use, as well as the rich tholos tombs around the Kastro, interregional exchange both on and off Crete had become considerably more complex. Crete probably played an important role as a meeting and provisioning place for merchants and craftsmen who were traveling in search of new markets and new resources. The people of the Kavousi area may have had little direct personal contact with people of the wider Aegean world, Cyprus, or the Levant, but there is much evidence to support the idea that foreigners from these regions were a regular presence on the island (e.g., at Knossos and Kommos; Wallace 2018, 407–411).

Cosmological or Eschatological Beliefs

Without written records, cosmological beliefs are generally impossible to deduce from burial remains, and there is no direct evidence for such beliefs at Vronda. While the choice of Vronda for the cemetery might be seen as part of a pattern of ancestor worship, there is no evidence for any religious building or activities involving ancestor veneration on the site. It seems likely that the population believed that the dead joined the ancestors and enjoyed social positions and powers with them, but there is no physical evidence for a cult of the dead.

Some scholars have tried to determine notions about the soul from burial remains. Bo Gräslund (1994), for example, examined remains from cremations in prehistoric northern Europe and made deductions about beliefs concerning the soul based on the presence of grave goods. He proposed that goods that are cremated with the body are indications of a belief that the soul was multifaceted and that at least part of it survived the physical death of the body and needed provisions of food or other goods on the journey or in the afterlife (Gräslund 1994, 19–20; McKinley 2006, 86). We cannot know for certain why certain types of grave goods were deposited in the Vronda burials, but the predominance of drinking vessels in the grave assemblages suggests they were used in a part of the burial ritual that included feasting and drinking. Meat may have been placed on the pyre with the deceased, and it could represent either sustenance for the journey or food for the afterlife. Like the human bodies, animals were transformed by the fire and may have been food for the deceased during or after transformation. The fact that when the cremation was complete the remains were simply covered and in subsequent uses of the enclosures they were pushed aside suggests the transition of the deceased to another form of existence was finished when the flesh was consumed. The bodily remains and grave goods no longer had much significance; they could be removed, if only accidentally, or pushed to the sides, although some effort seems to have been made to keep them within the enclosure or at least nearby. Perhaps seeing the calcined bones of the dead and the metal objects buried with them reinforced people's memories of past events and past individuals. The physical remains are mute, however, about how the afterlife was conceived or what deities were imagined to have been a part of it. All we can say is that the change in burial rite during the eighth century from inhumation to cremation involved a difference in the time scale in the transformation of the remains of the dead, but not necessarily a major change in beliefs.

Conclusions

Soon after the abandonment of the settlement in the 11th century, Vronda became the site of burial in two discrete cemeteries, an earlier one characterized by inhumations in tholos tombs and a later one with cremations in stone-lined enclosures.

The tholoi were used by a group of people who probably lived on the Kastro, perhaps the families and descendants of those who had previously resided at Vronda and who still had living memories of the village and its population. It is likely that members of the burying group were asserting their own collective identity in the newly nucleated Kastro settlement by burying their dead where their ancestors had once lived. The dead were inhumed around the periphery of the former settlement in small tholos tombs, a form of burial that was popular in LM and EIA eastern Crete. The chronology of the tholos tombs spans the SM–PG periods, but the tombs seem to have been used sporadically rather than continuously. Although there is some evidence for eighth century burials, the tholoi were probably not used much during the ninth and earlier eighth centuries. Because of later disturbance and looting, the tholos tombs do not provide much information about the society of the burying population. They seem to have contained family burials, and the tombs themselves may have been arranged in clusters representing larger clan or corporate groups. Grave goods included pottery, bronze jewelry, and a few iron weapons and tools.

Sometime after the middle of the eighth century, in the LG period, an entirely new cemetery came into use. Stone-lined enclosures were constructed within the decaying buildings of the former settlement and used for multiple cremation burials. These enclosures lasted into the third quarter of the seventh century, or the LO period. Although it is likely that the same kinship groups were using these new burial features, given the amount of time that had elapsed since the abandonment of the settlement at Vronda and the regular use of the tholoi, it is not reasonable to suppose that the burying population had real memories about the place. Rather, these graves seem to be an example of social memory that was probably more fictive than real.

The enclosure graves are unusual because they served both as the pyre site and as the final resting place of the deceased. The enclosures seem to have been family graves, containing both sexes and all ages, and some hereditary traits observed on skeletal remains found in particular clusters of graves suggest that the clusters represent extended families or clans. The most common ceramic vessels found in the graves were large cups, which may be the remains of drinking rituals that occurred over the many hours it took to complete the cremation. Male burials were usually accompanied by iron weapons (spears and daggers or dirks) and sometimes tools that might have been personal possessions. Women were buried with jewelry but no other identifiable personal possessions. This variation in gender treatments suggests different roles for women in life and different attitudes toward their deaths. Another important gender difference can be seen in the shorter life expectancy of women relative to that of men. Women were often buried with infants or children, and a number of them were pregnant at the time of death. It is likely that childbearing carried significant dangers for the women, and perhaps this is one reason why they were treated differently in death. Children could be cremated or occasionally inhumed, and there is evidence that they experienced a high mortality rate. Although cremation was the primary form of disposal of the dead, there were some other forms of burial, namely, inhumations and secondary cremations placed in pits or in vessels within the enclosures, generally without many accompanying grave goods.

The advent of cremation, which had been the most common form of burial in mainland Greece and Central Crete for centuries, marks a major change in burial practice in the Kavousi area. Even as it was adopted at Vronda, other members of the Kastro community continued to inhume their dead with rich and exotic objects in large tholos tombs near the Kastro peak. The Vronda burials were not as wealthy as those found around the Kastro, and their grave assemblages lacked many of the high status goods found with the Kastro burials. The choice of some social groups to bury their dead at Vronda may have resulted from a need to reinforce their identity as being different from that of other members of the Kastro community. They made this difference widely visible with long-lasting and dramatic cremations on territory that they were claiming as their own.

When the Kastro was finally abandoned toward the end of the seventh century and Azoria became the dominant site in the area, there was a major break in the use of the landscape. The cremations on Vronda stopped, and the tholos tombs around the Kastro ceased to be used. Whatever tensions there had been within the Kastro community, or between that community and others, which led to contrasting practices of theatrical cremation on Vronda and burial in elaborate built tombs around the Kastro apparently no longer existed. The members of the new Azoria community, with their communal dining and rituals, no longer looked to the past to establish their identities or claim agricultural and pastoral resources. Perhaps there was a greater sharing of power and resources among the people than had been the case when there was competition among elite groups living on the Kastro (Haggis 2014). Whatever social, political, and economic forces were at work, the members of the new community no longer valued their long established connections to the past, and they abandoned the earlier sites of habitation and burial ritual. Although the remains of past activities continued to be visible, Vronda and the Kastro were both deserted, and burials were made elsewhere.

Appendix A

Estimates of Vessel Capacities

Kevin T. Glowacki

The potential capacity of each vessel listed in Table 28 has been calculated as a fluid volume using the method described in *Kavousi* IIC (Day et al. 2016) for the Late Minoan IIIC pottery from Vronda (Glowacki 2016, 241–242). As in that previous study, each capacity estimate is an indirect measurement derived from an AutoCAD model of the vessel's interior, based upon a single profile drawing. This process results in an axially symmetric, three-dimensional solid whose volume can be calculated using the mass properties (MASSPROP) command in AutoCAD. For vessels that are noticeably asymmetrical, either as a result of the manufacturing process or from a deformation at some later stage (e.g., warping caused by severe heat in a pyre), the estimates are based on the average of two profiles. Averages were used for several vessels: **GR3 P1, GR3 P4, GR3 P7, GR3 P9, GR3 10, GR4 P16, GR6 P3, GR6 P9, GR6 P23, GR9 P16, GR12 P4, GR12 P6, GR12 P7, GR16 P6, GR17 P1, GR19 P5, GR19 P8, GR27 P1, GR28 P4–GR28 P8, GR28 P11, GR30 P6, GR36 P2, IX P2, IX P28, IX P31, IX P50, IX P59, IX P60**. In the case of one extremely warped vessel (**GR12 P20**), the volume was calculated based on the average of four profiles.

All calculations represent the theoretical maximum capacity as measured to the top of the rim or point of overflow. While it is important to recognize that this capacity measurement is not the same as the effective capacity (that is, the maximum level to which the vessel was most likely filled during use in order avoid spilling), it does reflect an objective physical property that can be measured and compared by independent investigators (Senior and Birnie 1995, 320–321). Studies that attempt to calculate effective capacity often employ different and sometimes subjective criteria based on morphology, such as the curvature of the interior profile (Karasik and Smilansky 2006) or other physical characteristics specific to each shape, in order to estimate where the body of the vessel ends and the neck or rim begins (Tsatsaki 2003; Kotsonas 2008). Moreover, the level at which each vessel was considered effectively full may have been determined by any number of factors, such as cultural conventions, the nature of the occasion, the substance being consumed, or even the personal preferences of the participants.

All of the indirect measurements presented here should be considered approximate. Due to the fragile state of the artifacts, direct measurements (that is, actually filling the restored vessels with a measurable amount of water or dry material) were not attempted. Only vessels whose complete profiles were preserved or could be reconstructed have been included in this sample.

The cups, footed cups, mug-like cups, and widemouthed jugs possibly used for drinking from the graves at Vronda range in size from 0.049 L (**GR4 P17**) to 1.758 L (**GR4 P1**). As suggested by the scatter plots of capacities (Charts 13, 14), some vessel sizes clearly stand out, especially at the lower and upper ends of the range. These vessels can be categorized broadly as "extra small" and "extra large," respectively. Between these extremes, however, the overall capacities of the cups increase in size in a nearly linear trajectory from 0.263 to 1.072 L, making the distinction between meaningful size groups more difficult to discern. Nevertheless, by isolating clusters of vessels of similar capacities and trajectories, it is possible to refine this linear distribution into approximate size categories, within which there can be distinguished several possible subgroups.

On the basis of the available data, the cups, footed cups, mug-like cups, drinking cups, skyphoi, and kraters may be categorized according to the sizes described below.

Cups

Only four cups and one footed cup fall into the extra small category (0.049–0.178 L; n=5; avg. 0.147 L). The smallest preserved cup (**GR4 P17**), with a maximum potential capacity of 0.049 L (or 1.657 US fluid ounces), could be classified as a miniature. It is approximately one-third the size of the next smallest vessel. The next size category among cups is small (0.263–0.423 L; n=24; avg. 0.355 L). Possible subgroups within this size category are: 0.263–0.267 L, 0.294–0.343 L, and 0.364–0.423 L. Medium cups have volumes ranging from 0.448 to 0.515 L (n=13; avg. 0.485 L). The volume of medium-large cups ranges from 0.531 to 0.609 L (n=9; avg. 0.568 L). Possible subgroups within this size category are: 0.531–0.550 L and 0.586–0.609 L. Large cups range from 0.636 to 0.919 L (n=37; avg. 0.771 L). Possible subgroups within this size category are: 0.636–0.676 L, 0.696–0.782 L, 0.810–0.828 L, 0.848–0.879 L, and 0.915–0.919 L. Extra large cups have volumes between 0.976 and 1.758 L (n=17; avg. 1.096), with possible subgroups in the following ranges: 0.976–0.994 L, 1.024–1.072 L, 1.153–1.220 L, and 1.758 L. Fifteen cups from enclosure graves, one footed cup from a tholos tomb (**IX P4**) and one mug-like cup from an enclosure (**GR4 P1**), are represented in this category.

Single-handled, stemless cups are the most common vessel represented in the sample (n=88; avg. 0.648 L). They are associated with both tholos tombs and enclosure graves. Capacities range from extra small (0.049 L) to extra large (1.176 L). Footless cups found in the tholos tombs (n=10) tend to cluster in the small range of sizes (0.263–0.423 L), with only one (**IX P31**) in the medium range (0.474 L). This last vessel is an anomaly in many ways and may also represent one of the latest cups, associated with the Geometric amphora (**IX P58**) from Tomb IX (see this vol., Ch. 2, pp. 38, 44). The generally small sizes of cups from the tholos tombs, in comparison with the much larger ones from the enclosures, support the argument that there is a change in size over time, a phenomenon also noted at Knossos and Eleutherna, where cups get progressively larger, probably reaching a peak in the late eighth century (Coldstream 2001, 57; Kotsonas 2008, 207). In contrast, several examples found in enclosure graves can be categorized as extra large, ranging in net capacity from 0.976 L (**GR9 P13**) to 1.220 L (**GR6 P12**). The unique kantharos **G5 P11** (0.981 L) also falls within the extra large range. Footed cups in the sample (n=3; avg. 0.584 L) are attested only from Tholos IX. They range in vessel volume from extra small (**IX P34**; 0.168 L), to medium (**IX P2**; 0.546 L), to extra large (**IX P4**; 1.037 L).

Mug-like cups (n=8; avg. 0.742 L) range in maximum capacity from 0.380 to 1.758 L, corresponding to small, medium-large, large, and extra-large sizes. A mug-like cup from Grave 4 (**GR4 P1**), which also contained the smallest vessel in the sample (**GR4 P17**), is substantially larger than any other drinking vessel included in this study (1.758 L).

Wide-mouthed jugs (n=5; avg. 0.420) range in capacity from 0.294 to 0.531 L, with examples only in the small, medium, and medium large size categories.

Skyphoi and Kraters

Skyphoi (n=27; avg. 0.665 L) are the second most common shape represented in the Vronda sample. The clusters of sizes seen in the scatter plot of their capacities (Chart 15) indicate slightly different size categories than those proposed for the other drinking vessels. The small size category ranges from 0.242 to 0.276 L (n=3; avg. 0.264 L). The medium category has a range of 0.330 to 0.486 L (n=9; avg. 0.421 L). Large skyphoi have volumes between 0.571 and 0.805 L (n=8; avg. 0.703 L). The extra large examples fall within the range of 0.950 to 1.247 L (n=7; avg. 1.107).

None of the skyphoi in the sample can be classified as extra small, at least when compared to the cups, but in general they reflect the same overall range of capacities as the other drinking vessels (0.242–1.247 L; Chart 13). Stemless skyphoi (n=23; avg. 0.683 L) have the greatest range of capacities, varying from small to extra large. Stemmed skyphoi (n=4; avg. 0.559 L), however, fall only in the medium to large range of skyphoi.

Only two kraters were preserved well enough to be included in this study. The smallest (**GR4 P16**) has a maximum vessel volume of 5.375 L, over 4.3 times the capacity of the largest skyphos (**GR4 P15**, 1.247 L), which also happens to come from the same grave. The second krater (**GR6 P27**) is much larger and has a maximum potential capacity of 34.643 L, which is over 43 times the capacity of the largest skyphos (**GR6 P23**; 0.805 L) and 28.4 times the capacity of the largest cup (**GR6 P12**; 1.220 L) from the same grave.

Appendix B

Metallographic and Analytical (SEM-EDAX) Investigation of Metalwork from Early Iron Age Kavousi

Effie Photos-Jones

Excavations at the EIA cemeteries at Vronda produced a large collection of iron objects, including knives, daggers/dirks, spearheads, and arrowheads, along with tools and jewelry. The nearby settlement on the Kastro has produced blooms and slags, irrefutable evidence for iron making on site, perhaps even some of the artifacts from the graves (for the Kastro, see Coulson et al. 1997). The aim of the present study is to illuminate aspects of early iron metallurgy in Crete in the period from the late eighth to later seventh centuries B.C. The study is based on the examination, with the metallographic microscope as well as the scanning electron microscope attached to an energy-dispersive X-ray analyzer (SEM-EDAX), of small sections removed from the objects; it also provides microhardness testing of these sections.

Table 29 lists the objects for which permission to sample was granted by the Greek Archaeological Service. They derive from both the Vronda cemeteries and the Kastro. The ones from Kastro are associated with iron-making processes—that is, they are blooms/smithing hearth bottoms (SHBs). The Vronda cemeteries, as expected, held only finished objects; among those examined here are included iron axeheads and spearheads; also objects made of bronze. With the two sets of artifacts, from Kastro and Vronda, we are afforded a glimpse of the entire iron-making process from raw material to finished product.

Overall, 28 objects were sampled, and from them 40 samples were prepared as polished blocks (PBs); they are numbered KAV1–KAV40. Of the 40 PBs, only 15 were found to contain remaining metal (see column "Metallic?", Table 29). The main questions addressed are: what type of metal (wrought iron or steel) was produced at Kastro? Did the Kavousi smith prepare the "right" metal for the intended use of the object produced? We observe that the Kastro blooms and billets tend to be made of malleable, low carbon iron while carburization was introduced at the object forming stage and when deemed necessary. As mentioned in the Preface, this appendix represents work undertaken and completed in the late 1990s.

Iron Production Using the Bloomery Process

This section gives a brief account of the workings of the bloomery (iron making) furnace and the type of iron that was produced within. The aim is to set the Kavousi analytical results discussed in the sections below within the framework of that technology, which, for Europe and the Mediterranean, was the main method for making iron until the preindustrial period. The bloomery process, which continued in use well into the 19th century, but for specialized ironwork only, has often been called the "direct" process, because the conversion from iron ore to iron metal takes place directly, or in one step. This step involves the reduction (loss of oxygen) of the iron oxide (magnetite, hematite, limonite) to metallic iron plus slag. The latter consists of all unwanted ore impurities, namely silica, alkali and alkaline soils, and other ore impurities. The bloomery furnace comprised a shaft furnace, no higher than 2 m (but often much lower than that); the ore was charged from the top, and there was a small outlet at the bottom. Figure 175 provides a schematic illustration of such a furnace, as well as a breakdown of temperatures and conditions within. Ore and fuel (charcoal) were loaded in a layered manner from the top of the furnace. Most early bloomery furnaces were operated with hand-driven bellows, but from the Medieval period onward in Europe, low shaft furnaces became taller and used waterpower to drive their bellows. This led to the development of the blast furnace, which generated molten iron, evenly carburized throughout (2%–4% carbon). In Europe, the blast furnace was introduced, as already mentioned, at the end of the post-Medieval period, but in China it already was known much earlier and by the end of the first millennium B.C.

In the bloomery furnace, iron oxide is converted to iron metal while in the solid state, with only the slag being molten (ca. 900°–1,100°C). The slag represents all the non-ferrous minerals present in the original charge. The melting point of iron is ca. 1,500°C, a temperature range well beyond what could be achieved in the bloomery. It follows that iron was never molten (other than in small localized spots and near the hottest zone of the furnace). Bloomery iron was low in carbon (less than 0.1%) because the carbon, in the form of carbon monoxide originating from the burning of fuel, was absorbed by the iron metal as it formed, the diffusion rate being relatively slow. Because conditions varied within different parts of the furnace, it also follows that the metal formed would end up with an uneven distribution of carbon throughout its matrix.

The solid lump of iron metal produced in the bloomery furnace was called the bloom, and it formed physically just below the area of the tuyère (the ceramic tube connecting the furnace interior with the hand driven bellows; Fig. 175). The bloom consisted of a mixture of metal and slag trapped within. That slag had to be physically "squeezed out" by hammering while it lay hot in a hearth, usually set up separate from the smelting furnace. The bloom was consolidated into a billet (a lump of iron relatively free of slag carried over from the smelting furnace) and then shaped into a bar. These bars were then worked into functional objects by smiths. It has been assumed blooms and billets were manufactured at smelting sites, usually away from urban areas, and that iron metal was exchanged in the shape of bars. This model is, however, rather generalized and does not need to be applied to Crete in the Early Iron Age.

Unlike slag, which can be ubiquitous in archaeological sites, bloomery furnaces and smithing hearths usually leave very few material remains, and as such they tend to be rare. Bloomery iron making in northern Greece has received attention from the present author both in terms of metals analyses—for example, the metallographic analysis of iron artifacts from Vergina (Photos 1992) as well as Eastern Macedonia in the EIA and later periods (Photos 1987, 1989; Photos, Koukouli-Chrysanthaki, and Gialoglou 1987; Photos et al. 1989)—and more recently and in summary form by Nerantzis Nerantzis (2015, 52–59) and Giorgos Sanidas and colleagues (2016). This short appendix was compiled in 1999, and it does not cover recent research on EIA iron making in Crete or in other parts of Greece. Neither does it attempt to place early iron metallurgy in Crete in a broader cultural context; instead, it is simply reporting on the finds analyzed. In reference to Crete, and for the later periods, it is worth consulting the work by Eleni Filippaki, Yannis Bassiakos, and Barbara Hayden (2014) on mainly Late Roman–Byzantine iron slag from Priniatikos Pyrgos, near Hagios Nikolaos in East Crete.

As mentioned above, the solid lump of iron, the bloom, would almost invariably contain unevenly distributed amounts of carbon throughout its matrix. Metallurgically, it would consist of wrought iron (<0.1% carbon) to low carbon steel (0.3%–0.8% carbon). Steel, as a material, reflects both a carbon content as well as a method of manufacturing. The latter involves fast cooling or quenching of the artifact from a particular temperature range, ca. 720°C, to room temperature; in the process a hard phase, martensite, is formed. Consistent presence of martensite in metallographic sections suggests that the metalworkers had an understanding of how to manufacture steel.

In iron-carbon alloys the following phases, which are mentioned in the text below, can be discerned:

(1) Ferrite is a magnetic form of iron, soft and almost devoid of carbon (ca. 0.01% carbon) but capable of containing various amounts of other elements, such as phosphorus.

(2) Cementite, iron carbide (Fe_3C), is a very hard and brittle phase.

(3) Pearlite is a mixture of ferrite and cementite with carbon, usually laminated in form but also spheroidized. Spheroidization occurs when lamellar pearlite is heated for a prolonged period near or below 700°C.

(4) Martensite is a phase resulting from the quenching (rapid cooling) of carbon containing iron from temperatures of ca. 720°C to room temperature or above. As this phase is very brittle, it is usually necessary to soften the hard and brittle constituent by heating it for a short time at temperatures between 100° and 650°C. This process is called tempering, by which a combination of properties are achieved: namely hardness (the ability to withstand indentation) and toughness (the ability to withstand cracking; Verhoeven 2007, 9–19). If the total composition of carbon within the iron is 0.4%, the section will appear to contain equal amounts of ferrite and pearlite. At 0.8% carbon the entire section consists of pearlite only.

While the Fe-C alloy forms within the bloomery furnace, another early iron alloy, Fe-P, can form naturally from phosphorus-rich iron ores. Phosphorus (P) is a common impurity in many iron ores and is seen in sections of tools and weapons dating to the pre-Roman and Roman Iron Age (600 B.C. to A.D. 300; Kaloyeros and Ehrenreich 1990). Cold hammering of low phosphorus iron increases the hardness of the metal. However, the presence of phosphorus in steel increases the tensile strength, but at the cost of reducing ductility and shock resistance (Rostoker and Bronson 1990, 22; Tylecote 1992, 144). Phosphorus is thought to distribute within the metal, but it has been shown that it can be carried in slag inclusions in metal artifacts, where it can occur in high concentrations.

As will be demonstrated below (see Table 31), there is no strong corroborative evidence for the use of phosphorus-rich iron ores at Kavousi, nor is there evidence for deliberate manufacture of steel. As we shall demonstrate, Kavousi iron was largely ferritic iron.

Iron Objects from Vronda and Kastro and Their Examination with Optical and Scanning Electron Microscopy and Microhardness Testing

Forty samples from 28 objects from both Vronda and the Kastro (KAV1–KAV40; Table 29) were prepared as polished blocks (see below) for examination and analysis. This means that for some objects there was more than one sample removed. Most of the 40 samples revealed an advanced state of corrosion, and therefore little can be said about the type and quality of metal produced. Only 13 samples deriving from 10 objects showed clear signs of metal being present and therefore were examined closely both optically as well as with the SEM-EDAX. They can be divided into four groups:

Group I, comprising blooms/billets, includes PBs KAV1, KAV14, KAV16, and KAV17 (Table

29); also to that group belong samples KAV4 and KAV10, deriving from one object (K 20014). All five originate from the Kastro (Table 29) and form one group, since they reflect iron-making processes. The other three groups derive from Vronda. Group II, axe-heads, includes PBs KAV11 and KAV26, both from one object (**GR9 M40**; Table 29). Group III, spearheads, includes KAV33 and KAV35 (**GR26 M3** and **GR26 M2**, respectively; Table 29). Finally, Group IV, miscellany, includes PBs KAV15, KAV21 (both from object **GR 9 M2**), and PB KAV29 (**GR26 M4**; Table 29).

Wedge-shaped sections were removed from the sampled objects and mounted on resin for the preparation of polished blocks. The sections were ground with silicon carbide papers (of increasing fineness: 260, 400, 800, 1200 grades) and polished with a diamond paste of increasingly small size (6 μm, 3 μm, 1 μm grades). The polished sections were etched with a solution of 4% nital, a solution of nitric acid and alcohol, which helps reveal the microstructure of iron and steel.

The results are presented in Table 30 and Plates 76A–83B, which should be read in tandem. They are based on the study of metallographic sections seen under the optical (metallographic) microscope as well as their examination with the scanning electron microscope. The latter was a Jeol instrument, located at Glasgow University's Geographical and Earth Sciences Department. The SEM images of the sections under examination shown in the plates were obtained either in the back scattered (BS) or secondary emission (SE) modes. Microhardness testing was carried out at the former metallurgy department of Strathclyde University on a Vickers Hardness tester. Values are registered in H_v units and reflect the indentation made by a load tipped with diamond on the surface of the metal. The depth and size of indentation is an indication of the resistance of the metal to the load. The higher the H_v value, the harder the metal, with ferrite being softer than pearlite. Table 31 presents compositional analyses (on a phase-by-phase basis) of slag inclusions trapped within the metal.

Results and Discussion

The cremation cemetery at Vronda and the settlement at the Kastro have produced a total of 172 iron objects dating from the late eighth to late seventh centuries B.C. As noted above, on the basis of the metallographic investigation of only a small number of PBs (of the 40 PBs prepared only a small percentage thereof were suitable for analysis), the Kavousi iron metalwork can be divided into four groups.

Group I includes 6 samples from 5 objects, all from the Kastro: KAV1 (Pl. 76A), KAV4 (Pls. 76B, 76C), KAV10 (Pls. 77A, 77B), KAV14 (Pls. 78A, 78B), KAV16 (Pl. 79A), and KAV17 (Pl. 79B). The Kastro blooms and billets are unique finds because of the scarcity of their occurrence and the fact that they were found within several rooms (44, 47, 56; see Coulson et al. 1997, 316, fig. 1). Their find spots may indicate "slag scatter" or may be associated with one or more bloom smithing hearths within the corresponding rooms. We have no data as to the type and amounts of slag found within these rooms; neither do we know whether there has been evidence for fired clay fragments or scorched areas on the room floor.

Metallographically, the blooms/billets are characterized by varied amounts of metallic iron and slag phases consisting of crystalline phases (iron oxide) and fayalite (iron silicate), and a glassy phase consisting of calcium iron silicate. Samples KAV1, KAV4, and KAV10 are metallic throughout, making them more akin to "billets" (metal that is in the process of being shaped into a bar), while KAV14, KAV16, and KAV17 are primarily a combination of metallic iron with various slag phases, making them more akin to products of the stage before billet making—namely, bloom smithing. Samples KAV1, KAV4, and KAV10 are characterized by varied amounts of carbon within the iron. Sample KAV1 is primarily ferritic, while samples KAV4 and KAV10 have a higher carbon content, which may have been imparted following working at the hearth. At the smithing hearth, the bloom can either be further carburized or decarburized according to the smith's skill and/or requirements.

The presence of copper-tin inclusions (ca. 5% and in roughly equal amounts) within the metallic iron phase of KAV1 (see Table 31) suggests that the hearth may have been used for additional purposes, such as bronze making or working. The ratio of copper to tin varies from ca. 1:1 to 9:1 (the usual ratio for a bronze alloy), a proportion that suggests "contamination" of the hearth by metallic tin in the presence of metallic copper (see, e.g., "unusual" phases [SnO/SnS] in KAV21). Therefore, we cannot be confident as to the origin of these nonferrous inclusions. Nevertheless, the presence of copper, albeit in very small amounts, is a recurring theme within the Kavousi artifacts.

It is important to emphasize that the metallic and non-metallic phases analyzed with SEM-EDAX reflect the localized conditions of temperature and the CO/CO_2 ratios prevailing within the furnace/hearth. It can be safely argued that the metal coming out of the bloomery process, albeit inherently non-homogeneous, was iron with a low carbon content. As such, it would have been worked quite easily.

Group II consists of shaped artifacts primarily made of ferrite, which are evident in an axe-head consisting of soft ferrite with long nitride needles (KAV11 and KAV26). Ferritic iron is soft iron. Nitride needles tend to form during prolonged heating in a reducing environment. It is not possible to discern whether that reducing environment was present in the smithing hearth while the object was being shaped or at any later stage (e.g., had the object been placed in a cremation pyre). In any case, nitride needles do not increase the hardness of the object by any substantial amount. Consequently, this ferritic iron would not have been very useful as a cutting edge; the action of an axe head is mostly on impact. Samples KAV11 and KAV26 could have been produced from a section of the bloom similar to KAV1, but following removal of high carbon areas and with only the ferritic areas involved.

We come now to Group III, the spearheads (KAV-33, KAV35). These samples also consist of ferrite iron, but they have a multitude of slag inclusions. Again, extensive nitriding of the surface is evident. Spearheads and arrowheads were primarily made of ferritic iron, their effectiveness relying on penetration or piercing as a result of the throwing action rather than on a cutting edge. What is of concern here is the presence of many slag inclusions following the line of working, as shown in Plate 81.

Group IV consists of iron-carbon alloys, pearlite, and ferrite. The dagger KAV29 is the only highly carburized object. Carburization is spread throughout and not restricted to the edge, suggesting that the object would have been brittle on impact. It is possible the dagger was ceremonial. It may have derived from highly carburized sections of the bloom like KAV4 and KAV10, or it may have been further carburized while in the hearth. The consistent use of ferritic iron for axe-heads and spearheads and of highly carburized iron for dirks or daggers suggests a good empirical understanding of the properties of the iron-carbon alloy on the part of the Early Iron Age Cretan smith. In summary, and on the basis of the available evidence, it can be argued that the Kavousi iron smith knew how to suit his metal to the intended function of the finished object.

The final group includes copper/bronze metalwork, as in the case of KAV15 and KAV21, both PBs deriving from the same object (**GR9 M2**). The X-ray radiography of the same object (see Pl. 34) shows a uniform metallic content (leaded bronze) throughout, also observed in Plate 82A where the metallic matrix appears sound and relatively corrosion free. Plate 82C shows a close-up of the matrix with corrosion growing at the grain boundaries. Alternately, KAV15, the PB of a section removed from another area of the same artifact, shows two metals, bronze and iron (Plate 82B). Plate 82D shows the bronze alloy to be "enveloped" in iron. This unique object may suggest a familiarity on the part of Kavousi smiths in working with a combination of metals, either as part of an original design or as part of a mending operation. Copper-iron metalwork has been documented elsewhere in Greece, in Thasos (Photos 1992) and Macedonia (Photos, Koukouli-Chrysanthaki, and Gialoglou 1987), as well as at EIA Lefkandi (Jones 1979–1980).

Iron and Copper Ores: Sources

The question of where the iron ore sources were located, and whether they are associated with phosphrus-rich deposits that occur, for example, in West Crete (Varoufakis 1989), cannot be answered with confidence. The P_2O_5 values in Table 31 do not strongly support the use of phosphorus-rich iron ores.

It has been argued that Crete has no substantial deposits of copper ore (Muhly and Kassianidou 2012, 121). Faure (1966) has documented the existence of small-scale deposits, many of which, significantly, are associations of copper and iron minerals such as primary sulfide with chalcopyrite and magnetite, as well as with secondary minerals such as malachite or azurite with limonite. Examples of such deposits in East Crete occur in the areas near Katharo and Milatos (both in the Lasithi district to the west of Kavousi), the former area having copper and iron sulfides associated with volcanic rocks (Faure 1966, 49). Iron minerals include limonite, siderite, ankerite, hematite, and magnetite, as well as the sulfides pyrite and chalcopyrite. Copper minerals include chalcopyrite, copper sulfides, and malachite or azurite.

Appendix C

Concordance of Excavation Inventory Numbers with Catalog Numbers and Museum Numbers

Inventory Number	Catalog Number	Ierapetra Museum Number	Hagios Nikolaos Museum Number	Herakleion Museum Number
V81.1	IX P55	—	—	—
V84.64a	GR1 M2	—	HNM 15729	—
V84.64b	GR1 M4	—	HNM 15729	—
V84.64c	GR1 M3	—	HNM 15729	—
V84.64d	GR1 M5	—	HNM 15729	—
V84.65a	GR1 M6	—	HNM 15730	—
V84.65b	GR1 M7	—	HNM 15730	—
V84.65c	GR1 M8	—	HNM 15730	—
V84.65d	GR1 M9	—	HNM 15730	—
V84.65e	GR1 M10	—	HNM 15730	—
V84.65f	GR1 M11	—	HNM 15730	—
V84.65g	GR1 M12	—	HNM 15730	—
V84.65h	GR1 M13	—	HNM 15730	—
V84.66a	GR1 M14	—	HNM 15731	—
V84.66b+g	GR1 M15	—	HNM 15731	—
V84.66c	GR1 M16	—	HNM 15731	—
V84.66d	GR1 M17	—	HNM 15731	—
V84.66f	GR1 M18	—	—	—
V84.67	GR1 S1	IM 1013	—	—
V84.68	GR1 M1	—	—	—
V84.77	GR1 P1	—	—	—

Inventory Number	Catalog Number	Ierapetra Museum Number	Hagios Nikolaos Museum Number	Herakleion Museum Number
V84.78	GR1 P2	—	—	—
V87.13	GR3 ST1	IM 852	—	—
V87.14	GR4 TC1	IM 853	—	—
V87.21	GR3 TC1	IM 860	—	—
V87.32	GR3 P18	IM 874	—	—
V87.33	GR3 P19	IM 875	—	—
V87.34	GR3 P16	IM 924	—	—
V87.35	GR3 P1	IM 963	—	—
V87.36	GR3 P9	IM 925	—	—
V87.43	GR3 P5	IM 926	—	—
V87.64	GR6 TC1	IM 890	—	—
V87.68	GR4 P17	IM 965	—	—
V87.69	GR4 P3	IM 964	—	—
V87.80	GR5 ST1	IM 897	—	—
V87.81	GR6 ST1	IM 898	—	—
V87.83	GR4 P25	—	—	—
V87.84	GR4 P7	IM 966	—	—
V87.89	GR4 P20	—	—	—
V87.90	GR4 P1	—	—	—
V87.91	GR4 P12	—	—	—
V87.92	GR3 P2	IM 974	—	—
V87.93	GR3 M1	IM 899	HNM 15732	—
V87.94	GR4 M1	IM 900	HNM 15733	—
V87.95	GR4 M2	IM 901	HNM 15734	—
V87.96	GR5 M7	IM 936	HNM 15735	—
V87.97	GR5 M11	IM 937	—	—
V87.98a	GR5 M2	IM 938	—	—
V87.98b	GR5 M3	IM 938	—	—
V87.99	GR5 M10	IM 939	—	—
V87.100	GR5 M12	IM 940	—	—
V87.101	GR5 M4	IM 941	—	—
V87.102	GR5 M7	IM 942	HNM 15735	—
V87.103	GR5 M9	IM 943	—	—
V87.104	GR5 M8	IM 944	—	—
V87.105	GR3 M3	IM 945	—	—
V87.106	GR6 M4	IM 946	—	—
V87.107	GR6 M8	IM 947	—	—
V87.108	GR6 M10	IM 948	HNM 15737	—
V87.109	GR6 M8	IM 950	—	—
V87.110	GR6 M8	IM 949	—	—
V87.111	GR6 M7	IM 951	—	—
V87.112	GR6 M15	IM 952	—	—
V87.113	GR6 M14	IM 953	HNM 15738	—
V87.114	GR6 M17	IM 954	HNM 15739	—
V87.115	GR6 M18	IM 955	—	—

APPENDIX C. CONCORDANCE OF EXCAVATION INVENTORY NUMBERS

Inventory Number	Catalog Number	Ierapetra Museum Number	Hagios Nikolaos Museum Number	Herakleion Museum Number
V87.116	**GR6 M17**	IM 956	HNM 15739	—
V87.117	**GR6 M5**	IM 957	—	—
V87.118	**GR6 M13**	IM 958	HNM 15740	—
V87.119	**GR6 M6**	IM 959	—	—
V87.120	**GR6 M7**	IM 960	—	—
V87.121	**GR6 M11**	IM 961	HNM 15741	—
V87.122a	**GR6 M19**	IM 962	—	—
V87.122e	**GR6 M20**	IM 962	—	—
V87.123	**GR6 P5**	IM 929	—	—
V87.127	**GR4 P13**	IM 968	—	—
V87.128	**GR5 P2**	IM 969	—	—
V87.134	**GR3 P6**	IM 975	—	—
V87.135	**GR3 P20**	IM 973	—	—
V87.137	**GR3 M2**	IM 978	—	—
V87.138	**GR5 M1**	IM 979	—	—
V87.140	**GR6 M9**	—	—	—
V87.141	**GR6 M12**	—	—	—
V87.142a	**GR6 M21**	—	—	—
V87.142b	**GR6 M22**	—	—	—
V87.144	**GR6 M16**	—	—	—
V88.4	**GR16 ST1**	—	—	—
V88.55	**GR16 P14**	—	—	—
V88.56	**GR17 P3**	—	—	—
V88.57	**GR16 P3**	—	—	—
V88.58	**GR16 P2**	—	—	—
V88.59	**GR9 P38**	—	—	—
V88.60	**GR17 P7**	—	—	—
V88.66	**GR17 P2**	—	—	—
V88.68	**GR16 P3**	—	—	—
V88.70	**GR16 P6**	—	—	—
V88.71	**GR16 P15**	—	—	—
V88.74	**GR12 TC1**	IM 1003	—	—
V88.76	**GR19 TC1**	IM 1005	—	—
V88.77	**GR9 S1**	IM 1004	—	—
V88.84	**GR9 P6**	—	—	—
V88.85	**GR16 M6**	—	—	—
V88.86	GR12 M37	—	HNM 15752	—
V88.87	**GR16 M3**	—	—	—
V88.88	**GR16 M7**	—	—	—
V88.89	**GR12 M5**	—	HNM 15753	—
V88.90	**GR12 M6**	—	HNM 15754	—
V88.91	**GR16 M2**	—	—	—
V88.92	**GR12 M31**	—	HNM 15755	—
V88.93	**GR12 M28**	—	—	—
V88.94	**GR17 M6**	—	—	—

Inventory Number	Catalog Number	Ierapetra Museum Number	Hagios Nikolaos Museum Number	Herakleion Museum Number
V88.95	GR12 M24	—	—	—
V88.96	GR12 M27	—	—	—
V88.97	GR12 M25	—	—	—
V88.98	GR12 M26	—	—	—
V88.99	GR17 M4	—	—	—
V88.100	GR12 M35	—	—	—
V88.101	GR12 M21	—	—	—
V88.102	Uncataloged	—	—	—
V88.103	GR17 M7	—	HNM 15765	—
V88.104	GR17 M5	—	—	—
V88.105	GR12 M10	—	HNM 15756	—
V88.106	GR12 M20	—	HNM 15757	—
V88.107	GR12 M11	—	HNM 15758	—
V88.108	GR12 M7	—	HNM 15759	—
V88.109	GR12 M9	—	HNM 15760	—
V88.110	GR12 M13	—	—	—
V88.111	GR12 M32	—	—	—
V88.112	GR12 M22	—	—	—
V88.113	GR9 M46	IM 1186	—	—
V88.114	GR12 M29	—	—	—
V88.115	GR12 M42	—	—	—
V88.116	GR12 M12	—	—	—
V88.117	GR12 M33	—	—	—
V88.118	GR12 M34	—	—	—
V88.119a	GR16 M4	—	—	—
V88.119b	GR16 M5	—	—	—
V88.121	GR12 M8	—	HNM 15761	—
V88.122	GR12 M17	—	—	—
V88.123	GR12 M16	—	—	—
V88.124	GR12 M15	—	—	—
V88.126a	GR12 M38	—	—	—
V88.126b	GR12 M40	—	—	—
V88.127	GR12 M23	—	—	—
V88.128	GR12 M41	—	—	—
V88.129	GR12 M14	—	—	—
V88.130	GR9 M2	IM 1184	—	—
V88.131a	GR12 M18	—	—	—
V88.131b	GR12 M19	—	—	—
V88.132a	GR12 M39	—	—	—
V88.132b	GR12 M44	—	—	—
V88.133	GR12 M30	—	—	—
V88.134	GR12 M36	—	HNM 15762	—
V88.135	GR12 M43	—	—	—
V88.136	GR12 M1	—	HNM 15763	—
V88.137	GR17 M3	—	—	—

APPENDIX C. CONCORDANCE OF EXCAVATION INVENTORY NUMBERS

Inventory Number	Catalog Number	Ierapetra Museum Number	Hagios Nikolaos Museum Number	Herakleion Museum Number
V88.139	GR17 M1	—	—	—
V88.140	VIII M1	—	—	—
V88.141	GR12 M4	—	—	—
V88.144	IV M7	—	—	—
V88.145	GR12 M2	—	HNM 15764	—
V88.150	GR20 B1	IM 1008	—	—
V88.151	IV S2	IM 1009	—	—
V88.155	GR9 M19	IM 1195	HNM 15742	—
V88.156	GR9 M20	—	—	—
V88.157	GR9 M18	IM 1201	HNM 15743	—
V88.158	GR9 M1	IM 1176	—	—
V88.159	GR9 M45	IM 1187	—	—
V88.169	GR9 M3	IM 1199	—	—
V88.170	GR9 M13	IM 1182	—	—
V88.171	GR9 M48	IM 1183	—	—
V88.172	GR9 M4	—	—	—
V88.173	GR9 M22	IM 1188	—	—
V88.174	GR9 M26	IM 1189	—	—
V88.175	GR9 M39	IM 1190	—	—
V88.178	GR9 M30	IM 1198	—	—
V88.179	GR9 M14	IM 1191	—	—
V88.180	GR9 M17	IM 1200	—	—
V88.181	GR9 M44	IM 1177	HNM 15745	—
V88.182	Uncataloged	—	—	—
V88.183	GR9 M15	IM 1185	—	—
V88.184	GR9 M35	IM 1193	HNM 15744	—
V88.186	GR9 M33	IM 1194	HNM 15746	—
V88.187	GR9 M38	IM 1196	—	—
V88.188	GR9 M28	IM 1180	—	—
V88.189	GR9 M25	IM 1181	—	—
V88.190	GR9 M7	—	—	—
V88.191	GR9 M27	IM 1178	—	—
V88.192	GR9 M43	IM 1179	—	—
V88.193	GR9 M32	IM 1204	—	—
V88.194	GR9 M31	IM 1203	—	—
V88.195	GR9 M24	IM 1192	—	—
V88.196	GR9 M40	IM 1202	HNM 15747	—
V88.197	GR9 M42	IM 1197	HNM 15748	—
V88.198	GR9 M29	IM 1212	—	—
V88.199	GR9 M23	IM 1206	—	—
V88.200	GR9 M49	IM 1210	—	—
V88.201	GR9 M21	IM 1213	HNM 15749	—
V88.202	GR9 M41	IM 1205	HNM 15750	—
V88.203	GR9 M8	IM 1218	—	—
V88.204	GR9 P31	—	—	—

Inventory Number	Catalog Number	Ierapetra Museum Number	Hagios Nikolaos Museum Number	Herakleion Museum Number
V88.206	**GR9 M34**	IM 1215	—	—
V88.207	**GR9 M11**	IM 1216	—	—
V88.208	**GR9 M9**	IM 1217	—	—
V88.209	**GR9 M8**	IM 1218	—	—
V88.210	**GR9 M5**	IM 1219	—	—
V88.211	**GR9 M6**	—	—	—
V88.212	**GR9 M10**	IM 1220	—	—
V88.213	**GR9 M37**	IM 1208	—	—
V88.214	**GR9 M25**	IM 1211	—	—
V88.215	**GR9 M51**	IM 1209	—	—
V88.216	**GR9 M36**	IM 1207	—	—
V88.217	**GR9 M16**	IM 1214	—	—
V88.222	**GR17 M2**	—	—	—
V88.223	**GR16 M1**	—	—	—
V88.224	**GR12 P13**	—	—	—
V88.226	**GR9 M47**	—	HNM 15751	—
V88.227a	**GR9 M52**	—	—	—
V88.227b	**GR9 M53**	—	—	—
V88.228	**GR9 M54**	—	—	—
V88.229	**GR9 M55**	—	—	—
V88.230	**GR20 M8**	IM 1221	—	—
V88.231	**GR20 M9**	IM 1222	HNM 15736	—
V88.232	**GR20 M7**	IM 1223	—	—
V88.233	**GR20 M10**	—	—	—
V88.235	**GR20 M4**	—	—	—
V88.236	**GR20 M3**	—	—	—
V88.237	**GR20 M1**	—	—	—
V88.238	**GR20 M2**	—	—	—
V88.241	**GR20 S1**	—	—	—
V88.242	**GR12 P27**	—	—	—
V88.249	**GR12 M45**	—	—	—
V88.250	**GR12 M46**	—	—	—
V88.251	**GR9 M50**	—	—	—
V88.252	**GR9 M12**	—	—	—
V88.253	**GR20 M5**	—	—	—
V88.254	**GR20 M6**	—	—	—
V88.255	**GR12 M3**	—	—	—
V89.26	**GR23 S1**	IM 1001	—	—
V89.27	**GR23 S2**	IM 1002	—	—
V89.28	**GR21 S1**	—	—	—
V89.29	**VIII M2**	—	—	—
V89.30	**GR28 P2**	IM 1242	—	—
V89.37	**GR21 P11**	IM 1244	—	—
V89.38	**GR26 P13**	IM 1237	—	—
V89.39	**GR23 P3**	IM 1239	—	—

APPENDIX C. CONCORDANCE OF EXCAVATION INVENTORY NUMBERS

Inventory Number	Catalog Number	Ierapetra Museum Number	Hagios Nikolaos Museum Number	Herakleion Museum Number
V89.46	GR28 S1	—	—	—
V89.48	GR23 ST1	—	—	—
V89.52	GR28 P26	IM 1238	—	—
V89.53	GR28 P4	IM 1248	—	—
V89.54	GR28 P22	IM 1246	—	—
V89.55	GR28 P19	IM 1241	—	—
V89.56	GR21 P9	IM 1243	—	—
V89.57	GR21 P12	IM 1240	—	—
V89.65	GR28 P3	IM 1245	—	—
V89.66	GR28 M5	—	—	—
V89.67	GR28 M6	—	—	—
V89.68	GR21 P8	IM 1249	—	—
V89.71	GR29 M1	—	—	—
V89.73	GR23 M2	—	—	—
V89.74	GR23 M1	—	—	—
V89.76	GR23 M3	—	—	—
V89.77	GR32 M1	—	—	—
V89.78	GR28 M1	—	—	—
V89.79	GR28 P9	—	—	—
V89.81	GR28 P7	—	—	—
V89.82	GR28 P11	—	—	—
V89.84	GR28 P5	—	—	—
V89.85	GR28 P6	—	—	—
V89.86	GR28 P8	—	—	—
V89.87	GR30 P33	—	—	—
V89.91	GR28 M4	—	—	—
V89.92	GR21 M3	—	—	—
V89.93	GR21 M1	—	—	—
V89.94	GR21 M2	—	—	—
V89.95	GR27 M1	—	—	—
V89.96	GR23 M4	—	—	—
V89.97	GR28 M2	—	—	—
V89.98	GR28 M3	—	—	—
V90.37	GR30 TC1	IM 989	—	—
V90.39	GR30 TC2	IM 983	—	—
V90.50	GR26 TC1	IM 996	—	—
V90.55	GR36 S1	IM 986	—	—
V90.58	GR32 P1	IM 1231	—	—
V90.85	GR36 ST1	—	—	—
V90.116	GR36 TC1	IM 991	—	—
V90.117	GR36 TC2	IM 992	—	—
V90.118	GR36 TC3	IM 990	—	—
V90.119	GR36 TC4	IM 993	—	—
V90.120	GR36 TC5	IM 994	—	—
V90.123	GR36 B1	IM 987	—	—

Inventory Number	Catalog Number	Ierapetra Museum Number	Hagios Nikolaos Museum Number	Herakleion Museum Number
V90.126	GR36 G1	—	—	—
V90.134	GR32 G1	—	—	—
V90.135	GR26 M3	—	—	—
V90.136	GR26 M1	—	—	—
V90.137	GR26 M2	—	—	—
V90.138a	GR26 M4	—	—	—
V90.138b	GR30 M10	—	—	—
V90.139	GR30 M12	—	—	—
V90.140	GR30 M8	—	—	—
V90.141	GR30 M4	—	—	—
V90.142	GR30 M14	—	—	—
V90.143	GR30 M1	—	—	—
V90.144	GR30 M3	—	HNM 15766	—
V90.145	GR30 M6	—	—	—
V90.146	GR30 M2	—	—	—
V90.147	GR30 M15	—	—	—
V90.148	GR30 M7	—	—	—
V90.149	GR30 M11	—	—	—
V90.153	GR36 M1	—	—	—
V90.154	GR36 M2	—	—	—
V90.155	GR36 M3	—	—	—
V90.156	GR30 M5	—	—	—
V98.1	GR4 P16	—	—	—
V98.43	IX P10	—	—	—
V98.44	IX P11	—	—	—
V98.45	IX P24	—	—	—
V98.46	IX P49	—	—	—
V98.71	GR21 P13	—	—	—
V98.81	GR4 P16	—	—	—
V98.82	GR6 P2	—	—	—
V98.83	GR6 P3	—	—	—
V98.84	GR6 P23	—	—	—
V98.85	GR6 P29	—	—	—
V98.86	GR9 P36	—	—	—
V98.87	GR9 P37	—	—	—
V98.88	GR9 P39	—	—	—
V98.89	GR10 P1	—	—	—
V98.90	GR9 P13	—	—	—
V98.91	GR9 P14	—	—	—
V98.92	GR9 P15	—	—	—
V98.93	GR9 P16	—	—	—
V98.94	GR12 P20	—	—	—
V98.95	GR6 P29	—	—	—
V98.96	GR12 P2	—	—	—
V98.97	GR12 P4	—	—	—
V98.99	GR12 P5	—	—	—

APPENDIX C. CONCORDANCE OF EXCAVATION INVENTORY NUMBERS 393

Inventory Number	Catalog Number	Ierapetra Museum Number	Hagios Nikolaos Museum Number	Herakleion Museum Number
V98.100	GR12 P6	—	—	—
V98.101	GR12 P7	—	—	—
V98.102	GR23 P2	—	—	—
V98.103	GR16 P17	—	—	—
V98.104	GR16 P18	—	—	—
V98.105	GR16 P4	—	—	—
V98.106	GR16 P7	—	—	—
V98.107	GR16 P5	—	—	—
V98.108	GR19 P3	—	—	—
V98.109	GR19 P2	—	—	—
V98.110	GR19 P7	—	—	—
V98.111	GR19 P8	—	—	—
V98.112	GR19 P5	—	—	—
V98.113	GR19 P15	—	—	—
V98.114	GR19 P13	—	—	—
V98.115	GR20 P7	—	—	—
V98.116	GR20 P1	—	—	—
V98.117	GR30 P6	—	—	—
V98.118	GR30 P7	—	—	—
V98.119	GR30 P28	—	—	—
V98.120	GR30 P5	—	—	—
V98.121	GR26 P4	—	—	—
V98.122	GR26 P20	—	—	—
V98.123	GR26 P23	—	—	—
V98.124	GR26 P22	—	—	—
V98.125	GR32 P2	—	—	—
V98.126	GR36 P6	—	—	—
V98.127	GR36 P1	—	—	—
V98.128	GR36 P4	—	—	—
V98.129	GR36 P5	—	—	—
V98.130	GR36 P9	—	—	—
V98.131	GR36 P2	—	—	—
V98.132	GR36 P8	—	—	—
V98.204	GR26 P7	—	—	—
V98.205	GR26 P8	—	—	—
V98.206	GR26 P9	—	—	—
V98.207	GR26 P10	—	—	—
V98.208	GR26 P11	—	—	—
V98.209	GR26 P5	—	—	—
V98.210	GR26 P14	—	—	—
V98.211	GR26 P15	—	—	—
V98.212	GR26 P12	—	—	—
V98.213	GR26 P6	—	—	—
V98.214	GR26 P17	—	—	—
—	GR M1	—	—	HM 12
—	Chondrovolakes 1	—	—	HM 1977

Inventory Number	Catalog Number	Ierapetra Museum Number	Hagios Nikolaos Museum Number	Herakleion Museum Number
—	II-VII-VIII P1	—	—	HM 3693
—	II-VII-VIII P2	—	—	HM 1019
—	II P1	—	—	HM 1972
—	IV P1	—	—	HM 1971
—	IV P2	—	—	HM 1969
—	IV P3	—	—	HM 1963
—	IV P4	—	—	HM 1965
—	IV P5	—	—	HM 1966
—	IV P6	—	—	HM 1976
—	IV P7	—	—	HM 1975
—	IV P8	—	—	HM 1962
—	IV P9	—	—	HM 1959
—	IV P10	—	—	HM 1961
—	IV M1	—	—	HM 519
—	IV M2	—	—	HM 520
—	IV M3	—	—	HM 521
—	IV M4	—	—	HM 522
—	IV M5	—	—	HM 523
—	VII P1	—	—	HM 3692
—	VII P2	—	—	HM 1970
—	VII P3	—	—	HM 1964
—	VII P4	—	—	HM 1960 bis
—	VII M1	—	—	HM 518
—	VIII P1	—	—	HM 1968
—	IX P2	IM 552	—	—
—	IX P4	IM 551	—	—
—	IX P6	IM 117	—	—
—	IX P7	IM 154	—	—
—	IX P12	IM 763	—	—
—	IX P13	IM 175	—	—
—	IX P16	IM 162	—	—
—	IX P18	IM 757	—	—
—	IX P19	IM 548	—	—
—	IX P20	IM 546	—	—
—	IX P21	IM 549	—	—
—	IX P22	IM 592	—	—
—	IX P27	IM 759	—	—
—	IX P28	IM 789	—	—
—	IX P29	IM 786	—	—
—	IX P34	IM 812	—	—
—	IX P42	IM 767	—	—
—	IX P45	IM 685	—	—
—	IX P50	IM 788	—	—
—	IX P53	IM 547	—	—
—	IX P58	IM 550	—	—
—	IX P59	IM 153	—	—

References

Abbreviations follow the conventions of the *American Journal of Archaeology*.

Abrahams, P.H., S.C. Marks, and R.T. Hutchings. 2003. *McMinn's Color Atlas of Human Anatomy*, 5th ed., Edinburgh.

Agelarakis, A.P. 2005. *The Anthropology of Tomb A1K1 of Orthi Petra in Eleutherna: A Narrative of the Bones. Aspects of the Human Condition in Geometric–Archaic Eleutherna*, Athens.

Alcock, S.E. 2002. *Archaeologies of the Greek Past: Landscape, Monuments, and Memories*, Cambridge.

Andreadaki-Vlasaki, M. 1987. "An Early Greek Child Burial at Gavalomouri," *SMEA* 26, pp. 307–335.

———. 1991. "The Khania Area, ca. 1200–700 B.C.," in *La transizione dal Miceneo all'Alto Arcaismo: Dal palazzo alla città. Atti del Convegno Internazionale, Roma, 14–19 marzo 1988* (*Monografie scientifiche*), D. Musti, A. Sacconi, M. Rocchi, L. Rocchetti, E. Scafa, L. Sportiello, and M.E. Giannotta, eds., Rome, pp. 403–423.

———. 2004. "Η Κυδωνία της Δυτικής Κρήτης στα Πρώιμα Χρόνια του Σιδήρου," in Stampolides and Giannikouri, eds., pp. 21–34.

Angel, J.L. 1942. "A Preliminary Study of the Relations of Race to Culture, Based on Ancient Greek Skeletal Material," Ph.D. diss., Harvard University.

———. 1954. "Human Biology, Health, and History in Greece from First Settlement until Now," *Yearbook of the American Philosophical Society* 1954, pp. 168–172.

———. 1966. "Porotic Hyperostosis, Anemias, Malarias, and Marshes in the Prehistoric Eastern Mediterranean," *Science* 153, pp. 760–763.

———. 1971. *The People of Lerna: Analysis of a Prehistoric Aegean Population*, Princeton.

———. 1975. "Paleoecology, Paleodemography and Health," in *Population, Ecology and Social Evolution* (*World Anthropology*), S. Polgar, ed., The Hague, pp. 167–190.

———. 1978. "Porotic Hyperostosis in the Eastern Mediterranean," *Medical College of Virginia Quarterly* 14, pp. 10–16.

Angel, J.L., and S.C. Bisel. 1986. "Health and Stress in an Early Bronze Age Population," in *Ancient Anatolia:*

Aspects of Change and Cultural Development. Essays in Honor of Machteld J. Mellink, J.V. Canby, E. Porada, B.S. Ridgway, and T. Stech, eds., Madison, pp. 12–30.

Asmussen, B. 2009. "Intentional or Incidental Thermal Modification? Analysing Site Occupation via Burned Bone," *JAS* 36, pp. 528–536.

Åström, P. 1987. "Intentional Destruction of Grave Goods," in Thanatos: *Les coutumes funéraires en Egée à l'âge du Bronze. Actes du colloque de Liège (21–23 avril 1986)* (*Aegaeum* 1), R. Laffineur, ed., Liège, pp. 213–219.

Aufderheide, A.C., and C. Rodríguez-Martín. 1998. *The Cambridge Encyclopedia of Human Paleopathology*, Cambridge.

Avila, R.A.J. 1983. *Bronzene Lanzen- und Pfeilspitzen der griechischen Spätbronzezeit* (*Prähistorische Bronzefunde* V [1]), Munich.

Banks, P., and A. Brown. 2001. *Fractures of the Facial Skeleton*, Edinburgh.

Barber, E.W. 1991. *Prehistoric Textiles: The Development of Cloth in the Neolithic and Bronze Ages, with Special Reference to the Aegean*, Princeton.

Barber, G., I. Watt, and J. Rogers. 1997. "A Comparison of Radiological and Palaeopathological Diagnostic Criteria for Hyperostosis Frontalis Interna," *International Journal of Osteoarchaeology* 7, pp. 157–164.

Barnes, E. 1994. *Developmental Defects of the Axial Skeleton in Paleopathology*, Boulder.

Bass, G.F. 1961. "The Cape Gelidonya Wreck: Preliminary Report," *AJA* 65, pp. 267–276.

———. 1967. *Cape Gelidonya: A Bronze Age Shipwreck* (*TAPS*, n.s., 57 [8]), Philadelphia.

Bass, W.M., and R.L. Jantz. 2004. "Cremation Weights in East Tennessee," *Journal of Forensic Sciences* 49, pp. 901–904.

Bavazzano, A., P.L. del Bianco, E. del Bene, and V. Leoni. 1970. "A Statistical Evaluation of the Relationships between Headache and Internal Frontal Hyperostosis," *Research and Clinical Studies in Headache* 3, pp. 191–197.

Belcastro, M.G., A. Todero, G. Fornaciari, and V. Mariotti. 2011. "Hyperostosis Frontalis Interna (HFI) and Castration: The Case of the Famous Singer Farinelli (1705–1782)," *Journal of Anatomy* 219, pp. 632–637.

Betancourt, P.P. 2008. *The Bronze Age Begins: The Ceramics Revolution of Early Minoan I and the New Forms of Wealth that Transformed Prehistoric Society*, Philadelphia.

Bikaki, A.H. 1984. *Keos IV: Ayia Irini. The Potters' Marks*, Mainz.

Binford, L.R. 1971. "Mortuary Practices: Their Study and Their Potential," in *Approaches to the Social Dimensions of Mortuary Practices* (*Memoirs of the Society for American Archaeology* 25), J.A. Brown, ed., Washington, D.C., pp. 6–29.

Blandin, B. 2007. *Les pratiques funéraires d'époque géométrique à Érétrie: Espace des vivants, demeures des morts* (*Eretria* XVII), Lausanne.

Blegen, C.W. 1952. "Two Athenian Grave Groups of about 900 B.C.," *Hesperia* 21, pp. 279–294.

Blinkenberg, C. 1926. *Lindiaka V: Fibules grecques et orientales* (*Kongelig Danske videnskabernes selskab. Historosk-filologiske meddeleiser* XIII [1]), Copenhagen.

Boardman, J. 1960. "Protogeometric Graves at Agios Ioannis near Knossos (Knossos Survey 3)," *BSA* 55, pp. 128–148.

———. 1961. *The Cretan Collection at Oxford: The Dictaean Cave and Iron Age Crete*, Oxford.

———. 1971. "Ship Firedogs and Other Metalwork from Kavousi," *CretChron* 23, pp. 5–8.

Boileau, M.-C., and J. Whitley. 2010. "Patterns of Production and Consumption of Coarse to Semi-Fine Pottery at Early Iron Age Knossos," *BSA* 105, pp. 225–268.

Borgna, E., I. Caloi, F.M. Carinci, and R. Laffineur, eds. 2019. Μνημη/Mneme: *Past and Memory in the Aegean Bronze Age. Proceedings of the 17th International Aegean Conference, University of Udine, Department of Humanities and Cultural Heritage, Ca' Foscari University of Venice, Department of Humanities, 17–21 April 2018* (*Aegaeum* 43), Leuven and Liège.

Bourbou, C. 2010. *Health and Disease in Byzantine Crete (7th–12th centuries AD)*, Farnham, UK.

Bouzek, J. 1974. "Attic Dark Age Incised Ware," *Sborník Národního Muzea v Praze. Acta musei nationalis Pragae* 28 (1), pp. 1–55.

———. 1994. "Late Bronze Age Greece and the Balkans: A Review of the Present Picture," *BSA* 89, pp. 217–234.

———. 1997. *Greece, Anatolia and Europe: Cultural Interrelations during the Early Iron Age* (*SIMA* 122), Jonsered.

Bowman, S., and S. Needham. 2007. "The Dunaverney and Little Thetford Flesh-Hooks: History, Technology and Their Position within the Later Bronze Age Atlantic Zone Feasting Complex," *AntJ* 87, pp. 53–108.

Boyd, H.A. 1901. "Excavations at Kavousi, Crete, in 1900," *AJA* 5, pp. 125–157.

———. 1904. "Gournia. Report of the American Exploration Society's Excavations at Gournia, Crete,

1901–1903," in *Transactions of the Department of Archaeology, Free Museum of Science and Art, University of Pennsylvania* I (1), Philadelphia, pp. 7–44.

Boyd, M.J. 2015. "Destruction and Other Material Acts of Transformation in Mycenaean Funerary Practice," in Harrell and Driessen, eds., 2015, pp. 155–165.

———. 2016. "Fields of Action in Mycenaean Funerary Practices," in Dakouri-Hild and Boyd, eds., 2016, pp. 57–87.

Bradley, R. 2002. *The Past in Prehistoric Societies*, London.

Branigan, K. 1974. *Aegean Metalwork of the Early and Middle Bronze Age* (*Oxford Monographs on Classical Archaeology*), Oxford.

Brickley, M., and R. Ives. 2008. *The Bioarchaeology of Metabolic Bone Disease*, Boston.

Brock, J.K. 1957. *Fortetsa: Early Greek Tombs near Knossos* (*BSA* Suppl. Paper 2), Cambridge.

Brooks, S.T., and J.M. Suchey 1990. "Skeletal Age Determination Based on the Os Pubis: A Comparison of the Acsádi-Nemeskéri and Suchey-Brooks Methods," *Human Evolution* 5, pp. 227–238.

Brown, J.A. 1981. "The Search for Rank in Prehistoric Burials," in Chapman, Kinnes, and Randsborg, eds., 1981, pp. 25–37.

———. 1995. "On Mortuary Analysis—with Special Reference to the Saxe-Binford Research Program," in *Regional Approaches to Mortuary Analysis* (*Interdisciplinary Contributions to Archaeology*), L.A. Beck, ed., New York, pp. 3–26.

Brown, J.A., ed. 1971. *Approaches to the Social Dimensions of Mortuary Practices* (*Memoirs of the Society for American Archaeology* 25), Washington, D.C.

Buchholz, H.-G. 1962. "Der Pfeilglätter aus dem VI. Schachtgrab von Mykene und die helladischen Pfeilspitzen," *JdI* 77, pp. 1–58.

Buikstra, J. E., and M. Swegle. 1989. "Bone Modification Due to Burning: Experimental Evidence," in *Bone Modification*, R.B. Bonnichsen and M.H. Sorg, eds., Orono, ME, 247–258.

Buikstra, J.E., and D.H. Ubelaker, eds. 1994. *Standards for Data Collection from Human Skeletal Remains* (*Arkansas Archeological Survey Research Series* 44), Fayetteville, AR.

Burnett, S.E. 2016. "Crown Wear: Identification and Categorization," in *A Companion to Dental Anthropology* (*Blackwell Companions to Archaeology* 29), J.D. Irish and G.R. Scott, eds., Malden, MA, pp. 413–432.

Cadogan, G., M. Iacovou, K. Kopaka, and J. Whitley, eds., 2012. *Parallel Lives: Ancient Island Societies in Crete and Cyprus. Papers Arising from the Conference in Nicosia Organised by the British School at Athens, the University of Crete and the University of Cyprus, in November–December 2006* (*BSA* Studies 20), London.

Callaghan, P.J., and A.W. Johnston. 2000. "The Iron Age Pottery from Kommos: The Pottery from the Greek Temples at Kommos," in Shaw and Shaw, eds., 2000, pp. 210–301.

Carington Smith, J. 1975. "Spinning, Weaving, and Textile Manufacture in Prehistoric Crete from the Beginning of the Neolithic to the end of the Mycenaean Age, with Particular Reference to the Evidence Found on Archaeological Excavations," Ph.D. diss., University of Tasmania.

Carr, C. 1995. "Mortuary Practices: Their Social, Philosophical-Religious, Circumstantial, and Physical Determinants," *Journal of Archaeological Method and Theory* 2, pp. 105–200.

Catling, H.W. 1964. *Cypriot Bronzework in the Mycenaean World* (*Oxford Monographs on Classical Archaeology*), Oxford.

———. 1968. "Late Minoan Vases and Bronzes in Oxford," *BSA* 63, pp. 89–131.

———. 1995. "Heroes Returned? Subminoan Burials from Crete," in *The Ages of Homer. A Tribute to Emily Townsend Vermeule*, J.B. Carter and S.P. Morris, eds., Austin, pp. 123–136.

———. 1996a. "The Dark Age and Later Bronzes," in Coldstream and Catling, eds., 1996, pp. 543–574.

———. 1996b. "The Objects Other Than Pottery in the Subminoan Tombs," in Coldstream and Catling, eds., 1996, pp. 517–537.

———. 1996c. "The Subminoan Phase in the North Cemetery at Knossos," in Coldstream and Catling, eds., 1996, pp. 639–649.

———. 1996d. "The Subminoan Pottery," in Coldstream and Catling, eds., 1996, pp. 295–310.

Catling, H.W., and E. Catling. 1979–1980. "Objects of Bronze, Iron, and Lead," in Popham, Sackett, and Themelis, eds., 1979–1980, pp. 231–264.

Catling, R.W.V., and D.G.J. Shipley. 1989. "Messapian Zeus: An Early Sixth-Century Inscribed Cup from Lakonia," *BSA* 84, pp. 187–200.

Cavanagh, W.G. 1996. "The Burial Customs," in Coldstream and Catling, eds., 1996, pp. 651–675.

Cavanagh, W.G., and C. Mee. 1998. *A Private Place: Death in Prehistoric Greece* (*SIMA* 125), Jonsered.

Chapman, R. 2013. "Death, Burial, and Social Representation," in Tarlow and Stutz, eds., 2013, pp. 47–57.

Chapman, R., I. Kinnes, and K. Randsborg, eds. 1981. *The Archaeology of Death* (*New Directions in Archaeology*), Cambridge.

Chesson, M.S. 2001. "Social Memory, Identity, and Death: An Introduction," in Chesson, ed., 2001, pp. 1–10.

Chesson, M.S., ed. 2001. *Social Memory, Identity, and Death: Anthropological Perspectives on Mortuary Rituals* (*Archaeological Papers of the American Anthropological Association* 10), Arlington.

Chlouveraki, S., E. Nodarou, K. Zervaki, G. Kostopoulou, and M. Tsipopoulou. 2010. "Technological Observations on the Manufacture of the Late Minoan Goddesses from Halasmenos, East Crete, as Revealed during the Process of Conservation," in *Conservation and the Eastern Mediterranean. Contributions to the Istanbul Congress, 20–24 September 2010* (*The International Institute for Conservation of Historic and Artistic Works. Studies in Conservation* 55, Suppl. 2), C. Rozeik, A. Roy, and D. Saunders, eds., London, pp. 190–194.

Christakis, K.S. 2005. *Cretan Bronze Age Pithoi: Traditions and Trends in the Production and Consumption of Storage Containers in Bronze Age Crete* (*Prehistory Monographs* 18), Philadelphia.

Cocking, J.M. 1996. "Textile Remains," in Coldstream and Catling, eds., 1996, pp. 613–620.

Coldstream, J.N. 1968. *Greek Geometric Pottery: A Survey of Ten Local Styles and Their Chronology*, London.

———. 1972. "Knossos 1951–61: Protogeometric and Geometric Pottery from the Town," *BSA* 67, pp. 63–98.

———. 1973. "Knossos 1951–61: Orientalizing and Archaic Pottery from the Town," *BSA* 68, pp. 33–63.

———. 1990. "Cycladic and Euboean Imports in the North Cemetery of Knossos," in *ΕΥΜΟΥΣΙΑ: Ceramic and Iconographic Studies in Honour of Alexander Cambitiglou* (*Mediterranean Archaeology* Suppl. 1), J.-P. Descoeudres, ed., Sydney, pp. 25–30.

———. 1992. "Early Hellenic Pottery," in Sackett, ed., 1992, pp. 67–87.

———. 1996. "The Protogeometric and Geometric Pottery," in Coldstream and Catling, eds., 1996, pp. 311–420.

———. 2001. "The Early Greek Period: Subminoan to Late Orientalizing," in *Knossos Pottery Handbook: Greek and Roman* (*BSA Studies* 7), J.N. Coldstream, L.J. Eiring, and G. Forster, London, pp. 21–76.

Coldstream, J.N., and H.W. Catling, eds. 1996. *Knossos North Cemetery: Early Greek Tombs* (*BSA* Suppl. 28), London.

Coldstream, J.N., and E.M. Hatzaki 2003. "Knossos: Early Greek Occupation under the Roman Villa Dionysos," *BSA* 98, pp. 279–306.

Coldstream, J.N., and M.S.F. Hood. 1968. "A Late Minoan Tomb at Ayios Ioannis near Knossos," *BSA* 63, pp. 205–218.

Coldstream, J.N., and L.H. Sackett. 1978. "Knossos: Two Deposits of Orientalizing Pottery," *BSA* 73, pp. 45–60.

Cook, R.M. 1998. "Ionian Cups," in *East Greek Pottery*, R.M. Cook and P. Dupont, London, pp. 129–131.

Coulson, W.D.E., D.C. Haggis, M.S. Mook, and J.L. Tobin. 1997. "Excavations on the Kastro at Kavousi: An Architectural Overview," *Hesperia* 66, pp. 315–390.

Coulson, W.D.E., and M. Tsipopoulou. 1994. "Preliminary Investigations at Halasmenos, Crete, 1992–93," *Aegean Archaeology* 1, pp. 65–97.

Courtois, J.-C. 1984. *Alasia III: Les objets des niveaux stratifiés d'Enkomi (Fouilles C.F.A. Schaeffer 1947–1978)* (*Mission archéologique d'Alasia* 6; *Éditions Recherche sur les civilisations, mémoire*, 32), Paris.

Crielaard, J.P. 1998. "Surfing on the Mediterranean Web: Cypriot Long-Distance Communications during the Eleventh and Tenth Centuries B.C.," in *Eastern Mediterranean: Cyprus-Dodecanese-Crete, 16th–6th cent. B.C. Proceedings of the International Symposium, Rethymnon, 13–16 May 1997*, V. Karageorghis and N.C. Stampolides, eds., Athens, pp. 187–206.

Crowe, A. 2019. "Old Things, New Contexts: Bronze Age Objects in Early Iron Age Burials at Knossos," in Borgna et al., eds., 2019, pp. 481–486.

Csapo, E., A.W. Johnston, and D. Geagan. 2000. "The Iron Age Inscriptions," in Shaw and Shaw, eds., 2000, pp. 101–134.

Curtin, A.J. 2008. "Putting Together the Pieces: Reconstructing Mortuary Practices from Commingled Ossuary Cremains," in Schmidt and Symes, eds., 2008, pp. 201–209.

Dabney, M.K. 2019. "Heirlooms for the Living, Heirlooms for the Dead," in Borgna et al., eds., 2019, pp. 507–510.

D'Agata, A.L. 1999. "Defining a Pattern of Continuity during the Dark Age in Central-Western Crete: Ceramic Evidence from the Settlement of Thronos/Kephala (Ancient Sybrita)," *SMEA* 41, pp. 181–218.

———. 2003. "Late Minoan IIIC–Subminoan Pottery Sequence at Thronos/Kephala and Its Connections with the Greek Mainland," in *LH IIIC Chronology and Synchronisms. Proceedings of the International Workshop Held at the Austrian Academy of Sciences at Vienna, May 7th and 8th, 2001* (*DenkschrWien* 310; *Veröffentlichungen der Mykenischen Kommission* 20), S. Deger-Jalkotzy and M. Zavadil, eds., Vienna, pp. 23–36.

———. 2007. "Evolutionary Paradigms and Late Minoan III: On a Definition of LM IIIC Middle," in *LH IIIC Chronology and Synchronisms II: LH IIIC Middle. Proceedings of the International Workshop Held at the Austrian Academy of Sciences at Vienna, October 29th and 30th, 2004* (DenkschrWien 362; Veröffentlichungen der Mykenischen Kommission 28), S. Deger-Jalkotzy and M. Zavadil, eds., Vienna, pp. 89–118.

———. 2011. "Subminoan: A Neglected Phase of the Cretan Pottery Sequence," in *Our Cups Are Full: Pottery and Society in the Aegean Bronze Age. Papers Presented to Jeremy B. Rutter on the Occasion of His 65th Birthday* (BAR-IS 2227), W. Gauss, M. Lindblom, R.A.K. Smith, and J.C. Wright, eds., Oxford, pp. 51–69.

Davis, B., E. Banou, L.A. Hitchcock, and A.P. Chapin. 2019. "Curation in the Bronze Age Aegean: Objects as Material Memories," in Borgna et al., eds., 2019, pp. 435–441.

Day, L.P. 1984. "Dog Burials in the Greek World," *AJA* 88, pp. 21–32.

———. 1995. "The Geometric Cemetery at Vronda, Kavousi," in Πεπραγμένα του Ζ′ Διεθνούς Κρητολογικού Συνεδρίου Α′ (2), Rethymnon, pp. 789–796.

———. 2011a. "Appropriating the Past: Early Iron Age Mortuary Practices at Kavousi, Crete," in Mazarakis Ainian, ed., 2011, vol. II, pp. 745–757.

———. 2011b. *The Pottery from Karphi: A Reexamination* (BSA Studies 19), London.

———. 2017. "Identifying Family Structures in Early Iron Age Crete," in *Mediterranean Families in Antiquity: Households, Extended Families, and Domestic Space*, S.R. Huebner and G. Nathan, eds., Chichester, pp. 29–43.

Day, L.P., W.D.E. Coulson, and G.C. Gesell 1986. "Kavousi, 1983–1984: The Settlement at Vronda," *Hesperia* 55, pp. 355–387.

Day, L.P., H.M.C. Dierckx, K. Flint-Hamilton, G.C. Gesell, K.T. Glowacki, N.L. Klein, D.S. Reese, and L.M. Snyder. 2016. *Kavousi IIC: The Late Minoan IIIC Settlement at Vronda. Specialists Reports and Analyses* (Prehistory Monographs 52), Philadelphia.

Day, L.P., and K.T. Glowacki. 2012. *Kavousi IIB: The Late Minoan IIIC Settlement at Vronda. The Buildings on the Periphery* (Prehistory Monographs 39), Philadelphia.

Day, L.P., N.L. Klein, and L.A. Turner. 2009. *Kavousi IIA: The Late MinoanSettlement at Vronda. The Buildings on the Summit* (Prehistory Monographs 26), Philadelphia.

Day, P.M, L. Joyner, V. Kilikoglou, and G.C. Gesell. 2006. "Goddesses, Snake Tubes, and Plaques: Analysis of Ceramic Ritual Objects from the LM IIIC Shrine at Kavousi," *Hesperia* 75, pp. 137–175.

Day, P.M., L. Joyner, E. Kiriatzi, and M. Relaki. 2005. "Petrographic Analysis of Some Final Neolithic–Early Minoan II Pottery from the Kavousi Area," in Haggis 2005, pp. 177–195.

Del Papa, M.C., and S.I. Perez. 2007. "The Influence of Artificial Cranial Vault Deformation on the Expression of Cranial Nonmetric Traits: Its Importance in the Study of Evolutionary Relationships," *American Journal of Physical Anthropology* 134, pp. 251–262.

Denoyelle, M. 1994. *Chefs-d'œuvre de la céramique grecque dans les collections du Louvre*, Paris.

Desborough, V.R.d'A. 1952. *Protogeometric Pottery*, Oxford.

———. 1964. *The Last Mycenaeans and their Successors: An Archaeological Survey, c. 1200–c. 1000 B.C.*, Oxford.

———. 1972. "Bird Vases," *CretChron* 24, pp. 245–277.

———. 1979–1980. "The Dark Age Pottery (SM–SPG III) from Settlement and Cemeteries," in Popham, Sackett, and Themelis, eds., 1979–1980, pp. 281–354.

Deshayes, J. 1960. *Les outils de bronze, de l'Indus au Danube (IVe ou IIe millénaire)* (BAHBeyrouth Bibliothèque Archéologie et Historique 71), Paris.

Dibble, F. 2017. "Politika Zoa: Animals and Social Change in Ancient Greece (ca. 1600–300 B.C.)," Ph.D. diss., University of Cincinnati.

Dickinson, O.T.P.K. 1983. "Cist Graves and Chamber Tombs," *BSA* 78, pp. 55–67.

———. 2006. *The Aegean from Bronze Age to Iron Age: Continuity and Change between the Twelfth and Eighth Centuries BC*, London.

Dierckx, H.M.C. 2016. "The Ground and Chipped Stone Implements from the Settlement," in Day et al. 2016, pp. 137–153.

Dierckx, H.M.C., and B. Tsikouras. 2007. "Petrographic Characterization of Rocks from the Mirabello Bay Region, Crete, and Its Application to Minoan Archaeology: The Provenance of Stone Implements from Minoan Sites," *Proceedings of the 11th International Congress, Athens, May, 2007* (Bulletin of the Geological Society of Greece 37), Athens, pp. 1768–1779.

DiGangi, E.A., and J.T. Hefner. 2013. "Ancestry Estimation," in *Research Methods in Human Skeletal Biology*, E.A. DiGangi and M.K. Moore, eds., Oxford, pp. 117–150.

Dikaios, P. 1969–1971. *Enkomi: Excavations from 1948–1958*, 3 vols., Mainz.

D'Onofrio, A.M. 2011. "Athenian Burials with Weapons: The Athenian Warrior Grave Revisited," in Mazarakis Ainian, ed., 2011, vol. II, pp. 645–673.

Dooijes, R., and O.P. Nieuwenhuyse. 2007. "Ancient Repairs: Techniques and Social Meaning," in *Konservieren oder restaurieren: Die restaurierung griechischer Vasen von der Antike bis heute* (*Beihefte zum Corpus vasorum antiquorum* 3), M. Bentz and U. Kästner, eds., Munich, pp. 15–20.

Driessen, J. 2015. "Fragmented Souvenirs: Introduction to the Volume," in Harrell and Driessen, eds., 2015, pp. 15–20.

Droop, J.P. 1905–1906. "Some Geometric Pottery from Crete," *BSA* 12, pp. 24–62.

Eaby, M.S. 2007. "Mortuary Variability in Early Iron Age Cretan Burials," Ph.D. diss., University of North Carolina, Chapel Hill.

———. 2010. "Ένας θολωτός τάφος από τον Αζοριά Καβουσίου," in *Αρχαιολογικό Έργο Κρήτης 1: Πρακτικά της 1ης συνάντησης, Ρέθυμνο, 28–30 Νοεμβρίου 2008*, M. Andrianakis and I. Tzachili, eds., Rethymnon, pp. 170–178.

———. 2011. "Regionalism in Early Iron Age Cretan Burials," in *Prehistoric Crete: Regional and Diachronic Studies on Mortuary Systems*, J.M.A. Murphy, ed., Philadelphia, pp. 165–202.

Effinger, M. 1996. *Minoischer Schmuck* (*BAR-IS* 646), Oxford.

Eiring, L.J. 2001. "The Hellenistic Period," in *Knossos Pottery Handbook: Greek and Roman* (*BSA* Studies 7), J.N. Coldstream, L.J. Eiring, and G. Forster, London, pp. 91–134.

Ekengren, F. 2013. "Contextualizing Grave Goods: Theoretical Perspectives and Methodological Implications," in Tarlow and Stutz, eds., 2013, pp. 173–192.

Ekroth, G. 2017. "Bare Bones: Zooarchaeology and Greek Sacrifice," in *Animal Sacrifice in the Ancient Greek World*, S. Hitch and I. Rutherford, eds., Cambridge, pp. 15–47.

Englezou, M. 2011. "Κεραμική γεωμετρικής: Πρώιμης ανατολίζουσας περιόδου από την περιοχή της Λιγόρτυνος Μονοφατσίου," in *Identità culturale, etnicità, processi di transformazione a Creta fra Dark Age e Arcaismo. Per i cento anni dello scavo di Priniàs 1906–2006. Convegno di studi, Atene 9–12 novembre 2006* (*Studi e materiali di archeologia greca* 10), G. Rizza, ed., Catania, pp. 281–308.

Erickson, B.L. 2010. *Crete in Transition: Pottery Styles and Island History in the Archaic and Classical Periods* (*Hesperia* Suppl. 45), Princeton.

Eustathiou, M. 2001. "Το νεκροταφείο Οίας στη Θήρα: Ταφές καύσης," in Stampolides, ed., 2001, pp. 301–320.

Evans, A. 1928. *The Palace of Minos at Knossos* II, vol. 1, London.

Evely, R.D.G. 1993. *Minoan Crafts: Tools and Techniques. An Introduction* I (*SIMA* 92 [1]), Göteborg.

———. 1996. "Other Materials," in Coldstream and Catling, eds., 1996, pp. 621–636.

———. 2000. *Minoan Crafts: Tools and Techniques. An Introduction* II (*SIMA* 92 [2]), Jonsered.

Fairgrieve, S.I. 2008. *Forensic Cremation: Recovery and Analysis*, Boca Raton.

Fantalkin, A. 2001. "Low Chronology and Greek Protogeometric and Geometric Pottery in the Southern Levant," *Levant* 33, pp. 117–125.

Fantalkin, A., I. Finkelstein, and E. Piasetzky. 2011. "Iron Age Mediterranean Chronology: A Rejoinder," *Radiocarbon* 53, pp. 179–198.

Farnham, S. 2016. "Pollution and Purity in the Argolid and Corinthia during the Early Iron Age: The Burials," in Dakouri-Hild and Boyd, eds., 2016, pp. 361–388.

Faure, P. 1966. "Les minerais de la Crète antique," *RA*, n.s., 1, pp. 45–78.

Fazekas, I.G., and F. Kosa. 1978. *Forensic Fetal Osteology*, Budapest.

Filippaki, E., Y. Bassiakos, and B. Hayden. 2014. "Metalworking at Priniatikos Pyrgos, Mirabello Gulf, Crete," in *A Cretan Landscape through Time: Priniatikos Pyrgos and Environs* (*BAR-IS* 2634), B.P.C. Molloy and C.N. Duckworth, eds., Oxford, pp. 105–112.

Finkelstein, I., and E. Piasetzsky. 2011. "The Iron Age Chronology Debate: Is the Gap Narrowing?" *NEA* 74, pp. 50–54.

Finkelstein, I., D. Ussishkin, and B. Halpern, eds. 2000. *Megiddo III: The 1992–1996 Seasons* (Tel Aviv University Monograph Series of the Sonia and Marco Nadler Institute of Archaeology 18), 2 vols., Tel Aviv.

Flint-Hamilton, K. 2016. "The Palaeoethnobotany of Vronda," in Day et al., 2016, pp. 181–193.

Fortenberry, C.D. 1990. "Elements of Mycenaean Warfare," Ph.D. diss., University of Cincinnati.

Fox, S.C. 2005. "Health in Hellenistic and Roman Times: The Case Studies of Paphos, Cyprus, and Corinth, Greece," in *Health in Antiquity*, H. King, ed., London, pp. 59–82.

Gagarin, M., and P. Perlman. 2016. *The Laws of Ancient Crete c. 650–400 BCE*, Oxford.

Gaignerot-Driessen, F. 2016. *De l'occupation postpalatiale à la cité-état grecque: Le cas du Mirambello (Crète)* (*Aegaeum* 40), Leuven and Liège.

———. 2019. "From Peak Sanctuaries to Hilltop Settlements: Reshaping a Landscape of Memory in Late Minoan Crete," in Borgna et al., eds., 2019, pp. 65–70.

Gaignerot-Driessen, F., M. Anastasiadou, P. Baudain, G. Enry, C. Judson, A. Lattard, R. Machavoine, O. Vanwalleghem, and V. Vlachos. 2020. "Fouilles de l'Anavlochos II: La nécropole de Lami, le sanctuaire de Kako Plaï et ses abords, le dépôt votif 1 et ses abords, les terrasses du sommet Nord-Ouest," *Bulletin archéologique des Écoles françaises à étranger, Grèce* 2020, accessed April 25, 2023, https://doi.org/10.4000/baefe.1348.

Gaignerot-Driessen, F., P. Baulain, G. Erny, B. Jagou, C. Judson, A. Lattard, R. Machavoine, and A. Paillard. 2022. "Fouilles de l'Anavlochos IV: L'agglomération urbaine du vallon central et la nécropole," *Bulletin archéologique des Écoles françaises à l'étranger, Grèce* 2022, accessed March 31, 2023, https://doi.org/10.4000/baefe.5863.

Galloway, A. 1999. *Broken Bones: Anthropological Analysis of Blunt Force Trauma*, Springfield, IL.

Garland, R. 1985. *The Greek Way of Death*, London.

Gesell, G.C. 1985. "New Light on the Iron Age Tombs at Kavousi," in Πεπραγμένα τοῦ Ε' Διεθνοῦς Κρητολογικοῦ Συνεδρίου Α', Herakleion, pp. 131–137.

Gesell, G.C., W.D.E. Coulson, and L.P. Day 1991. "Excavations at Kavousi Crete, 1988," *Hesperia* 60, pp. 145–177.

Gesell, G.C., L.P. Day, and W.D.E. Coulson. 1983. "Excavations and Survey at Kavousi, Crete, 1978–1981," *Hesperia* 52, pp. 389–420.

———. 1985. "Kavousi, 1982–1983: The Kastro," *Hesperia* 54, pp. 327–355.

———. 1988. "Excavations at Kavousi, Crete, 1987," *Hesperia* 57, pp. 279–301.

———. 1995. "Excavations at Kavousi, Crete, 1989 and 1990," *Hesperia* 64, pp. 67–120.

Gillespie, S.D. 2001. "Personhood, Agency, and Mortuary Ritual: A Case Study from the Ancient Maya," *JAnthArch* 20, pp. 73–112.

Gjerstad, E. 1948. *The Swedish Cyprus Expedition* IV. Part 2: *The Cypro-Geometric, Cypro-Archaic, and Cypro-Classical Periods*, Stockholm.

Glencross, B.A. 2011. "Skeletal Injury Across the Life Course: Towards Understanding Social Agency," in *Social Bioarchaeology*, S.C. Agarwal and B.A. Glencross, eds., Chichester, pp. 390–409.

Glowacki, K.T. 2007. "House, Household and Community at LM IIIC Vronda, Kavousi," in *Building Communities: House, Settlement and Society in the Aegean and Beyond. Proceedings of a Conference Held at Cardiff University, 17–21 April 2001* (*BSA* Studies 15), R. Westgate, N. Fisher, and J. Whitley, eds., London, pp. 129–139.

———. 2016. "Estimates of Vessel Capacities of LM IIIC Pottery from Vronda," in Day et al. 2016, pp. 241–245.

Glowacki, K.T., and N.L. Klein. 2011. "The Analysis of 'Dark Age' Domestic Architecture: The LM IIIC Settlement at Kavousi Vronda," in Mazarakis Ainian, ed., 2011, vol. I, pp. 451–461.

Godart, L., and Y. Tzedakis. 1992. *Témoignages archéologiques et épigraphiques en Crète occidentale, du Néolithique au Minoen Récent IIIB* (*Incunabula Graeca* 93), Rome.

Goldstein, L.G. 1976. "Spatial Structure and Social Organization: Regional Manifestations of Mississippian Society," Ph.D. diss., Northwestern University.

Gräslund, B. 1994. "Prehistoric Soul Beliefs in Northern Europe," *PPS* 60, pp. 15–26.

Grethlein, J. 2008. "Memory and Material Objects in the *Iliad* and *Odyssey*," *JHS* 128, pp. 27–51.

Grinsell, L.V. 1961. "The Breaking of Objects as a Funerary Rite," *Folklore* 72, pp. 475–491.

Grossman, C.B., and D.G. Potts. 1974. "Arachnoid Granulations: Radiology and Anatomy," *Radiology* 113, pp. 95–100.

Haggis, D.C. 2005. *Kavousi I: The Archaeological Survey of the Kavousi Region* (*Prehistory Monographs* 16), Philadelphia.

———. 2014. "Excavations at Azoria and Stratigraphic Evidence for the Restructuring of Cretan Landscapes ca. 600 BCE," in *Cultural Practices and Material Culture in Archaic and Classical Crete. Proceedings of the International Conference, Mainz, May 20–21, 2011*, O. Pilz and G. Seelentag, eds., Berlin, pp. 11–39.

Haggis, D.C., and M.S. Mook. 1993. "The Kavousi Coarse Wares: A Bronze Age Chronology for Survey in the Mirabello Area, East Crete," *AJA* 97, pp. 265–293.

———. 2015. "Stratigraphic Excavations at Azoria in 2015," *KENTRO: The Newsletter of the INSTAP Study Center for East Crete* 18, pp. 18–23.

Haggis, D.C., M.S. Mook, T. Carter, and L.M. Snyder. 2007a. "Excavations at Azoria, 2003–2004, Part 2: The Final Neolithic, Late Prepalatial, and Early Iron Age Occupation," *Hesperia* 76, pp. 665–716.

Haggis, D.C., M.S. Mook, R.D. Fitzsimons, C.M. Scarry, and L.M. Snyder. 2007b. "Excavations at Azoria, 2003–2004, Part 1: The Archaic Civic Complex," *Hesperia* 76, pp. 243–321.

Haggis, D.C., M.S. Mook, R.D. Fitzsimons, C.M. Scarry, L.M. Snyder, and W.C. West. 2011a. "Excavations in the Archaic Civic Buildings at Azoria in 2005–2006," *Hesperia* 80, pp. 1–70.

Haggis, D.C., M.S. Mook, R.D. Fitzsimons, C.M. Scarry, and L.M. Snyder. 2011b. "Excavations of the Archaic Houses at Azoria in 2005–2006," *Hesperia* 80, pp. 431–489.

Haggis, D.C., M.S. Mook, C.M. Scarry, L.M. Snyder, and W.C. West. 2004. "Excavations at Azoria, 2002," *Hesperia* 73, pp. 339–400.

Hall, E. 1914. *Excavations in Eastern Crete: Vrokastro* (University of Pennsylvania, The University Museum Anthropological Publications 3 [2]), Philadelphia.

Hall, J.M. 1997. *Ethnic Identity in Greek Antiquity*, Cambridge.

Hallager, B.P. 2007. "Problems with LM/LH IIIC Synchronisms," in *LH IIIC Chronology and Synchronisms II: LH IIIC Middle. Proceedings of the International Workshop Held at the Austrian Academy of Sciences at Vienna, October 29th and 30th, 2004* (DenkschrWien 362; Veröffentlichungen der Mykenischen Kommission 28), S. Deger-Jalkotzy and M. Zavadil, eds., Vienna, pp. 189–202.

———. 2010. "The Elusive Late IIIC and the Ill-Named Subminoan," in *Cretan Offerings: Studies in Honour of Peter Warren* (BSA Studies 18), O. Krzyskowska, ed., London, pp. 141–155.

Hallager, E., and B.P. Hallager, eds. 1997. *The Greek-Swedish Excavations at the Agia Aikaterini Square, Kastelli, Khania, 1970–1987. I: From the Geometric to the Modern Greek Period* (ActaAth 4°, 47 [I]), Stockholm.

———, eds. 2000. *The Greek-Swedish Excavations at the Agia Aikaterini Square, Kastelli, Khania, 1970–1987. II: The Late Minoan IIIC Settlement* (ActaAth 4°, 47 [II]), Stockholm.

Halstead, P. 1977. "The Bronze Age Demography of Crete and Greece: A Note," *BSA* 72, pp. 107–111.

Hamilakis, Y. 2013. *Archaeology of the Senses: Human Experience, Memory, and Affect*, Cambridge.

Hamilakis, Y., and S. Sherratt. 2012. "Feasting and the Consuming Body in Bronze Age Crete and Early Iron Age Cyprus," in Cadogan et al., eds., 2012, pp. 187–207.

Harcourt, R.A. 1974. "The Dog in Prehistoric and Early Historic Britain," *JAS* 1, pp. 151–175.

Harrell, K. 2015. "Piece Out: Comparing the Intentional Destruction of Swords in the Early Iron Age and the Mycenae Shaft Graves," in Harrell and Driessen, eds., 2015, pp. 143–153.

Harrell, K., and J. Driessen, eds. 2015. *THRAVSMA: Contextualising the Intentional Destruction of Objects in the Bronze Age Aegean and Cyprus* (Aegis 9), Louvain.

Harrison, T.P. 2004. *Megiddo 3: Final Report on the Stratum VI Excavations* (OIP 127), Chicago.

Hatzaki, E. 2007. "Final Palatial (LM II–LM IIIA2) and Postpalatial (LM IIIB–LM IIIC Early): The MUM South Sector, Long Corridor Cists, MUM Pits (8, 10–11), Makritikhos 'Kitchen,' MUM North Platform Pits, and SEX Southern Half Groups," in *Knossos Pottery Handbook: Neolithic and Bronze Age (Minoan)* (BSA Studies 14), N. Momigliano, ed., 2007, London, pp. 197–251.

Hayden, B.J. 1995. "Rural Settlement of the Orientalizing through Early Classical Period: The Meseleroi Valley, Eastern Crete," *Aegean Archaeology* 2, pp. 93–144.

———. 2003. *Reports on the Vrokastro Area, Eastern Crete 1: Catalogue of Pottery from the Bronze and Early Iron Age Settlement of Vrokastro in the Collections of the University of Pennsylvania Museum of Archaeology and Anthropology and the Archaeological Museum, Herakleion, Crete* (University Museum Monograph 113), Philadelphia.

———. 2004. *Reports on the Vrokastro Area, Eastern Crete 2: The Settlement History of the Vrokastro Area and Related Studies* (University Museum Monograph 119), Philadelphia.

———. 2005. *Reports on the Vrokastro Area, Eastern Crete 3: The Vrokastro Regional Survey Project. Sites and Pottery* (University Museum Monograph 123), Philadelphia.

Hayden, B.J., J.A. Moody, and O. Rackham. 1992. "The Vrokastro Survey Project, 1986–1989: Research Design and Preliminary Results," *Hesperia* 61, pp. 293–353.

Hayden, B.J., and M. Risser. 2005. "Early Iron Age–Hellenistic Pottery Catalogue," in Hayden 2005, pp. 51–90.

Hayes, J.W. 1983. "The Villa Dionysos Excavations, Knossos: The Pottery," *BSA* 78, pp. 97–169.

Hesse, B., and P. Wapnish. 1985. *Animal Bone Archaeology: From Objectives to Analysis*, Washington, D.C.

Hillson, S. 1996. *Dental Anthropology*, Cambridge.

———. 2008. "Dental Pathology," in *Biological Anthropology of the Human Skeleton*, M.A. Katzenberg and S.R. Saunders, eds., 2nd ed., Hoboken, pp. 301–340.

———. 2009. "The World's Largest Infant Cemetery and Its Potential for Studying Growth and Development," in Shepartz, Fox, and Bourbou, eds., 2009, pp. 137–154.

Höckmann, O. 1980. "Lanze und Speer in spätminoischen und mykenischen Griechenland," *JRGZM* 27 [1982], pp. 13–158.

Hodder, I. 1982. *Symbols in Action: Ethnoarchaeological Studies of Material Culture (New Studies in Archaeology)*, Cambridge.

Holck, P. 2008. *Cremated Bones: A Medical-Anthropological Study of Archaeological Material on Cremation Burials*, reprint of 3rd ed., Oslo.

Hood, M.S.F., and J. Boardman. 1961. "Early Iron Age Tombs at Knossos (Knossos Survey 25)," *BSA* 56, pp. 68–80.

Hood, M.S.F., G. Huxley, N. Sandars, and A.E. Werner. 1958–1959. "A Minoan Cemetery on Upper Gypsades (Knossos Survey 156)," *BSA* 53–54, pp. 194–262.

Hutchinson, R.W., and J. Boardman. 1954. "The Khaniale Tekke Tombs," *BSA* 49, pp. 215–228.

Iezzi, C.A. 2005. "Regional Differences in the Health Status of Late Bronze Age Mycenaean Populations from East Lokris, Greece," Ph.D. diss., State University of New York at Buffalo.

I.G.S.R. 1959. Geological Map of Greece: Kato Chorion (Ierapetra) Sheet. 1:50,000. Institute for Geology and Subsurface Research, Athens.

Jackes, M. 2000. "Building the Bases for Paleodemographic Analysis: Adult Age Determination," in *Biological Anthropology of the Human Skeleton*, 1st ed., M.A. Katzenberg and S.R. Saunders, eds., New York, pp. 417–466.

Jacobsthal, P. 1956. *Greek Pins and Their Connexions with Europe and Asia (Oxford Monographs on Classical Archaeology)*, Oxford.

Janes, S. 2014. "An Entangled Past: Island Interactions, Mortuary Practices and the Negotiation of Identities on Early Iron Age Cyprus," in Knapp and van Dommelen, eds., 2014, pp. 571–584.

Johannowsky, W. 2002. *Il santuario sull'acropoli di Gortina II (Monografie della Scuola archeologica italiana di Atene e delle Missioni italiane in Oriente* 16), Athens.

Johnston, A.W. 1979. *Trademarks on Greek Vases*, Warminster.

———. 2000. "Building Z at Kommos: An 8th-Century Pottery Sequence," *Hesperia* 69, pp. 189–226.

———. 2005. "Kommos: Further Iron Age Pottery," *Hesperia* 74, pp. 309–393.

———. 2006. *Trademarks on Greek Vases: Addenda*, Oxford.

Jones, A. 2007. *Memory and Material Culture (Topics in Contemporary Archaeology)*, Cambridge.

Jones, R.E. 1979–1980. "Analyses of Bronze and Other Base Metal Objects from the Cemeteries," in Popham, Sackett, and Themelis, eds., 1979–1980, pp. 447–459.

Kaiser, I. 2013. *Kretisch geometrische Keramik: Form und Dekor. Entwicklung aus Tradition und Rezeption*, Möhnesee.

Kaloyeros, A.E., and R.M. Ehrenreich. 1990. "The Distribution of Phosphorus in Romano-British Ironwork," *Materials Research Society Proceedings* 185, p. 725.

Kanta, A. 1980. *The Late Minoan III Period in Crete: A Survey of Sites, Pottery, and Their Distribution (SIMA* 58), Göteborg.

———. 2001. "The Cremations of Olous and the Custom of Cremation in Bronze Age Crete," in Stampolides, ed., 2001, pp. 59–68.

———. 2003. "Aristocrats–Traders–Emigrants–Settlers: Crete in the Closing Phases of the Bronze Age," in Stampolides and Karageorghis, eds., 2003, pp. 173–186.

Kanta, A., and K. Davaras. 2004. "The Cemetery of Krya, District of Seteia: Developments at the End of the Late Bronze Age and the Beginning of the Early Iron Age in East Crete," in Stampolides and Giannikouri, eds., 2004, pp. 149–157.

Karageorghis, V. 1974. *Excavations at Kition* I: *The Tombs*, Nicosia.

———. 1975. *Alaas: A Protogeometric Necropolis in Cyprus*, Nicosia.

———. 1983. *Palaepaphos-Skales: An Iron Age Cemetery in Cyprus (Ausgrabungen in Alt-Paphos auf Cypern* 3), Konstanz.

Karageorghis, V., A. Kanta, N.C. Stampolides, and Y. Sakellarakis. 2014. *Kypriaka in Crete: From the Bronze Age to the End of the Archaic Period*, Nicosia.

Karasik, A., and U. Smilansky. 2006. "Computation of the Capacity of Pottery Vessels Based on Drawn Profiles," in *Excavations at Tel Beth Shean 1989–1996* I: *From the Late Bronze Age IIB to the Medieval Period (The Beth-Shean Valley Archaeological Project Publication* 1), A. Mazar, ed., Jerusalem, pp. 392–394.

Kaufman, B., and D.A. Scott. 2015. "Fuel Efficiency of Ancient Copper Alloys: Theoretical Melting

Thermodynamics of Copper, Tin and Arsenical Copper and Timber Conservation in the Bronze Age Levant," *Archaeometry* 57, pp. 1,009–1,024.

Keswani, P. 2004. *Mortuary Ritual and Society in Bronze Age Cyprus* (*Monographs in Mediterranean Archaeology*), London.

Khung, S., J.-F. Budzik, E. Amzallag-Bellenger, A. Lambiliote, G. Soto Ares, A. Cotton, and N. Boutry. 2013. "Skeletal Involvement in Langerhans Cell Histiocytosis," *Insights into Imaging* 4, pp. 569–579.

Kilian-Dirlmeier, I. 1984. *Nadeln der frühelladischen bis archaischen Zeit von der Peloponnes* (*Prähistorische Bronzefunde* XIII [8]), Munich.

———. 1993. *Die Schwerter in Griechenland (ausserhalb der Peloponnes), Bulgarien und Albanien* (*Prähistorische Bronzefunde* IV [12]), Stuttgart.

Klein, N.L., and K.T. Glowacki. 2016. "The Architecture of Vronda," in Day et al. 2016, pp. 1–46.

Knapp, A.B., and S.W. Manning. 2016. "Crisis in Context: The End of the Late Bronze Age in the Eastern Mediterranean," *AJA* 120, pp. 99–149.

Knapp, A.B., and P. van Dommelen, eds. 2014. *The Cambridge Prehistory of the Bronze and Iron Age Mediterranean*, Cambridge.

Konigsberg, L.W., L.A. Kohn, and J.M. Cheverud. 1993. "Cranial Deformation and Nonmetric Trait Variation," *American Journal of Physical Anthropology* 90, pp. 35–48.

Kotsonas, A. 2008. *The Archaeology of Tomb A1K1 of Orthi Petra in Eleutherna: The Early Iron Age Pottery*, Herakleion.

———. 2011a. "Ceramic Variability and Drinking Habits in Iron Age Crete," in Mazarakis Ainian, ed., 2011, vol. II, pp. 943–953.

———. 2011b. "Foreign Identity and Ceramic Production in Early Iron Age Crete," in *Identità culturale, etnicità, processi di transformazione a Creta fra Dark Age e Arcaismo. Per i cento anni dello scavo di Priniàs 1906–2006. Convegno di studi (Atene 9–12 novembre 2006)* (*Studi e materiali di archeologia greca* 10), G. Rizza, ed., Catania, pp. 133–155.

———. 2012. "'Creto-Cypriot' and 'Cypro-Phoenician' Complexities in the Archaeology of Interaction between Crete and Cyprus," in *Cyprus and the Aegean in the Early Iron Age: The Legacy of Nicolas Coldstream. Proceedings of an Archaeological Workshop Held in Memory of Professor J.N. Coldstream (1927–2008)*, M. Iacovou, ed., Nicosia, pp. 155–181.

———. 2016. "Politics of Periodization and the Archaeology of Early Greece," *AJA* 120, pp. 239–270.

———. 2017. "Ceramics, Analytical Scales and Cultural Histories of 7th Century Crete," in *Interpreting the Seventh Century B.C.: Tradition and Innovation*, X. Charalambidou and C. Morgan, eds., Oxford, pp. 15–23.

———. 2018. "Homer, the Archaeology of Crete and the 'Tomb of Meriones' at Knossos," *JHS* 138, pp. 1–35.

Kourou, N. 1999. Ἀνασκαφές Νάξου: Τὸ νότιο νεκροταφεῖο τῆς Νάξου κατὰ τῇ γεωμετρικὴ περίοδο. Ἔρευνες τῶν ἐτῶν 1931–1939 (Βιβλιοθήκη τῆς ἐν Ἀθήναις Ἀρχαιολογικῆς Ἑταιρείας 193), Athens.

Kumar, V., A.K. Abbas, and N. Fausto. 2005. *Robbins & Cotran Pathologic Basis of Disease*, 7th ed., Philadelphia.

Kurtz, D.C., and J. Boardman. 1971. *Greek Burial Customs*, London.

Labrude, A. 2016. "Aegean Late Bronze and Early Iron Age Burials in the Ruins of Rulers' Dwellings: A Legitimisation of Power?" in Dakouri-Hild and Boyd, eds., 2016, pp. 297–314.

Larsen, C.S. 2015. *Bioarchaeology: Interpreting Behavior from the Human Skeleton* (*Cambridge Studies in Biological Anthropology*), 2nd ed., Cambridge.

Lawton, C.L. 2007. "Children in Classical Attic Votive Reliefs," in *Constructions of Childhood in Ancient Greece and Italy* (*Hesperia* Suppl. 41), A. Cohen and J.B. Rutter, eds., Princeton, pp. 41–60.

Lebessi, A. 1970. "Ἀνασκαφικαὶ ἔρευναι εἰς Ἀνατολικὴν Κρήτην: Μασταμπᾶς Ἡρακλείου," *Prakt* 125 [1972], pp. 270–297.

Lemos, I.S. 1994. "Birds Revisited," *Cyprus in the 11th Century B.C. Proceedings of the International Symposium Organized by the Archaeological Research Unit of the University of Cyprus and the Anastasios G. Leventis Foundation, Nicosia 30–31 October 1993*, V. Karageorghis, ed., Nicosia, pp. 229–236.

———. 2002. *The Protogeometric Aegean: The Archaeology of the Late Eleventh and Tenth Centuries BC*, Oxford.

Levi, D. 1927–1929. "Arkades: un città cretese all'alba della civiltà ellenica," *ASAtene* 10–12 [1931], pp. 1–723.

Lewis, M.E. 2007. *The Bioarchaeology of Children: Perspectives from Biological and Forensic Anthropology*, Cambridge.

———. 2018. *Paleopathology of Children: Identification of Pathological Conditions in the Human Skeletal Remains of Non-Adults*, London.

Liston, M.A. 1993. "The Human Skeletal Remains from Kavousi, Crete: A Bioarchaeological Analysis," Ph.D. diss., University of Tennessee, Knoxville.

———. 2007. "Secondary Cremation Burials at Kavousi Vronda, Crete: Symbolic Representation in Mortuary Practice," *Hesperia* 76, pp. 57–71.

———. 2017. "The Human Skeletal Remains," in Papadopoulos and Smithson 2017, pp. 503–560.

Liston, M.A., and L.P. Day. 2009. "It Does Take a Brain Surgeon: A Successful Trepanation from Kavousi, Crete," in Schepartz, Fox, and Bourbou, eds., 2009, pp. 57–73.

Liston, M.A., and S.I. Rotroff. 2013. "Babies in the Well: Archaeological Evidence for Newborn Disposal in Hellenistic Greece," in *The Oxford Handbook of Childhood and Education in the Classical World*, J.E. Grubbs and T. Parkin, eds., Oxford, pp. 62–82.

Lloyd, M. 2015. "Death of a Swordsman, Death of a Sword: The Killing of Swords in the Early Iron Age Aegean (ca. 1050 to ca. 690 B.C.E.)," in *Ancient Warfare: Introducing Current Ressearch* I, G. Lee, H. Whittaker, and G. Wrightson, eds., New Castle upon Tyne, pp. 14–31.

Lochner, M., and F. Ruppenstein, eds. 2013. *Brandbestattungen von der mittleren Donau bis zur Ägäis zwischen 1300 und 750 v. Chr. Akten des internationalen Symposiums an der Österreichischen Akademie der Wissenschaften in Wien, 11.-12. Februar 2010* (*DenkschrWien* 448; *Mitteilungen der Prähistorischen Kommission* 77; *Veröffentlichungen der Mykenischen Kommission* 32), Vienna.

Lovejoy, C.O., R.S. Meindl, T.R. Pryzbeck, and R.P. Mensforth. 1985. "Chronological Metamorphosis of the Auricular Surface of the Ilium: A New Method for the Determination of Adult Skeletal Age at Death," *American Journal of Bioilogical Anthropology* 68, pp. 15–28.

Luschey, H. 1939. *Die Phiale*, Bleicherode am Harz.

Lyman, R.L. 1987. "Zooarchaeology and Taphonomy: A General Consideration," *Journal of Ethnobiology* 7, pp. 93–117.

Macdonald, C.F. 1992. "The Iron and Bronze Weapons," in *La nécropole d'Amathonte VI: Tombes 113–367. Bijoux, armes, verre, astragales et coquillages, squelettes* (*Études Chypriotes* XIV), V. Karageorghis, O. Picard, and C. Tytgat, eds., Nicosia, pp. 43–99.

Maggidis, C. 2019. "The Palace Throne of Mycenae: Constructing Collective Historical Memory and Power Ideology," in Borgna et al., eds., 2019, pp. 165–172.

Manning, S.W. 1998. "Changing Pasts and Socio-political Cognition in Late Bronze Age Cyprus," *WorldArch* 30, pp. 39–58.

Maran, J. 2012. "Ceremonial Feasting Equipment, Social Space and Interculturality in Post-Palatial Tiryns," in *Materiality and Social Practice: Transformative Capacities of Intercultural Encounters*, J. Maran and P.W. Stockhammer, eds., Oxford, pp. 121–136.

Marinatos, S. 1931–1932. "Πρωτογεωμετρικὰ καὶ γεωμετρικὰ εὑρήματα ἐκ κεντρικῆς καὶ Ἀνατολικῆς Κρήτης," *ArchDelt* 14 [1935], pp. 1–11.

May, H., N. Peled, G. Dar, J. Abbas, B. Medlej, Y. Masharawi, and I. Hershkovitz. 2010. "Hyperostosis Frontalis Interna and Androgen Suppression," *The Anatomical Record: Advances in Integrative Anatomy and Evolutionary Biology* 293, pp. 1,333–1,336.

Mazar, A. 2011. "The Iron Age Chronology Debate: Is the Gap Narrowing? Another Viewpoint," *NEA* 74, pp. 105–111.

Mazarakis Ainian, A., ed. 2011. *The "Dark Ages" Revisited. Acts of an International Symposium in Memory of William D.E. Coulson at the University of Thessaly, Volos, Greece, 14–17 June, 2007*, Volos.

McKinley, J.I. 2006. "Cremation . . . the Cheap Option?" in *Social Archaeology of Funerary Remains* 1, R. Gowland and C. Knüsel, eds., Oxford, pp. 81–88.

———. 2013. "Cremation: Excavation, Analysis, and Interpretation of Materials from Cremation-Related Contexts," in Tarlow and Stutz, eds., 2013, pp. 147–171.

Meindl, R.S., and C.O. Lovejoy. 1989. "Age Changes in the Pelvis: Implications for Paleodemography," in *Age Markers in the Human Skeleton*, M.Y. Işcan, ed., Springfield, IL, pp. 137–168.

Melas, E.M. 1984. "The Origins of Aegean Cremation," *Anthropologika* 5, pp. 21–36.

Meskell, L.M. 2003. "Memory's Materiality: Ancestral Presence, Commemorative Practice and Disjunctive Locales," in Van Dyke and Alcock, eds., 2003, pp. 34–55.

Metcalf, P., and R. Huntington. 1991. *Celebrations of Death: The Anthropology of Mortuary Ritual*, Cambridge.

Milner, G.R., J.W. Wood, and J.L. Boldsen. 2000. "Paleodemography," in *Biological Anthropology of the Human Skeleton*, 1st ed., M.A. Katzenberg and S.R. Saunders, eds., New York, pp. 467–497.

Moignard, E. 1996. "The Orientalizing Pottery," in Coldstream and Catling, eds., 1996, pp. 421–462.

Molloy, B.P.C. 2012. "Martial Minoans? War as Social Process, Practice and Event in Bronze Age Crete," *BSA* 107, pp. 87–142.

Moody, J. 2012. "Hinterlands and Hinterseas: Resources and Production Zones in Bronze Age and Iron Age Crete," in Cadogan et al., eds., 2012, pp. 233–271.

Mook, M.S. 1993. "The Northwest Building: Houses of the Late Bronze and Early Iron Ages on the Kastro at Kavousi, East Crete," Ph.D. diss., University of Minnesota, Minneapolis.

———. 2004. "From Foundation to Abandonment: New Ceramic Phasing for the Late Bronze Age and Early Iron Age on the Kastro at Kavousi," in *Crete Beyond the Palaces. Proceedings of the Crete 2000 Conference* (*Prehistory Monographs* 10), L.P. Day, M.S. Mook, and J.D. Muhly, eds., Philadelphia, pp. 163–179.

———. 2005. "The Kavousi Fabrics: A Typology for Coarse Pottery in the Mirabello Region of Eastern Crete," in Haggis 2005, pp. 167–176.

———. 2011. "The Settlement on the Kastro at Kavousi in the Late Geometric Period," in Mazarakis Ainian, ed., 2011, vol. I, pp. 477–488.

Mook, M.S., and L.P. Day 2009. "Kavousi Coarse Ware Fabrics," in Day, Klein, and Turner 2009, pp. 163–167.

Morris, I. 1987. *Burial and Ancient Society: The Rise of the Greek City-State* (*New Studies in Archaeology*), Cambridge.

———. 1992. *Death-Ritual and Social Structure in Classical Antiquity* (*Key Themes in Ancient History*), Cambridge.

Müller-Karpe, H. 1962. "Metallbeigahen der Früheisenzeitlichen Kerameikos-Gräben," *JdI* 77, pp. 59–129.

Muhly, J.D., and V. Kassianidou. 2012. "Parallels and Diversities in the Production, Trade, and Use of Copper and Iron in Crete and Cyprus from the Bronze Age to the Iron Age," in Cadogan et al., eds., 2012, pp. 119–140.

Munsell Color. 1998. *Munsell Soil Color Charts*, rev. ed., New York.

———. 2000. *Munsell Soil Color Charts*, rev. washable ed., New York.

Murphy, E.M., ed. 2008. *Deviant Burial in the Archaeological Record* (*Studies in Funerary Archaeology* 2), Oxford.

Musgrave, J.H. 1996. "The Human Bones," in Coldstream and Catling, eds., 1996, pp. 677–702.

———. 2005. "An Anthropological Assessment of the Inhumations and Cremations from the Early Iron Age Cemetery at Torone," in Papadopoulos 2005, pp. 243–315.

Nadalini, G. 2007. "Restauri antichi su ceramiche greche: Differenziazione dei metodi," in *Konservieren oder Restaurieren: Die Restaurierung griechischer Vasen von der Antike bis heute* (*Beihefte zum Corpus vasorum antiquorum* 3), M. Bentz and U. Kästner, eds., Munich, pp. 29–34.

Nagy, G. 1983. "Sêma and Nóesis: Some Illustrations," *Arethusa* 16, pp. 35–55.

Nayyar, S., M. Quirno, S. Hasan, L. Rybak, and R.J. Meislin. 2011. "Rupture of the Distal Biceps Tendon Combined with a Supinator Muscle Tear in a 51-Year-Old Woman: A Case Report," *Case Reports in Radiology* 2011, accessed April 25, 2023, https://doi.org/10.1155/2011/515912.

Needham, S.P., and S. Bowman. 2005. "Flesh-Hooks, Technological Complexity and the Atlantic Bronze Age Feasting Complex," *EJA* 8, pp. 93–136.

Neeft, C.W. 1987. *Protocorinthian Subgeometric Aryballoi* (*Allard Pierson Series* 7), Amsterdam.

Nerantzis, N.X. 2015. *Rhesus' Gold, Heracles' Iron: The Archaeology of Metals Exploitation in NE Greece*, Glasgow.

Nodarou, E. 2010. "Petrographic Analysis of the LM III Pottery Assemblage," in *Mochlos IIB: Period IV. The Mycenaean Settlement and Cemetery: The Pottery* (*Prehistory Monographs* 26), R.A.K. Smith, Philadelphia, pp. 3–14.

———. 2022. "'Εδώ στο Νότο': South Coast Fabrics and Patterns of Pottery Production in South-Southeast Crete," in *South by Southeast: The History and Archaeology of Southeast Crete from Myrtos to Kato Zakros*, E. Oddo and K. Chalikias, eds., Oxford, pp. 92–100.

Nodarou, E., and J. Moody. 2014. "'Mirabello' Fabric(s) Forever: An Analytical Study of the Granodiorite Pottery of the Vrokastro Area from the Final Neolithic Period to Modern Times," in *A Cretan Landscape through Time: Priniatikos Pyrgos and Environs* (*BAR-IS* 2634), B.P.C. Molloy and C.N. Duckworth, eds., Oxford, pp. 91–98.

Nodarou, E., and C. Rathossi. 2008. "Petrographic Analysis of Selected Animal Figurines from Syme Viannou," in *The Sanctuary of Hermes and Aphrodite at Syme Viannou IV: Animal Images of Clay. Handmade Figurines, Attachments, Mouldmade Plaques* (Βιβλιοθήκη της εν Αθήναις Αρχαιολογικής Εταιρείας 256), P. Muhly, Athens, pp. 165–182.

Noy, D. 2000. "'Half-Burnt on an Emergency Pyre': Roman Cremations which Went Wrong," *Greece & Rome* 47, 186–196.

Onar, V., and O. Belli. 2005. "Estimation of Shoulder Height from Long Bone Measurement on Dogs

Unearthed from the Van-Yoncatepe Early Iron Age Necropolis in Eastern Anatolia," *Revue de médecine vétérinaire* 156, pp. 53–60.

Ortner, D.J. 2003. *Identification of Pathological Conditions in Human Skeletal Remains*, 2nd ed., San Diego.

Ortner, D.J., and W.G.J. Putschar. 1985. *Identification of Pathological Conditions in Human Skeletal Remains* (Smithsonian Contributions to Anthropology 28), Washington, D.C.

O'Shea, J.M. 1981. "Social Configurations and the Archaeological Study of Mortuary Practices: A Case Study," in Chapman, Kinnes, and Randsborg, eds., 1981, pp. 39–52.

———. 1984. *Mortuary Variability: An Archaeological Investigation* (Studies in Archaeology), New York.

Pader, E.-J. 1982. *Symbolism, Social Relations and the Interpretation of Mortuary Remains* (BAR-IS 130), Oxford.

Panagiotopoulos, D. 2012. "Encountering the Foreign: (De-)constructing Alterity in the Archaeologies of the Bronze Age Mediterranean," in *Materiality and Social Practice: Transformative Capacities of Intercultural Encounters*, J. Maran and P.W. Stockhammer, eds., Oxford, pp. 51–60.

———. 2019. "From 'Tradition' to 'Cultural Memory:' Towards a Paradigm Shift in Aegean Archaeology," in Borgna et al., eds., 2019, pp. 363–369.

Papadaki, C., and K. Galanaki. 2012. "Τὸ δένδρον ἴσα τῷ θεῷ σέβειν. Μία ΥΓ: Ἀπεικόνιση 'Δέντρου τῆς Ζωῆς' ἀπό τα Αϊτάνια Πεδιάδος," in *Athanasia: The Earthly, the Celestial, and the Underworld in the Mediterranean from the Late Bronze and the Early Iron Age* (International Archaeological Conference, Rhodes, 28–31 May, 2009), N.C. Stampolides, A. Kanta, and A. Giannikouri, eds., Herakleion, pp. 335–340.

Papadimitriou, G. 2008. "The Technological Evolution of Copper Alloys in the Aegean during the Prehistoric Period," in *Aegean Metallurgy in the Bronze Age. Proceedings of an International Symposium Held at the University of Crete, Rethymnon, Greece, November 19–21, 2004*, I. Tzachili, ed., Rethymnon, pp. 271–287.

Papadimitriou, N. 2016. "Structuring Space, Performing Rituals, Creating Memories: Towards a Cognitive Map of Early Mycenaean Funerary Behaviour," in Dakouri-Hild and Boyd, eds., 2016, pp. 335–360.

Papadopoulos, J.K. 1994. "Early Iron Age Potters' Marks in the Aegean," *Hesperia* 63, pp. 437–507.

———. 1998. "A Bucket, by Any Other Name, and an Athenian Stranger in Early Iron Age Crete," *Hesperia* 67, pp. 109–123.

———. 2005. *The Early Iron Age Cemetery at Torone* (Monumenta Archaeologica 24), Los Angeles.

———. 2014. "Greece in the Early Iron Age: Mobility, Commodities, Polities, and Literacy," in Knapp and van Dommelen, eds., 2014, pp. 178–195.

———. 2017. "To Write and to Paint: More Early Iron Age Potters' Marks in the Aegean," in *Panhellenes at Methone: Graphê in Late Geometric and Protoarchaic Methone, Macedonia (ca. 700 BCE)* (Trends in Classics Suppl. Vol. 44), J.S. Clay, I. Malkin, and Y.Z. Tzifopoulos, eds., Berlin, pp. 36–104.

Papadopoulos, J.K., B.N. Damiata, and J.M. Marston. 2011. "Once More with Feeling: Jeremy Rutter's Plea for the Abandonment of the Term Submycenaean Revisited," in *Our Cups Are Full: Pottery and Society in the Aegean Bronze Age. Papers Presented to Jeremy B. Rutter on the Occasion of His 65th Birthday* (BAR-IS 2227), W. Gauss, M. Lindblom, R.A.K. Smith, and J.C. Wright, eds., Oxford, pp. 187–202.

Papadopoulos, J.K., and E.L. Smithson. 2017. *The Early Iron Age: The Cemeteries* (Athenian Agora XXXVI), Princeton.

Papadopoulos, T.J. 1998. *The Late Bronze Age Daggers of the Aegean I: The Greek Mainland* (Prähistorische Bronzefunde VI [11]), Stuttgart.

Papathanasiou, A. 2001. *A Bioarchaeological Analysis of Neolithic Alepotrypa Cave, Greece.* (BAR-IS 961), Oxford.

———. 2005. "Health Status of the Neolithic Population of Alepotrypa Cave, Greece," *American Journal of Physical Anthropology* 126, pp. 377–390.

Parker Pearson, M. 1982. "Mortuary Practices, Society, and Ideology: An Ethnoarchaeological Study," in *Symbolic and Structural Archaeology* (New Directions in Archaeology), I. Hodder, ed., Cambridge, pp. 99–114.

———. 1984. "Economic and Ideological Change: Cyclical Growth in the Pre-state Societies of Jutland," in *Ideology, Power, and Prehistory* (New Directions in Archaeology), D. Miller and C. Tilley, eds., Cambridge, pp. 69–92.

———. 1993. "The Powerful Dead: Archaeological Relationships between the Living and the Dead," *CAJ* 3, pp. 203–229.

———. 1999. *The Archaeology of Death and Burial*, College Station, TX.

Parkin, T.G. 1992. *Demography and Roman Society: Ancient Society and History*, Baltimore.

———. 2013. "The Demography of Infancy and Early Childhood in the Ancient World," in *The Oxford*

Handbook of Childhood and Education in the Classical World, J.E. Grubbs and T. Parkin, eds., Oxford, pp. 40–61.

Peebles, C.S. 1971. "Moundville and Surrounding Sites: Some Structural Considerations of Mortuary Practices II," in *Approaches to the Social Dimension of Mortuary Practices* (Society for American Archaeology Memoir 25), J.A. Brown, ed., Washington, D.C., pp. 68–91.

Pendlebury, H.W., J.D.S. Pendlebury, and M.C. Money-Coutts. 1937–1938. "Excavations in the Plain of Lasithi III. Karphi: A City of Refuge of the Early Iron Age in Crete," *BSA* 38, pp. 57–145.

Pendlebury, J.D.S. 1939. *The Archaeology of Crete: An Introduction*, London.

Photos, E. 1987. "Early Extractive Iron Metallurgy in N Greece: A Unified Approach to Regional Archaeometallurgy," Ph.D. diss., University of London.

———. 1989. "Metallographic Investigation of Iron Artefacts from EIA Cemetery at Vergina, Appendix 1," in "Neue Funde aus der eisenzeitlichen Hugelnekropole von Vergina, griechisch Makedonien," K. Romiopoulou and I. Kilian-Dirlmeier, *PZ* 64, pp. 146–149.

———. 1992. "Late Bronze Age–Early Iron Age Copper and Iron Slags from Kastri and Palaiokastro on Thasos," in Πρωτοϊστορική Θάσος: Τα νεκροταφεία του οικισμού Καστρί (Υπουργείου Πολιτισμού δημοσιεύματα του Αρχαιολογικού Δελτίου 45), C. Koukouli-Chrysanthi, Athens, pp. 795–801.

Photos, E., C. Koukouli-Chrysanthaki, and G. Gialoglou. 1987. "Iron Metallurgy in Eastern Macedonia: A Preliminary Report," in *The Crafts of the Blacksmith. Essays Presented to R.F. Tylecote at the 1984 Symposium of the UISPP Comité pour la sidérurgie ancienne, Held in Belfast, N. Ireland, 16th–21st September 1984*, B.G. Scott and H. Cleere, eds., Belfast, pp. 113–120.

Photos-Jones, E., C. Koukouli-Chrysanthaki, R.F. Tylecote, and G. Gialogou. 1989. "Precious Metals Extraction in Palaia Kavala, N.E. Greece," in *Archäometallurgie der Alten Welt. Proceedings of the International Symposium "Old World Archaeometallurgy"*, A. Hauptmann, E. Pernicka, and G.A. Wagner, eds., Bochum, pp. 179–190.

Platon, N. 1951. "Χρονικά," *CretChron* 5, pp. 438–449.

———. 1954. "Χρονικά," *CretChron* 8, pp. 506–517.

———. 1955. "Ἀνασκαφαὶ περιοχῆς Σητείας," *Prakt* 110 [1960], pp. 288–297.

Popham, M.R. 1965. "Some Late Minoan III Pottery from Crete," *BSA* 60, pp. 316–342.

———. 1992. "The Sub-Minoan Pottery," in Sackett, ed., 1992, pp. 59–66.

Popham, M.R., and I.S. Lemos. 1996. *Lefkandi III: The Toumba Cemetery. The Excavations of 1981, 1984, 1986, and 1992–4. Plates* (*BSA* Suppl. 29), London.

Popham, M.R., L.H. Sackett, and P. Themelis, eds. 1979–1980. *Lefkandi I: The Iron Age Settlement. The Cemeteries* (*BSA* Suppl. 11), London.

Prent, M. 2003. "Glories of the Past in the Past: Ritual Activities at Palatial Ruins in Early Iron Age Crete," in Van Dyke and Alcock, eds., 2003, pp. 81–103.

———. 2014. "Ritual and Ideology in Early Iron Age Crete: The Role of the Past and the East," in Knapp and van Dommelen, eds., 2014, pp. 650–664.

Rabinowitz, A. 2014. "Drinkers, Hosts, or Fighters? Masculine Identities in Pre-Classical Crete," in *Cultural Practices and Material Culture in Archaic and Classical Crete. Proceedings of the International Conference, Mainz, May 20–21, 2011*, O. Pilz and G. Seelentag, eds., Berlin, pp. 91–119.

Rathbun, T.A., and J.E. Buikstra, eds. 1984. *Human Identification: Case Studies in Forensic Anthropology*, Springfield, IL.

Reed, N.B. 1976. "Griffins in Post-Minoan Cretan Art," *Hesperia* 45, pp. 365–379.

Reese, D.S. 2000. "The Marine Invertebrates," in Shaw and Shaw, eds., 2000, pp. 571–642.

———. 2004. "The Fauna," in *Mochlos IC: Period III. Neopalatial Settlement on the Coast: The Artisans' Quarter and the Farmhouse at Chalinomouri. The Small Finds* (Prehistory Monographs 9), J. S. Soles, C. Davaras, J. Bending, T. Carter, D. Kondopoulou, D. Mylona, M. Ntinou, A.M. Nicgorski, D.S. Reese, A. Sarpaki, W.H. Schoch, M.E. Soles, V. Spatharas, Z.A. Stos-Gale, D.H. Tarling, and C. Witmore, Philadelphia, pp. 118–121.

Reinhard, K.J., and T.M. Fink. 1982. "The Multi-Individual Cremation Phenomenon of the Santa Cruz Drainage," *The Kiva* 47, pp. 151–161.

Reitz, E.J., and E.S. Wing. 1999. *Zooarchaeology* (Cambridge Manuals in Archaeology), Cambridge.

Renfrew, C. 1976. "Megaliths, Territories, and Population," in *Acculturation and Continuity in Atlantic Europe, Mainly during the Neolithic Period and the Bronze Age. Papers Presented at the IVth Atlantic Colloquium, Ghent, 1975* (Dissertationes archaeologicae Gandenses XVI), S.J. De Laet, ed., Bruges, pp. 198–220.

Resnick, D., and G. Niwayama. 1995. "Enostosis, Hyperostosis, and Periostitis," in *Diagnosis of Bone and Joint Disorders* 6, 3rd ed., D. Resnick, ed., Philadelphia, pp. 4,396–4,466.

Rethemiotakis, G., and M. Englezou. 2010. *Το γεωμετρικό νεκροταφείο της Έλτυνας*, Herakleion.

Rivera, F., and M. Mirazon Lahr. 2017. "New Evidence Suggesting a Dissociated Etiology for *Cribra Orbitalia* and Porotic Hyperostosis," *American Journal of Physical Anthropology* 164, pp. 76–96.

Rizza, G., and V. Santa Maria Scrinari. 1968. *Il Santuario sull'Acropoli di Gortina* I (*Monographie dello Scuola Missioni Italiane in Oriente* II), Rome.

Rizzotto, L.-C. 2015. *"Sein Zum Tode . . .": Untersuchungen zu den gesellschaftlichen Strukturen anhand der Nekropolen und Gräber der protogeometrischen und geometrischen Epoche aus Mittel-und Ostkreta* (BAR-IS 2749), Oxford.

Rocchetti, L. 1967–1968. "Il deposito protogeometrico di Petrokephali presso Festòs," *ASAtene* 45–46, pp. 181–209.

———. 1974–1975. "La ceramica dell'abitato geometrico di Festòs a occidente del palazzo minoico," *ASAtene* 52–53, pp. 169–300.

———. 1988–1989. "La ceramica della necropoli di Curtes," *ASAtene* 66–67, pp. 173–257.

Rostoker, W., and B. Bronson. 1990. *Pre-Industrial Iron: Its Technology and Ethnology* (*Archaeomaterials Monograph* 1), Philadelphia.

Rowlands, M. 1993. "The Role of Memory in the Transmission of Culture," *WorldArch* 25, pp. 141–151.

Ruscillo, D. 2005. "Marine Remains and Land Mollusks from Terrace V," in Papadopoulos 2005, pp. 321–338.

———. 2017. "Faunal Remains," in Papadopoulos and Smithson 2017, pp. 561–573.

Rutter, J.B. 1978. "A Plea for the Abandonment of the Term 'Submycenaean'," in *Studies of New and Little Known Materials from the Aegean Bronze Age. A Symposium Sponsored by the Department of Art History, Temple University, Philadelphia, Pennsylvania on March 3, 1978* (*TUAS* 3), P.P. Betancourt, ed., Philadelphia, pp. 58–65.

Sackett, L.H., ed. 1992. *Knossos: From Greek City to Roman Colony. Excavations at the Unexplored Mansion* II (*BSA* Suppl. 21), London.

Sackett, L.H., and J. Musgrave. 1976. "A New Figured Krater from Knossos," *BSA* 71, pp. 117–129.

Sakellarakis, I. 1986. "Πρωτογεωμετρική-γεωμετρική κεραμική ἀπὸ τὶς Ἀρχάνες," *CretChron* 26, pp. 7–50.

Sandars, N.K. 1955. "The Antiquity of the One-Edged Bronze Knife in the Aegean," *PPS* 21, pp. 174–197.

Sanidas, G.M, Y. Bassiakos, M. Georgakopoulou, E. Filippaki, B. Jagou, and N. Nerantzis. 2016. "Polykmetos Sideros: À propos du fer en Grèce antique," *Revue archéologique* 62, pp. 279–301.

Sapouna-Sakellaraki, E. 1978. *Die Fibeln der griechischen Inseln* (*Prähistorische Bronzefunde* XIV [4]), Munich.

Saxe, A.A. 1970. "Social Dimensions of Mortuary Practices," Ph.D. diss., University of Michigan, Ann Arbor.

Schaefer, M., S. Black, and L. Scheuer. 2009. *Juvenile Osteology: A Laboratory and Field Manual*, Amsterdam.

Schepartz, L.A., S.C. Fox, and C. Bourbou, eds. 2009. *New Directions in the Skeletal Biology of Greece* (*Hesperia* Suppl. 43), Princeton.

Scheuer, L., and S. Black. 2000. *Developmental Juvenile Osteology*, San Diego.

Schlotzhauer, U. 2000. "Die südionischen Knickrandschalen. Formen und Entwicklung der sogenannten Ionischen Schalen in archaeischer Zeit," in *Die Agais und des westliche Mittelmeer. Beziehungen und Wechselwirkurgen 8. bis 5. Jh. V. Chr., Wein, 24. bis 27. März 1999* (*DenkschrWien* 288; *AF* 4), F. Krinzinger, ed., Vienna, pp. 407–416.

Schmidt, C.W., and S.A. Symes, eds. 2008. *The Analysis of Burned Human Remains*, New York.

Schütte-Maischatz, A. 2011. *Die Phiale: zur zeichenhaften Funktion eines Gefässtyps* (*Wissenschaftliche Schriften der WWU Münster* X [9]), Münster.

Senior, L.M., and D.P. Birnie. 1995. "Accurately Estimating Vessel Volume from Profile Illustrations," *AmerAnt* 60, pp. 319–334.

Shanks, M., and C. Tilley. 1982. "Ideology, Symbolic Power and Ritual Communication: A Reinterpretation of Neolithic Mortuary Practices," in *Symbolic and Structural Archaeology* (*New Directions in Archaeology*), I. Hodder, ed., Cambridge, pp. 129–154.

Shaw, J.W., and D. Harlan. 2000. "Bronze and Iron Tools and Weapons," in Shaw and Shaw, eds., 2000, pp. 363–373.

Shaw, J.W., and M.C. Shaw, eds. 2000. *Kommos* IV: *The Greek Sanctuary*, Princeton.

She, R., and J. Szakacs. 2004. "Hyperostosis Frontalis Interna: Case Report and Review of Literature," *Annals of Clinical & Laboratory Science* 34, pp. 206–208.

Shepherd, G. 2013. "Ancient Identities: Age, Gender, and Ethnicity in Ancient Greek Burials," in Tarlow and Stutz, eds., 2013, pp. 542–557.

Sherratt, S. 2004. "Feasting in Homeric Epic," in "The Mycenaean Feast," J.C. Wright, ed., special issue, *Hesperia* 73 (2), pp. 301–337.

Shipman, P., G. Foster, and M. Schoeninger. 1984. "Burnt Bones and Teeth: An Experimental Study of Color, Morphology, Crystal Structure and Shrinkage," *JAS* 11, pp. 307–325.

Simantoni-Bournia, E. 2004. *La céramique grecque à reliefs: Ateliers insulaires du VIIIe au VIe Siècle Avant J.-C.* (*Hautes Études du monde Gréco-Romain* 32), Geneva.

Smithson, E.L. 1961. "The Protogeometric Cemetery at Nea Ionia, 1949," *Hesperia* 30, pp. 147–178.

———. 1974. "A Geometric Cemetery on the Areopagus: 1897, 1932, 1947," *Hesperia* 43, pp. 325–390.

Snodgrass, A.M. 1964. *Early Greek Armour and Weapons, from the End of the Bronze Age to 600 B.C.*, Edinburgh.

———. 1996. "Iron," in Coldstream and Catling, eds., 1996, pp. 575–597.

Snoeck, C., J.A. Lee-Thorp, R.J. Schulting. 2014. "From Bone to Ash: Compositional and Structural Changes in Burned Modern and Archaeological Bone," *Palaeogeography, Paleoclimatology, Paleoecology* 416, pp. 55–68.

Snyder, L.M. 2016. "The Animal Bones," in Day et al. 2016, pp. 169–177.

Snyder, L.M., and W.E. Klippel. 2000. "Dark Age Subsistence at the Kastro Site, East Crete: Exploring Subsistence Change and Continuity during the Late Bronze Age–Early Iron Age Transition," in *Paleodiet in the Aegean. Papers from a Colloquium Held at the 1993 Meeting of the Archaeological Institute of America in Washington, D.C.* (*Wiener Laboratory Monograph* 1), S.J. Vaughan and W.D.E. Coulson, eds., Oxford, pp. 65–84.

———. 2003. "From Lerna to Kastro: Further Thoughts on Dogs as Food in Ancient Greece; Perceptions, Prejudices and Reinvestigations," in *Zooarchaeology in Greece: Recent Advances* (*BSA* Studies 9), E. Kotjabopoulou, Y. Hamilakis, P. Halstead, C. Gamble, and P. Elefanti, eds., London, pp. 221–231.

Sørensen, T.F., and M. Bille. 2008. "Flames of Transformation: The Role of Fire in Cremation Practices," *WorldArch* 40, pp. 253–267.

Spagnoli, F. 2010. *Cooking Pots as an Indicator of Cultural Relations between Levantine Peoples in Late Bronze and Iron Ages: Origins, Diffusion and Typological Development of Cooking Ware in Levantine and Cypriot Repertoires (14th–7th Centuries B.C.)* (*Quaderni di Archeologia Fenicio-Punica* IV), Rome.

Stampolides, N.C. 1990. "Eleutherna on Crete: An Interim Report on the Geometric-Archaic Cemetery," *BSA* 85, pp. 375–403.

———. 1996. *"Ἀντίποινα": Συμβολή στη των ηθών και των εθίμων της γεωμετρικής-αρχαϊκής περιόδου* (*Eleutherna* Sector 3 [3]), Rethymnon.

———. 2001. "Οι ταφικές πυρές στην αρχαία Ελεύθερνα," in Stampolides, ed. 2001, pp. 189–199.

———. 2008. *Ancient Eleutherna: West Sector*, Athens.

Stampolides, N.C., ed. 2001. *Καύσεις στην εποχή του Χαλκού και την πρώιμη εποχή του Σιδήρου. Πρακτικά του Συμποσίου. Ρόδος, 29 Απριλίου–2 Μαΐου 1999*, Athens.

———, ed. 2004. *Ελεύθερνα: Πόλη-ακρόπολη-νεκρόπολη*, Athens.

Stampolides, N.C., and A. Giannikouri, eds. 2004. *Το Αιγαίο στην πρώιμη εποχή του Σιδήρου. Πρακτικά του Διεθνούς Συμποσίου, Ρόδος, 1–4 Νοεμβρίου 2002*, Athens.

Stampolides, N.C., and V. Karageorghis, eds. 2003. *ΠΛΟΕΣ—Sea Routes: Interconnections in the Mediterranean 16th–6th c. B.C. Proceedings of the International Symposium Held at Rethymnon, Crete, September 29th–October 2nd, 2002*, Athens.

Steele, D.G., and C.A. Bramblett. 1988. *The Anatomy and Biology of the Human Skeleton*, College Station.

Stone, R.J., and J.A. Stone. 1990. *Atlas of the Skeletal Muscles*, Dubuque.

Stravopodi, E., S.K. Manolis, S. Kousoulakos, V. Aleporou, and M.P. Schultz. 2009. "Porotic Hyperostosis in Neolithic Greece: New Evidence and Further Implications," Schepartz, Fox, and C. Bourbou, eds., 2009, pp. 257–270.

Symes, S.A., C.W. Rainwater, E.N. Chapman, D.R. Gipson, and A.L. Piper. 2008. "Patterned Thermal Destruction of Human Remains in a Forensic Setting," in Schmidt and Symes, eds., 2008, pp. 15–54.

Tainter, J.A. 1978. "Mortuary Practices and the Study of Prehistoric Social Systems," in *Advances in Archaeological Method and Theory* 1, M.B. Schiffer, ed., New York, pp. 105–141.

Tarlow. S., and L.N. Stutz, eds. 2013. *The Oxford Handbook of the Archaeology of Death and Burial*, Oxford.

Tegou, E. 2001. "Θόλωτος τάφος της πρώιμης εποχής του Σιδήρου στην Παντάνασσα Αμαρίου Ν. Ρεθύμνης," in Stampolides, ed., 2001, pp. 121–153.

Thompson, T. 2015. "Fire and the Body: Fire and the People," in *The Archaeology of Cremation: Burned*

Human Remains in Funerary Studies (Studies in Funerary Archaeology 8), T. Thompson, ed., Oxford, pp. 1–17.

Todd, T.W. 1920. "Age Changes in the Pubic Bone I: The Male White Pubis," *American Journal of Physical Anthropology* 3, pp. 285–334.

———. 1921. "Age Changes in the Pubic Bone," *American Journal of Physical Anthropology* 4, pp. 1–70.

Toffolo, M.B., A. Fantalkin, I.S. Lemos, R.C.S. Felsch, W.-D. Niemeier, G.D.R. Sanders, I.Finkelstein, and E. Boaretto. 2013. "Towards an Absolute Chronology for the Aegean Iron Age: New Radiocarbon Dates from Lefkandi, Kalapodi and Corinth," *PLoS ONE* 8(12): e83117, accessed April 25, 2023, https://doi.org/10.1371/journal.pone.0083117.

Tsatsaki, N. 2003. "Μετρολογική προσέγγιση της υπομινωικής έως ανατολίζουσας κεραμικής από την Κνωσό υπομινωική έως ανατολίζουσα περίοδος," Ph.D. diss., University of Crete, Rethymnon.

Tsipopoulou, M. 1984. "Τάφοι της πρώιμης εποχής του Σιδήρου στην ανατολική Κρήτη: Συμπλήρωμα," *ArchDelt* 39 (Α') [1990], pp. 232–245.

———. 1997. "Phatsi-Droggara: Un dépôt de céramique de la fin de l'Âge du Bronze et du début de l'Âge du Fer provenant de Crète orientale," in *La Crète mycénienne. Actes de la Table Ronde internationale organisée par l'École française d'Athènes, 26–28 mars 1991* (*BCH* Suppl. 30), J. Driessen and A. Farnoux, eds., Paris, pp. 455–484.

———. 2004. "Μια περίπτωση πρώιμων συμποσίων ή απλώς ηρωολατρείας: Γεωμετρική ανακατάληψη στο Χαλασμένο Ιεράπετρας," in Stampolides and Giannikouri, eds., 2004, pp. 127–142.

———. 2005. *Η ανατολική Κρήτη στην πρώιμη εποχή του Σιδήρου*, Herakleion.

———. 2013. "Eteocretan Geometric Revisited: The Pottery from the Burial Cave at Kephala, Piskokephalo, Siteia," in *Kreta in der geometrischen und archaischen Zeit. Akten des Internationalen Kolloquiums am Deutsche Archäologischen Institut, Abteilung Athen 27.–29. Januar 2006* (Athenaia 2), W.-D. Niemeier, O. Pilz, and I. Kaiser, eds., Munich, pp. 133–156.

Tsipopoulou, M., and D. Rupp. 2019. "The Pre- and Protopalatial Cemetery at Petras-Kephala: A Persistent Locale as an Arena for Competing Cultural Memories," in Borgna et al., eds., 2019, pp. 81–94.

Tsipopoulou, M., L. Vagnetti, and M.A. Liston. 2003. "New Evidence for the Dark Ages in Eastern Crete: An Unplundered Tholos Tomb at Vasiliki," *SMEA* 45, pp. 85–124.

Tufnell, O. 1953. *Lachish (Tell ed Duweir) III: The Iron Age (The Wellcome-Marston Archaeological Research Expedition to the Near East* III), Oxford.

Tylecote, R.F. 1992. *A History of Metallurgy*, London.

Ubelaker, D.H. 1999. *Human Skeletal Remains: Excavation, Analysis, Interpretation*, 3rd ed., Washington, D.C.

Ubelaker, D.H., T.W. Phenice, and W.M. Bass. 1969. "Artificial Interproximal Grooving of the Teeth in American Indians," *American Journal of Physical Anthropology* 30, pp. 145–149.

Ubelaker, D.H., and J.L. Rife. 2008. "Approaches to Commingling Issues in Archeological Samples: A Case Study from Roman Era Tombs in Greece," in *Recovery, Analysis, and Identification of Commingled Human Remains*, B.J. Adams and J.E. Byrd, eds., Totowa, NJ, pp. 97–122.

Van Dyke, R.M., and S.E. Alcock, eds., 2003. *Archaeologies of Memory*, Malden, MA.

Varoufakis, G.J. 1989. "Greece: An Important Metallurgical Centre of Iron in Antiquity," in *Archaeometallurgy of Iron. International Symposium of the Comité pour la sidérugie ancienne de l'UISPP*, R. Pleiner, ed., Prague, pp. 279–286.

Vasilakis, A. 2004. "Πρωτογεωμετρικός οικισμός στη Γριά Βίγλα Μοιρών στη νότια Κρήτη," in Stampolides and Giannikouri, eds., 2004, pp. 93–104.

Velho, G. 2008. "Retour sur les 'Bone Enclosures' de Vrokastro: Éléments de datation et pratiques funéraires," *CretAnt* 9, pp. 209–243.

Verhoeven, J.D. 2007. *Steel Metallurgy for the Non-Metallurgist*, Materials Park, OH.

Villotte, S., and C.J. Knüsel. 2013. "Understanding Entheseal Changes: Definition and Life Course Changes," *International Journal of Osteoarchaeology* 23, pp. 135–146.

Wahl, J. 2008. "Investigations on Pre-Roman and Roman Cremation Remains from Southwestern Germany: Results, Potentialities and Limits," in Schmidt and Symes, eds., 2008, pp. 145–161.

Walker, P.L. 2001. "A Bioarchaeological Perspective on the History of Violence," *Annual Review of Anthropology* 30, pp. 573–596.

Walker, P.L., R.R. Bathhurst, R. Richman, T. Gjerdrum, and V.A. Andrushko. 2009. "The Causes of Porotic Hyperostosis and Cribra Orbitalia: A Reappraisal of the Iron-Deficiency-Anemia Hypothesis," *American Journal of Physical Anthropology* 139, pp. 109–125.

Wallace, S.A. 2010. *Ancient Crete: From Successful Collapse to Democracy's Alternatives, Twelfth–Fifth Centuries* BC, Cambridge.

———. 2018. *Travellers in Time: Imagining Movement in the Ancient Aegean World* (*Routledge Studies in Archaeology*), London.

Warren, P.M. 1982–1983. "Knossos: Stratigraphical Museum Excavations, 1978–82. Part II," *AR* 29, pp. 63–87.

———. 1969. *Minoan Stone Vases* (*Cambridge Classical Studies*), Cambridge.

Warren, P.M., and V. Hankey. 1989. *Aegean Bronze Age Chronology*, Bristol.

Webb, P.A., and J.M. Suchey. 1985. "Epiphyseal Union of the Anterior Iliac Crest and Medial Clavicle in a Modern Multiracial Sample of American Males and Females," *American Journal of Physical Anthropology* 68, pp. 457–466.

Webb, V.E.S. 1996. "Faience and Glass," in Coldstream and Catling, eds., 1996, pp. 599–610.

Węcowski, M. 2012. "When Did the *Symposion* Rise: Some Archaeological Considerations Regarding the Emergence of the Greek Aristocratic Banquet," Αρχαιογνωσία 16, pp. 19–48.

Weiss-Krejci, E. 2008. "Unusual Life, Unusual Death and the Fate of the Corpse: A Case Study from Dynastic Europe," in Murphy, ed., 2008, pp. 169–190.

Weninger, B., and R. Jung. 2009. "Absolute Chronology of the End of the Aegean Bronze Age," in *LH IIIC Chronology and Synchronisms III: LH IIIC Late and the Transition to the Early Iron Age. Proceedings of the International Workshop Held at the Austrian Academy of Sciences at Vienna, February 23rd and 24th, 2007* (*DenkschrWien* 384; *Veröffentlichungen der Mykenischen Kommission* 30), S. Deger-Jalkotzky and A.E. Bächle, eds., Vienna, pp. 373–416.

West, W.C. 2015. "Informal and Practical Uses of Writing on Potsherds from Azoria, Crete," *ZPE* 193, pp. 151–163.

Whitbread, I.K. 1995. *Greek Transport Amphorae: A Petrological and Archaeological Study* (*Fitch Laboratory Occasional Paper* 4), Athens.

Whitelaw, T.M., P.M. Day, E. Kiriatzi, V. Kilikoglou, and D.E. Wilson. 1997. "Ceramic Traditions at EM IIB Myrtos Fournou Korifi," in *TEXNH: Craftsmen, Craftswomen and Craftsmanship in the Aegean Bronze Age. Proceedings of the 6th International Aegean Conference, Philadelphia, Temple University, 18–21 April 1996* (*Aegaeum* 16), R. Laffineur and P.P. Betancourt, eds., Liège, pp. 265–274.

Whitley, J. 2002. "Objects with Attitude: Biographical Facts and Fallacies in the Study of Late Bronze Age and Early Iron Age Warrior Graves," *CAJ* 12, pp. 217–232.

———. 2009. "Crete," in *A Companion to Archaic Greece*, K. Raaflaub and H. van Wees, eds., Chichester, pp. 273–293.

———. 2011. "Praisos V: A Preliminary Report on the 2007 Excavation Season," *BSA* 106, pp. 3–45.

———. 2016. "Burning People, Breaking Things: Material Entanglements, the Bronze Age/Iron Age Transition and the Homeric Dividual," in *An Archaeology of Prehistoric Bodies and Embodied Identities in the Eastern Mediterranean*, M. Mina, S. Triantaphyllou, and Y. Papadatos, eds., Oxford, pp. 215–223.

Williams, H. 2004. "Death Warmed Up: The Agency of Bodies and Bones in Early Anglo-Saxon Cremation Rites," *Journal of Material Culture* 9, pp. 263–291.

———. 2005. "Keeping the Dead at Arm's Length: Memory, Weaponry and Early Medieval Mortuary Technologies," *Journal of Social Archaeology* 5, pp. 253–275.

———. 2013. "Death, Memory, and Material Culture: Catalytic Commemoration and the Cremated Dead," in Tarlow and Stutz, eds., 2013, pp. 194–208.

Wright, J. 2013. "Land Ownership and Landscape Belief: Introduction and Contexts," in Tarlow and Stutz, eds., 2013, pp. 405–419.

Yermán, L., H. Wall, J. Carrascal, A. Browning, D. Chandraratne, C. Nguyen, A. Wong, T. Goode, D. Kyriacou, M. Campbell, J. Cao, T. Do, D. Casimiro-Soriguer, A. Lucherini, S. Zárate, H.K. Wyn, A. Bolanos, A. Solarte, C. Górska, B.-D. Le, S. Tran, Q. Le, and J.L. Torero. 2018. "Experimental Study on the Fuel Requirements for the Thermal Degradation of Bodies by Means of Open Pyre Cremation," *Fire Safety Journal* 98, pp. 63–73.

Yon, M. 1971. *Salamine de Chypre* II: *La Tombe T.I du XIe s. av. J.-C.*, Paris.

Young, R.S. 1949. "An Early Geometric Grave near the Athenian Agora," *Hesperia* 18, pp. 275–297.

Zimhoni, O. 1997. *Studies in the Iron Age Pottery of Israel: Typological, Archaeological and Chronological Aspects* (*Journal of the Institute of Archaeology at Tel Aviv University Occasional Papers* 2), Tel Aviv.

Index

abscess, 140, 152, 175, 224, 229, 230
adolescent, 31, 63, 68, 76, 222, 224, 227, 338, 343, 346
adornment. *See* bead; bronze, sheeting
Adromyloi, 23, 34, 44, 55, 72, 78, 100, 103, 118, 119, 126, 143, 178, 197
age at death, 203, 221, 223
age estimation, 31, 94, 130, 140, 152, 222
alabastron, 126, 288
    straight sided, 126, 288
Aloni/Skala, 158, 223, 246, 359, 363, 367
amphora, 6, 9, 23, 24, 25, 37, 38, 42, 43, 44, 50, 55, 57, 62, 78, 79, 80, 84, 86, 96, 97, 99, 100, 102, 103, 104, 115, 119, 121, 129, 130, 131, 133, 140, 143, 146, 147, 148, 150, 154, 156, 162, 163, 164, 165, 168, 169, 171, 172, 174, 176, 177, 178, 182, 183, 192, 250, 267, 269, 277, 279, 281–284, 286, 287, 288, 289, 290, 293, 294, 298, 299, 322, 332, 333, 334, 335, 336, 338, 342, 343, 345, 346, 348, 349, 351, 353, 355, 363, 368, 376
    amphoriskos, 26, 34, 37, 43, 51, 52, 99, 177, 262, 264, 281, 284, 285, 288, 293
Anavlochos, 39, 171, 328, 333, 342, 346
anemia, 63, 68, 75, 94, 95, 113, 135, 145, 153, 203, 225–226
Angel, J.L., 220, 223, 225, 226
animal bones. *See* bones, animal
antemortem tooth loss (AMTL), 195, 229–230
antiques. *See* heirlooms or antiquities
Aphrati, 266, 333, 367

architecture
    tholos tomb, 17–18, 20, 27, 28, 31, 35, 45, 48, 49, 246, 247, 328
    enclosure, 53, 60, 61, 67, 73, 82, 90, 92, 109, 111, 124, 125, 127, 129, 134, 139, 144, 151, 157, 161, 163, 168, 173, 182, 184, 192, 194, 198, 200, 201, 216, 248–249, 251, 331, 332
Argos, 276
arrowhead. *See* iron, weapon, arrowhead
arthritis, arthritic, 95, 185, 226
aryballos, 24, 39, 63, 64, 65, 66, 69, 70, 71, 78, 79, 96, 102, 115, 117, 119, 120, 130, 131, 132, 136, 137, 138, 141, 142, 167, 176, 179, 187, 188, 193, 195, 196, 209, 271–272, 275, 276, 277, 278, 293, 294, 342, 343, 344, 351, 353, 368, 371
askos, 23, 24, 25, 371. *See also* bird askos/bird vase
Athenian Agora, 224, 225, 226, 333
Athens, Attica, 11, 23, 38, 79, 106, 117, 222, 224, 225, 232, 243, 254, 255, 261, 276, 308, 313, 317, 333, 363, 367, 369, 371
auricular surface, 32, 76, 83, 93, 94, 140, 152, 186, 199, 222
Avila, R., 312, 314
awl. *See* bronze, tool; iron, tool
axe/axe-head. *See* iron, tool
Azoria, 12, 57, 69, 117, 188, 190, 237, 241, 263, 291, 295, 328, 332, 339, 357, 358, 359, 360, 374

basin, 9, 104, 136, 138, 196, 199, 200, 265, 267, 270, 271, 293, 342, 343
basket handle, 43, 273, 288, 289
basket vase, 34, 96, 99, 100, 159, 160, 288, 293, 343
bead(s). *See* glass bead; ivory/bone object; lead object; stone object; terracotta object
bedrock, 31, 46, 47, 48, 49, 60, 67, 247
    breccia (brecciated dolomite), 62, 67, 73, 74, 81, 82, 92, 109, 110, 112, 125, 129, 134, 135, 136, 139, 144, 157, 169, 173, 181, 182, 193, 202, 215, 227, 246, 249
    tsakali, xv, 17, 18, 21, 27, 28, 29, 45, 246
bench, 139, 173, 174, 198, 200, 248
bimetallic object(s), 98, 105, 107, 116, 123, 150, 154, 156, 191, 305, 306, 310, 314
bird askos/bird vase, 23, 24, 25, 36, 37, 43, 45, 46, 47, 273, 274, 371
Bikaki, A., 296
bloomery, xi, 380–381
bone/antler objects, 85, 90, 114, 116, 154, 156, 169, 170, 171, 239, 240, 241, 321
bones, animal, 235–241. *See also* calcined bone, animal
    bird, 237
    cat, 46, 231
    cattle/cow, 32, 46, 50, 77, 182, 186, 193, 236, 238, 241, 331
    deer, 54, 84, 85, 90, 114, 116,153, 154, 156, 169, 170, 171, 193, 199, 236, 238, 239, 240, 241, 350, 353, 368, 370
    dog, 29, 32, 44, 46, 60, 77, 110, 153, 236, 237, 331, 356
    horse, 331
    mouse/shrew, 95, 176, 236
    pig, 32, 46, 68, 77, 84, 114, 136, 146, 153, 162, 182, 186 195, 204, 236, 237, 238, 331, 350, 353
    rabbit/hare, 29, 32, 68, 95, 110, 130, 146, 236, 237, 331
    sheep/goat, 17, 19, 22, 27, 29, 32, 46, 49, 50, 54, 60, 68, 77, 84, 91, 95, 110, 114, 128, 146, 153, 158, 162, 164, 169, 182, 186, 193, 195, 199, 236, 237, 238–240, 241, 331, 350, 353
    snake, 95, 236
bosses
    as decoration on pottery, 65, 79, 102, 169, 170, 171, 258
    as decoration on pins, 306, 307, 308, 311
botanical remains
    grain, 154, 216, 242, 243, 318, 350
    grape, 96, 128, 146, 154, 158, 164, 176, 186, 204, 216, 242, 243, 345, 350
    legume, 114, 154, 164, 176, 216, 242, 243, 350
    lentil, 96, 114, 136, 242, 243, 350
    olive, 96, 146, 154, 158, 216, 242, 243, 350, 353
    pea, 110, 158, 242, 243
    pistachio, 146, 154, 216, 242, 243, 350

bowl, 7, 29, 30, 34, 38, 39, 42, 48, 63, 66, 133, 136, 138, 190, 195, 196, 197, 260, 265, 300
    deep bowl, 19, 20, 22, 23, 24, 27, 28, 32, 33, 34, 42, 47, 51, 128, 165
Boyd (Hawes), H., ix, xi, xii, 1, 2, 3, 5, 15, 17, 19, 20, 21, 29, 31, 48, 51, 209, 246, 248, 305, 367
Brock, J., 9, 11
bronze
    jewelry, 13, 216, 330, 333, 340, 341, 345, 351, 373
        bracelet, 13, 20, 23, 26, 309, 330, 340, 349, 351
        earring, 13, 18, 19, 23, 26, 29, 32, 309, 330, 340
        fibula, 13, 20, 21, 23, 25, 29, 30, 32, 47, 56, 58, 97, 98, 99, 105, 116, 147, 148, 150, 159, 160, 165, 168, 174, 177, 178, 180, 187, 188, 190, 194, 196, 197, 305, 306, 307–308, 311, 330, 335, 336, 340, 345, 346, 349, 351, 352, 367, 368, 372
        pin, 26, 32, 33, 45, 47, 63, 64, 66, 69, 72, 78, 80, 115, 116, 122, 131, 133, 136, 138, 147, 159, 160, 216, 306–307, 308, 311, 330, 335, 336, 345
        ring, 13, 18, 19, 23, 26, 29, 32, 309, 330, 340
    sheeting, 13, 97, 98, 105, 116, 138, 147, 148, 150, 187, 191, 204, 305, 306, 309–310, 330, 334, 340, 372
    tool, 105, 122, 306, 310, 319
Buchholz, H.-G., 312
building
    A-B, ix, 2, 3, 208, 209, 248, 334, 360, 361
    C, 59, 67, 73, 77, 144
    D, 67, 182, 192, 193, 201, 205
    E East, 208
    E West, 53, 54, 334, 345
    F, ix, 14, 162, 165, 194
    G (Shrine), x, 81, 139, 140, 141, 162, 163, 168, 193, 248, 249, 297, 301, 332, 334, 335, 336, 337, 347, 361, 366
    I, 90, 127, 173, 183, 184, 200
    J, 5, 92, 109, 110, 111, 134, 144, 151, 233, 257, 274, 282, 344, 361
    K, 129, 233
    L, 16, 31, 32, 33, 245, 328, 357
    N, 172, 174, 198
    O, 157, 161, 172, 173, 183, 198, 200, 250
    P, ix
    Q, ix
    R, ix, 14, 21, 112, 134
building complex/building
    C-D, ix, 81, 233, 334, 335, 337, 347, 366, 367
    E, ix, 53, 54, 208, 334, 345
    I-O-N, ix, 16, 48, 156, 157, 183, 184, 233, 334, 335, 337, 347
    J-K, ix, 113, 233, 334, 335, 337, 345, 347, 366, 367
    L-M, ix, 16, 31, 32, 245

building materials
  breccia, 17, 18, 21, 27, 28, 31, 36, 45, 49, 109, 111, 129, 134, 144, 157, 163, 169, 184, 202, 246, 249
  limestone, 17, 18, 19, 20, 21, 27, 28, 31, 36, 45, 49, 53, 62, 73, 82, 92, 109, 111, 129, 134, 144, 151, 157, 163, 169, 184, 194, 202, 212, 246, 249, 332, 353
burial
  cremation, primary, 2, 5, 6, 54, 62, 63, 68, 74, 76, 82, 83, 93, 94, 95, 112, 113, 114, 128, 130, 135, 140, 145, 146, 153, 157, 158, 164, 169, 174, 175, 176, 177, 185, 186, 193, 194, 195, 198, 199, 202, 203, 212, 214, 215, 331, 333, 334, 335, 337, 338, 351, 353, 363
  cremation, secondary, 6, 9, 91, 152, 164, 174, 175, 176, 215, 290, 328, 331, 333, 335, 337, 338, 339, 342, 345, 346, 349, 351, 353, 355, 363, 374
  experimental pig cremation, 212–215, 340
  inhumation, 2, 6, 9, 17, 19, 21, 22, 24, 31, 32, 36, 46, 49, 73, 74, 76, 77, 78, 82, 83, 84, 109, 110, 152, 157, 158, 159, 161, 201, 220, 221, 224, 225, 228, 230, 327, 328, 331, 333, 334, 335, 336, 337, 338, 339, 346, 347, 348, 351, 353, 354, 359, 363, 364, 365, 370, 373, 374
  ritual. See funerary ritual
butchery, 182, 239, 369
Byzantine
  metalworking, xi, 380
  Byzantine period, 226
  pottery, 28, 48

cairn, 17, 19
calcined bone,
  animal, 54, 68, 77, 84, 90, 95, 114, 130, 153, 171, 182, 186, 193, 199, 203, 236, 238, 239, 240, 241, 341, 350
  human, 54, 60, 62, 63, 68, 74, 75, 82, 83, 94, 95, 113, 114, 125, 128, 130, 135, 140, 145, 146, 153, 157, 158, 164, 169, 175, 176, 182, 185, 186, 193, 195, 198, 199, 202, 203, 212, 213, 215, 232, 373
capacities of vessels, x, xii, 7, 64, 178, 254, 256, 257, 258, 259, 261, 262, 263, 264, 268, 278, 286, 375–377
Cape Gelidonya, 318
carbon/charcoal, 112, 124, 173, 213, 341, 353, 356, 380
  carbon in iron working, 380, 381, 382, 383
carburization, 311, 318, 383
caries, 175, 229, 230
Catling, H., 307, 308, 309, 311, 312, 318, 358
centaur, 188, 190
Chalasmenos, 117, 177, 263, 266, 299, 301, 302, 303, 304, 357, 358, 361

Chamaizi area, 300, 303, 304
  Chamaizi Phatsi, 11, 34, 38, 55, 293
  Skopi Droggara, 34
Chania, 22, 99, 154, 188, 240
child/children, subadult, 2, 5, 6, 31, 36, 46, 69, 95, 109, 114, 152, 157, 161, 162, 164, 165, 177, 199, 201, 202, 203, 219, 220, 221, 223, 224, 225, 226, 230, 231, 232, 233, 247, 248, 250, 260, 272, 274, 278, 290, 296, 307, 308, 311, 322, 324, 329, 331, 332, 333, 334, 335, 337, 338, 339, 343, 344, 346, 347, 353, 359, 363, 368, 370, 374
chromosome, 224
chronology/dating, 7, 11–13, 14, 16, 18, 19, 22, 24, 27, 30, 32, 37, 47, 50, 56, 60, 64, 69, 78, 85, 91, 99, 110, 116, 126, 128, 131, 136, 141, 147, 154, 159, 162, 165, 170, 177, 183, 187, 193, 196, 199, 201, 205, 208, 255, 259, 297, 306, 333, 350, 355–358, 373
cist grave, xv, 2
clans, 364, 366, 373, 377
clusters
  tholos tombs, 245, 328, 331, 362, 366, 373
  enclosures, 233, 248, 257, 282, 283, 334–337, 338, 339, 344, 347, 349, 359, 366, 367, 368, 373
Coldstream, J.N., x, xiii, 9, 30, 117, 273, 285, 286, 287
construction techniques. See architecture
Corinth, 69, 213, 214, 271, 272, 276, 278, 280, 288, 371
cremation
  primary. See burial
  secondary. See burial
  discard deposits, 6, 60, 67, 73, 74, 77, 91, 92, 93, 96, 109, 127, 151, 152, 156, 182, 183, 184, 185, 186, 194, 195, 201, 215, 225, 235, 248, 250, 331, 338, 339
  visibility of cremations, 332, 364, 365, 366, 367, 374
cribra orbitalia, 68, 75, 94, 95, 135, 152, 153, 203, 225, 226
cup, 16, 23, 34, 35, 36, 37, 38, 47, 48, 49, 55, 64, 126, 254–261, 264, 267, 271, 293, 299, 300, 301, 302, 330, 343, 344, 351, 353, 354, 355, 363, 369, 273, 376–377
  footed, 37, 38, 42, 261, 376
  Ionian, 70, 263
  ledge-rim, 96, 97, 99, 101, 147, 148, 149, 155, 182, 257, 259, 280, 293, 302, 363
  mug like, 64, 69, 70, 105, 117, 118, 130, 131, 132, 155, 173, 176, 177, 179, 260–261, 278, 343, 376
  surface treatment
    decorated, 23, 24, 37, 38, 46, 55, 56, 64, 69, 84, 86, 97, 99, 102, 115, 117, 120, 130, 131, 132, 136, 137, 141, 143, 146, 147, 148, 154, 155, 159, 165, 169, 170, 183, 187, 188, 195, 196, 208, 254–255, 256, 292, 294, 295, 330
    dipped/blob, 8, 9, 22, 34, 37, 38, 52, 148, 254, 261, 262, 288, 293

cup, surface treatment, cont.
            monochrome, 41, 43, 44, 50, 55, 57, 58, 60, 61,
                62, 63, 64, 65, 66, 67, 68, 69, 71, 72, 78, 79, 84,
                85, 86, 87, 91, 96, 97, 99, 100, 101, 102, 103, 104,
                105, 115, 119, 121, 125, 126, 128, 130, 132, 133,
                136, 138, 141, 142, 143, 146, 147, 148, 149, 154,
                155, 156, 159, 160, 164, 166, 169, 171, 173, 174,
                176, 177, 178, 179, 182, 186, 187, 188, 189, 190,
                195, 197, 199, 204, 205, 206, 207, 208, 255–
                260, 275, 290, 293, 303, 334, 336, 343, 344,
                355, 368, 371
            plain, 71, 44, 51, 71, 84, 88, 156, 179, 189, 260
cup or skyphos, 20, 23, 26, 36, 42, 47, 50, 51, 55, 57, 58, 65,
    87, 88, 101, 102, 118, 120, 121, 126, 127, 129, 130, 131,
    133, 142, 143, 148, 149, 155, 159, 160, 170, 171, 179, 187,
    189, 190, 197, 200, 264. See also skyphos/cup
Cyclades, Cycladic, 117, 254, 258, 261, 264, 269, 283, 367,
    371, 372
Cyprus, Cypriot, 22, 55, 165, 170, 171, 196, 269, 270, 274,
    275, 276, 285, 288, 295, 307, 308, 312, 313, 314, 317, 318,
    320, 336, 363, 367, 371, 372

deep bowl. See bowl, deep bowl
demographic analysis, 219, 220, 221
dental attrition, 229
dentition, 29, 31, 32, 46, 110, 130, 140, 175, 221, 228, 230
Desborough, V.R.d'A., 11, 16, 22, 273
Deshayes, J., 317, 318
deviant burials, 338
disease, 63, 145, 158, 220, 225, 228, 231, 233. See also hyperostosis frontalis interna, joint disease, Langerhans cell histiocytosis (LCH), linear enamel hypoplasia (LEH), periodontal disease, porotic hyperostosis
DNA analysis, 224, 232, 358
Dreros, 34, 55, 159, 328, 333
drinking ritual. See ritual, drinking ritual
dromos. See pseudo-dromos

Eaby, M. xi, 2, 20, 247
Early Iron Age (EIA), xi, 1, 11, 46, 136, 212, 223, 224,
    225, 226, 240, 242, 243, 247, 250, 253, 255, 256, 261,
    266, 268, 270, 274, 278, 286, 291, 295, 302, 304, 314,
    316, 317, 318, 320, 322, 324, 331, 333, 334, 344, 346,
    348, 349, 350, 351, 355, 357, 360, 362, 366, 369, 370,
    373, 379, 380, 383
Early Minoan (EM), 1, 17, 26, 138, 247, 286, 297, 298,
    299, 303, 322, 332, 349, 360
Early Orientalizing (EO), 8, 11, 13, 14, 30, 34, 46, 47, 55,
    56, 57, 60, 64, 69, 70, 71, 72, 78, 84, 85, 99, 115, 117, 119,
    136, 137, 138, 154, 155, 159, 160, 165, 170, 171, 188, 189,
    196, 197, 209, 225, 253, 255, 257, 258, 259, 260, 263,
    264, 266, 267, 269, 270, 272, 276, 277, 288, 289, 291,
    294, 298, 306, 307, 308, 331, 335, 336, 337, 342, 343,
    356, 359, 366

Early Protoarchaic (EPAR), 137, 196
earring. See bronze, jewelry
economy, 304, 364, 379–372, 374. See also exchange/trade
Eleutherna, 23, 55, 64, 78, 85, 99, 137, 141, 148, 154, 165,
    196, 205, 257, 258, 259, 260, 261, 264, 265, 266, 267,
    268, 269, 272, 277, 278, 280, 281, 284, 286, 328, 333,
    349, 350, 367, 376
elite(s), 233, 316, 344, 359, 360, 361, 364, 365, 366, 367,
    368, 369, 372, 374
Eltyna, 11, 23, 98, 116, 279, 282, 284, 309, 320, 331, 346,
    370
enclosure grave, 2–3, 53–209, 245–250
    construction, 53, 67, 73, 82, 92, 109, 111–112, 127,
        129, 134, 139, 144, 151, 157, 163, 169, 173, 184,
        194, 198, 202, 249, 332
    date, 56, 64, 69–70, 73–74, 82, 99, 110, 116–117, 126,
        128, 131, 136–137, 141, 147–148, 154–155, 159,
        165, 170, 178, 187–188, 196, 205, 208, 356
    definition, xv
    evidence for burning, 215
        fractured/fissured limestone, 53, 62, 73, 82, 109,
            111, 129, 134, 144, 151, 157, 169, 184, 194, 202,
            249
        calcined breccia, 67, 82, 92, 111, 112, 134, 144,
            173, 184, 193, 194, 249
    excavation and recording of, 3–5, 6
    floors, 62, 73, 82, 92, 109, 112, 127, 129, 134, 139,
        144, 151, 157, 163, 169, 173, 184, 194, 198, 202,
        249
    incorporation of earlier walls, 53, 67, 92, 109, 111,
        127, 134, 139, 144, 157, 173, 198, 201, 216, 248
    other Cretan examples, 333
    orientation, 6, 61, 67, 73, 82, 92, 109, 111, 129, 134,
        139, 144, 151, 157, 163, 169, 173, 184, 194, 198,
        201
    origins, 332–334
    shape, 248
    size, 53, 61, 67, 73, 82, 92, 109, 111, 127, 129, 134,
        139, 144, 151, 157, 163, 169, 173, 184, 194, 198,
        201, 212, 216, 248
    stratigraphy, 5, 7, 54, 60, 62, 67, 82, 92–93, 110, 112,
        127, 129–130, 135, 139, 144, 152, 157, 163, 169,
        173–174, 184, 192, 194, 198, 199, 202
enthesopathy, enethesopathies, 83, 227
ethnicity, 362
Evans, A., 1, 253, 367
Evans, M., 92
Evely, D., 316, 318, 319, 320
exchange/trade, 293, 304, 348, 367, 371, 372. See also
    economy
experimental pig cremation. See cremation

fabric types, ceramic, main discussions, 9–10, 11, 291–
    293, 297–304, 371

family, 36, 225, 232–233, 247, 296, 306, 334, 336, 337, 338, 339, 340, 345, 346, 347, 349, 359, 360, 362, 366, 368, 369, 370, 373. *See also* clans; kinship groups
faunal remains. *See* bones, animal
feasting, 23, 164, 239, 320, 332, 340, 342, 344, 348, 350, 352, 353, 359, 360, 365, 367, 369, 373
fetus, fetal, 5, 68, 91, 92, 94, 95, 111, 112, 113, 114, 127, 128, 139, 140, 145, 151, 152, 153, 199, 221, 222, 223, 224, 225, 232, 239, 250, 308, 324, 334, 335, 336, 337, 338, 346, 347, 353, 354, 370
fibula. *See* bronze, jewelry; iron, jewelry
fill (in graves), 3, 7, 16, 21, 32, 33, 45, 46, 47, 49, 50, 84, 129, 134, 146, 148, 155, 216, 237, 238, 247, 249, 328, 372. *See also* rock/stone tumble
flask, 19, 23, 24, 25, 35, 36, 37, 39, 40, 61, 62, 63, 66, 68, 275, 276, 280, 293, 294, 329, 330, 343, 344, 351, 353, 367, 371
floral remains. *See* botanical remains
Fortenberry, D., 313, 314, 315
Fortetsa, 55, 115, 165, 242, 295, 307, 311, 317, 370
fracture, 75, 94, 152, 186, 226, 227, 228, 283
funerary/burial ritual. *See* ritual

Gaignerot-Driessen, F., 2, 12, 328, 333, 342, 346, 360, 361, 382
gender, 223, 224, 307, 340, 343, 345, 347, 348, 366, 370, 374
genetic anomalies, 113, 153, 232, 334, 335, 336, 338
Geometric
    ceramic phase/styles, 12, 16, 22, 38, 92, 96, 97, 99, 131, 140, 148, 151, 152, 182, 193, 196, 208, 209, 259, 276, 279, 281, 285, 294, 355, 258, 376
    Geometric period, 2, 5, 12, 21, 28, 38, 50, 141, 181, 193, 224, 256, 266, 280, 282, 297, 298, 301, 308, 313, 321, 331, 356, 358, 359
glazed wares, 37, 43, 44, 45, 47, 48
glass bead, 196, 197, 205, 207, 321–322, 335
Gournia, 298
Gortyn law code, 327
granodiorite/granitic-dioritic fabric, 72, 79, 87, 103,104, 117, 119, 121, 133, 156, 276, 297, 298, 300–301, 303, 304
grave
    goods, ix, 2, 3, 4, 5, 6, 7, 46, 73, 109, 113, 181, 192, 193, 202, 215, 225, 233, 243, 248, 250, 328, 329–331, 335, 338, 340–350, 351, 352, 353, 354, 362, 365, 366, 368, 372, 373, 374
    marker, 6, 9, 19, 55, 62, 96, 97, 112, 115, 129, 130, 131, 140, 187, 246, 249, 250, 271, 282, 283, 284, 332, 334, 335, 336, 337, 340, 342, 344, 345, 349, 351, 352, 353, 361, 363
Gulf of Mirabello, 1, 301, 303

Haggis, D., 10
Hagios Ioannis, 22, 37, 55, 254, 323
Hall, E., 209, 333, 362
health, 219, 220, 221, 225–232, 233. *See also* disease
heirlooms or antiques, 12, 14, 28, 32, 33, 131, 141, 148, 177, 268, 271, 274, 306, 308, 309, 322, 323, 348–350, 355, 357, 362, 367
Höckmann, O., 314
Homer, 260, 361, 364, 367
hormone deficiency, 64, 224
hunter, hunting, 222, 236, 241, 310, 313, 321, 340, 350, 368, 369, 370
hydria, 26, 50, 84, 115, 121, 136, 138, 165, 167, 171, 182, 183, 195, 196, 197, 268, 279, 280–281, 284, 290, 293, 343, 344
hyperostosis frontalis interna, 63, 75, 230, 231

identity, 344, 345, 360, 361, 362, 365, 368–370, 373, 374
infant, 4, 5, 68, 69, 75, 76, 81, 83, 84, 92, 95, 111, 135–136, 157–158, 183, 184, 186, 187, 194, 195, 201, 202–203, 204, 213, 214, 219, 221, 222, 223, 224, 225, 229, 230, 231, 250, 260, 278, 283, 288, 296, 308, 311, 324, 335, 338, 339, 343, 344, 345, 346, 347, 353, 368, 370, 374
infection, 75, 77, 146, 158, 175, 195, 223, 228, 230, 231
incised decoration, 22, 23, 24, 27, 28, 37, 44, 48, 64, 67, 69, 72, 84, 88, 116, 124, 160, 165, 168, 179, 183, 191, 204, 206, 207, 208, 258, 279, 280, 308, 322, 323, 324
inflammation, 76, 83, 220, 228, 230, 232
inhumation. *See* burial
Ionian cup. *See* cup
iron
    tool, 2, 13, 78, 81, 85, 89, 90, 97, 98, 107, 108, 116, 124, 147, 170, 171, 173, 177, 181, 187, 191, 216, 310, 314, 319, 320, 330, 334, 335, 336, 340, 341, 342, 345, 346, 347–348, 351, 353, 357, 359, 362, 368, 370, 373, 374, 379
    awl, 13, 56, 59, 85, 88, 89, 90, 98, 108, 116, 124, 147, 150, 310, 318, 319, 321, 348
    axe/axe-head, 13, 85, 89, 98, 108, 177, 181, 187, 191, 209, 310, 311, 318, 336, 346, 348, 367, 370, 379, 382, 383
    chisel, 13, 85, 89, 98, 108, 116, 124, 131, 134, 177, 181, 191, 310, 318–319, 321, 348, 368
    file, 13, 85, 89, 116, 123, 124, 319, 348, 368
    fire dog, 316, 320, 348, 359, 367
    flesh hook, 13, 98, 108, 109, 116, 124, 310, 320, 348, 359, 368
    knife, 13, 23, 26, 27, 37, 44, 78, 80, 81, 89, 98, 107, 108, 114, 116, 123, 136, 138, 147, 150, 171, 173, 174, 177, 181, 187, 191, 241, 310, 316–318, 321, 330, 336, 346, 348, 368, 370, 379

iron, tool, cont.
>needle, 131, 134, 159, 160, 187, 191, 306, 319, 320, 336, 348, 368
>punch or hammer, 13, 89, 310, 319, 320, 348
>saw, 116, 123, 318, 348
>scraper, 13, 78, 81, 98, 108, 131, 134, 310, 319, 348
>sickle/sickle-shaped knife, 27, 56, 78, 81, 108, 116, 123, 136, 138, 187, 191, 316, 317, 348
>spatulate tool, 98, 116, 124, 319
>spit, 78, 98, 170, 171, 316, 320, 348, 359, 367
>tongs, 13, 85, 89, 310, 320, 348, 368
>tweezers, 13, 78, 81, 310, 320, 348
>weapon, 2, 13, 37, 44, 64, 78, 81, 83, 85, 97, 98, 107, 114, 152, 165, 196, 209, 216, 225, 228, 236, 283, 305, 310, 313, 314, 315, 316, 317, 318, 328, 330, 333, 334, 335, 336, 337, 340, 341, 342, 344, 345, 346, 347, 348, 350, 351, 353, 359, 362, 366, 367, 368, 369, 370, 373, 374, 381
>>arrowhead, 13, 53, 54, 56, 58, 59, 103, 116, 122–123, 310, 311, 312–313, 316, 334, 336, 346, 347, 350, 367, 368, 369, 370, 379, 383
>>dagger, 13, 85, 89, 97, 98, 107, 165, 166, 187, 191, 306, 310, 311, 315–316, 321, 334, 336, 346, 368, 370, 374, 379, 383
>>dirk/short sword, 13, 32, 85, 89, 97, 98, 107, 116, 123, 131, 134, 154, 156, 165, 168, 187, 191, 209, 310, 315–316, 330, 334, 335, 336, 346, 374, 379, 383
>>spear/spearhead, 13, 23, 32, 34, 37, 44, 56, 78, 80, 85, 88, 89, 97, 98, 103, 106–107, 115, 116, 123, 131, 134, 136, 138, 147, 150, 154, 156, 165, 168, 170, 173, 177, 180, 181, 187, 191, 306, 310, 313–315, 316, 324, 330, 334, 335, 336, 341, 346, 347, 367, 368, 369, 370, 374, 379, 382, 383
>>sword, 13, 98, 171, 209, 241, 306, 315, 316, 330, 347, 367, 368, 370

isthmus of Ierapetra, 1, 299, 301, 302, 304, 360, 365
ivory/bone object
>bead, 147, 150, 205, 207, 321
>tool, 85, 90, 114, 116, 240, 241

Jacobsthal, P., 307
jar, 9, 17, 18, 23, 26, 34, 41, 55, 57, 84, 86, 177, 180, 199, 200, 288, 329
>necked, 9, 23, 24, 25, 26, 29, 30, 36, 37, 38, 39, 50, 51, 63, 65, 77, 78, 79, 96, 102, 116, 119, 126, 136, 137, 146, 147, 148, 149, 150, 154, 155, 164, 167, 172, 176, 177, 180, 204, 205, 206, 268, 270, 284–287, 288, 290, 293, 294, 295, 296, 300, 343, 349, 354, 368
>stirrup, 23, 24, 26, 29, 30, 32, 33, 36, 37, 39, 45, 46, 7, 51, 52, 100, 196, 273, 274–275, 276, 280, 293, 294, 330, 343, 349, 351, 357

javelin. *See* iron, weapon, spear/spearhead
joint disease, 75, 95, 153, 185, 220, 226
jug, 22, 23, 29, 30, 34, 36, 37, 38, 40, 41, 43, 50, 57, 64, 69, 78, 80, 84, 85, 91, 96, 97, 99, 100, 102, 104, 115, 119, 120, 128, 129, 143, 146, 149, 154, 155, 159, 160, 165, 166, 167, 170, 171, 174, 176, 177, 178, 179, 182, 183, 187, 189, 190, 269, 276, 277–278, 279, 280, 284, 294, 295, 300, 302, 343, 344, 368
>juglet, 20, 22, 23, 24, 35, 36, 37, 39, 51, 52, 55, 57, 84, 85, 86, 96, 104, 136, 189, 195, 197, 199, 200, 202, 204, 207, 272–273, 275, 277, 280, 293, 295, 296, 330, 343, 344
>wide mouthed, 55, 56, 63, 65, 96, 101, 115, 118, 120, 126, 127, 141, 142, 146, 149, 260, 278, 295, 343, 368, 377
juvenile. *See* child/children, subadult

kalathos, 17, 18, 23, 26, 32, 33, 57, 96, 99, 100, 115, 116, 118, 146, 149, 154, 155, 165, 167, 179, 204, 205, 206, 267–268, 290, 293, 294, 295, 296, 329, 343, 344
kantharos, 55, 78, 79, 261, 370
Kanta, A., 2
Karphi, 12, 18, 21, 22, 50, 247, 331, 357, 358, 360
Kastro
>settlement, x, xi, 1, 2, 10, 11, 12, 14, 34, 37, 51, 99, 110, 128, 154, 158, 170, 182, 188, 223, 225, 227, 237, 241, 251, 253, 256, 257, 259, 264, 266, 281, 291, 293, 294, 311, 316, 320, 321, 327, 332, 339, 348, 352, 356, 357, 358, 359, 360, 364, 365, 366, 367, 371, 372, 373, 374, 379, 381, 382
>tombs, x, 1, 281, 295, 359, 363, 366, 367, 368, 372, 374. *See also* Aloni/Skala; Plai tou Kastrou; Skouriasmenos
Kilian-Dirlmeier, I., 316
killed weapons, 106, 346, 347
kinship groups, 148, 233, 296, 334, 336, 358, 359, 362, 366, 368, 373. *See also* clans
knife. *See* iron, tool
knobs
>as decoration on fibulae, 180, 197
>as handles for lids, 26, 288, 289
>as omphalos on tray, 206, 266, 267
>at end of dirk, 123
>on top of false spouts of stirrup jars, 24, 30, 33, 52, 274
>on top of metal pins, 72, 80, 134, 138, 150, 160, 191, 207, 306
Knossos, 9, 11, 12, 17, 22, 24, 27, 28, 30, 34, 37, 38, 47, 55, 60, 64, 69, 77, 78, 84, 85, 97, 98, 99, 116, 117, 131, 136, 137, 141, 147, 148, 154, 155, 159, 165, 170, 177, 187, 188, 196, 205, 240, 242, 243, 253, 254, 255, 256, 257, 258, 260, 261, 262, 263, 264, 265, 266, 267, 268, 269, 270, 272, 274, 275, 276, 277, 278, 279, 280, 281, 282, 283, 284

Knossos, cont.
285, 287, 288, 289, 293, 295, 302, 306, 308, 309, 311, 312, 313, 314, 316, 317, 321, 322, 323, 324, 341, 344, 349, 350, 355, 356, 358, 363, 367, 368, 369, 370, 371, 372, 376

Kommos, 37, 38, 84, 85, 117, 261, 277, 283, 295, 312, 313, 317, 349

Kotsonas, A., x, 1, 9, 11, 13, 128, 137, 159, 178, 188, 255, 264, 270, 271, 275, 284, 304

krater, 9, 17, 18, 23, 24, 26, 30, 38, 42, 45, 48, 49, 50, 51, 55, 69, 71, 85, 88, 96, 102, 115, 116, 117, 118, 119, 121, 146, 147, 149, 159, 160, 169, 170, 174, 176, 177, 180, 189, 247, 260, 263, 265, 268–271, 293, 299, 329, 334, 335, 342, 343, 344, 345, 365, 367, 369, 370, 371, 377

    bell krater, 17, 30, 50, 117, 118, 119, 263, 268, 269, 271

    krateriskos, 34, 36, 37, 263, 264

kylix, 199, 200, 323, 335

Langerhans cell histiocytosis (LCH), 161, 231–232, 338

Late Geometric (LG) period/ceramic style, 2, 3, 5, 11, 12, 13, 14, 20, 22, 23, 24, 28, 34, 35, 38, 39, 41, 44, 47, 48, 50, 51, 55, 56, 57, 58, 60, 61, 64, 65, 66, 69, 70, 71, 72, 77, 78, 79, 80, 85, 86, 87, 88, 91, 96, 97, 99, 100, 101, 102, 103, 104, 105, 110, 115, 116, 117, 118, 119, 120, 121, 125, 126, 127, 128, 129, 131, 132, 133, 136, 137, 138, 141, 142, 143, 147, 148, 149, 150, 154, 155, 156, 159, 160, 165, 166, 167, 168, 170, 171, 176, 177, 178, 179, 180, 183, 187, 188, 189, 190, 196, 197, 199, 200, 204, 205, 206, 207, 208, 209, 225, 245, 253, 254, 255, 256, 257, 258, 259, 260, 261, 263, 264, 265, 266, 269, 271, 275, 276, 277, 278, 280, 281, 282, 285, 288, 289, 294, 295, 308, 323, 327, 331, 333, 335, 337, 342, 348, 349, 351, 355, 356, 358, 359, 360, 362, 363, 366, 373

Late Geometric–Early Orientalizing period (LG–EO), 26, 28, 56, 61, 65, 69, 70, 71, 72, 77, 78, 79, 80, 96, 100, 117, 118, 119, 120, 129, 137, 138, 143, 154, 155, 156, 160, 165, 171, 187, 188, 189, 190, 191, 196, 197, 258, 260, 266, 268, 272, 276, 277, 280, 284, 307, 308, 333, 361, 367

Late Minoan (LM), 274, 301, 309

    LM IIIC, 46, 161, 211, 375

Late Orientalizing period (LO), 2, 8, 11, 13, 14, 69, 70, 78, 99, 120, 129, 155, 159, 160, 188, 190, 196, 205, 209, 245, 253, 255, 258, 264, 269, 271, 272, 291, 293, 327, 335, 336, 337, 339, 349, 358, 373

lead object, 182, 183, 321

Lefkandi, 195, 196, 197, 265, 267

lekane, 17, 18, 271

lekanis, 195, 196, 197, 265, 267

lekythos, 23, 24, 34, 50, 69, 70, 71, 72, 78, 96, 128, 129, 171, 187, 188, 190, 199, 200, 204, 205, 206, 274, 275, 277, 278, 279, 293, 330, 343, 344, 351, 371

    Creto-Cypriot lekythos/aryballos, 20, 25, 35, 69, 70, 136, 137, 276, 367, 371

    Praisos-type lekythos, 69, 70, 72, 78, 276, 294

Lerna, 224, 226

lid, 37, 38, 42, 45, 46, 47, 60, 61, 69, 72, 100, 103, 136, 143, 146, 147, 148, 149, 165, 166, 167, 172, 174, 176, 177, 179, 186, 187, 188, 190, 195, 197, 204, 260, 266, 267, 268, 287, 288–290, 293, 294, 296, 329, 335, 343, 354

linea aspera, 83, 94, 95, 227

linear enamel hypoplasia (LEH), x, 110, 230

lintel block, 17, 18, 19, 20, 21, 27, 28, 29, 31, 45, 49, 246, 247, 328

Medieval–Modern era, 36, 37, 38, 45, 46, 47, 162, 329, 356, 380

memory, 348, 360–362, 365, 373

metal objects. *See* bronze; iron; lead object

methodology, 3–5, 221

metopal panels on pottery, 38, 39, 56, 66, 80, 86, 100, 117, 118, 131, 133, 137, 141, 142, 154, 156, 166, 178, 190, 205, 206, 254, 262, 264, 266, 267, 268, 272, 273, 278, 279, 282, 283, 286, 294

metopic suture, 36, 113, 152, 153, 202, 203, 232, 233, 235, 366

Middle Minoan (MM), 163

Mirabello fabrics. *See* granodiorite fabrics

monochrome decoration

    on beads, 85, 90, 192, 208, 323

    on pottery, 8, 10, 26, 33, 37, 39, 42, 43 ,47, 58, 66, 71, 72, 80, 87, 88, 96, 104, 120, 133, 149, 160, 167, 168, 179, 180, 189, 190, 197, 265, 267, 270, 271, 272, 273, 278, 279, 287, 289, 293. *See also* cup; cup or skyphos

Mook, M., x, 10, 11, 12, 110, 170, 291, 358

motifs on pottery

    bands, 20, 22, 24, 25, 26, 28, 30, 33, 38, 39, 40, 41, 43, 52, 57, 66, 70, 71, 72, 79, 85, 86, 88, 97, 99, 103, 118, 119, 120, 121, 132, 136, 137, 141, 142, 148, 149, 155, 156, 160, 166, 170, 171, 183, 188, 197, 206, 209, 254, 255, 261, 263, 264, 268, 270, 271, 272, 273, 274, 275, 277, 278, 279, 280, 282, 283, 285, 286, 287, 288, 289, 294

    bands as main decoration, 30, 39, 66, 70, 100, 102, 104, 117, 118, 119, 120, 131, 133, 141, 154, 156, 188, 190, 205, 255, 265, 277, 278

motifs on pottery, cont.
  checkerboard, 100, 104, 119, 143, 149, 154, 155, 255, 267, 280, 283, 284, 294
  chevron, 40, 52, 55, 56, 104, 136, 188, 190, 255, 274, 287, 289
  circles, 20, 25, 30, 33, 35, 39, 52, 57, 69, 71, 72, 80, 99, 100, 103, 116, 117, 118, 119, 121, 136, 137, 148, 150, 155, 168, 170, 171, 177, 180, 190, 196, 209, 255, 263, 267, 269, 272, 274, 275, 276, 282, 283, 284, 285, 286, 287, 289, 294, 295, 371
  cross-hatching, 154, 155, 168, 206, 255, 281, 282, 284, 295
    on hourglass/butterfly, 66, 180, 263, 370
    on lozenges, 25, 28, 38, 39, 47, 86, 149, 159, 160, 188, 196, 197, 255, 267, 285, 287, 288, 294
    on meanders, 103, 121, 131, 132, 261, 283
    on panels, 30, 34, 131, 133, 160, 166, 294
    on triangles, 24, 25, 28, 30, 39, 40, 47, 51, 52, 100, 132, 188, 261, 263, 272, 273, 274, 278, 279, 285, 294, 371
  curved bands, 170, 269
  curved strokes, 40, 133, 282
  dots, 25, 33, 71, 72, 119, 188, 209, 263, 273, 280, 281, 289, 294
  dotted loops/semicircles, 64, 171, 260, 269, 287
  guilloche, 47, 71, 100, 190, 255, 277, 284
  hourglass/butterfly, 39, 66, 104, 117, 118, 143, 180, 263, 270, 273, 283, 294
  leaf, 70, 79, 103, 268, 283
  meander/meander hook, 23, 28, 38, 44, 80, 103, 121, 131, 132, 143, 170, 171, 261, 269, 281, 283, 294
  oblique strokes, 27, 48, 65, 85, 88, 100, 103, 133, 142, 156, 160, 168, 170, 178, 206, 263, 264, 267, 268, 273, 278, 283, 285
  rosettes, 72, 209, 276
  running dog, 56, 177, 178, 264, 282, 294
  scroll, 37, 43, 279
  S-pattern, 47, 86, 100, 133, 147, 166, 182, 183, 261, 264, 282, 283, 284, 289, 294
  spiraliform, 7, 24, 69, 72, 171, 190, 196, 263, 273, 284
  triangle, 24, 30, 33, 78, 143, 273, 280, 285, 294, 295
  vertical/upright strokes, 24, 39, 69, 78, 86, 99, 103, 118, 132, 141, 142, 148, 149, 155, 170, 206, 254, 260, 261, 263, 268, 273, 276, 278, 282, 283, 294
  wavy line, 25, 30, 37, 38, 39, 40, 43, 70, 97, 133, 155, 180, 254, 261, 267, 279, 286, 294
  zigzag, 48, 52, 65, 72, 78, 86, 102, 118, 131, 133, 137, 141, 143, 160, 165, 167, 171, 178, 254, 255, 261, 264, 267, 276, 280, 282, 284, 286, 288
mug-like cup. *See* cup

necked jar. *See* jar
necklace, 147, 205, 322, 323, 324, 348

needle. *See* iron, tool
Neefe, C., 209
Neolithic, 7, 136, 226, 240, 241
nonmetric traits, 232, 233, 336, 338

obsidian, 14, 78, 81, 90, 91, 131, 134, 322, 335, 336, 351
oinochoe, 19, 22, 23, 26, 35, 36, 37, 38, 40, 41, 42, 43, 51, 52, 84, 85, 88, 96, 97, 99, 102, 115, 119, 120, 121, 154, 155, 159, 160, 164, 165, 168, 205, 261, 276, 277, 278, 279–280, 293, 295, 299, 300, 330, 343, 344
osteoarthritis, osteoarthritic, 75, 77, 84, 94, 95, 130, 146, 152, 153, 176, 220, 221, 222, 226, 228
osteomyelitis, 77, 228
osteopenia, osteoporosis, 77, 91, 94, 226
Ottoman period, 45, 47

paint on pottery
  added white, 8, 41, 69, 72, 79, 148, 188, 196, 197, 263, 277, 286, 289
  bichrome, 119, 170, 269, 367, 371
Papadopoulos, J., 295, 296, 307, 333, 365
Papadopoulos, T., 315
pavements associated with enclosures, 21, 62, 82, 163, 249–250, 344, 353
paving associated with tholos tombs, 18, 19, 48, 246, 328, 332, 352
periodontal disease, 140, 145, 229–230
periosteal bone, 63, 76, 83, 146, 175, 186, 195, 220, 228–229, 230, 231
petrographic groups
  Fabric Group 1, phyllite-quartzite, 298–299
  Fabric Group 2, phyllite-quartzite, 299
  Fabric Group 3, phyllite-quartzite, 299–300
  Fabric Group 4, grano dioritic/Mirabello, 300–301
  Fabric Group 5, south coast, 301–302
  Fabric Group 6, south coast, 301–302
  Gabric Group 7, south coast, 302
  other, 302–303
phyllite ceramic fabrics, 20, 26, 33, 34, 51, 56, 57, 58, 65, 66, 71, 80, 87, 88, 100, 102, 103, 104, 105, 115, 120, 121, 126, 133, 138, 143, 149, 150, 156, 160, 180, 189, 196, 200, 205, 206, 207, 209, 297, 298, 300, 301, 303
pin. *See* bronze, jewelry; iron, jewelry
pit, 3, 4, 15, 17, 18, 19, 21, 27, 28, 31, 32, 44, 45, 46, 47, 48, 49, 50, 73, 74, 92, 93, 110, 112, 124, 125, 151, 152, 162, 163, 172, 173, 174, 176, 178, 181, 183, 184, 192, 201, 235, 247, 331, 338, 347, 331, 333, 339. *See also* pseudo-dromos.
  burial, 2, 90–91, 248, 250, 332, 335, 337, 354, 374

pithos
- burial, 6, 8, 9, 17, 19, 23, 24, 90, 109, 110, 151, 152, 153, 154, 192, 225, 230, 248, 250, 268, 290, 315, 322, 328, 331, 332, 333, 334, 335, 337, 338, 344, 346, 352, 353, 363, 370
- ceramic shape, 2, 3, 20, 21, 23, 25, 28, 37, 43, 63, 69, 72, 80, 90, 103, 109, 110, 115, 119, 137, 143, 151, 154, 156, 184, 187, 188, 190, 193, 204, 207, 266, 270, 284, 288, 290–292, 293, 296, 300, 336, 343

Plai tou Kastrou, 1, 24, 64, 131, 187, 266, 281, 289, 290, 310, 358, 359, 367

plants. *See* botanical remains

platform, 61, 62, 163, 169, 198, 249. *See also* pavements associated with enclosures

Platon, N., 15, 35

Pliny the Elder, 224

polis, 271, 359

political organization, 304, 361, 365, 374

porotic hyperostosis, 62, 94, 95, 135, 175, 176, 199, 225, 226

post-funerary rituals, 21, 30, 50, 165, 169, 246, 247, 249, 271, 275, 328, 329, 332, 340, 342, 343, 344, 352, 353

Postpalatial Crete, 247

pot stand, 62, 115, 249, 250, 344

potters' mark, 294–296
- incised, 204, 206, 207, 268, 294, 295, 296
- painted, 255, 294, 295, 296

pottery
- clusters, 4, 81, 82, 139, 141, 165
- pottery/ceramic fabrics, general discussions, 9–10, 291–293, 303
- pottery shapes. *See* individual shapes passim
- ware groups, 8–9, 9–10, 11, 36, 63, 68, 96, 97, 136, 291, 297, 303, catalog entries passim

Praisos, 35, 38, 55, 159, 263, 285, 295, 310, 331, 333

pregnancy, pregnant women, 68, 91, 114, 222, 226, 230, 233, 234, 324, 337, 339, 343, 345, 374

primary cremation. *See* cremation

Prinias, 333, 346, 367

prothesis, 327

Protogeometric (PG)
- period, 11, 12, 17, 18, 20, 22, 24, 25, 26, 30, 32, 33, 34, 35, 37, 38, 39, 40, 41, 42, 43, 44, 45, 46, 47, 48, 50, 51, 52, 55, 57, 97, 98, 99, 116, 117, 119, 121, 126, 132, 149, 154, 159, 176, 177, 180, 208, 245, 256, 257, 259, 261, 262, 263, 264, 266, 268, 271, 273, 274, 275, 277, 279, 280, 281, 282, 286, 288, 306, 308, 323, 324, 327, 333, 344, 346, 356, 357, 358, 359, 363
- style, 11, 12, 28, 30, 35, 50, 51, 55, 72, 99, 100, 104, 126, 131, 133, 147, 148, 154, 180, 205, 253, 254, 256, 293, 294, 349, 355, 35

pseudo-dromos, xv, 3, 15, 16, 18, 19, 20, 21, 27, 28, 29, 31, 32, 33, 45, 48, 49, 50, 51, 247, 328, 329, 332, 352, 364

Psychro Cave, 182, 321

pubic symphysis, 113, 146, 152, 222

pyre
- construction, 5, 67, 82, 112, 135, 157, 163, 174, 176, 202, 212–213, 214, 216, 248–249, 332, 333, 352–353
- pyre site, 2, 91, 124, 125, 126, 192, 200, 213, 215, 248, 250, 332, 333, 334, 336, 337, 338, 341, 351, 373

pyxis, pyxides, 9, 22, 23, 28, 35, 37, 38, 41, 42, 55, 69, 70, 71, 84, 86, 102, 110, 126, 136, 137, 147, 165, 167, 186, 187, 188, 190, 195, 196, 197, 263, 265, 268, 271, 284, 285, 286, 287–288, 290, 293, 301, 343, 349, 351, 363

quartz/quartzite, 26, 56, 57, 72, 88, 104, 121, 207, 301. *See also* petrographic groups, Fabric Groups 1–3; phyllite ceramic fabrics

radiocarbon dates, 45, 331, 356

ratios, 224, 274, 330, 344, 383
- height to diameter of rim (H/DR) of cups, xiv, 254, 255, 256, 257, 258, 259, 260, 262, 263, 264, 267, 268

regionalism, 11, 12

relief decoration, 188, 190, 336

religious beliefs, 372–373

religious practices. *See* ritual, activities

ring. *See* bronze, jewelry

ritual
- activities, 21, 23, 36, 47, 61, 62, 63, 130, 176, 212, 238, 239, 241, 247, 253, 254, 267, 268, 274, 277, 280, 290, 296, 327, 329, 330, 342, 343, 344, 347, 352, 360, 362, 364, 369, 373, 374
- drinking, 23, 36, 47, 50, 62, 63, 247, 261, 268, 271, 278, 280, 296, 328, 330, 343, 344, 351, 352, 353, 365, 368, 369, 373, 374
- funerary/burial, 23, 130, 176, 238, 247, 250, 254, 277, 281, 290, 294, 296, 327, 329, 330, 332, 339, 342, 343, 344, 345, 347, 350, 351, 352, 354, 361, 362, 369, 371, 373, 374
- objects, 241, 267, 297, 298, 301, 304

rock crystal, 202, 203, 205, 207, 321, 322, 323, 248

rock or stone wall tumble, 60, 61, 67, 73, 81, 82, 84, 90, 92, 93, 140, 157, 161, 162, 163, 164, 168, 169, 172, 174, 176, 179, 183, 184, 192, 193, 194, 195, 196, 198, 201, 208, 249

roofing material/clay, 48, 49, 54, 60, 67, 73, 74, 90, 92, 93, 124, 125, 139, 151, 161, 162, 173, 181, 183, 184, 192, 193, 198, 216, 246, 247, 249, 250, 338, 354

sacrifice, 95, 96, 114, 146, 186, 239, 240, 353, 350, 365
secondary cremation. *See* cremation, secondary
seeds. *See* botanical remains
Sekadakis, G., 35
sex
    estimation, 7, 224
    distribution, 221, 223–224, 247, 329, 336, 338, 339, 366, 367
sheeting. *See* bronze, sheeting
shield, 306, 309, 310, 367
shell
    snail, 5, 67, 82, 92, 93, 110, 111, 112, 124, 125, 129, 144, 151, 152, 162, 194, 201, 202, 339
    marine, 7, 242, 331, 340, 350
        dog cockle (*glycymeris*), 22, 36, 331
        limpet (*patella*), 32, 186, 204, 331
        murex (*hexaplex*), 46, 176, 331
        topshell (*phorcus*), 32, 331
        trough shell (*mactra*), 32, 331
        vermetid, 54
Shrine. *See* Building, G
Siteia, 196, 262, 295
Sklavoi, 35, 55, 295
Skouriasmenos, 51, 246, 255, 268, 281, 309, 310, 313, 331, 359, 363, 367
skyphos/cup, 42, 56, 78, 105, 120, 190. *See also* cup or skyphos
skyphos/skyphoi, 17, 19, 27, 30, 36, 45, 46, 47, 48, 50, 55, 60, 61, 77, 78, 84, 85, 96, 115, 126, 131, 154, 165, 177, 186, 188, 205, 255, 258, 261–264, 265, 268, 293, 294, 295, 299, 343, 351, 376, 377
    bell, 17, 18, 22, 23, 27, 34, 37, 38, 42, 254, 261, 262, 264, 270
    deep, 99, 120, 263
    low based, 55, 57, 60, 63, 65, 66, 69, 70, 71, 84, 85, 86, 87, 88, 96, 97, 99, 104, 115, 118, 128, 129, 131, 132, 133, 136, 137, 138, 141, 146, 148, 164, 165, 166, 187, 189, 190, 204, 205, 207, 262–264, 294, 295, 296
    stemmed/footed, 32, 38, 55, 56, 85, 86, 141, 174, 177, 178, 264
    surface treatment
        decorated, 38, 66, 70, 84, 85, 86, 96, 99, 115, 117, 118, 130, 131, 132, 133, 141, 146, 148, 164, 166, 174, 177, 204, 205, 262–263
        dipped, 22, 37, 262
        monochrome, 42, 48, 50, 55, 57, 61, 64, 65, 69, 71, 78, 84, 87, 88, 96, 104, 115, 117, 120, 128, 129, 136, 137, 138, 165, 166, 187, 188, 189, 190, 207, 262, 263
        plain, 84, 164, 167, 204, 264
Snodgrass, A., 97, 98, 116, 147, 310, 313, 314, 315, 317

society, 7, 223, 227, 338, 362, 373
    social identity, 221, 365, 368–370, 374
    social memory, 360, 365, 373
    social organization/structure, 224, 225, 260, 271, 287, 304, 337, 339, 351, 352, 361, 362, 364, 365, 366, 368, 369, 374
    social status/differentiation, 63, 64, 148, 221, 222, 246, 260, 264, 271, 287, 338, 347, 348, 359, 360, 362, 364, 365, 366–368, 369
spear or javelin. *See* iron, weapon
spindle whorl. *See* terracotta object, bead
stamped decoration, 111, 124, 208, 323, 295
stirrup jar. *See* jar, stirrup
stomion, xv, 3, 15, 16, 17, 18, 19, 20, 21, 27, 28, 29, 31, 32, 33, 36, 45, 46, 47, 48, 50, 246, 247, 328, 331, 352
    blocking, 17, 19, 21, 27, 29, 31, 48, 49, 50, 328
stone object
    bead, 13, 24, 27, 56, 59, 109, 147, 150, 160, 161, 202, 203, 205, 207, 321, 322, 334, 336
    lid, 13, 14, 24, 26, 151, 154, 156, 172, 174, 176, 181, 322, 330, 349, 351
    tool, x, 2, 8, 14, 66, 205, 322
    vessel/lid, 24, 151, 154, 156, 172, 174, 181, 268, 322, 330, 349
storage, 243, 299, 302, 304, 328, 329, 330, 343, 345, 351. *See also* amphora; amphora, amphoriskos; jar; jar, necked; pithos; pyxis
strainer, 55, 58, 60, 167, 290, 367
straight-sided alabastron. *See* alabastron, straight sided
subadult. *See* child/children, subadult
Subgeometric period (SubG), 307
Subminoan period (SM), 2, 11, 12, 18, 19, 20, 22, 24, 25, 26, 27, 30, 32, 33, 34, 35, 37, 39, 45, 46, 47, 52, 78, 116, 147, 148, 245, 247, 253, 261, 271, 273, 275, 280, 285, 286, 288, 306, 307, 308, 312, 327, 348, 349, 358, 369
Subminoan–Protogeometric (SM–PG), 13, 16, 18, 19, 22, 25, 34, 37, 38, 43, 50, 51, 52, 99, 100, 126, 147, 150, 168, 182, 261, 262, 267, 268, 274, 275, 281, 293, 307, 309, 351, 356, 357, 358, 366, 373
Subprotogeometric (SubPG), 12, 13, 117, 131, 154, 256, 257, 259
suprameatal pit/spine, 233
sword. *See* iron, weapon
Sybrita/Thronos, 11, 12

terracotta object
    bead, 24, 63, 64, 67, 69, 72, 85, 90, 116, 124, 141, 143, 165, 168, 191, 192, 202, 203, 208, 323–324, 334, 335, 336
    kylix stem used as spindle whorl, 199, 200, 323

terrace, 17, 29, 37, 44, 61, 82, 90, 156, 157, 172, 181, 182, 183, 188, 236, 245, 246, 248, 332, 334, 361
    terrace wall, 5, 21, 44, 45, 48, 49, 61, 73, 140, 162, 163, 168, 169, 173, 181, 182, 184, 186, 193, 198, 200, 201, 202, 248
textile remains, xi, 89, 238, 320, 324–325, 341, 342
tholos tombs, 15–52
    architecture, 17, 18, 20, 21, 27, 28, 29, 31, 32–33, 35–36, 45, 48–49, 245–246
    date, 2–3, 12, 14, 18, 19, 24, 30, 37–38, 47, 50, 356–358, 360, 362
    definition, xv
    excavation, 1–2, 3
    floors, 17, 18, 21, 27, 31, 49
    orientation, 17, 18, 20, 31, 45, 49, 246
    origins, 247
    shape, 17, 20, 21, 27, 28, 31, 35, 45, 48, 246
    size, 17, 20, 21, 27, 28, 31, 35, 45, 48, 246
    stomion, 17, 18, 20, 21, 27, 28, 31, 45, 48, 246
    stratigraphy, 17, 18–19, 21, 27–28, 29, 31, 36, 45, 49
tools. *See* bronze, tool; iron, tool; stone object, tool
tray, 63, 66, 115, 116, 117, 120, 165, 166, 204, 205, 206, 265–267, 293, 294, 295, 296, 343, 344, 368
trauma, 75, 114, 175, 227–228, 229
trepanation, 74, 228, 231, 319
tsakali bedrock. *See* bedrock, *tsakali*
Tsipopoulou, M., x, 30, 258, 285, 333

Vasiliki, 11, 182, 321
Vasiliki Kefala, 299, 301, 302, 303, 304

Venetian era, 5, 14, 37, 38, 43, 44, 45, 47, 48, 134, 140, 162, 165, 193, 194, 195, 337
vessel capacities. *See* capacities of vessels
visibility of cremations. See cremation
Vrokastro, 117, 147, 159, 165, 170, 188, 209, 266, 276, 291, 293, 304, 308, 312, 314, 328, 332, 333, 350, 363, 371

warrior, 315, 320, 321, 340, 346, 368, 369, 370
    graves/burials, 335, 336, 366, 369, 370
water sieve, 4, 5, 11, 60, 81, 83, 91, 94, 95, 109, 111, 116, 122, 126, 127, 135, 139, 140, 145, 147, 151, 152, 157, 186, 195, 201, 202, 211, 214, 224, 229, 231, 235
water uses
    fire control, 213, 344, 353
    mixing with wine, 260, 268, 271, 280, 344
    ritual cleansing/purification, 344
Whitley, J., 369
wine, 60, 213, 260, 268, 271, 280, 282, 344, 353, 369
wood
    for pyres, 96, 125, 173, 202, 212, 213, 214, 216, 249, 316, 328, 332, 340, 352, 353, 356, 363, 364
    oak, 159, 176, 216, 353
    olive, 96, 216, 243, 353
    used on objects or in crafts, 44, 89, 97, 98, 108, 124, 309, 310, 316, 317, 318, 319, 324
wool, 238, 311, 321

Xerambela, 15, 37